DISTRIBUTED SYSTEMS

Vol. II:

Distributed Data Base Systems

The Artech House Computer Library

Techniques in Data Communications by Ralph Glasgal
Advances in Computer Communications and Networking, Wesley Chu, ed.
Advances in Computer System Security, Rein Turn, ed.
Advances in Computer System Security, Vol. II, Rein Turn, ed.
Advances in Microprogramming, Efrem Mallach and Norman Sondak, eds.
Proceedings, Conference on Advanced Research in VLSI, 1982, MIT
Graphical and Binary Image Processing and Applications, J.C. Stoffel, ed.
Error-Control Coding and Applications by Djimitri Wiggert

RELATED TITLES

Communications

Microcomputer Tools for Communication Engineering by S.T. Li, J.C. Logan, J.W. Rockway, and D.W.S. Tam
Error-Control Coding and Applications by Djimitri Wiggert
Antenna Design Using Personal Computers by David M. Pozar
Radar Calculations Using Personal Computers by William A. Skillman

Business

Electronic Information Processing by W.V. Smith
Micrographics Handbook by Charles Smith

Technology in Medicine

Computers in Nutrition by C. Maloff and R.W. Zears
Management and Clinical Engineering, C.A. Caceres, ed.
The Management of Technology in Health and Medical Care, C.A. Caceres, ed.
Computers in Medical Administration, Norman Sondak and Florence Kavaler, eds.
Computers and Medicine, Vernon Sondak, Howard Schwartz, and Norman Sondak, eds.
Evaluating Telecommunication Technology in Medicine by David Conrath, Earl Dunn, and Christopher Higgins

DISTRIBUTED SYSTEMS

Vol. II:

Distributed Data Base Systems

Wesley W. Chu, Editor

ARTECH HOUSE, INC.
610 Washington Street
Dedham, MA 02026

International Standard Book Number (Vol. II): 0-89006-213-7
International Standard Book Number (2 vols.): 0-89006-214-5
Library of Congress Catalog Card Number: 86-70445

86 87 10 9 8 7 6 5 4 3 2 1

PREFACE

During the past decades, both VLSI and computer communications have provided the foundation to accelerate the development of distributed systems in the 80's. With the advent of VLSI, low cost microprocessor and memory chips become available. Thus, distributed processing systems become economically feasible. Further, with the advent of computer communication and networking during the past decade, remote terminals and computers are commonly connected together to allow resource sharing of hardware, software, and data bases.

Since a distributed processing system consists of many processors, it has several advantages over single processor systems, such as providing higher availability, flexibility, and improved response time. However, it also creates many new and complex design issues such as how to partition an application task into modules and allocate to the set of processors, and methods for providing efficient interprocess communication, and efficient task scheduling. Other issues that need to be considered are how to provide user transparency and how to provide fault tolerance to processors and data bases in a distributed environment and methods for debugging and maintaining software systems in distributed systems.

The sharing of data bases among a set of computers also adds new dimensions to the data base design problem. Technical issues that need solutions are techniques to partition, distribute, and allocate files and data bases; methods to organize an efficient integrated directory system; integrating views from different data bases; solutions for efficient data translation among heterogeneous data bases; techniques to provide data consistency among the set of replicated data bases; and optimal query processing that requires accessing data from different sites.

A large body of knowledge and techniques concerning distributed systems has been developed during the past decades. This information is scattered in various conference proceedings, transactions, and journals. A textbook to summarize these results is very desirable, since there is a critical need in the technical community for textbooks as well as reference materials. However, due to the time required to prepare such a text, the time usually required for publication, and the rapid technological changes and growth in this field, publishing a book containing up-to-date information as well as technical depth in computer communications at this time is very difficult, if not impossible. Therefore, we have taken a different approach. We have selected a set of reprints representing significant advances in distributed systems during the past decades. We have organized them into this book with the objective of answering some of the questions which have arisen about the planning and designing of distributed processing systems and distributed data base systems.

Since distributed processing systems and distributed data base systems are closely related, they are considered together in this volume. This book consists of two major integral volumes: distributed processing systems and distributed data base systems. For the distributed processing systems (Volume I), it covers such topics as task allocation, distributed operating systems, interconnection networks, distributed system design methodology, fault tolerant design, cache memory for distributed systems, and case studies of commercial distributed systems. For the distributed data base systems (Volume II), it covers such issues as distributed data base design methodology, concurrency control, query optimization, fault tolerant design, interconnection of heterogeneous data base systems, and case studies of operational distributed data base systems.

This collection of reprints can be used as texts or reference books for a graduate course in distributed systems. It is an outgrowth of a short course entitled "Distributed Data Base Systems," which has been offered at UCLA for a period of five years. Most of the papers in these volumes have also been used in a first year graduate course entitled "Distributed Processing and Distributed Data Base Systems." These books are also a valuable reference source for engineers or scientists who are engaged in the design and development of distributed processing and distributed data base systems.

Considering the large number of fine papers available, and the limited number that we can collect into this set of books, the selection of the set of papers for these volumes has been a difficult task. Many excellent papers that could not be included here are mentioned in the list of references.

Several authors have added comments on and corrections to their papers. This material is appended to their papers.

We wish to express our appreciation to all of the authors and publishers for permission to reprint the papers in this book. The majority of the papers are publications of the IEEE, ACM, VLDB, and AFIPS. We have also received helpful comments from J.F. Bartlett, J. Gray, T. Lang, B. Lindsay, and G. Wiederhold in selecting the materials for this book.

WESLEY W. CHU
Los Angeles, California

TABLE OF CONTENTS

Vol. II: DISTRIBUTED DATA BASE SYSTEMS

Chapter 1

DESIGN METHODOLOGY FOR DISTRIBUTED DATA BASE SYSTEMS

From a technical viewpoint, distributed data base technology is the marriage of computer communication networking with data base technology. From a user viewpoint, it is an application of computer communication networking and provides an efficient means of sharing data bases. With the advent of data communication technology for computer networking, there is a need by users for integrating and communicating with remotely located data bases. There is also a demand for the construction of distributed data bases for the geographically separated user community.

In this chapter, we shall present design methodology for distributed data base systems. The first paper provides the various directory distribution strategies and their cost-performance trade-offs. The second paper by Wah presents a survey of the file placement on distributed computer systems. The third paper presents a file allocation model for distributed systems. The fourth paper by Navathe, Ceri, Wiederhold, and Dou addresses the vertical partitioning of a set of logical records or relations into fragments. Vertical partitioning subdivides attitudes into groups and assigns each group to a physical object. Fragments consist of smaller records and, therefore, provide efficient access for transaction processing. The fifth paper by Sacca and Wiederhold discusses the partitioning and allocation of data base problems over the set of processors. A heuristic algorithm for assigning fragment to processors is presented. Chan, *et al.*, describes an implementation approach for supporting logical pointers between distributed entities. The access structures used to support entity-to-entity pointers in a data model facilitates the maintenance of referential integrity across sites and also provides efficient access paths for distributed query processing. Bertino, Haas, and Lindsay present the implementation and management of views in distributed relational DBMS. The last paper by Lu and Carcy presents some experimental results on the performance of a distributed join algorithm in a local network. The results obtained indicate that the pipeline join method outperforms sequential methods over a wide range of join queries.

Much work has been done in the area of file allocation. For further information, the interested reader should refer to the extensive references of Wah's survey paper. For a formulation for estimating the average delay for distributed data base systems that use packet switched network, see [CHU 84]. For more information about integrated dictionary/directory systems, refer to [ALLE 82]. For reading about the concept and characteristics of transaction processing, the interested reader should refer to [GRAY 81].

Performance of file directory systems for data bases in star and distributed networks*

by WESLEY W. CHU
University of California, Los Angeles
Los Angeles, California

ABSTRACT

Three classes of file directories for distributed data bases are studied: The centralized directory system, the local directory system, and the distributed directory system. The parameters considered are communication cost, storage cost, code translation cost, query rate, update rate, directory size, and directory response time. This study reports the cost performance tradeoffs of these three classes of directory systems in star and distributed networks and provides a guide in the design of file directory systems when operating in these network environments.

INTRODUCTION

In the automation of large information systems, a major portion of the planning is concerned with methods of storing, updating, retrieving, and distributing large quantities of information in an information processing system. Examples of such efforts are found in business, medicine, library and management information systems. These systems, which may consist of several geographically separate divisions, need to process information files in common and thus form a network information processing system known as a distributed data base. One of the significant advantages of this network environment is the resource sharing capability. Problems that arise in the design of distributed data bases include file allocation policy,[1,2,3] avoidance of file deadlock,[4] file directory design, file partitioning policy, file reliability, privacy, and security issues, and interfacing considerations. This paper concerns itself with the allocation of directories in a distributed data base.

A directory is a listing of files available to the users of the network. Such a directory will enable a user at any node to determine where in a network a specific sharable file exists. One can consider such a directory to be similar to a card catalog of a public library. These sharable files are referred to as public files. Users at each node may offer to list their files in this directory of public files for sharing purposes. A user may interrogate this list to determine its contents or to obtain information on where a specific sharable file exists. The list of non-shared files is assumed to be stored at the computer that is known to its users and, therefore, is not considered here. Further, we assume that each computer has its own local directory which consists of all the public files stored in that computer. To locate a file that is not in the local computer, the user must consult the file directory.

There are several ways to design the file directory: centralized file directory, local file directory and distributed file directory. Based on the computer network topology, operating cost (communication cost, storage cost, and code translation cost), directory query rate and directory update rate, we use mathematical models to study the operating cost and response time of these directory systems as a function of directory query rate, directory update rate, and the ratio of storage cost to communication cost. Two numerical examples are given (one with a star network topology, the other with a distributed network topology) to illustrate the applications of the models. The results provide us with insights on how to optimally plan for a file directory for a distributed data base.

THE MODEL

In this section, several mathematical models are introduced to study the performance of file directory systems for operating in the star network and distributed network topologies. Let us first consider the centralized file directory system.

Centralized file directory system

Single master directory

In the centralized file directory system, a master directory is located at one of the computers. When a

* This research was supported by the U.S. Office of Naval Research, Contract No. N00014-75-C-0650.

user requires a file that is not stored at his local directory, he consults the master directory to find out the location or content of that file. The centralized directory must be updated when there is a change in the storage location or contents of a file, or a creation of a new version of the file. Directory updating in such a system is relatively easy. However, there are communication costs incurred for each transaction. The operating cost for such a system per unit time is

$$C_c = \underbrace{\sum_{\substack{i=1\\i\neq d}}^{n} C_{id}{}^{t} s_{id} l_i \sum_{j=1}^{m_i} q_{ij}(2+p_{ij})}_{\text{communication cost}} + \underbrace{\sum_{\substack{i=1\\i\neq d}}^{n}\sum_{j=1}^{m_i}[T_i q_{ij}(2+P_{ij})]}_{\text{translation cost}} + \underbrace{C_d{}^{s}F}_{\text{storage cost}} \quad (1)$$

Where: m_i = total number of files in the ith computer

n = total number of computers in the network

d = location of the master directory

$C_{id}{}^{t}$ = transmission cost per character and per unit distance from the ith computer to the master directory

s_{id} = distance between the ith computer to the master directory.

l_i = average record length in characters for each transaction at the ith computer, $i=1, 2, \ldots, n$

q_{ij} = directory query rate by the jth file at the ith computer per unit time. $j=1, 2, \ldots, m$.

P_{ij} = normalized directory update rate (the ratio of directory update rate to directory query rate) of the jth file generated by the ith computer. $0 \leq P_{ij} \leq 1$.

T_i = code translation cost per transaction by the ith computer at the master directory.

$C_d{}^{s}$ = storage cost per character per unit time at the master directory

F = size of the master file directory in characters.

The first term in Equation (1) represents the transmission cost for querying and updating the file directory, the second term represents the code translation cost (due to non-uniform information representations) for transactions (querying and updating) performed by all the computers at the directory, and the last term is the cost for storing the master file directory.

To simplify the notation in Equation (1), we let $q_i = \sum_{j=1}^{m_i} q_{ij}$. The q_i is the total number of queries generated per unit time by the ith computer for the directory. Further, we assume that all the files at the ith computer have the same directory update; that is, $P_{ij}=P_i$ for all j. Equation (1) then reduces to

$$C_c = \sum_{\substack{i=1\\i\neq d}}^{n} C_{id}{}^{t} s_{id} l_i q_i (2+p_i) + \sum_{\substack{i=1\\i\neq d}}^{n} T_i q_i (2+P_i) + C_d{}^{s}F \quad (2)$$

Extended centralized directory

In a centralized file directory, once the user finds the location or description of a file, he can append this information onto his local directory. Should the user use this file again, the directory information for this file can be obtained from his local directory, thereby reducing the communication cost as well as time for querying the master directory. However, when the information of that file at the master directory is updated, we also require updating of the information of that file in the local directories. Therefore, for notification of future updates in the master directory, the list of local directories that have appended file information is recorded in the master directory. The operating cost of such a system is:

$$C_{EC} = \sum_{\substack{i=1\\i\neq d}}^{n} C_{id}{}^{t} s_{id} l_i q_i p_i + \sum_{\substack{i=1\\i\neq d}}^{n} q_i p_i T_i + C_d{}^{s}(F+F_e) + \sum_{\substack{i=1\\i\neq d}}^{n} \alpha_i C_i{}^{s} F + \sum_{\substack{i\neq k\\i=1}}^{n} \sum_{\substack{k\neq d\\k=1}}^{n} q_i p_i \beta_{ki} (C_{dk}{}^{t} s_{dk} l_k + T_{dk}) \quad (3)$$

where α_i = fraction of the master directory being appended at the local directory of the ith computer, $0 \leq \alpha_i \leq 1$ $i=1, 2, \ldots, n$.

β_{ki} = probability that a file at the kth computer has a transaction at the ith computer, $0 \leq \beta_{ki} \leq 1$, $i=1, 2, \ldots, n$ and $k=1, 2, \ldots, n$.

T_{dk} = translation cost for the master directory to perform a transaction with the kth computer.

F_e = the size of the list of all the files stored at the master directory that requires notification for directory updates (in characters).

We assume that compared with the overall operating cost, the first cost of locating a file in the master directory is negligible. The first term in Equation (3) is the transmission cost for updating the master directory, the second term is the code translation cost for updating the master directory, the third term is the cost for storing the directory and the list of the transaction records for notification of future file directory updates, the fourth term is the cost for storing the extended file directories at all the local directories, and the last term is the communication cost and translation cost for the master directory to update the relevant appended local directories.

Multiple master directories

When the computers in a network are clustered in groups, it is often cost effective to provide a master directory at each of these clusters. The savings in communication cost for a multiple master directory system could far outweigh the cost of storing and updating the file directories. We can partition the n computers in the system into r clusters ($r \leq n$) such that

$$\sum_{j=1}^{r} n_j = n$$

where n_j is the number of computers in the jth cluster. During normal operation, the computers in the jth cluster will query the jth directory which is a member of the jth cluster. One way to partition the n computers into r groups is to base on the network topology such that the partitioned clusters yield minimum communication costs. Another way is to base the clusters on directory query rate and directory update rate to achieve minimum response time. The operating cost for such a system is:

$$C_M = \sum_{k=1}^{r} \left\{ \sum_{\substack{\{i\} \epsilon d_k \\ d_k \neq i}} C_{id_k}{}^t s_{id_k} l_i q_i (2+p_i) + \sum_{\substack{\{i\} \epsilon d_k \\ i \neq d_k}} T_i q_i (2+p_i) \right\}$$
$$+ \sum_{k=1}^{r} C_{d_k}{}^s F \quad \sum_{\substack{g=1 \\ k \neq g}}^{r} \sum_{k=1}^{r} \sum_{\{i\} \epsilon d_k} (C_{d_k d_g}{}^t \cdot s_{d_k d_g} \cdot l_i + T_{d_k d_g}) p_i q_i \qquad (4)$$

where $r =$ number of master directories in the system

$d_k =$ the kth master directory, $k = 1, 2, \ldots, r$.

$\{i\} \epsilon d_k =$ the set of computers that uses the kth master directory

$C_{d_k}{}^s =$ storage cost per character per unit time of the kth master directory

$C_{id_k}{}^t =$ transmission cost per character per unit distance from the ith computer to the kth master directory, $i = 1, 2, \ldots, n$ and $k = 1, 2, \ldots, r$.

The last term of (4) is the communication cost and translation cost for updating the rest of the multiple directories in the system. For the single master directory case ($r=1$), Equation (4) reduces to (2).

Local file directory system

In the local directory case, there is no master directory in the system. When a requested file is not stored in the user's local directory, the user queries all the other local directories in the system until the requested file has been located. Such a directory system requires high communication cost and translation cost, as well as search time for locating the file. For a system of n computers, it requires an average of (n-1)/2 directory queries to locate a file. Assuming the directory can only be updated by its owner, updating is done at its local directory which does not require communications cost. The operating cost for such a system is

$$C_L = \tfrac{1}{2} \Bigg[\underbrace{2 \sum_{\substack{i=1 \\ i \neq k}}^{n} \sum_{k=1}^{n} C_{ik}{}^t s_{ik} l_i \sum_{j=1}^{m_i} q_{ij}}_{\text{Communication Cost}} + \underbrace{2 \sum_{\substack{i=1 \\ i \neq k}}^{n} \sum_{k=1}^{n} T_{ik} \sum_{j=1}^{m_i} q_{ij}}_{\text{Translation Cost}} \Bigg] \qquad (5)$$

where T_{ik} is the code translation cost per transaction for the ith computer at the kth computer. The first term of Equation (5) is the expected communication costs for querying to and replying from all the local directories for those files that are not stored in the local computer, and the second term is the expected code translation costs for transactions with all the local directories in the system. The factor 1/2 is for taking the average operating cost. Since there is no master directory in such a system, there is no storage cost in Equation (5).

For simplicity in notation, we let $q_i = \sum_{j=1}^{m_i} q_{ij}$. Eq. (5) becomes

$$C_L = \sum_{i=1}^{n} \sum_{\substack{k=1 \\ k \neq i}}^{n} [C_i{}^t s_{ik} l_i + T_{ik}] \; q_i \qquad (6)$$

Let us consider the case where each of the computers contains a routing table which routes the directory query directly to the other computers rather than returning the negative query reply to the sender. As a result, the expected total communication cost can be greatly reduced, particularly if the routing sequence takes into consideration the probability of finding the file in the directory. The total operating cost reduces to

$$C_L{}' = \gamma \sum_{\substack{i=1 \\ i \neq k}}^{n} \sum_{k=1}^{n} [C_{i_k}{}^t s_{ik} l_i q_i + T_{ik} q_i] + \sum_{i=1}^{n} C_{ik}{}^t s_{ik} l_i q_i \qquad (7)$$

where $0 < \gamma < 0.5$. The value of γ depends on the network topology and the policy used in the routing table. The last term of Eq. (7) is the communication cost for replying to the queries.

Distributed file directory system

In the distributed directory case, each computer in the system has a master directory. The advantage of this system is its fast response time. The disadvantage of this system is the cost of storing master file directories at each computer as well as the communication cost for updating all these directories. The operating cost per unit time of such a system is

$$C_D = \underbrace{\sum_{\substack{i=1 \\ i \neq k}}^{n} \sum_{k=1}^{n} C_{ik}{}^t s_{ik} l_i \sum_{j=1}^{m_i} q_{ij} p_{ij}}_{\text{Communication Cost}}$$
$$+ \underbrace{\sum_{\substack{i=1 \\ i \neq k}}^{n} \sum_{k=1}^{n} T_{ik} \sum_{j=1}^{m_i} q_{ij} p_{ij}}_{\text{Translation Cost}} + \underbrace{\sum_{i=1}^{n} C_i{}^s F}_{\text{Storage Cost}} \qquad (8)$$

The first term of Equation (8) is the communication cost for updating all the distributed master directories in the system, the second term is the translation cost associated with the updating of all the distributed directories, and the last term is the cost for storing all the master directories. If we assume that the directory update rates of all the files at the ith computer are identical, then $P_{ij}=P_i$. Again for simplicity in notation, we let $q_i=\sum_{j=1}^{m_i} q_{ij}$. Then (8) reduces to

$$C_D=\sum_{\substack{i=1\\i\neq k}}^{n}\sum_{k=1}^{n}(C_{ik}{}^t s_{ik} l_i+T_{ik})\,p_i q_i+\sum_{i=1}^{n} C_i{}^s F \qquad (9)$$

OPERATING COST TRADEOFFS OF DIRECTORY SYSTEMS

The intersection of two operating cost curves $C_x(P)$ and $C_y(P)$ (Figures 1 and 2) represent the cost tradeoff point (in terms of update rate) for directory systems x and y. If we assume that all the computers in the system have identical directory update rates, then the operating cost is a linear function of the normalized update rate P. Thus $C_x(P)$ and $C_y(P)$ can be expressed as:

$$C_x(P)=a_xP+b_x$$
$$\text{and}\quad C_y(P)=a_yP+b_y$$

where a_x and a_y are incremental costs for directory updates and b_x and b_y are fixed directory operating costs. The intersection point of $C_x(p)$ and $C_y(P)$, $P(x,y)$, satisfies

$$P(x,y)=\frac{b_y-b_x}{a_x-a_y} \qquad (10)$$

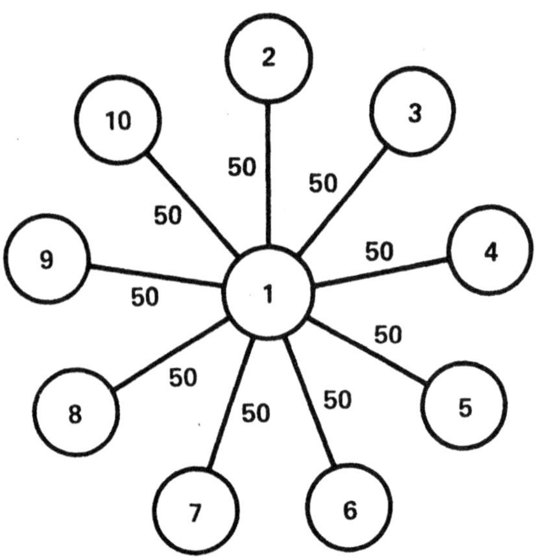

DISTANCES IN MILES

Figure 1—Performance of directory systems for a star network $C^t/C^s=10$ month/mile—(a) A star network

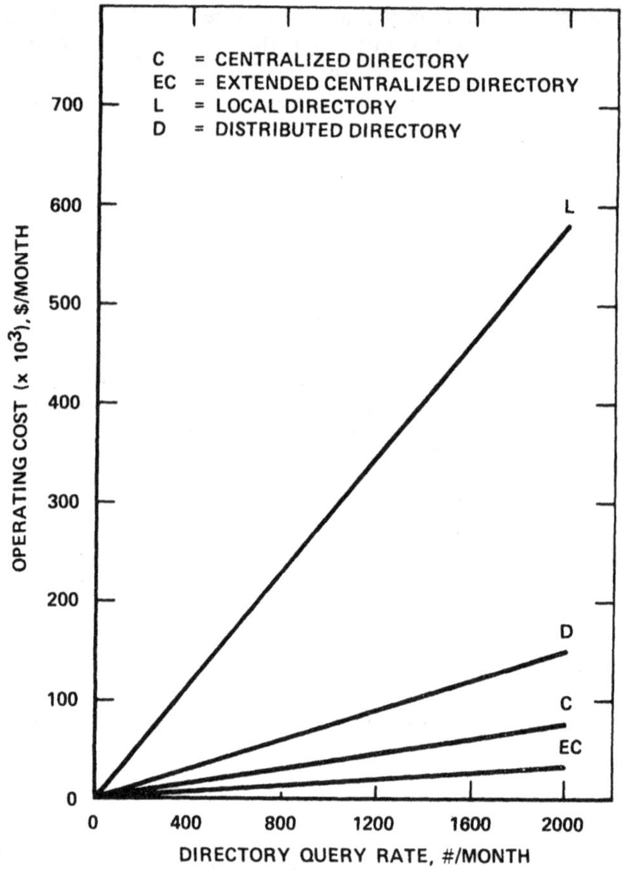

(b) Directory operating cost vs. directory query rate

Let us now consider the intersection of the cost curves for the centralized and extended centralized directory systems. From Equation (2), we have

$$a_c=\sum_{\substack{i=1\\i\neq d}}^{n} C_{id}{}^t s_{id} l_i q_i+\sum_{\substack{i=1\\i\neq d}}^{n} T_i q_i$$

$$b_c=\sum_{\substack{i=1\\i\neq d}}^{n} 2C_{id}{}^t s_{id} l_i q_i+\sum_{\substack{i=1\\i\neq d}}^{n} 2T_i q_i+C_d{}^s F$$

From (3), we have

$$a_{EC}=\sum_{\substack{i=1\\i\neq d}}^{n} C_{id}{}^t s_{id} l_i q_i+\sum_{\substack{i=1\\i\neq d}}^{n} q_i T_i+\sum_{\substack{i\neq k\\i=1}}^{n}\sum_{\substack{k\neq d\\k=1}}^{n} q_i \beta_{ki}(C_{dk}{}^t s_{dk} l_k+T_{dk})$$

$$b_{EC}=C_d{}^s(F+F_e)+\sum_{\substack{i=1\\i\neq d}}^{n} \alpha_i C_i{}^s F$$

Substituting a_c, a_{EC}, b_c, and b_{EC} into (10) and simplifying, we have

$$P(c,EC)=\frac{C_d{}^s F_e-\sum_{\substack{i=1\\i\neq d}}^{n} \alpha_i C_i{}^s F+\sum_{\substack{i=1\\i\neq d}}^{n} 2T_i q_i+\sum_{\substack{i=1\\i\neq d}}^{n} 2C_{id}{}^t s_{id} l_i q_i}{\sum_{\substack{i\neq k\\i=1}}^{n}\sum_{k\neq d}^{n} q_i \beta_{ki}(C_{dk}{}^t s_{dk} l_k+T_{dk})} \qquad (11)$$

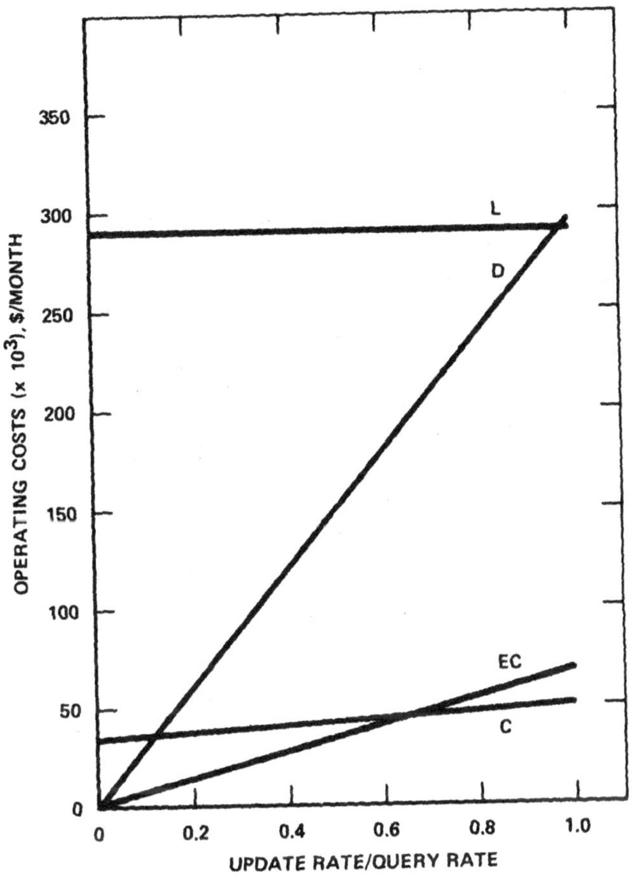

(c) Directory operating cost vs. normalized directory update rate. Query rate=1000/month

In order to simplify equation (11), we assume that (1) the communication cost is much higher than the storage cost so that the storage cost becomes negligible, (2) all the computers in the system are using the same software code, thus translation cost is not required; that is, $T_i=0$, and (3) $\beta_{ki}=\beta$, $l_i=1$, and $q_i=q$ for all i, then (11) reduces to

$$P(c,EC) \doteq \frac{2}{(n-1)\cdot\beta} \qquad (12)$$

For example, if $n=10$ and $\beta=1/3$, then $P(c,EC)=2/3=0.667$. Thus for a network with ten computers operated in the above stated environment, when the directory update rate of each computer is less than 67 percent of its query rate, the extended centralized directory system yields a lower operating cost than that of the centralized directory system.

We shall now consider the directory operating cost tradeoff between the centralized directory system and the distributed directory system. From (9), we have

$$a_D = \sum_{\substack{i=1 \\ i\neq k}}^{n} \sum_{k=1}^{n} (C_{ik}{}^t s_{ik} l_i + T_{ik})\, q_i$$

$$b_D = \sum_{i=1}^{n} C_i{}^s F$$

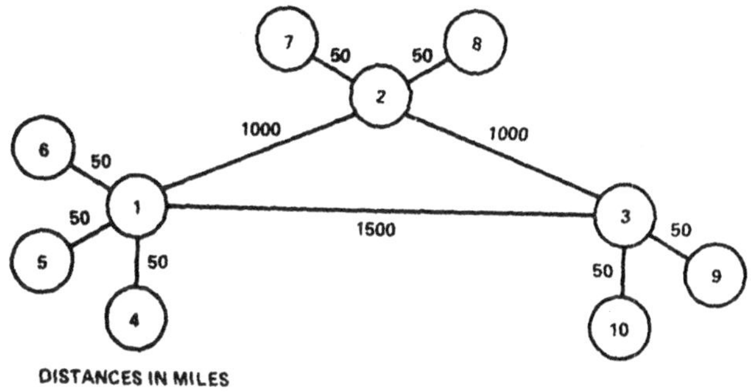

Figure 2—Performance of directory system for a distributed network. $C^t/C^s=10$ month/mile—(a) A distributed network

Substituting a_C, a_D, b_C, and b_D into (10), we have

$$P(c,D) = \frac{-\sum\limits_{\substack{i=1 \\ i\neq d}}^{n} C_i{}^s F + \sum\limits_{\substack{i=1 \\ i\neq d}}^{n} 2C_{id}{}^t s_{id} l_i q_i + \sum\limits_{\substack{i=1 \\ i\neq d}}^{n} 2T_i q_i}{\sum\limits_{\substack{i=1 \\ i\neq k}}^{n} \sum\limits_{\substack{k=1 \\ i\neq d}}^{n} (C_{ik}{}^t s_{ik} l_i + T_{ik})\, q_i} \qquad (13)$$

Compared with the communication cost, the storage cost again can be assumed to be negligible. Further we

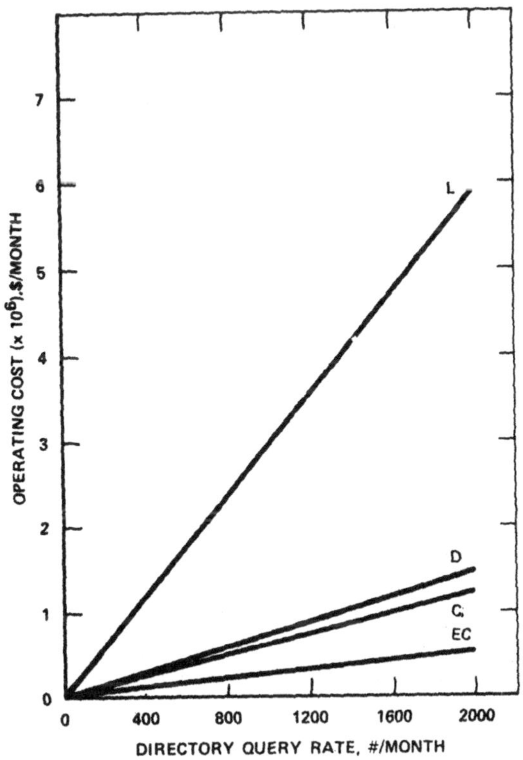

(b) Directory operating cost vs. directory query rate. Normalized directory update rate=0.25

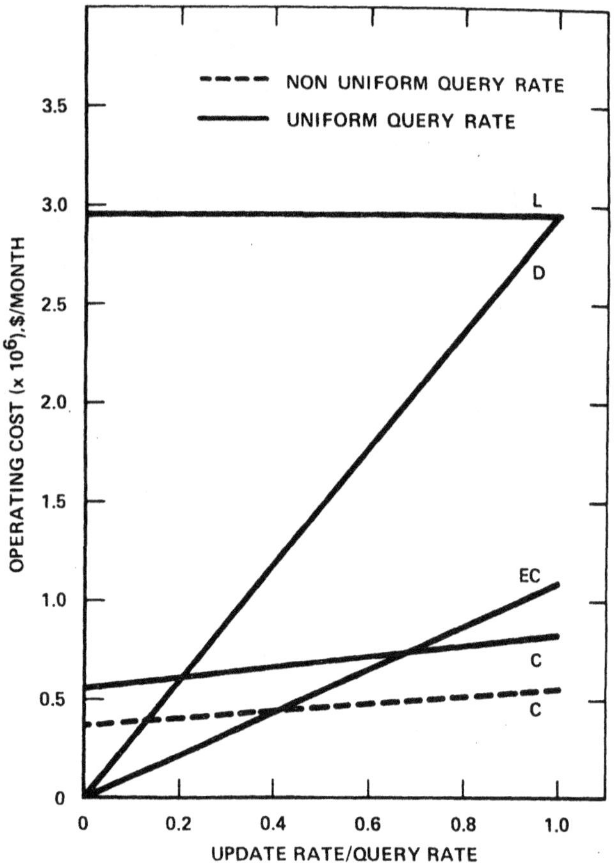

(c) Effect of query rate on operating cost. Master directory at computer 1. Uniform query rate query case: $q_i=1000$ queries/month, $i=1, 2, \ldots, 10$; Non-uniform Query Case: $q_i=1500$ queries/month $i=1, 2, \ldots, 5$ and $q_j=500$ queries/month, $j=6, 7, \ldots, 10$

assume that $l_i=1$, $q_i=q$, for $i=1,2, \ldots, n$; $C_{ik}{}^t s_{ik} \doteq C_{id}{}^t s_{id}$ and $T_i=T_{ik}=0$. Then (13) reduces to

$$P(c,D) \doteq \frac{2}{(n-1)} \tag{14}$$

For a network with ten computers operated in the above stated environment, from (14) we know that $P(C,D) \doteq 0.22$ which implies that when the directory update rate is less than 22 percent of its query rate, the distributed file directory yields a lower operating cost than the centralized file directory.

We shall now consider the intersection of the local file directory cost curve $C_L(P)$ with the distributed file directory cost curve $C_D(P)$. From (6), we have

$$a_L=0$$

$$b_L=\sum_{i=1}^{n}\sum_{\substack{k=1\\ i\neq k}}^{n}[C_{ik}{}^t s_{ik} l_i q_i + T_{ik} q_i]$$

Substituting a_L, a_D, b_L and b_D into (10), we have

$$P(L,D)=\frac{-\sum_{i=1}^{n} C_i{}^s F+\sum_{i=1}^{n}\sum_{\substack{k=1\\ i\neq k}}^{n}(C_{ik}{}^t s_{ik} l_i+T_{ik})q_i}{\sum_{i=1}^{n}\sum_{\substack{k=1\\ i\neq k}}^{n}(C_{ik}{}^t s_{ik} l_i+T_{ik})q_i} \tag{15}$$

When $C_{ik}{}^t \gg C_i{}^s$, $P(L,D)\rightarrow 1$. This implies that when the communication cost is high as compared to the storage cost and when the directory update rate is less than the directory query rate, the distributed file directory system yields a lower operating cost than that of the local file directory system.

Comparing the approximate results obtained from Equations (12), (14), and (15) with those from direct computation as shown in Figure 3, we note that they agree quite well at high communication cost. Therefore (12), (14), and (15) may be used to estimate the approximate operating cost tradeoffs for high communication cost cases.

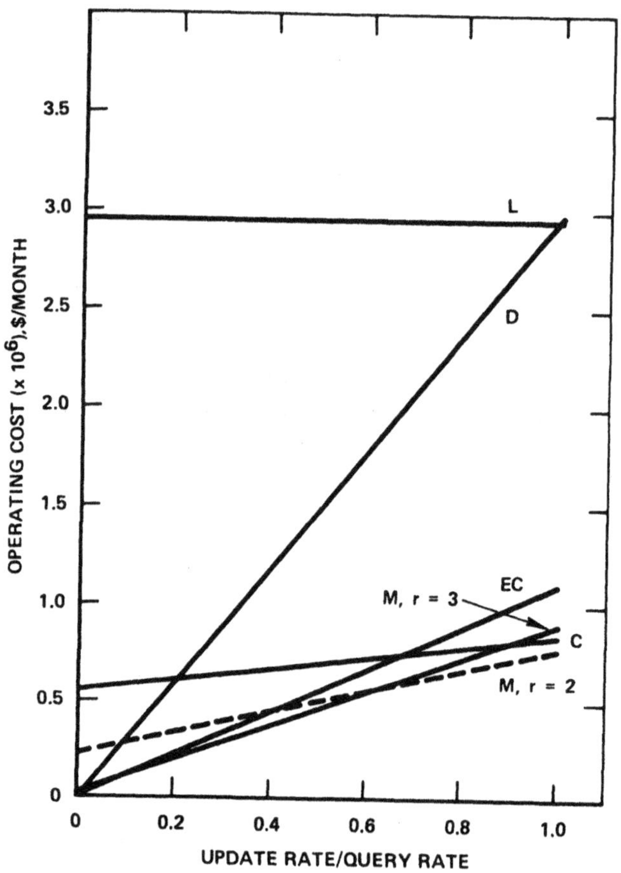

Figure 3—Performance of multiple directory systems for the distributed network. $C^t/C^s=10$ month/mile, and query rate $=1000$ queries/month. For $r=2$, master directories at computers 1 and 2; For $r=3$, master directories at computers 1, 2, and 3

DIRECTORY QUERY RESPONSE TIME

In this section, we shall consider the query response time for various directory systems. The expected response time for the ith computer to query its directory is defined as from initiation of a query at the ith computer to the directory until the start of its reception. The expected response time consists of the waiting time at the input queue of the directory for processing the query $t_1(i)$, the waiting time at the output queue of the directory for transmission $t_2(i)$, the time to transmit the query to and its reply from the directory $t_3(i)$, and the directory processing time $t_4(i)$. The processing time consists of code translation, searching, and accessing. It depends on the file structure of the directory as well as the access time of the storage device and could be different from one system to another and should be known to the users. Here, therefore, we only consider the delay incurred at the input queue and output queue(s) of the directory, and the time to transmit the query on the communication channel. Let us denote the sum of these components as $t_{i,d}$, known as the directory query response time from the ith computer to the directory; thus

$$t_{i,d}=t_1(i)+t_2(i)+t_3(i) \tag{16}$$

Clearly, the real query response time incurred by the users, $t^r_{i,d}$, is equal to the sum of $t_{i,d}$ and $t_4(i)$.

The arrivals at the input queue of the directory are the queries and updates generated by all the computers. The arrivals at the output queue(s) of the directory are the query replies generated at the directory. We shall assume these query arrivals can be approximated by a Poisson Process. The time between interrupts by the computer to process directory queries is $1/\mu_1$. Since the communication line transmits at a constant rate of R characters/second, the time to transmit (send or reply) a query of l character is $1/\mu_2=l/R$. Under these conditions, the waiting time can be computed from known queuing theory results. The average waiting time for a single server queuing system with Poisson arrivals and constant service time,[5] M/D/1, is

$$W=\frac{1}{\mu}\cdot\frac{\lambda}{2(\mu-\lambda)}$$

where

$1/\mu$ = time to service a query in seconds

λ = average number of queries arrived/second

Assuming that queries and their replies generated at the directory input and output queues can be approximated as a Poisson process, then the query response time equals

$$t_{i,d}=t_1(i)+t_2(i)+t_3(i)=\frac{\lambda_1}{2\mu_1(\mu_1-\lambda_1)}+\frac{\lambda_2}{2\mu_2(\mu_2-\lambda_2)}+2/\mu_2 \tag{18}$$

Let us first consider the centralized directory system. The total number of queries arriving at the directory, λ_d, consists of directory queries and their updates from all the computers in the system. Thus $\lambda_1=\lambda_d=\sum_{i=1}^{n}q_i(1+p_i)$. Since the directory does not have to reply to update traffic, and since each destination has its own output queue, the arrival rate at the output queue for the ith computer is equal to $\lambda_2=\lambda_{di}=q_i$. By substituting λ_1 and λ_2 into (18), we have

$$t_{i,d}=\frac{\sum_{i=1}^{n}q_i(1+p_i)}{2\mu_1\left[\mu_1-\sum_{i=1}^{n}q_i(1+p_i)\right]}+\frac{lq_i}{2R[R/l-{}_iq]}+\frac{2l}{R} \tag{19}$$

For the computer that stores the master directory, $t_2(d)=t_3(d)=0$. The expected query response time $t_{d,d}=t_1(d)$.

Let us now consider the extended centralized directory system. For those files that have not yet been queried at the directory by the ith computer, the response time is similar to (19) except that the directory query rate is much smaller and the directory output queue for the ith computer should also include the update traffic (generated by all the computers) for the ith computer. For those files whose directory information has already been appended to the local directory at the ith computer, there is no need for the ith computer to consult the master directory about these files. Thus the query response time reduces to $t_{i,d}=t_1(i)$.

For multiple master directory systems, since the directory queries are shared by the multiple master directories, the waiting time for processing the directory queries at each master directory is much lower than the single master directory system. Therefore, the response time for the multiple master directory is lower than that of the single master directory system. The query arrival rate at the kth master directory d_k is $\lambda_1=\lambda_{d_k}=\sum_{\{i\}\epsilon d_k}q_i+\sum_{i=1}^{n}p_iq_i$ and the query reply rate at the output queue for the ith computer is $\lambda_2=q_i$. Thus the response time for the ith computer to the kth master directory can be computed from (19) by replacing the $\sum_i q_i(1+p_i)$ in the first term of (19) by $\sum_{\{i\}\epsilon d_k}q_i+\sum_{i=1}^{n}p_iq_i$. When directory queries are generated by those computers that store the master directories, these query replies do not require transmission. Thus the response time equals $t_1(d)$.

For the local directory system whose replies are returned directly to the sender (i.e., without routing), the ith computer may locate the information of the file before reaching the kth local directory. Therefore on the average only half of the queries generated at the ith computer will reach the kth computer. Thus the query arrival rate at the input queue of the kth local directory is $\lambda_1=\frac{1}{2}\sum_{i=1}^{n}q_i$, where q_i = directory query rate generated by the ith computer. Assuming there is an output queue for each destination at the kth computer, then the arrival rate at the output designated for the ith computer is $\lambda_2 = q_i$. Substituting λ_1 and λ_2 into (18), we have

$$t_{i,k} = \frac{\sum_{i=1}^{n} q_i}{4\mu_1\left(\mu_1 - \frac{1}{2}\sum_{i=1}^{n} q_i\right)} + \frac{lq_i}{2R[R/l - q_i]} + \frac{2l}{R} \quad (20)$$

Because the local directory system uses routing, queries are passed around from one directory to another rather than sent directly to the sender. With a carefully designed routing strategy, the input traffic rate λ could be greatly reduced. Further the third term of (20) reduces to half of its value. Therefore, the query response time for the system with routing could be much smaller than that without routing.

Assuming all the files in the data base are equally likely to be stored in any local directory system, the time to locate a file by the ith computer is

$$t_i = \frac{1}{2}\sum_{k=1}^{n} t_{i,k} \quad (21)$$

and the real expected directory response time for the ith computer is

$$t_i^r = \frac{1}{2}\sum_{k=1}^{n} [t_{ik} + t_4(k)]$$

For the distributed directory system, each computer has a master directory. Public file information can be obtained from the file directory at the user's computer. Thus, $t_2(i) = t_3(i) = 0$. The query arrival rate at the directory input queue is $\lambda_1 = q_i\left(1 + \sum_{k=1}^{n} p_k\right)$. The expected directory query response time reduces to

$$t_{i,i} = t_1(i) = q_i\left(1 + \sum_{k=1}^{n} p_k\right) \Big/ \left\{2\mu_1\left[\mu_1 - q_i\left(1 + \sum_{k=1}^{n} p_k\right)\right]\right\} \quad (22)$$

NUMERICAL COMPUTATIONS

From the models we developed in the last section, we know that the operating cost of the directory system depends on many parameters such as network topology, transmission cost, storage cost, translation cost, directory query rate, directory update rate, and directory size. Although the models are formulated in general terms and can be applied to different parameter values, in order to draw some meaningful conclusions as well as limit the number of study cases, we shall select two types of network topologies: a star network which has the property that the distances from the center node to all the computers are equal, and a distributed network of computers that forms clusters, the distances among these clusters being unequal. In our example we assume that all the computers in the system have the same storage cost, code translation cost, and directory update rate; the size of the master file directory is directly proportional to the number of computers in the system; all communication channels have full duplex capabilities and the same communication cost. First, we study the star network as shown in Figure 1a. We computed the monthly operating cost as a function of file directory query rate and directory update rate for various directory systems. Numerical results are shown in Figures 1b and 1c. The parameters used in this example are: $C^t/C^s = 10$ month/mile, $T/C^s = 2000$ byte month/transaction, $C^s = 7.0 \times 10^{-5}$ \$/byte month, $F = 6 \times 10^5$ bytes, $F_1 = 3 \times 10^3$ bytes, $l = 50$ bytes, $\alpha = 0.1$, $\beta = 1/3$, and $q = q_i = 1000$ queries/month. The directory update rate is expressed in terms of the normalized directory update rate which is the ratio of directory update rate to directory query rate.

In the same manner, we study the distributed network which consists of ten computers that forms into three clusters as shown in Figure 2(a). Using the same parameter values as for the star network, we compute the monthly operating cost as a function of directory query rate and normalized directory update rate. The results are given in Figures 2(b) and 2(c).

So far we have assumed that each computer has the same directory query rate. We shall now relax this assumption and let the query rate at each computer be different. In order to compare with the uniform query rate case, we let the total number of directory queries generated from all the computers remain the same but vary the query rates among the computers. For example, we let computers 1, 2, 3, 4, and 5 have a rate of 1500 queries/month and others 500 queries/month. The results reveal that the operating cost of the centralized directory system with the above stated query rate is lower than that of the case that 1000 queries/month generated from each computer (Figure 2(c)). On the other hand, if we interchange the directory query rate of computers 1 to 5 with computers 6 to 10, then the operating cost of the centralized directory system with the above non-uniform query rate is higher than that of the uniform query rate case.

Next, we study the operating cost characteristics of the multiple master directories system. According to the distance among computers, we partitioned the ten computers into three groups in which each computer belongs to one of the three master directories. We evaluate the monthly operating costs as a function of directory update rate from Equation (5) and compare them with those of the extended centralized directory system, the local file directory system, and the distributed directory system as shown in Figure 3.

Figure 4 shows the operating cost trade-offs for file directory systems as a function of the ratio of communication cost to storage cost. The results are obtained from the intersection of the operating cost curves un-

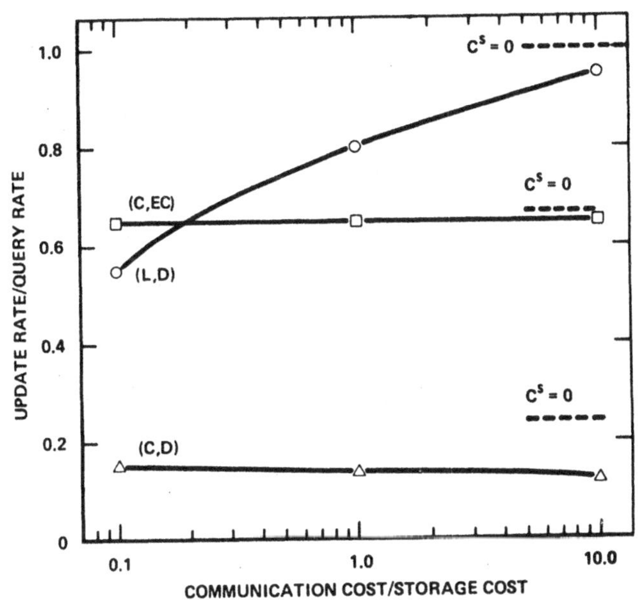

Figure 4—Cost trade-offs for various directory systems. (x,y) = cost trade-offs for directory systems x and y—(a) Star network

der various communication cost to storage cost ratios.

Finally, we study the query response time for the three classes of directories. The time between interrupts to process the directory is assumed to be equal to the time required to transmit the query; that is, $1/\mu_1 = 1/\mu_2 = 1/R$, where R is the transmission rate of the communication channel. Numerical results of the

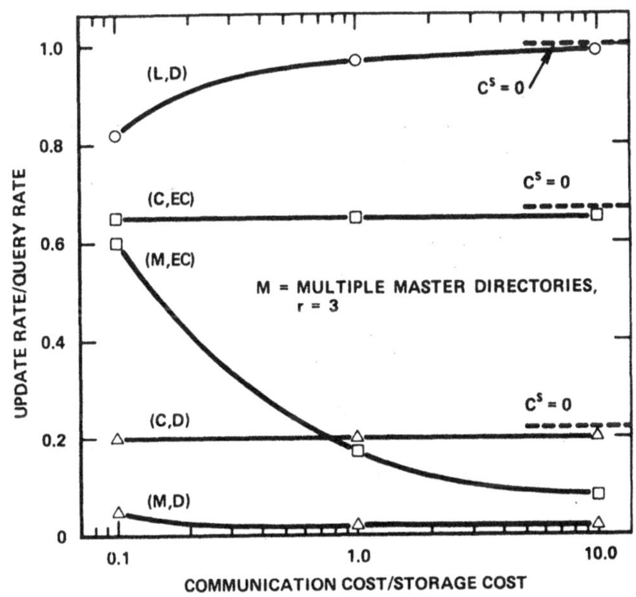

(b) Distributed network

delay occurring at the directory input queues, directory query response time, and the traffic intensities with R = 960 char/sec are portrayed in Figure 5.

DISCUSSION OF RESULTS

From the numerical examples studied in the last section we notice that the operating cost of the file directory depends greatly on the directory query rate and the directory update rate. Because of the large amount of data communication and translation associated with the directory updates in the distributed directory system, the rate of increase in operating cost with respect to directory update rate for the distributed directory system is higher than that of the centralized directory system. In the local directory system, we only need to update the local directory that generates the update and no transmission is required. Therefore, the operating cost is independent of the directory update rate. For a given network topology the operating costs of the local directory systems are higher than the centralized directory systems.

Assuming that the transmission cost is higher than the storage cost, our study reveals that when the directory update rate is low (e.g., less than 10% of the query rate), the distributed directory system yields lower operating costs than the centralized directory system. As directory update rate increases, the oper-

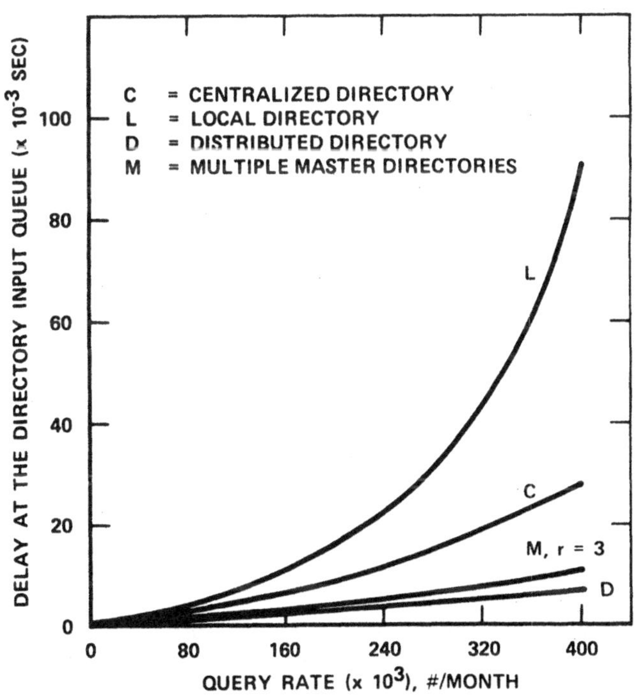

Figure 5—Expected queuing delay time for various directory systems—(a) Expected delay at the directory input queue vs. directory query rate. Normalized directory update rate = 0.5

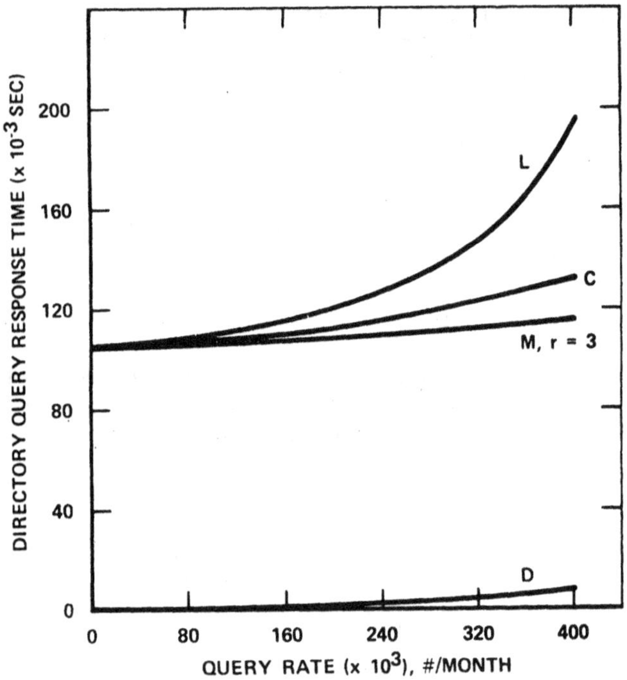

(b) Expected directory query response time vs. directory query rate. Normalized directory update rate=0.5

ating cost of the centralized directory system yields lower operating costs than the distributed directory system.

Comparing the two types of centralized directory systems, the extended centralized directory yields lower operating costs than the centralized directory at low directory updating (less than 50% of the query rate), and the performance reverses at high directory update rates. This is because of the excessive data communications required in the extended centralized directory system to update all the extended local directories. The exact cross-over point of the operating cost curves for these two types of directory systems depends on network topology and such parameters as storage cost, transmission costs, translation costs, etc. As the directory update rate increases, the performance characteristics of the extended centralized directory system become similar to that of the distributed directory system.

We also studied the influence of the distribution of the directory query traffic on the operating cost. In order to provide a common base for comparison, we kept the total number of queries generated by the computers to be a constant, and varied the query traffic among the computers. We found that the traffic distribution does not have an effect on the directory operating cost when all the computers are equal distances from each other, and does have an effect on the operating cost when the distances among the computers are different.

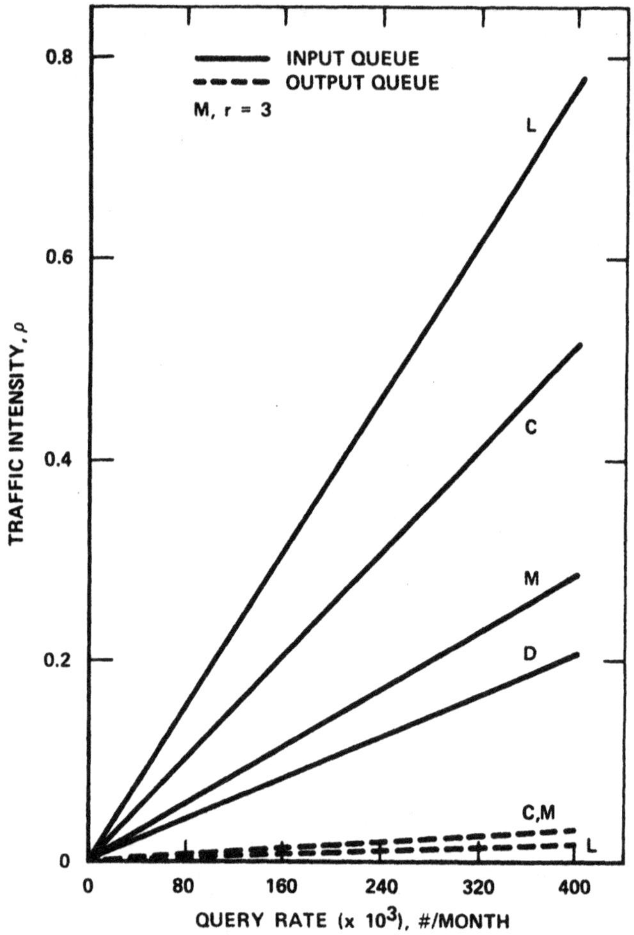

(c) Traffic intensity vs. directory query rate. Normalized directory update rate=0.5

When a network of computers forms in clusters (Figure 2(a)) and when their directory update rates are low, our studied example reveals that installing a master directory at each cluster requires less communication cost and therefore yields better performance than the extended centralized directory system as shown in Figure 3.

Figure 5(a) displays the queuing delay occurring at the input of the directory. The queuing delay increases as the query rate increases. Except in the local directory case, the queuing delay increases as the directory update rate increases. This is because the update messages are considered as input traffic to the directory. Since the input traffic to the multiple master directory system is shared among the master directories, it yields lower queuing delay than the centralized directory system. In the distributed directory system, the input traffic consists only of queries generated from its initiator and the directory updates generated from the rest of the computers in the system. Therefore such systems have the lowest delay at the directory input queue. Figure 5(b) displays the query response time for different types of directory systems. For the range of query rates that we have studied, the time spent in transmission to and from the directories constitutes a large portion of the delay. Since the distributed directory system does not require such transmission, it yields the lowest query response time. In the extended centralized directory system, the directory output traffic also has to include directory update traffic; therefore, the query response time of the extended centralized directory system has similar characteristics but slightly higher than those of the distributed directory system. Figure 5(c) displays the traffic intensity of the directory input queue and the directory output queue as a function of query rate. The traffic intensity provides an indication of the level of traffic at input queue and output queue(s) at the directory.

CONCLUSION

Based on the computer network topology, communication cost, storage cost, code translation cost, directory query rate, and directory update rate, we studied the cost-performance tradeoffs of the three classes of directory systems. Assuming that the transmission cost is much higher than the storage cost, our study reveals that for low directory update rates (less than 10% of the query rate), the distributed file directory yields a lower operating cost than the centralized directory system. When the update rate is greater than about 15% of the query rate, the centralized directory yields a lower operating cost than the distributed file directory system and also the local directory system. The extended centralized file directory system yields a lower operating cost than the centralized directory systems at low directory update rate (for example, less than 50% of the query rate). For a system which has a very low directory update, for example, less than 5-10% of query rate, the extended centralized directory system should be used. When a network topology forms in clusters and when directory updating is greater than 5-10% of the query rate, multiple directories systems with a master directory at each cluster yield a lower operating cost and directory response time than the extended centralized file directory system.

In the local directory system, because of the large amount of communication costs associated with searching a file when it is not stored in the user's local file directory, the operating cost is much higher than that of the centralized directory system. However, when the directory update rate is very high (greater than 50% of the query rate) and when communication cost is lower than the storage cost, the local directory system yields a lower operating cost than the distributed directory system. Since the local directory system requires a large amount of communications as well as search time for locating a file, efficient routing strategy could greatly reduce the operating cost and query response time in such systems.

We have also studied the cost tradeoffs when the storage cost is equal to or greater than the communication cost. Our study reveals that the cost curves are similar to the cases where the communication cost is higher than the storage cost except the intersection points of these cost curves differ as shown in Figure 4.

Since the distributed directory system and the extended centralized directory system (assuming that the requested file resides in the appended local directory at the user's computer) do not require communication for querying the directory, they yield lower file query response time than those of the centralized directory system and the localized directory system. When using the multiple master directories, the queries generated by the users are shared by the master directories in the system. Therefore, the directory query response time for the multiple directory system is lower than that of the single master directory system.

For a given network topology and operating environment, we can use the models developed in this paper to study the operating cost tradeoffs and directory response time for various directory systems. Such investigation provides us with a guide in designing directory systems for distributed data bases.

ACKNOWLEDGMENTS

The author wishes to thank E. E. Nahouraii of IBM for his stimulating discussion in the formulation of the model and David Lee and Shaila V. Kinariwala of UCLA for their assistance in performing the computation.

REFERENCES

1. Chu, W. W., "Optimal File Allocation in a Multiple Computer System," *IEEE Transactions on Computers*, October 1969, pp. 885-889.
2. Whitney, V. K. M., *A Study of Optimal File Assignment and Communication Network Configuration*, Ph.D. dissertation, University of Michigan, 1970.
3. Casey, R. G., "Allocation of Copies of a File in an Information Network," *SJCC 1972*, AFIPS Press, Vol. 40, 1972.
4. Chu, W. W. and G. Ohlmacher, "Avoiding Deadlock in Distributed Data Bases," *Proceedings of the ACM National Symposium*, Vol. 1, March 1974, pp. 156-160.
5. Kleinrock, L., "Queuing Systems," Vol. 1, *Theory*, Wiley-Interscience, 1975 pp. 188-190.

Errata for "Performance of File Directory Systems for Data Bases in Star and Distributed Networks" by Wesley W. Chu, AFIPS Conference Proceedings, Vol. 45. 1975.

1. p. 578, Equation (1). Replace P_{ij} with p_{ij}.

2. p. 578, below Equation (1). Replace the parameter definitions as follows:

   m_i = total number of files used by site i requiring queries to the directory by site i.

   l_i = average length of messages sent from the ith computer to the directory and from the directory to the ith computer, i=1,2,...,n.

   q_{ij} = directory query rate generated by the ith computer for information on the jth file per unit time, $j=1,2,...,m_i$.

   p_{ij} = normalized directory update rate (the ratio of directory update rate to directory query rate) generated by the ith computer for directory information on the jth file. $0 < p_{ij} < 1$.

3. p.578, left column. Replace the last sentence with: Further, we assume that all the files whose directory entries are used by the ith computer have the same directory update rate; that is, $p_{ij}=p_i$ for all j.

4. p.578, Equation (2). Replace P_i with p_i.

5. p.578. Replace parameter definitions under equation (3):

   β_{ki} = probability that the extended centralized directory at the kth computer requires updating given that the ith computer has updated the master directory.

6. p.579, Equation (6). Replace $C_i{}^t$ with $C_{ik}{}^t$.

7. p.579, Equation (7). Replace $Ci_k{}^t$ with $C_{ik}{}^t$.

8. p.580. Section entitled "Operating Cost Tradeoffs...". Change first paragraph, 2nd sentence: "If we assume that all the computers in the system have identical normalized update rates, ...".

9. p. 580, Equation (11). The summation limits in the denominator should be changed to:

$$\sum_{\substack{i \neq k \\ i=1}}^{n} \sum_{\substack{k \neq d \\ k=1}}^{n}$$

10. Replace Figure 5 (a), (b), and (c) on p. 585 and 586 by the following new figure 5(a), (b) , and (c):

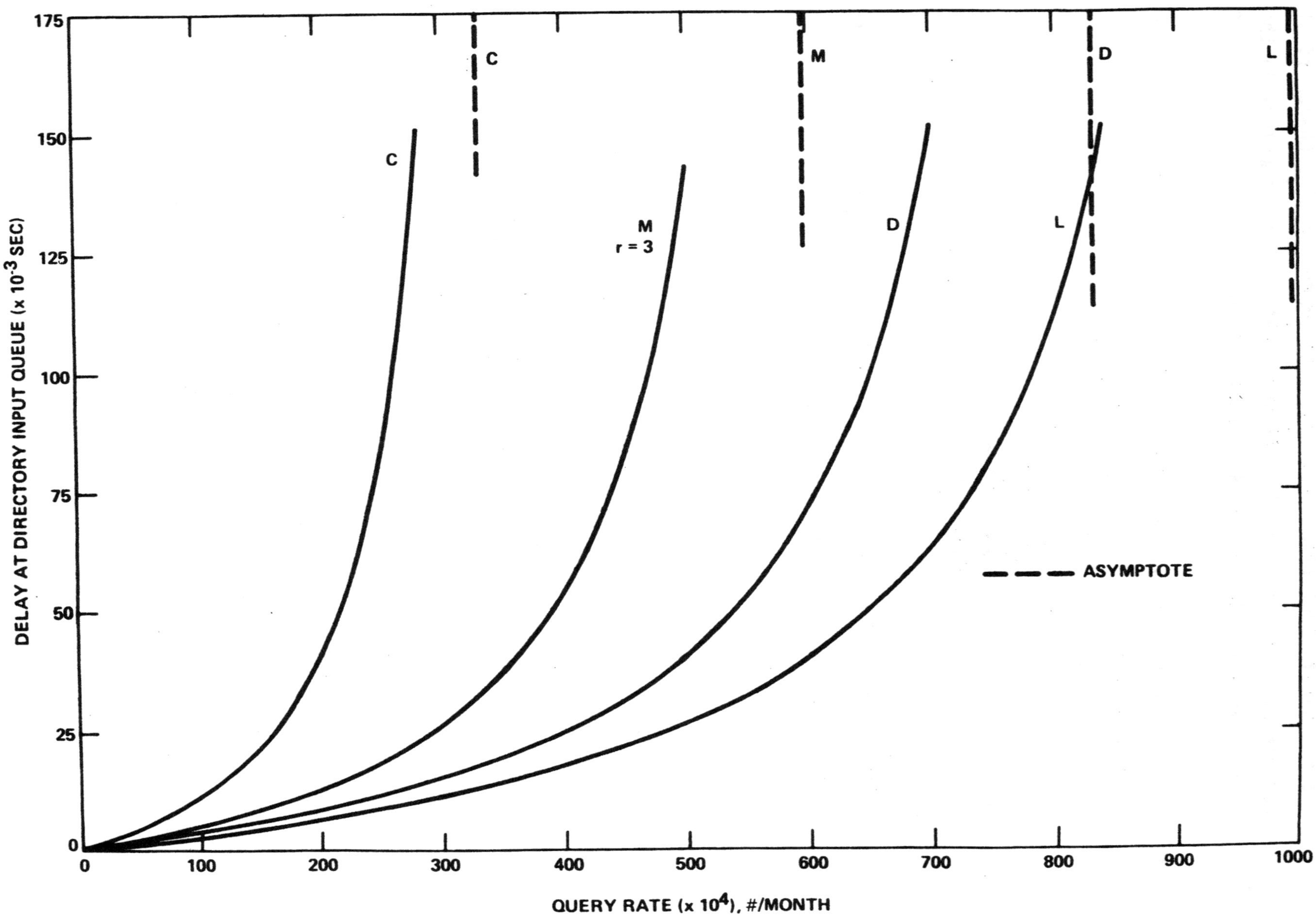

Figure 5 - Expected queuing delay time for various directory systems - (a) Expected delay at the directory input queue vs. directory query rate. Normalized directory update rate = 0.5

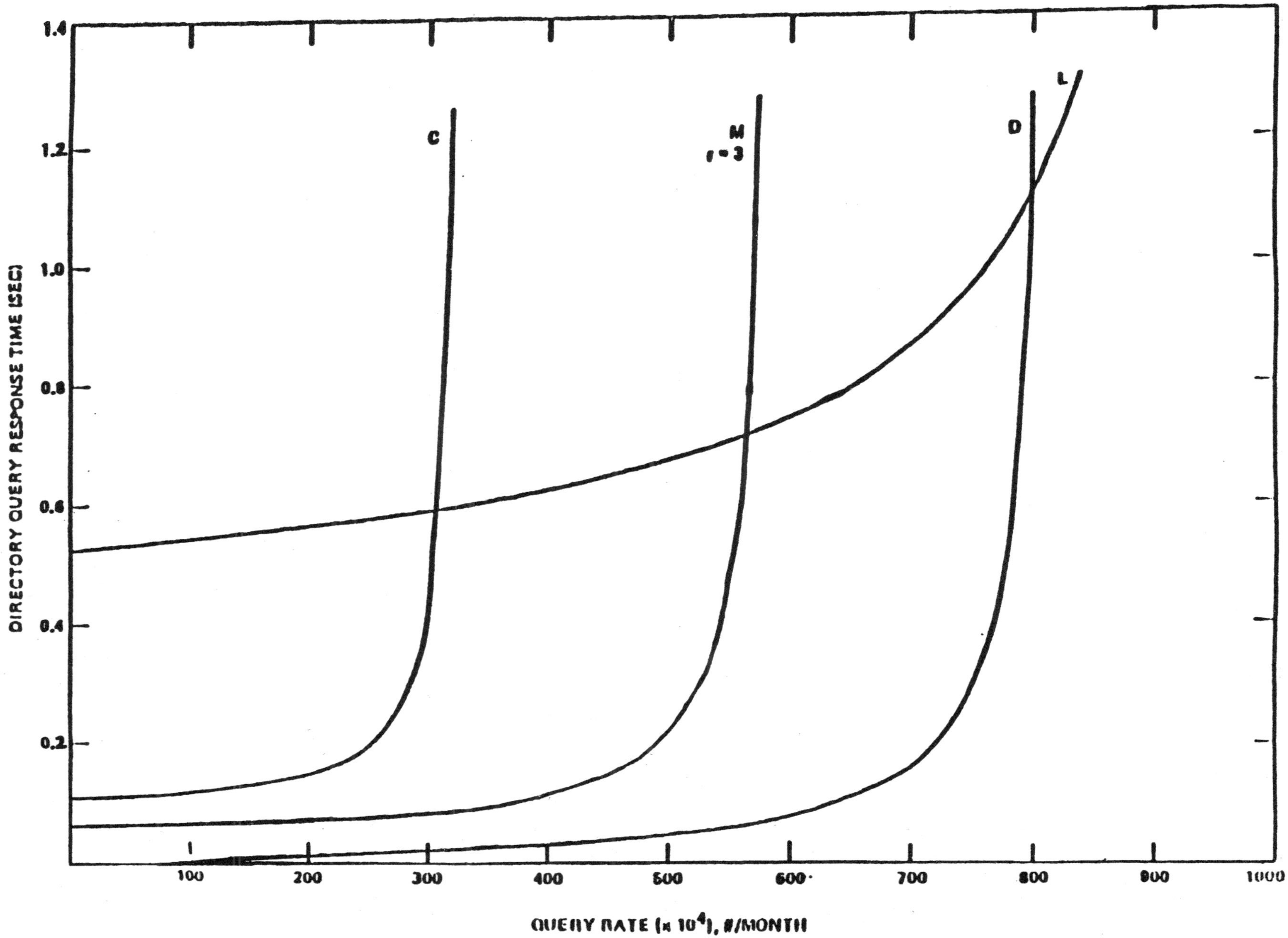

Figure 5b - Expected directory query response time vs. directory query rate. Normalized directory update rate. Normalized directory update rate = 0.5

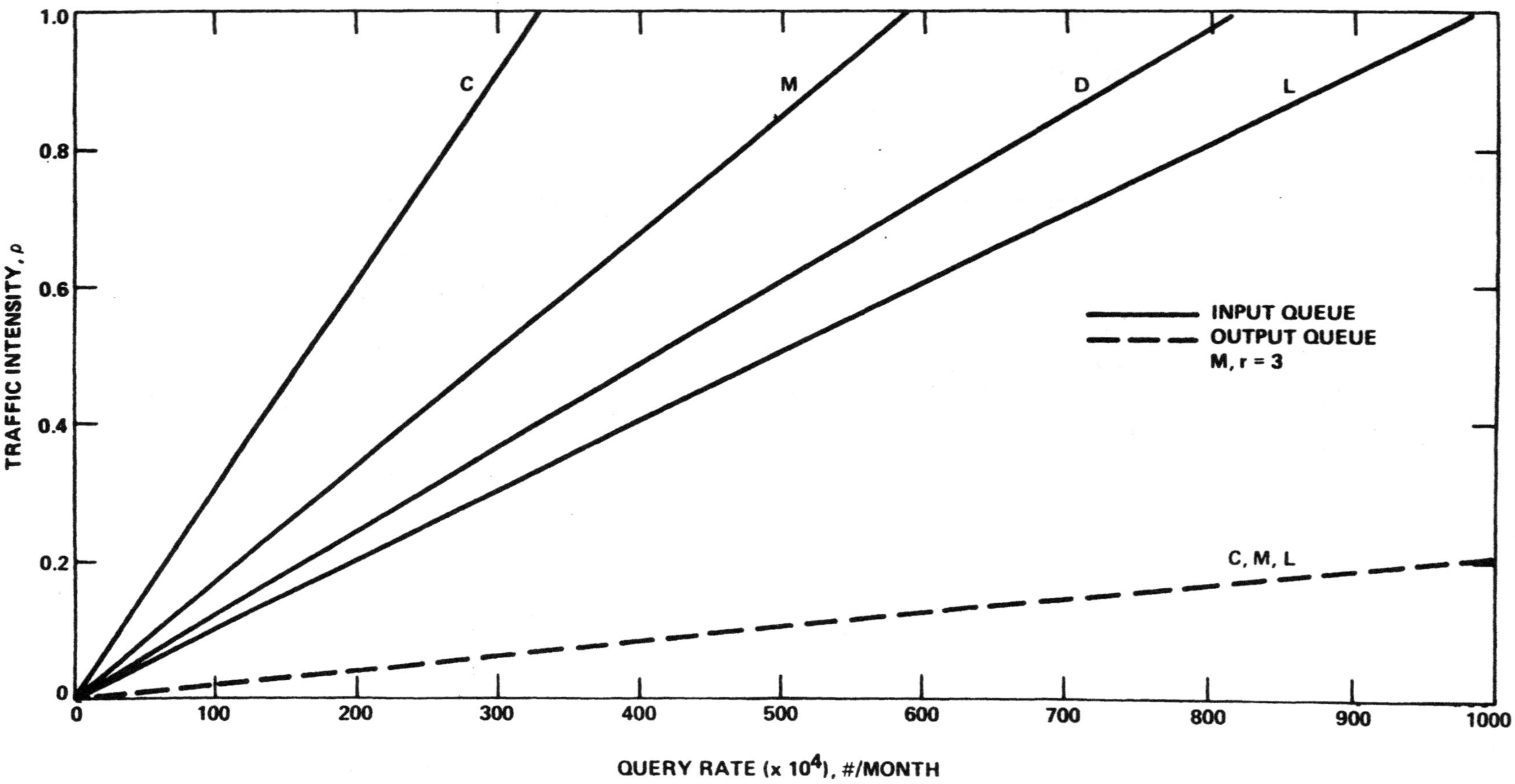

Figure 5C - Traffic intensity vs. directory query rate. Normalized directory update rate = 0.5

Systems communications delays obstruct optimal file allocation and migration, but heuristics provide practical, approximate solutions.

File Placement on Distributed Computer Systems

Benjamin W. Wah, Purdue University

Advances in large-scale integrated logic and communication technology coupled with the applications explosion have led to distributed architectures. A *distributed computer system* is basically an interconnection of processing elements, each having certain capabilities, communicating with other elements through a network, and working on a set of related or unrelated jobs. DCS architecture is implemented in global systems such as Arpanet, local computer networks such as C_m*, and office information systems.

One important DCS characteristic is localized information processing by a subset of the processing elements. A piece of information may be processed repeatedly within a local subsystem before it changes locality. For example, a seat assignment file in an airline reservation system is very heavily used first at the airport where passengers are preparing to board. Then, as the plane flies to another airport, the use locality changes. To maximize the efficiency of the system, the file should be distributed so that it is accessible at the locality of first use and should be allowed to migrate as the need changes.

The distribution of DCS information is the distribution design problem.[1] In general, information is partitioned into fragments (files) and placed in appropriate locations. In some systems, the files are uniquely defined, and no partitioning is necessary. But often databases must be partitioned horizontally, when the instances of an object are divided into fragments, or vertically when the attributes are divided into possibly overlapping fragments. After the fragments are partitioned, the FAP, or (optimal) file allocation problem, distributes files and fragments on a DCS to satisfy system objectives, such as availability, reliability, and delay constraints, and if the constraints and needs change dynamically, the files are allowed to migrate. The optimal file migration problem adjusts the file migration sequence to assure efficient adaptation to changing needs.

Solutions to the distribution design problems depend on the operations performed on the information. In the simplest form, an operation is a file access from a specified origin. In a database distributed on a DCS, an operation or query may originate in a program located anywhere in the system. It may access multiple files assembled at a single node before it is processed, or the query and the intermediate results created in each step may be sent sequentially through the files. A combination of the two strategies is also possible. In addition, query processing is related to file placement, concurrency control, and communication network design, as shown in Figure 1, since files are partitioned and placed according to the network characteristics and query characteristics in the system. It is very difficult to solve these problems as whole units for real databases, so the designer usually decomposes them into independent problems.

The FAP was originally isolated and investigated by Chu[2] who studied it with respect to multiple files on a multiprocessor system. Current work lies in the integration of the query processing, file partitioning, concurrency control, and network design problems with the file placement problem. This article examines recent developments in these areas.

Simple file allocation

Problem formulation. The basic file placement problem is the allocation of multiple copies of a single file. It assumes that average query and update rates can be assessed for each node, that each query accesses only one copy of the file, and that all copies must be accessed by an update. Queries, updates, and data storage are represented as system costs, which must be minimized. The problem addresses the most basic attributes of query, update and storage costs, and omits operational features, such as the delay of return traffic and system reliability. This was called the file allocation problem, but after studies with different design requirements for optimization, it was renamed the simple file allocation problem. There is a corresponding simple file migration problem.

The solution can be formulated as a linear integer program. The cost function is expressed as a combination of query, storage, and update costs over the multiple copies of the single file when the nearest file copy is accessed.[4]

The problem is to find an index set

$$I = \{Y_k = 0 \text{ or } 1, k = 1, \ldots, n\}$$

such that the cost function is minimized, where $Y_k = 1$ if a copy exists at node k (0 otherwise) and n is the number of nodes. This is an NP-hard problem[3]: it belongs to a class of problems for which there is no known optimal algorithm, and computation time increases at least exponentially with the size of the problem.[5] The computation times for all known optimal algorithms for this class increase at least exponentially with the problem size, so if n represents the size of the problem, then the computation time increases at least as fast as k^n where $k > 1$. These algorithms are, therefore, very expensive to run in realtime.

For large problems, heuristics offer "reasonable" polynomial time search strategies, which, however, do not guarantee precision. They are generally interactive algorithms that generate feasible solutions. A decision algorithm then decides whether or not to improve the solution and how to improve it. Since heuristics do not always generate optimal solutions and the analytical average and worst-case behaviors are difficult to evaluate, evaluations are generally made by simulating sample cases.

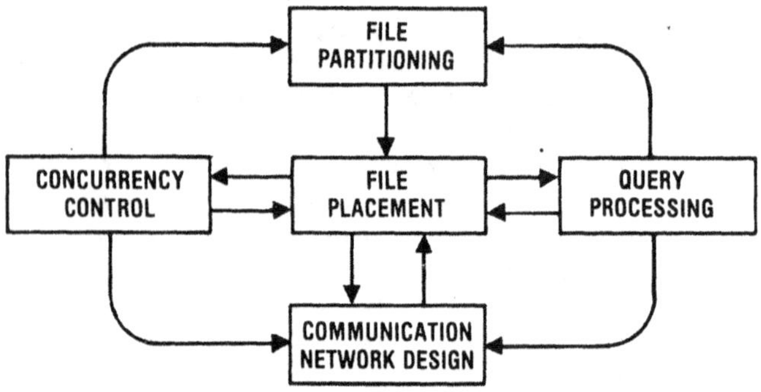

Figure 1. Problems related to file placement. Arrows indicate information flow.

Table 1.
Mapping between simple file allocation and single-commodity warehouse location.

SIMPLE FILE ALLOCATION PROBLEM	SINGLE COMMODITY WAREHOUSE LOCATION PROBLEM
Locations of computers	Possible warehouse sites
Locations of file	Locations of warehouse
Access for a file	Commodity flow
Unit cost of communicating one query unit from j to k	Unit cost of shipping commodity from plant to warehouse j and from warehouse j to customer k
File storage cost + multiple update cost for file at node k	Fixed cost of opening a warehouse at site k
File migration	Warehouse relocation
Cost of migraing a copy of the file from j to k	Cost of relocating a warehouse from site j to site k

Isomorphism in simple file allocation. The SFAP and SFMP have been shown to be isomorphic to two well-known problems in operations research, the Single Commodity Warehouse Location Problem and the Single Commodity Dynamic Warehouse Location Problem.[4] In the SCWLP, a set of warehouses has to be located for given sets of factories and customers so that the fixed and operational costs of the system are minimal. In the dynamic version of the same problem, plant or warehouse locations are allowed to change over multiple periods to adapt to the changing demands of customers. SFAP and SCWLP mapping parameters are shown in Table 1.

Isomorphism permits many techniques developed for the SCWLP and SCDWLP to solve SFAP and SFMP. Optimal algorithms developed for the SCWLP belong to two types: the branch-and-bound type,[6] which exhaustively enumerates possible solutions to obtain the optimal allocations; and the direct-search or implicit-enumeration type, which allows the search to be terminated with predefined conditions. Heuristic solutions, on the other hand, are usually of the add-drop type and alter feasible allocation in order to generate a better solution.[7] And dynamic programming[4] assigns dynamic warehouse locations with specified access requirements at fixed time intervals. Conversely, SCWLP and SCDWLP can be solved by techniques developed for SFAP and SFMP—the hypercube technique;[8,9] the clustering technique;[10] and the dynamic programming method,[9] which is used to solve for the optimal migration sequence.[4]

Similar to SFAP is the Stone problem of allocating processes to interconnected network of computers.[11] There is a fixed allocation cost, and the objective is to minimize assignments and communications costs. The Stone problem differs from SFAP in that it has multiple processes of one copy each and its process communication is initiated from another process, not from a fixed computer (in simple file allocation, there are multiple copies of a single file, and accesses and updates are initiated from fixed locations). The process allocation problem can be shown to be isomorphic to the single commodity quadratic assignment problem.[4] In the SCQAP, there is a set of possible plant locations and plants that require the exchange of fixed quantities of a single type commodity. The problem is to assign the plants to locations to minimize the total cost of the system. The isomorphism is in associating processes with plants, accesses with commodity flows, and in locating computers and plants.

Branch-and-bound algorithms. All feasible SFAP solutions are successively partitioned into smaller and smaller subsets by branch-and-bound algorithms.[6] Both lower and upper bounds are calculated for solutions within each subset. Newly created subsets are rejected if their lower bounds lie above the least upper bound of all subsets. Then the partitioning continues until the process finds a solution with a value equal to or less than the lower boundary of any subset.

The state of the partitioning process at any time can be represented as a partial tree. Each terminal node in the tree represents a partition, called a subproblem, which branches into even smaller partitions. Three search strategies are available to select a branching node: the breadth-first search, the depth-first search, and the best-first search.

- In a breadth-first search, tree nodes are examined at various levels. Nodes at a lower depth will always be examined before nodes at a higher depth. This search always yields a goal node nearest the root. However the sequence of nodes examined is predetermined, so the search is "blind."
- The depth-first search is similar, except that it generates complete subtrees before generating and examining others. In both algorithms, the next node to be examined is known, so the unique state of the parent node is easily found. Since the memory space required for storing the state is very small, these two algorithms save space.
- The best-first search stores all active subproblems as intermediate data. The total number of nodes expanded is minimal, since branching operations governed by this strategy are also performed under other strategies, provided the lower bounds are unique. However, it has the disadvantage of requiring large storage space.

Once a node has been selected for partitioning, a problem parameter with an undetermined value must also be selected, alternative parameters defined, and multiple subproblems created. In SFAP, the alternative parameters are a set of unassigned computers. In expanding a subproblem, the algorithm selects an unassigned computer and creates two alternatives, one with an allocated copy and another without. Expansion parameters are usually chosen to suit specific problem needs, and the computer with the highest query traffic can be selected for branching.

The lower boundary is usually furnished by the same problem with relaxed constraints: The integrality constraint on Y_k is disregarded, and the overall cost optimization is solved as a linear program. A closed form has been derived by Efroymson and Ray.[6] The upper bound is updated when a feasible solution is found.

To simplify computation of the simple file allocation, rules have been developed to decide, without any enumeration, whether a copy of the file should be placed at a node. Table 2 informally lists the four principal rules, which can be applied during the evaluation of the branch-and-bound algorithm to reduce the complexity of search algorithms.[4]

Casey's five-node example[8] illustrates the algorithm in the best-first search strategy. The lower bound of a subproblem is computed by Efroymson and Ray's equation.[6] Suppose the following matrix represents the query and update costs for a five-node system:

$$\text{query costs} = \text{update costs} = \begin{bmatrix} 0 & 6 & 12 & 9 & 6 \\ 6 & 0 & 6 & 12 & 9 \\ 12 & 6 & 0 & 6 & 12 \\ 9 & 12 & 6 & 0 & 6 \\ 6 & 9 & 12 & 6 & 0 \end{bmatrix}$$

Let query rates = [24,24,24,24,24],
update rates = [2,3,4,6,8], and
storage costs = [0,0,0,0,0].

The branch-and-bound tree is shown in Figure 2, where the state vector shows the state of the allocation. The state of a node i can be 0 ($Y_i=0$), 1 ($Y_i=1$), or U (Y_i = unassigned). The number below each vertex is the linear-programming lower bound. The corresponding conditions of Table 2 are shown on the edges. (See Ramaroorthy and Wah[4] for calculations.) The order of traversal is shown within each vertex. Since the minimum lower bound criterion is used, (UU011) is expanded. Then, there are three subproblems, (U0011), (U1011), and (UU111) with lower bounds 693, 657, and 567, respectively. Subproblem (UU111) with the minimum

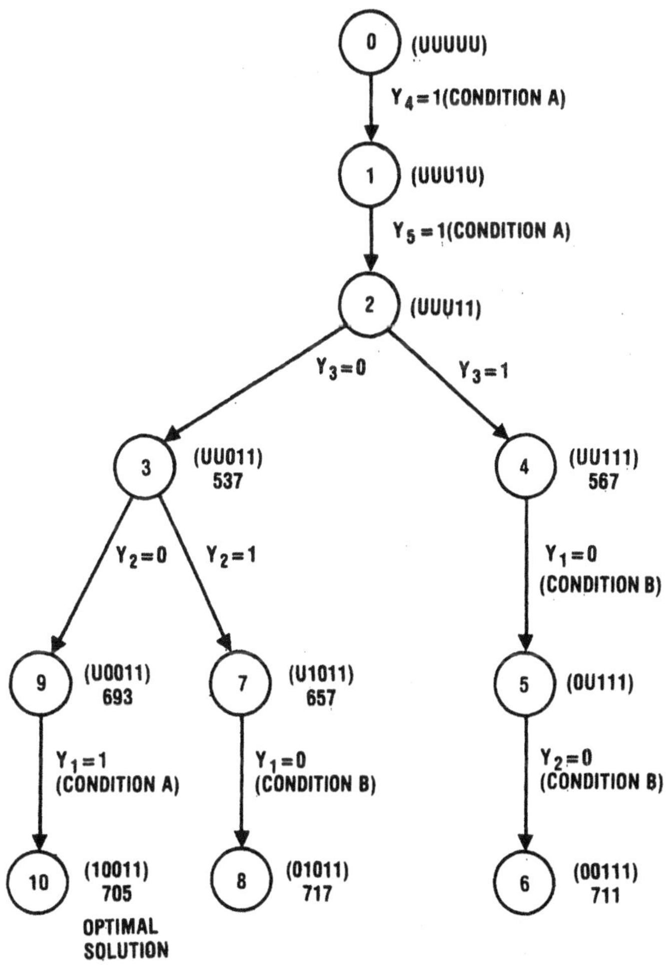

Figure 2. Application of branch-and-bound algorithm and conditions of Table 2 for Casey's five-node example. *U* indicates that a node is unassigned; the integer outside each node is the lower bound or actual cost.

lower bound is selected for expansion in the next iteration. The vertex obtained after step 9 gives the optimal solution.

Besides branch-and-bound algorithms, other enumerative approaches are also available. For example, Casey has developed a technique that shows all possible assignments in a hypercube.[8] He found that, if the total system cost decreases when a new copy is introduced, it is worthwhile to introduce one, but unnecessary to introduce further copies otherwise. Although the size of the enumerations is reduced, the complexity of the problem still increases exponentially. In other words, enumerations are impractical when the problem is large.

Fast heuristics for simple file allocation. Branch-and-bound and other enumerative algorithms are time-consuming because they backtrack on previous decisions, once it is determined that the current path may not lead to an optimal solution. To speed up processing, backtracking is limited or eliminated, but at the risk of reducing the quality of the solution.

A fast heuristic can be extended from the branch-and-bound algorithm discussed earlier. The set of unassigned nodes K_2 is selected, one node at a time, and the current assignment is extended by the selected node. There are two possibilities: either to assign or not to assign a copy of the file. Then there are 2 $|K_2|$ possible extended assignments. The linear programming lower bounds are calculated for each of these. A criterion for deciding which node to extend is to select the extended assignment with the minimum lower bound. The effect of the heuristic applied on Casey's five-node example is shown in Figure 3.

Another effective heuristic is the add-drop algorithm,[7] which begins by finding a feasible allocation. It then tries to reduce the total system cost by successive addition or deletion of file copies. When a feasible, lower cost solution is found, the algorithm adopts it as a new starting solution, and the process continues. Eventually, it reaches a local optimum in which addition or deletion does not reduce the cost. The whole procedure can be repeated with a different starting solution to produce another local optimum. The final solution is obtained by taking the minimum over all the local optima. The heuristic is illustrated in Figure 4, which shows an initial copy assignment to every node. Copies are successively dropped until costs can no longer be reduced. Then copies can be added to the assignment to test for further improvement.

Extensive evaluations of the first heuristic on sample SFAP and SCWLP cases confirm its reliability.[4] Of the 22 cases evaluated, 14 show optimal assignments. As a comparison, the application of the add-drop algorithm results in nine optimal assignments, but the error percentage for the add-drop algorithm is smaller (0.10 vs. 0.22 percent). Since both heuristics have polynomial time complexity,—$O(n^4)$ in both cases—they can be applied simultaneously to take advantage of the benefits of each.

Although the NP-hardness produces exponential time optimal algorithms, some special cases can be solved optimally in polynomial time. Coffman et al.,[9] for instance, derived a simple formula to achieve the maximum READ throughputs where there are infinite READs and updates arriving stochastically. Whitney[10] considered the allocation of a fixed number of copies without the update effects on a network modeled by a linear graph and found that the computational complexity is $O((n-q)^q)$ where q is the given number of copies. Ghosh[11] developed polynomial time algorithms for distributing a database so that multiple segments satisfying a query can be retrieved in parallel. These special cases are hard to generalize, however, and suboptimal heuristics prevail in the general file allocation problem.

Table 2.
Summary of conditions for placement and non-placement of a file at an unassigned node *i*.

CONDITION	RULE	USE
A	Y_i = 1 if the cost of a local copy at node i is smaller than the smallest possible access cost increase without a copy at node i.	Preassignment in each iteration
B	Y_i = 0 if the cost of a local copy at node i is greater than the maximum possible access cost increase.	Preassignment in each iteration
C	The number of possible users who can access a copy at an unassigned node should be reduced by 1 if it is more cost-effective to access an already existing copy.	Evaluating linear programming lower bound
D	Y_i = 0 if there exists a "better" site nearby.	Initial preassignment

General file allocation

FAP, the general file allocation problem, allocates single or multiple files with design requirements such as delay, storage capacity, parallelism, and availability, and in the presence of program accesses and specialized hardware. Its objective functions are storage and communication costs. The communication cost is further broken down for queries and updates. The optimization problem is to locate copies that (1) minimize the cost function and (2) satisfy all the accesses. More complicated cost functions can also be written. For example, the cost of a query can be separated into the cost of the request and the cost of data return.

In the absence of other constraints, the optimization problem can be decomposed into multiple optimization problems—one for each file, since all the files are independent. Techniques described in the previous section can solve individual optimization problems. When delay, availability, and capacity constraints are taken into account, their effects are usually represented in constraint equations. Then one file may affect the allocation of other files and preclude decomposition.

An interesting decomposition problem was investigated by Morgan and Levin.[9] In their model, queries and updates were processed by the corresponding programs before they were sent to databases. Query traffic from programs to databases could not be determined for each node, however, because the locations of programs are not fixed. And if the problem assigns negligible costs to program storage, programs can be duplicated in every node. For a given placement of a file, the route taken to access the file from a node through a program was fixed. Because of the fixed routing, file independence, and freedom from delay and storage constraints, the optimization could be handled as multiple problems, one for each file.

Delay constraints. The delay in accessing is an important factor in determining file placement, but individual access or update delays are not analyzed. Rather, many simplifications are made, and an average delay for all transactions is calculated. We examine some of the methods here.

Chu modeled the traffic between two points of a network as an M/D/1 queueing process.[2] By evaluating the arrival and service rates of transactions and by neglecting the overhead of sending requests to files, he found a closed formula for the average delay. He calculated the average delay for sending file *f* from node *j* to node *k* and added it as a constraint to the optimization problem so that it was less than the maximum allowable retrieval time.

In their model, Mahmoud and Riordon[12] assumed that the query and query-return traffic for a request originating from the same node are equally divided among all the copies in the system. By using a fixed routing, the traffic along a link in the network could be evaluated. The delay along a link was modeled by an M/M/1 queueing process. It was assumed that all intermediate messages were independent and exponentially distributed. The average delay in the network was the average delay for all messages.

Irani and Khabbaz[13] produced the most accurate analytical evaluation of delay. They used the same M/M/1 queueing model for a link as Mahmoud and Riordon, but they accounted for the effects of routing and congestion more accurately. They showed that the flow along a link depends on the placement of copies, network connectivity, and diameter. Adaptive routing schemes were used, and flow was directed along paths with the least congestion.

Since analytical delay equations may not fully represent the effects of adaptive routing procedures and flow control techniques, Laning and Leonard developed a simulation model to evaluate the delays in each step of an iterative heuristic.[14] Their evaluation time may be long, so it is difficult to apply this technique in real time.

In updating multiple copies of a file, the updates can be issued sequentially or in parallel. When multiple, concurrent updates are issued by different users, all except one has to be blocked, then reissued. Queries are also delayed when updates are made. Detailed update effects are excluded, first, because the model was already fairly complicated and second, because the dynamic, interaction of updates would probably not be a significant factor in determining the allocation.

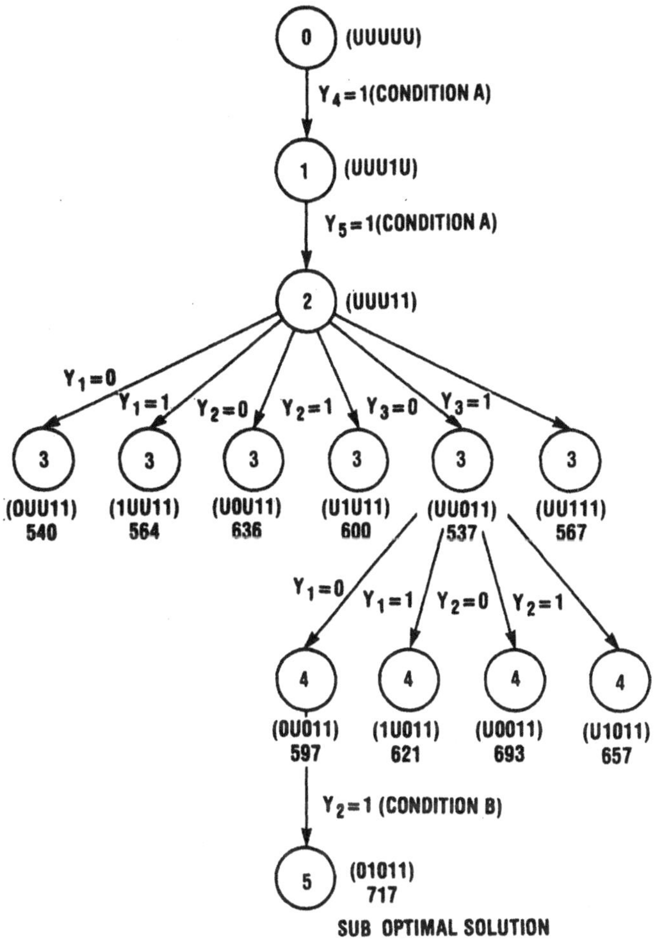

Figure 3. Application of heuristic and conditions of Table 2 on Casey's five-node example. *U* indicates that node is unassigned; the integer outside each node is the lower bound or actual cost.

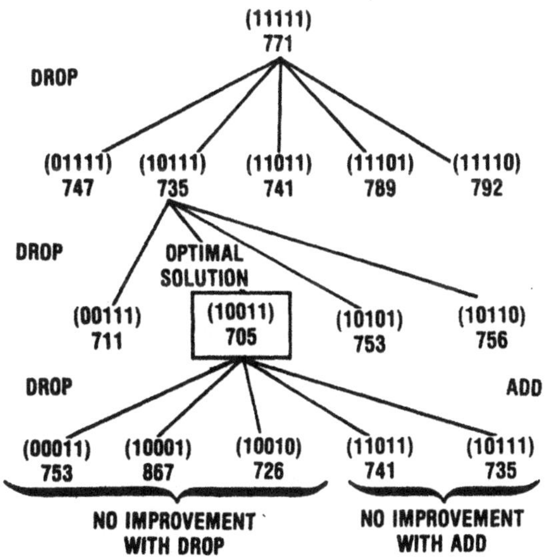

Figure 4. Application of add-drop heuristic on Casey's five-node example.

Availability constraint. Multiple copies of a file must be kept to insure that at least one copy is readily accessible if the network or a computer fails. The availability of a given file is defined as the probability that it is accessible through the storage location of the file. The reliability of a file is the probability that at least one intact copy is maintained. High reliability can be achieved by maintaining a large number of copies on the system, but high availability cannot because it depends on the network configuration.

The availability requirement is a constraint to establish the minimum acceptable availability for file f (α^f). It should be less than or equal to the average availability as evaluated from the file distribution and network configuration ($\overline{\alpha}^f$).

Mahmoud and Riordon evaluated $\overline{\alpha}^f$ as the average availability of file f accessed from node j, $\overline{\alpha}^f_j$, weighted over the total traffic demand with adjustments, for the total traffic demand for file f at node j.[15] Since static routing was assumed in the model, α^f_j was approximated in terms of the availability of a fixed set of network paths leading to copies weighted by the network connectivity. Similar availability constraints were used by Laning and Leonard.[17]

The general problem allocates files with design requirements while controlling program accesses and specialized hardware.

Irani and Khabbaz expressed availability as the probability that the network is connected and that at least one computer can make a copy available.[13] Network reliability is a function of the network diameter, degree of connectivity, and site and link reliabilities. Copies can be correctly updated only if the network is connected, and when the network is partitioned, updates within a partition cannot be communicated to other partitions.

Other constraints. Other constraints can be added for capacity, privacy/security and parallelism. The capacity constraint has been used by Chu,[2] but other researchers excluded it, since storage cost is very low and virtually unlimited storage capacity can be provided at any node. Morgan and Levin felt that the network management should provide storage transparent to network users.[2] The capacity constraint is perhaps important only for some small microcomputer-based systems, and since the size of files may grow, it is difficult to anticipate future capacity needs at design time. Consequently, the designer need distinguish only between expandable nodes and unexpandable nodes.

For file security, it may be necessary to preclude the storage of copies at some nodes. The constraint $Y^f_k=3$ prevents the storage of file f at node k. And to take advantage of special processing capabilities of nodes and to allow maximum parallelism, a constraint may be needed for copies in a subset of nodes or for copies of two files on different computers.[10]

Heuristic solution techniques. Constraints increase the complexity of the problem. The conditions of Table 2 are no longer applicable because they reflect no restrictions. In addition, delay and availability constraints prevent the decomposition of optimization for multiple files, so the most reliable method for solving placement problems is exhaustive enumeration, such as branch-and-bound algorithms.[18]

Heuristics including the add-drop heuristic,[15] clustering algorithm,[13] steepest ascent and subgradient method, and greedy algorithm[13] have been used effectively in sample cases. Simulations have also been used iteratively to search for a feasible solution.[17] A linear-programming, lower bound without the integrality constraints can be developed, but it cannot be put into a closed form as in SFAP,[6] and the linear program must be evaluated each time. Other integer-programming algorithms can also be applied,[2,12] but the size of solvable problems is very restricted.

General file allocation with network design

Optimal file allocation parallels network design. Besides placing programs and files at appropriate locations, the capacities of communication lines are assigned,[15,16] computer processing power is chosen,[18] and a network with maximal connection and minimal diameter is designed.[16] The general form of the optimization problem is

minimized cost = storage cost + link cost

subject to network reliability constraints, database availability constraints, and access delay constraints, and others.

Among objective functions, Mahmoud and Riordon considered costs of file storage and leasing communication links.[15] To these, Irani added the termination cost of a link.[16] Both formulations sought optimal link capacities, and query and update effects were included in the delay constraint.

A complicated objective function was developed by Loomis and Popek,[13] who included the specialized needs of a query, the extent of specialization of a node, local memory accessibility, transmission delay time, and the possibility of accessing two objects in parallel. An equally elaborate objective function was also used by Chen and Akoka,[18] who considered the costs for database software, computer equipment, communication line installation, database storage, and communication of query/update from users to programs and from programs to databases. Their goal here was to simultaneously optimize the distribution of processing power, the allocation of programs and databases, and the assignment of communication link capacities on a system in which queries and updates were sent along static routes.

In a heuristic approach, a feasible file allocation is first generated, and the communication network is designed with the given file allocation and the delay and availability constraints. The files are reallocated, and design steps are iterated until no further improvement in cost is possible.[15,16] The cost function includes storage and network. Queries and updates affect only the delay in the network. This approach is an improvement over problems discussed earlier, which model the effects of queries and updates as system costs. It is not appropriate, however, when file migration is allowed because link capacities cannot be changed dynamically. An optimization suitable for investigating file migration should have the following form:

minimized cost = storage cost

subject to access delay contraints, database availability constraints and others.

Here, link capacities are assumed to be statically chosen.

General file allocation with query processing

In general, a query may access multiple files. A query processing strategy schedules the order that the files are accessed. To solve the query processing problem, file locations must be known, while solutions to the file allocation problem require a query processing strategy. All the studies described so far assume that a query or update is directed toward a single file and that queries and updates originate from a known location. Morgan and Levin have assumed a more general query or update originating from a given node, which must be processed by a program before it is sent to a file.[12]

Solving combined query and allocation problems is extremely complex, especially when delay and availability constraints are also included. Apers proposed a solution based on the assumption that the overhead of communication depends on the amount of data sent and that the cost of communication per unit data is constant in the network.[19] The two problems can then be solved independently. First, the query processing order is optimized independently for each query or update providing that distinct copies of files are used. Distinct copies are located at virtual sites and the file allocation becomes the mapping of the virtual sites to physical sites so that the total communication costs are minimal. It is assumed that the cost of communication within a physical site is zero. The optimization can be formulated as a nonlinear integer program. Branch-and-bound algorithms and heuristics have been proposed to solve the combined query and allocation problem, and network configuration would not enter into the optimization.

Optimization is further complicated when the communication cost is not uniform in the network because the query processing order and file allocation must be optimized together. Future research will have to establish conditions that permit the two problems to be studied independently.

File migration

The problem of file migration arises from the dynamic nature of accesses. Although there may be a locality of access for a file, there are occasionally very few activities inside the locality, and the file is accessed outside its locality. Moreover, the locality of access may be time-varying, as in global networks distributed over different time zones. Then it is more efficient to allow the file to migrate to major access points.

A typical migration method involves the application of a static algorithm. Access rates are set initially, and migrations occur at fixed intervals. At the end of each interval, either migrations take place or they do not. Therefore, over a period of t intervals, there are a minimum of 2^t possible alternatives.

To simplify evaluation of the file allocation algorithm in each iteration, additional conditions are set to eliminate unnecessary enumerations.[12] If I_t is the index set of allocation in period t and $F(I_t)$ is the query and storage costs with allocations I_t, then

$$\bar{F}(I_t) = F(I_t) + M_{t+1}(I_t, I_{t+1}),$$

where $M_{t+1}(I_t, I_{t+1})$ is the migration cost from I_t to I_{t+1} at the beginning of period $t+1$. Only alternatives with $F(I_t) \leq F(I_t - \{i\})$ and $\bar{F}(I_{t-1}) \leq \bar{F}(I_{t-1} - \{i\})$ have to be considered in the file allocation algorithm.

Dynamic programming, both static and stochastic, has also been used in solving optimal migration sequences. In static dynamic programming, it is assumed that time is divided into periods during which the access rates remain constant. In the stochastic version, the access rate is modeled as a continuous random variable with a fixed number of different values that vary according to a Markov model.[20] These assumptions permit solutions, but they do not correspond to conditions in real systems.

Optimal allocation places programs and files at appropriate locations and assigns communications capacities.

Porcar has studied user behavior of file systems collected on traces and proposed synthetic generation of user accesses.[21] He observed that users access files at independently variable rates but in a rather precise order. Basically, they tend to access files that have been recently accessed in the working set. Heuristics for file migration were proposed and were verified by simulations.

Current models are based on the user-file relationship and on the assumption that access rates can be predicted or collected accurately in real time. Future studies should concentrate on the characterization of database behavior and modeling of systems with long access delays, in which the collection of accurate access rates is difficult. A model has been investigated to determine the complexity of migration detection. The NP-hardness of the problem makes enumerative algorithms impractical for real time applications. Furthermore, the access characteristics are dynamic and unpredictable and, therefore, cannot be used by the same dynamic programming that precomputes the migration sequence. A polynomial time heuristic proves to be very efficient for coping with the transient nature of accesses.

Assuming that the access rates are set beforehand, determining when to migrate multiple copies of a single file in the time interval $[0,t]$ to minimize the cost is NP-hard. This fact can be proved by showing that the corresponding decision problem—whether or not there is a migration sequence such that the total operating cost equals B— is reducible from the knapsack decision problem.* A special form of the problem in which migrations can be initiated at discrete times is used to determine the NP-hardness of the general problem.

This knapsack decision problem is reducible to the above decision problem. Given an instance of the knapsack problem with inputs $a_1, a_2, \ldots, a_n, A$, we can construct in polonimial time an instance of the migration problem by selecting the parameters as follows:

Let

$$x_i = \begin{array}{l} 0 \text{ (no migration is initiated at } t_i) \\ 1 \text{ (migration is initiated at } t_i) \end{array}$$

a_i = the number of file movements at t_i (assuming that each file movement incurs a unit cost).

$A = B$ (the total migration cost).

There are no other costs associated with the operation of the system.

The knapsack decision problem is, therefore, reducible to selecting the migration points. Since the knapsack problem is NP-complete, the file migration problem is also NP-hard, as are more general forms of the file migration problems. It is clear that, even when the access rates are known, exhaustive enumeration, such as in Levin's approach,[12] is necessary to determine the optimal migration sequence.

In general, specific access rates are rarely constant, although the average access rate over a relatively long interval is usually predictable. When there is a transient increase in the access rate at a node without a copy, it may be desirable to allow a copy of the file to migrate there,

*The knapsack decision problem has been shown to be NP-complete.[5] In this problem, a set of integers $a_1, a_2, \ldots, a_n$, and A are given. It is necessary to find a set $\{x_i: x_i \in \{0,1\}, i=1, \ldots, n\}$ such that $\sum a_i x_i = A$.

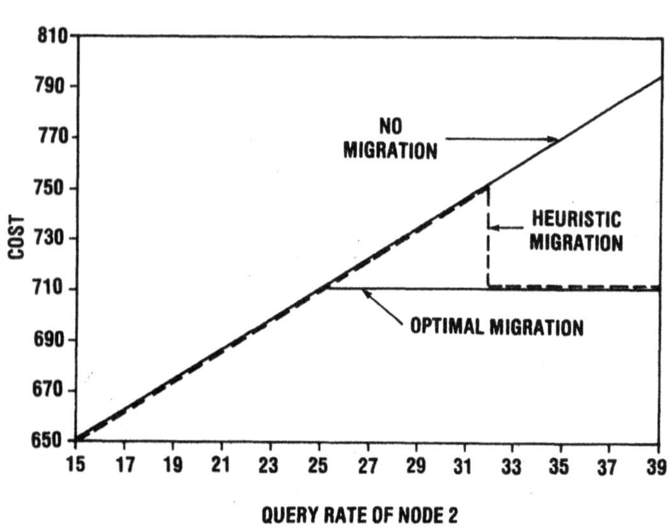

Figure 5. An illustration of heuristic migration detection using Casey's five-node example (only query rate of node 2 is changing)

then eliminate it when the accesses cease. Experience shows

- Access rates are not predictable in a short time interval, and there may be transient variations. It is difficult to extrapolate trends from past behavior.
- Communication overhead and the transient nature of accesses make it difficult to collect changes in access rates to a central computer in real time and to determine the optimal migration sequence. It is best for each node to determine in a distributed fashion whether or not to permit migration.
- The file allocation algorithm (optimal or heuristic) is time-consuming when executed locally each time the access rate changes. A simpler criterion should be used by each node to determine whether migration is needed.

These observations suggest a simple heuristic that permits limited migration in the locality of node j and determines when migration should be carried out. Let $d_{j,k}$ be the cost per unit size of query from j to k, I^f be the index set of nodes with a copy of file f, and λ^f_j be the query load originating at node j for file f per unit time. Suppose k is a node in the locality of j containing a copy of file f, such that

$$d_{j,k} = \min_{l \in I^f} d_{j,l} \text{ and}$$

$$J^f_k = \{x \mid d_{x,k} = \min_{l \in I^f} d_{x,l}\} \text{ with ties broken accordingly.}$$

J^f_k is the set of nodes in the locality of j which also accesses the copy of file f at node k. Note that

$$j, k \in J^f_k.$$

Suppose each node initiates migrations for the neighboring nodes based on the local change in access rates. When λ^f_j is changed to $\lambda^f_j{}'$ and the access rates of other nodes remain constant, the copy at node k is allowed to migrate to any of the remaining $|J^f_k| - 1$ nodes; or the copy at node k is eliminated, and all the nodes in J^f_k will access other copies in the system. Whenever migration is necessary, the static file allocation algorithm is called to find the optimal allocations. This detection procedure requires $|J^f_k| + 1$ evaluations of the cost function and is relatively simple even with delay and availability constraints.

As an illustration, the detection procedure can be applied on Casey's five-node example, where there is one file and where index f is dropped. As evaluated before, the optimal cost is 705 with allocations at nodes 1, 4 and 5. The copy at node 1 is shared between nodes 1 and 2, that is

$$J_1 = \{1,2\}$$

Figure 5 shows a plot of the cost function when λ_2 is increasing, and the cost for migrating the copy from node 1 to node 2 is negligible. The algorithm detects that migration should be initiated at $\lambda_2 = 32.05$. At this point, the static file allocation algorithm is called to find that the optimal allocations are at nodes 3, 4, and 5, but for the system to operate optimally, migrations should be initiated when λ_2 reaches 25.05.

The advantage of the above scheme is that migration is not initiated until after it is first needed to avoid transient increase in the access rate. Moreover, the detection procedure is relatively simple to execute in real time. But if the access rate does not reach a threshold, migration will not be initiated and the system will be operating suboptimally. A more accurate estimation algorithm may have to be used.

File migration requires that access rates be assessed in real time at each node, which may be difficult for queries that have not been executed. The assessment can be made by estimating the access rate from the average access rate in a previous time window. The size of the window is application-dependent, but should not be so large that transients are filtered out. The estimated access rate should be transmitted regularly to other nodes.

Special file migration detection

Although the previous section shows that the detection problem for file migration is NP-hard, some special cases of the problem can be solved in polynomial time. The Engineering Computer Network at Purdue University, provides the capability of virtual terminal access. It allows a user to connect directly to a remote host while the terminal acts as though it were connected physically to the remote host. Basically, the local host relays information between the user and the remote host without interpreting the information. Many users can share the link and access remote files through the Unix high-level operating system.

In a virtual terminal access approach, the processes that access remote files are executed on the remote host. A user editing a remote file actually communicates with an alternative is to edit on the local host and communicate over the network with the remote file. This approach is rarely effective, however, because a large part ciate over the network with the remote file. This approach is rarely effective, however, because a large part of the file may have to be searched in executing an editor command. The last alternative migrates the file to the local host, edits locally, and writes the file back at the end of the session. These three techniques are illustrated in Figure 6.

Using the first or the third approach, we can determine precisely when migration should be initiated. Let x be the amount of information transferred between a user and the editor on a remote file. It includes requests sent and the results returned. $G(x)$ is the distribution function of x and

$$\bar{x}=\int_0^\infty x\,[dG(x)]$$

is the mean of x.

Let S be the size of the remote file. We want to find a threshold T such that, whenever x exceeds T, the file should be migrated to the local host for editing.

The information transfer is

$$\int_0^T x\,[dG(x)]+\int_T^\infty 2S\,[dG(x)]$$

It assumes that the file size is unchanged at the end of the editing session. To find the value of T such that the amount of information transfer is minimal, we can rewrite the amount as

$$\bar{x}+\int_T^\infty (2S-x)\,[dG(x)]$$

We note that the integral is minimum when we start the integration at $T=2S$. In this case, the integrand is always negative and the minimum of the integral is obtained.

For this example, the detection of migration is simple and unique. At the beginning of the editing session, if $x>2S$, the file should be migrated immediately to the local host; otherwise, remote editing should be done. Of course, the value of x is unknown until the editing session is completed. In this case, an estimated x, such as $\bar{x}$, will be used.

Besides the editor process, this migration detection is applicable to other processes in the system. For instance, if the overhead of remote execution is greater than the overhead of migration and rewriting, migration is beneficial. Still the workload of the local and remote computers cannot be overlooked, and if the local computer is seriously overloaded, it may be advisable to execute the processes remotely.

File migration is more difficult to solve than the file allocation problem mainly because of the dynamic

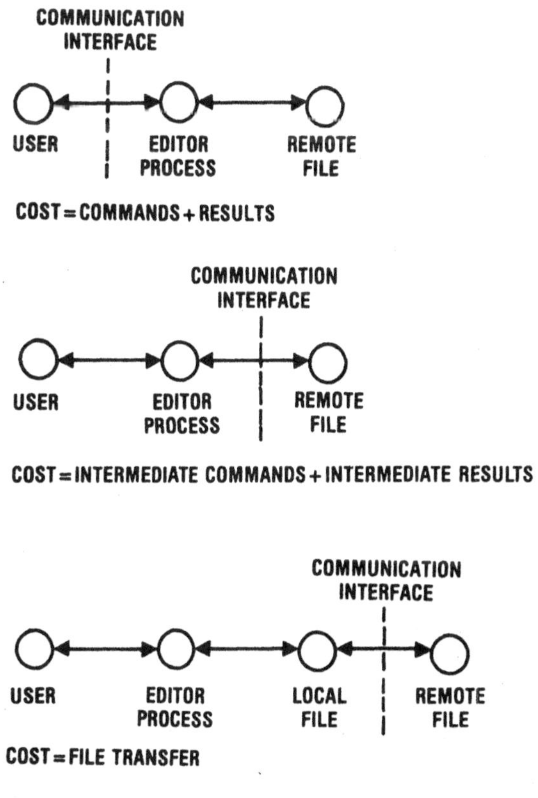

Figure 6. Three techniques of editing a remote file.

nature of accesses and the infeasibility of collecting accurate information in real time. Heuristics seem to be appropriate for most applications, but adjusting parameters for these heuristics is application-dependent and must be verified by experiments. The important feature of a real-time file migration algorithm is to detect when migrations should be carried out. The detection problem is NP-hard, and a heuristic should determine the time for migration. Long-term prediction of the access rates may be feasible, but will not contribute to the optimal system performance. Current research is in a combination of file placement, query processing, file partitioning, and network design problems. Most studies make very simple assumptions about the other problems in order to make the file placement problem solvable. The future trend lies in the relaxation of these assumptions while keeping the file placement problem mathematically tractable. ■

Acknowledgments

This research was partially supported by National Science Foundation grant ECS81-05968 and by CIDMAC, a research unit sponsored by Purdue University, Cincinnati Milicron Corporation, Control Data Corporation, Cummins Engine Company, Ransburg Corporation, and TRW.

References

1. S. Ceri, and S. B. Navathe, " A Methodology for the Distribution Design of Databases," *Proc. Compcon 83,* Feb. 1983, pp. 426-431.
2. W. W. Chu, "Multiple File Allocation in a Multiple Computer System," *IEEE Trans. Computers,* Vol. C-18, No. 10, Oct. 1969, pp. 885-889.
3. K. P. Eswaran, "Placement of Records in a File and File Allocation in a Computer Network," *Information Processing 74,* IFIPS, 1974, pp. 304-307.
4. C. V. Ramamoorthy and B. W. Wah, "The Isomorphism of Simple File Allocation," *IEEE Trans. Computers,* Vol. C-32, No. 3, Mar. 1983, pp. 221-232.
5. M. R. Garey and D. S. Johnson, *Computers and Intractability: A Guide to the Theory of NP-Completeness,* W. H. Freeman and Company, 1979.
6. M. A. Efroymson and T. C. Ray, "A Branch and Bound Algorithm for Plant Location," *Operations Research,* May-June 1966, pp. 361-368.
7. A. A. Keuhn and M. J. Hamburger, "A Heuristic Program for Locating Warehouses," *Management Science,* Vol. 9, No. 4, July 1963, pp. 643-666.
8. R. G. Casey, "Allocation of Copies of a File in an Information Network," *SJCC,* 1972, pp. 617-625.
9. E. G. Coffman, Jr., et al, "Optimization of the Number of Copies in a Distributed Database," *IEEE Trans. Software Engineering,* Vol. SE-7, No. 1, Jan. 1981, pp. 78-84.
10. V. Whitney, "A Study of Optimal File-Site Assignment and Communication Network Configuration in Remote-Access Computer-Message-Processing and Communication Systems," PhD thesis, Univ. of Michigan, 1970.
11. S. P. Ghosh, "Distributing a Database with Logical Associations on a Computer Network for Parallel Searching," *IEEE Trans. Software Engineering,* Vol. SE-2, No. 2, June 1976, pp. 106-113.
12. H. L. Morgan and K. D. Levin, "Optimal Program and Data Locations in Computer Networks," *Comm. ACM,* Vol. 20, No. 5, May 1977, pp. 315-322.
13. M. E. S. Loomis and G. J. Popek, "A Model for Data Base Distribution," *Computer Networks: Trends and Applications,* 1976, IEEE Press, New York, pp. 162-169.
14. H. S. Stone, "Multi-processor Scheduling with the Aid of Network Flows," *IEEE Trans. Software Engineering,* Vol. SE-3, No. 1, Jan. 1977, pp. 85-93.
15. S. Mahmoud and J. S. Riordon, "Optimal Allocation of Resources in Distributed Information Networks," *ACM Trans. DataBase Systems,* Vol. 1, No. 1, Mar. 1976, pp. 66-78.
16. K. B. Irani, and N. G. Khabbaz, "A Methodology for the Design of Communication Networks and the Distribution of Data in Distributed Supercomputer Systems," *IEEE Trans. Computers,* Vol. C-31, No. 5, May 1982, pp. 419-434.
17. L. J. Laning and M. S. Leonard, "File Allocation in a Distributed Computer Communication Network," *IEEE Trans. Computers,* Vol. C-32, No. 3, Mar. 1983, pp. 232-244.
18. P. P. S. Chen and J. Akoka, "Optimal Design of Distributed Information Systems," *IEEE Trans. Computers,* Vol. C-29, No. 12, Dec. 1980, pp. 1068-1080.
19. P. M. G., Apers, "Centralized or Decentralized Data Allocation," *Distributed Data Sharing Systems,* R. P. van de Riet and W. Litwin, eds., North-Holland, New York, 1982.
20. A. Segall, "Dynamic File Assignment in the Computer Network," part 1, *IEEE Trans. Automatic Control,* Vol. AC-24, no. 5, Oct. 1979.
21. J. M. Porcar, "File Migration in Distributed Computer Systems," PhD thesis, Univ. of California, Berkeley, 1982.

Benjamin W. Wah is an assistant professor of electrical engineering at Purdue University. He received his BS and MS degrees in electrical engineering and computer science from Columbia University in 1974 and 1975, and MS degree in computer science and the PhD degree in engineering from the University of California at Berkeley in 1976 and 1979, respectively. His current research interests include parallel computer architecture, distributed computer systems, and theory of computing.

Wah's address is, School of Electrical Engineering, Purdue University, West Lafayette, IN 47907.

Optimal File Allocation in a Multiple Computer System

WESLEY W. CHU, MEMBER, IEEE

Abstract—A model is developed for allocating information files required in common by several computers. The model considers storage cost, transmission cost, file lengths, and request rates, as well as updating rates of files, the maximum allowable expected access times to files at each computer, and the storage capacity of each computer. The criterion of optimality is minimal overall operating costs (storage and transmission). The model is formulated into a nonlinear integer zero-one programming problem, which may be reduced to a linear zero-one programming problem. A simple example is given to illustrate the model.

Index Terms—Computer communication, linear integer programming, multicomputer information system, multiprocessor, nonlinear integer programming, optimal file allocation.

Introduction

IN THE AUTOMATION of large information systems, a major portion of the planning is concerned with storing large quantities of information in a computer system. This requires study of information storage, modification, and transmission. Examples of such efforts are found in business, medical, library, and management information systems. These systems, which may consist of several geographically separated divisions (subsystems), need to process information files in common.

It is apparent that when a given information file is required in common by several computers, it may be stored in at least one of them and accessed by the others when needed. The overall operating cost related to the files is considered to consist of transmission and storage costs. The problem is the following. Given a number of computers that process common information files, how can one allocate the files so that the allocation yields minimum overall operating costs subject to the following constraints: 1) the expected time to access each file is less than a given bound, 2) the amount of storage needed at each computer does not exceed the available storage capacity.

The Model

The file allocation problem can be formulated as an integer (0 or 1) programming model.

Let X_{ij} indicate that the jth file is stored in the ith computer:

$$X_{ij} = \begin{cases} 1 & j\text{th file stored in the } i\text{th computer} \\ 0 & \text{otherwise} \end{cases} \tag{1}$$

where

$i = 1, 2, \cdots, n$

$j = 1, 2, \cdots, m$

n = total number of computers in the multicomputer system

m = total number of distinct files in the multicomputer system.

For storing r_j redundant copies of the jth in the information system, we have

$$\sum_i X_{ij} = r_j \qquad \text{for } 1 \le j \le m. \tag{2}$$

To assure that the storage capacity of each computer is not exceeded, we have

$$\sum_j X_{ij} L_j \le b_i \qquad \text{for } 1 \le i \le n \tag{3}$$

where

L_j = length of the jth file,

b_i = available memory size of the ith computer.

The expected time for the ith computer to retrieve the jth file from the kth computer (from initiation of request till start of reception) is denoted as a_{ijk}. The maximum allowable retrieval time of the jth file to the ith computer is T_{ij}. We required that a_{ijk} be less than T_{ij}, i.e.,

$$(1 - X_{ij}) X_{kj} a_{ijk} \le T_{ij} \qquad \text{for } i \ne k, \qquad 1 \le j \le m. \tag{4}$$

When $r_j = 1$ for all j, then from (2) we know that $X_{ij} X_{kj} = 0$ for $i \ne k$. Thus (4) reduces to

$$X_{kj} a_{ijk} \le T_{ij} \qquad \text{for } i \ne k, \qquad 1 \le j \le m. \tag{5}$$

Now, a_{ijk} is equal to the sum of the expected queuing delay at the ith computer for the channel to the kth computer[1] $w_{ik}^{(1)}$, the expected queuing delay at the kth computer for the channel to the ith computer $w_{ki}^{(2)}$, and the expected computer access time to the jth file t_{kj}. In most cases, the quantity t_{kj} is much smaller than $w_{ik} = w_{ik}^{(1)} + w_{ki}^{(2)}$ and can be neglected. Hence,

$$a_{ijk} \doteq w_{ik}. \tag{6}$$

[1] The number in the superscripts of $w_{ik}^{(\cdot)}$ and $w_{ki}^{(\cdot)}$ denotes the priority class of the messages that are transmitted between the ith and kth computers, which will be discussed shortly.

Manuscript received July 12, 1968; revised May 29, 1969. This is a generalized version of the paper entitled "Optimal file allocation in a multicomputer information system," presented at the IFIP Congress 68, Edinburgh, Scotland, August 5–10, 1968.

The author was with Bell Telephone Laboratories, Inc., Holmdel N. J. He is now with the Computer Science Department, University of the City of Los Angeles, Los Angeles, Calif.

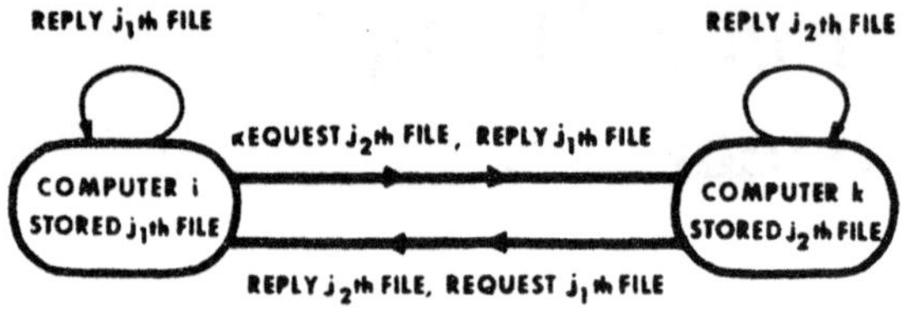

Fig. 1. Transmission paths between each pair of computers.

Next we will discuss the mechanism involved in the queuing delay. Each pair of computers is assumed to be able to transmit information in both directions simultaneously. This is known as single-channel full-duplex operation. Further, the files can be accessed by the local and remote computers at the same time. One pair of transmission paths links each pair of computers; one of these paths carries *requests* for the files from the ith computer to the kth computer, and *reply* messages (files) from the ith computer to the kth computer, whereas the other path carries *requests* for files from the kth computer to the ith computer, and *reply* messages from kth to the ith computer (Fig. 1). In most cases, the request message is much shorter than the reply message. Therefore, we shall assign a higher priority to request messages than to reply messages. Messages of the same priority are served in the order of their arrival. Assume, for example, a reply message is being transmitted on a particular transmission path at the time a new request is initiated. The request will interrupt the current reply and the computer will transmit the request first. After finishing transmission of that new request, the computer resumes transmitting the previous reply. Such preemptive-resume priority servicing faciltates optimization, since the queuing delay will be minimum if the shortest messages are serviced first [1], [2]. Recalling that the requested message length is much shorter than that of the reply message, the delay due to the request message can be neglected.[2] Under these conditions, the queuing system can be viewed as a single server queue with constant service time.

In many cases, it is reasonable to model the file accessing process as a Poisson process. Then the rate of requests from the ith computer to the kth computer (arrival rate) λ_{ik} is the sum of the rates of request of those files not stored in the ith computer but stored in the kth computer. The requested file length may be less than the entire storage file length and is defined as the length of each transaction; that is, the length of each transaction of the jth file l_j should be less or equal to the entire jth file length L_j. The average time required to transmit the reply from the kth computer to the jth computer $1/\mu_{ik}$ (i.e., service time) is dependent on l_j and λ_{ik}. Clearly, both λ_{ik} and $1/\mu_{ik}$ depend on the file allocation, yet the allocation is unknown in advance. Hence, we shall express λ_{ik} and $1/\mu_{ik}$ in terms of the X_{ij}'s:

$$\lambda_{ik} = \sum_j u_{ij}(1 - X_{ij})X_{kj} \tag{7}$$

where

u_{ij} = the request rate[3] of the entire or part of the jth file at the ith computer per unit time.

The average time required to transmit a reply message from the kth to the ith computer via a line with transmission rate R is

$$1/\mu_{ik} = \frac{1}{\lambda_{ik}} \sum \frac{1}{\mu_j} u_{ij}(1 - X_{ij})X_{kj} \tag{8}$$

where

$1/\mu_j = l_j/R$ = required time to transmit each transaction of the jth file.

Equation (8) states that $1/\mu_{ik}$ is equal to the time required for the kth computer to reply all the messages requested from the ith computer divided by the total number of requests initiated from the ith computer to the kth computer. Since the l_j's and R are constants, μ_j and μ_{ik} are also constants.

The traffic intensity from the kth to the ith computer ρ_{ik} measures the degree of congestion of the line that provides the transmission path between the kth and ith computer, or the fraction of time that the line is busy. It is defined as

$$\rho_{ik} = \lambda_{ik}/\mu_{ik} = \sum_j \frac{1}{\mu_j} u_{ij}(1 - X_{ij})X_{kj}. \tag{9}$$

Since physically it is impossible for the transmission line to be 100 percent busy, the traffic intensity is less than unity, i.e., $\rho_{ik} < 1$.

When only a single copy of the file is stored in the information system, then $X_{ij}X_{kj} = 0$ for $i \neq k$. Hence

$$\lambda_{ik} = \sum_j u_{ij}X_{kj} \qquad \text{for } i \neq k \tag{10}$$

and

$$1/\mu_{ik} = \frac{1}{\lambda_{ik}} \sum_j u_{ij} \frac{1}{\mu_j} X_{kj} \qquad \text{for } i \neq k \tag{11}$$

when all the $\mu_j = \mu$; then (11) reduces to

$$1/\mu_{ik} = 1/\mu. \tag{12}$$

The average waiting time [1], [2] from the initiation of a request at the ith computer to the receipt of the requested message from the kth computer, with the above assumptions (single server queue with Poisson arrivals and constant service time), is

[2] Preemptive priority servicing permits the assumption that $w_{ik} \doteq w_{ki}^{(2)}$. Note that the file retrieval time constraint as shown in (4) also applies to the nonpremptive priority case, but a more complex expression would be required for w_{ik} since $w_{ik}^{(1)}$ can no longer be neglected.

[3] In general, the request rate may be time dependent. In the analysis here, we are concerned with the request rate of the busy period.

$$w_{ik} \doteq w_{ki}^{(2)} = \frac{1}{\mu_{ik}} \frac{\rho_{ik}}{2(1 - \rho_{ik})} \qquad \text{for } i \neq k \tag{13}$$

where $1/\mu_{ik}$ and ρ_{ik} are functions of X_{ij}'s as given by (8) and (9). The variance and probability distribution of w_{ik} for a specific allocation can be computed from its ρ_{ik} and μ_{ik} [1], [2].

Substituting (13) into (6) and (4), we have

$$(1 - X_{ij})X_{kj}\frac{1}{\mu_{ik}} \frac{\rho_{ik}}{2(1 - \rho_{ik})} \leq T_{ij},$$

which can be rearranged into the form

$$(1 - X_{ij})X_{kj}\lambda_{ik} - 2\mu_{ik}(\mu_{ik} - \lambda_{ik})T_{ij} \leq 0. \tag{14}$$

For the special case that $\mu_{ik} = \mu$ and $r_j = 1$, (14) reduces to

$$\sum_{\substack{j_1 \\ j \neq j_1}} u_{ij}X_{kj_1}X_{kj} + 2T_{ij}\mu \sum_{j_1} u_{ij_1}X_{kj_1} + u_{ij}X_{kj} - 2\mu^2 T_{ij} \leq 0. \tag{15}$$

Finally, we shall express the operating cost (objective function) in terms of the allocation (X_{ij}'s). Suppose we know the storage cost of the jth file per unit length and unit time at the ith computer C_{ij}, the transmission cost from the kth computer to the ith computer per unit time C_{ik}', the request rate for the entire or part of the jth file at the ith computer per unit time u_{ij}, the frequency of modification of the jth file at the ith computer after each transaction P_{ij}, the length of each transaction for the jth file l_j, and the number of redundant copies of the jth file stored in the system r_j. Then the overall operating cost per unit time C for processing m distinct files required in common by n computers is

$$C = \underbrace{\sum_{i,j} C_{ij}L_jX_{ij}}_{\text{storage cost}} + \underbrace{\sum_{i,j,k} \frac{1}{r_j} C_{ik}'l_ju_{ij}X_{kj}(1 - X_{ij}) + \sum_{i,j,k} C_{ik}'l_ju_{ij}X_{kj}P_{ij}}_{\text{transmission cost}},$$

which can be rearranged into the form

$$= \sum_{i,j} D_{ij}X_{ij} - \sum_{i,j,k} E_{ijk}X_{kj}X_{ij} \quad \text{where} \quad D_{ij} > 0, \quad E_{ijk} > 0 \tag{16}$$

when $r_j = 1$, $1 \leq j \leq m$; then $X_{kj}X_{ij} = 0$ for $k \neq i$, and $C_{ii}' = 0$. Under this case, (16) reduces to

$$C = \sum_{i,j} D_{ii}X_{ij}. \tag{17}$$

We want to minimize (16) subject to storage and access time requirements constraints given in (1), (2), (3), and (14). As X_{ij}'s take on value zero or one, the allocation problem becomes solving a nonlinear zero-one programming problem. In the next section, we shall introduce a technique to reduce the nonlinear zero-one equations to the linear zero-one equations. With this technique, the allocation problem can be then solved by standard linear zero-one programming techniques [3], [4].

Reduction of Zero–One Nonlinear Programming Problems to Zero–One Linear Programming Problems[4]

Because nonlinear programming problems are so complex, we are able to obtain a global optimal solution only for special cases (e.g., convexity). Therefore, it is desirable to reduce the nonlinear zero-one programming problems to the linear zero-one programming problems. We shall now show such a reduction, which is derived from the integer (0 or 1) property.

Suppose we want to minimize an arbitrary cost function (which need not be convex)

$$C = \min_X F(X_1, X_2, \cdots, X_k) \tag{18}$$

subject to a set of nonconvex constraint equations

$$G_i(X_1, X_2, \cdots, X_k) \leq B_i \qquad i = 1, 2, \cdots, N \tag{19}$$

where the X_i's are zero-one variables, F and G_i are polynomials of the X_i's with constant coefficients, and B_i is a constant. Clearly, $X_i^q = X_i$ (q = positive integer). Let the coefficient of the product terms in (18) or (19), $X_iX_j, \cdots, X_uX_v$, be denoted as $C_{ij\cdots uv}$.

To reduce the above nonlinear zero-one problem to a linear zero-one problem, first we consider the objective function (18). Let us define

$$X_{ij\cdots uv} = \underbrace{X_iX_j \cdots X_uX_v}_{q} \qquad q = 2, \cdots, Q \tag{20}$$

which takes value zero or one where Q is the highest degree of nonlinearity. We then represent each nonlinear term in (18) by terms of the form (20) and then examine its coefficient. If the coefficient of the nonlinear term is positive, we introduce the following constraint equation:

$$\underbrace{X_i + X_j \cdots + X_u + X_v}_{q} - q + 1 \leq X_{ij\cdots uv}. \tag{21}$$

[4] A similar but less general result has also been obtained independently by Watters [5].

If the coefficient of the nonlinear term is negative, we introduce the following constraint equation:

$$\underbrace{X_i + X_j + \cdots + X_u + X_v}_{q} \geq qX_{ij\ldots uv}. \tag{22}$$

If all the X's in left side of (21) have value one, then $X_{ij\ldots uv}=1$. If one or more of the X's have value zero, then $X_{ij\ldots uv}$ may be either zero or one, but the coefficient of $X_{ij\ldots uv}$ in (18), $C_{ij\ldots uv}$, is positive. Thus minimizing (18) under X assures that $X_{ij\ldots uv}=0$. If we substitute (20) for each nonlinear term in (18) that has positive coefficient and introduce the additional constraint (21), then the X's in the transformed linear equations take on the same values as the original ones. Similarly, if one or more of the X's in (20) have value zero, then $X_{ij\ldots uv}=0$. If all the X's have value one, then $X_{ij\ldots uv}$ may either be zero or one, but the coefficient of $X_{ij\ldots uv}$ in (18), $C_{ij\ldots uv}$, is negative. Thus minimizing (18) under X assures that $X_{ijkl\ldots uv}=1$. If we substitute (20) for each nonlinear term in (18) that has negative coefficient and introduce the additional constraint (22), then the X's in the transformed linear equations take on the same values as the original ones. Thus, we have linearized the objective function (18).

To linearize the constraint equations, we represent the nonlinear terms in (19) by (20) and introduce its corresponding *two* additional constraint equations (21) and (22). If one or more of the X's in (20) have value zero, then $X_{ij\ldots uv}=0$; this condition is also satisfied by (21) and (22). If all the X_{ij}'s have value one in (20), then $X_{ij\ldots uv}$ is one. Similarly, from (21) $X_{ij\ldots uv}$ may be either zero or one, but from (22) $X_{ij\ldots uv}$ is one. Thus (21) and (22) assure that $X_{ij\ldots uv}=1$. Substituting (20) and introducing the additional constraint (21) and (22) for each nonlinear term in (19) satisfy all the relationships of X's. Thus, we have also linearized the nonlinear constraints equations.

With this reduction technique,[5] nonlinear zero-one programming problems may be transformed into solution of linear zero-one programming problems. Using available linear integer programming techniques [3], [4], we can obtain the global optimal solutions.

Linearization of the Objective Function and Access Time Constants

To apply the above technique to linearize the objective function (16), we let $X_{ij}X_{kj}=X_{ijkj}$. Since the coefficients of X_{ijkj} in (16) are negative, for each X_{ijkj}, we introduce the additional constraint equation

[5] This reduction technique can be easily extended to the case when the X_i's in (18) or (19) are real numbers. In this case, we shall express each X_i in terms of binary variables X_{ij}'s as follows:

$$X_i = \sum_{l=1}^{\alpha_i+\beta_i} (X_{il})2^{\alpha_i-l}$$

where α_i is chosen large enough for 2^{α_i-1} to be an upper bound on the value of X_i, while β_i is chosen large enough for $2^{-\beta_i}$ to be the maximum allowable accuracy tolerance on the value of X_i. Thus (18) or (19) is reduced from a nonlinear equation to a nonlinear zero–one equation.

$$X_{ij} + X_{kj} \geq 2X_{ijkj}. \tag{23}$$

Next, we shall linearize the constraint equation (15). We let $X_{kj_1}X_{kj}=X_{kj_1kj}$. For each X_{kj_1kj}, we introduce two additional constraint equations

$$\begin{cases} X_{kj_1} + X_{kj} \geq 2X_{kj_1kj} \\ X_{kj_1} + X_{kj} - 1 \leq X_{kj_1kj} \end{cases} \quad \text{for } j \neq j_1. \tag{24}$$

In the same manner, we can linearize (14). Hence, solution to the optimal file allocation problem is reduced to: minimize (16) subject to (1), (2), (3), (14) or (15), (20), (23), and (24) which is a linear zero–one programming problem.

File Allocation in a Multiprocessor

Let us consider a multiprocessor with virtual memory system that operates in a paging environment. One of the important problems in such a system is how to allocate files to various types of available storage systems such as thin films, cores, disks, drums, data cells, tapes, etc., so that the operating cost is minimum yet the access time requirements are satisfied for each file, and the storage limitation of each storage system is not exceeded. The model developed in this paper can be directly applied to this problem by letting the distances between computers equal to zero. Clearly, under this condition, a multiple computer system becomes a multiprocessor.

Example

Consider a specific computer communication system consisting of three computers that process five information files in common, as shown in Fig. 2. These computers are located about 20 miles from each other. The transmission facility between each pair of computers has a rate of $R=5\times10^3$ char/second. The cost of each such facility is \$1050 per month or \$$1.4\times10^{-7}$/char (based on 100 hours per week and 4.2 weeks per month). The first cost of storage is 35 cents per character or \$$5.8\times10^{-7}$/char second.[6] Table I gives the lengths of each file, file length for each transactions, the request rate of these files at each computer, the rate of modification of these files at each computer after each transaction, the available storage capacity of each computer, and the maximum allowable retrieval time of each file. Using the linearized model developed above and the Gomory cutting technique [3], [4] for solving the integer linear programming problem, the example was solved on the IBM 360/65. Table II lists the optimal allocation for the case of no redundant files. The computation time required for this example is about 25 seconds.

Some characteristics of the optimum allocation are worthy of note. File 4 is stored in computer 2 as it is only used by that computer. File 1 has highest request

[6] The calculation is based on 40 months of machine life operating at 100 hours per week and 4.2 weeks per month.

TABLE I

DATA OF EXAMPLE FOR FILE ALLOCATION

File j	L_j	l_j	P_j	Computer 1 u_{1j}	Computer 1 T_{1j}	Computer 2 u_{2j}	Computer 2 T_{2j}	Computer 3 u_{3j}	Computer 3 T_{3j}
1	100×10^3	500	0.5	5	30	2	10	0	0
2	10×10^3	500	0.5	0	0	2	30	5	1
3	10×10^3	500	0.5	3	10	0	0	4	1
4	10×10^3	500	0.5	0	0	4	0.1	0	0
5	100×10^3	500	0.5	1	1	1	1	5	1

P_j = the frequency of modification of the jth file after each transaction.
L_j = length of the jth file in characters.
l_j = file length (in characters) of each transaction for the jth file.
u_i = average hourly request rate of the entire or part of the jth file at the ith computer. Request arrivals are assumed to be Poisson distributed.
T_{ij} = maximum allowable average retrieval time in seconds for the jth file to the ith computer.
C_{ij} = (storage cost) = \$$0.58\times10^{-8}$/char second.
C_{ik}' = (transmission cost) = \$$1.4\times10^{-7}$/char.
b_i = (available storage capacity of the ith computer) = 110×10^3 char for i = 1, 2, 3.
$1/\mu = l/R$ (the time required to transmit the reply message) = 0.1 second.

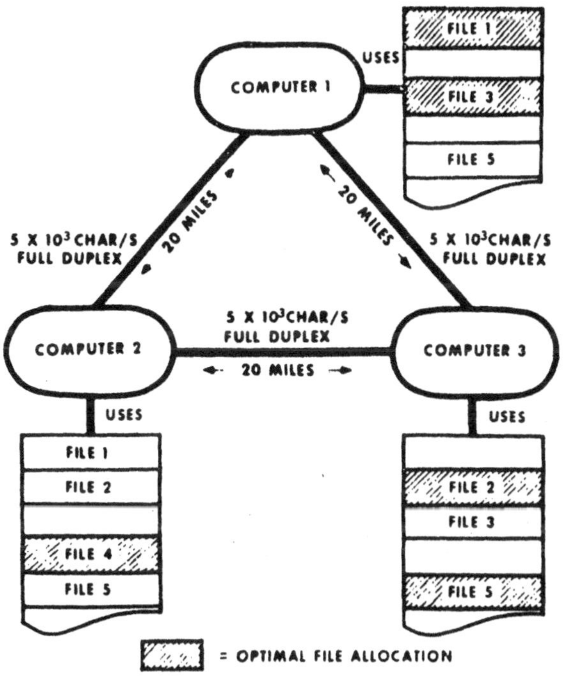

Fig. 2. A specific multiple computer system.

rate at computer 1; to minimize the transmission cost, it is stored in computer 1. For the same reason, Files 2 and 5 are stored in computer 3. Although File 3 has a high request rate at computer 3, the available storage size of computer 3 (110×10^3 char) forced File 3 to be stored in computer 1. The overall operation cost under the optimal allocation is \$3620 per month. If each file is stored at the computer where it is used, the total operating cost under such arrangement is \$6670 per month. The higher operating cost is due to the extra storage cost and the file updating cost.

CONCLUSION

The file allocation problem can be formulated into a nonlinear zero–one programming problem. By adding additional constraint equations, these nonlinear terms

TABLE II

OPTIMAL FILE ALLOCATION FOR EXAMPLE

File j	X_{ij} Computer 1	Computer 2	Computer 3
1	1	0	0
2	0	0	1
3	1	0	0
4	0	1	0
5	0	0	1

in the objective and constraint equations can be reduced to linear equations. Thus, solution of the optimal allocation requires solving a linear zero–one programming problem. The model introduced in this paper provides a common denominator for analysis and comparison of various proposed information system configurations, a tool to study the sensitivity of various parameters and constraints to the operating cost, and a method for evaluating the growth potential of information systems. However, some related problems still require further studies, such as file reliability, privacy, file partition, etc. All these problems are important considerations for optimal file allocation in multicomputer information systems.

ACKNOWLEDGMENT

The author would like to thank E. Fuchs of Bell Telephone Laboratories for his stimulating discussions.

REFERENCES

[1] D. R. Cox and W. L. Smith, *Queues, Methnen's Statistical Monographs.* London, England: Spottiswoode, Ballantyne, and Co., 1961, pp. 50–59.
[2] T. L. Saaty, *Elements of Queuing Theory.* New York: McGraw-Hill, 1961, pp. 153–161.
[3] R. Gomory, "All-integer integer programming algorithm," *Industrial Scheduling*, Muth and Thompson, Eds. Englewood Cliffs, N. J.: Prentice-Hall, 1963, pp. 195–206.
[4] J. Haldi and L. M. Isaacson, "Linear integer programming," Graduate School of Business, Stanford University, Stanford, Calif., working paper 45, December 1964.
[5] L. J. Watters, "Reduction of integer polynomial programming problems to zero–one linear programming problems," *Operations Res.*, vol. 15, pp. 1171–1174, November–December 1967.

Vertical Partitioning Algorithms for Database Design

SHAMKANT NAVATHE, STEFANO CERI, GIO WIEDERHOLD, AND JINGLIE DOU
Stanford University

This paper addresses the vertical partitioning of a set of logical records or a relation into fragments. The rationale behind vertical partitioning is to produce fragments, groups of attribute columns, that "closely match" the requirements of transactions.

Vertical partitioning is applied in three contexts: a database stored on devices of a single type, a database stored in different memory levels, and a distributed database. In a two-level memory hierarchy, most transactions should be processed using the fragments in primary memory. In distributed databases, fragment allocation should maximize the amount of local transaction processing.

Fragments may be nonoverlapping or overlapping. A two-phase approach for the determination of fragments is proposed; in the first phase, the design is driven by empirical objective functions which do not require specific cost information. The second phase performs cost optimization by incorporating the knowledge of a specific application environment. The algorithms presented in this paper have been implemented, and examples of their actual use are shown.

1. INTRODUCTION

Partitioning in database design is the process of assigning a logical object (relation) from the logical schema of the database to several physical objects (files) in a stored database. *Vertical partitioning* subdivides attributes into groups and assigns each group to a physical object. *Horizontal partitioning* subdivides object instances (tuples) into groups, all having the same attributes of the original object. We refer to the physical objects that are a result of vertical or horizontal partitioning as *horizontal* or *vertical fragments*.

This paper considers the vertical partitioning problem. We use the term *vertical partitioning* somewhat loosely, in the sense that we allow fragments to overlap, so that partitions are not necessarily disjoint. The term *clusters* has been used in the literature (e.g., [11]) to refer to nondisjoint fragments; but for the sake of convenience we shall use the term *partitioning* to refer to both the disjoint and nondisjoint cases.

This work was performed at Stanford University as part of the Knowledge Base Management Systems Project, supported by the Defense Advanced Research Projects Agency contract N39-80-G-0132. S. Ceri's work was supported in part by a grant from the Italian National Research Council.
Authors' addresses: S. Navathe and S. Ceri, Dipartimento di Elettronica, Politecnico di Milano, Milan, Italy; G. Wiederhold, Dept. of Computer Science, Stanford University, Stanford, CA 94305; J. Dou, Dept. of Computer and Information Sciences, University of Florida, Gainesville, FL 32611.

ACM Transactions on Database Systems, Vol. 9, No. 4, December 1984. Pages 680–710.

Vertical partitioning is used during the design of a database to improve the performance of transactions: fragments consist of smaller records, and therefore fewer pages in secondary memory are accessed to process a transaction. When allocating data to a memory hierarchy, vertical partitioning is used to store the attributes that are most heavily accessed in the fastest memory. In the design of a multiple-site distributed database, fragments are allocated, and possibly replicated, at the various sites.

Vertical fragments are ultimately stored in the database by using some physical file structure; the actual implementation of storage structures for fragments is not discussed in this paper.

In order to obtain improved performance, fragments must be "closely matched" to the requirements of the transactions. The ideal case occurs when each transaction "matches" a fragment, because the transaction has to access that fragment only. If certain sets of attributes are always processed together by transactions, the design process is trivial. But in real-life applications one rarely comes across such trivial examples; hence, for objects with tens of attributes, we need to develop a systematic approach to vertical partitioning. As pointed out in [11], an object with m attributes can be partitioned into $B(m)$ different ways, where $B(m)$ is the mth Bell number; for large m, $B(m)$ approaches m^m; for $m = 15$, it is $\approx 10^9$, for $m = 30$, it is $\approx 10^{23}$.

Not may previous attempts to solve this problem have been reported, and none of them has considered all the possible applications of vertical partitioning. The main contributions of our paper are in the following areas:

(i) We extend the work of Hoffer and Severance [13]. They defined an algorithm in which attributes of an object were permuted in such a way that attributes with "high affinity" were clustered together. Affinity among attributes expresses the extent to which they are used together in processing. Starting from the algorithm in [13], several algorithms are developed in this paper for determining the grouping of attributes into nonoverlapping or overlapping fragments.

(ii) We consider the application of partitioning to databases that use one level of memory or a memory hierarchy. We also consider the application of vertical partitioning to distributed databases by determining the allocation of fragments to different sites, allowing nonreplicated or replicated fragments. Thus, we apply vertical partitioning to a much more general environment in comparison to the previous work.

(iii) A unique feature of our approach is the two-step design of fragments. During the first step, vertical partitioning is governed by an empirical notion of partitioning, where one expects that the need for a transaction to visit multiple fragments should be minimized; this step does not require detailed cost factors. During the second step, the design of fragments can be further refined by incorporating estimated cost factors, which reflect the physical environment in which the fragments are eventually stored. Cost factors are based on "logical" performance measures; such measures are not tied to particular access methods or transaction processing strategies.

Our computational experience with the vertical partitioning algorithms has been very encouraging. In this paper we present examples of the partitioning of objects in various ways, using different algorithms under different application environments. Results are supported by intuitive reasoning, to the extent possible.

1.1 Problem Description

We refer to a logical record or a relation as an *object* to be partitioned; each object consists of a set of attributes. An object can be vertically partitioned by considering its projections onto different sets of attributes as new objects, called *fragments*.

A *binary vertical partitioning* (BVP) generates two fragments. A BVP is said to be *nonoverlapping* if the intersection of the two fragments is empty, otherwise it is said to be *overlapping*.

The following is a general statement of the *vertical partitioning problem* (VPP):

Database and Transaction Specification. A database consisting of a set of objects is given in terms of a schema definition. Each object has a set of attributes with given lengths. A set of transactions is defined a priori for the database; our assumption of knowing important transactions a priori is consistent with the common practice of distributed applications and with the notion of precompiled transactions of the R* Distributed Database System [24], or of transaction classes in SDD-1 [19]. The transaction specification relevant to the vertical partitioning of an object consists of the following information:

(i) the frequency (per unit time period) of occurrence of the transaction; when the same transaction can be issued at multiple sites in a distributed database, the frequency at each site is specified;
(ii) the subset of the attributes used for retrieval or update by the transaction;
(iii) the total number of instances of the object selected on the average by one occurrence of the transaction.

This information is typically available after the "logical design" phase of the overall database design activity (see [14, 22] and [23] for a discussion of the overall database design process).

Approach. To place the VPP problem, as defined in this paper, in proper perspective, one may refer to three kinds of decisions:

(i) logical decisions, concerning the structure and composition of the fragments of an object;
(ii) distribution and allocation decisions, concerning the placement of fragments at various storage devices or sites;
(iii) physical decisions, concerning the storage structure (file organization) and access methods for each fragment.

The use of the terms *logical* and *physical* above is only for convenience: it is difficult to argue where the exact boundary lies between these two types of decisions. This paper concentrates on the logical and distribution decisions, assuming that the physical decisions will be taken in a later phase of the design. This, however, does allow the designer to use some "a priori" knowledge about physical cost factors in performing the above two decisions.

Figure 1 shows the overall approach to the VPP problem in this paper. Vertical partitioning will be addressed in two phases:

(1) Empirical design of fragments based on the specified logical access frequencies of the transactions.

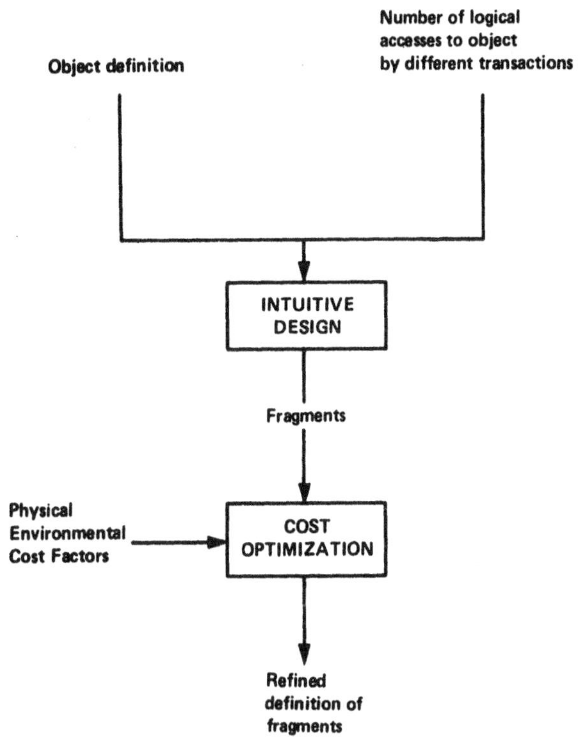

Fig. 1. An overall approach to solving the vertical partitioning problem (VPP).

(2) Design based on cost factors related to the physical environment; this produces a refinement of fragmentation and, if applicable, the allocation of fragments to multiple levels of a memory hierarchy or to multiple sites of a distributed database.

Phase 1 allows the designer to make "reasonable" decisions in the absence of detailed information about the cost factors; of course, phase 1 can be skipped if this cost information is available at the beginning of the design. The early determination of a "reasonable" fragmentation can be used for determining cost factors experimentally, which in turn allows us to refine the design in phase 2. Finally, in some cases, no adequate cost measures are available, and the first approach is the only feasible one.

In the design decisions of phase 1, we use the notion of a "logical access" to a record occurrence made by a transaction. This notion models the observation that in current database systems it is in general not possible to retrieve into main memory individual attributes, and, therefore, whenever a record occurrence is accessed, all attributes within it are accessed. After the fragments have been defined (and allocated), the physical decisions will be made so that the logical accesses of the most important transactions can be performed efficiently.

In the design decisions of phase 2, we use cost factors that do not depend on features of specific file or database system organizations. We realize that our model can be enhanced by using the specific information from a given DBMS, such as the available storage structures, file organizations, access methods, transaction processing strategies, and so on. But such a specific model can only be used for a particular environment. We address the problem in a general way, so that our method yields a general, yet reasonable, solution.

Identification of Occurrences Within Fragments. In an environment where a single object is fragmented and allocated to one or more sites, it is necessary that every object occurrence (tuple) in fragments be fully identified. This can be done in two ways:

(i) by replicating the primary key of the object in every fragment;
(ii) by using tuple identifiers (TID), that is, system controlled identifiers for each tuple of the original object, which are replicated into all the fragments.

If solution (i) is used, the attributes constituting the primary key are not considered by the following optimization procedure, and are simply prepended to each fragment after the optimization; if solution (ii) is used, then the attributes constituting the primary key are treated like any other attributes.

1.2 Previous Related Work

The previous work on vertical partitioning can be grouped into two major categories. In the first, an optimal solution of the problem is attempted, typically under restrictive assumptions; in the second, a heuristic approach is used. We are not aware of any systematic work on the vertical partitioning with overlapping fragments and of its application in the context of distributed databases.

Hoffer [12] developed a nonlinear, zero–one program for the solution of the vertical partitioning problem which minimizes a linear combination of storage, retrieval, and update costs, under capacity constraints assigned to each subfile. Babad [1] formulated the less restricted vertical partitioning problem for variable length attributes as a nonlinear, zero–one program. In his model, one subrecord is designated as the primary record, and all requests are addressed to that subrecord and "dispatched" to other subrecords later. It is revealing that the final example considered four attributes only, as the problem soon becomes unmanageable.

The simpler problem of partitioning a record between a fast, primary memory and a slow, secondary memory has been formulated by Eisner and Severance in [9]. The authors show the isomorphism of this problem with the mincut–max flow network problem, which can be solved by the standard Ford/Fulkerson algorithm. A disadvantage of the method is that the graph requires a number of nodes and edges proportional to the sum of all attributes, users, and individual attributes required by each user; this number can become very large in real-life problems. In a follow-up paper, March and Severance [16] extended the previous model to incorporate block factors for both primary and secondary memories.

Schkolnick [20] considered the problem of clustering records within an IMS-type hierarchical structure, and determined an efficient solution method whose complexity is linear in the number of nodes of the hierarchical tree.

Papers of the second category describe heuristic approaches to the attribute partitioning problem. We agree with Hammer and Niamir [11] that the general vertical partitioning problem is "heuristic in nature," and that optimal methods cannot deal with it adequately.

Hoffer and Severance [13] measured the "affinity between pairs of attributes," and used the bond energy algorithm (BEA), developed in [17], to cluster attributes according to their affinity. Their attribute similarity function uses the notion of an attribute being "required for processing," or "required only if the record is selected," or finally "not required." We feel that in database systems the first and the second cases cannot be distinguished because all attributes of the same record are accessed together; therefore, we prefer the notion of logical accesses. We do, however, distinguish between retrieval and update accesses because, when an attribute is replicated in different fragments, an update transaction involving that attribute has to visit all fragments. In [13] attribute length is used in the evaluation of affinity—on the grounds that it should be less appealing to store attributes together as their length increases and more appealing as their length decreases; we do not consider length as a factor in determining affinity.

Hammer and Niamir [11] summarize the problems left unsolved by the approach in [12] in the following two points:

(i) The BEA determines an ordering of attributes, but it is still left to the subjective judgment of the designer to decide how to "clump" the attributes together to form fragments.

(ii) Similarity of pairs of attributes can be inadequate if the similarity among larger groups of attributes is not taken into account.

Our present paper extends the results of [13] by giving algorithms for the design of fragments that perform the activity at point (i) automatically and by taking into account in our algorithms "blocks" of attributes with similar properties, addressing point (ii).

Hammer and Niamir [11] developed two heuristics to be used in combination. The "grouping" heuristic starts by assigning each attribute to a different partition; at each step, all groupings of partitions of the current candidate solution are considered, and the one that represents the greatest improvement over the current candidate grouping becomes the new candidate. The process iterates until no improvement is found over the current candidate. The "regrouping" heuristic attempts to move attributes from their current partition to another partition. Grouping and regrouping are iterated until no further benefit can be achieved. When the set of all partitions is viewed as a lattice, grouping moves attributes "up" and regrouping moves attributes "sideways" [11].

The major criticism of this approach is regarding the direction in which to explore the lattice—while Hammer and Niamir proceed "up" by grouping, we proceed "down" by splitting. The rationale behind this approach is that the "optimal" solution, in our opinion, is much closer to the group composed of all attributes, assumed to be our starting point, than to groups that are single-attribute partitions, as assumed in [11]. A typical solution will not incur too much splitting because of the disadvantage of storing too many small subrecords. Thus, in our approach, the "moves" along the lattice will be in a direction that promises optimality; Hammer and Niamir, on the contrary, recognized that their approach introduces many discrepancies at the first iterations (in fact, they introduced the regrouping heuristics to get rid of these discrepancies).

Some other research is related to the present paper. Chang and Cheng discussed both horizontal and vertical partitioning [6]. Their paper uses the term *horizontal partitions* for the issues addressed here (usually called *vertical partitioning*). They developed a methodology for the decomposition of an object into fragments, but did not give a precise evaluation of the factors that should guide the decomposition. Dayal and Bernstein [8] have studied the fragmentation problem from a more theoretical viewpoint, giving rules through which objects can be lossless decomposed into fragments.

Ceri, Negri, and Pelagatti [3] analyzed the horizontal partitioning problem, dealing with the specification of partitioning predicates and the application of horizontal partitioning to different database design problems. Ceri, Navathe, and Wiederhold [4] have proposed a model for designing distributed database schemas that incorporates the notion of horizontal partitioning. The paper describes a linear integer formulation of the horizontal partitioning problem without replication and then presents heuristic algorithms for the decomposition of the problem into smaller subproblems and the introduction of replication, assuming the nonreplicated solution as a starting point. The present paper complements our past work on horizontal partitioning.

Finally, several papers have addressed the general problem of allocating database objects over multiple sites, without taking object partitioning into consideration; among them are [7, 10, 15, 18].

1.3 Algorithms for the Vertical Partitioning Problem—Organization of the Paper

In this section we provide an overview of the structure of the paper by discussing the various algorithms that are used to solve the VPP. The algorithms are discussed in detail in Sections 2 and 3.

As shown in Figure 2, the input to the algorithms is twofold:

(a) The *logical accesses* of transactions to the object.
(b) The *relevant design parameters*, such as cost of storage, cost of accessing a record occurrence, cost of transmission.

Input (a) is required for phase 1 of the VPP; input (b) for phase 2.

The given information about the usage of attributes by transactions is initially converted into a square matrix, called the *attribute affinity matrix*. This matrix is diagonalized by the algorithm CLUSTER, described in Section 2.1, which is essentially the bond energy algorithm [17]. In that paper the algorithm has been shown to be useful in partitioning a set of interacting variables into subsets such that the subsets either do not interact or interact minimally.

We distinguish the following three environments for the vertical partitioning problem:

(a) single site with one memory level;
(b) single site with several memory levels (i.e., devices of different speeds, capacities, and costs); and
(c) multiple sites.

Problem (a) can be solved by using either nonoverlapping or overlapping fragments. These are produced by the use of the algorithms SPLIT_NONOVERLAP and SPLIT_OVERLAP, respectively—described in Sections 2.2 and 2.3; these two algorithms automate the manual grouping of attributes required in [13]. The algorithms are invoked repeatedly (see Section 2.6) until no further partition

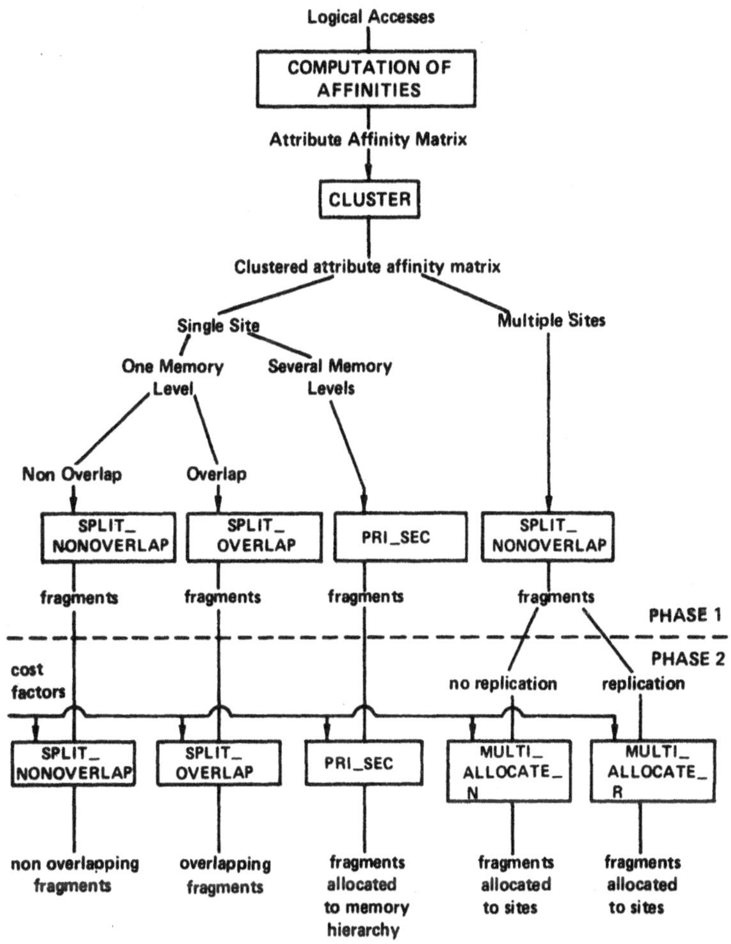

Fig. 2. Algorithms for solving the vertical partitioning problem in different application environments.

occurs; they can use empirical objective functions for phase 1, described in Sections 2.2 and 2.3, or objective functions based on cost factors for phase 2, described in Section 3.2.

Problem (b) is a special application of the VPP, where an object may be resident on secondary memory and only a "highly active" part of it will be stored in primary (fast) memory. This problem uses the PRI_SEC algorithm, described in Section 2.4, in place of the SPLIT algorithms mentioned above. The PRI_SEC algorithm can also use either an empirical objective function for phase 1, described in Section 2.4, or an objective function based on cost factors, described in Section 3.3. If the fragments have to be allocated among multiple levels of memory, the PRI_SEC algorithm needs to be applied at each level (see Section 3.3).

Problem (c) considers the VPP problem in a distributed database environment. The SPLIT_NONOVERLAP algorithm is used to design the fragments in phase 1; the allocation of fragments to sites requires cost factors and must be done in phase 2. Algorithms MUTLI_ALLOCATE_N and MULTI_ALLOCATE_R, described in Sections 3.4 and 3.5, respectively, determine the allocation of fragments to sites with and without replication.

Variations of the algorithm are described throughout Section 2; in particular, the algorithm SHIFT, which produces the pairwise permutation of the first row and column of the clustered affinity matrix with the last rows and columns, and the algorithm CLUSTER, which recomputes affinity after producing intermediate partitionings, can be used at every iteration of the SPLIT algorithms. We anticipate that these algorithms will be used in a highly interactive setting, where the designer can select the best combination of algorithms. Conclusions and further research problems are described in Section 4.

2. ALGORITHMS BASED ON EMPIRICAL OBJECTIVE FUNCTIONS

Vertical partitioning algorithms require the specification of data and transaction parameters shown in Tables I and II.

Table I presents the parameters that refer to a database object having ten attributes on a single site. The 0/1 entries in the ATTRIBUTE USAGE (AU) matrix show whether or not a given attribute is used by a given transaction. The ACCESS column shows for each transaction the frequency of access to object instances per unit time period (e.g., a day). The ATTRIBUTE LENGTH (AL) row gives the number of bytes of each attribute. The TYPE column shows the type of the transaction, depending upon whether the transaction retrieves (R) or updates (U) it. In this paper, for ease of notation, we give the same treatment to attributes within one transaction (i.e., all attributes are considered to be either retrieved or updated). In an actual environment some attributes may be retrieved and some may be updated; this calls for recording some additional information for transactions that involve updates. Dealing with this general case, however, does not change the basic structures of the algorithms.

Table II shows the parameters for a multiple-site problem with four sites. The access column is now transformed into an ACCESS MATRIX, giving the number of transaction accesses from each site.

In the single object (file) VPP problem all the attributes of the object appear in the attribute usage matrix and attribute length row; in a database VPP problem, one can either imagine one data usage per object or a global data usage table of all the transactions against all the attributes. From a global table, one would select the relevant columns for a given object and all transactions that utilize at least one attribute from the object, and construct individual data usage tables.

2.1 Affinity Among Attributes

The first step in the design of a vertical partition is to construct an ATTRIBUTE AFFINITY (AA) matrix. Figure 1 shows an example of an attribute affinity matrix derived from the attribute usage in Table I. AA is a symmetric square matrix which records the affinity among the attributes $a_{i'}$ and $a_{i''}$ as a single number, $\text{aff}_{i'i''} (= \text{aff}_{i''i'})$, defined below.

Let the following parameters be defined for each transaction k:

$u_{ki} = 1$ if transaction k uses attribute a_i
$= 0$ otherwise (u_{ki} is an element of matrix AU).

Table I. Parameters for a Single Site VPP

Attribute usage matrix											Type	Single site accesses per time period
Attribute	1	2	3	4	5	6	7	8	9	10		
T 1	1	0	0	0	1	0	1	0	0	0	Type 1 = R	Acc 1 = 25
T 2	0	1	1	0	0	0	0	1	1	0	Type 2 = R	Acc 2 = 50
T 3	0	0	0	1	0	1	0	0	0	1	Type 3 = R	Acc 3 = 25
T 4	0	1	0	0	0	0	1	1	0	0	Type 4 = R	Acc 4 = 35
T 5	1	1	1	0	1	0	1	1	1	0	Type 5 = U	Acc 5 = 25
T 6	1	0	0	0	1	0	0	0	0	0	Type 6 = U	Acc 6 = 25
T 7	0	0	1	0	0	0	0	0	1	0	Type 7 = U	Acc 7 = 25
T 8	0	0	1	1	0	1	0	0	1	1	Type 8 = U	Acc 8 = 15
Attribute length vector												
	10	8	4	6	15	14	3	5	9	12		

Table II. Additional Parameters for a Multiple Site VPP

	Multiple site accesses per time period			
Site	1	2	3	4
T 1	10	15	0	0
T 2	10	20	10	10
T 3	0	0	15	10
T 4	10	15	0	10
T 5	5	10	5	5
T 6	10	5	5	5
T 7	5	10	5	5
T 8	5	5	2	3

type_k = 'r' (retrieval transactions)
= 'u' (update transactions).
n_k = number of accesses to object instances for one occurrence of transaction k (single site).
n_{kj} = number of accesses to object instances for one occurrence of transaction k at site j (multiple sites).
freq_k = frequency of occurrence of transaction k (single site).
freq_{kj} = frequency of occurrence of transaction k at site j (multiple sites).
$\text{acc}_k = n_k \text{freq}_k$ (single site)
$= \sum_j n_j \text{freq}_{kj}$ (multiple sites).

acc_k measures the number of accesses of transaction k to the object instances per time period.

The affinity measure is

$$\text{aff}_{i'i''} = \sum_{k \mid u_{ki'}=1 \wedge u_{ki''}=1} \text{acc}_k.$$

The attribute affinity defined above measures the strength of an imaginary bond between the two attributes, on the basis of the fact that attributes are used together by transactions. Note that affinity as defined here is *not* site specific; we use affinity information for determining the composition of fragments. In Section 3 we shall discuss how the site-specific access measures can be employed to determine the allocation of fragments in distributed databases.

The algorithms developed below will cluster groups of attributes with high affinity in the same fragment, and keep attributes with low affinity in separate fragments. One may refine the notion of affinity to take different factors into account; the elaborate formulation of affinity given in [13] could be used. We stress that the particular definition of affinity has no bearing whatsoever on the design of the subsequent algorithms; all they presuppose is that the affinity matrix has been defined.

2.2 Clustering of Attributes

The AA matrix is processed by the algorithm CLUSTER. The algorithm employs the bond energy algorithm (BEA) of [17], which is a general procedure for permuting rows and columns of a square matrix in order to obtain a semiblock diagonal form. The algorithm is typically applied to partition a set of interacting variables into subsets which interact minimally.

The objective function used by the BEA tends to surround large values of the matrix with large values, and the small ones with small values. It maximizes the following expression:

$$\sum_{ij} \text{aff}_{ij}(\text{aff}_{i,j-1} + \text{aff}_{i,j+1} + \text{aff}_{i-1,j} + \text{aff}_{i+1,j})$$

where

$$\text{aff}_{i,0} = \text{aff}_{0,j} = \text{aff}_{i,n+1} = \text{aff}_{n+1,j} = 0.$$

The algorithm is heuristic, and it considers only a small number of the possible permutations of the columns; it has a complexity $O(n^2)$. The algorithm takes advantage of the following features:

(i) the AA matrix is symmetric, and hence allows a pairwise permutation of rows and columns, which reduces the complexity;

(ii) because of the definition of $\text{aff}_{i'i''}$, the initial AA matrix is already semiblock diagonal, in that each diagonal element has a greater value of any element along the same row or column ($\text{aff}_{i'i'} \geq \text{aff}_{i'i''}$ and $\text{aff}_{i'i'} \geq \text{aff}_{i''i'}$, for any i' and i''). This feature motivates, from a practical point of view, the definition of diagonal elements of the matrix, which have no physical meaning.

The application of the CLUSTER algorithm to the initial AA matrix of Figure 3a produces the new AA matrix in Figure 3b. The blocks along the main diagonal of AA correspond to groups of jointly accessed data items which are candidates for constituting vertical fragments.

So far our procedure is similar to that of [13]. After diagonalizing the AA matrix, Hoffer and Severance suggest a tentative assignment of groups of attributes to fragments. We have designed the three basic algorithms: SPLIT_NON_OVERLAP, SPLIT_OVERLAP, and PRI_SEC in order to perform a less subjective clustering of attributes into fragments for the single-site, binary partitioning problems;[1] extensions of the basic algorithms allow one to deal with n-ary partitions and multiple sites.

2.3 Partitioning an Object Into Nonoverlapping Fragments

The SPLIT_NON_OVERLAP algorithm uses the clustered affinity matrix to partition an object into two nonoverlapping fragments. Assume that a point x is fixed along the main diagonal of the clustered AA matrix, as shown in Figure 3c. The point x defines two blocks U (for "upper") and L (for "lower"). Each block defines a vertical fragment given by the set of attributes in that block.

Starting from the attribute usage matrix, we define $A(k)$ as the set of attributes used by transaction k as follows:

$$A(k) = \{i \mid u_{ki} = 1\}.$$

[1] These algorithms were proposed by S. Ceri and implemented by J. Dou and S. Ceri.

Attribute	1	2	3	4	5	6	7	8	9	10
1	75	25	25	0	75	0	50	25	25	0
2	25	110	75	0	25	0	60	110	75	0
3	25	75	115	15	25	15	25	75	115	15
4	0	0	15	40	0	40	0	0	15	40
5	75	25	25	0	75	0	50	25	25	0
6	0	0	15	40	0	40	0	0	15	40
7	50	60	25	0	50	0	85	60	25	0
8	25	110	75	0	25	0	60	110	75	0
9	25	75	115	15	25	15	25	75	115	15
10	0	0	15	40	0	40	0	0	15	40

(a)

Attribute	5	1	7	2	8	3	9	10	4	6
5	75	75	50	25	25	25	25	0	0	0
1	75	75	50	25	25	25	25	0	0	0
7	50	50	85	60	60	25	25	0	0	0
2	25	25	60	110	110	75	75	0	0	0
8	25	25	60	110	110	75	75	0	0	0
3	25	25	25	75	75	115	115	15	15	15
9	25	25	25	75	75	115	115	15	15	15
10	0	0	0	0	0	15	15	40	40	40
4	0	0	0	0	0	15	15	40	40	40
6	0	0	0	0	0	15	15	40	40	40

(b)

Attribute	5	1	7	2	8	3	9	10	4	6
5	75	75	50	25	25	25	25	0	0	0
1	75	75	50	25	25	25	25	0	0	0
7	50	50	85	60	60	25	25	0	0	0
2	25	25	60	110	110	75	75	0	0	0
8	25	25	60	110	110	75	75	0	0	0
3	25	25	25	75	75	115	115	15	15	15
9	25	25	25	75	75	115	115	15	15	15
10	0	0	0	0	0	15	15	40	40	40
4	0	0	0	0	0	15	15	40	40	40
6	0	0	0	0	0	15	15	40	40	40

(c)

Fig. 3. (a) Initial attribute affinity matrix (AA); (b) attribute affinity matrix in semiblock diagonal form; (c) nonoverlapping splitting of AA into two blocks L and U.

Using $A(k)$, it is possible to compute the following sets:

$$T = \{k \mid k \text{ is a transaction}\}$$

$$LT = \{k \mid A(k) \subseteq L\}$$

$$UT = \{k \mid A(k) \subseteq U\}$$

$$IT = T - \{LT \cup UT\}$$

T represents the set of all transactions; LT and UT represent the set of transactions that "match" the partitioning, as they can be entirely processed using attributes in the lower or upper block, respectively; IT represents the set of transactions that needs to access both fragments.

$$CT = \sum_{k \in T} \text{acc}_k$$

$$CL = \sum_{k \in LT} \text{acc}_k$$

$$CU = \sum_{k \in UT} \text{acc}_k$$

$$CI = \sum_{k \in IT} \text{acc}_k$$

CT counts the total number of transaction accesses to the considered object. CL and CU count the total number of accesses of transactions that need only one fragment; CI counts the total number of accesses of transactions that need both fragments. We consider $n - 1$ possible locations of point x along the diagonal, where n is the size of the matrix (i.e., the number of attributes). A nonoverlapping partition is obtained by selecting the point x such that the following goal function z is maximized:

$$\max z = CL \times CU - CI^2. \tag{1}$$

The partitioning that corresponds to the maximal value of the z function is accepted if z is positive, and is rejected otherwise.

The above objective function comes from an empirical judgment of what should be considered a "good" partitioning. The function is increasing in CL and CU and decreasing in CI. For a given value of CI, it selects CL and CU in such a way that the product $CL \times CU$ is maximized. This results in selecting values for CL and CU that are as nearly equal as possible. Thus, the above z function will produce fragments that are "balanced" with respect to the transaction load. Notice that in Section 2.5, where we deal with memory hierarchies, we present a goal function that attains the opposite result (i.e., produces "unbalanced" partitionings).

Recalling that $CT = CL + CU + CI$ is a constant value, it is possible to visualize the z surface in the space of CL and CU (see Figure 4). Notice that $z = 0$ in absence of a partitioning, where either ($CL = 0$ and $CU = CT$) or ($CU = 0$ and $CL = CT$) and $CI = 0$; z takes its minimum feasible value at (0, 0), where it is $z = -CT^2$, and its maximum feasible value at ($CT/2$, $CT/2$), where it is $z = CT^2/4$. Figure 4 also shows the intersection of z with the $z = 0$ plane; partitions corresponding to points in the dashed area are accepted (because it is $z \geq 0$).

The proposed algorithm has the disadvantage of not being able to partition an object by selecting out an embedded "inner" block. For example, consider the clustering of attributes shown in the AA matrix in Figure 5a, which is a reasonable result for the bond energy algorithm (the example was actually produced by applying the BEA algorithm). The best binary partition in this case is the one that places the attributes between points $x1$ and $x2$ on the diagonal into one fragment, and all other attributes into the other; this solution is not one of those considered by the SPLIT_NON_OVERLAP algorithm.

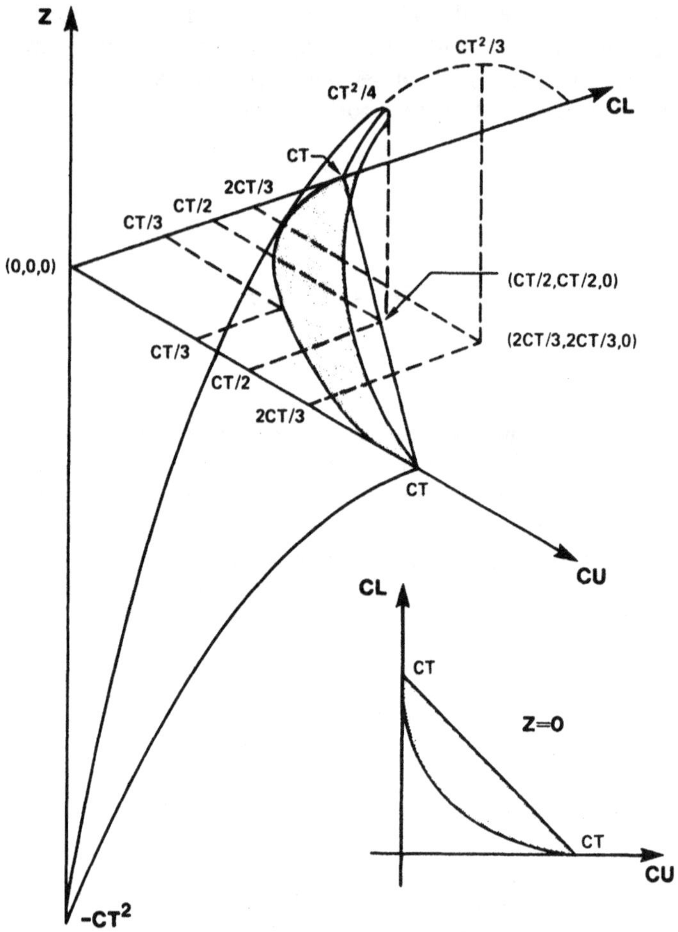

Fig. 4. A surface representing the function z used by the SPLIT_NON_OVERLAP algorithm.

This disadvantage can be avoided by using the procedure SHIFT, which moves the leftmost column of the AA matrix to the extreme right, and the topmost row of the matrix to the bottom (see Figure 5b). SHIFT is called a total of n times, so that every diagonal block gets the opportunity of being brought to the upper left corner in the matrix; the SPLIT_NON_OVERLAP algorithm is used to select the best partition after each application of SHIFT. Figure 5c shows the AA matrix in which, by applying SHIFT three times, the "inside" block of Figure 5a has been taken to the upper left corner. When the SHIFT procedure is used, the complexity of the algorithm increases by factor n. Experience has shown that the use of the SHIFT procedure improves the solution of the BVP problem in several cases.

2.4 Partitioning an Object Into Overlapping Fragments

A binary overlapping splitting consists of two clusters of attributes with a nonempty intersection. A representation of overlapping clusters on the AA matrix

Attribute	3	2	1	7	6	4	5	10	8	9
3	10	10	10	0	0	0	0	0	0	0
2	10	10	10	0	0	0	0	0	0	0
1	10	10	10	0	0	0	0	0	0	0
			$x1$							
7	0	0	0	50	50	50	50	0	0	0
6	0	0	0	50	50	50	50	0	0	0
4	0	0	0	50	50	50	50	0	0	0
5	0	0	0	50	50	50	50	0	0	0
							$x2$			
10	0	0	0	0	0	0	0	10	10	10
8	0	0	0	0	0	0	0	10	10	10
9	0	0	0	0	0	0	0	10	10	10

(a)

Attribute	2	1	7	6	4	5	10	8	9	3
2	10	10	0	0	0	0	0	0	0	10
1	10	10	0	0	0	0	0	0	0	10
7	0	0	50	50	50	50	0	0	0	0
6	0	0	50	50	50	50	0	0	0	0
4	0	0	50	50	50	50	0	0	0	0
5	0	0	50	50	50	50	0	0	0	0
10	0	0	0	0	0	0	10	10	10	0
8	0	0	0	0	0	0	10	10	10	0
9	0	0	0	0	0	0	10	10	10	0
3	10	10	0	0	0	0	0	0	0	10

(b)

Attribute	7	6	4	5	10	8	9	3	2	1
7	50	50	50	50	0	0	0	0	0	0
6	50	50	50	50	0	0	0	0	0	0
4	50	50	50	50	0	0	0	0	0	0
5	50	50	50	50	0	0	0	0	0	0
10	0	0	0	0	10	10	10	0	0	0
8	0	0	0	0	10	10	10	0	0	0
9	0	0	0	0	10	10	10	0	0	0
3	0	0	0	0	0	0	0	10	10	10
2	0	0	0	0	0	0	0	10	10	10
1	0	0	0	0	0	0	0	10	10	10

(c)

Fig. 5. (a) Clustering of attributes with a block "inside" the matrix; (b) the SHIFT procedure after one iteration; (c) the best nonoverlapping split at the third iteration of the SHIFT procedure.

is given in Figure 6: notice that now two points x_1 and x_2 are needed along the diagonal. The upper fragment comprises the attributes from the first one up to x_2, and the lower comprises the attributes from x_1 to the last one; attributes between x_1 and x_2 constitute the intersection.

Attribute	5	1	7	2	8	3	9	10	4	6
5	75	75	50	25	25	25	25	0	0	0
1	75	75	50	25	25	25	25	0	0	0
7	50	50	85	60	60	25	25	0	0	0
2	25	25	60	110	110	75	75	0	0	0
8	25	25	60	110	110	75	75	0	0	0
					$x1$					
3	25	25	25	75	75	115	115	15	15	15
9	25	25	25	75	75	115	115	15	15	15
							$x2$			
10	0	0	0	0	0	15	15	40	40	40
4	0	0	0	0	0	15	15	40	40	40
6	0	0	0	0	0	15	15	40	40	40

Fig. 6. Overlapping splitting into two blocks L and U.

In the algorithm SPLIT_OVERLAP we consider the $n \times (n-1)/2$ possible combinations of locating points x_1 and x_2 along the main diagonal. The case with $x_1 = x_2$, corresponding to nonoverlapping splittings, is also considered.

The same objective function is used as in Eq. (1) above, but with a different evaluation of sets LT and UT. Transactions that update attributes from the intersection $I = L \cap U$ have to be directed to both fragments in order to preserve the consistency of replicated data. On the other hand, by sharing the attributes from I in both L and U, more read transactions can be satisfied by either L or U alone, as compared with the nonoverlapping case. As before, LT and UT represent the set of transactions that "match" the two fragments, while IT represents the set of transactions that need to access both fragments. We have

$$LT = \{k \mid (\text{type}_k = \text{'r'} \wedge A(k) \subseteq L) \vee (\text{type}_k = \text{'u'} \wedge A(k) \subseteq (L - I))\}$$

$$UT = \{k \mid (\text{type}_k = \text{'r'} \wedge A(k) \subseteq U) \vee (\text{type}_k = \text{'u'} \wedge A(k) \subseteq (U - I))\}$$

$$IT = T - (LT \cup UT).$$

From the above sets, we compute the counts CL, CU, CI as before and use them in the goal function (1). To keep the formulation free of cost factors in the empirical design phase, we do not incorporate the additional storage cost of attributes in I here. This cost factor is instead taken into account in the cost optimization phase of Section 3.

Notice that $LT \cap UT$ is not void (it includes the retrieval transactions that use attributes from the intersection I only (i.e., $(A(k) \subseteq I)$), and therefore the equation $CT = CL + CU + CI$ does not hold any more.

It is also possible to use the SHIFT procedure described in the previous section in the SPLIT_OVERLAP algorithm. As before, the complexity of the problem increases by factor n.

2.5 Partitioning Into Primary and Secondary Fragments

The PRI_SEC algorithm is designed to produce a "biased" partitioning into a primary and a secondary fragment. It is applicable to the problem of allocating an object to multiple-storage devices.

Attribute	5	1	7	2	8	3	9	10	4	6
5	75	75	50	25	25	25	25	0	0	0
1	75	75	50	25	25	25	25	0	0	0
7	50	50	85	60	60	25	25	0	0	0
2	25	25	60	110	110	75	75	0	0	0
8	25	25	60	110	110	75	75	0	0	0
3	25	25	25	75	75	115	115	15	15	15
9	25	25	25	75	75	115	115	15	15	15
10	0	0	0	0	0	15	15	40	40	40
4	0	0	0	0	0	15	15	40	40	40
6	0	0	0	0	0	15	15	40	40	40

Fig. 7. Splitting into a primary (U) and a secondary (L) fragment.

Consider a BVP where a logical object is to be partitioned into two blocks U and L; U is the block containing the "more important" attributes (i.e., those used more frequently) and L is the block containing the "less important" ones. Attributes in U will typically be assigned to the faster (PRImary) memory, while those in L (or the entire object) to a slower (SECondary) memory.

The PRI_SEC algorithm partitions the clustered AA matrix into two nonoverlapping blocks L and U that meet the above criteria. To do so, it is necessary to bring the "less important" block to the bottom right corner of the matrix (see Figure 7). This is accomplished by the procedure SHIFT, described in Section 2.3, called by PRI_SEC. Also in this case, SHIFT is called a total of n times, so that every block gets the opportunity of being brought to the lower right corner in the matrix. After each shift of the AA matrix, every point x along the main diagonal is considered for defininig L and U; thus, $(n-1) \times n$ possible solutions are examined.

Let the following parameters and counts be defined:

l_i: length of attribute i,

$TL = \sum_i l_i$: total length of the object,

$UL = \sum_{i \in U} l_i$: length of attributes in the upper block.

CT and CU are computed as in the nonoverlapping problem (see Section 2.3).

The partition evaluation function needs to be asymmetric in order to maximize the number of transactions that are satisfied by using just the attributes of U. By the very fact that we are considering this problem, we have assumed that the entire object cannot be conveniently stored in primary memory. Hence, a counteracting objective is to keep the size of U, in terms of the total length of attributes in it, to a minimum. This effect is produced by maximizing the following objective function:

$$\max z = \frac{CU}{CT} - \frac{UL}{TL}. \tag{2}$$

The splitting that corresponds to the maximal value of the z function is accepted if z is positive, and rejected otherwise.

In this function, CU/CT is the ratio of the transaction volume satisfied by the upper block (U) to the total transaction volume; UL/TL is the ratio of the size of the fragment defined by U to the size of the object. Whenever z is positive, the former ratio exceeds the latter, implying that the primary block (U) is able to carry a fraction of the transaction load that is higher in comparison to its relative size. Maximizing this function intuitively selects a "good" block U. The above objective function was selected in preference to several other candidates—one worth mentioning, which gives similar results, is

$$\max z = \frac{CU \times TL}{CT \times UL}. \tag{2'}$$

2.6 Repetitive Use of Binary Partitioning

The solution of the general VPP problem may consist of several fragments; thus the algorithms that we have presented for the BVP problem have to be extended from binary to n-ary partitioning. Consider the AA matrix in Figure 8; assume that the three well-defined blocks shown in the figure correspond to the final fragmentation. If a nonoverlapping n-ary partitioning is to be accomplished by an algorithm, the algorithm in general has to try using 1 or 2 or ... $n - 1$ points along the diagonal as candidate break points to define the partitions. The complexity of such algorithm would be $O(2^n)$. The complexity of an algorithm for the overlapping problem would be even greater.

To avoid the combinatorial complexity, we propose solving the VPP problem by repetitively applying the BVP algorithms. At each iteration the fragments produced by the algorithms are considered as two distinct objects, and the BVP algorithm is applied to further partition each of them. This generates two distinct subproblems. In each subproblem only those transactions are considered by the SPLIT algorithms that have some intersection with the considered fragment, and all other transactions are disregarded; thus, decisions about further splitting are not influenced by irrelevant transactions.[2] The process terminates when no further partitioning is indicated.

This approach is suboptimal compared to the general n-ary partitioning, but it drastically reduces the complexity of the computation of the n-ary VPP; for large n, the overall complexity can be considered equivalent to the complexity of the first application of SPLIT. The approach is not only computationally very attractive, but it takes advantage of the following two facts:

(i) The selection of the best partition at each binary split corresponds to taking the most promising decision; to this extent, the approach can be classified as a "greedy" heuristic.

(ii) At each iteration of the solution procedure, new fragments are generated which give rise to a new BVP for each fragment. These subproblems are totally independent, in the sense that each considers a fragment as an object in its own right. Each new subproblem considers all the relevant

[2] A slight error is introduced in the overlapping case for retrieval transactions that use attributes from intersection I only (i.e., $A(k) \subseteq I$), because these transactions are considered in both problems, while a transaction will eventually use one of the fragments only; this error can be avoided by arbitrarily assigning these transactions to one of the two fragments.

Attribute	5	1	7	2	8	3	9	10	4	6
5	75	75	50	25	25	25	25	0	0	0
1	75	75	50	25	25	25	25	0	0	0
7	50	50	85	60	60	25	25	0	0	0
2	25	25	60	110	110	75	75	0	0	0
8	25	25	60	110	110	75	75	0	0	0
3	25	25	25	75	75	115	115	15	15	15
9	25	25	25	75	75	115	115	15	15	15
10	0	0	0	0	0	15	15	40	40	40
4	0	0	0	0	0	15	15	40	40	40
6	0	0	0	0	0	15	15	40	40	40

Fig. 8. A *n*-ary partitioning.

Attribute Part*	5	1	7	2	8	3	9	10	4	6	Iteration level
1	X	X	X								2
2				X	X	X	X				2
3								X	X	X	1

Attribute Part*	5	1	7	2	8	3	9	10	4	6	Iteration level
1	X	X	X								2
2			X	X	X						2
3			X	X	X						2
4				X	X	X	X				3
5								X	X	X	3

Attribute	5	1	7	2	8	3	9	10	4	6	Iteration level
PRI	X	X	X	X	X	X	X				1
SEC								X	X	X	
PRI	X	X	X	X	X						2
SEC						X	X	X	X	X	
PRI	X	X	X	X							3
SEC					X	X	X	X	X	X	

* abbreviates partition in all subsequent figures.

Fig. 9. Results of repetitive application of SPLIT_NON_OVERLAP, SPLIT_OVERLAP, and PRI_SEC.

transactions that use attributes of the fragment, without any loss of information from the original problem.

Figure 9 shows the output of the repeated application of the algorithms SPLIT_NON_OVERLAP, SPLIT_OVERLAP, and PRI_SEC to the partitioning problem whose input parameters are shown in Table I.

In Figures 9a and 9b, the output includes the final fragmentation produced by the SPLIT algorithm. Each fragment in the final solution is associated with the iteration level in the binary split tree at which that fragment was produced. For example, in Figure 9a, the fragment including attributes 10, 4, and 6 was produced at the first iteration, and the remaining fragment including attributes 5, 1, 7, 2, 8, 3, and 9 was further divided into two fragments, including attributes 5, 1, 7 and 2, 8, 3, 9, respectively, at the second iteration.

In Figure 9c, the output includes the solutions produced at each iteration of the BVP problem using the PRI_SEC algorithm; the final solution is to have attributes 5, 1, 7, and 2 in the primary memory.

In the nonoverlapping and overlapping algorithms, the iterative approach can take advantage of the following two options in the BVP algorithms:

(i) the evaluation of the affinity measures can be repeated for each subproblem independently, by considering only the relevant transactions. Procedure CLUSTER is then applied to produce the semiblock diagonal form of the new affinity matrix.

(ii) the procedure SHIFT can be called by the SPLIT algorithms; notice that the use of the procedure SHIFT is mandatory in the case of the PRI_SEC algorithm.

Computational experience has shown that the repetitive application of CLUSTER improves the performance of the partitioning algorithms, because decisions that are made at each iteration rely on current values of attribute affinity. On the other hand, the application of SHIFT does not substantially improve the performance of partitioning algorithms. Recall the discussion in Section 2.3 about the need of selecting blocks "inside" the affinity matrix for the BVP. In the VPP, without applying SHIFT, it is likely that "inside" blocks are selected after some iterations, thus the two versions of SPLIT algorithms, with and without SHIFT, lead to the same result with a different sequence of splittings. Notice that the use of SHIFT at the first iteration is very expensive, since it increases the overall complexity of the VPP problem by factor n.

It is possible to enforce some constraints on the partitioning process:

(i) Impose a limitation on the number of partitions that can be produced; this constraint is motivated by the limitation on the overall number of files that can be supported by the system.

(ii) Impose a minimum size on fragments; this constraint can prevent partitioned records from becoming too small.

These constraints and the appropriate use of CLUSTER and SHIFT procedures can be properly controlled by a knowledgeable designer. We contemplate the use of an interactive design tool in which all these procedures are available to the designer, intermediate results are shown, and the designer is able to direct the design sequence.

3. VERTICAL PARTITIONING BASED ON COST OPTIMIZATION

In the previous section we have given algorithms that use empirical objective functions, suggested by our intuition of the problem. The disadvantage of the approach is in its lack of precision; such an approach is attractive, however, as it

Problem type	Cost factors			
	$C1$	$C2$	$C3$	$C4$
S	M	H	L	—
H	L	H	H	—
M	L	M	M	H

Fig. 10. The relative importance (L = low, M = medium, H = high) of coefficients $C1$, $C2$, $C3$, and $C4$ in different application environments (S = single site; H = single site, several memory levels; M = multiple sites).

is possible to evaluate the convenience of partitioning without requiring absolute measurements of costs, which are seldom available or accurate.

As we suggested in Figure 1, the empirical design should be followed by a cost optimization phase. For each of the three application environments of VPP defined in Section 1.3, it is possible to estimate the total cost of vertical partitioning in terms of certain cost factors. They are

$C1$. cost of irrelevant attributes accessed within a fragment (per byte);
$C2$. cost of accessing fragments for retrieval and updates (per access);
$C3$. storage cost (per byte);
$C4$. transmission cost (per byte).

Note that the above cost factors are relative and that they represent an estimate of the design parameters associated with a particular physical environment. Figure 10 shows the relative importance (low, medium, or high) of these cost factors in the three types of application environments, as expressed in the database design literature in general [23] and as it applies to present-day systems. The relative importance of the factors stems from the following:

(a) *Single site with one memory level.* The costs $C1$ and $C2$ are both related to unnecessary I/O. The cost $C2$ also includes the CPU cost of putting the data from the fragments together and of applying updates simultaneously to fragments. Hence, $C2$ is the most important cost factor, followed by $C1$. In comparison, $C3$ is less important because storage is becoming less and less expensive, and $C4$ is not applicable.

(b) *Single site with several memory levels.* In this case, the costs of accessing fragments and of storage are both equally important, since there is a trade-off between them. $C1$ is relatively less important, and $C4$ is not applicable.

(c) *Multiple sites.* In the case of a distributed database, the transmission cost is dominant [2, 5]; however, local access and storage costs cannot be disregarded [21]. Therefore, we have shown $C4$ as having high importance, $C2$ and $C3$ as having medium importance, and $C1$ as having low importance.

In the following, we give simple expressions for weighing these cost factors in the three types of problems. The objective function we will consider throughout the rest of the paper is

$$\min z = \sum_{1 \le i \le 4} w_i c_i. \tag{3}$$

The VPP and solution algorithms for a specific problem are identified by a five-character subscript: $i1, i2, i3, i4, i5$

$i1$: S = single site, one memory level
H = single site, several memory levels (heterogeneous devices)
M = multiple sites
$i2$: N = multiple sites, nonreplicated
R = multiple sites, replicated
— = single site
$i3$: N = nonoverlapping
O = overlapping
— = several memory levels
$i4$: S = algorithm SHIFT used
— = algorithm SHIFT not used
$i5$: C = algorithm CLUSTER used
— = algorithm CLUSTER not used

Fig. 11. Classification of the VPP and of options within algorithms.

This objective function can be used in the SPLIT_NONOVERLAP, SPLIT_OVERLAP, and PRI_SEC algorithms instead of the empirical objective functions (1) and (2) described in Section 2.

3.1 Notation and Definitions

This subsection is devoted to the definition of some additional notation. It includes a summary of some notation from Section 2, which is retained. To denote one particular problem and solution method, we use five "switches," explained in Figure 11. Subscripts $i1$, $i2$, $i3$ define the nature of the problem, while subscripts $i4$, $i5$ define the choice of algorithms used for the solution. In Figures 12, 13, 15, and 16 the "problem type" column on the left contains this five-character subscript.

In a BVP problem, the sets LT and UT include the transactions that can be entirely processed in the upper (U) or lower (L) block; their definition is the same as in Section 2.4 (overlapping fragments), and it applies also to the nonoverlapping and the primary–secondary fragments, where the intersection $I = L \cap U$ is void. The set IT includes transactions that need to access both fragments.

$$LT = \{k \mid (\text{type}_k = \text{'r'} \land A(k) \subseteq L) \lor (\text{type}_k = \text{'u'} \land A(k) \subseteq (L - I))\}$$

$$UT = \{k \mid (\text{type}_k = \text{'r'} \land A(k) \subseteq U) \lor (\text{type}_k = \text{'u'} \land A(k) \subseteq (U - I))\}$$

$$IT = T - (LT \cup UT)$$

The set S_k includes the blocks required by a given transaction k; it is

$$S_k = \{L\} \text{ if } k \in LT$$

$$S_k = \{U\} \text{ if } k \in UT$$

$$S_k = \{L, U\} \text{ if } k \in IT$$

The counts CL and CU weigh all transactions that need to access either block L or block U; the count CI weighs transctions that need to access both blocks.

$$CL = \sum_{k \in LT} \text{acc}_k$$

$$CU = \sum_{k \in UT} \text{acc}_k$$

$$CI = \sum_{k \in IT} \text{acc}_k$$

In the multiple site problem, we use F to denote a fragment being allocated and alloc_F to denote the allocation sites for fragment F; alloc_F may contain either a single site in nonreplicated VPP or multiple sites in the replicated VPP.

3.2 The VPP for a Single Site with One Memory Level

The partitioning of an object on a single site with homogeneous devices requires the repeated use of the SPLIT algorithms, introduced in Sections 2.3, 2.4, and 2.6.

The specific weight factors for this problem, to be used in the objective function (3), are

$$w1 = \sum_k \text{acc}_k \sum_{F \in S_k} \sum_{(i \in F) \wedge (i \notin A(k))} l_i$$

$$w2 = CL + CU + 2 \times CI$$

$$w3 = \sum_{i \in I} l_i$$

The weight $w1$ sums the length of irrelevant attributes accessed by transactions; it evaluates the inefficiency of the transfer from mass memory to main memory, where only relevant attributes will be used.

The weight $w2$ counts the number of accesses made by transactions to all the partitions; it evaluates the number of input–output operations that are required, assuming that this number is proportional to the total number of the records accessed.

The weight $w3$ counts the amount of memory that is necessary to store the overlapping attributes, which are replicated on both partitions.

Figure 12 shows an application of the VPP for a single site, overlapping partitioning with one memory level which uses the goal function (3); the cost factors were set as follows: $C1 = 1$, $C2 = 1000$, $C3 = 100$. In the figure, the result of all possible combinations of use of the SHIFT and CLUSTER procedures is shown. Notice that the use of CLUSTER reduces the number of partitions in the result.

3.3 The VPP for a Single Site with Multiple Memory Levels

The partitioning of an object between a fast (and costly) and a slow (and cheap) memory device requires the repeated use of the PRI_SEC algorithm, described in Sections 2.5 and 2.6. The cost $C1$ is deemed irrelevant to this problem; the

Problem type: S-O--	Attribute Part	5	1	7	2	8	3	9	10	4	6	Iteration level
	1	X	X	X								2
	2			X	X							2
	3			X	X	X						2
	4				X	X	X	X	X	X	X	2

Problem type: S-OS-	Attribute Part	5	1	7	2	8	3	9	10	4	6	Iteration level
	1	X	X	X								2
	2			X	X							2
	3			X	X	X						2
	4				X	X	X	X	X	X	X	2

Problem type: S-O-C	Attribute Part	6	10	4	9	3	8	5	7	1	2	Iteration level
	1	X	X	X			X		X	X	X	2
	2							X	X	X	X	2
	3				X	X	X	X	X	X	X	1

Problem type: S-OSC	Attribute Part	5	1	8	9	10	4	7	6	2	3	Iteration level
	1	X	X					X				2
	2							X		X		2
	3			X	X	X	X	X	X	X	X	1

Fig. 12. The use of the objective function (3) in the SPLIT_OVERLAP problem, combining in all possible ways the use of SHIFT and CLUSTER procedures.

weight factors to be used in the objective function (3) are

$$w2 = CL$$

$$w3 = \sum_{i \in U} l_i$$

The weight $w2$ counts the number of accesses made by transactions to the secondary memory, while $w3$ counts the amount of data in the fast memory.

A generalization of the primary–secondary memory allocation problem, the *memory hierarchy allocation problem* (MHAP), is defined as follows: "Partition an object into m levels of memory such that data is allocated from level 1 to level m, 1 being the costliest and m being the cheapest memory, so as to minimize the total cost of storage and processing for that object."

The proposed solution method consists of invoking PRI_SEC $m - 1$ times; each time a pair of memories is considered, starting from the two levels m and $m - 1$. After having solved the first problem, the primary partition is temporarily assigned to memory $m - 1$ and the secondary partition is assigned to memory m. Then, memories $m - 2$ and $m - 1$ are considered, and the fragment assigned to memory $m - 1$ is evaluated for further partitioning. If at some iteration i no partition is assigned to the memory at level $i - 1$, the solution method proceeds considering the two noncontiguous levels of i and $i - 2$. The procedure terminates when level 1 is reached.

Problem type: H	Attribute	3	9	2	8	7	5	1	10	4	6	Iteration level
levels 1 and 2	PRI	X	X	X	X	X						1
	SEC						X	X	X	X	X	
levels 2 and 3	PRI	X	X	X	X							1
	SEC					X						

Fig. 13. The use of the PRI_SEC algorithm to solve the MHAP problem.

Clearly, each partitioning problem is characterized by a different value of the coefficients $C2$ and $C3$, which reflect the differences in price and performances of the considered pairs of memories. Figure 13 shows an example of the MHAP problem with three levels. The cost factors between level 1 and 2 were set to $C1 = 100$, $C2 = 1$; those between levels 2 and 3 were set to $C1 = 20$, $C2 = 3$. Note that at each iteration for the given two levels of memory it is important to consider the ratio of costs, and not the absolute cost.

3.4 The VPP on Multiple Sites with Nonreplicated Allocation

The VPP on multiple sites with nonreplicated allocation is solved by a repetitive use of the MULTI_ALLOCATE_N algorithm described in Figure 14a. The algorithm applies to an object O and produces a nonoverlapping binary split into two blocks L and U; the splitting process is the same as in the SPLIT_NONOVERLAP algorithm, and can take advantage of the use of SHIFT or CLUSTER algorithms as described before.

For each possible partition L and U, the algorithm attempts all possible fragment allocations (i.e., m^2 cases for m sites) and selects the pair with the least cost. The weight factors $w1$, $w2$, and $w3$ are computed in the same way as for the single-site, homogeneous devices VPP (see Section 3.2). However, in a multiple-site problem the transmission cost $C4$ is predominant; the weight factor $w4$ is given by

$$w4 = \sum_k \sum_{F \in S_k} \sum_{j \mid \text{alloc}_F \neq j} n_{kj} \text{freq}_{kj} \sum_{i \in (F \cap A(k))} l_i.$$

The weight $w4$ counts the number of bytes selected from records on remote sites that need to be transmitted to the transaction site.[3]

A table of partitions versus allocations is maintained, which stores the allocation sites for each fragment produced by the algorithm. If an object O is split into two objects L and U by the algorithm, then the entry for O is deleted, and two entries for L and U are inserted. The process of splitting is repeated until no partition may be split with any further gain.

Figure 15a shows the solution of the nonreplicated, multiple-site VPP problem, whose input parameters are specified in Tables I and II. Cost factors were set as follows: $C_1 = 1$, $C_2 = 100$, $C_3 = 10$, and $C_4 = 1000$.

[3] This simple transaction model applies to typical applications using distributed file systems or unsophisticated distributed databases, where the system collects the information at the site of the transaction and then executes the transaction there. A more complicated transaction model, which is more realistic for advanced systems, is in [4].

```
procedure MULTI_ALLOCATE_N (0)
  begin
  for all points x on the diagonal of clustered matrix AA (determining L and U) do
    for all possible allocations j1 of L do
      for all possible allocations j2 of U do
        begin
        evaluate z(L, U, j1, j2)
        if there is improvement then remember L, U, j1, j2
        end
  if there was improvement then
    begin
    delete ⟨0, j0⟩
    store ⟨L, j1⟩
    store ⟨U, j2⟩
    MULTI_ALLOCATE_N (L)
    MULTI_ALLOCATE_N (U)
    end
  end
```

Table of partitions and allocations

Partition	Allocation
0	j0

Fig. 14(a). Algorithm MULTI_ALLOCATE_N.

```
procedure MULTI_ALLOCATE_R(F)
  begin
  start from alloc_F = nonreplicated solution of MULTI_ALLOCATE_N
  repeat
    try all sites not in alloc_F
    let j be the most beneficial
    alloc_F = alloc_F ∪ j
  until
    no further benefit
  end
```

Fig. 14(b). Algorithm MULTI_ALLOCATE_R.

3.5 The VPP on Multiple Sites with Replicated Allocation

To consider the replicated allocation in the multiple-site case, we first solve the problem of nonreplicated partitioning using the algorithm MULTI_ALLOCATE_N; then we apply the algorithm MULTI_ALLOCATE_R to each fragment in the solution of that problem independently. The algorithm MULTI_ALLOCATE_R is shown in Figure 14b.

The MULTI_ALLOCATE_R algorithm applies to each normalized fragment F individually, and proceeds by allocating it to the sites that are not in $alloc_F$, until no further benefit is obtained. The algorithm can be classified as a "greedy" heuristic, as at each iteration the most convenient site is selected for replication.

The objective function considers only those costs that depend on the degree of replication of a single fragment F; cost $C1$ is irrelevant, and the following weight

Problem type:	Attribute Part	5	1	7	2	8	3	9	10	4	6	Allocation 1	2	3	4	Depth level
MNN—3	1	X	X	X	X	X	X	X					X			1
	2								X	X	X				X	1

Fig. 15(a). Results of the application of the algorithm MUTLI_ALLOCATE_*N*.

Problem type:	Attribute Part	5	1	7	2	8	3	9	10	4	6	Starting allocation 1	2	3	4	Final allocation 1	2	3	4
MRN—3	1	X	X	X	X	X	X	X					X				X		
	2								X	X	X				X			X	X

Fig. 15(b). Results of the application of the algorithm MULTI_ALLOCATE_*R*.

factors are computed:

$$w2 = \sum_{k \mid (\text{type}_k = \text{`u'}) \wedge (A(k) \cap F \neq \Phi)} \sum_j n_{kj} \text{freq}_{kj}$$

$$w3 = \sum_{i \in P} \mid \text{alloc}_F \mid \sum_{i \in P} l_i$$

$$w4 = \sum_{k \mid A(k) \cap F \neq \Phi} \sum_{j \mid j \notin \text{alloc}_F} n_{kj} \text{freq}_{kj} \sum_{i \in (F \cap A(k))} l_i.$$

The weight $w2$ counts the number of update operations that have to be applied to each copy of the replicated fragment in order to preserve their mutual consistency.

The weight $w3$ counts the amount of memory that is required for storing the replicated copies. The weight $w4$ counts the number of bytes that need to be transmitted to the site of the transaction, as in Section 3.4.

Notice that retrieval transactions are now likely to find a local copy of the required information, thus $w4$ decreases with the increase of replication; however, update and storage costs, represented by $w2$ and $w3$, grow with the number of copies, thus establishing a trade-off.

Figure 15b shows the results produced by applying the MULTI_ALLOCATE_R algorithm to the solution of the nonredundant allocation problem shown in Figure 15a. It shows that the algorithm finds it profitable to allocate an additional copy of fragment 2 at site 3.

4. CONCLUSIONS

In this paper we have presented several algorithms for determining vertical fragments and discussed their application to the design of databases. All the algorithms described in the paper have been implemented in PASCAL; the run for the final example shown in Figure 16, with 20 attributes and 15 variables, used only 1 second of CPU time on a DEC-2060 system.

Our approach is similar to that of Hoffer and Severance [13], in that we use the notion of affinity of attributes to permute them and produce an initial clustering. However, we have designed algorithms for an automatic selection of vertical fragments, which substitutes for the designer's subjective judgment, as proposed in [13].

Attribute usage matrix																					Type	Single site frequency
Attribute	1	2	3	4	5	6	7	8	9	10	11	12	13	14	15	16	17	18	19	20		
T 1	1	0	0	1	1	1	0	1	0	0	0	0	0	0	0	0	0	0	0	0	1 = R	1 = 50
T 2	0	1	0	0	0	0	0	0	1	0	0	1	1	1	0	0	0	0	0	0	2 = R	2 = 50
T 3	0	0	1	0	0	0	1	0	0	1	1	0	0	0	0	0	1	1	0	0	3 = R	3 = 50
T 4	0	0	0	0	0	0	0	0	0	0	0	0	0	0	1	1	0	0	1	1	4 = R	4 = 50
T 5	1	0	0	0	1	0	0	1	0	0	0	0	0	0	0	0	0	0	0	0	5 = R	5 = 15
T 6	1	0	0	0	0	0	0	1	0	1	1	0	0	0	0	0	0	0	0	0	6 = R	6 = 15
T 7	0	0	1	0	0	0	1	0	0	1	1	0	0	0	0	0	1	0	0	0	7 = R	7 = 15
T 8	0	1	0	0	0	0	0	0	0	0	0	1	1	1	1	1	0	1	0	1	8 = R	8 = 15
T 9	0	1	0	0	1	0	0	0	0	0	1	0	0	1	0	0	0	0	1	0	9 = R	9 = 10
T10	1	0	0	0	0	0	0	0	1	0	0	0	0	0	0	1	0	1	0	0	10 = R	10 = 10
T11	1	1	1	0	1	1	0	0	1	0	0	1	1	0	0	0	0	0	0	0	11 = U	11 = 10
T12	0	0	0	1	0	0	1	0	0	1	0	0	0	1	0	0	0	0	1	1	12 = U	12 = 10
T13	0	0	0	0	0	0	0	1	0	0	1	0	0	0	1	1	1	1	0	0	13 = U	13 = 10
T14	1	1	1	1	1	1	1	1	1	0	0	0	0	0	0	0	0	0	0	0	14 = U	14 = 5
T15	0	0	0	0	0	0	0	0	0	0	0	0	0	0	1	1	1	1	1	1	15 = U	15 = 5

Fig. 16(a). Parameters for the final example, with 20 attributes and 15 transactions.

Clustering of attributes on affinity matrix

Attribute	4	6	8	1	5	9	13	12	2	14	18	17	11	10	3	7	19	20	15	16
4	65	55	55	55	55	5	0	0	5	10	0	0	0	10	5	15	10	10	0	0
6	55	65	55	85	65	15	10	10	15	0	0	0	0	0	15	5	0	0	0	0
8	55	55	95	85	70	5	0	0	5	0	10	10	25	15	5	5	0	0	10	10
1	55	65	85	105	80	25	10	10	15	0	10	0	15	15	15	5	0	0	0	10
5	55	65	70	80	90	15	10	10	25	10	0	0	10	0	15	5	10	0	0	0
9	5	15	5	25	15	75	60	80	65	50	10	0	0	0	15	5	0	0	0	10
13	0	10	0	10	10	60	75	75	75	65	15	0	0	0	10	0	0	15	15	15
12	0	10	0	10	10	60	75	75	75	65	15	0	0	0	10	0	0	15	15	15
2	5	15	5	15	25	65	75	75	90	75	15	0	10	0	15	5	10	15	15	15
14	10	0	0	0	10	50	65	65	75	85	15	0	10	10	0	10	20	25	15	15
18	0	0	10	10	0	10	15	15	15	15	90	65	60	50	50	50	5	20	30	40
17	0	0	10	0	0	0	0	0	0	0	65	60	75	65	65	65	5	5	15	15
11	0	0	25	15	10	0	0	0	10	10	80	75	100	80	85	85	10	0	10	10
10	10	0	15	15	0	0	0	0	0	10	50	85	80	90	65	75	10	10	0	0
3	5	15	5	15	15	15	10	10	15	0	50	65	65	65	80	70	0	0	0	0
7	15	5	5	5	5	5	0	0	5	10	50	65	65	75	70	80	10	10	0	0
19	10	0	0	0	10	0	0	0	10	20	5	5	10	10	0	10	75	65	55	55
20	10	0	0	0	0	0	15	15	15	25	20	5	0	10	0	10	85	80	70	70
15	0	0	10	0	0	0	15	15	15	15	30	15	10	0	0	0	55	70	80	80
16	0	0	10	10	0	10	15	15	15	15	40	15	10	0	0	0	55	70	80	90

Problem type: S-N

Attribute Part	4	6	8	1	5	9	13	12	2	14	18	17	11	10	3	7	19	20	15	16	Iteration level
1	X	X	X	X	X																1
2						X	X	X	X	X											2
3											X	X	X	X	X	X					3
4																	X	X	X	X	3

Fig. 16(b). Solution of the final example (single site, nonoverlapping VPP).

The algorithms do not require very sophisticated input data. In fact, according to the well-known 20–80 rule, a limited number of important transactions (20 percent) typically account for most of the use of the database (80 percent), and therefore it is sufficient to collect input data for them. Moreover, we have kept the required information about the database usage to a minimum; we require only the specification as to whether an attribute is used by a transaction and the number of logical accesses to the object being considered.

We postulate the integration of these algorithms into an interactive design tool. With such a tool, the designer will typically be able to select a proper mix of algorithms and to use partial results to steer the design appropriately. This tool is applied for the initial design of the database, or for the reconfiguration of the database at an intermediate stage of its life cycle.

Further extensions of this work will be in the direction of developing site-specific affinity measures for distributed databases, of incorporating different transaction processing strategies, and of considering new applications of vertical partitioning, such as parallel processing of transactions.

ACKNOWLEDGMENTS

Many colleagues have participated in discussions on vertical partitioning, and have inspired some of the concepts used here. Particular thanks are due to Sheldon Finkelstein, Arthur Keller, Don Batory, and to the anonymous referees.

REFERENCES

1. BABAD, M.J. A record and file partitioning model. *Commun. ACM 20*, 1 (Jan. 1977).
2. BERNSTEIN, P.A., GOODMAN, N., WONG, E., REEVE, C.L., AND ROTHNIE, J.B., JR. Query processing in a system for distributed databases (SDD-1). *ACM Trans. Database Syst. 6*, 4 (Dec. 1981), 602–625.
3. CERI, S., NEGRI, M., AND PELAGATTI, G. Horizontal data partitioning in database design. In *Proceedings ACM SIGMOD International Conference on Management of Data* (Orlando, Fla., 1982), ACM, New York.
4. CERI, S., NAVATHE, S.B., AND WIEDERHOLD, G. Distribution design of logical database schemas. *IEEE Trans. Softw. Eng. SE-9*, 3 (July 1983).
5. CERI, S., AND PELAGATTI, G. The allocation of operations in distributed database access. *IEEE Trans. Comput. TC-32*, 2 (1982).
6. CHANG, S.K., AND CHENG, W.H. A methodology for structured database decomposition. *IEEE Trans. Softw. Eng. SE-6*, 2 (Mar. 1980).
7. CHEN, P.P.S., AND AKOKA, J. Optimal design of distributed information systems. *IEEE Trans. Comput. C-29*, 12 (Dec. 1980).
8. DAYAL, U., AND BERNSTEIN, P.A. The fragmentation problem: Lossless decomposition of relations into files. Tech. Rep. CCA-78-13, Computer Corporation of America, Cambridge, Mass.
9. EISNER, M.J., AND SEVERANCE, D.G. Mathematical techniques for efficient record segmentation in large shared databases. *J. ACM 23*, 4 (Oct. 1976).
10. FISHER, M.L., AND HOCHBAUM, D.S. Database location in computer networks. *J. ACM 27*, 4 (Oct. 1980), 718–735.
11. HAMMER, M., AND NIAMIR, B. A heuristic approach to attribute partitioning. In *Proceedings ACM SIGMOD International Conference on Management of Data* (Boston, Mass., 1979), ACM, New York.
12. HOFFER, J.A. An integer programming formulation of computer database design problems. *Inf. Sci. 11* (July 1976), 29–48.
13. HOFFER, J.A., AND SEVERANCE, D.G. The use of cluster analysis in physical database design. In *Proceedings 1st International Conference on Very Large Databases* (Framingham, Mass., 1975).
14. LUM, V.Y. The 1978 New Orleans Database Design Workshop Report. In *Proceedings 5th International Conference on Very Large Databases* (Rio de Janeiro, Oct. 1979).
15. MAHMOUD, S., AND RIORDON, J.S. Optimal allocation of resources in distributed information networks. *ACM Trans. Database Syst. 1*, 1 (1976).
16. MARCH, S.T., AND SEVERANCE, D.G. The determination of efficient record segmentations and blocking factors for shared data files. *ACM Trans. Database Syst. 2*, 3 (Sept. 1977).
17. MCCORMICK, W.T., SCHWEITZER, P.J., AND WHITE, T.W. Problem decomposition and data reorganization by a clustering technique. *Oper. Res. 20*, 5 (Sept. 1972), 993–1009.
18. MORGAN, H.L., AND LEVIN, J.D. Optimal program and data location in computer networks. *Commun. ACM 20*, 1 (Jan. 1977).
19. ROTHNIE, J.B., JR., ET AL. Introduction to a system for distributed databases (SDD-1). *ACM Trans. Database Syst. 6*, 4 (Dec. 1980), 431–466.
20. SCHKOLNICK, M. A clustering algorithm for hierarchical structure. *ACM Trans. Database Syst. 2*, 1 (Mar. 1977).
21. SELINGER, P.G., AND ADIBA, M.E. Access path selection in distributed database management systems. In *Proceedings of the International Conference on Databases* (Aberdeen, Scotland, July 1980), British Computer Society.
22. YAO, S.B., NAVATHE, S.B., AND WELDON, J.L. An integrated approach to logical database design. In *Proceedings NYU Symposium on Database Design, 1978*. Lecture Series in Computer Science, No. 132, Springer-Verlag, New York, 1982.
23. WIEDERHOLD, G. *Database Design*. 2nd ed., McGraw-Hill, New York, 1983.
24. WILLIAMS, R., ET AL. R*, an overview of the architecture. In *Proceedings 2nd International Conference on Databases: Improving Usability and Responsiveness*. P. Scheuermann, Ed., Academic Press, New York, 1981.

Received January 1983; revised August 1983; accepted February 1984

Database Partitioning in a Cluster of Processors

DOMENICO SACCÀ AND GIO WIEDERHOLD
IBM Research Laboratory, San Jose

In a distributed database system the partitioning and allocation of the database over the processor nodes of the network can be a critical aspect of the database design effort. In this paper we develop and evaluate algorithms that perform this task in a computationally feasible manner. The network we consider is characterized by a relatively high communication bandwidth, considering the processing and input output capacities in its processors. Such a balance is typical if the processors are connected via busses or local networks. The common constraint that transactions have a specific root node no longer exists, so that there are more distribution choices. However, a poor distribution leads to less efficient computation, higher costs, and higher loads in the nodes or in the communication network so that the system may not be able to handle the required set of transactions.

Our approach is to first split the database into fragments which constitute appropriate units for allocation. The fragments to be allocated are selected based on maximal benefit criteria using a greedy heuristic. The assignment to processor nodes uses a first-fit algorithm. The complete algorithm, called GFF, is stated in a procedural form.

The complexity of the problem and of its candidate solutions are analyzed and several interesting relationships are proven. Alternate benefit metrics are considered, since the execution cost of the allocation procedure varies by orders of magnitude with the alternatives of benefit evaluation. A mixed benefit evaluation strategy is eventually proposed.

A model for evaluation is presented. Two of the strategies are experimentally evaluated, and the reported results support the discussion. The approach should be suitable for other cases where resources have to be allocated subject to resource constraints.

Categories and Subject Descriptions: H.2.2 [**Database Management**]: Physical Design; H.2.4 [**Database Management**]: Systems; D.4.2 [**Operating Systems**]: Storage Management; G.1.6 [**Numerical Analysis**]: Optimization; C.2.4 [**Computer-Communication Networks**]: Distributed Systems; D.2.8 [**Software Engineering**]: Metrics

General Terms: Algorithms, Design, Theory

Additional Key Words and Phrases: Allocation, database, multiprocessor, greedy method, first-fit method, partitioning

1. INTRODUCTION

In a distributed database system the partitioning and allocation of the database over the processor nodes of the network can be a critical aspect of the database

An earlier version of this paper appeared as IBM Research Report RJ4076(45454), October 1983; an abstract of this paper was published in the Proceedings on Very Large Data Bases, 9, 1983. G. Wiederhold's work was supported in part by ARPA contract N39-82-C-0250.
Authors' current addresses: D. Saccà, CRAI, Via Bernini 5, 87030 Rende, Italy; G. Wiederhold, Stanford University, Computer Science Dept., Stanford, CA 94305.

design effort. In networks that have only a limited communication capability, local processing of transactions dominates. When a system using a network of processors has a high communication bandwidth, a high shared utilization of its processors becomes possible. A cluster of processors can also provide high reliability and availability, this aspect is presented in [21]. To the user, the cluster appears as if it were a high-quality centralized processor.

The shared database should be partitioned so that the system throughput is maximal. The partitioning of the database has to be such that the transactions using the database are executed efficiently, while the capacity constraints of all the processors and limits of the communication network are observed. A poor partitioning of the database can lead to higher processing costs in the nodes or to greater demands on the communication network, so that the system may not be able to handle the required set of transactions.

We are investigating, in this context, the optimal nonredundant partitioning of databases in a system where a number of processors are clustered and connected via a high-capacity network. Given is a set of source relations of the database and their attributes and a set of transactions which are to be executed during some period of interest. A transaction performs operations on some subset of the database.

The database resides on multiple processors which are connected using a dense and reliable communication network. The contents of the database are assigned to the processor nodes. Associated with every transaction is an initial network node. Since the user is not connected to any prespecified node, the initial network node is to be assigned as part of the design.

The capacity limits of each of the processors may be given in terms of processor cycle capacity and IO-block move capacity per unit time. The capacity limit of the network is given in terms of aggregate block transfer capacity per unit time. The demands of the transactions are then given using the same measures.

We model the content of the database as a collection of relations. The given conceptual relations may be too large to be effectively assigned to single processors. We initially consider how the relations can be fragmented, and then allocate those fragments to the processor nodes. In the designed database, each transaction accesses some subset of the tuples and the attributes of each original relation. In order to complete transactions that do not find all their data on the same processor, a scheduling algorithm is invoked which optimizes the processing over the network. We do not investigate this scheduling algorithm, but simply assume that it exists, and that we can use it in order to obtain the costs for the execution of a given transaction over a proposed database allocation for some specified but fictitious processor network.

In Section 2 of this paper we discuss previous and related work on this topic. In Section 3 we formulate our problem precisely, and then study the intrinsic complexity of the problem in Section 4. Section 5 develops the heuristic *greedy with first-fit* (GFF) algorithms that we propose, and proves statements about their behavior. In Section 6 we present alternate computations for the estimation of the benefits which drive the greedy selection algorithm. Section 7 contains a model and reports on some experimental evaluations. The conclusions we draw from this work are presented in Section 8.

2. OVERVIEW OF THE DATABASE PARTITIONING AND ALLOCATION PROBLEM

Comprehensive software for distributed database systems has been only recently introduced, and only a few systems using a flexible allocation strategy are in operation. As a consequence, the problem of partitioning and allocating databases in a network of computers has not been the subject of many studies. In fact, most of the available literature is related to problems of allocating files [2, 5, 9, 20] or to the problem of vertically partitioning and clustering attributes within a single file [12–14]. An excellent overview is presented in [8].

The problem of partitioning databases both horizontally and vertically into subrelations or fragments, and of allocating the fragments obtained in a network of computers, has been studied only recently in [1] and [4]. In [1], several algorithms have been proposed to solve this problem in the case of unlimited capacities of processors. The case with limited capacities has been studied in [4] by considering horizontal partitioning of databases only. We note that in [4] a set of possible alternative horizontal partitions of the relations are considered as the input of the problem, and the optimal partition is given as a solution of the problem together with the allocation. This approach cannot be extended to vertical partitioning because of the large number of possible vertical partitions of a relation.

In the analyses cited, including the ones concerned with the file allocation problem, it has always been supposed that the starting point of every transaction is given as input of the problem, so that every transaction is assigned to a predefined processor. This assumption is very reasonable in many cases. However, in the case of clustered processors, in which the transaction may start from any processor, this assumption cannot be accepted, since the optimal allocation of the transaction becomes as important as the allocation of the relations fragments. We point out that any attempt to adapt the algorithms proposed in the literature to this extension leads to useless results. For instance, if we try to use some of the algorithms prescribed in [1] for the database partitioning and allocation problem in a cluster of processors, we obtain the trivial solution that all relations are allocated in only one processor. Nevertheless, by starting from the results obtained in some of thc previous work, we shall propose algorithms for the solution of the problem of partitioning in a cluster of processors.

3. FORMULATION OF THE DATABASE PARTITIONING PROBLEM

3.1 The General Database Partitioning Problem

We investigate the optimal nonredundant partitioning and allocation of a database in a cluster of processes. Given that $\mathbf{P} = \{P_1, \ldots, P_p\}$ is a small set of processor nodes of a densely and reliably interconnected network. Associated with every processor P_i of $\mathbf{P}$ is the input-output capacity CI_i, expressed in terms of the maximum number of blocks that can be processed, and the processsor capacity CC_i, expressed in terms of the maximum number of cycles of the processor. Furthermore, associated with each pair of processors (P_i, P_j) is the communication capacity $\mathbf{CM}_{ij}$, expressed in terms of the maximum volume of messages that can be transmitted between the two processors.

We also have a set of source relations $\mathbf{R} = \{R_1, \ldots, R_r\}$. We denote the set of attributes of each relation R_i of $\mathbf{R}$ by A_i. We can split the relations into fragments for allocation to processors in order to satisfy the capacity constraints of those processors.

Replication and Vertical and Horizontal Partitioning

Traditional terminology in allocation for distributed systems uses the notions of replication and of vertical and horizontal partitioning. Vertical partitioning allocates columns of a relation over distinct nodes. Horizontal partitioning allocates rows of a relation over distinct nodes. A partition of a relation may be referred to as a fragment of a relation. In this analysis we do not consider replication of relations, since in this particular architecture all data are already kept in duplicate on each component processor to provide reliability and availability [21]. Note that tuple identifiers (TIDs) will be further replicated as a byproduct of vertical partitioning.

Horizontal partitioning. A horizontal partitioning of a relation R_i in $\mathbf{R}$ is a set of relation fragments $fh(R_i) = \{R_{i_1} \ldots, R_{i_h}\}$ such that all tuples are complete and represented only once:

(i) for all R_{i_q} in $fh(R_i)$, $A_{i_q} = A_i$;
(ii) for all tuples t in R_i there is exactly one fragment in $fh(R_i)$ that contains t;
(iii) for all R_{i_q} in $fh(R_i)$ and for all tuples t of R_{i_q}, R_i contains t.

The specification of a horizontal partitioning of a relation R_i is given by providing predicate expressions on some attribute of A_i. Each predicate specifies a candidate partitioning into two or more horizontal fragments. The total number of such horizontal fragments for one relation R_i is equal to the product of the candidate partition cardinality for each attribute that provides a candidate partitioning rule.

For example, during a preanalysis phase, an employee relation which may be partitioned into four geographic and three age categories will be submitted to this analysis as twelve distinct relation fragments. A postanalysis phase may combine any relation fragments of the same source relation which were allocated to the same node.

Vertical partitioning. If different subsets of attributes of one relation are mainly seen at one node it may be desirable to partition the relations vertically. A vertical partitioning of a relation R_i in R is a set of relation fragments $fv(R_i) = \{R_{i_1}, \ldots, R_{i_h}\}$ such that all attributes are represented only once and all fragments have tuples corresponding to each of the source relation tuples:

(i) $\cup_{q=1}^{h} (A_{i_q}) = A_i$;
(ii) for all R_{i_p}, R_{i_q} in $fv(R_i)$, $A_{i_p} \cap A_{i_q} = \emptyset$;
(iii) for all R_{i_q} in $fv(R_i)$, there is a bisection φ from the tuples of R_{i_q} to the tuples of R_i for which a tuple t of R_{i_q} is equal to the projection of $\varphi(t)$ on A_{i_q}.

More than one vertical partitioning can be defined in this manner by defining different subsets of A_i.

Notice that although our analysis does not consider replication of relations, the tuple identifiers (TIDs) [6] will be replicated as a by-product of a vertical partitioning. The database management system has the responsibility of managing the TIDs properly. If a relation is vertically partitioned into a number of fragments, and a tuple is inserted into the relation, all fragments must be updated with the TID and its assigned fields, even if all the fields in a fragment are null.

Fragments. By combining vertical and horizontal partitioning, we can associate to any relation R_i of **R** a set of fragments $F(R_i) = \{F_{i_1}, \ldots, F_{i_h}\}$, obtained by letting $F(R_i) = fv(fh(R_i))$. Note that $fh(fv(R_i))$ leads to a less general, but perhaps easier to manage, partitioning.

Given a set of fragments $F(R_i)$ for all R_i in **R**, we denote by $\mathbf{F} = \{F_1, \ldots, F_f\}$ a set of fragments such that

$$\mathbf{F} = \bigcup_{i=1}^{r} (F(R_i)).$$

Since we may define several different fragmentations of any relation R_i in **R** (for instance, by choosing different subsets of A_i for the vertical partitioning or by providing different predicate expressions on some attribute of A_i for horizontal partitioning), there could be several sets of fragments **F** associated with **R**. In Section 3.2 we present conditions for an appropriate fragmentation.

Transactions. A set of transactions $\mathbf{T} = \{T_1, \ldots, T_t\}$ performs some operations on **R** (or on **F** if we refer to a set of fragments of **R**). Each transaction T_i of **T** is executed during some period of interest with frequency q_i and performs operations op_i on some subset $\mathbf{X}_i$ of **R** (or **F**). In general, a transaction T_i in **T** will access only some rows and some columns of each relation (or fragment) X_{i_j} in $\mathbf{X}_i$; thus it performs operations on a fragment of X_{i_j} only. Associated with each transaction T_i in **T** is an initial network node P_{T_i}, which is not prespecified but is to be assigned as part of the design.

Allocation. Given the set of transactions **T** and a suitable set of fragments **F**, let $\mathbf{O} = \mathbf{T} \cup \mathbf{F}$ be the set of objects to be allocated on the network. Furthermore, given a set of fictitious processor nodes $\mathbf{N} = \{N_1, \ldots, N_n\}$, where **N** does not necessarily equal **P**, an allocation of **O** to **N**, denoted by $\mathbf{L}_N(\mathbf{O})$, is a mapping of **O** into **N**. In the case where $\mathbf{N} = \mathbf{P}$, the allocation $\mathbf{L}_P(\mathbf{O})$ represents a possible real allocation of the objects (fragments and transactions) to the processors **P** of the network.

Objective

The objective of this analysis is to find an allocation design $\mathbf{L}_P$ for the set of fragments **F** and the set of transaction **T**, so that the aggregate cost function is minimized, while the capacity constraints {**CI**, **CC**, **CM**} are observed, where $\mathbf{CI} = \{CI_1, \ldots, CI_p\}$, $\mathbf{CC} = \{CC_1, \ldots, CC_p\}$, and $\mathbf{CM} = \{CM_{11}, \ldots, CM_{pp}\}$. The elements of the cost are the load parameters as produced at execution time by a transaction optimizer as part of its planning. The analysis model is limited by the capability of the optimizer, as it should be: no design will be produced that employs a transaction processing strategy that will not be generated by the optimizer.

Cost evaluation. In order to evaluate the cost of processing some allocation, we invoke at design time the program that, at execution time, is used for the optimization of transaction execution. Processing cost estimates are produced by a transaction optimizer (like the optimzer in System R* [23]) prior to execution of the transactions. Such a program determines the total cost for each transaction T_i in **T** and, in the process, computes the execution load components. We assume that these load values are scaled relative to each other, just as required for the internal decision-making of the optimizer. This optimizer is the basis for the cost evaluator used to design a specific database allocation. How the optimizer is used to provide the cost evaluation function is explained in Section 6.

The sum of the costs of all individually optimized transactions for one proposed allocation is the measure of the goodness of that allocation. We do not compute, however, the costs for all or many possible allocations over the network of available processors and then select the best alternative. Rather, we use the transaction-optimizing program to provide us with the component costs for a fictitious network of fragments and use these values to direct us step-by-step to the desired solution.

For generality, in our model we refer to a cost evaluation function *Cef*, which is formally a mapping and is defined as follows: Given a set **F** of fragments of **R**, a set **N** of nodes (not necessarily equal to **P**), the set of objects $\mathbf{O} = \mathbf{T} \cup \mathbf{F}$, and an allocation $\mathbf{L}_N(\mathbf{O})$, $Cef(\mathbf{L}_N(\mathbf{O}))$ is the triple (**vi, vc, vm**), where

(i) $\mathbf{vi} = \{vi_1, \ldots, vi_n\}$, and vi_i is the load in terms of the number of block accesses required in the node N_i.

(ii) $\mathbf{vc} = \{vc_1, \ldots, vc_n\}$, and vc_i is the load in terms of the number of processor cycles consumed by the node N_i.

(iii) $\mathbf{vm} = \{vm_{ij} \mid 1 \le i, j \le n\}$, and $vm_{i,j}$ is the load due to the message traffic generated between the nodes N_i and N_j or, more generally, to the communication cost between the two nodes.

Notice that **vi, vc, vm** represent the costs necessary to execute the transactions in **T** on the fictitious network of nodes **N**.

Objective function. The problem of database partitioning in a cluster of processors is the following:

The DBPCP problem over relations. Let **R** be a set of relations, **T** a set of transactions, **P** a set of **p** processors, and *Cef* a cost evaluation function. Find a set **F** of fragments of **R** and an allocation $\mathbf{L}_P(\mathbf{O})$, where $\mathbf{O} = \mathbf{T} \cup \mathbf{F}$, such that the cost

$$\sum_{i=1}^{p} (vi_i + vc_i) + \sum_{i=2}^{p} \sum_{j=1}^{i-1} vm_{ij} \quad \text{is minimum,}$$

subject to

(i) $vi_i \le CI_i$ for all P_i in P,

(ii) $vc_i \le CC_i$ for all P_i in P,

(iii) $vm_{ij} \le CM_{ij}$ for all P_i, P_j in P,

where $(\mathbf{vi}, \mathbf{vc}, \mathbf{vm}) = Cef(\mathbf{L}_P(\mathbf{O}))$.

We note that this problem is different from the database partitioning problems treated in the literature (see, for instance, [1] and [4]). In particular, in this case, the initial network node of each transaction is not predefined. This means that we cannot neglect the capacity constraint, as it was assumed in previous papers, because if we do we would find a trivial solution, that is, one allocating all transactions and relations in only one processor. We discuss differences in allocation heuristics further in Section 5.1.

A reviewer has pointed out, correctly, that these optimizations do not optimize response times. It is clear that specific transaction response constraints have to be considered prior to aggregate optimization [22; Fig. 7-27]. Such constraints can be satisfied by combining fragments and transactions prior to application of the optimization procedure. The ability in this architecture to allocate transactions to any node should provide a better balance of response times than seen in systems where transactions are bound to an entry node. Priority transactions might be handled by binding them to a node with a low utilization, reflected by reduced load constraints. Since these decisions precede the aggregate optimization process, we can now continue with the methods specifically addressed in this paper.

3.2 The Database Partitioning Problem with a Defined Set of Fragments

We note that the DBPCP problem considers any possible fragmentation of the relations in **R**. If we assume that a set **F** of fragments is given, a variant of the DBPCP problem is the following.

The DBPCP problem over fragments. Let **F** be a set of fragments of a given set of relations **R**. Let **T** be a set of transactions, **P** a set of **p** processors, and *Cef* a cost evaluation function. Find an allocation $\mathbf{L}_P(\mathbf{O})$, where $\mathbf{O} = \mathbf{T} \cup \mathbf{F}$, such that

$$\sum_{i=1}^{p} (vi_i + vc_i) + \sum_{i=2}^{p} \sum_{j-1}^{i-1} vm_{ij} \quad \text{is minimum,}$$

subject to constraints (i), (ii), and (iii) of the DBPCP problem over relations.

We note that in general the solution of this second problem is not a solution of the general problem. However, if the initial set of fragments contains units of allocation (i.e., elementary objects of allocation that cannot be further fragmented), then the solution of the DBPCP problem over a set of predefined fragments is also the solution of the DBPCP problem over relations.

This means that since the transactions cannot be fragmented, we have to find an initial set **F** of fragments such that each fragment in **F** will not be further partitioned but only (eventually) combined.

In [1], a method is proposed to obtain the initial units of allocation. In particular, the elementary fragments of the relations are determined on the basis of the fragments defined by the transactions. Using the same approach, we can define the set **F** of elementary fragments, which we call functional elementary objects, of relations in the following way:

(i) For each fragment F_i in **F** and each transaction T_j in **T**, either T_j accesses all rows and columns of F_i or T_j does not perform any operation on F_i.

(ii) The property (i) does not hold for all sets **F**′ of fragments obtained from **F** by combining any two fragments of the same source relation.

We note that a similar definition of elementary fragments for the case of horizontal partitioning only is given in [3]. We must point out that the functional elementary objects defined above do not yet represent real units of allocations, as they are for the problem considered in [1]. Since in our problem capacity constraints have a fundamental role, it might be that a functional elementary object is further horizontally partitioned in an optimal solution of the DBPCP problem in order to respect capacity constraints, even though the object is seen as a unitary object from all transactions. Atomic units of allocation should perhaps be fragments composed by one row and one column only. Considering the size of the input necessary to represent such extensive fragmentation, this approach cannot be proposed. We can, however, propose that any functional elementary object—which is a large fraction of the database, considering the number of available processors—should be further fragmented prior to the allocation phase.

From now on we consider as input of the DBPCP problem over fragments either a set of functional elementary objects or whatever set of fragments has been predefined by the database designer. The size of the set of fragments is polynomially bound by the size of the input of the DBPCP problem over relations. Our conjecture is that even with fewer fragments, due to the natural granularity provided by query predicates or the designer, an optimal or suboptimal solution of the DBPCP problem over these fragments is also a good suboptimal solution of the DBPCP problem over fully fragmented relations. Furthermore, since the optimal solution of both problems cannot be found in a reasonable amount of time, as we prove in the next section, the above assumption is the only one suitable to provide polynomial-time heuristic algorithms.

Before concluding with the formulation of the database partitioning problems, we point out that after the solution to the problems is found, a postanalysis will recombine any fragments of the same source relations that are allocated into the same processor.

4. COMPLEXITY OF DATABASE PARTITIONING PROBLEMS

Problems of optimal allocation tend to be hard, even if the cost function to be minimized is simple. In our case, where the cost function has an unknown behavior for any pattern of proposed allocations, the problems appear to be harder yet.

The solution of the two database partitioning problems introduced in the previous section is strongly dependent on the cost evaluation function *Cef*. It is obvious that if the computation of such a function requires exponential time in the size of the relations in **R** and the transactions in **T**, we do not have any hope of finding a solution, even a suboptimal one, in a reasonable amount of time.

In this paper we suppose that the cost evaluation function computes the costs in polynomial time. This is not a strong assumption, since the transaction optimizer, invoked by the cost evaluation function, must be practical if it is to be useful during query execution. It must compute the cost of transactions in a reasonable amount of time. However, we have to point out that such a computation cannot be considered as an elementary computer operation. The transaction optimizer itself will have to execute a high number of operations, and will have to use heuristics to achieve its goal in polynomial time.

To deal with this aspect in our complexity analysis, we evaluate how many times the cost evaluator function is invoked separately from the evaluation of the number of simple operations. In Section 6 we consider how often the cost evaluator has to evoke the transaction optimizer. Note that the cost of executing the optimizer even once will vary with number of objects and nodes to be considered; and this number is initially quite large.

Despite the simplifying assumption about the polynomial complexity of the cost evaluator, the complexity of the DBPCP problem over relations is still hard. In fact, we prove not only that there is no polynomial-time algorithm to solve the problem, unless $P = NP$ [10], but also that no polynomial-time algorithm is able to find a feasible solution to the problem.

THEOREM 1. *Finding a feasible solution of the DBPCP problem over relations is NP-hard.*

PROOF. To prove the theorem it is sufficient to show that any instance of a known NP-complete problem can be transformed in polynomial time into an instance of a DBPCP problem. Let us consider the minimum cut into bounded set (MCBS) problem, which was shown to be NP-complete in [11]. Any instance of the MCBS problem is the following:

Graph $G = (V, E)$, weight $w(e) \in Z^+$ for each $e \in E$, specified vertices v_s, $v_t \in V$, positive integer $B < |V|$, positive integer k.

The question now is: Is there a partition of V into disjoint sets V_1 and V_2 such that $v_s \in V_1$, $v_t \in V_2$, $|V_1| \leq B$, $|V_2| \leq B$, and such that the sum of the weights of the edges of E that have one endpoint in V_1 and one endpoint in V_2 is no more than k?

Let us suppose, for simplicity, that any instance of the above problem is such that $B = |V|/2$ and $w(e) = 1$ for all $e \in E$. This variant of the MCBS problem remains NP-complete.

We associate a relation R_i of $\mathbf{R}$ with each node v_i of V. We assume that each relation has one row and one column only, for which no further fragmentation is possible. We associated a transaction T_i of $\mathbf{T}$ with each edge e_i of E in such a way that T_i performs operations only on the two relations corresponding to the endpoints of the edge e_i. The network is composed of two processors only, P_1 and P_2. The components of the processors' capacity are

$$CI_1 = CI_2 = \infty$$
$$CC_1 = CC_2 = (B - 1) \times a + b + k$$
$$CM_{12} = \infty$$

where $a = (|V^2| + 1) \times 2$ and $b = |V^2| + 1$.

We now define the cost evaluation function, *Cef*, for costs due to the CPU load only—because of unlimited IO and communication capacity—in the following way:

(i) $vc_i = d_i \times a - (c_s + c_t) \times b + m$, where
   d_i is the number of relations allocated in processor P_i;
   c_s is equal to 1 if the relation R_s, associated with the node v_s of V, is allocated in the processor P_1, and 0 otherwise;
   c_t is equal to 1 if the relation R_t, associated with the node v_t of V, is allocated in the processor P_2, and 0 otherwise; and

m is the number of edges whose endpoints correspond to relations allocated in two different processes, for all allocations of **R** to **P** and for all P_i in **P**.

Let us suppose that there is a solution of the MCBS problem. It is then easily seen that there is also a feasible solution of the associated DBPCP problem. Let us now suppose that the DBPCP problem has a feasible solution. Hence, by considering CPU constraints, the relations R_s and R_t are allocated in two different processors. Furthermore, the quantity m defined above is less or equal to k. Hence, the MCBS problem has a solution. Finally, considering that the transformation of any instance of the MCBS problem into one instance of the DBPCP problem can obviously be done in polynomial time, finding a feasible solution of the DBPCP problem is NP-hard. □

Since finding an optimal solution is bound to be at least as difficult as finding a feasible solution, we can also state:

THEOREM 1′. *Finding an optimal solution of the DBPCP problem over relations is NP-hard.*

We do not give a formal proof here, but go on to consider fragments.

By considering the proof of Theorem 1, we note that the instance of the DBPCP problem over relations constructed in that proof is also an instance of the DBPCP problem over fragments. Hence, the following property also holds:

PROPOSITION 1. *Finding a feasible or optimal solution of the DBPCP problem over fragments is NP-hard.*

From Theorem 1 and Proposition 1, we see that we cannot find a solution to the database partitioning problem, even a feasible, and not an optimal, solution, in a reasonable amount of time without using heuristic procedures.

Feasible and Optimal Solutions

We conjecture that the capacity constraints in practical systems are not overly restrictive. Requirements in terms of system response times prohibit designs that are close to their capacity limits. Then, many feasible solutions exist. With reasonable heuristics one of the feasible, although suboptimal, solutions should be found in polynomial time.

There is unfortunately no way to tell initially if there exists any feasible solution. Use of an arbitrary heuristic, say a random allocation of transactions and relations over the processor nodes $P_i \in \mathbf{P}$, might yield a solution; but, if this procedure does not yield a solution, we cannot tell if this failure occurred because there is no feasible solution or because we were unlucky.

A good initial heuristic is required to minimize the probability of not finding a feasible solution. Experience with databases tells us that the choice between poor strategies and good strategies can easily make a difference by a factor of 100 in performance. With an arbitrary heuristic, the probability of failure is quite high. Feasible and optimal solutions share the same characteristic: allocation should generate a low demand on the available capacity.

In the next sections we give heuristic algorithms for the solution of the DBPCP problem, based on the greedy method [16] and on the first-fit algorithm [18].

Since a feasible solution of the DBPCP problem over fragments is also a feasible solution of the DBPCP problem over relations, and since starting from a predefined set of elementary fragments is a more suitable way to provide heuristic algorithms, we consider the DBPCP problem over fragments only.

5. HEURISTIC ALGORITHMS FOR THE DBPCP PROBLEM OVER FRAGMENTS

To find a solution to the DBPCP problem, we considered heuristic algorithms based on the greedy method, on branch-and-bound strategies, and on algorithms used for bin-packing. We developed an approach, GFF, which combines the greedy method and first-fit bin-packing in a novel manner.

5.1 The Greedy and the First-Fit Algorithms

Our task is to select fragments from a large set of fragments and allocate them to the processors. Fragments should be combined if this leads to great benefits in terms of reduction of communication, IO, or CPU load. Combining a transaction and a fragment into a processor leads to similar benefits. Objects (fragments and transactions) have to be placed into processor nodes subject to capacity constraints.

Greedy selection of objects. Selecting objects suggests using a greedy method; that is an algorithm that, in stages, considering two objects at a time, selects pairs of objects for allocation [16]. Here the input is the set of benefits obtained for all candidate combinations. At each stage, an optimal "local" solution is found by combining the two objects whose combination leads to the greatest benefit, that is, the greatest reduction in aggregate load. A pair, after allocation, is considered as a single, new object for the next stage of the algorithm. Such solutions may or may not lead to the optimal solution of the problem. However, most of the time such a method will result in algorithms that generate good suboptimal solutions. In our case, the greedy method reduces to the following algorithm.

We start from the set **O** of **o** objects (transactions and relation fragments), and we consider a set of **n** nodes **N** such that $\mathbf{n} = \mathbf{o} - 1$. For all pairs of objects O_i, O_j, we consider an allocation on $\mathbf{L}_N(\mathbf{O})$ such that [illegible]$_h$ of **N** contains the combination of two objects O_i, O_j, and that e [illegible] 109 [illegible] remaining nodes contains only one object of $\mathbf{O} - \{O_i, O_j\}$. Let $\mathbf{vt}_{ij}$ be the total cost of this allocation,

$$\mathbf{vt}_{ij} = \sum_{i=1}^{n} (vi_i + vc_i) + \sum_{i=2}^{n} \sum_{j=1}^{i-1} vm_{ij},$$

where $(\mathbf{vi}, \mathbf{vc}, \mathbf{vm}) = Cef(\mathbf{L}_N(\mathbf{O}))$.

We select the pair of nodes O_i, O_j for which $\mathbf{vt}_{ij}$ is minimum and the capacity constraints of the problem are satisfied. We then modify the set of objects **O** by replacing the object O_i, O_j with the compound object. In a further stage, we repeat the above step by considering the modified set of objects **O** and by reducing the number of nodes by one. Eventually, the algorithm stops when either the number of nodes is reduced to the number of available processors $\mathbf{n} = \mathbf{p}$ or no two nodes can be combined further. If the algorithm reaches the stage where $\mathbf{n} = \mathbf{p}$, the compound objects in **O** define the final allocation of the objects in the processors. The greedy method fails if it reaches the point where no nodes can be combined while **n** > **p**; although a feasible solution to the problem may exist.

We note that the same algorithm was proposed in [1] for the solution of a database partitioning problem without capacity constraints but with a predefined starting site of each transaction. In that paper it was shown that such an application gives a good suboptimal solution to the problem. Substantial communication benefits are gained by allocating fragments at the entry site of the transactions that use them. Unfortunately, it appears that this algorithm is unlikely to give a feasible solution of the allocation phase for our problem, where the entry sites are not predetermined.

Note that without any load constraints, Apers' algorithm will achieve the optimum by allocating all fragments and transactions at a single site. If we do have to consider load constraints, finding a feasible solution corresponds to solving the bin-packing problem, where the fragments are the items to be inserted in the bins, represented by the processors. It is known in the literature (for instance, [10] and [18]) that any algorithm that starts a new bin before all the nonempty bins are full, gives a very bad solution to the bin-packing problem. A new bin corresponds here to the entry site of the transaction.

In general, any "good" heuristic allocation algorithm must at least be a "first-fit" algorithm. We further have to consider that the IO and CPU loads associated with the fragments are also not independent of the allocation of the fragments, since accesses and program functions may be shared. Our problem is therefore more complex than the traditional bin-packing problems, which consider items to have predetermined size. Nevertheless, in this case, a first-fit approach is also necessary to satisfy the constraints. The greedy method remains responsible for the goodness of the solution.

First-fit allocation. Let us review the basic greedy algorithm described above. Any time it combines two objects, which were never combined before, it starts what amounts to a new bin, although there are bins not yet full. Hence, we have to modify the allocation phase of the greedy algorithm in order to meet the above-mentioned property of first-fit algorithms. Notice that we could use some other, better algorithm for the bin-packing problem (such as the "first-fit decreasing" algorithm in [17]). However, in such a case the selection phase would be driven only by the capacity constraints during allocation, not by the optimality objective used for selection. In the case of the simple first-fit algorithm we have the freedom to select fragment combinations on the basis of the greedy method, since the only constraint is to never introduce too many bins. In particular, there should never be more bins than the number of available processors. Since we believe that in reality the capacity constraints are not too restrictive, a first-fit allocation approach should permit the constraints to be respected.

5.2 The Case of Processors with Equal Capacity

Let us assume, for simplicity, that all **P** processors have the same CPU capacity **CC**, while the other capacities (IO and message traffic) are unlimited. We analyze the case in which processors have differing capacities in Section 5.3; the case in which IO capacities are considered in Section 5.4; and the general case in which message traffic is also considered in Sections 5.5 and 5.6.

A greedy selection algorithm, combined with a first-fit assignment algorithm, for finding an approximate solution of the predefined DBPCP problem follows.

Greedy First-Fit (GFF) Algorithm

```
/* Data Structures
O is the set of o source elementary objects (transactions + fragments).
D = {D_1, ..., D_p}, where D_i corresponds to the processor P_i and is a subset of the objects
   of O.
d is the number of nonempty elements in D.
CC is the CPU capacity of each processor.
O', O^1, O^2 are sets of elementary and compound objects.
N is a set of n fictitious processor nodes such that n = o'.
L_N(O') is an assignment of the elements in O' to the nodes in N.
Cef is the cost evaluation function.
⟨vi, cv, vm⟩ = Cef(L_N(O')) are loads of assignment L_N(O') and Vt is the total cost due
   to these loads.
Vtm = current total minimum cost.
Ob_1, Ob_2 is the current object pair whose merging gives Vtm */
/* Algorithm
At every step the algorithm uses the greedy technique to select two objects to be merged.
Following the first-fit constraint, it creates up to p compound objects, where p is the actual
number of processors. */
begin
(a)  Set D_i := ∅ forall D_i ∈ D
     Set there_is_a_solution := true
(b)  while there_is_a_solution do
       Set there_is_a_solution := false
(c)    Set O^1 := O ∪ {D_i | D_i is not empty}
(d)    if d < p then Set O^2 := O^1
                else Set O^2 := {D_i | D_i is not empty}
       Set Vtm := ∞.
(e)    forall O^1_i in O^1 and O^2_j in O^2 | O^1 ≠ O^2 do
         Let O_ij be the compound object obtained by combining
           O^1_i and O^2_j
(f)      Set O' := (O^1 − {O^1_i, O^2_j}) ∪ {O_ij}.
(g)      Set ⟨vi, vc, vm⟩ := Cef(L_N(O'))
           and let Vt be the total cost.
         Set constraints_satisfied := true
(h)      forall D_i in D do
           if vc_i > CC then constraint_satisfied := false
(i)      if constraint_satisfied and Vt < Vtm then
             Set Vtm := Vt
             Set Ob_1 := O^1_i and Ob_2 := O^2_j
             Set there_is_a_solution := true
         endif
         end forall
(j)        if there_is_a_solution then
(k)        case
             :both Ob_1 and Ob_2 are elementary objects:
               Set O := O − {Ob_1, Ob_2}.
               Set D := D ∪ {{Ob_1, Ob_2}}.
             :both Ob_1 and Ob_2 are compound elements:
               Set D := (D − {Ob_1, Ob_2}) ∪ (Ob_1 ∪ Ob_2}.
             Otherwise (let us suppose that Ob_1 is elementary):
               Set O := O − {Ob_1}
               Set D := (D − {Ob_2}) ∪ {{Ob_1} ∪ Ob_2}.
           end
```

```
endwhile
if O is empty then /* Combine object pair and allocate */
  D gives the allocation of the initial set of objects O to the nodes of P.
end
```

Let us first of all show that the GFF algorithm never introduces more than **p** bins, where **p** is the number of processors. In fact, as soon as all the bins in **D** are not empty, the algorithm (see statement (d)) no longer merges two elementary objects into a new bin, but merges either two compound objects only or an elementary and a compound object. In other words, either two bins are combined or an item is inserted into a nonempty bin.

Nevertheless, the algorithm still uses the greedy method for selecting objects to be combined. Let us now prove that the GFF algorithm runs in polynomial time.

PROPOSITION 2. *The GFF algorithm for equal capacity processors runs in* $O(\mathbf{o}^3\mathbf{p})$ *time, where* **o** *is the number of objects to be allocated and* **p** *is the number of processors.*

PROOF. Let us suppose at this point that the operations involving the optimizer are simple operations; we discuss the complexity of such operations in Section 6.2.

Let **o** be the number of initial elementary objects (fragments and transactions). The innermost loop, step (h), is performed at most $O(\mathbf{p})$ times, since constraints have to be checked for the nodes receiving allocations only. The enclosing loop through the fragment combinations, step (e), is performed $O(\mathbf{o}^2)$ times. Step (b) is performed $O(\mathbf{o})$ times, since, any time the step is performed, the set $\mathbf{O}^1$, computed by statement (c), is reduced by one, and because, in the beginning, there are **o** elements in $\mathbf{O}^1$. Let us now compute how many operations are performed in step (e).

All statements but statement (h) require $O(1)$ time, while statement (h) requires $O(\mathbf{p})$ time.

Statements (c), (d), and (k) inside step (b) require only $O(\mathbf{o})$ time. Hence, there are $O(\mathbf{o}^3\mathbf{p})$ operations to be performed. □

We note that the number of calls to the cost evaluation function *Cef* are $O(\mathbf{o}^3)$. This cost is more critical than the effect of the factor **p** incurred within the algorithm. We point out in Section 6.2 that any time the evaluator executes statement (g), the cost evaluation function invokes the transaction optimizer $O(t)$ times, where **t** is the number of transactions, and its own cost is a function of the number of objects addressed by the transaction.

In conclusion, considering that step (e) is actually performed $O(\mathbf{o}^2\mathbf{f})$ times, where **f** is the number of fragments, and since there is no benefit from combining two transactions, the number of calls to the optimizer is $O(\mathbf{o}^2\mathbf{ft})$ times.

In general, a database designer cannot afford so many calls to the optimizer. In Section 6 we show how to reduce the number of such calls.

5.3 The Case of Differing CPU Processor Capacities

Let us now consider the case of a network of processors **P** with differing CPU capacities (i.e., there is a set $\mathbf{CC} = \{CC_1, \ldots, CC_p\}$ such that processors P_i, P_j of

P have a CPU capacity $CC_i \neq CC_j$). We continue to assume that the IO capacity and the communication capacity are unlimited.

We observe that the GFF algorithm is to be changed only in statement (h), where the capacity constraints are checked. This means that the number of calls to the cost evaluator function remains unchanged. We prove that in this case also the GFF algorithm runs in polynomial time.

PROPOSITION 3. *The GFF algorithm for differing capacity processors runs in* $O(\mathbf{o}^3\mathbf{p} \log \mathbf{p})$ *time.*

PROOF. We modify statement (h) of the GFF algorithm, from the previous section, by checking whether the CPU constraints are satisfied, in the following way.

Let us consider the CPU capacities $\mathbf{CC} = \{CC_1, \ldots, CP_p\}$ of the **p** processors in **P** computed by statement (g). Considering how the algorithm works, only the nodes of the subset **D** of **N**, where $\mathbf{d} \leq \mathbf{p}$, contain more than one object. In other words, we are filling nodes **D** of **N** only; and only these are subject to exceeding constraint limits. Let $\mathbf{vc}' = \{vc_1', \ldots, vc_d'\}$ be the CPU load assigned to the nodes of **D**.

We sort the **p** elements in **CC** in ascending order in $O(\mathbf{p} \log \mathbf{p})$ time, and the elements in $\mathbf{vc}'$ in $O(\mathbf{d} \log \mathbf{d})$ time. Then we perform the allocation step as follows: For each element vc_i' in **vc**, taken in sorted order, we mark the first element CC_j in **CC**, not already marked, such that $vc_i' \leq CC_j$.

CPU constraints are satisfied if and only if the step succeeds for all elements in **vc**. Since this step can be easily implemented in $O(\mathbf{p})$ time, the overall complexity of testing CPU constraint is $O(\mathbf{p} \log \mathbf{p})$. Hence, the GFF algorithm runs in $O(\mathbf{o}^3\mathbf{p} \log \mathbf{p})$ time. □

5.4 The Case of Limited IO Processor Capacities

In this section we address the assumptions that IO and CPU capacities are limited, while communication capacity is still unlimited. The GFF algorithm is again to be changed in statement (h) only, where the capacity constraints are checked.

First of all, we note that if the IO capacity is equal for all processors, we only need to check in $O(\mathbf{p})$ time whether all IO loads of the **d** assigned nodes are less or equal to IO capacity. We still check in $O(\mathbf{p} \log \mathbf{p})$ time whether the CPU constraints are satisfied. Hence, the GFF algorithm will require $O(\mathbf{o}^3\mathbf{p} \log \mathbf{p})$ time.

Let us now suppose that the IO capacities are not equal for all processors (i.e., there is a set $\mathbf{CI} = \{CI_1, \ldots, CI_p\}$ such that the processor P_i has the IO capacity CI_i).

We prove that in this case also the GFF algorithm runs in polynomial time.

PROPOSITION 4. *The GFF algorithm for differing capacity processors and IO capacities runs in* $O(\mathbf{o}^3\mathbf{p}^{5/2})$ *time.*

PROOF. We modify the GFF algorithm in statement (h) only, by checking whether the IO and CPU constraints are satisfied, in the following way. Let us consider IO loads $\mathbf{vi}' = \{vi_1', \ldots, vi_d'\}$ and CPU loads $\mathbf{vc}' = \{vc_1', \ldots, vc_d'\}$ of the

d fictitious nodes in **D**, where **D** is the subset of nodes in **N** that contain more than one object. Notice that $\mathbf{d} \le \mathbf{p}$. We construct an undirected graph $G = (V, E)$, where V is the set vertices and E is the set of edges, in the following way.

Let $V = \mathbf{D} \cup \mathbf{P}$ and let $E = \{(D_i, P_j) \mid vc_i' \le CC_j \text{ and } vi_i' \le CI_j\}$. The graph G is bipartite, since V can be partitioned into two sets **D** and **P** such that each edge in E joins a vertex in **D** with a vertex in **P**. A matching of G is a set $E' \subseteq E$ such that no vertex in V is incident with more than one edge in E'. A maximum matching of G is a matching of maximum cardinality. It is easy to see that the IO and CPU constraints are satisfied if and only if the cardinality of a maximum matching of G is equal to **d**. In fact, the above constraints are satisfied if and only if there is an injection φ: $\mathbf{D} \rightarrow \mathbf{P}$ such that for all D_i in **D**, $vi_i \le CI_j$, and $vc_i' \le CC_j$, where $j = \varphi(i)$. In [15] an algorithm that computes the maximum matching of a bipartite graph which runs in $O(|V|^{5/2})$ time is presented. This translates in our case to $O(\mathbf{p}^{5/2})$ time. Hence, the GFF algorithm runs in $O(\mathbf{o}^3\mathbf{p}^{5/2})$ time. Notice that maximum matching establishes the assignment of the fictitious nodes to the actual processors. □

5.5 The Case with Limited but Homogeneous Communication Capabilities

Let us now consider that the capacities of the communication network between processors are also limited. In networks that provide complete interconnection, the limits are typically determined by an aggregate capability of the network, or are equal for all $\mathbf{p}(\mathbf{p} - 1)$ links in the network.

The first case applies to shared bus or cable systems. If the communication capacity is limited in the aggregate to **CM**, the test that $\sum_i \sum_j vm_{ij} < \mathbf{CM}$ can be performed in $O(\mathbf{p}^2)$ time.

In fully interconnected networks with distinct links of equal communication capacity, the test that loads do not exceed any of the capacities between every pair of fictitious nodes can also be performed link-by-link in $O(\mathbf{p}^2)$ time.

PROPOSITION 5. *The GFF algorithm for differing processor and input-output capacities, and equal communication capacity, runs in* $O(\mathbf{o}^3\mathbf{p}^{5/2})$ *time.*

PROOF. We have already shown that checking the communication capacity requires $O(\mathbf{p}^2)$ time. Since checking whether IO and CPU capacities are satisfied still requires $O(\mathbf{p}^{5/2})$ time (see Proposition 4), the GFF algorithm still requires $O(\mathbf{o}^3\mathbf{p}^{5/2})$ time. □

We point out that, in practice, either situation is quite frequent. Local networks among heterogeneous nodes provide equal communication capacities. The input-output capacity may differ, depending on local needs.

5.6 The General Case

For complete generality, let us consider that communication capacities are not equal for all pairs of processors (i.e., $\mathbf{CM} = \{CM_{1,1}, CM_{1,2}, \ldots, CM_{p-1,p}, CM_{p,p}\}$ is such that the communication between the processor pair P_i, P_j is CM_{ij}). This case mainly occurs in incompletely interconnected long-distance networks. We prove that in this case the GFF algorithm cannot run in polynomial time unless $P = NP$.

Proposition 6. *The GFF algorithm for the general case runs in nondeterministic time, but not in deterministic polynomial time, unless $P = NP$.*

Proof. The GFF algorithm runs in nondeterministic polynomial time, since all steps except the step of checking capacity constraints require (deterministic) polynomial time and since we can test capacity constraints in nondeterministic polynomial time as follows. We just guess an assignment of fictitious nodes of the subset **D** of nodes of **N** containing more than one object to the actual processors in **P**. Then we check in $O(p^2)$ all capacity constraints. Let us now prove that the algorithm cannot run in polynomial time unless $P = NP$. We show that any instance of a known NP-complete problem can be transformed into an instance of the problem of checking capacity constraints. Let us consider the subgraph isomorphism (SI) problem, which was shown to be NP-complete in [7]. An instance of the SI problem is the following:

$$\text{Graphs } G^1 = (V^1, E^1), \quad G^2 = (V^2, E^2).$$

The question is: Does G^2 contain a subgraph isomorphic to G^1, that is, a subset $V \subseteq V^2$ and a subset $E \subseteq E^2$ such that $|V| = |V^1|$, $|E| = |E^1|$, and there is a bijection $\varphi: V \rightarrow V^1$ for which the edge (i, j) is in E if and only if $(\varphi(i), \varphi(j))$ is in E^1?

We associate a fictitious node D_i of **D** with each vertex i of V^1 and a processor node P_j of **P** with each vertex j of V^2. Furthermore, for each edge (i, j) in E^1 the communication load vm_{ij} between the two fictitious nodes D_i and D_j is equated to 1, while all communication loads that do not correspond to any edge in E^1 are equated to 0. Similarly, for each edge (i, j) in E^2 the communication capacity CM_{ij} between the two fictitious processors P_i and P_j is equated to 1, while all capacities that do not correspond to any edge in E^2 are equated to 0.

Finally, we suppose that the IO and CPU capacities of all processors are unlimited; that is, they can support any IO and CPU loads for which, as far as they are concerned, any fictitious node could be assigned to any processor. Hence, only communication constraints must be respected. It is easily seen that such constraints are satisfied if and only if the graph G^1 (corresponding to **D**) is isomorphic to a subgraph of G^2 (corresponding to **P**). Since the transformation of any instance of the SI problem to an instance of the problem of testing the communication capacities can obviously be done in polynomial time, we have proven that the GFF algorithm cannot run in polynomial time unless $P = NP$. □

5.7 Conclusion

We have shown that the proposed GFF algorithm runs in all but the most general case in $O(\mathbf{o}^3\mathbf{p}^{5/2})$ time. The general case where the algorithm does not appear to run in polynomial time occurs when the network is not homogeneous. Such networks, having links of unequal capacity or, more likely, absent links between processor pairs are common in long-haul networks. These are not the type of networks that are addressed in our analysis, since for these networks the initial assumption that the entry point for the transaction can be assigned arbitrarily is highly unlikely.

We also note that typically the set of candidate fragments and transactions $\mathbf{o} \gg \mathbf{p}$, so that the cost of all cases $O(\mathbf{o}^3\mathbf{p}^{5/2}) \approx O(\mathbf{o}^3)$. We point out that the calls to the cost evaluation function are $O(\mathbf{o}^3)$ in all cases. We still have to consider the complexity of the unit cost for an evaluation, since step (g) in the algorithm requires use of the optimizer.

6. TECHNIQUES FOR GREEDY SELECTION

During the selection of a fragment pair for allocation, we evaluate a cost evaluation function *Cef*. The results, in Section 5, give the order of complexity for the invocation of the cost evaluation function. We now consider the complexity of candidate cost evaluation functions themselves.

6.1 Cost Estimation Using the Optimizer

In order to obtain cost estimates, the cost evaluation function invokes the transaction optimizer with a proposed design. The result is the execution load of a given transaction. We build a *cost estimator* by invoking the transaction optimizer, such as the one used in System R*, once for each transaction, and by letting the sum of costs of the individual transactions be the cost estimate.

The proposed design can contain $\mathbf{n} < \mathbf{o}$ fictitious processor nodes **N**. The knowledge available to the cost estimator for a specific design proposed by the allocation program is

(1) The set of **t** transactions **T**, with their frequency q, their operations *op*, and the set of relation fragments $\mathbf{F}(T_i)$ that they access.
(2) The proposed assignment of a transaction entry node in **N** for all **t** transactions in **T**.
(3) Estimates of the fragment sizes.
(4) The allocation **O** of relation fragments to the pseudonodes **N**.
(5) The existence of indexes and many system parameters.

One call to the optimizer will return an execution load for one $T_i \in \mathbf{T}$. This load is aggregated by the cost estimator for all transactions in **T** in order to obtain the load (**vi, vc, vm**) for the given design $\mathbf{L}_N(\mathbf{O})$, where

vi_k is the number of block accesses required for each processor P_k;
vc_k is the number of processor cycles consumed by each processor P_k;
vm_{kl} is the volume of message traffic generated between each pair of processors P_k, P_l.[1]

The set of nodes **N** is a fictitious set, created only to provide a network image to the optimizer for the transactions. All objects **O**—fragments and transactions—are assigned to the nodes. Some of the nodes ($\mathbf{P} \subseteq \mathbf{N}$) are candidates for processing nodes. The set of all nodes contains pseudonodes to hold unassigned relation fragments and the processor nodes which have been used in an assignment. The allocation strategies reduce the subset of fictitious nodes, and alloca-

---

[1] We note that the current R* optimizer does not return vm_{kl}, but does return the aggregate load $\sum vm$. However, it does actually compute the detail loads internally, but aggregates the message loads phase by phase rather than by link k, l.

tion is complete when the pseudonodes **N** coincide with an actual set of candidate processor nodes **P**.

6.2 Techniques

This section deals with the techniques for choosing the objects to be combined during the execution of the GFF algorithm, described in the previous sections. In this algorithm, and all variations of it, we drive the greedy selection of the two objects whose combination appears to give the best benefit by calling the cost evaluator function $O(\mathbf{o}^3)$ times, where **o** is the number of objects (transactions and fragments). We use the term *dynamic* to illustrate that, as the configuration changes, all previous results produced by the costs estimator may change.

The cost evaluation function is best computed by invoking the cost estimator to recompute all benefits. One execution of the cost estimator requires the optimization of **t** transactions, and hence that many invocations of the optimizer. Each single optimization of a transaction requires extensive computation itself, since it has to consider all fragments and nodes involved in the transaction. We believe that generally the database designer cannot afford a large number of calls to the optimizer. In order to reduce the amount of computation, we present three techniques which reduce the number of invocations of the cost estimator, and hence the optimizer, when computing the cost evaluation function. We use the terms: *static*, *semistatic*, and *semidynamic* to identify these techniques, as distinct from the most costly, the *dynamic*, technique.

The results of the cost evaluation functions are used by the first-fit allocation part of the GFF algorithm to assure that nodes are not loaded beyond their constraints. They are also used to compute the benefit matrix that drives the greedy selection part of the GFF algorithm. Any of these four techniques can be used for either part, but we assume that only one is chosen at one time. We concentrate on greedy selection in our discussions. We illustrate below the available alternatives by using pseudocode.

```
GFF algorithm: /* heuristics */
  Allocate each Object to its own fictitious Node;
  Call Cost_Estimator to obtain initial load-estimates;
  Forall Object pairs
    Begin
    Propose combined allocation;
    Call Cost_Estimator;
    End;
Compute benefit-matrix;
Select best Object-pair and make it the New-object;
Call First_Fit to allocate the Object pair together;
Forall Objects until they fit into the actual Processors
  Begin iteration;
  Invoke Cost_Evaluator:
  Case (dynamic):      Obtain load-estimates for selected pair;
                       Forall object pairs
                         Begin
                         Propose combined allocation;
                         Call Cost_Estimator;
                         End;
                       Compute benefit_matrix;
```

```
        (semidynamic): Obtain load-estimates for selected pair;
                       Forall New-object-Object pairs
                         Begin
                         Propose combined allocation;
                         Call Cost_Estimator;
                         Update benefit_matrix;
                         End;
        (semistatic):  Begin
                         Call Cost_Estimator;
                         Forall New-object-Object pairs
                           correct benefit-matrix by new
                             cost versus sum of old costs;
                       End;
        (static):      Forall New-object-Object pairs
                         set loads to sum of old loads and
                           benefits to sum of old benefits:
   Select best Object-pair and make it the New-object;
   Call First_Fit to allocate the Object pair together;
   End iteration;
Done.
```

The actual total complexity of the GFF algorithm is the product of the number of cost evaluation function calls required, as determined in Section 5, and the cost of its invocation in terms of cost estimator calls as presented here.

In all cases, the cost estimator is invoked once, and immediately, for the initial allocation of **o** objects to **n** fictitious nodes. This establishes a base load $\mathbf{Vt}^0$ for all components (IO, CPU, and communication). Then the cost estimator is invoked $O(\mathbf{o}^2)$ times for all possible pairs of objects to be combined. The benefit matrix **BM** is computed by setting the value of the benefit BM_{ij} of combining two objects O_i, O_j equal to the difference of the base load $\mathbf{Vt}^0$ and the load after allocating O_i and O_j to the same fictitious node. After each iteration the number of objects remaining to be allocated is reduced by one.

The greedy algorithm chooses the best combination according to the values in **BM** and allocates it to a new node. Correspondingly, the benefit matrix must be changed by adding one new row and one new column, corresponding to the benefits for combinations involving the new combined object, while the two rows and columns corresponding to the pair of objects that were combined are dropped.

Static

In the initialization of the GFF algorithm, the loads and benefits of allocating all objects to **n** separated fictitious nodes are computed using the cost estimator as presented above. For all further iterations, the loads and benefits for the successive allocations are computed by modifying the original load and benefit elements without calling the cost estimator function again.

Loads are estimated for the new object, say O_{ij}, created by combining two objects O_i, O_i, by setting its IO and CPU loads for to the sum of the values, since that is where the work will now be performed: $vi_{ij} := vi_i + vi_j$, $vc_{ij} := vc_i + vc_j$. For the communication load matrix **vm**, the communication loads at the intersection $vm_{i,j}$ disappear, and the values associated with the old rows and old columns are computed by summing the values of the loads of the old rows and columns: $vm_{ij},_* := vm_i,_* + vm_j,_*$, $vm_*,_{ij} := vm_*,_i + vm_*,_j$.

Similarly, a corrected benefit matrix of size $\mathbf{o} \times (\mathbf{o} - \mathbf{t}')$, **BM**, is generated by setting the value of the benefits of the combined row and column $BM_{ij,*}$, $BM_{*,ij}$, created by combining two objects O_i, O_j, to the sum of the values in the old rows $BM_{i,*}$, $BM_{j,*}$ and old columns $BM_{*,i}$, $BM_{*,j}$. The difference $\mathbf{t}'$ accounts for the yet unassigned transactions. The communication benefits at the intersection $BM_{i,j}$ disappear, since they have been taken and, in effect, reduce the new total **Vt**. The IO and CPU benefits of the new row and column should be incremented by the values of the element at the intersection $BM_{i,j}$. The rows and columns corresponding to the old objects are dropped.

This recomputation implements the assumption that the benefits of a co-assignment of two objects are equal to the communication load vm_{ij} between the two fictitious nodes in which the two objects were allocated. The change in IO and CPU benefits due to combining fragments is null. If the benefits of IO and CPU allocations are wholly ignored, then we consider the benefits of combining nodes proportional to their intercommunication load.

After the initial calls to the cost estimator to set the benefit matrix, there are no further calls to the estimator during execution of the cost evaluating function; $Cost = O(1)$ calls.

Semistatic

Initially, the cost estimator is invoked for the initial state as presented above. After each combination at two objects, the cost estimator is invoked in order to obtain the new loads of the fictitious nodes. The remainder of the load estimate is retained.

The benefit matrix is still estimated by $\mathbf{BM} = \mathbf{vm}$, as it was in the static case; however, its values are recomputed during each iteration using the results of the one call to the cost estimator. Reductions of IO and CPU costs for the pair are applied to the sum of all IO and CPU costs for this pair and the other objects. Hence, there are at most **o** calls to the estimator; $Cost = O(\mathbf{o})$.

Semidynamic

Again, an initial benefit matrix is computed. As soon as the initial selection of the first two objects O_i, $O(j)$ has been made and the new design $\mathbf{L}_N(\mathbf{O})$ is known, the benefit matrix **BM** is corrected for all directly involved object pairs. The cost estimator is invoked for the new **o** row elements and $\mathbf{o} - \mathbf{t}'$ column elements $O(\mathbf{o})$ times.

The benefit matrix **BM** is now updated as follows: The two rows $BM_{*,i}$, $BM_{*,j}$ and the two columns $BM_{i,*}$, $BM_{j,*}$ are dropped and a new row and column is set with values found by the cost estimator. Secondary effects on elements of **BM** not specified above are ignored.

In each of the $O(\mathbf{o})$ further iterations, the new row objects to be combined are chosen on the basis of the corrected benefit matrix, and, after each combination of two objects, the entire cost evaluator function is invoked at most 2 **o** times. This means that the cost estimator is invoked $O(\mathbf{o}^2)$ times; $Cost = O(\mathbf{o}^2)$.

Dynamic

Here we again use the benefit matrix **BM** by using **Vt**, which includes IO, CPU, and communication loads. In the fully dynamic technique we recompute the entire benefit matrix **BM** at each iteration of the greedy selection algorithm, rather than applying corrections to the directly affected rows and columns only. The cost estimator is invoked $O(\mathbf{o}^2)$ times per iteration. Now, all effects of interactions are accounted for as well; this matrix matches as precisely as the data allow the situation actually seen by the query optimizer at execution time.

Now all of the benefit matrix **BM** is recomputed in each iteration; *Cost* = $O(\mathbf{o}^3)$.

6.3 The Validity of Using the Alternate Techniques

We note that in the two static cases the only cost associated with a combination of relation fragments or transaction sites is due to the communication load. This means that the optimization heuristic is driven solely by the communication load, and implies the assumption that all benefits of coassignment fragments are proportional to the communication load. This assumption is reasonable under the following conditions:

(1) The communication cost dominates, and communications are a major capacity constraint on the network, so that optimization of IO and CPU costs are secondary.

(2) The major fraction of the IO and CPU loads incurred is associated with operations that incur a data communications load as well. This is probably typically true in the initial stages of the algorithm, where every join, union, or intersection operation requires communication with another fictitious processor node. As the algorithm progresses, the fragments that had high intercommunication loads are merged into candidate processor nodes. These nodes now have a high disk IO and internal CPU loads for their joins, and the remaining communication load is relatively less important. The communication loads in this phase are probably less indicative of the potential IO and CPU load benefits of an assignment.

(3) The static technique assumes that the IO and CPU loads for two separate nodes are similar to the IO and CPU loads incurred when the nodes are combined. If the nodes contain fragments of the same relations, then more effective processing methods may be used within the new node. The semistatic scheme permits capturing of these benefits. This scheme is also appropriate if the global message traffic over the network is reorganized as the fragment distribution over the nodes changes.

Dynamic techniques permit the selection for assignment to be driven by any of the IO, CPU, and message benefits. Benefits are now measured by estimates of the difference in before- and after-costs.

(4) The semidynamic technique avoids a complete recomputation of the benefit matrix by making the assumption that recomputation of the loads for the directly affected nodes provides an adequate estimate for selecting nodes for merging in further iterations.

(5) The fully dynamic technique provides for a full recomputation of the benefit matrix at every step. If the optimizing techniques can drastically change as the node configuration and fragment assignment changes, this technique will provide the appropriate estimates.

In the section above, we find, not surprisingly, that the most economical technique in terms of computational complexity (the static approach) is also the one that has the least precise information for choosing the best candidate.

However, more economical techniques appear reasonable in the earlier stages of the iterative assignment process. During the assignment process the value of **o**, the number of objects to be considered for assignment changes, eventually becomes **p**, where **p** is a relatively small number compared to the initial value of **o**. This means that in the later stages a more complex technique can be used with a considerably smaller penalty.

We can thus suggest the following:

(1) Initially, use the static technique. Recomputation of the IO, CPU, and communication loads is performed by step (g) of the GFF algorithm, without invoking the cost estimator.

(2) When capacity constraints begin to be encountered, the semistatic technique should be used. A single call after every assignment step to the cost estimator will recompute the IO, CPU, and communication loads for the current configuration.

(3) If it now seems that either the aggregate IO or the CPU loads of the transactions have not yet been reduced to a level below the aggregate IO or CPU capacity constraints of the processors, that is,

$$\sum_{i=1}^{o} vi_i > \sum_{j=1}^{p} CI_j$$

$$\sum_{i=1}^{o} vc_i > \sum_{j=1}^{p} CC_j,$$

then it is important to select those remaining unassigned nodes with the greatest actual IO or CPU benefits. Now the semidynamic technique is initiated so that the true IO or CPU capacity can become the driving criterion of the selection phase of our heuristic.

We note that performing the initial step of the semidynamic technique at this point is equivalent to doing one step of the fully dynamic technique.

Whether more than one fully dynamic step is needed is not simple to determine without more experience. If the transaction optimizer is apt to switch to radically different global strategies for query processing, then the full reevaluation provided by the dynamic technique may be wise. Since many transactions are quite constraining in an execution sequence, such a requirement does not appear likely.

7. EXPERIMENTAL WORK

A model for further experimental work has been designed, and a subset of that model was implemented and used to evaluate the two static techniques.

7.1 Estimation Model

The underlying model is based on the following notions: Our files are modeled by **r** relations **R**. These have been split into **f** fragments F_i of cardinality S_i and width W_i. In order to test the schemes in the absence of an operating system, which could give estimates of transaction costs, we construct a simple model based on assumptions of typical transaction behavior. The model we propose here is not related to the actual system optimizers.

Assumptions. We recapitulate assumptions made in our model of the **R*** optimizer used to conceptually verify our approach. These assumptions are based on discussions with implementors of the optimizer, although the assumptions cannot reflect improvements made concurrently. An actual design tool should use the actual optimizer to assure that database distribution designs reflect a current status of the actual system.

(1) The load of primitive IO, CPU, and communication operations is determined solely by the volume of data moved or transferred from those relations, namely, s_i tuples of width a_i. The values of s_i are computed as shown below. The values of a_i are either A_i or 1 for the first transfer in a semijoin.

(2) Operations between nodes involve joins, rather than union or intersection operations. The join of two fragments F_q, F_q is performed by an algorithm similar in performance to a semijoin, so that its performance in terms of IO accesses is proportional to $s_r \log s_r + s_q \log s_q$, and is asymmetric in its behavior.

(3) The queries have given restriction factors rf_i, applied to their source relations. These are specified for each relation-fragment I participating in the relation. The factor rf_i $(0 < rf_i < 1)$ is applied to each relation fragment size S_i prior to estimating the join cost, so that $s_i = rf_i \times S_i$. The default for rf_i is 1.

(4) For each join among two fragments F_q, F_r, a join selectivity factor jf_{qr} is specified in the query description. The size of a join result can range from the crossproduct $s_q s_r$ to 0. We assume that joins are most common along $1{:}n$ connections, and that these joins generate $s_j = jf_{qr} \times s_q \times (s_r/s_q) = jf_{qr} \times s_r$ tuples, where s_r is the larger of $\{s_q, s_r\}$ and s_q is the other. The default is 1, but jf_{qr} can range from s_q to 0.

(5) The communication cost for a join among two fragments F_q, F_r depends on the size of the join column from fragment F_q, which has to be transmitted to the other node to execute the join, and the volume of data needed to create the result relation.

The volume of the single join column of fragment F_q is estimated as $s_q \times 1$. The volume of the tuples to be transmitted also depends on the size of the tuples of relation fragment F_r, a_r, and is estimated as

$$cf_{qr}(s_q + jf_{qr}\, s_r a_r),$$

cf_{qr} is 0 or 1, depending on whether $\{F_q$ and $F_r\}$ reside on the same node or on distinct nodes. The assignment of the join direction between the two participating fragments F_q, F_r is made by the optimizer.

(6) When relation fragments are combined, two cases might be considered:

(a) Fragments come from the same source relation. When such fragments are combined, no join will take place between the fragments, although the transaction included both fragments. The size of the result is the simple sum, corresponding to a join factor of 1. The restriction factors may be averaged (they were probably equal).

(b) Fragments come from distinct source relations. When such fragments are combined, a join is typical and the appropriate join factor should be applied. The restriction factors apply to both fragments and should be multiplied.

The cost of the join is higher than the cost of the union in case 1.
We propose for now to treat cases (a) and (b) identically. The proper setting of join factors can be used to provide reasonable descriptions. The error introduced by averaging restriction factors is somewhat offset by not counting local join costs.

(7) The only cost associated with the transaction site is the final transfer of the final join result to the transaction node. If those are identical (a reasonable goal for an optimizer), this cost is made zero by getting $cf = 0$.

Input and Results. The required data are now:

(1) For each relation fragment F_i, the cardinality S_i and the width A_i;
(2) For each transaction $T_h \in \mathbf{T}$, an execution sentence

$$T_h: F_i rf_i F_k rf_k jf_{ik} F_l rf_l jf_{lm} \ldots F_p rf_p,$$

where each $F_i \in \mathbf{F}$.
(3) Each object O_i (fragment or transaction) is assigned to a fictitious node N_j. The term b_i of vector **b** denotes the node to which O_i is assigned. The initial assignment is, of course, $b_i = i$, for $F_i \in \mathbf{F}$.

Computations. The computation consists of an iteration to select candidates for merging and recomputation of the cost of the new configuration. Each iteration step assigns one object O_i or (initially two objects) to a processor node $P_q \in \mathbf{P}$ and sets $b_i \rightarrow P_q$.

The optimizer, in estimating the cost, rearranges the execution sequence; combined objects are always treated together. Specifically, in order to estimate the benefits of merging, it must do the following: For all $\{F_i, F_k\}$ where $b_i = b_k$ it will compute

$$S_{ik} = S_i + S_k \qquad A_{ik} = \frac{A_i S_i + A_k S_k}{S_{ik}}$$

$$rf_{ik} = \frac{(rf_i S_i + rf_k S_k)}{S_{ik}} jf_{ik} \qquad jf_{ik} \text{ is no longer needed,}$$

and produce a communication load of 0 by setting $cf_{ik} = 0$.

However, the evaluation model does not rearrange the execution sequence as an actual optimizer might. Also, we do not directly handle transactions that use the same fragment more than once. These differences do not affect the validity of the evaluation of the GFF method.

For the static technique, described in Section 6.1, the values of the IO and CPU loads VI_{ik}, VC_{ik} are computed (without calling the optimizer or this estimation) as the sums $VI_i + VI_k$, $VC_i + VC_k$. The other techniques require that the results from the estimator be summed into load vectors VI, VC for the IO and the CPU loads, and into a cost matrix **COM** for the communication load. Elements for storage are determined by the assignment value b_i given for each object O_i. Actually, we simplified the recomputation for the semistatic method as shown in Section 7.2.

The computational sequence for evaluating the cost of one configuration is then as follows:

(1) Assign relations and transactions as desired by using assignment vector **b**.
(2) Zero result vectors, matrix as appropriate.
(3) For each transaction, do (4).
(4.1) Combine all relation fragments assigned to the same node.
(4.2) Create a new transaction sentence to reflect the combined relation fragments.
(4.3) Determine the join direction for each join in the sentence.
(4.4) Compute the IO load for each relation fragment F_i and add into assigned slot VI_{b_i}.
(4.5) Compute the CPU load for each relation fragment F_i and add into assigned slot VC_{b_i}.
(4.6) Compute data transmission load for each join of two fragments F_i, F_j and add into assigned element of matrix $COM_{b_i b_j}$.
(5) Done.

7.2 Results

A simulation was performed on the static and semistatic techniques. The simulation was written in Pascal, and executed to demonstrate the correctness and the performance of the GFF algorithm versus the greedy-only algorithm. We used only the static technique, and considered only constant IO and CPU capacity constraints, while assuming unlimited communication capacity among all processors. We also analyzed the behavior of our algorithm with respect to an exact branch-and-bound algorithm and to a greedy algorithm that does not use the first-fit strategy for allocating objects.

We tested the algorithms using five different samples of processor clusters, having 5, 10, 15, 20, and 30 nodes; for each cluster we considered three different capacity constraints. A heavy load was used to stress the algorithms, the transaction demands on the nodes were 0.62, 0.66, and 0.77 of the aggregate node capacity; the test considered fifteen cases. The greedy algorithm found a feasible solution for only two cases out of fifteen, while the GFF algorithm found a feasible solution for thirteen out of fifteen cases; the capacity constraints for the two cases left were very restrictive. The solutions found were 10 to 20 percent below the optimum.

Static versus semistatic technique. We tested the semistatic technique by slightly modifying the fifteen cases described above. We increased the aggregate load by approximately 10 percent, and, whenever two nodes were combined, we made the combined load equal to 95 percent of the sum of the two loads, in order to account for the efficiency gained by avoiding distributed processing. It turned out that while the static technique found a feasible solution for seven cases only, the semistatic technique was able to find a feasible solution for twelve out of fifteen cases. The solutions found in these cases were also 10 to 20 percent below the optimum. Our conclusion is that the fully static technique should be used only until some capacity constraints are violated.

8. CONCLUSION

We have addressed the problem of distributing a database over a fixed number of processors. The processors and the network connecting them have limited processing and transmission capacities. The relations of the database are fragmented to provide suitable units of allocation. The entry point of the query transactions is not constrained. The complexity of the general problem is shown to be NP-hard, so that a heuristic algorithm is called for. This algorithm should not only provide a feasible solution, but a solution that is near to optimal as well; these two criteria are related, since, without finding a low cost solution, no solution that satisfies the processor constraints may be found.

The analysis shows that the intrinsic high complexity of the partitioning problem over a distributed database can be overcome by heuristic approaches. The approaches we investigate use the query optimization program of the database management system over a hypothetically defined network in order to obtain the information needed to make design decisions. The approach of using the systems' cost-evaluation program makes the methods shown here independent of implementation assumptions. The database is fragmented prior to the analysis so that an appropriate granularity for distribution is obtained.

A new heuristic algorithm, GFF, for assigning fragments to processors is presented and analyzed. It combines a greedy algorithm for the selection of candidate fragments to be assigned with a first-fit bin-packing algorithm for the allocation of selected fragments to processor nodes.

Four alternate tactics of implementing the cost-evaluation program are considered and ranked. A strategy of beginning with a very simple estimation, but using costlier and more informative tactics as the design progresses is recommended. Experimental results are reported that verify the analytical results presented in this paper.

We believe that the GFF method will have applications in other situations in which complex design constraints arise.

ACKNOWLEDGMENTS

This work was performed in the context of a larger research project on "A Highly Available Transaction Support System" at the IBM San Jose Research Laboratory, under the leadership of Mario Schkolnick. We profited greatly from discussions with members of the Laboratory. Jayne Pickering helped with entering the text into the TEX system [19], which was used to prepare the original paper.

The referees of VLDB and ACM TODS have contributed greatly to the clarity of this paper by raising many relevant questions. Any mysteries remaining must be blamed on the authors.

REFERENCES

1. APERS, P.M.G. Redundant allocation of relations in a communication network. In *Berkeley Workshop 5* (San Francisco, Feb. 1981), 245–258. Final results to appear in *ACM Trans. Database Syst.*
2. CASEY, R.G. Allocation of copies of a file in an information network. In *Proceedings 1972 Spring Joint Computer Conference*, AFIPS Vol. 40, 617–625.

3. CERI, S., NEGRI, M., AND PELAGATTI, G. Horizontal data partitioning in database design. *ACM-SIGMOD 82,* (Orlando, Fla., 1982), M. Schkolnick, Ed., ACM, New York.
4. CERI, S., NAVATHE, S., AND WIEDERHOLD, G. Distribution design of logical database schemas. *IEEE Trans. Softw. Eng. SE-9* (July 1983), 487–563.
5. CHU, W. W. Optimal file allocation in a multiple computer system. *IEEE Trans. Comput. C-18,* 10 (Oct. 1969), 885–889.
6. CODD, E.F. Extending the database relational model to capture more meaning. *ACM Trans. Database Syst. 4,* 4 (Dec. 1979), 397–434.
7. COOK, S.A. The complexity of theorem-proving procedure. In *Proceedings 3rd Annual ACM Symposium on the Theory of Computing,* (1971), ACM, New York, 151–158.
8. DOWDY, L.W., AND FOSTER, D.V. Comparative models of the file assignment problem. *ACM Comput. Surv. 14,* 2 (June 1982), 287–313.
9. ESWARAN, K.P. Placement of records in a file and file allocation in a computer network. In *Information Processing 74, Proceedings IFIP Congress,* North-Holland, Amsterdam, 1974.
10. GAREY, M.R., AND JOHNSON, D.S. *Computers and Intractibility—A guide to the Theory of NP-Completeness,* W.H. Freeman, San Francisco, 1979.
11. GAREY, M.R., JOHNSON, D.S., AND STOCKMEYER, L. Some simplified NP-complete graph problems. *Theor. Comput. Sci. 1* (1976), 237–267.
12. HAMMER, M., AND NIAMIR, B. A heuristic approach to attribute partitioning. In *ACM-SIGMOD 79,* Bernstein, Ed., ACM, New York, 1979, 93–100.
13. HOFFER, J.A. A clustering approach to the generation of subfiles for the design of a computer database. Ph.D. dissertation, Cornell Univ., Ithaca, N.Y., Jan. 1975.
14. HOFFER, J.A., AND SEVERANCE, D.G. The use of cluster analysis in physical database design. In *Very Large Data Bases 1,* Kerr, Ed., IEEE, New York, 1975, 69–86.
15. HOPCROFT, J.E., AND KARP, R.M. An $n^{5/2}$ algorithm for maximum matchings in bipartite graphs. *SIAM J. Comput.* 2 (1973), 225–331.
16. HOROWITZ, E., AND SAHNI, S. *Fundamentals of Computer Algorithms.* Computer Science Press, Rockville, Md., 1978.
17. JOHNSON, D.S. Approximation algorithms for combinatorial problems. *JCSS 9* (1974), 256–278.
18. JOHNSON, D.S., DEMERS, A., ULLMAN, J.D., GAREY, M.R., AND GRAHAM, R.L. Worst-case performance bounds for simple one-dimensional packing algorithms. *SIAM J. Comput. 3* (1974), 299–325.
19. KNUTH, D.E. *TEX and METAFONT. New Directions in Typesetting.* Digital Press, Bedford, Mass., 1979.
20. MORGAN, H.L., AND LEVIN, K.D. Optimal program and data locations in computer networks. *Commun. ACM 20,* 5 (May 1977), 315–322.
21. SCHKOLNICK, M., ET AL. A multiprocessor system for high availability. In *Proceedings IEEE COMPSAC,* (San Francisco, Calif., 1983).
22. WIEDERHOLD, G. *Database Design.* 2nd ed., McGraw-Hill, New York, 1984.
23. WILLIAMS, R., DANIELS, D., HAAS, L., LAPIS, G., LINDSAY, B., NG, P., OBERMARK, R., SELINGER, P., WAKER, A., WILMS, P., AND YOST, R. R*: An overview of the architecture. In *Proceedings International Conference on Database Systems,* (Jerusalem, June 1982).

Received October 1983; revised October 1984; accepted January 1985

Supporting a Semantic Data Model in a Distributed Database System

Arvola Chan
Umeshwar Dayal
Stephen Fox
Daniel Ries

Computer Corporation of America
4 Cambridge Center
Cambridge, Massachusetts 02142

Abstract

Existing distributed database systems are based mostly on the relational model. Furthermore, it has been argued that the relational model is the model best suited for distributed databases. This paper describes an implementation approach for supporting logical pointers between distributed entities. This approach is being employed in a distributed database system that supports a semantically rich data model and that currently is under implementation. The access structures used to support entity-to-entity pointers in this data model facilitate the maintenance of referential integrity across sites. At the same time, they provide efficient access paths for distributed query processing. To make use of these access structures the extensions required of existing query processing techniques are quite straightforward.

The research reported in this paper is supported jointly by the Advanced Research Projects Agency of the Department of Defense (DARPA) and the Naval Electronics Systems Command (NAVELEX) under contract N00039-82-C-0226. The views and conclusions contained in this paper are those of the authors and should not be interpreted as necessarily representing the official policies, either expressed or implied, of DARPA, NAVELEX, or the U.S. Government.

1. Introduction

Existing distributed database systems for the most part have been based on the relational data model [SN77] [RBFG80] [WDHL82]. Furthermore, it has been argued that the relational model is the model best suited for distribution [CODD82]. There are two properties of the relational model that facilitate its support for distribution. First, all of the relationships between records or types of objects are value-based; there is no need to support logical pointers across sites. Second, a high level language is available for specifying processing on sets of data; there is no need to follow record-at-a-time navigational links across sites.

This paper describes an implementation approach for supporting logical pointers across sites. This approach is currently being used in the implementation of the Distributed Database Manager (DDM) [CDFG83a] [CDFG83b], a distributed database system that supports the semantically rich Daplex data model [SHIP81]. Similar approaches could be used for distributed systems that support high level access based on the entity-relationship model [CHEN76] and the network model [MP82], or in relational systems that support physical links between tuples stored at different sites.

In order to extend effectively the relational distributed database technology to these models, three important problems should be addressed. First, it should be possible to control the placement of data that is based on relationships between data objects. Assume, for example, that information about university departments is distributed according to the building in which each department is housed. Now suppose we want to store information about each of the courses with information about the department that is offering the course. In relational systems such as distributed INGRES [SN77], SDD-1 [RBFG80], and R* [WDHL82], the course relation must include redundant information about the building that is housing the department offering the course, and the distribution criteria for the course relation would have to be based on the redundant building information. In the DDM, it is possible to fragment courses by department, and to group together related courses and departments.

The second problem is the maintenance of referential integrity across sites. If there is an integrity constraint that requires every course to have an offering department (i.e., the offering function from course to department is total), then even if course and department information are stored at different sites, the DDM will prevent the insertion of information for a new course for which there is no corresponding department. Similarly, the DDM will prevent the deletion of a department that is still referenced by an existing course. Furthermore, the DDM maintains this integrity constraint without requiring cross-site checking on each insertion or deletion. In a relational system, such integrity requirements would have to be specified by general integrity constraints [EC75] [HS78] [BCC81] [KP81]. The efficient support of such constraints for distributed relational databases remains an open problem.

The key to efficient distributed query processing in relational systems is the provision for set-at-a-time operations on distributed data. Thus, the third problem is how to use links that relate data across sites effectively. These links can augment physical access paths as in a single-site relational system like System R, or they can represent logical relationships. The DDM uses pointers across sites(1) to provide faster access to sets of records and to reduce data movement from one site to another during distributed query processing. These intersite pointers identify the logical entities and their residing sites only. Thus, they are unaffected by the relocation of physical records (representing entities) within a site. Furthermore, they are used by high level set-at-a-time operations. Hence, a network message is not incurred for following each such pointer.

Section 2 provides an overview of the semantic data model, Daplex, that is supported by the DDM. Section 3 addresses the first of the three problems stated above by describing the database fragmentation facilities of the DDM. Section 4 addresses the second problem by presenting the auxiliary data structures that are used to enforce referential integrity and to provide faster multi-site query processing. Section 5 addresses the third problem by discussing query processing operations that can make use of the presented structures. Finally, Section 6 summarizes our conclusions about data models and distributed databases.

---

(1) These pointers identify only the logical entity and the site where the entity is to be found. They do not have to be updated when an entity is relocated within a site.

2. The Daplex Data Model

The Daplex data model that is supported by the DDM originally was described in [SHIP81]. Its basic constructs are entities and functions. Entities are intended to represent conceptual objects and functions correspond to the properties of conceptual objects. Entities that have the same set of generic properties are grouped together into entity sets. Each function, when applied to an entity of an appropriate entity set, returns a specific property of that entity. Each property is represented either by a single value or a set of values. Such values can be drawn from scalar data types and character strings, or they can refer to other entities stored in the database as values.

Consider a university database modelling students, instructors, departments, and courses. Figure 2.1 is a graphical representation of the logical definition for such a database in Daplex. The big rectangles depict entity types and the small rectangles indicate scalar data types and character strings. The single- and double-headed arrows represent respectively single-valued and set-valued functions that map entities from their domain types into their corresponding range types.

One notable difference between the Daplex data model and the relational data model is that referential constraints [DATE81], which are extremely fundamental in database applications (but not easily specifiable in relational contexts), are directly supported in Daplex. For example, in the above database, the database system will ensure that students are assigned valid instructors as advisors. Likewise, the database system will allow an update action that removes an instructor from the database to go through, but only if this will not result in dangling references from student entities that remain in the database. (Unlike general integrity constraints that are enforced only at the end of transactions, referential integrity is enforced at the data manipulation language statement level since it is considered an integral part of the data model.)

Another important semantic concept related to distribution is the notion of a generalization hierarchy of overlapping entity types. In relational systems, a real-world entity that plays several roles in an application environment typically is represented by tuples in a number of relations. In the university database, we might have an instructor named John Doe and a student also named John Doe, who are in fact the same person in real life. In this case, we might want to impose the constraint that the age of John Doe as an instructor should agree with the age of John Doe as a student. This constraint can be more succinctly expressed in Daplex by declaring a new entity type called person and indicating that student and instructor are subtypes of per-

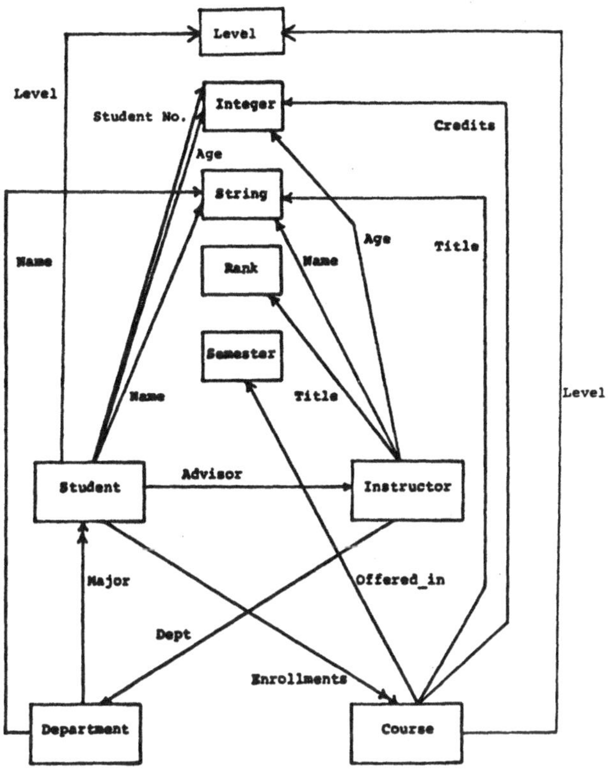

Figure 2.1 A Daplex Database

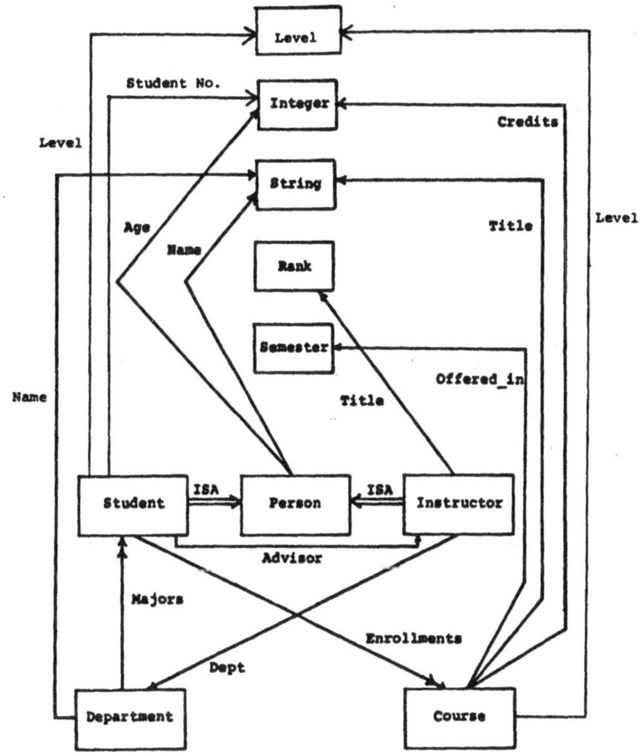

Figure 2.2 A Daplex Database with Type Overlap

son, and that age is a function applicable to person. The function inheritance semantics of Daplex automatically guarantee the consistency of age information on student and age information on instructor, since age is a function inherited from the supertype person. At the same time, inherited functions can be applied directly to an entity in data manipulation constructs in Daplex, without the need for tedious explicit joining operations. Figure 2.2 is a graphical representation of the revised database definition. The double-edged arrows represent is-a relationships (e.g., each student is-a person). The entity types person, student, and instructor are said to form a generalization hierarchy. Since every entity in this generalization hierarchy also must be a person, the type person is referred to as the root of the generalization hierarchy.

The implications of the need to efficiently enforce referential integrity and type overlap constraints on storage and access structures, for a centralized environment, have been discussed in [CDFL82]. In this paper, we focus on the implications of these fundamental integrity constraints for distributed database design.

3. Fragmentation and Grouping

The DDM provides complete physical data independence to end users. A separate interface is provided for database administrators (DBAs) for the purpose of specifying physical design parameters. An important design option available to DBAs is the allocation and replication of data to different sites in the network.(2) This section discusses the choice of allocation units in the DDM.

The database fragmentation options supported in the DDM are somewhat different from those found in previous systems like distributed INGRES [SN77], SDD-1 [RBFG80], and R* [WDHL82], which are based on the relational data model.(3) This

(2) The purpose of distributing and replicating data over different sites is to maximize locality of reference (i.e., to ensure that most transactions can be run using local data) and to provide resiliency against site failures.

(3) The typical unit for allocation in these systems is a fragment of a relation (i.e., a logically subset defined by a local predicate).

is necessitated by our support for entity-valued functions in Daplex. Essentially, Daplex allows for "direct" pointers that point from one entity to another. The semantics of Daplex requires that insertion and deletion of entities to and from the database do not result in dangling pointers. In order to simplify the maintenance of "direct" inter-entity pointers, we introduce the notion of a fragment group. A fragment group consists of a collection of fragments, each of which is a logically defined subset of a generalization hierarchy. Each fragment group is a unit for allocation and replication. Fragment groups can be designed to "localize" interentity references. This localization simplifies the enforcement of deletion dependencies and improves the efficiency of query processing. We expect that most databases can be designed in such a way that frequently followed interentity references (from entities within each fragment group) can be localized. This will eliminate the cumbersome maintenance of nonlocal pointers. It is important to note that we do not require fragment groups to be defined in such a way that all interentity references are localized.

Our support for generalization hierarchies in Daplex leads us to forgo vertical partitioning,(4) an option that is provided in SDD-1 [RBFG80] and R* [WDHL82]. Our decision here has been influenced mostly by simplicity and efficiency considerations. Had we supported vertical fragmentation, we would have the additional problem of deciding how interentity pointers should be represented. When accessing an entity of a given type, Daplex allows for access to attributes (functions) that are defined from the viewpoint of any overlapping type. In order to provide efficient support for such accesses, we require that all functions/attributes of an entity, regardless of being primitively defined or inherited, be accessible from the same site. Thus, our objects for fragmentation in the DDM are the generalization hierarchies within databases.

The fragmentation of entities within a generalization hierarchy may be defined in terms of function values, subtype memberships, subtype nonmemberships, and one-to-many relationships induced by single-valued entity functions. Since we have ruled out the possibility of vertical fragmentation of entities within a generalization hierarchy across sites, we permit the disjoint partitioning of base entity types (i.e., roots of generalization hierarchies) only. Partitioning of entities within a subtype can be implicitly defined by partitioning the corresponding base entity type. Each fragment of a base entity type is defined by a conjunction of conditions. The DBA assigns a unique identifier to each fragment in order to permit the definition of one fragment to be dependent on that of another fragment. Each defining condition can be in one of the following forms:

1. e is in "subtype" (where e is an entity in the base type and "subtype" is contained in the base type).

2. e not in "subtype" (where e is an entity in the base type and "subtype" is contained in the base type).

3. f(e) "comparison operator" "constant" (where e is an entity in the base type; f is a single-valued scalar function that is applicable to an entity that satisfies the type membership conjuncts forming part of the defining predicate in question; and "comparison operator" is one of "=", "/=", "<=", ">=", "<", ">").

4. f(e) is in F (where e is an entity in the base type; F is a previously defined fragment; and f is a single valued function that ranges over entities in F.(5)

Figure 3.1 illustrates one feasible fragmentation and grouping scheme for the example database from Section 2. Four fragment groups are defined under this particular scheme. The first fragment group stores department entities located on the first-floor, along with the courses offered by these first-floor departments and the instructors who work in these first-floor departments. The second fragment group stores second-floor departments and the associated courses and instructors. The third fragment group stores departments located on other(6) floors, along with the associated courses and instructors. Finally, the fourth fragment group stores only a single fragment that consists of persons who are not instructors.

4. Access Structures

In this section, we discuss auxiliary data structures used in the DDM for supporting the maintenance of referential integrity constraints, and for facilitating the processing of transactions that span fragment group boundaries. Our

---

(4) That is, representing individual entities by multiple distributed records.

(5) We do impose the restriction that if fragment A's definition depends on that of fragment B, then fragment B must be assigned to the same fragment group as fragment A.

(6) The predicate "others" in Figure 3.1 is interpreted by the DDM system as a shorthand for the complement of the disjunction of the other fragment defining predicates on the generalization hierarchy in question.

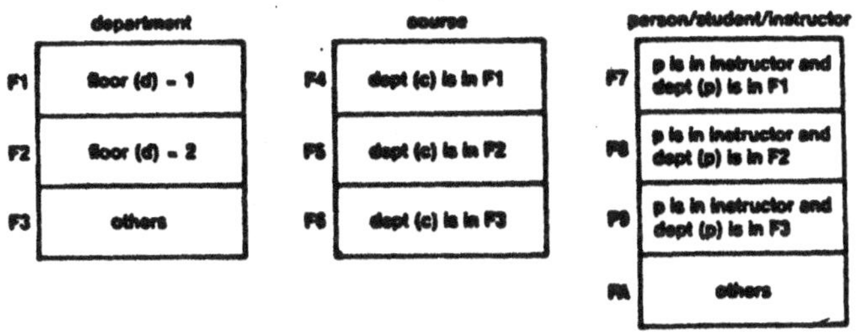

fragment group 1 = {F1, F4, F7}
fragment group 2 = {F2, F5, F8}
fragment group 3 = {F3 F6 F9}
fragment group 4 = {FA}

Figure 3.1 A Feasible Fragmentation and Grouping Scheme

principal objectives in designing these structures are:

1. To enforce referential integrity constraints that apply to entities stored across multiple sites without requiring updates across sites each time a reference is added or removed.

2. To provide fast access paths for traversals based on entity-valued functions.

3. To support efficient associative access to entities based on selection criteria that are orthogonal to those used in fragment definitions.

4. To facilitate the dynamic addition/removal of fragment group copies.

We have introduced two new types of access structures in the DDM. The first type of structure is a fragment group entity directory. One or more fragment group entity directories are automatically maintained for each fragment group. This is required to support semantics of the Daplex data model. Each directory is associated with a single fragment group. It is used to resolve references to entities stored in the fragment group and to identify the other fragment groups that store nonlocal entities referenced by entities in the fragment group. The second type of structure is a distribution index. Its maintenance is optional, and its applicability is not restricted to the Daplex data model. Each distribution index, whose maintenance is specified by the DBA, is associated with a single entity type and function. It pinpoints the fragment groups that contain entities that have specific values of that function.

Since each fragment group entity directory is associated with a single fragment group, it is actually considered part of the representation for entities in that fragment group. When specifying a distribution index for maintenance, a DBA can specify its placement in any previously defined fragment groups or in a new fragment group of its own. The replication of a distribution index is thus governed by the replication of the fragment group in which it is placed. The maintenance of these two types of structures are further explained below.

4.1 Fragment Group Entity Directory

Like the Local Database Manager [CFLR81] [CDFL82] which supports centralized Daplex databases, we maintain entity directories in the DDM in order to facilitate the resolution of interentity references and the enforcement of referential and type overlap constraints. In general, for a given fragment group we maintain a fragment group entity directory for each generalization hierarchy that is either stored in the fragment group or potentially referenced (as specified in the logical schema) by entities stored within the fragment group.

Two kinds of entries may be stored in a fragment group entity directory. A primary entry is one that pertains to an entity that is stored in the fragment group. A secondary entry is for an entity that is referenced but not stored in the fragment group.

A primary entry for an entity contains typing information, local reference count(s), physical record pointer(s), and one or more sets of nonlocal fragment group identifiers. A fragment group's identifier is in one set if it contains entities that reference the given entity from the viewpoint of a specific entity type in the generalization hierarchy. The local reference counts keep track of local references from within the fragment group, one for each entity type to which the entity belongs. A secondary entry contains typing information and a reference count for each entity type to which the nonlocally stored (but referenced) entity belongs. This reference count indicates the number of times the designated entity is being referenced (from the viewpoint of a specific type) from entities stored within this fragment group.

Figure 4.1 illustrates a fragmentation and grouping scheme for the course and person entity types. Note that the entity to entity references are not completely localized. In this scheme, undergraduate courses are grouped with undergraduate students in FG_1, and graduate courses are grouped with graduate students in FG_2. However,

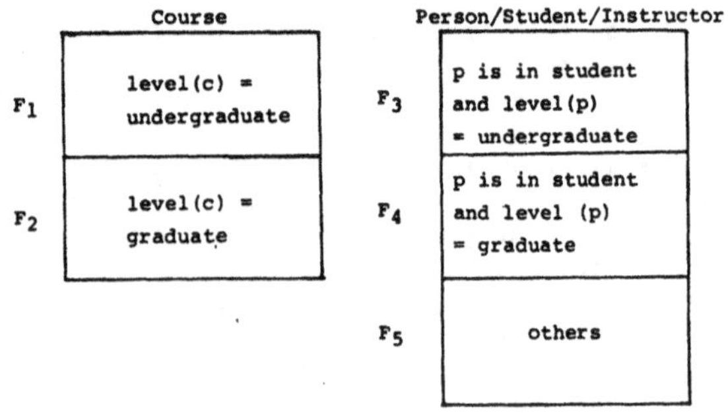

fragment group 1 = {F1, F3}
fragment group 2 = {F2, F4}
fragment group 3 {F5}

Figure 4.1 A Course/Person Fragmentation Schema

undergraduates can take graduate courses and graduates can take undergraduate courses. Figure 4.2 shows the set of courses taken by each student in the database. Figure 4.3 shows the corresponding fragment group entity directories for the (degenerate) course generalization

$S_1, \ldots, S_4$ = undergrad students
$S_5, \ldots, S_8$ = graduate students

S_1 (C_1, C_2, C_5, C_6)	S_5 (C_5, C_6, C_1, C_2)
S_2 (C_1, C_2, C_5, C_6)	S_6 (C_5, C_6, C_1, C_2)
S_3 (C_1, C_2, C_3, C_4)	S_7 (C_5, C_6, C_7, C_8)
S_4 (C_1, C_2, C_3, C_4)	S_8 (C_5, C_6, C_7, C_8)

Figure 4.2 Enrollment of Students in Courses

hierarchy. Courses C_1 through C_4 are undergraduate courses and have primary entries in FG_1's directory for course entities. For these courses, the directory maintains local reference counts, local physical pointers, and indicates that some entities in FG_2 point to C_1 and C_2 (i.e., graduate students are taking these courses). Graduate courses C_5 and C_6 are not stored in FG_1 but are referenced (twice) by entities stored within FG_1.

Essentially, we have separated the reference counts for an entity from different fragment groups and stored the counts with the fragment groups where the references are made. Our motivation is to minimize update cost. The primary entry will be affected by nonlocal updates (on another fragment group) only if the update results in the addition of a "new" secondary entry or the removal of an "old" secondary entry in the foreign fragment group's corresponding entity directory (i.e., if the nonlocal reference count goes from 0 to 1, or from 1 to 0, in a secondary entry).

fragment group 1: entity directory for courses

entity id	fragment group id	local reference count	non-local references from fragment groups	physical ptr
C1	FG1	4	{FG2}	→
C2	FG1	4	{FG2}	→
C3	FG1	2	{}	→
C4	FG1	2	{}	→
C5	FG2	2		
C6	FG2	2		

fragment group 2: entity directory for courses

entity id	fragment group id	local reference count	non-local references from fragment groups	physical ptr
C5	FG2	4	{FG1}	→
C6	FG2	4	{FG1}	→
C7	FG2	2	{}	→
C8	FG2	2	{}	→
C1	FG1	2		
C2	FG1	2		

Figure 4.3 Fragment Group Entity Directories

Similarly, the entity directory for courses in FG_2 contains primary entries for graduate courses C_5 through C_8 and secondary entries for C_1 and C_2. If another graduate student enrolls in C_1, only the reference count in FG_2 needs to be incremented. If graduate students were no longer enrolled in C_7 as a result of updates, its local reference count would become zero. Since C_7 is not referenced by entities in any other fragment group, the deletion of C_7 would be allowed. The legality of the deletion can always be determined by checking only the appropriate primary entry in the local entity directory.

4.2 Distribution Index

In distributed databases, it is often necessary to access all entities with a specific function value: entities that potentially could be stored in any fragment group. In order to facilitate such accesses, we introduce the notion of a distribution index. Each entry in a distribution index identifies the logical fragment groups that store entities that have a given indexed value. In order to maintain a distribution index efficiently, we require that corresponding local secondary indices be maintained for each fragment group where entities of the indexed entity type reside. (A local secondary index contains only entries for entities that are locally stored within a fragment group.) Without such local indices, it would be difficult to determine if an insertion or deletion operation has any effect on the distribution index. With the local indices, we know that the distribution index has to be updated whenever an update operation causes the creation or deletion of an entry in a local secondary index.

Figure 4.4 illustrates a distribution index that could be maintained for the students in the fragment groups identified in figure 4.1. While this example distribution index is based on a unique function (i.e., each student has a unique student number), distribution indices in general can involve nonunique functions and combinations of functions.

Student No.	F G
77446	{FG1}
78550	{FG2}
79450	{FG2}
---	--
---	--
---	--

Student No. Index

Figure 4.4 A Distribution Index

The distribution index on student number can be used to locate a specific student regardless of whether the student is a graduate or an undergraduate. That index is updated only when students enter or leave the university or change undergraduate/graduate status. No specific physical location information is maintained in the distribution index to shield it from changes of the student record within a fragment group.

In systems such as SDD-1, R*, and Distributed INGRES, both fragments would have to be searched based on student number. Alternately, these systems would allow a fragmentation criterion based on student number. However, the specification of ranges of student numbers as fragmentation criteria violates the important principle of separating logical and physical database designs: student numbers would have to be assigned based on where the records should be stored. On the other hand, the specification of an individual distribution criterion for each student number is cumbersome and would require updates to the distribution criteria (which normally can be performed only by a DBA) for each change in student status. The distribution index seems like a more natural extension to single-site secondary indices for locating data.

4.3 Implications of Replication

The DDM supports data replication [CDFG83a] [CDFG83b], and fragment groups are used as the units for allocation to sites in the system. However, it is important to note that all nonlocal references used in the representation of entity functions, in entity directories, and in distribution indices, refer to logical fragment groups and not to sites that stores copies of those fragment groups. This serves to simplify pointer maintenance significantly. At the same time, it facilitates our compilation approach to the generation of access plans for repetitive transactions. The same plan would be usable, regardless of which copy of a given fragment group is dynamically selected for executing the transaction. At run time, each logical fragment group must be bound to a physically available site for reading purposes. (That is, for each logical fragment group that must be read during the execution of the transaction, a site that stores a copy of the fragment group must be used.)

In fact, our implementation scheme for fragment group entity directories has been influenced strongly by the desire for the capability to add and remove fragment group copies dynamically. The allocation and replication parameters of a fragment group can be changed without requiring update operations on entity directories. For example, a new fragment group copy can be added simply by obtaining an image of an existing copy. Conceivably, we could have chosen a more compact representation for the fragment group entity directories by collapsing the directories for different fragment group copies if they happened to be stored at the same site. However, this would have brought major upheavals when the allocation and replication parameters of fragment groups have to be changed for performance reasons.

5. Distributed Query Processing

An overview of our two-stage approach to optimizing repetitive transactions has been presented in [CDFG83b]. The selection of a processing strategy treats each fragment group as a logical site and is performed at compile time. The result of compilation is a plan that prescribes the local operations to be performed on data stored within individual fragment groups and the movement of data resulting from these local operations. Optimization at compile time is essentially based on a worst case analysis, since it assumes that different fragment groups are stored at different sites. At run time, the binding of logical fragment groups to physical sites is performed. That is, a set of sites is selected for following the compile time plan. The optimization during site selection for each fragment group takes into consideration which sites are operational (and thus which copies of a needed fragment group are accessible), and which fragment groups are potentially needed for running the transaction.

The presence of distributed access structures discussed in Section 4 affects the set of cross-site operations that are included in the access plan generated at compile time. At run time, they are used to reduce the set of fragment groups that potentially contain the desired data to the set of fragment groups that are actually required. We discuss the uses of fragment group entity directories and distribution indices for query processing below.

5.1 Use of Fragment Group Entity Directories

In addition to providing direct support for referential integrity maintenance, fragment group entity directories support fast access from individual entities to the entities they reference. Consider the fragmentation and grouping scheme illustrated in Figure 4.1. The enrollments function of a given student is represented by a collection of pointers to course entities. As explained in [CDFL82], either logical pointers or hybrid pointers can be used for the representation of entity functions. A logical pointer consists of the entity's unique identifier that was assigned at the time of its creation. A hybrid pointer combines a logical pointer with a physical pointer. The physical pointer portion of a hybrid pointer depends on whether the referenced entity is local or foreign. The physical pointer to a local entity points to a single local record representing the entity from a specific viewpoint (i.e., the range type of the entity-valued function). The physical pointer to a foreign entity is represented as an indirection flag only. It simply indicates that the entity is foreign, and that an appropriate entry in the local fragment group entity directory should be consulted to determine the fragment group that stores the foreign entity. (See [CDFL82] for discussions on hybrid pointer maintenance and validation.) A request can then be passed on to the site chosen during site binding for the identified fragment group in order to access the desired entity. The fragment group entity directory at this foreign fragment group is used to obtain the physical pointer(s) to the record(s) that represent the referenced entity. Thus, fragment group entity directories provide efficient support for "small" transactions that typically access a single entity of one type, along with related entities from other types.

At the same time, it is possible to make use of entity directories to process "large" transactions that perform joining operations on entire entity types. Consider a joining operation between student and course types based on the enrollments function. Assume that students who are not enrolled in any course, and courses that are not taken by any student, do not qualify for output in this transaction.

Now, assume that the database is fragmented as shown in Figure 4.1, that FG_1 and FG_2 are available at different sites, and that the transaction is originated at a third site. The most straightforward processing strategy is to transfer all student and course information from both FG_1 and FG_2 to the transaction's home site, reconstruct the student entity type by taking the union of undergraduate students and graduate students, reconstruct the course entity type by taking the union of undergraduate courses and graduate courses, and then compute the desired join between students and courses.

An often used strategy for reducing the amount of data that have to be transferred to the transaction's home site is to make use of semi-join operations [BGWR81]. Typically, this would involve projecting one of the operands on its joining field, and transferring this projection to the site of the second operand in order to reduce the size of the latter. With fragmented operands, the semi-join operation becomes more complicated. (For example, see [YCTB83] for discussions on how semi-joins can be performed on fragmented operands.)

However, with the presence of fragment group entity directories, a faster processing strategy is readily available. Let SU and CU represent undergraduate students and undergraduate courses in FG_1. Let SG and CG represent the graduate students and graduate courses in FG_2. A possible processing strategy, selected at compile time, is illustrated in figure 5.1.

At a site that stores FG_1, we perform the join based on enrollments between SU and CU and store the result in a temporary T_1. By examining entities in SU and the entity directory for courses in FG_1, we also can determine locally those undergraduate students who are taking graduate courses (SU semi-joined by CG) and those undergraduate courses being taken by graduate students (CU semi-joined by SG). These operations result in temporaries T_2 and T_3 respectively. Similarly, the temporaries T_4, T_5, and T_6 can be formed locally at a site that contains FG_2. At step 2, only some of the courses and students need to be joined. T_7 represents undergraduates taking graduate courses, and T_8 represents graduates taking undergraduate courses. The unions at step 3 thus do not need to remove duplicates.

	Site FG1	Site FG2
Step 1:	T_1 = SU Join CU	T_4 = SG Join CG
	T_2 = SU Semi-Join CG	T_5 = SG Semi-Join CU
	T_3 = CU Semi-Join SG	T_6 = CG Semi-Join SU
	Site X	
Step 2:	T_7 = T_2 Join T_6	
	T_8 = T_5 Join T_3	
	Site X	
Step 3:	Result = T1 U T4 U T7 U T8	

Figure 5.1 Use of Entity Directories

We say that this compile time plan specifies that the join is to be distributed over the union operations and that double semi-join reductions are to be used to reduce the amount of data that has to be transferred. At run time further reductions become apparent automatically (T_7 (or T_8) would be empty if T_2 and T_6 (or T_5 and T_3) were empty). Note that T_2 would be empty if and only if T_6 were empty.

With the above processing strategy, we are minimizing the amount of computation cost that will have to be incurred during step 2. If the intermediate results obtained during step 1 must individually be transferred to a different final site before step 2 is carried out, then it may be preferrable to perform semi-joins between SU and CU to form temporaries T_{1a} and T_{1b}, and between SG and CG to form temporaries T_{2a} and T_{2b}, and postpone all joining operations until step 2. At the same time, since T_{1a} may overlap with T_2, and T_{1b} may overlap with T_3, it may be preferrable to represent these temporaries with sets of entity identifiers, and to send information concerning entities that belong to multiple overlapping temporaries to the final site only once.(7)

5.2 Use of Distribution Indices

As previously mentioned, one obvious use for distribution indices is processing selection operations. Assume a distribution index on the age of students is kept for the previous example database. Consider a query that asks for all students who are 17 years old. Without a distribution index, it would be necessary to issue two subqueries, one on each of the two fragment groups, in order to retrieve all of the desired students. However, a distribution index may indicate that there are no 17 year old students in FG_2, thus eliminating the futile access to FG_2 that otherwise would have to be made.

Another potential use for distribution indices is for the processing of valued-based joining operations. Consider a query that joins suppliers and projects based on their respective cities. If we have available distribution indices on both the city function of suppliers and on the city function of projects, we can use the distribution index to identify the fragment groups that actually have matching entities. For each supplier fragment we can identify the cities for which there will be a matching project. We can then use the list of cities to perform a semi-join on that supplier fragment. Similarly, we can collect a list of qualifying cities for each project fragment. At compile time, the optimizer will decide to use neither, one, or both of the semi-join reductions. At run time, it may be determined that entire fragments need not be accessed.

6. Conclusions

The design of the DDM has led us to three important conclusions. The first conclusion is that it is indeed possible to build distributed database systems that support a semantically rich data model like Daplex, the entity-relationship model, and other models that support explicit relationships between different types of objects. The distributed database management system that supports these models must support a high level, set-at-a-time data manipulation facility. With such a facility, the support for distribution should allow for the placement of data that is based on the relationships between the types of data, maintain referential integrity between data stored at different sites, and use distribution access paths along with relational like operations to support query processing.

The second conclusion we have reached is that in addition to the increased functionality of the semantically rich data model, a distributed system like the DDM actually can improve performance over a distributed relational database system. The distributed access structures used to maintain referential integrity also can be used in query processing to locate and limit the number of fragments that need to be accessed and to reduce the amount of data that needs to be shipped between sites. Furthermore, these structures can be designed so that multiple-site checking and updating is not required for individual entity insertions and deletions.

The third conclusion we have reached is that the required extension to relational distributed database technology is straightforward. The extensions described in this paper do not seem significantly more difficult than the implementa-

(7) Likewise, T_{4a} may overlap with T_5, and T_{4b} may overlap with T_6.

tions required for a distributed relational system. In fact, the extensions, particularly the query processing extensions, are built on relational query processing techniques. Furthermore, these extensions are orthogonal to other aspects of the DDM implementation such as directory management, (inter-transaction) concurrency control, reliability, and recovery.

7. References

[BCC81]
Bernstein, P.A., B.T. Blaustein, and E.M. Clarke, "Fast Maintenance of Semantic Integrity Assertions Using Redundant Aggregate Data," VLDB Conference Proceedings, 1981.

[BGWR81]
Bernstein, P.A., N. Goodman, E. Wong, C. Reeve, and J.B. Rothnie, "Query Processing in a System for Distributed Databases (SDD-1)," ACM Transactions on Database Systems, Vol. 6, No. 4, December 1981.

[CDFG83a]
Chan, A., U. Dayal, S. Fox, N. Goodman, D. Ries, and D. Skeen, "DDM: An Ada Compatible Database Manager," IEEE COMPCON Digest of Papers, 1983.

[CDFG83b]
Chan, A., U. Dayal, S. Fox, N. Goodman, D. Ries, and D. Skeen, "Overview of an Ada Compatible Distributed Database Manager," ACM SIGMOD Conference Proceedings, 1983.

[CDFL82]
Chan, A., S. Danberg, S. Fox, W.K. Lin, A. Nori, and D. Ries, "Storage and Access Structures to Support a Semantic Data Model," VLDB Conference Proceedings, 1982.

[CHEN76]
Chen, P.P., "The Entity Relationship Model -- Towards a Unified View of Data," ACM Transactions on Database Systems, Vol. 1, No. 1, March 1976.

[CFLR81]
Chan, A., S. Fox, W.K. Lin, and D. Ries, "The Design of an Ada Compatible Local Database Manager (LDM)," Technical Report CCA-81-09, Computer Corporation of America, November, 1981.

[CODD82]
Codd, E.F., "Relational Database: A Practical Foundation for Productivity," ACM Communications, Vol. 25, No. 2, February 1982.

[DATE81]
Date, C.J., "Referential Integrity," VLDB Conference Proceedings, 1981.

[EC75]
Eswaran, K.P., and D.D. Chamberlin, "Functional Specification of a Subsystem for Database Integrity," VLDB Conference Proceedings, 1975.

[HS78]
Hammer, M., and S. Sarin, "Efficient Monitoring of Database Assertions," ACM SIGMOD Conference Proceedings Supplement, 1978.

[KP81]
Koenig, S., and R. Paige, "A Transformational Framework for the Automatic Control of Derived Data," VLDB Conference Proceedings, 1981.

[MP82]
Manola, F., and A. Pirotte, "CQLF -- A Query Language for CODASYL-type Databases," ACM SIGMOD Conference Proceedings, 1982.

[RBFG80]
Rothnie, J.B., P.A. Bernstein, S. Fox, N. Goodman, M. Hammer, T.A. Landers, C. Reeve, D.W. Shipman, and E. Wong, "Introduction to a System for Distributed Databases (SDD-1)," ACM Transactions on Database Systems, Vol. 5, No. 1, March 1980.

[SHIP81]
Shipman, D., "The Functional Data Model and the Data Language Daplex," ACM Transactions on Database Systems, Vol. 6, No. 1, March 1981.

[SN77]
Stonebraker, M., and E. Neuhold, "A Distributed Database Version of INGRES," Proceedings of the Berkeley Workshop on Distributed Data Management and Computer Networks, 1977.

[WDHL82]
Williams, R., D. Daniels, L. Haas, G. Lapis, B. Lindsay, P. Ng, R. Obermarck, P. Selinger, A. Walker, P. Wilms, and R. Yost, "R*: An Overview of the Architecture," Proceedings of the 2nd International Conferences on Databases: Improving Usability and Responsiveness, 1982.

[YCTB83]
Yu, C.T., C.C. Chang, M. Templeton, D. Brill, and E. Lund, "On the Design of a Query Processing Strategy in a Distributed Database Environment," ACM SIGMOD Conference Proceedings, 1983.

VIEW MANAGEMENT IN DISTRIBUTED DATA BASE SYSTEMS

E. BERTINO, L.M. HAAS, B.G. LINDSAY

IBM San Jose Research Lab
5600 Cottle Road
SAN JOSE, CA95193 USA

1. Introduction

The structure of data to be stored by a Data Base Management System (DBMS) is usually decided by a database administrator. Individual users and applications are generally interested in only a subset of the data stored in the database. Often, they wish to see this subset structured in a way which reflects their particular needs. Since it is not generally possible to structure a database so as to please all of its users, some mechanism is needed whereby each user can view the data according to his (her) own requirements. The representation of the data structure as seen by a user is often referred to as an external schema; the view mechanism is a means by which a DBMS can support various external schemas.

Besides providing users with tailored views of the data, the view mechanism contributes to [Chamberlin75]:

- Data independence: giving applications a logical view of data, thereby isolating them from data reorganization.

- Data isolation: giving the application exactly that subset of data it needs, thereby minimizing error propagation.

In a relational DBMS, a view is defined as a "virtual table" derived by a specific query on one or more base tables. The relational operations join, restrict and project as well as statistical summaries of tables may be used to define a view. Access rights may be granted and revoked on views just as though they were ordinary tables. This allows users to selectively share data, preventing unauthorized users from reading sensitive information.

SQL/DS [SQL81] and INGRES [Stonebraker76] are examples of relational DBMS's that provide the view facility.

In this abstract, the implementation of views in distributed relational DBMS's is discussed. Section 2 briefly reviews view management in a single-site DBMS. In section 3, the view concept is extended to a distributed DBMS (DDBMS) and two types of views are introduced: shorthand views and protection views. Finally section 4 outlines view management in a DDBMS.

2. Views in Single-Site Database Systems

A DBMS must construct and store an internal representation for each view that it supports. This occurs at view definition time. In systems such as SQL/DS, this internal representation is a parse tree for the view definition statement. When a view is later referenced in a query, a view composition operation is performed to combine the view's parse tree with the query parse tree. The result is a composite parse tree which only contains references to real stored tables.

In creating the internal representation of a view, names in the view definition statement are bound to the specific objects they reference, namely tables and other views. A view is therefore logically dependent on the continued existence of all objects that it references. If an object is dropped or substantially changed (for example, if the columns of a table are rearranged or a view is redefined) then the views referencing those objects must be invalidated.

In addition, since at view usage time the operations performed on the view will be translated into operations on the underlying objects, the view must have the necessary privileges on those objects. The privileges are granted to the view by the view definer. The view definer must therefore have the necessary privileges on the objects referenced in the view definition to be able to define the view. This allows users who do not have privileges on the underlying objects, but who do have privileges on the view, to access those objects through the view, according to protection requirements expressed by the view. If all privileges on an underlying object are revoked from the view definer, the view is no longer valid.

To be certain that a view is valid, the DBMS must keep track of dependencies of views upon all objects they reference. At view definition time, the system determines the set of objects referenced by the view, and the set of authorizations needed by the view. Records of the form <view name>

depends on <object name> and <view name> *possesses* <authorization> *on* <object name> are stored in special system catalogs. If an object is dropped or substantially changed, or if an authorization is revoked, the catalogs can be searched to find the views affected by the change, and the views can be marked invalid.

The next time the view is used in a query, the system notes the invalid state of the view, and drops the view. Alternatively, it could attempt to revalidate the view, by redefining the view against the current database. Note that revalidation will not always succeed: if an object referenced by the view has been dropped, the view cannot be defined. If, however, the object has merely been changed, and the changes are compatible with the view definition, the view can be revalidated (for example this might happen if the columns of a table have been reordered).

3. Views in Distributed Database Systems

Within the last few years, distributed database management systems (DDBMS) have become a rapidly growing field of investigation and a number of implementations have been reported [Williams81,Rothnie80,Stonebraker77]. Among the numerous goals of a DDBMS, two have been recognized as key objectives: site autonomy and data distribution transparency.

Site autonomy means that each site can operate on its own data as a stand-alone, single-site DBMS, and that each site retains local control of its own data, even if the site participates in the execution of a distributed query. This guarantees better resiliency to failures of sites and communication lines, since there are no centralized functions or services, such as a global dictionary or centralized deadlock detector. Further, each site performs all operations on its own local data, including authorization checking and, of course, database accesses and updates.

The second objective, distribution transparency, means that users are shielded from the physical distribution and redundancy of data and are able to interact with the distributed system as easily as with a conventional centralized one. This ensures logical independence of applications.

Any extension of views to a DDBMS must preserve the appearance of views as virtual tables. This presents many problems due to the fact that views in a DDBMS may be defined using tables which are not local to the view definition site and/or using other views defined at remote sites. Views defined using non-local objects are themselves distributed objects, which requires that the operations of creating, dropping and using a view be distributed operations.

The issue of authorization on views also has major implications for the implementation. When a view is used in a query, view composition must take place in order to derive an execution strategy for the query. If views are not objects of authorization, this composition can take place at any site. If views are objects of authorization, site autonomy considerations require that the view definition site maintain control over the materialization of the view. In particular, view composition must take place at the view definition site. (Actually any "trusted" site will do, but the "trusted" set should default to the view definition site). If view composition is allowed to occur at any site, a malicious site could pervert the view definition by dropping restrictions or projections in the view definition.

Forcing view composition at the view definition site can have negative effects on performance. If the definition site of a view is not the site at which a query using the view is submitted (the query master site), then it may not be possible for a single site to produce a complete execution strategy for the query, because the view definition may only be composed into the query at the view definition site. Further, in systems which separate planning a query from its execution, the execution strategy must include accessing the view definition site to check that the user is still authorized to use the view. This must be done at execution time even if no tables referenced in the fully composed query are stored at the view definition site.

For these reasons, the execution strategy for a query referencing a remotely defined view is unlikely to be optimal, and a performance penalty may be incurred. If views were not objects of authorization the query site could produce a complete execution strategy, which would not require accessing the view definition site unless some table were actually stored there.

Hence, two types of views are recognized. Shorthand views provide the data hiding, data conversion, typing elimination and renaming functions associated with views, but are not objects of authorization. The user posing queries against a shorthand view must be authorized to access the objects referenced by the view. Protection views provide the same semantics as shorthand views and in addition are objects of authorization. Authorization to access the objects referenced by the protection view belongs to the view and the user of the view only needs the privilege to use the protection view. Queries referencing remotely defined shorthand views will in general execute more efficiently than identical queries with shorthand views replaced by protection views.

4. Distributed View Management

As mentioned in the previous section, views are defined in terms of queries which may reference local and non-local tables and views. Queries may be imbedded in programs, which are precompiled by (D)DBMS's such as System R [Astrahan76] and R* [Wiliams81]. The result of precompilation is a set of access modules, defining the execution plan for the query, which are stored in the (distributed) database. Precompilation also creates dependencies (as described in section 2) for the program on the tables and views referenced in the program. Thus, if a table is dropped or a view redefined, the program must be invalidated. At execution time of a program, the system checks whether the program is valid. If the program is still valid, the system loads and executes the necessary access modules. If the program has been invalidated, the system may try to recompile the program; if recompilation succeeds, the program is executed, otherwise an error is reported [Ng82].

Since distribution transparency requires that the system have the same behavior with respect to users as a centralized DBMS, a correct implementation of views in DDBMS must ensure that views are dependent on the objects they reference, and that programs referencing views are dependent on those views. These requirements ensure a consistent usage of views by users.

In addition, site autonomy requires that each site be able to perform any action on local (non-distributed) objects, such as dropping local tables or purely local views, without notifying any other site. In particular, it should not be necessary to contact other sites at which programs or views referencing the local objects are stored or defined.

These two requirements suggest that dependency recording should be distributed among the sites of those objects on which the view (or program) depends. In other words, view or program dependencies on remote tables should be recorded at the sites where those tables are stored. This allows local invalidation of distributed programs or remotely defined views if a local table is dropped or changed.

Actually the situation is somewhat more complicated. Programs and views may depend on remotely defined protection and shorthand views, as well as remotely stored tables. Dependencies on protection views are recorded at the view definition site. In fact this site will be accessed at execution time, since the view is materialized at that site.

If the dependency of a program on a shorthand view is recorded at the view definition site, and that view is later dropped, it may not be possible to invalidate the program. This will happen if no table referenced by either program or view is stored at the view definition site. In this situation, the program has no need to access the view definition site at execution time and hence it will not discover that the view has been dropped.

To invalidate a program in these circumstances, dependencies on shorthand views are recorded at other sites, chosen in such a way that any program referencing the view must access these sites at execution time. In fact, those sites are the sites at which tables referenced by the view are stored.

An obvious consequence of these distributed dependencies is that view definition and view drop are distributed operations. At view definition time, the dependency of a view on remote tables must be recorded at the table store sites. When dropping a view, remote sites storing view dependencies must be accessed in order to delete these dependencies and, at the same time, invalidate programs and views depending upon the dropped view. Note that remote sites are only accessed when the view is a distributed object. Local views are still dropped locally.

5. Conclusions

In this paper, the implementation of views in a DDBMS has been discussed. Two kinds of views have been introduced: shorthand views and protection views.

The approach chosen for view implementation has many advantages. Programs using views depend upon them; thus they always correctly incorporate the current semantics of any view referenced by the programs. If the views are dropped or changed, the programs will be invalidated. Views also depend on the objects referenced in the view definition statements; this allows invalidation of views when one of these objects is dropped or changed.

View definition and drop view are distributed operations, involving all sites that store objects referenced in the view definition statement. Since the actions of defining and dropping views are expected to occur relatively infrequently, this is not a high price to pay for good query performance with these semantics.

REFERENCES

[Chamberlin75] Chamberlin,D.D., Gray,J.N. and Traiger,I.L. , "Views, Authorization and Locking in a Database System", Proc. AFIPS NCC, Vol. 44, 1975.

[Ng82] Ng, P., "Distributed Compilation and Recompilation of Database Queries", IBM Research Laboratory RJ3375 San Jose, Calif., January 1982.

[Rothnie80] Rothnie,J.B, Bernstein,P.A., Fox,S.A, Goodman,N., Hammer,M.M., Landers, T.A., Reeve,C.L., Shipman,D.W. and Wong,E., "A system for distributed database (SDD-1)", ACM Transactions on Database System, March 1980.

[SQL81] IBM Corp., "SQL/Data System: Application Programming", SH24-5018, 1981.

[Stonebraker76] Stonebraker,M., Wong,E.,Kreps,P., and Held, G., "The Design and Implementation of INGRES", ACM Trans. Database Syst. 1,3 (Sept.1976).

[Stonebraker77] Stonebraker,M., Neuhold,E., "A Distributed Version of INGRES", Proc. 2nd Berkeley Workshop Distributed Data Management and Computer Networks, May 1977.

[Wiliams81] Wiliams,R. et Al. "R*: An Overview of the Architecture" Proceedings of the international Conference on Database Systems, Jerusalem, Israel, June 1982. Published in Improving Database Usability and Responsiveness, P.Scheuermann, ed. Academic Press, N.Y.

SOME EXPERIMENTAL RESULTS ON DISTRIBUTED JOIN ALGORITHMS IN A LOCAL NETWORK

Hongjun Lu
Michael J. Carey

Computer Sciences Department
University of Wisconsin
Madison, WI 53706

ABSTRACT

This paper presents some experimental results on the performance of distributed join algorithms in a local network. Eight different join methods have been implemented in an experimental distributed system, the Crystal multicomputer, and tested for join queries with a variety of relation sizes, join selectivities, and join column value distributions. The results obtained indicate that pipelined join methods outperform sequential methods over a wide range of join queries. It was also found that the communications costs in a local network environment are not a dominant factor with respect to performance, and that shipping a whole relation from one site to another is not an unreasonable decison as long as it is done in the framework of pipelined algorithms. Two pipelined variants of a centralized nested loops join algorithm (with an index) were found to perform well for many of the queries tested.

1. INTRODUCTION

In relational database systems, queries are typically posed in a high-level, nonprocedural query language based on the relational calculus such as QUEL or SQL [Ullm82]. It is the task of the query optimizer to decompose the query into primitive relational operations such as selection, projection and join. The join operator has attracted a great deal of research interest since the costs of available join methods tend to vary widely with the characteristics of the data and the available access paths [Blas76, Seli79, DeWi82a, Brab84, DeWi85]. The join operation and join orders have also been the primary focus of many query optimization algorithms for centralized database systems [Wong76, Seli79]. The distribution of data in distributed database systems further increases the complexity and tradeoffs associated with the join operation. A great deal of research work has gone into the problem of developing distributed query processing algorithms, particularly into finding good methods for performing distributed joins. A new operation, the semijoin, was introduced as a way of minimizing the communications cost for performing distributed joins, and a number of researchers have addressed the problem of finding optimal semijoin sequences for various classes of queries [Bern81a, Bern81b]. A related method, known as "fetch the inner tuple as needed", is among the algorithms used for processing distributed joins in System R^* [Seli80, Lohm84].

Along with the development of new join algorithms has come research on the performance of the various algorithms. Four methods for processing a general select-project-join query in a centralized database system were investigated analytically and their performance was compared in [Blas76]. They found that, in most cases, either the nested loops algorithm or the sort-merge algorithm offered the best (or close to the best) performance. Other researchers have analyzed alternative centralized join algorithms as well [Nieh76, Yao78, Yao79, Brab84]. There have also been a few studies of distributed query processing performance issues. Epstein and Stonebraker tested 14 versions the of Distributed INGRES query processing algorithms [Epst80]. Their results indicated that exhaustive search performs consistently better than limited search, that dynamic optimization is beneficial, and that using a "worst case"

This research was partially supported by the Wisconsin Alumni Research Foundation, National Science Foundation Grant Number DCR-8402818, and an IBM Faculty Development Award.

estimate for intermediate relation sizes is overly pessimistic. Some simulation results on the performance of different join strategies for a distributed database system based on a star computer network were presented in [Kers82], and the effects of join selectivity and communications speed on the optimal algorithm choice were investigated in this context. Some results on query processing in a locally distributed system were reported in [Page83], where query processing costs for the INGRES database system were analyzed in the context of the LOCUS distributed operating system.

Compared to the number of distributed query processing *algorithm* papers in the literature, relatively few papers have addressed the *performance* of distributed join algorithms. This is one of the major motivations which lead us to perform this study. We have implemented eight different distributed two-way join methods in an experimental locally distributed computer system at the University of Wisconsin. The join methods examined in our study include methods based on both traditional joins and semijoins using several different access methods and data transfer strategies. The work reported here differs from most of the work mentioned above in the sense that it is an *empirical* study — we present measurements of actual response times, disk activity, and message transfers for the join algorithms that we consider.

The organization of the remainder of the paper is as follows. The eight different join algorithms that we studied are described in section 2. Section 3 provides an overview of our experimental environment. Our experiments are described and the results are presented in Section 4. Section 5 summarizes what we have learned from this study and its influence on what we plan to do in the future.

2. DISTRIBUTED JOIN METHODS

Given an equi-join query $R_a[A=B]R_b$ in a distributed database system, where R_a and R_b reside at (different) sites S_a and S_b, respectively, there are a number of distributed join methods available for processing it. Considering all of the possible combinations of access paths, local processing algorithms, execution paradigms, etc., would lead to a prohibitively large search space for an empirical investigation. Thus, to reduce the number of experiments necessary we categorize distributed join methods along three dimensions and consider the following options in each:

(1) General approach — "traditional" join methods versus semijoin-based methods.

(2) Execution paradigm — sequential versus pipelined execution for the pair of sites involved.

(3) Local join processing — sort-merge versus nested loops (with an index).

In the remainder of this section we elaborate on each of these dimensions, and we then present descriptions of our implementations of eight join algorithms that are produced by combining options from these dimensions.

2.1. Join Versus Semijoin

The semijoin operator was introduced as a primitive for processing distributed queries with less data transfer than traditional join methods [Bern79a, Bern79b, Bern81a, Bern81b]. Using the semijoin method, only the join column values of one relation and then the matching tuples of the second relation need to be transferred between the two sites. If intersite data transfer is expensive, the join field width is relatively small compared to the width of an entire tuple, and there are not many matching tuples, the use of semijoins can result in a significant savings. In local area networks, however, the data transfer rate between sites is much higher — on the same order of magnitude as that between memory and a local disk. It is questionable whether or not semijoins will be beneficial in such an environment, as using them requires multiple scans of one of the source relations and therefore more disk accesses.

2.2. Sequential Versus Pipelined Processing

When an operation at a site requests remote data, as in a distributed join, a choice exists — the two sites can work in either a sequential fashion or in a pipelined fashion. If the sites work sequentially, the site receiving data will not begin its processing until all of the required data has arrived. In the pipelined case, processing will begin at the receiving site as soon as the first tuple or packet of data has arrived. One advantage of the pipelined approach is its parallelism — the two sites work in parallel, so the elapsed time for the query will be reduced in proportion to the amount of overlapped processing. Second, and perhaps more important, is the fact that the receiving site doesn't actually store the incoming data in a temporary relation, thus saving the time and disk accesses required to store and then re-retrieve the data received from the remote site.

2.3. Sort-Merge Versus Nested Loops Join

Since any distributed join involves local processing, the join algorithm and associated access methods are still important factors in a distributed database system. For centralized joins, it was found in [Blas76] that, except for very small relations, the nested loops join or sort-merge join methods were always optimal or near optimal. We thus chose these two local join methods to implement for our distributed join experiments. For the nested loops join method, we assume the availability of a B+ tree index on the join column of the inner relation, as would likely be the case in System R^* [Seli80, Lohm84].[1] If the inner relation is shipped to the outer relation's site, a B+ tree index is constructed for the inner relation at the outer site. Because the WiSS system [Chou83] does not support clustered indexes on non-unique (i.e., non-key) attributes, and in addition it is not always reasonable to assume that the join column will have a clustered index available, our implementation uses secondary (i.e., non-clustered) indexes.

2.4. Join Algorithm Details

As described earlier, we have implemented eight join algorithms for our study. The algorithms, classified according to the three dimensions presented above, are SJSM, SJNL, PJSM, PJNL, SSSM, SSNL, PSSM, and PSNL. For the first letter, "S" stands for sequential and "P" stands for pipelined. The second letter, "J" or "S", is used to represent "traditional join" versus semijoin. The last two letters indicate either sort-merge ("SM") or nested loops ("NL") join. In the remainder of this section we describe each of these methods in turn. In our tests, site S_a initiates the join query and is both the join site and the result site.

2.4.1. SJSM and SJNL

The sequential join methods SJSM and SJNL are the simplest of the distributed join methods. The remote relation R_b is shipped to join site S_a as a whole. The two relations are then joined at site S_a using either the sort-merge method (SJSM) or the nested loops method (SJNL). For SJSM, the two relations are each sorted at their local sites first to increase parallelism. For SJNL, a B+ tree index is built on the join column of the received relation at site S_a before performing the local join.

2.4.2. PJSM and PJNL

Like SJSM and SJNL, the PJSM and PJNL algorithms transfer the whole relation R_b from site S_b to site S_a. The difference is that R_b is not stored as a temporary relation at site S_a. Instead, tuples of R_b are joined with R_a tuples on the fly as they arrive. Using the PJSM method, both relations are sorted first. Then, when a group (packet) of R_b tuples arrives at site S_a, a scan cursor on R_a is incremented to find matching tuples. Matches are merged with the tuples from the R_b group and written to the result relation. The scan cursor is then reset to the its last starting point in R_a and the process is repeated for the next group of R_b tuples. In the PJNL case, since no temporary relation for R_b is stored at site S_a, the local relation R_a always serves as the inner relation and the remote relation R_b serves as the outer relation. Both PJSM and PJNL can be viewed as distributed executions of centralized join algorithms.

2.4.3. SSSM and SSNL

SSSM and SSNL are two implementations of the semijoin method. One variation in our implementation is that the join column $R_a.A$, which is sent from site S_a to site S_b, is not stored on disk at site S_b — the incoming values are processed on the fly as they arrive. Similarly, the relation R_b', which is transferred back to site S_a, is processed on the fly as it arrives at S_a instead of being stored there as a temporary relation. Although there is therefore some limited pipelining involved in the SSSM and SSNL execution strategies, we still categorize them as being sequential as compared to the truly pipelined PSSM and PSNL algorithms to be described next.

2.4.4. PSSM and PSNL

The pipelined semijoin methods, referred to as "fetch the inner tuple as needed" in System R^* [Seli80], were the most complicated join methods to implement. Relation R_a is scanned in a tuple-by-tuple manner (conceptually), and join column values $R_a.A$ are sent to site S_b. Upon receiving an $R_a.A$ value, site S_b selects the matching tuples from R_b and sends them to S_a; a null message is sent if there are no matching tuples. These tuples are then merged with the corresponding tuple of R_a, which is waiting for them (still in main memory). Our implementation actually processes R_a tuples in one-page batches, so one buffer page is allocated for keeping the tuples from R_a.

2.5. Discussion

The eight distributed join methods described in this section represent a range of possible methods. The sequential join methods, pipelined join methods, and pipelined semijoin methods are all among the methods used System R^* [Seli80, Lohm84], although our implementation may differ in minor ways. Of these methods, sequential join methods are attractive for their simplicity and the pipelined methods are attractive because they allow more concurrency and avoid the cost of storing and retrieving tuples from a temporary relation. The pipeline methods, of course, require some synchronization of the two processing sites (in the form of flow control, so the receiving site can indeed avoid having to

[1] The cost of a nested loops join without an index for relations of reasonable size is usually prohibitive [Bitt83], so we do not consider this possibility.

store incoming tuples). One limitation of PJNL (the pipelined nested loops join method) is that R_a must be the inner relation, regardless of how its size compares to that of R_b, as the inner relation has to be available for multiple scans. The semijoin methods are attractive because they reduce communications costs. The main difference between the pipelined and sequential semijoin methods is related to duplicates — since the pipelined version simply scans R_a instead of projecting on $R_a.A$, it will send duplicate join column values if they are present in R_a; however, the sequential semijoin method requires multiple scans of R_a, increasing the local processing cost. Clearly, there are tradeoffs among all of these algorithms — these are the tradeoffs to be empirically investigated in Section 4.

3. THE EXPERIMENTAL TESTBED

Figure 3.1 depicts the testbed system used for our performance study. A collection of test programs were written to implement (hard-wired) distributed join queries using the different methods described in section 2. These programs access a synthetic database, the Wisconsin database [Bitt83], via WiSS (the Wisconsin Storage System) [Chou83]. The programs run on a pair of node machines from the Crystal multicomputer, an experimental distributed computer system [DeWi84]. Monitor programs run on a VAX/Unix host machine to initiate test program execution and to collect performance statistics after the test programs terminate. For communications between node machines, or between node machines and the host, we used a Crystal communications package called the Simple Application Package (SAP). In this section we briefly describe each of these components of the system.

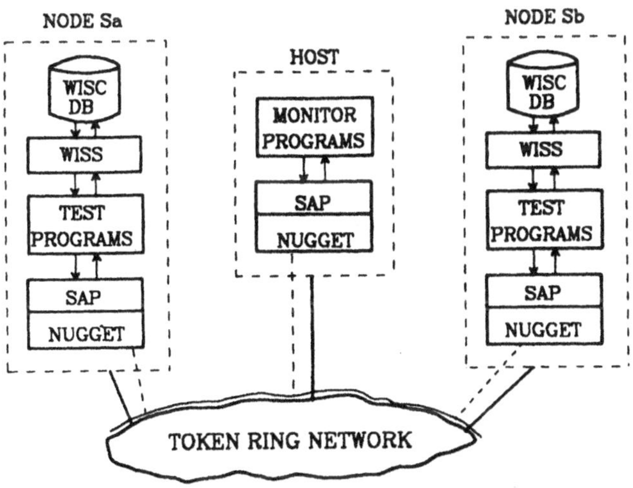

Figure 3.1: Distributed Join Method Testbed.

3.1. The Crystal Multicomputer

The Crystal multicomputer [DeWi84] currently consists of 20 DEC VAX 11/750's interconnected via a 10-Mb/sec Proteon token ring network. The ring network is also connected to several of the Computer Science Department's research VAXes, each of which can serve as a host machine. Crystal multicomputer users can claim a number of node machines as a partition. The partitions of different users in the system are logically isolated from each other — each partition is basically a virtual distributed computer system. For our distributed join algorithm experiments, we used a partition of two node machines with 2 megabytes memory and 160 megabyte Fujitsu disks to create a distributed database system testbed.

There are several levels of software available on Crystal. We used two of the lowest levels, the Crystal Nugget and the Simple Applications Package (SAP), to avoid unnecessary overhead. The Nugget is a simple communications kernel that resides permanently on each node machine, providing low-level message-passing primitives and enforcing the logical isolation of partitions. SAP is a set of subroutines that sit on top of the Nugget, providing buffered communications using two queues, one for incoming messages and other for outgoing messages. It provides a somewhat higher-level message facility for our applications.

3.2. The Wisconsin Storage System

The Wisconsin Storage System, or WiSS, is an access-method level data storage system that can run either on top of Unix or directly on top of a "raw" disk [Chou83]. For our experiments, it was installed on the Crystal node machines and accessed their disks directly. WiSS manages devices, deals with physical storage allocation, manages buffer pages, and provides a primitive concurrency control mechanism. At its highest level, WiSS implements the access methods of sequential scan, index scan, and long data item scan. This level also provides routines for creating and destroying files, indexes and long data items. Some explicit control over scans, such as the capability to reset a scan cursor (search pointer), is also provided. Our test programs interface with WiSS at this level.

3.3. The Wisconsin Database

The Wisconsin Database was designed for use in systematically benchmarking relational database systems [Bitt83]. There are four basic relations in the database, called "thoustup", "twothoustup", "fivethoustup", and "tenthoustup". These relations contain 1000, 2000, 5000, and 10,000 tuples, respectively. Tuples in all of these relations are 182 bytes long, each consisting of thirteen 2-byte integer attributes and three 52-byte string attributes. All of the integer attributes have uniformly distributed values, but the range of their distributions varies in order to provide for different selectivities and projectivities. The string attributes were not used in our study, so we do not discuss them here.

4. EXPERIMENTS AND RESULTS

4.1. Some Considerations

The first problem that arose in designing our tests was the issue of choosing an appropriate set of test queries. In their classic study of join methods for centralized database systems, Blasgen and Eswaren used a query that selected a subset of tuples from two relations, joined these together, and finally projected out a subset of the resulting fields as a general query for their analyses [Blas76]. Our initial inclination was to do the same for our study of distributed joins. However, since we are more interested in the effects of data distribution on the various join options, and adding the two pre-join selections and a post-join projection would only increase the fraction of the execution time due to local processing, we decided to use the simple two-site join of Figure 4.1 for our test queries. The sizes of relations R_a and R_b, the size of the result relation R, and the value distributions of the join attributes are varied in our experiments to observe their respective effects on performance.

```
range a is Ra at Sa
range b is Rb at Sb
retrieve into R(a.all,b.all) at Sa
where (a.A = b.B)
```

Figure 4.1: General Form of the Test Query.

Our choice of source relations followed the methodology presented in [Bitt83]. There are several considerations here. First, relation sizes should be large enough to be realistic. The basic relations used in our tests have 1,000 tuples and 10,000 tuples (the "thoustup" and "tenthoustup" relations of the Wisconsin database), occupying about 46 and 456 pages, respectively. Second, random attribute value distributions are desirable in order to provide an unbiased treatment of each of the join methods. This was particularly important in the sort-merge join case. Third, in order to insure that the results of the various tests were not biased by preceeding ones, we had to ensure that no test query was likely to find useful pages sitting in the buffer from its predecessors. We used a technique described in [Bitt83], where two copies of source relations are maintained (at each site in our case), and alternate queries use alternate copies of the source relations.

Another important decision for our study was the choice of an appropriate set of performance metrics and a reasonable measurement approach. For our experiments, the elapsed time of a query was the main metric measured. This time is defined as the time interval beginning when site S_a initiates the query and ending when the result is completely stored at site S_a. The Crystal Nugget provides a timing procedure that is accurate to the nearest 10 milliseconds; this procedure was used for our elapsed time measurements. For each query, we also measured the number of disk accesses performed and the number of messages sent. Our disk access measurements were taken using a special version of WiSS that is instrumented to trace disk operations. For each disk access, the start and completion times of the access are recorded. An analysis of the trace records from our experiments indicates that an average disk access in our test environment takes about 25.5 milliseconds (for a 4K-byte page). To measure network traffic, we counted messages in our own communications interface routines. To measure the actual message send and receive times, we ran separate tests to send and receive a large number of single-packet "null" messages between two node machines using the same communications interface routines used for our test queries. Our results indicate that the average message transfer time is about 16.6 milliseconds (for a 2K-byte packet). Finally, while we would also like to have measured the CPU time used by our test queries, this was not easily done at the level at which our experiments ran (i.e., stand-alone on Crystal nodes).

4.2. The Experiments and Results

We designed test queries to investigate the effects of a number of different factors on the performance of the alternative distributed join algorithms. The factors investigated include the sizes of the source relations and the join selectivity (i.e., the result relation size and the distributions of the join column values). We describe our experiments and the results that we obtained in this section. First, however, we describe the results of one of our distributed join executions in great detail in order to illustrate the costs and benefits of the various approaches and to provide the reader with useful background knowledge for later discussions.

4.2.1. Query Resource Demands: A Detailed Example

The example that we will examine in this section involves a query where both R_a and R_b are "thoustup" relations and the result relation has 100 tuples.

Figure 4.2 shows the elapsed time for the example query processed using the different join methods. The elapsed time for site S_a is the actual elapsed time for the

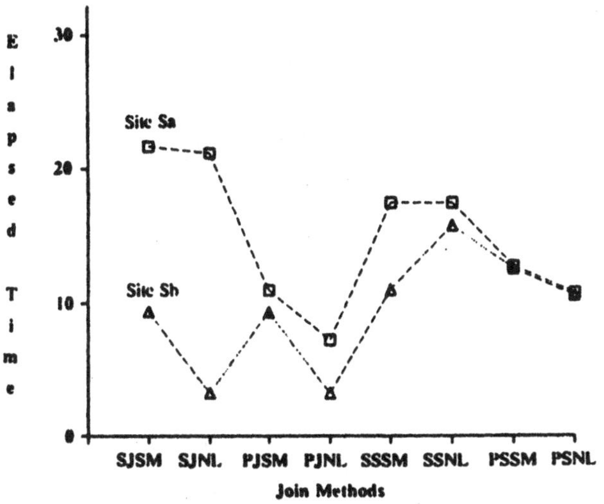

Figure 4.2: Elapsed Time.

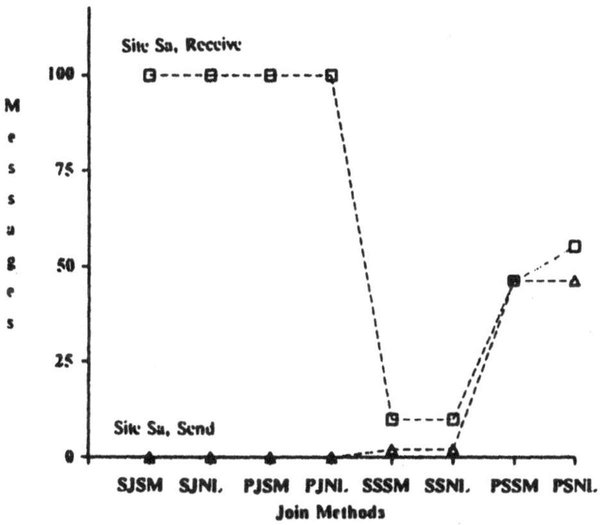

Figure 4.3: Number of Messages.

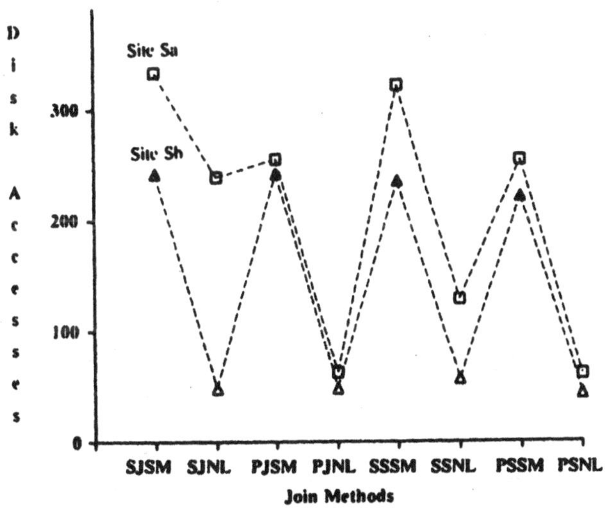

Figure 4.4: Number of Disk Accesses.

query, and the elapsed time for site S_b shows the portion of time during which S_b was involved in the query. The general trend is that the pipelined join methods — PJSM, PSSM, PJNL, and PSNL — executed the join more quickly than the sequential methods did. Of the pipelined methods, the nested loops join method outperformed the sort-merge method for this example. (That is, PJNL did better than PJSM, and PSNL did better than PSSM). This can be explained by taking a look at the resource demands of the various join methods.

Figure 4.3 shows the number of messages that were required to transfer data between the two sites S_a and S_b (measured at site S_a), illustrating the communications cost of each of the join methods. For each of the traditional join methods (SJNL, SJSJ, PJSM and PJNL), all of relation R_b is shipped to site S_a, and site S_a sends no data to site S_b. For the sequential semijoin methods (SSNL and SSSM), site S_a sends its join column values to site S_b, and site S_b sends back its matching tuples. In our example, since the total size of the join column values of R_a is only 2000 bytes (just exceeding the size of a single message packet with control information), and the semijoin selectivity is 0.1, the communications cost of the sequential semijoin methods is much lower than that of the other join methods. However, it is important to realize that the fractional communications cost (i.e., communications cost as a portion of the total elapsed time) is not high in any of the join methods. For the non-semijoin methods, 100 messages were required in all, yielding a total message time of about 1.65 seconds.

The message cost analysis for the pipelined semijoin methods (PSNL and PSSM) is a bit more complicated for our implementation. First of all, the number of messages for PSNL and PSSM is affected both by the buffer space size that is allocated at site S_a for holding R_a tuples, and also by the message packet size. Our implementation allocates only one buffer page (22 tuples) for scanning R_a, so we sent only 22 join column values each time. That is, we were limited by buffer space, so the message packets were not fully used. (This may indicate that, since one message packet can hold many join column values, it may be better in practice to select the number of R_a buffer pages used according to the number of join column values that fit in one message packet.) Another complication involved in the pipelined semijoin message analysis is that the number of messages received by site S_a is influenced by the distribution of the join column values. For some messages sent by S_a, many values will be returned, but other messages may simply say "no matches" or may contain just a few tuples. This is in contrast to the sequential semijoin case, which will totally fill all but the last of the messages returned from S_b to S_a. For all

GQ1			QG2					
			QG2.a			QG2.b		
$\|R_a\|$	$\|R_b\|$	$\|R\|$	$\|R_a\|$	$\|R_b\|$	$\|R\|$	$\|R_a\|$	$\|R_b\|$	$\|R\|$
10,000	10,000	10,000	10,000	1,000	1,000	1,000	10,000	1,000
1,000	1,000	1,000	10,000	100	100	100	10,000	100
500	500	500	10,000	10	10	10	10,000	10
100	100	100	10,000	1	1	1	10,000	1

Figure 4.5: Sizes of Relations in Query Groups QG1 and QG2.

of the reasons cited above, then, the number of messages for the PSSM and PSNL algorithms usually exceeds the number for SSSM and SSNL, as is the case in Figure 4.3. (Again, however, we remind the reader that the message cost is far from being the dominant cost factor here.)

The number of disk accesses for a join method depends on the number of different pages accessed during the operation (of course), but it also depends strongly on the available buffer space, on the page replacement policy used by the buffer manager, and on the physical allocation of pages in each relation. Figure 4.4 shows the measured number of disk accesses for the example query, and provides insight into the disk usage of the various distributed join methods. At site S_b, the sort-merge join methods (SJSM and SJNL) both require the same number of disk accesses — this number is the sum of the accesses required for sorting relation R_b and those needed to scan R_b once to send its tuples to S_a. The sort-merge semijoin methods (SSSM and PSSM) require a similar number of disk accesses. For the nested loops join methods (SJNL and PJNL), just one scan of R_b is required at S_b (to send it to S_a). For the nested loops semijoin methods (SSNL and PSNL), the number of disk accesses at site S_b depends on the semijoin selectivity of the query. SSNL requires somewhat more disk accesses at S_b because it has to store the intermediate semijoin result $R_a.A[A=B]R_b$ and then retrieve it again to send it back to S_a. Similar trends are observed at site S_a. As observed in the measurements at S_b, the sort-merge methods require more disk accesses than the nested loops methods due to sorting. Among the nested loops methods, the sequential ones have higher disk costs than the pipelined methods due to the storage and retrieval of the received relation; this is especially true for the sequential join case (SJNL), which builds an index on the received relation at S_a.

4.2.2. The Effect of Relation Sizes

Two groups of queries, QG1 and QG2, were tested to investigate the behavior of the different join methods as the relation sizes were varied. QG1 consists of joins between two relations of the same size; the result relation in QG1 is the same size as the source relations (making the join selectivity simply the inverse of the source relation size). QG2 consists of joins between two relations of various differing sizes; the join selectivity is kept constant in query group QG2 (at a value of 10^{-4}). Since the two sites in these queries are asymmetrical, QG2 is further divided into two subgroups of queries, QG2.a and QG2.b. In QG2.a, the site having the larger relation was chosen as the join site; in QG2.b, the smaller relation resided at the join site. (As before, the result site is taken to be the join site for these tests.) These query groups are listed in Figure 4.5.

Figure 4.6 shows the elapsed time measured for each of the QG1 queries. For the join of the two "tenthoustup" relations, all of the nested loops methods lost to the sort-merge methods even though the sort-merge methods must sort these large relations. This is because the amount of work saved through sorting significantly outweighs the work required to perform the sorts. This is illustrated by Figure 4.9, which shows the measured elapsed times and disk accesses for sorting the "tenthoustup", "thoustup" and "hundredtup" relations, and by the following analysis. Figure 4.9 shows that it takes 64.89 seconds to sort the "tenthoustup" relation, and that this involves 1911 disk accesses. This constitutes the per-join "overhead" portion of the sort-merge methods for this case. After sorting, the merge phase accesses each page of each relation just once. In contrast, for the nested loops join using a nonclustered index, the number of disk accesses is much larger; this is due to the number of data pages (randomly) accessed. Figure 4.7 shows this clearly. Of the four nested loops methods, three of them required more than 10,000 disk accesses, which is what was chosen as an upper limit for the number of disk accesses traced due to space considerations. The one exception was PSNL (pipelined semijoin-based nested loops), which keeps tuples in memory at site S_a, scanning R_a only once. However, this method involved a large number of disk accesses at site S_b (not shown), where R_b is searched using the index to find the matching tuples for the 10,000 join attribute values sent by R_a. The elapsed time was

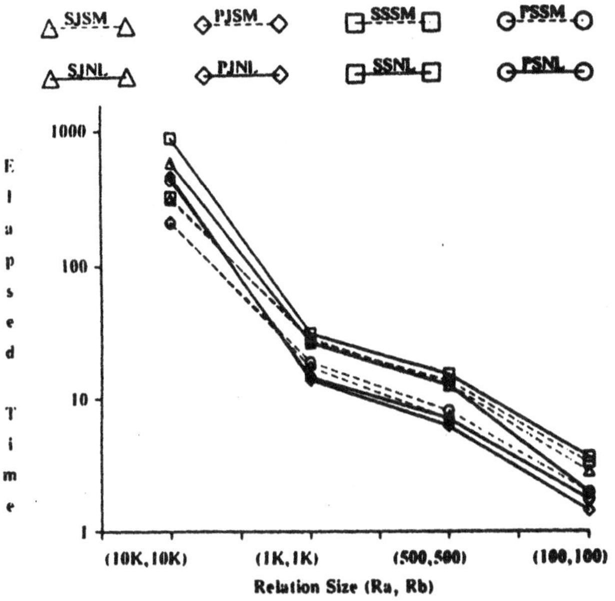

Figure 4.6: Elapsed Time (QG1).

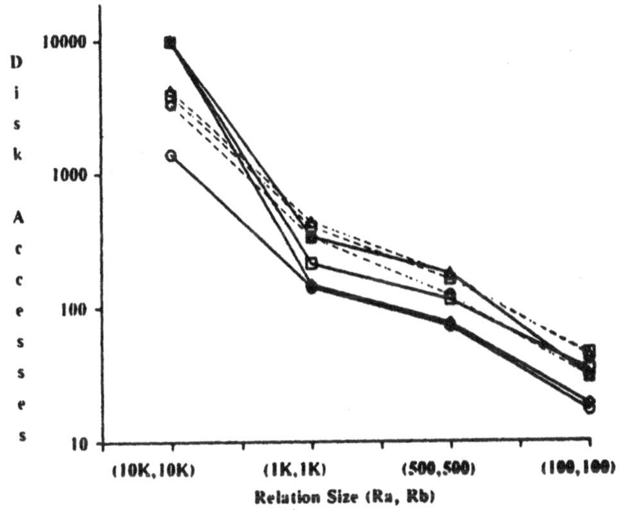

Figure 4.7: Number of Disk Accesses (QG1).

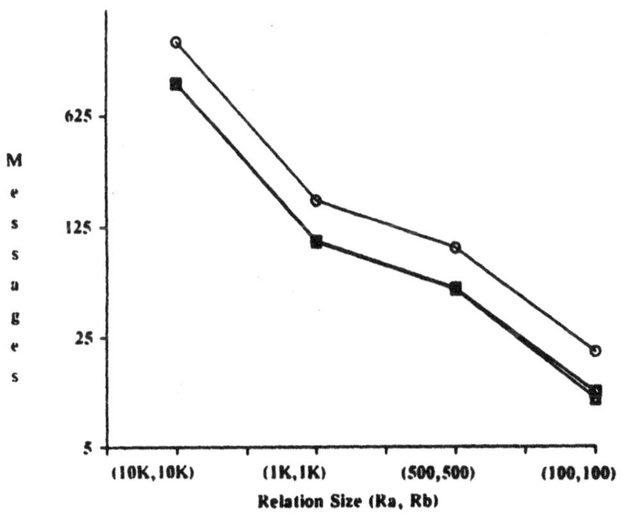

Figure 4.8: Number of Messages (QG1).

Relation	Elapsed Time	Number of Disk Accesses		
		Total	Reads	Writes
hundredtup	0.54	13	6	7
thoustup	6.46	196	97	99
tenthoustup	64.89	1911	955	956

Figure 4.9: Sorting Times Versus Relation Size.

mainly determined by the processing rate at site S_b in this case, which explains its elapsed time as compared to the sort-merge methods.

Figure 4.6 shows that, as the relation sizes are decreased, the cost of sorting the relations begins to outweigh the cost of performing an inner relation disk access per outer relation tuple. With smaller relation sizes, Figure 4.7 shows that the total numbers of disk accesses for the the pipelined nested loops methods (PJNL and PSNL) are lower than those for the sort-merge methods. Thus, the pipelined nested loops methods are the best performers except at the largest relation size tested for QG1.

Figure 4.8 shows the total number of messages involved in executing each of the eight join methods tested. Only three curves are evident. The highest cost here is for the pipelined semijoin methods, the next highest cost is for the sequential semijoin methods, and the lowest among the message costs are the non-semijoin methods. This is because, in this case, the join is a "one-to-one join" — each tuple of R_a joins with one and only one tuple of R_b. Thus, the use of semijoins here does not reduce the amount of data ultimately transferred to the join site; rather, it increases the overall message cost by the amount of data sent to the remote site from the join site initially. In all cases, given our packet transfer time of 16.6 milliseconds, the overall message time is never more than about 5-10% of the overall elapsed time. (Also, the effect of the message time is even less significant for the pipelined algorithms, as there is processing going on while messages are in transit.)

Figures 4.10 and 4.11 give the measured elapsed times for the queries in query groups QG2.a and QG2.b. These results clearly illustrate the differences between the various join methods tested. The diversity of the results can be explained based on the discussion of the detailed example and analysis given in Section 4.2.1. It is evident from the figures that the nested loops join methods are more sensitive to relation size differences than the sort-merge methods, particularly at the larger relation sizes. This is because the sort-merge methods have a fixed component of their costs due to

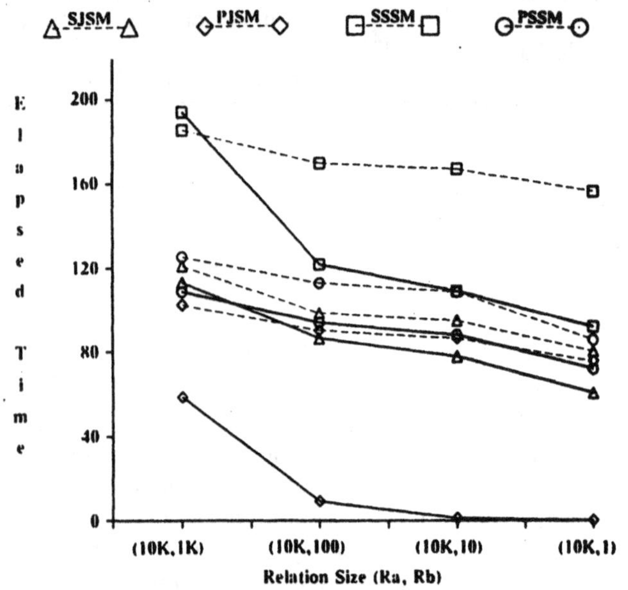

Figure 4.10: Elapsed Time (QG2.a).

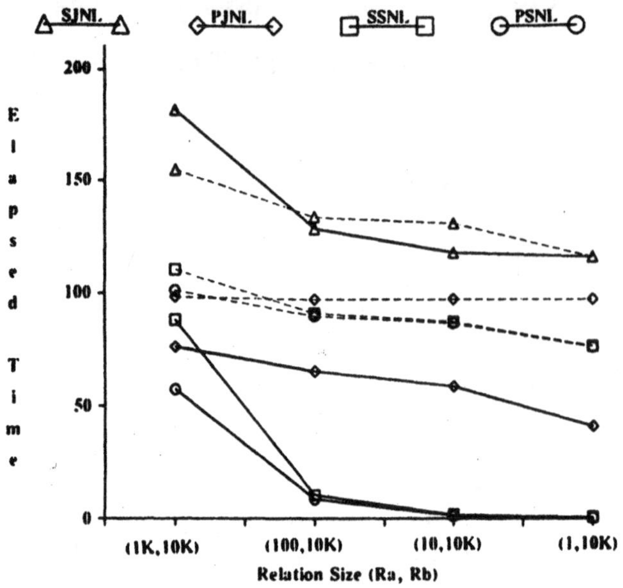

Figure 4.11: Elapsed Time (QG2.b).

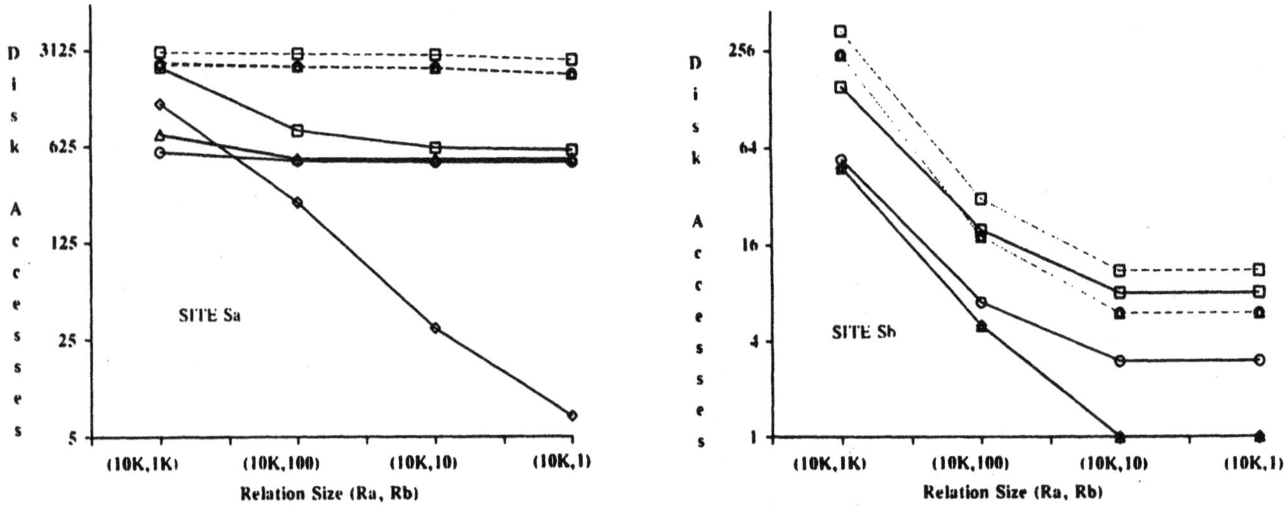

Figure 4.12: Number of Disk Accesses (QG2.a).

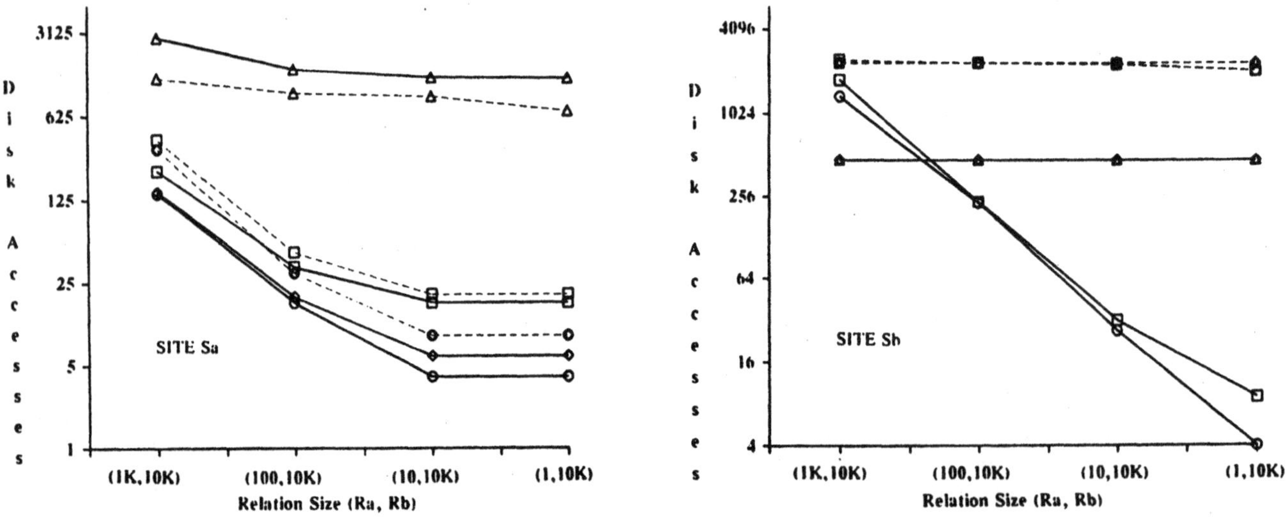

Figure 4.13: Number of Disk Accesses (QG2.b).

sorting the "tenthoustup" relation (see Figure 4.9 for this cost). An extreme case is illustrated in Figure 4.11 for the the pipelined join case (PJSM). With the smaller relation site as the join site, its cost remains nearly constant over the whole size range investigated. The main components of the cost of PJSM are sorting R_b at site S_b and scanning R_b to send it to site S_a. (These two factors alone account for about 90% of the elapsed time.) The sort merge methods can never execute faster than the time it takes to sort and scan the larger of its relations. The nested loops join methods are different, however. When the size of one of the source relations decreases, the number of disk accesses decreases dramatically for at least one of the nested loops methods in both query groups, as shown in Figures 4.12 and 4.13. This is due to the absence of sorting overhead and the effectiveness of the index for smaller outer relation sizes. The winner for query group QG2.a is the pipelined join version of nested loops (PJNL). The winner for query group QG2.b is the pipelined semijoin version of nested loops (PSNL); the sequential semijoin method ((SSNL) is the next best choice, with nearly identical performance for the smaller relation sizes. While the message counts are not given here, they represent an insignificant portion of the overall query processing cost (as in the previous cases examined).

One note here: It seems to us that the queries in QG2 are representative of a class of queries that is likely to arise in real database systems — that is, queries with a small number of tuples in one relation (the result of a selection) being joined with tuples from a much larger relation. An important observation from the tests covered by query groups QG1 and QG2 is that, when one relation is small, the pipelined nested loops join methods perform much better than their sequential counterparts or any of the sort-merge methods. When both relations are large, however, as when both were "tenthoustup" relations in our tests, the optimal methods will be the pipelined sort-merge methods.

4.2.3. The Effects of Join Selectivity

Join selectivity, which is the ratio of the size of the result relation to the product of the sizes of the source relations, is an influential factor with respect to join algorithm performance. To see just how various join selectivities affect performance, we ran tests on the eight distributed join methods using two relations each with 1,000 tuples. These were not the "thoustup" relations from the Wisconsin database, however. Rather, the join selectivity was varied to produce result sizes of 1000 tuples, 100 tuples, 10 tuples, and 1 tuple in the following way. A result size of N tuples was obtained by selecting R_a from the "tenthoustup" relation with

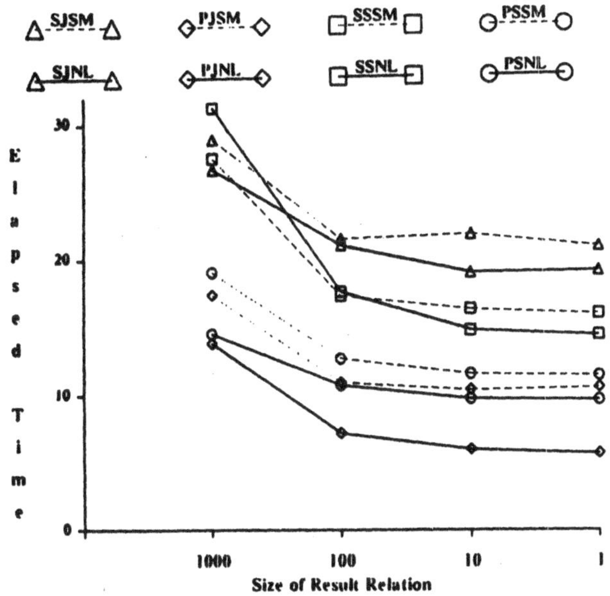

Figure 4.14: Effect of Join Selectivity.

"unique1" values in the range [4500..5499], while choosing N of R_b's tuples from the "tenthoustup" relation randomly in the same range and choosing the remainder of R_b's tuples randomly from outside this range.

Figure 4.14 shows the measured elapsed times for the different join methods for the various join selectivities tested. Higher join selectivities (i.e. smaller result relations) mean that fewer tuples will match during the join, which leads to several cost savings. First, the result relation is smaller, so fewer disk accesses are needed to write out the result. Second, fewer data pages are accessed for the indexed nested loops join methods. Third, fewer tuples will be retrieved from the remote site for the semijoin methods, so the communications cost is reduced in their case. The pipelined nested loops join and semijoin methods were the winners in this experiment, with the semijoin method doing somewhat worse than the join-based method. Their pipelined sort-merge counterparts were next best in terms of elapsed time here.

4.2.4. The Effects of Duplicate Attribute Values

Another factor which can influence the performance of a join method is the degree of join column value duplication. In the merge phase of a sort-merge join, duplicate join attribute values can cause multiple scans of pages of one relation. Perhaps more significant is the effect of duplicates on sequential versus pipelined semijoin performance. In semijoin methods, site S_a sends the join column values of R_a to site S_b, and site S_b uses the values to fetch and return any matching tuples in relation R_b. In the sequential variant of the semijoin method, duplicate $R_a.A$ values are removed,

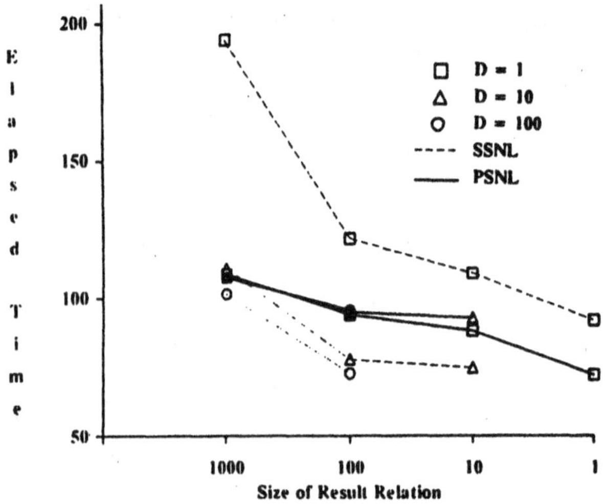

Figure 4.15: Effect of Duplicate Values.

which has two effects. First, less data is sent — duplicate join column values are avoided in messages from S_a to S_b, and (as a result) each matching R_b tuple is sent to S_a just once. Second, and related, is the avoidance of multiple disk accesses in R_b for a given $R_a.A$ value. These two savings reduce both the communications cost and the local processing cost. We tested a group of queries which join two relations on an attribute with duplicate values in this experiment.

We use the *duplication factor D* of attribute A of relation R_a to quantitatively describe the degree of duplication. This factor is defined as the ratio of the number of tuples in relation R_a to the number of distinct values of attribute A. Figure 4.15 shows the effects of duplicates on the sequential and pipelined semijoin methods (SSNL and PSNL). In all tests, both source relations have 1000 tuples. Join columns in R_a are chosen with D = 1, 10, and 100, respectively. It can be seen from the figure that duplicates have almost no effect on PSNL. For SSNL, however, an increase in the duplication factor moves it from being much worse than PSNL to being much better. Obviously, the benefit due to the elimination of duplicates outweighs the usual disadvantages of the sequential methods when the duplication factor is high.

4.2.5. Summary of Test Results

There are a few observations that we would like to make here. First, if we set the issue of join site selection aside, Figures 4.10 and 4.11 show that the three nested loops methods PJNL, SSNL and PSNL provide the best performance when joining a large relation with a small one. For "medium" similar size relation joins, such as those shown in Figure 4.14, PJNL and PSNL

$\vert R\vert$, $\vert R_b\vert$	Elapsed Time (seconds)		
	local	distributed	degeneration
1000	55.8739	58.6128	4.90%
100	8.0877	9.3826	16.00%
10	0.9503	1.1164	17.48%
1	0.3500	0.3895	11.29%

Figure 4.16: Local versus Distributed Join ($|R_a|$ = 10K).

also perform the best, and the sequential SSNL algorithm becomes worse than the two pipelined sort-merge methods (PJSM and PSSM). This leads to the conclusion that pipelined join and semijoin methods seem to be the most promising of the distributed join methods tested. To join very large relations of similar size, the pipelined sort-merge methods seem to be the best choices, as shown in Figure 4.6. These conclusions hold for the entire range of queries that we investigated.

Another general conclusion of this study is that the communications cost did not play a significant role in determining algorithm performance in our environment. The contribution of communications costs to the overall measured elapsed times was typically around 10-15%. As an illustrative example, to transfer a "tenthoustup" relation from one site to another requires about 1000 messages, but it only takes about 16-17 seconds for this transmission. In queries where such a transfer might be useful, however, the processing cost may be as high as several hundred seconds. The relatively poor performance of the sequential semijoin method is also evidence that communication cost savings alone does not help much. As a more concrete example, Figure 4.16 compares local join costs with distributed join costs in our environment. In all cases, $|R_a|$ = 10K, and the local and distributed join methods used were those that gave the least elapsed time. It is clear from the example that the message cost is not the major determining factor for performance.

The last point to be made is that choosing the right combination of a join processing site and a join method is important. Figures 4.10 and 4.11 indicate that, if the two relations to be joined have different sizes, the pipelined nested loops join method (PJNL) needs the site with larger relation to be the join site (i.e., it needs the outer relation to be the smaller of the two source relations). In contrast, the semijoin nested loops methods (PSNL and SSNL) perform much better when the smaller relation site is chosen as the join site (i.e., they also need the outer relation to be the smaller of the two). The intuition behind these results is fairly simple, in retrospect: PJNL and PSNL are basically the same algorithm if communications cost is zero, both being distributed executions of a simple nested loops join; they have the same local processing costs. The outer relation should be the smaller of the two in the centralized case as well [Blas76, Seli79]. Note also that in a low communications cost environment such as this, we can switch our join site choice with little or no significant impact on performance. For example, suppose that R_a is a small relation, R_b is a large relation, that S_a is to be the result site, and therefore that the pipelined semijoin (PSNL) method is the best choice. In this case, S_a ends up being the join site. If we would prefer to have S_b be the join site for some reason, such as load balancing considerations [Care85], we can accomplish this by doing a pipelined join (PJNL) at site S_b and shipping the results back to site S_a.

5. CONCLUSIONS

In this paper, we have studied the performance of a number of different join methods for a distributed database system. Eight different methods were implemented on top of the Wisconsin Storage System and run on an experimental distributed computer system, the Crystal multicomputer, at the University of Wisconsin. Join queries with various sizes, join selectivities, and attribute value distributions were tested. Our results have shown that, in a local network, communication cost is not the dominant factor. Shipping an entire relation from one site to another site is a reasonable way to process a distributed join query — as long as it is done correctly. Correctly in this case means that a pipelined join algorithm, where the outer relation is shipped to the join site (the inner site) in parallel with the local join processing itself, is employed. Although traditional (sequential) semijoin methods can reduce the communications cost, and they perform well in cases where the join column duplication factor is high (many matching inner relation tuples per outer relation tuple), pipelined semijoin methods were found to be preferable in most of the test cases examined. These results hold over a wide range of query characteristics. For the case where two very large relations are to be joined, pipeline sort-merge methods are recommended. We also found that the combination of the join method and the join site are important, that it is very important to ensure that the outer relation for the join is the smaller of the two source relations (as in centralized database systems).

Our results are related to several other pieces of work on distributed query processing techniques. First, the pipelined semijoin methods that we implemented are the ones used in System R^*, known there as the "fetch the inner tuple as needed" methods [Seli80]. They opted to use the pipelined version of semijoin over the more traditional sequential version because they believed that it would tend to win in most situations due to lower local processing costs. Our results indicate that this is indeed the case in a local network. Our results also concur with the claims of Page, which indicate that, in a distributed database system based on a local network, it is far more important that joins be done in the correct order and with the correct inner and outer relations than that they be done at the site which minimizes communications [Page83]. The key difference between Page's results and ours are that his conclusions were based on a cost analysis of the INGRES database system and the LOCUS distributed operating system, whereas ours were obtained from measuring the performance of a number of actual distributed join queries. Finally, earlier analytical studies have indicated that pipelined query evaluation techniques provide the best performance in centralized database systems [Smit75, Yao79]. Our results in favor of pipelined join methods can be viewed as showing experimentally that pipelining is still the method of choice in a locally distributed database system.

There are several directions that can be taken from here in terms of future research on query processing methods for locally distributed database systems. One direction that we are actively pursuing is the incorporation of load balancing techniques into a distributed database system [Care85]. We intend to use the results obtained here to guide the design of query processing algorithms that incorporate such techniques. We also plan to use our detailed measurements to drive a simulation model that we have developed for research in this area. Another direction that one might pursue is a study of the performance of processing strategies for n-way joins (where $n > 2$). While we feel that our results paint a fairly complete picture of the relative merits of the alternative join methods for our environment, we have not taken an exhaustive look at all possibilities.

ACKNOWLEDGEMENTS

The authors wish to acknowledge helpful discussions with David DeWitt. We must also thank Hong-Tai Chou, who provided us with the instrumented version of WiSS used in these experiments. We also want to thank Bart Miller, who helped us learn about Unix/IPC for an earlier implementation of the distributed join methods. Finally, we wish to acknowledge the NSF-sponsored Crystal multicomputer project at the University of Wisconsin, which provided the experimental environment for this work and a helpful group of staff members to aid us in learning how to work in the Crystal environment.

REFERENCES

[Bern79a] Bernstein, P. A. and Goodman, N. *The theory of semijoins*, Tech. Rep. CCA-79-27, Computer Corp. of America, 1979.

[Bern79b] Bernstein, P. A. and Goodman, N. "Full reducers for relational queries using multi-attribute semi-joins," in *Proc. 1979 NBS Symp. on Comp. Network.*, December 1979.

[Bern81a] Bernstein, P. A., and Chiu, D. W. "Using semijoins to solve relational queries," *J. ACM. 28*, 1 January 1981, 25-40.

[Bern81b] Bernstein, P. A., and Goodman, N. "The power of natural semijoins," *SIAM J. Comput. 10*, 4, Nov. 1981, 751-771.

[Bitt83] Bitton, D., DeWitt, D. J., and Turbyfill, C. "Benchmarking database systems: a systematic approach", *Proc. 9th Int'l Conf. on Very Large Data Bases*, October, 1983.

[Blas76] Blasgen, M. W., and Eswaren, K. P. "On the evaluation of queries in a relational data base system," IBM Research Rep. RJ1745, April 1976.

[Brab84] Brabergsengen, K. "Hashing methods and relational algebra operations", *Proc. 10th Int'l Conf. on Very Large Data Bases*, September 1984.

[Care85] Carey, M. J., Livny, M., and Lu, H. "Dynamic task allocation in a distributed database system", *Proc. 5th Int'l Conf. on Distributed Computing Systems*, May 1985.

[Chou83] Chou, H.T., DeWitt, D.J., Katz, R. H., and Klug, A. C. *Design and implementation of the Wisconsin storage system*, Technical Report, Computer Sciences Department, University of Wisconsin-Madison, November 1983.

[DeWi84] DeWitt, D. J., Finkel, R., and Solomon, M. *The Crystal multicomputer: design and implementation experience*, Technical Report, Computer Sciences Department, University of Wisconsin-Madison, September 1984.

[DeWi85] DeWitt, D.J. and Gerber, R, *Partitioned hashing algorithms*, Technical Report #583, Computer Sciences Department, University of Wisconsin-Madison, February 1985

[Epst80] Epstein, R., and Stonebraker, M "Analysis of distributed database processing Strategies" *Proc. 6th Int'l Conf. on Very Large Data Bases*, October 1980, 82-101.

[Kers82] Kerschberg, L., Ting, P. D., and Yao, S. B. "Query optimization in star computer networks," *ACM Trans. Database Syst. 7*, 4, December 1982, 678-711.

[Lohm84] Lohman, G. M., Mohan, C., Haas, L. M., Lindsay, B. G., Selinger, P. G., Wilms, P. F., and Daniels, D., "Query Processing in R^* ", IBM Research Report, RJ 4272, April 1984.

[Nieb76] Niebuhr, K. E. and Smith, S. E. "N-ary joins for processing Query by Example", *IBM Tech. Disclosure Bull. 19*, 6, 1976, 2377-2381.

[Page83] Page, T. W. Jr., "Distributed query processing in local network databases", Master Thesis, University of California, Los Angeles, 1983.

[Seli79] Selinger, P., et al, "Access path selection in a relational database management system", *Proc. of the ACM-SIGMOD Int'l Conf. on Management of Data*, June 1979.

[Seli80] Selinger, P., and Adiba, M., "Access path selection in distributed database management systems", *Proc. 1st Int'l Conf. on Distributed Data Bases*, Aberdeen, 1980.

[Smit75] Smith, J. M. and Chang, P. Y. T., "Optimizing the performance of a relational algebra database interface", *Commun. ACM 18*, 10, October 1975, 568-579.

[Ullm82] Ullman, J. D. *Principles of Database Systems*, Computer Science Press, Rockville, Maryland, 1982.

[Wong76] Wong, E., and Youssefi, K. "Decomposition -- A strategy for query processing," *ACM Trans. Database Syst. 1*, 3 (September 1976), 223-241

[Yao78] Yao, S. B., and DeJong, D. "Evaluation of database access paths", *Proc. of the ACM-SIGMOD Int'l Conf. on Management of Data*, 1978, 66-77.

[Yao79] Yao, S. B. "Optimization of query evaluation algorithms," *ACM Trans. Database Syst. 4*, 2, June 1979, 133-155

Chapter 2

CONCURRENCY CONTROL OF MULTIPLE COPY DATA BASES

To improve the availability and response time of distributed data bases, multiple copies of files may be stored in the distributed data base system. Therefore, the loss of a processor or channel link will not result in the loss of the entire data base, and storing data at those sites that use it frequently provides faster access. However, storing multiple copies of files in the system creates the problem of synchronization of concurrent updates.

Every transaction that causes a change in any data item stored in the data base must be followed by update messages to all sites that have a copy of the data. Each site has a data base management system which applies those updates to the data it maintains. Besides the problem of mutual consistency of the redundant copies of the data base, we also must consider the preservation of invariant relations among items within the data base. This is called internal consistency or data integrity.

In this chapter, Bernstein and Goodman propose to decompose the concurrency control into two subproblems: read-write and write-write synchronization. They present a series of techniques for solving each subproblem and show how to combine those techniques into algorithms for solving the entire concurrency control problem. Kohler surveyed the related problems of synchronization and recovery in decentralized computer systems. Stonebraker presented a primary site locking (PSL) for ensuring the consistency of a distributed data base for handling multiple concurrent updates. A mechanism to update multiple copies correctly and to continue operations when the system has a partial failure is discussed. Carey and Stonebraker present the performance of centralized concurrency control algorithms. The algorithms studied include four locking algorithms, two time stamp algorithms, and one optimistic algorithm. The study shows that in general, locking algorithms perform better. Chu and Hellerstein propose two low cost concurrency control algorithms, exclusive writer protocol (EWP) and exclusive writer protocol with locking (EWL), for real time distributed systems. Analytical models are developed to study the response time and compare to that of basic time stamp and primary site locking, and conclude that if limited serial access is acceptable, EWP should be used due to its simplicity and short response times, which have great appeal for real time distributed processing systems. Otherwise, EWL is popular because it performs well over a wide range of parameters and dynamic switching with PSL to improve performance further.

For further information on distributed concurrency control of updating replicated data bases, interested readers should refer to [GELE 78, THOM 78, BADA 80, GARD 80, TRAI 82, BERN 84].

Concurrency Control in Distributed Database Systems

PHILIP A. BERNSTEIN AND NATHAN GOODMAN

Computer Corporation of America, Cambridge, Massachusetts 02139

In this paper we survey, consolidate, and present the state of the art in distributed database concurrency control. The heart of our analysis is a decomposition of the concurrency control problem into two major subproblems: read-write and write-write synchronization. We describe a series of synchronization techniques for solving each subproblem and show how to combine these techniques into algorithms for solving the entire concurrency control problem. Such algorithms are called "concurrency control methods." We describe 48 principal methods, including all practical algorithms that have appeared in the literature plus several new ones. We concentrate on the structure and correctness of concurrency control algorithms. Issues of performance are given only secondary treatment.

Keywords and Phrases: concurrency control, deadlock, distributed database management systems, locking, serializability, synchronization, timestamp ordering, timestamps, two-phase commit, two-phase locking

CR Categories: 4.33, 4.35

INTRODUCTION

The Concurrency Control Problem

Concurrency control is the activity of coordinating concurrent accesses to a database in a multiuser database management system (DBMS). Concurrency control permits users to access a database in a multiprogrammed fashion while preserving the illusion that each user is executing alone on a dedicated system. The main technical difficulty in attaining this goal is to prevent database updates performed by one user from interfering with database retrievals and updates performed by another. The concurrency control problem is exacerbated in a distributed DBMS (DDBMS) because (1) users may access data stored in many different computers in a distributed system, and (2) a concurrency control mechanism at one computer cannot instantaneously know about interactions at other computers.

Concurrency control has been actively investigated for the past several years, and the problem for nondistributed DBMSs is well understood. A broad mathematical theory has been developed to analyze the problem, and one approach, called *two-phase locking*, has been accepted as a standard solution. Current research on nondistributed concurrency control is focused on evolutionary improvements to two-phase locking, detailed performance analysis and optimization, and extensions to the mathematical theory.

Distributed concurrency control, by contrast, is in a state of extreme turbulence. More than 20 concurrency control algorithms have been proposed for DDBMSs, and several have been, or are being, implemented. These algorithms are usually complex, hard to understand, and difficult to prove correct (indeed, many are incorrect). Because they are described in different terminologies and make different assumptions

CONTENTS

about the underlying DDBMS environment, it is difficult to compare the many proposed algorithms, even in qualitative terms. Naturally each author proclaims his or her approach as best, but there is little compelling evidence to support the claims.

To survey the state of the art, we introduce a standard terminology for describing DDBMS concurrency control algorithms and a standard model for the DDBMS environment. For analysis purposes we decompose the concurrency control problem into two major subproblems, called read-write and write-write synchronization. Every concurrency control algorithm must include a subalgorithm to solve each subproblem. The first step toward understanding a concurrency control algorithm is to isolate the subalgorithm employed for each subproblem.

After studying the large number of proposed algorithms, we find that they are compositions of only a few subalgorithms. In fact, the subalgorithms used by all practical DDBMS concurrency control algorithms are variations of just two basic techniques: two-phase locking and timestamp ordering; thus the state of the art is far more coherent than a review of the literature would seem to indicate.

Examples of Concurrency Control Anomalies

The goal of concurrency control is to prevent interference among users who are simultaneously accessing a database. Let us illustrate the problem by presenting two "canonical" examples of interuser interference. Both are examples of an on-line electronic funds transfer system accessed via remote *automated teller machines* (*ATMs*). In response to customer requests, ATMs retrieve data from a database, perform computations, and store results back into the database.

Anomaly 1: Lost Updates. Suppose two customers simultaneously try to deposit money into the same account. In the absence of concurrency control, these two activities could interfere (see Figure 1). The two ATMs handling the two customers could read the account balance at approximately the same time, compute new balances in parallel, and then store the new balances back into the database. The net effect is incorrect: although two customers deposited money, the database only reflects one activity; the other deposit is lost by the system.

Anomaly 2: Inconsistent Retrievals. Suppose two customers simultaneously execute the following transactions.

Customer 1: Move $1,000,000 from Acme Corporation's savings account to its checking account.
Customer 2: Print Acme Corporation's total balance in savings and checking.

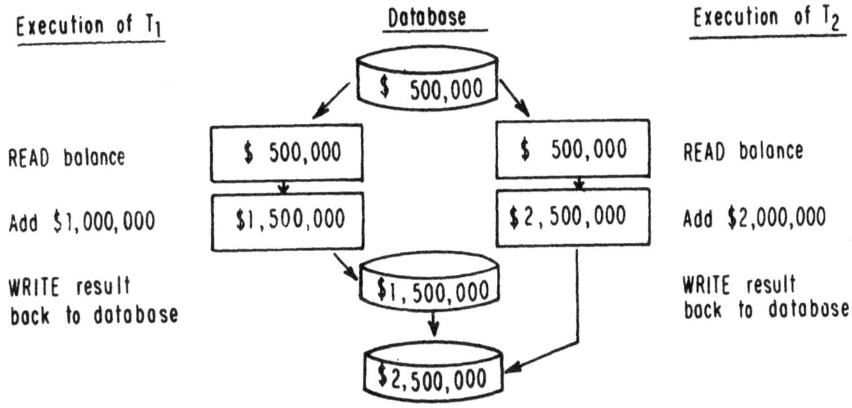

Figure 1. Lost update anomaly.

In the absence of concurrency control these two transactions could interfere (see Figure 2). The first transaction might read the savings account balance, subtract $1,000,000, and store the result back in the database. Then the second transaction might read the savings and checking account balances and print the total. Then the first transaction might finish the funds transfer by reading the checking account balance, adding $1,000,000, and finally storing the result in the database. Unlike Anomaly 1, the final values placed into the database by this execution are correct. Still, the execution is incorrect because the balance printed by Customer 2 is $1,000,000 short.

These two examples do not exhaust all possible ways in which concurrent users can interfere. However, these examples are typical of the concurrency control problems that arise in DBMSs.

Comparison to Mutual Exclusion Problems

The problem of database concurrency control is similar in some respects to that of mutual exclusion in operating systems. The latter problem is concerned with coordinating access by concurrent processes to system resources such as memory, I/O devices, and CPU. Many solution techniques have been developed, including locks, semaphores, monitors, and serializers [BRIN73, DIJK71, HEWI74, HOAR74].

The concurrency control and mutual exclusion problems are similar in that both are concerned with controlling concurrent access to shared resources. However, control schemes that work for one do not necessarily work for the other, as illustrated by the following example. Suppose processes P_1 and P_2 require access to resources R_1 and R_2 at different points in their execution. In an operating system, the following interleaved execution of these processes is perfectly acceptable: P_1 uses R_1, P_2 uses R_1, P_2 uses R_2, P_1 uses R_2. In a database, however, this execution is not always acceptable. Assume, for example, that P_2 transfers funds by debiting one account (R_1), then crediting another (R_2). If P_2 checks both balances, it will see R_1 after it has been debited, but see R_2 *before* it has been credited. Other differences between concurrency control and mutual exclusion are discussed in CHAM74.

1. TRANSACTION-PROCESSING MODEL

To understand how a concurrency control algorithm operates, one must understand how the algorithm fits into an overall DDBMS. In this section we present a simple model of a DDBMS, emphasizing how the DDBMS processes user interactions. Later we explain how concurrency control algorithms operate in the context of this model.

1.1 Preliminary Definitions and DDBMS Architecture

A distributed database management system (DDBMS) is a collection of sites interconnected by a network [DEPP76,

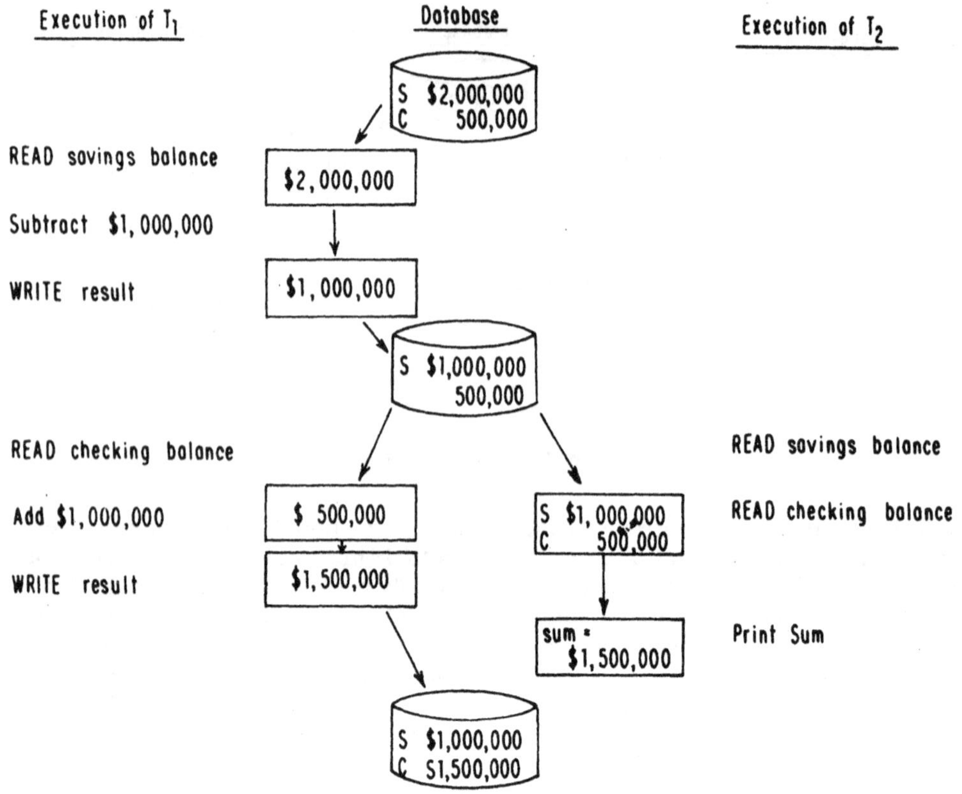

Figure 2. Inconsistent retrieval anomaly.

ROTH77]. Each *site* is a computer running one or both of the following software modules: a transaction manager (TM) or a data manager (DM). *TMs* supervise interactions between users and the DDBMS while *DMs* manage the actual database. A *network* is a computer-to-computer communication system. The network is assumed to be perfectly reliable: if site A sends a message to site B, site B is guaranteed to receive the message without error. In addition, we assume that between any pair of sites the network delivers messages in the order they were sent.

From a user's perspective, a *database* consists of a collection of *logical data items*, denoted X, Y, Z. We leave the granularity of logical data items unspecified; in practice, they may be files, records, etc. A *logical database state* is an assignment of values to the logical data items composing a database. Each logical data item may be stored at any DM in the system or redundantly at several DMs. A stored copy of a logical data item is called a *stored data item*. (When no confusion is possible, we use the term *data item* for stored data item.) The stored copies of logical data item X are denoted $x_1, \ldots, x_m$. We typically use x to denote an arbitrary stored data item. A *stored database state* is an assignment of values to the stored data items in a database.

Users interact with the DDBMS by executing *transactions*. Transactions may be on-line queries expressed in a self-contained query language, or application programs written in a general-purpose programming language. The concurrency control algorithms we study pay no attention to the computations performed by transactions. Instead, these algorithms make all of their decisions on the basis of the data items a transaction reads and writes, and so details of the form of transactions are unimportant in our analysis. However we do assume that transactions represent complete and correct computations; each transaction, if ex-

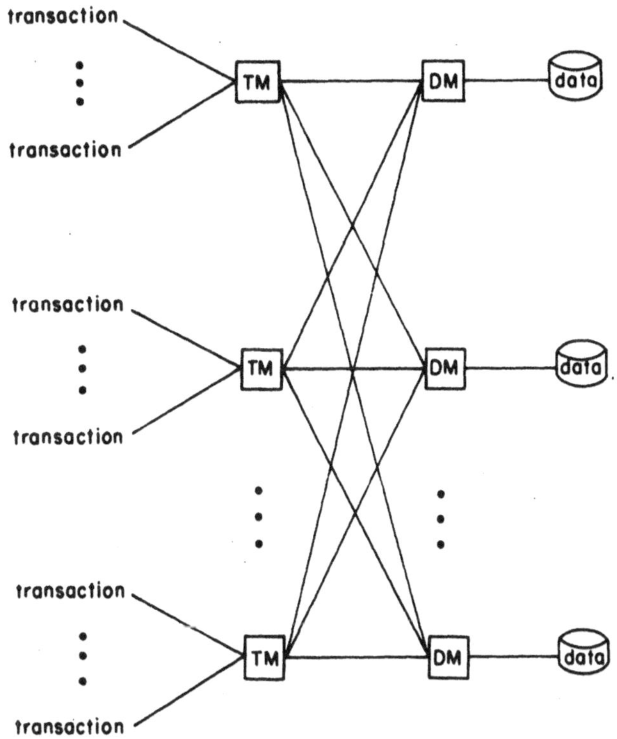

Figure 3. DDBMS system architecture.

ecuted alone on an initially consistent database, would terminate, produce correct results, and leave the database consistent. The *logical readset* (correspondingly, *writeset*) of a transaction is the set of logical data items the transaction reads (or writes). Similarly, *stored readsets* and *stored writesets* are the stored data items that a transaction reads and writes.

The correctness of a concurrency control algorithm is defined relative to users' expectations regarding transaction execution. There are two correctness criteria: (1) users expect that each transaction submitted to the system will eventually be executed; (2) users expect the computation performed by each transaction to be the same whether it executes alone in a dedicated system or in parallel with other transactions in a multiprogrammed system. Realizing this expectation is the principal issue in concurrency control.

A DDBMS contains four components (see Figure 3): transactions, TMs, DMs, and data. Transactions communicate with TMs, TMs communicate with DMs, and DMs manage the data. (TMs do not communicate with other TMs, nor do DMs communicate with other DMs.)

TMs supervise transactions. Each transaction executed in the DDBMS is supervised by a *single* TM, meaning that the transaction issues all of its database operations to that TM. Any distributed computation that is needed to execute the transaction is managed by the TM.

Four operations are defined at the transaction–TM interface. READ(X) returns the value of X (a logical data item) in the current logical database state. WRITE(X, new-value) creates a new logical database state in which X has the specified new value. Since transactions are assumed to represent complete computations, we use BEGIN and END operations to bracket transaction executions.

DMs manage the stored database, functioning as backend database processors. In response to commands from transactions, TMs issue commands to DMs specifying stored data items to be read or written. The details of the TM–DM interface constitute the core of our transaction-processing model and are discussed in Sections 1.2 and 1.3. Section 1.2 describes the TM–DM interaction in a centralized database environment, and Section 1.3 extends the discussion to a distributed database setting.

1.2 Centralized Transaction-Processing Model

A centralized DBMS consists of one TM and one DM executing at one site. A transaction T accesses the DBMS by issuing BEGIN, READ, WRITE, and END operations, which are processed as follows.

BEGIN: The TM initializes for T a *private workspace* that functions as a temporary buffer for values read from and written into the database.

READ(X): The TM looks for a copy of X in T's private workspace. If the copy exists, its value is returned to T. Otherwise the TM issues *dm-read*(x) to the DM to retrieve a copy of X from the database, gives the retrieved value to T, and puts it into T's private workspace.

WRITE(X, new-value): The TM again checks the private workspace for a copy of X. If it finds one, the value is updated to new-value; otherwise a copy of X with the new value is created in the workspace. The new value of X is *not* stored in the database at this time.

END: The TM issues *dm-write*(x) for each logical data item X updated by T. Each dm-write(x) requests that the DM update the value of X in the stored database to the value of X in T's local workspace. When all dm-writes are processed, T is finished executing, and its private workspace is discarded.

The DBMS may *restart* T any time before a dm-write has been processed. The effect of restarting T is to obliterate its private workspace and to reexecute T from the beginning. As we will see, many concurrency control algorithms use transaction restarts as a tactic for attaining correct executions. However, once a single dm-write has been processed, T cannot be restarted; each dm-write permanently installs an update into the database, and we cannot permit the database to reflect partial effects of transactions.

A DBMS can avoid such partial results by having the property of *atomic commitment*, which requires that either all of a transaction's dm-writes are processed or none are. The "standard" implementation of atomic commitment is a procedure called *two-phase commit* [LAMP76, GRAY78].[1] Suppose T is updating data items X and Y. When T issues its END, the *first phase* of two-phase commit begins, during which the DM issues *prewrite* commands for X and Y. These commands instruct the DM to copy the values of X and Y from T's private workspace onto secure storage. If the DBMS fails during the first phase, no harm is done, since none of T's updates have yet been applied to the stored database. During the *second phase*, the TM issues *dm-write* commands for X and Y which instruct the DM to copy the values of X and Y into the stored database. If the DBMS fails during the second phase, the database may contain incorrect information, but since the values of X and Y are stored on secure storage, this inconsistency can be rectified when the system recovers: the recovery procedure reads the values of X and Y from secure storage and resumes the commitment activity.

We emphasize that this is a *mathematical model* of transaction processing, an approximation to the way DBMSs actually function. While the implementation details of atomic commitment are important in designing a DBMS, they are not central to an understanding of concurrency control. To explain concurrency control algorithms we need a model of transaction execution in which atomic commitment is visible, but not dominant.

1.3 Distributed Transaction-Processing Model

Our model of transaction processing in a distributed environment differs from that in a centralized one in two areas: handling private workspaces and implementing two-phase commit.

[1] The term "two-phase commit" is commonly used to denote the distributed version of this procedure. However, since the centralized and distributed versions are identical in structure, we use "two-phase commit" to describe both.

In a centralized DBMS we assumed that (1) private workspaces were part of the TM, and (2) data could freely move between a transaction and its workspace, and between a workspace and the DM. These assumptions are not appropriate in a DDBMS because TMs and DMs may run at different sites and the movement of data between a TM and a DM can be expensive. To reduce this cost, many DDBMSs employ *query optimization procedures* which regulate (and, it is hoped, reduce) the flow of data between sites. For example, in SDD-1 the private workspace for transaction T is distributed across all sites at which T accesses data [BERN81]. The details of how T reads and writes data in these workspaces is a query optimization problem and has no direct effect on concurrency control.

The problem of atomic commitment is aggravated in a DDBMS by the possibility of one site failing while the rest of the system continues to operate. Suppose T is updating x, y, z stored at DM_x, DM_y, DM_z, and suppose T's TM fails after issuing dm-write(x), but before issuing the dm-writes for y and z. At this point the database is incorrect. In a centralized DBMS this phenomenon is not harmful because no transaction can access the database until the TM recovers from the failure. However, in a DDBMS, other TMs remain operational and can access the incorrect database.

To avoid this problem, prewrite commands must be modified slightly. In addition to specifying data items to be copied onto secure storage, prewrites also specify which other DMs are involved in the commitment activity. Then if the TM fails during the second phase of two-phase commit, the DMs whose dm-writes were not issued can recognize the situation and consult the other DMs involved in the commitment. If any DM received a dm-write, the remaining ones act as if they had also received the command. The details of this procedure are complex and appear in HAMM80.

As in a centralized DBMS, a transaction T accesses the system by issuing BEGIN, READ, WRITE, and END operations. In a DDBMS these are processed as follows.

BEGIN: The TM creates a private workspace for T. We leave the location and organization of this workspace unspecified.

READ(X): The TM checks T's private workspace to see if a copy of X is present. If so, that copy's value is made available to T. Otherwise the TM selects some stored copy of X, say x_i, and issues dm-read(x_i) to the DM at which x_i is stored. The DM responds by retrieving the stored value of x_i from the database, placing it in the private workspace. The TM returns this value to T.

WRITE(X, new-value): The value of X in T's private workspace is updated to new-value, assuming the workspace contains a copy of X. Otherwise, a copy of X with the new value is created in the workspace.

END: Two-phase commit begins. For each X updated by T, and for each stored copy x_i of X, the TM issues a prewrite (x_i) to the DM that stores x_i. The DM responds by copying the value of X from T's private workspace onto secure storage internal to the DM. After all prewrites are processed, the TM issues dm-writes for all copies of all logical data items updated by T. A DM responds to dm-write(x_i) by copying the value of x_i from secure storage into the stored database. After all dm-writes are installed, T's execution is finished.

2. DECOMPOSITION OF THE CONCURRENCY CONTROL PROBLEM

In this section we review concurrency control theory with two objectives: to define "correct executions" in precise terms, and to decompose the concurrency control problem into more tractable subproblems.

2.1 Serializability

Let E denote an execution of transactions $T_1, \ldots, T_n$. E is a *serial execution* if no transactions execute concurrently in E; that is, each transaction is executed to completion before the next one begins. Every serial execution is defined to be *correct*, because the properties of transactions (see Section 1.1) imply that a serial execution terminates properly and preserves database consistency. An execution is *serializable* if it is computationally equivalent to a serial execution, that is, if it produces the same output and has the same effect on the database as some serial execution. Since serial executions are correct and every serializable execution is equivalent to a serial one, every serializable execution is also correct. The

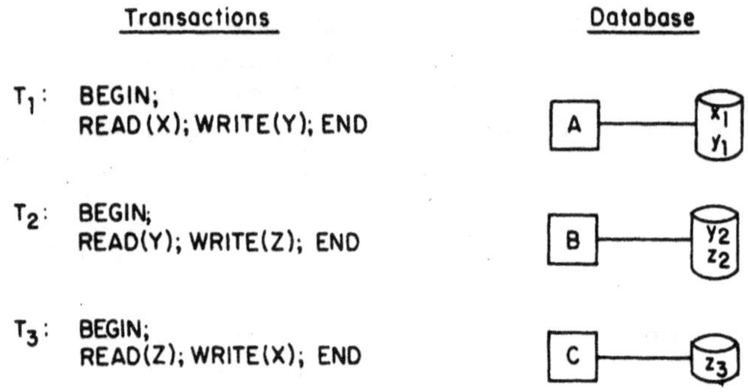

One possible execution of T_1, T_2, and T_3 is represented by the following logs. (Note: $r_i[x]$ denotes the operation dm-read(x) issued by T_i; $w_i[x]$ denotes a dm-write(x) issued by T_i.)

Log for DM A: $r_1[x_1]w_1[y_1]r_2[y_1]w_3[x_1]$
Log for DM B: $w_1[y_2]w_2[z_2]$
Log for DM C: $w_2[z_3]r_3[z_3]$

Figure 4. Modeling executions as logs.

- The execution modeled in Figure 4 is serial. Each log is itself serial; that is, there is no interleaving of operations from different transactions. At DM A, T_1 precedes T_2 precedes T_3; at DM B, T_1 precedes T_2; and at DM C, T_2 precedes T_3. Therefore, T_1, T_2, T_3 is a total order satisfying the definition of serial.
- The following execution is not serial. The logs themselves are not serial.

  DM A: $r_1[x_1]r_2[y_1]w_3[x_1]w_1[y_1]$
  DM B: $w_2[z_2]w_1[y_2]$
  DM C: $w_2[z_3]r_3[z_3]$
- The following execution is also not serial. Although each log is serial, there is no total order consistent with all logs.

  DM A: $r_1[x_1]w_1[y_1]r_2[y_1]w_3[x_1]$
  DM B: $w_2[z_2]w_1[y_2]$
  DM C: $w_2[z_3]r_3[z_3]$

Figure 5. Serial and nonserial loops.

goal of database concurrency control is to ensure that all executions are serializable.

The only operations that access the stored database are dm-read and dm-write. Hence it is sufficient to model an execution of transactions by the execution of dm-reads and dm-writes at the various DMs of the DDBMS. In this spirit we formally model an execution of transactions by a set of *logs*, each of which indicates the order in which dm-reads and dm-writes are processed at one DM (see Figure 4). An execution is *serial* if there is a total order of transactions such that if T_i precedes T_j in the total order, then all of T_i's operations precede all of T_j's operations in every log where both appear (see Figure 5). Intuitively, this says that transactions execute serially and in the same order at all DMs.

Two operations *conflict* if they operate on the same data item and one of the operations is a dm-write. The order in which operations execute is computationally significant if and only if the operations conflict. To illustrate the notion of conflict, consider a data item x and transactions T_i and T_j. If T_i issues dm-read (x) and T_j issues dm-write(x), the value read by T_i will (in general) differ depending on whether the dm-read precedes or follows the dm-write. Similarly, if both transactions issue dm-write(x) operations, the final value of x depends on which dm-write happens last. Those conflict situations are called *read-write* (*rw*) *conflicts* and *write-write* (*ww*) *conflicts*, respectively.

The notion of conflict helps characterize the equivalence of executions. Two executions are *computationally equivalent* if (1) each dm-read operation reads data item values that were produced by the same dm-writes in both executions; and (2) the final dm-write on each data item is the same in both executions [PAPA77, PAPA79]. Condition (1) ensures that each transaction reads the same input in both executions (and therefore performs the same computation).

Combined with (2), it ensures that both executions leave the database in the same final state.

From this we can characterize serializable executions precisely.

Theorem 1 [PAPA77, PAPA79, STEA76]

Let T = {$T_1, \ldots, T_m$} *be a set of transactions and let E be an execution of these transactions modeled by logs* {$L_1, \ldots, L_m$}. *E is serializable if there exists a total ordering of T such that for each pair of conflicting operations O_i and O_j from distinct transactions T_i and T_j (respectively), O_i precedes O_j in any log $L_1, \ldots, L_m$ if and only if T_i precedes T_j in the total ordering.*

The total order hypothesized in Theorem 1 is called a *serialization order*. If the transactions had executed serially in the serialization order, the computation performed by the transactions would have been identical to the computation represented by E.

To attain serializability, the DDBMS must guarantee that all executions satisfy the condition of Theorem 1, namely, that conflicting dm-reads and dm-writes be processed in certain relative orders. *Concurrency control* is the activity of controlling the relative order of conflicting operations; an algorithm to perform such control is called a *synchronization technique*. To be correct, a DDBMS must incorporate synchronization techniques that guarantee the conditions of Theorem 1.

2.2 A Paradigm for Concurrency Control

In Theorem 1, rw and ww conflicts are treated together under the general notion of conflict. However, we can decompose the concept of serializability by distinguishing these two types of conflict. Let E be an execution modeled by a set of logs. We define several binary relations on transactions in E, denoted by → with various subscripts. For each pair of transactions, T_i and T_j

(1) $T_i \rightarrow_{rw} T_j$ if in some log of E, T_i reads some data item into which T_j subsequently writes;
(2) $T_i \rightarrow_{wr} T_j$ if in some log of E, T_i writes into some data item that T_j subsequently reads;
(3) $T_i \rightarrow_{ww} T_j$ if in some log of E, T_i writes into some data item into which T_j subsequently writes;
(4) $T_i \rightarrow_{rwr} T_j$ if $T_i \rightarrow_{rw} T_j$ or $T_i \rightarrow_{wr} T_j$;
(5) $T_i \rightarrow T_j$ if $T_j \rightarrow_{rwr} T_j$ or $T_i \rightarrow_{ww} T_j$.

Intuitively, → (with any subscript) means "in any serialization must precede." For example, $T_i \rightarrow_{rw} T_j$ means "T_i in any serialization must precede T_j." This interpretation follows from Theorem 1: If T_i reads x before T_j writes into x, then the hypothetical serialization in Theorem 1 must have T_i preceding T_j.

Every conflict between operations in E is represented by an → relationship. Therefore, we can restate Theorem 1 in terms of →. According to Theorem 1, E is serializable if there is a total order of transactions that is consistent with →. This latter condition holds if and only if → is acyclic. (A relation, →, is *acyclic* if there is no sequence $T_1 \rightarrow T_2, T_2 \rightarrow T_3, \ldots, T_n\text{-}1 \rightarrow T_n$ such that $T_1 = T_n$.) Let us decompose → into its components, $\rightarrow_{rwr}$ and $\rightarrow_{ww}$, and restate the theorem using them.

Theorem 2 [BERN80a]

Let $\rightarrow_{rwr}$ and $\rightarrow_{ww}$ be associated with execution E. E is serializable if (a) $\rightarrow_{rwr}$ and $\rightarrow_{ww}$ are acyclic, and (b) there is a total ordering of the transactions consistent with all $\rightarrow_{rwr}$ and all $\rightarrow_{ww}$ relationships.

Theorem 2 is an immediate consequence of Theorem 1. (Indeed, part (b) of Theorem 2 is essentially a restatement of the earlier theorem.) However, this way of characterizing serializability suggests a way of decomposing the problem into simpler parts. Theorem 2 implies that rw and ww conflicts can be synchronized independently except insofar as there must be a total ordering of the transactions consistent with both types of conflicts. This suggests that we can use one technique to guarantee an acyclic $\rightarrow_{rwr}$ relation (which amounts to *read-write synchronization*) and a different technique to guarantee an acyclic $\rightarrow_{ww}$ relation (*write-write synchronization*). However, in addition to both $\rightarrow_{rwr}$ and $\rightarrow_{ww}$ being acyclic, there must also be *one* serial order consistent with *all* → relations. This serial order is the cement that binds together the rw and ww synchronization techniques.

Decomposing serializability into rw and ww synchronization is the cornerstone of our paradigm for concurrency control. It will be important hereafter to distinguish algorithms that attain either rw or ww synchronization from algorithms that solve the entire distributed concurrency control problem. We use the term *synchronization technique* for the former type of algorithm, and *concurrency control method* for the latter.

3. SYNCHRONIZATION TECHNIQUES BASED ON TWO-PHASE LOCKING

Two-phase locking (2PL) synchronizes reads and writes by explicitly detecting and preventing conflicts between concurrent operations. Before reading data item x, a transaction must "own" a *readlock on* x. Before writing into x, it must "own" a *writelock on* x. The ownership of locks is governed by two rules: (1) different transactions cannot simultaneously own *conflicting locks*; and (2) once a transaction surrenders ownership of a lock, it may never obtain additional locks.

The definition of *conflicting lock* depends on the type of synchronization being performed: for rw synchronization two locks *conflict* if (a) both are locks on the same data item, and (b) one is a readlock and the other is a writelock; for ww synchronization two locks *conflict* if (a) both are locks on the same data item, and (b) both are writelocks.

The second lock ownership rule causes every transaction to obtain locks in a *two-phase* manner. During the *growing phase* the transaction obtains locks without releasing any locks. By releasing a lock the transaction enters the *shrinking phase*. During this phase the transaction releases locks, and, by rule 2, is prohibited from obtaining additional locks. When the transaction terminates (or aborts), all remaining locks are automatically released.

A common variation is to require that transactions obtain all locks before beginning their main execution. This variation is called *predeclaration*. Some systems also require that transactions hold all locks until termination

Two-phase locking is a correct synchronization technique, meaning that 2PL attains an acyclic $\rightarrow_{rwr}$ ($\rightarrow_{ww}$) relation when used for rw (ww) synchronization [BERN79b, ESWA76, PAPA79]. The serialization order attained by 2PL is determined by the order in which transactions obtain locks. The point at the end of the growing phase, when a transaction owns all the locks it ever will own, is called the *locked point* of the transaction [BERN79b]. Let E be an execution in which 2PL is used for rw (ww) synchronization. The $\rightarrow_{rwr}$ ($\rightarrow_{ww}$) relation induced by E is identical to the relation induced by a *serial* execution E′ in which every transaction executes at its locked point. Thus the locked points of E determine a serialization order for E.

3.1 Basic 2PL Implementation

An implementation of 2PL amounts to building a *2PL scheduler*, a software module that receives lock requests and lock releases and processes them according to the 2PL specification.

The basic way to implement 2PL in a distributed database is to distribute the schedulers along with the database, placing the scheduler for data item x at the DM were x is stored. In this implementation readlocks may be implicitly requested by dm-reads and writelocks may be implicitly requested by prewrites. If the requested lock cannot be granted, the operation is placed on a waiting queue for the desired data item. (This can produce a *deadlock*, as discussed in Section 3.5.) Writelocks are implicitly released by dm-writes. However, to release readlocks, special lock-release operations are required. These lock releases may be transmitted in parallel with the dm-writes, since the dm-writes signal the start of the shrinking phase. When a lock is released, the operations on the waiting queue of that data item are processed first-in/first-out (FIFO) order.

Notice that this implementation "automatically" handles redundant data correctly. Suppose logical data item X has copies $x_1, \ldots, x_m$. If basic 2PL is used for rw synchronization, a transaction may read any copy and need only obtain a readlock on the copy of X it actually reads. However, if a transaction updates X, then it must update all copies of X, and so must obtain writelocks on all copies of X (whether basic 2PL is used for rw or ww synchronization).

3.2 Primary Copy 2PL

Primary copy 2PL is a 2PL technique that pays attention to data redundancy [STON79]. One copy of each logical data item is designated the *primary copy;* before accessing any copy of the logical data item, the appropriate lock must be obtained on the primary copy.

For readlocks this technique requires more communication than basic 2PL. Suppose x_1 is the primary copy of logical data item X, and suppose transaction T wishes to read some other copy, x_i, of X. To read x_i, T must communicate with two DMs, the DM where x_1 is stored (so T can lock x_1) and the DM where x_i is stored. By contrast, under basic 2PL, T would only communicate with x_i's DM. For writelocks, however, primary copy 2PL does not incur extra communication. Suppose T wishes to update X. Under basic 2PL, T would issue prewrites to all copies of X (thereby requesting writelocks on these data items) and then issue dm-writes to all copies. Under primary copy 2PL the same operations would be required, but only the prewrite (x_1) would request a writelock. That is, prewrites would be sent for $x_1, \ldots, x_m$, but the prewrites for $x_2, \ldots, x_m$ would not implicitly request writelocks.

3.3 Voting 2PL

Voting 2PL (or *majority consensus 2PL*) is another 2PL implementation that exploits data redundancy. Voting 2PL is derived from the majority consensus technique of Thomas [THOM79] and is only suitable for ww synchronization.

To understand voting, we must examine it in the context of two-phase commit. Suppose transaction T wants to write into X. Its TM sends prewrites to each DM holding a copy of X. For the voting protocol, the DM always responds immediately. It acknowledges receipt of the prewrite and says "lock set" or "lock blocked." (In the basic implementation it would not acknowledge at all until the lock is set.) After the TM receives acknowledgments from the DMs, it counts the number of "lockset" responses: if the number constitutes a majority, then the TM behaves as if all locks were set. Otherwise, it waits for "lockset" operations from DMs that originally said "lock blocked." Deadlocks aside (see Section 3.5), it will eventually receive enough "lockset" operations to proceed.

Since only one transaction can hold a majority of locks on X at a time, only one transaction writing into X can be in its second commit phase at any time. All copies of X thereby have the same sequence of writes applied to them. A transaction's locked point occurs when it has obtained a majority of its writelocks on each data item in its writeset. When updating many data items, a transaction must obtain a majority of locks on every data item before it issues any dm-writes.

In principle, voting 2PL could be adapted for rw synchronization. Before reading any copy of X a transaction requests readlocks on all copies of X; when a majority of locks are set, the transaction may read any copy. This technique works but is overly strong: Correctness only requires that a single copy of X be locked—namely, the copy that is read—yet this technique requests locks on all copies. For this reason we deem voting 2PL to be inappropriate for rw synchronization.

3.4 Centralized 2PL

Instead of distributing the 2PL schedulers, one can centralize the scheduler at a single site [ALSB76a, GARC79a]. Before accessing data at any site, appropriate locks must be obtained from the central 2PL scheduler. So, for example, to perform dm-read(x) where x is not stored at the central site, the TM must first request a readlock on x from the central site, wait for the central site to acknowledge that the lock has been set, then send dm-read(x) to the DM that holds x. (To save some communication, one can have the TM send both the lock request and dm-read (x) to the central site and let the central site directly forward dm-read(x) to x's DM; the DM then responds to the TM when dm-read (x) has been processed.) Like primary copy 2PL, this approach tends to require more communication than basic

Transactions | **Database**

T_1: BEGIN;
READ(X); WRITE(Y); END

T_2: BEGIN;
READ(Y); WRITE(Z); END

T_3: BEGIN;
READ(Z); WRITE(X); END

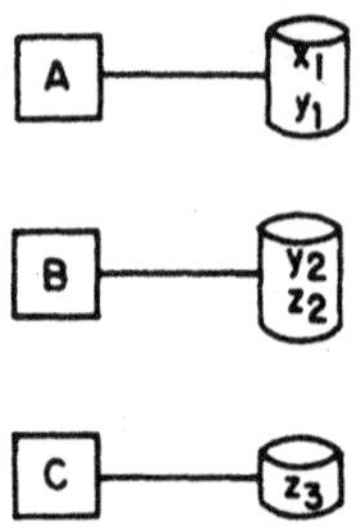

- Suppose transactions execute concurrently, with each transaction issuing its READ before any transaction issues its END.
- This partial execution could be represented by the following logs.

DM A: $r_1[x_1]$
DM B: $r_2[y_2]$
DM C: $r_3[z_3]$

- At this point, T_1 has readlock on x_1
  T_2 has readlock on y_2
  T_3 has readlock on z_3
- Before proceeding, all transactions must obtain writelocks.
  T_1 requires writelocks on y_1 and y_2
  T_2 requires writelocks on z_2 and z_3
  T_3 requires writelock on x_1
- But

  T_1 cannot get writelock on y_2, until T_2 releases readlock
  T_2 cannot get writelock on z_3, until T_3 releases readlock
  T_3 cannot get writelock on x_1, until T_1 releases readlock

  This is a deadlock.

Figure 6. Deadlock.

2PL, since dm-reads and prewrites usually cannot implicitly request locks.

3.5 Deadlock Detection and Prevention

The preceding implementations of 2PL force transactions to wait for unavailable locks. If this waiting is uncontrolled, deadlocks can arise (see Figure 6).

Deadlock situations can be characterized by *waits-for graphs* [HOLT72, KING74], directed graphs that indicate which transactions are waiting for which other transactions. Nodes of the graph represent transactions, and edges represent the "waiting-for" relationship: an edge is drawn from transaction T_i to transaction T_j if T_i is waiting for a lock currently owned by T_j. There is a deadlock in the system if and only if the waits-for graph contains a *cycle* (see Figure 7).

Two general techniques are available for deadlock resolution: *deadlock prevention* and *deadlock detection.*

3.5.1 Deadlock Prevention

Deadlock prevention is a "cautious" scheme in which a transaction is restarted when the system is "afraid" that deadlock might occur. To implement deadlock prevention, 2PL schedulers are modified as follows. When a lock request is denied, the scheduler tests the requesting transaction (say T_i) and the transaction that currently owns the lock (say T_j). If T_i and T_j pass the test, T_i is permitted to wait for T_j as usual. Otherwise, one of the two is aborted. If T_i is restarted, the deadlock prevention algorithm is called *nonpreemptive*; if T_j is restarted, the algorithm is called *preemptive.*

The test applied by the scheduler must

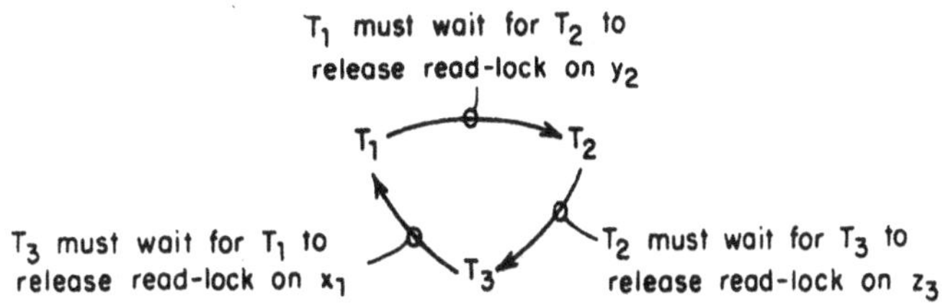

Figure 7. Waits-for graph for Figure 6.

guarantee that if T_i waits for T_j, then deadlock cannot result. One simple approach is never to let T_i wait for T_j. This trivially prevents deadlock but forces many restarts.

A better approach is to assign *priorities* to transactions and to test priorities to decide whether T_i can wait for T_j. For example, we could let T_i wait for T_j if T_i has lower priority than T_j (if T_i and T_j have *equal* priorities, T_i cannot wait for T_j, or vice versa). This test prevents deadlock because, for every edge $\langle T_i, T_j \rangle$ in the waits-for graph, T_i has lower priority than T_j. Since a cycle is a path from a node to itself and since T_i cannot have lower priority than itself, no cycle can exist.

One problem with the preceding approach is that *cyclic restart* is possible—some unfortunate transaction could be continually restarted without ever finishing. To avoid this problem, Rosenkrantz et al. [ROSE78] propose using "timestamps" as priorities. Intuitively, a transaction's timestamp is the time at which it begins executing, so old transactions have higher priority than young ones.

The technique of ROSE78 requires that each transaction be assigned a *unique* timestamp by its TM. When a transaction begins, the TM reads the local clock time and appends a unique TM identifier to the low-order bits [THOM79]. The resulting number is the desired timestamp. The TM also agrees not to assign another timestamp until the next clock tick. Thus timestamps assigned by different TMs differ in their low-order bits (since different TMs have different identifiers), while timestamps assigned by the same TM differ in their high-order bits (since the TM does not use the same clock time twice). Hence timestamps are unique throughout the system. Note that this algorithm does not require clocks at different sites to be precisely synchronized.

Two timestamp-based deadlock prevention schemes are proposed in ROSE78. *Wait-Die* is the nonpreemptive technique. Suppose transaction T_i tries to wait for T_j. If T_i has lower priority than T_j (i.e., T_i is younger than T_j), then T_i is permitted to wait. Otherwise, it is aborted ("dies") and forced to restart. It is important that T_i not be assigned a new timestamp when it restarts. *Wound-Wait* is the preemptive counterpart to *Wait-Die*. If T_i has higher priority than T_j, then T_i waits; otherwise T_j is aborted.

Both Wait-Die and Wound-Wait avoid cyclic restart. However, in Wound-Wait an old transaction may be restarted many times, while in Wait-Die old transactions never restart. It is suggested in ROSE78 that Wound-Wait induces fewer restarts in total.

Care must be exercised in using preemptive deadlock prevention with two-phase commit: a transaction must not be aborted once the second phase of two-phase commit has begun. If a preemptive technique wishes to abort T_j, it checks with T_j's TM and cancels the abort if T_j has entered the second phase. No deadlock can result because if T_j is in the second phase, it cannot be waiting for any transactions.

Preordering of resources is a deadlock avoidance technique that avoids restarts altogether. This technique requires predeclaration of locks (each transaction obtains all its locks before execution). Data items are numbered and each transaction requests locks one at a time in numeric order. The priority of a transaction is the number of the highest numbered lock it owns. Since a transaction can only wait for transactions with higher priority, no deadlocks can occur. In addition to requiring predeclaration, a principal disadvantage of this technique is that it forces locks to be obtained sequentially, which tends to increase response time.

- Consider the execution illustrated in Figures 6 and 7.
- Locks are requested at DMs in the following order:

DM A	DM B	DM C
readlock x_1 for T_1	readlock y_2 for T_2	readlock z_3 for T_3
writelock y_1 for T_1	writelock z_2 for T_2	
*writelock x_1 for T_3	*writelock y_2 for T_1	*writelock z_3 for T_2

- None of the "starred" locks can be granted and the system is in deadlock. However, the waits-for graphs at each DM are acyclic.

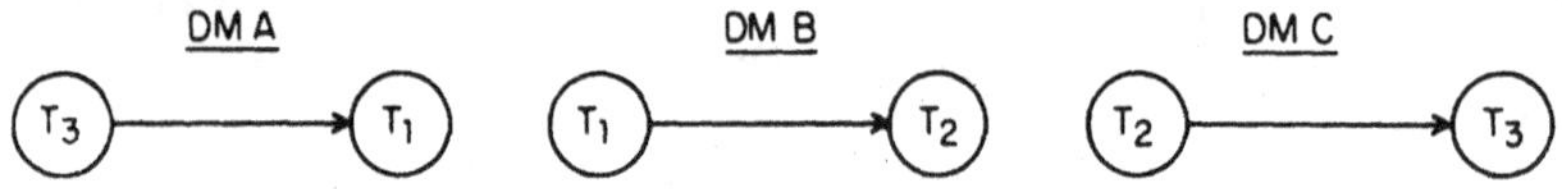

Figure 8. Multisite deadlock.

3.5.2 Deadlock Detection

In *deadlock detection*, transactions wait for each other in an uncontrolled manner and are only aborted if a deadlock actually occurs. Deadlocks are detected by explicitly constructing the waits-for graph and searching it for cycles. (Cycles in a graph can be found efficiently using, for example, Algorithm 5.2 in AHO75.) If a cycle is found, one transaction on the cycle, called the *victim*, is aborted, thereby breaking the deadlock. To minimize the cost of restarting the victim, victim selection is usually based on the amount of resources used by each transaction on the cycle.

The principal difficulty in implementing deadlock detection in a distributed database is constructing the waits-for graph efficiently. Each 2PL scheduler can easily construct the waits-for graph based on the waits-for relationships local to that scheduler. However, these local waits-for graphs are not sufficient to characterize all deadlocks in the distributed system (see Figure 8). Instead, local waits-for graphs must be combined into a more "global" waits-for graph. (Centralized 2PL does not have this problem, since there is only one scheduler.) We describe two techniques for constructing global waits-for graphs: centralized and hierarchical deadlock detection.

In the *centralized* approach, one site is designated the deadlock detector for the distributed system [GRAY78, STON79]. Periodically (e.g., every few minutes) each scheduler sends its local waits-for graph to the deadlock detector. The deadlock detector combines the local graphs into a system-wide waits-for graph by constructing the union of the local graphs.

In the *hierarchical* approach, the database sites are organized into a hierarchy (or tree), with a deadlock detector at each node of the hierarchy [MENA79]. For example, one might group sites by *region*, then by *country*, then by *continent*. Deadlocks that are local to a single site are detected at that site; deadlocks involving two or more sites of the same region are detected by the regional deadlock detector; and so on.

Although centralized and hierarchical deadlock detection differ in detail, both involve periodic transmission of local waits-for information to one or more deadlock detector sites. The periodic nature of the process introduces two problems. First, a deadlock may exist for several minutes without being detected, causing response-time degradation. The solution, executing the deadlock detector more frequently, increases the cost of deadlock detection. Second, a transaction T may be restarted for reasons other than concurrency control (e.g., its site crashed). Until T's restart propagates to the deadlock detector, the deadlock detector can find a cycle in the waits-for graph that includes T. Such a cycle is called a *phantom deadlock*. When the deadlock detector discovers a phantom deadlock, it may unnecessarily restart a transaction other than T. Special precautions are also needed to avoid unnecessary restarts for deadlocks in voting 2PL.[2]

[2] Suppose logical data item X has copies x_1, x_2, and x_3, and suppose using voting 2PL T_i owns write-locks on x_1 and x_2 but T_i's lock request for x_3 is blocked by T_j.

A major cost of deadlock detection is the restarting of partially executed transactions. Predeclaration can be used to reduce this cost. By obtaining a transaction's locks before it executes, the system will only restart transactions that have not yet executed. Thus little work is wasted by the restart.

4. SYNCHRONIZATION TECHNIQUES BASED ON TIMESTAMP ORDERING

Timestamp ordering (T/O) is a technique whereby a serialization order is selected a priori and transaction execution is forced to obey this order. Each transaction is assigned a unique timestamp by its TM. The TM attaches the timestamp to all dm-reads and dm-writes issued on behalf of the transaction, and DMs are required to process *conflicting operations* in timestamp order. The timestamp of operation O is denoted ts(O).

The definition of conflicting operations depends on the type of synchronization being performed and is analogous to conflicting locks. For rw synchronization, two operations *conflict* if (a) both operate on the same data item, and (b) one is a dm-read and the other is a dm-write. For ww synchronization, two operations *conflict* if (a) both operate on the same data item, and (b) both are dm-writes.

It is easy to prove that T/O attains an acyclic $\rightarrow_{rwr}$ ($\rightarrow_{ww}$) relation when used for rw (ww) synchronization. Since each DM processes conflicting operations in timestamp order, each edge of the $\rightarrow_{rwr}$ ($\rightarrow_{ww}$) relation is in timestamp order. Consequently, all paths in the relation are in timestamp order and, since all transactions have unique timestamps, no cycles are possible. In addition, the timestamp order is a valid serialization order.

4.1 Basic T/O Implementation

An implementation of T/O amounts to building a *T/O scheduler*, a software module that receives dm-reads and dm-writes and outputs these operations according to the T/O specification [SHAP77a, SHAP77b]. In practice, prewrites must also be processed through the T/O scheduler for two-phase commit to operate properly. As was the case with 2PL, the basic T/O implementation distributes the schedulers along with the database [BERN80a].

If we ignore two-phase commit, the basic T/O scheduler is quite simple. At each DM, and for each data item x stored at the DM, the scheduler records the largest timestamp of any dm-read(x) or dm-write(x) that has been processed. These are denoted R-ts(x) and W-ts(x), respectively. For rw synchronization, scheduler S operates as follows. Consider a dm-read(x) with timestamp TS. If TS < W-ts(x), S *rejects* the dm-read and aborts the issuing transaction. Otherwise S outputs the dm-read and sets R-ts(x) to max(R-ts(x),TS). For a dm-write(x) with timestamp TS, S rejects the dm-write if TS < R-ts(x); otherwise it outputs the dm-write and sets W-ts(x) to max(W-ts(x),TS). For ww synchronization, S rejects a dm-write(x) with timestamp TS if TS < W-ts(x); otherwise it outputs the dm-write and sets W-ts(x) to TS.

When a transaction is aborted, it is assigned a new and larger timestamp by its TM and is restarted. Restart issues are discussed further below.

Two-phase commit is incorporated by timestamping prewrites and accepting or rejecting prewrites instead of dm-writes. Once a scheduler accepts a prewrite, it must guarantee to accept the corresponding dm-write no matter when the dm-write arrives. For rw (or ww) synchronization, once S accepts a prewrite(x) with timestamp TS it must not output any dm-read(x) (or dm-write(x)) with timestamp greater than TS until the dm-write(x) is output. The effect is similar to setting a writelock on x for the duration of two-phase commit..

To implement the above rules, S *buffers* dm-reads, dm-writes, and prewrites. Let min-R-ts(x) be the minimum timestamp of any buffered dm-read(x), and define min-W-ts(x) and min-P-ts(x) analogously. Rw synchronization is accomplished as follows:

1. Let R be a dm-read(x). If ts(R) < W-ts(x), R is rejected. Else if ts(R) > min-P-ts(x), R is buffered. Else R is output.

Insofar as x_3's scheduler is concerned, T_i is waiting for T_j. However, since T_i has a *majority* of the copies locked, T_i can proceed without waiting for T_j. This fact should be incorporated into the deadlock resolution scheme to avoid unnecessary restarts.

Let R = dm-read (x).
Let W = dm-write (x).
R is *ready* if it precedes the earliest prewrite request:
if ts(R) < min-P-ts(x).
W is *ready* if it precedes the earliest dm-read request:
if ts (W) < min-R-ts(x).
When a dm-write(x) arrives, do the following:

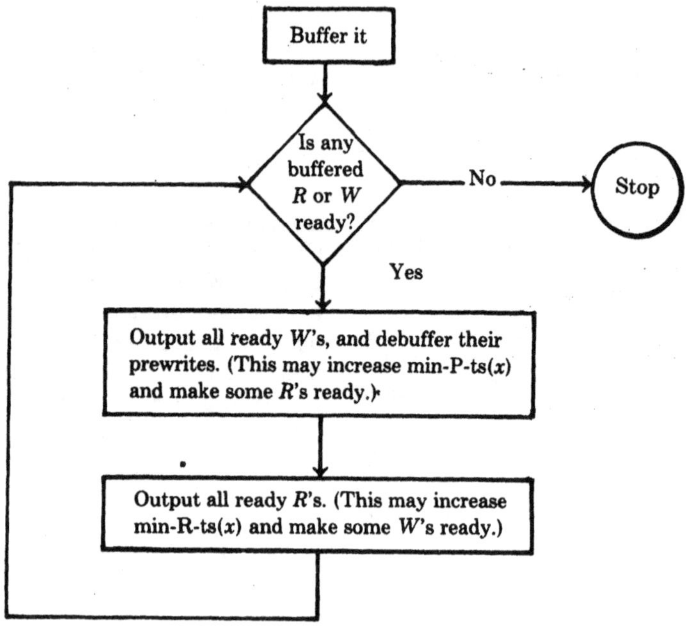

Figure 9. Buffer emptying for basic T/O rw synchronization.

2. Let P be a prewrite(x). If ts(P) < R-ts(x), P is rejected. Else P is buffered.
3. Let W be a dm-write(x). W is never rejected. If ts(W) > min-R-ts(x), W is buffered. (If W were output it would cause a buffered dm-read(x) to be rejected.) Else W is output.
4. When W is output, the corresponding prewrite is debuffered. If this causes min-P-ts(x) to increase, the buffered dm-reads are retested to see if any of them can be output. If this causes min-R-ts(x) to be increased, the buffered dm-writes are also retested, and so forth. This process is diagramed in Figure 9.

Ww synchronization is accomplished as follows:

1. Let P be a prewrite(x). If ts(P) < W-ts(x), P is rejected; else P is buffered.
2. Let W be a dm-write(x). W is never rejected. If ts(W) > min-P-ts(x), W is buffered; else W is output.
3. When W is output, the corresponding prewrite is debuffered. If this causes min-P-ts(x) to be increased, the buffered dm-writes are retested to see if any can now be output. See Figure 10.

As with 2PL, a common variation is to require that transactions *predeclare* their readsets and writesets, issuing all dm-reads and prewrites before beginning their main execution.[3] If all operations are accepted,

[3] These prewrites are nonstandard relative to the definition in Section 1.4. Since new values for the data items in the writeset are not yet known, these prewrites do *not* instruct DMs to store values on secure storage; instead, prewrite (x) merely "warns" the DM to expect a dm-write (x) in the near future. However, these prewrites are processed by synchronization algorithms exactly as "standard" ones are.

When a dm-write(x) arrives, do the following:

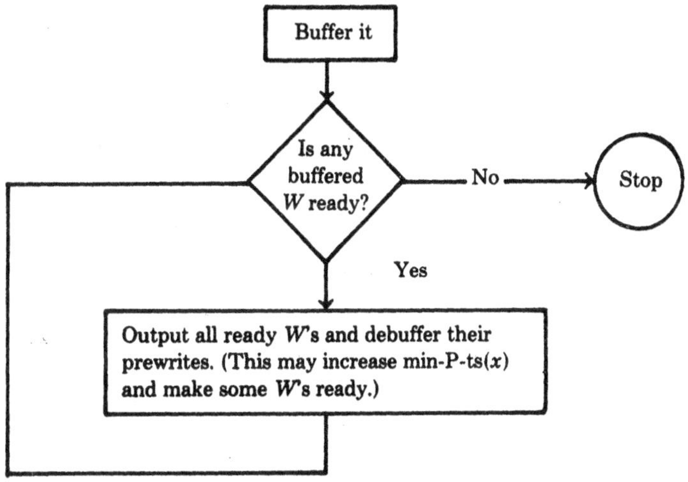

Figure 10. Buffer emptying for basic T/O ww synchronization.

the transaction is guaranteed to execute without danger of restart. Another variation is to *delay* the processing of operations to wait for operations with smaller timestamps. The extreme version of this heuristic is *conservative T/O*, described in Section 4.4.

4.2 The Thomas Write Rule

For ww synchronization the basic T/O scheduler can be optimized using an observation of THOM79. Let W be a dm-write(x), and suppose ts(W) < W-ts(x). Instead of rejecting *W we can simply ignore it.* We call this the *Thomas Write Rule (TWR)*. Intuitively, TWR applies to a dm-write that tries to place obsolete information into the database. The rule guarantees that the effect of applying a set of dm-writes to x is identical to what would have happened had the dm-writes been applied in timestamp order.

If TWR is used, there is no need to incorporate two-phase commit into the ww synchronization algorithm; the ww scheduler always accepts prewrites and never buffers dm-writes.

4.3 Multiversion T/O

For rw synchronization the basic T/O scheduler can be improved using *multiversion data items* [REED78]. For each data item x there is a *set* of R-ts's and a set of ⟨W-ts, value⟩ pairs, called *versions*. The R-ts's of x record the timestamps of all executed dm-read(x) operations, and the versions record the timestamps and values of all executed dm-write(x) operations. (In practice one cannot store R-ts's and versions forever; techniques for deleting old versions and timestamps are described in Sections 4.5 and 5.2.2.)

Multiversion T/O accomplishes rw synchronization as follows (ignoring two-phase commit). Let R be a dm-read(x). R is processed by reading the version of x with largest timestamp less than ts(R) and adding ts(R) to x's set of R-ts's; see Figure 11a. R is never rejected. Let W be a dm-write(x), and let *interval*(W) be the interval from ts(W) to the smallest W-ts(x) > ts(W);[4] see Figure 11b. If any R-ts(x) lies in interval(W), W is rejected; otherwise W is output and creates a new version of x with timestamp ts(W).

To prove the correctness of multiversion T/O, we must show that every execution is equivalent to a serial execution in timestamp order [BERN80b]. Let R be a dm-read(x) that is processed "out of order"; that is, suppose R is executed after a dm-write(x) whose timestamp exceeds ts(R). Since R ignores all versions with time-

[4] Interval(W) = (ts(W),∞) if no W-ts(x) > ts (W) exists.

(a) Let us represent the versions of a data item x on a "time line":

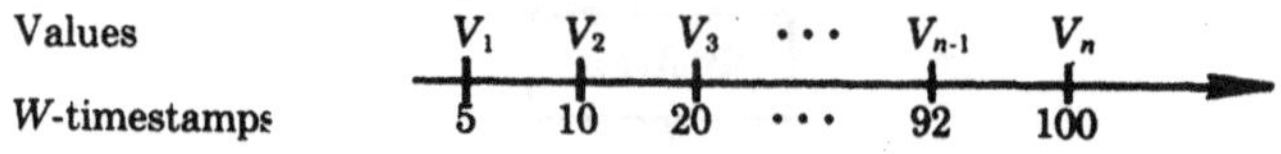

To process a dm-read(x) with timestamp 95, find the biggest W-timestamp less than 95; in this case 92. That is the version you read. So in this case, the value read by the dm-read is V_{n-1}.

(b) Let us represent the R-timestamps of x similarly:

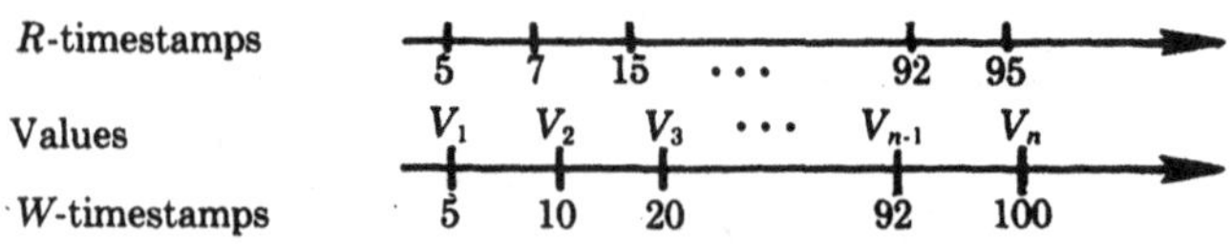

Let W be dm-write(x) with timestamp 93. Interval(W) = (93,100).

To process W we create a new version of x with that timestamp.

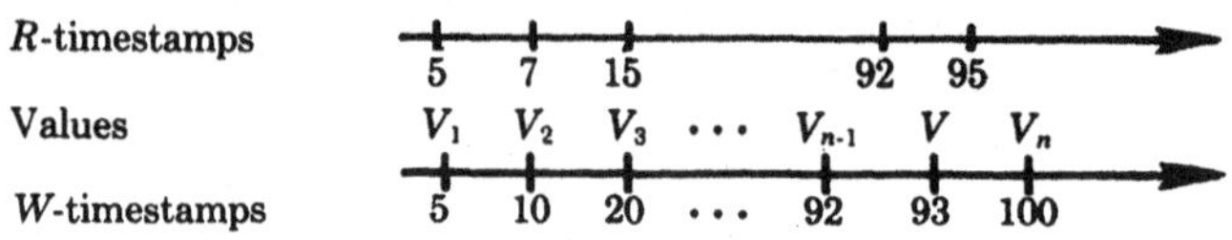

However, this new version "invalidates" the dm-read of part (a), because if the dm-read had arrived after the dm-write, it would have read value V instead of V_{n-1}. Therefore, we must reject the dm-write.

Figure 11. Multiversion reading and writing.

stamps greater than ts(R), the value read by R is identical to the value it would have read had it been processed in timestamp order. Now let W be a dm-write(x) that is processed "out of order"; that is, suppose it is executed after a dm-read(x) whose timestamp exceeds ts(W). Since W was not rejected, there exists a version of x with timestamp TS such that ts(W) $<$ TS $<$ ts(dm-read). Again the effect is identical to a timestamp-ordered execution.

For ww synchronization, multiversion T/O is essentially an embellished version of TWR. A dm-write(x) always creates a new version of x with timestamp ts(dm-write) and is never rejected.

Integrating two-phase commit requires that dm-reads and prewrites (but not dm-writes) be buffered as in basic T/O. Let P be a buffered prewrite(x): *interval*(P) is the interval from ts(P) to the smallest W-ts(x) $>$ ts(P). Rw synchronization is performed as follows:

1. Let R be a dm-read(x). R is never rejected. If ts(R) lies in interval(prewrite(x)) for some buffered prewrite(x), then R is buffered. Else R is output.
2. Let P be a prewrite(x). If some R-ts(x) lies in interval(P), P is rejected. Else P is buffered.
3. Let W be a dm-write(x). W is always output immediately.
4. When W is output, its prewrite is debuffered, and the buffered dm-reads are retested to see if they can now be output. See Figure 12.

Two-phase commit is not an issue for ww synchronization, since dm-writes are never rejected for ww synchronization.

Let R = dm-read(x). R is *ready* if ts(R) $\notin$ interval (P), where P is any buffered prewrite(x).

When a dm-write arrives do the following:

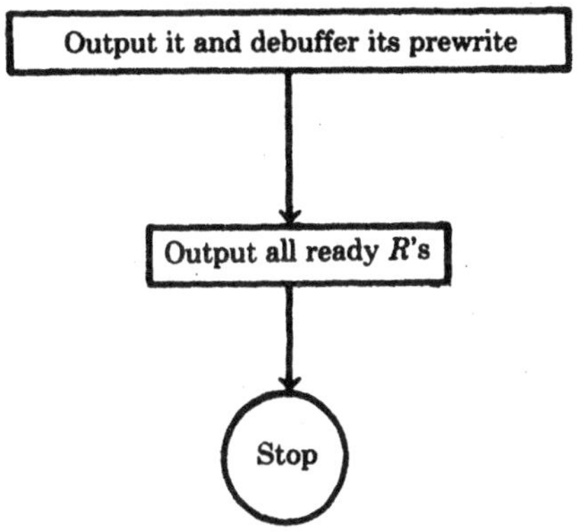

Figure 12. Buffer emptying for multiversion T/O.

4.4 Conservative T/O

Conservative timestamp ordering is a technique for eliminating restarts during T/O scheduling [BERN80a]. When a scheduler receives an operation O that might cause a future restart, the scheduler *delays* O until it is sure that no future restarts are possible.

Conservative T/O requires that each scheduler receive dm-reads (or dm-writes) from each TM in timestamp order. For example, if scheduler S_j receives dm-read(x) followed by dm-read(y) from TM_i, then ts(dm-read(x)) $\leq$ ts(dm-read(y)). Since the network is assumed to be a FIFO channel, this timestamp ordering is accomplished by requiring that TM_i *send* dm-reads (or dm-writes) to S_j in timestamp order.[5]

Conservative T/O buffers dm-reads and dm-writes as part of its normal operation. When a scheduler buffers an operation, it remembers the TM that sent it. Let min-R-ts(TM_i) be the minimum timestamp of any buffered dm-read from TM_i, with min-R-ts(TM_i) = $-\infty$ if no such dm-read is buffered. Define min-W-ts(TM_i) analogously.

Conservative T/O performs rw synchronization as follows:

1. Let R be a dm-read(x). If ts(R) > min-W-ts(TM) for any TM in the system, R is buffered. Else R is output.
2. Let W be a dm-write(x). If ts(W) > min-R-ts(TM) for any TM, W is buffered. Else W is output.
3. When R or W is output or buffered, this may increase min-R-ts(TM) or min-W-ts(TM); buffered operations are retested to see if they can now be output.

The effect is that R is output if and only if (a) the scheduler has a buffered dm-write from every TM, and (b) ts(R) < minimum timestamp of any buffered dm-write. Similarly, W is output if and only if (a) there is a buffered dm-read from every TM, and (b) ts(W) < minimum timestamp of any buffered dm-read. Thus R (or W) is output if and only if the scheduler has received every dm-write (or dm-read) with smaller timestamp that it will ever receive.

Ww synchronization is accomplished as follows:

1. Let W be a dm-write(x). If ts(W) > min-W-ts(TM) for any TM in the system, W is buffered; else it is output.
2. When W is buffered or output, this may increase min-W-ts(TM); buffered dm-writes are retested accordingly.

The effect is that the scheduler waits until it has a buffered dm-write from every TM and then outputs the dm-write with smallest timestamp.

Two-phase commit need not be tightly integrated into conservative T/O because dm-writes are never rejected. Although prewrites must be issued for all data items updated, these operations are not processed by the conservative T/O schedulers.

The above implementation of conservative T/O suffers three major problems: (1) If some TM never sends an operation to some scheduler, the scheduler will "get stuck" and stop outputting. (2) To avoid the first problem, every TM must communicate regularly with every scheduler; this is infeasible in large networks. (3) The im-

[5] This can be implemented by requiring that TMs process transactions serially. Alternatively, we can require that transactions issue all dm-reads before beginning their main execution, and all dm-writes after terminating their main execution. Then transactions can execute concurrently, although they must terminate in timestamp order.

- A *class* is defined by a readset and a writeset. For example,

  C_1: readset = $\{x_1\}$, writeset = $\{y_1, y_2\}$
  C_2: readset = $\{x_1, y_2\}$, writeset = $\{y_1, y_2, z_2, z_3\}$
  C_3: readset = $\{y_2, z_3\}$, writeset = $\{x_1, z_2, z_3\}$

- A transaction is a member of a class if its readset is a subset of the class readset and its writeset is a subset of the class writeset. For example,

  T_1: readset = $\{x_1\}$, writeset = $\{y_1, y_2\}$
  T_2: readset = $\{y_2\}$, writeset = $\{z_2, z_3\}$
  T_3: readset = $\{z_3\}$, writeset = $\{x_1\}$

- T_1 is a member of C_1 and C_2
- T_2 is a member of C_2 and C_3
- T_3 is a member of C_3

Figure 13. Transaction classes.

plementation is overly conservative; the ww algorithm, for instance, processes *all* dm-writes in timestamp order, not merely conflicting ones. These problems are addressed below.

Null Operations. To solve the first problem, TMs are required to periodically send timestamped *null operations* to each scheduler in the absence of "real" traffic. A null operation is a dm-read or dm-write whose sole purpose is to convey timestamp information and thereby unblock "real" dm-reads and prewrites. An impatient scheduler can prompt a TM for a null operation by sending a "request message." For example, for rw synchronization suppose scheduler S wants to process a dm-read with timestamp TS, but does not have a buffered dm-write from TM_i. S can send a message to TM_i requesting a null-dm-write with timestamp greater than TS.

A variation is to use null operations with *very large* (perhaps infinite) timestamps. For example, if TM_i rarely needs to issue dm-reads to S, TM_i can send S a null-dm-read with infinite timestamp signifying that TM_i does not intend to communicate with S until further notice.

Transaction Classes. Transaction classes [BERN78a, BERN80d] is a technique for reducing communication in conservative T/O and for supporting a less conservative scheduling policy. As in predeclaration, assume that every transaction's readset and writeset are known in advance. A *class* is defined by a readset and a writeset (see Figure 13). Transaction T is a *member* of class C if readset(T) is a subset of readset(C) and writeset(T) is a subset of writeset(C). (Classes need not be disjoint.)

Class definitions are not expected to change frequently during normal operation of the system. Changing a class definition is akin to changing the database schema and requires mechanisms beyond the scope of this paper. We assume that class definitions are stored in static tables that are available to any site requiring them.

Classes are associated with TMs. Every transaction that executes at a TM must be a member of a class associated with the TM. If a transaction is submitted to a TM that has no class containing it, the transaction is forwarded to another TM that does. We assume that every class is associated with exactly one TM, and vice versa. The class associated with TM_i is denoted C_i. To execute transactions that are members of class C at two TMs, we define another class C′ with the same definition as C and associate C with one TM and C′ with the other. To execute transactions that are members of two classes at one site, we multiprogram two TMs at that site.

Classes are exploited by conservative T/O schedulers as follows. Consider rw synchronization and suppose scheduler S wants to output a dm-read(x). Instead of waiting for dm-writes with smaller timestamps from all TMs, S need only wait for dm-writes *from those TMs whose class writeset contains x*. Similarly, to process a dm-write (x), S need only wait for dm-reads with smaller timestamp from those TMs whose class readset contains x. Thus communication requirements are decreased, and the level of concurrency in the system is increased. Ww synchronization proceeds similarly.

Conflict Graph Analysis. Conflict graph analysis is a technique for further improving the performance of conservative T/O with classes. A *conflict graph* is an undirected graph that summarizes potential conflicts between transactions in different classes. For each class C_i the graph contains two nodes, denoted r_i and w_i, which represent the readset and writeset of C_i. The edges of the graph are defined as follows (see Figure 14): (1) For each class

Define C_1, C_2, C_3 as in Figure 13.

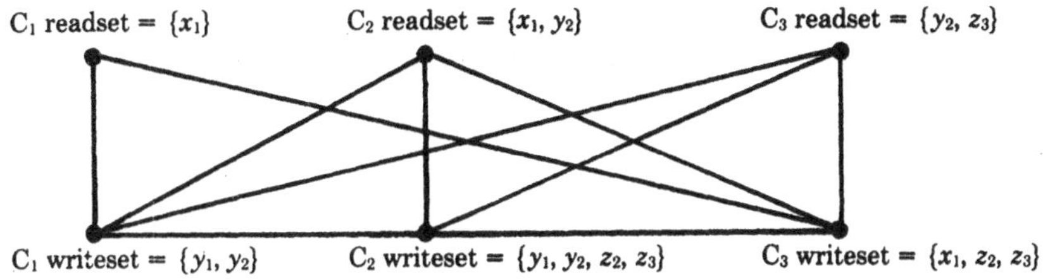

Figure 14. Conflict graph.

C_i there is a *vertical edge* between r_i and w_i; (2) for each pair of classes C_i and C_j (with $i \neq j$) there is a *horizontal edge* between w_i and w_j if and only if writeset(C_i) intersects writeset(C_j); (3) for each pair of classes C_i and C_j (with $i \neq j$) there is a *diagonal edge* between r_i and w_j if and only if readset(C_i) intersects writeset(C_j).

Intuitively, a horizontal edge indicates that a scheduler S may be forced to delay dm-writes for purposes of ww synchronization. Suppose classes C_i and C_j are connected by a horizontal edge (w_i, w_j), indicating that their class writesets intersect. If S receives a dm-write from C_i, it must delay the dm-write until it receives all dm-writes with smaller timestamps from C_j. Similarly, a diagonal edge indicates that S may need to delay operations for rw synchronization.

Conflict graph analysis improves the situation by identifying interclass conflicts that cannot cause nonserializable behavior. This corresponds to identifying horizontal and diagonal edges that do not require synchronization. In particular, schedulers need only synchronize dm-writes from C_i and C_j if either (1) the horizontal edge between w_i and w_j is embedded in a *cycle* of the conflict graph; or (2) portions of the intersection of C_i's writeset and C_j's writeset are stored at two or more DMs [BERN80c]. That is, if conditions (1) and (2) do not hold, scheduler S need not process dm-writes from C_i and C_j in timestamp order. Similarly, dm-reads from C_i and dm-writes from C_j need only be processed in timestamp order if either (1) the diagonal edge between r_i and w_j is embedded in a cycle of the conflict graph; or (2) portions of the intersection of C_i's readset and C_j's writeset are stored at two or more DMs.

Since classes are defined statically, conflict graph analysis is also performed statically. The analysis produces a table indicating which horizontal and vertical edges require synchronization and which do not. This table, like class definitions, is distributed in advance to all schedulers that need it.

4.5 Timestamp Management

A common criticism of T/O schedulers is that too much memory is needed to store timestamps. This problem can be overcome by "forgetting" old timestamps.

Timestamps are used in basic T/O to reject operations that "arrive late," for example, to reject a dm-read(x) with timestamp TS_1 that arrives after a dm-write(x) with timestamp TS_2, where $TS_1 < TS_2$. In principle, TS_1 and TS_2 can differ by an arbitrary amount. However, in practice it is unlikely that these timestamps will differ by more than a few minutes. Consequently, timestamps can be stored in small tables which are periodically purged.

R-ts's are stored in the *R-table* with entries of the form $\langle x, \text{R-ts}\rangle$; for any data item x, there is at most one entry. In addition, a variable, *R-min*, tells the maximum value of any timestamp that has been purged from the table. To find R-ts(x), a scheduler searches the R-table for an $\langle x, \text{TS}\rangle$ entry. If such an entry is found, R-ts(x) = TS; otherwise, R-ts(x) ≤ R-min. To err on the side of safety, the scheduler assumes R-ts(x) = R-min. To update R-ts(x), the scheduler modifies the $\langle x, \text{TS}\rangle$ entry, if one exists. Otherwise, a new entry is created and added to the table. When the R-table is full, the scheduler selects an appropriate value for R-min and deletes all entries from the table with smaller timestamp. W-ts's are managed similarly, and analogous techniques can be devised for multiversion databases.

Maintaining timestamps for conservative T/O is even cheaper, since conservative T/O requires only timestamped operations, not timestamped data. If conservative T/O is used for rw synchronization, the R-ts's of data items may be discarded. If conservative T/O is used for both rw and ww synchronization, W-ts's can be eliminated also.

5. INTEGRATED CONCURRENCY CONTROL METHODS

An integrated concurrency control method consists of two components—an rw and a ww synchronization technique—plus an interface between the components that attains condition (b) of Theorem 2: a total ordering of the transactions consistent with all $\longrightarrow_{rwr}$ and $\longrightarrow_{ww}$ relationships. In this section we list 48 concurrency control methods that can be constructed using the techniques of Sections 3 and 4.

Approximately 20 concurrency control methods have been described in the literature. Virtually all of them use a *single* synchronization technique (either 2PL or T/O) for both rw and ww synchronization. Indeed, most methods use the same *variation* of a single technique for both kinds of synchronization. However, such homogeneity is neither necessary nor especially desirable.

For example, the analysis of Section 3.2 suggests that using basic 2PL for rw synchronization and primary copy 2PL for ww synchronization might be superior to using basic 2PL (or primary copy 2PL) for both. More outlandish combinations may be even better. For example, one can combine basic 2PL with TWR. In this method ww conflicts never cause transactions to be delayed or restarted; multiple transactions can write into the same data items concurrently (see Section 5.3).

In Sections 5.1 and 5.2 we describe methods that use 2PL and T/O techniques for both rw and ww synchronization. The concurrency control methods in these sections are easy to describe given the material of Sections 3 and 4; the description of each method is little more than a description of each component technique. In Section 5.3 we list 24 concurrency control methods that combine 2PL and T/O techniques. As we show in Section 5.3, methods of this type have useful properties that cannot be attained by pure 2PL or T/O methods.

5.1 Pure 2PL Methods

The 2PL synchronization techniques of Section 3 can be integrated to form 12 *principal 2PL methods*:

Method	rw technique	ww technique
1	Basic 2PL	Basic 2PL
2	Basic 2PL	Primary copy 2PL
3	Basic 2PL	Voting 2PL
4	Basic 2PL	Centralized 2PL
5	Primary copy 2PL	Basic 2PL
6	Primary copy 2PL	Primary copy 2PL
7	Primary copy 2PL	Voting 2PL
8	Primary copy 2PL	Centralized 2PL
9	Centralized 2PL	Basic 2PL
10	Centralized 2PL	Primary copy 2PL
11	Centralized 2PL	Voting 2PL
12	Centralized 2PL	Centralized 2PL

Each method can be further refined by the choice of deadlock resolution technique (see Section 3.5).

The interface between each 2PL rw technique and each 2PL ww technique is straightforward. It need only guarantee that "two-phasedness" is preserved, meaning that *all* locks needed for both the rw and ww technique must be obtained before any lock is released by *either* technique.

5.1.1 Methods Using Basic 2PL for rw Synchronization

Methods 1–4 use basic 2PL for rw synchronization. Consider a logical data item X with copies $x_1, \ldots, x_m$. To read X, a transaction sends a dm-read to *any* DM that stores a copy of X. This dm-read implicitly requests a readlock on the copy of X at that DM. To write X, a transaction sends prewrites to *every* DM that stores a copy of X. These prewrites implicitly request writelocks on the corresponding copies of X. For all four methods, these writelocks conflict with *readlocks* on the same copy, and may also conflict with other *writelocks* on the same copy, depending on the specific ww synchronization technique used by the method.

Since locking conflict rules for writelocks will vary from copy to copy, we distinguish three types. An *rw writelock* only conflicts with readlocks on the same data item. A *ww writelock* only conflicts with ww writelocks on the same data item. And an *rww writelock* conflicts with readlocks, ww writelocks, and rww writelocks. Thus, using basic 2PL for rw synchronization, every prewrite sets rw writelocks, and may set stronger locks depending on the ww technique.

Method 1: *Basic* 2*PL for ww synchronization.* All writelocks are rww writelocks; that is, for $i = 1, \ldots, m$, a writelock on x_i conflicts with either a readlock or a writelock on x_i. This is the "standard" distributed implementation of 2PL.

Method 2: *Primary copy* 2*PL for ww synchronization.* Writelocks only conflict on the primary copy. An rww writelock is used on the primary copy, while rw writelocks are used on the others.

Method 3: *Voting* 2*PL for ww synchronization.* A DM responds to a prewrite(x_i) by *attempting* to set an rww writelock on x_i. However, if another transaction already owns an rww writelock on x_i, the DM only sets an rw writelock and leaves a request for an rww writelock pending. A transaction can write into any copy of X after it obtains rww writelocks on a majority of copies. This is similar to the method proposed in GIFF79.

Method 4: *Centralized* 2*PL for ww synchronization.* To write into X, a transaction must first explicitly request a ww writelock on X from a centralized 2PL scheduler. The rw writelocks set by prewrites *never* conflict with each other.

In all four methods, readlocks are explicitly released by lock releases while writelocks are implicitly released by dm-writes. Lock releases may be transmitted in parallel with dm-writes. In Method 4, *after all* dm-writes have been executed, additional lock releases must be sent to the centralized scheduler to release writelocks held there.

5.1.2 Methods Using Primary Copy 2PL for rw Synchronization

Methods 5–8 use primary copy 2PL for rw synchronization. Consider a logical data item X with copies $x_1, \ldots, x_m$, and assume x_1 is the primary copy. To read X, a transaction must obtain a readlock on x_1. It may obtain this lock by issuing a dm-read(x_1). Alternatively, the transaction can send an explicit lock request to x_1's DM; when the lock is granted the transaction can read *any* copy of X.

To write into X, a transaction sends prewrites to *every* DM that stores a copy of X. A prewrite(x_1) implicitly requests an rw writelock. Prewrites on other copies of X may also request writelocks depending on the ww technique.

Method 5: *Basic* 2*PL for ww synchronization.* For $i = 2, \ldots, m$, prewrite(x_i) requests a ww writelock. Since the writelock on x_1 must also conflict with readlocks on x_1, prewrite(x_1) requests an rww writelock.

Method 6: *Primary copy* 2*PL for ww synchronization.* Prewrite(x_1) requests an rww writelock on x_1. Prewrites on other copies do not request any locks. This method was originally proposed by STON79 and is used in Distributed INGRES [STON77].

Method 7: *Voting* 2*PL for ww synchronization.* When a scheduler receives a prewrite(x_i) for $i \neq 1$, it tries to set a ww writelock on x_i. When it receives a prewrite(x_1), it tries to set an rww writelock on x_1; if it cannot, then it sets an rw writelock on x_1 (if possible) before waiting for the rww writelock. A transaction can write into every copy of X after it obtains a ww (or rww) writelock on a majority of copies of X.

Method 8: *Centralized* 2*PL for ww synchronization.* Transactions obtain ww writelocks from a centralized 2PL scheduler. Thus a prewrite(x_1) requests an rw writelock on x_1; for $i = 2, \ldots, m$, prewrite(x_i) does not request any lock.

Lock releases for Methods 5–8 are handled as in Section 5.1.1.

5.1.3 Methods Using Centralized 2PL for rw Synchronization

The remaining 2PL methods use centralized 2PL for rw synchronization. Before reading (or writing) any copy of logical data item X, a transaction must obtain a readlock (or rw writelock) on X from a centralized 2PL scheduler. Before writing X, the transaction must also send prewrites to every DM that stores a copy of X. Some of these prewrites implicitly request ww writelocks on copies of X, depending on the specific method.

Method 9: *Basic 2PL for ww synchronization.* Every prewrite requests a ww writelock.

Method 10: *Primary copy 2PL for ww synchronization.* If x_1 is the primary copy of X, a prewrite(x_1) requests a ww writelock. Prewrites on other copies do not request any writelocks.

Method 11: *Voting 2PL for ww synchronization.* Every prewrite *attempts* to set a ww writelock. A transaction can write into every copy of X after it obtains ww writelocks on a majority of copies of X.

Method 12: *Centralized 2PL for ww synchronization.* All locks are obtained at the centralized 2PL scheduler. Before writing into any copy of X, an rww writelock on X is obtained from the centralized scheduler. Prewrites set no locks at all. Method 12 is the "standard" implementation of centralized 2PL (called *primary site* in ALSB76a).

Lock releases for Methods 9–12 are handled as in Section 5.1.1.

5.2 Pure T/O Methods

The T/O synchronization techniques of Section 5 can also be integrated to form 12 *principal T/O methods*:

Method	rw technique	ww technique
1	Basic T/O	Basic T/O
2	Basic T/O	Thomas Write Rule (TWR)
3	Basic T/O	Multiversion T/O
4	Basic T/O	Conservative T/O
5	Multiversion T/O	Basic T/O
6	Multiversion T/O	TWR
7	Multiversion T/O	Multiversion T/O
8	Multiversion T/O	Conservative T/O
9	Conservative T/O	Basic T/O
10	Conservative T/O	TWR
11	Conservative T/O	Multiversion T/O
12	Conservative T/O	Conservative T/O

(That there are also 12 2PL methods is coincidental.)

Each T/O method that incorporates a conservative component can be refined by including classes and conflict graph analysis (see Sections 4.4.2 and 4.4.3).

The interface between rw and ww synchronization techniques is even simpler for T/O methods than for 2PL. The only requirement is that both techniques use the *same* timestamp for any given transaction.

5.2.1 Methods Using Basic T/O for rw Synchronization

Methods 1–4 use basic T/O for rw synchronization. All four methods require R-ts's for each data item. Methods 1, 2, and 4 require W-ts's, while in Method 3 each data item has a set of timestamped versions; for Method 3, let W-ts(x) denote x's largest timestamp. Each method buffers dm-reads and prewrites for two-phase commitment purposes; let min-R-ts(x) and min-P-ts(x) be the minimum timestamps of any buffered dm-read(x) and prewrite(x), respectively.

These methods can be described by the following steps. Let R be a dm-read(x), P a prewrite(x), and W a dm-write(x).

1. If ts(R) $<$ W-ts(x), R is rejected. Else if ts(R) $>$ min-P-ts(x), R is buffered. Else R is output and R-ts(x) is set to max(R-ts(x), ts(R)).
2. If ts(P) $<$ R-ts(x) or *condition (A)*[6] holds, P is rejected. Else P is buffered.
3. If ts(W) $>$ min-R-ts(x) or *condition (B)*[6] holds, W is buffered. Else W is output and W-ts(x) is set to max(W-ts(x), ts(W)). For Method 3, a new version of x is created with timestamp ts(W).
4. When W is output, its prewrite is debuffered and the buffered dm-reads and dm-writes are retested to see if any can now be output.

Method 1: *Basic T/O for ww synchronization.* Condition (A) is ts(P) $<$ W-ts(x) and condition (B) is ts(W) $>$ min-P-ts(x). Note that min-R-ts(x) $>$ min-P-ts(x), since R is buffered only if ts(R) $>$ min-P-ts(x). Also, when W is output, ts(W) $>$ W-ts(x), since condition (B) forces dm-writes on a given x to be output in timestamp order. Thus step 3 simplifies to

3. If ts(W) $>$ min-P-ts(x), W is buffered. Else W is output and W-ts(x) is set to ts(W).

Method 2: *TWR for ww synchronization.* Conditions (A) and (B) are null. However,

[6] Conditions (A) and (B) are determined by the new technique. See the following.

if ts(W) < W-ts(x), W has no effect on the database.

Method 3: *Multiversion T/O for ww synchronization.* Like Method 2 except that W always creates a new version of x.

Method 4: *Conservative T/O for ww synchronization.* Condition (A) is null. For each TM, let min-W-ts(TM) be the minimum timestamp of any buffered dm-write from that TM. Condition (B) is ts(W) > min-W-ts(TM) for some TM. As in Method 1, this causes dm-writes on a given x to be output in timestamp order, and step 3 simplifies to

3. If ts(W) > min-R-ts(x) or ts(W) > min-W-ts(TM) for some TM, W is buffered. Else W is output and W-ts(x) is set to ts(W).

5.2.2 Methods Using Multiversion T/O for rw Synchronization

Methods 5–8 use multiversion T/O for rw synchronization and require a set of R-ts's and a set of versions for each data item. These methods can be described by the following steps. Define R, P, W, min-R-ts, min-W-ts, and min-P-ts as above; let interval(P) be the interval from ts(P) to the smallest W-ts(x) > ts(P).

1. R is never rejected. If ts(R) lies in interval(prewrite(x)) for some buffered prewrite(x), then R is buffered. Else R is output and ts(R) is added to x's set of R-ts's.
2. If some R-ts(x) lies in interval(P) or *condition* (A) holds, then P is rejected. Else P is buffered.
3. If *condition* (B) holds, W is buffered. Else W is output and creates a new version of x with timestamp ts(W).
4. When W is output, its prewrite is debuffered, and buffered dm-reads and dm-writes are retested.

Method 5: *Basic T/O for ww synchronization.* Condition (A) is ts(P) < max-W-ts(x) and condition (B) is ts(W) > min-P-ts(x). Condition (A) implies that interval(P) = (ts(P), ∞); some R-ts(x) lies in that interval if and only if ts(P) < maximum R-ts(x). Thus step 2 simplifies to

2. If ts(P) < max W-ts(x) or ts(P) < max R-ts(x), then P is rejected. Else it is buffered.

Because of this simplification, the method only requires that the maximum R-ts(x) be stored.

Condition (B) forces dm-writes on a given data item to be output in timestamp order. This supports a systematic technique for "forgetting" old versions. Let max-W-ts(x) be the maximum W-ts(x) and let min-ts be the minimum of max-W-ts(x) over all data items in the database. No dm-write with timestamp less than min-ts can be output in the future. Therefore, insofar as update transactions are concerned, we can safely forget all versions timestamped less than min-ts. TMs should be kept informed of the current value of min-ts and queries (read-only transactions) should be assigned timestamps greater than min-ts. Also, after a new min-ts is selected, older versions should not be forgotten immediately, so that active queries with smaller timestamps have an opportunity to finish.

Method 6: *TWR for ww synchronization.* This method is *incorrect.* TWR requires that W be ignored if ts(W) < max W-ts(x). This may cause later dm-reads to be read incorrect data. See Figure 15. (Method 6 is the only incorrect method we will encounter.)

Method 7: *Multiversion T/O for ww synchronization.* Conditions (A) and (B) are null. Note that this method, unlike all previous ones, never buffers dm-writes.

Method 8: *Conservative T/O for ww synchronization.* Condition (A) is null. Condition (B) is ts(W) > min-W-ts(TM) for some TM. Condition (B) forces dm-writes to be output in timestamp order, implying interval(P) = (ts(P), ∞). As in Method 5, this simplifies step 2:

2. If ts(P) < max R-ts(x), P is rejected; else it is buffered.

Like Method 5, this method only requires that the maximum R-ts(x) be stored, and it supports systematic "forgetting" of old versions described above.

5.2.3 Methods Using Conservative T/O for rw Synchronization

The remaining T/O methods use conservative T/O for rw synchronization. Methods

- Consider data items x and y with the following versions:

- Now suppose T has timestamp 50 and writes $x := 50$, $y := 50$. Under Method 6 the update to x is ignored, and the result is

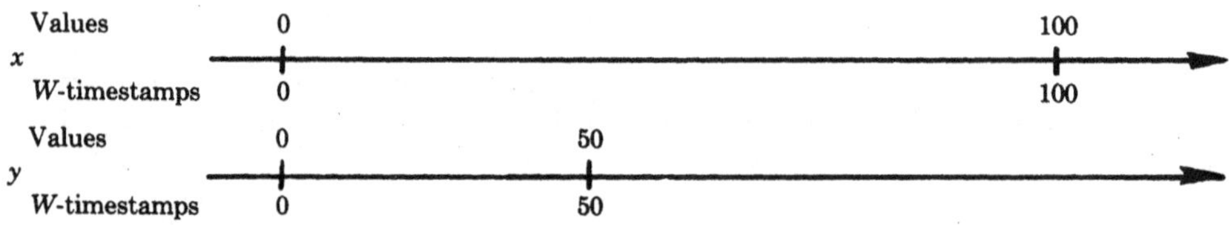

- Finally, suppose T′ has timestamp 75 and reads x and y. The values it will read are $x = 0, y = 50$, which is incorrect. T′ *should* read $x = 50$, $y = 50$.

Figure 15. Inconsistent retrievals in Method 6.

9 and 10 require W-ts's for each data item, and Method 11 requires a set of versions for each data item. Method 12 needs no data item timestamps at all. Define R, P, W and min-P-ts as in Section 5.2.1; let min-R-ts(TM) (or min-W-ts(TM)) be the minimum timestamp of any buffered dm-read (or dm-write) from TM.

1. If ts(R) > min-W-ts(TM) for any TM, R is buffered; else it is output.
2. If *condition (A)* holds, P is rejected. Else P is buffered.
3. If ts(W) > min-R-ts(TM) for any TM or *condition* (B) holds, W is buffered. Else W is output.
4. When W is output, its prewrite is debuffered. When R or W is output or buffered, buffered dm-reads and dm-writes are retested to see if any can now be output.

Method 9: *Basic T/O for ww synchronization.* Condition (A) is ts(P) < W-ts(x), and condition (B) is ts(W) > min-P-ts(x).

Method 10: *TWR for ww synchronization.* Conditions (A) and (B) are null. However, if ts(W) < W-ts(x), W has no effect on the database.

This method is essentially the SDD-1 concurrency control [BERN80d], although in SDD-1 the method is refined in several ways. SDD-1 uses classes and conflict graph analysis to reduce communication and increase the level of concurrency. Also, SDD-1 requires predeclaration of read-sets and only enforces the conservative scheduling on dm-reads. By doing so, it forces dm-reads to wait for dm-writes, but does not insist that dm-writes wait for all dm-reads with smaller timestamps. Hence dm-reads can be rejected in SDD-1.

Method 11: *Multiversion T/O for ww synchronization.* Conditions (A) and (B) are null. When W is output, it creates a new version of x with timestamp ts(W). When R is output it reads the version with largest timestamp less than ts(R).

This method can be optimized by noting the multiversion T/O "automatically" prevents dm-reads from being rejected, and makes it unnecessary to buffer dm-writes. Thus step 3 can be simplified to

3. W is output immediately.

Method 12: *Conservative T/O for ww synchronization.* Condition (A) is null; condition (B) is ts(W) > min-W-ts(TM) for some TM. The effect is to output W if the scheduler has received *all* operations with timestamps less than ts(W) that it will ever receive. Method 12 has been proposed in CHEN80, KANE79, and SHAP77a.

5.3 Mixed 2PL and T/O Methods

The major difficulty in constructing methods that combine 2PL and T/O lies in developing the interface between the two techniques. Each technique guarantees an acyclic $\rightarrow_{rwr}$ (or $\rightarrow_{ww}$) relation when used for rw (or ww) synchronization. The interface between a 2PL and a T/O technique must guarantee that the combined $\rightarrow$ relation (i.e., $\rightarrow_{rwr} \cup \rightarrow_{ww}$) remains acyclic. That is, the interface must ensure that the serialization order induced by the rw technique is consistent with that induced by the ww technique. In Section 5.3.1 we describe an interface that makes this guarantee. Given such an interface, *any* 2PL technique can be integrated with *any* T/O technique. Sections 5.3.2 and 5.3.3 describe such methods.

5.3.1 The Interface

The serialization order induced by any 2PL technique is determined by the locked points of the transactions that have been synchronized (see Section 3). The serialization order induced by any T/O technique is determined by the timestamps of the synchronized transactions. So to interface 2PL and T/O we *use locked points to induce timestamps* [BERN80b].

Associated with each data item is a *lock timestamp*, L-ts(x). When a transaction T sets a lock of x, it simultaneously retrieves L-ts(x). When T reaches its locked point it is assigned a timestamp, ts(T), greater than any L-ts it retrieved. When T releases its lock on x, it updates L-ts(x) to be max(L-ts(x), ts(T)).

Timestamps generated in this way are consistent with the serialization order induced by 2PL. That is, ts(T_j) < ts(T_k) if T_j must precede T_k in any serialization induced by 2PL. To see this, let T_1 and T_n be a pair of transactions such that T_1 must precede T_n in any serialization. Thus there exist transactions $T_1, T_2, \ldots, T_{n-1}, T_n$ such that for $i = 1, \ldots, n-1$ (a) T_i's locked point precedes T_{i+1}'s locked point, and (b) T_i released a lock on some data item x before T_{i+1} obtained a lock on x. Let L be the L-ts(x) retrieved by T_{i+1}. Then ts(T_i) < L < ts(T_{i+1}), and by induction ts(T_1) < ts(T_n).

5.3.2 Mixed Methods Using 2PL for rw Synchronization

There are 12 principal methods in which 2PL is used for rw synchronization and T/O is used for ww synchronization:

Method	rw technique	ww technique
1	Basic 2PL	Basic T/O
2	Basic 2PL	TWR
3	Basic 2PL	Multiversion T/O
4	Basic 2PL	Conservative T/O
5	Primary copy 2PL	Basic T/O
6	Primary copy 2PL	TWR
7	Primary copy 2PL	Multiversion T/O
8	Primary copy 2PL	Conservative T/O
9	Centralized 2PL	Basic T/O
10	Centralized 2PL	TWR
11	Centralized 2PL	Multiversion T/O
12	Centralized 2PL	Conservative T/O

Method 2 best exemplifies this class of methods, and it is the only one we describe in detail. Method 2 requires that every stored data item have an L-ts and a W-ts. (One timestamp can serve both roles, but we do not consider this optimization here.)

Let X be a logical data item with copies $x_1, \ldots, x_m$. To read X, transaction T issues a dm-read on any copy of X, say x_i. This dm-read implicitly requests a readlock on x_i, and when the readlock is granted, L-ts(x_i) is returned to T. To write into X, T issues prewrites on every copy of X. These prewrites implicitly request rw writelocks on the corresponding copies, and as each writelock is granted, the corresponding L-ts is returned to T. When T has obtained all of its locks, ts(T) is calculated as in Section 5.3.1. T attaches ts(T) to its dm-writes, which are then sent.

Dm-writes are processed using TWR. Let W be dm-write(x_j). If ts(W) > W-ts(x_j), the dm-write is processed as usual (x_j is updated). If, however, ts(W) < W-ts(x_j), W is *ignored*.

The interesting property of this method is that *writelocks never conflict with writelocks*. The writelocks obtained by prewrites are only used for rw synchronization, and only conflict with readlocks. This permits transactions to execute concurrently to completion even if their writesets intersect. Such concurrency is never possible in a pure 2PL method.

5.3.3 *Mixed Methods Using T/O for rw Synchronization*

There are also 12 principal methods that use T/O for rw synchronization and 2PL for ww synchronization:

Method	rw technique	ww technique
13	Basic T/O	Basic 2PL
14	Basic T/O	Primary copy 2PL
15	Basic T/O	Voting 2PL
16	Basic T/O	Centralized 2PL
17	Multiversion T/O	Basic 2PL
18	Multiversion T/O	Primary copy 2PL
19	Multiversion T/O	Voting 2PL
20	Multiversion T/O	Centralized 2PL
21	Conservative T/O	Basic 2PL
22	Conservative T/O	Primary copy 2PL
23	Conservative T/O	Voting 2PL
24	Conservative T/O	Centralized 2PL

These methods all require *predeclaration of writelocks.* Since T/O is used for rw synchronization, transactions must be assigned timestamps before they issue dm-reads. However, the timestamp generation technique of Section 5.3.1 requires that a transaction be at its locked point before it is assigned its timestamp. Hence every transaction must be at its locked point before it issues any dm-reads; in other words, every transaction must obtain all of its writelocks before it begins its main execution.

To illustrate these methods, we describe Method 17. This method requires that each stored data item have a set of R-ts's and a set of ⟨W-ts, value⟩ pairs (i.e., versions). The L-ts of any data item is the maximum of its R-ts's and W-ts's.

Before beginning its main execution, transaction T issues prewrites on every copy of every data item in its writeset.[7] These prewrites play a role in ww synchronization, rw synchronization, and the interface between these techniques.

Let P be a prewrite(x). The ww role of P is to request a ww writelock on x. When the lock is granted, L-ts(x) is returned to T; this is the interface role of P. Also when the lock is granted, P is buffered and the rw synchronization mechanism is informed that a dm-write with timestamp greater than L-ts(x) is pending. This is its rw role.

When T has obtained all of its writelocks, ts(T) is calculated as in Section 5.3.1 and T begins its main execution. T attaches ts(T) to its dm-reads and dm-writes and rw synchronization is performed by multiversion T/O, as follows:

1. Let R be a dm-read(x). If there is a buffered prewrite(x) (other than one issued by T), and if L-ts(x) < ts(T), then R is buffered. Else R is output and reads the version of x with largest timestamp less than ts(T).
2. Let W be a dm-write(x). W is output immediately and creates a new version of x with timestamp ts(T).
3. When W is output, its prewrite is debuffered, and its writelock on x is released. This causes L-ts(x) to be updated to max(L-ts(x), ts(T)) = ts(T).

One interesting property of this method is that restarts are needed only to prevent or break deadlocks caused by ww synchronization; rw conflicts never cause restarts. This property cannot be attained by a pure 2PL method. It can be attained by pure T/O methods, but only if conservative T/O is used for rw synchronization; in many cases conservative T/O introduces excessive delay or is otherwise infeasible.

The behavior of this method for queries is also interesting. Since queries set no writelocks, the timestamp generation rule does not apply to them. Hence *the system is free to assign any timestamp it wishes to a query.* It may assign a small timestamp, in which case the query will read old data but is unlikely to be delayed by buffered prewrites; or it may assign a large timestamp, in which case the query will read current data but is more likely to be delayed. No matter which timestamp is selected, however, *a query can never cause an update to be rejected.* This property cannot be easily attained by any pure 2PL or T/O method.

We also observe that this method creates versions in timestamp order, and so sys-

[7] Since new values for the data items in the writeset are not yet known, these prewrites do not instruct DMs to store values on secure storage; they merely "warn" DMs to "expect" the corresponding dm-writes. See footnote 3.

tematic forgetting of old versions is possible (see Section 5.2.2). In addition, the method requires only *maximum* R-ts's; smaller ones may be instantly forgotten.

CONCLUSION

We have presented a framework for the design and analysis of distributed database concurrency control algorithms. The framework has two main components: (1) a system model that provides common terminology and concepts for describing a variety of concurrency control algorithms, and (2) a problem decomposition that decomposes concurrency control algorithms into read-write and write-write synchronization subalgorithms.

We have considered synchronization subalgorithms outside the context of specific concurrency control algorithms. Virtually all known database synchronization algorithms are variations of two basic techniques—two-phase locking (2PL) and timestamp ordering (T/O). We have described the principal variations of each technique, though we do not claim to have exhausted all possible variations. In addition, we have described ancillary problems (e.g., deadlock resolution) that must be solved to make each variation effective.

We have shown how to integrate the described techniques to form complete concurrency control algorithms. We have listed 47 concurrency control algorithms, describing 25 in detail. This list includes almost all concurrency control algorithms described previously in the literature, plus several new ones. This extreme consolidation of the state of the art is possible in large part because of our framework set up earlier.

The focus of this paper has primarily been the *structure* and *correctness* of synchronization techniques and concurrency control algorithms. We have left open a very important issue, namely, performance.

The main performance metrics for concurrency control algorithms are system throughput and transaction response time. Four cost factors influence these metrics: intersite communication, local processing, transaction restarts, and transaction blocking. The impact of each cost factor on system throughput and response time varies from algorithm to algorithm, system to system, and application to application. This impact is not understood in detail, and a comprehensive quantitative analysis of performance is beyond the state of the art. Recent theses by Garcia-Molina [GARC79a] and Reis [REIS79a] have taken first steps toward such an analysis but there clearly remains much to be done.

We hope, and indeed recommend, that future work on distributed concurrency control will concentrate on the performance of algorithms. There are, as we have seen, many known methods; the question now is to determine which are best.

APPENDIX. OTHER CONCURRENCY CONTROL METHODS

In this appendix we describe three concurrency control methods that do not fit the framework of Sections 3–5: the certifier methods of Badal [BADA79], Bayer et al. [BAYE80], and Casanova [CASA79], the majority consensus algorithm of Thomas [THOM79], and the ring algorithm of Ellis [ELLI77]. We argue that these methods are not practical in DDBMSs. The certifier methods look promising for *centralized* DBMSs, but severe technical problems must be overcome before these methods can be extended correctly to distributed systems. The Thomas and Ellis algorithms, by contrast, are among the earliest algorithms proposed for DDBMS concurrency control. These algorithms introduced several important techniques into the field but, as we will see, have been surpassed by recent developments.

A1. Certifiers

A1.1 The Certification Approach

In the certification approach, dm-reads and prewrites are processed by DMs first-come/first-served, with no synchronization whatsoever. DMs do maintain summary information about rw and ww conflicts, which they update every time an operation is processed. However, dm-reads and prewrites are never blocked or rejected on the basis of the discovery of such a conflict.

Synchronization occurs when a transaction attempts to terminate. When a transaction T issues its END, the DBMS decides whether or not to *certify*, and thereby commit, T.

To understand how this decision is made, we must distinguish between "total" and "committed" executions. A *total execution* of transactions includes the execution of all operations processed by the system up to a particular moment. The *committed execution* is the portion of the total execution that only includes dm-reads and dm-writes processed on behalf of committed transactions. That is, the committed execution is the total execution that would result from aborting all active transactions (and not restarting them).

When T issues its END, the system tests whether the committed execution augmented by T's execution is serializable, that is, whether after committing T the resulting committed execution would still be serializable. If so, T is committed; otherwise T is restarted.

There are two properties of certification that distinguish it from other approaches. First, synchronization is accomplished entirely by restarts, never by blocking. And second, the decision to restart or not is made *after* the transaction has finished executing. No concurrency control method discussed in Sections 3–5 satisifies both these properties.

The rationale for certification is based on an optimistic assumption regarding run-time conflicts: if very few run-time conflicts are expected, assume that most executions are serializable. By processing dm-reads and prewrites without synchronization, the concurrency control method never delays a transaction while it is being processed. Only a (fast, it is hoped) certification test when the transaction terminates is required. Given optimistic transaction behavior, the test will usually result in committing the transaction, so there are very few restarts. Therefore certification simultaneously avoids blocking and restarts in optimistic situations.

A certification concurrency control method must include a *summarization algorithm* for storing information about dm-reads and prewrites when they are processed and a *certification algorithm* for using that information to certify transactions when they terminate. The main problem in the summarization algorithm is avoiding the need to store information about already-certified transactions. The main problem in the certification algorithm is obtaining a *consistent* copy of the summary information. To do so the certification algorithm often must perform some synchronization of its own, the cost of which must be included in the cost of the entire method.

A1.2 Certification Using the → Relation

One certification method is to construct the → relation as dm-reads and prewrites are processed. To certify a transaction, the system checks that → is acyclic [BADA79, BAYE80, CASA79].[8]

To construct →, each site remembers the most recent transaction that read or wrote each data item. Suppose transactions T_i and T_j were the last transactions to (respectively) read and write data item x. If transaction T_k now issues a dm-read(x), $T_j \rightarrow T_k$ is added to the summary information for the site and T_k replaces T_i as the last transaction to have read x. Thus pieces of → are distributed among the sites, reflecting run-time conflicts at each site.

To certify a transaction, the system must check that the transaction does not lie on a cycle in → (see Theorem 2, Section 2). Guaranteeing acyclicity is sufficient to guarantee serializability.

There are two problems with this approach. First, it is in general not correct to delete a certified transaction from →, even if all of its updates have been committed. For example, if $T_i \rightarrow T_j$ and T_i is active but T_j is committed, it is still possible for $T_j \rightarrow T_i$ to develop; deleting T_j would then cause the cycle $T_i \rightarrow T_j \rightarrow T_i$ to go unnoticed when T_i is certified. However, it is obviously not feasible to allow → to grow indefinitely. This problem is solved by Casanova [CASA79] by a method of encoding information about committed transactions in space proportional to the number of active transactions.

A second problem is that *all* sites must be checked to certify *any* transaction. Even

[8] In BAYE80 certification is only used for rw synchronization whereas 2PL is used for ww synchronization.

sites at which the transaction never accessed data must participate in the cycle checking of →. For example, suppose we want to certify transaction T. T might be involved in a cycle $T \rightarrow T_1 \rightarrow T_2 \rightarrow \cdots \rightarrow T_{n-1} \rightarrow T_n \rightarrow T$, where each conflict $T_k \rightarrow T_{k+1}$ occurred at a different site. Possibly T only accessed data at one site; yet the → relation must be examined at n sites to certify T. This problem is currently unsolved, as far as we know. That is, any *correct* certifier based on this approach of checking cycles in → must access the → relation at *all* sites to certify each and every transaction. Until this problem is solved, we judge the certification approach to be impractical in a distributed environment.

A2. Thomas' Majority Consensus Algorithm

A2.1 The Algorithm

One of the first published algorithms for distributed concurrency control is a certification method described in THOM79. Thomas introduced several important synchronization techniques in that algorithm, including the Thomas Write Rule (Section 3.2.3), majority voting (Section 3.1.1), and certification (Appendix A1). Although these techniques are valuable when considered in isolation, we argue that the overall Thomas algorithm is not suitable for distributed databases. We first describe the algorithm and then comment on its application to distributed databases.

Thomas' algorithm assumes a fully redundant database, with every logical data item stored at every site. Each copy carries the timestamp of the last transaction that wrote into it.

Transactions execute in two phases. In the first phase each transaction executes locally at one site called the transaction's *home site*. Since the database is fully redundant, any site can serve as the home site for any transaction. The transaction is assigned a unique timestamp when it begins executing. During execution it keeps a record of the timestamp of each data item it reads and, when its executes a write on a data item, processes the write by recording the new value in an *update list*. Note that each transaction must read a copy of a data item before it writes into it. When the transaction terminates, the system augments the update list with the list of data items read and their timestamps at the time they were read. In addition, the timestamp of the transaction itself is added to the update list. This completes the first phase of execution.

In the second phase the update list is sent to every site. Each site (including the site that produced the update list) *votes* on the update list. Intuitively speaking, a site votes yes on an update list if it can certify the transaction that produced it. After a site votes yes, the update list is said to be *pending* at that site. To cast the vote, the site sends a message to the transaction's home site, which, when it receives a majority of yes or no votes, informs all sites of the outcome. If a majority voted yes, then all sites are required to commit the update, which is then installed using TWR. If a majority voted no, all sites are told to discard the update, and the transaction is restarted.

The rule that determines when a site may vote "yes" on a transaction is pivotal to the correctness of the algorithm. To vote on an update list U, a site compares the timestamp of each data item in the readset of U with the timestamp of that same data item in the site's local database. If any data item has a timestamp in the database different from that in U, the site votes *no*. Otherwise, the site compares the readset and writeset of U with the readset and writeset of each pending update list at that site, and if there is no rw conflict between U and any of the pending update lists, it votes *yes*. If there is an rw conflict between U and one of those pending requests, the site votes *pass* (abstain) if U's timestamp is larger than that of all pending update lists with which it conflicts. If there is an rw conflict but U's timestamp is smaller than that of the conflicting pending update list, then it sets U aside on a *wait queue* and tries again when the conflicting request has either been committed or aborted at that site.

The voting rule is essentially a certification procedure. By making the timestamp comparison, a site is checking that the readset was not written into since the transaction read it. If the comparisons are satisfied, the situation is as if the transaction had locked its readset at that site and held the locks until it voted. The voting rule is thereby guaranteeing rw synchronization with a certification rule approximating rw 2PL. (This fact is proved precisely in BERN79b.)

The second part of the voting rule, in which U is checked for rw conflicts against pending update lists, guarantees that conflicting requests are not certified concurrently. An example illustrates the problem. Suppose T_1 reads X and Y, and writes Y, while T_2 reads X and Y, and writes X. Suppose T_1 and T_2 execute at sites A and B, respectively, and X and Y have timestamps of 0 at both sites. Assume that T_1 and T_2 execute concurrently and produce update lists ready for voting at about the same time. Either T_1 or T_2 must be restarted, since neither read the other's output; if they were both committed, the result would be nonserializable. However both T_1's and T_2's update lists will (concurrently) satisfy the timestamp comparison at both A and B. What stops them from both obtaining unanimous yes votes is the second part of the voting rule. After a site votes on one of the transactions, it is prevented from voting on the other transaction until the first is no longer pending. Thus it is not possible to certify conflicting transactions concurrently. (We note that this problem of concurrent certification exists in the algorithms of Section A1.2, too. This is yet another technical difficulty with the certification approach in a distributed environment.)

With the second part of the voting rule, the algorithm behaves as if the certification step were atomically executed at a primary site. If certification were centralized at a primary site, the certification step at the primary site would serve the same role as the majority decision in the voting case.

A2.2 Correctness

No simple proof of the serializability of Thomas' algorithm has ever been demonstrated, although Thomas provided a detailed "plausibility" argument in THOM79. The first part of the voting rule can correctly be used in a centralized concurrency control method since it implies 2PL [BERN79b], and a centralized method based on this approach was proposed in KUNG81. The second part of the voting rule guarantees that for every pair of conflicting transactions that received a majority of yes votes, all sites that voted yes on both transactions voted on the two transactions in the same order. This makes the certification step behave just as it would if it were centralized, thereby avoiding the problem exemplified in the previous paragraph.

A2.3 Partially Redundant Databases

For the majority consensus algorithm to be useful in a distributed database environment, it must be generalized to operate correctly when the database is only partially redundant. There is reason to doubt that such a generalization can be accomplished without either serious degradation of performance or a complete change in the set of techniques that are used.

First, the majority consensus decision rule apparently must be dropped, since the voting algorithm depends on the fact that all sites perform exactly the same certification test. In a partially redundant database, each site would only be comparing the timestamps of the data items stored at that site, and the significance of the majority vote would vanish.

If majority voting cannot be used to synchronize concurrent certification tests, apparently some kind of mutual exclusion mechanism must be used instead. Its purpose would be to prevent the concurrent, and therefore potentially incorrect, certification of two conflicting transactions, and would amount to locking. The use of locks for synchronizing the certification step is not in the spirit of Thomas' algorithm, since a main goal of the algorithm was to avoid locking. However, it is worth examining such a locking mechanism to see how certification can be correctly accomplished in a partially redundant database.

To process a transaction T, a site produces an update list as usual. However, since the database is partially redundant, it may be necessary to read portions of T's readset from other sites. After T terminates, its update list is sent to every site that contains part of T's readset or writeset. To certify an update list, a site first sets local locks on the readset and writeset, and then (as in the fully redundant case) it compares the update list's timestamps with the database's timestamps. If they are identical, it votes yes; otherwise it votes no. A unanimous vote of yes is needed to commit the updates. Local locks cannot be released until the voting decision is completed.

While this version of Thomas' algorithm for partially redundant data works correctly, its performance is inferior to standard 2PL. This algorithm requires that the same locks be set as in 2PL, and the same deadlocks can arise. Yet the probability of restart is higher than in 2PL, because even after all locks are obtained the certification step can still vote no (which cannot happen in 2PL).

One can improve this algorithm by designating a primary copy of each data item and only performing the timestamp comparison against the primary copy, making it analogous to primary copy 2PL. However, for the same reasons as above, we would expect primary copy 2PL to outperform this version of Thomas' algorithm too.

We therefore must leave open the problem of producing an efficient version of Thomas' algorithm for a partially redundant database.

A2.4 Performance

Even in the fully redundant case, the performance of the majority consensus algorithm is not very good. First, repeating the certification and conflict detection at each site is more than is needed to obtain serializability: a centralized certifier would work just as well and would only require that certification be performed at one site. Second, the algorithm is quite prone to restarts when there are run-time conflicts, since restarts are the only tactic available for synchronizing transactions, and so will only perform well under the most optimistic circumstances. Finally, even in optimistic situations, the analysis in GARC79a indicates that centralized 2PL outperforms the majority consensus algorithm.

A2.5 Reliability

Despite the performance problems of the majority consensus algorithm, one can try to justify the algorithms on reliability grounds. As long as a majority of sites are correctly running, the algorithm runs smoothly. Thus, handling a site failure is free, insofar as the voting procedure is concerned.

However, from current knowledge, this justification is not compelling for several reasons. First, although there is no cost when a site fails, substantial effort may be required when a site recovers. A centralized algorithm using backup sites, as in ALSB76a, lacks the symmetry of Thomas' algorithm, but may well be more efficient due to the simplicity of site recovery. In addition, the majority consensus algorithm does not consider the problem of atomic commitment and it is unclear how one would integrate two-phase commit into the algorithm.

Overall, the reliability threats that are handled by the majority consensus algorithm have not been explicitly listed, and alternative solutions have not been analyzed. While voting is certainly a possible technique for obtaining a measure of reliability, the circumstances under which it is cost-effective are unknown.

A3. Ellis' Ring Algorithm

Another early solution to the problem of distributed database concurrency control is the ring algorithm [ELLI77]. Ellis was principally interested in a proof technique, called *L systems*, for proving the correctness of concurrent algorithms. He developed his concurrency control method primarily as an example to illustrate L-system proofs, and never made claims about its performance. Because the algorithm was only intended to illustrate mathematical techniques, Ellis imposed a number of restrictions on the algorithm for mathematical convenience, which make it infeasible in practice. Nonetheless, the algorithm has received considerable attention in the literature, and in the interest of completeness, we briefly discuss it.

Ellis' algorithm solves the distributed concurrency control problem with the following restrictions:

(1) The database must be fully redundant.
(2) The communication medium must be a ring, so each site can only communicate with its successor on the ring.

(3) Each site-to-site communication link is pipelined.
(4) Each site can supervise no more than one active update transaction at a time.
(5) To update any copy of the database, a transaction must first obtain a lock on the entire database at all sites.

The effect of restriction 5 is to force all transactions to execute *serially*; no concurrent processing is ever possible. For this reason alone, the algorithm is fundamentally impractical.

To execute, an update transaction migrates around the ring, (essentially) obtaining a lock *on the entire database at each site*. However, the lock conflict rules are nonstandard. A lock request from a transaction that originated at site A conflicts at site C with a lock held by a transaction that originated from site B if B = C and either A = B or A's priority < B's priority. The daisy-chain communication induced by the ring combined with this locking rule produces a deadlock-free algorithm that does not require deadlock detection and never induces restarts. A detailed description of the algorithm appears in GARC79a.

There are several problems with this algorithm in a distributed database environment. First, as mentioned above, it forces transactions to execute serially. Second, it only applies to a fully redundant database. And third, the daily-chain communication requires that each transaction obtain its lock at one site at a time, which causes communication delay to be (at least) linearly proportional to the number of sites in the system.

A modified version of Ellis' algorithm that mitigates the first problem is proposed in GARC79a. Even with this improvement, performance analysis indicates that the ring algorithm is inferior to centralized 2PL. And, of course, the modified algorithm still suffers from the last two problems.

ACKNOWLEDGMENT

This work was supported by Rome Air Development Center under contract F30602-79-C-0191.

REFERENCES

AHO75 AHO, A. V., HOPCROFT, E., AND ULLMAN, J. D. *The design and analysis of computer algorithms*, Addison-Wesley, Reading, Mass., 1975.

ALSB76a ALSBERG, P. A., AND DAY, J. D. "A principle for resilient sharing of distributed resources," in *Proc. 2nd Int. Conf. Software Eng.*, Oct. 1976, pp. 562–570.

ALSB76b ALSBERG, P. A., BELFORD, G.C., DAY, J. D., AND GRAPLA, E. "Multi-copy resiliency techniques," Center for Advanced Computation, AC Document No. 202, Univ. Illinois at Urbana-Champaign, May 1976.

BADA78 BADAL, D. Z., AND POPEK, G. J. "A proposal for distributed concurrency control for partially redundant distributed data base system," in *Proc. 3rd Berkeley Workshop Distributed Data Management and Computer Networks*, 1978, pp. 273–288.

BADA79 BADAL, D. Z. "Correctness of concurrency control and implications in distributed databases," in *Proc. COMPSAC 79 Conf.*, Chicago, Ill., Nov. 1979.

BADA80 BADAL, D. Z. "On the degree of concurrency provided by concurrency control mechanisms for distributed databases," in *Proc. Int. Symp. Distributed Databases*, Versailles, France, March 1980.

BAYE80 BAYER, R., HELLER, H., AND REISER, A. "Parallelism and recovery in database systems," *ACM Trans. Database Syst.* **5**, 2 (June 1980), 139–156.

BELF76 BELFORD, G. C., SCHWARTZ, P. M., AND SLUIZER, S. "The effect of back-up strategy on database availability," CAC Document No. 181, CCTCWAD Document No. 5515, Center for Advanced Computation, Univ. Illinois at Urbana-Champaign, Urbana, Feb. 1976.

BERN78a BERNSTEIN, P. A., GOODMAN, N., ROTHNIE, J. B., AND PAPADIMITRIOU, C. A. "The concurrency control mechanism of SDD-1: A system for distributed databases (the fully redundant case)," *IEEE Trans. Softw. Eng.* **SE-4**, 3 (May 1978), 154–168.

BERN79a BERNSTEIN, P. A., AND GOODMAN, N. "Approaches to concurrency control in distributed databases," in *Proc. 1979 Natl. Computer Conf.*, AFIPS Press, Arlington, Va., June 1979.

BERN79b BERNSTEIN, P. A., SHIPMAN, D. W., AND WONG, W. S. "Formal Aspects of Serializability in Database Concurrency Control," *IEEE Trans. Softw. Eng.* **SE-5**, 3 (May 1979), 203–215.

BERN80a BERNSTEIN, P. A., AND GOODMAN, N. "Timestamp based algorithms for concurrency control in distributed database systems," *Proc. 6th Int. Conf. Very Large Data Bases*, Oct. 1980.

BERN80b BERNSTEIN, P. A., GOODMAN, N., AND LAI, M. Y. "Two Part Proof Schema for Database Concurrency Control," in *Proc. 5th Berkeley Workshop Distributed Data Management and Computer Networks*, Feb. 1980.

BERN80c BERNSTEIN, P. A., AND SHIPMAN, D. W. "The correctness of concurrency control mechanisms in a system for distributed databases (SDD-1)," in *ACM Trans. Database Syst.* **5**, 1 (March 1980), 52–68.

BERN80d BERNSTEIN, P., SHIPMAN, D. W., AND ROTHNIE, J. B. "Concurrency control in a system for distributed databases (SDD-1)," in *ACM Trans. Database Syst.* **5**, 1 (March 1980), 18–51.

BERN81 BERNSTEIN, P. A., GOODMAN, N., WONG, E., REEVE, C. L., AND ROTHNIE, J. B. "Query processing in SDD-1," *ACM Trans. Database Syst.* **6**, 2, to appear.

BREI79 BREITWIESER, H., AND KERSTEN, U. "Transaction and catalog management of the distributed file management system DISCO," in *Proc. Very Large Data Bases*, Rio de Janerio, 1979.

BRIN73 BRINCH-HANSEN, P. *Operating system principles*, Prentice-Hall, Englewood Cliffs, N. J., 1973.

CASA79 CASANOVA, M. A. "The concurrency control problem for database systems," Ph.D. dissertation, Harvard Univ.; Tech. Rep. TR-17-79, Center for Research in Computing Technology, 1979.

CHAM74 CHAMBERLIN, D. D., BOYCE, R. F., AND TRAIGER, I. L. "A deadlock-free scheme for resource allocation in a database environment," *Info. Proc.* **74**, North-Holland, Amsterdam, 1974.

CHEN80 CHENG, W. K., AND BELFORD, G. C. "Update Synchronization in Distributed Databases," in *Proc. 6th Int. Conf. Very Large Data Bases*, Oct. 1980.

DEPP76 DEPPE, M. E., AND FRY, J. P. "Distributed databases: A summary of research," in *Computer networks*, vol. 1, no. 2, North-Holland, Amsterdam, Sept. 1976.

DIJK71 DIJKSTRA, E. W. "Hierarchical ordering of sequential processes," *Acta Inf.* **1**, 2 (1971), 115–138.

ELLI77 ELLIS, C. A. "A robust algorithm for updating duplicate databases," in *Proc. 2nd Berkeley Workshop Distributed Databases and Computer Networks*, May 1977.

ESWA76 ESWARAN, K. P., GRAY, J. N., LORIE, R. A., AND TRAIGER, I. L. "The notions of consistency and predicate locks in a database system." *Commun. ACM* **19**, 11 (Nov. 1976), 624–633.

GARC78 GARCIA-MOLINA, H. "Performance comparisons of two update algorithms for distributed databases," in *Proc. 3rd Berkeley Workshop Distributed Databases and Computer Networks*, Aug. 1978.

GARC79a GARCIA-MOLINA, H. "Performance of update algorithms for replicated data in a distributed database," Ph.D. dissertation, Computer Science Dept., Stanford Univ., Stanford, Calif., June 1979.

GARC79b GARCIA-MOLINA, H. "A concurrency control mechanism for distributed data bases which use centralized locking controllers," in *Proc. 4th Berkeley Workshop Distributed Databases and Computer Networks*, Aug. 1979.

GARC79c GARCIA-MOLINA, H. "Centralized control update algorithms for fully redundant distributed databases," in *Proc. 1st Int. Conf. Distributed Computing Systems* (IEEE), New York, Oct. 1979, pp. 699–705.

GARD77 GARDARIN, G., AND LEBAUX, P. "Scheduling algorithms for avoiding inconsistency in large databases," in *Proc. 1977 Int. Conf. Very Large Data Bases* (IEEE), New York, pp. 501-516.

GELE78 GELEMBE, E., AND SEVCIK, K. "Analysis of update synchronization for multiple copy databases," in *Proc. 3rd Berkeley Workshop Distributed Databases and Computer Networks*, Aug. 1978.

GIFF79 GIFFORD, D. K. "Weighted voting for replicated data," in *Proc. 7th Symp. Operating Systems Principles*, Dec. 1979.

GRAY75 GRAY, J. N., LORIE, R. A., PUTZULO, G. R., AND TRAIGER, I. L. "Granularity of locks and degrees of consistency in a shared database," IBM Res. Rep. RJ1654, Sept. 1975.

GRAY78 GRAY, J. N. "Notes on database operating systems," in *Operating Systems: An Advanced Course*, vol. 60, *Lecture Notes in Computer Science*, Springer-Verlag, New York, 1978, pp. 393–481.

HAMM80 HAMMER, M. M., AND SHIPMAN, D. W. "Reliability mechanisms for SDD-1: A system for distributed databases," *ACM Trans. Database Syst.* **5**, 4 (Dec. 1980), 431–466.

HEWI74 HEWITT, C. E. "Protection and synchronization in actor systems," Working Paper No. 83, M.I.T. Artificial Intelligence Lab., Cambridge, Mass., Nov. 1974.

HOAR74 HOARE, C. A. R. "Monitors. An operating system structuring concept," *Commun. ACM* **17**, 10 (Oct. 1974), 549–557.

HOLT72 HOLT, R. C. "Some deadlock properties of computer systems," *Comput. Surv.* **4**, 3 (Dec. 1972) 179–195.

KANE79 KANEKO, A., NISHIHARA, Y., TSURUOKA, K., AND HATTORI, M. "Logical clock synchronization method for duplicated database control," in *Proc. 1st Int. Conf. Distributed Computing Systems* (IEEE), New York, Oct. 1979, pp. 601–611.

KAWA79 KAWAZU, S., MINAMI, ITOH, S., AND TERANAKA, K. "Two-phase deadlock detection algorithm in distributed databases," in *Proc. 1979 Int. Conf. Very Large Data Bases* (IEEE), New York.

KING74 KING, P. F., AND COLLMEYER, A. J. "Database sharing—an efficient method for supporting concurrent processes," in *Proc. 1974 Nat. Computer Conf.*, vol. 42, AFIPS Press, Arlington, Va., 1974.

KUNG79 KUNG, H. T., AND PAPADIMITRIOU, C. H. "An optimality theory of concurrency control for databases," in *Proc. 1979*

ACM-SIGMOD Int. Conf. Management of Data, June 1979.

KUNG81 KUNG, H. T., AND ROBINSON, J. T. "On optimistic methods for concurrency control," *ACM Trans. Database Syst.* **6**, 2, (June 81), 213–226.

LAMP76 LAMPSON, B., AND STURGIS, H. "Crash recovery in a distributed data storage system," Tech. Rep., Computer Science Lab., Xerox Palo Alto Research Center, Palo Alto, Calif., 1976.

LAMP78 LAMPORT, L. "Time, clocks and ordering of events in a distributed system," *Commun. ACM* **21**, 7 (July 1978), 558–565.

LELA78 LELANN, G. "Algorithms for distributed data-sharing sytems which use tickets," in *Proc. 3rd Berkeley Workshop Distributed Databases and Computer Networks*, Aug. 1978.

LIN79 LIN, W. K. "Concurrency control in multiple copy distributed data base system," in *Proc. 4th Berkeley Workshop Distributed Data Management and Computer Networks*, Aug. 1979.

MENA79 MENASCE, D. A., AND MUNTZ, R. R. "Locking and deadlock detection in distributed databases," *IEEE Trans. Softw. Eng.* **SE-5**, 3 (May 1979), 195–202.

MENA80 MENASCE, D. A., POPEK, G. J., AND MUNTZ, R. R. "A locking protocol for resource coordination in distributed databases," *ACM Trans. Database Syst.* **5**, 2 (June 1980), 103–138.

MINO78 MINOURA, T. "Maximally concurrent transaction processing," in *Proc. 3rd Berkeley Workshop Distributed Databases and Computer Networks*, Aug. 1978.

MINO79 MINOURA, T. "A new concurrency control algorithm for distributed data base systems," in *Proc. 4th Berkeley Workshop Distributed Data Management and Computer Networks*, Aug. 1979.

MONT78 MONTGOMERY, W. A. "Robust concurrency control for a distributed information system," Ph.D. dissertation, Lab. for Computer Science, M.I.T., Cambridge, Mass., Dec. 1978.

PAPA77 PAPADIMITRIOU, C. H., BERNSTEIN, P. A., AND ROTHNIE, J. B. "Some computational problems related to database concurrency control," in *Proc. Conf. Theoretical Computer Science*, Waterloo, Ont., Canada, Aug. 1977.

PAPA79 PAPADIMITRIOU, C. H. "Serializability of concurrent updates," *J. ACM* **26**, 4 (Oct. 1979), 631–653.

RAHI79 RAHIMI, S. K., AND FRANTS, W. R. "A posted update approach to concurrency control in distributed database systems," in *Proc. 1st Int. Conf. Distributed Computing Systems* (IEEE), New York, Oct. 1979, pp. 632–641.

RAMI79 RAMIREZ, R. J., AND SANTORO, N. "Distributed control of updates in multiple-copy data bases: A time optimal algorithm," in *Proc. 4th Berkeley Workshop Distributed Data Management and Computer Networks*, Aug. 1979.

REED78 REED, D. P. "Naming and synchronization in a decentralized computer system, Ph.D. dissertation, Dept. of Electrical Engineering, M.I.T., Cambridge, Mass., Sept., 1978.

REIS79a REIS, D. "The effect of concurrency control on database management system performance," Ph.D. dissertation, Computer Science Dept., Univ. California, Berkeley, April 1979.

REIS79b REIS, D. "The effects of concurrency control on the performance of a distributed database management system," in *Proc. 4th Berkeley Workshop Distributed Data Management and Computer Networks*, Aug. 1979.

ROSE79 ROSEN, E. C. "The updating protocol of the ARPANET's new routing algorithm: A case study in maintaining identical copies of a changing distributed data base," in *Proc. 4th Berkeley Workshop Distributed Data Management and Computer Networks*, Aug. 1979.

ROSE78 ROSENKRANTZ, D. J., STEARNS, R. E., AND LEWIS, P. M. "System level concurrency control for distributed database systems," *ACM Trans. Database Syst.* **3**, 2 (June 1978), 178–198.

ROTH77 ROTHNIE, J. B., AND GOODMAN, N. "A survey of research and development in distributed databases systems," in *Proc. 3rd Int. Conf. Very Large Data Bases* (IEEE), Tokyo, Japan, Oct. 1977.

SCHL78 SCHLAGETER, G. "Process synchronization in database systems." *ACM Trans. Database Syst.* **3**, 3 (Sept. 1978), 248–271.

SEQU79 SEQUIN, J., SARGEANT, G., AND WILNES, P. "A majority consensus algorithm for the consistency of duplicated and distributed information," in *Proc. 1st Int. Conf. Distributed Computing Systems* (IEEE), New York, Oct. 1979, pp. 617–624.

SHAP77a SHAPIRO, R. M., AND MILLSTEIN, R. E. "Reliability and fault recovery in distributed processing," in *Oceans '77 Conf. Record*, vol. II, Los Angeles, 1977.

SHAP77b SHAPIRO, R. M., AND MILLSTEIN, R. E. "NSW reliability plan," Massachusetts Tech. Rep. 7701-1411, Computer Associates, Wakefield, Mass., June 1977.

SILB80 SILBERSCHATZ, A., AND KEDEM, Z. "Consistency in hierarchical database systems," *J. ACM* **27**, 1 (Jan. 1980), 72–80.

STEA76 STEARNS, R. E., LEWIS, P. M. II, AND ROSENKRANTZ, D. J. "Concurrency controls for database systems," in *Proc. 17th Symp. Foundations Computer Science* (IEEE), 1976, pp. 19–32.

STEA81 STEARNS, R. E., AND ROSENKRANTZ, J. "Distributed database concurrency controls using fore-values," in *Proc. 1981 SIGMOD Conf.* (ACM).

STON77 STONEBRAKER, M., AND NEUHOLD, E. "A distributed database version of INGRES," in *Proc. 2nd Berkeley Workshop Distributed Data Management and Computer Networks*, May 1977.

STON79 STONEBRAKER, M. "Concurrency control and consistency of multiple copies of data in distributed INGRES, *IEEE Trans. Softw. Eng.* **SE-5,** 3 (May 1979), 188–194.

THOM79 THOMAS, R. H. "A solution to the concurrency control problem for multiple copy databases," in *Proc. 1978 COMPCON Conf.* (IEEE), New York.

VERH78 VERHOFSTAD, J. S. M. "Recovery and crash resistance in a filing system," in *Proc. SIGMOD Int. Conf. Management of Data* (ACM), New York, 1977, pp. 158–167.

A Partial Index of References

1. *Certifiers*: BADA79, BAYE80, CASA79, KUNG81, PAPA79, THOM79
2. *Concurrency control theory*: BERN79b, BERN80c, CASA79, ESWA76, KUNG79, MINO78, PAPA77, PAPA79, SCHL78, SILB80, STEA76
3. *Performance*: BADA80, GARC78, GARC79a, GARC79b, GELE78, REIS79a, REIS79b, ROTH77
4. *Reliability*
   General: ALSB76a, ALSB76b, BELF76, BERN79a, HAMM80, LAMP76
   Two-phase commit: HAMM80, LAMP76
5. *Timestamp-ordered scheduling (T/O)*
   General: BADA78, BERN78a, BERN80a, BERN80b, BERN80d, LELA78, LIN79, RAMI79
   Thomas' Write Rule: THOM79
   Multiversion timestamp ordering: MONT78, REED78
   Timestamp and clock management: LAMP78, THOM79
6. *Two-phase locking (2PL)*
   General: BERN79b, BREI79, ESWA76, GARD77, GRAY75, GRAY78, PAPA79, SCHL78, SILB80, STEA81
   Distributed 2PL: MENA80, MINO79, ROSE78, STON79
   Primary copy 2PL: STON77, STON79
   Centralized 2PL: ALSB76a, ALSB76b, GARC79b, GARC79c
   Voting 2PL: GIFF79, SEQU79, THOM79
   Deadlock detection/prevention: GRAY78, KING74, KAWA79, ROSE78, STON79

Received April 1980; final revision accepted February 1981.

A Survey of Techniques for Synchronization and Recovery in Decentralized Computer Systems

WALTER H. KOHLER

Corporate Research Group, Digital Equipment Corporation and Department of Electrical and Computer Engineering, University of Massachusetts, Amherst, Massachusetts

Two related and fundamental problems in designing decentralized systems which support an object model of computation are introduced, and proposed solution techniques are surveyed. The first problem is synchronizing access to shared objects while allowing a high degree of concurrency. The second is the recovery of objects in spite of user errors, application errors, or partial system failure. The synchronization problem is a generalization of the concurrency control problem which arises in database and transaction-processing systems. Concurrency control methods which use locking, timestamps, circulating permit, tickets, conflict analysis, and reservations are presented and compared. The proposed approach to solving the recovery problem is based on a software structuring abstraction called the atomic action, a type of generalized transaction. Requirements and techniques for implementing atomic actions in a decentralized environment are discussed.

Keywords and Phrases: decentralized system, object model, access synchronization, concurrency control, crash recovery, atomic action

CR Categories: 4.32, 4.33, 4.35

INTRODUCTION

During the 1980s the marriage of computers and communications will play an increasingly important role in the automation of service and manufacturing industries. Business forecasters project that electronic funds transfer will revolutionize banking, word processing and electronic mail will become commonplace in the office environment, and sophisticated robots will join, if not control, production lines. All of these typically benefit from the emerging distributed processing technology. As essential production, distribution, and service functions are automated, business can be halted by the failure of critical systems. The high economic cost of system failure has already created a significant demand for fault-tolerant, general-purpose computer systems [BART77, KATZ77].

This paper is a survey of techniques that have been proposed to address two fundamental problems in the design of reliable decentralized computer systems: (1) *synchronization of access* to shared objects while supporting a high degree of concurrency, and (2) *recovery of objects* in spite of user errors, application errors, or partial system failure. While these problems must be treated in the design of all complex multiserver systems, they are of particular interest in decentralized systems that must reliably support distributed data-management applications [ROTH80, ECKH78, PEEB78, SHAP78, RAND78].

Randell, Lee, and Treleaven have recently surveyed the issues involved in achieving high reliability from complex computing systems [RAND78]. Their definitions help to distinguish between relia-

CONTENTS

bility and availability, and among failures, errors, and faults. They state that

> The *reliability* of a system is taken to be a measure of the success with which the system conforms to some authoritative specification of its behavior. Without such specification, nothing can be said about the reliability of the system. When the behavior deviates from that which is specified for it, this is called a *failure*. A failure is thus an event, with the reliability of the system being inversely related to the frequency of such events. Various formal measures related to a system's *reliability* can be based on the actual (or predicted) incidence of failures, and their consequences. ... These measures include Mean Time Between Failures (MTBF), Mean Time To Repair (MTTR), and *availability*, that is, the fraction of the time that a system meets its specification.... We term an internal state of a system an *erroneous state* when the state is such that there exist circumstances (within the specification of the use of the system) in which further processing, by the normal algorithms of the system, will lead to a failure which we do not attribute to a subsequent fault. ... The term *error* is used to designate that part of the state which is incorrect. ... A *fault* is the mechanical or algorithmic cause of an error, while a *potential fault* is a mechanical or algorithmic construction within a system such that (under some circumstances within the specification of the system) the construction will cause the system to assume an erroneous state.... We hope it will now be clear that the generality of our definitions of failure and fault enables the notion of fault to encompass design inadequacies such as a mistaken choice of component, a misunderstood or inadequate specification (of either the component or the service required from the system), or an incorrect interrelationship among components (such as wrong or missing interconnections in the case of hardware systems, or a program bug in software systems), as well as, say, hardware component failure due to aging....
>
> The significance of the distinction between faults and errors may be seen by considering the repair of a database system. Repair of a fault may consist of the replacement of a failing program (or hardware) component by a correctly functioning one. Repair of an error requires that the information in the database be changed from its currently erroneous state to one which will permit the correct operation of the system. In most systems, recovery from errors is required, but repair of faults which cause these errors, although very desirable, is not necessarily essential for continued operation. [RAND78, pp. 126, 127]

The authors point out that it can be very difficult to attribute a given failure to a specific fault, since a detected error is only a symptom of the fault that caused it. This is particularly true of software faults stemming from unmastered complexity in the system design. As discussed later, reliability of a physical system can never be proved formally and a perfectly reliable system can never be achieved. We must be content with developing hardware and software techniques for improving reliability.

In this survey we do not review all the standard techniques for improving the fault tolerance of computer systems; this material has been comprehensively treated by Randell et al. [RAND78]. We instead focus on those software structuring techniques that can be used to achieve error recovery in decentralized systems.

We assume the now-popular model of a decentralized system as consisting of a loose confederacy of cooperating autonomous nodes supporting an object-oriented model of computation [PEEB78, SALT78, JONE79, WATS79]. An *object* is any passive element of a computation whose state can only be modified by members of a well-defined set of *operations* or *functions*. The behavior of an object is completely determined by its set of permissible operations. Jones [JONE79] uses the example of an elevator as an abstract object on which only three operations are defined: install, which initializes its state, and up and down, used by passengers to change floors. As in programming methodology, objects with the same set of defined operations are said to constitute a *type*. In the operating-system context, named objects are generally associated with memory segments, and access is controlled by means of a capability. We assume that objects can be referenced by a unique systemwide name. (Mechanisms for supporting this functionality, though a topic of current research, are beyond the scope of this survey.) The encapsulation provided by the object abstraction appears to be a promising approach to the design of fault-tolerant and protected operating systems [DENN76].

In the object model all computation is performed by invoking *functions* on *objects*. A form of abstraction, called *aggregation* in the database literature, provides a natural means of building high-level abstract objects and functions from lower level primitives [LEDG77, SMIT77a, SMIT77b]. This is related to the layered system approach advocated by operating system designers, where every layer interface can be represented by a collection of abstract objects and possible operations on them. Information on the internal structure of the objects and operations is inaccessible to their users.

Our model of a decentralized system is consistent with the class of systems Enslow calls "distributed data processing systems" [ENSL78]. The nodes are typically individual processors with their own local set of data and computational resources to control. These nodes are interconnected by a communications network to enable applications to share, with the support of a unified high-level network operating system, distributed data and computational resources. Network operating systems are an active topic of current research, with a significant portion of the work being directed toward the support of distributed data management [BERN78, GARC79, GRAY79, HAMM78, LAMP76, LAMP79, LELA78, LIN79, MENA79, MILE79, PEEB78, PEEB80, REED78, REED79b, ROSE78, ROTH80, SHAP78, STON79, THOM79, WATS79].

In the next section we develop a more precise statement of the synchronization and recovery problems that are of interest. This is followed by two sections containing surveys of techniques relevant to the solution of these problems.

1. STATEMENT OF PROBLEMS

The term *synchronization* is used to refer to the solution of either of two distinct but related problems:

(1) specification and control of the joint activity of cooperating sequential processes, or
(2) serialization of concurrent access to shared objects by multiple processes.

Since cooperating sequential processes can be synchronized by means of mutually exclusive operations on a common data object, proposed solutions frequently address both problems.

Conventional programming-language and operating-system solutions to the specification and control problem include semaphores, conditional critical regions, and monitors. Event counts, synchronizers, path expressions, and object managers are proposed new approaches compatible with the object model. The latter two have been reviewed by Lagally for use in the context of a layered distributed system of cooperating sequential processes [LAGA79]. Event counts and sequencers were recently formalized by Reed and Kanodia [REED79a], and Lomet showed that a simple wait operation on a Boolean expression of synchronizing variables was adequate [LOME77].

We, however, concentrate on the second problem, the serialization of access to objects by multiple processes, also referred to in the database literature as concurrency control.

1.1 Concurrency Control

The term *transaction*, in database circles, is used to describe a sequence of operations on one or more database objects (files, records, etc.) that transforms a current consistent state of the system into a new consistent state [ESWA76]. When a valid transaction completes successfully, the new state of the database is by this definition *consistent*. Assertions regarding the valid interrelationships among object values could in theory be used to define a set of formal

```
Initial Balance in Accounts
   A contains a balance of $200
   B contains a balance of $100
   C contains a balance of $50

Transactions
   T1
      begin
   1    read account A obtaining A-Balance
   2    read account B obtaining B-Balance
   3    write A_Balance - $100 to account A
   4    write B_Balance + $100 to account B
      end
   T2
      begin
   1    read account B obtaining B_Balance
   2    read account C obtaining C_Balance
   3    write B-Balance - $50 to account B
   4    write C-Balance + $50 to account C
      end
```

Figure 1. Concurrent transactions.

consistency constraints. Proposed changes to the database then could be checked against these constraints before they are accepted. However, in real systems it is possible that the constraints cannot be checked, specified, or known by the database system or even by the application program.

During the processing of a transaction, before all changes have been made, the consistency constraints may not be satisfied. For example, during a transaction that moves money from one bank account to another there will be some time during which one account has been debited and the other not yet credited. In general, therefore, other transactions that involve the modified objects must be prevented from executing until the in-progress transaction is complete and a consistent state is guaranteed.

To understand the problems associated with running transactions concurrently, consider a simple system used to maintain checking account balances. Suppose there are three accounts (objects) called *A*, *B*, and *C*, which initially contain balances of $200, $100, and $50, respectively. There are two transactions, T1 and T2, to be processed. T1 is designed to transfer $100 from account *A* to account *B* and T2 is designed to transfer $50 from account *B* to account *C*. The situation is illustrated in Figure 1.

The obvious consistency constraint is that the sum of the account balances must be constant and in this example equal to $350. Although when considered alone both T1 and T2 preserve consistency, they have the following properties [ESWA76]:

- *Temporary Inconsistency.* After the first write operation of T1 or T2, the sum of the account balances is inconsistent.
- *Conflict.* If transaction T2 is scheduled to run between the first and second write operations of T1, then the sum of the account balances will be set to $400 rather than $350, which comprises an inconsistent state.

Temporary inconsistency is inherent in all sequential computations, and for this reason consistency requirements cannot generally be enforced before the end of a transaction. However, conflict can and must be avoided to achieve consistency.

One solution would be to require transactions to run serially, that is, one at a time in any order. Since each transaction when run alone is assumed to take a consistent state into a new consistent state, the final state after a sequence of two or more transactions must also be consistent. However, this prohibits the temporal interleaving of transaction steps and may thereby severely reduce performance.

We are interested in synchronization techniques which will enable nonconflicting steps to be interleaved so that transactions can proceed with maximal concurrency. The interleaved ordering of the steps of a set of transactions is called a *schedule.* Following Eswaran et al., a schedule which gives each transaction a consistent view of the state is called a *consistent schedule* [ESWA76]. A sufficient condition for a schedule to be a consistent schedule is that the effect of running the schedule is the same as if the transactions had been run serially. A consistent schedule satisfying this condition is called a *serializable* or *linearized schedule* [BERN79, ROSE78].

One example of a serializable schedule for the banking transactions just intro-

Time	Transaction	Step	Action
1	T1	1	**read** *account A obtaining A_Balance*
2	T2	1	**read** *account B obtaining B_Balance*
3	T2	2	**read** *account C obtaining C_Balance*
4	T2	3	**write** *B_Balance* – $50 *to account B*
5	T1	2	**read** *account B obtaining B_Balance*
6	T2	4	**write** *C_Balance* + $50 *to account C*
7	T1	3	**write** *A_Balance* – $100 *to account A*
8	T1	4	**write** *B_Balance* + $100 *to account B*

Figure 2. Serializable schedule.

duced is given in Figure 2. For further discussion and formal analysis of the problem of consistency in a transaction environment, refer to the papers by Eswaran et al. [Eswa76] and Bernstein, Shipman, and Wong [Bern79].

The concurrency control problem is a special case of the deadlock problem associated with shared serially reusable resources [Coff71]. In addition to being deadlock-free, a schedule must also preserve consistency. Techniques similar to those used to solve the deadlock problem (avoidance, detection and recovery, and prevention) can be used to solve the concurrency control problem. As an indication of the difficulty of the general problem, Papadimitrio has shown that the problem of determining whether an arbitrary schedule is serializable is NP-complete [Papa70].

The literature dealing with concurrency control generally considers the problem from either a general operating-system perspective (physical and logical resources) or from a database transaction-processing perspective (database entities). In the latter case, objects are database entities directly associated with physical or logical records or files; the basic operations on these objects are read and write.

While we are interested in designing mechanisms that support extensible objects and operations, the concurrency control techniques proposed for current database systems are relevant and represent our current level of knowledge. We survey these approaches in Section 2, but first we provide background information on the related problem of object recovery.

1.2 Atomic Actions and Recovery

An abstraction that is central to the structuring of fault-tolerant systems involving multiple interacting processes is the *atomic action*. Lomet was the first to formalize the concept [Lome77], but he points out that ideas similar to atomic actions had been suggested earlier by Dijkstra and Brinch Hansen for general computations and by Eswaran et al. [Eswa76] for a transaction-processing environment. Lampson and Sturgis [Lamp76] developed a similar approach to crash recovery, apparently independently.

The important properties of atomic actions were first stated in three equivalent ways by Lomet and later expanded by Randell to the following four:

> 1. An action is atomic if the process (processes) performing it is (are) not aware of the existence of any other active processes, and no other process is aware of the activity of the process (processes) during the time the process is (processes are) performing the action.
> 2. An action is atomic if the process (processes) performing it does (do) not communicate with other processes while the action is being performed.
> 3. An action is atomic if the process (processes) performing it can detect no state changes except those performed by itself (themselves) and if it does (they do) not reveal its (their) state changes until the action is complete.
> 4. Actions are atomic if they can be considered, so far as other processes are concerned, to be indivisible and instantaneous, such that the effects on the system are as if they were interleaved as opposed to concurrent. [Rand79, pp. 299, 300]

The concept of atomic action in the context of system structuring was described by Reed [Reed79b] as a "computation that, although composed of primitive computational steps executed at different times and in different places, cannot be decomposed from the point of view of computations outside of the atomic action. Intermediate states of data objects that arise during the execution of atomic actions... will never be observed by computations outside of the atomic action." Lomet proposed a programming construct called an *action procedure* to express an operation that is to be performed as an atomic action [LOME77]. As later pointed out by Randell [RAND79], an atomic action is a generalization of the concept of transaction introduced by database designers.

Atomic actions may involve multiple processes since a process executing an atomic action may temporarily create one or more processes for assistance. It is important to recognize that "atomicity" must be viewed as relative rather than absolute in the sense that high-level atomic actions may be built from lower ones. The critical constraint is that all constituent atomic operations be hierarchically nested.

The relevance of atomic actions to the design of fault-tolerant systems is that they provide a simple conceptual framework for error detection and recovery. It follows from the definition of atomic action that if a failure occurs which prevents the successful completion of an atomic action, then the state of all objects that the atomic action has modified must be restored to their state prior to the atomic action. Randell terms this *backward error recovery* [RAND79]. Otherwise, failures would allow intermediate states of objects resulting from partial execution to be observable by processes outside the atomic action [REED79b]. It is the job of the synchronization mechanism to prohibit access to the objects by other independent atomic actions until recovery is completed.

Randell [RAND75], Anderson and Lee [ANDE76], Anderson, Lee, and Shrivastava [ANDE78], Shrivastava and Banatre [SHRI78], and others associated with the Computing Laboratory at the University of Newcastle-upon-Tyne, England, have investigated extensively a related backward error recovery mechanism (the recovery block) for centralized systems. A *recovery block* is a program structure for adding software redundancy, in the form of standby spares, to computer programs. If an error is detected by a programmer-defined consistency check, the computation is rolled back to an earlier state and then continued, using an alternate algorithm.

Verhofstad has surveyed the standard recovery mechanisms used in database systems [VERH78]. Rather than attempt to duplicate that material, we encourage the reader to consult the original article. The overview article by Randell et al. [RAND78] provides additional background information on reliability issues in computer system design.

Techniques that have been proposed for implementing atomic actions in decentralized systems are discussed in Section 3; Section 2 concentrates on proposed solutions to the synchronization problem.

2. SYNCHRONIZATION TECHNIQUES

Given that the system has not failed, all concurrency control mechanisms must ensure that

(1) consistency of objects is preserved, and
(2) each atomic action is completed in finite time.

In addition, a good concurrency control mechanism for decentralized systems should

(1) be resilient to node and communication network failure,
(2) permit parallelism to the extent necessary to satisfy system performance requirements,
(3) incur modest computational and storage overhead,
(4) perform satisfactorily in a network environment that has significant communication delay, and
(5) place few constraints on the structure of the atomic actions.

Below we describe, and to some extent evaluate, the major approaches that have been used or proposed to solve the concurrency control problem in transaction-processing systems, a special case of our more general environment. Although many of these methods are hybrids, for the purpose of discussion they have been divided into five categories according to their most distinguishing feature: locking, timestamps, circulating permit and tickets, conflict analysis, and reservations.

2.1 Locking

Most solutions to the access synchronization problem are based on some explicit or implicit *locking* scheme [EswA76, GRAY79]. A transaction or atomic action may lock objects to ensure their inaccessibility while in a temporarily inconsistent state. In the simplest case each object has a unique lock which is held by at most one transaction at a time. (The case of shared access is discussed later.) If a transaction attempts to lock an object that is already locked, it must either wait, abort itself, or preempt the other transaction. (Each object already locked and modified by an aborted or preempted transaction must be restored to the state it was in prior to the transaction's beginning. Then it can be unlocked.) When two or more transactions are waiting, they may be involved in a deadlock. Deadlock is resolved by preempting at least one of the transactions. Methods for representing, detecting, and avoiding deadlock are reviewed later in this section.

In an environment where each transaction can potentially modify any object it accesses, Eswaran et al. [EswA76] have proved that all transactions must be well-formed and two-phase in order to guarantee consistency. A transaction is well-formed if it

(1) locks an object before accessing it,
(2) does not lock an object which is already locked, and
(3) before it completes, unlocks each object it locked.

It is *two-phase* if no object is unlocked before all objects are locked.

Consider the transaction example of Figure 1 as modified in Figure 3 to include explicit *lock* and *unlock* operations. Although *lock* and *unlock* operations are shown here as part of the *user-level* code, some transaction-processing systems automatically generate these requests at the *system level* in response to user *read* and *write* requests. Observe that both transactions are well-formed and two-phase.

Transactions

```
T1
    begin
      lock account A
      read account A obtaining A_Balance
      lock account B
      read account B obtaining B_Balance
      write A_Balance - $100 to account A
      unlock account A
      write B_Balance + $100 to account B
      unlock account B
    end

T2
    begin
      lock account B
      read account B obtaining B_Balance
      lock account C
      read account C obtaining C_Balance
      write B_Balance - $50 to account B
      unlock account B
      write C_Balance + $50 to account C
      unlock account C
    end
```

Figure 3. Well-formed, two-phase transactions.

The *lock* and *unlock* operations impose an additional constraint on the interleaving of transaction steps to form a schedule: in particular, a schedule is *legal* only if it does not lock an object currently locked by some other transaction. Consistent legal schedules can be constructed dynamically by observing the lock protocol that a transaction attempting to lock an already locked object must wait.

For the purpose of illustration, the *lock* operation is divided into two actions, *request* and *assignment.* Figure 4 shows a legal consistent schedule. Note that the request by transaction T1 at time 7 to lock account *B* is not granted until after transaction T2 unlocks account *B* at time 12; in the interim, transaction T1 must wait. The assignments and waiting requests at time 10 are illustrated by the resource allocation graph of Figure 5. Objects and transactions are represented by nodes, lock requests by directed arcs from transaction nodes to object nodes, and lock assignments by directed arcs from object nodes to transaction nodes.

The assignment edge from resource *B* to transaction T2 will disappear at time 12, and the request edge from T1 to *B* will change to an assignment edge from *B* to T1

Time	Transaction	Step	Action
1	T1	1A	**request lock** *account A*
2	T2	1A	**request lock** *account B*
3	T1	1B	**assigned lock** *account A*
4	T2	1B	**assigned lock** *account B*
5	T1	2	**read** *account A obtaining A_Balance*
6	T2	2	**read** *account B obtaining B_Balance*
7	T1	3A	**request lock** *account B*
8	T2	3A	**request lock** *account C*
9	T2	3B	**assigned lock** *account C*
10	T2	4	**read** *account C obtaining C_Balance*
11	T2	5	**write** *B_Balance* – $50 *to account B*
12	T2	6	**unlock** *account B*
13	T1	3B	**assigned lock** *account B*
14	T1	4	**read** *account B obtaining B_Balance*
15	T2	7	**write** *C_Balance* + $50 *to account C*
16	T1	5	**write** *A_Balance* – $100 *to account A*
17	T2	8	**unlock** *account C*
18	T1	6	**unlock** *account A*
19	T1	7	**write** *B_Balance* + $100 *to account B*
20	T1	8	**unlock** *account B*

Figure 4. A legal consistent schedule.

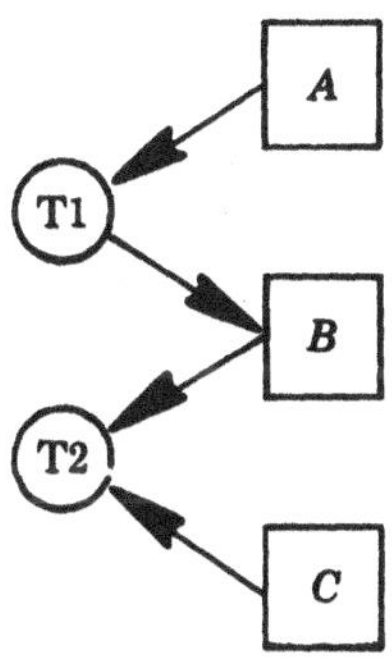

Figure 5. Resource allocation graph.

at time 13. Under different schedules T1 will be required to wait for T2, or vice versa, but they will never be deadlocked waiting for one another. Deadlock cannot occur in this example but is examined later in this section.

We can now illustrate how a global concurrency control mechanism based on local locking can be implemented in a distributed environment. Suppose that our system consists of two nodes, N1 and N2, and that account objects *A* and *B* used in Figure 3 are located on node N1 and account object *C* is on node N2. Each node has a local lock manager which controls the locks associated with objects stored at that site. Since transactions must *lock* objects before accessing them, transaction T1 must communicate with the local lock manager at node N1 to request and obtain locks on account objects *A* and *B*. Transaction T2 must communicate with the lock manager at node N1 to request and obtain the lock on account *B* and the lock manager at N2 to request and obtain the lock on account *C*.

When a lock manager grants (assigns) a lock to a transaction, it gives the transaction exclusive access to the object until the lock is released by an *unlock* operation. After obtaining all required locks, a transaction can read and modify objects without any interference from other transactions. Once all locks are obtained, we assume that each transaction will complete in some finite but not necessarily bounded time and release (unlock) all locks that it holds.

Some interleaved legal schedules for concurrent transactions may lead to deadlock. In a distributed system which uses local lock managers, the managers must cooperate to detect global deadlock. Deadlock has been shown to be equivalent to a cycle in the system allocation graph in which each request edge is followed by an assignment edge [COFF71, RYPK79]. In this case two or more transactions are blocked, each waiting

```
T3
   begin
     lock account C
     read account C obtaining C_Balance
     lock account A
     read account A obtaining A_Balance
     write C_Balance - $25 to account C
     write A_Balance + $25 to account A
     unlock account C
     unlock account A
   end
```

Figure 6. Additional transaction.

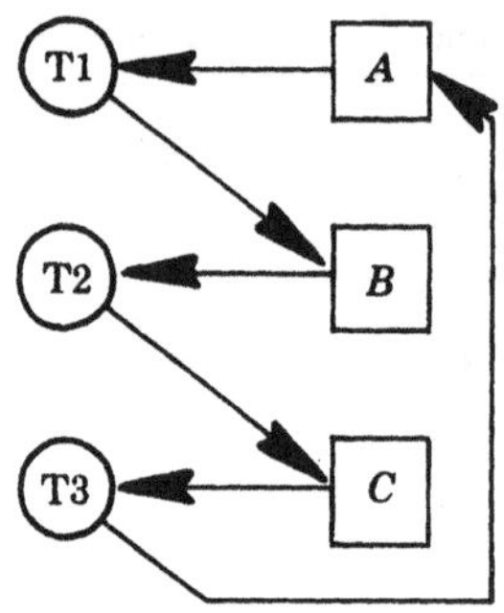

Figure 7. Deadlock situation.

for another blocked transaction to release a lock.

A third transaction is added to our example to illustrate this situation. Transaction T3 of Figure 6 is designed to transfer $25 from account *C* to account *A*. Schedules in which each transaction locks its first object before any lock their second will produce deadlock, as depicted in Figure 7.

Deadlock detection schemes based on algorithms for locating cycles in a centralized allocation graph are well known, and recent research by Menasce and Muntz [MENA79] has shown one way to implement this approach in a decentralized environment without maintaining a centralized graph. Gligor and Shattuck [GLIG80] have shown that many of the proposed "distributed protocols" for deadlock detection, including that of Menasce and Muntz, are in fact incorrect. And although it is possible to correct them, their poor performance then renders them impractical. Once deadlock is detected, the cycle may be broken by preempting one or more transactions. Under the assumption that the cost of preempting each member of a set of deadlocked actions is known, the problem of selecting a minimum total-cost deadlock-breaking set has been shown to be NP-complete [LEUN79].

Deadlock can also be broken by using *time-outs* to revoke waits after a specified time interval. However, in practice it may be difficult to pick a workable time-out interval. When a wait is revoked, the waiting transaction is rolled back before it is restarted. (As discussed in Section 3, rollback (also called backup) involves first restoring the prior state of all objects the transaction has already modified and then unlocking each object the transaction has locked.) As the time-out interval is made shorter, more transactions that are not deadlocked will be restarted unnecessarily. As the time-out interval is made longer, more time will be wasted by deadlocked transactions before being timed out and restarted. Furthermore, as the system becomes more congested more time-outs occur, which in turn adds to further congestion.

Distributed INGRES, a proposed distributed version of a relational database system developed and implemented by researchers at the University of California at Berkeley, will use a form of distributed locking. Concurrency control will be done by local locking and deadlock controllers which cooperate with a centralized controller (the SNOOP) for global deadlock detection [STON79].

Garcia-Molina discusses a different concurrency control mechanism for distributed databases which uses an independent centralized locking controller for each replicated fragment of data [GARC79]. The proposed mechanism is based on a two-phase commit protocol for performing updates. (Two-phase commit is discussed in Section 3.2.) It is designed to preserve database consistency and continue to operate in spite of node and controller failure. Global deadlock must be detected and eliminated by some additional mechanism. Alsberg and Day [ALSB76], Ellis [ELLI77], and Lampson and Sturgis [LAMP76] were among the first to propose techniques for reliably updating multiple copy databases.

The major disadvantage of deadlock detection methods is that the objects held by preempted transactions must be backed up to their original consistent state. To avoid unnecessary backup, deadlock avoidance methods can sometimes be used. These usually require transactions to preclaim all objects that will be accessed before any are assigned [RYPK79]. In these systems the possibility of deadlock is determined before the objects are assigned, and only safe assignments are granted. Preclaiming strategies reduce the possibility of concurrency and are not feasible in environments where the objects to be accessed are computed dynamically. This is particularly true for systems designed to support concurrent user transactions that are allowed to query and update objects interactively. SDD-1 is a distributed database system which takes advantage of application knowledge to precompute conflict [BERN78], but, although it reduces the cost of synchronization, it does not limit the type of transactions that can be accepted. This is discussed in Section 2.3.

Rosenkrantz, Stearns, and Lewis have pointed out that deadlock is only one of four possible cases in which a transaction may wait forever [ROSE78]:

(1) deadlock,
(2) infinite chain of distinct waiting transactions,
(3) waiting for a transaction that runs forever,
(4) waiting for an infinite number of new transactions, each of which completes or aborts.

(In the second case an infinite chain of waits occurs if one transaction waits for a second, which waits for a third, etc., and the number increases without limit as new transactions enter the system.) Although we do not discuss this further, an acceptable control algorithm must be guaranteed to eliminate all four possibilities.

An important issue that has not yet been discussed is the choice of *lockable objects* and their relationship to one another. So far we have treated objects as independent entities representing a common level of abstraction. However, the power of the object model as a system-structuring technique is based on its ability to support multiple levels of abstraction. For example, consider a specific bank customer object consisting of a specific savings account object, a specific checking account object, and a specific loan account object. An operation, such as an automatic loan payment, may need to lock the entire customer object in order to first transfer money from the checking account to pay the loan and then transfer money from the savings account to the checking account if the checking account balance is below some prespecified minimum. Other operations may only need to lock a single component from several different customer objects, as in the case of a check written by customer X to be deposited in customer Y's savings account.

In many cases a low-level object will be part of more than one high-level object. The savings account object for customer X is part of a customer X object, as well as an object consisting of all savings accounts at a particular bank. Database designers would say that the model must simultaneously support multiple *views* of the data objects.

Figure 8 shows one possible relationship between the following objects: bank customers, bank checking accounts, bank savings accounts, bank loan accounts, customer X, customer Y, checking account X, checking account Y, savings account X, savings account Y, and loan account X. The illustration is an example of a directed acyclic graph (dag). Directed edges connect high-level objects to lower level components.

Gray, Lorie, and Putzolu have proposed a method for locking objects that are organized as simple hierarchies (trees) or general dags [GRAY75, GRAY79]. Their goal was to achieve efficient locking at several granularities by implicitly locking entire subtrees or subgraphs. When an object is locked, all component objects that are descendants of the object are locked implicitly. They introduced the concept of an *intention mode* lock to signify that locking is being done at a lower level. All ancestors of a node to be locked are first "tagged" in intention mode. If an ancestor is found to be locked already by another transaction, the request will not be granted.

For example, in order to lock checking account X in Figure 8, the following higher level objects must first be tagged in inten-

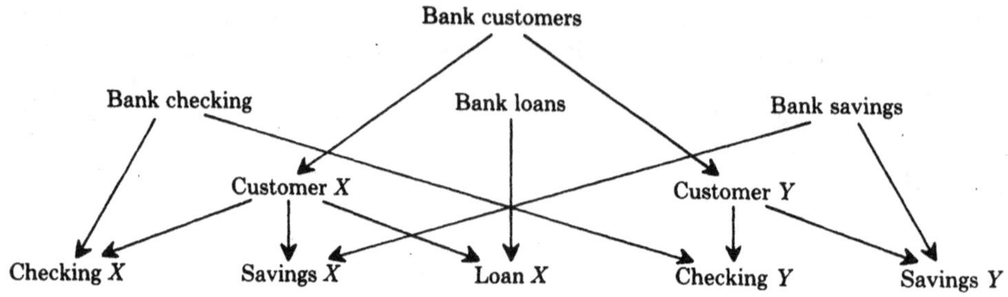

Figure 8. Graph representation of object relationships.

tion mode: customer X, bank customers, and bank checking. The lock will not be granted if any one of the higher level components is already locked. The intention mode tag is used to prevent transactions from locking objects which contain locked components; if customer X is tagged in intention mode, then a request to lock customer X would be denied since it has a locked component.

Silberschatz and Kedem have recently examined hierarchical locking of records in a database environment where records are organized as nodes of a tree [SILB80]. Their model differs from that of Gray et al. in that they assume that all locking is done at the record level and descendants of locked nodes are not locked implicitly when an ancestor is locked. This model does not conveniently support the notion of layered abstraction.

Ries and Stonebraker used a simulation model to examine the effects of locking granularity in the performance of a centralized database system [RIES79]. They ran a series of simulations to compare computer utilization as a function of lock granularity (as measured by the percent of the database locked by each lock operation). The sensitivity of these results to the placement of locks (number needed to cover all entities to be locked), the lock request strategy (preclaim or dynamic acquisition), and the lock hierarchy (single or two-level) were investigated. They concluded that the optimum granularity is application-dependent and gave guidelines for choosing between fine and coarse granularity or a two-level hierarchy. Since the simulation model is based on many simplifying assumptions and has not been validated by comparison with any real system, their results should be accepted with caution.

Table 1. Mode Compatibility

	Mode of current lock	
Mode of request	Share	Exclusive
Share	Compatible	Conflict
Exclusive	Conflict	Conflict

So far we have assumed that an object has a unique lock which is held by at most one transaction at a time. Additional requests are handled by either waiting or aborting, or preempting another transaction. However, in some cases concurrency can be increased without sacrificing consistency by permitting multiple transactions to hold a lock. Lock requests for the same object by different transactions are said to be *compatible* if they can be granted concurrently while preserving consistency [GRAY75, GRAY79, RYPK79]. In database and transaction-processing systems the concept of *mode* is used to specify a class of permitted uses of an object. Compatibilities among modes derive from their semantics. For example, the simplest extension would involve only two modes, share and exclusive. Objects locked in *share* mode are assumed to be locked for the purpose of reading only, while objects locked in *exclusive* mode can be read or modified. Compatibility among these two modes is shown in Table 1.

If a transaction re-requests the same object in the same or a new mode, this is called a *conversion* and is handled in much the same way as a new request. One mode is said to be *convertible* to another if the first may be transformed to the second

Table 2. Mode Convertibility

Mode of request	Mode of current lock	
	Share	Exclusive
Share	Compatible	Compatible
Exclusive	Conflict	Compatible

without violating the compatibility relations that hold for the first.

Convertibility in the case of share and exclusive modes is shown in Table 2. In this case an object locked in share mode by a transaction can be relocked in share mode but not in exclusive mode, whereas an object locked in exclusive mode can be relocked in either. For a more complete treatment of the problem in a database environment, including the case of intention mode and hierarchical locking, refer to the excellent work by Gray et al. [GRAY75, GRAY79]. In a more general object environment that includes functions other than read and write, modes and mode compatibility will be more difficult to specify and control.

Eswaran et al. have analyzed an alternate locking method called *predicate locks*, in which all objects whose values satisfy a specified predicate are locked implicitly [ESWA76]. To return to our example, all bank charge accounts with a balance below zero might constitute a predicate. When a set of locks is requested (by specifying a new predicate), all existing predicates must be tested for possible conflict. The general problem of determining conflicts is known to be recursively unsolvable, and consequently practical systems must be restricted to use a class of simple predicates for which conflict can be tested easily. This method appears to have sufficiently severe practical limitations, particularly in a decentralized environment, that we do not consider it further in this survey.

2.2 Timestamps

A *timestamp* is a unique number which is assigned to a transaction or object and is chosen from a monotonically increasing sequence which is often a function of the time of day. In a decentralized system where each node has a unique identifier, a timestamp can be generated by concatenating the local time with the local identifier. This timestamp mechanism is an example of what Rosenkrantz, et al. call a *valid numbering method*. It has the property that once an entity (transaction or object) has been assigned a timestamp, only a finite (bounded) number of other entities can be assigned a smaller (earlier) timestamp [ROSE78]. Timestamps can be used to avoid deadlock in systems which lock objects or as a substitute for locks altogether.

First we discuss one example of their use in conjunction with locks. In this case each transaction or atomic action is assigned a timestamp to indicate when it was initiated. Since timestamps are unique, they specify a total ordering of all the transactions in the system. As before, we assume that each transaction when run by itself will eventually terminate, providing a new consistent state. Access to objects is assumed to be requested in one of two modes: *read* (share) mode or *update* (exclusive) mode. If a transaction conflicts with another transaction, then it must either wait, abort itself, or preempt the other transaction.

Rosenkrantz et al. have proved that a concurrency control mechanism based on timestamps and locking can be used in a distributed environment to avoid deadlocks, as well as other infinite waiting conditions [ROSE78]. In their model of a distributed database system each transaction is assumed to be composed of sequential steps that may need to access and update data objects at different sites in a network. The objects are assumed to be independent, representing separately modifiable entities. Concurrency control is performed at the system level by local controllers and is invisible to the user. Transactions do not contain explicit *lock* and *unlock* statements since the system performs this function for all data objects.

When a request conflicts with an existing transaction, the concurrency control takes one of the following two actions:

1. *Wait*. The requesting transaction is made to wait until the transaction (or transactions) with which it is in conflict terminates (completes) or is aborted.
2. *Restart*. Either the requesting transaction or some of the transactions it is in

conflict with can be restarted. Restarting a transaction means first aborting it and then beginning the process again at its original site. The abort operation must return all modified data to its original value.

Restarting is initiated by the local concurrency control using one of the following primitives:

1. *Die.* The transaction making the request is restarted.
2. *Wound.* The requesting transaction waits while a transaction in conflict with the request is tagged as *wounded* and a message is sent to all the sites the wounded process has visited saying that it is wounded. If the message is received before the transaction has initiated termination (committed some of the changes made), the concurrency control at that site initiates an abort of the transaction. If the transaction has already initiated termination, the *wound* message is ignored. The original requesting transaction proceeds after the wounded transaction completes termination or abortion. If the wounded transaction is aborted, it will be restarted again at its initial site.

The choice of a particular action by the concurrency controller is based on a comparison of the timestamps of the requesting and conflicting transactions.

Rosenkrantz et al. proposed and analyzed two protocols, which they call WAIT-DIE and WOUND-WAIT:

1. *WAIT-DIE.* If the requester is older (has an earlier timestamp), then the requester *waits*; otherwise the requester *dies*.
2. *WOUND-WAIT.* If the requester is older, then the requester *wounds*; otherwise the requester *waits*.

Both protocols produce consistent schedules and guarantee that no transaction will wait forever. They also give priority to older transactions.

In the WAIT-DIE scheme, an older transaction is permitted to wait for a resource held by a younger transaction. This is preferable to dying and restarting, the fate of a younger transaction. In the WOUND-WAIT scheme an older transaction wounds a younger transaction and waits for the wound to take effect. After the desired object is rolled back and unlocked, the older transaction can lock it. An undesirable property of the WAIT-DIE system is that a transaction which dies and is restarted may again cause a conflict with the same transaction and be forced to die again. On the other hand, it has the desirable property, not shared by the WOUND-WAIT system, that once a transaction has accessed all the required database entities for the first time, it will not be forced to restart. Thus, if a transaction is organized to access all database entities before interacting with external devices, it is guaranteed not to be restarted in the middle of output.

The WAIT-DIE and WOUND-WAIT systems were designed for use in a decentralized network environment. Deadlock and other infinite waiting conditions are avoided by using timestamps to order conflicting requests. However, since no system-wide resource allocation graph is maintained, transactions not involved in deadlock may be restarted unnecessarily. For instance, consider transactions T1 and T2 in Figure 1 again; assume that both are in progress and that T2 is older than T1. If T1 were to request to *read* account B after T2 had already accessed it, a conflict would occur. The WAIT-DIE protocol would require T1 (the requester) to *die*, even though no deadlock would occur if it were to wait. Similar situations can be constructed for the WOUND-WAIT protocol.

Recognizing this limitation, Rosenkrantz, et al. proposed several other alternatives to increase concurrency:

(1) a *centralized scheme* based on the detection of potential cycles in a global allocation graph, from which a global "CAN-WAIT-FOR" relation is computed for all pairs of transactions (T1 CAN-WAIT-FOR T2 if and only if it will not result in a deadlock condition);
(2) two *hybrid WAIT-DIE* and *WOUND-WAIT* schemes which compute local CAN-WAIT-FOR relations and use separate restart protocols for local and global (distributed) transactions.

These methods should improve concurrency and may reduce restarts at the expense of an unknown amount of additional overhead to update the CAN-WAIT-FOR relations.

Thomas has proposed a decentralized concurrency control scheme based on timestamps and voting that does not require objects to be locked explicitly [THOM79]. The scheme was proposed as part of the solution to the problem of synchronizing the update of database entities which are replicated at multiple sites. In a computer network envirnoment it may be desirable to maintain duplicate copies at several or all nodes to ensure data accessibility in case of site failure, to improve response time by accessing a local copy, and to distribute the computational load.

In Thomas's model the database is assumed to consist of a collection of independent named elements (objects) which are duplicated at every site. Each object has a value and a timestamp, obtained from a centralized or synchronized clock, which represents the time the current value was assigned. The timestamps are used to ensure internal database consistency and to guarantee mutual consistency of an object's duplicate copies. (The protocol used to do this is discussed below.) *Mutual consistency* means that all copies of an object must converge to the same value and would be identical if update activity ceased. Queries and updates are assumed to be the two primitive operations on all data objects. Query requests are satisfied by returning the value and timestamp associated with an object. Those objects queried for the purpose of updating an object are called the *base variables* for the update.

Concurrency control is based on a distributed voting scheme which employs a *majority consensus* algorithm. Before accepting an update request, the local controllers ask to compare timestamps to determine whether a given controller's copy of any base variable has been modified by another transaction since the original query. If no variables have been changed, then as far as the local controller can determine, the update can proceed since no conflicting requests have been accepted. However, if any base variable has been modified, the premises for the update are no longer valid and the local controller must vote to reject the request.

Each controller communicates its vote to other controllers, waits for replies, and then uses a majority consensus request resolution rule to determine the outcome of the vote. The *resolution rule* accepts the request only if a majority of controllers vote to accept. Since a majority is required, any two requests that are accepted must have at least one local controller that voted for both, thereby guaranteeing that they cannot be in conflict. The outcome of each vote must be resolved and all local updates made before a new update request can be processed by a controller.

This approach has the advantage that it will continue to function in the presence of site and communication failures as long as a majority of sites are operational and connected. Furthermore, it does not require transactions to preclaim objects. However, to ensure correct behavior under all circumstances, the actual voting and resolution rules are much more complicated than described here. Parallelism among concurrent transactions is limited by the number of rejected transactions whose common base variables have been modified by another transaction. If many transactions conflict and are repeatedly rejected, the throughput performance of the algorithm degenerates.

Bernstein et al. have shown by means of a simple model that this scheme provides less concurrency than two-phase locking [BERN79]. Using a detailed simulation model of the fully redundant database environment, Garcia-Molina found that centralized locking performs considerably better than distributed voting for a wide variety of measures, except in high-load cases where both perform poorly [GARC78]. Storage costs may be increased dramatically since timestamps must be permanently stored with each data object. Extension to the partially redundant case is possible, but this would severely complicate the update resolution rule. In its present form this model does not allow for hierarchically structured objects. Also, since there is no provision for rollback of an updated object, if more than one object is to be updated by a transaction, all objects must be voted on and accepted at the same time.

2.3 Circulating Permit and Tickets

LeLann also has investigated the joint problems of concurrency control and mutual consistency in distributed database systems [LeLa78]. He proposes a distributed approach based on a *circulating permit* or control token. The basic scheme can be described as follows. Nodes are linked together to form a virtual communication ring on which a unique control token circulates. Each node is assumed to be the agent for a single user transaction. Transactions are distinguished as one of two types, query or update. Only the node owning the token is allowed to initiate an update transaction. When the update is complete, the token is passed to the successor on the ring. The circulating token serializes the update requests. Resiliency is obtained by an algorithm that monitors the ring, reconfigures it, and regenerates lost tokens in case of failure. The drawback of this simple approach is that there is no parallelism even when transactions modify separate objects.

Extensions of the circulating permit mechanism to provide for parallelism are also described by LeLann. In this case the database is assumed to be partitioned into r independent parts, where access to each part is monitored by a database controller. (Extensions to the case of n replicated copies of each part are also outlined.) The circulating control token now carries r sequence numbers or *ticket values*, one for each database partition.

An update transaction must request and obtain the next consecutive ticket for each partition it will access before proceeding. Tickets can only be obtained from the control token when it visits the node on which the transaction is running. The controller for the rth partition will grant access to an update transaction with ticket value $t(r)$ only after the transaction with ticket value $t(r)-1$ is finished. Thus the circulating token no longer needs to wait for the transaction to complete before being passed to the successor on the ring, since access is serialized by the consecutive tickets. In effect, the circulating control token with ticketing implements a form of centralized timestamp mechanism in a distributed environment.

Various resilient algorithms for distributing tickets have been proposed, but their performance is still unknown. However, the basic ticketing mechanism is prone to infinite waiting whenever a node crashes without using its tickets. Because of the need to preclaim the partitions to be accessed, this approach is not suitable for interactive transactions. Also, since each update transaction locks at least one database partition, the maximum degree of parallelism is limited by the number of partitions and not by the conflicts between objects. This may be a reasonable approach for some systems, but it does not have the flexibility of a generalized lock scheme.

2.4 Conflict Analysis

SDD-1, a System for Distributed Databases, is currently under development at the Computer Corporation of America [Roth80]. It consists of a collection of database sites interconnected through a communications network. In the general configuration each site may contain a portion of the overall database, and some parts may be stored redundantly at several sites. A recent paper by Bernstein, Shipman, and Rothnie contains a comprehensive description of the concurrency control technique used in SDD-1 [Bern80b]. Their synchronization technique is designed to preserve internal and mutual database consistency while minimizing intercomputer-synchronization overhead. When copies of the data are stored redundantly at all sites (fully redundant case), the mechanism is somewhat simplified.

The SDD-1 mechanism does not assume that every transaction requires synchronization as strong as global locking. The method, which we call *conflict analysis*, is based on an analysis of how distributed transactions can conflict with each other and how the conflicts can be avoided. For the fully redundant case, each transaction is assumed to be executed in two stages:

1. *Local Execution.* The transaction accesses the local copy and keeps a list of changes. Local synchronization and locking is used to avoid conflict with other local transactions and to delay conflicting updates from remote sites.

2. *Global Update.* When local execution is completed, the local site broadcasts its list of changes to all other sites. Update messages from site i to site j are assumed to be received at j in the order in which they were sent from i.

The notation $L(t, m)$ is used to denote the local execution of transaction t at site m and $U(t, n)$ the processing of the global update message from transaction t at receiving site n. If the system contained three sites, then a single transaction t at site 1 would generate the actions $L(t, 1)$, $U(t, 2)$, $U(t, 3)$. These can be legally time ordered as either $L(t, 1)$, $U(t, 2)$, $U(t, 3)$ or $L(t, 1)$, $U(t, 3)$, $U(t, 2)$. A single transaction t consists of one L action followed by as many U actions as there are other sites. The processing of each L and U action is assumed to be atomic.

Since the system is processing many transactions concurrently, each with its own set of local execution and global update actions, many different interleaved execution histories (schedules) are possible. It is the job of the synchronization mechanism to guarantee that only consistent schedules are allowed.

The methodology used in SDD-1 groups together similar transactions into *transaction classes* for the purpose of determining the level of synchronization required to avoid conflict and guarantee a serializable schedule. These classes are determined statically, at the time of system design. The ith transaction class associated with site s, denoted by $C(i, s)$, is characterized by its read set and write set. All transactions in class $C(i, s)$ read exclusively from data items (objects) contained in the *read-set*, $RS(C(i, s))$, and update exclusively members of the *write-set*, $WS(C(i, s))$. These sets are not necessarily disjoint.

The concept of conflicting transaction classes can now be precisely stated. Concurrent transactions from classes $C(i, s)$ and $C(j, u)$ are defined to be *conflicting* if and only if

$$RS(C(i, s)) \wedge WS(C(j, u)) \neq \emptyset,$$

or

$$WS(C(i, s)) \wedge RS(C(j, u)) \neq \emptyset$$

or

$$WS(C(i, s)) \wedge WS(C(j, u)) \neq \emptyset.$$

Concurrent transactions are not conflicting if only their read sets intersect.

Mutual consistency of redundant copies is achieved by associating a unique locally generated timestamp with each transaction and updated object. (In a related study, Lin has proposed a protocol that does not require timestamps on data objects [LIN79].) The values of the local clocks are kept synchronized by advancing the local time if a message with a later timestamp is received. The timestamp of transaction t, $TS(t)$, is sent to each site n as a part of t's update message $U(t, n)$. For each object listed in the update message, site n updates its local copy if and only if the timestamp on its current copy is older (smaller) than $TS(t)$. Updated objects are given the new timestamp. Note that since timestamp comparison and update are performed on an object-by-object basis, some objects specified in $U(t, n)$ will be updated while others, whose updates are already outdated, will not. The timestamp mechanism ensures that the update operations in $U(t, n)$ appear to occur at each site in the same order as the corresponding $L(t, m)$ actions occurred.

Bernstein et al. have proved that mutual consistency is preserved by this timestamping and update mechanism [BERN78, BERN80a]. They use the following argument to prove that all copies of each object would converge to the same value once all transactions were completed:

> Suppose that all transaction processing did cease. For each data item X we construct a set T_X of transactions that have updated X in the history of the database system. If T_X is empty, then X was never updated. Else, there must be a transaction t_X in T_X such that $TS(t_X)$ is maximum in T_X. Hence, once the U for t_X has been processed at all sites, the value of X will be identical at all sites, and will never subsequently change. [BERN78, p. 157]

The synchronization mechanism used by SDD-1 to maintain the internal consistency of each database copy distinguishes it from the other approaches. The serializability of an interleaved schedule of local executions and global updates is based on two central components:

1. *Synchronization Protocol.* The synchronization protocols specify those messages that a site s must send and/or receive before it may begin executing a given local transaction $L(t, s)$, and those messages that it must send upon completion of $L(t, s)$. SDD-1 uses four protocols which vary in

the degree of synchronization required and cost of use.

2. *Protocol Selector Function.* The protocol selector function determines which protocol must be used on the basis of an analysis of the potential conflict between transaction types. The transaction classes and their corresponding read and write sets are used in this decision.

The least expensive protocol is intended for transactions that cannot interfere, such as reading the database to generate a sales slip through a point-of-sale terminal. The strongest and most expensive protocol is reserved for "unanticipated" transactions that are not known members of any of the predefined classes.

Bernstein et al. [BERN79] have shown that their conflict analysis approach allows more concurrency than the classical locking approach. As is true of most database concurrency control methods, the SDD-1 approach assumes that all database items (objects) are independent (common level of abstraction) and bases its determination of transaction classes and the protocol selector function on this assumption. Although when used in a known environment this approach should prove to be an efficient synchronization technique, its performance in a more general or unknown environment and its resiliency to node and communication failure are open questions.

2.5 Reservations

Milenkovic has recently proposed a new variation based on the use of a *reservation list* associated with each active individually reservable database entity [MILE79]. He has devised separate algorithms for centralized and distributed database systems, both of which allow transactions to use one of two compatible synchronization protocols. One protocol requires a transaction to preclaim and reserve its resources in exchange for the guarantee that it will not be preempted by another transaction once started. The other protocol allows a transaction to dynamically request resources but does not guarantee that in case of conflict it might not be required to restart. Both protocols use timestamps to avoid deadlock, thus eliminating the overhead of deadlock detection. Only the algorithm for the distributed fully redundant database environment is presented here. The generalization to the partially redundant case and the related algorithm for the centralized environment can be found in MILE79.

In the fully redundant case it is assumed that all objects required by a transaction can be found at a single database site. Each transaction is assigned a unique and nondecreasing timestamp by the database controller at the site where it is initiated. Although not mentioned directly by Milenkovic, the local clocks must be kept synchronized by advancing the local time if a message with a later timestamp is received. (Lamport has formally analyzed the problem of defining a total ordering of events in a distributed system and proposes a method for synchronizing clocks [LAMP78].) Furthermore, the synchronization protocol assumes that all messages sent from one site to another are delivered, after some variable but finite delay, in the order in which they were sent. The above assumptions are similar to those made by SDD-1; the distinguishing characteristic is a local reservation list which is associated with each active individually reservable database entity.

The synchronization scheme allows transactions to use one of two compatible protocols. Protocol P (for pessimistic) requires transactions to preclaim and reserve database objects prior to execution, while under protocol O (for optimistic) the transaction is first tentatively executed locally with updates made permanent and propagated only if there are no consistency conflicts. As described by Milenkovic, when a transaction T is submitted for execution to the database controller residing at a site Si, the following set of rules constitute protocol P:

1. *Timestamping.* Si assigns a unique timestamp, derived from Si's clock and unique identifier, to the transaction T, TS(T).

2. *Internal Reservation.* Si reserves entities from T's read-set, RS(T) and write-set, WS(T), internally. If any of those entities is already reserved, T's request is entered in the associated reservation list according to its timestamp: after all older reservations' requests (whose timestamps

are smaller that TS(*T*)), and in front of the younger ones.

3. *Global Reservation.* Si broadcasts a reservation message on behalf of *T*. The reservation message has the following format:

Reserve; sender's ID: Si,
timestamp: TS(*T*),
identity of entities
to be reserved: WS(*T*).

All reservation broadcasts sent by a site must be ordered according to the timestamps of the transactions themselves; they must contain increasing, although not necessarily consecutive, timestamps.

4. *Acknowledgments.* Each site *j*, upon receipt of the transaction broadcast, reserves entities contained in WS(*T*) in its respective copy of the database, according to rule 2. When this process is completed, an acknowledgment is sent back to the site Si. The acknowledgment format is

Acknowledgment; responder's ID: *j*,
transaction: *T*.

5. *Execution.* Transaction *T* is executed, using Si's copy of the database, when the following conditions are met.

(a) An acknowledgment of the reservation broadcast is received from each database site, and
(b) *T*'s reservations become the oldest in Si's reservation lists associated with the entities contained in RS(*T*) and WS(*T*).

6. *Update Broadcast.* Si applies updates of *T*, WS(*T*), to its copy of the database, removes internal reservations made on behalf of *T*, and broadcasts the following update message to all other sites:

Update; values of the entities
to be updated: WS(*T*).

7. *Completion.* Upon receipt of the update message, each site applies the specified updates to its copy of the entities contained in WS(*T*) as soon as the reservations set on behalf of *T* becomes the oldest in the related reservation lists. Each such reservation is subsequently removed.

Note that if we assume that remote clocks are synchronized by the reservation messages broadcast in step 3, step 5(a) ensures that no additional earlier reservations from remote sites can be received once execution of transaction *T* begins. Like the ticketing mechanism of LeLann [LeLa78], ths protocol totally orders conflicting requests but does not constrain the parallelism of nonconflicting requests. Protocol P also does not require permanent storage of timestamps, and a reservation list is only maintained for active objects. Since objects are stored redundantly, only updates are globally communicated and reserved.

A second compatible protocol, protocol O, was designed to remove the restriction that entities must be preclaimed and reserved before execution can begin. This should improve the efficiency of transactions that would otherwise have to reserve large portions of the database just to guarantee that all objects that are needed have been preclaimed. For the sake of brevity, only protocol O is outlined here. Under protocol O the objects required by a transaction are locked locally at the initiating site and reserved at all others in timestamp order using a lock/reservation list. Updates are tentative until it is confirmed that they cannot be rendered obsolete by an older transaction. Milenkovic [Mile79] states: "Protocol P should be used for transactions that are long and/or expensive to run in order to avoid undesirable restarts. Protocol O, on the other hand, should be used for transactions that are known to have low probability of conflicts, or for which preclaiming of resources is inefficient."

The disadvantage of protocol O is that transactions which use it may be restarted indefinitely. To maintain compatibility with protocol P, restarted transactions are given a new (younger) timestamp. Since younger transactions have lower priority, they cannot be guaranteed to run until all older conflicting transactions have completed. A simple remedy is to keep track of the number of restarts and switch to protocol P if this number exceeds a threshold. Milenkovic also proposed several refinements to reduce unnecessary messages and generalized protocol P for use in partially redundant systems.

His refined approach is a clever hybrid based on aspects of locking, timestamps, and tickets. Compared with SDD-1 the basic protocols are more straightforward, but nevertheless too complex for simple analysis and proof of correctness. Informal proofs and a performance comparison based on message traffic can be found in MILE79, but additional analysis and confirmation are necessary. Since reservation lists and locks are associated with database entities (objects), this approach can be directly extended to more general hierarchical structures. While the detection of node and communication failure was not discussed by Milenkovic, the proposed reservation protocol is based on a broadcast/acknowledgment mechanism which can be adapted to detect failures and request reconfiguration when necessary. An approach which uses a two-phase commit protocol is discussed in Section 3.2.2.

2.6 General Comments

There are many other interesting and important synchronization algorithms and variations that have not been discussed or referenced in this survey. New proposals appear regularly in the database and distributed processing literature.

All of the concurrency control mechanisms we have surveyed were designed for use in a distributed transaction-processing environment. With the exception of hierarchical locking, objects were assumed to be independent database entities directly associated with physical or logical storage units (pages, records, or files). Transactions were assumed to consist of a sequence of read and write operations intermixed with local computation. In their present form, none of these mechanisms can support concurrency control in a general object-based distributed environment.

The locking approach shows the most promise for extension. It can support the notions of object hierarchies and compatibility between multiple concurrent operations. A useful mechanism must be extensible to user- and application-defined objects and operations. This is a topic for future research. Satisfactory mechanisms will probably be hybrids based on approaches similar to those surveyed above. In the next section we discuss the atomic action as the basis for a recovery strategy and its relationship to the synchronization problem.

3. RECOVERY TECHNIQUES

In this section we discuss techniques that have been proposed for implementing recoverable atomic actions. As stated by Lomet [LOME77], in order for atomic actions to be recoverable their implementation must be such that

1. Updated objects are not released until the action is completed. Once a modified object is released, recovery can no longer be assured, as another independent atomic action may use the object and become dependent on it.
2. The initial states of all objects modified by the action can be reconstructed. This usually involves maintaining an incremental log of all changes to objects on nonvolatile storage.

Mechanisms for implementing atomic actions rely on a fault-tolerant synchronization mechanism to "lock" all updated objects until the atomic action is successfully completed. Candidates for this were discussed in the previous section.

As pointed out by Gray [GRAY78], in order to design a recovery system it is essential to have a clear notion of what kinds of errors can be expected and with what probabilities. This is discussed next, followed by a survey of mechanisms that have been proposed to implement atomic actions.

3.1 Failures, Errors, and Reliability

At the beginning of this paper *reliability* was defined as a measure of the success with which a system conforms to some authoritative specification of its behavior. An evaluation of the reliability should be made by testing the behavior of the physical system against its specification under all possible conditions. Of course, this exhaustive testing approach is not feasible for the types of systems we have in mind. A common alternative approach is to compare the specification with a model of the system behavior. In theory at least, a system model can be derived from models of the physical components and from the algorithms used

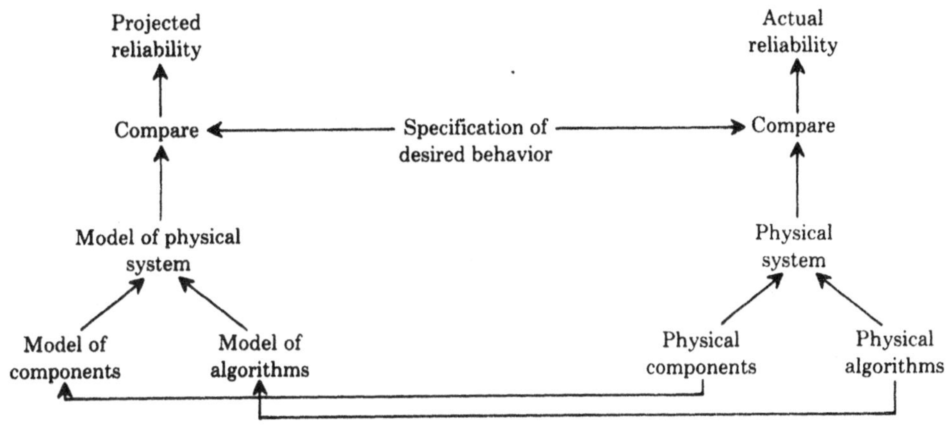

Figure 9. Determining system reliability.

to control and transform these components into a system. Figure 9 shows the relationship between actual and projected reliability, the system specification, the model, and the actual physical system.

In the modeling approach, system reliability is determined by formally comparing the specification with the system model, itself derived from the component and algorithm models which are based on their real physical counterparts. However, as pointed out by Lampson and Sturgis [LAMP79], the inherent flaw in this approach is that the validity of the models themselves cannot be established by proof. Lampson and Sturgis argue that since physical systems like disk storage, processors, and communications links do not have formal properties, their relationship to a formal model cannot be formally shown. The best we can do is to claim that the physical system will behave like the formal system with some high probability, and the correctness of this claim can only be established by experience.

Nevertheless, models are important in identifying potential failure mechanisms and establishing techniques for correcting their undesired effects.

Expanding on their earlier work [LAMP76], Lampson and Sturgis proposed a hierarchy of more reliable abstract machines as an approach to implementing atomic transactions [LAMP79]. Transactions are assumed to consist of a sequence of read and write commands sent by a client to the file system. In developing their model, they divided the events that occur into two categories: *desired* and *undesired*. In a fault-free system only desired events will occur. Undesired events are further divided into *expected* and *unexpected*.

The central theme of their approach is that algorithms should be designed to work in the presence of any bounded number of expected events. They denote by p the probability of an unexpected event (which may lead to a failure). In terms of our earlier discussion, p is the probability that the physical system will not behave like the formal model. The value of p can only be estimated by an exhaustive enumeration of possible failure mechanisms. Their approach to designing a reliable system is that, while errors may occur, all expected errors will be detected and corrected before they cause a failure. The probability of unexpected errors must be reduced to an acceptable level by accounting for the important failure modes.

We now present Lampson and Sturgis' comprehensive model [LAMP79] for the three main physical components of a decentralized system: disk storage, processors with volatile memory, and communications. Following this we cite an example of how they have proposed to handle undesired but expected events for the case of disk storage.

Disk storage is modeled as a set of *addressable pages*, where each page contains a *status* which may be good or bad, and a block of *data*. If the status is bad, the data are assumed to be meaningless.

A processor can communicate with the disk by two operations:

procedure *Put(at: Address, data: Dblock)*
procedure *Get(at: Address)*
returns(*status*:
(good, looksBad), data:
Dblock)

There are three kinds of events associated with processor action *Get(at: a)*:

Desired
Normal operation: If page *a* is (*good, d*), then returns (*good, d*). If page *a* is *bad*, then returns *looksBad*.
Undesired Expected
Soft read error: If page *a* is *good*, then returns *looksBad*. However, repeating *Get* a bounded number of times will result in (*good, d*).
Undesired Unexpected
Undetected error: If page *a* is *bad*, then returns *good*, or if page *a* is (*good, d*), then returns (*good, d'*) with $d' \neq d$, that is, returns the wrong page.

The effects of a *Put(at: a, data: d)* are classified as

Desired
Normal operation: Page *a* becomes (*good, d*).
Undesired Expected
Write error: Page *a* is unchanged, or page *a* becomes *bad*.

Other undesired events called *decays* are introduced to model various kinds of accidents. Collections of pages that may be damaged by a single decay event are grouped together into *decay sets*. For example, all pages on a cylinder or surface might form a single decay set. Disk pages are also assumed to be partitioned into *units* such that each decay set is wholly contained in one unit and within each unit each page can be paired with another page from a different decay set. A time interval TD, called the *unit decay time*, is also associated with each unit. Units will be used to construct more reliable storage from regular disk storage. A *decay* is then defined to be a spontaneous event in which some set of pages, all within one characteristic decay set, changes status from good to bad.

The *spontaneous events* are further classified as

Undesired Expected
Infrequent decay: A decay preceded and followed by time intervals of duration at least TD, during which there is no other decay in the same unit and the only bad *Puts* on that unit are to pages in the characteristic set of the decay.
Undesired Unexpected
Frequent decay: Two decays in the same unit within an interval TD.
Undetected error: Some pages change from *bad* to *good*, or from (*good, d*) to (*good, d'*), with $d' \neq d$.

By combining these spontaneous events with the earlier events associated with *Get* and *Put*, many other events can be included in the model. For example, writing the correct data *d* into the wrong page address *a'* is an unexpected event in which page *a* is unchanged by a *Put* (*at: a, data: d*) operation followed by the spontaneous event which changes page *a'* from (*good, d'*) to (*good, d*).

Lampson and Sturgis modeled a *processor* as a collection of processes with some shared state, where each process has local state as well and executes instructions (changes state) at some finite rate. Instructions can read and write the shared state (using a local synchronization primitive), as well as the local state of the process. The *state* of the processor consists of the union of the shared state and process states of all processes. A processor interacts with disk storage using *Put* and *Get* operations and with other processors through the communications system using *Send* and *Receive* (described next). The following events are associated with processors:

Desired
Normal operation: Instructions are executed without error.
Undesired Expected
Crash: The state of the processor is reset to some standard value, which means the previous *volatile* state was lost unless stored elsewhere. A crash does not propagate errors to the storage or communication units. (This may not be a realistic assumption.)
Undesired Unexpected
All other events not explicitly included above, including undetected propagation of errors to storage and communication units.

In systems designed to recover from a

crash, a processor will examine its disk storage and communicate with other processors to restore its state to some mutually consistent value.

Finally, *communications* is modeled as a set of messages, where each message contains a status (*good, bad*), a block of data, and a destination which is a processor. The two operations used to communicate with another processor are

procedure *Send* (*to*: *Processor*, *data*: *Mblock*)
procedure *Receive* **returns** (*status*: (*good*, *bad*), *data*: *Mblock*)

The possible results of a *Send*(*to*: *q*, *data*: *d*) are categorized as

Desired
Normal operation: Creates a message (*good, d, q*).
Undesired
These events are accounted for by spontaneous events to be discussed below.

When a *Receive* is executed by a processor *p*, the following events are possible:

Desired
Normal operation: If a message (*good*, *d*, *p*) exists, *p* returns (*good*, *d*) and destroys the message. If a bad message exists, *p* returns *bad* and destroys the message. Note that there may be an arbitrary delay before the return.
Undesired
Again, these events are accounted for by spontaneous events.

Undesired spontaneous events associated with communications include the following:

Undesired Expected
Loss: Some message is destroyed.
Duplication: Some message identical to an existing message is created.
Decay: Some message changes from *good* to *bad*.
Undesired Unexpected
Undetected error: Some message changes from *bad* to *good*, or from (*good*, *d*, *q*) to (*good*, *d'*, *q'*), with $d' \neq d$ or $q' \neq q$.

As before, other undesired events can be described as combinations of those given above.

To illustrate how Lampson and Sturgis propose to build reliable systems by constructing a hierarchy of more reliable virtual machines, we discuss their *stable storage system*. It was designed to provide operations that are equivalent to *Put* and *Get* but to eliminate all the undesired expected events associated with the physical disk. Their stable storage is actually built by first constructing another intermediate abstraction called *careful disk storage*, which eliminates two of the original undesired expected events. Careful disk storage looks the same as physical storage except that the only undesired expected events are a disk write error followed by a processor crash and infrequent disk decay. (Note that combinations of storage, processor, and communications events must now be considered.) The other expected events are eliminated later by appropriate control algorithms.

Careful disk storage is built using *careful disk pages*, where each careful page is represented by a physical disk page. The only difference is that instead of performing the standard *Get* and *Put* operations, careful disk storage uses *CarefulGet* and *CarefulPut*. *CarefulGet* repeatedly performs a *Get* until it gets a good status or until it has tried *n* times, where *n* is specified as the bound on soft read errors. Soft read errors are eliminated by this standard technique and all remaining read errors can be classified as due to undesired and unexpected spontaneous events. Similarly, *CarefulPut* repeatedly performs a *Put* followed by a *Get* until the *Get* returns a good status. This common read-after-write technique eliminates write errors which either do not change the page or leave a bad page, provided there is no processor crash during the *CarefulPut*.

Stable storage is constructed from careful storage by introducing the notion of a *stable page* and a new operation called *Cleanup*. A stable page consists of a pair of careful disk pages chosen from the same storage unit but not in the same decay set. Consequently, the spontaneous decay of both pages during interval TD is an undesired unexpected event.

One page is designated as the primary and its value is used unless its status is bad. Of course, a write operation must update both copies as an atomic action. In particular, a *StablePut* performs a *CarefulPut* on each of the pair in turn, with the *CarefulPut* on the backup page not started until the first is complete. If a crash occurs during the primary *CarefulPut*, the second one will not be started. (This case is discussed below.) However, if the secondary *CarefulPut* is started, the primary must have completed with no write error. A *StableGet* is implemented by doing a *CarefulGet* from one member of the page pair and, if the status is bad, doing a *CarefulGet* on the other page.

The final element required to guarantee that all the original undesired expected events associated with physical storage have been eliminated, in spite of processor crash, is a recovery and refresh operation called *Cleanup*. It is applied to each stable page during crash recovery and at least every unit decay time TD thereafter. *Cleanup* performs the following steps:

Do a *CarefulGet* from each of the two pages;
if *both return good and the same data*
  then *do nothing*
  else if *one returns bad*
    then {one of the two pages has decayed or has suffered a bad write error in a *CarefulPut* which was interrupted by a crash}
      do a CarefulPut of the data block from the good to the bad address
  else if *both return good but different data*
    then {a crash occurred between the *CarefulPuts* of a *StablePut*}
      choose either one of the pages and do a CarefulPut of the data to the other.

Lampson and Sturgis presented an informal proof that their stable storage works properly for all expected events, both desired and undesired. A formal invariant (statement of requirements and properties) could be defined and it could then be formally validated under all possible combinations of events. This is a tedious and error-prone procedure, even for the simple model used here, but it is the only thorough way to validate it. We have presented one of the many idealized virtual machines from the hierarchy proposed by Lampson and Sturgis. Other more complex abstractions are necessary for the complete system.

In spite of its complexity, this layered virtual machine approach is the only reasonable means of expressing and accounting for the important underlying assumptions and their influence on system behavior. When this approach is not used, we run the risk of inadvertently removing some of the harder problems to a level where they might be forgotten rather than solved. Randell calls the approach the multilevel error recovery approach [RAND79].

Many authors have proposed mechanisms to create virtual components that are more reliable than the original basic component, HAMM78, LORI77, and SEVE76, for example, but few [LAMP79, GRAY79] have considered how these components interact or can be integrated into a complete system. In the next section we discuss proposed mechanisms for implementing atomic actions. The proper functioning of these mechanisms relies on the support of different underlying virtual machines, which we are unable to develop in detail. We consider recovery at the transaction level and assume that all required lower level recovery mechanisms have already been implemented.

3.2 Implementing Atomic Actions

We begin by presenting the main ideas of a method proposed by Gray [GRAY79], which is apparently based to a large extent on work done by himself and colleagues at the IBM Research Laboratory, San Jose, Calif., while developing System R. System R is an experimental relational database system designed to support transaction processing. We should note, however, that the techniques discussed here are not all implemented in System R. As stated by Gray:

> The system provides a set of objects and actions on these objects along with a set of primitives which allow groups of actions to be collected into atomic transactions. It guarantees no consistency on the objects beyond the atomicity of the actions. That is, an action will either successfully complete or it will not modify the system state at all. Furthermore, if two actions are performed on an object then the result will be equivalent to the serial execution of the two actions. . . . The notion of transaction is introduced to provide a similar abstraction above the system interface. Transactions are an all or nothing thing, either they happen completely or all trace of them (except in the log) is erased. [GRAY79, pp. 421–422]

BEGIN	BEGIN	BEGIN
action	action	action
action	action	action
⋮	⋮	⋮
action	action	action
COMMIT	ABORT	ABORT ⇒
Successful transaction	Suicidal transaction	Murdered transaction

Figure 10. Transaction outcomes.

Before a transaction completes it may be *aborted* and its updates to recoverable data *undone*. The abort may be self-inflicted (suicide) as a result of bad input data, user cancel, etc., or from outside (murder) because of deadlock, time-out, system crash, or some other external cause. However, once a transaction *commits* (successfully completes), the effects of the transaction can only be undone by running another transaction to correct the data. This is called *compensation*, and it is assumed to be the responsibility of the user and application rather than the system.

A transaction instance is implemented by a collection of processes (called *cohorts*), which may execute on different network nodes. A transaction instance is created by the arrival of a message or request which causes a process to be built from a transaction descriptor. The *transaction descriptor* provides complete instructions on how to build an instance, including which cohort processes are required, how to schedule the transaction, what recovery and locking options should be used, and so on.

Every instance starts by issuing a BEGIN action which establishes a recovery unit. It then issues a series of actions (operations) on database objects, some of which may change the database state. Finally, it issues a COMMIT action to cause the changes to be made permanent and public. Figure 10 shows the three possible outcomes of a transaction instance.

Since complete rollback and restart may involve undoing and then redoing many actions, it is desirable to provide an additional mechanism to allow a transaction to back up and continue from some predefined intermediate point. The notion of a *save point* is introduced to allow enough intermediate state to be saved so that processing can be resumed at that step. For example, an interactive (conversational) transaction could establish save points after each user message is processed. If bad input is discovered when the action is being processed, it would then be sufficient to back up to the previous save point and re-request the last input information rather than undo the entire transaction.

These options are assumed to be provided by two additional recovery actions: SAVE, which establishes a save point, and BACKUP, which undoes the effects of a transaction to an earlier save point. The SAVE action does not commit the changes that have been made, so complete rollback is still possible if necessary. The system must also maintain a separate *checkpoint* action to save the entire system state and a restart procedure to coordinate system recovery.

3.2.1 Lock Requirements

Transactions are assumed to be well-formed and two-phase as discussed in Section 2.1. Furthermore, when objects are locked, they are locked in one of two modes, share or exclusive, by local lock managers, which cooperate to detect and resolve deadlock. Under this model a transaction is said to be *recoverable* if its updates can be undone before it has completed the commit step without undoing other transactions' updates.

This independence from other transactions is important since otherwise an ABORT action could have a domino effect on other transactions, some of which may have completed. To eliminate this possibility and meet the requirements of recoverability, all locks on updated objects (exclusive mode locks) must be held until the transaction has committed. Furthermore, if the transaction is to be *repeatable*—that is, to reproduce the original result if rerun following recovery—then all share mode (read) locks must also be held.

Gray used the diagram shown in Figure 11 to illustrate the possible scenarios associated with system crash recovery. We assume that each transaction (T1, T2, T3, T4, T5) is well-formed, two-phase, and recoverable. The *normal* fault-free operation of the

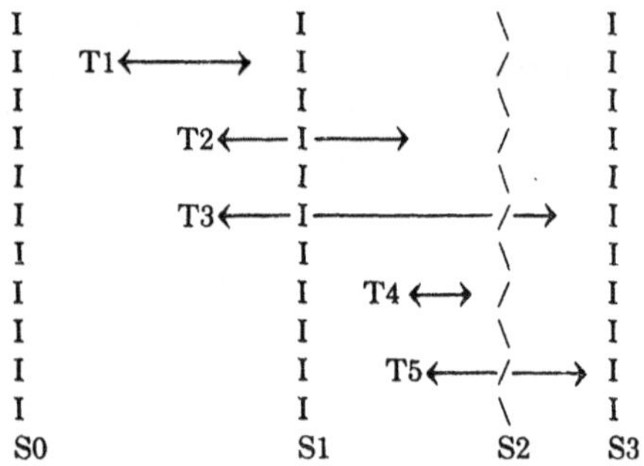

Figure 11. Scenarios for system crash recovery.

system takes the original consistent database state S0 into the final consistent state S3. S1 depicts a system checkpoint state and S2 the current database state after a crash. States S1 and S2 may be inconsistent since transactions were in progress, and state S2 may contain errors as well.

Database recovery after a system crash means returning the database to a consistent state. To eliminate the need to rerun transactions that completed successfully before the crash, the restored database state should reflect all changes made by completed transactions and no changes made by in-progress transactions.

Under the assumption that transactions aborted by the crash (T3 and T5) will not be restarted automatically by the recovery process, Gray suggests the following ways to restore a consistent state:

(a) Start from state S2 and *undo* all actions of transactions in progress at the time of the crash. (For the Figure 11 example, this could be done by aborting T3 and T5.)
(b) Start from checkpoint state S1 and undo all actions of transactions in progress at the time of the crash. (Abort transaction T3.) Then *redo* all actions of transactions which completed after S1 and before the crash. (Complete T2 and restart T4.)
(c) Start at state S0 and *redo* all transactions which completed before the crash. (Restart T1, T2, and T4.)

In illustration of the fact that recovery cannot be guaranteed unless each transaction holds its update locks until after its commit point, suppose T3 updates object *A* and releases the lock immediately, whereupon T4 reads *A*'s value, updates object *B*, and terminates successfully before the crash at S2. Under recovery protocol (a), T3 will be undone but T4 will not, even though its output may depend on T3's update. The effects of transaction crash can be illustrated using a similar approach.

3.2.2 Recovery Management

Database recovery after transaction or system crash depends on the interaction between many system components and protocols. The following four protocols are central to the approach described by Gray [GRAY79]:

(1) consistency lock;
(2) DO-UNDO-REDO log;
(3) write-ahead log;
(4) two-phase commit.

Transactions meet Gray's consistency lock protocol if they are well-formed and two-phase, as discussed in Section 2.1. The remaining protocols are discussed below.

The *DO-UNDO-REDO* log protocol is used to recover committed and uncommitted actions. It is based on keeping an *incremental log* of changes to the database; each action that updates an object writes a record entry on the log (also called audit trail or journal) giving the old and new value of the object. The entry must contain enough information to allow the action to be completely undone or redone. The entries are aggregated by transaction and collected in a common system log, which is stored on *stable storage* (assumed never to fail). In particular, every recoverable action must have the following log entries and operations [GRAY79]:

(1) a DO operation that does the action and also records a log entry sufficient to undo and redo the action;
(2) an UNDO operation that undoes the action given the log entry written by the DO operation;
(3) a REDO operation that redoes the action given the log entry written by the DO operation;
(4) optionally, a DISPLAY operation that translates the log into a human-readable format.

The UNDO and REDO operations must work properly even if another crash occurs during crash recovery. The write-ahead log protocol is designed to help solve this type of problem.

If an object update is recorded in stable database storage before the log entry for the object is recorded in the stable log, then the update cannot be undone if a crash occurs before the log is completed. Similar problems occur when updates to a collection of objects must be committed together. Consequently, the log entry must be recorded in the stable log before the object update is recorded.

The *write-ahead log* protocol consists of the following steps:

(1) Before recording uncommitted updates of recoverable objects in stable storage, force the relevant undo entry to be written to the stable log.
(2) Before committing an update of a recoverable object, the redo and undo log entries must be written on the stable log. (This is necessary for transaction commit, which is discussed next.)

Additional discussion and some implementation details can be found in GRAY79.

The *two-phase commit* protocol is the final element of the recovery scheme. It coordinates the networkwide commit actions of all cohorts participating in a transaction. The protocol may be implemented by a centralized *commit coordinator* which communicates with all cohorts. To process a COMMIT request issued by a transaction, the commit coordinator performs the following steps (with some of Gray's original terms renamed to clarify the description):

Commit Coordinator

Phase 1:

(1) Send a PREPARE message to each cohort. (Each cohort will send a reply only after it has completed its part of the transaction and written the appropriate UNDO-REDO log on stable storage.)
(2) Wait for a reply from each cohort.
    (a) If any cohort sends a negative reply (ABORTED) or a time-out expires, then broadcast ABORT to all cohorts, write ABORT in the log, and terminate after receiving acknowledgments from cohorts. (This will undo the transaction and terminate the coordinator.)
    (b) If a positive reply (PREPARED) is received from all cohorts, then start Phase 2.

Phase 2:

(1) Write a COMMIT entry in the log.
(2) Send a COMMIT message to each cohort.
(3) Wait for a positive acknowledgment (ACK_COMMIT reply) from each cohort. (Retransmit COMMIT message if timeout expires.)
(4) Write a COMPLETE entry in log and terminate.

The proposal for each *cohort* can be described as follows:

Cohort

Phase 1:

(1) Wait for PREPARE message from the commit coordinator.
(2) After completing, write UNDO-REDO log on stable storage.
(3) If successful, then write COMPLETE in log and send PREPARED message to commit coordinator else send ABORTED.

Phase 2:

(1) Wait for verdict from coordinator.
(2) Send reply as follows:
    (a) If verdict is ABORT, then UNDO transaction, release locks, and send abort acknowledgment (ACK_ABORT) to commit coordinator.
    (b) If verdict is COMMIT, then release locks and send commit acknowledgment (ACK_COMMIT) to coordinator.

The three possible interactions between a coordinator and an individual cohort are shown in Fig. 12. Note that the commit coordinator may have to abort a cohort which has successfully completed and is prepared to commit (Case 3), since another cohort may have aborted.

The centralized approach presented here is the simplest to understand. Other variations that reduce somewhat the number of messages required have also been proposed.

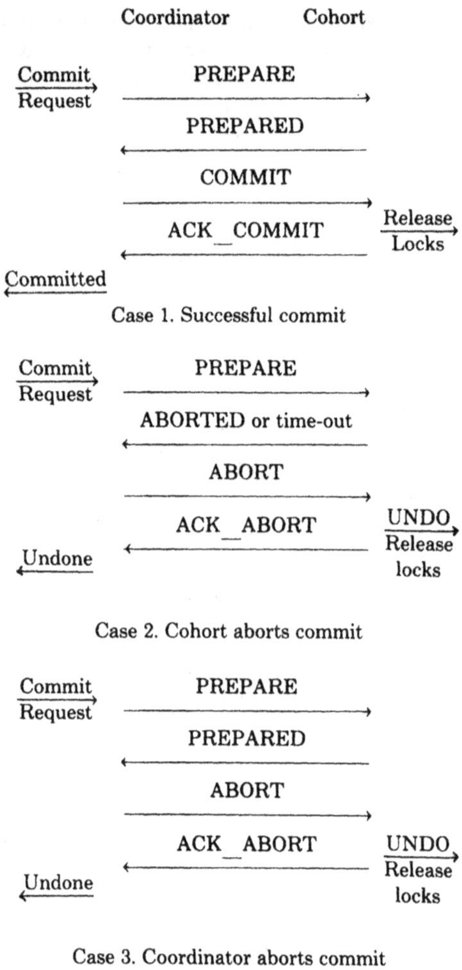

Figure 12. Possible coordinator–cohort interactions.

There is one more protocol that must be specified before the two-phase commit logic is complete. In the event of system crash and restart, the *recovery manager* must obey the following rules:

(1) If the commit coordinator crashes before completing step 1 of Phase 2 (coordinator log does not contain a COMMIT entry), then send an ABORT message to each cohort.
(2) If the commit coordinator crashes after step 1 of Phase 2 but before step 4 (coordinator log contains COMMIT but not COMPLETE), then send a COMMIT message to each cohort.
(3) If the commit coordinator crashes after step 4 of Phase 2 (coordinator log contains COMPLETE entry), then the transaction is already committed and the job of the commit coordinator is complete. Restart can be ignored.

In addition, we see that if any cohort aborts or crashes, causing time-out, then the entire transaction will be aborted. If a cohort crashes during its Phase 2, then the recovery manager can either undo or redo the transaction instance since the required information was written to the log during Phase 1. (The REDO and UNDO operations must be *idempotent*, i.e., repeatable any number of times, since restart may be retried.)

The net effect of the two-phase commit protocol is that either all the cohorts commit or that none of them commit (all are undone), thus satisfying the atomicity requirement. While no formal proof was given [GRAY79], Gray says that a more precise argument has been formulated. Lampson and Sturgis first developed a similar approach independently [LAMP76] and later expanded it [LAMP79]. Therein the central idea is that

> a transaction is made atomic by performing it in two *phases*:
>
> First, record the information necessary to do the writes in a set of *intentions*, without changing the data stored by the system. The last action taken in this phase is said to *commit* the transaction.
>
> Second, do the writes, actually changing the stored data.
>
> If a crash occurs after the transaction is committed but before all the changes to stored data have been done, the second phase is restarted. This restart happens as many times as necessary to … get all the changes made. [LAMP79, p. 18]

Lampson and Sturgis take a formal approach based on a hierarchy of virtual machines, while Gray's model is strongly influenced by an actual implementation.

Reed has recently proposed an alternate approach to implementing atomic actions in decentralized systems [REED78, REED79b]. It explicitly recognizes the interrelationship between the synchronization of access to shared objects and the recovery of objects in the case of failures, and is designed to solve both problems simultaneously. Reed describes the basic philosophy as follows [REED79b]: "Updating an object will be thought of as creating a new version, while reading an object will be thought of as selecting the proper version and obtaining its value." The synchronization and recovery problems associated with implementing atomic actions are reduced to the problem of creating, maintaining, and providing access to the collection of object versions.

The underlying implementation uses a modified timestamp mechanism, rather than explicit locks, to synchronize access to objects, and a two-phase commit protocol to achieve atomic update of a collection of objects. Two unique binary fractions, called *pseudotimes*, are associated with each version of an object. (Pseudotime values are constructed by concatenating two locally generated timestamps.) The first pseudotime value represents the time of the write that created the version and the second the time of the last read that accessed it.

Each atomic action is assigned a pseudotime value when it is started, which is used as the basis for accepting or rejecting (synchronizing) read and write requests. In particular, if a write with a pseudotime less than an already executed read arrives for an object, it cannot be executed, for that would invalidate the later read. The write must be rejected and the atomic action of which it is a part aborted.

Deadlock and inconsistency are avoided by having reads abort writes. Changes made by an atomic action (called *tokens*) are tagged as tentative until the atomic action completes successfully, at which time all the changes are committed simultaneously (using a modified two-phase commit mechanism) and each token becomes a new *version*. If completion of the atomic action is prevented because of system failure or an abort request, all tokens it has created are erased. Changes that have not been committed are not visible outside the atomic action. Additional details on possible implementation mechanisms can be found in REED78 and REED79a.

Reed's approach has several apparent drawbacks. One of the most obvious is that each update (write) generates a new object version. While in theory all versions of an object may need to be stored forever, Reed has proposed several acceptable ways to prune all but a few recent versions. This may cause some atomic actions to be aborted owing to missing object versions, but they can be restarted. Nevertheless, if object granularity is large (many pages or a whole file), considerable storage may be necessary to store even a modest number of past versions and current tokens.

A more serious limitation is that the proposed synchronization mechanism restricts the degree of concurrency more than alternative mechanisms. All concurrency control protocols must guarantee that the observable behavior of the system is the same as some serial schedule of the atomic actions.

The locking schemes discussed in Section 2.1 support the notion of compatible concurrent operations (like reads) on objects by independent atomic actions. Compatible operations on shared objects may be interleaved in real time. Since Reed's model does not incorporate the concept of compatible access modes, any two concurrent atomic actions accessing the same object (even for the purpose of reading) are forced to execute serially in real time, with the younger (in pseudotime) waiting for the older to complete or abort. Furthermore, as discussed above, a previous read may force a current write to be rejected and cause the entire atomic action to be aborted and restarted. Once restarted, there is no guarantee that this will not happen again, even indefinitely.

Finally, in the proposed implementation the abstract objects supported by the synchronization and recovery mechanism must be independent with separate physical representations and only two primitive access operations, read and write. In its present form this approach lacks the generality to support composite abstract objects (hierarchies and dags) and user-defined functions.

4. CONCLUSION

We have surveyed the related problems of synchronization and recovery in decentralized systems designed to support an object model of computation. Possible techniques for solving these problems have also been presented. Similar problems arise in all systems in which access to shared data must be controlled to preserve the data's consistency, and loss of critical data must be prevented to permit recovery. In fact, most of the techniques were first developed for use in distributed database and transaction-processing systems. Few have been fully implemented and tested even experimentally.

Distributed locking combined with deadlock detection or avoidance appears to be the most general and powerful concurrency control approach. However, in their present form none of the mechanisms can support arbitrary user- and application-defined object structures and access operations (functions). This capability must be provided to make the object model abstraction mechanism a usable high-level software structuring tool for distributed systems.

The atomic action has been introduced as the conceptual framework for error detection and recovery. This abstraction requires that the state of objects involved in an aborted or failed atomic action be backed up to some previously consistent state. Mechanisms for implementing atomic transactions (a form of atomic action specific to the database environment) have also been presented.

The real challenge, we find, is to design and implement an integrated system that provides the enhanced functionality necessary in a general object-based environment. This challenge is currently being addressed by university and industrial research groups. Their results should provide a deeper understanding of both the problems and solution techniques.

ACKNOWLEDGMENTS

This report was prepared while the author was on sabbatical at Digital Equipment Corporation, Maynard, Mass., and was supported in part by a Sabbatical Research Grant.

The author is indebted to Digital Equipment Corporation for financial support and the opportunity to be part of the Corporate Research Group while on sabbatical from the University of Massachusetts. Rick Peebles encouraged me to work in this area and prepare this report, and Tom Dopirak was kind enough to proofread my first draft thoroughly. I would also like to acknowledge the contribution of the referees, whose comments and suggestions helped to correct and enhanced the technical content, and the ACM editor whose many small but important grammatical and structural changes improved the style of the final version.

ANNOTATED BIBLIOGRAPHY

(Note. MENA78, RUSS77, SCHL76, and WULF75 were not referred to in text.)

ALSB76 ALSBERG, P. A., AND DAY, J. D. "A principle for resilient sharing of distributed resources," in *Proc. Int. Conf. Software Engineering*, San Francisco, Calif., Oct. 1976, pp. 562–570. A single primary, multiple backup strategy is proposed to support resilient distributed resource sharing. Update message protocol to support resiliency and restructuring is discussed.

ANDE76 ANDERSON, T., AND KERR, R. "Recovery blocks in action: A system supporting high reliability," in *Proc. Int. Conf. Software Engineering*, San Francisco, Calif., Oct. 1976, pp. 447–457. The recovery block scheme for providing software fault tolerance is reviewed and a new architectural device called the "recovery cache" is proposed to support the required state restoration in centralized systems. An improved implementation of the cache mechanism is described

ANDE78 ANDERSON, T., LEE, P. A., AND SHRIVASTAVA, S. K. "A model of recoverability in multilevel systems," *IEEE Trans. Softw. Eng.* **SE-4,** 6 (Nov. 1978), 486–494. The issues involved in supporting backward error recovery for abstract objects in layered multilevel interpretive systems are examined. Two recovery schemes (disjoint and inclusive) are presented for implementing recoverable objects.

BART77 BARTLETT, J. F., "A 'non stop' operating system," Tandem Computers Inc., Cupertino, Calif., 1977. The design of Guardian, the operating system for a fault-tolerant, general-purpose, multiple-computer commercial system, is discussed. Guardian is constructed from processes which communicate via messages. Fault tolerance is achieved by duplicating hardware and software components and checkpointing state changes so that a backup process may take over in the case of a failure.

BERN78 BERNSTEIN, P. A., ROTHNIE, J. B. JR., GOODMAN, N., AND PAPADIMITRIOU, C. A. "The concurrency control mechanism of SDD-1: A system for distributed databases. (the fully redundant case)," *IEEE Trans. Softw. Eng.* **SE-4,** 3 (May 1978), 154–168. This paper describes a method for updating data stored redundantly in a network of database management systems. The overhead of always locking all copies of data being updated is avoided by predefining transaction classes that require different levels of synchronization.

BERN79 BERNSTEIN, P. A., SHIPMAN, D. W., AND WONG, W. S. "Formal aspects of serializability in database concurrency control," *IEEE Trans. Softw. Eng.* **SE-5,** 3 (May

1979), 203–216. A formal model based on the use of a log of transaction read and write steps is developed for analyzing and comparing the behavior of different database concurrency control mechanisms. A simple centralized system that permits one read operation and one write operation per transaction is assumed for the analysis. Several proposed mechanisms that do not explicitly lock entities are shown to be equivalent to locking but to allow less concurrency than the conflict analysis method used in SDD-1.

BERN80a BERNSTEIN, P. A., AND SHIPMAN, D. W. "The correctness of concurrency control mechanisms in a system for distributed databases (SDD-1)," *ACM Trans. Database Syst.* **5**, 1 (March 1980), 52–68. The database supported by SDD-1 is distributed over multiple sites, and portions of the database may be replicated at individual locations. By means of formal analysis, the concurrency control strategy used in SDD-1 is shown to guarantee database consistency.

BERN80b BERNSTEIN, P. A., SHIPMAN, D. W., AND ROTHNIE, J. B. JR. "Concurrency control in a system for distributed databases (SDD-1)," *ACM Trans. Database Syst.* **5**, 1 (March 1980), 18–25. The mechanisms used in SDD-1 to preserve internal and multiple copy database consistency while supporting concurrent user transaction update requests are discussed in detail. The method is based on timestamps and the preanalysis of transactions into conflict classes. Implementation and reliability issues are also treated.

COFF71 COFFMAN, E. G. JR., ELPHIC, M. J., AND SHOSHANI, A. "System deadlocks," *Comput. Surv.* **3**, 2 (June 1971), 36–46. An early survey on the problem of deadlocks in multiprogramming systems. The necessary conditions for deadlock are characterized, and the approaches to treating the problem are discussed and categorized into three classes: prevention, detection and recovery, and avoidance.

DENN76 DENNING, P. J. "Fault-tolerant operating systems," *Comput. Surv.* **8**, 4 (Dec. 1976), 359–390. Capability-based architectures are examined as the basis for the design of reliable operating systems. The capability architecture is shown to support a high degree of error confinement.

ECKH78 ECKHOUSE, R. H. JR., AND STANKOVIC, J. A. "Issues in distributed processing—An overview of two workshops," *Computer* **11**, 1 (Jan. 1978), 22–26. A summary of two workshops on distributed computing held at Brown University in 1976 and 1977. The workshops had three broadly defined goals: (1) to define the field of distributed processing more precisely, (2) to examine the state of the art, and (3) to identify problem areas for future research.

ELLI77 ELLIS, C. "A robust algorithm for updating duplicate databases," in *Proc. 2nd Berkeley Workshop on Distributed Management of Data and Computer Networks,* Berkeley, Calif., May 1977, pp. 146–158. Two algorithms, centralized and decentralized, for updating a distributed multiple copy database are formally specified using evaluation nets, a modified form of Petri net. The decentralized solution is robust with respect to node failure.

ENSL78 ENSLOW, P. H. JR. "What is a 'distributed' data processing system?" *Computer* **11**, 1 (Jan. 1978), 13–21. Since the term "distributed processing" has become overused and misused, this paper is an attempt to specify the characteristics of a new class of systems to be called "distributed data processing systems." These systems are characterized along three dimensions: hardware decentralization, control decentralization, and database decentralization. The systems of interest exhibit a high degree of distribution in all dimensions, as well as a high degree of cooperative autonomy in their overall operation.

ESWA76 ESWARAN, K. P., GRAY, J. N., LORIE, R. A., AND TRAIGER, I. L. "The notions of consistency and predicate locks in a database system," *Commun. ACM* **19**, 11 (Nov. 1976), 624–633. The notions of transaction, consistency, and locking are formally defined by an abstract data model. It is then shown that consistency requires that transactions be two-phase and well-formed, and conversely that if all transactions are well-formed and two-phase they are consistent. Logical locking based on predicates is shown to solve the problem of locking nonexistent or phantom records in a database environment.

GARC78 GARCIA-MOLINA, H. "Performance comparison of two update algorithms for distributed databases," in *Proc. 3rd Berkeley Workshop on Distributed Data Management and Computer Networks*, Berkeley, Calif., 1978, pp. 108–119. A detailed set of simulations is used to compare the performance of two update algorithms: centralized locking and distributed voting. The database is assumed to be fully replicated at each site, and updates are the only access operations. The results show that centralized locking performs considerably better than distributed voting on a wide variety of measures except in high-load cases where both perform poorly.

GARC79 GARCIA-MOLINA, H. "A concurrency control mechanism for distributed databases which uses centralized locking controllers," in *Proc. 4th Berkeley Conf. Distributed Data Management and Computer Networks*, Berkeley, Calif., Aug. 1979, pp. 113–124. A concurrency control mechanism based on independent centralized controllers which operate without explicit backup is proposed. A modified two-phase commit protocol that requires only a majority of acknowledgments from copies is used to perform updates.

GLIG80 GLIGOR, V. D., AND SHATTUCK, S. H. "On deadlock detection in distributed systems," *IEEE Trans. Softw. Eng.* **SE-6,** 5 (Sept. 1980), 435–440. A counterexample is used to show that one of the two deadlock detection protocols proposed by Menasce and Muntz [MENA79], the distributed protocol, is incorrect. Furthermore, it is argued that even a corrected version of this or any similar distributed protocol will be impractical due to performance considerations.

GRAY75 GRAY, J. N., LORIE, R. A., AND PUTZOLU, G. R. "Granularity of locks in a shared data base," in *Proc. Int. Conference Very Large Data Bases*, Sept. 1975, vol. 1, no. 1, pp. 428–451. A method for locking sets of resources described by tree and directed acyclic graph hierarchies is presented. The protocol allows simultaneous locking at various granularities and is based on the introduction of additional lock modes that are assigned to the ancestor nodes.

GRAY79 GRAY, J. N. "Notes on data base operating systems," in *Operating systems: An advanced course*, R. Bayer, R. M. Graham, and G. Seegmuller, Eds., Springer-Verlag, New York, 1979, pp. 393–481. After an overview presentation on database management and data communications, the report focuses on the problems of locking and recovery in a transaction environment. A detailed and unified design is presented and compared with alternative approaches. This design is based largely on ideas developed and implemented by members of the System R group at IBM Research, San Jose, Calif.

HAMM78 HAMMER, M., AND SHIPMAN, D. "An overview of reliability mechanisms for a distributed data base system," in *COMPCON Spring '78 Proc*, Feb. 1978, pp. 63–65. Mechanisms to create a reliable network that guarantees the eventual delivery of messages and the broadcast of messages to a number of sites are discussed. This approach is being used to support the redundant update mechanisms of SDD-1, a distributed database system being designed and implemented by the Computer Corporation of America.

JONE79 JONES, A. K. "The object model: A conceptual tool for structuring software," in *Operating systems: An advanced course*, R. Bayer, R. M. Graham, and G. Seegmuller, Eds., Springer-Verlag, New York, 1979, pp. 8–16. This introductory chapter gives a general explanation of the object model and considers some of its ramifications with respect to operating system design.

KATZ77 KATZMAN, J. A. "A fault-tolerant computing system," Tandem Computers, Inc., Cupertino, Calif., 1977. The hardware architecture of a fault-tolerant commercially available computer system is described. The design goals were (1) to provide continuous operation through any single hardware failure, and (2) to be able to repair failures while the system remains on-line.

LAGA79 LAGALLY, K. "Synchronization in a layered system," in *Operating systems: An advanced course*, R. Bayer, R. M. Graham, and G. Seegmuller, Eds., Springer-Verlag, New York, 1979, pp. 253–281. Five mechanisms (semaphores, conditional critical regions, monitors, path expressions, and object managers) for synchronizing access to shared objects in a layered system of cooperating sequential processes are reviewed and compared. Solutions to the "Readers and Writers" and "Five Dining Philosophers" synchronization problems are presented using each mechanism. The object manager solution, while not without fault, is the only one that can be easily adapted for use in a distributed system.

LAMP78 LAMPORT, L. "Time, clocks, and the ordering of events in a distributed system," *Commun. ACM* **21,** 7 (July 1978), 558–565. The relationship of physical time and event ordering in distributed systems is examined. The concept of one event happening before another is shown to define a partial ordering of the events which can be associated with a system of logical clocks implemented by counters. A protocol for extending this partial ordering to a total ordering which can be used to synchronize events is given and then applied to the problem of synchronizing physical clocks.

LAMP76 LAMPSON, B. W., AND STURGIS, H. E. "Crash recovery in a distributed storage system," unpublished paper, Computer Science Lab., Xerox Palo Alto Research Center, Palo Alto, Calif., 1976. An algorithm for maintaining the consistency of a distributed file system in the presence of individual crashes is presented. The algorithm is based on the use of an "intentions list" to implement atomic transactions.

LAMP79 LAMPSON, B. W., AND STURGIS, H. E. "Crash recovery in a distributed storage system," unpublished paper, Computer Science Lab., Xerox Palo Alto Research Center, Palo Alto, Calif., 1979. A revised and expanded algorithm is presented for maintaining the consistency and reliable storage of data in a distributed system when different portions of the database are updated as a single transaction. The approach is based on implementing a hierarchy of abstract machines.

LEDG77 LEDGARD, H. F., AND TAYLOR, R. W. "Two views of data abstraction," *Commun. ACM* **20**, 6 (June 1977), 382-384. An introduction to a collection of selected papers from the ACM Conference on Data: Abstraction, Definition and Structure, presented at Salt Lake City, Utah, March 1976. It is argued that work on data abstraction has proceeded in two directions: in the language area, where the emphasis is on type definition facilities for new languages, and in the database area, where the research is focused on using abstraction as an aid to understanding and controlling complexity.

LELA78 LE LANN, G. "Algorithms for distributed data-sharing systems which use tickets," in *Proc. 3rd Berkeley Workshop on Distributed Data Management and Computer Networks*, Berkeley, Calif., Aug. 1978, pp. 259-272. A virtual ring with circulating tickets is proposed as a solution to the problem of synchronizing access to shared data in a distributed system. Four distributed algorithms are described for acquiring tickets. The scheme is shown to survive failures of the ring controllers.

LEUN79 LEUNG, J. Y. T., AND LAI, E. K. "On minimum cost recovery from system deadlock," *IEEE Trans. Comput.* **C-28**, 9 (Sept. 1979), 671-677. Under the assumption that the cost of aborting each member of a set of deadlocked jobs is known, the problem of selecting a minimum total cost deadlock breaking set is shown to be NP-complete. Three fast heuristics are proposed, and their worst case performance is analyzed.

LIN79 LIN, W. K. "Concurrency control in a multiple copy distributed database system," in *Proc. 4th Berkeley Conf. Distributed Data Management and Computer Networks*, Berkeley, Calif., Aug. 1979, pp. 207-220. Modifications to the concurrency control mechanism of SDD-1 are proposed which eliminate the need for timestamps on data items and weaken the constraints of some of the read-write protocols.

LOME77 LOMET, D. B. "Process structuring, synchronization, and recovery using atomic actions," in *Proc. Conf. on Language Design for Reliable Software*, (ACM) *SIGPLAN Notices*, vol. 12, no. 3, March 1977, pp. 128-137. Atomic actions are explored as means of structuring and controlling concurrent computations. Action procedures are proposed as ways of specifying atomic actions in a programming language, and it is shown that synchronization can be achieved by means of an await statement. As an example, these mechanisms are used to implement recovery blocks.

LORI77 LORIE, R. A. "Physical integrity in a large segmented database," *ACM Trans. Database Syst.* **2**, 1 (March 1977), 91-104. A recovery mechanism based on maintaining two versions of modified pages, the current page and previous page, is presented. The overhead required to maintain the pages is shown to be quite low.

MENA78 MENASCE, D. A., POPEK, G. R., AND MUNTZ, R. R. "A locking protocol for resource coordination in distributed databases," in *Proc. SIGMOD Int. Conf. on Management of Data*, Austin, Texas, 1978 (supplement), pp. 1-14. A locking protocol based on a centralized lock table with local backup copies is proposed and shown to be resilient to node and communication failures. Recovery mechanisms are given and proved to be robust. Bounds on the performance are presented. A hierarchy of lock controllers is proposed as method of improving performance where lock requests exhibit strong locality.

MENA79 MENASCE, D. A., AND MUNTZ, R. R. "Locking and deadlock detection in distributed data bases," *IEEE Trans. Softw. Eng.* **SE-5**, 3 (May 1979), 195-201. Two protocols for deadlock detection based on the detection of cycles in the transaction-wait-for graph are presented and analyzed. The first is based on a hierarchy of lock controllers and the second on a partitioning of the resources by decentralized local controllers.

MILE79 MILENKOVIC, M. "Update synchronization in multiaccess database systems," Ph.D. dissertation, Dep. of Electrical and Computer Engineering, Univ. Massachusetts, Amherst, May 1979. A unified reservation mechanism for synchronizing concurrent updates in single- and multiple-copy distributed database systems is proposed. The approach is based on the use of two compatible protocols that match the requirements of different types of transactions. The first is required to preclaim all the entities required by the transaction but is guaranteed not to be preempted, while the second is allowed to dynamically lock database entities but may be preempted and required to roll back a finite number of times.

PAPA79 PAPADIMITRIOU, C. H. "Serializability of concurrent database updates," *J. ACM* **26, 4** (Oct. 1979), 631-653. The serializability of a general sequence of interleaved transactions is proved to be an NP-complete problem. Existing concurrency control protocols are shown to generate special classes of schedules that can be detected efficiently.

PEEB78 PEEBLES, R., AND MANNING, E. "System architecture for distributed data management," *Computer* **11,** 1 (Jan.

1978), 40–47. The architectures for distributed data management systems are classified as either (1) integrated or loosely coupled multiprocessors, (2) homogeneous federation, or (3) heterogeneous federation. Five fundamental problems that must be addressed by any data management system are then discussed: (1) how to provide an integrated database, (2) where to store data in the system, (3) how to locate data, (4) how to control concurrent access, and (5) how to provide security and integrity.

PEEB80 PEEBLES, R., AND DOPIRAK, T. "ADAPT: A guest system," in *COMPCON Spring '80 Proc.*, Feb. 1980. This paper describes the kernel of a distributed operating system that runs on top of existing single host operating systems that are networked together. The purpose of the kernel is to transform the network of individual systems into a single unified system that will be easier for application programmers to use.

RAND75 RANDELL, B. "System structure for software fault tolerance." *IEEE Trans. Softw. Eng.* **SE-1,** 2 (June 1975), 220–232. A method of achieving software fault tolerance by means of standby sparing is proposed. The goal is to provide dependable error detection and recovery facilities by using a system structuring technique called the recovery block, which is used to specify an acceptance test and alternate spare program components. Reliable systems are implemented by building multilevel interpretive virtual machines.

RAND78 RANDELL, B., LEE, P. A., AND TRELEAVEN, P. C. "Reliability issues in computing system design," *Comput. Surv.* **10,** 2 (June 1978), 123–165. This paper surveys the various problems involved in achieving high reliability from complex computing systems, and discusses the relationship between system structuring techniques and techniques of fault tolerance. Topics covered include (1) redundancy in hardware and software, (2) the use of atomic actions to structure the activity of a system to limit information flow and provide recovery points, (3) strategies for locating and dealing with faults and for assessing the damage they have caused, and (4) forward and backward error recovery techniques. Three case studies of the use of these techniques in actual systems are presented.

RAND79 RANDELL, B. "Reliable computing systems," in *Operating systems: An advanced course*, R. Bayer, R. M. Graham, and G. Seegmuller, Eds., Springer-Verlag, New York, 1979, pp. 282–391. A somewhat expanded version of the report by Randell, Lee, and Treleaven [RAND78].

REED78 REED, D. P. "Naming and synchronization in a decentralized computer system," Ph.D. dissertation; Tech. Rep. TR-205, M.I.T. Lab. for Computer Science, Sept. 1978. A new approach to the synchronization of accesses to shared data objects is developed. Modifiable objects are treated as a sequence of versions, where each version is the state of the object after an update. Synchronization is achieved by a mechanism that names the proper version to be read, based on a pseudotime associated with its state.

REED79a REED, D. P., AND KANODIA, R. K. "Synchronization with eventcounts and sequencers," *Commun. ACM* **22,** 2 (Feb. 1979), 115–123. Synchronization mechanisms which are based on observing and signaling the occurrence of events associated with abstract objects called eventcounts and sequencers are defined. Eventcounts are suggested as an alternative synchronization mechanism for processes in a distributed system that do not require mutually exclusive access to shared objects. For those cases where a total ordering is necessary, the use of a ticketing operation on a sequencer object is proposed. Implementation of the sequencer requires some underlying arbitration mechanism to achieve mutual exclusion.

REED79b REED, D. P. "Implementing atomic actions on decentralized data" (abstract), in *Proc. 7th Symposium on Operating System Principles* (ACM), Dec. 1979. (Paper will appear in *Commun. ACM*). The problems of synchronizing accesses to shared data and recovering the state of such data in the case of failures are shown to be two related aspects of the same problem—implementing atomic actions. A unified mechanism that solves both problems in the context of a decentralized system is introduced. This paper contains the basic ideas developed in the author's Ph.D. dissertation.

RIES79 RIES, D.R., AND STONEBRAKER, M. R. "Locking granularity revisited," *ACM Trans. Database Syst.* **4,** 2 (June 1979), 210–227. A stimulation model is used to examine the effects of locking on the performance of a centralized database system. Computer utilization is determined as a function of the lock granularity, as measured by the percent of the database locked by each lock operation. The sensitivity of the results to the placement of locks, lock request strategy, and lock hierarchy is investigated.

ROSE78 ROSENKRANTZ, D. J., STEARNS, R. E., AND LEWIS, P. M. "System level concurrency control for distributed database systems," *ACM Trans. Database Syst.* **3,** 2 (June 1978), 178–198. Several system-level concurrency control protocols for distributed database systems are formally presented and compared. The methods are based on a logical timestamp ordering of the requests. Two protocols called WAIT-DIE and WOUND-WAIT are suggested for implementation in decentralized systems.

ROTH80 ROTHNIE, J. B. JR., BERNSTEIN, P. A., FOX, S., GOODMAN, N., HAMMER, M., LANDERS, T. A., REEVE, C., SHIPMAN, D. W., AND WONG, E. "Introduction to a system for distributed databases (SDD-1)," *ACM Trans. Database Syst.* **5,** 1 (March 1980), 1–17. An overview of the design of SDD-1, a distributed database management system being developed by Computer Corporation of America, is presented. Users interact with SDD-1 as if it were a centralized single-user database system. SDD-1 handles all the issues arising from the distribution and concurrent access of data. Solutions to the following issues are discussed: distributed concurrency control, distributed query processing, resiliency to component failure, and distributed directory management.

RUSS77 RUSSEL, D. L. "Process backup in producer–consumer systems," in *Proc. 6th Conference on Operating System Principles* (ACM), Nov. 1977, reprinted in *Oper. Syst. Rev.* **11,** 5, 151–157. The problem of managing state restoration during process recovery is discussed, and a technique for limiting the domino effect is described. The method is based on the fact that when process interactions are asymmetric (producer–consumer situations), it is not necessary to back up both processes.

RYPK79 RYPKA, D. J., AND LUCIDO, A. P. "Deadlock detection and avoidance for shared logical resources," *IEEE Trans. Softw. Eng.* **SE-5,** 5 (Sept. 1979), 465–471. Modes are used to specify the manner in which processes may concurrently access logical resources. Mode compatibility is defined and used to specify deadlock detection and avoidance strategies.

SALT78 SALTZER, J. H. "Research problems of decentralized systems with largely autonomous nodes," *Oper. Syst. Rev.* **12,** 1 (Jan. 1978), 43–52. Research problems associated with the design of decentralized computer systems consisting of a loose confederacy of cooperating autonomous nodes are discussed informally. Topics covered include use of the object model of computation, reliability, integrity, responsibility for protection, the naming problem, atomic updates, and the provision for "close" rather than "correct" results.

SCHL76 SCHLAGETER, G. "The problem of lock by value in large data bases," *Comput. J.* **19,** 1 (Feb. 1976), 17–20. The concept of lock by value in multiple-access database systems is developed, and a lock system to support this approach is proposed. The problems of implementing lock by value are discussed.

SEVE76 SEVERANCE, D. G., AND LOHMAN, G. M. "Differential files: Their application to the maintenance of large databases," *ACM Trans. Database Syst.* **1,** 3 (Sept. 1976), 256–267. The use of differential files to represent modified data is described, and the advantages of using this representation are presented.

SHAP78 SHAPIRO, R. M., AND MILLSTEIN, R. E. "Failure recovery in a distributed data base system," in *COMPCON Spring '78 Proc.*, Feb. 1978, pp. 66–70. A mechanism for maintaining the consistency of redundant copies of a database in the event of a crash of one or more of the sites is presented. Each site maintains a recent update history which is used to restore the crashed site.

SHRI78 SHRIVASTAVA, S. K., AND BANATRE, J. P. "Reliable resource allocation between unreliable processes," *IEEE Trans. Softw. Eng.* **SE-4,** 3 (May 1978), 230–241. Error recovery problems associated with interacting processes are discussed, and an argument for using separate recovery mechanisms for cooperative and competitive processes is put forward. A recovery mechanism based on new programming language features (recoverable monitors and ports) is developed for processes which compete for the use of shared resources. This work extends the recovery block approach.

SILB80 SILBERSCHATZ, A., AND KEDEM, Z. "Consistency in hierarchical database systems," *J. ACM* **27,** 1 (Jan. 1980), 72–80. The problems of locking and consistency in database systems consisting of records organized hierarchically as a tree are studied. A record locking protocol that is deadlock-free and ensures consistency is presented. This approach does not implicitly lock all the nodes of a subtree when the root is locked.

SMIT77a SMITH, J. M., AND SMITH, D. C. P. "Database abstractions: Aggregation," *Commun. ACM* **20,** 6 (June 1977), 405–413. Aggregation, a data abstraction which transforms a relationship between several objects into a higher level object, is introduced and defended as necessary for real-world applications. A new data type, called aggregate, is developed to support aggregation abstractions.

SMIT77b SMITH, J. M., AND SMITH, D. C. P. "Database abstractions: Aggregation and generalization," *ACM Trans. Database Syst.* **2,** 2 (June 1977), 105–133. Two types of abstraction (aggregation and generalization) are put forward as being fundamental in database design and usage. Aggregation is an abstraction which turns a relationship between objects into an aggregate object. Generalization is an abstraction which turns a class of objects into a generic object.

STON79 STONEBRAKER, M. "Concurrency control and consistency of multiple copies of data in distributed INGRES," *IEEE Trans. Softw. Eng.* **SE-5,** 3 (May 1979), 180–194. Distributed INGRES is a proposed distributed version of a relational database system designed and implemented by researchers at the University of California, Berkeley. This paper describes the design philosophy and presents rough outlines of the algorithms proposed for concurrency control, consistency of multiple copies of data, and system crash recovery. Concurrency control is based on the use of local locking and deadlock controllers which cooperate with a centralized controller (the SNOOP) for global deadlock detection.

THOM79 THOMAS, R. H. "A majority consensus approach to concurrency control for multiple copy databases," *ACM Trans. Database Syst.* **4,** 2 (June 1979), 180–209. An algorithm based on the timestamping mechanism and a "majority consensus" procedure at voting sites is proposed for the synchronization of updates in multiple-copy databases. The approach utilizes distributed control and is shown to be resilient in the presence of communication and database site failures.

VERH78 VERHOFSTAD, J. S. M. "Recovery techniques for database systems," *Comput. Surv.* **10,** 2 (June 1978), 167–195. This paper surveys the techniques used to implement backing out, crash recovery, crash resistance, and consistency in database file systems. The techniques are categorized according to the environment in which they are used and the purpose for which they are applied.

WATS79 WATSON, R. W., AND FLETCHER, J. G. "An architecture for support of network operating system services," in *Proc. 4th Berkeley Conf. on Distributed Data Management and Networks,* Aug. 1979, pp. 18–50. It is argued that network architectures should be designed explicitly to support a coherent network operating system. The suggested model has three levels of protocol: an interprocess communication layer, a service support layer, and a layer of standard services.

WULF75 WULF, W. A. "Reliable hardware/software architecture," *IEEE Trans. Softw. Eng.* **SE-1,** 2 (June 1975), 233–240. A strategy used to achieve reliability in a hardware/software system is discussed. The proposed approach is based on an extension of modular programming methodology to include dynamic error detection and recovery. Each module is responsible for maintaining the integrity of the abstraction it implements.

Received May 1980; final revision accepted March 1981.

Concurrency Control and Consistency of Multiple Copies of Data in Distributed INGRES

MICHAEL STONEBRAKER

Abstract—This paper contains algorithms for ensuring the consistency of a distributed relational data base subject to multiple, concurrent updates. Also included are mechanisms to correctly update multiple copies of objects and to continue operation when less than all machines in the network are operational. Together with [4] and [12], this paper constitutes the significant portions of the design for a distributed data base version of INGRES.

Index Terms—Concurrency control, crash recovery, distributed data bases, multiple copies, synchronization.

I. INTRODUCTION

THIS PAPER contains a collection of algorithms to handle concurrency control, crash recovery, and the update of multiple copies of relations in a distributed data base system. Together with [4] and [12], this suggests the heart of the design for a distributed version of the relational data base system, INGRES. Earlier thoughts on the same subject are presented in [17], [19].

The algorithms presented herein are based on what might be called the "primary site" model [1], [17] for copies. As such, these algorithms borrow notions from the work in [1]. Hence, each object possesses a known primary site to which all updates in the network for that object are first directed. It should be clearly noted that different objects may have different primary sites.

In our environment an object is a subset of the rows of a relation (a so-called fragment [14]). Consequently, a relation is partitioned into fragments, each with a primary site and some number of redundant copies. The syntax by which fragments, primary sites, and copies are specified is given in [12].

Concurrency control is, of course, a problem with which to contend. Unlike D. A. Menasce *et al.* [8], who proposes a centralized "GOD" called the lock controller to maintain lock tables and detect and resolve deadlock, we propose to handle locking in a distributed fashion. Deadlock detection and resolution can also be distributed, but we propose allocating these tasks to one machine called the SNOOP. It will be seen that extremely low lock overhead can be achieved using our scheme.

Lastly, crash recovery entails two tasks: 1) handling the failure of a single node in the network, and 2) dealing with a failure that partitions the network. It will be seen that both situations can be handled by very simple algorithms.

In the next section we point out some fundamental assumptions we have made and explain the environment in which distributed data management takes place, Then, in Sections III and IV, we present the algorithms for concurrency control and consistency of multiple copies, respectively. Lastly, in Section V, we examine our proposal in light of those in [3], [8], [13], and [18].

Throughout this paper we only sketch our algorithms and make no attempt at formal proofs. Arguments along the lines of [7] and [8] can be applied to our situation without difficulty, but for the sake of brevity, they are omitted.

II. THE ASSUMED ENVIRONMENT

Our work is based on the four following basic assumptions. (The reader can think of these as global assumptions about the "state of the world." For environments where these are not true, our proposals may not be appropriate.)

1) Locality: At least 95 percent of the traffic to be processed by a distributed data base system is *local.* By this we mean that all data to successfully process an interaction are resident at the site where the interaction originates. Moreover, this statement holds even if there are no redundant copies of objects. We make this assumption based on our belief that other architectural choices (namely centralization or tightly coupled networks with a notion of "GOD") become cost effective when traffic is not predominantly local.

2) Reliability: Computer hardware (and perhaps software) is becoming more reliable. Hence, when possible, mechanisms should make normal processing faster at the expense of lengthened crash recovery time.

3) Closeness: The main performance consideration when processing an interaction is whether it is *local* or not. Nonlocal interactions are not expected to be scaled on "closeness," and the notion of a "nearby" site is not assumed to be meaningful. This is a reasonable approximation of most real networks that we are familiar with.

4) Types of Networks: The algorithms should work well for both "broadcast" networks and "point-to-point" networks. Hence, they should be able to utilize the capabilities of a network where the cost to send a message to all sites is almost equal to the cost to communicate it to one site. Likewise, the algorithms should also perform well if only point-to-point communication is possible. To a first approximation, we

Manuscript received February 6, 1978; revised November 1, 1978. This research was supported in part by the Naval Electronics Systems Command under Grant N00039-78-C-0013 and by the National Science Foundation under Grant MCS75-03839-A01.

The author is with the Electronics Research Laboratory, University of California, Berkeley, CA 94720.

think of the ETHERNET [9] and the ARPANET [10] as generic examples of these two cases.

The algorithms we propose must exist within the context of the query processing done by a distributed INGRES in handling transactions. We now give necessary information on distributed query processing.

A transaction T in our environment consists of ONE QUEL command which is either a RETRIEVE or an UPDATE (APPEND, DELETE, REPLACE). There is no extra algorithmic complexity in handling the more general case where a transaction consists of an arbitrary collection of such commands. The only problem is that crash recovery will be decomposed into local crash recovery followed by some extra processing. Current INGRES one-site crash recovery software can only handle the smaller transactions, and we do not plan to rewrite it to be more general.

In the discussion to follow, the reader should note that while we present the restricted context, our algorithms will work for the general case if one pretends that the local notions of "commit transaction" and "recover transaction" handle the general case for a one-site environment.

Such a transaction originates from a user process (application program or interactive terminal monitor) at some site i in the network. A "master" or coordinating collection of INGRES processes is invoked at site i. This master creates "slave" INGRES processes at other sites and ensures that each slave knows the identity of all other slaves. Although slaves need be created only at sites where processing will take place, it may be convenient to pretend that they exist at all sites. Hence, we make no further note of creating or destroying slaves. As discussed in [4], a master can send two commands to slaves: 1) run the (local) interaction I at a subset of the sites, and 2) send a copy of fragment R_j to a subset of the sites in the network.

The slaves eventually return a "done." By a sequence of such commands the master ensures that the user interaction is eventually processed. The details on how such a sequence is generated appear in [4].

If T is a RETRIEVE command then it can be equally thought of as a sequence $I_1, \cdots, I_n$ of interactions where each I_j is either a local RETRIEVE command or a SEND command to be executed on a subcollection of the sites.

If T is an update, the master first generates a RETRIEVE command to figure out what to do. This command is processed as above and (eventually) generates a deferred update list of the changes to be made. As noted in [4], these lists of updates may not always be at the site where the tuples to be updated reside. Consequently, the lists may have to be appropriately shuffled so that each slave has a complete deferred update list for its site. Since each slave knows the identity of all other slaves, it can simply wait for a message from all other sites containing the appropriate tuples. Alternatively, the master site knows the collection of sites where deferred update is possible. It can send this information to the slaves with some interaction I. Each slave, in this case, need only expect a message from this subset of sites.

When all is appropriately arranged, a "commit transaction" message must be sent by the master to all slaves. Hence, an update transaction is a sequence of local interactions $I_1, \cdots, I_n$, followed by some shuffling and a "commit transaction." The detailed protocols to be followed on updates will be explained presently.

It should be noted that $I_1, \cdots, I_n$ for RETRIEVES and updates is always a collection of local RETRIEVES and SENDS. For updates, however, the local RETRIEVES that isolate changes to be made sometimes contain a "tuple identifier" as part of the requested data. In this way, the deferred update list will have an indication of exactly which tuples must be modified. The "tuple identifier" also indicates that the current RETRIEVE is really isolating tuples which will later be changed. Hence, for some local locking algorithms (such as [5]), these must be considered writes rather than reads.

III. Concurrency Control Algorithm

If T is a RETRIEVE command, proceed according to step 1 or step 2.

Step 1: (High performance but has data integrity problems.) The master directs each interaction I to the local copy of each object. If one does not exist, he directs it to the primary copy. Section IV indicates how the identity of the primary copy is determined.

Step 2: (Lower performance but no "surprises.") The master directs each I to the primary copy of each object. (We will discuss in Section IV what the "surprises" are and when step 1 can be safely chosen.) Alternatively, if T is an update, the master must direct each I to the primary copy of the object without exception.

Note that the choice of step 1 or step 2 will affect whether a particular interaction is local or not. Hence, it may affect the sequence of interactions which is chosen by the master during distributed decomposition.

A local concurrency controller (CC) runs at each site. This CC sees a transaction T as consisting of a collection of interactions $I_1, \cdots, I_n$, each local to that site which it receives one by one from the master. It is assumed that level 3 consistency [5] for such a transaction is satisfied. How CC performs this task is of no concern here. All that matters is that the response to each interaction I, which a master sends to a slave, is a "done" (indicating that it is complete) or no response (indicating that it is either still processing or is waiting for permission from the CC to proceed further).

Since the sequence of interactions may not be known in advance, deadlock may occur. If it happens within one machine, the CC picks a victim and performs local backout. The appropriate slave sends a "reset" message to his master which in turn resets all other slaves. This accomplishes backing out T.

However, deadlock may happen in such a way that it involves multiple machines. We suggest the following mechanism to deal with this problem. Whenever an interaction is run at a node it will either run to completion or wait, due to a lock conflict. Say transaction T_j holds a lock for which transaction T_k waits. When CC detects such a condition, it sends identifiers for T_j and T_k to an agreed on machine (the SNOOP). The SNOOP then detects deadlock by ordinary analysis of the global "wait for" graph, which it can generate from all such messages. When a master completes a transaction, it sends a "done" to the SNOOP, who can appropriately update his "wait for" graph.

In summary, each site has a CC that handles concurrency control for local transactions (using some technique). The lock tables each CC creates and uses are *local* to its site and are present nowhere else. Only the SNOOP needs to be informed of "wait for" conditions.

In the absence of crashes, it is clear that such a scheme can work correctly. We now turn to control of multiple copies and crash recovery.

IV. Copies and Crash Recovery

There are two algorithms to handle copies and crash recovery. One is called the "performance" algorithm. It processes updates with the minimum possible delay (i.e., fastest possible response time). However, it will be seen to have a data consistency problem since transactions can be lost and relations can become inconsistent if certain sorts of crashes happen. In the absence of crashes, however, there are no consistency problems.

This algorithm will require the notion of a "copy INGRES." This is an invocation of INGRES that can receive a complete deferred update list from a slave INGRES for some object and performs the update on a copy of that object. A copy INGRES must exist for every copy of the object which is not the primary copy.

The other algorithm is called the "reliability" algorithm. It ensures that there is never a data consistency problem. However, there may be a substantial response time penalty in order to guarantee this.

In this section we make the following assumptions.

1) Crashes of a single node can happen. Service is restored after some delay. Local crash recovery procedures will automatically be run and will guarantee that local transactions, which were "committed" before the crash but whose effects were not completely merged into the local data base, are correctly committed.

2) Communication failures can happen. They will either be transparent or will partition the network into subsets that cannot communicate with each other.

3) Every message sent is reliably received if the recipient is "up" and the sender does not crash inopportunely. If the recipient is down, the sender can queue the message for later delivery. Presumably, it is queued at the sender's site so that subsequent delivery can only happen if the sender is "up."

In this section we will indicate several algorithms that must be run by the various actors under various circumstances. The data structures used in the algorithms are the following.

A. Data Structures

Each machine in the network maintains the following information.

1) A State Flag: This is either "normal," indicating normal operation, or "restructure," which means the network is dynamically adjusting to a crash or restoration of service.

2) An Up-List: This is a list of sites that the given node thinks are in operation. These sites form a "logical partition" [8] of the network that may lag in time behind the actual physical state of the network.

3) The Identity of the Current SNOOP: This is an identifier for the machine that performs deadlock detection. If the up-list changes in such a way that the current SNOOP is not in the up-list, there is a globally agreed upon procedure for choosing a new SNOOP.

Moreover, each master INGRES must have the following.

4) A Commit Flag: This flag is set by the master when it thinks that a transaction is committed. It is reset otherwise.

Each slave INGRES must have the following.

5) A Ready Flag: This flag is set if the slave has the proper deferred update list and is ready to commit a transaction. It is reset otherwise.

6) A Commit Flag: This is set when the slave believes that his transaction is committed and is reset otherwise.

Lastly, the location of all copies for each object is known (by an examination of some system catalogs whose composition will not concern us here). In addition, there is a known linear ordering of all these copies. As a result, any site can always access its up-list and find the particular copy which is lowest in the ordering among those at sites in the up-list. This is by definition the PRIMARY COPY of the object.

Now, if the network is currently partitioned, nodes in different partitions will disagree on the identity of the primary copy. Obviously, chaos would result if more than one partition was allowed to independently update a given object, since there would be no possible way to make the objects consistent when the network was repaired. The easiest way to avoid this situation is to allow a primary copy to exist *only* if a majority of all copies are at sites in the up-list. Otherwise, the object is inaccessible.

However, it should be clearly noted that a problem arises in the case where there are exactly two copies of an object. In this (presumably very common) situation, any network partition will make both copies inaccessible. To handle this, one must be able to tell the difference between 1) a crash of a single site and 2) a network partition that leaves each copy in a different partition. In the former case we wish the backup copy to become the primary, while in the latter case we do not. If these two situations cannot be differentiated, the backup copy is worthless.

There are six algorithms to be presented. In order to assist the reader we first outline the general flow of control before proceeding with the details.

ALGORITHM MASTER, SLAVE, and COPY are executed, respectively, by master, slave, and copy INGRES's. The key point is that a master has a "commit point" when it sets its commit flag. Before that point, it will back out a transaction if a failure occurs. After that point it will ensure that the transaction is correctly committed. The tactics used amount to a "two-phase" commit protocol [6] and are similar to the proposal of [7].

Each slave responds to directives from the master. It uses the local commit flag to indicate whether it thinks that the transaction is committed. On crashes, local recovery examines the flag to decide whether to back out or complete the local transaction. When a slave commits a transaction, it in turn directs copy INGRES's to correctly update the auxiliary copies.

The final three algorithms are run in the context of failures. ALGORITHM LOCAL RECOVERY performs "local cleanup" and is run when a site wishes to resume service. ALGORITHM RECONFIGURE is used to adjust the up-list after a failure or a service restoration. It allows the network to continue with less than all sites operational or even in a partitioned state. Lastly, ALGORITHM SLAVE PROMOTE is run when a master crashes. Its purpose is to allow the slaves to correctly finish or backout the transaction in question.

B. The Performance Algorithms

The reader is again cautioned that data integrity problems exist in the algorithms which are now presented.

1) ALGORITHM MASTER: This is the algorithm to be used by a master INGRES when it receives an update transaction T from a user process.

m1) Refuse T unless state = "normal."

m2) Examine the up-list and calculate the primary site for each object involved in T. Refuse T if the primary site of any object is inaccessible.

m3) Supervise distributed decomposition for T and coordinate getting a correct local deferred update list (DU) to each slave.

m4) Wait for a "I am ready" message from each slave. If not all respond, go to m8).

m5) Set commit flag. Send a "commit" message to all slaves. Send a "done" to the user process.

m6) Wait for a "done" from all sites. If not all respond, go to m9).

m7) Send a "done" to the application program (if it is more convenient to wait until master processing is complete). Send a "done" to the SNOOP. Go to m1).

m8) Send "reset" to all slaves, the user process, and the SNOOP. Queue this message for later delivery to the nonresponding machines. Send a "reconfigure" message to each site. Go to m1).

m9) Queue a "commit" message and a "potential trouble" message for the down machine(s). Send a "reconfigure" message to each site. Go to m1).

2) ALGORITHM SLAVE: This algorithm is to be run by each slave which assists a master in processing a transaction T.

s1) Execute interactions at the request of the master and assemble a DU list for the local site. When it is correct, set the ready flag.

s2) Send "I am ready" to the master.

s3) Wait for "commit" or "reset."

s4) If a "commit" is received, then set local commit flag. Commit the transaction. Respond "done" to the master when completed. Spawn a process to execute steps s6) to s8). Go to s1).

s5) If a "reset" is received, run ALGORITHM LOCAL RECOVERY. When complete, go to s1).

s6) Send DU to each copy INGRES for the object being updated that is operational. Queue DU for later delivery to nonresponding sites.

s7) Wait for a "done" from each copy INGRES. If not all respond, queue a DU message for the nonrespondents and send a "reconfigure" message to all sites.

s8) Terminate.

3) ALGORITHM COPY: This algorithm is run by each copy INGRES that is assisting in processing a transaction T.

c1) Wait for DU.

c2) Perform update and respond "done."

4) ALGORITHM LOCAL RECOVERY: This algorithm must be run when a site restores service or when a transaction wishes to "reset."

r1) Read all outstanding (i.e., queued) messages and perform appropriate local actions.

r2) If a local commit flag is set (either for the transaction in question or for all transactions), commit the update. If not, correctly back out the transaction. Techniques for doing r2) for "soft" crashes, (i.e., ones in which data are not lost from secondary storage), are well known [2], [7], [16] and easily implementable. A more elaborate (and tedious) restoration must be done for hard crashes where data may be lost.

r3) If this is a service restoration, then proceed; otherwise, send a "done" to master and terminate.

r4) Send a "reconfigure" message to all sites.

r5) Execute ALGORITHM RECONFIGURE.

5) ALGORITHM RECONFIGURE: This algorithm must be executed whenever a "reconfigure" message is received by a site. Its purpose is to dynamically alter the up-list.

f1) Set state = "reconfigure." Instruct each master INGRES at the local site to back out or complete the current transaction. Go to f2) when the site is quiescent.

f2) Send "I am up" to all sites.

f3) Wait for a predetermined interval for replies and set the up-list equal to the set of all respondants.

f4) If current machine is the lowest in a predetermined ordering of all machines in the up-list, go to f5); otherwise, go to f8).

f5) Send up-list to all sites in the up-list.

f6) Wait for "I agree" from everybody. If any do not respond (or respond with "disagree"), send a "reconfigure" message to each site and go to f1).

f7) Set state = "normal." Send "normal" to all sites on the up-list and go to f11).

f8) Wait for up-list from some other site.

f9) Compare with local up-list and respond with "agree" or "disagree."

f10) Wait for "normal." When received, set state = "normal."

f11) If current SNOOP is in the up-list, resume normal operation. Otherwise, calculate the new SNOOP by the prearranged algorithm and send local conflict graph to that site. Resume normal operation.

It should be noted that step f1) will take a varied amount of time and an operational site may not send an "I am up" message within the "predetermined interval" of step f3). This problem can be handled by a straightforward (but tedious) extension of the algorithm.

It should also be noted that various, multiple, crash conditions can leave all up sites at step f8) in the algorithm. This can be detected and handled by a time-out and algorithm restart mechanism.

6) ALGORITHM SLAVE PROMOTE: This algorithm is executed by any slave that cannot communicate with its master.

p1) Invoke execution of ALGORITHM RECONFIGURE.

p2) Wait for state = "normal."

p3) Examine up-list to see whether all other slaves are up. (If not, there may be a data consistency problem which is discussed in the sequel.)

p4) If the slave is the lowest one in a predetermined ordering of the slaves in the up-list, go to p5); otherwise, go to p9).

p5) Send "is there a commit flag on" to all other up slaves.

p6) Wait for all replies.

p7) If there are no commits, send a "reset" to all slaves, the SNOOP, and the user process. Queue this message to down sites.

p8) If there is one or more commits, send a "commit" to all slaves and go to m6) of the ALGORITHM MASTER.

p9) Wait for "is there a commit" message.

p10) Reply "yes" or "no" and go to step s3) of the ALGORITHM SLAVE.

C. Data Integrity Problems with the Performance Algorithms

This collection of algorithms has the following three "features."

1) Transactions may be lost: This situation will normally be detected by a received "potential trouble" message. If a slave crashes after it has set its local commit flag but before it has reliably communicated DU to any copy INGRES, the following situation arises. No copy of the object in question has received the update. However, ALGORITHM LOCAL RECOVERY will ensure that a service restoration at the crashed site will commit the update. Hence, when service is restored and the network is reconfigured, one copy will not agree with the others because it will have had an extra update performed. This "phantom" is lost until service restoration, at which point it generates a consistency problem.

Of course, the slave can make this possibility very remote. However, there is another serious case to consider. Suppose a slave crashes after the master has set its commit flag. In this case, other slaves associated with the same master will proceed with the update, and the crashed site will not. Moreover, no copy of the object at the crashed site will ever be updated. This generates the following feature.

2) The data base may be inconsistent: According to the above scenario, a user process could be giving a 10-percent raise to all system programmers. If system programmers appear at fifteen sites, then fifteen slaves will be processing. A crash of one of them at an inopportune time will leave the update committed at fourteen sites and undone at the other. Hence, some system programmers got the raise and some did not.

3) Messages can get lost: The algorithms all assume that a down machine recovers by (among other things) reading its outstanding messages. However, some outstanding messages may be on machines that are currently down. This may mean, for example, that DU messages that were queued are not delivered before a machine resumes normal operation. Depending on the composition of the lost messages, the result can be benign or catastrophic.

D. Reasons for Tolerating Data Inconsistency

Obviously, these are serious drawbacks. Moreover, it is not clear what a user process can do to deal with these problems. However, there appear to be cases where a user might be willing to tolerate such "surprises." Three examples are suggested.

1) Update transactions always affect only one fragment of a relation: In this case, problem 2 cannot arise, and problem 1 can be easily recovered from. If machines are reasonably reliable, problem 3 may not be an issue. (It only arises if at least two machines are simultaneously out of service.)

2) Almost all updates are local: With the above algorithms, a "done" can be given to the user process for a local transaction after *only* local processing. Hence, the response time can be (more or less) the same as for a centralized system. To alleviate any of the above problems would require at least one other machine be signaled before a "done" could be sent to the user process. This may degrade response time substantially (by perhaps an order of magnitude, depending on the speed of the network). There may be situations where such a degraded response time is unacceptable.

3) Almost all updates can be decomposed into a sequence of interactions, each of which is local to some machine. Again, response time may be substantially degraded by any mechanism dealing with the above problems: As a result, a data base administrator can decide if better response time is worth the above headaches. For administrators who answer "no," we offer a collection of much more reliable (and expensive) algorithms.

E. The Reliable Algorithms

The previous algorithms may be made more reliable by making the following changes.

1) Treat each copy INGRES identically as the slave for which it is updating a backup copy. Hence, each copy INGRES will receive a correct DU before a transaction is committed. All messages which are sent to slaves are also sent to copy INGRES's.

2) ALGORITHM COPY is no longer necessary.

3) Steps s6) to s8) of ALGORITHM SLAVE are no longer necessary.

4) At every step where the instruction to queue a message for a process at a nonresponding site occurs, change it to queue the message at K sites, $K > 1$.

With these modifications it is easy to show that all three problems mentioned above are avoided if less than K machines are down at any one time and if there are at least K copies of each object.

The cost of this scheme is, of course, that a "done" cannot be signaled to the user process until a correct DU is received reliably at *all* sites where a copy resides. Clearly, substantial network traffic (and delay) will be required to perform this.

It is obvious that there is no possible scheme which can guarantee that there will be no "surprises" if K-1 machines crash, unless that scheme ensures that any update is reliably received at K sites before committing the update. Whether users are willing to pay the cost in response time for such a guarantee is unknown.

F. Accesses to the Local Copy

We are now in a position to discuss when a RETRIEVE can be reliably directed to the local copy (step 1 from Section III). Clearly a RETRIEVE can be directed to the local copy of an object (step 1) if it accesses only one fragment of any relation. If a RETRIEVE accesses multiple fragments of the same relation, then the possibility exists that the local copies of each fragment are not consistent. This will happen if there is an update which spans multiple fragments (such as the previously discussed 10-percent update to all system programmers), and some local fragments have received the update and the others have not (since copies are updated asynchronously). This will be termed the "multiple-fragment read problem."

Moreover, it is possible to create situations where the update messages from two different transactions arrive in the opposite order that they were performed at the primary site. If these updates conflict and the performance algorithm is used to update copies, then there will be time periods in which a local copy is inconsistent.

It appears that consistency of local copies can be guaranteed by time-stamping each transaction and including this time-stamp with all DU messages. Then modifications to copies could be performed strictly in time-stamp order. There is no extra message overhead to do this, and the details are straightforward.

In summary, a one-fragment RETRIEVE can always use a local copy if one exists. Other RETRIEVEs can use the local copy of data, but consistency is only guaranteed if the above time-stamping is done and there is a local copy of *all* needed data. Otherwise, the primary copy of all needed data must be accessed. Since it is a performance winner to access local fragments if possible, we plan to allow the user to set a flag indicating that he wishes to "take a chance" and use a local copy for those RETRIEVE commands for which consistency cannot be guaranteed.

V. Comparison with Other Schemes

We now examine our scheme in comparison with the updating schemes proposed by [3], [8], [13], [18].

In [8] a centralized concurrency control scheme is proposed. Moreover, to successfully handle arbitrary crashes, the lock table for this centralized controller must be fully redundant (i.e., present at each of N sites). Therefore, each interaction I in our model–using their scheme–requires $3*N - 1$ messages to correctly alert all N copies of the lock table. Our scheme only requires one message (the interaction I) to be sent to a SUBCOLLECTION of the sites. Moreover, this message must be sent anyway. Only if a "wait for" condition is generated must a second message be sent to the SNOOP. Moreover, equal robustness on crashes is achieved by our scheme with far less messages. In addition, our recovery algorithms are much simpler because the lock table is not redundant (and hence cannot be inconsistent with copies of itself).

Rosenkrantz *et al.* [13] propose a concurrency control scheme that avoids using the SNOOP by having time-stamps on transactions to resolve deadlock in a distributed fashion. However, that scheme may abort a transaction without a deadlock existing. Our scheme, on the other hand, backs out a transaction only if a deadlock actually occurs. Whichever scheme has less overhead is application dependent, and a simulation model (perhaps along the lines of an extension to [11]) would have to resolve the issue.

In [18] a scheme is presented for updating multiple copies of objects based on majority voting. In this proposal, a "done" cannot be given to a user until $n/2$ copies are serially updated. Only when this number is achieved can the transaction be sure that it will not be backed out due to conflict. Clearly, our performance algorithms generate a "done" much sooner. However, our reliability algorithms (in essence) require all copies to be updated before a commitment is signaled. On the other hand, we deal robustly with arbitrary crashes. Reference [18] does not contain a crash recovery proposal (and would have to be extended to do so). Without adding crash recovery procedures to the algorithms of [18], there is nothing more that we can say.

We now consider the proposal of [3]. In environments where traffic is not predominantly local, it appears to be a desirable (but complex) solution. Our scheme, on the other hand, is directed toward environments where there is high locality (assumption 1 from Section II).

Without giving the details of [3], we simply note that it proposes doing conflict resolution (if possible) at data base design time. If transactions do not conflict, each can update the copies of an object in any order. The preferred order is to update the local copy first and give a "done" to the user process when this is complete. Hence, excellent response time can be guaranteed. Transactions that cannot be shown to be nonconflicting do not have this freedom. For such transactions more extensive coordination must be done. In general this will require communicating with multiple sites, although in fortuitous circumstances a site will send the right sort of a message without being requested to.

Comparing our scheme with that of [3], we first presume that an equal number of copies of objects exist at the same sites for either situation. Also, we note that the algorithms in [3] are not robust on machine crashes. Providing such a feature will require additional mechanisms. Hence, it appears appropriate to compare [3] with our performance algorithms, which also fail to make robustness guarantees. Lastly, [3] avoids the "multiple-fragment read problem" mentioned earlier by requiring that a transaction only send *one* write message to each site. This will ensure that all fragments of objects at a given site are updated atomically and requires extra synchronization effort of the same flavor as the time-stamping scheme mentioned previously. Hence, we presume that both proposals make local copies consistent.

The comparison to follow is based on the number of sites which must be communicated with. This is a crude approximation to response time and allows a simple analysis. Of course, the actual overhead of the two schemes depends on what is counted, is stochastic in nature, and would require additional study to quantify. The comparison is based on the following cases.

CASE	PROBABILITY	NUMBER OF SITES TO BE COMMUNICATED WITH PER UPDATE ([3])	NUMBER OF SITES TO BE COMMUNICATED WITH PER UPDATE (OUR PROPOSAL)
4	XY	0	0
5	$X(1-Y)$	c	0
6	$Y(1-X)$	0	c
7	$(1-X)(1-Y)$	c	c

Fig. 1. A comparison of our scheme with [3].

1) The transaction is a RETRIEVE, *and there is a local copy of each referenced object:* Here both proposals can access the local object, and response time is the same either way.

2) The transaction is a RETRIEVE, *and there is a local copy of some (but not all) required data:* In this case we must obtain the primary copy of all objects, while [3] only requires nonlocal copies of some objects. We will assume that the extra cost which our algorithm incurs in this case is exactly offset by the untallied extra cost required by [3] in case 6).

3) The transaction is a RETRIEVE, *and 1) and 2) are not satisfied:* In either case, a nonlocal copy is accessed. By our assumptions concerning closeness (assumption 3), it does not matter which copy is used, and the number of sites communicated with is the same for each proposal.

4) The transaction is an update, and the primary copy of all objects is local, and the transaction is one which can be preanalyzed by [3] as a "nonconflict" one: Both algorithms will generate a "done" after local processing only.

5) The transaction is an update, and its primary copy of all objects is local, and it is not in the "nonconflict" category: Here, [3] requires that a message be sent to several sites and a response received. The exact number of sites is stochastic in nature and depends on query traffic and the details of the data base design. For this analysis, we will assume that the average number of such sites is some constant c. On the other hand, our scheme requires only local processing.

6) The transaction is an update and is "nonconflicting" but not local: Here, [3] requires no messages (but only if there is a local copy of all objects. We assume that the cases where this is not true balance in cost the cases in 2) which were not counted). Our scheme requires communicating with the primary site of each nonlocal object. The number of such sites depends on the data base design and the query. To a first approximation, we will assume it is equal to the constant c from 5).

7) Other cases: This is the same as 5) for [3] and 6) for our proposal.

Suppose X percent of the update transactions are local for our algorithm and Y percent are "nonconflicting" for [3]. Fig. 1 indicates the number of sites which must be communicated with for each scheme in cases 4)-7).

Clearly, [3] will win only if $Y > X$. To support the plausibility of a high Y, an example is presented in [15] where $Y = 0.9925$. However, for the identical example, an interested reader can ascertain that $X = 0.9925$ also. It is left as an open question whether there exist applications for which Y can be made large but which do not have the possibility of making X large also. A more detailed analysis of the two collections of algorithms (preferably by a disinterested third party) is also clearly in order.

REFERENCES

[1] P. A. Alsberg, and J. D. Day, "A principle for resilient sharing of distributed resources," Center for Advanced Computation, University of Illinois, Urbana, IL, 1976.

[2] M. M. Astrahan *et al.*, "System R: A relational approach to database management," *TODS*, vol. 2, p. 2, June 1976.

[3] P. A. Bernstein *et al.*, "The concurrency control mechanism of SSD-1: A system for distributed data bases," Comput. Corp. of America, Cambridge, MA, Dec. 1977.

[4] R. S. Epstein *et al.*, "Distributed query processing in a relational data base system," in *Proc. 1978 ACM-SIGMOD Conf. on Management of Data*, (Austin, TX), May 1978.

[5] J. Gray *et al.*, "Granularity of locks and degrees of consistency in a shared data base," IBM Research, San Jose, CA, RJ 1849, July 1976.

[6] J. Gray, "Notes on data base operating systems," unpublished course notes, July 1977.

[7] B. Lampson and H. Sturgis, "Crash recovery in a distributed system," Xerox Palo Alto Res. Ctr., 1976.

[8] D. A. Menasce *et al.*, "A locking protocol for resource coordination in distributed systems," in *Proc. 1978 ACM-SIGMOD Conf. on Management of Data* (Austin, TX), May 1978.

[9] R. M. Metcalfe and D. R. Bogs, "Ethernet: Distributed packet switching for local computer networks," *Commun. Ass. Comput. Mach.*, vol. 19, no. 7, July 1976.

[10] L. Roberts and B. Wessler, "Computer network development to achieve resource sharing," in *Proc. 1970 Spring Joint Comput. Conf.*, 1970.

[11] D. Ries and M. Stonebraker, "A study of the effect of locking granularity in a relational data base system," *TODS*, vol. 3, no. 3, Sept. 1977.

[12] D. Ries and R. Epstein, "Specification of the distribution criteria for a distributed data base system," Electron. Res. Lab., University of California, Berkeley, CA, Memo M78-25.

[13] D. J. Rosenkrantz *et al.*, "A system level concurrency control for distributed database systems," in *Proc. 2nd Berkeley Workshop on Distributed Data Bases and Comput. Networks* (Berkeley, CA), May 1977.

[14] J. B. Rothnie and N. Goodman, "An overview of the preliminary design of SDD-1: A system for distributed data bases," in *Proc. 2nd Berkeley Workshop on Distributed Data Bases and Comput. Networks* (Berkeley, CA), May 1977.

[15] J. B. Rothnie *et al.*, "The redundant update methodology of SDD-1: A system for distributed databases," Computer Corporation of America, Cambridge, MA, June 1977.

[16] M. Stonebraker *et al.*, "The design and implementation of INGRES," *TODS*, vol. 2, no. 3, Sept. 1976.

[17] M. Stonebraker and E. Neuhold, "A distributed data base version of INGRES," in *Proc. 2nd Berkeley Workshop on Distributed Data Bases and Comput. Networks* (Berkeley, CA), May 1977.

[18] R. H. Thomas, "A solution to the update problem for multiple copy data bases which use distributed control," BBN Rep. 3340, July 1975.

[19] E. Wong, "Retrieving dispersed data from SSD-1: A system for distributed data bases," in *Proc. 2nd Berkeley Workshop on Distributed Data Bases and Comput. Networks* (Berkeley, CA), May 1977.

Michael Stonebraker was born in Newburyport, MA, on October 11, 1943. He received the B.S.E. degree from Princeton University, Princeton, NJ, and the Ph.D. degree from the University of Michigan, Ann Arbor, in 1971.

Since that time he has been teaching at the University of California, Berkeley, where he is now an Associate Professor. His research interests center around relational database management systems and he has been one of the designers of the INGRES system.

THE PERFORMANCE OF CONCURRENCY CONTROL ALGORITHMS FOR DATABASE MANAGEMENT SYSTEMS

Michael J. Carey

Computer Sciences Department
University of Wisconsin
Madison, WI 53706

Michael R. Stonebraker

Electronics Research Laboratory
University of California
Berkeley, CA 94720

ABSTRACT

This paper describes a study of the performance of centralized concurrency control algorithms. An algorithm-independent simulation framework was developed in order to support comparative studies of various concurrency control algorithms. We describe this framework in detail and present performance results which were obtained for what we believe to be a representative cross-section of the many proposed algorithms. The basic algorithms studied include four locking algorithms, two timestamp algorithms, and one optimistic algorithm. Also, we briefly summarize studies of several multiple version algorithms and several hierarchical algorithms. We show that, in general, locking algorithms provide the best performance.

1. INTRODUCTION

1.1. Background

Much research on algorithm construction has been done in the area of concurrency control for both centralized (single-site) and distributed database systems. This research has led to the development of many concurrency control algorithms, most of which are based on one of three mechanisms: *locking* [Mena78, Rose78, Gray79, Lind79, Ston79], *timestamps* [Reed78, Thom79, Bern80, Bern81], and commit-time *validation* (also called optimistic concurrency control or certification) [Bada79, Casa79, Baye80, Kung81, Ceri82]. Bernstein and Goodman [Bern81] survey many of these algorithms and describe how new algorithms can be created by combining these mechanisms.

Given the ever-growing number of available concurrency control algorithms, the database system designer is faced with a difficult decision: Which concurrency control algorithm should be chosen? Several recent studies have evaluated concurrency control algorithm performance using qualitative, analytical, and simulation techniques. Bernstein and Goodman performed a comprehensive qualitative study which discussed performance issues for several distributed locking and timestamp algorithms [Bern80]. Results of analytical studies of locking performance have been reported by Irani and Lin [Iran79], Potier and Leblanc [Poti80], and Goodman et al [Good83]. Simulation studies of locking done by Ries and Stonebraker provide insight into granularity versus concurrency tradeoffs [Ries77, Ries79a, Ries79b]. Analytical and simulation studies by Garcia-Molina [Garc79] provide some insight into the relative performance of several distributed variants of locking as well as a voting algorithm and a "ring" algorithm. Simulation studies by Lin and Nolte [Lin82, Lin83] provide some comparative performance results for several distributed locking and timestamp algorithms. A thesis by Galler [Gall82] provides a new analysis technique for locking, a qualitative method for comparing distributed algorithms, and some simulation results for distributed locking versus timestamps (which contradict those of Lin and Nolte). A study by Robinson [Robi82a, Robi82c] includes some experimental results on locking versus serial validation. Finally, Agrawal and Dewitt recently completed a performance study of several integrated concurrency control and recovery algorithms based on a combination of analytical and simulation techniques [Agra83a, Agra83b].

These performance studies are informative, but they fail to offer definitive results regarding the choice

This research was supported by AFOSR Grant AFOSR-78-3596, NESC Contract NESC-N00039-81-C-0569, and a California MICRO Fellowship at the University of California, Berkeley.

of a concurrency control algorithm for several reasons. First, the analytical and simulation studies have mostly examined only one or a few alternative algorithms. Second, the underlying system models and assumptions vary from study to study. Examples include whether transaction sizes are fixed or random, whether there is one or several classes of transactions, which system resources are modeled and which are omitted, and what level of detail is used in representing resources which are included in the models. It is thus difficult to arrive at general conclusions about the many alternative algorithms. Third, the models used are in some cases insufficiently detailed to reveal certain important effects. For example, some models group the I/O, CPU, and message delay times for transactions into a single random delay [Lin82, Lin83], in which case the performance benefit of achieving CPU-I/O overlap cannot be revealed. Finally, the few comprehensive studies of alternative algorithms which have been performed were of a non-quantitative nature.

1.2. Our Work

The remainder of this paper describes a comprehensive quantitative study of the performance of centralized concurrency control algorithms. An algorithm-independent simulation framework was developed in order to support fair comparative studies of various concurrency control algorithms. We describe this framework in detail and present performance results which were obtained for what we claim to be a representative cross-section of the many proposed algorithms. The basic concurrency control algorithms studied include four locking algorithms, two timestamp algorithms, and one optimistic algorithm. Also, we briefly summarize the results of studies of several multiple version algorithms and several hierarchical algorithms. We show that, in general, locking algorithms provide the best performance.

2. THE SIMULATION MODEL

This section outlines the structure and details of the simulation model which was used to evaluate the performance of the algorithms. The model was designed to support performance studies for a variety of centralized concurrency control algorithms [Care83c], so the design was made to be as algorithm-independent as possible.

2.1. The Workload Model

An important component of the simulation model is a transaction workload model. When a transaction is initiated from a terminal in the simulator, it is assigned a readset and a writeset. These determine the objects that the transaction will read and write during its execution. Two transaction classes, *large* and *small*, are recognized in order to aid in the modeling of realistic workloads. The class of a transaction is determined at transaction initiation time and is used to determine the manner in which the readset and writeset are to be assigned. Transaction classes, readsets, and writesets are generated using the workload parameters shown in Table 1.

The parameter *num_terms* determines the number of terminals, or level of multiprogramming, for the workload. The parameter *restart_delay* determines the mean of an exponential delay time required for a terminal to resubmit a transaction after finding that its current transaction has been restarted. The parameter *db_size* determines the number of objects in the database, and *gran_size* determines the number of objects in each granule of the database. When a transaction reads or writes an object, any associated concurrency control request is made for the granule which contains the object. To model read and write requests, objects and granules are given integer names ranging from 1 to *db_size* and 1 to $\lceil db\_size / gran\_size \rceil$, respectively. Object i is contained in granule number $\lceil (i-1)/gran\_size \rceil + 1$.

The readset and writeset for a transaction are lists of the numbers of the objects to be read and written, respectively, by the transaction. These lists are assigned at transaction startup time. When a terminal initiates a transaction, *small_prob* is used to randomly determine the class of the transaction. If the class of the transaction is small, the workload parameters *small_mean*, *small_xact_type*, *small_size_dist*, and *small_write_prob* are used to choose the readset and writeset for the transaction as described below. Readsets and writesets for the class of large transactions are determined in the same manner using the *large_mean*, *large_xact_type*, *large_size_dist*, and *large_write_prob* parameters.

Workload Parameters	
num_terms	level of multiprogramming
restart_delay	mean xact restart delay
db_size	size of database
gran_size	size of granules in database
small_prob	Pr(xact is small)
small_mean	mean size for small xacts
small_xact_type	type for small xacts
small_size_dist	size distribution for small xacts
small_write_prob	Pr(write X | read X) for small xacts
large_mean	mean size for large xacts
large_xact_type	type for large xacts
large_size_dist	size distribution for large xacts
large_write_prob	Pr(write X | read X) for large xacts

Table 1: Workload parameters for simulation.

The readset size distribution for small transactions is given by *small_dist*. It may be constant, uniform, or exponential. If it is constant, the readset size is simply *small_mean*. If it is uniform, the readset size is chosen from a uniform distribution on the range from 1 to 2**small_mean*. The exponential case is not used in the experiments of this paper. The particular objects accessed are determined by the parameter *small_xact_type*, which determines the type (either random or sequential) for small transactions. If they are random, the readset is assigned by randomly selecting objects without replacement from the set of all objects in the database. In the sequential case, all objects in the readset are adjacent, so the readset is selected randomly from among all possible collections of adjacent objects of the appropriate size. Finally, given the readset, the writeset is determined as follows using the *small_write_prob* parameter: It is assumed that transactions read all objects which they write ("no blind writes"). When an object is placed in the readset, it is also placed in the writeset with probability *small_write_prob*.

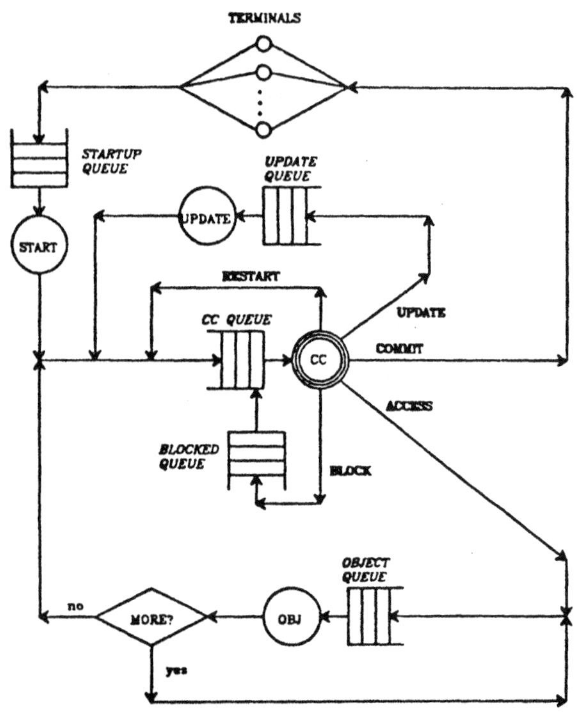

Figure 1: Logical database queuing model.

2.2. The Queuing Model

Central to the detailed simulation approach used here is the closed queuing model of a single-site database system shown in Figure 1. This model is an extended version of the model of Ries [Ries77, Ries79a, Ries79b]. There are a fixed number of terminals from which transactions originate. When a new transaction begins running, it enters the *startup queue*, where processing tasks such as query analysis, authentication, and other preliminary processing steps are performed. Once this phase of transaction processing is complete, the transaction enters the *concurrency control queue* (or *cc queue*) and makes the first of its concurrency control requests. If this request is granted, the transaction proceeds to the *object queue* and accesses its first object. If more than one object is to be accessed prior to the next concurrency control request, the transaction will cycle through this queue several times. (An example of this is when there are several objects per granule.) When the next concurrency control request is required, the transaction re-enters the concurrency control queue and makes the request. It is assumed for convenience that transactions which read and write objects perform all of their reads before performing any writes.

If the result of a concurrency control request is that the transaction must block, it enters the *blocked queue* until it is once again able to proceed. If a request leads to a decision to restart the transaction, it goes to the back of the concurrency control queue after a randomly determined restart delay period of mean *restart_delay*; it then begins making all of its concurrency control requests and object accesses over again. Eventually, the transaction may complete and the concurrency control algorithm may choose to commit the transaction. If the transaction is read-only, it is finished. If it has written one or more objects during its execution, however, it must first enter the *update queue* and write its deferred updates into the database.

Underlying the logical model of Figure 1 are two physical resources, the CPU and I/O (disk) resources. Associated with each logical service depicted in the figure (startup, concurrency control, object accesses, etc.) is some use of each of these two resources — each involves I/O processing followed by CPU processing. The amounts of CPU and I/O per logical service are specified as simulation parameters. All services compete for portions of the global I/O and CPU resources for their I/O and CPU cycles. The underlying physical system model is depicted in Figure 2. As shown, the physical model is simply a collection of terminals, a CPU server, and an I/O server. Each of the two servers has one queue for concurrency control service and another queue for all other service.

The scheduling policy used to allocate resources to transactions in the concurrency control I/O and CPU queues of the underlying physical model is FCFS (first-come, first-served). Concurrency control requests are thus processed one at a time, as they would be in an actual implementation. The resource allocation policies used for the normal I/O and CPU service queues of the physical model are FCFS and round-robin scheduling, respectively. These policies are again chosen to approximately model the characteristics which a real database system implementation would have. When requests for both concurrency control service and normal service are present at either resource, such as when one or more lock requests are pending while other transactions are processing objects, concurrency control service is given priority.

The parameters determining the service times (I/O and CPU) for the various logical resources in the model are given in Table 2. The parameters *startup_io* and *startup_cpu* are the amounts of I/O and CPU associated

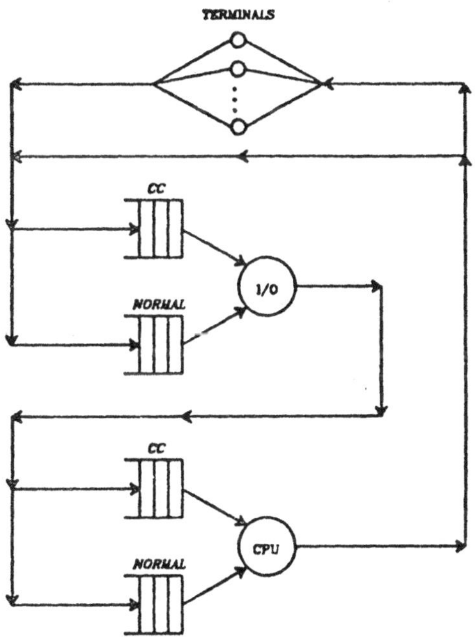

Figure 2: Physical database queuing model.

System Parameters	
startup_io	I/O time for transaction startup
startup_cpu	CPU time for transaction startup
obj_io	I/O time for accessing an object
obj_cpu	CPU time for accessing an object
cc_io	basic unit of concurrency control I/O time
cc_cpu	basic unit of concurrency control CPU time
stagger_mean	mean of exponential randomizing delay

Table 2: System parameters for simulation.

with transaction startup. Similarly, *obj_io* and *obj_cpu* are the amounts of I/O and CPU associated with reading or writing an object. Reading an object takes resources equal to *obj_io* followed by *obj_cpu*. Writing an object takes resources equal to *obj_cpu* at the time of the write request and *obj_io* at deferred update time, as it is assumed that transactions maintain deferred update lists in buffers in main memory. The parameters *cc_io* and *cc_cpu* are the amounts of I/O and CPU associated with a concurrency control request. All these parameters represent constant service time requirements rather than stochastic ones for simplicity. Finally, *stagger_mean* is the mean of an exponential time distribution which is used to randomly stagger transaction initiation times from terminals (not to model user thinking) each time a new transaction is started up. All parameters are specified in internal simulation time units, the unit of CPU time allocated to a transaction in one sweep of the round-robin allocation code for the simulator.

2.3. Algorithm Descriptions

Concurrency control algorithms are described for simulation purposes as a collection of four routines. These are: *Init_CC_Algorithm*, *Request_Semantics*, *Commit_Semantics*, and *Update_Semantics*. Each routine is written in SIMPAS, a simulation language based on extending PASCAL with simulation-oriented constructs [Brya80], the language in which the simulator is implemented. *Init_CC_Algorithm* is called when the simulation starts up, and it is responsible for initializing all algorithm-dependent data structures and variables. The other three routines are responsible for implementing the semantics of the concurrency control algorithm being modeled. *Request_Semantics* handles concurrency control requests made by transactions before they reach their commit point. *Commit_Semantics* is invoked when a transaction reaches its commit point. *Update_Semantics* is called after a transaction has finished writing its deferred updates. Each of the latter three routines returns information to the simulator about how much simulation time to charge for CPU and I/O associated with concurrency control processing.

2.4. Some Other Details

In this section, we briefly discuss two issues which are relevant to the results presented in the remainder of the paper. We outline the way that concurrency control costs are modeled and the statistical methods used to analyze the experimental results.

2.4.1. Concurrency Control Costs

In order to simulate concurrency control algorithms, it is necessary to make some assumptions about their costs. To evaluate them fairly and determine how their blocking and restart decisions affect performance, the assumptions made for each of the algorithm simulations are consistent. It is assumed that the unit costs for concurrency control operations in locking, timestamps, and validation are all the same, *cc_cpu* and *cc_io*, as a first-order approximation. This is reasonable since the basic steps in each algorithm, such as setting a lock or checking a timestamp, involve doing one or two table lookups per request. Thus, the costs of processing requests in the various algorithms are not likely to differ by more than small constant factors. (This is borne out by the cost results reported in [Care83b].)

To illustrate how concurrency control costs are modeled, let us take as an example the 2PL algorithm to be described subsequently. In this algorithm, transactions set read locks on items which they read, and they later upgrade read locks to write locks for items which they also write. Consider a transaction which makes N_r granule read requests and N_w granule write requests. A CPU cost of *cc_cpu* and an I/O cost of *cc_io* are assessed each time the transaction makes a read or write lock request for a granule. For 2PL, then, the total concurrency control CPU and I/O costs for the transaction in the absence of restarts are $(N_r + N_w)cc\_cpu$ and $(N_r + N_w)cc\_io$, respectively. The concurrency control costs for other locking algorithms, timestamp algorithms, and validation algorithms are determined similarly (see [Care83c] for details).

Of course, if the transaction is restarted, it will incur the additional costs involved in executing again from the beginning. These include all the costs associated with reading and writing the objects that the transaction accesses, plus the costs for making all of its concurrency control requests over again.

2.4.2. Statistical Analysis

In the simulation experiments reported here, the performance metric used is the transaction throughput rate. Mean throughput results and 90% confidence intervals for these results were obtained from the simulations using a variant of the *batch means* [Sarg76] approach to simulation output analysis. The approach used is due to Wolf [Wolf83]; it differs from the usual batch means approach in that an attempt is made to account for the correlation between adjacent batches. Briefly, we assume that adjacent batches are positively correlated, that non-adjacent batches are not correlated, and that the correlation between a pair of adjacent batches is independent of the pair under consideration. We then estimate this correlation and use it in computing a confidence interval for the mean throughput. In the remainder of this paper, we present only the mean throughput results. However, we point out only performance differences which are significant in the sense that their confidence intervals do not overlap. More information and data on the statistical approach used in our experiments may be found in Appendix 3 of [Care83c].

3. BASIC CONCURRENCY CONTROL ALGORITHMS

In this section, we describe our performance results for *basic* concurrency control algorithms. The class of basic concurrency control algorithms consists of those algorithms which operate using the most recent version of each data granule and a single level of granularity. A later section will summarize results for *multiple version* algorithms, which use older versions of data items to provide greater potential concurrency (usually for large, read-only transactions), and *hierarchical* algorithms, which use a hierarchy of two or more granule sizes (e.g., files and pages) in an attempt to trade lower concurrency for reduced concurrency control costs.

3.1. Algorithms Studied

Given the large number of proposed concurrency control algorithms, it is not possible to study all (or even a significant fraction) of them. Thus, we chose to study a collection of algorithms which we believe to be a representative cross-section of the proposals. We believe our collection of algorithms to be representative because it contains algorithms which use a range of blocking and restarts in resolving conflicts: Some just use blocking, some just use restarts, and some use a mix of these two tactics. Also, the algorithms vary as to when conflicts are detected and dealt with.

Our study of basic concurrency control algorithms includes seven algorithms: four locking algorithms, two timestamp algorithms, and one optimistic algorithm. We describe each of the algorithms briefly below.

Dynamic Two-Phase Locking (2PL). Transactions set read locks on granules which they read, and these locks are later upgraded to write locks for granules which they also write. If a lock request is denied, the requesting transaction is blocked. A waits-for graph of transactions is maintained [Gray79], and deadlock detection is performed each time a transaction blocks. If a deadlock is discovered, the transaction which just blocked and caused the deadlock is chosen as the victim and restarted. (This may not be the best victim choice, but it was selected initially for ease of implementation.)

Wait-Die Two-Phase Locking (WD). This algorithm is like 2PL, except that wait-die deadlock prevention [Rose78] is used instead of deadlock detection. When a lock request from transaction T_i conflicts with a lock held by T_j, T_i is permitted to wait only if it started running before T_j. Otherwise, T_i is restarted.

Dynamic Two-Phase Locking, No Upgrades (2PLW). The only difference between this algorithm and 2PL is that, if a transaction both reads and writes a granule x, it does not request a read lock and then later upgrade it to a write lock. Rather, for granules which are eventually written, write locks are requested the first time the granule is accessed, eliminating upgrades. Full deadlock detection is employed as before.

Exclusive Preclaimed Two-Phase Locking (PRE). In this algorithm, all granules read or written by a transaction are locked in exclusive (write) mode at transaction startup time. If a transaction cannot obtain all required locks, it blocks without obtaining any of its locks and waits until all required locks are available. The use of only exclusive locks will result in more blocking than would occur using both read and write locks; this will aid in establishing later performance results about the effects of blocking.

Basic Timestamp Ordering (BTO). This algorithm is described by Bernstein and Goodman [Bern81]: Each transaction T has a timestamp, $TS(T)$, which is issued when T begins executing. Each data granule x in the database has a read timestamp, $R\text{-}TS(x)$, and a write timestamp, $W\text{-}TS(x)$, which record the timestamps of the latest reader and writer (respectively) for x. A read request from T for x is granted only if $TS(T) \geq W\text{-}TS(x)$, and a write request from T for x is granted only if both $TS(T) \geq R\text{-}TS(x)$ and $TS(T) \geq W\text{-}TS(x)$. Transactions whose requests are not granted are restarted. In the version of the algorithm tested here, read requests are checked dynamically; writes, however, go to a deferred update list, and write timestamps are all checked together at commit time.

Basic Timestamp Ordering, Thomas Write Rule (TWW). This is BTO with a slight modification [Bern81]: When a transaction T makes a write request for an object x and $TS(T) \geq R\text{-}TS(x)$ but $TS(T) < W\text{-}TS(x)$, BTO will restart T. In this algorithm, T's request is instead granted, but the actual (outdated) write is ignored. In all of our experiments, TWW and BTO always performed identically. This is due to the fact that, under the "no blind writes" assumption which underlies the mechanism by which writesets are assigned in our simulations, TWW is identical to BTO [Care83c]. Thus, results for TWW are not presented separately.

Serial Validation (SV). This is the optimistic concurrency control algorithm of Kung and Robinson [Kung81]. Transactions record their read and write sets, and a transaction is restarted when it reaches its commit point if any granule in its readset has been written by a transaction which committed during its lifetime. Our version differs from the original algorithm in that we use startup and commit timestamps to enforce the semantics of the algorithm (instead of keeping old write sets around and explicitly checking for readset/writeset intersections) [Care83d]. However, transactions committed (restarted) using our version would be committed (restarted) by the original algorithm as well, so the change in implementation strategy does not affect the outcome of our performance experiments. (The only difference is a slight reduction in concurrency control costs using our scheme.)

3.2. Performance Experiments and Results

We performed six different performance experiments on these basic concurrency control algorithms. In this section we present some of the more interesting experimental data and summarize the remainder of our results. All of the experiments reported in this section were run with settings of $batch\_time$ = 50,000 and $num\_batches$ = 20 (for a total of 1,000,000 simulation time units) in order to obtain tight confidence intervals. One simulation time unit represents one millisecond of simulated time for these experiments, so the length of each experiment was 1,000 seconds of simulated time.

3.2.1. Experiment 1: Transaction Size

The first experiment examined the performance characteristics of the basic algorithms under homogeneous workloads of fixed-size transactions. Parameters varied in this experiment were the granularity of the database and the size of transactions. The purpose of this experiment was to observe the behavior of the algorithms of interest under various conflict probabilities and transaction sizes.

The system parameter settings for this experiment are given in simulated time in Table 3. The relevant workload parameter settings are given in Table 4.

System Parameter	Time (Milliseconds)
startup_io	35
startup_cpu	10
obj_io	35
obj_cpu	10
cc_io	0
cc_cpu	1
stagger_mean	20

Table 3: System parameters for experiment 1.

Workload Parameters	
db_size	10000 objects
gran_size	varied from 1 to 10000 objects/granule
num_terms	10
restart_delay	1 second
small_prob	1.0
small_mean	varied from 1 to 30 objects
small_xact_type	random
small_size_dist	fixed
small_write_prob	0.5

Table 4: Workload parameters for experiment 1.

(These database and granularity parameters might correspond, for example, to a 40 megabyte database where objects are 4K byte pages and granules are groups of one or more pages.) Transactions read a fixed number of objects selected at random from among all objects in the database; this number was set at 1, 2, 5, 10, 15, and 30 for different simulation runs in the experiment. Transactions update each object that they read with 50% probability.

Tables 5 and 6 show the throughput results (in transactions/second) and the number of transactions restarted for transactions of size 2. Tables 7 and 8 give these figures for transactions of size 10. A number of observations can be made from these results. Examining Table 5, there is no significant performance difference between the algorithms when database is organized as many granules. This also holds for Table 7. The implication of this is that all algorithms perform equally well when the probability of conflicts is low. As the probability of conflicts increases, however, differences do begin to appear. This is visible in the results for coarser granularities in the two tables. We also observed differences at finer granularities as the transaction size parameter was increased to 15 and then 30.

Examining the coarser granularity results in both Tables 5 and 7, we see that the PRE and 2PLW algorithms yield the best performance. Tables 6 and 8 show that these are the two algorithms which caused the fewest restarts*. No restarts occurred with PRE, as it is deadlock free, and few occurred with 2PLW. In Table 5, 2PL is the next best algorithm, followed by WD, and then finally by SV and BTO. An examination of Table 6 shows that the ordering of the algorithms by throughput corresponds closely to the opposite of their ordering by restart counts. This implies that having more restarts leads to poorer performance, and therefore that restarts should be avoided if possible. Further

Throughput versus Granularity						
Grans	2PL	WD	2PLW	PRE	BTO	SV
1	3.400	3.638	6.479	6.241	2.595	3.634
10	5.974	5.790	7.096	7.161	5.119	5.231
100	7.039	6.966	7.161	7.163	6.906	6.714
1000	7.152	7.149	7.161	7.161	7.138	7.113
10000	7.159	7.159	7.160	7.161	7.158	7.158

Table 5: Throughput, *small_mean* = 2.

Restart Counts versus Granularity						
Grans	2PL	WD	2PLW	PRE	BTO	SV
1	6311	7638	0	0	7594	6529
10	2366	4633	242	0	4071	3844
100	247	706	3	0	508	879
1000	20	73	0	0	51	102
10000	2	11	0	0	4	9

Table 6: Restarts, *small_mean* = 2.

Throughput versus Granularity						
Grans	2PL	WD	2PLW	PRE	BTO	SV
1	0.281	0.240	1.518	1.425	0.001	0.336
10	0.074	0.234	0.432	1.415	0.004	0.355
100	0.827	0.701	1.414	1.759	0.235	0.784
1000	1.676	1.599	1.784	1.790	1.473	1.480
10000	1.776	1.770	1.788	1.788	1.763	1.749

Table 7: Throughput, *small_mean* = 10.

Restart Counts versus Granularity						
Grans	2PL	WD	2PLW	PRE	BTO	SV
1	2351	4142	0	0	2855	2323
10	2816	3837	4223	0	2848	2293
100	1543	2360	769	0	2482	1612
1000	180	388	7	0	501	485
10000	16	31	0	0	38	56

Table 8: Restarts, *small_mean* = 10.

evidence supporting this conclusion was observed in the other cases tested, and we will see more evidence in the remainder of these experiments as well. The main trend observed as transaction size was increased to 15 and 30, since restarts are more costly for large transactions, was that performance differences among the algorithms are more pronounced for larger transactions.

In Table 7, 2PL outperforms WD and SV under low conflicts, but it does worse than WD and SV at higher conflict probabilities (when *Grans* = 10, for example). The poor performance of 2PL occurs because its simplistic deadlock victim selection policy can lead to thrashing-like restart behavior when conflicts are likely [Care83c]. This same effect occurred for 2PLW when the transaction size parameter was set

*The one exception to this statement, which occurs in Table 8, will be discussed shortly.

at 15 and 30. BTO performs the worst here, especially at higher conflict probabilities. Its poor performance is due to a problem with the BTO algorithm: It is possible to have "cyclic restarts", with two or more conflicting transactions becoming involved in cycles where they continuously restart each other instead of making progress [Date82, Care83c, Ullm83]. At the coarsest granularities, SV actually outperforms WD. This is because, using WD, a transaction which is restarted due to a conflict can actually be restarted several times before the conflict disappears [Rose78]; this does not happen in SV, so SV is in some sense more "stable" than WD.

Comparing Tables 7 and 8, we again see that higher numbers of restarts result in lower throughputs in most cases. There are a few exceptions, however. One example is WD, which seems to have performed better than its number of restarts would imply. This occurs because WD restarts the younger transaction when a conflict occurs, and thus tends to restart transactions which have completed less work (wasting fewer resources in the process). This implies that it is better to restart a transaction which has done little work if a restart is unavoidable. Another example is the performance of 2PL versus that of 2PLW at *Grans* = 10. 2PLW outperforms 2PL even though it causes more restarts because, in 2PLW, all restarts occur as locks are set in response to read requests. In 2PL, restarts can still occur as write requests are processed. Thus, the average 2PL restart wastes more resources than a 2PLW restart.

3.2.2. Experiment 2: Access Patterns

This experiment investigated the performance characteristics of the seven concurrency control algorithms under two workloads consisting solely of large transactions. One workload consisted of random transactions of mean size 30, and the other workload consisted of sequential transactions of mean size 30. In both cases, transaction sizes were chosen from a uniform distribution. The granularity of the database was varied in order to vary the probability of conflicts. The objective of this experiment was to observe the effects of random versus sequential object access patterns on algorithm performance.

The results of this experiment were similar to those of Experiment 1. Again, restart behavior determined performance. The main performance difference observed between the random and sequential transaction cases was that the 2PLW and 2PL locking algorithms had even more of a performance advantage with sequential transactions. This is because, with sequential transactions, 2PLW becomes deadlock-free (like PRE), and the only source of deadlocks for 2PL in this case is when read locks are upgraded to write locks. Thus, fewer restarts occurred for these algorithms in the sequential case, resulting in better performance.

3.2.2.1. Experiment 3: Mixed Workload

This experiment investigated the performance characteristics of the seven concurrency control algorithms under a workload consisting of a mix of large and small transactions. The fraction of small transactions in the mix was varied in steps of 20% to investigate algorithm performance under different combinations of small and large transactions. The granularity of the database was also varied in order to vary the probability of conflicts. Table 9 gives the relevant workload parameters for this experiment.

Tables 10 and 11 give the throughput results obtained for the cases of 80% small transactions and 20% small transactions, respectively. The locking algorithms are again seen to outperform the alternatives. In particular, SV rarely outperforms a locking algorithm in these cases, only beating 2PL at very coarse granularities where 2PL's bad victim selection criteria causes it to perform poorly. As before, PRE and 2PLW are the dominant algorithms.

3.2.3. Experiment 4: Multiprogramming Level

This experiment investigated the effects of the multiprogramming level on the results of the previous experiments. A portion of Experiment 3 was repeated with the multiprogramming level set to 5 and then 20 transactions. It was found that the multiprogramming level affects performance in an *absolute* sense, as changing it changes the probability of conflicts, but the *relative* performance of the basic concurrency control algorithms was not affected by changes in the multiprogramming level. Also, the effect of the level of multiprogramming on throughput without a concurrency control algorithm was investigated for the same portion

Workload Parameters	
db_size	10000 objects
gran_size	varied from 1 to 10000 objects/granule
num_terms	10
restart_delay	1 second
small_prob	varied from 0.2 to 0.8
small_mean	2 objects
small_xact_type	random
small_size_dist	fixed
small_write_prob	0.5
large_mean	30 objects
large_xact_type	sequential
large_size_dist	uniform
large_write_prob	0.1

Table 9: Workload parameters for experiment 3.

Throughput versus Granularity						
Grans	2PL	WD	2PLW	PRE	BTO	SV
1	0.101	0.450	2.521	2.371	0.022	0.333
10	0.853	1.551	2.830	2.860	0.338	0.963
100	2.352	2.580	2.865	2.861	1.246	2.185
1000	2.675	2.752	2.859	2.864	2.415	2.504
10000	2.803	2.777	2.860	2.864	2.634	2.554

Table 10: Throughput, *small_prob* = 0.8.

Throughput versus Granularity						
Grans	2PL	WD	2PLW	PRE	BTO	SV
1	0.066	0.091	0.919	0.771	0.000	0.111
10	0.464	0.517	0.967	0.963	0.124	0.450
100	0.883	0.894	0.966	0.964	0.691	0.858
1000	0.930	0.945	0.966	0.969	0.775	0.905
10000	0.942	0.944	0.966	0.967	0.874	0.913

Table 11: Throughput, *small_prob* = 0.2.

of Experiment 3. It was found that having 4 or more non-conflicting transactions ready to run was sufficient to allow the system to reach its maximum throughput capacity.

3.2.4. Experiment 5: System Balance

This experiment investigated the effects of system balance on the results of the previous experiments. A portion of Experiment 3 was repeated with the system parameters set to yield I/O-boundedness, CPU-boundedness, and then good balance. It was found that system balance is another factor which is not significant with respect to the relative performance of the algorithms.

3.2.5. Experiment 6: Concurrency Control Cost

In this experiment, a portion of Experiment 3 was repeated with the concurrency control cost parameters modified to investigate their importance. Experiments were run with concurrency control being free (*cc_cpu* = 0, *cc_io* = 0), expensive in terms of CPU cost (*cc_cpu* = 5 milliseconds, *cc_io* = 0), and expensive in terms of I/O cost (*cc_cpu* = 1 millisecond, *cc_io* = 35 milliseconds). We found that the effects of concurrency control cost are negligible as long as they are small compared to the costs associated with accessing objects (i.e., when *cc_io* = 0). In the last case, where concurrency control was very expensive, we observed results similar to those of Ries [Ries77]: A medium granularity was optimal for all algorithms rather than the finest granularity, as coarse granularities led to high conflict probabilities and fine granularities led to high concurrency control overhead. The relative performance of the algorithms, however, was not affected by changes in the concurrency control cost parameters.

4. MULTIPLE VERSION AND HIERARCHICAL ALGORITHMS

In addition to the basic concurrency control algorithm studies which have been described, studies were performed on several multiple version algorithms and several hierarchical algorithms. Space precludes a detailed description of these studies, but the main results are summarized in this section. The interested reader can find a detailed description of these experiments and results in [Care83c].

4.1. Multiple Version Algorithms

The multiple version algorithms which were studied include the CCA version pool algorithm [Chan82], which is based on locking, the multiple version timestamp ordering algorithm of Reed [Reed78], and a multiple version optimistic algorithm [Care83d]. In modeling the costs associated with these algorithms, we made the simplistic assumption that the cost of accessing any version of a granule is the same as the cost of accessing its most recent version. We intend to investigate algorithm performance using a more realistic cost model in the future.

We performed several experiments, comparing the performance of the multiple version algorithms with each other and with their single version counterparts. For workloads consisting of large read-only transactions and small update transactions, all of the multiple version algorithms performed alike, enabling transactions to execute with little interference. Multiple versions did little to improve the performance of locking for the cases studied, but they did help improve performance both for timestamp ordering and optimistic concurrency control. The performance of mixes with mostly small update transactions and a small fraction of large read-only transactions was improved the most using multiple versions.

4.2. Hierarchical Algorithms

The hierarchical algorithms studied include hierarchical variants of preclaimed exclusive locking, basic timestamp ordering, serial validation, and multiversion timestamp ordering. Descriptions of the latter three hierarchical algorithms may be found in [Care83a]. The performance of the algorithms in a two-level granularity hierarchy was investigated under the assumption that the cost of processing a concurrency control request for fine granules was twice that for coarse granularity requests.

We performed several experiments, comparing the performance of the hierarchical algorithms with each other and with their single granularity counterparts for a mix of large and small transactions. No performance improvements were obtained using the hierarchical algorithms under normal concurrency control costs (i.e., those used in evaluating the basic concurrency control algorithms). However, under very high concurrency control cost settings, all four of the hierarchical algorithms improved system performance by reducing concurrency control costs. Hierarchical preclaimed locking performed the best of the algorithms examined.

5. CONCLUSIONS

We have described a study of the performance of centralized concurrency control algorithms. An algorithm-independent simulation framework was presented and used to study the performance of a number of basic algorithms: four locking algorithms, two timestamp algorithms, and one optimistic algorithm. All were found to perform equally well when conflicts are rare. When conflicts are not rare, it was shown that blocking is the preferred tactic for handling conflicts, as restarts waste resources and consequently lead to poorer performance. Hence, locking algorithms appear to be the concurrency control method of choice for centralized database systems. Preclaimed locking (PRE) consistently outperformed the other alternatives, and dynamic two-phase locking without lock upgrades (2PLW) also performed very well.

In some systems, especially those in which concurrency control is handled entirely at the physical data level, it may be impossible to accurately preclaim only the required locks or to predict writes at the time when reads are performed. In such systems, PRE and 2PLW will not be viable. Based on our results, dynamic two-phase locking (2PL) is recommended in this situation. However, the simple "pick the current blocker" criteria for deadlock victim selection is not recommended, as it led to poor performance under high conflict probabilities*. Instead, our results indicate that better policies will choose transactions which have completed little work. In situations where deadlock-free locking protocols are a feasible alternative [Silb80, Kort82, Moha82], such protocols are of course recommended.

The results of studies of the performance of several multiple version and hierarchical algorithms were summarized. For workloads consisting of large read-only transactions and small update transactions, the multiple version algorithms studied performed alike. Multiple versions did little to improve the performance of locking for the cases studied, but they were beneficial for timestamp ordering and optimistic concurrency control. Of the hierarchical algorithms examined, hierarchical locking performed the best. However, none of the hierarchical algorithms studied were beneficial under normal concurrency control costs.

A number of questions remain for future research. First of all, our results only apply directly to centralized database systems. We hypothesize that locking algorithms will also provide the best performance in distributed database systems, and we plan to investigate this hypothesis through further simulation modeling and experimentation. Second, it appears worthwhile to make a thorough study of alternative deadlock-handling strategies for database systems. We intend to use our current simulation environment to perform such a study. Finally, we would like to verify our simulation results by adding an algorithm-independent concurrency control module to WiSS (the Wisconsin Storage System) [Chou83] and running performance experiments on this actual system.

*This also applies to victim selection for 2PLW.

ACKNOWLEDGEMENTS

Discussions with Rakesh Agrawal influenced the cost modeling aspects of this work. David DeWitt and Toby Lehman made suggestions that helped to improve the presentation.

REFERENCES

[Agra83a] Agrawal, R., and DeWitt, D., "Integrated Concurrency Control and Recovery Mechanisms: Design and Performance Evaluation", Technical Report No. 497, Computer Sciences Department, University of Wisconsin-Madison, February 1983.

[Agra83b] Agrawal, R., "Concurrency Control and Recovery in Multiprocessor Database Machines: Design and Performance Evaluation", Ph.D. Thesis, Computer Sciences Department, University of Wisconsin-Madison, 1983.

[Bada79] Badal, D., "Correctness of Concurrency Control and Implications in Distributed Databases", Proceedings of the COMPSAC '79 Conference, Chicago, Illinois, November 1979.

[Baye80] Bayer, R., Heller, H., and Reiser, A., "Parallelism and Recovery in Database Systems", ACM Transactions on Database Systems 5(2), June 1980.

[Bern80] Bernstein, P., and Goodman, N., "Fundamental Algorithms for Concurrency Control in Distributed Database Systems''. Technical Report. Computer Corporation of America. 1980.

[Bern81] Bernstein. P.. and Goodman. N.. ''Concurrency Control in Distributed Database Systems''. ACM Computing Surveys 13(2). June 1981.

[Brya80] Bryant. R.. ''SIMPAS — A Simulation Language Based on PASCAL''. Technical Report No. 390. Computer Sciences Department. University of Wisconsin. Madison. June 1980.

[Care83a] Carey. M.. ''Granularity Hierarchies in Concurrency Control''. Proceedings of the Second ACM SIGACT-SIGMOD Symposium on Principles of Database Systems. Atlanta. Georgia. March 1983.

[Care83b] Carey. M., ''An Abstract Model of Database Concurrency Control Algorithms''. Proceedings of the ACM SIGMOD International Conference on Management of Data, San Jose. California. May 1983.

[Care83c] Carey, M.. ''Modeling and Evaluation of Database Concurrency Control Algorithms''. Ph.D. Thesis. Computer Science Division (EECS). University of California, Berkeley. September 1983.

[Care83d] Carey. M.. ''Multiple Versions and the Performance of Optimistic Concurrency Control''. Technical Report No. 517. Computer Sciences Department. University of Wisconsin. Madison. October 1983.

[Casa79] Casanova. M.. ''The Concurrency Control Problem for Database Systems''. Ph.D. Thesis. Computer Science Department. Harvard University. 1979.

[Ceri82] Ceri. S.. and Owicki. S.. ''On the Use of Optimistic Methods for Concurrency Control in Distributed Databases''. Proceedings of the Sixth Berkeley Workshop on Distributed Data Management and Computer Networks. February 1982.

[Chan82] Chan. A.. Fox. S.. Lin. W.. Nori. A.. and Ries. D.. ''The Implementation of An Integrated Concurrency Control and Recovery Scheme''. Proceedings of the ACM SIGMOD International Conference on Management of Data. March 1982.

[Chou83d] Chou. H.. DeWitt. D.. Katz. R.. and Klug. A.. ''Design and Implementation of the Wisconsin Storage System''. Technical Report No. 524. Computer Sciences Department. University of Wisconsin. Madison. November 1983.

[Date82] Date. C.. An Introduction to Database Systems (Volume II). Addison-Wesley Publishing Company. 1982.

[Elli77] Ellis. C.. ''A Robust Algorithm for Updating Duplicate Databases''. Proceedings of the 2nd Berkeley Workshop on Distributed Databases and Computer Networks, May 1977.

[Gall82] Galler. B.. ''Concurrency Control Performance Issues'' Ph.D. Thesis. Computer Science Department. University of Toronto. September 1982.

[Garc79] Garcia-Molina. H.. ''Performance of Update Algorithms for Replicated Data in a Distributed Database''. Ph.D. Thesis. Computer Science Department. Stanford University. June 1979.

[Good83] Goodman. N.. Suri. R.. and Tay. Y.. ''A Simple Analytic Model for Performance of Exclusive Locking in Database Systems''. Proceedings of the Second ACM SIGACT-SIGMOD Symposium on Principles of Database Systems. Atlanta. Georgia. March 1983.

[Gray79] Gray. J.. ''Notes On Database Operating Systems''. in Operating Systems: An Advanced Course. Springer-Verlag. 1979.

[Iran79] Irani. K.. and Lin. H.. ''Queuing Network Models for Concurrent Transaction Processing in a Database System''. Proceedings of the ACM SIGMOD International Symposium on Management of Data. 1979.

[Kort82] Korth. H.. ''Deadlock Freedom Using Edge Locks''. ACM Transactions on Database Systems 7(4). December 1982.

[Kung81] Kung. H.. and Robinson. J.. ''On Optimistic Methods for Concurrency Control''. ACM Transactions on Database Systems 6(2). June 1981.

[Lin82] Lin. W.. and Nolte. J.. ''Distributed Database Control and Allocation: Semi-Annual Report''. Technical Report. Computer Corporation of America. Cambridge, Massachusetts. January 1982.

[Lin83] Lin. W.. and Nolte. J.. ''Basic Timestamp. Multiple Version Timestamp. and

Two-Phase Locking''. Proceedings of the Ninth International Conference on Very Large Data Bases. Florence, Italy, November 1983.

[Lind79] Lindsay. B., Selinger. P., Galtieri. C., Gray. J., Lorie. R., Price. T., Putzolu. F., Traiger. I., and Wade. B., ''Notes on Distributed Databases''. Report No. RJ2571. IBM San Jose Research Laboratory. 1979.

[Mena78] Menasce. D., and Muntz. R., ''Locking and Deadlock Detection in Distributed Databases''. Proceedings of the Third Berkeley Workshop on Distributed Data Management and Computer Networks. August 1978.

[Moha82] Mohan. C., Fussel. D., and Silberschatz. A., ''Compatibility and Commutativity in Non-Two-Phase Locking Protocols''. Proceedings of the ACM SIGACT-SIGMOD Symposium on Principles of Database Systems. Los Angeles. California. March 1982.

[Poti80] Potier, D., and LeBlanc, P., ''Analysis of Locking Policies in Database Management Systems''. Communications of the ACM 23(10), October 1980.

[Reed78] Reed. D., ''Naming and Synchronization in a Decentralized Computer System''. Ph.D. Thesis. Department of Electrical Engineering and Computer Science. Massachusetts Institute of Technology. 1978.

[Ries77] Ries. D., and Stonebraker. M., ''Effects of Locking Granularity on Database Management System Performance''. ACM Transactions on Database Systems 2(3), September 1977.

[Ries79a] Ries. D., ''The Effects of Concurrency Control on Database Management System Performance''. Ph.D. Thesis. Department of Electrical Engineering and Computer Science. University of California at Berkeley. 1979.

[Ries79b] Ries. D., and Stonebraker. M., ''Locking Granularity Revisited''. ACM Transactions on Database Systems 4(2), June 1979.

[Robi82a] Robinson. J., ''Design of Concurrency Controls for Transaction Processing Systems''. Ph.D. Thesis. Department of Computer Science. Carnegie-Mellon University. 1982.

[Robi82b] Robinson. J., ''Separating Policy from Correctness in Concurrency Control Design''. Report No. RC9308. IBM Thomas J. Watson Research Center. March 1982.

[Robi82c] Robinson. J., ''Experiments with Transaction Processing on a Multi-Microprocessor''. Report No. RC9725. IBM Thomas J. Watson Research Center. December 1982.

[Rose78] Rosenkrantz. D., Stearns. R., and Lewis. P., ''System Level Concurrency Control for Distributed Database Systems''. ACM Transactions on Database Systems 3(2), June 1978.

[Sarg76] Sargent. R., ''Statistical Analysis of Simulation Output Data''. Proceedings of the Fourth Annual Symposium on the Simulation of Computer Systems. August 1976.

[Silb80] Silberschatz, A., and Kedem. Z., ''Consistency in Hierarchical Database Systems''. Journal of the ACM 27(1). January 1980.

[Ston79] Stonebraker. M., ''Concurrency Control and Consistency of Multiple Copies of Data in Distributed INGRES''. IEEE Transactions on Software Engineering 5(3). May 1979.

[Thom79] Thomas. R., ''A Majority Consensus Approach to Concurrency Control for Multiple Copy Databases''. ACM Transactions on Database Systems 4(2). June 1979.

[Ullm83] Ullman. J., Principles of Database Systems, Second Edition. Computer Science Press. Rockville. Maryland. 1983.

[Wolf83] Wolff. R., personal communication.

The Exclusive-Writer Approach to Updating Replicated Files in Distributed Processing Systems

WESLEY W. CHU, FELLOW, IEEE, AND JOSEPH HELLERSTEIN

Abstract —**Consistency control protocols can be classified as either pessimistic or optimistic. Pessimistic protocols check for conflicting file accesses before a transaction references shared files; this prevents transaction restarts but adds *intercomputer synchronization delays* to execution response times T_E. Optimistic protocols avoid intercomputer synchronization delays for T_E, but existing optimistic protocols repeatedly restart a transaction until it executes without conflict. Repeated restarts lengthen the time to finalize an update T_U, and can saturate the computing and communication resources.**

We present two new optimistic protocols that avoid repeated restarts: the *exclusive-writer protocol (EWP)* and the *exclusive-writer protocol with locking option (EWL)*. EWP has no transaction restarts, database rollbacks, or deadlocks due to shared data access. But EWP ensures only a limited form of serializability. EWL is an extension of EWP that ensures full serializability. EWL has no database rollbacks. Also, EWL can guarantee that a transaction will be restarted at most once. To further reduce restarts, each site can independently and dynamically switch between primary site locking (PSL), which has no restarts, and EWL. Such switching requires no additional messages or delays to synchronize protocol selection.

Analytic models are developed to study the response times (i.e., T_E and T_U) of EWP, EWL, PSL, and basic timestamps (BTS). Our study reveals that EWP and EWL have the smallest T_E since neither requires update-log maintenance (unlike BTS) nor intercomputer synchronization delays for T_E (unlike PSL). EWP has the smallest T_U unless the cost of communicating and processing updates is high. T_U(BTS) is larger than T_U(PSL) and/or T_U(EWL) over a wide range of parameter values due to the overhead of BTS update-log maintenance, database rollbacks, distributed conflict checking, and repeated restarts. Choosing between EWL and PSL for T_U depends on several parameters. T_U(EWL) increases with update message costs and restart probability, while T_U(PSL) is unaffected by these parameters. However, T_U(PSL) increases more rapidly than T_U(EWL) with waiting time for file locks and control message costs.

We conclude that if limited serializability is acceptable, EWP should be used due to its simplicity and short response times. Otherwise, EWL has much appeal since it has good performance over a wide range of parameter values and permits dynamic switching with PSL to further improve performance.

Index Terms —**Concurrency control, distributed database, distributed processing, exclusive-writer, locking, multiple copy update, real time, response time models, timestamps.**

I. INTRODUCTION

DISTRIBUTED processing has commonly been used because of its flexibility, reliability, and cost effectiveness. Distributed processing has many design implications. One of these is preserving file consistency, which arises when two or more transactions (or *transaction modules, TM*) concurrently access the same file in a conflicting manner (i.e., at least one access is a write). This problem is further complicated since files may be replicated to reduce read access times and to improve reliability.

To preserve file consistency, *consistency control protocols (CCP's)* are used (see surveys in [3] and [11]). Distributed processing systems need CCP's with short response times. Such response times are measured from the transaction's arrival to when its file updates are available. In some applications, file updates need only be tentative (e.g., radar tracking in which object positions are continuously changing). So, we use the following response time measure.

Execution Response Time (T_E): the time from the transaction's arrival until it has completed its first execution, thereby making available tentative file updates. For other applications (e.g., banking), a transaction must be assured that previous updates to its input files are finalized (i.e., will not be undone due to database rollbacks) before the files can be used. Here we use the following.

Update Finalization Response Time[1] *(T_U):* the time from the transaction's arrival until its update is known to be finalized at some site.

CCP's can be characterized by whether they check for conflicting file accesses *before* or *after* transactions access shared files. Protocols that check after shared files are accessed (e.g., [9], basic timestamps [3], and the majority vote algorithm [14]) are seen as *optimistic* since they are optimistic that a conflict will not occur. Conversely, protocols that check before permitting shared file accesses (e.g., primary site locking [13], SDD-1 timestamp protocols [2], and centralized locking [6]) are called *pessimistic*. Pessimistic protocols delay completing a transaction's first execution, or execution response time T_E, until messages are exchanged

Manuscript received April 11, 1984; revised October 20, 1984. This work was supported by the Ballistic Missile Defense Advanced Technology Center under Contract DASG60-83-C-0019.

W. W. Chu is with the Department of Computer Science, University of California, Los Angeles 90024.

J. Hellerstein is with the IBM T. J. Watson Research Center, Yorktown Heights, NY 10598.

[1]The site that first knows an update is finalized depends on the CCP. In particular, for some CCP's this site may not be the transaction's execution site. Our reason for not always using the transaction's execution site relates to the fact that distributed processing applications are often performed by a sequence of transactions (e.g., [8]). So, communication delays are reduced by assigning a transaction to the site which first knows that the updates of its predecessor transaction have been finalized.

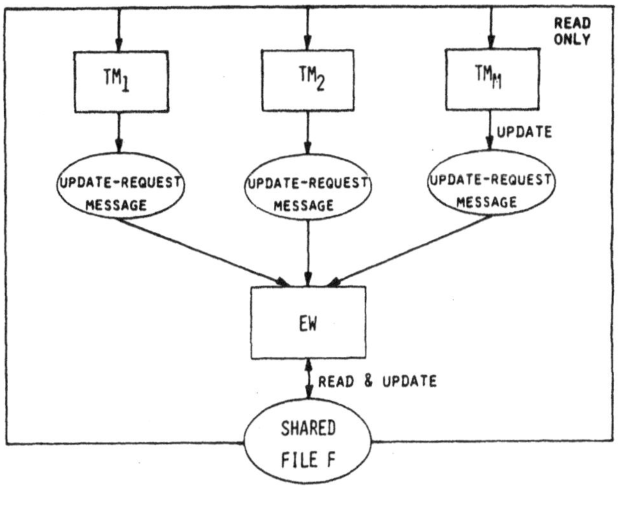

$TM_1, \ldots, TM_M$ ARE TRANSACTIONS

Fig. 1. The exclusive-writer approach.

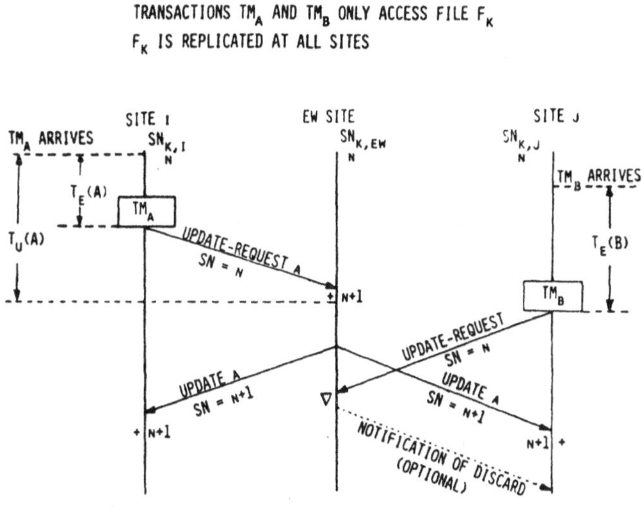

$SN_{K,I}$ = UPDATE SEQUENCE NUMBER FOR THE COPY OF FILE F_K AT SITE I

□ = TRANSACTION EXECUTION
T_E = TRANSACTION EXECUTION RESPONSE TIME
T_U = UPDATE CONFIRMATION RESPONSE TIME
\+ = UPDATE IS WRITTEN
▽ = UPDATE-REQUEST IS DISCARDED

Fig. 2. Timing diagram for exclusive-writer protocol (EWP).

for conflict checking, which causes *intercomputer synchronization delays*. Optimistic protocols avoid such delays for T_E. But existing optimistic protocols repeatedly restart a transaction until it executes without conflict, which can cause long delays to finalize a transaction's update T_U, and can saturate the computing and communication resources. Also, for many existing optimistic protocols, a transaction restart may force files to be rolled back to a previous state (referred to as *database rollback*).

In this paper, we present two new optimistic protocols: the exclusive-writer protocol (EWP) and the exclusive-writer protocol with a locking option (EWL). We describe the operation and implementation of EWP in Section II and EWL in Section III. In Section IV, we study the response times of EWP, EWL, primary site locking (PSL), and basic timestamps (BTS). Our conclusions are presented in Section V.

II. The Exclusive-Writer Protocol (EWP)

The EWP is a low-cost and special-purpose optimistic protocol for updating replicated files. Under EWP, each replicated file is controlled by a special transaction referred to as its *exclusive-writer (EW)*; all copies of a file have the same EW. Only a file's EW can write (update) the file. A non-EW transaction sends to the file's EW an update-request message which includes the proposed update (see Fig. 1). A non-EW transaction knows that its update request has been accepted when the transaction's site receives an update message corresponding to the transaction's update request. Conflicts are detected by the use of *update sequence numbers (SN)*. An SN is attached to each file copy, and update requests include the SN of the file copy read by the requesting transaction. If an EW accepts an update request, it increments the SN of its file copy and distributes the update with the new SN (see Fig. 2). Updates are written in the order of their SN's. A file's EW accepts an update request if the SN in the update request is identical to the SN of the EW's file copy since the requesting transaction read the most current file copy. Otherwise, a conflict occurred, and the transaction is said to have "lost the conflict." An *update request that loses a conflict is discarded*, and, if required, the requesting transaction is notified.

TRANSACTION *TM* HAS JUST COMPLETED ITS EXECUTION AT SITE *i*

1. *RMSG.SN* := $SN_{k,i}$
2. *RMSG.UP* := *TM*'s update to F_k
3. send *RMSG* to EW_k

AN UPDATE-REQUEST MESSAGE (*RMSG*) WAS RECEIVED AT EW_k's SITE

1. if *RMSG.SN* = $SN_{k,j}$ (* No Conflict *)
   a. $SN_{k,j}$:= $SN_{k,j}$ + 1
   b. update $F_{k,j}$ based on *RMSG.UP*
   c. *UMSG.SN* := $SN_{k,j}$
   d. *UMSG.UP* := *RMSG.UP*
   e. broadcast *UMSG* to all other sites with a copy of F_k
2. otherwise (* Conflict *)
   a. discard *RMSG*
   b. if required, notify the requesting transaction

AN UPDATE MESSAGE (*UMSG*) WAS RECEIVED AT SITE *i*

1. once *UMSG.SN* = $SN_{k,i}$ + 1 (* Wait until in sequence *)
   a. $SN_{k,i}$:= *UMSG.SN*
   b. update $F_{k,i}$ based on *UMSG.UP*

Fig. 3. EWP operation at site i for file F_k.

Fig. 3 presents an algorithm for EWP operation at site i for file F_k. Let EW_k be F_k's EW, $SN_{k,i}$ be the SN of F_k at site i, and RMSG be an update-request message. We use the programming language notation for records to indicate fields in messages: RMSG.SN is the SN field in the update-request message and RMSG.UP is the proposed update. UMSG is defined similarly for an update message. The symbol ":=" is used to indicate an assignment statement, and text enclosed in "(* · · · *)" are comments. The algorithm operates under the following assumptions: transactions only access file F_k, which is both read and written; at each site, transaction and protocol control processing are performed atomically (i.e., conflicting file accesses are prevented by using local consistency control techniques such as semaphores); SN fields have a sufficient number of bits so that an update to F_k will be written at all sites before the same SN value is assigned to another update for F_k; there are no site failures; the network guarantees that messages are eventually received without error; and when the system begins operation, copies of the same file are identical, and their SN's have the same value.

EWP preserves mutual consistency and the serializability of successful transactions (i.e., those whose updates are distributed). The latter property is called *limited serializability* since it is limited to transactions whose updates are distributed. Limited serializability implies internal consistency, if the database is initially internally consistent and each transaction preserves internal consistency, since only transactions whose updates are distributed affect the database, and these transactions are serializable. We note that consecutive updates to F_k are assigned consecutive SN's. This is due to EW_k always incrementing its SN for F_k before an F_k update is broadcast. Mutual consistency follows from the fact that consecutive F_k update messages receive consecutive SN's, and updates are written in order of their SN. Hence, the same updates are written in the same order to all copies of F_k.

To establish limited serializability, we present a serial order for executing successful transactions which results in the same values for F_k as when transactions execute under EWP. Let TM(m) be the mth successful transaction for F_k. We show that TM(m + 1) read a copy of F_k to which TM(m)'s updates were the last to be written, or TM(m + 1) *read from* TM(m). (This is equivalent to a serial execution in which TM(m) executed to completion, then TM(m + 1) began execution and read TM(m)'s updates.) Since UMSG(m + 1) (TM(m + 1)'s update message) is the (m + 1)st F_k update, UMSG(m + 1).SN = m + 1. So, TM(m + 1)'s update-request message (RMSG(m + 1)) must have had RMSG(m + 1).SN = m. Since a copy of F_k with an SN of m was last written by TM(m), TM(m + 1) read from TM(m). Hence, EWP preserves limited serializability.

EWP has much appeal for distributed processing systems. Foremost, EWP is simple to implement. Since it does not use locking, *EWP has no deadlocks due to shared data access*. Also, because an update is not written until the EW accepts it, *EWP has no database rollbacks*. Since update requests that lose a conflict are discarded, *EWP has no transaction restarts*. EWP has no intercomputer synchronization delays for T_E since EWP is optimistic. In addition, T_U(EWP) is small even when conflicts are frequent since the only source of intercomputer synchronization is checking update requests at the EW's site, and T_U never includes a wait for transaction restart. While EWP can preserve internal consistency, EWP is not a general-purpose protocol since it only ensures a limited form of serializability.

A. EWP Application Areas

For many applications, discarding update requests that lose a conflict is not acceptable. However, EWP has much appeal for applications such as 1) real time feedback control in which a conflict occurs only when a real time constraint has been violated, and 2) data collection in which occasionally discarding an update request has little overall effect.

For example, EWP is currently used in the distributed processing architecture design (DPAD) [8] for updating radar tracking data. In the DPAD, a record is maintained in the track file for each object detected by radar. Periodically for each object, a radar beam is sent which results in a radar return. Track file records are updated only as a result of radar returns for the object. The *real time constraint* of concern here is that *updates to an object's track record must be completed before a new radar beam is sent for the same object*. (The intent is to direct a radar beam based on the object's most recent sighting so that the beam encounters the correct object.) Thus, a conflict occurs only when the real time constraint is violated (e.g., track processing for record k was not completed prior to scheduling a radar beam for the object associated with record k). By discarding an update request that loses a conflict for the track file, system load is reduced, which facilitates meeting real time constraints. Of course, information is lost when an update request is discarded. However, this information can be recovered from future radar returns which, hopefully, will arrive when the system is not so heavily loaded. Thus, under the very extreme conditions of violating a real time constraint, discarding update requests that lose a conflict has appeal.

B. EWP with Basesets that Have Multiple Files

The files a transaction reads (i.e., readset) and writes (i.e., writeset) are referred to as its *baseset* (readset plus writeset). When a transaction's baseset consists of several files which have the same EW, the update request should include the SN for each file in the baseset. The EW accepts the update request if the SN for each file in the update request is identical to the SN of the EW's file copy; otherwise, all of the update requests are discarded. When an update request is accepted, the SN of each file written is incremented, and file updates are distributed.

If a transaction's baseset includes files with different EW's, a separate update request is sent to *each* EW. An update request is accepted only if the SN for each EW's file copy is the same as the file's SN in the update request. For real time applications, the communication costs and time delays required for EW's to inform one another that an update request has been accepted may be excessive. Thus, it is desirable for the transaction's entire baseset to have the same EW.

C. EWP Implementation Considerations

When a transaction reads a file that is not replicated at its execution site, a copy of the required file data must be obtained along with the file copy's SN. The SN of the remote copy is inserted in the transaction's update request in the same manner as if the site had a local file copy.

How transactions should be assigned to sites (referred to as task assignment in [4]) is affected by utilization due to transaction executions and intertransaction (or intermodule) communication [5]. Assigning an EW to a transaction's execution site increases the site's utilization due to EW executions. However, such an assignment can decrease communication overhead since a transaction does not send an update-request message for a file whose EW is assigned to the transaction's execution site.

In EWP, non-EW transactions cannot directly modify files. Instead, writing updates is deferred until the EW has checked them for conflicts. Referred to as *deferred update writing*, this approach requires providing a transaction with a temporary copy of the file data it modifies and writing a transaction's update to the site's permanent file copy once the EW has accepted the transaction's update request. Deferring file updates can be accomplished with little additional overhead if shadow file copies are used for site fault tolerance [7]. With this technique, the operating system creates a temporary copy of file data whenever a transaction first writes the data; after the transaction finishes executing, the temporary copy becomes the site's permanent file copy. Deferred update writing can be achieved by not modifying the permanent file copy until the EW has accepted the transaction's update request.

EWP message volume can be reduced as follows. For a point-to-point network, site i retains a copy of all update-request messages it sends. If an EW accepts a site i update request, an update-accepted *control message* is sent to site i (instead of an update message), and site i writes the update based on the saved update request. Thus, message volume is reduced since update messages should always be larger than control messages. This approach can be applied to broadcast networks by broadcasting update requests and update-accepted messages to all sites.

Since sites may fail, it is desirable that EWP: 1) preserve database consistency when sites fail; and 2) permit resumption of database operations at sites that have recovered. Regarding 1), if sites write updates atomically, only the failure of an EW site affects consistency since the EW site for F_k could fail before an update message has been sent to all copies of F_k. This can be resolved by having for each EW a backup that assumes control if the current EW site fails.[2] For 2), we can either maintain a log of updates missed by the failed site, or the site can, after recovery, obtain (via a remote read) a current copy of the data it requires.

III. Exclusive-Writer Protocol with Locking Option (EWL)

We extend EWP so that it preserves full serializability by not discarding update requests that lose a conflict, and this is done in a way that minimizes transaction restarts. Our approach is to add a locking option, which is used only when a conflict occurs. In essence, we combine EWP with PSL [13].

We begin by describing the operation of PSL. PSL ensures serializability by requiring transactions to get permission from the file's primary site (PS) before accessing the file as shown in Fig. 4. Specifically, when the transaction arrives, a lock-request message is sent to the file's PS. The transaction waits until the PS replies with a lock-grant message. This message includes the SN of the most current copy of the file. After the transaction executes, the file's SN is incremented, and the transaction's updates are distributed with the new SN. Updates are written in order of their SN's. The PS treats an update message as an implicit lock release.

EWL combines EWP and PSL as shown in Fig. 5. When a transaction arrives, it executes under EWP. EWL's operation is the same as EWP's if the transaction's update request is accepted. Otherwise: 1) the file's EW site becomes its PS; 2) the update request is treated as a PSL lock request and is placed in a lock queue; and 3) the transaction is restarted under PSL.[3] The criteria for accepting an F_k update request are the following.

1) The SN for F_k in the update request is identical to the SN of the file copy at EW_k's site.

2) F_k is not locked.

Fig. 6 contains an algorithm for EWL operation at site i for file F_k. We use the same notation and assumptions as for the EWP algorithm with the additional assumption that a transaction's baseset does not change when it is restarted.

We show that the algorithm in Fig. 6 preserves mutual consistency and serializability. First note that consecutive updates to F_k are assigned consecutive SN's. This is a consequence of: 1) at most one transaction has the authority to distribute updates at any instant (i.e., the EW distributes updates if F_k is not locked and the current lock holder distributes updates if F_k is locked), and this transaction keeps update distribution authority until its updates have been received by EW_k; 2) a transaction with update distribution authority does not execute until its copy of F_k (and hence F_k's SN) is identical to EW_k's copy; and 3) F_k's SN is always incremented before its updates are distributed. Mutual consistency is assumed since updates are written in the same order to all copies of a file.

To establish serializability, let TM(m) be the mth transaction for F_k to have its updates distributed. We show that the same value for F_k would have been obtained by a serial execution of the transactions in the order in which their updates were distributed. Specifically, TM$(m+1)$ read a copy of F_k to which TM(m)'s updates were the last to be written, or TM$(m+1)$ *read from* TM(m). Let RMSG$(m+1)$ be TM$(m+1)$'s update-request message, UMSG$(m+1)$ be its update message, and i be its site of execution. By definition of TM$(m+1)$, UMSG$(m+1)$.SN $= m + 1$. If TM$(m+1)$ was not restarted, EW_k distributed UMSG$(m+1)$. So,

$$\text{RMSG}(m+1).\text{SN} = \text{UMSG}(m+1).\text{SN} - 1 = m .$$

So, TM$(m+1)$ read from TM(m). Now suppose that TM$(m+1)$ was restarted. Let SN(k, i, t) be the SN of F_k at

[2]A single backup can be extended to N-site resiliency as in [1].

[3]A site learns that a transaction will be restarted as follows. If transaction TM executes at site i and updates F_k with SN $= n$, then site i knows that TM will be restarted if site i receives an update for F_k with SN $= n + 1$ but the update was not made by TM.

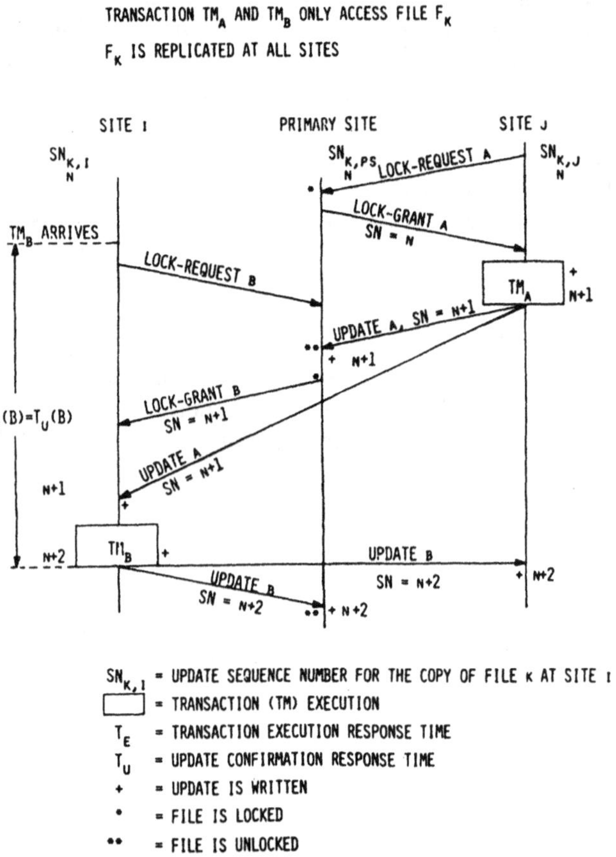

Fig. 4. Timing diagram for primary site locking (PSL).

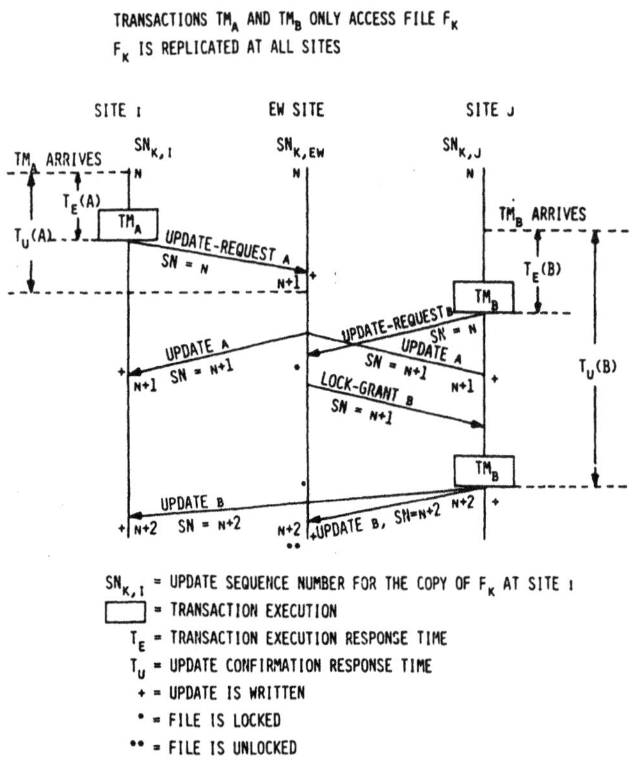

Fig. 5. Timing diagram for exclusive-writer protocol with locking option (EWL).

TRANSACTION *TM* HAS JUST COMPLETED ITS EXECUTION AT SITE *i*

1. if *TM* was restarted
   a. $SN_{k,i} := SN_{k,i} + 1$
   b. update $F_{k,i}$ based on *TM*'s update
   c. $UMSG.SN := SN_{k,i}$
   d. $UMSG.UP :=$ *TM*'s update to F_k
   e. broadcast *UMSG* to all other sites with a copy of F_k
2. otherwise
   a. $RMSG.SN := SN_{k,i}$
   b. $RMSG.UP :=$ *TM*'s update to F_k
   c. send *RMSG* to EW_k

AN UPDATE-REQUEST (*RMSG*) MESSAGE WAS RECEIVED AT EW_K'S SITE

1. if $RMSG.SN = SN_{k,i}$ and F_k is not locked (* No Conflict *)
   a. $SN_{k,i} := SN_{k,i} + 1$
   b. update $F_{k,i}$ based on *RMSG.UP*
   c. $UMSG.SN := SN_{k,i}$
   d. $UMSG.UP := RMSG.UP$
   e. broadcast *UMSG* to all other sites with a copy of F_k
2. otherwise (* Conflict *)
   a. put *RMSG* at the end of F_k's lock queue
   b. if *RMSG* is the first entry in F_k's lock queue
      i. lock F_k
      ii. $LMSG.SN := SN_{k,i}$ (* *LMSG* is a lock-grant message *)
      iii. send *LMSG* to the transaction with the first entry in F_k's lock queue (* Delegate Update Distribution Authority *)

A LOCK-GRANT MESSAGE (*LMSG*) WAS RECEIVED FOR TRANSACTION *TM* AT SITE *i*

1. once $LMSG.SN = SN_{k,i}$ (* Wait until $F_{k,i}$ is current *)
   a. schedule *TM* for restart execution

AN UPDATE MESSAGE (*UMSG*) WAS RECEIVED AT SITE *i*

1. once $UMSG.SN = SN_{k,i} + 1$ (* Wait until in sequence *)
   a. $SN_{k,i} := UMSG.SN$
   b. update $F_{k,i}$ based on *UMSG.UP*
2. if EW_k resides at site *i* (* F_k is currently locked *)
   a. remove the first entry in F_k's lock queue and unlock F_k
   b. if F_k's lock queue is not empty
      i. lock F_k
      ii. $LMSG.SN := SN_{k,i}$ (* *LMSG* is a lock-grant message *)
      iii. send *LMSG* to the transaction with the first entry in F_k's lock queue (* Delegate Update Distribution Authority *)

Fig. 6. EWL operation at site *i* for file F_k.

site *i* when TM$(m + 1)$ was scheduled for execution at time *t*. Since F_k's SN is incremented after TM$(m + 1)$ executes and before UMSG$(m + 1)$ is distributed,

$$m + 1 = \text{UMSG}(m + 1).\text{SN} = \text{SN}(k, i, t) + 1 .$$

Hence, $\text{SN}(k, i, t) = m$. So, TM$(m + 1)$ read from TM(m).

EWL is more difficult to implement than EWP. However, unlike EWP, EWL ensures serializability. EWL has no database rollbacks. Since it restarts transactions under a pessimistic protocol, *EWL restarts a transaction at most once* if the transaction's baseset does not change when it is restarted. T_E(EWL) has no intercomputer synchronization delays. The intercomputer delays for T_U(EWL) are similar to those for T_U(EWP) if the transaction is not restarted, and similar to those for T_U(PSL) if the transaction is restarted.

A. EWL with Basesets that Have Multiple Files

If all files in the transaction's baseset have the same EW, the EW accepts the update request if for each file the SN in the update request is identical to the SN of the EW's file copy and the file is not locked; otherwise, all of the transaction's update requests are discarded. If a transaction's baseset includes files with different EW's, a separate update request is sent to each EW. An update request is accepted only if for each file in the baseset the file's EW has the same SN for its file copy as the SN in the update request, and the file is not locked. For real time applications, the communication costs and time delays required for EW's to inform one another that an update request has been accepted may be excessive. Thus, as with EWP, all files in the transaction's baseset should have the same EW.

The criteria for granting a lock must consider the possibility of deadlock. Thus, some form of deadlock management, such as avoidance, prevention, or detection, is required.

There may be files in a transaction's baseset that are read but not written. If the transaction is restarted, the EW for such a file will not receive an update to indicate that the file's lock should be released. So, after a transaction completes its restart execution, a lock-release message should be sent to the EW of each file which is read but not written.

B. Dynamic Switching Between PSL and EWL

EWL's performance can degrade due to transaction restarts which increase load and lengthen T_U. EWL improves on existing optimistic protocols since EWL can guarantee that a transaction will be restarted at most once. However, when restarts are frequent, pessimistic protocols are preferred since they have no transaction restarts. Ideally, we should use an optimistic protocol when restarts are rare and not too costly and use a pessimistic protocol when restarts are frequent and/or costly. A very appealing aspect of EWL is that each site can independently and dynamically choose whether to execute a transaction under EWL (which is optimistic) or PSL (which is pessimistic). Further, unlike other approaches to dynamic protocol selection (e.g., [2] and [12]), *dynamic switching between EWL and PSL is done without additional messages or delays to synchronize protocol selection.* This feature results from being able to use EWL and PSL concurrently for the same shared file (see Fig. 7). Recall that EWL already requires implementing PSL. So, a PSL lock request is treated as a rejected EWL update request. Specifically, a lock request received by EW_k is placed in F_k's lock queue until EW_k selects it. Then, EW_k sends a lock grant to the requesting transaction, and the transaction executes. EW_k treats the transaction's update message as an implicit lock release. While switching between PSL and EWL requires no message or delay to synchronize protocol selection, overhead may be required for sites to gather the information necessary to choose which protocol to use.

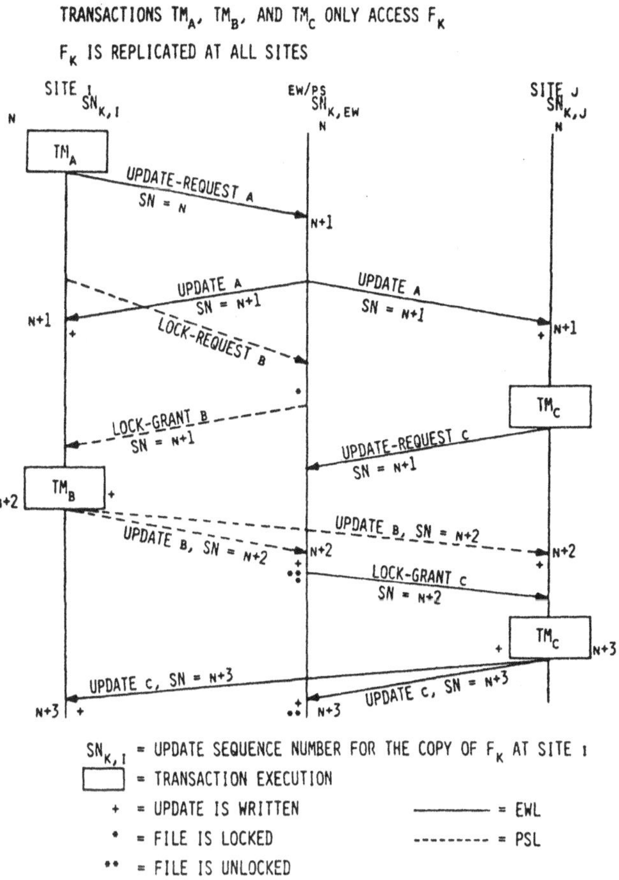

Fig. 7. Concurrent use of EWL and PSL for the same shared file.

C. EWL Implementation Considerations

Except for fault tolerance, the same implementation considerations mentioned for EWP also apply to EWL. In addition, using EWL has implications for transactions whose basesets change when they are restarted.

EWL can be made fault tolerant by employing an existing scheme for fault tolerance which is applicable to PSL (e.g., [15]). The EWL update request is viewed as a PSL lock request. If the update request is accepted, this is immediately followed by a lock release. If the update request is not accepted, EWL's operation becomes the same as that of PSL.

In general, a transaction's baseset may be different when it is restarted since file access patterns can be data dependent. This can be resolved by the transaction sending a lock-release message to all EW's from which it received a lock grant and sending an update-request message to the EW of each file in its new baseset. Thus, if there is a high probability that a transaction's baseset changes when it is restarted, EWL might perform poorly since it would have delays for locking and repeated transaction restarts. Dynamic switching to PSL could alleviate this problem by using PSL for those transactions that have a high probability of being restarted with a different baseset.

IV. Response Time Studies

Here, we compare the response times of EWP and EWL to PSL and BTS, an optimistic timestamp protocol[4] [3]. We first develop analytic models for T_E and T_U, then derive crossover points for the response times of the protocols, then perform numerical studies, and finally discuss our results.

Let us describe the BTS protocol (see Fig. 8). BTS preserves mutual consistency and serializability by assigning globally unique timestamps to transactions and their updates and by requiring updates to be written in the order of their timestamp. Since BTS is optimistic, after a transaction arrives it executes without any intercomputer synchronization delay. Then the transaction's updates are written to the database at its execution site. An *update log* is maintained in case updates are not written in timestamp order and must be removed by performing a *database rollback*. BTS uses *distributed conflict checking*. That is, the transaction's updates are sent to all other sites, and each site checks that the updates are in timestamp order. If the updates are in timestamp order, an acknowledgment indicating acceptance is returned to the sending site. Otherwise, an acknowledgment indicating rejection is returned to the sending site. Transactions whose updates are rejected are restarted in the same manner as their original execution. The first site to know that an update has been finalized is the transaction's execution site when it has received an acknowledgment with acceptance from all other sites.

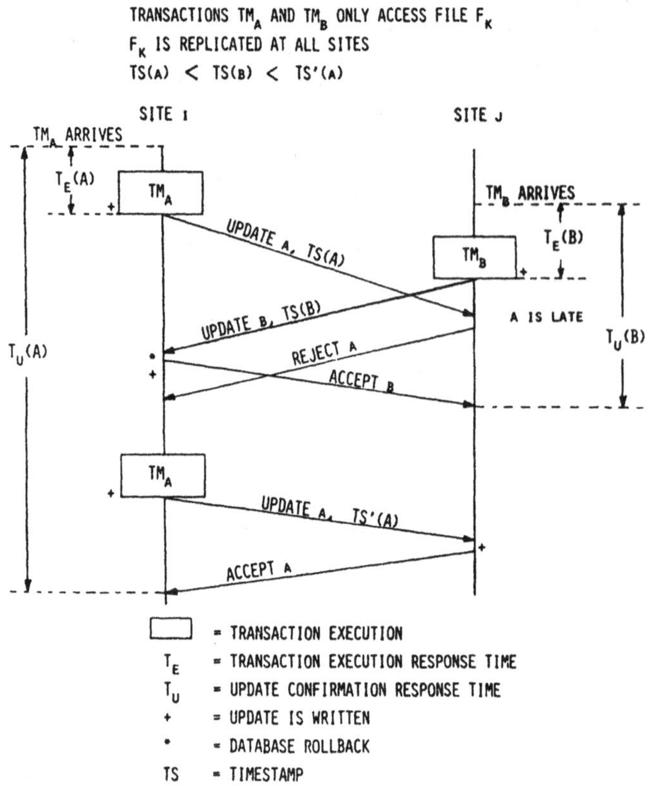

Fig. 8. Timing diagram for basic timestamps (BTS).

A. Response Time Models

To construct our response times models, we assume the following.

1) A transaction's baseset does not change if the transaction is restarted.

2) All files in a transaction's baseset have the same PS for PSL and the same EW site for EWP and EWL.

3) Transaction file requirements are known in advance.

4) The communication network is reliable, and sites do not fail.

T_E(PSL) includes time from the transaction's arrival until its lock request is placed in the lock queue; wait in the lock queue; time from lock grant processing at the PS until the transaction is placed in its site execution queue; transaction's wait for execution; and execution of the transaction (see Fig. 9). Thus,

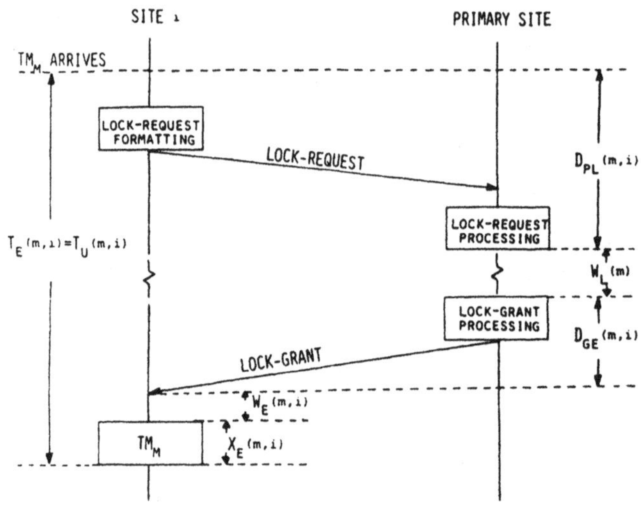

Fig. 9. Timing diagram for PSL response times.

$$T_E(\text{PSL}; m, i) = D_{PL}(m, i) + W_L(m) + D_{GE}(m, i) + W_E(m, i) + X_E(m, i) \quad (1)$$

where

$T_E(\text{PSL}; m, i)$ = PSL execution response time for transaction m at site i;

$D_{PL}(m, i)$ = prelock processing delay for transaction m at site i from transaction arrival at site i to enqueueing all of the transaction's lock requests;

$W_L(m)$ = waiting time for file locks for transaction m starts when the transaction's last lock request is enqueued and ends when its last lock is granted;

$D_{GE}(m, i)$ = delay starting from lock grant processing of transaction m to when the transaction enters the execution queue at site i;

$W_E(m, i)$ = waiting time for executing transaction m at site i;

$X_E(m, i)$ = service time for executing transaction m at site i.

Since PSL is a pessimistic protocol, updates are known to be finalized after the transaction's first execution.

$$T_U(\text{PSL}; m, i) = T_E(\text{PSL}; m, i) \quad (2)$$

[4]The algorithm in [3] only applies to single copy database systems. However, extensions to multiple copy databases are assumed in our analysis.

where

$T_U(\mathrm{PSL}; m, i)$ = PSL update finalization response time for transaction m at site i.

Next consider the response times for BTS. Since BTS has no intercomputer synchronization delay for T_E, $T_E(\mathrm{BTS})$ consists of only the transaction's wait for execution, transaction execution time, and time for update-log maintenance (see Fig. 10).

$$T_E(\mathrm{BTS}; m, i) = W_E(m, i) + X_E(m, i) + Y_M(m, i) \quad (3)$$

where

$Y_M(m, i)$ = service time for update-log maintenance after transaction m executes at site i.

Under BTS, transactions are repeatedly restarted until they execute without conflict. Let $q(m, i)$ be the probability of restarting transaction m at site i. Assuming a geometric distribution, the number of times transaction m executes for each arrival instance is

$$N_E(m, i) = \frac{1}{1 - q(m, i)}. \quad (4)$$

To compute $T_U(\mathrm{BTS})$, note that each time a transaction executes there are delays for execution response time, conflict checking (i.e., wait for *all* sites to check the timestamp of the updates and return an acknowledgment), and database rollbacks if the transaction is restarted.

$$\begin{aligned} T_U(\mathrm{BTS}; m, i) = N_E(m, i)[&T_E(\mathrm{BTS}; m, i) \\ &+ \max_j \{D_{EC}(m, i, j) + D_{CA}(m, j, i)\} \\ &+ q(m, i) Y_R(m, i)]. \end{aligned} \quad (5)$$

$D_{EC}(m, i, j)$ = delay from completing the execution of transaction m at site i to completion of checking the timestamp ordering of its updates at site j;

$D_{CA}(m, j, i)$ = delay from checking the timestamp ordering of transaction m's updates at site j until completion of processing of site j's acknowledgment at site i;

$Y_R(m, i)$ = service time for database rollback of updates made by transaction m at site i.

We now consider response times for EWP. $T_E(\mathrm{EWP})$ only consists of the transaction's wait for execution and transaction execution time (see Fig. 11).

$$T_E(\mathrm{EWP}; m, i) = W_E(m, i) + X_E(m, i). \quad (6)$$

$T_U(\mathrm{EWP})$ has update-request processing by the EW. Thus, update finalization response time is

$$T_U(\mathrm{EWP}; m, i) = T_E(\mathrm{EWP}; m, i) + D_{ER}(m, i) \quad (7)$$

where

$D_{ER}(m, i)$ = delay from completing the execution of transaction m at site i until update-request processing has been completed for all of the transaction's update requests.

From the discussion of EWL in Section III, $T_E(\mathrm{EWL})$ is identical to $T_E(\mathrm{EWP})$. Thus,

$$T_E(\mathrm{EWL}; m, i) = T_E(\mathrm{EWP}; m, i). \quad (8)$$

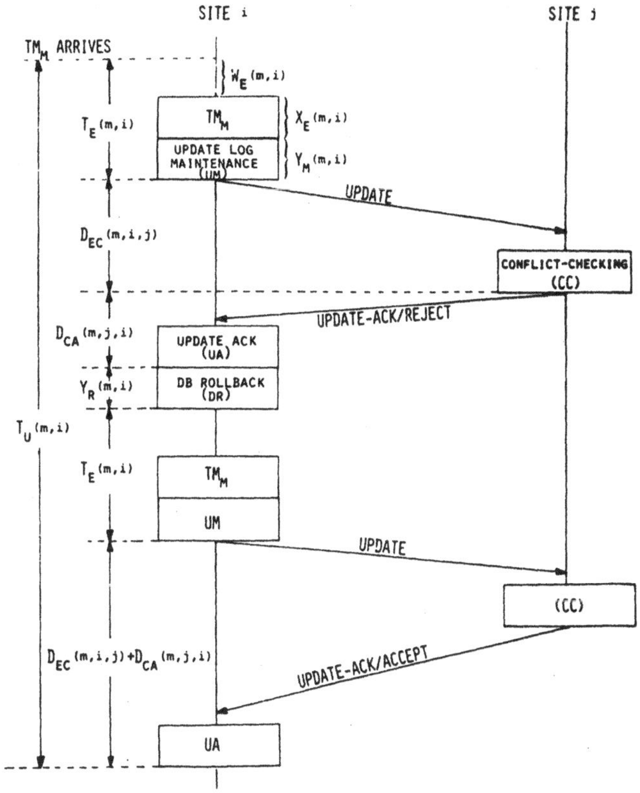

Fig. 10. Timing diagram for BTS response times.

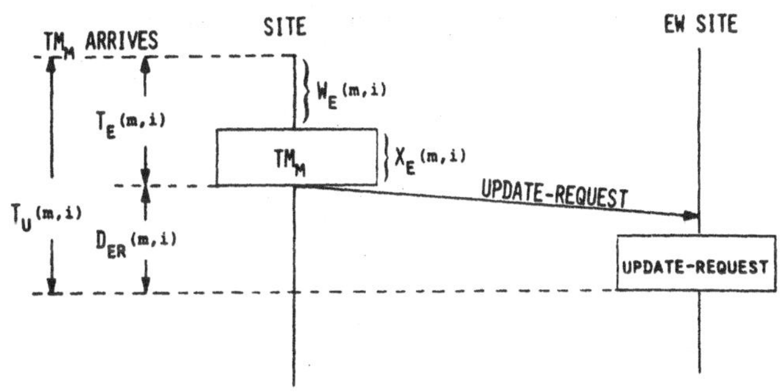

Fig. 11. Timing diagram for EWP response times.

To estimate $T_U(\mathrm{EWL})$, there are two cases. If the transaction is not restarted, $T_U(\mathrm{EWL})$ is the same as $T_U(\mathrm{EWP})$. Otherwise, there are delays due to execution response time, time from the transaction's execution until update requests have been placed in lock queues, wait for file locks, time from lock-grant processing until the transaction enters the execution queue at its site, and another execution response time. The time components for the restart case are shown in Fig. 12.

$$\begin{aligned} T_U(\mathrm{EWL}; m, i) = &T_E(\mathrm{EWL}; m, i) \\ &+ (1 - q(m, i)) D_{ER}(m, i) \\ &+ q(m, i)[D_{EL}(m, i) + W_L(m) \\ &+ D_{GE}(m, i) + T_E(\mathrm{EWL}; m, i)] \end{aligned} \quad (9)$$

where

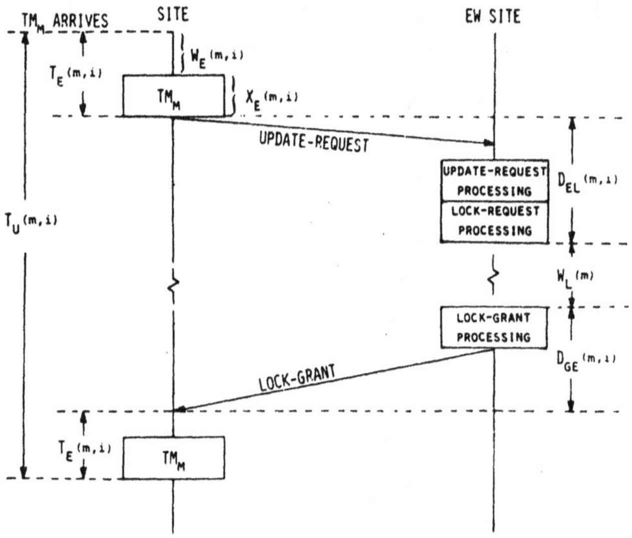

Fig. 12. Timing diagram for EWL response times.

$D_{EL}(m, i)$ = delay from completing the execution of transaction m at site i until all its lock requests have been enqueued.

For EWL and BTS, we obtain a quadratic equation when comparing (5) and (9). Solving for both roots, we determine that $T_U(\text{EWL}; m, i) \leq T_U(\text{BTS}; m, i)$ when either (14a) or (14b) holds.

$$q(m, i) \leq \frac{b(m, i) - [b^2(m, i) - 4a(m, i)c(m, i)]^{1/2}}{2a(m, i)} \tag{14a}$$

$$q(m, i) \geq \frac{b(m, i) + [b^2(m, i) - 4a(m, i)c(m, i)]^{1/2}}{2a(m, i)} \tag{14b}$$

where

$$a(m, i) = D_{EL}(m, i) - D_{ER}(m, i) + W_E(m, i) + X_E(m, i) + W_L(m) + D_{GE}(m, i)$$

$$b(m, i) = W_L(m) + D_{GE}(m, i) + D_{EL}(m, i) - 2D_{ER}(m, i) - Y_R(m, i)$$

$$c(m, i) = Y_M(m, i) + \max_j \{D_{EC}(m, i, j) + D_{CA}(m, j, i)\} - D_{ER}(m, i).$$

Comparing (2) and (5), we have $T_U(\text{BTS}; m, i) \leq T_U(\text{PSL}; m, i)$ when

$$q(m, i) \leq \frac{D_{PL}(m, i) + W_L(m) + D_{GE}(m, i) - Y_M(m, i) - \max_j\{D_{EC}(m, i, j) + D_{CA}(m, j, i)\}}{D_{PL}(m, i) + W_L(m) + D_{GE}(m, i) + W_E(m, i) + X_E(m, i) + Y_R(m, i)}. \tag{15}$$

B. Crossover Points for Protocol Response Times

By comparing the protocol response time equations, we derive crossover points for the response time measures.[5] Let us first consider execution response times. From (8), EWP and EWL have the same execution response times, so it suffices to compare PSL, BTS, and EWL. From (1) and (8), we have $T_E(\text{EWL}; m, i) \leq T_E(\text{PSL}; m, i)$ when

$$0 \leq D_{PL}(m, i) + W_L(m) + D_{GE}(m, i). \tag{10}$$

From (3) and (8), we have $T_E(\text{EWL}; m, i) \leq T_E(\text{BTS}; m, i)$ when

$$0 \leq Y_M(m, i). \tag{11}$$

Comparing (1) and (3), we have $T_E(\text{BTS}; m, i) \leq T_E(\text{PSL}; m, i)$ when

$$0 \leq D_{PL}(m, i) + W_L(m) + D_{GE}(m, i) - Y_M(m, i). \tag{12}$$

We observe that optimistic protocols have much appeal for execution response times. Specifically, *EWP and EWL have the smallest* T_E. $T_E(\text{BTS})$ will also be small if the cost of update-log maintenance, Y_M, is small.

Next, we consider update finalization response times. By comparing (2) and (9), we have $T_U(\text{EWL}; m, i) \leq T_U(\text{PSL}; m, i)$ when

$$q(m, i) \leq \frac{D_{PL}(m, i) + W_L(m) + D_{GE}(m, i) - D_{ER}(m, i)}{D_{EL}(m, i) - D_{ER}(m, i) + W_L(m) + D_{GE}(m, i) + W_E(m, i) + X_E(m, i)}. \tag{13}$$

From (7) and (9), we have $T_U(\text{EWP}; m, i) \leq T_U(\text{EWL}; m, i)$ when

$$0 \leq q(m, i)[D_{EL}(m, i) - D_{ER}(m, i) + W_L(m) + D_{GE}(m, i) + W_E(m, i) + X_E(m, i)]. \tag{16}$$

We observe from (13) and (15) that $T_U(\text{PSL})$ is smaller than $T_U(\text{BTS})$ or $T_U(\text{EWL})$ when the restart probability q is large since BTS and EWL have restarts but PSL does not. From (14b), $T_U(\text{EWL})$ is smaller than $T_U(\text{BTS})$ for large q, due to BTS repeated transaction restarts. Since $D_{EL} \geq D_{ER}$, (16) indicates that $T_U(\text{EWP}) \leq T_U(\text{EWL})$.

C. Numerical Studies

To better illustrate the interrelationships of parameters for T_U, numerical studies are presented. To simplify our studies, we make several assumptions. First, all sites are identical, and all transactions are identical. Thus, $W_E = W_E(m, i)$, $X_E = X_E(m, i)$, $q = q(m, i)$, and $W_L = W_L(m)$. Second, the average delay for communicating and processing an update message is the same for all types of update messages. Thus, $D = D_{ER}(m, i) = D_{EL}(m, i) = D_{EC}(m, i, j)$. Third, the delay for communicating and processing a control message is the same for all types of control messages. Thus, $D' = D_{PL}(m, i) = D_{GE}(m, i) = D_{CA}(m, j, i)$. Fourth, the

[5]For simplicity, we assume parameter values are independent of the protocol used.

time for update-log maintenance is the same as the time for database rollbacks. Thus, $Y = Y_M(m, i) = Y_R(m, i)$. Fifth, we define R_{max} as the relative delay for conflict checking of the slowest site and assume that R_{max} is the same for all transactions and sites. Let D_{EC} be the average value for $D_{EC}(m, i, j)$ and D_{CA} be the average value for $D_{EC}(m, j, i)$. Since $D = D_{EC}$ and $D' = D_{CA}$, $R_{max} = (\max_j\{D_{EC}(m, i, j) + D_{CA}(m, j, i)\})/(D + D')$. We define site response time as the sum of the waiting time for transaction execution and the transaction execution time. To further simplify our studies, time is normalized with respect to site response time.

Fig. 13 presents T_U as a function of restart probability q for selected values of the times for processing and communicating update messages, D, and the times for processing and communicating and control messages, D'. T_U(PSL) is unaffected by q since PSL has no restarts. Also, PSL is not affected by D since under PSL no update message is sent prior to the update being finalized. T_U(PSL) increases linearly with D' at a rate of 2 since for each transaction two control messages are required (i.e., lock request and lock grant). T_U(BTS) increases geometrically with q due to repeated transaction restarts [see (4)]. Also T_U(BTS) increases linearly at a rate of $R_{max}/(1 - q)$ with both D and D' due to distributed conflict checking and repeated restarts. T_U(EWL) increases linearly with q. T_U(EWL) increases linearly with D at a rate of 1, due to the update-request message. T_U(EWL) increases linearly with D' at a rate of q since a control message (i.e., lock grant) is required only when a transaction is restarted.

We consider four cases for comparing T_U(PSL), T_U(BTS), and T_U(EWL) in Fig. 13. When D and D' are both small, T_U is primarily affected by the other parameters. If D is small and D' is large, EWL has the smallest T_U since EWL has the lowest rate of increase with D'. For D large and D' small, PSL has the smallest T_U since T_U(PSL) is unaffected by D. When both D and D' are large, T_U(EWL) is the smallest for small q and T_U(PSL) for large q.

Fig. 14 plots T_U against q for selected values of the wait in the lock queue, W_L, with four selected pairs of D and D' values. T_U(BTS) is unaffected by W_L; T_U(PSL) increases linearly with W_L at a rate of 1 since all transactions wait in the lock queue; T_U(EWL) increases linearly with W_L at a rate of q since locking is used only when a transaction is restarted. Thus, BTS is preferred when W_L is large but q, D, and D' are small since BTS is unaffected by W_L, but T_U(BTS) grows rapidly with the other parameters. Of the three protocols, PSL has the lowest T_U when W_L and D' are small and q is large since both T_U(BTS) and T_U(EWL) increase with q and D, but PSL is unaffected by either q or D. EWL has a lower T_U than BTS for larger values of q and has lower T_U than PSL for larger values of W_L.

Fig. 15 plots T_U against q for selected values of update-log maintenance and database rollbacks, Y, as well as the relative delay for conflict checking of the slowest site, R_{max}, with four selected pairs of D and D' values. PSL and EWL are unaffected by Y and R_{max}, and thus are preferred as Y and R_{max} increase. T_U(BTS) increases with both Y and R_{max}, especially with larger q (due to repeated restarts). Further, the effect of R_{max} is greatest with larger D and D' since the cost of distrib-

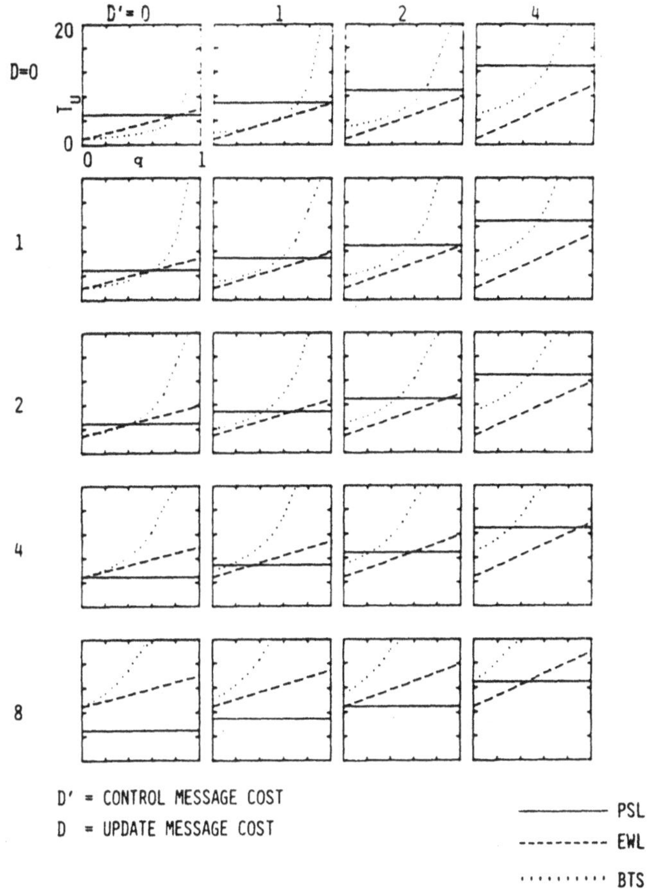

Fig. 13. Effect of D' and D on T_U ($W_L = 4$, $R_{max} = 1$, $Y = 0$).

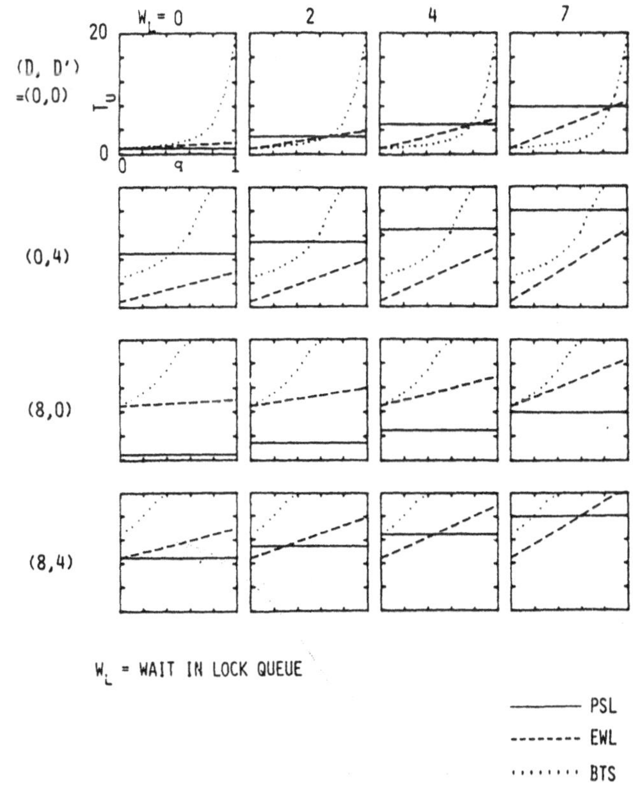

Fig. 14. Effect of W_L on T_U ($R_{max} = 1$, $Y = 0$).

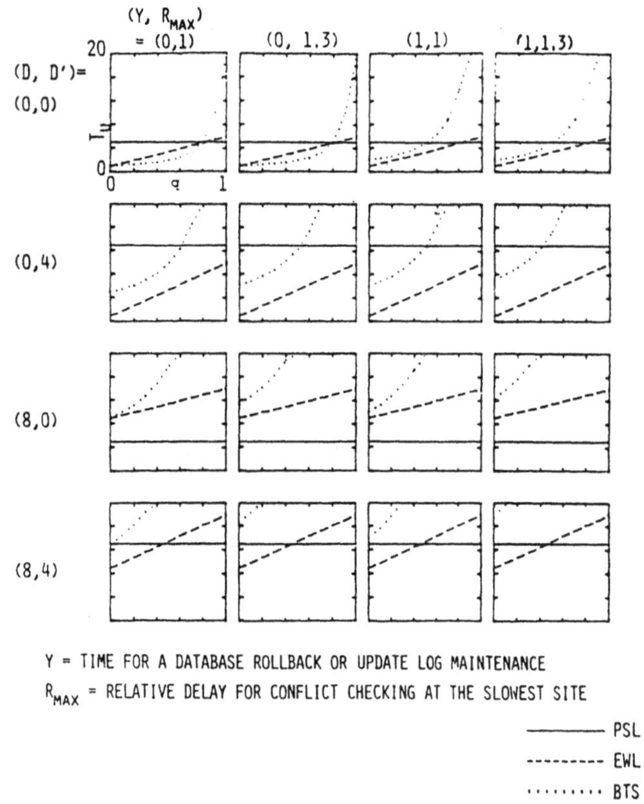

Fig. 15. Effect of Y and $R_{\max}$ on T_U (W_L = 4).

uted conflict checking increases with longer delays for message communication and processing.

D. Discussions

We observe that optimistic protocols, such as BTS, EWP, and EWL, have smaller execution response times T_E than pessimistic protocols (such as PSL) since optimistic protocols have no intercomputer synchronization delays before the transaction's first execution. However, optimistic protocols which require an update log, such as BTS, lengthen T_E for update-log maintenance (i.e., Y_M).

For update finalization response times T_U, BTS performs poorly for several reasons. First, BTS has overhead for update-log maintenance and database rollbacks. Second, BTS uses distributed conflict checking; thus, T_U(BTS) grows with the relative delay of conflict checking for the slowest site (i.e., $R_{\max}$). Finally, BTS has repeated transaction restarts, which further lengthens T_U(BTS) and can saturate the computing and communication resources.

Choosing between EWL and PSL for T_U depends on several parameters. T_U(EWL) increases with delays for communicating and processing update messages, D, since EWL's update-request message contains the proposed update. Also, T_U(EWL) increases with q, the probability of a restart. T_U(PSL) is unaffected by both D and q. However, T_U(PSL) increases more rapidly than T_U(EWL) with delays for communicating and processing control messages, D', since PSL exchanges two control messages (i.e., lock request and lock grant) and EWL only requires a single control message (i.e., lock grant) when a transaction is restarted. Also, T_U(PSL) increases more rapidly than T_U(EWL) with waiting times for file locks, W_L, since PSL always has such waits while EWL incurs them only when a transaction is restarted.

Since EWP is a simplification of EWL, the response times for EWP should be less than those for EWL. Specifically, T_U(EWL) increases with q, W_L, and D' while T_U(EWP) is unaffected by these parameters.

Choosing among PSL, BTS, and EWL requires knowledge of the relationships between the waiting times for file locks, W_L, and the probability of a transaction restart, q. Intuitively, BTS provides a distributed queueing system in which transactions are queued at their execution site but are delayed (via restarts) by transactions at other sites. Because a transaction accesses the same files regardless of the protocol used, one might expect a transaction in this distributed queueing system to wait for as many other transactions as if PSL had been used. However, the site waiting times W_E for BTS will be longer than those for PSL due to BTS repeated transaction restarts, which increase site loads. Thus, we expect in general, T_U(BTS) will be larger than T_U(PSL). EWL has restarts but can guarantee that a transaction will be restarted at most once. Hence, site waiting times for EWL will be lower than those for BTS but higher than those for PSL. However, EWL waiting times for file locks may be smaller than those for PSL. Specifically, let λ_{TM} be the external arrival rate of transactions and λ_L be the arrival rate at the lock queue. Under PSL, $\lambda_L(\text{PSL}) = \lambda_{TM}$ since all transactions enter the lock queue. However, for EWL, locking is required only when a transaction is restarted, so $\lambda_L(\text{EWL}) = q\lambda_{TM}$. Thus, the utilization of the lock queue under EWL may be smaller than that for PSL; as a result, W_L(EWL) may be less than W_L(PSL).

V. Conclusions

Optimistic protocols have appeal for distributed processing systems since they avoid intercomputer synchronization delays for execution response times T_E. However, existing optimistic protocols have repeated transaction restarts, which lengthen update finalization response times T_U and can saturate the computing and communication resources.

EWP and EWL are optimistic protocols that avoid repeated restarts. EWP has no restarts or database rollbacks and avoids deadlocks due to shared data access. However, EWP is not a general-purpose protocol since it preserves only a limited form of serializability. EWL is a fully serializable extension of EWP. Although deadlocks are possible under EWL, EWL has no database rollbacks. EWL restarts a transaction at most once if the transaction's baseset does not change when it is restarted. To further reduce restarts, each site can independently and dynamically switch between PSL, which has no restarts, and EWL. Such switching requires no additional messages or delays to synchronize protocol selection.

Analytic models were developed to study the response times T_E and T_U of EWP, EWL, PSL, and BTS. The performance of these protocols depends on several parameters: q (the probability of restarting a transaction), D (delay for communicating and processing an update message), D' (delay for communicating and processing a control message), W_L (waiting time in the lock queue), Y (time for update-log maintenance and database rollbacks), and $R_{\max}$ (relative delay for the slowest site to do conflict checking). EWP and EWL have the smallest T_E since neither requires update-log maintenance (unlike BTS) or has intercomputer synchronization delays for T_E (unlike PSL). Unless D is quite large, T_U(EWP) has the smallest T_U since EWP has no transaction restarts or lock queue waits. T_U(PSL) is unaffected by q, but it increases linearly with W_L and D'. T_U(EWL) grows linearly with q and D, but is less affected than T_U(PSL) by either W_L or D' since these costs are incurred only when a transaction is restarted. T_U(BTS) grows geometrically with q due to repeated transaction restarts, increases with Y since update-log maintenance is required for each transaction execution and database rollbacks occur whenever a transaction is restarted, and increases with D, D', and R_{max} due to distributed conflict checking. Although T_U(BTS) is unaffected by W_L, in general we expect that delays due to repeated transaction restarts will exceed W_L.

We conclude that if limited serializability is acceptable, EWP should be used due to its simplicity and short response times, which have great appeal for distributed processing systems. Otherwise, EWL has much appeal since it has good performance over a wide range of parameters and permits dynamic switching with PSL to further improve performance.

Acknowledgment

The authors thank Prof. H. Garcia-Molina at Princeton University for stimulating discussions on EWP and M. T. Lan, J. M. An, and K. K. Leung for a careful reading of an early draft of this paper.

References

[1] P. A. Alsberg and J. D. Day, "A principle for resilient sharing of distributed resources," *Second Int. Conf. Software Eng.*, San Francisco, CA, Oct. 13–15, 1976, pp. 562–570.

[2] P. A. Bernstein, J. B. Rothnie, N. Goodman, and C. A. Papadimitriou, "The concurrency control mechanism of SDD-1: A system for distributed databases (The fully redundant case)," *IEEE Trans. Software Eng.*, vol. SE-4, pp. 154–168, May 1978.

[3] P. A. Bernstein and N. Goodman, "Concurrency control in distributed database systems," *ACM Comput. Surv.*, vol. 13, no. 2, pp. 185–222, June 1981.

[4] W. W. Chu, L. J. Holloway, M.-T. Lan, and K. Efe, "Task allocation in distributed data processing," *IEEE Comput. Mag.*, pp. 57–69, Nov. 1980.

[5] W. W. Chu, M.-T. Lan, and J. Hellerstein, "Estimation of intermodule communication (IMC) and its applications in distributed processing systems," *IEEE Trans. Comput.*, vol. C-33, pp. 691–699, Aug. 1984.

[6] H. Garcia-Molina, "Performance comparison of two update algorithms for distributed databases," *Third Berkeley Workshop Distributed Data Management Comput. Networks,* Aug. 29–31, 1978, pp. 108–119.

[7] J. Gray, P. McJones, M. Balsgen, B. Lindsay, R. Lorie, T. Price, F. Putzolu, and I. Traiger, "The recovery manager of the system *R* database manager," *ACM Comput. Surv.*, vol. 13, no. 2, pp. 223–242, June 1981.

[8] M. L. Green *et al.*, "A distributed real time operating system," in *Proc. Symp. Distributed Data Acquisition, Comput., Contr.*, Dec. 1980.

[9] H. T. Kung and J. T. Robinson, "On optimistic methods for concurrency control," in *Proc. Very Large Database Conf.*, Rio de Janeiro, Brazil, Oct. 1979.

[10] B. Lampson, Ed., "Distributed systems-architecture and implementation," in *Lecture Notes on Computer Science*. Berlin, West Germany: Springer-Verlag, 1981.

[11] W.-T. Lin, J. Nolte, P. Bernstein, and N. Goodman, *Distributed Database System Designer Handbook*, Comput. Corp. America, Contract F30602-81-C-0028.

[12] M. Milenkovic, *Update Synchronization in Multiaccess Systems.* Ann Arbor, MI: Univ. Michigan Research Press, 1981.

[13] M. Stonebraker, "Concurrency control and consistency of multiple copies of data in distributed INGRES," *IEEE Trans. Software Eng.*, vol. SE-5, pp. 188–194, May 1979.

[14] R. Thomas, "A solution to the concurrency control problem for multiple copy data bases," in *Proc. COMPCON'78*, Feb. 28–Mar. 3, 1978, pp. 56–62.

[15] B. Walker, G. Popek, R. English, C. Kline, and G. Thiel, "The LOCUS distributed operating system," in *Proc. 9th Symp. Oper. Syst. Principles*, Oct. 10–13, 1983, pp. 49–70.

Wesley W. Chu (S'62–M'67–SM'74–F'78) received the B.S. and M.S. degrees from the University of Michigan, Ann Arbor, in 1960 and 1961 and the Ph.D. degree in electrical engineering from Stanford University, Stanford, CA, in 1966.

From 1961 to 1962 he worked on switching circuit design at the General Electric Computer Department (now Honeywell), Phoenix, AZ; from 1964 to 1966 he worked on the design of large-scale computers at IBM, Menlo Park and San Jose, CA; and from 1966 to 1969 he researched computer communications at Bell Laboratories, Holmdel, NJ. He joined the University of California, Los Angeles (UCLA), in 1969, and is currently a Professor in the Department of Computer Science. He directs a research group at UCLA in the areas of computer communications and networking, distributed processing, and distributed databases. He is also a consultant to government agencies and private industries. He is a member of the Technical Review Committee for the Western Union Telegraph Co., NJ, where he reviews various technical programs related to computer networking and distributed processing systems. He has authored or coauthored more than 70 articles on information processing systems and computer communications and has edited two textbooks: *Advances in Computer Communications* (Dedham, MA: Artech House, 1st ed., 1974, and 2nd revised ed., 1977) and *Centralized and Distributed Database Systems* (coedited with P. P. Chen) (IEEE Computer Society, 1979).

Dr. Chu is a member of Tau Beta Pi, Eta Kappa Nu, Phi Tau Phi, and Sigma Xi. He was an ACM National Lecturer from 1972 to 1973, IEEE Distinguished Visitor from 1973 to 1974, Chairman of the ACM SIGCOMM from 1973 to 1977, a member of the IEEE Technical Committee on Computer Communications, Chairman of the 1975 ACM Interprocess Communication Workshop, Technical Program Chairman of the Fourth Data Communication Symposium in 1975, and Chairman of the IEEE Lake Arrowhead Workshop on Computer Networking and Distributed Databases in 1977. He was an Associate Editor for the IEEE TRANSACTIONS ON COMPUTERS for the field of computer networking and distributed processing systems (1978–1982) and received a meritorious award for his service to IEEE in 1983. He is currently a member of the Editorial Board of *Computer Networks* and the *International Journal on Computers and Electrical Engineering* and an Associate Editor for the *Journal of Computer Networks*.

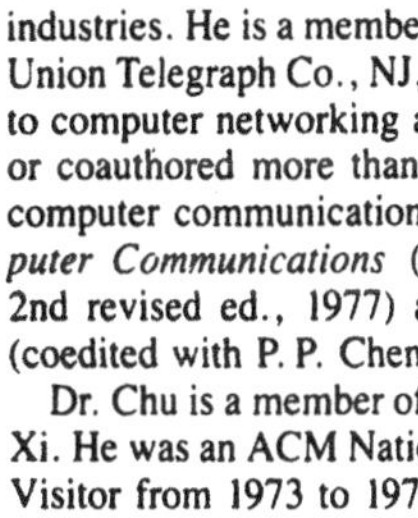

Joseph Hellerstein was born in Indianapolis, IN, in 1952. He received the B.A. degree in mathematics, with honors, from the University of Michigan, Ann Arbor, in 1974 and the M.S. and Ph.D. degrees in computer science from the University of California, Los Angeles (UCLA), in 1979 and 1984, respectively.

From 1974 to 1978 he worked as a Software System Designer for Honeywell, developing communications, operating systems, and network software. From 1978 to 1984 he was a Research Assistant working on the ARPA Packet Radio contract and the Ballistic Missile Defense Distributed Processing contract. His research interests include computer systems performance modeling, distributed processing systems, and distributed database systems.

Chapter 3

QUERY OPTIMIZATION POLICY FOR DISTRIBUTED DATA BASES

Query optimization determines the sequence of operations and the locations of operations to process a query on a distributed data base so that the total operating cost is minimized and user constraints such as response time, security, and reliability are satisfied. The problem is complicated by the fact that query processing policy depends not only on the structure of the query, but also on the operational parameters associated with the query.

The paper by Wong presents an algorithm for efficient retrieval of data from a relational distributed data base. The paper by Chu and Hurley assumes that a complex query can be decomposed into subqueries that require operations at geographically separated data bases. Algorithms are developed to determine the sequence and the sites for performing this set of operations such that the operating cost (communication cost and processing cost) for processing this query is minimized. The paper by Apers, Hevner, and Yao presents two classes of algorithms: one for minimizing the response time by emphasizing parallel transmission, and another for minimizing total time by emphasizing serial transmission. Then, depending on run time factors, such as system load and query complexity, the system select the optimization objective. The paper by Lohman, *et al.*, describes how to optimize nested queries in SQL language in a distributed relational data base. The last paper by King describes how knowledge of the semantics of data can be used for query optimization. With the knowledge of the data base structure and processing methods, semantic transformation can be applied effectively to improve significantly processing data base queries. Further research in this area is needed.

For further information in query processing, the interested reader should refer to [EPST 78, APER 80, BERN 81b, CHAN 82, HEVN 85].

Retrieving Dispersed Data from SDD-1: A System for Distributed Databases*

Eugene Wong
University of California, Berkeley
and
Computer Corporation of America
575 Technology Square
Cambridge, Massachusetts 02139

Abstract

In this paper we present an algorithm for efficient retrieval from a distributed database. By adopting a succession of relational "views" of the data, we are able to isolate those problems of query processing unique to a distributed system. The resulting strategy of query processing becomes two tiered, consisting of a strategy of data transfer (distribution) interwoven with a strategy of local processing (decomposition). The remainder of the paper is concerned with finding an optimal distribution strategy.

The distribution strategy is developed by a sequential optimization procedure which can be represented by a binary decision tree. Each node of the tree corresponds to a query and a set of parallel "moves" for that query. The leaf nodes of the tree from left to right represent the optimal sequence of sets of moves, and the query that remains after the moves of the right-most leaf is a purely local query that requires no further data transfer. The only problems which remain are those of purely local processing, the most difficult of which is the estimation of costs and sizes of results for local processing.

The algorithm presented here is used by SDD-1, A System for Distributed Databases, which is being developed by Computer Corporation of America.

---

* This research was supported by the Advanced Research Projects Agency of the Department of Defense under contract no. N00039-77-C-0074. The views and conclusions contained in this document are those of the authors and should not be interpreted as necessarily representing the official policies, either expressed or implied, of the Advanced Research Projects Agency or the U.S. Government.

1. INTRODUCTION

This paper presents a plan for efficient retrieval of data from a distributed database system. The method presented here is used by SDD-1, A System for Distributed Databases, which is under development by Computer Corporation of America. SDD-1 is described further in [ROTHNIE and GOODMAN] and [ROTHNIE et al].

SDD-1 permits the storage of data in a dispersed and redundant manner so as to improve the responsiveness and reliability of the overall system. Architecturally SDD-1 is composed of a collection of database sites, each of which contains a portion of the database. In addition, portions of the database may be stored redundantly at two or more sites in order to increase its availability.

A basic strategy of SDD-1 is to separate the problem of retrieving dispersed data from the problem of maintaining redundant copies of the data. To accomplish this we specify sub-sets of the total database that are to be in effect during the processing of given queries. These sub-sets are called "materializations" and each consists of exactly one copy of each portion of the database (cf [ROTHNIE and GOODMAN]); each materialization thus represents a distributed but non-redundant version of the database being managed by SDD-1.

The method described here for the retrieval of dispersed data always operates in the context of a specified materialization, and thus from its point of view the database appears to be distributed but non-redundant. That the database is, in fact, redundant is of no concern to our retrieval technique and hereafter will not be considered. (The methodology used by SDD-1 to maintain redundant database copies is described in [ROTHNIE et al] and [BERNSTEIN et al].)

A central constraint on our retrieval algorithm is that communication between database sites in SDD-1 is via relatively slow channels. Using the Arpanet as the archtypical communication channel in SDD-1, the bandwidth between sites is some 50-100 times slower than the bandwidth between each computer and its local disk storage. Consequently the minimization of data transfer from site to site is the primary objective in optimization though not the only one.

The retrieval method is based on a number of assumptions which can be stated as follows:

a. For the duration of any one query, the data model remains fixed and is a <u>relational</u> model. Since the method operates in the context of one materialization, there are no redundantly stored relations in the model. For expository convenience we assume that each relation resides at a single site; there is no loss of generality in this assumption and the extension to relations fragmented among several sites is straightforward.

b. Only fragments of relations in the data model are moved from one site to another, a <u>fragment</u> being a subrelation, a projection, or a combination of these two operations.

c. It is a matter of indifference as to where the final result is produced, as long as it is produced at a single site.

Given a query which references data distributed over several sites, our goal is to reduce it to a sequence of local queries with data transfer between local processing steps, and to do it in a way so as to minimize the combined communication and processing cost.

To fix ideas, let us consider a specific example to which we shall refer throughout the remainder of this paper:

<u>Example 1.1</u>

<u>Relation (Domains)</u>	<u>Site</u>	<u>Variable in Query</u>
Supplier (S#, City)	A	S
Availability (S#, P#, QOH)	A	V
Parts (P#, Pname)	B	P
Projects (J#, City)	C	J
Supply (J#, S#, P#, Qty)	C	Y

<u>Query</u>

```
RETRIEVE (S.S#)
WHERE (S.S# = V.S#) AND (S.City = J.City)
  AND (S.S# = Y.S#) AND (V.P# = P.P#)
  AND (V.QOH > Y.Qty) AND (P.P# = Y.P#)
  AND (P.Pname = 'Bolts') AND (J.J# = Y.J#)
  AND (Y.Qty > 1000)
```

Stated verbally, the query asks for the S# for those suppliers who supply bolts to projects located in the same city in quantity greater than 1000 and for whom the quantity-on-hand is larger than the quantity supplied. It is useful to have a graphical representation for the query as is done in Figure 1.1 where lines represent linking terms.

Graphical Represenation of Example 1.1 Figure 1.1

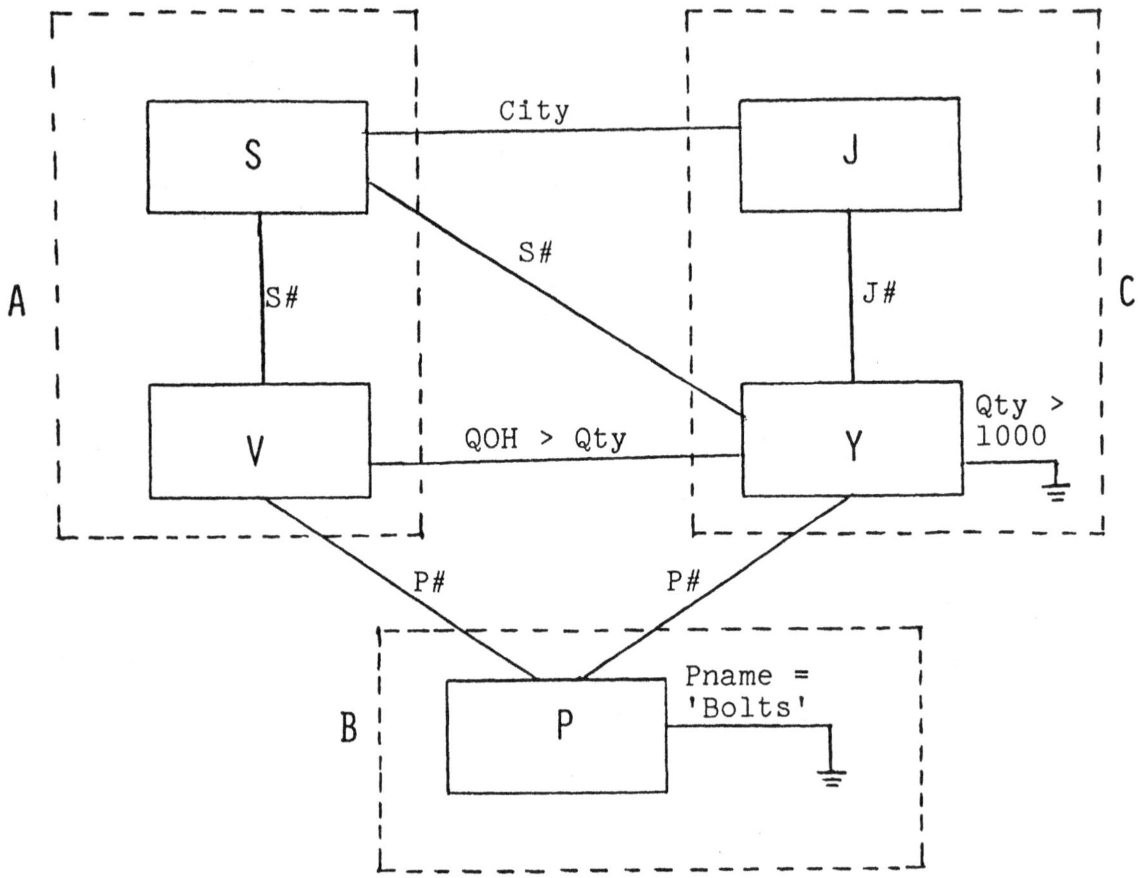

2. A DIFFERENCE OF VIEW

The added dimension in dispersed retrieval as compared to retrieval from a centralized database is the necessity to transfer data between database sites. As a first step in query processing it seems desirable to separate the complexity inherent in the query from the added difficulty due to distribution. This can be rather neatly done by adopting a series of "views" of the database as follows:

V_1: <u>The User View</u>

This consists of the data model, plus possibly some or all of the distribution information.

V_2: <u>The Distribution View</u>

This view consists of a collection of relations, one per site, each being the cartesian product of all the relations at one site. For the example in section 1 V_2 consists of the following relations:

<u>Example 2.1</u>

RELA (SS#, SCity, VS#, VP#, VQOH)
RELB (PP#, PPname)
RELC (JJ#, JCity, YJ#, YS#, YP#, YQty)

Our convention in renaming is self-explanatory.

V_3: <u>The Local Views</u>

There is one local view per site, consisting of all the relations of the data model at that site.

We observe that in the distribution view (V_2) the most prominent features are precisely the boundaries of data dispersion. Expressed in V_2, a query gives explicit display to its multilocational nature. A query is local (i.e., of single site) if and only if its V_2 expression is one-variable. This suggests that the concept of <u>decomposition</u> (reducing a multivariable query to a sequence of one-variable queries) (cf [STONEBRAKER et al], [WONG and YOUSSEFI]) be adapted to reduce a distributed query to a series of local queries.

The overall plan of query processing that we propose can be separated into the following steps:

1. <u>conversion</u> V_1 query --> V_2 query
2. <u>distribution</u> multivariable V_2 query --> one-variable V_2 queries
3. <u>reconversion</u> one-variable V_2 query --> multivariable V_3 query
4. <u>decomposition</u> multivariable V_3 query --> one-variable V_3 queries
5. <u>local one-variable query processing</u>

Conversion and reconversion (steps 1 and 3) are both mechanical and fast so that nothing further about them needs to be said. Step 4 does not involve the distributed nature of the database in any way. While the optimization problem of decomposition is by no means completely solved, the focus of our attention in this paper is on the distributed nature of the database, and purely local optimization problems will not be considered further. What remains then is the problem of optimizing the reduction of a distributed query into local queries (step 2), a procedure that we call distribution.

Example 2.2 Suppose that we consider the query in section 1 to be a V_1 query. The corresponding V_2 query takes on the form:

```
RANGE OF (A, B, C) IS (RELA, RELB, RELC)

RETRIEVE (A. SS#)
WHERE (A.SS# = A.VS#) AND (A.SCity = C.JCity)
  AND (A.SS# = C.YS#) AND (A.VP# = B.PP#)
  AND (A.VQOH > C.YQty) AND (B.PP# = C.YP#)
  AND (B.PPname = 'Bolts') AND (C.JJ# = C.YJ#)
  AND (C.YQty > 1000)
```

3. THE BASIC TACTICS OF DISTRIBUTION

The basic tactics proposed in [WONG and YOUSSEFI] to decompose a multivariable query into one-variable queries are the following:

a. One-Variable Subqueries: Portions of the query may entail reducing single relations by restriction and/or projection. These one-variable operations should always be performed first.

b. Reduction: When a query can be separated into two parts with only a single overlapping variable; it is often advantageous to do so.

c. Tuple Substitution: One of the variables is successively replaced by the actual tuples in the range relation of the variable.

Since distribution is decomposition in V_2, it is of interest to interpret these tactics in terms of the distributed database.

a. A V_2 one-variable query is a local query. It seems clear that what can be processed locally to reduce the sizes of the relations should always be done first. Hence, <u>one-variable subquery processing</u> should be retained as a tactic in distribution.

b. Interpreted in terms of the distributed database, reduction means a partition of the network into subsets which overlap at a single site. This could be advantageous, but the algorithm that we shall present makes no use of this tactic.

c. Tuple substitution in V_2 implies the transfer of data one V_2-tuple at a time between sites. However, bulk transfer of data is undoubtedly more efficient than tuple-at-a-time transfers. Therefore if a variable is to be tuple-substituted, it is often better to move the entire relation. There are situations where not every tuple needs to be substituted, but on balance we decide in favor of moving relations rather than tuples. Consequently we replace tuple-substitution as a tactic by:

   <u>Move relation</u> R from site A to site B

   Observe that the application of the "move" tactic is restricted, by assumption, to only fragments of the relations in the data model. The role played by "move" in distribution is quite similar to that of "tuple-substitute" in decomposition, each being a necessary but undesirable operation. Like tuple-substitution in decomposition, repeated "moves" will completely distribute any query. However, the object of optimization in distribution will be to move as little as possible.

4. A STRATEGY OF MOVES

A distribution strategy consists of a series of <u>move relation</u> tactics with local processing between them. Since communication costs are assumed to be high relative to local processing, the optimization of a distribution strategy depends principally on the optimization of its move tactics, and the optimization of moves can be undertaken largely independently of local processing optimization. We make use of this independence in designing our algorithms, although the cost of local processing is not entirely ignored.

For any query Q, one strategy that is always possible is the following:

(4.1) Do all the local processing that can be done with no data transfer at all.

(4.2) Then, make the minimum moves which would render the residual V_2-query one-variable without further local processing.

In such a strategy the moves are all made in parallel without intervening local processing. For this reason, it is in general far from optimal. However, it does represent an initial strategy that we can refine in successive steps.

Let M(Q) denote the set of moves defined by (4.2). Each element in M(Q) is of the form: m = "Move R from A to B".

Example 4.1 For the query in our example, define

R_1 = (Parts {Pname = 'Bolts'}) [P#]

R_2 = (Supplier (S# = S#)
(Availability {QOH > 1000}))
[S#, City]

R_3 = (Supplier (S# = S#)
(Availability {QOH > 1000}))
[S#, P#, QOH]

where R[A] denotes the projection of R on domain A, R{predicates} the restriction of R defined by the predicate and R(A = B)S the equijoin of R and S on A and B.

One possible value for M(Q) is the following:

$$M(Q) = \begin{Bmatrix} m_1 = \text{"move } R_1 \text{ from B to C"} \\ m_2 = \text{"move } R_2 \text{ from A to C"} \\ m_3 = \text{"move } R_3 \text{ from A to C"} \end{Bmatrix}$$

The actual value of M(Q) would depend on the sizes of the various relations.

The general plan now is to replace M(Q) by two sets of moves, M_1 and M_2, that are to be executed sequentially with local processing between them. The objective in selecting M_1 and M_2 is for the total cost of the moves together with the cost of any additional local processing to be less than the cost of M.

Example 4.2 M(Q) is the same as before.

M_1 = {m_4 = "move R_1 from B to A"}

Define R_2' and R_3' by the same formulas as R_2 and R_3 respectively, except that the relation "Availability" is replaced by its join with R_1. The construction of this join constitutes the local processing between M_1 and M_2.

Now set

$$M_2 = \begin{Bmatrix} m_5 = \text{"move } R_2' \text{ from A to C"} \\ m_6 = \text{"move } R_3' \text{ from A to C"} \end{Bmatrix}$$

Observe that since $R_3'[P\#] = R_1$ there is no need to include "move R_1 from A to C" in M_2.

Because $R_2' \subset R_2$ and $R_3' \subset R_3$, $M_1 + M_2$ clearly entails moving less than M(Q) if we assume that moving R_1 from B to A costs no more than moving it from B to C. We can represent the transformation M(Q) --> (M_1 followed by M_2) graphically as follows:

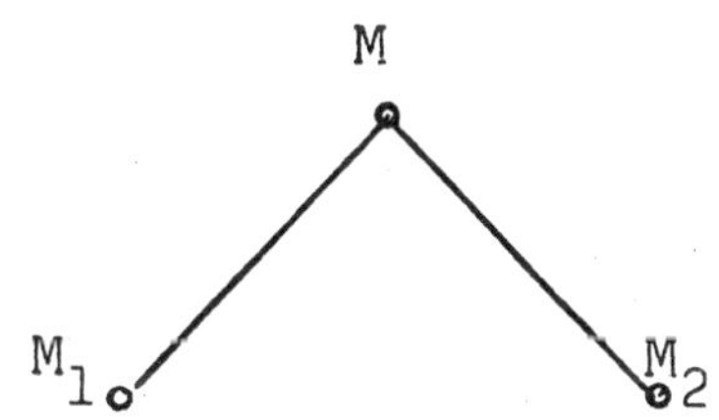

where it is understood that the left offspring always precedes the right with local processing in between.

It is possible that we can continue to split the nodes, and in general end up with a binary tree where the leaf nodes represent all the moves that are to be undertaken. The moves within one leaf can be made in parallel and the leaves are executed sequentially from left to right. The criterion for node splitting is as follows:

A node N is split into N_1 and N_2 if and only if

a. the combined cost of N_1 and N_2 is less than N alone, and
b. the pair (N_1, N_2) is minimum in cost among all pairs satisfying (a).

The resulting algorithm might be termed a "greedy" algorithm. In general it cannot be optimum, since it can never climb a hill surrounded by valleys, nor is it guaranteed to seek the highest peak if there are more than one. The algorithm could, in theory, be expanded by permitting condition (a) to attempt more global minimization. However, such an extension greatly increases the number of candidate splits which would have to be considered.

In the overall scheme that we have outlined, any relation which is the result of local operations is a candidate to be moved. Potentially, the number of such relations is enormous. The strategy that we have presented is designed to: (a) severely limit the number of such candidates that need to be considered, and (b) make the optimization recursive so that the overall algorithm can be expressed in terms of what is to be done at a single step.

There are only two basic ingredients in the algorithm: determination of M(Q) and splitting a node in the strategy tree. In section 5 we explain how M(Q) is determined; section 6 then explores node splitting.

5. DETERMINATION OF M(Q)

As described in section 4, M(Q) represents a first cut at obtaining a good distribution strategy for processing a query Q. M(Q) is obtained by limiting the local processing to operations that can be performed in the database prior to any moves of M(Q).

To determine M(Q) we first determine what local processing is possible before any moves. The effect of this local processing is to reduce the sizes of the fragments that must be moved. Then we compute the cost of moving all the reduced size fragments to a given destination site S_{DEST} for all posible values of S_{DEST}. M(Q) is then the set of moves associated with the minimum-cost S_{DEST}.

We begin by expressing the query Q in a conjunctive form. In this form the condition expressed by every clause must be satisfied, and therefore, any clause which is one-variable (in V_2) represents local processing which is possible prior to any moves.

The first question that arises is this: are the one-variable clauses the only local operations that are possible at this point? The answer is clearly no. It is possible to generate additional local operations by Transitivity. For example, in example 2.2 the clauses

```
        (A.VQOH > C.YQty) AND (C.YQty > 1000)
imply
        (A.VQOH > 1000)
```

which is a local operation (at site A) not represented in the original query. It follows, therefore, that we should close Q under transitivity. For example 2.2, the transitive closure has the form

Example 5.1

```
RETRIEVE (A.SS#)
WHERE (A.SS# = A.VS#) AND (A.SS# = C.YS#)
  AND (A.VS# = C.YS#) AND (A.VP# = B.PP#)
  AND (B.PP# = C.YP#) AND (A.VP# = C.YP#)
  AND (A.VQOH  > C.YQty) AND (C.YQty > 1000)
  AND (A.VQOH > 1000) AND (A.SCity = C.JCity)
  AND (B.PPname = 'Bolts') AND (C.JJ# = C.YJ#)
```

Given the transitive closure of Q (call it Q_1) we strip it of all local clauses (V_2 one-variable) and call the resulting query Q_2. Q_2 depicts the inter-site linkages in the original query Q and thus indicates the information that must be moved by the distribution strategy. In particular Q_2 specifies what columns of the V_2 relation at each site have to be retained in the distribution.

For Q_1 given by example 5.1, Q_2 is

Example 5.2

```
RETRIEVE (A.SS#)
WHERE (A.SS# = C.YS#) AND (A.VS# = C.YS#)
  AND (A.VP# = B.PP#) AND (B.PP# = C.YP#)
  AND (A.VP# = C.YP#) AND (A.VQOH > C.YQty)
  AND (A.SCity = C.JCity)
```

The columns to be retained are indicated below:

Example 5.3

Site	Columns to be Retained
A	(A.SS#, A.SCity, A.VS#, A.VQOH)
B	(B.PP#)
C	(C.YS#, C.YP#, C.YQty, C.JCity)

Now, we have assumed that only fragments of the original relations of the data model can be moved. In general, local operations at each site do not automatically yield such fragments. In example 5.3, the columns for sites A and C come from more than one original relation. Therefore, we need to perform the necessary projections to find the fragments which comprise M.

Example 5.4

Site	Fragments and Their Definition	
A	ASupplier (A.SS#, A.SCity) AAvailability (A.VS#, A.VP#, A.VQOH)	WHERE (A.SS# = A.VS#) AND (A.VQOH > 1000)
B	BParts (B.P#)	WHERE (B.PPname = 'Bolts')
C	CSupply (C.YS#, C.YP#, C.YJ#, C.YQty) CProject (C.JJ#, C.JCity)	WHERE (C.YQty > 1000) AND (C.JJ# = C.YJ#)

Note that the J# column has to be retained in CSupply and CProject in order to preserve the joining information C.JJ# = C.YJ#. The requirement that only fragments be moved implies that some joining operations would have to be repeated, hence those V_2 one-variable clauses have to be retained, e.g., the clauses (A.SS# = A.VS#) and (C.JJ# = C.YJ#) in example 5.4.

We can now readily determine M(Q), the minimum set of moves that can assemble all the data needed by Q at a single site with no further processing. Take each site in turn, and consider the cost of moving all the fragments not at that site.

Example 5.5

Final Destination	Fragments to be Moved
A	BParts, CSupply, CProject
B	ASupplier, AAvailability, CSupply, CProject
C	ASupplier, AAvailability, BParts

It is obvious that in example 5.5 B would never be chosen as the final destination. It is also likely that the fragment CSupply is very large since it involves the interrelationship among supplies, parts and projects. Therefore, for our example, the final destination is probably C and

$$M(Q) = \begin{Bmatrix} m_1 = \text{"move ASupplier from A to C"} \\ m_2 = \text{"move AAvailability from A to C"} \\ m_3 = \text{"move BParts from B to C"} \end{Bmatrix}$$

We can now summarize the algorithm for determining M(Q) as follows:

1. Put Q in conjunctive form.
2. Close Q under transitivity.
3. Perform local processing corresponding to V_2-one-variable clauses.
4. Identify the fragments at each site. And
5. Determine M(Q) by comparing costs.

6. NODE SPLITTING IN THE STRATEGY TREE

The preceding section explained how M(Q), an initial distribution strategy is obtained. In this section we describe how M(Q) is successively refined.

The central step in the optimization procedure takes a proposed set of parallel moves, M, and replaces it by two successive sets of parallel moves, M_1 and M_2. As described in section 4, the procedure is first applied to the initial set of moves, M(Q), and then recursively to each move that replaces M(Q) and so forth. The procedure thus generates a binary tree whose nodes represent proposed sets of moves and whose leaves represent a sequence of moves that can be taken to process the query. The procedure terminates when it is not possible to replace any node in the tree by two sons whose total cost is less than the parent's cost.

The remainder of this section explores in greater detail the criteria for splitting a node, M, into two sons M_1 and M_2.

A node M which is not the root of the tree (i.e. a node which does not represent the initial set of moves, M(Q)) operates on a sub-query of the initial query Q. Let us call the sub-query which M is operating on, Q_1. Observe that Q_1 retains any clause which involves more than one fragment and not merely multivariable clauses.

Example 6.1

$$M = \begin{Bmatrix} m_1 = \text{"move ASupplier from A to C"} \\ m_2 = \text{"move AAvailability from A to C"} \\ m_3 = \text{"move BParts from B to C"} \end{Bmatrix}$$

Q_1 is:

```
RETRIEVE (A.SS#)
WHERE (A.SS# = A.VS#) AND (A.SS# = C.YS#)
  AND (A.VS# = C.YS#) AND (A.VP# = B.PP#)
  AND (B.PP# = C.YP#) AND (A.VP# = C.YP#)
  AND (A.VQOH > C.YQty) AND (A.SCity = C.JCity)
  AND (C.JJ# = C.YJ#)
```

The optimization procedure dictates that M is split only if there is an immediate improvement. This implies that if M is split then the cost of at least one of the moves in M can be reduced. And the only way that can be done is through a clause involving the fragment of that move. Hence, the first thing that we do is to identify the V_2 multivariable clauses which involve each of the fragments in M.

Example 6.2

move	fragment	clauses
m_1	ASupplier	(A.SS# = C.YS#) AND (A.SCity = C.JCity)
m_2	AAvailability	(A.VS# = C.YS#) AND (A.VP# = C.YP) AND (A.VP# = B.PP#) AND (A.VQOH > C.YQty)
m_3	BParts	(A.VP# = B.PP#) AND (B.PP# = C.YP#)

The possible moves which might reduce each m_i are given by

move	potential reducing moves
m_1	m_{11} = CSupply [S#] from C to A,
	m_{12} = CProject [City] from C to A
m_2	m_{21} = CSupply [S#, P#, Qty] from C to A
	m_{22} = BParts [P#] from B to A
m_3	m_{31} = AAvailability [P#] from A to B
	m_{32} = CSupply [P#] from C to B

In order that a potential reducing move be included in M_1, its cost must be less than the reduction it effects.

Example 6.3

candidate	cost	reduction
m_{11}	CSupply [S#]	ASupplier reduced to (ASupplier(S#=S#)CSupply) [S#,City]
m_{12}	CProject [City]	ASupplier reduced to (ASupplier (City=City) CProject) [S#,City]
m_{21}	CSupply [S#, P#, Qty]	ASupplier reduced to (ASupplier(S#=S#)CSupply) [S#,City] and AAvailability reduced to (AAvailability (S#=S#,P#=P#,QOH>Qty) CSupply) [S#,P#,QOH]
m_{22}	BParts	AAvailability reduced to (AAvailability (P#=P#) BParts) [S#,P#,QOH]

m_{31}	AAvailability [P#]	BParts reduced to (BParts (P#=P#) AAvailability) [P#]
m_{32}	CSupply[P#]	BParts reduced to (BParts(P#=P#)CSupply) [P#]

It is obvious that m_{31} and m_{32} are bad moves, and m_{22} is an excellent move. It is likely that m_{21} is also a bad move since CSupply [S#, P#, Qty] is probably as large as AAvailability and much larger than the total reduction it effects. It is not clear as to whether m_{11} and m_{12} are worthwhile moves, and the precise answer would have to be provided by our estimate of the relative costs. Let's say that for our example m_{12} is worthwhile but m_{11} is not.

Now, we have determined certain moves which are not in M but which should be in M_1. Take these moves together with the moves of M not affected by them, and these comprise M_1. The remaining moves in M as modified by M_1 constitute M_2.

At this point we have to say something about whether multiple copies of a fragment are kept at different sites. For example, if we execute m_{22} = "move BParts from B to A", should BParts be retained at site B? If we do, m_3 in M is unaffected by m_{22}. If not, then m_3 becomes m_3' = "move BParts from A to C".

Example 6.4

For our example, M_1 is given by

$$M_1 = \left\{ \begin{array}{l} m_{22} = \text{"move BParts from B to A"} \\ m_{12} = \text{"move CProject [City] from C to A"} \end{array} \right\}$$

The candidates to be included in M_2 are

m_1' = move (ASupplier(City=City)CProject) [S#,City] from A to C

m_2' = move (AAvailability(P#=P#)BParts) [S#,P#,QOH] from A to C

m_3' = move BParts from A to C

But m'_3 can be considered to be redundant since it is a part of m'_2. Hence,

$$M_2 = \{m'_1, m'_2\}$$

After the application of M_1 the residual query Q_2 is given by

```
RETRIEVE (A.SS#)
WHERE (A.SS# = A.VS#) AND (A.SS# = C.YS#)
  AND (A.VS# = C.YS#)AND (A.VP# = A.PP#)
  AND (A.PP# = C.YP#) AND (A.VP# = C.YP#)
  AND (A.VQOH > C.YQty) AND (A.SCity = A.JCity)
  AND (C.JJ# = C.YJ#)
```

where the clauses which have been changed from Q_1 are underlined.

If we do not make the move m'_3 but subsume it in m'_2, then it is tantamount to replacing (A.P# = C.YP#) by (A.VP# = C.YP#), which is already present in the query and hence can be eliminated.

The general procedure for node splitting can be summarized as follows:

a. The state at each node is represented by a V_2-query Q_1 and a proposed set of moves M on the fragments referenced by Q_1.
b. For each element m in an M we determine the set R_m of moves which would reduce the fragment referenced by m.
c. Take the union $\bigcup_m R_m$ and eliminate redundancy. Denote the resulting set by R.
d. Let M_1 be the set consisting of (i) any move in R which reduces more than it costs, and (ii) any move in M unaffected by the moves of category (i).
e. M is replaced by M_1 followed by
   M_2 = {the remaining moves of M as modified by M_1}.
   If $M=M_1$ the splitting stops.
f. Let Q_2 denote the query resulting from modifying Q_1 by M_1.
g. The node (M, Q_1) is replaced by ((M_1, Q_1), (M_2, Q_2)) or

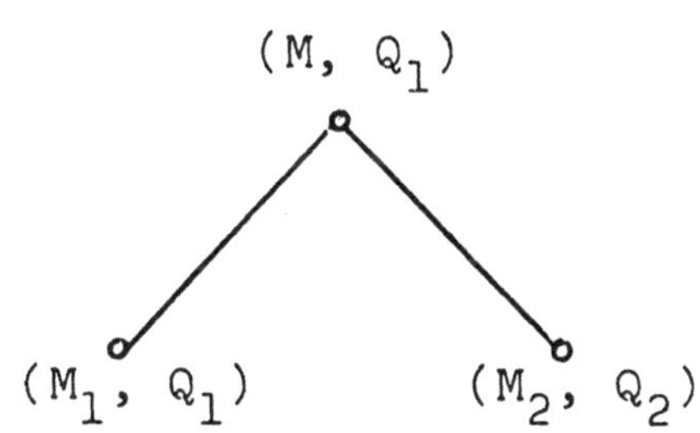

7. CONCLUSION

The final piece, and it is an important one, in the strategy that we have proposed is the estimation of costs and benefits. Consider examples 6.2 and 6.3 once again. The move m_1 involves moving the fragment ASupplier from site A to C, and it is possible to reduce the fragment by moving CProject [City] from C to A. The question is: should this be done? Here, the costs are given by:

C_1 = cost of projecting CProject on the domain City
C_2 = cost of moving CProject [City] from C to A
C_3 = cost of forming a new fragment
ASupplier2 =
(ASupplier(City=City)CProject)
[S#,City]
at Site A.

and the benefit is

B = the savings resulting from moving ASupplier2 instead of ASupplier.

We can assume in the above example, that ASupplier and CProject are fragments which have already been formed. We can also assume that the communication cost as a function of data volume and sites is known. What we must estimate in order to determine C_1, C_2, and C_3, and B are the costs of the local operations indicated in C_1 and C_3 <u>and</u> the sizes of the resulting fragments.

The remaining problems in our strategy, then, are those of estimating the costs of local operations and the sizes of relations resulting from local operations. These are problems inherent in query processing and have nothing whatever to do with the dispersed nature of data. Insofar as we have limited ourselves in this paper to those aspects of retrieval unique to a distributed database system, our task can be considered complete.

REFERENCES

[BERNSTEIN et al]
Bernstein, P. A.; Rothnie, J. B.; Goodman N. Technical Report in progress.

[ROTHNIE et al]
Rothnie, J. B.; Goodman, N.; Bernstein, P. A.; and Papadimitriou, C. A. "The Redundant Update Methodology of SDD-1: A System for Distributed Databases", Technical Report no. CCA-77-02, Computer Corporation of America, February 15, 1977.

[ROTHNIE and GOODMAN]
Rothnie, J. B.; and Goodman, N. "An Approach to Updating In a Redundant Distributed Database Environment", Technical Report no. CCA-77-01, Computer Corporation of America, February 15, 1977.

[STONEBRAKER et al]
Stonebraker, M.; Wong, E.; Kreps, B.; and Held, G. "The Design and Implementation of INGRES", ACM Transactions on Database Systems, vol. 1, no. 3, September 1976, pp.189-272.

[WONG and YOUSSEFI]
Wong, E.; and Youssefi, K. "Decomposition - A Strategy for Query Processing", ACM Transactions on Database Systems, vol. 1, no. 3, September 1976, pp.223-241.

Optimal Query Processing for Distributed Database Systems

WESLEY W. CHU, FELLOW, IEEE, AND PAUL HURLEY

Abstract—A model is developed for determining the optimal policy for processing a given relational model query. The model is based on operating cost (processing cost and communication cost), which is a function of selection of sites for processing query operations, sequence of operations, file size, and data reduction functions. The optimal policy specifies the site selection and sequence of operations that yield minimum operating cost.

The query is first decomposed into a set of relational algebra operations whose precedence relationships are expressed as a query tree. Additional query trees may be generated by permuting these operations. A set of query processing graphs is then generated for a given query tree. Each node of a query processing graph represents the execution of a set of operations at a single site. Since the neighboring nodes represent distinct processing sites, the arcs between nodes represent the communication cost among sites.

Theorems based on the cost model and the query processing graphs are developed for determining the optimal sites for processing the operations and for selecting the local optimal graphs from the set of query processing graphs. Use of these theorems greatly reduces the computation requirements in determining the optimal query processing policy. An example is given to illustrate the model.

Index Terms—Distributed database, local operation group, optimal query processing, query operating cost, query processing graph, query tree, relational algebra, relational database.

I. INTRODUCTION

OPTIMAL query processing is an important concern in the field of distributed databases. The main problem is the following: if a query can be decomposed into subqueries that require operations at geographically separated databases, determine the sequence and the sites for performing this set of operations such that the operating cost (communication cost and processing cost) for processing this query is minimized. The problem is complicated by the fact that query processing not only depends on the operations of the query, but also on the parameter values associated with the query.

Most previous works in query processing are for queries that use only SELECTION, PROJECTION, and JOIN operations. Further, the algorithms emphasize minimizing communication cost. In [1], a heuristic algorithm was proposed to find a query processing policy with a low volume of data communication among sites for processing a query. In [2], Epstein *et al.* proposed a method to minimize either processing time (based on the size of relations) or network traffic. Their model optimizes each query operation locally. However, such local optimization may not necessarily yield the global optimal policy. Hevner and Yao [3] proposed to use volume of data communication as an optimization criterion. They proposed a solution for a restricted class of queries (that reference a set of relations that have a common domain) and they proposed a heuristic method for queries with SELECTION, PROJECTION, and EQUI-JOINS.

Query processing, in general, involves both communication cost and processing cost. In fact, they are closely interrelated. Therefore, in this paper we shall propose a method for generating the optimal query processing policy that jointly optimizes the communication and processing cost. Further, our method includes a variety of relational algebra query operations. We shall first discuss the representation of a query by a set of query trees and describe their properties, then we will present a method for generating the set of query processing graphs from a given query tree. Next, theorems are derived for optimal selection of sites for performing the operations and for selecting local optimal query processing policies among the query processing graphs. Finally, a mathematical model is developed to compute the operating cost (communication and processing cost) for a given query processing policy. An example is also given to illustrate the procedure for determining the optimal policy for processing a given query.

II. QUERY OPTIMIZATION PROCEDURE

In this section, we provide an overview of the procedure for generating the optimal processing policy for a given query. This overview can also serve as an aid for reading the paper. We assume that a sequence of operations and their precedence relationships are given and are represented by a tree called the initial query tree. Based on permutability properties of the relational algebra, we derive the set of feasible query trees that will yield the same query result. Next, we optimize volume of data transfer by proper placement of unary operations in the query trees (see Section III).

We collect sets of connected operations (local operation groups) in each query tree which are candidates to be performed at a single site. Based on the local operation groups, we transform each query tree into a graph representation that explicitly shows communication between operations at different sites. This representation results in a set of query pro-

Manuscript received August 18, 1981; revised April 23, 1982. This work was supported by the National Science Foundation under Contract IST 80 02671.

W. W. Chu is with the Department of Computer Science, School of Engineering and Applied Science, University of California, Los Angeles, CA 90024.

P. Hurley was with the Department of Computer Science, University of California, Los Angeles, CA 90024. He is now with Bell Laboratories, Holmdel, NJ 07733.

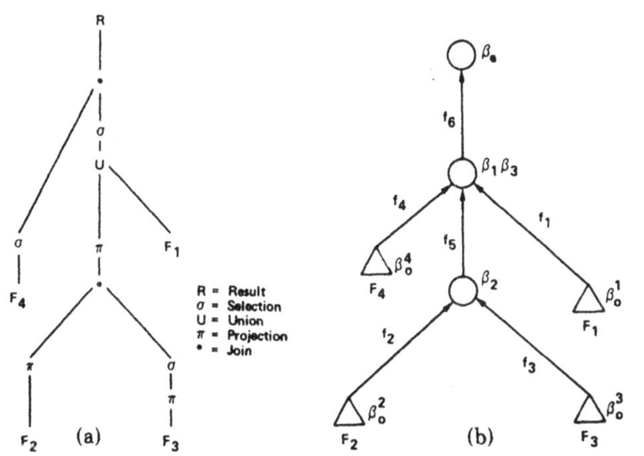

Fig. 1. A query tree and one of its query processing graphs. (a) A query tree. (b) A query processing graph for (a).

Notation: The PROJECTION π_d projects its operand onto the set of attributes d. The SELECTION σ_p has selection condition p. The JOIN $*p$ has join condition p.

Fig. 2. Operation permutability in query trees.

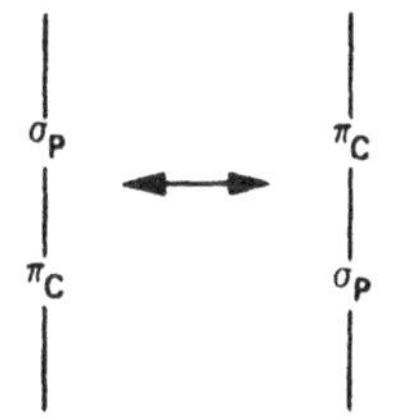

The right-to-left transformation can be performed only if all of the attributes of condition p are contained in set c.

Fig. 2. (a) Two adjacent unary operations.

cessing graphs for each query tree. A set of theorems is applied to the query graphs for eliminating nonoptimal graphs, and for site selection for performing operations (see Section IV). At this point, each query processing graph defines a sequence of operations and the sites for the operations; therefore, it becomes a query processing policy.

Next, we compute the communication cost for each policy (3). Based on Theorem 7, we select the set of local optimal policies from the set of query graphs with site selection for operations. Finally, we use (3) to compute the total operating cost (communication cost and processing cost) of all the local optimal query processing policies. By comparing the operating cost among the local optimal policies, we select the global optimal query processing policy.

III. Query Trees

We assume that a given query can be decomposed into a sequence of operations with series and parallel relationships, which will yield the correct result. We shall use a query tree as shown in Fig. 1(a) to express these relationships. For example, in Fig. 1(a), the PROJECTION operation on F_2 and the PROJECTION and SELECTION operations on F_3 are performed in parallel and then input to the JOIN and PROJECTION operations which are performed serially. The output from these operations together with F_1 are processed by the UNION and SELECTION operations serially, etc. In general, for a given query, there are many query trees that will produce the correct result of the query. We shall call these the set of feasible query trees for this query. Based on commutativity, associativity, and distributivity of operations we can generate the set of feasible query trees for a given query.

A. Generation of the Feasible Query Trees

In a centralized database system, one approach of optimal query processing is to minimize the cost of local processing of a query; that is, to select the query tree from the set of feasible query trees that has the minimum volume of data flow from the bottom to the top. However, in a distributed database system, the operations may be performed at different sites which introduces cost for communication among sites. As a result, it is no longer sufficient to minimize the flow of data volume from the bottom to the top of the tree. Rather, we shall minimize the operating cost which is a function of allocation, communication cost, and processing cost.

Since many query operations are commutative, associative, or distributive, for a given query tree we are able to generate a set of feasible query trees that produce the correct answer for the query.

B. Commutativity, Associative, and Distributivity Properties of Query Operations

1) *Unary Operations:* The permutability properties of unary operations and of unary operations with binary operations were reported in [4]. We shall summarize their results in Fig. 2(a) and (b), respectively.

a) *Two Adjacent Unary Operations:* Let us consider the SELECTION and PROJECTION operations. A set of neighboring SELECTION operations or a set of neighboring PROJECTION operations can be trivially combined together into a single SELECTION operation or a single PROJECTION operation, respectively. When a PROJECTION operation precedes a SELECTION operation, because the SELECTION operation does not eliminate any information needed to perform the PROJECTION, these two operations are always permutable. When a SELECTION operation precedes a PROJECTION operation, they can then be interchanged only if the set of attributes (columns) removed by the PROJECTION operations does not intersect the set of attributes referenced by the SELECTION operation. This is because if they do intersect, the PROJECTION operation eliminates attributes that are referenced by the SELECTION. Therefore, the SELECTION operation could not be performed after a permutation with the PROJECTION.

b) *Adjacent Unary and Binary Operations:* These cases occur when a SELECTION or PROJECTION operation has a neighboring binary operation in a query tree. The permutation properties of the unary operations with unary operations and of the unary operations with the binary operations are used for moving the unary operations downward to the lowest possible level in a query tree. It can be shown that this is a necessary condition to obtain the optimal query processing policy (see Theorem 1).

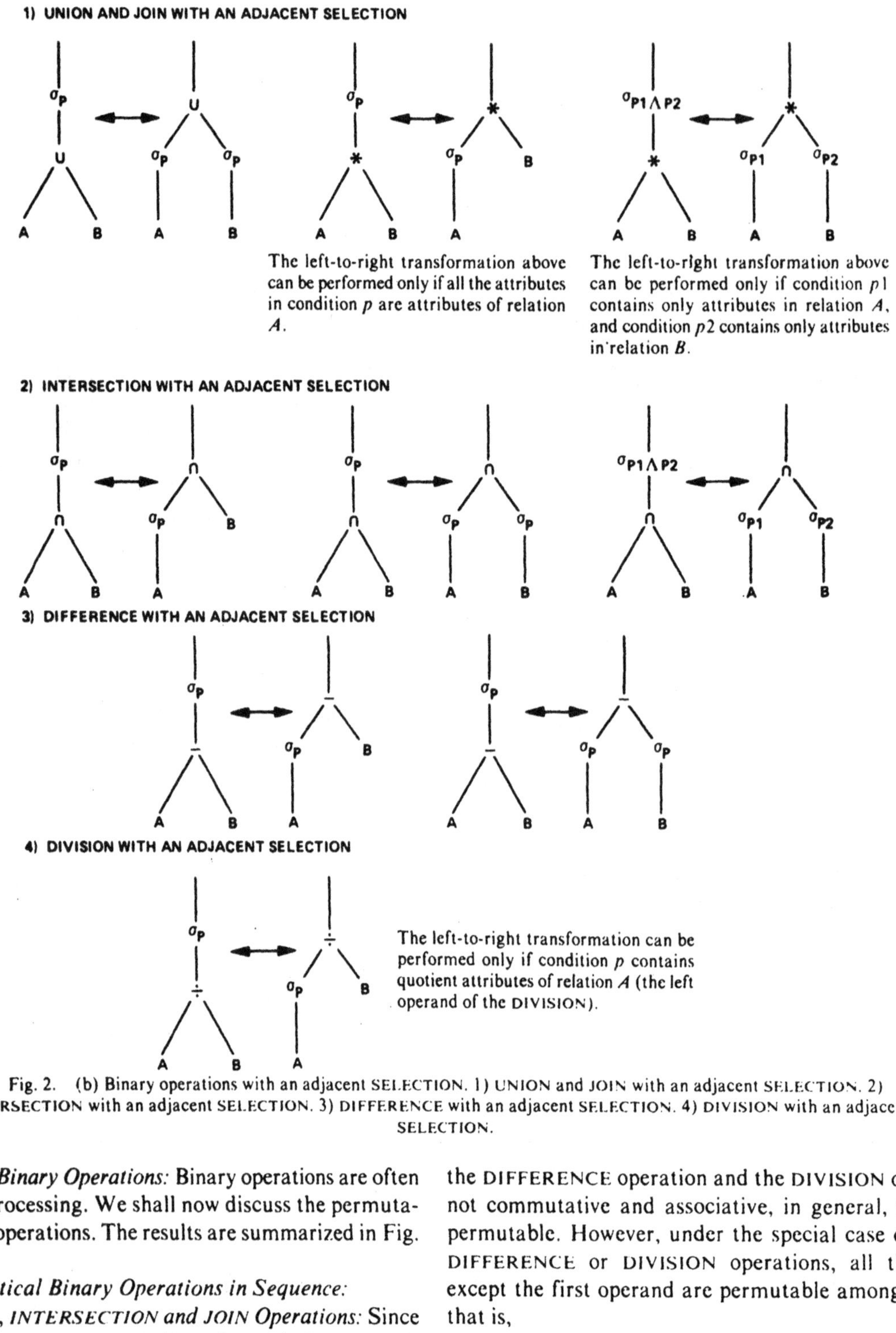

Fig. 2. (b) Binary operations with an adjacent SELECTION. 1) UNION and JOIN with an adjacent SELECTION. 2) INTERSECTION with an adjacent SELECTION. 3) DIFFERENCE with an adjacent SELECTION. 4) DIVISION with an adjacent SELECTION.

2) *Adjacent Binary Operations:* Binary operations are often used in query processing. We shall now discuss the permutability of binary operations. The results are summarized in Fig. 2(c).

a) *Two Identical Binary Operations in Sequence:*

1) *UNION, INTERSECTION and JOIN Operations:* Since UNION operations are commutative and associative, any pair of adjacent UNIONS may be permuted. Likewise, the INTERSECTION operation as well as the JOIN operation are commutative and associative, therefore, adjacent JOIN[1] operations as well as adjacent INTERSECTION operations are permutable.

2) *DIFFERENCE and DIVISION Operations:* Since both the DIFFERENCE operation and the DIVISION operation are not commutative and associative, in general, they are not permutable. However, under the special case of a chain of DIFFERENCE or DIVISION operations, all the operands except the first operand are permutable among themselves; that is,

$$A - B - C = A - C - B$$

$$A \div B \div C = A \div C \div B.$$

b) *Two Different Binary Operations in Sequence:*

1) *UNION Operations:* Let us consider the permutability of JOIN and INTERSECTION when immediately following the UNION operation. JOIN as well as INTERSECTION are distributive over UNION (that is, $(A \cup B) * C = (A * C) \cup (B * C)$ and $(A \cup B) \cap C = (A \cap C) \cup (B \cap C)$). Therefore, UNION and JOIN as well as UNION and INTERSECTION are

[1] Adjacent JOIN operations can be permuted only if the attributes in the JOIN condition of each JOIN in the permuted sequence are attributes of the operands of that JOIN.

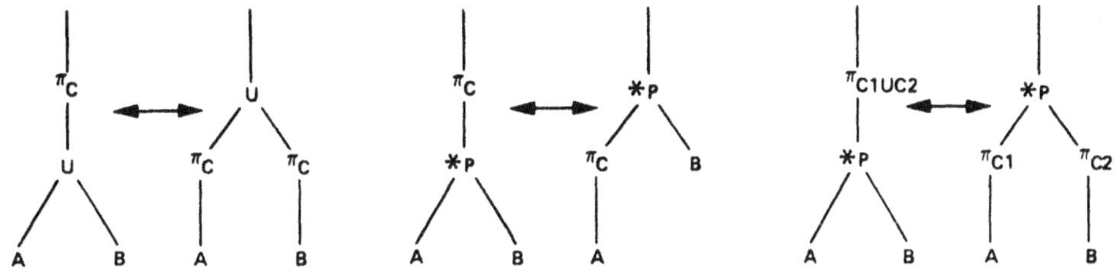

The left-to-right transformation above can be performed only under the following two conditions: 1) the attributes in condition p from relation A are all in the set c and 2) the attributes in set c are all attributes of relation A.

The left-to-right transformation above can be performed only under the following three conditions: 1) the attributes in condition p are all in the set $c1 \cup c2$, 2) the attributes in set $c1$ are all attributes of relation A, and 3) the attributes in set $c2$ are all attributes of relation B.

Fig. 2. (c) Binary operations with an adjacent PROJECTION.

permutable. The resultant query tree has two parallel JOIN operations or two parallel INTERSECTION operations.

Let us consider the permutability of the DIFFERENCE operation when it immediately follows the UNION operation. The DIFFERENCE is distributive with the UNION operation when the result produced from the UNION operation is the left operand of the DIFFERENCE operation. That is, $(A \cup B) - C = (A - C) \cup (B - C)$. The permuted tree yields two parallel subtrees with DIFFERENCE operations.

When the result produced from the UNION operation is the right operand of the DIFFERENCE operation, then the UNION and DIFFERENCE are not permutable. However, they can be transformed to produce the following different operations.

$$A - (B \cup C) = A - B - C = A - C - B = (A - B) \cap (A - C)$$

Let us consider the permutability of the DIVISION operation when it follows the UNION operation. Since the DIVISION operation is based on the relationships between the values of different set of attributes in an entire relation, it cannot be permuted with the preceding UNION, since such a permutation would cause the division to be performed on a subset of one of its original operands, thus changing the final result of the two operations.

2) *JOIN Operations:* Since the result of the JOIN operation usually has a different set of attributes than its operands, JOIN usually cannot be permuted with subsequent binary operations.

Let us consider the case where the JOIN operation is an EQUIJOIN whose result has the same set of attributes as one of its operands. Let that operand be operand A. In this restrictive case, the JOIN can be permuted with a subsequent DIFFERENCE[2] or INTERSECTION but cannot be permuted with a UNION or DIVISION; that is,

$$(A * B) \cap C = (A \cap C) * B$$

$$(A * B) - C = (A - C) * B.$$

In the same restrictive case, and when the JOIN is followed by an INTERSECTION or DIFFERENCE, that sequence of operations can be transformed as follows:

$$(A * B) \cap C = (A * B) \cap (B * C)$$

$$(A * B) - C = (A * B) - (C * B)$$

$$(A * B) \cap C = (C * B) \cap A.$$

If the JOIN operation is permuted with a subsequent UNION, the UNION creates a larger set of tuples for the JOIN than if we perform the JOIN first, which will cause the JOIN to produce a larger result. If the JOIN operation is permuted with a subsequent DIVISION, the result of the two operations will have fewer tuples than if the JOIN precedes the DIVISION, because the DIVISION eliminates some tuple values from an operand of the JOIN. Therefore, JOIN cannot be permuted with a subsequent UNION or DIVISION.

3) *INTERSECTION Operations:* Let us consider the case when INTERSECTION is followed by UNION or JOIN. Since the UNION or JOIN is distributive over INTERSECTION, either operation can be permuted with the INTERSECTION operation in a query tree and yields two parallel subtrees of UNION or JOIN, respectively, that is,

$$(A \cap B) \cup C = (A \cup C) \cap (B \cup C) \text{ and}$$

$$(A \cap B) * C = (A * C) \cap (B * C).$$

Let us consider the case when INTERSECTION is followed by a DIFFERENCE operation. When the result of the INTERSECTION is the left operand of the DIFFERENCE operation, the DIFFERENCE operation is distributive over the INTERSECTION, that is, $(A \cap B) - C = (A - C) \cap (B - C)$, and yields two parallel subtrees of the DIFFERENCE operation.

If the result of the INTERSECTION is the right operand of the DIFFERENCE operation, then the two operations can be transformed to a set of different operations with two parallel subtrees of DIFFERENCE operations, that is, $A - (B \cap C) = (A - B) \cup (A - C)$.

Let us consider INTERSECTION followed by the DIVISION. If the result of the INTERSECTION is the left operand of the DIVISION, the DIVISION is distributive over the INTERSECTION and yields two parallel subtrees of DIVISION operations, that is, $(A \cap B) \div C = (A \div C) \cap (B \div C)$.

[2] The DIFFERENCE can be permuted with the JOIN only if the result of the JOIN is the left operand of the DIFFERENCE.

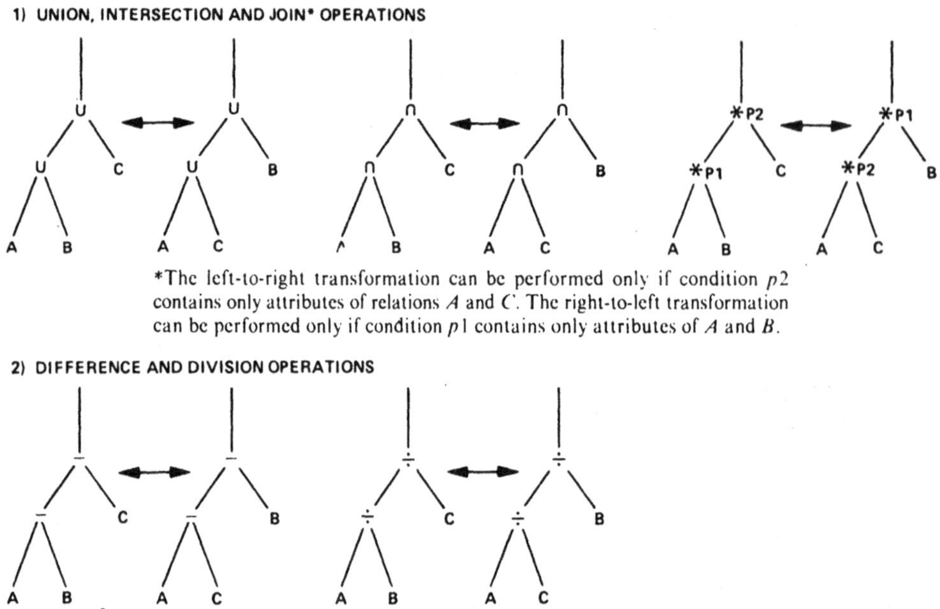

Fig. 2. (d) Two identical binary operations in sequence. 1) UNION, INTERSECTION, and JOIN* operations. 2) DIFFERENCE and DIVISION operations.

4) *DIFFERENCE Operation:* Let us consider the DIFFERENCE operation followed by JOIN or INTERSECTION. Since JOIN and INTERSECTION are distributive over the DIFFERENCE, they are permutable with the DIFFERENCE operation and yield two parallel subtrees of JOIN or INTERSECTION operations, respectively. That is,

$$(A - B) * C = (A * C) - (B * C)$$

$$(A - B) \cap C = (A \cap C) - (B \cap C).$$

When the DIFFERENCE operation is followed by the UNION operation, the operations cannot be permuted. This is because a sequence of UNION and DIFFERENCE operations is a sequence of additions and removals of tuples in relations. If the additions and removals are performed in different orders, the final results will be different.

When the DIFFERENCE operation is followed by a DIVISION operation, the operations cannot be permuted. This is because if the DIFFERENCE is performed after the DIVISION, the DIFFERENCE will be undefined unless the DIVISION is first performed on both of the original operands of the DIFFERENCE. In that case, the final result will be different, since the DIVISION removes rows from both of those operands.

5) *DIVISION Operation:* DIVISION cannot be permuted with a subsequent UNION, JOIN, INTERSECTION, or DIFFERENCE, because DIVISION removes both columns (attributes) and rows (tuples) from its left operand and the rows removed depend on the contents of its right operand. If the order of DIVISION and a subsequent binary operation is changed, then either the DIVISION operation will be undefined, or in general, the quotient will be different.

C. *Algorithm for Generation of Feasible Query Trees*

Let us present the algorithm for generating the set of feasible query trees from a given query tree. We use the permutability properties of the relational algebra operations (discussed in Section II-B) to modify the structure of the given tree to produce the set of feasible trees that produce the same query results.

The permutability properties used to transform a given query tree can be identified by a pattern-matching technique based on the permutability properties discussed in Section II-B as shown in Fig. 2. The transformations may change the relative positions of operations, operands, and/or subtrees of a given query tree. The relations (A, B, C, etc.) in the discussion in Section II-B may represent temporary files produced by a set of operations in a subtree of the query tree. If a permutability transformation causes these to change position, the corresponding subtrees change position in the query tree. Further, based on Theorem 1, the unary operations are placed at their lowest possible positions in the query tree which eliminates many of the transformations.

The permutability transformations change the sequence of operations that have father-son(s) relationships in the query tree, i.e., they are adjacent and located at different levels. For example, the transformation in Fig. 2(e).1(a), in the left-to-right direction, which converts a UNION followed by a JOIN into two parallel JOINS followed by a UNION, may be applied to such operations in any query tree. The corresponding transformation in the right-to-left direction converts two parallel JOINS followed by a UNION into a UNION followed by a JOIN, and may be applied to any query tree in which a UNION occurs as the father of two parallel JOINS, provided that the two JOINS have a common operand.

In order to indicate the permutations that are applicable, we first determine the set of operations, and their relationships, which are necessary for each specific transformation [e.g., a father–son combination consisting of JOIN and UNION, respectively, for the transformation of Fig. 2(e).1(a)]. The operations and their relationship information can be used as a "key pattern" for the transformation, and it includes the

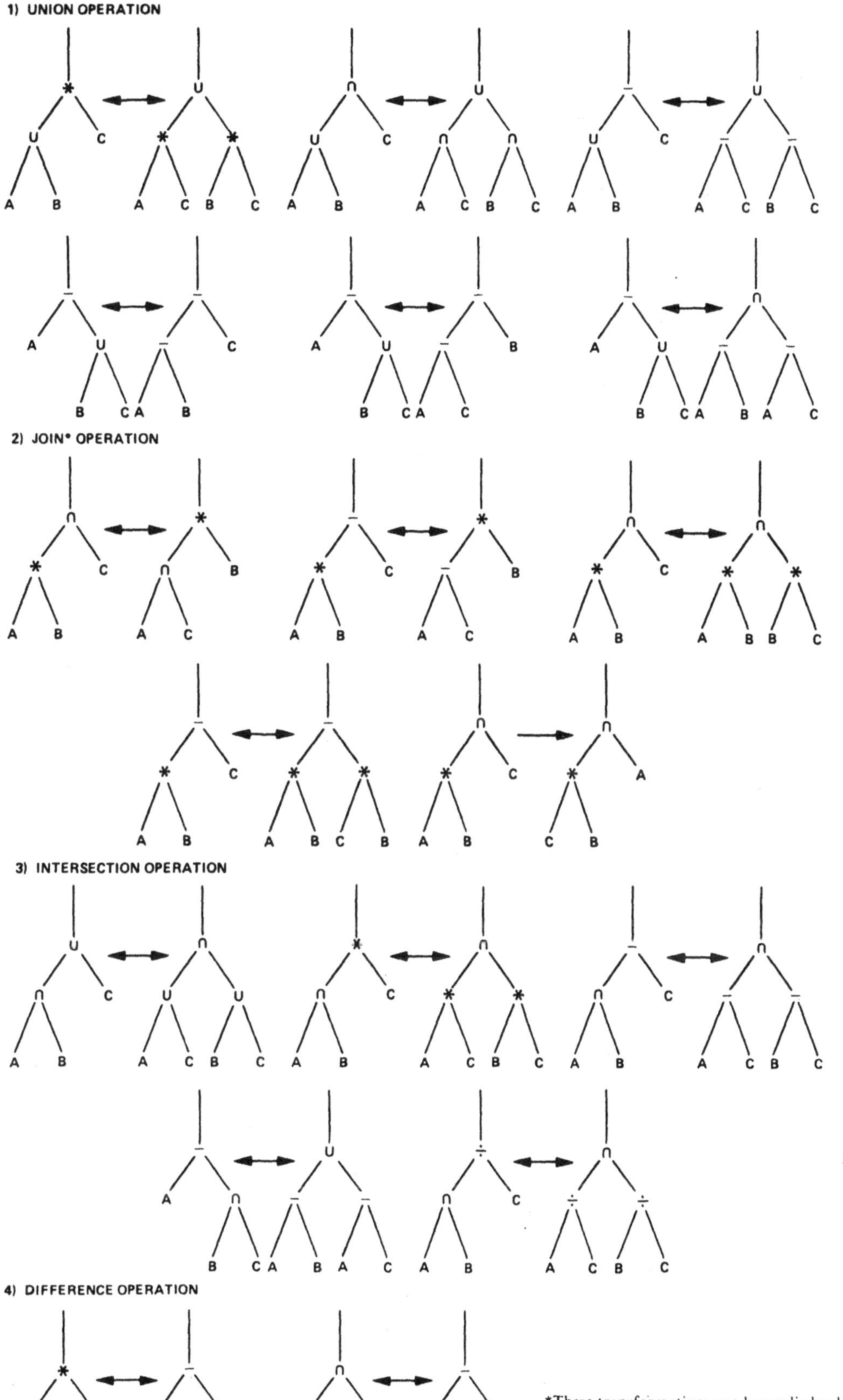

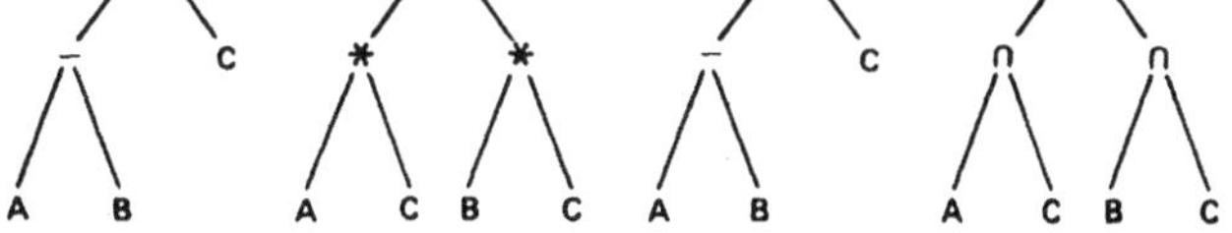

*These transformations can be applied only if the JOIN operation is an EQUIJOIN such that the set of attributes in the result of the JOIN is identical to the set of attributes in operand A.

Fig. 2. (c) Two different binary operations in sequence. 1) UNION operation. 2) JOIN* operation. 3) INTERSECTION operation. 4) DIFFERENCE operation.

necessary restrictions on the type of operation or the attributes of the relations. (For example, in Fig. 2(e).2, the JOIN operation must be a specific type of EQUIJOIN.) Given a query tree, it is necessary to search the tree for operations that match the key patterns. This can be done by a standard tree traversal.

For each match to a key pattern found in the query tree, the corresponding transformation can be performed to produce a new query tree. We repeat the same procedure for each new query tree. This process terminates when all the distinct feasible query trees have been generated. Since this algorithm applies all possible transformations to a query tree, it generates the complete set of feasible query trees.

D. Optimal Placement of Unary Operations in Query Tree

A large number of query trees can be generated by varying the placement of their unary operations. The following theorem provides optimal placement of the unary operations in a query tree, which reduces the number of feasible query trees.

Theorem 1: If the unit communication cost between any two sites in the distributed database is the same, and the processing cost of a given operation is the same for all computers and is proportional to the volume of data, then placing each unary operation at the lowest possible position in a query tree is a necessary condition to obtain the optimal query processing policy.

Proof: In a unary operation, the output volume of data is always less than or equal to the input volume of data. Therefore, if we move a unary operation to a lower position and leave the rest of the operations at the original position, such a placement will yield lower or equal volume of data flow from the bottom to the top through the query tree. As a result it either reduces or does not change communication and processing cost for all subsequent operations in the query tree. Therefore, any other query trees that have the unary operation higher than the lowest possible position, with the remaining operations in their original positions, will yield equal or higher communication and processing cost. Thus, this placement of the unary operation is a necessary condition for achieving optimal query processing.

Corollary: If the optimal placement of a unary operation is adjacent to two binary operations, then a necessary condition to obtain the optimal query processing policy is to process the unary operation at the same site as the binary operation that has the lower position in the tree (i.e., processed earlier).

IV. Query Processing Graphs

To reduce communication cost in distributed data base systems, it is often desirable to perform a group of operations at a single site and then transmit the results to other site(s) for further processing. Therefore, we collect sets of connected operations in the query tree into groups (local operation groups). These groups have the property that any pair of operations in a group can be linked by a path in the query tree such that all the operations on the path are in the group. These groups may be selected as candidates to be performed at a single site. Further, under such arrangements the communication cost for processing this query becomes the algebraic sum of the communication cost among the selected groups. Therefore, this motivates us to transform the query tree into a graph representation. We shall call this new representation the query processing graph.

There are three types of operations in a query processing graph: initial operations, intermediate operations, and final operations. Initial operations are designated by β_0^i, $i = 1, \cdots, s$, which mainly involve SELECTIONS and PROJECTIONS performed at the site that stores the file. Therefore, the initial operation selects the desired subset of the file for query processing. Intermediate operations are designated by β_i which is either a single binary operation or a binary operation combined with one or more adjacent unary operations from a query tree to be executed at a single site. The final operation β_e presents the query result to the query initiator.

The query processing graph consists of execution nodes, storage nodes, and arcs as shown in Fig. 1(b). The execution node (denoted by circles) represents execution of a local operation group (either a single operation β_j or multiple operations, $\beta_i \cdots \beta_j$) which are performed at a single site. The sites for execution by two neighboring execution nodes are distinct. Therefore, the arcs connecting the execution nodes represent data communication between sites. The storage node (denoted by triangles) represents a file permanently stored at a specific site. The arcs connecting storage nodes to execution nodes represent input data to the execution nodes. Therefore, a query processing graph not only represents a sequence of operations for processing the query, but also provides the information about a single operation or groups of operations to be performed at the same site or at different sites.

For example, β_2, an intermediate operation, in the query processing graph [Fig. 1(b)] represents the JOIN and PROJECTION operations of the query tree [Fig. 1(a)] which are to be performed at a single site. β_0^3 in the query processing graph represents the initial operations of PROJECTION and SELECTION on file F_3 of the query tree. Files $f_1, \cdots, f_6$ are intermediate files. The transfer of intermediate file f_5 is represented by an arc between the site that performs β_2 and the site that performs β_1 and β_3. This graph represents the operation sequence $\beta_2\beta_1\beta_3\beta_e$ such that β_2 is executed at one site, followed by β_1 and β_3 at a second site, followed by β_e at the query originating site which presents the final result file f_6 to the query initiator.

Since there are many possible ways for selecting local operation groups, there are many possible query graphs for a given query tree.

A. Transformation from Query Trees to Query Processing Graphs

Based on Theorem 1, we assume that all the query trees have the unary operations placed in their optimal positions (i.e., at the lowest possible level in the tree). To generate the set of query processing graphs from a given query tree, we first generate the set of local operation groups, and according to the sequence of operations in the query tree, we then construct the query processing graphs from the set of local operation groups.

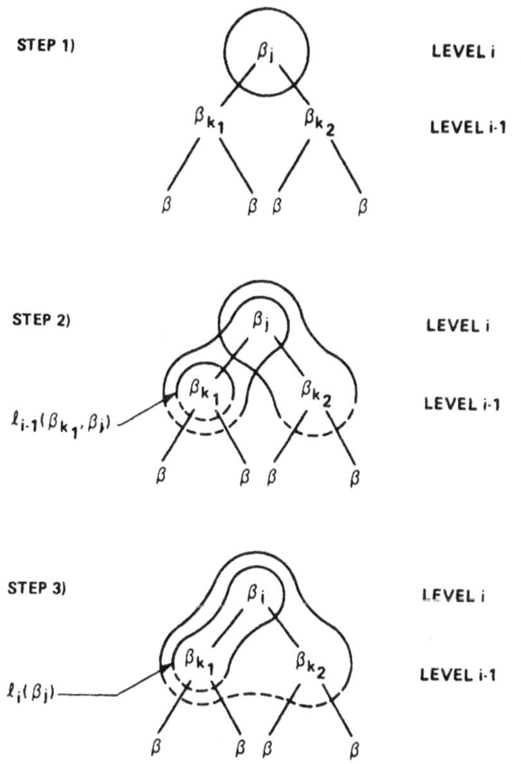

Fig. 3. The Iterative Construction Method for generating local operation groups.

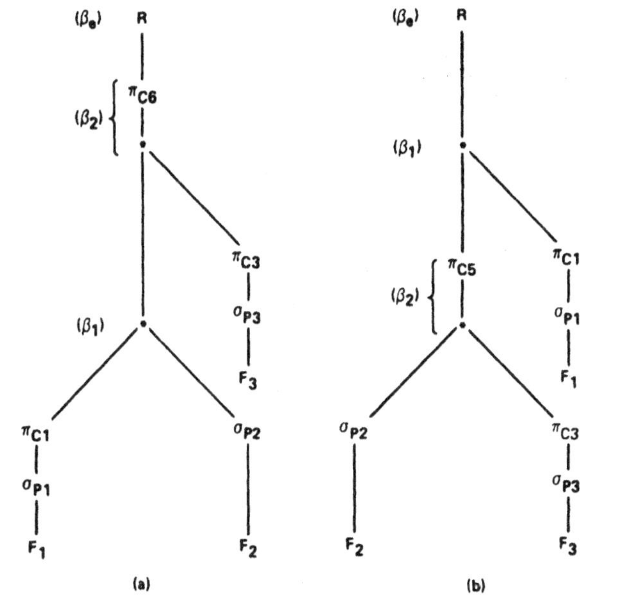

Fig. 4. Feasible query trees for the example.

B. Generation of the Set of Local Operation Groups

We shall use the following Iterative Construction Method (ICM) to generate the set of local operation groups. Let us number the levels of the query tree from the bottom to the root of the tree. Level 1 is the lowest level that has operations. The set of local operation groups can be generated at each level of the tree by combining adjacent operations in the query tree. When a unary operation and an adjacent binary operation are to be processed at the same site, they shall be combined into the same local operation group (corollary to Theorem 1). The set of local operation groups can be systematically generated by starting at the lowest level and then moving up the tree one level at a time until we reach the highest level of the tree.

We consider only the portion of the query tree that consists of operations. This portion consists of the root node and the branch nodes of the query tree, i.e., the entire tree except for the storage nodes. Let L_i be the set of local operation groups of a query tree which contain an operation at level i and no operation at any levels higher than i. An element of L_i is known as a local operation group at level i. Let L_r be the set of local operation groups that contain the root node. Consider a tree at level i which has a binary operation β_j at its root. We shall construct $L_i(\beta_j)$, the set of local operations groups at level i that includes β_j, from the following three steps as shown in Fig. 3.

1) β_j is a local operation group. 2) Select the subset $\{l_{i-1}, (\beta_k, \beta_j)\}$ in L_{i-1} such that $l_{i-1}(\beta_k, \beta_j)$ contains a node β_k at level $i - 1$ which is adjacent to β_j. Then for each $l_{i-1}(\beta_k, \beta_j)$ we combine it with β_j to form a new local operation group $l_i(\beta_j)$. Thus we have formed a set $l_i(\beta_j, \beta_k)$ of local operation groups. We repeat this step for the other β_k node (if it exists) at level $i - 1$ which is adjacent to β_j. 3) When there are two operations β_{k1} and β_{k2} at level $i - 1$ adjacent to β_j, combine elements from the sets $\{l_{i-1}(\beta_j, \beta_{k1})\}$ and $\{l_{i-1}(\beta_j, \beta_{k2})\}$ with β_j to form a new set of local operation groups $L_i(\beta_j, \beta_{k1}, \beta_{k2})$. The set of local operation groups generated by steps 1) to 3) for operation β_j is $L_i(\beta_j)$. We shall repeat steps 1) to 3) for all β_j at level i. Then $L_i = \bigcup_j L_i(\beta_j)$ is the set of local operation groups at level i. By repeating this process for all levels of the query tree, working from the lowest level of operations ($i = 1$) to the highest level (the root of the query tree), we construct the set of all local operation groups for the given query tree, $L = \bigcup_i L_i \cup L_r$.

For example, for the query tree in Fig. 4(a), we have two operations β_1 and β_2. At the lowest level, $i = 1$, we have a subtree that consists of the β_1 operation and some unary operations. Operation β_1 is the only operation for the tree at level 1, $L_1(\beta_1) = L_1 = \{\beta_1\}$. Next, for the tree at level 2 consisting of β_2, β_1, and some unary operations, the set of local operation groups containing β_2 is $L_2(\beta_2) = L_2 = \{\beta_2, \beta_1\beta_2\}$. Finally, the set of local operation groups that contains the root is $L_r = \{\beta_e, \beta_2\beta_e, \beta_1\beta_2\beta_e\}$. Therefore, the set of local operation groups for this query tree is $L = \bigcup_{i=1}^{2} L_i \cup L_r = \{\beta_1, \beta_2, \beta_e, \beta_1\beta_2, \beta_2\beta_e, \beta_1\beta_2\beta_e\}$.

C. Completeness Proof for the Query Processing Graph Construction Procedure

The set of local operation groups generated by the ICM is used for the execution nodes of the query processing graphs. We shall prove by induction that the ICM generates the complete set of local operation groups.

Theorem 2: The set of local operation groups for a given query tree generated by the Iterative Construction Method (ICM) is complete.

The proof of this theorem is contained in the Appendix.

D. Properties of Query Processing Graphs

The operating cost for processing a query with a given policy consists of communication cost and processing cost. To apply a query processing graph to a given distributed database, we assume that the communication cost between each pair of computers is proportional to the volume of data, the unit communication costs among different pairs of computers are the same, and that the processing cost for all computers depends on the operation performed and on the volume of data. For a given operation the unit processing cost is the same for all the computers. Under these circumstances, we obtained the following theorems for site selection and computation reduction for the query processing graph.

Theorem 3: For a given query processing graph, if the unit communication costs among different pairs of computers are the same, and the processing cost for a given operation is the same for all the computers, then for each execution node of the graph, selecting the storage node site that sends the largest amount of data (for single copies of files) to that execution node as the site for performing its operations yields minimum operating cost for that graph.

Proof: The operating costs consist of communication cost and processing cost. For a given graph, the sequence of operations is fixed, which implies that the input volume to each operation is fixed. Since the unit processing cost for a given operation is the same for all sites in the network, the total processing cost is constant. Therefore, to minimize operating cost, we need only minimize communication cost.

The communication cost of the given graph consists of two parts: 1) the communication cost of transmission between the execution node sites and 2) the communication cost of transmission from storage node sites to execution node sites. Since all unit communication costs are the same, and since the operations of adjacent execution nodes must be executed at different sites, cost 1) is constant for a given graph. Therefore, minimizing cost 2) minimizes communication cost.

For a given execution node N_a, we select the storage node site that sends the largest volume of data to N_a as the site for performing its operations. This site selection minimizes the volume of data transmitted from storage node sites to the site of N_a, and since unit communication costs are the same between any pair of computers, such a selection minimizes communication cost 2) for N_a. Since site selection does not affect the volume of output data generated by the operations, the site selections of the remaining execution nodes are independent of the site selection of N_a, and the sites of the remaining execution nodes in the graph can be selected one at a time in the same manner. Since the set of execution nodes is fixed for the graph, using this theorem for site selection minimizes communication cost 2), thus minimizing operating cost.

Corollary: Theorem 3 also holds for a distributed database system with multiple copies of files, except that in computation of the volume of data sent by a site to a given execution node, we must include all the files that reside at the site and are required by the execution node.

If this site selection method generates an inconsistent site selection (selects the same site for two adjacent execution nodes of a graph), then the graph can be reduced to a simpler graph (one that has a lesser number of execution nodes) that yields a lower operating cost than that of the orignal graph as will be shown in Theorem 4.

Theorem 4: If the unit communication costs among different pairs of computers in the distributed database are the same, and the processing cost for a given operation is the same for all the computers, if the site selection for a given query processing graph based on Theorem 3 is inconsistent, then that graph can be reduced to a simpler graph (one with a lesser number of nodes) which has the same sequence of operations. Further, the reduced graph yields lower operating cost than that of the original graph.

Proof: If the site selection based on Theorem 3 is inconsistent, we combine the two adjacent execution nodes causing the inconsistency into one node. The resultant graph performs the same set of operations in the same sequence. As a result, the processing cost of the two graphs is the same. Therefore, it will suffice to show that the communication cost of the reduced graph is lower than that of the original graph.

Let the two execution nodes that caused the inconsistency be denoted as node N_a and node N_b. The difference in communication between the original graph and the reduced graph is: 1) the communication cost of data transferred between the sites of nodes N_a and N_b and 2) the communication cost of data transferred from storage node sites to the sites of N_a and N_b. Communication cost 1) is eliminated in the reduced graph because nodes N_a and N_b are combined into one node and thus their operations are executed at the same site. As shown in the proof of Theorem 3, communication cost 2) for an execution node is minimized by executing the operation(s) at the storage node site S_k that sends the largest amount of data to the site of that execution node. In this case, because of the inconsistent site selection, that storage node site S_k is the site selected for performing the operations of both nodes N_a and N_b. Since S_k is the site that sends the largest amount of data both to node N_a and to node N_b, site S_k is selected for performing the operations of the combined node (N_a, N_b) in the reduced graph. Thus, the communication cost 2) of the reduced graph and of the original graph (when site selection is based on Theorem 3) are identical. This implies that total communication cost of the reduced graph is lower than that of the original graph.

Theorem 5: If a query processing graph has an execution node that has no adjacent storage nodes, then this graph cannot produce the optimal query processing policy.

Proof: When the execution node N_a has no adjacent storage nodes, this implies that it processes only intermediate files and does not process any permanently stored files; thus, there is no need to assign a new site for processing the operations of N_a. Therefore, N_a can be combined with either of its adjacent execution nodes to form a *multioperation execution node* (an execution node that consists of more than one operation) that reduces communication cost. Since the processing cost of a fixed sequence of operations is the same at different sites, the total operating cost for processing the query from the original graph would be larger than that of the graph that has node N_a combined with one of its adjacent execution nodes.

Theorem 6: For a given query processing graph that contains a multioperation execution node consisting of a set of operations $\{\beta_i \cdots \beta_j\}$, the sequence of operations from this set which has least processing cost is used by the policy that has least operating cost for this graph.

Proof: the set of operations $\{\beta_i \cdots \beta_j\}$ is performed at a single site and its output volume is independent of its sequence. Therefore, for any two policies for this graph,, if their only difference is in the sequence of the set of operations $\{\beta_i \cdots \beta_j\}$, then their communication costs will be the same. Therefore the sequence of the set $\{\beta_i \cdots \beta_j\}$ that has least processing cost is used by the policy that has least operating cost for the graph.

Corollary: Theorem 6 is true for a query processing graph with more than one multioperation execution node.

Proof: Since the output volume of each multioperation execution node is fixed regardless of the sequence of the operations of that node, the sequence of operations of each multioperation execution node can be optimized independently. Therefore, we can apply Theorem 6 to each of the multioperation execution nodes.

Theorem 7: If the processing cost for a given operation is the same for all the computers in the distributed database and, further, if the sequence of operations for processing a given query is fixed, then the query processing policy that minimizes the communication cost (total volume of traffic for the case of the communication cost among each pair of computers being equal) yields the lowest operating cost among the set of policies that uses this fixed sequence of operations.

Proof: For a given query, if the sequence of operations is fixed, the output volume of each individual operation will be the same for all the policies that use this sequence of operations. Since the unit processing cost for each operation is the same for all the computers, the total processing cost for all policies using this fixed sequence of operations is the same. This implies that the policy that requires the lowest communication cost (total volume of traffic for the case of identical unit communication cost) yields lowest operating cost.

Theorems 3, 4, and 5 together with the known file allocation information provide guidelines in site selection for performing operations. Theorem 6 can be used to select local optimal query processing policies from certain query processing graphs that have multioperation execution nodes and Theorem 7 provides a way of locating local optimal query processing policies from the set of policies that perform a given fixed sequence of operations (that is, the set of query processing graphs generated from the same query tree). As will be discussed in the following section, using these theorems greatly reduces the computation requirements for determining the optimal query processing policy.

E. Reduction of Computational Cost

In this section, we discuss the computational requirements of the proposed query processing model and compare with that of using an exhaustive random search method. Consider a distributed database with n_s sites which is to execute a query with n_t feasible query trees, with an average of n_p operations per tree. Using an exhaustive search to find the optimal query processing policy, we must calculate both communication cost and processing cost for each possible site assignment for each operation, and then repeat this process for each query tree. Let C_1 represent the cost of calculating either communication cost or processing cost for a candidate query processing policy. Then the total cost is $C_{ES} = 2C_1 n_t n_s{}^{n_p}$.

Now let us determine the computational requirements of using our model and theorems. For a given query tree, the entire set of query processing graphs can be generated by making a binary decision independently for each operation of the query tree: the decision of whether or not to associate that operation with its father (each operation has a unique father) in the same local operation group. Thus, for a query tree with n_p operations, 2^{n_p} query processing graphs will be generated. Site selection on a given query graph requires a small amount of computation: for an execution node with one adjacent storage node, the choice of site is made immediately, while for an execution node with more than one adjacent storage node, a small number of comparisons must be made between different data volume values. Thus the cost of this computation is less than that of calculating communication cost for a query processing policy (which involves summing up all volumes of intersite data transfers). Therefore, it is reasonable to assume that the computational cost for site selection on a query processing graph is $C_1/2$. Then the total cost of site selection on all the graphs generated from a given query tree is $(C_1/2) \cdot 2^{n_p}$.

After site selection is completed, we use Theorem 7 to obtain local optimal query processing policies by calculating the communication cost for $n_t \cdot 2^{n_p}$ graphs. This step reduces the set of $n_t \cdot 2^{n_p}$ graphs to n_t graphs. Based on a calculation of the processing cost of the remaining n_t query graphs, we obtain optimal query processing policy.

Now let us evaluate the further reductions obtainable using Theorem 6. Such reductions apply only if we have more than one query tree for the query. Consider the minimal reduction case in which only one permutation is possible, where two adjacent operations in the original (initial) query tree can be permuted to generate another query tree. One of the two sequences of operations will have higher processing cost; therefore, one of the query trees will have a higher processing cost for these two operations. Among the query processing graphs generated from that query tree, half of them will have an execution node for a local operation group that includes both operations. Theorem 6 allows us to eliminate all of these graphs from consideration; thus $\frac{1}{4}$ of the graphs generated for this query can be eliminated. It can be shown that if more permutations of query operations are possible, a larger set of graphs can be eliminated; thus $\frac{1}{4}$ represents a lower bound on the portion of the set of query graphs that can be eliminated by using Theorem 6.

Therefore, the computational cost for obtaining the optimal query processing policy using the proposed model is

$$C_m = \frac{3}{4}\left(\frac{C_1}{2} \cdot n_t \cdot 2^{n_p} + C_1 n_t \cdot 2^{n_p}\right) + C_1 \cdot n_t = \frac{3}{4} C_1 n_t \left(\frac{3}{2} \cdot 2^{n_p} + \frac{4}{3}\right). \quad (1)$$

The first term of (1) represents the cost of computing site selections; the second term represents the cost of computing communication cost for each graph, and the third term represents the cost of computing processing cost for the local optimal query processing graphs.

The ratio of the cost of applying the model to the cost of the exhaustive search is

$$\frac{C_m}{C_{ES}} = \frac{\frac{3}{4} C_1 n_t \left(\frac{3}{2} \cdot 2^{n_p} + \frac{4}{3}\right)}{2C_1 n_t n_s^{n_p}}$$

$$= \frac{9}{16}\left(\frac{2}{n_s}\right)^{n_p} + \frac{1}{2} \cdot \frac{1}{n_s^{n_p}}$$

$$= \frac{9}{16}\left(\frac{2}{n_s}\right)^{n_p} \quad \text{for large } n_s \text{ and } n_p. \tag{2}$$

From (2), we know that the reduction factor depends on n_p and n_s. For example, if $n_s = 5$, and $n_p = 4$, 5, and 6, the corresponding computation reduction factor is 0.014, 0.0058, and 0.0023, respectively.

V. Query Operating Cost Model

The operating cost for processing a query consists of communication cost and processing cost. The communication cost depends partially on the sites selected for the operations. Both the communication and processing costs depend on the data reduction functions, sequence of operations, and on the data volumes of the files involved. The data reduction function $\alpha(\beta_j, \overline{F}, \overline{\gamma})$ is the ratio of the output data volume to the input data volume for the operation β_j, input files $\overline{F}$, and the query operation parameter $\overline{\gamma}$. The data reduction function further depends on the previous operations. The data reduction function of operation β_i preceded by operations $\overline{\beta}$ with input files $\overline{F}$ and query operation parameter $\overline{\gamma}$ is denoted as $\alpha(\beta_i | \overline{\beta}, \overline{F}, \overline{\gamma})$. $\alpha(\beta_j, \overline{F}, \overline{\gamma})$ permits us to estimate the output temporary file length $l(f_i)$ for operation β_j from its input file size. Such data reduction functions may be estimated by simulation or measurement on a distributed database [5] and their values are stored in the directory system.

Let C_o^i be the processing cost for operation β_o^i, and C_j be the processing cost for operation β_j per unit input file data (byte). Further, let C'_{ij} be the communication cost for transmitting a unit of data (byte) from the site that outputs file f_i to the site of operation β_j. We will further define two indicating functions, Y_{ij} and Z_{ij}. We use Y_{ij} for indicating whether temporary file f_i is an input to operation β_j; that is,

$$Y_{ij} = \begin{cases} 1 & \text{if } f_i \text{ is an input to operation } \beta_j \\ 0 & \text{otherwise.} \end{cases}$$

We use Z_{ij} for indicating whether f_i is available for processing at the site for performing β_j; that is,

$$Z_{ij} = \begin{cases} 1 & \text{if file } f_i \text{ is needed but is not available for processing at the site for performing } \beta_j \\ 0 & \text{otherwise.} \end{cases}$$

Thus if $Z_{ij} = 1$, it is required to transmit file f_i to the site for performing β_j. Z_{ij} is determined from the file allocation and the query processing policy. The operating cost for processing a query with policy ψ equals

$$C(\psi) = \sum_{i=1}^{s} C_o^i l(F_i) + \sum_{j=1}^{k} C_j \sum_{i=1}^{q} l(f_i) Y_{ij} + \sum_{j=1}^{k} C'_{ij} \sum_{i=1}^{q} l(f_i) Z_{ij} + \delta_{ez} \cdot C'_{qe} \cdot l(f_q) \tag{3}$$

where

$l(F_i)$ = file length of F_i

$l(f_i)$ = file length of temporary file f_i

q = total number of temporary files required for processing of a given query

k = total number of operations β_j, $j > 0$, required for completing processing of a given query

$$\delta_{ez} = \begin{cases} 1 & \text{if } \beta_e \text{ is not at the same site of the last operation of } \psi, \beta_z \\ 0 & \text{otherwise} \end{cases}$$

C'_{qe} = unit communication cost for transmitting the query result to the originating site.

f_q = the result of the query.

The first term of (3) is for the cost of the set of initial operations $\{\beta_o^i, i = 1, \cdots, s\}$ on the set of files $\{F_i, i = 1, \cdots, s\}$. The second term represents the total processing cost for performing operations $\beta_j, j = 1, \cdots, k$, the third term represents the total communication cost for transmitting temporary files f_i, $i = 1, \cdots, q$, to the sites of operations $\beta_j, j = 1, \cdots, k$, and the last term represents the cost of transferring the final query result file to the result destination site. The δ_{ez} function indicates whether this transfer is necessary.

Different query processing policies yield different sequences of query operations, as well as different locations for processing these operations. As a result, different policies yield different operating costs for processing a given query on a distributed data base. Equation (3) computes the operating cost for a given query processing policy. With the aid of the theorems described in the last section and the use of (3), we can determine the optimal policy that yields minimum operating cost for processing a given query.

VI. Example

Consider a four site computer network (Fig. 5) which contains an inventory relational data model and a database consisting of three relations stored as files. The allocation and the descriptions of the files are given in Table I.

The following query is initiated as site 4: "generate a listing of part number, supplier name, quantity for all 'calculators' produced in Los Angeles in a quantity greater than 1000 by any one supplier."

From this query an algorithm may be used to derive the required operations to construct the query tree and after moving the unary operations to the lowest possible positions

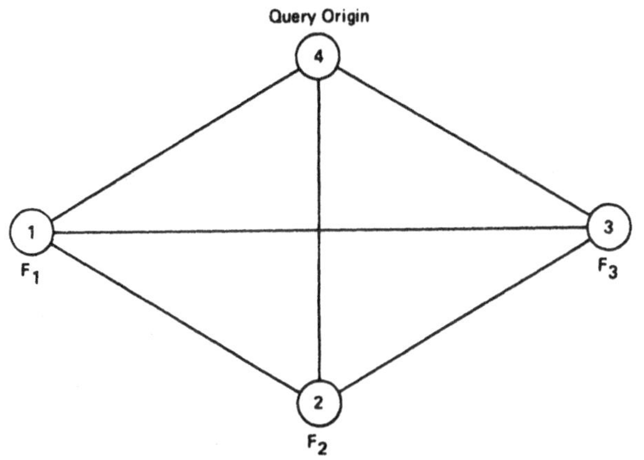

Fig. 5. Computer network for the example.

TABLE I
FILE CHARACTERISTICS OF A DISTRIBUTED DATABASE FOR THE EXAMPLE

File	Location	Contents	Length (in bytes)
F_1	1	(Part #, Part Name)	10^5
F_2	2	(Supplier #, Part #, Quantity)	10^5
F_3	3	(Supplier #, Supplier Name, City)	10^4

(to generate an optimal query tree as specified by Theorem 1), we have the tree as shown in Fig. 4(a). Based on the permutability of operations in the query tree (i.e., adjacent JOIN operations are permutable), we can construct an additional tree for this query as shown in Fig. 4(b). Let us now generate the query graphs from each of the query trees.

In generating the processing query graphs from a query tree, we first generate the set of local operation groups from the operations in the query tree. Each of the local operation groups may be performed at an execution node in a query processing graph. Then we select the elements of the set of local operating groups and cascade them according to the sequence of operations in the query tree. The operations from the query trees are

- $\beta_0^1 = \sigma_{p_1}\pi_{c_1}$ are the initial SELECTION and PROJECTION operations on F_1
- $\beta_0^2 = \sigma_{p_2}$ is the initial SELECTION operation on F_2
- $\beta_0^3 = \sigma_{p_3}\pi_{c_3}$ are the initial SELECTION and PROJECTION operations on F_3
- β_1 is a JOIN on part number
- β_2 is a JOIN operation on supplier number and a PROJECTION operation that eliminates the supplier number column
- β_e is the operation that presents the query result to the query initiator.

The set of local operation groups for the query tree of Fig. 4(a) is $\{\beta_1, \beta_2, \beta_1\beta_2, \beta_e, \beta_2\beta_e, \beta_1\beta_2\beta_e\}$. The set of query processing graphs that are constructed is shown in Fig. 6(a). The query processing graph for policy ψ_1 represents the policy of transmitting the files f_1, f_2, and f_3 resulting from the initial operations β_0^1, β_0^2, and β_0^3 to site 4 and processing them there by performing operation β_1 followed by β_2. The graph for policy ψ_2 represents performing the same sequence of operations, $\beta_1\beta_2$, at either site 1, 2, or 3 and then transmitting the query result to site 4. The graph for policy ψ_3 corresponds to performing operation β_1 at either site 1, 2, or 3, and then performing operation β_2 at site 4. The graph for policy ψ_4 represents performing operation β_1 and β_2 separately at two of the sites 1, 2, and 3, by performing operation β_1 at one site, then transmitting its result file to another site for processing by β_2, and then sending the final result to site 4.

In the same manner, the set of local operation groups for the query tree of Fig. 4(b) is $\{\beta_2, \beta_1, \beta_2\beta_1, \beta_e, \beta_1\beta_e, \beta_2\beta_1\beta_e\}$. The set of query processing graphs constructed from this set is shown in Fig. 6(b). The query processing graph for policy ψ_5 represents the policy of transmitting the intermediate files f_1, f_2, and f_3 to site 4 for processing by operating β_2 followed by β_1. The graph for policy ψ_6 corresponds to performing operation β_2 followed by β_1 at one of the sites 1, 2, or 3, then transmitting the result of operation β_1 (the query result) to site 4. The graph for policy ψ_7 represents first performing operation β_2 at one of the sites 1, 2, or 3, then transmitting its result to site 4 for processing by operation β_1. Finally, the graph for policy ψ_8 corresponds to performing operations β_2 and β_1 at separate locations among sites 1, 2, and 3 by performing β_2 first, transmitting its result to the site for β_1, performing operation β_1, and finally transmitting the query result to site 4.

The operations β_0^i, $i = 1, 2, 3$, reduce the files F_1, F_2, and F_3 to f_1, f_2, and f_3, respectively. The temporary file sizes $l(f_i) = \alpha(\beta_0^i, F_i, \overline{\gamma}) \cdot l(F_i)$ for $i = 1, 2, 3$. These temporary files have the characteristics summarized in Table II.

We will study the example under three different cases by varying the parameter values. In all three cases, we assume that the unit communication cost is the same for all pairs of sites i and j and that the unit processing cost for each operation is the same for all the computers. Since file f_2 is an input to both operations, for simplicity we express the data reduction functions for operations β_1 and β_2 in terms of the length of file f_2.

We will first consider case A. The data reduction function values are $\alpha(\beta_0^i, F_i, \overline{\gamma})$ for $i = 1, 2, 3$ as given in Table II, $\alpha(\beta_1, f_2, \overline{\gamma}) = 10^{-1}$, $\alpha(\beta_2, f_2, \overline{\gamma}) = 2 \times 10^{-1}$, and $\alpha(\beta_2|\overline{\beta}, f_2, \overline{\gamma}) = \alpha(\beta_1|\overline{\beta}, f_2, \overline{\gamma}) = 5 \times 10^{-2}$. The unit communication cost value is $C'_{ij} = C' = \$10^{-3}$/byte and the unit processing cost values are $C_o^i = C_o = \$10^{-6}$/byte for $i = 1, 2, 3$, and $C_1 = C_2 = \$0.5 \times 10^{-3}$/byte.

The query-processing graphs for policies ψ_2 and ψ_6 have a multioperation execution node that performs a set of operations, $\{\beta_1, \beta_2\}$, such that this set of operations can be executed in either of the sequences $\beta_1\beta_2$ or $\beta_2\beta_1$. It can be shown that the processing cost of the sequence of operations $\beta_1\beta_2$ is lower than that of the sequence $\beta_2\beta_1$. Therefore, based on Theorem

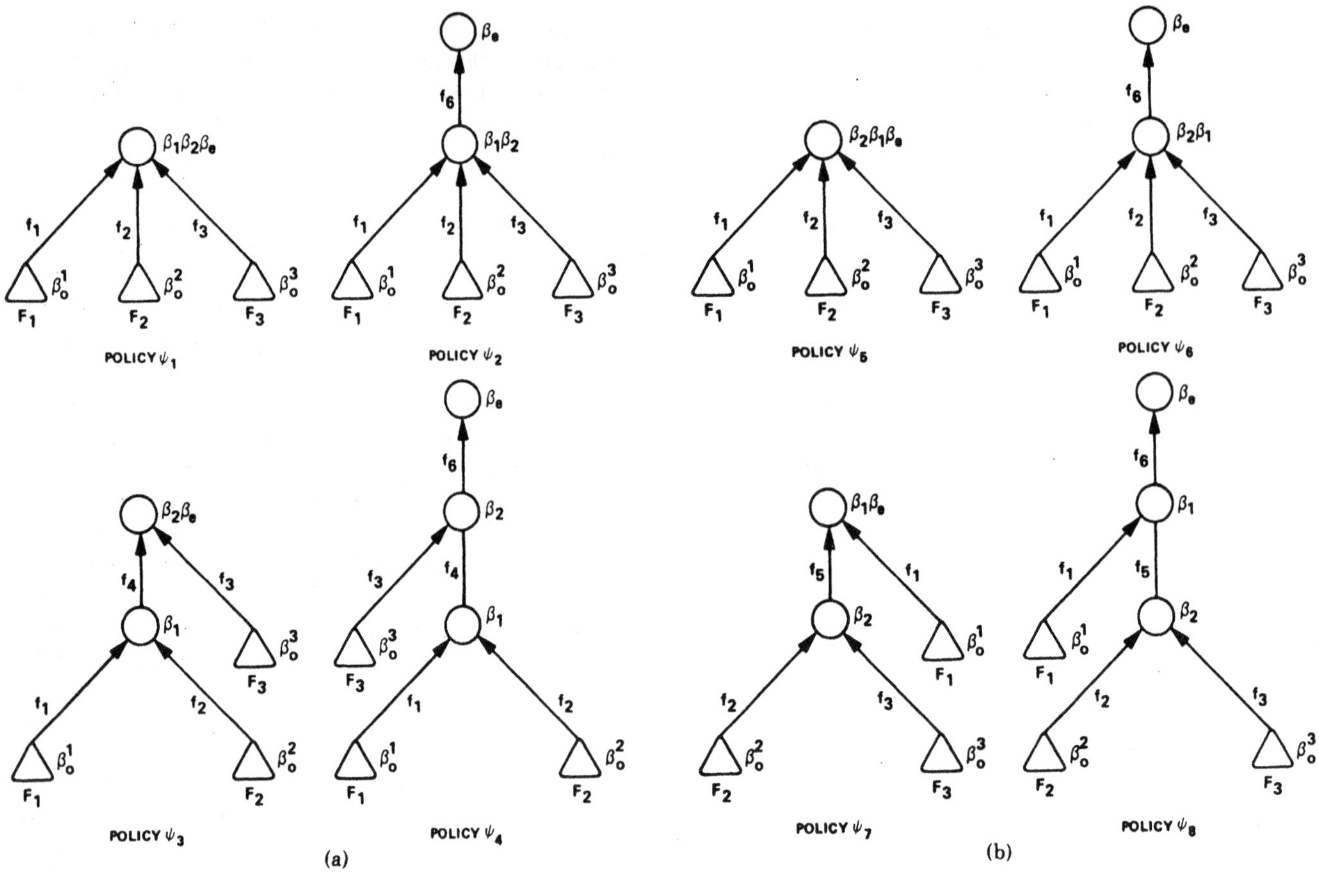

Fig. 6. Query graphs for the example. (a) Query graphs for the query tree of Fig. 4(a). (b) Query graphs for the query tree of Fig. 4(b).

TABLE II
TEMPORARY FILE CHARACTERISTICS

f_i Contents	$\bar{\gamma}$ for β_0^i	$\alpha(\beta_0^i, F_i, \bar{\gamma})$	$l(f_i)$ in bytes
f_1 Part #	Part Name is "Calculators"	0.05	0.5×10^4
f_2 Supplier #, Part #, Quantity	Quantity > 1000	0.1	1×10^4
f_3 Supplier #, Supplier Name	City is Los Angeles	0.3	0.3×10^4

TABLE III
OPTIMAL SITES FOR OPERATIONS

Policy	Site for β_1	Site for β_2	Site for β_e
ψ_1	4	4	4
ψ_2	2	2	4
ψ_3	2	4	4
ψ_4	2	3	4
ψ_7	4	2	4
ψ_8	1	2	4

6, we chose the policy ψ_2 over ψ_6. Likewise, we choose the sequence $\beta_1\beta_2\beta_e$ over $\beta_2\beta_1\beta_e$ thus choosing policy ψ_1 over ψ_5.

Next, we use Theorem 3 to select the sites of all the execution nodes in a given graph. This determines the optimal query processing policy for that graph. Table III displays the optimal sites selected for operations for all the query processing graphs.

All the policies in the set $\{\psi_1, \psi_2, \psi_3, \psi_4\}$ have the sequence of operations $\beta_0^1\beta_0^2\beta_0^3\beta_1\beta_2\beta_e$. Both of the policies in the set $\{\psi_7, \psi_8\}$ have the sequence of operations $\beta_0^1\beta_0^2\beta_0^3\beta_2\beta_1\beta_e$. In order to find the best policy within each of these sets, we need to compute the total communication cost $C'(\psi)$ for each policy in the set as follows:

$$C'(\psi_1) = C' \cdot [l(f_1) + l(f_2) + l(f_3)] = 18$$

$$C'(\psi_2) = C' \cdot [l(f_1) + l(f_3) + l(f_6)]$$
$$= C' \cdot [l(f_1) + l(f_3) + \alpha(\beta_2|\bar{\beta}, f_2, \bar{\gamma}) \cdot l(f_2)] = 8.5$$

$$C'(\psi_3) = C' \cdot [l(f_1) + l(f_3) + l(f_4)]$$
$$= C' \cdot [l(f_1) + l(f_3) + \alpha(\beta_1, f_2, \bar{\gamma}) \cdot l(f_2)] = 9$$

$$C'(\psi_4) = C' \cdot [l(f_1) + l(f_4) + l(f_6)]$$
$$= C' \cdot [l(f_1) + \alpha(\beta_1, f_2, \bar{\gamma}) \cdot l(f_2) + \alpha(\beta_2|\bar{\beta}, f_2, \bar{\gamma}) \cdot l(f_2)] = 6.5$$

$$C'(\psi_7) = C' \cdot [l(f_1) + l(f_3) + l(f_5)]$$
$$= C' \cdot [l(f_1) + l(f_3) + \alpha(\beta_2, f_2, \bar{\gamma}) \cdot l(f_2)] = 10$$

$$C'(\psi_8) = C' \cdot [l(f_3) + l(f_5) + l(f_6)]$$
$$= C' \cdot [l(f_3) + \alpha(\beta_2, f_2, \bar{\gamma}) \cdot l(f_2) + \alpha(\beta_1|\bar{\beta}, f_2, \bar{\gamma}) \cdot l(f_2)] = 5.5$$

Since $C'(\psi_4) < C'(\psi_2) < C'(\psi_3) < C'(\psi_1)$, based on Theorem 7, ψ_4 is the optimal policy among the set of policies $\{\psi_1,$

$\psi_2, \psi_3, \psi_4\}$. Likewise, ψ_8 is the optimal policy among the set of policies $\{\psi_7, \psi_8\}$.

Finally, we use (3) to compute the operating cost of policies ψ_4 and ψ_8. Based on policy ψ_4 and the file allocation information in Table I, we construct the following indicating functions:

$$Y(\psi_4) = \begin{vmatrix} 1 & 0 \\ 1 & 0 \\ 0 & 1 \\ 0 & 1 \\ 0 & 0 \\ 0 & 0 \end{vmatrix} \qquad Z(\psi_4) = \begin{vmatrix} 1 & 0 \\ 0 & 0 \\ 0 & 0 \\ 0 & 1 \\ 0 & 0 \\ 0 & 0 \end{vmatrix}$$

Substituting the parameters into (1), we have

$$\begin{aligned} C(\psi_4) &= C_0 \cdot [l(F_1) + l(F_2) + l(F_3)] + C_1 \cdot [l(f_1) \\ &\quad + l(f_2)] + C_2 \cdot [l(f_3) + l(f_4)] + C'(\psi_4) \\ &= 9.71 + 6.5 = 16.21. \end{aligned}$$

Likewise, for policy ψ_8, we have

$$Y(\psi_8) = \begin{vmatrix} 1 & 0 \\ 0 & 1 \\ 0 & 1 \\ 0 & 0 \\ 1 & 0 \\ 0 & 0 \end{vmatrix} \qquad Z(\psi_8) = \begin{vmatrix} 0 & 0 \\ 0 & 0 \\ 0 & 1 \\ 0 & 0 \\ 1 & 0 \\ 0 & 0 \end{vmatrix}$$

In the same manner, the operating cost of ψ_8 equals

$$\begin{aligned} C(\psi_8) &= C_0 \cdot [l(F_1) + l(F_2) + l(F_3)] + C_1 \cdot [l(f_1) \\ &\quad + l(f_5)] + C_2 \cdot [l(f_2) + l(f_3)] + C'(\psi_8) \\ &= 10.21 + 5.5 = 15.71. \end{aligned}$$

We note that $C(\psi_8) < C(\psi_4)$; therefore, ψ_8 is the optimal query processing policy for case A (see Table IV).

Let us now consider case B. All the parameter values remain the same as for case A except that the unit processing cost for operation β_1, C_1, has been reduced from \$0.5 $\times 10^{-3}$/byte to \$0.25 $\times 10^{-3}$/byte. The communication costs $C'(\psi_i)$ for $i = 1, 2, \cdots, 8$ of case A remain the same for case B. Therefore, based on Theorems 3, 6, and 7, policies ψ_4 and ψ_8 remain as the two local optimal policies for processing the query. The reduction in unit processing cost C_1 results in $C(\psi_4) < C(\psi_8)$. Therefore, ψ_4 becomes the optimal policy for processing the query as shown in Table IV.

Finally, let us consider case C. The unit processing costs C_o^i and $C_j, j = 1, 2$, the unit communication costs C'_{ij}, and the data reduction functions for operations β_o^i, $\alpha(\beta_o^i, F_i, \overline{\gamma})$, remain the same as for case B. However, the data reduction functions for operations β_1 and β_2 have been increased. Their new values are: $\alpha(\beta_1, f_2, \overline{\gamma}) = 0.3$, $\alpha(\beta_2, f_2, \overline{\gamma}) = 0.45$, and $\alpha(\beta_2 | \overline{\beta}, f_2, \overline{\gamma}) = \alpha(\beta_1 | \overline{\beta}, f_2, \overline{\gamma}) = 0.4$. From Theorem 3 we know that site selections for the execution nodes are independent of the data reduction functions for operations β_1 and β_2. Therefore, the sites for performing β_1 and β_2 remain the same as in cases A and B.

Due to the increase in the data reduction functions for operations β_1 and β_2, the output data volumes from these operations have increased. As a result, policy ψ_3 yields the lowest total communication cost among the set of policies $\{\psi_1, \psi_2, \psi_3, \psi_4\}$. Therefore, by Theorem 7, ψ_3 is the optimal policy among that set of policies. Likewise, policy ψ_8 is the optimal policy among the set of policies $\{\psi_7, \psi_8\}$. Comparing ψ_3 and ψ_8, we note that $C(\psi_3) < C(\psi_8)$. Thus the policy ψ_3 is the optimal policy for case C.

TABLE IV
OPERATING COSTS OF THE THREE CASES FOR THE EXAMPLE

Case	Policy	Communications Cost	Processing Cost	Operating Cost
A	ψ_4	6.5	9.71	16.21
	ψ_8	5.5	10.21	15.71
B	**ψ_4**	6.5	5.96	12.46
	ψ_8	5.5	8.46	13.96
C	**ψ_3**	11.0	6.96	17.96
	ψ_8	11.5	9.08	20.58

The optimal policy is shown circled.

VII. DISCUSSIONS

A. *Integration of Low-Level Operations into the Model*

The proposed cost model is based on high-level relational operations. We shall now consider the integration of it with the lower level operations that are provided by most storage systems.

When a high-level operation is partitioned into set of low-level operations, there may be several ways to implement it using different sequences of low-level access operations. Since the model is based on an equal processing cost for a given operation at all sites, we assume that each file has the same access methods available at all sites. Thus, to implement a unary operation we choose the best access strategy and apply that to any site where the operation may be executed.

On the other hand, for a binary operation, the operand files may originate at different sites; in these cases, the choice of access path for executing the operation affects both communication cost and processing cost. For example, in a join operation, the presence of indexes to the operand files and the order of accessing the files affects the processing cost [6]. If both operands are present in the site where the join is performed, then we choose an access path that minimizes processing cost. However, if one or both of the operand files are produced at a site different from the joining site, then communication cost is also affected, and therefore, the optimal access path may be different from the one that would be used if both files were available at a single site. In order to apply the proposed model to these cases where low-level access strategy impacts both communication cost and processing cost, we treat the high-level operation implemented by different access strategies as different types of operation with a normalized processing cost. (The normalized cost includes both the processing and communication cost for the operation.) In this way, a binary operation in a query tree may be represented as different types of operations with normalized processing costs in the query processing graphs. This enables us to use the assumption that the processing cost of a given operation is the same at all sites, and simultaneously integrate the lower level operations into the model.

B. Reduction of the Set of Feasible Query Trees

In the cases where there is a large number of operations in the initial query tree, or where a large number of transformations can be applied to the tree, a great deal of time and space may be necessary to generate and process the complete set of feasible query trees. In such a case, in order to reduce the amount of computation, a heuristic may be used to select a subset from the complete set of feasible trees for evaluation. Such a heuristic may be based on detection of duplicated operations in a tree, duplicated subtrees, or repeated accesses to the same operand. For example, several joins involving the same relation may occur among the lower levels of a generated query tree. The heuristic might instead be based on the breadth and depth of the generated trees. If we consider executing a very broad and deep query tree on a network, the query processing will either involve a large number of communications between sites, or large numbers of operations clustered in the same sites. Thus, trees that have both large breadth and large depth may not yield the optimal solution. Thus the selection of such trees may be avoided. Further research in this direction may be desirable.

VIII. Conclusions

A model is presented for determining the optimal query processing policy based on selecting the sequence and the sites for executing a set of subquery operations to yield minimum operating cost. The model considers communication cost, processing cost, query processing sequences, sites for processing the operations, file length, and the data reduction function. The communication and processing cost are assumed to be proportional to the volume of traffic flow. The data reduction function provides an estimate of input/output volumes for a given operation. This information is useful for estimating the output file length(s) which is used to compute the operating cost of a query processing policy.

Given a query to be optimized, we partition it into subqueries expressed by relational algebra operations and represent their serial and parallel relationships and their processing sequences in a query tree. Based on the permutability of adjacent operations in the tree, a set of trees may be generated such that processing any of these query trees will yield the same result.

Based on the topology of the query tree, we collect operations together into local operation groups to be processed on a single site. According to the sequence expressed by the query tree, the set of local operation groups can be used to generate a set of query processing graphs for that query tree.

Theorems based on the operating cost model are developed to determine the best sites for executing the operations of a given query processing graph and to identify the graphs representing local optimal policies. Such theorems greatly reduce computational requirements as compared to exhaustive search for determining the optimal query processing policy for a given query.

Appendix

Theorem 2: The set of local operation groups for a given query tree generated by the Iterative Construction Method (ICM) is complete.

Proof: Consider a one-level tree that has a root β_e and a binary operation β_j at level 1 which is connected to two files. At level 1 the ICM generates one local operation group, $\theta_1 = \beta_j$. At the root level, the ICM generates the set of local operation groups $\theta_r = \{\beta_e, \beta_j\beta_e\}$ using steps 1) and 2), respectively. Since there is only one operation β_j at level 1, and no lower levels, $L_1 = \beta_j$. Thus clearly $\theta_1 = L_1$. The elements of θ_r are $\beta_j\beta_e$ and β_e. Since there is one operation β_e at the root level, and only one adjacent operation β_j at a lower level of this tree, $L_r = \{\beta_e, \beta_j\beta_e\}$. Therefore, $L_r = \theta_r$. Thus we have shown that the set of local operation groups constructed from the ICM for the one-level tree $L = L_1 \cup L_r$ is complete.

An n-level query tree consists of a root and n levels of binary operations, where $n \geq 2$. First we will consider the set of local operation groups for the n levels of binary operations, that is,

$$L(n) = \bigcup_{i=1}^{n} L_i = L - L_r.$$

Assuming that the ICM correctly generates $L(n-1)$, we shall prove that it also correctly generates $L(n)$. Consider an n-level tree. Such a tree has only a single operation at level n. Let us call this operation β_j. The n-level tree has two $(n-1)$-level subtrees, both adjacent to β_j. We know from the induction assumption that the set of local operation groups constructed for each of the two $(n-1)$-level subtrees is complete. Since the ICM works from bottom to top, on the n-level tree it first constructs the local operation groups $L_1, L_2, \cdots, L_{n-1}$ for the two $(n-1)$-level subtrees. Since the subtrees are not connected with each other, the sets $L_1, L_2, \cdots, L_{n-1}$ are correctly generated by the ICM. The remaining local operation groups for the n-level tree are those of the set L_n.

Let θ_n be the set of local operation groups at level n generated by the ICM. To complete our proof, we must show that $\theta_n = L_n$.

First we show that $\theta_n \subseteq L_n$. Let us consider the three subsets of θ_n, namely $\theta_n^1, \theta_n^2, \theta_n^3$ constructed by steps 1), 2), and 3) of the ICM, respectively. θ_n^1 is the local operation group that contains β_j. Clearly, this local operation group satisfies the definition of L_n. θ_n^2 is the set of local operation groups formed by combining β_j with an element $l_{n-1}(\beta_k, \beta_j)$ of L_{n-1}. Thus, θ_n^2 is a subset of L_n. Finally, θ_n^3 is formed by combining operation β_j with two local operation groups $l_{n-1}(\beta_{k_1}, \beta_j)$ and $l_{n-1}(\beta_{k_2}, \beta_j)$. The combination of β_j with the two local operation groups at level $n-1$ forms a local operation group at level n. Thus, θ_n^3 is a subset of L_n. This completes the proof that $\theta_n \subseteq L_n$.

Now we will show that $L_n \subseteq \theta_n$. Since the n-level tree has exactly one operation at level n, namely β_j, β_j must be a member of each element of L_n. Since β_j is at level n of the tree, L_n consists of all the local operation groups that can be formed by combining β_j with other operations at levels below n. Thus β_j is an element of L_n and belongs to θ_n^1. The other members of L_n must consist of β_j, plus some operations at levels below n. For each of these local operation groups, if we remove β_j

from the group, there are two cases: 1) the remaining operations of that group are connected (they are from one $(n-1)$-level subtree); 2) the remaining operations are disconnected (they are from both $(n-1)$-level subtrees). For the first case, the set of operations without β_j must be a local operation group at level $n-1$, l_{n-1}. Further, it includes exactly one node at level $n-1$, since the only path between the two nodes at level $n-1$ includes β_j. Thus, the elements of L_n formed by adding β_j to such a member of L_{n-1} are $l_n(\beta_j, \beta_k)$ which are local operation groups belonging to θ_n^2.

For the second case, the path connecting the two disconnected local groups must include β_j. However, β_j is adjacent to only two operation nodes at level $n-1$, that is, β_{k_1} and β_{k_2}. Therefore these two disconnected groups are members of $L_{n-1}(\beta_{k_1})$ and $L_{n-1}(\beta_{k_2})$, respectively. Thus the local operation groups formed by $l_{n-1}(\beta_{k_1}, \beta_j) \cup l_{n-1}(\beta_{k_2}, \beta_j) \cup \beta_j$ is a member of θ_n^3. Therefore, we have proved that $L_n \subseteq \theta_n$. Thus, $L_n = \theta_n$, and the ICM correctly generates $L(n)$.

Now we will consider θ_r, the set of local operation groups generated at the root level by the ICM.

Since β_e is the root, and β_i at level n is the only operation connected to it, in the same manner as above, we can show that $L_r = \theta_r$.

Since both $L(n)$ and L_r are completely generated by ICM, the set $L = L(n) \cup L_r$ constructed by the ICM is complete.

References

[1] E. Wong, "Retrieving dispersed data from SSD-1: A system for distributed databases," in *Proc. 2nd Berkeley Workshop Distributed Data Management Comput. Networks*, May 1977, pp. 217-235.

[2] R. Epstein, M. Stonebraker, and E. Wong, "Distributed query processing in a relational data base system," in *Proc. SIGMOD*, May 1978, pp. 169-180.

[3] A. R. Hevner and S. B. Yao, "Query processing in distributed database systems," *IEEE Trans. Software Eng.*, vol. SE-5, pp. 177-187, May 1979.

[4] J. M. Smith and P. Y. Chang, "Optimizing the performance of a relational algebra database interface," *Commun. Ass. Comput. Mach.*, vol. 18, pp. 568-579, Oct. 1975.

[5] D. Small and W. W. Chu, "A distributed data base architecture for data processing in a dynamic environment," in *Proc. COMPCON*, Mar. 1979.

[6] P. G. Selinger, and M. Adiba, "Access path selection in distributed database systems," IBM Res. Rep RJ2883, Aug. 1980.

Wesley W. Chu (S'62-M'67-SM'74-F'78) received the B.S. and M.S. degrees from the University of Michigan, Ann Arbor, in 1960 and 1961, respectively, and the Ph.D. degree in electrical engineering from Stanford University, Stanford, CA, in 1966.

From 1961 to 1962 he worked on switching circuit design at the General Electric Computer Department (now Honeywell), Phoenix, AZ, from 1964 to 1966 he worked on the design of large-scale computers at IBM, Menlo Park and San Jose, CA, and from 1966 to 1969 he worked on research in computer communications at Bell Laboratories, Holmdel, NJ. He is currently a Professor in the Department of Computer Science, School of Engineering and Applied Science, University of California, Los Angeles. He directs a research group at UCLA in the areas of computer communications and networking, distributed processing, and distributed databases. He is also a consultant to government agencies and private industries.

Dr. Chu is a member of Tau Beta Pi, Eta Kappa Nu, Phi Tau Phi, and Sigma Xi. He was an ACM National Lecturer from 1972 to 1973, IEEE Distinguished Visitor from 1973 to 1974, Chairman of the ACM SIGCOMM from 1973 to 1977, a member of the Technical Committee of IEEE Computer Communications, Chairman of the 1975 ACM Interprocess Communication Workshop, Technical Program Chairman of the 4th Data Communication Symposium in 1975, and the IEEE Lake Arrowhead Workshop Chairman on Computer Networking and Distributed Databases in 1977. He has authored or coauthored more than 60 articles on information processing systems and computer communications and has edited two textbooks: *Advances in Computer Communications*, Artech House (1st ed., 1974; 2nd ed., 1976; and 2nd revised ed., 1977), and *Centralized and Distributed Data Base Systems* (coedited with P. P. Chen), IEEE Computer Society, 1979. He is a member of the Editorial Board of *Computer Networks* and the *International Journal on Computers and Electrical Engineering* and an Associate Editor of the *Journal of Computer Networks*.

Paul Hurley received the S.B. degree in mathematics from the Massachusetts Institute of Technology, Cambridge, in 1973, and the M.S. and Ph.D. degrees in computer science from the University of California, Los Angeles, in 1976 and 1982, respectively.

He is now a member of the Technical Staff of Bell Laboratories, Holmdel, NJ. His interests include distributed processing architecture and database management systems.

Optimization Algorithms for Distributed Queries

PETER M. G. APERS, ALAN R. HEVNER, AND S. BING YAO

Abstract—The efficiency of processing strategies for queries in a distributed database is critical for system performance. Methods are studied to minimize the response time and the total time for distributed queries. A new algorithm (Algorithm GENERAL) is presented to derive processing strategies for arbitrarily complex queries. Three versions of the algorithm are given: one for minimizing response time and two for minimizing total time. The algorithm is shown to provide optimal solutions under certain conditions.

Index Terms—Computer network, database, distributed database systems, distributed processing strategy, heuristic algorithms, query processing, relational data model, system modeling.

I. Introduction

IN a distributed database, we have the ability to decentralize data that are most heavily used by end users at geographically dispersed locations and, at the same time, to combine data from different sources by means of queries. The decentralization of data will result in better response times and, if multiple copies are used, in a more reliable system.

The retrieval of data from different sites in a network is known as distributed query processing. The difference between query processing in a centralized database and a distributed database is the potential for decomposing a query into subqueries which can be processed in parallel, and their intermediate results can be sent in parallel to the required computers. Finding an efficient way of processing a query is important. If a query is processed inefficiently, it not only takes a long time before the end user gets his answer, but it might also decrease the performance of the whole system because of network congestion. We will investigate two optimization objectives: the minimization of response time and of total time. Which of these two objectives is better for a specific system depends upon the system's characteristics.

Distributed query processing has received a great deal of attention [15], [19]. The initial research in this area was done by Wong [24]. He proposed an optimization method based on a greedy heuristic that produces efficient, but not necessarily optimal query processing strategies. An enhanced version of this method is implemented in the SDD-1 system [5]. Epstein *et al.* [9] developed an algorithm based on the query optimization technique of decomposition [23]. This algorithm is implemented in the distributed INGRES database system. Performance studies of this algorithm are reported in [10]. A dynamic optimization algorithm for the POLYPHEME system has been proposed by Toan [17]. Further research on dynamic optimization algorithms has been done by Baldissera *et al.* [3] and Takizawa [22].

Work by Chu and Hurley [7] defined the solution space of feasible processing strategies for distributed queries. They presented an optimal, although inherently exponential, optimization algorithm. The use of the semi-join operation has led to the development of full-reduction methods of processing a

Manuscript received October 1, 1980; revised January 4, 1982 and April 1, 1982.

P.M.G. Apers is with the Informatica Wiskundig Seminarium, Vrije Universiteit, de Boelelaan 1081, HV Amsterdam, The Netherlands.

A. R. Hevner and S. B. Yao are with the College of Business and Management, University of Maryland, College Park, MD 20742.

distributed query [6], [11], [25], [4]. These methods are applicable for a special class of queries known as tree queries. Pelagatti and Schreiber [18] use an integer programming technique to minimize cost in distributed query processing. Kershberg *et al.* [16] apply query optimization to a database allocated on a star network and study the system performance.

For a special class of simple queries, Hevner and Yao developed algorithms PARALLEL and SERIAL [12] that find strategies with, respectively, minimum response time and total time. In [14], they extended these algorithms to Algorithm G that processes general distributed queries. Apers [1] showed that this algorithm had some serious drawbacks. Its complexity for worst case queries does not have a polynomial bound. Also, the analysis of the quality of the derived processing strategies is difficult. Both Hevner [13] and Apers [2] recognized these problems and developed improved algorithms. Here we present this improved algorithm, Algorithm GENERAL. It is more clearly understood and more usable as a distributed query optimization algorithm than Algorithm G.

This paper is organized as follows. In Section II, we will briefly repeat the query processing model described in [13]. Three versions of Algorithm GENERAL, for response time and total time, are presented and analyzed in Section III.

II. Definitions and Distributed System Model

A distributed database system is characterized by the distribution of the system components of hardware, control, and data. For this research, a distributed system is a collection of independent computers interconnected via point-to-point communication lines. Each computer, known as a node in the network, has a processing capability, a data storage capability, and is capable of operating autonomously in the system. Each node contains a version of a distributed DBMS.

The database is viewed logically in the relational data model [8]. The database is allocated across system nodes in units of relations (without loss of generality, relation fragments may be considered as relations for distribution). The relation distribution allows a general manner of redundancy. The only allocation constraint is that all data must be either locally or globally accessible from any system node. The distribution of data on the network is invisible to the user.

We assume that we know the following information about the relations.

For each relation R_i, $i = 1, 2, \cdots, m$,

- n_i: number of tuples,
- α_i: number of attributes,
- s_i: size (e.g., in bytes).

For each attribute d_{ij}, $j = 1, 2, \cdots, \alpha_i$ of relation R_i,

- p_{ij}: selectivity,
- b_{ij}: size (e.g., in bytes) of the data item in attribute d_{ij}.

The selectivity p_{ij} of attribute d_{ij} is defined as the number of different values occurring in the attribute divided by the number of all possible values of the attribute. Thus, $0 < p_{ij} \leqslant 1$.

To process a query in a relational database, we only need the operations restriction, projection, and join [8]. In a distributed database, we may need to compute joins on relations which are located at different sites. Instead of computing these joins immediately, we will first reduce the sizes of the relations wherever possible by restrictions and projections. A relation, which is one of the operands of a join, can be made smaller by deleting the tuples that cannot play a role in the join. An operation called a *semi-join* [4] deletes these tuples of the relation. If relation R_i has a semi-join with attribute d_{kl} on attribute d_{ij}, then the parameters of relation R_i are changed in the following way:

$$s_i \leftarrow s_i * p_{kl},$$

$$p_{ij} \leftarrow p_{ij} * p_{kl},$$

$$b_{ij} \leftarrow b_{ij} * p_{kl}.$$

The selectivity and size of only the joining attribute are reduced because of an assumption of attribute independence within each relation in our model.

To compute a semi-join, the unique values of the joining attribute of one relation are sent to the other relation: It is cheaper to compute this semi-join than the complete join. In the result node, the complete join will be computed after the reduced relations have arrived by concatenating matching tuples on the joining attributes. The data transmissions used for reducing a relation and the transmission of the reduced relation to the query computer form a *schedule* for this relation. An example of a schedule for relation R_i can be seen below.

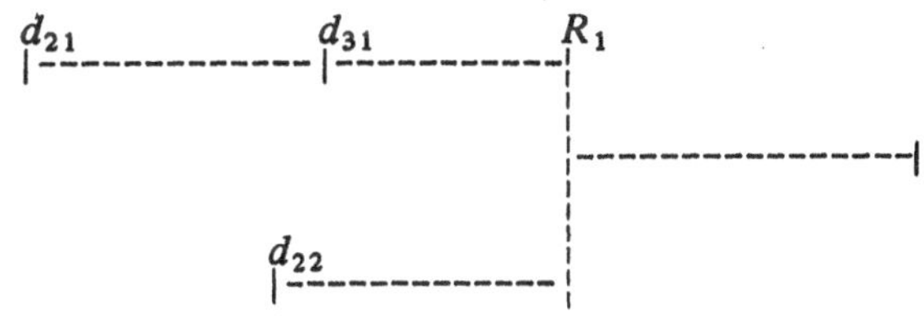

Attribute d_{21} is sent to attribute d_{31}. A semi-join is performed on relation R_3. The reduced d_{31} attribute is sent to relation R_1 in parallel with attribute d_{22}. Further relational operations reduce the size of relation R_1. Finally, the reduced relation R_1 is sent to the result node.

It is also possible to construct a schedule for an attribute instead of a relation. A schedule for an attribute is constructed to send the attribute to a relation upon which a semi-join will be computed—for example, attribute d_{31} in the above schedule.

We assume that the *transmission cost* of the data is the same between any two computers and is a linear function of the size of the data. This function will be denoted by $C(X) \leftarrow C_0 + C_1X$ where X is the amount of data transmitted. The *response time* of a schedule is the time elapsed between the start of the first transmission and the time at which the relation (attribute) arrives at the required computer. The *minimum response time* of a relation (attribute) is the minimum response time among all possible schedules for this relation (attribute). The *total time* of a schedule is the sum of the costs of all transmissions required in the schedule.

The *incoming selectivity* of a schedule for a relation (or attribute) is the product of selectivities of all the attributes in the schedule (more than one occurrence of an attribute in a schedule can contribute only one instance of its selectivity) excluding the attributes of the relation (or in the case of an attribute, the attribute itself).

A *distribution strategy* for a query consists of the schedules for all relations which do not reside in the result node and are used in the query. With the assumption that data transmission costs are significantly greater than local processing costs in the system, the cost of processing a query is determined by the transmission costs in its distribution strategy. Another implicit assumption that we make throughout this paper is that the query processing strategy is run on a dedicated system in order to achieve minimum execution times. Dynamic system factors such as communication line contention and subsequent queueing delays are not considered in our static query optimization algorithms.

In a distributed database, it is, in general, better to do local processing first because it reduces the amount of data to be transmitted. With local processing, we mean the computation of restrictions, projections, and semi-joins between relations that reside in the same node. After the initial processing, each node that has query data will be considered to contain only one "integrated" relation. The relations at each node remain distinct (i.e., no Cartesian product relation is formed). However, by reformatting the query so that each node becomes a variable, the distribution aspects of the query are emphasized [24]. Without loss of generality, this assumption provides a distribution abstraction to the problem and simplifies the understanding of our following algorithms.

Initial local processing results in the following parameters:

m: number of relations in the remaining query,

α_i: number of attributes in relation R_i,

β_i: number of internodal joining attributes in relation R_i.

In [12] and [14], Hevner and Yao introduced and investigated algorithms, PARALLEL and SERIAL, which, respectively, compute minimum response and total time schedules for simple queries. Queries are called *simple* if, after initial local processing, the relations contain only one attribute: the joining attribute. Thus, $\alpha_i = \beta_i = 1$ for $i = 1, 2, \cdots, m$.

Algorithm PARALLEL

1) Order relations R_i such that $s_1 \leqslant s_2 \leqslant \cdots \leqslant s_m$.

2) Consider each relation R_i in ascending order of size.

3) For each relation $R_j (j < i)$, construct a schedule to R_i that consists of the parallel transmission of the relation R_j and all schedules of relations $R_k (k < j)$. Select the schedule with minimum response time.

Algorithm SERIAL

1) Order relations R_i such that $s_1 \leqslant s_2 \leqslant \cdots \leqslant s_m$.

2) If no relations are at the result node, then select strategy:

$$R_1 \to R_2 \to \cdots \to R_n \to \text{result node.}$$

Or else if R_r is a relation at the result node, then there are two strategies:

$$R_1 \to R_2 \to \cdots \to R_r \to \cdots \to R_n \to R_r \quad \text{or}$$

$$R_1 \to R_2 \to \cdots \to R_{r-1} \to R_{r+1} \to \cdots \to R_n \to R_r.$$

Select the one with minimum total time.

The complexity of algorithm PARALLEL is $O(m^2)$ and that of algorithm SERIAL is $O(m \log_2 m)$ where m is the number of required relations in the query [14].

III. Algorithm GENERAL

A *general query* is characterized by $\alpha_i \geqslant \beta_i \geqslant 1$ for $i = 1, 2, \cdots, m$. This means that a relation can contain more than one joining attribute. Let σ represent the number of joining attributes in a query. Therefore, such a relation can be reduced in size by semi-joins on different joining attributes.

To illustrate our query optimization methods, we will use a database consisting of the following relations:

PARTS($P\#$, PNAME)
ON-ORDER($S\#$, $P\#$, QTY)
S-P-J($S\#$, $P\#$, $J\#$).

The query represented by Fig. 1 is: "List the $P\#$, PNAME, and total quantity for all parts that are currently on order from suppliers who supply that part to jobs 10 or 20."

In this query, there are two joining attributes, $P\#$ and $S\#$. Assume that each relation is located at a different node and that the result is required at a fourth node. After performing the restriction on the *S-P-J* relation, the required attributes in each relation are projected. The resulting size and selectivity parameters are given in Table I.

Let $C(X) = 20 + X$.

The response time and total time costs of the different query processing strategies for this query will be compared for the response time and total time versions of algorithm GENERAL.

A simple way of processing a query is to perform initial local processing, followed directly by the transmissions of all remaining data to the result node, where centralized query processing builds the result. This will be called the Initial Feasible Solution (IFS).

R_1: ON-ORDER R_1 1020
|---------|

R_2: *S-P-J* R_2 2020
|------------------|

R_3: PARTS R_3 3020
|----------------------------|

Response time = 3020. Total time = 6060.

We now present an outline of Algorithm GENERAL. Minimization of response time and total time is done by three different versions of the algorithm, which are discussed in the next three sections.

Algorithm GENERAL

1) *Do all initial local processing.*

2) *Generate candidate relation schedules.* Isolate each of the σ joining attributes, and consider each to define a *simple query* with an undefined result node.

a) To minimize *response time*, apply Algorithm PARALLEL to each simple query. Save all candidate schedules for integration in step 3.

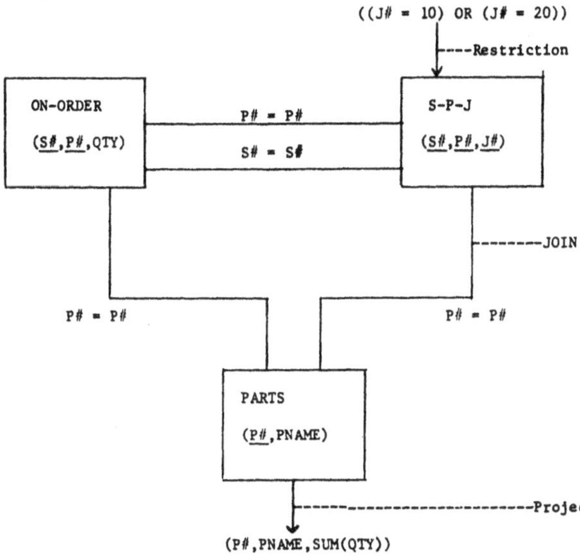

Fig. 1. Example query 1.

TABLE I

Relation R_i	Size s_i	$d_{i1} = P\#$ b_{i1}	p_{i1}	$d_{i2} = S\#$ b_{i2}	p_{i2}
R_1: ON-ORDER	1000	400	0.4	100	0.2
R_2: *S-P-J*	2000	400	0.4	450	0.9
R_3: PARTS	3000	900	0.9	–	–

b) To minimize *total time*, apply Algorithm SERIAL to each simple query. This results in one schedule per simple query. From these schedules, the candidate schedules for each joining attribute are extracted. Consider joining attribute d_{ij}. Its candidate schedule is identical to the schedule produced by Algorithm SERIAL, applied to the simple query in which d_{ij} occurs, up to the transmission of d_{ij}. All transmissions after that are deleted from the schedule.

3) *Integrate the candidate schedules.* For each relation R_i, the candidate schedules are integrated to form a processing schedule for R_i. The integration is done by procedure RESPONSE for response time minimization and by procedure TOTAL or procedure COLLECTIVE for total time minimization.

4) *Remove schedule redundancies.* Eliminate relation schedules for relations which have been transmitted in the schedule of another relation.

Algorithm GENERAL derives a query processing strategy for either response time or total time minimization by using the procedures RESPONSE, TOTAL, and COLLECTIVE.

A. Response Time Version

To minimize the response time of a relation R_k, we have to test whether transmitting an attribute d_{ij} to R_k is cost beneficial. Therefore, we have to know how long it takes to get d_{ij} to the site where R_k is located. Algorithm PARALLEL derives minimum response time schedules for joining attributes. In fact, there is no procedural difference between computing the minimum response time schedules for joining attributes whether they are sent to a result node or the node where R_k is located. Therefore, in step 2 of Algorithm GENERAL, Algorithm PARALLEL is applied to each joining attribute individually to compute a minimum response time schedule for each. All these candidate schedules are saved for integration by procedure RESPONSE.

Procedure RESPONSE

1) *Candidate schedule ordering.* For each relation R_i, order the candidate schedules on joining attribute $d_{ij}, j = 1, 2, \cdots, \sigma$ in ascending order of arrival time. Let ART_l denote the arrival time of candidate schedule CSCH_l. (For the d_{ij} joining attributes not in R_i, disregard the corresponding candidate schedules.)

2) *Schedule integration.* For each candidate schedule CSCH_l in ascending order, construct an integrated schedule for R_i that consists of the parallel transmission of CSCH_l and all CSCH_k with $k < l$. Select the integrated schedule with minimum response time.

Applying Algorithm GENERAL (response time) to the previous example, after the initial processing, two simple queries are formed, one having $d_{i1} = P\#$ as a common joining attribute and the other having $d_{i2} = S\#$. Running Algorithm PARALLEL on the $P\#$ query, the resulting candidate schedules are

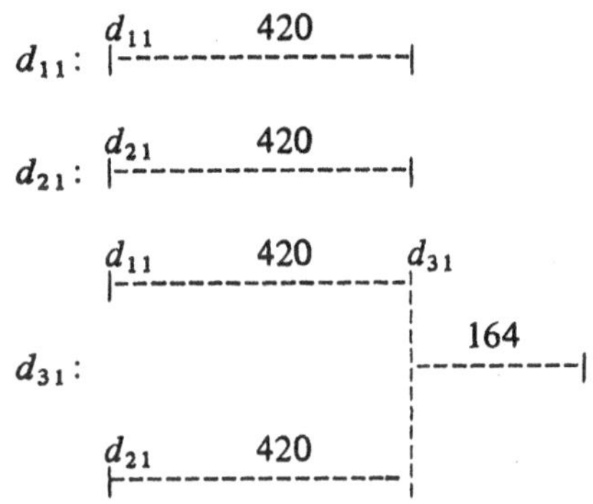

Applying Algorithm PARALLEL to the $S\#$ query, the candidate schedules are

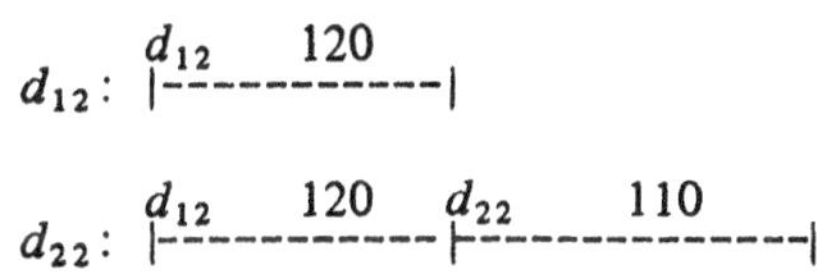

The construction of the schedule for R_1 will be given in detail. In step 1 of Procedure RESPONSE, the schedules of attributes that can be applied to relation R_1 are ordered on their arrival time in the node where R_1 is located. This gives the following result:

Attribute d_k	Arrival Time ART_k
d_{22}	330
d_{21}	420
d_{31}	584

In step 2, for each of these attributes d_k, an integrated schedule for R_1 is constructed, consisting of the parallel transmission of all attributes having an arrival time less than or equal to ART_k. The following three integrated schedules are constructed:

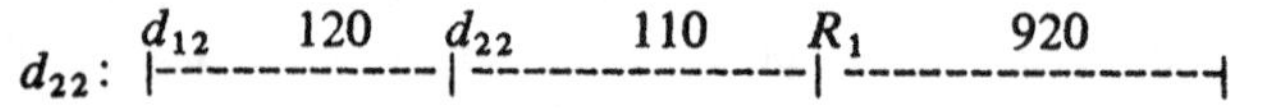

$$\text{Response time} = C(100) + C(0.2 * 450) + C(0.9 * 1000) = 120 + 110 + 920 = 1150.$$

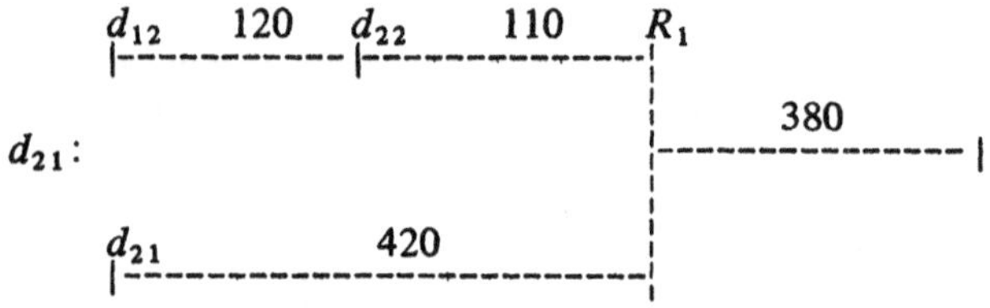

$$\text{Response time} = C(400) + C(0.9 * 0.4 * 1000) = 420 + 380 = 800.$$

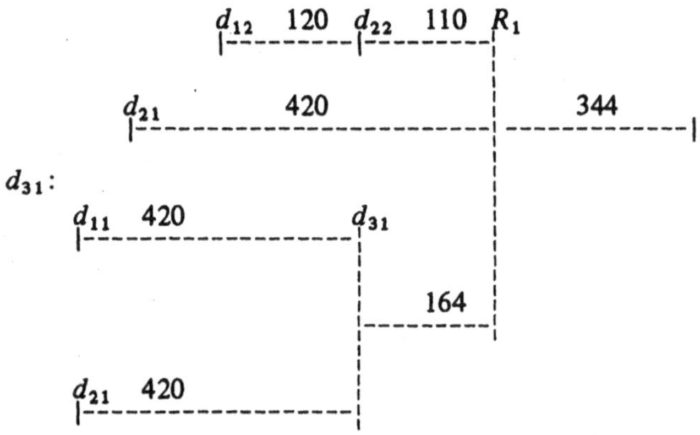

$$\text{Response time} = C(400) + C(0.4 * 0.4 * 900) + C(0.9 * 0.4 * 0.9 * 1000) = 420 + 164 + 344 = 928.$$

From these three schedules for R_1 and the Initial Feasible Solution for R_1, the schedule with the minimum response time is chosen. This is the second schedule and its response time is 800.

The schedules for R_2 and R_3 are constructed in a similar way. The Algorithm GENERAL (response time) query processing strategy for the example query is

A comparison to the response time of the IFS shows a considerable cost reduction.

Procedure RESPONSE is given the minimum response time schedules of all joining attributes. In step 2 of Algorithm GENERAL, Algorithm PARALLEL is applied to σ different simple queries. Therefore the minimum response time schedules for one common joining attribute are given in order of response time. This means that putting the candidate schedules in order of arrival time will take at most $O(\sigma m \log_2 \sigma)$, which is the merging complexity.

In step 2 of Algorithm GENERAL, Algorithm PARALLEL is applied σ times and its complexity is $O(m^2)$. However, the cost of applying procedure RESPONSE for every relation R_i is $O(\sigma m^2 \log_2 \sigma)$. Therefore, the complexity of Algorithm GENERAL (response time) is $O(\sigma m^2 \log_2 \sigma)$.

Now we will investigate the quality of the derived schedules. The schedules produced by algorithm PARALLEL for the joining attributes have a minimum response time. From this fact, we now can prove that each relation schedule has a minimum response time and, consequently, that the total query processing strategy has a minimum response time. Implicit within our proofs, we require the model assumption of attribute independence within each relation. Initial studies indicate that the effect of this assumption on the performance of the resulting query processing strategies may not be significant [20].

Theorem 1: Procedure RESPONSE derives a minimum response time integrated schedule for R_i.

Proof: The candidate schedules used in procedure RESPONSE are all minimum response time schedules because of the optimality of Algorithm PARALLEL [13]. Procedure RESPONSE puts these candidate schedules in ascending order of arrival time, and it only considers integrated schedules for relation R_i that consist of the parallel transmission of joining attributes with arrival time less than or equal to the arrival time of a certain CSCH_k. We will show that no other integrated schedule needs to be considered.

Assume that we are given a minimum response time schedule for R_i. This schedule contains the transmissions of some joining attribute which arrives last (i.e., has the greatest value of ART_k in the schedule). The corresponding integrated schedule (based on ART_k as the largest ART value) considered

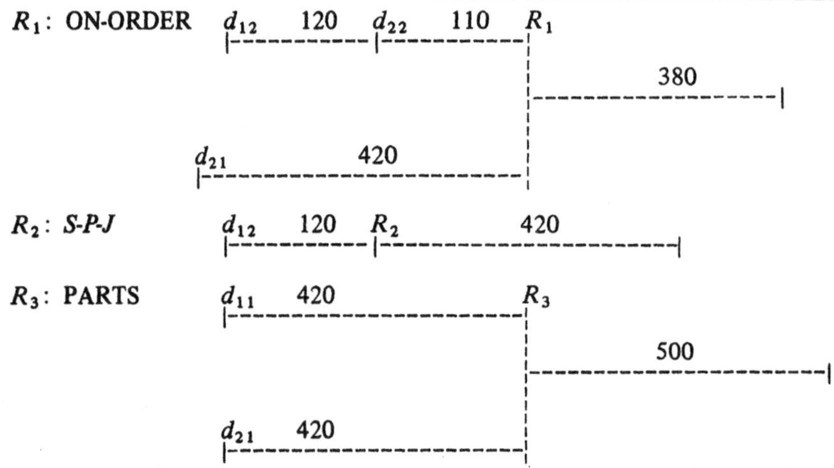

Response time = 920. Total time = 2910.

by procedure RESPONSE contains at least as many transmissions of joining attributes as the previous schedule and, therefore, its selectivity is at least as small. Hence, its response time must be less than or equal to that of the minimum response time schedule.

Theorem 2: Algorithm GENERAL (response time) derives a minimum response time processing strategy for any distributed query.

Proof: The response time of a processing strategy is the maximum response time of the relation schedules in the strategy. Theorem 1 showed that these relation schedules have minimum response time. Hence, the theorem follows.

B. Total Time Version

The motivation for using the minimization of the total time as the objective of Algorithm General comes from the use of the algorithm in a multiprocessing environment. Minimizing response time leads to an increased number of parallel data transmissions in the query processing strategy. In multiprocessing systems, under moderate to heavy loads, these extra transmissions may lead to significant queueing delays and synchronization delays, delays which may cause poor query response time. By minimizing the total time in a query processing strategy, fewer transmissions will be included and improved actual response times may result in certain system environments.

The candidate schedules produced in step 2 of Algorithm GENERAL (total time) look very much like the schedules produced by Algorithm SERIAL. Algorithm SERIAL produces minimum total time schedules for simple queries. In its optimality proof [14], it is shown that parallel transmissions of common joining attributes can be avoided. Therefore, we will do the same in Algorithm GENERAL (total time). Only parallel transmissions of *different* joining attributes are allowed. This means that in constructing a schedule for relation R_i, we will consider only one candidate schedule per joining attribute of R_i. This candidate schedule will be the one that minimizes the total time of transmitting R_i if only that one joining attribute is considered.

In [1], it was shown that it is not sufficient to just look at the candidate schedules produced in step 2 of Algorithm GENERAL. For every candidate schedule *to* relation R_i containing a transmission of a joining attribute *from* the same relation R_i, we have to add another candidate schedule, namely, one without the transmission of this joining attribute. This is necessary since the size of relation R_i cannot be reduced by the selectivity of its own attribute. Thus, this data transmission in the incoming schedule may not be cost beneficial. Among this extended set of candidate schedules, we select the schedule which minimizes the total time of transmitting R_i if only one joining attribute is considered. This selected schedule for relation R_i considering joining attribute d_{ij} will be called BEST_{ij}.

We define SLT_{ij} to be the accumulated attribute selectivity of the BEST_{ij} candidate schedule into R_i. Note that j may take on values from 1 to σ only if the common joining attributes d_{ij} appear in R_i.

Procedure TOTAL

1) *Adding candidate schedules.* For each relation R_i and each candidate schedule CSCH_l, do the following.

If this schedule contains a transmission of a joining attribute of R_i, say d_{ij}, then add another candidate schedule which is the same as CSCH_l except that the transmission of d_{ij} is deleted.

2) *Select the best candidate schedule.* For each relation R_i and for each joining attribute $d_{ij}(j = 1, 2, \cdots, \sigma)$, select the candidate schedule which minimizes total time for transmitting R_i if only the joining attributes are considered which can be joined with d_{ij}.

3) *Candidate schedule ordering.* For each relation R_i, order the candidate schedules BEST_{ij} on joining attributes d_{ij}, $j = 1, 2, \cdots, \sigma$, so that $\text{ART}_{i1} + C(s_1 * \text{SLT}_{i1}) \leqslant \cdots \leqslant \text{ART}_{i\sigma} + C(s_i * \text{SLT}_{i\sigma})$. (For the joining attributes not in R_i, disregard BEST_{ij}.) ART_{ij} denotes the arrival time of the BEST_{ij} schedule.

4) *Schedule integration.* For each BEST_{ij} in ascending order of j, construct an integrated schedule to R_i that consists of the parallel transmission of candidate schedule BEST_{ij} and all schedules BEST_{ik} where $k < j$. Select the integrated schedule that results in the minimum total time value

$$\text{TOTT}_i = \sum_{k=1}^{j} \left[\text{ART}_{ik} + C\left(s_i * \prod_{k=1}^{j} \text{SLT}_{ik}\right)\right].$$

Applying Algorithm GENERAL (total time) to the example, two simple queries are formed on the following joining attributes, $d_{i1} = P\#$ and $d_{i2} = S\#$ in the example query. In step 2 of Algorithm GENERAL (total time), the following serial candidate schedules are formed.

For $P\#$,

```
      d11    420
d11:  |-----------|

      d11    420    d21    180
d21:  |-----------|-----------|

      d11    420    d21    180    d31    164
d31:  |-----------|-----------|-----------|
```

For $S\#$,

```
      d12    120
d12:  |-----------|

      d12    120    d22    110
d22:  |-----------|-----------|
```

Again, the construction of the schedule for R_1 will be discussed in detail. We will treat the two attributes of R_1 in turn.

Attribute d_{11}

In step 1 of Procedure TOTAL, the following two schedules are added to the above schedules for $P\#$. The first one is obtained by deleting the transmission of d_{11} from the schedule for d_{21}, and the second one by deleting d_{11} from the schedule for d_{31}:

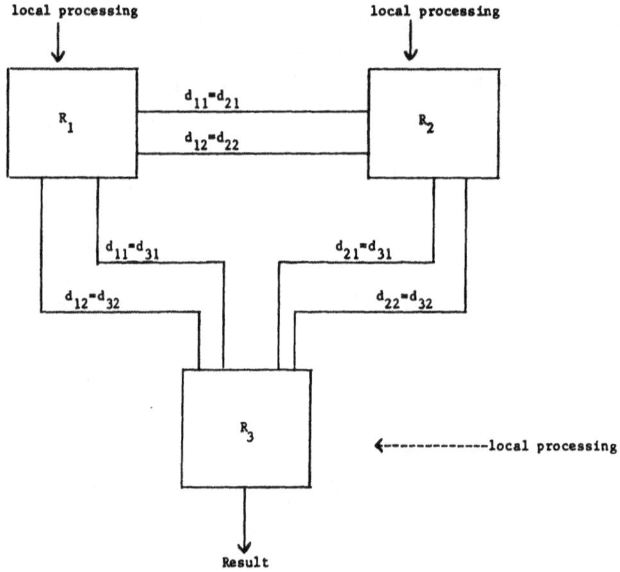

Fig. 2. Example query 2.

d_{21}^1: d_{21} 420 |————|

d_{31}^1: d_{21} 420 |————| d_{31} 380 |————|

Thus, there are five schedules that only contain transmissions of the $P\#$ attribute. Four of them will be tested. The transmission of d_{11} to R_1 is meaningless as a schedule.

TABLE II

Relation R_i	Size s_i	d_{i1} b_{i1}	d_{i1} p_{i1}	d_{i2} b_{i2}	d_{i2} p_{i2}
R_1	1000	300	0.6	300	0.25
R_2	2000	100	0.2	900	0.75
R_3	2000	400	0.8	600	0.5

d_{21}: d_{11} 420 |————| d_{21} 180 |————| R_1 420 |————|

Total time = $C(400) + C(0.4 * 400) + C(0.4 * 1000)$
= 420 + 180 + 420
= 1020.

d_{31}: d_{11} 420 |————| d_{21} 180 |————| d_{31} 164 |————| R_1 380 |————|

Total time = $C(400) + C(0.4 * 400) + C(0.4 * 0.4 * 900) + C(0.4 * 0.9 * 1000)$
= 420 + 180 + 164 + 380
= 1144.

d_{21}^1: d_{21} 420 |————| R_1 420 |————|

Total time = $C(400) + C(0.4 * 1000)$
= 420 + 420
= 840.

d_{31}^1: d_{21} 420 |————| d_{31} 380 |————————————| R_1 380 |————|

Total time = $C(400) + C(0.4 * 900) + C(0.4 * 0.9 * 1000)$
= 420 + 380 + 380
= 1180.

Because the schedule of d_{21}^1 has the smallest total time, it is chosen as the BEST_{11} schedule.

Attribute d_{12}

In step 2 of Procedure TOTAL, only one schedule is added to the above schedules for attribute $S\#$.

d_{22}^1: d_{22} 470 |————|

Each of the schedules for $S\#$ is applied to R_1. Again, transmitting d_{12} to R_1 is not considered.

```
       d12    120    d22     110    R1         920
d22:  |-----------|-----------|-----------------|
```

Total time $= C(100) + C(0.2 * 450) + C(0.9 * 1000)$
$= 120 + 110 + 920$
$= 1150.$

```
       d22          470              R1    920
d22^1: |-----------------------------|-----------|
```

Total time $= C(450) + C(0.9 * 1000)$
$= 470 + 920$
$= 1390.$

Because the schedule of d_{22} has the smallest total time, it is chosen as the BEST_{12} schedule.

In steps 3 and 4 of the Procedure TOTAL, the above obtained BEST_{1j} schedules are ordered on their total time, and the following two integrated schedules are constructed:

```
d21    420                  R1            420
|---------------------------|---------------------|

d21    420                  R1
|---------------------------|
                            |
                            |            380
                            |--------------------|
                            |
         d12   120   d22 110|
         |-----------|------|
```

The first of these two has the smallest total time; it is chosen as the solution of Algorithm GENERAL for R_1.

The schedules for R_2 and R_3 are constructed in a similar way. The Algorithm GENERAL (total time) query processing strategy for the example query is

```
R1: ON-ORDER   d21       420      R1      420
               |----------------|----------------|

R2: S-P-J      d12     120    R2     420
               |-----------|-----------|

R3: PARTS      d11       420      d21  180  R3        500
               |----------------|---------|-------------------|
```

Response time = 1100. Total time = 2480.

The total time of this strategy is considerably smaller than the total time of the IFS. Also, the response time of its strategy for the example query is not much larger than the response time of the strategy produced by the response time version of Algorithm GENERAL, although it only tries to minimize total time.

Algorithm GENERAL (total time) has a slightly better worst case complexity than the response time version, $O(\sigma m^2)$. Again, assume that a general query requires data from m relations, and all m relations are joined on σ joining attributes. In step 2, algorithm SERIAL is applied to each simple query. The complexity of this is $O(\sigma m \log_2 m)$ because the joining attributes have to be ordered by size.

The complexity of the procedure TOTAL is $O(\sigma m^2)$. In step 1, no more than $O(\sigma m)$ candidate schedules are added. This means that for every relation, the procedure has to determine the BEST_{ij} schedule among $O(\sigma m)$ candidate schedules. Hence, the cost of step 2 is $O(\sigma m^2)$. This means that for an arbitrary general distributed query, Algorithm GENERAL (total time) has a processing complexity no worse than $O(\sigma m^2)$.

The quality of the resulting query processing strategies is much harder to analyze than those for minimizing response time. The BEST_{ij} schedules were shown to be the best possible schedules for minimizing the total transmission time of relation R_i if only one common joining attribute is considered [1]. However, the optimality is lost during the integration of the different BEST_{ij} schedules. In [13], it was shown that finding the minimum total time schedule is equivalent to a problem which is proved to be NP-hard.

C. Handling Redundant Data Transmissions

A major reason why the query processing strategy derived by Algorithm GENERAL (total time) is not optimal is that procedure TOTAL does not consider the existence of redundant data transmissions in separate relation schedules. (Note that such redundant transmissions between relation schedules do not effect the minimum response time strategies of Section III-A. This is because Algorithm GENERAL (response time) minimizes the response time of each relation schedule separately.)

This example illustrates the benefit of redundant data transmissions. A database contains three relations: R_1, R_2, and R_3. The query represented by Fig. 2 is entered in a distributed database system wherein each relation is located at a separate node and the result of the query is required at a different node.

The sizes and selectivities for each d_{ij}, after local processing, are given in Table II. Assume the cost function for the system to be $C(X) = 25 + X$.

By applying Algorithm GENERAL (total time) to this example query (the derivation appears in the Appendix), the resulting processing strategy is

```
d21     125    R1     225
|-----------|-----------|

d12     325          d32     175    R2          275
|----------------|-----------|----------------|

d21     125    d11     85     R3  265
|-----------|-----------|----------------|
```

Total time = 1600.

The first redundant transmission one can clearly recognize is the transmission of the attribute d_{21} towards R_1. This transmission will physically take place only once, so its cost (125) should be accounted for only once as well. We might visualize this removal as follows:

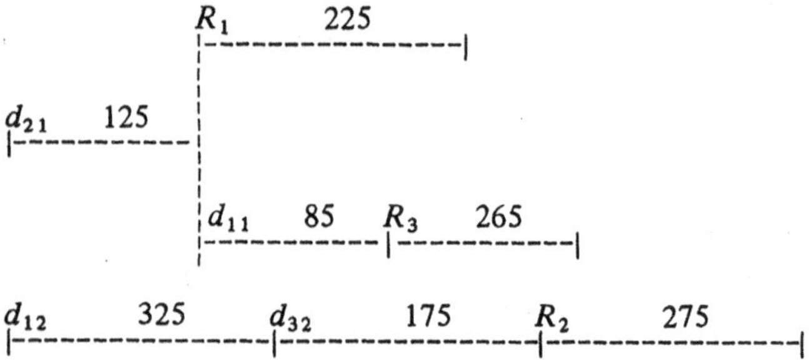

Total time = 1475.

Apart from this type of direct transmission redundancy, it is possible to discern a somewhat more complicated type. It might happen that the transmission of d_{ij} towards the node of R_k is part of some schedule, while it does not occur in the schedule of R_k itself. Because the values of this attribute d_{ij} are available for a semi-join with R_k, it seems fair enough to assume that this semi-join will actually take place, and that the cost for the final transmission of R_k will subsequentially decrease. In such a case, it is clear that R_k cannot be transmitted before all attributes have arrived, which means that the schedule must be synchronized. This could lead to an increased response time. In our example, we can also detect such a case.

In the R_2 schedule, d_{12} is sent to d_{32}. So d_{12} is available for R_3, although it is not part of the R_3 schedule. The final transmission of R_3 will only cost $C(0.6 * 0.2 * 0.25 * 2000) = 85$ instead of 265. Again we try to illustrate this:

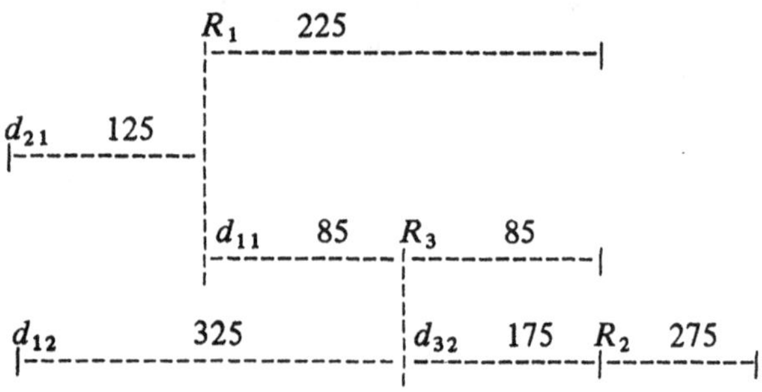

Total time = 1295.

(Note that R_3 can be sent at time $t = 325$, instead of at time $t = 210$.)

As these aspects are not considered during the selection of the final schedules, a few beneficial strategies will not be found by Algorithm GENERAL (total time). This is mainly due to the characteristic that a best schedule is separately chosen for each relation, without regarding the "collective" benefits. It means that for some R_k, a schedule might be just too expensive and thus rejected, while it had many transmissions in common with selected schedules of other relations, and thus would have been a very good choice for the strategy as a whole.

In order to test the above statements, we developed an alternative version of Algorithm GENERAL (total time) called Algorithm GENERAL (collective), completely based on redundant transmissions. It is simpler in that it constructs only one basic strategy for the entire query, after which a few variations are tried out. The schedules of the basic strategy include as many semi-joins as possible for each relation. This tends towards a large number of redundant transmissions. The investments for such an extended integrated schedule are shared, as it were, by all R_k. The strategy is then perturbed by subsequentially trying to drop schedule components (i.e., linear parts of an integrated schedule) for some relation R_k, and finally to drop such a component, which actually stands for the semi-joins on one particular attribute, from the entire strategy.

Algorithm GENERAL (collective) performs step 2b) in Algorithm GENERAL. The candidate schedule integration is performed in step 3 by the following procedure.

Procedure COLLECTIVE

1) *Select candidate schedule.* For each relation R_i and for each joining attribute $d_{ij}(j = 1, 2, \cdots, \sigma)$, select the minimum cost candidate schedule that contains the transmission of all components of attribute j with selectivities <1.

2) *Build processing strategy.* For each relation R_i, define the schedule to be the parallel transmission of all d_{ij} candidate schedules to R_i.

3) *Test variations of strategy.* Using a removal heuristic, derive new strategies by removing the most costly data transmissions. Compare the total time cost of the new and old strategies. Maintain the less costly strategy. Continue testing until no cost benefit can be obtained.

Consider the state of the relations R_1, R_2, and R_3 in Table III after local processing for the query in Fig. 3. The transmission cost function is $C(X) = 10 + X$.

The schedule components for the three attributes are

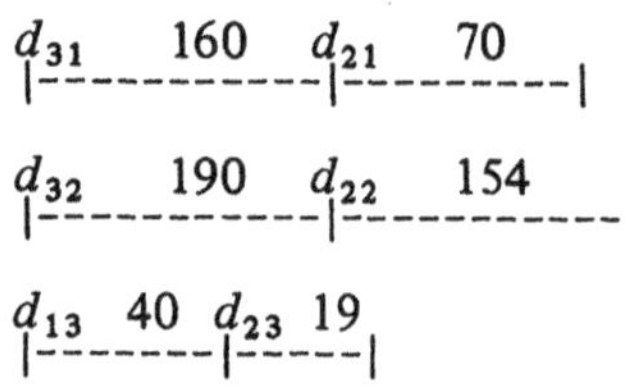

leading to the basic strategy (integrating as much as possible)

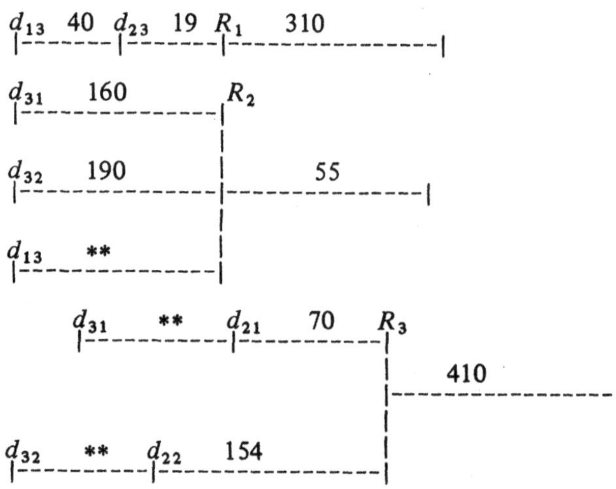

Total Time = 1408.

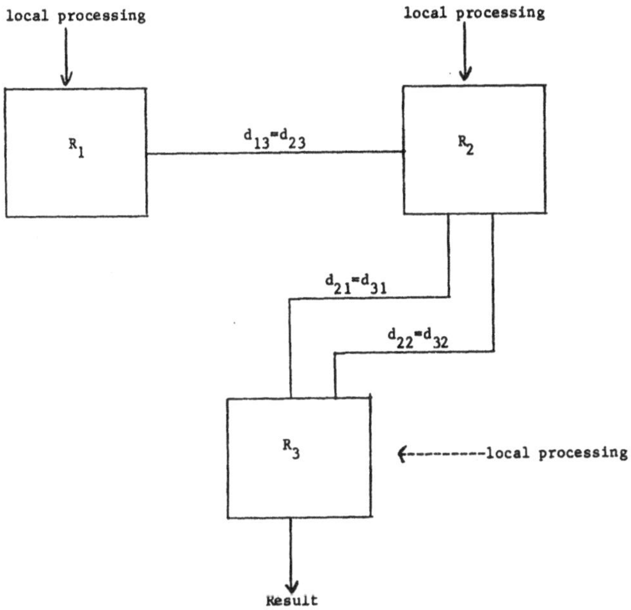

Fig. 3. Example query 3.

TABLE III

Relation R_i	Size s_i	d_{i1} b_{i1}	d_{i1} s_{i1}	d_{i2} b_{i2}	d_{i2} s_{i2}	d_{i3} b_{i3}	d_{i3} s_{i3}
R_1	1000	–	–	–	–	30	0.1
R_2	2500	200	0.4	240	0.8	90	0.3
R_3	1250	150	0.3	180	0.6	–	–

(Here ** stands for transmissions, which are already accounted for.)

During the variation trials, it turns out that it is beneficial to drop the component of attribute 2 from the schedule for R_3. This saves 154 time units, while the cost for the transmission of R_3 will increase: $C(0.4 * 1250) = 510$. Together this means a gain of 54. In the second variation round, it is found that it is better to leave out the component of attribute 2 at all relations.

Thus, the final solution of the "COLLECTIVE" algorithm for this example is

```
d13   40    d23   19   R1    310
|-----  -----|---------|-------------|

d31      160       R2
|---------------|
                |       85
                |----------------|
d13    **       |
|---------------|

d31    **        d21   70   R3    510
|----------------|---------|-----------------|
```

Total time = 1194.

Algorithm GENERAL (collective) has the same worst case complexity as Algorithm GENERAL (total time) since the complexity of procedure COLLECTIVE is $O(\sigma m^2)$. In step 1, for every relation (m possibilities) and for every joining attribute (σ possibilities), the desired candidate schedule must be selected from m possible schedules. The optimization of step 3 is a greedy heuristic procedure with linear order.

For a significant number of queries, the collective version of Algorithm GENERAL will produce a smaller total time strategy than will the total time version. Such improvement is due to the recognition and inclusion of redundant data transmissions among separate relation schedules in the overall query processing strategy.

IV. Conclusions

We claim Algorithm GENERAL to be an efficient algorithm of polynomial complexity that derives close to optimal query processing strategies on distributed systems. The algorithm was designed as a straightforward extension of the processing tactics found optimal for simple queries in Algorithm PARALLEL and Algorithm SERIAL.

There are two primary versions of Algorithm GENERAL. To minimize response time of a processing strategy, parallel data transmissions are emphasized by the use of Algorithm PARALLEL and Procedure RESPONSE. Algorithm GENERAL (response time) can be proved to derive minimum response time strategies under the assumption of attribute independence within query relations. To minimize the total time of a processing strategy, serial time transmissions are emphasized by the use of Algorithm SERIAL and Procedure TOTAL in Algorithm GENERAL (total time).

Recognizing the existence of identical data transmissions in different relation schedules may lead to a further reduction in the total time of a query processing strategy. We develop a third version of Algorithm GENERAL (collective) that uses Algorithm SERIAL and Procedure COLLECTIVE to produce strategies with increased data transmission redundancy among schedules. In many cases, the total time of these strategies is less than the total time of strategies produced by Algorithm GENERAL (total time).

Algorithm GENERAL can be applied to any general distributed query environment. It is relatively simple to program and has the added flexibility that all versions can be implemented together. Then, depending upon run-time factors, such as system load or query complexity, the optimization objective can be changed by a simple switch in the program.

Appendix

The derivation of the query processing strategy using Algorithm GENERAL (total time) on the database state found in Table II proceeds as follows.

Two simple queries are formed on the joining attributes d_{i1} and d_{i2}. In step 2 of Algorithm GENERAL (total time), the following serial candidate schedules are formed.

For attribute d_{i1}:

```
d11:  d21       125       d11   85
      |--------------|---------|

d21:  d21       125
      |--------------|

d31:  d21       125       d11   85      d31   73
      |--------------|----------|--------|
```

For attribute d_{i2}:

```
d12: d12    135
     |--------------|

d22: d12    325       d32   175            d22  137
     |--------------|---------------|----------|

d32: d12    325       d32   175
     |--------------|---------------|
```

Entering Procedure TOTAL, the $BEST_{i1}$ and $BEST_{i2}$ schedules are determined as follows:

the linear schedules (i.e., the first in the $BEST_{ij}$ ordering) are the cheapest solutions. Thus, our strategy will be

```
d21   125   R1     225
|-----------|-------------|

d12   325          d32   175   R2   275
|---------------|-----------|-------------|

d21   125   d11   85   R3    265
|-----------|-----------|-------------|
```

Total Time = 1600

	Total Time:
`d21 125 R1 225` `|-----------|----------------|`	→ 350
`d21 125 d11 85 d31 73 R1 185` `|-----------|-----------|-----------|-----------|`	→ 568
`d21 125 d31 105 R1 185` `|-----------|----------|---------------|`	→ 415

The first schedule becomes our $BEST_{11}$.

For $BEST_{12}$, we have to choose among

`d12 325 d32 175 R1 525` `|---------------|-----------|---------------|`	→ 1025
`d12 325 d32 175 d22 137 R1 400` `|---------------|-----------|-----------|-----------|`	→ 1037
`d32 625 R1 525` `|--------------------|-----------------|`	→ 1150
`d32 625 d22 425 R1 400` `|--------------------|-----------|----------|`	→ 1450

The first schedule thus will be our $BEST_{12}$.

In the same way, we find

$BEST_{21}$:	`d21 125 d11 85 d31 73 R2 985` `|-----------|---------|-------------|---------------|`	→ 1268
$BEST_{22}$:	`d12 325 d32 175 R2 275` `|--------------|---------|-------------|`	→ 775
$BEST_{31}$:	`d21 125 d11 85 R3 265` `|-----------|--------|-------------|`	→ 475
$BEST_{32}$:	`d12 325 R3 525` `|--------------|----------------|`	→ 850

By now we can determine the solution for each R_i.

For example, for R_1, there are two possibilities, which are

I)

```
d21   125   R1    225
|-----------|------------|                          → 350
```

and

II)

```
                              d21    125
                              |-------------|
                                            |R1    125
                                            |-------------|   → 750
d12   325            d32     175            |
|---------------|-------------|
```

We conclude that the first schedule is superior.

For the other relations, it also (coincidentally) turns out that

References

[1] P. M. G. Apers, "Critique on and improvement of Hevner and Yao's distributed query processing algorithm G," Vrije Univ., Amsterdam, The Netherlands, IR 48, Feb. 1979.

[2] —, "Distributed query processing: Minimum response time schedules for relations," Vrije Univ., Amsterdam, The Netherlands, IR 50, Mar. 1979.

[3] C. Baldissera, G. Bracchi, and S. Ceri, "A query processing strategy for distributed data bases," in *Proc. EURP-IFIP 79*, 1979, pp. 667-678.

[4] P. A. Bernstein and D. W. Chiu, "Using semi-joins to solve relational queries," *J. Ass. Comput. Mach.*, vol. 28, Jan. 1981.

[5] P. A. Bernstein, N. Goodman, E. Wong, C. L. Reeve, and J. Rothnie, "Query processing in a system for distributed databases (SDD-1)," *ACM Trans. Database Syst.*, vol. 6, Dec. 1981.

[6] D. Chiu and Y. Ho, "A methodology for interpreting tree queries into optimal semi-join expressions," in *Proc. ACM SIGMOD Conf.*, Santa Monica, CA, 1980.

[7] W. W. Chu and P. Hurley, "A model for optimal processing for distributed databases," in *Proc. 18th IEEE COMPCON*, Spring 1979, pp. 116-122.

[8] E. F. Codd, "A relational model of data for large shared data banks," *Commun. Ass. Comput. Mach.*, vol. 13, pp. 377-387, June 1970.

[9] R. Epstein, M. R. Stonebraker, and E. Wong, "Distributed query processing in a relational data base system," in *Proc. ACM-SIGMOD*, May 1978, pp. 169-180.

[10] R. Epstein and M. Stonebraker, "Analysis of distributed data base processing strategies," in *Proc. Int. Conf. Very Large Data Bases*, Montreal, P.Q., Canada, 1980.

[11] N. Goodman and O. Shmueli, "Hierarchies of database state reductions," Aiken Computation Lab., Harvard Univ., Cambridge, MA, Tech. Rep. TR-18-80, 1980; also, *ACM Trans. Database Syst.*, to be published.

[12] A. R. Hevner and S. B. Yao, "Query processing in distributed database systems," in *Proc. 3rd Berkeley Workshop on Distributed Data Management and Comput. Networks*, Berkeley, CA, 1978.

[13] A. R. Hevner, "The optimization of query processing on distributed database systems," Ph.D. dissertation, Database Syst. Res. Cen., Dep. Comput. Sci., Purdue Univ., W. Lafayette, IN, Rep. DB-80-02, Dec. 1979.

[14] A. R. Hevner and S. B. Yao, "Processing in distributed database systems," *IEEE Trans. Software Eng.*, vol. SE-5, pp. 177-187, May 1979.

[15] A. R. Hevner, "Data allocation and retrieval in distributed systems," in *Advances in Database Management, Vol. II*, P. Fisher, Ed. New York: Wiley, 1983.

[16] L. Kershberg, P. Ting, and S. B. Yao, "Query optimization in a Star network," Bell Lab. Tech. Rep., 1979; also, *ACM Trans. Database Syst.*, to be published.

[17] N. G. Toan, "Decentralized dynamic query decomposition for distributed database systems," in *Proc. ACM Pacific Conf.*, San Francisco, CA, 1980.

[18] G. Pelagatti and F. A. Schreiber, "Evaluation of transmission requirements in distributed database access," in *Proc. ACM SIGMOD Conf.*, Boston, MA, 1979.

[19] G. M. Sacco and S. B. Yao, "Query optimization in distributed database systems," in *Advances in Computers, Vol. 21*. New York: Academic, 1982.

[20] P. G. Selinger, M. M. Astrahan, D. D. Chamberlin, R. A. Lorie, and T. G. Price, "Access path selection in a relational database management system," in *Proc. ACM SIGMOD Conf.*, Boston, MA, 1979.

[21] M. Stonebraker and E. Neuhold, "A distributed version of INGRES," in *Proc. 2nd Berkeley Workshop Distributed Data Management and Comput. Networks*, May 1977, pp. 19-36.

[22] M. Takizawa, "Operational query decomposition algorithm in distributed databases," Japan Inform. Processing Develop. Cen. Rep. TR80/2, 1980.

[23] E. Wong and K. Youssefi, "Decomposition–A strategy for query processing," *ACM Trans. Database Syst.*, vol. 1, Sept. 1976.

[24] E. Wong, "Retrieving dispersed data from SDD-1: A system for distributed databases," in *Proc. 2nd Berkeley Workshop Distributed Data Management and Comput. Networks*, May 1977, pp. 217-235.

[25] Z. Ozsoyoglu, "Query processing in distributed relational databases," Ph.D. dissertation, Univ. Alberta, 1980.

Peter M. G. Apers, photograph and biography not available at the time of publication.

Alan R. Hevner received the Ph.D. degree in computer science in 1979 from Purdue University, West Lafayette, IN.

He is currently an Assistant Professor of Information Systems at the University of Maryland, College Park. His research interests include database systems design, distributed database systems, database performance evaluation, and office information systems.

Dr. Hevner is a member of the Association for Computing Machinery and the IEEE Computer Society. He is an Associative Editor of *Database Engineering*, a publication of the IEEE Technical Committee on Database Engineering. He edited the December 1982 special issue of that publication on current research on distributed database systems.

S. Bing Yao received the Ph.D. degree from the University of Michigan, Ann Arbor, in 1974.

He is currently an Associate Professor of Business Management and Computer Science and is Director of the Database Systems Research Group at the University of Maryland, College Park. He is involved in the design and implementation of several database management systems and tools including XQL, a relational database system. He has authored over 50 technical papers on database storage structures, database performance optimization, database design, distributed database systems, database machines, and office automation. He is Editor of *Data Base Design Techniques* (Springer-Verlag, 1982) and *Principles of Data Base Design* (Prentice-Hall, 1982). He is founder of Software Systems Technology, a computer form specializing in database systems and machines. His international consulting clients include Bell Laboratories, IBM, and the Swedish Technical Development Board. He is an Editor of the *ACM Transactions on Office Information Systems*, is on the Editorial Board of the *ACM Transactions on Data Systems*, was Program Chairman of the 4th International Conference on Very Large Data Bases and the NYU Symposium on Database Design, and is the Conference Chairman of the 9th International Conference on Very Large Data Bases.

Optimization of Nested Queries in a Distributed Relational Database

Guy M. Lohman†, Dean Daniels‡, Laura M. Haas†, Ruth Kistler†, Patricia G. Selinger†

†IBM Almaden Research Center
‡Carnegie-Mellon University

1. Abstract

This paper describes how nested queries in the SQL language are processed by R*, an experimental adaptation to the distributed environment of the well-known centralized relational DBMS, System R. Nested queries are queries in which a predicate references the result of another query block (SELECT...FROM...WHERE...), called a subquery block (subQB). SubQBs may themselves contain one or more subQBs. Depending upon whether a subQB references values in other query blocks, it is processed differently, as either an Evaluate-at-Open or Evaluate-at-Application subQB type. Three tasks comprise execution of each query block: initiation, evaluation, and application. When the query's tables are distributed among multiple sites, optimization of nested queries requires determining for each subQB: the site to perform each task, the protocols controlling interactions between those tasks, and the costs of each option, so that a minimal-cost plan can be chosen. R* optimizes each query block independently, "bottom up", using only the cost, cardinality, and result site of the subQB in the optimization of its containing query block.

2. Introduction

One of the principal advantages of relational query languages is that they are "closed" in the mathematical sense, i.e. that the result of a query against one or more relations (tables) is itself a relation and referenceable in another query. Some relational query languages, such as SQL [SQL] permit this nesting of one query within another as a single, unified query. This nesting of queries permits the specification of very complex queries in a structured way that aids understanding by the user and optimization of the nested queries as a unified whole. For example, the following query retrieves the names of all employees assigned to the (presumably unique) shipping department located in Denver[1]:

```
SELECT E.NAME                              QB 1
FROM   EMPLOYEES E
WHERE  E.DEPT =                                    (A)
  (SELECT D.DEPT#                          QB 2
   FROM   DEPARTMENTS D
   WHERE  D.LOCATION = 'DENVER'
     AND  D.NAME = 'SHIPPING'  );
```

Each SELECT...FROM...WHERE... sequence is called a **query block** (hereafter abbreviated QB). Query blocks are numbered in the order in which they are specified, and are referred to by number throughout this paper. The QB within the parentheses in (A) above (QB 2) returns a single DEPT# of DEPARTMENTS that has LOCATION = 'DENVER' and NAME = 'SHIPPING', and this (single) value is then substituted as though it were a literal for the right-hand side of the E.DEPT predicate that will be used to test each instance of the EMPLOYEES table. While this same query may be expressed without nested queries as:

```
SELECT E.NAME                              QB 1
FROM   EMPLOYEES E, DEPARTMENTS D                  (B)
WHERE  E.DEPT = D.DEPT#
  AND  D.LOCATION = 'DENVER'
  AND  D.NAME = 'SHIPPING';
```

not all nested queries may be so transformed without changing the semantics that are implicit in the nested query structure, and it may not be optimal to do so (e.g., evaluate-at-open QBs need be evaluated less often, as discussed in Section "3.2. Types of Nested Queries" below). In addition, the nested form is often easier for the user to formulate and to understand. Finally we wished to maintain compatibility in R* with as much of System R's SQL as possible. It was for these reasons that we implemented nested queries in R*.

There has been very little discussion of nested queries in the literature on query optimization, and virtually no discussion on nested query optimization for distributed databases (e.g., [EPST 78], [YAO 79], [EPST 80], [NGUY 80], [BERN 81], [CHU 82], [KAMB 82], [KERS 82], [APER 83], [CHAN 83], [YU 83], etc.). Selinger [SELI 79] discusses the internal processing of nested que-

1 Table qualifiers are added to column names in the examples for clarity only: they are required in SQL only to resolve ambiguity. Similarly, indentation of QBs is not required but done here only for readability.

ries in the (centralized) DBMS System R, particularly the order of execution of QBs within a nested query, and how values are passed between QBs. Only Kim [KIM 82] addresses the optimization of nested queries. His goal is to transform nested queries into a single QB involving joins, as was done in Examples (A) and (B) above, in order to utilize existing join optimization techniques for a single-site database. However, he does not consider the consequences of these transformations when tables that are involved in the query are stored in different databases.

This paper discusses the optimization of *distributed* nested queries in the distributed database management system R*, a prototype distributed DBMS that was developed and implemented at IBM San Jose Research Laboratory [HAAS 82, WILL 82, LOHM 85]. The terminology, types, and execution tasks of nested queries are introduced in Section 2. In Section 3, the problems of optimizing nested queries against a distributed database are contrasted with those of centralized databases. Section 4 provides a detailed description of how sites are selected for the three major tasks in nested query processing. The lower-level protocols between processes performing these tasks, and the cost estimates of each, are presented in Section 5. Section 6 suggests some further refinements to minimize the traffic between sites, for certain types of distributed nested queries. Section 7 discusses some difficulties encountered while implementing nested queries in R*. Section 8 concludes with a summary of the current status of, and future plans for, the R* optimizer.

To avoid lengthy reviews, we assume that the reader is familiar with the relational database model, the relational query language SQL [SQL], and System R [ASTR 76, BLAS 81, CHAM 81b]. As in System R, query compilation -- of which optimization is a part -- is essential to efficient R* execution of SQL queries that are embedded in an application program [CHAM 81a]. The R* optimizer has been adapted from the System R optimizer [SELI 79] to permit tables referenced in a single query to reside at distinct sites. And as in System R, for each QB in the query, the optimizer enumerates all "reasonable" combinations of alternative access paths to an individual table (e.g., via an index scan or relation scan) and join methods (i.e., nested-loop and merge join), incrementally adding tables and permuting the order in which tables are joined while avoiding joins that require a Cartesian product. Intermediate alternatives that produce identical results (i.e., the same set of tuples at the same site in the same order) are compared, and only the one with minimal cost is retained [LOHM 85]. In R*, costs have been extended to include a linear combination of the number of inter-site messages and the length of inter-site messages, as well as the System R cost components of CPU (number of instructions executed) and I/O (pages accessed) [DANI 82, LOHM 85]. Including site processing costs as well as inter-site communication costs has been justified based upon an analysis of the relative costs of actual communications, disk, and CPU resources consumed for typical queries [SELI 80], and distinguishes R* optimization from most other distributed database optimizers [LOHM 85].

Examples used to illustrate this paper are drawn from the following simplified database of three tables:

```
EMPLOYEES( EMP#,NAME,SAL,MGR,DEPT,HIREDATE,JOB# )
DEPARTMENTS( DEPT#,LOCATION,NAME,MANAGER )
JOBS( JOB#,TITLE )
```

Each employee has a (unique) identifying employee number, a name, salary, the employee number of his manager, the (unique) identifying number of his department, his date of hire, and the (unique) number of his job. Each department has a (unique) number, location, name, and the employee number of its manager. Each job classification has a (unique) number and name associated with it.

3. Nested Queries

3.1. Nomenclature

The fundamental syntactic structure of the SQL query language is the query block (hereafter abbreviated as **QB**):

```
SELECT select-list
FROM   from-list
<WHERE  predicate>
```

The SELECT-list is a list of expressions involving columns of tables that are contained in the FROM-list, and the optional predicate contains one or more simple Boolean predicates. A **nested predicate** is a simple predicate that takes any one of the following three forms:

```
col-expr OP query-block
EXISTS      query-block
NOT EXISTS  query-block
```

where "col-expr" is an expression involving zero or more columns, and OP may be a scalar comparison operator (=, ¬=, <, <=, >, >=), a set membership operator (IN, NOT IN), or a set comparison operator (OP ALL or OP ANY, where OP is a scalar comparison operator). Scalar comparison operators require that the QB evaluates to a single value, whereas set operators allow the QB to return one or more values [SQL]. A query containing one or more nested predicates is referred to as a **nested query**, and the QB in the predicate is called a **subquery block (subQB)** or **nested query block** of the containing or **parentQB** whose predicate formed the nesting.[2]

A subQB may itself have nested predicates, so that QBs may be nested to a (theoretically) arbitrary level. Also, a QB may have several subQBs, but only one parentQB. Hence the parentQB/subQB relationship forms a tree, the root of which is the first QB. The first QB and all of its descendant subQBs will be referred to collectively as one **query**.

3.2. Types of Nested Queries

If a subQB contains a reference in its predicate to a column from some table in the FROM-list of one of its ancestor QBs, then it is said to be **correlated** to that ancestor by that column. The subQB must be re-evaluated for each candidate value of the correlated column in the ancestor QB. A subQB that is correlated to its parentQB is referred to as an **evaluate-at-application (EAA)** subQB,[3] because the subQB must be newly evaluated for each application of the predicate in the parentQB that contains that

2 Note that this use of the term "subquery" is different from that of [WONG 76] and [ONUE 83], in which a "subquery" may be any isolatable step in the execution of the query, i.e., that has at most one column in common with the rest of the query.

subQB. Re-evaluation is necessary because the correlation changes the results of the subQB. This re-evaluation must be done before the correlated subQB's parentQB predicate can be tested for acceptance or rejection of the candidate tuple [SELI 79]. For example, consider the following query to retrieve all employees who work in Denver and are managers of their department:

```
SELECT E.NAME                              QB 1
FROM   EMPLOYEES E
WHERE  E.DEPT IN                                    (C)
   (SELECT D.DEPT#                         QB 2
    FROM   DEPARTMENTS D
    WHERE  D.LOCATION = 'DENVER'
    AND    D.MANAGER = E.EMP#    );
```

For each candidate row of the EMPLOYEES table, the EMP# value is used for evaluating QB 2. The result is a set of DEPARTMENTS that is then used to test the "E.DEPT IN" predicate.

If, on the other hand, a subQB and all of its descendant QBs are not correlated to any tables in the FROM-list of its parentQB, then it is called an **evaluate-at-OPEN (EAO)** subQB, because absence of references to values from its parentQB's tables permit it to be evaluated at the time of OPEN (when it begins processing) of its parentQB or one of its ancestor QBs. For example, suppose the correlating predicate (D.MANAGER = E.EMP#) in query (C) above were removed:

```
SELECT E.NAME                              QB 1
FROM   EMPLOYEES E
WHERE  E.DEPT IN                                    (D)
  (SELECT D.DEPT#                          QB 2
   FROM   DEPARTMENTS D
   WHERE  D.LOCATION = 'DENVER');
```

QB 2 (on DEPARTMENTS) can be evaluated *once* upon OPEN of QB 1 (on EMPLOYEES), and the resulting set of department numbers (DEPT#) can be stored temporarily for use in evaluating the nested predicate of QB 1 for each EMPLOYEE.

If a QB, J, is correlated to an ancestor QB other than its immediate parentQB, i.e. is separated from the QB to which it is correlated by one or more intermediate QBs, then QB J may be evaluated-at-OPEN of the "highest" (in terms of ancestry) of the intermediate QBs. For example:

```
SELECT E.NAME                              QB 1
FROM   EMPLOYEES E
WHERE  E.SAL >
  (SELECT AVG(F.SAL)                       QB 2
   FROM   EMPLOYEES F                               (E)
   WHERE  F.DEPT IN
     (SELECT D.DEPT#                       QB 3
      FROM   DEPARTMENTS D
      WHERE  D.LOCATION = 'DENVER'
      AND    D.MANAGER = E.EMP#    ) );
```

Here evaluation of the last QB (QB 3) requires a specific value for E.EMP# (from the EMPLOYEES table of QB 1). Since QB 3 contains no references to any tables in QB 2, it is evaluated once for each new QB 1 candidate tuple from EMPLOYEES, but not for every QB 2 candidate tuple from EMPLOYEES. So QB 3 is correlated to QB 1 by column E.EMP#, but is an EAO QB because it is evaluated at OPEN time of processing QB 2.

A QB, J, acquires the correlations of all of its subQBs, even if they are evaluated at QB J's OPEN, because those correlations change the value of some of QB J's predicates (those containing the correlated subQBs). If any of QB J's subQBs are correlated to QB J's parentQB, then QB J must be EAA. For example, in query (E) above, QB 2 is correlated to QB 1 because its child (QB 3), which is EAO of QB 2, must be re-evaluated for each new value of E.EMP#, and that may alter the right-hand-side of the "F.DEPT IN..." predicate. Hence QB 2 must be EAA. If we were to remove the correlating predicate, "D.MANAGER = E.EMP#", in QB 3, then both QB 2 and QB 3 would be EAO.

For more examples and a detailed discussion of how subQBs are processed in a centralized database, see [SELI 79].

3.3. Tasks in SubQB Execution

Processing any subQB requires three successive tasks:

1. **Initiation:** detects that a predicate is eligible to be evaluated; provides from ancestor QBs any values for correlated columns that are needed for that evaluation; and, for EAO QBs only, causes a temporary relation to be created on disk in which to store the set of results returned by the evaluation step.

2. **Evaluation:** uses the values provided by initiation to evaluate the subQB, and returns the results to the application step. Note that this may involve processing one or more subQB sequences.

3. **Application (Parent):** uses the results to apply the predicate to candidate tuples in the parentQB.

For EAO subQBs, initiation and evaluation are performed once (at OPEN of the QB at whose OPEN it can be evaluated, i.e., the parentQB or an ancestor QB), and application is repeated once per candidate tuple of the parentQB by simply reading the results from the temporary relation. For EAA QBs, initiation and application are always performed within the parentQB, and all three steps are repeated for each candidate tuple of the parentQB.

4. Optimization of Nested Query Blocks

4.1. Dependencies Between Query Blocks

When all tables in the query are at a single site, optimization of a nested query is fairly simple, because optimization of a subQB does not depend upon that of its parentQB, and optimization of the parentQB depends upon that of its subQBs in a very limited way. Three attributes of a subQB might affect the cost of evaluating its parentQB: the subQB's estimated cost, its estimated cardinality, and the order of its result. The first, the subQB's cost, affects the parentQB's cost because the cost of a subQB's evaluation contributes

---

3 [SELI 79] and [SQL] refer to this as a "correlated subquery", but as we shall see in query (E) below, a QB must be correlated to its *parentQB* to be of this type.

to the cost of evaluating the parentQB. The second attribute, the subQB's cardinality, affects the parentQB's cost because each subQB predicate restricts which tuples satisfy the parentQB, so the estimated cardinality of the subQB is used to estimate the selectivity of the predicate containing that subQB. Thirdly, the order of a subQB is important because, if the column on the left-hand-side of the nested predicate is in a particular order, and the subQB is EAA, we could save re-evaluating the subQB each time the same column value occurred. However, System R (and the distributed database management system, R*) ignores the limited possible savings of enforcing such an ordering[4], so that the parentQB can be optimized once an estimate has been made for the cost and for the number of values returned by each of its subQBs. Thus, QBs in a query may be optimized independently, starting with the most nested QB and working "bottom up" through the family tree of QBs, with each subQB passing to its parentQB an estimate of its cost and the number of values that it returns.

For a nested query in a *distributed* database, the major difficulty posed in optimizing it is that we can no longer optimize its QBs independently in a simple bottom-up fashion, passing up only each subQB's cost and cardinality. This is because the choice of sites at which the QB result is materialized introduces another dependency between QBs, *in addition to* the ones relevant in a centralized database. Specifically, the site to which a subQB delivers its result -- its **delivery site** -- must necessarily be the site to which the predicate containing the subQB is applied -- its **application site**. Since the predicate involves tables belonging to the parentQB, selection of the application site must be decided during optimization of the *parentQB*, and thus is not yet known when the *subQB* is being optimized. Ideally we would optimize QB 1 to deliver its result to the site to which the query was submitted (the **master site**), and its optimization would dictate the site at which each of its subQBs would be applied, and so on. However, this "top-down" processing conflicts with the "bottom-up" dependence of QB optimization upon the cardinality and cost estimates of its subQBs, as described in the previous paragraph.

R* resolves this "top down" versus "bottom up" dependency conflict by postponing selection of the delivery site of a subQB until its parentQB has been optimized. The optimizer essentially keeps its delivery site options open as it optimizes each QB, permitting it once again to optimize QBs bottom up. The result of optimizing each QB, S, is a number of candidate plans, each the best plan to deliver S's result to its "natural" result sites, plus a "to-be-determined-later" site (these are defined below). Then, during optimization of S's parentQB, P, each candidate plan for P determines an application site to which S's result should be delivered and uses the best plan for S to deliver its result to that application site. We say that the parentQB **resolves** the postponed decision on the delivery site of its subQB, once it chooses an application site in this way. The process of generating all possible site options, and selecting the best one for each QB, will be discussed in more detail in Section "5. Site Selections for Nested QBs".

4.2. Master vs. Apprentice Planning

When a query references objects such as tables or views at multiple sites, compilation (and optimization) involves multiple sites. In R*, the site to which the query is submitted and any site having a table or view involved in a query must participate in the planning process for that query as the master or an apprentice. The site to which the query was originally presented, the master site, is responsible for developing a global plan containing all *inter-site* decisions, including the site at which all operations (especially, joins) are to be performed, the method of join, the order in which the tables/composites are joined, and the required order of the result [DANI 82, LOHM 85]. For nested queries, the master site also decides the site at which subQBs are to be applied (which dictates the site to which its results should be delivered) and initiated, as will be described in detail in Section "5. Site Selections for Nested QBs" below.

All other sites participating in the compilation of a query compile it as an **apprentice site**. Compilation by each apprentice site is initiated by receiving from the master site a copy of the global plan and the original query, which it re-parses. Each apprentice must (1) find the portions of the global plan that are relevant to it, and (2) develop a local plan for itself within the constraints imposed upon it by the global plan. It does this by traversing the global plan and re-creating its own version of the global plan, using the global plan for direction on inter-site matters and for making some shortcuts [DANI 82, LOHM 85]. For example, the apprentice uses the global plan to decide at which sites to apply subQBs, and thus the site at which each subQB is to deliver its result. So, unlike the master planner, the apprentice can choose the optimal plan for a QB to result at the dictated site only, and need not "keep its options open". This significantly streamlines apprentice planning.

An apprentice site is granted latitude in planning decisions affecting only its tables (e.g., alternative access paths, join methods, and permutations of *its* tables to join). The only decision involving nested queries over which the apprentice retains jurisdiction is deciding the order in which to apply multiple subQBs that the master dictates should be applied at that site, subject to the requirement that all correlated columns have values when their predicates are applied. Therefore, because the interesting decisions for QBs is at which site they are applied and initiated, we will be concerned only with master planning for the remainder of this paper.

5. Site Selections for Nested QBs

This section describes the master's procedure for determining at which site(s) to perform the three tasks -- initiation, evaluation, and application -- involved in executing each subQB in a query statement, in order to minimize the total cost of executing the entire query statement. In a distributed query, each of these three tasks may be executed at different sites, depending upon where the tables referenced in that query are stored, and where the master's optimizer chooses to join tables, apply predicates, etc. (see [DANI 82]). Each task may be executed by one or more processes, as follows:

1. **Initiation** usually requires only a single process, which we will call the **initiator**. In cases where the initiator's site is different from the applier's site (discussed below), initiation also requires some work to be done at the applier's site. The initiator spawns an agent process, called INIT′, to perform this work

4 See Section "7.1. Exploit ParentQB's Order" for more discussion of this decision.

(see Section "6. Evaluation Protocols and Costs" for more detailed protocols between sites).

2. **Evaluation** may require any number of processes. However, all of these processes are subordinate to a single, first process that OPENs processing of the QB and that receives the final results of the QB, i.e., the **result site** of that QB. This "chief process of the QB" is the only process with which the initiator and applier process interact, and will be referred to as the **evaluator** process.

3. **Application** never requires more than one process, called the **applier**.

We now discuss in more detail how the procedure chooses the sites for the evaluator, applier, and initiator processes, in that order.

5.1. Evaluator's Site Selection

The evaluator's (delivery) site is chosen from the "natural" result sites of that QB, plus a "to-be-determined-later" site, as described below.

5.1.1. Result Sites

To join two tables at different sites, R* generates candidate plans to perform the join at three different sites [DANI 82, LOHM 85]:

```
(J1) the inner table's site,
(J2) the outer table's site, and
(J3) an unknown site (or, more accurately,
     a "to-be-determined-later" site,
     designated here as "??".
```

To illustrate, consider the following distributed version of the query of example (B):

```
SELECT E.NAME
FROM   EMPLOYEES@SF E, DEPARTMENTS@NY D
WHERE  E.DEPT = D.DEPT#                          (F)
  AND  D.LOCATION = 'DENVER'
  AND  D.NAME = 'SHIPPING';
```

where table EMPLOYEES@SF is stored at site SF and table DEPARTMENTS@NY is stored at site NY.[5] When DEPARTMENTS@NY is the outer table and EMPLOYEES@SF is the inner table of the join in a candidate plan, then the three different site options for performing this join would be:

```
(J1) Ship DEPARTMENTS@NY to SF
     and join at SF (result site = SF).
(J2) Ship EMPLOYEES@SF to NY
     and join at NY (result site = NY).
(J3) Ship EMPLOYEES@SF and DEPARTMENTS@NY to
     some other site, ??, and join them there.
```

If this query originated in SF, option (J1) is likely to be optimal, whereas option (J2) would be favored by a query originating in NY. The third option is generated in case the query originated at some third site, say LA, or in case the result of the join is to be joined later with a third table at another site, perhaps KC. At the time EMPLOYEES@SF and DEPARTMENTS@NY are joined, however, the possible third sites are not yet known. So the third join site is left "to be determined later".

By generating all combinations of inner and outer tables, R* will generate a distinct optimal plan for a QB to result at each site having one or more tables in the FROM-list of that QB, or in the FROM-lists of its descendant QBs, plus site ??. We call sites other than ?? the **natural result sites** for a QB.

5.1.2. Resolving the Evaluation Site of a QB

Once the delivery site X of a subQB is chosen by the parentQB (as described earlier), we say that its evaluation site is **resolved** (to be X). From the set of all plans for the subQB, each of which result at one of the subQB's result sites as described above, R* picks the cheapest of the following three candidates for the best plan to deliver the subQB's result to X:

```
(P1) The best plan to result at site X.
     (This option is viable only if site
     X is a natural result site of the subQB.)
(P2) The best plan that results at ??,
     where ?? is replaced by X.
(P3) The best overall plan for the subQB,
     independent of result site, shipped
     from its natural result site, Y,
     to the dictated delivery site, X.
```

As discussed above, the delivery site for QB 1 is the site at which the query was presented (the master site), and the delivery site for any other QB is the application site chosen by its parentQB. We next discuss how this choice is made.

5.2. Application Site Selection

As each table in the parentQB is retrieved and joined to the outer table (or composite of outer tables), columns are added to the parentQB composite tuple that may be needed to apply the subQB's predicate. A predicate therefore becomes **eligible** for application only when the last table containing columns referenced by the predicate is joined to the composite as the inner table. So, for a given choice of a (possibly composite) outer table and an inner table, one or more subQB predicates may become eligible. The problem is at which site(s) should they be applied? Deciding this determines (resolves) the desired delivery site for that subQB.

5.2.1. Application Site Options

A subQB may ultimately be applied, i.e., used to evaluate the predicate of which it is a part, at sites other than its natural result sites. The application site is decided by the subQB's parentQB, which has to consider the interactions between sites at which its tables are located and possibly the natural result sites of its other subQBs. In this section, we discuss which sites are reasonable sites for the parentQB to consider applying nested predicates.

Consider the following variation of example query (F) having a subQB (QB 2), in which the two tables of QB 1 and the one table of QB 2 are each at different sites:

---

5 The site name embedded in the table name does *not* change, even if the table is moved to another site. The current store site of each table and its name agree here *only for expository reasons*. See [LIND 81] for a complete description of R* table-naming conventions.

```
SELECT E.NAME                                    QB 1
FROM   EMPLOYEES@SF E, DEPARTMENTS@NY D
WHERE  E.DEPT = D.DEPT#
  AND  D.LOCATION = 'DENVER'
  AND  D.NAME = 'SHIPPING'
  AND  E.JOB# =                                   (G)
    (SELECT J.JOB#                               QB 2
     FROM   JOBS@LA
     WHERE  J.TITLE = 'CLERK');
```

This query requests the names of all employees that are clerks and work in the shipping department in Denver. Note that the predicate containing QB 2 becomes eligible with the addition of table EMPLOYEES@SF, because its column E.JOB# is referenced in that predicate.

For any given set of tables already joined as composite C and any given table T in the parentQB, J, the procedure considers three (possibly redundant) classes of application sites for a subQB K whose predicate becomes eligible for application only when table T is joined to the set:

(A1) Site of table T
(A2) Site of any partial or final computation for QB J (e.g., a join between outer composite C and inner table T, or delivery of QB J's final result, or application of another subQB to QB J).
(A3) SubQB K's possible result sites (natural + ??)

with the following qualifications:

- Option (A1) is viable only if the nested predicate containing subQB K references only columns of table T (or none at all) and columns of tables in QBs that are ancestors of QB J. Table T could be any table (inner or outer) in a join. For example, the predicate containing QB 2 in example query (G) references only EMPLOYEES@SF, so option (A1) is viable when EMPLOYEES@SF is table T.

- Options (A2) and (A3) apply the predicate to the result of joining T to C (if C is not empty) before any final computations for ordering or grouping QB J's result.

- Option (A3), when applied to a plan for QB J with result site ??, will cause the ?? to be replaced by subQB K's result site (which might also be ??).

- Redundant application site options are not re-evaluated. For example, if the join site is the inner site (i.e., for option (J1)) and if the predicate references only the inner table, then options (A1) and (A2) are equivalent: only one of the two options need be evaluated. Similarly, subQB result sites that have already been covered by options (A1) or (A2) are redundant.

For our example query (G) above, when (again) table DEPARTMENTS@NY is the outer table and EMPLOYEES@SF is the inner table and our table T of interest, options (J1) through (J3) have the following sub-options for applying the predicate that contains QB 2:

(J1) Join site = SF (i.e., ship DEPARTMENTS@NY to SF)
  - (A1) Apply subQB predicate to EMPLOYEES@SF before join
  - (A2) Apply subQB predicate at SF (same as (A1))
  - (A3) Apply subQB predicate at subQB's result sites =
    - (R1) LA (i.e., ship composite after join to LA, then apply)
    - (R2) ?? (i.e., ship composite after join to ??, then apply)

(J2) Join site = NY (i.e., ship EMPLOYEES@SF to NY to join)
  - (A1) Apply subQB predicate to EMPLOYEES@SF before shipping it to NY for join
  - (A2) Apply subQB predicate at join site = NY
  - (A3) Apply subQB predicate at subQB's result sites =
    - (R1) LA (i.e., ship composite after join to LA, then apply)
    - (R2) ?? (i.e., ship composite after join to ??, then apply)

(J3) Join site = ?? (ship both DEPARTMENTS@NY and EMPLOYEES@SF to ??)
  - (A1) Apply subQB predicate to EMPLOYEES@SF before shipping it to ?? to join
  - (A2) Apply subQB predicate at join site = ?? (i.e., do every- thing at site ??)
  - (A3) Apply subQB predicate at subQB's result sites =
    - (R1) LA (fill in ?? to be LA, i.e., do everything at LA)
    - (R2) ?? (redundant of option (J3)-(A2) above)

Option (J1)-(A2) is equivalent to (J1)-(A1) in this example because the predicate containing QB 2 references only the inner table (EMPLOYEES@SF), and we always apply predicates as soon as they become eligible (i.e., there is nothing to gain by waiting to apply the predicate to the composite after the join). Note also that option (J3)-(A3)-(R1) could be derived by setting ?? = LA in option (J3)-(A2).

The above options and suboptions are exhaustive and may all be reasonable possibilities, depending upon the sizes of the tables and the ratio of intra-site costs (CPU and I/O) to communications costs.

For this example, the natural result sites for each QB are as follows:

```
QB 2: LA
QB 1: NY, SF, LA
```

Note that optimization of QB 1 is likely to choose a delivery site for QB 2 that is not one of its natural result sites, in which case the ?? plan for QB 2 will be used.

5.2.2. Applying SubQB Predicates Simultaneously

Two subQBs that have the same parentQB *and* that reference one or more columns of the same table(s) in the ancestor QBs become eligible to be applied simultaneously. In such cases, order of application of these subQBs is unimportant, unless one subQB is sufficiently more restrictive than the other *and* we choose an option that ships the composite to both of the subQBs' (different) result sites. In that case, the more restrictive predicate is applied first to reduce the volume of data shipped between the two subQB result sites.

5.3. Initiation Site Selection

For EAA subQBs, selection of the applier's site necessarily selects the initiator's site, since by definition they must be the same. Thus, selection of the applier's site chooses a single plan for that subQB.

For EAO subQBs, however, the initiator and the applier may have different sites and even different QBs. The site at which an EAO subQB K is initiated is the delivery site of the QB at whose OPEN QB K is initiated. So, for any given plan for the initiating QB, its delivery site dictates the initiator's site for each EAO subQB, thus choosing a single, optimal plan for it.

5.4. Summary of Global Optimization

An overview of the algorithm for global optimization of distributed nested queries is given in Figure 1. The portions newly introduced for nested queries are shown in bold italics.

6. Evaluation Protocols and Costs

The protocols between sites and the cost for evaluating a QB depends upon: (a) whether an individual subQB is EAA or EAO, and (b) in the latter case, whether the initiator's site and the applier's site are chosen to be the same. A discussion of the protocols between sites and the evaluation costs for each of the three possible cases follows.

6.1. Evaluate-at-Application SubQB

This is the simplest case, because initiation and application always take place at the same point in the parentQB, and therefore at the same site, with only evaluation of the subQB intervening (refer to Figure 2 and Figure 3). So both the initiator and applier processes

```
FOR EACH query block, H (bottom up):

  Generate tree of possible subsets of tables of H
  FOR EACH subset of tables:

    Generate tree of possible plans
    FOR EACH possible plan:

      FOR set of ALL subQBs of H eligible simultaneously:

        Generate tree of subQB application sites
        FOR EACH set of subQB application sites:
          FOR EACH subQB J in the set:

            FOR EACH subQB K of QB J
              IF subQB K is Evaluated-at-OPEN of QB J
              THEN
                Resolve initiation site of subQB K
                Add cost of initiating and evaluating subQB K to cost of QB J
            Find best plan for subQB J to be delivered to dictated application
              site for subQB J (i.e., resolve application site for subQB J)
            Record best plan in plan for QB H
            Add costs of applying subQB J to costs of QB H
            IF subQB J is Evaluate-at-Application
            THEN add costs of initiating and evaluating subQB J to costs
              of QB H
        Find plan for QB H with a matching site & result order
        IF new plan cheaper
        THEN retain new plan

  Add sorts for GROUP BY, ORDER BY, etc., if needed
  Pick best plan resulting at each result site of QB H (natural and ??).

FOR TOP query block (QB 1):

  FOR EACH result site of QB 1 (i.e., for each plan for QB 1):

    FOR EACH subQB L in plan:
      IF subQB L is Evaluated-at-OPEN of QB 1
      THEN
        Resolve initiation site of subQB L to be master's site
        Add cost of initiating and evaluating subQB L to cost of QB 1

  Find best plan for delivery to master's site (resolve result site of QB 1)
  Distribute master plan to apprentices
  Generate access structures to perform plan (see [LOHM 85]).
```

Figure 1: Algorithm for Optimizing Nested Queries in R*

belong to the parentQB, QB J. For each candidate tuple in the parentQB J, site A sends to the evaluator at site B the values of all correlated columns for that tuple, and prepares to receive back the result. The evaluator receives the correlation values, evaluates the subQB K, and returns a single-valued result to site A. EAA QBs that might return multiple values (those QBs having a set membership or set comparison OP in the predicate containing that QB) can be transformed during optimization into an equivalent QB that returns only a single value -- EXISTS or NOT EXISTS (see Section 6.5 below). The initiator receives the result and passes it to the applier, which applies the results in the predicate and either accepts or rejects the candidate tuple.

The estimated cardinality and cost of evaluating QB K and delivering it to the applier at site A for each tuple of the parentQB (J) is obtained by dictating that QB K deliver its result to site A. This resolves the evaluator's site for QB K, yielding an optimal plan for QB K. Its cost, multiplied by the estimated cardinality of QB J, gives the total cost to apply this subQB in QB J. This total cost is added into the cost associated with all candidate plans for QB J that dictate delivering QB K to site A.

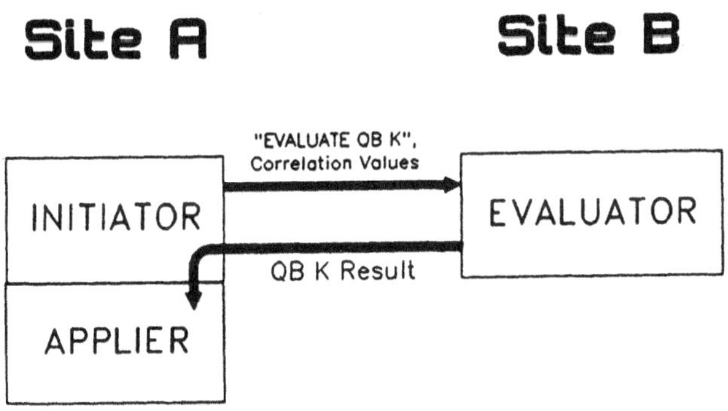

Figure 2: Evaluate-at-Application (EAA) subQB.

FOR EACH tuple of QB K's parentQB, QB J:

(1) Initiation: Initiator initiates Evaluator of QB K at Site B:

(1.1) Initiator detects eligibility of QB K's predicate
(1.2) Initiator sends values of correlated variables to Evaluator

(2) Evaluation: Evaluator evaluates QB K and returns results to Initiator at Site A, who passes them to Applier.

(3) Application: Applier applies results immediately in predicate in QB J that contains QB K

Note: Site A and Site B may be the same.

Figure 3: Procedure for Evaluate-at-Application (EAA) subQB.

6.2. Evaluate-at-Open SubQB, Applier's Site = Initiator's Site

EAO subQBs are initiated once, evaluated once at that time, and then sometime later applied repeatedly, once for each candidate tuple to which the predicate applies (refer to Figure 4 and Figure 5). In fact, as we saw in example query (E) above, initiation and application may (but need not) take place in different QBs. So the initiator process and applier process may belong to different QBs.

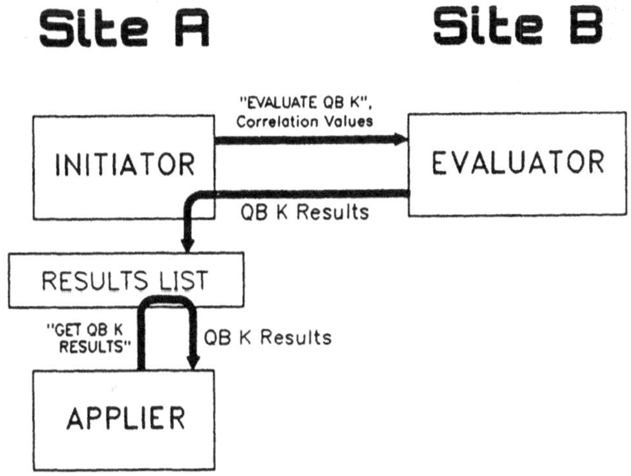

Figure 4: Evaluate-at-OPEN (EAO) subQB, Initiator's site = Applier's site.

(1) Initiation: Initiator initiates Evaluator at Site B:

(1.1) Initiator's OPEN triggers initiation of QB K processing
(1.2) Initiator creates a temporary relation to accept result(s) of QB K
(1.3) Initiator sends values of correlated variables, if any, to Evaluator at Site B

(2) Evaluation: Evaluator at Site B evaluates QB K:

(2.1) Evaluator evaluates QB K
(2.2) Evaluator returns result(s) to Initiator
(2.3) Initiator stores result(s) in temporary relation created in Step (1.2), enabling Application at a later time

(3) Application: FOR EACH tuple in QB K's parentQB, QB J, the predicate containing QB K is applied:

(3.1) Applier detects eligibility of QB K's predicate
(3.2) Applier reads QB K result(s) from temporary relation
(3.3) Applier applies predicate to its candidate tuple

Note:

- Site A and Site B may be the same.
- Initiator must be the first computation within its QB

Figure 5: Procedure for Evaluate-at-OPEN (EAO) subQB, Initiator's site = Applier's site.

For this case, however, we assume that the initiator and applier are at the same *site* (site A), even if they belong to different QBs. Recall that the initiator's site is defined to be the delivery site of the QB at whose OPEN the subQB is initiated.

At OPEN of the initiating query block, QB I, the initiator starts evaluation of QB K at site B by the evaluator, and receives back the results, which the initiator stores in a temporary relation at site A. Later, when the predicate containing QB K is encountered and needs to be applied, the applier process retrieves the results from the temporary relation to use in applying the predicate, once for each candidate tuple.

The cost of evaluating QB K and of shipping correlation values from A to B and subQB K's results from B to A is incurred only once: a significant savings. However, there are additional costs at site A for storing the result in the temporary relation and for reading from that relation each time. And because a temporary relation is not indexable in R*, retrieval from it cannot be in order or subsetted by a predicate without scanning the relation until the desired value is found. For purposes of optimization, the applier (QB J) is assessed only the cost of reading one half of the temporary table (on the average) N times, where N is the cardinality of QB J. The cost of initiating and evaluating QB K, and writing its results in the temporary relation at site A, is assessed to the initiator (QB I), not the applier. The reason that this cost assessment is different from that for EAA subQBs will become apparent when we contrast this case with case 3 below.

6.3. Evaluate-at-Open SubQB, Applier's Site ≠ Initiator's Site

It may happen that the initiator's site of an EAO query is not the same as the applier's site, in which case two sites are involved in initiation, as shown in Figure 6. Here site C is responsible for initiating the evaluation of QB K, but will not receive the results. So steps (1.2) and (1.3) of case 2 must be augmented into steps (1.2) through (1.4), as shown in Figure 7. The initiator INIT spawns an agent process at site A, called INIT′ in Figure 6 and Figure 7, which performs the usual functions of the initiator de-

Figure 7: Procedure for Evaluate-at-OPEN (EAO) subQB, Initiator's site ≠ Applier's site.

(1) Initiation: Initiator at Site C (INIT) initiates QB K at Site B:

- (1.1) INIT's OPEN triggers initiation of QB K
- (1.2) INIT sends values of correlated variables, if any, to an agent process, INIT′, that it spawns at Site A
- (1.3) INIT′ creates temporary relation to accept result(s) of QB K
- (1.4) INIT′ forwards values of correlated variables, if any, to Evaluator at Site B

(2) Evaluation: Evaluator at Site B evaluates QB K:

- (2.1) Evaluator evaluates QB K
- (2.2) Evaluator returns result(s) to INIT′ at Site A
- (2.3) INIT′ stores result(s) in temporary relation that was created in Step (1.3)
- (2.4) INIT′ acknowledges proper completion to INIT at Site C, enabling Application at a later time

(3) Application: FOR EACH tuple in QB J, predicate containing QB K is applied:

- (3.1) Applier detects eligibility of QB K's predicate
- (3.2) Applier reads QB K result(s) from temporary relation
- (3.3) Applier applies predicate to its candidate tuple

Note:

- Only Steps (1.2),(1.4), and (2.4) are different from case of Figure 4.
- Site A and Site B may be the same.
- When Site C = Site B, see previous case.
- Initiator must be the first computation within its QB

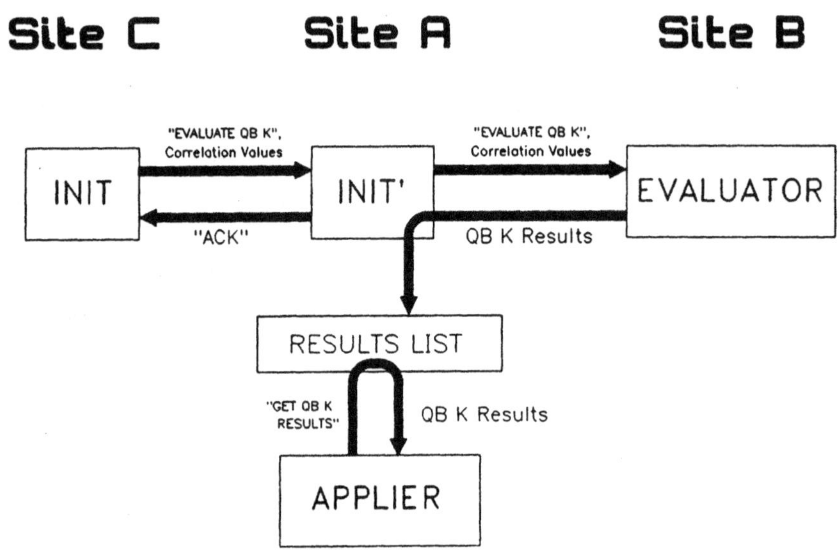

Figure 6: Evaluate-at-OPEN (EAO) subQB, Initiator's site ≠ Applier's site.

scribed in the second case. In addition, INIT′ must "close the loop" of communications that INIT started, by acknowledging the successful completion of evaluation (step (2.4)) to INIT at Site C.

As in case 2, the costs of initiation and evaluation are assessed to the initiating QB, but in this case there are additional communications costs for procedure steps (1.2) and (2.4).

One difficulty with EAO QBs is that the optimizer does not know whether case 2 or case 3 will happen until a delivery site is known for QB I, the initiating QB. Hence the plan for an EAO QB cannot be finalized until that QB's *initiating* QB -- not applying QB -- is optimized. Internally, the optimizer keeps different plans for both cases 2 and 3, with costs for each, so that when it optimizes QB I it can try both alternatives and choose the one having minimal cost.

7. Streamlining EAA Subquery Blocks

When the initiator and evaluator for an EAA subQB are at different sites, a great deal of inefficient communication traffic is generated: one exchange of correlation values and subQB results per parentQB tuple (see Figure 2). This section presents several possible ways to reduce this traffic, using the following distributed query that contains an EAA subQB:

```
SELECT E.NAME                          QB 1
FROM   EMPLOYEES@SF E
WHERE  E.DEPT =                              (H)
    (SELECT D.DEPT#                    QB 2
     FROM   DEPARTMENTS@NY D
     WHERE D.LOCATION = 'DENVER'
       AND D.NAME = 'SHIPPING'
       AND D.MANAGER = E.EMP#    );
```

7.1. Exploit ParentQB's Order

As suggested in Section "4.1. Dependencies Between Query Blocks", when the values for both the column in the nested predicate (E.DEPT in example (H)) *and* the correlation values of QB 1 (E.EMP#) are repeated in the next tuple, the evaluation of QB 2 will have the same result. Therefore, redundant evaluations as well as the communications to and from the initiator could be saved if the parentQB were ordered on those columns, so that duplicate values of those columns could be detected and redundant evaluation avoided. While R* in fact does exploit duplicate correlation values when it detects them, it does not *plan* it that way. The optimizer could trade off the estimated savings of enforcing a particular order for the parentQB against the higher costs of either sorting the composite or using an index scan (if one existed on the predicate and correlation columns) to achieve that order. The problem is that, given the statistics currently maintained for each table, it is very difficult to estimate reliably the number of tuples having duplicate values of just the predicate and correlation columns, and thus the potential savings. For this reason, the R* optimizer does not consider this option.

7.2. Transform Correlated QBs to Join

Kim has noted that EAA subQBs may be transformed to joins under certain circumstances [KIM 82]. For example, query (H) can be transformed to a single QB:

```
SELECT E.NAME
FROM   EMPLOYEES@SF E, DEPARTMENTS@NY
WHERE  E.DEPT = D.DEPT#                       (H1)
  AND  D.LOCATION = 'DENVER'
  AND  D.NAME = 'SHIPPING'
  AND  D.MANAGER = E.EMP#;
```

The benefit of such a transformation is that the optimizer is given more leeway in deciding how the query is to be processed. By placing the DEPARTMENTS@NY table in a subQB in query (H), the user effectively undermines the optimizer's function by *dictating* to the optimizer that a nested loop join with EMPLOYEES@SF as the outer table will be done. As transformed in (H1), existing mechanisms within the optimizer could evaluate alternative join methods (possibly exploiting orderings of both tables to do a merge scan join), storing the inner table at the join site to save re-shipping it, and using either EMPLOYEES@SF or DEPARTMENTS@NY as the outer table.

The difficulty is that (H1) is semantically not equivalent to (H) when the values of the SELECT-column of the subQB (D.DEPT) are not unique. As stated in Section "3.1. Nomenclature", the "=" operator in a nested predicate implies that a unique value is expected from the evaluation of the subQB, but there is no such implication in a join predicate. Furthermore, not all EAA subQBs may be so transformed. For example, in example (C) QB 2 cannot be transformed to a join with its parentQB because its nested predicate contains a set operator (...E.DEPT *IN*...) that is not expressible as a join with equivalent semantics when the subQB returns duplicate values matching E.DEPT: the nested query form would result in only one qualifying tuple, but the join form would result in one tuple per matching value found.

7.3. Move Correlations into Nesting Predicate

This transformation converts EAA subQBs to EAO subQBs by moving all correlation predicates into the nesting predicate, which now must permit more than one column to be specified. Query (H) thus becomes:

```
SELECT E.NAME                             QB 1
FROM   EMPLOYEES@SF E
WHERE  (E.DEPT, E.EMP#) =                       (H2)
    (SELECT D.DEPT#, D.MANAGER            QB 2
     FROM   DEPARTMENTS@NY D
     WHERE D.LOCATION = 'DENVER'
       AND D.NAME = 'SHIPPING');
```

Since QB 2 is now EAO, it need be evaluated only once, instead of once per tuple of EMPLOYEES@SF. On the other hand, the subQB's result in (H2) could be much bigger without the correlation predicate. So we might end up shipping *more* data from NY to SF *with* the transformation, but we save the multiple evaluations of the subQB and the communications overhead of a conversation between SF and NY for each new value of EMPLOYEES@SF. And as with the previous transformation, not all EAA subQBs can be transformed: for example, we cannot move the correlation predicate in query (C) because its scalar operator does not match the set operator of the nesting predicate. For this reason, and because allowing multiple columns in the nested predicate required significant changes to the semantics of SQL and the implementation of subQBs in R*, this transformation was also shelved.

7.4. Ship Subset of ParentQB to SubQB

Inspired by semijoins, this strategy still ships a subset of an entire table only once, but is the opposite of the previous transformation in that the parentQB -- not the subQB -- is the table to be shipped. For example, in query (H) we would ship EMPLOYEES@SF, projected on columns DEPT and EMP# (and restricted if there were other predicates on EMPLOYEES@SF), once to NY. At NY, each tuple in the subset would be re-read, used to evaluate the subQB, and either accepted or rejected by applying the nested predicate there. While this again reduces the number of conversations between SF and NY, it does not reduce the number of times the subQB is evaluated and has the added cost of storing and re-reading the subset of the parentQB if it does not fit in a buffer.

Note that the last two transformations would effectively be considered as alternative join options (shipping the inner table to the site of the outer, or *vice versa*) if Kim's transformation to a join predicate were done.

7.5. Return Only Single SubQB Result

The R* optimizer transforms the internal (parse-tree) representation of an EAA SubQB that may return a set of values into that of an equivalent subQB that returns exactly one value: FOUND or NOT FOUND. For example, when the nested predicate operator of example query (H) contains a set operator (IN) instead of a scalar operator (=):

```
SELECT E.NAME                             QB 1
FROM   EMPLOYEES@SF E
WHERE  E.DEPT IN                                  (I)
    (SELECT D.DEPT#                       QB 2
     FROM   DEPARTMENTS@NY D
     WHERE D.LOCATION = 'DENVER'
       AND D.NAME = 'SHIPPING'
       AND D.MANAGER = E.EMP#     );
```

it is modified to appear as:

```
SELECT E.NAME                               QB 1
FROM   EMPLOYEES@SF E
WHERE  E.DEPT IS NOT NULL                           (I1)
  AND EXISTS
    (SELECT <any columns>                   QB 2
     FROM   DEPARTMENTS@NY D
     WHERE D.LOCATION = 'DENVER'
       AND D.NAME = 'SHIPPING'
       AND D.MANAGER = E.EMP#
       AND E.DEPT = D.DEPT#     );
```

Because QB 2 returns only a single value rather than a potentially long set of values, communications volume may be substantially reduced. Evaluation of QB 2 may be cut short as soon as it finds a qualifying tuple in (I1), whereas in the original query the subQB had no hint from its nesting predicate that it need not scan all of DEPARTMENTS@NY to ensure that the subQB had a unique value. Finally, this transformation saved us having to implement new mechanisms for looping through multiple values of the right-hand-side of a predicate, looking for a match, for this type of predicate only.

8. Implementation Considerations

The extensions to R* to properly plan and execute nested queries required adding code to the optimizer: (1) to retain optimal plans for each natural result site of each QB plus the "unknown" site, rather than just the best overall plan for the QB; (2) to generate the application site alternatives ; (3) to evaluate the three possible cases for subQB execution; and (4) to determine for each apprentice those portions of the global plan pertaining to it. In addition, the run-time routines to execute the directives of the chosen plan had to be coded.

The additional bookkeeping required to keep track of optimal plans for each natural result site of each QB significantly increased the storage required and the code complexity. Because option (A3) adds a subQB's natural result sites to those of its parentQB (as described in Section "5.2.1. Application Site Options" above), the number of alternative application sites are compounded as the optimizer works its way up to the top QB. So the number of candidate plans may grow exponentially with the number of tables, if each table is at a different site *and* all tables are joined via a nested predicate. This problem was graphically illustrated by the simple example in Section "5.2.1. Application Site Options" (query (G)), which generated 10 different plans for joining two tables and applying one subQB, for a single join order, join method, and access method for each table. When the R* optimizer considers all feasible combinations of merge scan joins, alternative inner table transfer strategies (store the inner table at the join site versus re-fetch as needed), and EMPLOYEES as the outer table of the join (see [DANI 82] and [LOHM 85]), the costs of 48 different plans are evaluated. This is three times the number when no subquery is to be applied, and ten times the number of plans considered when all tables are at the same site. When the partial plans for single tables are included, the distributed query of example (G) considers 64 partial or complete plans. Each plan is composed of a "miniplan" for each table, inter-site transfer, or subQB application in the plan.

The plan storage problem has been somewhat ameliorated by restructuring the optimizer to store a plan only if it improves upon an existing plan to produce the same result (same tuples) in the same order at the same site, or if it provides a new result, order, or result site. Previously, all plans were allocated space that was not reclaimed even when the plan was later found to be dominated by another plan. Although evaluating all of the alternative plans sounds costly, in practice it is not noticeable to an interactive user, and for each alternative that is considered, one can construct cases in which it significantly out-performs all other alternatives. In addition, practical limits on the number of tables, and the inability of users to formulate queries that are nested sufficiently deep, should prevent the space and time demands from becoming too severe.

9. Conclusions

We have presented in this paper the problems associated with optimizing nested queries in a distributed relational database management system, and the approach used by R* to solve these problems. In particular, R* postpones determining the result site of a subQB until it optimizes its parentQB (applying QB), or, in the case of evaluate-at-open subQBs, its initiating QB. We have itemized the cases possible for both evaluate-at-application and evaluate-at-open types of QBs, and discussed algorithms for processing each case. In addition, we have presented the breakdown of work among sites cooperating in a distributed nested query, and how agreement upon plans for executing the query is coordinated by a master site while allowing the other (apprentice) sites a degree of site autonomy in matters pertaining to their own tables.

Nested queries for distributed databases have been implemented in R*, and have been tested for correct execution of complex queries involving up to five nested query blocks. To do this, we developed a test program that automatically varies the location of tables using SYNONYMs and tests the results of the queries against a table of expected results.

In the near future we intend to evaluate and validate the performance of the R* extensions to the System R optimizer, much as was done for System R by [ASTR 80], and in more detail than was done for Distributed INGRES [STON 82]. We also hope to improve the cost formulas to better conform to reality, and to isolate and improve situations for which bad plans are chosen or performance is anomalous. Sensitivity analyses will aid us in deciding where to concentrate improved detail in our modeling, and where the model can be simplified. Perhaps some heuristics or "rules of thumb" can be gleaned from this empirical analysis, which should help us to prune our enumeration tree of alternative plans further, without risking the omission of a truly optimal plan.

10. Acknowledgements

The authors are indebted to Morton Astrahan, Shel Finkelstein, Won Kim, Bruce Lindsay, Paul Wilms, and Bob Yost, who carefully and constructively reviewed an earlier draft of this paper. We also wish to acknowledge members of the R* project who also suggested some of the transformations of Section "7. Streamlining EAA Subquery Blocks": Elisa Bertino suggested the transformation of Section "7.3. Move Correlations into Nesting Predicate", and C. Mohan suggested that of Section "7.4. Ship Subset of ParentQB to SubQB".

11. References

[APER 83] P.M.G. Apers, A.R. Hevner, and S.B. Yao, "Optimizing Algorithms for Distributed Queries", *IEEE Transactions on Software Engineering, SE-9,* 1 (January 1983), pp. 57-68.

[ASTR 76] M.M. Astrahan et al., "System R: Relational Approach to Database Management", *ACM Transactions on Database Systems 1,* 2 (June 1976), pp. 97-137.

[ASTR 80] M.M. Astrahan, W. Kim, and M. Schkolnick, "Evaluation of the System R Access Path Selection Mechanism", *Proc. of 1980 IFIP Congress,* North-Holland Publishing, 1980. Also available as IBM Research Laboratory RJ2797, San Jose, Calif., April 1980.

[BERN 81b] P.A. Bernstein, N. Goodman, E. Wong, C.L. Reeve, J. Rothnie, "Query Processing in a System for Distributed Databases (SDD-1)", *ACM Transactions on Database Systems 6,* 4 (December 1981), pp. 602-625.

[BLAS 81] M.W. Blasgen, M.M. Astrahan, D.D. Chamberlin, J.N. Gray, W.F. King, B.G. Lindsay, R.A. Lorie, J.W. Mehl, T.G. Price, G.R. Putzolu, M. Schkolnick, P.G. Selinger, D.R. Slutz, H.R. Strong, I.L. Traiger, B.W. Wade, and R.A. Yost, "System R: An Architectural Overview", *IBM Systems Journal 20,* 1 (1981), pp. 41-62.

[CHAM 81a] D.D. Chamberlin, M.M. Astrahan, W.F. King, R.A. Lorie, J.W. Mehl, T.G. Price, M. Schkolnick, P. Griffiths Selinger, D.R. Slutz, B.W. Wade, and R.A. Yost, "Support for Repetitive Transactions and Ad Hoc Queries in System R", *ACM Transactions on Database Systems 6,* 1 (March 1981). Also available as IBM Research Laboratory RJ2551, San Jose, Calif., May 1979.

[CHAM 81b] D.D. Chamberlin, M.M. Astrahan, M.W. Blasgen, J.N. Gray, W.F. King, B.G. Lindsay, R. Lorie, J.W. Mehl, T.G. Price, F. Putzolu, P.G. Selinger, M. Schkolnick, D.R. Slutz, I.L. Traiger, B.W. Wade, R.A. Yost, "A History and Evaluation of System R", *Communications of the ACM, 24,* 10 (October 1981). Also available as IBM Research Laboratory RJ2843, San Jose, Calif., June 1980.

[CHAN 82] J-M. Chang, "A Heuristic Approach to Distributed Query Processing", *Procs. of the Eighth International Conference on Very Large Data Bases,* Mexico City, VLDB Endowment, Saratoga, CA, September 1982, pp. 54-61.

[CHAN 83] A. Chan, U. Dayal, S. Fox, N. Goodman, D. Ries, D. Skeen, "Overview of An ADA Compatible Distributed Database Manager", *Proc. SIGMOD 83,* May 1983.

[CHU 82] W.W. Chu and P. Hurley, "Optimal Query Processing for Distributed Database Systems", *IEEE Trans. on Computers, C-31*, 9 (September 1982), pp. 835-850.

[DANI 82] D. Daniels, P.G. Selinger, L.M. Haas, B.G. Lindsay, C. Mohan, A. Walker, P. Wilms. "An Introduction to Distributed Query Compilation in R*", *Proceedings Second International Conference on Distributed Databases*, Berlin, Sept. 1982. Also available as IBM Research Laboratory RJ3497, San Jose, Calif., June 1982.

[EPST 78] R. Epstein, M. Stonebraker, and E. Wong, "Distributed Query Processing in a Relational Data Base System", *Proceedings of ACM-SIGMOD*, Austin, TX, May 1978, pp. 169-180.

[EPST 80] R. Epstein and M. Stonebraker, "Analysis of Distributed Data Base Processing Strategies", *Procs. of the Sixth International Conference on Very Large Data Bases*, Montreal, IEEE, October 1980, pp. 92-101.

[HAAS 82] L. M. Haas, P. Selinger, E. Bertino, D. Daniels, B. Lindsay, G. Lohman, Y. Masunaga, C.Mohan, P. Ng, P. Wilms and R. Yost, "R*: A Research Project on Distributed Relational DBMS", *Database Engineering 5*, 4 (Dec. 1982), IEEE Computer Society, pp. 28-32.

[HEVN 79] A.R. Hevner and S.B. Yao, "Query Processing in Distributed Database Systems", *IEEE Trans. Software Engr., SE-5*, (May 1979), pp. 177-187.

[KIM 82] W. Kim, "On Optimizing an SQL-like Nested Query", *ACM Transactions on Database Systems 7*, 3 (September 1982), pp. 443-469. Also available as IBM Research Laboratory RJ3063, San Jose, Calif., February 1981.

[KERS 82] L. Kerschberg, P.D. Ting, S.B. Yao, "Query Optimization in Star Computer Networks", *ACM Transactions on Database Systems 7*,4 (December 1982).

[LIND 81] B. G. Lindsay, "Object Naming and Catalog Management for a Distributed Database Manager", *Proceedings 2nd International Conference on Distributed Computing Systems*, Paris, France, April 1981. Also available as IBM Research Laboratory RJ2914, San Jose, Calif., August 1980.

[LOHM 85] G. Lohman, C. Mohan, L. Haas, D. Daniels, B. Lindsay, P. Selinger, and P. Wilms, "Query Processing in R*", *Query Processing in Database Systems*, W. Kim, D. Reiner, and D. Batory (Eds.), Springer-Verlag (1985), pp.31-47.

[NGUY 80] G.T. Nguyen, "Decentralized Dynamic Query Decomposition for Distributed Database Systems", *Proc. ACM Pacific '80: Distributed Processing - New Directions for a New Decade*, San Francisco, November 1980.

[ONUE 83] E. Onuegbe, S. Rahimi, and A.R. Hevner "Local Query Translation and Optimization in a Distributed System", *Proceedings NCC 1983*, July, 1983, pp. 229-239.

[SELI 79] P.G. Selinger, M.M. Astrahan, D.D. Chamberlin, R.A. Lorie, T.G. Price, "Access Path Selection in a Relational Database Management System", *Proceedings of ACM-SIGMOD*, May 1979. Also available as IBM Research Laboratory RJ2429, San Jose, Calif., August 1979.

[SELI 80] P. G. Selinger and M. Adiba, "Access Path Selection in Distributed Database Management Systems", *Proceedings International Conference on Data Bases*, ed. Deen and Hammersly, University of Aberdeen, July 1980, pp. 204-215. Also available as IBM Research Laboratory RJ2883, San Jose, Calif., August 1980.

[SQL] IBM Corporation, SQL/Data System Concepts and Facilities, IBM Form No. GH24-5013.

[STON 82] M. Stonebraker, J. Woodfill, J. Ranstrom, M. Murphy, J. Kalash, M. Carey, K. Arnold, "Performance Analysis of Distributed Data Base Systems", *Database Engineering 5*, 4 (Dec. 1982), IEEE Computer Society, pp. 58-65.

[WILL 82] R. Williams, D. Daniels, L. Haas, G. Lapis, B. Lindsay, P. Ng, R. Obermark, P. Selinger, A. Walker, P. Wilms, R. Yost, "R*: An Overview of the Architecture", *Improving Database Usability and Responsiveness*, (Procs. International Conference on Databases, Jerusalem, Israel, June 1982), P. Scheuermann, ed., Academic Press, New York, 1982, pp. 1-27. Also available as IBM Research Laboratory RJ3325, San Jose, Calif., December 1981.

[WONG 76] E. Wong and K. Youssefi, "Decomposition -- a Strategy for Query Processing", *ACM Transactions on Database Systems 1*, 3 (September 1976), pp. 223-241.

[YAO 79] S.B. Yao, "Optimization of Query Algorithms", *ACM Transactions on Database Systems 4*, 2 (June 1979), pp. 133-155.

[YU 83] C.T. Yu, and C.C. Chang, "On the Design of a Query Processing Strategy in a Distributed Database Environment", *Proc. SIGMOD 83*, May 1983.

QUIST: A SYSTEM FOR SEMANTIC QUERY OPTIMIZATION IN RELATIONAL DATABASES

by Jonathan J. King

Computer Science Department
Stanford University*

Abstract

Semantic query optimization is an approach to query optimization that uses knowledge of the semantics of the data to transform a query into another query that has the same answer but can be processed more efficiently. However, the indiscriminate application of semantic transformations can itself be excessively costly when there are many semantic rules upon which transformations can be based. This paper describes a semantic query optimization system called QUIST (QUery Improvement through Semantic Transformation). QUIST demonstrates significant cost reductions for a class of relational database queries. At the same time, QUIST uses knowledge about relational database structures and processing methods to insure that semantic transformations are applied selectively. This knowledge reflects cost models and optimization techniques developed in recent query optimization research. To integrate semantic, structure, and processing knowledge, QUIST analyzes a query at several levels of detail, along the lines of the plan-generate-test paradigm of artificial intelligence systems.

Background

The technique of *semantic query optimization* (SQO) has been introduced by King ([King79] [King81a]) and independently by Hammer and Zdonik [Hammer80]. In contrast to what may be termed *conventional query optimization* methods that search for an efficient sequence of operations to be performed in the physical database for a particular query ([Selinger79] [Yao79] [Youssefi78]), semantic query optimization actually transforms the original query into a new one. The transformations are limited to those that yield a semantically equivalent query, one that produces the same answer as the original query in any state of the database. The semantic knowledge on which the transformations are based are the same *semantic integrity constraints* ([Stonebraker75] [Wilson80]) that are used to insure the semantic validity of database updates.

The great promise of SQO is that it makes possible significant reductions in the cost of query processing that are not otherwise available. In effect, SQO extends the usefulness of conventional optimization by creating new queries and therefore new opportunities to apply conventional optimization.

A framework for SQO is presented in [Hammer80] in the context of an entity-relationship style query language. Important issues for the design of an effective SQO system are indicated. Foremost among the issues is the need to control the number of transformations that the system performs. With an extensive collection of semantic knowledge about the database domain, there may be many possible ways to transform a query into equivalent ones, many possible transformations of those queries, and so forth. In order to maintain the overall efficiency of the system, it is necessary to perform only those transformations that may lead to reduced query processing costs. Hammer and Zdonik postulate a set of cost-reducing *techniques* to control transformations. One such technique would be *domain refinement*, the aim of which is to convert the domain of a restriction expression into a smaller one whose members are more readily accessible. To control the application of techniques, the idea of a multiprocesssing control structure is proposed. Methods for applying relevant techniques would be selected on the basis of heuristics that depend upon the query and upon the contents of the semantic knowledge base.

The central issue: interplay of knowledge sources

An effective SQO system is one that can make significant reductions in the cost of processing queries without incurring unacceptable costs in preprocessing analysis. But it is clear that the uncontrolled use of semantics for transformations makes preprocessing analysis too expensive. In order to control the process of query transformation, it is necessary to draw upon knowledge of database structures and access methods. The key questions are, what knowledge can be used, how should it be formulated, and how can it be applied so that only beneficial semantic transformations are attempted?

QUIST: A relational SQO system

In an effort to answer these questions, we have developed a system called QUIST (QUery Improvement through Semantic Transformation). The significance of QUIST's contribution is that it demonstrates, in a functioning system, that semantic transformations can significantly reduce the cost of processing queries, while showing just how knowledge of structures and access methods can be formulated and applied so that they control the use of semantic knowledge for useful query transformations.

Much recent research has focused on the processing of queries in relational database systems. As a result, there is a body of knowledge and shared assumptions about the important aspects of the problem and about the factors that influence the cost of processing. This

*Author's current address: Hewlett-Packard Laboratories, Palo Alto, California.

presents an opportunity to investigate SQO in a context in which the necessary query processing expertise exists. Because of this, we have chosen to have QUIST operate for an important class of relational database queries.

The class of queries

QUIST admits for possible semantic transformation a significant subset of restrict-join-project relational queries. The query language was chosen for simplicity, but could be easily extended to the complete relational calculus. The class of queries is very similar to those admitted by IDA [Sagalowicz77] and APPLE [Carlson76]. An IDA or APPLE query consists of a boolean combination of simple constraints on attributes, plus a list of attributes whose values are desired. This is made possible by predefining a single virtual relation in terms of joins of the real database relations. One and only one logical access path must exist between any two underlying relations. As an example, suppose a database contains two relations:

SHIP: (Shipname Shipclass Shiptype)

SHIPCLASS: (Class Type Length Draft)

where, for instance, Shipname is the name of a ship and Length is the length of any ship in a particular ship class. Assume the (only) permitted join between SHIP and SHIPCLASS is on Shipclass and Class, respectively. The query to request the length of a ship whose name is "Totor" is

(Shipname = "Totor"); (? Length).

The two attributes are on separate underlying relations, but this is hidden from the user.* The unique access path means that it is possible to represent only one kind of relationship between any two classes of entities represented as relations; in the example, ships and shipclasses cannot be related by common shiptypes. Moore discusses this and other limitations in [Moore79]. Nevertheless, as shown in the context of the LADDER natural language database access system [Hendrix78], such a query language admits a substantial and interesting class of queries.

Overview of system operation

In operational terms, QUIST starts with the constraints specified in the input query, and determines which database relations, if any, are *constraint targets*, or relations that have attributes on which additional constraints should be sought. If there are no targets, the process stops. Otherwise, QUIST repeats a cycle of operations that produce constraints until no more cycles can be carried out. During each cycle, QUIST retrieves relevant semantic rules. QUIST filters the rules according to structurally-based criteria (that is, the list of constraint targets), tests them for applicability against the current constraints, and asserts new constraints if possible. The process terminates when some cycle fails to generate new constraints. The semantically equivalent queries are then determined from the final set of constraints, both given and derived. Finally, QUIST estimates the cost of processing each of those queries and identifies the one with the lowest cost, using conventional query optimization and cost estimation procedures.

Levels of analysis: the plan-generate-test paradigm

The process by which QUIST seeks a lower cost version of a query exemplifies the *plan-generate-test* paradigm of artificial intelligence [Feigenbaum71] seen in such systems as Meta-Dendral [Buchanan76] and AM [Lenat76]. That is, the process operates at three levels. The planning level is the one at which constraint targets are established. At this level, the query is treated in very abstract terms. The query's only important characteristics are the names of the relation attributes that are constrained or from which output values are requested. At the planning level, QUIST divides the database's relations into those that should be targets for inference and those that should not, much in the way that the Dendral program [Feigenbaum71] divides fragments of chemical structures into those that should or should not be part of a desired complete structure.

At the generate level, QUIST moves through a space of semantically equivalent queries. Each move in this space is a query transformation based upon the inference of an additional constraint. Each inference is supported by a rule in the semantic knowledge base. Only plausible moves are generated in the sense that the constraint target list permits only those transformations which may possibly produce a lower cost query. The representation of the query at the generate level is less abstract than at the planning level. At the generate level, it is necessary to deal with the precise constraints on database attributes, not just with the names of the attributes that have been constrained.

The testing level views each query in the most detail. Here, estimates of actual processing cost are obtained. QUIST includes a conventional query optimizer to find the least expensive way to process each semantically equivalent query produced at the generate level. The sequence in which each part of the query is processed is an essential factor. Processing at this level can be regarded as carrying out moves in a space of physical realizations of a single logically expressed query produced at the level above.

QUIST's use of the query processing expertise developed in conventional query optimization research is seen in the relationship between the searches at the generate and testing levels. The testing level search of alternative processing sequences, which is nothing other than conventional query optimization, is guided by detailed models of the cost of data access. The generate level search of semantically equivalent queries is guided by the constraint target list. The heuristics that produce the constraint target are, in effect, summaries or abstract versions of the detailed cost models used at the testing level.

An illustration of QUIST at work

We now wish to illustrate this abstract description of QUIST in terms of a concrete example.* The example shows how QUIST analyzes a query posed to the following example database:

---

*The underlying query processing system determines the proper logical access path between the two relations.

*The example's only purpose is to explain the operation of the system.

SHIPS (Shipname Owner Shiptype Draft Deadweight Capacity Registry)

PORTS (Portname Country Depth Facilitytype)

CARGOES (Ship Destination Shipper Cargotype Quantity Dollarvalue Insurance)

OWNERS (Ownername Location Assets Business)

POLICIES (Policy Issuer Coverage)

INSURERS (Insurer Insurercountry Capitalization)

Figure 1: Example database relations

As indicated earlier, we must specify the unique logical access paths among the real relations. The implicit joins that underlie the logical access paths are:

1. OWNERS.Ownername = SHIPS.Owner
2. SHIPS.Shipname = CARGOES.Ship
3. CARGOES.Destination = PORTS.Portname
4. CARGOES.Insurance = POLICIES.Policy
5. POLICIES.Issuer = INSURERS.Insurer

which stand for, respectively,

1. A ship and its owner
2. A ship and a cargo it is carrying
3. A cargo and its destination port
4. A cargo and the policy that insures it
5. A policy and its issuing company

The database is assumed to be implemented by means of one file per relation. It is further assumed that the SHIPS file has a clustering index on its OWNER attribute. This means that the SHIPS file is clustered with respect to the OWNERS file; given a tuple in the OWNERS file, the corresponding tuples in the SHIPS file (that is, the ships owned by that owner) can be accessed much less expensively than by a sequential search of SHIPS. In addition, the OWNERS file is much smaller than the SHIPS file.

A very simple knowledge base of general semantic rules accompanies the database in this example. It includes the following rules:

- Rule R1. Every ship over 350 thousand tons deadweight can operate only at ports with offshore load/discharge capabilities.
- Rule R2. Only leasing companies own vessels that exceed 300 thousand tons deadweight.
- Rule R3. A cargo is never insured for more than its dollar value.
- Rule R4. A ship carries no more cargo than its rated capacity.
- Rule R5. Any cargo other than liquefied natural gas or refined petroleum products that is worth more than 500,000 dollars is handled only at general cargo ports.
- Rule R6. The only ships whose deadweight exceeds 150 thousand tons are supertankers.
- Rule R7. Cargoes worth over three million dollars and carried by supertankers are insured by policies issued by Lloyds.
- Rule R8. Ships owned by petroleum companies only carry liquefied natural gas, refined petroleum products, or crude oil.

which, because of the joinless form that QUIST supports, are represented in very simple terms:

R1: (Deadweight > 350) → (Facilitytype = "offshore")

R2: (Deadweight > 300) → (Business = "leasing")

R3: (Coverage ≤ Dollarvalue)

R4: (Quantity ≤ Capacity)

R5: (Cargotype ∉ {"LNG" "refined"}) ∧ (Dollarvalue > 500) → (Facilitytype = "general")

R6: (Deadweight > 150) → (Shiptype = "supertanker")

R7: (Dollarvalue > 3000) ∧ (Shiptype = "supertanker") → (Issuer = "Lloyds")

R8: (Business = "petroleum") → (Cargotype ∈ {"LNG" "refined" "oil"})

We choose an example query that is specifically arranged to illustrate semantic query optimization capabilities. It is not necessarily a typical query, but does help demonstrate what the system can do. The query is:

"List the destination of cargoes worth less than one million dollars being carried by supertankers over 400 thousand tons deadweight to ports with offshore load/discharge facilities."

The representation of this query to QUIST is:

(Deadweight > 400) ∧ (Shiptype = "supertanker") ∧ (Dollarvalue < 1000) ∧ (Facilitytype = "offshore"); (? Destination)

Three relations are involved in this query: SHIPS, CARGOES, and PORTS. Let us consider what kind of semantic optimization QUIST ought to do. We readily see that semantic rule R1 makes the constraint on Facilitytype superfluous. If this constraint is eliminated, then it won't be necessary to involve PORTS in the processing at all. Moreover, the constraint on Deadweight also makes it possible to infer a constraint on the Business attribute of the OWNERS file. Although this introduces a join to a new file, the database is structured so that this will be advantageous. This is because the join has, in effect, been precomputed and stored as the link from OWNERS to SHIPS. In addition, a constraint can be inferred on the Coverage attribute of the POLICIES relation by means of rule R3. However, it is not desirable to involve POLICIES in the query because the join to CARGOES is not supported by a prestored link or index. We want the system to avoid trying to make that inference.

Inference guiding heuristics

As its first step, the planning phase of plan-generate-test, QUIST establishes constraint targets. The three original files turn out to be targets, as does the OWNERS file. POLICIES and INSURERS are ruled out as targets.

Target selection is governed by a set of heuristics based on knowledge of query processing and file structures. The heuristics can be grouped into those that designate targets and those that designate nontargets. Target designation heuristics contemplate specific changes in underlying retrieval operations. While not necessarily a complete set, the target designation heuristics listed here are related to classes of transformations of queries that are important in terms of the effects they have on the cost of processing (see **[King81b]** for quantitative estimates of their effects). The heuristics are:

I. Heuristics that designate constraint targets.

H1. *Try to exploit a clustered index.* Try to obtain a constraint on an attribute of a relation which is restricted in the query and which has a clustered indexed attribute that is not restricted in the query.

This heuristic contemplates the replacement of a segment scan by a clustering index scan. We refer to this transformation as **index introduction.**

H2. *Push a constraint up a hierarchy.* A relation should be a constraint target if it has a clustering link into a much larger file that is constrained in the query, even if the relation itself is not in the original query.

This heuristic contemplates the addition of a join to the query, referred to as **join introduction**. The effect of the added join is similar to replacing a segment scan of the linked relation by a clustering index scan of that relation.

H3. *Move a constraint across a join boundary.* A relation involved in a join to a sufficiently strongly restricted relation is a target for constraints.

In this case, the objective is to reduce the number of inner scans of the join by obtaining additional restrictions prior to the cross referencing part of the operation. Hence, the transformation is called **scan reduction.**

H4. *Try to eliminate a dangling relation.* If a relation is joined to just one other relation and none of its attributes contribute to the output, then it is a target for constraints.

This heuristic is aimed at **join elimination.**

II. Heuristics that designate nontargets.

H5. *Do not introduce unlinked joins.* With the exception of the clustering link (hierarchical) case, do not generate constraints for relations that are not part of the original query.

H6. *Do not push a constraint down a hierarchy.* A relation should not be a target for constraints if it is joined to a restricted file from which it has a clustering link or equivalent index.

H7. *Use a strongly restricted clustered index.* If a file is strongly constrained* on an attribute with a clustered index, then it should not be a target for constraints.

SHIPS, PORTS, and CARGOES are each designated as a target by heuristic H3 (move a constraint across a join boundary) and because neither of the exceptions in heuristics H5 (don't push a constraint down a hierarchy) or H6 (use a strongly restricted clustered index) apply. Both SHIPS and PORTS are also designated as targets by heuristic H4 (try to eliminate a dangling relation) because both are joined just to CARGOES and neither has an attribute involved in the output. In addition, the OWNERS relation is designated as a constraint target by heuristic H2 (push a constraint up a hierarchy). The OWNERS file is much smaller than the SHIPS file and there is a clustering link from OWNERS to SHIPS. Finally, the POLICIES and INSURERS relations are designated as nontargets by heuristic H5 (don't introduce unlinked joins). The inclusion of either of these relations would introduce a costly join.

The use of heuristics in the inference process

The next step, the generation phase, is to infer new constraints. In the first cycle of constraint generation, the following new constraints are asserted:

From Rule R1: (Facilitytype = "offshore")

From Rule R2: (Business = "leasing")

The other rules are rejected by tests of two kinds: tests that show the rule can't be applied, and tests that suggest on heuristic grounds that the rule should not be applied because the resulting constraint does not lead to a reduction in query processing cost. Rules R4 and R7 are eliminated as inapplicable because the attributes they involve are not constrained in the query. Rule R5 does not assert a stronger constraint on Shiptype than the one already known, so R5 is eliminated as being ineffective (although QUIST notes that the restriction on Shiptype is derivable from other restrictions; this information is used in later estimating the cost of processing the query).

Rules R3 and R6 are eliminated because they are not heuristically promising. We don't wish to bring in constraints on the POLICIES relation. A rule is considered promising if and only if it may directly produce a constraint on an attribute associated with a constraint target relation. This formulation of the pruning heuristic leaves open the possibility that QUIST will fail to infer some cost-reducing constraint. This would happen if the inference chain contains a constraint on a non-target relation. The decision to formulate the heuristic this way reflects the belief that such inferences would be infrequent compared to those that involve only target relations. As we discuss below, the heuristic can substantially reduce the cost of inference.

---

*The constraint has an estimated *selectivity* ([Yao79]) close to zero.

After these tests, we are left with rules R1 and R2 that permit us to assert the constraints shown above.

In the second cycle of constraint generation, the major change is that rule R7 has become applicable owing to the new constaint on the Business attribute. However, R7's constraint on Business does not follow from what is known from rule R2. In fact, no other new constraints are asserted, so the process of constraint generation terminates.

Formulation of alternative queries

Alternative queries are now formulated. Some constraints must be part of the query while other constraints are optional. With some exceptions (which we will not detail here), a constraint is optional if it can be derived from other query constraints, and (again with some exceptions) the addition to a query of an optional constraint derived in the manner just sketched does not change the answer. In our example, the constraints on Deadweight, Shiptype, and Dollarvalue are necessary. The new constraint on Business is clearly optional. It turns out also that the constraint on Facilitytype is optional, because it is derivable from the constraint on Deadweight.

These movements of constraints support two of the operations contemplated by the target designation heuristics, namely join introduction and join elimination. We can bring OWNERS into the query, or drop PORTS from the query, or both, or neither. Four alternative queries result from these possibilities.

Estimation of the cost of alternative queries

The final step, the testing phase, is to estimate the retrieval cost for the alternatives. QUIST's query cost estimator is a simplified version of the System R access path selector [Selinger79]. QUIST's cost estimator differs from that of System R chiefly in assuming that a join is carried out by the nested loops method rather than choosing between that method and the merging scans method. Another difference is that QUIST's cost measure involves just the number of estimated page fetches rather than combining this with an estimate of CPU activity. However, results reported in [Astrahan80] suggest that the number of page fetches is a suitable cost measure for the class of queries admitted by QUIST.

Experiments with the system

System parameters including file sizes and access times (Figure 2) were chosen in order to make comparisons using QUIST's modified version of the System R cost model.

File	Size
SHIPS	20,000
CARGOES	25,000
PORTS	1,000
OWNERS	1000
POLICIES	25,000
INSURERS	500

Figure 2: Assumed File Sizes for Timing Experiments

It is assumed that there are twenty records per file page (the same value used in [Yao79]) and that the time per page fetch is thirty milliseconds (extrapolated from [Gotlieb75]). It is further assumed that the SHIPS file is physically clustered with respect to the OWNERS file. The experiments used a knowledge base of approximately thirty rules like the ones shown earlier. These rules were obtained in part from Couper's "Geography of Sea Transport" [Couper72]. The QUIST system is implemented in Interlisp [Teitelman78] on a Digital Equipment Corporation DECSystem20 model 60 computer.

The specific timing estimates that were obtained depend on the simplified cost model, on the chosen file sizes, and on the system implementation, so they should not be taken too literally. What is important, beyond the particular processing estimates, is that the results support the contention that semantic query optimization can bring about significant reductions in the cost of processing queries with an acceptable overhead for analysis. They also suggest the effectiveness of structurally-based inference-guiding heuristics.

For the example query shown earlier, QUIST's conventional query optimization subsystem determines that the original query in SHIPS, CARGOES, and PORTS can be processed in 439 seconds. The query in OWNERS, SHIPS, and CARGOES that results from join introduction and join elimination can be processed in just 19 seconds. The total time to perform this analysis is 2.1 seconds, including conventional optimization and cost estimation of the alternative queries. This striking result is due to the simultaneous application of join introduction and join elimination.*.

Other queries in which single transformations apply have less striking but still significant cost reductions, with even smaller overhead. In cases where QUIST determines that there are no constraint targets, or that the query conditions are not satisfiable, the analysis overhead is very low.

1. **Index introduction.**

   Query Q1: "List the owners of all ships with a deadweight greater than 200 thousand tons."

   Relevant rule: "Any ship over 150 thousand tons deadweight is a supertanker." (This is a change from example rule R6).

   Transformed query: "List the owners of all *supertankers* with a deadweight greater than 200 thousand tons."

   Result: A new constraint on the indexed Shiptype attribute of SHIPS.

2. **Join elimination.**

   Query Q2: "List the shipper and quantity of liquefied natural gas cargoes carried by pressurized tankers to Marseilles."

   Relevant rule: "Liquefied natural gas is always carried by pressurized tankers."

---

*The calculation of the cost of queries is shown in the Appendix

Transformed query: "List the shipper and quantity of liquefied natural gas cargoes carried to Marseilles."

Result: Elimination of the join with SHIPS because Shiptype constraint is superfluous.

3. **Scan reduction.**

Query Q3: "List the owners and the quantity of cargo of ships carrying refined petroleum products to Danish ports."

Relevant rule: "Refined petroleum products are carried by ships with deadweight under 60 thousand tons."

Transformed query: "List the owners and the quantity of cargo of ships *with deadweight under 60 thousand tons* carrying refined petroleum products to Danish ports."

Result: Constraint on Deadweight can be applied prior to cross matching step of join between SHIPS and CARGOES reducing the number of qualifying SHIPS tuples and therefore the number of scans of CARGOES.

4. **Join introduction.**

Query Q4: "List the owners of supertankers with deadweight over 350 thousand tons that are carrying cargoes to French ports."

Relevant rule: "Only leasing companies own vessels that exceed 300 thousand tons deadweight."

Transformed query: "List the *leasing company* owners of supertankers with deadweight over 350 thousand tons that are carrying cargoes to French ports."

Result: Addition of join between OWNERS and SHIPS has the effect of a more efficient scan of SHIPS.

5. **Detection of unsatisfiable conditions.**

Query Q5: "List the owners of all bulk cargo ships with deadweight over 200 thousand tons."

Relevant rule: "Any ship over 150 thousand tons deadweight is a supertanker."

Result: No transformed query. QUIST indicates that no items can satisfy the query conditions.

6. **Absence of opportunities for cost reducing semantic transformation.**

Query Q6: "List the owners of all refrigerated ships."

Result: Indexed attribute Shiptype is already constrained. No relevant rule. Query remains the same.

We now show the estimated processing times associated with these queries on the example database (Figure 3).

Query	Transformation	Est. Proc. Time Without SQO (sec.)	Est. Proc. Time With SQO (sec.)
Q0	join introduction & join elimination	439	19
Q1	index introduction	30	4
Q2	join elimination	313	37
Q3	scan reduction	1125	519
Q4	join introduction	348	112
Q5	(unsatisfiable)*	30	0
Q6	(SQO deemed useless)	3	3

Figure 3: Reduction in Processing Costs with SQO

The effectiveness of inference guiding heuristics is suggested by an example query that was tried with and without heuristics. Without heuristics, 33 rules were tried; these included 20 separate rules plus repetitions due to renewed eligibility as new constraints were inferred. Of these, 11 were actually found applicable and were used to infer new constraints. When heuristics were applied, only 8 rules were found eligible, and only 1 was used to infer a new constraint. Analysis without heuristics was even more inefficient because cost estimates had to be found for additional alternative queries. Further details on the effectiveness of inference guiding heuristics can be found in **[King81b]**.

Conclusion

The QUIST system supports the idea that semantic knowledge can be used to improve the efficiency of processing database queries. It brings out the interplay of semantic, structural, and processing knowledge in the context of relational database systems. Still to be investigated is the effectiveness of inference guiding heuristics in very large knowledge bases, although the confinement of inferences in most queries to a few relations suggests that the efficiency of the analysis can be maintained.

Acknowledgments

I wish to thank Gio Wiederhold and Daniel Sagalowicz for their valuable help with this paper. I also wish to thank the referees for their comments. The research described here was conducted as part of the Knowledge Base Management Systems Project, under contract N00039-80-G-0132 from The Defense Advanced Research Projects Agency of the United States Deparment of Defense. The views and conclusions contained in this document are those of the author and should not be interpreted as representative of the official policies of DARPA or the U.S. Government.

---

*The query is a null query. QUIST would not send it to the database for processing.

Appendix: Estimation of Query Processing Costs

In this appendix, we illustrate how QUIST estimates the cost of processing a query. The original query Q0 is represented in QUIST as

(Deadweight > 400) ∧ (Shiptype = "supertanker") ∧ (Dollarvalue < 1000) ∧ (Facilitytype = "offshore"); (? Destination).

The QUIST cost estimator determines that the least expensive way to carry out the query is first to join SHIPS and CARGOES, and then to join the result with PORTS. The SHIPS file is selected as the outer file of the first join. A sequential scan is used. There are 20,000 records in the SHIPS file and there are 20 records per page, so 1000 pages are scanned.

An important quantity in estimating processing cost is the estimated *selectivity* of the restrictions on the file. Selectivity is the fraction of tuples expected to meet the restrictions. In general, QUIST makes two simple assumptions: (1) the values of each attribute are uniformly distributed over their legal range; and (2) restrictions are independent, so that the selectivity of conjoined restrictions is the product of their independent selectivities.

The restrictions on SHIPS are (Deadweight > 400) and (Shiptype = "supertanker"). The valid ranges of all attributes are stored in the knowledge base. Deadweight ranges between 20 and 450. Shiptype has ten legal values. Thus, the estimated selectivity of the restriction (Deadweight > 400) is given by (450 - 400)/(450 - 20) or approximately 0.116. The estimated selectivity of (Shiptype = "supertanker") is 0.1.

However, QUIST determines that the Shiptype restriction is derivable from the Deadweight restriction (and hence is not independent of it). Therefore, the combined estimated selectivity of the restrictions on SHIPS is taken to be that of the Deadweight restriction alone, or 0.116. Thus, the number of qualifying SHIPS tuples is approximately 20,000 tuples multiplied by the estimated selectivity of 0.116, or about 2320 tuples.

For each of the qualifying SHIPS tuples, a scan is made on the CARGOES file. QUIST determines that the least expensive scan of CARGOES is the one using a nonclustering index on the SNAM attribute. The cost of a scan with a nonclustering index has three components: (1) traversal from the root of the index tree to the leaf level; (2) accessing of index leaf level pages; and (3) accessing of data pages via index pointers. For simplicity, QUIST assumes that the index tree is three levels deep. The other two components are estimated on the basis of the number of probed values. Following [Yao79], QUIST uses a system-wide constant ratio of five between the number of pointers that can fit on a leaf index page and the number of records that can fit on a data page. It is assumed that each file has twenty records per data page and 100 pointers per index page.

In the case of the join between SHIPS and CARGOES, there are 2320 qualifying SHIPS, hence 2320 scans of CARGOES. For each scan, the index tree is traversed at a cost of three pages, a single index leaf page is read, and an average of 1.25 data pages of the CARGOES file is read.* The last figure is based on the ratio of the number of tuples in CARGOES (25,000) to the number of tuples in SHIPS (20,000). Hence, the average cost of each scan is 5.25 pages. The total cost of scans of CARGOES is therefore 5.25 pages multiplied by 2320 occurrences, or about 12,180 pages.

The restriction on CARGOES is (Dollarvalue < $1,000). The legal range of this attribute is between 100 and 100,000, so the estimated selectivity is about 0.01. For the 2320 scans, about 2900 CARGOES tuples are read. Thus, the expected number of qualifying CARGOES tuples is about 29. This is the size of the resultant of the first join. The cost of the first join is the sum of the pages scanned in SHIPS (1,000) and the pages scanned in CARGOES (12,180), or about 13,180 pages.

The second join is with the PORTS file. QUIST determines that a sequential scan is the least expensive scan of PORTS. This is accomplished at a cost of 50 pages (1000 total records in the file at twenty records per page). The scan is repeated for each of the 29 resultants of the first join. Thus, the total cost is 29 multiplied by 50 pages, or 1450 pages.

Thus, the overall cost in pages for the query is the sum of the two joins, 13,180 pages plus 1450 pages, or 14,630 pages. The estimated time to read a page is 30 milliseconds, so the total processing time is estimated to be 14,630 pages multiplied by 0.03 seconds, or about 439 seconds.

References

[Buchanan76] Buchanan, Bruce G., *Scientific theory formation by computer*, in J.C.Simon (ed.), **Proc. of NATO Advanced Study Institute on Computer Oriented Learning Processes**, Noordhoff, Leyden, 1976.

[Carlson76] Carlson, C.R., and Kaplan, R.S., *A generalized access path model and its application to a relational data base system*, **Proc. 1976 ACM-SIGMOD** Conference, 143-154, May 1976.

[Couper72] Couper, A. D., **The geography of sea transport**, Hutchinson, London, 1972.

[Feigenbaum71] Feigenbaum, E.A., Buchanan, B.G., and Lederberg, J., *On generality and problem solving: a case study using the DENDRAL program*, in Meltzer and Michie (eds.), **Machine Intelligence 6**, American Elsevier, New York, 1971.

[Gotlieb75] Gotlieb, L., *Computing joins of relations*, **Proc. 1975 ACM-SIGMOD Conference**, 55-63.

[Hammer80] Hammer, Michael and Zdonik, Stanley B.Jr., *Knowledge-based query processing*, **Proc. Sixth Intl. Conf. on Very Large Data Bases**, Montreal, October 1980, 137-147.

[Hendrix78] Hendrix, Gary G. et. al., *Developing a natural language interface to complex data*, ACM Transactions on Database Systems, 3:2, (June 1978) 105-147.

---

*With a clustering index, consecutive values are assumed to fall most often on the same data page, so far fewer data page are fetched.

[King79] King Jonathan J., *Exploring the use of domain knowledge for query processing efficiency*, Stanford University Computer Science Department, Heuristic Programming Project Technical Report HPP-79-30, December 1979.

[King81a] King, Jonathan J., *Reasoning about access to knowledge*, in **Proceedings of the Workshop on Data Abstraction, Databases and Conceptual Modelling, Pingree Park, Colorado, June 1980,** SIGPLAN Notices 16:1, January 1981, 138-140.

[King81b] King, Jonathan J. *Query optimization by semantic reasoning*, Stanford University Computer Science Department, PhD. thesis.

[Lenat76] Lenat, Douglas B., *AM: an artificial intelligence approach to discovery in mathematics as heuristic search*, Stanford University Artificial Intelligence Laboratory Memo 286, July 1976.

[Moore79] Moore, Robert C., *Handling complex queries in a distributed data base*, SRI International Artificial Intelligence Center, Technical Note 170, October 1979.

[Sagalowicz77] Sagalowicz, Daniel, *IDA: An intelligent data access program*, **Proc. Third Intl.Conf. on Very Large Data Bases,** Tokyo, October 1977, 293-300.

[Selinger79] Selinger, P. Griffiths et. al. *Access path selection in a relational database management system*, **Proc. 1979 ACM-SIGMOD Conference**, 23-34, May 1979.

[Stonebraker75] Stonebraker, Michael. *Implementation of integrity constraints and views by query modification*, Proceedings of the ACM SIGMOD International Conference on the Management of Data, pp 65-78, May 1975.

[Teitelman78] Teitelman, Warren. *Interlisp Reference Manual*, Xerox Palo Alto Research Center, Palo Alto, California, October 1978.

[Wilson80] Wilson, Gerald A. *A conceptual model for semantic integrity checking*, Proc 1980 VLDB Conference, September 1980.

[Yao79] Yao, S. Bing, *Optimization of query evaluation algorithms*, **ACM Transactions on Database Systems,** 4:2 (June 1979) 133-155.

[Youssefi79] Youssefi, Karel A. Allen, and Wong, Eugene, *Query processing in a relational database management system*, **Proc. Fifth Intl. Conf. on Very Large Data Bases**, Rio de Janeiro, October 1979, 409-417.

Chapter 4

FAULT TOLERANT DISTRIBUTED DATA BASE DESIGN

One of the major advantages of distributed data base systems is their potential of achieving high availability if they are properly designed. There is a set of major problems that must be carefully considered during the design stage such as handling faults, commit point, network partitioning, reconfiguration, and node recovery. The main goal is for a system still to operate or operate in a degraded mode, in case failures occur. The designer should consider system requirements, the cost-performance of various fault tolerant algorithms and techniques, and then select the appropriate algorithm to be used for the system.

In this chapter, the first paper by Garcia-Molina provides an overview of reliability issues for fully replicated distributed data bases. The second paper by Parker, *et al.*, presents a method for detecting a single file, multiple copy mutual inconsistency efficiently in case of a network partitioned by failures. The third paper by Boor presents the fault tolerance design of a distributed data base for a loosely coupled multiple processor system. The fourth paper by Crus presents the various forms of data recovery provided by IBM Database 2, a data base management system that supports the relational model of data. The fifth paper presents a fault tolerant locking protocol for a tightly coupled distributed system for maintaining data consistency in case of failure during updating replicated record copies. The last paper by An and Chu discusses a low cost resilient protocol for real time systems which is based on one phase commit protocol with a back-up coordinator. This protocol ensures mutual consistency among file copies in case of multiple failures.

For more information on this subject, the interested reader is referred to [ALSB 76, ELLI 77, HAMM 80, SKEE 82, SKEE 81].

There are many types of failures possible in a fully replicated distributed database. This discussion of reliability divides design alternatives into seven broad categories.

Reliability Issues for Fully Replicated Distributed Databases

Hector Garcia-Molina, Princeton University

Reliability is commonly considered to be one of the main advantages of distributed databases, but there are problems that must be overcome before it can be achieved.

Exactly what is reliability? There are many types of failures, and we should know which types the system will be protected against. It is also necessary to define how the system will react to those failures. A considerable number of special protocols must be implemented with great care in order to realize the desired level of reliability.

The purpose of this article is to discuss the design alternatives and problems that must be solved in order to make a completely replicated distributed database reliable. A distributed database is completely replicated if a copy of the value of any data item is stored at every node (or site) in the system. A completely replicated distributed database is a special case of a general distributed database, and there are several reasons for studying the reliability issues in this limited context:

(1) Complete replication simplifies the problems. Making a distributed database reliable is not a simple matter, so as a first step we can try to understand a simplified specific case.

(2) Replicated data is the key to making data available after failures, so we will actually be concentrating on the critical component of distributed databases.

(3) Transaction processing (with no failures) in a completely replicated distributed database is well understood and a good number of papers have been written on the subject.[1-5]

Most of the research for reliable distributed databases has been performed in the context of particular transaction processing algorithms. (There are exceptions, however.[6,7]) This means that only the alternatives best suited to the transaction processing algorithm are considered. In this article this will be avoided by not advocating a particular transaction processing algorithm.

A person designing a reliable distributed database is faced with a set of choices. Here these choices are divided into seven broad categories and each category will be discussed in one of the following sections. For each choice that must be made by the designer, I will attempt to give the major alternatives available and then list the implications of these alternatives. Many of the mechanisms for reliable distributed databases that we will discuss have been presented in the literature. I would like to caution the reader that my division of choices is somewhat arbitrary and that the choices are not independent of each other.

Basic concepts

A completely replicated distributed database is a collection of named data items. Each item also has n values associated with it, where n is the number of nodes in the system. Each value for a given item is stored at a different node in the system. The values of an item should be the same, but due to the updating activity the values may be temporarily different. The values stored at a node are called the database of that node.

In addition to items and values, a distributed database has a collection of consistency constraints.[8] A consistency constraint is a predicate defined on the distributed database describing the relationships that must hold among the items and their values.

Operations on the data are grouped into transactions. Each transaction is a sequence of actions that preserve consistency. The following are examples of actions of a transaction: read the value of an item at a given node,

An earlier version of this article was published under the same title in *Proc. CompCon Fall 80*, Washington, DC, pp. 442-449.

write a new value of an item at a given node, lock an item, and lock a value of an item at a node.

A transaction processing algorithm (or concurrency control mechanism) must process transactions in a way that does not violate the consistency constraints. This last sentence may be interpreted in several ways, but a common interpretation[8] is that the effects on the distributed database of processing the transactions should be the same as the effect of executing the transactions one at a time (i.e., serially).

In order to prevent consistency violations, the transaction processing algorithm must monitor concurrently executing transactions to verify that they do not conflict. Two transactions conflict if their concurrent execution violates consistency. When the algorithm detects a conflict, it has two options: delay one of the transactions until the other conflicting transaction completes, or back out one of the two transactions. A transaction is backed out by undoing each of its actions so that the final effect is as if the transaction had never executed any of its actions. If the transaction that is backed out has written new values into the database, then the previous values of the modified items must have been saved in a log. And if another transaction has read the values produced by the transaction being undone, then that transaction too must be backed out. Notice that a transaction may also be backed out because of deadlocks, which are usually caused by conflicting transactions.

If the distributed database is to be reliable, the transaction processing algorithm should be capable of processing transactions without violating consistency, even in the face of failures. To make this statement more specific we must define what types of failures will be handled properly by the algorithm. This is actually the first choice faced by an algorithm designer and will be discussed in the next section. Guaranteeing consistency (i.e., equivalence to a serial execution of the transactions) in the face of failures is a common basic requirement for all algorithms, but in many cases the algorithm designer may have additional requirements. For example, it may also be required that if a single node fails or is isolated from the system, no transactions (other than those originating at the failed node) should be delayed indefinitely. Such requirements constitute additional decisions that must be made by the system designer and will be discussed later.

For a more complete discussion of basic concepts, see Eswaran et al.[8] and Gray.[9]

Types of failures

Protecting against all possible types of failures is in most cases impractical, so a first step in the design of a reliable transaction processing algorithm is to limit the types of failures that will be handled properly by the algorithm. Some failures that are expected to be rare or very hard to protect against will simply not be considered.

Let's look at the types of failures that could occur in a distributed database system.

• *Node failure.* This occurs when a node in the system "crashes" and temporarily ceases normal operation. Node failures can be further grouped into "soft" and "hard" failures. In a soft failure the node does not lose any vital state information or any values stored in its database. After a soft crash a node can usually recover by simply performing the updates it missed while it was down. In a hard failure the node loses some state information or data values. After a hard crash a node usually recovers by being placed in a previously saved safe state or checkpoint.

If the distributed database is to be reliable, the transaction processing algorithm should be capable of processing transactions without violating consistency, even in the face of failures.

• *Communication line failures.* These occur when messages between nodes are not transmitted properly. Let's assume that the protocol for sending a message from node X to node Y is as follows: Node X hands the message to the communications subsystem at time t, and d seconds later node X gets a response from the communications subsystem. (Here we use time in an intuitive fashion, but these concepts can be formalized.[10]) This response can either be positive ("message has been delivered") or negative ("message has not been delivered"). The delay d should be less than some predefined maximum acceptable delay d_m. At node Y there are several possible outcomes: the message may never be delivered; an erroneous message due to transmission errors may be delivered; the correct message may be delivered before $t+d$, but it may be out of sequence with respect to other X-Y messages; the correct message may be delivered in sequence before time $t+d$; the correct message may be delivered in sequence but after time $t+d$; and so on. This means that there are a large number of combined outcomes (e.g., no response at node X by time $t+d_m$ but message is delivered at Y in sequence before time $t+d_m$). Among all these outcomes, the only one not considered a communications failure is where node X gets a positive response before d_m seconds and the correct message is delivered at node Y in sequence and before time $t+d$. It is possible to protect against some of these failures by designing the communications subsystem properly (e.g., using sequence numbers to avoid out-of-order messages).

• *Malevolent failures.* A malevolent failure occurs when a node acts maliciously and does not follow the system protocols. An example would be if a node started generating and processing transactions that do not preserve consistency. Clearly, it is very hard to protect against such failures.

• *Multiple failures.* A multiple failure means that more than one of the failures we have discussed so far has occurred. If a transaction processing algorithm can still function properly after n failures, it is called n-resilient.[11] Algorithms that recover from multiple failures must guard against the situation where a failure occurs when the algorithm is recovering from a different failure.

- *Detectable failures.* If all nodes directly affected by a failure are able to recognize or discover that a failure has occurred, the failure is called detectable. But if the nodes continue to operate as if no failure has occurred, the failure is called undetected. For example, if a node's database is destroyed (e.g., by disk failure) and the node does not immediately recognize this, the hard node failure is called undetected. Clearly, this undefected failure can cause serious problems, as the failed node may attempt to modify other nodes' data based on its own erroneous data. Similarly, an undetected failure occurs when a node accepts as good a message that was altered by transmission errors. Another type of undetected communication failure occurs when a message's sender receives a positive response from the communication subsystem but the message is never delivered.

For another discussion of possible failures and their problems, see Rothnie and Goodman.[6]

As stated at the beginning of this section, the system designer may decide to ignore certain types of failures in order to simplify the job. There are two ways to do this: (1) Assume that the probability of a certain type of failure is so low that it will never occur, or (2) assume that some low-level mechanism will deal correctly with a certain type of failure so that the transaction processing algorithm will never encounter that failure.

Here are some of the more common assumptions that are made when designing transaction processing algorithms:

- No malevolent failures. Usually techniques from the area of security and protection are more useful in dealing with malevolent failures.
- No undetected failures. Data, state information, and messages can be coded so that errors can be detected (and possibly corrected) in most cases.
- No hard crashes. Local backup mechanisms such as logs and double-writing disk pages can make most hard crashes appear like soft crashes. Thus, hard crashes can be ignored in many cases.
- Maximum number of multiple node failures. In some systems it may be reasonable to assume that only a small number (e.g., one) of nodes may be down at any given time.
- No out-of-sequence messages. The communications subsystem can use sequence numbers to order messages so that they will never be delivered in the wrong order.
- No communication software failures. If the communications subsystem is thoroughly tested, most bugs can be eliminated. Thus, we may assume that a sending node will always get some response after d_m seconds and that if a positive response is given the message has been delivered.
- No communication failures. If the communication hardware is very reliable, we can assume that all messages will be delivered unless the destination node is down. For example, this may be a reasonable assumption for an Ethernet[12] or for a store-and-forward network with high connectivity.
- Communication failures only after node isolation. Another assumption may be that the communications subsystem is sufficiently robust so that only when a destination node is physically cut off or isolated from the source node will a message fail to be delivered.
- Consensus on failure identification. It is also possible to assume that once a node detects a failure, either node or communication, then all nodes connected to the detecting node will also identify the failure. Consider the following illustration. Node X is trying to send a message to node Y but gets a negative response from the communications subsystem. Then, if node X is able to communicate with another node, for example Z, and if there is a consensus on failure identification, then node X may assume that node Z cannot reach node Y either. This may be a reasonable assumption if the communication subsystem tries all communication paths from X to Y (including the one through Z) before giving the negative response to node X. Such an assumption simplifies the recovery protocols because it is impossible to have a group of connected nodes where some nodes say they can communicate with a node Y and the rest say they cannot.

Partitions

A partition of the distributed database occurs when the system is split into groups of isolated nodes. The nodes in each group can communicate with each other, but no node in the group is able to communicate with nodes in other groups. Notice that there may be only a single node in some groups.

The system designer must decide how the system will operate after a partition has occurred. There are three basic alternatives: (1) allow each group of nodes to process new transactions, (2) allow at most one group to process transactions, and (3) halt all transaction processing until the system is united again.

Since the idea behind complete data replication is to make the data accessible after failures, alternative 3 does not seem reasonable. As a matter of fact, since the data is replicated we see that any group has all the necessary data to process transactions; thus, alternative 1 may seem reasonable. Unfortunately, allowing more than one group to process transactions has some serious disadvantages. As each group processes different transactions and stores new values in the databases, the databases (i.e., the values at the nodes) will "diverge"; an item will have different values at different nodes. When the partition is eliminated, the distributed database will be inconsistent and corrective action must be taken.

There are two strategies for making the distributed database consistent after the partition ends. One strategy is to undo transactions. For example, for each item with different values, one of the values—let's call it v—is selected. The value of the item at all nodes is made equal to v. Then, any transaction is undone if, during the partition, it read or wrote the item at any of the nodes that did not have the value v. Any other transaction that read data produced by the undone transaction must also be undone, and this undoing requires the use of a detailed log. The undoing of transactions will be very time-consuming. Furthermore, users who submit transactions during a partition will not know if the values produced by their transaction are valid until the partition is corrected. In this case, transactions are unable to commit during a partition. (For a complete discussion of this strategy, see Davidson.[13])

A second strategy for making the distributed database consistent is to integrate the inconsistent values. As discussed by Rothnie and Goodman,[6] this is a very hard problem that requires semantic knowledge. For example, consider an item i that represents the deposits made into a bank account. If after a partition item i has values v_1 and v_2, then item i can be made to have the value $v_1 + v_2$ minus the value of i at partition time.

Since multiple operating groups after a partition lead to some very hard problems, alternative 2 is usually taken as a reasonable compromise. With only one operating group, recovery after the partition is simpler (i.e., nodes in the nonactive partitions must perform all updates they missed). The only problem now is how to guarantee that at most one group processes transactions. The solution is not hard. At system initiation time, a number of points are distributed to the nodes. Each node knows its number of points and also the total number of points P. Any group of nodes that has a majority of points can process new transactions because it knows that no other group can have a majority of points. (A majority is $P/2 + 1$ if P is even, $(P + 1)/2$ if P is odd.) This majority requirement guarantees that at most one group will process transactions during a partition.[5,14]

The number of points given to a node should reflect how important it is for the node to continue processing transactions during a partition. For example, a node that gets a majority of points by itself will always be able to operate. At the other extreme, if all nodes get an equal number of points, they will have equal weight in forming an operating group.

Notice that special read-only transactions can still be run in groups that are not in operation due to a partition. Users who submit such a special read-only transaction at a node isolated from the operating majority will get the desired values with a warning that the values may be out of date. The values read at the isolated nodes may also be inconsistent. This will depend on the concurrency control strategy used. If consistent data is required at the isolated nodes, care must be taken to select a concurrency control algorithm that can guarantee this.

Efficient operation after failures

The next important step in the design of a reliable transaction processing algorithm is to define the expected system performance after a failure. In particular, the designer must decide if it is acceptable for some or all transactions to be delayed until failures are repaired.

In the previous section we discovered that it is very hard to process transactions in more than one group of a partition. Therefore, it seems that some transactions, mainly those originating in the nonactive groups, will have to be delayed until the partition is repaired. In this section we will concentrate on the transactions originating in the active group of a partition and decide if they also may be delayed.

An equivalent situation occurs when some nodes fail but there is no partition. In this case we must also decide if the transactions submitted at the active nodes may be delayed because of the failed nodes. Both the partition and the node failure cases are equivalent because in both situations we have a group of nodes that know that no other node outside the group may process transactions. Thus, we consider both cases together here and call the nodes that may process transactions the active nodes or group.

The algorithm designer is faced with a basic choice: Either it is or it isn't acceptable for some transactions in the active group to be delayed. Allowing some (or possibly all) transactions to be delayed may be reasonable in some systems, and it simplifies the design of the transaction processing algorithm. For example, in systems where failures are very rare, where downtime of nodes and communication lines is brief, or where access to the data is not critical, it may be acceptable to allow some transactions in the active group to be delayed. The advantages of doing so should become clear as soon as we discuss all that is needed in order to guarantee that no transactions in the active group are delayed.

Detecting conflicts among transactions is the hardest part of transaction processing with missing nodes.

If transactions in the active group cannot be delayed they must be executed, even though some nodes may be inaccessible. There are basically four types of actions that must be executed by a transaction: read, compute, write, and synchronization (i.e., conflict detection). Read actions are no problem because the distributed database is completely replicated and the values needed by a transaction will be available in any group. Similarly, the computations can be done at any node in the system.

Since the data is replicated at all nodes, every transaction must write its results at all nodes. Unfortunately, after a failure some nodes may not be accessible. Therefore, if transactions are to be processed with inaccessible nodes, there is a need for a mechanism to guarantee that writes at the missing nodes will eventually occur—and in the proper order. The alternatives for such a mechanism will be discussed later when node recovery is explored.

Detecting conflicts among transactions is the hardest part of transaction processing with missing nodes. This problem will be treated in detail in the next three sections. Meanwhile, in order to understand the problem, it is first necessary to realize that in certain cases transactions will have to be undone because they cannot be completed and they interfere with the conflict detection process. That is, after a failure a transaction T may be left in a peculiar state where the active nodes are unable to complete T because some critical information was lost in the failure, or because the active nodes are unable to tell if T conflicts with other transactions. Furthermore, the unfinished transaction *T* may interfere with the processing of other transactions because *T* holds (synchronization) resources needed by the other transactions. In this case the unfinished transaction must be canceled and the resources it holds must be released.

To illustrate this situation, consider a transaction processing algorithm where transactions must lock all the values they reference before performing any other actions. Suppose that a transaction *T* is submitted at a node *X* and, after *T* obtains the required locks at all nodes, node *X* crashes. The remaining nodes are unable to complete *T* because the information about what *T* was going to do was at node *X*. Unless transaction *T* is canceled and the locks are reclaimed, other transactions that need those locks will be delayed until node *X* recovers. After transaction *T* is canceled, the system may try executing *T* at a later time.

Canceling a transaction is similar to backing out a transaction after a conflict is detected in that all actions of the transaction must be undone. However, when backing out a transaction after a conflict, all involved nodes are accessible and the action can be undone immediately. On the other hand, when canceling a transaction some nodes will not be accessible, making it necessary to design a mechanism to guarantee that the actions are eventually undone at the inaccessible nodes. This mechanism should also guarantee that when the inaccessible nodes rejoin the active group they will not attempt to finish a transaction that has been canceled. Therefore, we will use the term back out to mean undoing a transaction after a conflict is detected; the term cancel will mean undoing a transaction that cannot be completed due to failures in the system. Notice that many transaction processing algorithms do not need a backing-out protocol, but most algorithms (if not all) will need a canceling protocol.

The implementation of the canceling protocol is dependent on the commit strategy used, so further comments on transaction canceling will be deferred.

Commit point

As a transaction is performing its various actions, it is not sure that it will ever complete because at any time it may be backed out due to a conflict or canceled due to a failure. Furthermore, it may be a very long time before the transaction actually completes because some nodes where the transaction has to perform actions may be inaccessible. It would be desirable if at some time the transaction could know for sure if it was going to complete. This point, called the commit point, occurs when the transaction can guarantee that it will never be backed out or canceled. (The commit point is sometimes defined as the time when the values produced by a transaction first become available to other transactions.[7] However, in some algorithms[4] transactions may be backed out after they have given values to other transactions, so we prefer the first definition.)

When a transaction reaches its commit point, the transaction undo information in the log may be deleted or placed in some slow storage device, because it will not be needed. In addition, the user who submitted the transaction may be informed that the transaction has committed, and he will know that any values produced by this transaction will actually be recorded in the database.

The algorithm designer now has two choices: allow transactions to defer the commit decision until all nodes are accessible, or force transactions to commit (or to be canceled or backed out) even when nodes are inaccessible.

If the first choice is taken, users of the system may get responses like: "Your deposit of 10 dollars to account XXX has been processed. Your new balance is tentatively 110 dollars, but since some nodes are down it is not possible to confirm this balance until the failures are corrected." Such a response may be acceptable in some cases. Of course, when the failures are corrected, many transactions may have to be backed out. The faster the failures are repaired, the fewer transactions will be backed out.

If the commit decision can be delayed, the protocol for guaranteeing that a transaction will not be backed out or canceled is relatively simple. This protocol is called the *two-phase commit* protocol.[9] In this protocol, a coordinator node for a transaction *T* sends "prepare" messages to all nodes. A positive response to the prepare message from a node *X* means that, as far as that node *X* is concerned, *T* did not conflict with other transactions and *X* has sufficient information to complete *T* if necessary. When the coordinator for *T* gets positive responses from *all* nodes in the system (and this is where delays are introduced), *T* has reached its commit point. In the second phase, the coordinator sends "commit" messages to all nodes informing them that *T* has committed.

If the commit decision cannot be delayed until failures are repaired (the second choice), then the commit protocol is more complex. But before this more complex protocol is implemented, the algorithm designer must decide whether it is acceptable to reconfigure the system after a failure.

Reconfiguration

System reconfiguration after a failure involves taking some time out to clean up pending work and redefine what nodes are in charge of guaranteeing that transactions are not backed out or canceled. More specifically, reconfiguration generally consists of the following steps:

(1) Temporarily halt all transaction processing. When a node detects a failure, it goes into a special state where only reconfiguration is attempted. (Nodes may also enter the reconfiguration state voluntarily—for example, to admit a new node into the active group.)

(2) Forming a group. Each node will check to see what nodes are accessible; that is, each node will discover what other nodes are in its group. The nodes in a group should also agree among themselves as to what nodes are in the group. In addition, the nodes of the group elect a coordinator which manages the rest of the recovery. When this step completes there should be a single coordinator for each group, and all members should agree on the identity of this coordinator. Several protocols have

been suggested for group formation and coordinator election.[3, 15-17]

(3) Check for majority. The coordinator of each group should determine if its group has a majority of points. (See discussion of partitions.) If there aren't enough nodes in the group, the reconfiguration attempt is aborted and restarted at some later time. If a majority is obtained, the reconfiguration may proceed. (If this check for a majority of points is omitted, there may be multiple active groups. In this section and the next we are not interested in this case, since transactions cannot commit if there are several active groups.)

(4) Select new version number. At each reorganization, the operating group is assigned a version number that distinguishes the group from all other active groups. The version number selected is one plus the greatest previous version number reported by a member of the new group. The version number is very useful in identifying messages from nodes that are not aware that the reconfiguration has occurred. All messages carry the version number of the source node and are rejected if the destination node has a larger version number.

(5) Reconfigure. The distributed database is now defined to include only the nodes in the current active group. The version number mechanism allows all other nodes to be treated as if they did not exist. Later, if a "nonexistent" node wishes to join the group, another reconfiguration will be necessary. The strategy for detecting conflicts can be modified at this point. Even if the same strategy is followed, the number of nodes required to detect a conflict can be redefined, or the specific nodes that detect conflicts (e.g., a central controller node) can be selected. The total number of points, P, can also be reassigned among the nodes of the current group. If this is done, the definition of majority of points, given earlier, must be modified slightly. (Specifically, if a node has a version number smaller than any other version number in a group, then that node is defined to have zero points.) Note the implications. For example, in a three-node system each node can have one point. After one node fails, the two remaining nodes get two and one points. A second node could then fail and the remaining node could still continue processing transactions. This would not be possible without reconfiguration, or if the original system partitioned into three groups.

(6) Finish pending transactions. All pending (unfinished) transactions should either be committed or canceled. This can be done by the coordinator, which collects all information the other nodes have on pending transactions. Notice that all pending transactions that are unknown to the current group can be automatically canceled by the version number mechanism.

(7) Resume normal transaction processing. All nodes leave the special reconfiguration state and go into normal operation.

The reconfiguration protocol must be designed very carefully because failures may occur during a reconfiguration. For example, when the group coordinator finishes pending transactions (step 6), it may also encounter some transactions that were in the process of being canceled or committed by a previous group coordinator. Thus, a new coordinator must continue the work started by previous coordinators, so that the protocol converges even if multiple failures occur.[16,17]

The main advantage of having reconfigurations is that the system (actually, what remains of the system) will operate more efficiently while nodes are inaccessible. On the other hand, the reconfiguration itself will take some time, so reconfiguration will pay off only if the expected time between failures is relatively large. If failures are common, then it may be better to have a system that can operate properly through failures and without the need to reconfigure.

Implementation of the commit protocol

The most important protocol for a reliable distributed database is probably the commit protocol. A previous section described a two-phase commit protocol for the case where the commit decision could be delayed until all failures are repaired. If the commit decision cannot wait, the two-phase commit protocol must be modified, and the transaction processing algorithm designer has a large number of alternatives for doing this. Some of these choices will be outlined briefly.

A transaction T reaches its commit point when it is known for sure that T will not be backed out or canceled. Thus, we may think of the commit protocol as having two distinct steps: (1) guaranteeing that the transaction T will not be backed out (i.e., detecting conflicts) and (2) guaranteeing that T will not be canceled. Under the proper conditions these two steps can be combined into one, but for discussion purposes let's consider them as separate steps.

The main advantage of having reconfigurations is that the system will operate more efficiently while nodes are inaccessible.

Suppose that after some failures there is a single active majority group with n nodes out of the total of N nodes. The main requirement for steps 1 and 2 is that the number of nodes that participate in making sure that a transaction T is not backed out (step 1) or canceled (step 2) should be less than or equal to n; otherwise there would be delays.

For step 1 a large number of protocols have been suggested for detecting conflicts. These protocols can (1) use one or more specific nodes for detecting conflicts (e.g., a central synchronization node), (2) use all n nodes, or (3) use a majority mechanism similar to the one in the section on partitions.[5] If the majority mechanism is used, nodes are again given points, which we now call votes; and when a transaction T obtains commitments that T will not be backed out from a set of nodes with a majority of votes, then it is *known* that T will not be backed out. Notice that the votes assigned to nodes for this procedure can be different from the points used for forming active groups. Also notice that with this mechanism, reorganization will not be necessary until there are not enough votes in the active group to obtain a majority of votes.

If all *n* nodes participate in detecting conflicts, a reorganization will be necessary every time the active group loses any node. If one or more specific nodes are in charge of conflict detection, a reorganization will be needed any time one of these specific nodes becomes disconnected from the active group.

Notice that if all *n* nodes (alternative 2) or some specific nodes (alternative 1) are used for the protocol of step 1, then that protocol does not have to concern itself with failures. The moment that one of the specific nodes (case 1) or any node (case 2) fails, no more transactions will be processed by the protocol. Thus, after the failure, no transaction that received a guarantee that it would not be backed out will have to be backed out due to a conflict. Some transactions may have to be canceled because of the failure, but step 1 makes no promises about this. On the other hand, if a majority mechanism is used, the protocol for step 1 (i.e., conflict detection) can still operate after some failures. In this case, then, care must be taken to ensure that a guarantee that a transaction does not conflict will be honored as long as there are enough nodes in the active group so that the protocol may operate.

There are also many alternatives for step 2 of the commit protocol. To guarantee that a transaction *T* will never be canceled we need to make sure that any future active group knows that *T* does not conflict and that it has enough information to successfully complete *T*. This implies that out of the *k* nodes that will guarantee that *T* will not be canceled, at least one should be in any future active group. This can be achieved if the *k* nodes have at least a majority of the type of points used to form active groups.

These considerations lead to the following protocol,[7,16,18] which is based on the two-phase commit protocol mentioned earlier. A coordinator node for transaction *T* sends "prepare" messages to all active nodes. A positive response to this message is given by nodes that know *T* did not conflict (result of step 1) and know also that they can complete *T* if necessary (e.g., the nodes have copies of the new values produced by *T*). The nodes that give a positive response remember this and are said to be in a "prepared-for-*T*" state. (If nodes can forget their state information, the protocol gets more involved.) As the coordinator receives positive responses for *T*, it adds the total number of points for the nodes that have responded. When this sum becomes larger than a fixed value *p*, then *T* reaches its commit point. The value *p* is chosen by the designer but should always be larger than a majority of the total points *P*. The coordinator then sends "commit" messages to all nodes in the active group informing them that *T* has committed.

The choice of parameter *p* in step 2 involves the same trade-offs as the selection of the number of nodes that participate in step 1. If *p* is equal to *P*, then positive responses are required from all nodes in the active group. This makes reorganization mandatory whenever a node becomes inaccessible, but it simplifies the protocols that are related to the commit protocol (e.g., canceling protocol, reconfiguration, etc.). For example, if $p=P$, then transactions need only be canceled during reconfigurations. This means that the canceling protocol for this case can use the version number mechansim. If *p* is less than *P*, then transactions may have to be canceled any time, and a more complex protocol is needed.

In certain cases, complications may arise with the commit protocol. Suppose there is a node *X* in the active group that does not participate in either step 1 or step 2 of the commit protocol of transaction *T*. This node is not aware of the existence of *T* even though *T* has committed. Now suppose that a second transaction *S* reads some values produced by *T* (at a node other than *X*) and attempts to write some new values at node *X*. Simply writing these values can produce inconsistencies in the data because *T* has not completed at node *X*. Therefore, a special mechanism is needed to avoid the problems.

One solution is to use time stamps to ensure that out-of-order writes do not violate consistency, as in Thomas.[5] Or, when a central node is in charge of concurrency control, a second solution is to use "wait-for" lists.[16] The wait-for list for transaction *S* is a list of the transaction names of all transactions whose write actions must precede the write actions of *S*. The information needed to build wait-for lists is easily available at the central node. The wait-for list of *S* is appended to all messages that contain commands to execute write actions of *S* and can be used to avoid out-of-order writes. (In our example, the wait-for list of *S* would contain *T*, and thus node *X* would delay execution of the *S* actions until the missing *T* actions were performed.) These mechanisms are only needed when the number of nodes participating in steps 1 and 2 is less than the number of nodes in the active group, and this is one more factor to consider when choosing a commit protocol.

As mentioned earlier, steps 1 and 2 of the commit protocol can be combined in certain cases. So instead of the three phases suggested above (detect conflicts, prepare nodes, and inform nodes of commit), it may be possible to detect conflicts as nodes are prepared. However, if a node is allowed to respond positively to a prepared message for transaction *T* without knowing whether *T* conflicts, then after a failure it is possible to end up in a state where the active nodes know that *T* may have committed (and hence cannot be canceled) but do not know if *T* had conflicts (and hence *must* be canceled). So, steps 1 and 2 can only be combined if this can never occur—that is, if knowing that *T* may have committed implies that *T* does not conflict with other transactions.

For example, consider a system where each node has a single lock and is assigned one point. Suppose that a transaction *T* is processed as follows:

(1) *T* is submitted at node *X*.
(2) *T* is delayed until *X*'s lock is free. *X*'s lock is set and the values needed by *T* are read from the database at node *X*.
(3) The new values to be stored in the distributed database are computed by node *X*.
(4) Node *X* sends prepare messages with the new values to all nodes.
(5) When a node *Y* receives a prepare message for *T*, it checks its lock. If it is free, *Y* saves the values in a safe place, sets its lock, and gives a positive response. If *Y*'s lock is set, a negative response is given and *T* will be backed out.

(6) When node *X* gets positive responses from *all* active nodes, *T* is committed and commit messages are sent to all nodes. Node *X* stores the values produced by *T* in its database and releases its lock.

(7) When a node *Y* receives a commit message for *T*, the values that were saved are stored in the database and *Y*'s lock is released.

Notice that this sample algorithm has combined steps 1 and 2 of the commit protocol. After a failure and during reconfiguration, which is necessary after every failure, the active nodes can look at each pending transaction *T*. If at least one active node is not prepared for *T*, then *T* did not commit and may be canceled. If all active nodes are prepared for *T*, then *T* may have committed; fortunately *T* can be completed. The values produced by *T* are known, and the active nodes know that *T* holds locks at nodes with a majority of points (i.e., *T* does not conflict with any other transaction).

Notice that if step 6 of this sample algorithm is modified so that only a majority of positive responses is required for commitment, then it is possible to get into a state where a transaction cannot be canceled or completed. (An interesting exercise would be to show how one can get into this state.) Thus, in this example, if only a majority of nodes participate in the commit protocol, three phases are needed: request all locks, prepare nodes, and commit. Furthermore, in this case a mechanism like a wait-for list is needed to prevent inconsistencies. On the other hand, reconfigurations would not be necessary after every failure.

Before closing this section, I would like to make two additional comments. Notice that the commit and canceling protocols are highly dependent on each other and must be designed together. The commit protocol guarantees that a transaction will not be canceled, and the canceling protocol should guarantee (among other things) that a transaction will not commit. Hence, in addition to making sure that a transaction is undone, the canceling protocol must interact with the nodes that participate in step 2 of the commit protocol to make sure they do not commit the transaction.

Also notice that if we restrict the types of failures that can occur, the commit and canceling protocols can be simplified considerably. For example, if no communications failures can occur, then partitions will never occur and all protocols will be simpler.[19] Similarly, assuming that at most one node will be down at a given time will make the protocols less elaborate.

Node recovery

After failures are repaired, nodes that were isolated need to rejoin the active group and start processing transactions once more. This is made possible by the node recovery procedures. These procedures are highly dependent on the rest of the protocols we have discussed, but the algorithm designer still has some important new choices to make with respect to node recovery.

While a node is isolated from the active group, it does not perform any actions of the running transactions. Since the data is replicated at every node, all transactions must perform some actions at all nodes (i.e., write new values into the database); so when a node becomes accessible once more, all the actions that were missed must be performed. One question that must be answered is "What nodes are in charge of remembering the missed actions for a node that is inaccessible?" There are at least three answers to this question:

(1) No saving. If no node saves the missed actions, the recovering node will be unable to catch up by performing the actions it missed. Thus, the node must recover by requesting a complete up-to-date copy of the database from an active node. If failures are rare and databases small, this may be an acceptable solution.

(2) Save in log. The missed actions can be saved in a conventional type of log. There are many possible ways to do this: for example, there may be some distinguished logging nodes, all nodes may log all transactions, or each transaction may be logged at its originating node. If this solution is used, a transaction numbering or naming scheme is required. This way a recovering node can discover what transactions it missed, and the actions for these transactions can be requested from the log or logs. Sequence numbers assigned to transactions at some central node are especially useful, although not necessary.

(3) Persistent messages.[20] A third solution is to give the communications subsystem the responsibility for remembering the missed actions. In this case we assume that once a message is accepted by the communications subsystem, the subsystem guarantees eventual delivery of the message to the destination node. If this mechanism is available, every transaction can send a persistent message to all nodes with the new values that were produced by the transaction. As soon as a node is available again, the communications subsystem will deliver all the missed actions; in other words, it acts as an active log. Persistent messages are a powerful idea for "layering" the recovery protocols, but their use may introduce some inefficiencies. For example, logs may have to be kept in any case for hard-crash node recovery and backing out transactions, so the information saved by the communication subsystem may be duplicated.

If we restrict the types of failures that can occur, the commit and canceling protocols can be simplified considerably.

In addition to deciding where and how the missed actions are to be saved, the algorithm designer must construct the protocols for actually bringing a node up. In some cases it may be possible to add a node to an active group without interrupting the group's normal operation. For example, suppose that in an active group a node *X* is not needed for either step of the commit protocol. Then node *X* may fail and the active group may continue operation. When node *X* is repaired, it can simply start operating normally again. If a wait-for list mechanism is used, the missed actions will be automatically requested as new transactions arrive at node Y. If time stamps are used, node X can operate without the missed write actions. In other cases it may be necessary to perform a reconfiguration in order to add a node to an active group.

The protocols for joining an active group become more complex if the recovering node has lost any state information or if its database has been destroyed. For example, if nodes can forget that they are prepared for a transaction T, then in step 2 of the commit protocol it is not sufficient to obtain positive responses from nodes with a majority of points. If the protocol instead waits for positive responses from nodes with a majority plus q points, then it is possible to guarantee that a transaction will not be canceled, as long as no set of nodes with q or more combined points lose their state information.

Conclusions

We have discussed the major design alternatives faced by the designer of a reliable fully replicated distributed database. We can view these alternatives as forming a large "decision tree" where each node in the tree represents one of the choices to be made. We have analyzed some of the nodes close to the root of our tree, but, of course, there are many additional nodes dealing with specific implementation choices that we have not covered.

Each leaf in our decision tree represents a sequence of design choices leading to a specific reliable concurrency control algorithm with certain operating characteristics. A number of these algorithms have been studied in detail, but they represent a small minority of the leaves on the decision tree. There are actually entire unexplored sections in this tree. For example, algorithms that after a partition allow multiple groups of nodes to process update transactions have hardly been studied at all.

There is a cost associated with each leaf of the decision tree. This cost should take into account the complexity of the algorithm as well as the overhead incurred by the algorithm in sending extra messages and performing extra checks. As the tree is traversed, the designer should keep in mind the cost incurred by each decision and whether the cost can be justified. Reliability does not come for free; in many cases the distributed database designer may have to settle for algorithms that do not protect against some possible failures—or any failures at all. ■

References

1. P. A. Bernstein et al., "The Concurrency Control Mechanism of SDD-1: A System for Distributed Databases (The Fully Redundant Case)," *IEEE Trans. Software Eng.*, Vol. 4, No. 3, May 1978, pp. 154-168.
2. C. A. Ellis, "Consistency and Correctness of Duplicate Database Systems," *Sixth Symp. Operating System Principles*, Nov. 1977, pp. 67-84.
3. A. Kaneko et al., "Logical Clock Synchronization Method for Duplicated Database Control," *First Int'l Conf. Distributed Computing Systems*, Huntsville, Ala., Oct. 1979, pp. 601-611.
4. A. Takagi, "Concurrent and Reliable Updates of Distributed Databases," MIT Laboratory for Computer Science, Report MIT/LCS/TM-144, Nov. 1979.
5. R. H. Thomas, "A Majority Consensus Approach to Concurrency Control," *ACM Trans. Database Systems*, Vol. 4, No. 2, June 1979, pp. 180-209.
6. J. B. Rothnie and N. Goodman, "A Survey of Research and Development in Distributed Database Management," *Third VLDB Conf.*, Tokyo, 1977, pp. 48-62.
7. L. Svododova, "Reliability Issues in Distributed Information Processing Systems," *Ninth Symp. Fault Tolerant Computing*, Madison, Wis., June 1979, pp. 9-16.
8. K. P. Eswaran et. al., "The Notions of Consistency and Predicate Locks in a Database System," *Comm. ACM*, Vol. 19, No. 11, Nov. 1976, pp. 624-633.
9. J. N. Gray, "Notes on Database Operating Systems," Advanced Course on Operating Systems, Technical University Munich, July 1977.
10. L. Lamport, "Time, Clocks, and the Ordering of Events in a Distributed System," *Comm. ACM*, Vol. 21, No. 7, July 1978, pp. 558-564.
11. P. A. Alsberg and J. D. Day, "A Principle for Resilient Sharing of Distributed Resources," *Second Int'l Conf. Software Eng.*, San Francisco, 1976, pp. 562-570.
12. R. M. Metcalfe and D. R. Boggs, "Ethernet: Distributed Packet Switching for Local Computer Networks," *Comm. ACM*, Vol. 19, No. 7, July 1976, pp. 395-404.
13. S. Davidson, "An Optimistic Protocol for Partitioned Distributed Database Systems," PhD Thesis, EECS Department, Princeton University, July 1982.
14. D. K. Gifford, "Weighted Voting for Replicated Data," *Seventh Symp. Operating System Principles*, Dec. 1979, pp. 150-162.
15. M. Stonebraker, "Concurrency Control and Consistency of Multiple Copies of Data in Distributed INGRES," *IEEE Trans. Software Eng.*, Vol. SE-5, No. 3, May 1979, pp. 188-194.
16. H. Garcia-Molina, "Performance of Update Algorithms for Replicated Data in a Distributed Database," Report STAN-CS-79-744, Department of Computer Science, Stanford University, June 1979.
17. D. A. Menasce, G. J. Popek, and R. R. Muntz, "A Locking Protocol for Resource Coordination in Distributed Databases," *ACM Trans. Database Systems*, Vol. 5, No. 2, June 1980, pp. 103-138.
18. D. Skeen, "A Quorum-Based Commit Protocol," *Proc. Sixth Berkeley Workshop Distributed Data Management and Computer Networks*, Feb. 1982, pp. 69-80.
19. F. B. Schneider, "Synchronization in Distributed Programs," Technical Report TR 79-391, Department of Computer Science, Cornell University, Jan. 1980.
20. W. R. Sutherland, "Distributed Computation Research at BBN," Vol. III, Bolt, Beranek, and Newman Technical Report 2974, 1974.

Detection of Mutual Inconsistency in Distributed Systems

D. STOTT PARKER, JR., GERALD J. POPEK, GERARD RUDISIN, ALLEN STOUGHTON, BRUCE J. WALKER, EVELYN WALTON, JOHANNA M. CHOW, DAVID EDWARDS, STEPHEN KISER, AND CHARLES KLINE

Abstract—Many distributed systems are now being developed to provide users with convenient access to data via some kind of communications network. In many cases it is desirable to keep the system functioning even when it is partitioned by network failures. A serious problem in this context is how one can support redundant copies of resources such as files (for the sake of reliability) while simultaneously monitoring their mutual consistency (the equality of multiple copies). This is difficult since network failures can lead to inconsistency, and disrupt attempts at maintaining consistency. In fact, even the *detection* of inconsistent copies is a nontrivial problem. Naive methods either 1) compare the multiple copies entirely or 2) perform simple tests which will diagnose some consistent copies as inconsistent. Here a new approach, involving *version vectors* and *origin points*, is presented and shown to detect single file, multiple copy mutual inconsistency effectively. The approach has been used in the design of *LOCUS*, a local network operating system at UCLA.

Index Terms—Availability, distributed systems, mutual consistency, network failures, network partitioning, replicated data.

I. Introduction

A NUMBER of operating systems have been developed recently in which user files are distributed almost without restriction around a network. These systems range from network operating systems (NOS's) such as RSEXEC, NSW, ELAN [17], and DCS [4], to distributed database management systems (DDBMS's) like SDD-1 [5], [13] and INGRES [15]. These systems emphasize the uniform interfacing of multiple file systems. Files are to be accessible throughout the network, without regard to the accessor or file location.

Unfortunately, a file can be made inaccessible by network failures or crashes of the site where the file is located, so users may obtain randomly fluctuating views of the state of the network. To alleviate this problem, many of the systems propose to keep duplicate copies of files as a reliability mechanism. This solution engenders another problem. As soon as multiple copies of a file exist, the system must ensure the *mutual consistency* of these copies: when one copy of the file is modified, all must be modified correspondingly before an independent access can take place.

Much has been written about the problem of maintaining consistency in distributed systems, ranging from *internal* consistency methods (ways to keep a single copy of a resource looking consistent to multiple processes attempting to access it concurrently) to various ingenious updating algorithms which ensure mutual consistency [1], [2], [6], [8], [16], etc. We concern ourselves here with mutual consistency in the face of *network partitioning*, i.e., the situation where various sites in the network cannot communicate with each other for some length of time due to network failures or site crashes. This is a very real problem in most networks. For example, even in the Ethernet [10], gateways can be inoperative for significant lengths of time, while the Ether segments they normally connect operate correctly.

Network partitioning can completely destroy mutual consistency in the worst case, and this fact has led to a certain amount of restrictiveness, vagueness, and even nervousness in past discussions, of how it may be handled. In some environments it is desirable or necessary to permit users to continue modifying resources such as files when the network is partitioned. A network operating system would be a good example. In such environments mutual inconsistency becomes a fact of life which must be dealt with. This paper shows that in this case mutual inconsistency can be efficiently detected through the use of what we call *version vectors* and *origin points.* Once inconsistency is detected, some reconciliation steps are needed. In those cases where the semantics of the operations involved are straightforward, automatic reconciliation may be possible.

It is worth reflecting for a moment on the worth of keeping redundant copies. Although redundancy increases reliability and availability, and in most cases improves access time, it leads to mutual consistency problems when network partitions occur. When considering whether to store a file redundantly one must weigh the advantage of greater availability, the probability of a mutual inconsistency, and the ramifications of such an inconsistency. In many NOS environments, file update rates are moderate and "conflicts" would occur only rarely. However, in transaction-oriented DDBMS's update rates may be high, semantics of operations complex, and consistency extremely important.

Manuscript received November 11, 1980; revised November 13, 1981. This work was supported in part by ARPA Reseach Contract DSS MDA-903-77-C-0211 and in part by ONR Grant N00014-79-C-0866.

D. S. Parker, Jr., G. J. Popek, A. Stoughton, B. J. Walker, E. Walton, J. M. Chow, D. Edwards, and C. Kline are with the Department of Computer Science, University of California, Los Angeles, CA 90024.

G. Rudisin was with the Department of Computer Science, University of California, Los Angeles, CA 90024. He is now with the Systems Technology Center, Western Digital Company, Pittsburgh, PA 15213.

S. Kiser was with the Department of Computer Science, University of California, Los Angeles, CA 90024. He is now with Xerox Corporation, El Segundo, CA 90245.

The results of this paper may be nevertheless useful in any system where mutual inconsistency, presumably due to network partitioning, is tolerated. Since our application (*LOCUS* [12], [14], [18]) is concerned with files, we will restrict our discussion henceforth to mutual consistency of *files* rather than of general resources. It is clear, however, that all results here may be applied to more general contexts.

The paper is organized as follows. Section II briefly surveys previous research on the partitioning problem. Section III then lays the formal groundwork on inconsistency detection. An accurate and easily implemented technique for detecting mutual inconsistency is developed. Section IV points out briefly what must be done in the reconciliation of inconsistent copies. Although the reconciliation of these conflicts must necessarily be left to the user in some cases, it is also demonstrated that for certain kinds of files (mailboxes, directories) the reconciliation may be performed automatically by the system. Finally, conclusions are offered in Section V.

II. Previous Work on Partitioning

Network partitioning is the situation occurring when a network is broken into logically separate components because of site or link failures. There are many partitioning-related issues which *must* be addressed in the design of distributed file systems. These issues include the relative importance of availability over mutual consistency of files, what occurs when one finds a file has become inaccessible or out of date, and so forth.

To our knowledge, however, partitioning has not been investigated very thoroughly. It has been mentioned in several proposed methods for updating files in distributed systems. The most typical response has been to enforce consistency by permitting files to be accessed only in one partition. Unfortunately, effective implementation of this policy can often result in the files being accessible in *zero* partitions. We outline several existing proposals below.

Voting: In voting-based systems such as proposed by Thomas [16] and Menasce *et al.* [9], mutual consistency is guaranteed at the expense of availability. Users desiring to modify a file must lock it by obtaining majority assent in a vote. Since there can be at most one partition containing a majority of the sites, any file will be accessible in at most one partition. Unfortunately, it is possible that there will be no partition which contains a majority of the sites, so in this case no updates could occur anywhere.

Tokens: Here it is assumed that each file has a token associated with it, which permits the bearer to modify the file. Obtaining the token is another issue, reducible more or less to locking. In this model only sites in the partition containing the token are permitted to modify the file, so using tokens is less restrictive than using voting. However, the problem of recreating lost tokens is nontrivial. Moreover, when a partition occurs, the token may happen to be resident in a rarely used part of the network, effectively making the resource unavailable.

Primary Sites: Originally discussed by Alsberg and Day [1], this approach suggests that a single site be appointed responsible for a file's activities. Upon partitioning (possibly involving a primary site crash) either 1) a backup site is elected as the new primary site and consistency becomes a possible problem (the proposed approach), or else 2) the file becomes inaccessible in all but the primary site partition.

Reliable Networks and Optimism: Communications in the SDD-1 system are based on the use of a "reliable network" [5], which guarantees the eventual delivery of all messages even if partitioning occurs. This delivery depends on "spoolers" which save messages to be transmitted following a break in communications. No guarantee of postpartition consistency exists; as with the primary site model, assuming consistent data afterwards is "optimistic" [6] in the sense that it may work out, but quite possibly the work done in different partitions will have to be detected in some way as inconsistent, and then undone or coalesced somehow by users.

Disk Toting: In this approach, employed at Xerox Parc and other installations where very intelligent terminals are linked via a network, files are not stored redundantly but are kept on removable storage media which can be carried around during prolonged partitions. Thus, availability and consistency are simultaneously achieved, but they are not achieved automatically. This approach is clearly only useful for local networks with compatible portable storage media at each site, where the delay and inconvenience implied is acceptable.

Note that none of these approaches openly states either 1) how conflicting versions of files are detected or 2) what is to be done when these conflicting files are detected upon merge of several partitions. Either the possibility of conflict is precluded by restricting file availability, or else any seemingly conflicting files must be "rolled back" to the most recent point at which there was no conflict. We show in the next sections how, *without* restricted availability, we can ensure correct propagation of updates in all cases except when unavoidably conflicting file versions are found.

III. Detection of Mutual Inconsistency

One of the reasons the partition problem is so difficult is that each partition can break into subpartitions and/or merge with other partitions many times before the entire network finally becomes connected. Indeed, it is possible that the network will *never* be completely reconnected! However, all messages sent might be delivered eventually through dynamically changing partitions. In this unpleasant eventuality, how can one hope to guarantee mutual consistency of files without restricting file availability as in Section II? We now show how inconsistencies or "conflicts" in the file system can be accurately *detected* easily; this solves the major part of the problem. The next section will discuss how these inconsistencies may then be *reconciled.*

We must formalize what we mean by a file "conflict" which arises after a partition, and pinpoint the kinds of inconsistency which partitioning can cause. This is important since, as mentioned above, many basic systems principles are invalidated in systems subject to partitioning. First, the semantics of renaming, deletion, and even creation of redundantly stored files or resources in systems which are partitioned are totally unclear. Second, and worse, user-visible names of entities in the system may no longer be assumed to either uniquely specify, or even correctly specify, the entities themselves. After a partition, it may be discovered either that two files with the same name have been independently created, or that two independent updates to the same file have been made. In general, *names in one partition bear no relation to entities in another.* This is a principle reason for the difficulty in defining the semantics of renaming and deletion of files. We need some form of identification of system entities which is immune to partitioning. We achieve this below by using "origin points" and "version vectors."

A. File Conflict Types and Origin Points

A (network) *partition* is a set of sites which share a common, synchronized, view of some set of files.

An *origin point* OP(f) of a file f is a system wide unique identifier which is generated when f is created. It is an immutable attribute of f, although f's name is not (indeed f may have multiple system wide names). Thus, no number of modifications or renamings of f will change OP(f).

An origin point for a file might be something like a (creation time, creation site) pair. Now, just as names cannot uniquely specify files, origin points cannot either, but they do give us important information. Origin points tell us when two files are *based* on a common file, but do not tell us whether the two files are identical, since both could have been independently modified.

There are two types of conflicts that we wish to consider: *name conflicts* and *version conflicts.* A name conflict occurs when two files with different origin points have the same system wide name. In contrast, a version conflict occurs when two versions of the same file (same origin point) have been "incompatibly" modified. After some preliminaries, a version conflict occurrence is defined more precisely below.

A *modification id* for a version of a file f is a system wide unique identifier of a modification of f in some partition and at some time relative to that partition. A *modification history* for a version of a file f is the set of modification ids corresponding to the modifications of that version of f which have occurred. Two modification histories are *compatible* if they are identical or if one is an *initial history* of the other, and *incompatible* otherwise.

We define a version conflict to occur when two versions of the same file f (same origin point) have *incompatible modification histories.*

Note that when two versions of a file are not equal, their modification histories are always different. However, it *is* possible for two versions of a file to be equal yet have incompatible histories. For example, consider a file which contains a bank account balance. If the balance is \$20 million initially, and both partitions decrease it to \$0, then at partition merge time although both versions are \$0 a conflict *will* be indicated. Further, if the semantics of "decrease" mean "withdraw," a conflict intuitively *should* occur.

We claim that this definition of version conflict occurrence is a reasonable one given that nothing is known about the file content's semantics.

Clearly, name conflicts are easy to detect. Version conflicts, however, are more difficult to detect efficiently. This latter problem is addressed in the following sections: modifying, deleting, or renaming the various copies.

B. The Problem of Version Conflict Detection

One might think that a simple timestamp scheme could be used to detect possible version conflicts among files: every time a file is modified in a partition, one marks it with an update time and the previous update time. Upon partition merge, one checks whether the timestamps on the copies of a file are either all identical (no update on the file occurred), or one copy of the files differs from the others by a single update. Thus, no conflict is signaled when at most one update is made, but in any more complex situation a version conflict condition is raised. This approach is deficient in general, since some nonconflict situations will be handled as conflicts.

Let us describe the version conflict problem in the following way. Think of a partition *for a file* as a subset of sites in the network in which all copies of the file may be maintained with mutual consistency. Note that this definition is not strictly tied to the physical details of network failure. Instead, here partitions are defined relative to files and to the higher concept of consistency. Although two sites with different versions of a file f may be communicating for some time, we do not consider the sites to be in a common partition relative to f unless this difference in the two versions is resolved.

Definition: A *partition graph* $G(f)$ for any file f is a directed acyclic graph (dag) which is labeled as follows. The source node (and the sink node if it exists) is labeled with the names of all sites in the network having copies of file f, and all other nodes are labeled with a subset of this set of names. Each node can only be labeled with site names appearing on its ancestor nodes in the graph; conversely every site name on a node must appear on exactly one of its descendants. In addition, a node is marked with a "+" if f is modified one or more times within the corresponding partition, and/or a version conflict had to be *reconciled.*

We define this latter situation recursively as follows. Let P be a node in $G(f)$. A version conflict had to be reconciled at P if there are backward paths from P to distinct nodes $P1$ and $P2$ in $G(f)$, such that

1) an update to f and/or a version conflict reconciliation for f occurred at both $P1$ and $P2$, and

2) there is no ancestor node of P having two backward paths to both $P1$ and $P2$.

Each node in $G(f)$ thus corresponds to a partition for f, a period of time during which the labeled sites maintain "synchronized" information about f. All sites appearing in the node label resolve any differences that might exist among their copies of f. All connections in $G(f)$ between nodes indicate transitions of the network under partitions or merges.

The definition of conflict and reconciliation models the notions of Section III-A for the following reasons. First, any version conflict that is reconciled must have been generated by two prior partitions $P1$ and $P2$, giving incompatible modification sets. Second, and conversely, if a file modification of some kind (update or reconciliation of updates) occurs independently in two partitions $P1$ and $P2$, a version conflict must arise later whenever sites from these partitions inspect f. Condition 2) guarantees that partition P is the first point at which mutual consistency is again established.

An example of a partition graph is shown in Fig. 1. Here there are four sites, A, B, C, and D, which support f. Multiple partitions of these initially connected sites occur, so that at first sites A and B can communicate, but are isolated from sites C and D. Later A and B become isolated, as do C and D, but B and C resume communication. Ultimately, all four sites are reconnected in the bottom node of the graph. The file f is modified first in the $\{A, B\}$ partition, and subsequently in both the $\{A\}$ and $\{B, C\}$ partitions. Note that this sequence of modifications *should not* result in a version conflict in the *BC* or *BCD* partitions since site B at all times has the latest version of f; intelligent implementation of conflict detection should realize this fact and avoid notifying sites C or D that their f versions conflict with the current one. However, in the final *ABCD* partition a conflict *is* (and should be) reconciled, since in this case both versions of f have incompatible modification sets.

Now, as mentioned above it is simple to provide some mechanism which detects all *possible* version conflicts; a simple timestamp algorithm will be adequate. What is more difficult is to find a mechanism which detects version conflicts *only* when they are real. In Fig. 1, for example, even though the first update may have been initiated by site A, this information is transitively passed by site B without conflict to sites C and D.

C. Version Conflicts and Version Vectors

Many possible approaches exist for attacking the problem of accurately detecting version conflicts. More elaborate timestamp schemes are a possibility, and there are a number of methods based on "update log files" (sometimes referred to as "journaling"). Unfortunately, these approaches suffer from either or both 1) a need to maintain some kind of global network time (in itself nontrivial [7]) and 2) a need to store the entire partition graph—or its equivalent—someplace where it may be accessed later on. Since the partition graph may get arbitrarily large, the latter requirement is undesirable. We now present instead a straightforward solution to this problem based on a version numbering scheme encoding just the necessary characteristics of the history graph.

One maintains a vector with each copy of each file. Within every partition (unit of mutual consistency), these vectors keep an update history for the file. As partitions merge, these vectors for the possibly inconsistent files are compared. It turns out that version conflicts are signalled when, and only when, the vectors are "incompatible." We formalize this as follows.

Definition: A *version vector* for a file f is a sequence of n pairs, where n is the number of sites at which f is stored. The ith pair $(S_i: v_i)$ gives the index of the latest version of f made at site S_i. In other words, the ith vector entry counts the number v_i of updates to f made at site S_i. We will use leters $A, B, C, \cdots$ to designate site names, and vectors will be written as $\langle A{:}9, B{:}7, C{:}22, D{:}3\rangle$.

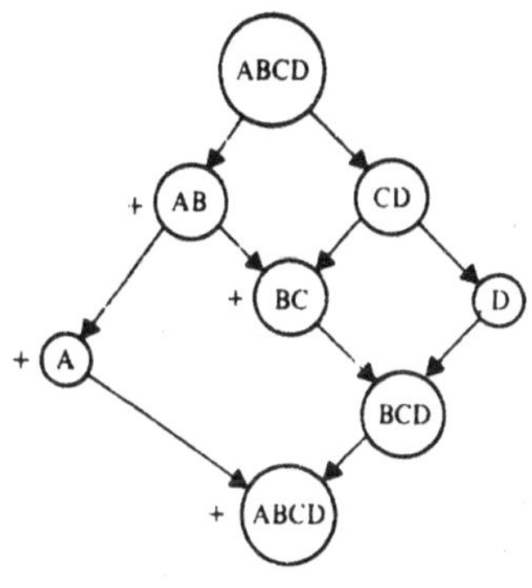

Fig. 1. Partition graph $G(f)$ for file stored redundantly at sites A, B, C, D.

Definition: A set of version vectors are *compatible* when one vector is at least as large as any other vector in every site component for which they each have entries. A set of vectors *conflict* when they are not compatible.

For example, the version vector $\langle A{:}1, B{:}2, C{:}4, D{:}3\rangle$ dominates $\langle A{:}0, B{:}2, C{:}2, D{:}3\rangle$ so the two are compatible; and $\langle A{:}1, B{:}2, C{:}4, D{:}3\rangle$ and $\langle A{:}1, B{:}2, C{:}3, D{:}4\rangle$ conflict, but $\langle A{:}1, B{:}2, C{:}4, D{:}3\rangle$, $\langle A{:}1, B{:}2, C{:}3, D{:}4\rangle$, and $\langle A{:}1, B{:}2, C{:}4, D{:}4\rangle$ do not conflict, since the third vector dominates the other two. In Fig. 2 version vectors are given for f in every partition of Fig. 1. The vector $\langle A{:}2, B{:}0, C{:}1, D{:}0\rangle$ associated with the node labeled *BCD*, indicates that f was modified twice at site A, once at site C, and nowhere else. Note in particular that during the $\{A, B\}$ partition, the file is modified twice at site A. The final merge results in a conflict.

We adopt the following *usage of version vectors.*

1) Each time an update to f originates at site S_i, we increment the S_ith component of f's version vector by one. The vector is committed with the updated file.

2) File deletion and renaming are treated as file updates. Deletion results in a version of the file of length zero, for example; when all versions of a file are of length zero, information on the file may be removed from the system.

3) When version conflicts are reconciled within a partition, the S_ith entry of the version vector for the reconciled file is set to be the maximum of the S_ith entries of all of its predecessors, and in addition the site initiating the reconciliation increments its entry. This ensures future compatibility with any old versions of the file still remaining on the network.

4) When copies of a file are subsequently stored at new sites, the version vector is augmented to include the new site information. The definition of compatibility above still applies in this case.

Point 4) states that the vectors are not required to be of fixed length, but may grow (or shrink, actually) as long as the relevant site information is maintained. If a copy of f is added at a site E during some partition, the vector in the partition where the copy was obtained is simply augmented to reflect the existence of the E copy. Thereafter, sites merging with this partition will be required to augment their vectors accordingly. Also, note that the version counts should be of variable length, so running out of space will not be a problem.

Version vectors serve basically to encode the partial order

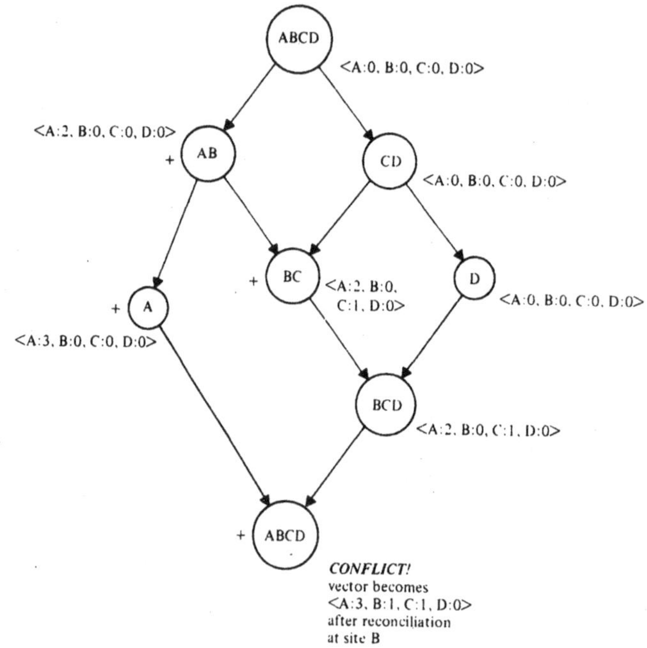

Fig. 2. Partition graph $G(f)$ for f with version vectors effective at the end of each partition.

defined by the partition graph: if one node in the graph "precedes" another, i.e., there is a path from the graph source through the former to the latter, then the version vectors of the two nodes will not conflict. This observation leads us to the following result, which shows us that version vectors are all we basically need to detect version conflicts.

Theorem: A version conflict must be reconciled at a node in $G(f)$ if and only if f's version vectors conflict at that point.

Proof: It is clear that if there is a conflict reconciliation at some node P in $G(f)$, then the version vectors will conflict at P. (Version vectors detect real conflicts just as well as the simple timestamp algorithm: what must be shown is that they detect only real conflicts.) Conversely, suppose that f's version vectors conflict at some node P. Then two of the vectors must conflict and not be dominated by any third vector. These two vectors were generated in two earlier partitions $P1$ and $P2$—both having paths to P—where f was modified independently. All that must be shown is that there is no ancestor P' of P which also has backward paths to $P1$ and $P2$. (Note P' could be either $P1$ or $P2$.) Suppose P' exists. We know that in this case the $P1$ and $P2$ version conflict will be reconciled at P', giving a version vector whose components are the maxima of the components from the vectors in $P1$ and $P2$. But this vector will dominate both the $P1$ and $P2$ vectors at P, removing their conflict. This contradicts our original assumption. Hence, P' cannot exist, so the partition graph conditions are satisfied and there is a conflict reconciliation at P. □

D. Conclusions on File Conflict Detection

The theorem above shows us that version vectors may be used to detect version conflicts and request user reconciliation of the conflicts. Version vectors will detect only "real" conflicts, i.e., situations in which versions of a file were modified independently in separate partitions. Thus, our work differs from previous research in that, where many people have developed mechanisms (e.g., timestamps) which detect *sufficient* conditions for a conflict to exist, we have striven to provide a mechanism detecting ***necessary and sufficient*** conditions for conflict.

It should be noted that if an identical update is made in two separate partitions, version vectors will indicate a file conflict even though there may be none. In some applications, then, it may be desirable to actually check a file for differences when several copies are found to have conflicting vectors. Indeed, this cross-checking of copies may have to be done eventually if the user is to resolve the file conflict.

It is also important to recognize that what has been presented here is applicable only when *single* files are being processed. Consider the following example (of Mark Brown) where two "transactions" $T1$ and $T2$ execute in different network partitions. Let

$$\text{readset}(T1) = \text{readset}(T2) = \{f, g\}$$

$$\text{writeset}(T1) = \{f\}$$

$$\text{writeset}(T2) = \{g\}$$

and assume that both $T1$ and $T2$ complete prior to reconnection of the network. Then a conflict (serialization error) should occur after reconnection, but it is easily seen that in this case version vectors will not detect anything amiss. Many appropriate extensions immediately suggest themselves; one is presented in [11]. Note, interestingly, that many of the "solutions" for providing mutual consistency mentioned in Section II also *do not* solve this problem. In particular, such conflicts can still occur with the Token and Primary Site approaches, unless *all* updates are constrained to occur within a single partition.

We have shown in this section that file conflicts, whether

they are name conflicts or version conflicts, can be accurately detected by maintaining just two pieces of information with each file f:

1) an origin point
2) a version vector.

In the following section we take up the question of how to resolve file conflicts, now that the problem of detection has been clarified.

IV. Resolution of Mutual Inconsistency

A conflict detection mechanism, while valuable, has increased effect if there is also a method for reconciling conflicts automatically. From several conflicting versions of a file, this method should produce a subsequent version that dominates these versions, while preserving the operations which were done to them. Although this is certainly not possible in general, there are many cases which admit automated reconciliation.

Clearly, conflict reconciliation must take into account the semantics of the operations which were done to the data objects in conflict. This has been noted by many researchers (e.g., [1, p. 568], [5, p. 65], [13, p. 57]). In those cases where the nature of the semantics is sufficiently constrained, straightforward reconciliation algorithms can be given. For example, consider two important types of files in *LOCUS*, directories and user mailboxes. In both of these cases, there are just two available operations:

- insert an item (e.g., create a file, or receive a message)
- remove an item (e.g., delete a file, or process a message).

Such files have the characteristic that version conflicts can be reconciled simply by taking the union of the entries in the component files, then removing any entries which had been deleted. Reconciliation for both of these file types is handled automatically in *LOCUS*.[1]

Automatic reconciliation applies in much more far-reaching contexts that on the systems level. An instructive example can be found in electronic funds transfer. Consider a checking account, as proposed earlier in Section III-A. Credits and debits can be made to different copies of the account. Resolution is straightforward so long as the ith copy is represented as

$$x + \delta_i(x)$$

where x was the original account balance before partition and $\delta_i(x)$ is the change in that partition. Then the new balance is

$$x + \sum_i \delta_i(x).$$

This approach may be improper if we require the balance to remain positive. However, there are many ways to deal with this problem. When x is the balance of a large corporation, presumably the problem will not occur. More generally, one may operate the system in a more constrained fashion when it is partitioned, either by limiting withdrawals in those cases where the customer is not trusted, or by imposing quota-like limits on withdrawals within each partition.

A number of existing applications permit automated reconciliation while still allowing robust operation during partition. Two cases which have been studied carefully are banking and airline reservation systems [3]. Extensive, although not full, operation of these systems is quite feasible while partitioned.

A desirable characteristic of system operation semantics, or of the reduced *partition semantics*, is that reconciliation of a data item not necessitate the alteration of many other data items. In order to keep automatic reconciliation cost low in a database, for example, one might insist that most transactions executed during partitions not require undoing and redoing when their read sets are subsequently altered during a reconciliation. This is the case today for portions of banking systems such as automated tellers.

In general, it is often possible to break the semantics of operations into classes, and for each class give rules by which the reconciliation algorithms can be constructed. Simple semantic classes permit reconciliation in a straightforward way without keeping much history. As the semantics become more complex, more history and work is required.

Of course, even when the semantics of operations are clear, automatic reconciliation can be very difficult, expensive, and in some cases impossible. Reconciliation cannot be performed in those cases where, as part of the system's activity, an external action has been taken that cannot be undone nor can a compensating action be taken. These cases are the same ones for which general purpose data management recovery is impossible too.

One suspects that in many systems, automatic reconciliation will be feasible for the large majority of data items. However, there will remain cases that require human intervention.

Independent of the degree of automatic reconciliation, a consistent system policy must be defined for each of the following questions.

- When and how are data conflicts detected?
- Is permission to access a data item altered by the fact that the item is in conflict? No alteration of permission raises the question of which version to make available, and leads to the possibility of propagating inappropriate values.
- How are users informed of conflicts?
- What support does the system provide the user for reconciling conflicts?

These questions raise a number of architectural issues, some of which are addressed in [12], [14], [18].

V. Conclusions

We have developed an effective method for detecting mutual inconsistency in distributed systems. Here inconsistency has been assumed to be caused by multiple users modifying different copies of a common file without mutually excluding one another. Such a situation would arise, for example, when network failures isolate these users in different partitions of the network. The technique also applies when partitions are artificially introduced; for example, when stations in a connected network delay their transmissions to take advantage of

[1] Most directory systems, and some mail systems, permit additional operations. Therefore the automatic recovery software in *LOCUS* for these file types is more involved than indicated here.

batching or lower communications rates at various times of day. The method used is simple, relying only on two newly introduced constructs, version vectors and origin points, for its operation. Although the method was discussed specifically in the context of file systems, it applies equally well to any class of resources for which occasional mutual inconsistency is tolerable for the sake of availability, or where the semantics of the allowed operations permit automated recovery.

The general problem of how to resolve mutual inconsistency of copies of a resource, once it is detected, is a complex question. We have only given it a summary treatment here, since it raises many design issues and can be answered thoroughly only when the semantics regarding the use of the resource are explicitly known. We have noted, however, that for some resources automatic reconciliation is straightforward to implement.

References

[1] P. A. Alsberg and J. D. Day, "A principle for resilient sharing of distributed resources," in *Proc. 2nd Int. Conf. Software Eng.*, Oct. 1976.

[2] C. A. Ellis, "A robust algorithm for updating duplicate databases," in *Proc. 2nd Berkeley Workshop Distributed Data Management and Comput. Networks*, 1977, pp. 1146-158.

[3] S. Faissol, "Operation of distributed database systems under network partitions," Ph.D. dissertation, Dep. Comput. Sci., UCLA, 1981.

[4] D. J. Farber and F. R. Heinrich, "The structure of a distributed computer system–The distributed file system," in *Proc. ICCC*, 1972.

[5] M. Hammer, and D. Shipman, "An overview of reliability mechanisms for a distributed data base system," in *Proc. Spring Compcon*, San Francisco, CA, Feb. 28-Mar. 3, 1978.

[6] H. T. Kung and J. R. Robinson, "On optimistic methods for concurrency control," *ACM TODS*, vol. 6, pp. 213-226, June 1981.

[7] L. Lamport, "Time, clocks, and the ordering of events in a distributed system," *Commun. Ass. Comput. Mach.*, vol. 21, pp. 558-565, July 1978.

[8] B. Lampson and H. Sturgis, "Crash recovery in a distributed data storage system," Tech. Rep., Xerox PARC, 1976.

[9] D. A. Menasce, G. J. Popek, and R. R. Muntz, "A locking protocol for resource coordination in distributed systems."

[10] R. M. Metcalfe and D. R. Boggs, "Ethernet: Distributed packet switching for local computer networks," *Commun. Ass. Comput. Mach.*, vol. 19, pp. 395-404, July 1976.

[11] D. S. Parker and R. Ramos, "A distributed file system architecture supporting high availability," in *Proc. 6th Berkeley Conf. Distributed Data Management & Comput. Networks*, Asilomar, CA, Feb. 1982.

[12] G. Popek, B. Walker, J. Chow, D. Edwards, C. Kline, G. Rudisin, and G. Thiel, "*LOCUS:* A network-transparent, high reliability distributed system," in *Proc. 8th Symp. Oper. Syst. Principles*, Asilomar, CA, Dec. 1981.

[13] J. B. Rothnie and N. Goodman, "A survey of research and development in distributed database management," in *Proc. 3rd VLDB*, Tokyo, Oct. 1977.

[14] G. J. Rudisin, "Architectural issues in a reliable distributed file system," M. S. thesis, Dep. Comput. Sci., UCLA, Rep. UCLA-ENG-8014 SDPS-80-001, Apr. 1980.

[15] M. Stonebraker, "Concurrency control and consistency of multiple copies of data in distributed INGRES," *IEEE Trans. Software Eng.*, vol. SE-5, pp. 188-194, May 1979.

[16] R. F. Thomas, "A solution to the concurrency control problem for multiple copy data bases," in *Proc. Spring COMPCON*, Feb. 28-Mar. 3, 1978.

[17] R. F. Thomas, R. H. Schantz, and H. C. Forsdick, "Network operating systems," Rome Air Develop. Cen., Tech. Rep. RADC-TR-78-117, May 1978.

[18] B. J. Walker, "Issues of network transparency and file replication in distributed systems: *LOCUS*," UCLA Tech. Rep., June 1981.

D. Stott Parker, Jr. received the A.B. degree in mathematics from Princeton University, Princeton, NJ, in 1974 and the M.S. and Ph.D. degrees in computer science from the University of Illinois, Urbana-Champaign, in 1976 and 1978, respectively.

Currently, he is an Associate Professor with the Department of Computer Science, University of California, Los Angeles. His main interests include distributed processing, algorithms, architecture, and logic programming.

Dr. Parker is a member of Sigma Xi and the Association for Computing Machinery.

Gerald J. Popek received the Ph.D. degree from Harvard University, Cambridge, MA, in 1972.

He then joined the faculty at the University of California, Los Angeles, where he is now Professor of Computer Science and in charge of the department's computing facilities. He is Principal Investigator of an ARPA contract, under which basic work in computer security was done, and which is now focused on distributed systems. He is the author of approximately 50 professional publications. He is also Vice President of Palyn Associates, Inc., and there has been responsible for major software efforts. Activities have focused on languages, operating systems, and distributed computing functions.

Gerard Rudisin received a B.S. degree from the Massachusetts Institute of Technology, Cambridge, in 1975 and the M.S. degree from the University of California, Los Angeles, in 1980, both in computer science.

He is currently a Ph.D. candidate in computer science at the University of California, Los Angeles, and also works for Western Digital Corporation's Systems Technology Center. His major research interests are local computer networks, operating systems, database technology, and Ada implementations and support environments.

Mr. Rudisin is a member of the Association for Computing Machinery and Sigma Xi.

Allen Stoughton received the B.S. degree in mathematics/computer science and the M.S. degree in computer science from the University of California, Los Angeles, in 1979 and 1981, respectively.

His current interests include operating system protection models and programming language semantics.

Bruce J. Walker received the B.Math degree from the University of Waterloo, Waterloo, Ont., Canada, in 1975 and the M.S. degree in computer science from the University of California, Los Angeles, in 1977.

He is currently finishing the Ph.D. degree at UCLA. The topic of his dissertation is the transparency and replication principles in distributed systems and in particular, LOCUS. Research interests also include computer security, about which he has published articles and a book.

Evelyn Walton was born in Little Rock, AR. She received the B.A. and M.S. degrees from the University of California, Los Angeles, in 1972 and 1975, respectively.

She has been working on research projects in the Department of Computer Science at UCLA since 1971. At present, she is working on the Ph.D. degree in computer science. Her research interests are in the areas of computer languages, systems, and networks.

ROBUSTNESS TO CRASH IN A DISTRIBUTED DATABASE: A NON SHARED-MEMORY MULTI-PROCESSOR APPROACH

Andrea Borr
Tandem Computers Incorporated
19333 Vallco Parkway
Cupertino, California 95014

ABSTRACT

Since attention first turned to the problem of database recovery following system crash, computer architectures have undergone considerable evolution. One direction such evolution has taken is toward fault-tolerant, highly available, distributed database systems. One such architecture is characterized by a single system composed of multiple independent processors, each with its own memory. This paper examines the inadequacy of both the traditional definition of system crash and the conventional approaches to crash recovery for this architecture. It describes an approach to recovery from failures which takes advantage of the multiple independent processor memories and avoids system restart in many cases.

INTRODUCTION

With the emergence of on-line update in transaction processing applications, log-based database recovery techniques have evolved to provide robustness to crash or system failure. Log-based crash recovery techniques have received considerable attention in the literature [4,5,8,9,10].

The strategies adopted by the proponents of these techniques fall into two basic categories. Both postulate the existence of two types of memory [4]:

i. main memory, which is volatile, hence does not survive system failure;

ii. secondary storage, which is stable or non-volatile, hence usually survives system failure.

In the first strategy, a transaction writes an intentions list rather than updating database pages in real-time. The application of a transaction's intended updates to the actual database pages is deferred until transaction commit, at which time the transaction's intentions list is written to a secondary storage log, following which the updates are applied to the actual database pages. If a failure occurs during the application of the intentions list, the recovery procedure consists of restarting the application of the intentions list from the beginning. This technique has been described by Lampson and Sturgis in [8].

In the second strategy, a transaction effects its database updates in real-time, but a so-called write-ahead log protocol governs the migration of the updated database pages from a memory buffer pool to secondary storage. According to this protocol, described by Gray in [4], no updated data page is permitted to be written to secondary storage before the log records describing the updates to that page have been written to the secondary storage log. At commit time, transaction recoverability is achieved by forcing to stable storage all log records related to the committing transaction.

Using either of the above strategies, database recovery following a crash is characterized by having recourse to the log stored on secondary storage in order to ensure that committed transactions are applied and uncommitted transactions are removed from the database. A difference between the two strategies lies in the type of log information required for crash recovery. In the case of deferred update, only redo information need be logged. In the case of real-time update with write-ahead log, both undo and redo information must be logged [6].

A RE-EXAMINATION OF THE TERM "CRASH"

Central to the strategies used in the conventional approaches to crash recovery is the definition of a crash or system failure as the loss of the contents of main memory [9]. The inadequacy of this definition of system failure becomes evident when applied to a non shared-memory multi-processor architecture. The concept of "main memory" as a unique and shared resource constituting a single point of failure is inappropriate for multi-computer systems. In a system architecture in which multiple independent processors, each with its own memory, are connected to form a single system or node via interprocessor buses or local area network, the use of the term "crash" to denote an all-or-nothing state of the system loses its validity. The term becomes even less meaningful when applied to a long-haul network consisting of multiple shared-memory nodes, or even of multiple multi-computer nodes. Such configurations raise the possibility of partial crashes caused by individual processor failures within a node or caused by node failures within a network. A fault-tolerant system design may allow certain failures within a node to be handled without requiring system restart. If a partial failure does not require system restart, neither should it require full database restart. However, the problem of the total failure or crash of a multi-computer node still remains and must be handled.

A corollary to the generalization of the concept of crash is the generalization of the concept of crash recovery. If, as in the above definition, secondary storage is viewed as the only storage which survives failures, then crash recovery must be based on a secondary storage log and system restart is required. If, on the other hand, a processor failure does not imply the failure of other processors, then recovery techniques not requiring system restart or recourse to secondary storage are possible. If a portion of the "log" were copied from the memory of one processor to that of another during normal processing, and one of these processors survived the failure of the other, then recovery from the partial system failure could be effected using the "log" information from the memory of a surviving processor while system operation continued "on-line".

Tandem Computers has implemented a multi-processor architecture using the above concepts. The next section presents a brief description of Tandem's system architecture in order to motivate a more general approach to identifying and recovering from both partial and total system failures. Subsequent sections define robustness to single and multiple processor failures in a Tandem system. A discussion of Tandem's implementation of fault tolerance and the evolution of its design follows.

ARCHITECTURAL OVERVIEW

The hardware architecture of a Tandem [TM] system is described in [7]. Illustrated in Figure 1, it is based on multiple independent processors which are interconnected by dual high-speed buses to form a single system (node). The goals of the architecture are fault-tolerance, high availability, and modularity. Hardware redundancy is provided such that the failure of a single module does not disable any other module or disable any inter-module communication. Normally, all components are active in processing the workload. However, when a component fails, the remaining system components automatically take over the workload of the failed component. Each of the (up to 16) processors in a system has its own power supply, memory, and I/O channel. Memory has battery backup power capable of saving system state for several hours in the event of power failure. Each I/O controller is connected to the I/O

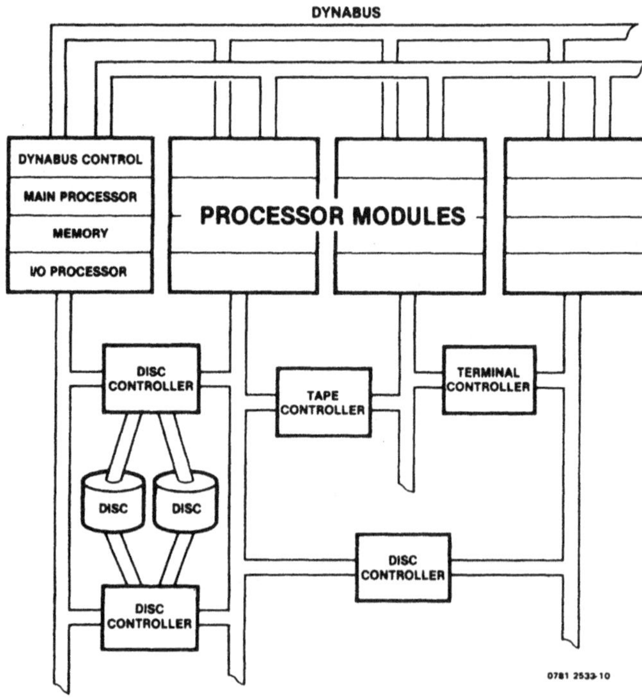

FIGURE 1
TANDEM HARDWARE ARCHITECTURE

channels of two processors, and each I/O device, such as a disc drive, may be connected to two controllers. A given disc volume is directly accessible from two processors. Disc volume availability, despite media failures, is provided by optional duplication, or mirroring of drives.

System resources are managed by a message-based operating system, described in [2]. The Message System, a component of the operating system, provides communication between processes executing in the same or different processors, making the distribution of hardware components transparent to processes. Through its Message and File Systems, the operating system makes the multi-computer structure appear as a unified multiprocessor to higher levels of software.

Built on this architecture is a distributed data management and transaction management system called ENCOMPASS [TM]. Described in [1], ENCOMPASS allows data to be distributed across multiple processors and discs within a single node, or even within multiple nodes of a Tandem long-haul network. It supports the transaction concept [6] in this distributed environment. The transaction concept is implemented by means of a log and real-time (as opposed to deferred) update. Transactions can span multiple discs (connected to multiple processors) within the same node or on multiple nodes of a Tandem long-haul network.

Updates to a file may or may not be protected by transaction auditing, depending on the value of the file attribute audited. (Henceforth, the terms "log/logging" and "audit trail/auditing" will be used interchangeably).

ENCOMPASS supports three kinds of structured file organizations:
  (1) key-sequenced;
  (2) relative-record;
  (3) entry-sequenced.
A key-sequenced file is organized as a B-tree on the primary key field. All three file organizations can have alternate keys. Alternate keys are implemented as separate key-sequenced files which "point" to primary file records via a field which contains the value of the primary key. Alternate key files and the primary files which they index can reside on separate disc volumes. Partitioning files -- by primary key value range -- across multiple disc volumes (possibly on multiple nodes) is also supported.

One of the basic implementation components of ENCOMPASS is a process which acts as a server for files on a particular disc volume. This process, designated the Discprocess, is an example of an I/O process-pair [3]. An I/O process-pair is a mechanism which provides fault-tolerant system-wide access to I/O devices. It consists of two cooperating processes which run in the two processors physically connected to a particular I/O device. One of these processes, designated the primary process, controls the I/O device, handling all requests to perform I/O on the device. The other process, designated the backup process, functions as a stand-by, ready to take over control of the device in case of failure of the primary path to the device. The processor in which the primary I/O process resides is an integral constituent of the primary path to the device. Should the primary's processor crash, the backup process must have information sufficient to take over control of the device. This critical information is sent from the primary process to the backup process during the course of normal processing in the form of so-called checkpoint messages. The process-pair which controls a disc volume is called the Discprocess-pair, or simply Discprocess. Its primary and backup members run in the "primary" and "backup" processors for the disc volume, respectively. The Discprocess has an active rather than a passive backup process. The term active backup process refers to the fact that the information which it receives via checkpoint messages drives its execution control flow. This is in contrast to a possible alternative design in which the backup process passively receives copies of recently-dirtied portions of the primary process' memory. The active backup concept is central to the design of single fault tolerance, as described below.

From the point of view of a given Discprocess, a "file" is a single partition of an ENCOMPASS "file" (if, indeed, the latter is partitioned). Partitions of key-sequenced primary data files and of alternate key files look alike to the Discprocess: each is structured as a single B-tree. The higher-level concept of a "file" with partitions and/or alternate keys is implemented by the File System. The File System is a set of user-callable procedures which execute in the environment of the user process. These procedures (e.g. OPEN, READ, KEYPOSITION, LOCKREC, WRITE, etc.) accomplish an operation by sending one or more request messages to the appropriate Discprocess(es). In a requester-server model, the invoker of the File System is the requester and the Discprocesses are servers.

The primary interface to the Discprocess is record-oriented, although a block-oriented interface is also provided. Most update requests result in the updating of a single record within a single block of a given file. In the case of key-sequenced files, however, the possibility that a single request message from the File System could cause a B-tree split or collapse means that the request may be executed as a series of micro update steps. Since an incomplete micro update step series leaves a file structurally inconsistent, robustness to crash requires a method of assuring its atomicity. This atomicity is provided for both audited and non-audited files, but the means differ, as explained later.

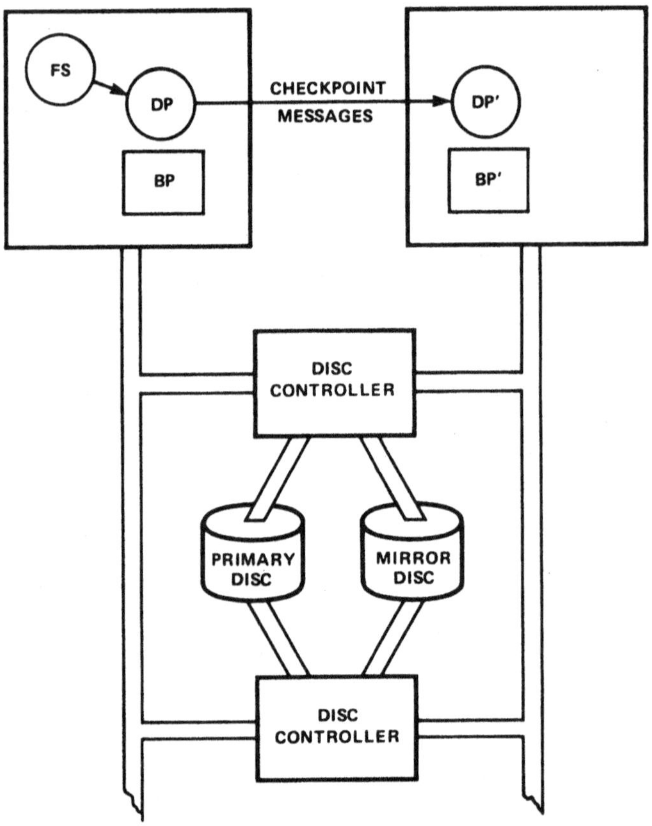

FIGURE 2

FS is the File System running in the user process environment. DP and DP' are the primary and backup Discprocesses for a mirrored disc volume. DP performs I/Os to move pages to and from its memory buffer pool, BP. Reads go to the closest disc; writes go to both discs. DP' maintains the backup buffer pool, BP', based on checkpoint messages received from DP.

FAILURE MODES

The system architecture described supports fault tolerance for a variety of failure modes other than processor crash. Fault tolerance extends from failures of single hardware components (discs, I/O channels, I/O controllers) to failures of system or application software (programmatic processor halt, user process error, transaction abort). The current discussion, however, will be limited to failures which result in the loss to a single multi-processor node of one or more of its constituent processors. "Loss" in this context means the invalidation of everything stored in the failed processor's memory. This could actually be caused by the failure of any hardware or software component associated with that processor.

The failure model supported can be characterized as fail fast. Consistency checks are an integral part of the system hardware and software. If such a check fails, the bad component is halted. This approach makes failures "clean" and makes it unlikely that a failed component will contaminate other components [3,6].

DEFINITION OF ROBUSTNESS TO SINGLE PROCESSOR FAILURE

The failure of a single processor in the described environment results in the takeover of its functions by the remaining processors. In particular, the failure of a primary Discprocess' processor results in the takeover of its function by the backup Discprocess' processor. If the failed processor contained other primary Discprocesses with different backup processors, then the failed processor may have its work taken over by several other processors.

The Discprocess is designed to provide robustness to single processor failure. This robustness is implemented by means of checkpoint messages sent from the primary process to the backup process during normal processing and a takeover algorithm described later.

The following elements constitute robustness to single processor failure:

(1) "Sessions" between the Discprocess and requesters calling the File System survive the failure of the Discprocess' primary processor. Thus, any file open before takeover still appears open after the takeover.

When updates are not protected by transaction auditing (i.e. updates to non-audited files), a mechanism of tagging messages between the File System and the Discprocess with sequence numbers can optionally be used to guarantee that a request message is never lost during the takeover and that a non-idempotent operation is never duplicated [3].

When updates are protected by transaction auditing (i.e. updates to audited files), the file open session survives the takeover, but updates executed under that open by a given transaction survive the takeover if and only if that transaction committed before the takeover.

The tolerance of sessions to single processor failure obviates the need to perform system restart in the event of such a failure. For non-audited files, the takeover is transparent to the caller of the File System. For audited files, the takeover is not transparent to the caller of the transaction management system (since transactions may be aborted), but higher-level software makes the abort and restart of such a transaction transparent to the end-user [1].

(2) The structural integrity of both audited and non-audited files on the volume is guaranteed. Thus, if the primary's processor fails in the middle of performing a series of micro update steps to a file, takeover processing restores the file's structure to a consistent state by backing out the steps performed before the failure.

(3) The transactional consistency of the database as a whole is guaranteed. Thus, if a transaction which was uncommitted at the time of takeover had updated audited files on the failed primary Discprocess' volume, takeover processing aborts the transaction and backs out its changes everywhere (on other volumes on this or other nodes). It should be noted that transaction backout does _not_ include undoing a _completed_ B-tree index operation. In this sense, transaction backout is _logical_ rather than _physical_.

DEFINITION OF ROBUSTNESS TO DISCPROCESS-PAIR CRASH

A _Discprocess-pair crash_ is defined as the simultaneous failure of both its primary and backup processors. The crash of a Discprocess-pair and the failure of its primary and backup processors are viewed as equivalent because the Discprocess is an integral part of the operating system, and as such becomes operational whenever the the processor is restarted. Conversely, whenever a Discprocess primary or backup process detects an internal consistency check failure, it halts its processor in accordance with the fail fast principle. While such a measure might be deemed Draconian in a conventional architecture, this aspect of the design is predicated on the principle that system availability is not compromised by the loss of a single processor. The underlying assumption is that processors fail independently, and that the primary and backup Discprocesses have independent failure modes. Of course, this assumption would be invalidated by the presence of a "hard" (i.e. non timing-dependent) algorithmic bug present in code which would inevitably be executed by either member of the process-pair. The elimination of such bugs has not proven to be an impractical goal, however. This might not be so were the primary and backup processors running in lock-step, or were the backup process passively receiving copies of recently-dirtied portions of the primary process' memory.

When a Discprocess-pair crashes, the situation is similar to the state described earlier as the crash of a shared-memory system. Information stored in memory (in this case the memories of _both_ primary and backup processors) is _lost_. Any method of recovery must resort to secondary storage. Furthermore, since "sessions" between the crashed Discprocess-pair and requesters calling the File System have been broken, there is the operational requirement of "restart". The analogy between the elements of robustness to single processor failure and robustness to Discprocess-pair crash is as follows:

(1) "Sessions" between the Discprocess and requesters calling the File System do not survive the Discprocess-pair crash.

(2) The structural integrity of both audited and non-audited files on the volume is guaranteed. Thus, if the Discprocess-pair crashes in the middle of performing a series of micro update steps to a file, crash recovery restores the file's structure to a consistent state.

(3) The transactional consistency of the database as a whole is guaranteed. Thus, if a transaction which was uncommitted at the time of the Discprocess-pair crash had updated audited files on the crashed Discprocess-pair's volume, crash recovery backs out that transaction's changes everywhere (on other volumes on this or other nodes). Conversely, if a transaction which was committed at the time of the Discprocess-pair crash had updated audited files on the crashed Discprocess-pair's volume, but those updates were still in memory buffers (rather than reflected in the corresponding database pages on secondary storage) at the time of the crash, crash recovery retrieves those updates (from the log) and applies them to the database pages on secondary storage. As in the single processor failure case, transaction backout does not undo completed B-tree index operations.

EVOLUTION OF THE DISCPROCESS DESIGN

The above description reflects a re-architecture of the Discprocess. The goals of the new design were to provide quick recovery from Discprocess-pair crash and less costly tolerance of single-processor failure. The old Discprocess provided robustness to single processor failure as described above. However the old implementation of single processor failure tolerance made a tradeoff in favor of fast takeover recovery from single processor failure at the expense of long recovery in the event of Discprocess-pair crash. The only method of recovery from Discprocess-pair crash was the time-consuming technique of re-loading previously-archived copies of audited database files and "rolling forward" these files to a state of transactional consistency by the application of after-images from the audit trail. The duration of volume unavailability implied by this procedure was justified by the assumption that double processor failure is rare. In actual fact however, double failures are more common than would be predicted by consideration of hardware mean-time-between-failures. Most processor failures are in fact caused by software bugs or operational errors.

Two characteristics of the original design dictated the "roll forward" approach to crash recovery and tolerated single processor failure at the expense of extra disc I/O's and extra checkpoint messages during normal processing. These were as follows:

i. the decision to synchronously <u>write through</u> to disc all updated database pages rather than buffering them in memory;

ii. the technique of <u>incremental checkpointing</u> (sending messages from primary to backup Discprocess during normal processing), which provided the backup process with the information needed in the event of the primary processor's failure to carry forward any interrupted series of micro update steps and to continue forward processing on transactions active on the disc volume.

The "write-through cache" was originally conceived as a means of simplifying the implemention of single processor failure tolerance. However it made the write-ahead log protocol [4] infeasible because unacceptable performance would result if every database update resulted in two writes: first, the before-image log necessary for undo in case of failure; second, the modified database page. The absence of write-ahead log made the fast crash recovery technique of in-place rollback of crashed transactions impossible. Writing-through every database update also had negative implications for throughput and response time. Rather than allowing the "piggy-backing" of several in-memory modifications on the same I/O, it meant that each time a page was "dirtied" in memory, it would be written out synchronously (while the application process waited).

Incremental checkpointing is necessary if the backup process is to be prepared -- in the event of the primary processor's failure at any instant -- to <u>carry forward</u> an interrupted series of micro update steps or an interrupted transaction. In the re-architected Discprocess, the approach to takeover is to provide the backup process with enough information to enable it to <u>back out</u> rather than to carry forward any interrupted series of micro update steps, and to abort rather than to continue processing forward any transaction active on the disc volume. With this approach, deferred checkpointing is possible. According to this technique, the information which would have been sent as synchronous incremental checkpoint messages in the old architecture is instead buffered on the primary process' side and sent as a batch at such times as transaction commit. This technique reduces considerably the cost of single processor failure tolerance in terms of number of messages. In particular, it saves sending checkpoint messages which inform the backup process of memory-only changes in the primary's processor which will not reach secondary storage and which will be backed out anyway in case of takeover. An example of such a change is a buffer dirtied in memory by a transaction which has not yet committed and for which the audit has not yet been forced. The backup process need have no knowledge of such a change since the transaction which caused it will be aborted and backed out (globally) in case the primary Discprocess' processor fails.

In order to explain the takeover algorithm used by the new Discprocess to recover from single processor failure, it is useful to draw an analogy between the use of log records by conventional crash recovery algorithms [4] and the use of checkpoint records during takeover processing. Checkpointing for the new Discprocess is analagous to logging to the backup process. Audit and checkpoint records have a common format; for this reason, they are known as audit/checkpoint records. A typical audit/checkpoint record contains identification of the file, page number within file, record number within page, and the before and after content of the changed record. A version number of the change is stored in both the page header and the audit/checkpoint record to provide idempotence during recovery. Just as conventional log-based crash recovery algorithms use the redo information in the log to bring the database pages up to date with the information which had been logged by the time the system crashed, so the takeover algorithm uses the redo information from checkpoint records received to bring the backup process' memory buffer pool up to date with the information which had been checkpointed by the time the primary's processor failed. Similarly, just as conventional crash recovery proceeds to use logged undo information to back out incomplete requests and uncommitted transactions, so the takeover algorithm uses checkpointed undo information to back out any incomplete series of micro update steps.

At this point, the takeover algorithm terminates and the former backup process begins operation as a primary process by accepting new request messages. Uncommitted transactions have not yet been recovered, however. Any partial micro update step series belonging to an uncommitted transaction has been backed out, and the transaction is prevented from continuing forward processing; but at the completion of takeover such a transaction's updates have not yet been backed out. Locks needed for backout are still held, however. Such a transaction will eventually be backed out by means of logically compensating Discprocess request messages sent by the Backout Process, a system process which extracts the information needed for such requests from the log. The logically compensating operations requested by the Backout Process are made idempotent by tolerating a "record not found" condition when deleting a record (compensating for an insert) or a "duplicate key" condition when inserting a record (compensating for a delete). Compensating update operations are automatically idempotent.

CRASH RECOVERY FOR THE RE-ARCHITECTED DISCPROCESS

The new Discprocess uses separate mechanisms to provide robustness to Discprocess-pair crash for non-audited and audited files. As previously stated, robustness to crash for non-audited files implies the restoration of structural integrity. For audited files, on the other hand, it implies not only the restoration of structural integrity to individual audited files, but in addition the guarantee of transactional consistency for the database as a whole.

In the case of non-audited files, updates are not protected by transaction auditing. However, loss of structural integrity due to a micro update step series interrupted by Discprocess-pair crash is prevented by use of the so-called Undo Area on the disc volume. This is a small pre-allocated area on the volume which is re-useable for every request. Before beginning a series of micro update steps on a non-audited file (e.g. B-tree block split), a highly-compacted encoding of the intended steps is written to the Undo Area using one

I/O. Then if the Discprocess-pair crashes before the operation completes, this undo information is used to back out the incomplete operation when the volume's processors are restarted.

The algorithm used to recover audited files from Discprocess-pair crash is summarized below. It is analagous to typical database crash recovery algorithms used for conventional architectures [4].

Following Discprocess-pair crash, the user first restarts the volume's primary and backup processors. He then initiates the Crash Recovery Process. Crash Recovery obtains a list of those audited files on the crashed volume which were open for write access at crash time. These are the files which are recovered from the log. Log processing during crash recovery consists of a forward and a backward pass.

The forward pass begins at the <u>redo start point</u>. This is a location in the log prior to which all logged updates (redo images) are guaranteed to be reflected in the database. Existence of such a point within a short distance of the end of the log is guaranteed by the periodic execution by each volume's Discprocess of <u>control points</u>. At each control point, currently dirty buffers are flagged. During any spare time between control points, flagged buffers are written out. At the occurrence of the next control point, any flagged buffers not yet written are forced out and newly-dirtied buffers are flagged. (Other systems term this mechanism a "checkpoint"; see [5]). The locations in the log of the latest two control point records are remembered at a known place on the disc volume.

When recovering a given crashed disc volume, Crash Recovery finds that volume's redo start point by obtaining the pointer to its next-to-last control point. When recovering a set of crashed volumes, Crash Recovery starts its forward pass of the log at the earliest redo start point for any of the crashed volumes. Crash Recovery then sends to the Discprocess of a crashed volume all redo log records it finds from that volume's redo start point through the end of the log.

After the redo phase, the backward pass begins. Reading the log backwards from the end, Crash Recovery sends to the appropriate Discprocess those undo log records which represent incomplete micro update step series. When all of the changes represented by these log records have been physically undone, all audited files open on the crashed volume(s) will have been restored to a state of structural integrity. During the same backward pass, Crash Recovery sends to the appropriate Discprocess those undo log records which represent logical operations on data blocks (e.g. record insert, modify, or delete) which were executed by transactions which were uncommitted at crash time. When all of the changes represented by these log records have been logically backed out (i.e. using compensating operations at Discprocess request level), global transactional integrity will have been achieved.

CONCLUSIONS

The concepts of "crash" and "crash recovery" have been seen to require generalization in order to find applicability to a non shared-memory multi-processor architecture, in which some processors may survive the crash of other processors in the system. The architecture of the Tandem computer system was described as a case in point. A technique of logging to another processor's memory was described which tolerates single-processor failure and obviates the need to perform system restart. An analogy was drawn between the technique used in a Tandem system to recover from a single-processor failure and conventional crash recovery techniques which rely on a secondary-storage-resident log.

ACKNOWLEGEMENTS

Many of the ideas incorporated into the new Discprocess design were originated by Franco Putzolu.

Thanks are due to Jim Gray, Chris Duke, and John Nauman for editorial suggestions whose implementation improved the presentation of this material.

REFERENCES

1. Borr, A. J., "Transaction Monitoring in ENCOMPASS: Reliable Distributed Transaction Processing", Seventh International Conference on Very Large Data Bases, September 1981.

2. Bartlett, J. F., "A 'NonStop' Operating System", Eleventh Hawaii International Conference on System Sciences, 1978.

3. Bartlett, J. F., "A NonStop Kernel", Proceedings of Eighth Symposium on Operating System Principles, ACM, 1981.

4. Gray, J. N., "Notes on Data Base Operating Systems", IBM Research Report: RJ 2188, February 1978.

5. Gray, J. N. et al., "The Recovery Manager of a Data Management System", IBM Research Report RJ 2623, August 1979.

6. Gray, J. N., "The Transaction Concept: Virtues and Limitations", Seventh International Conference on Very Large Data Bases, September 1981.

7. Katzman, J. A., "A Fault-Tolerant Computing System", Eleventh Hawaii International Conference on System Sciences, 1978.

8. Lampson, B. and Sturgis, H. E., "Crash Recovery in a Distributed Data Storage System", Xerox Palo Alto Research Center, 1976. Also appears as: Ch. 11, "Springer-Verlag Lecture Notes in Computer Science: Distributed Systems - Architecture and Implementation", Vol. 105, B. W. Lampson, Ed.,1981.

9. Menasce, D. A. and Landes, O. E., "On the Design of a Reliable Storage Component for Distributed Database Management Systems", Sixth International Conference on Very Large Data Bases", October 1980.

10. Verhofstad, J. S. M., "Recovery Techniques for Data Base Systems", Computer Surveys, Vol. 10, No. 2, June 1978

Data recovery in IBM Database 2

by R. A. Crus

This paper presents the various forms of data recovery provided by IBM Database 2 (DB2). It describes the DB2 recovery log, introduces the notion of a unit of recovery, and discusses the two-phase commit protocol used by DB2. Furthermore, it describes what type of information is logged, the DB2 checkpoint process, what a compensation log record is, and how DB2 handles undo/redo processing, media recovery, restart after abnormal system termination, and data unavailability.

Today, more and more organizations rely on data processing systems to manage data critical to the day-to-day operation of the organization. In some cases, if data is unavailable, it is impossible to proceed with normal business operations. If data is inconsistent or contains errors, such discrepancies can also seriously interfere with normal business operations. If Murphy's law holds true ("Anything that can go wrong will go wrong!"), and it seems from experience that it does, data will become unavailable and errors are going to be introduced into the data at one time or another.

If IBM's relational data base management system, IBM Database 2 (DB2), terminates abnormally prior to completing all work, the data that it manages becomes unavailable until DB2 can be restarted, which will return the data to a consistent state. A system failure can be caused by hardware problems, certain software problems, and even by power outages. It is important that DB2 be able to restart quickly after a failure; it is even more important that the data be made consistent after a system failure.

Data errors can be divided into two types, logical errors and physical errors. Logical errors include updates that should have been made to the data base but were not, updates that were made but should not have been, and updates that were made incorrectly. Errors of this type can be caused by system failure, errors in the data base manager, errors in various critical system components, and even errors in the application programs that use the Data Base Management System. Physical errors are caused by media or hardware malfunctions; e.g., data stored on disk cannot be read from the disk or written to it. What DB2 does to recover from logical and physical errors is addressed in the remainder of this paper.

The rest of the paper is divided into three parts in addition to some conclusions that the author has reached concerning data recovery in DB2. The first part is an overview of recovery. The second part describes DB2 logging, including what information is recorded in the log, when it is recorded, and for what purpose. The third part discusses the various DB2 recovery processes.

Overview

As noted in the introduction, data may be damaged in a variety of ways. The basic approach to recovery used by DB2 is to record all modifications made to data in the DB2 recovery log. When data is updated, both the way it looked before the modification and the way it looked after the modification are recorded in the log. The contents of the log can thus be used either to undo an update or to redo it. In this section, the DB2 recovery log and DB2 commit processing are described, and the notion of a "unit of recovery" is introduced.

The recovery log records both system status information and information describing changes made to data.

DB2 recovery log. The DB2 recovery log is used to record both system status information and information describing changes that are made to data. The DB2 recovery log consists of an active portion, an archive portion, and a special data set called the *Bootstrap Data Set* (BSDS). The active log resides in a set of log buffers in main storage and in a set of preallocated Virtual Storage Access Method (VSAM) entry-sequenced data sets. When an active log data set becomes full, an archive log data set is dynamically allocated, and the active log data set is off-loaded. The archive log is written via the Queued Sequential Access Method (QSAM) to standard label tapes, a direct access storage device (DASD), or a Mass Storage System. After the archive operation is complete, the VSAM data set is available for use as part of the active log again.

When log records are required for recovery, DB2 must determine which active or archive log data sets contain the records. This information is kept in the BSDS along with information used to help restart the system after it terminates either normally or abnormally. The BSDS itself is off-loaded during an archive operation along with the active log data set being archived.

Each portion of the log (i.e., the active log, the archive log, and the BSDS) may optionally be dual-copied. It is highly recommended that an installation maintain dual copies in all production environments, since one of the basic assumptions of recovery is that the integrity of the log can be depended upon.

Each log record written by DB2 has associated with it a Relative Byte Address (RBA), which is six bytes in length. The DB2 log is a linear address space of 2^{48} bytes, and each log record written begins at some offset from the beginning of the log. This offset is called the RBA of the log record. Note that an RBA can be likened to a point in time; that is, the event described by a log record whose RBA is x occurred prior to an event described by a log record whose RBA is $x + n$. Another basic assumption concerning the log and its use is that an RBA will never repeat. For all practical purposes this assumption is true, since if the DB2 log were to grow at a rate of 2^{34} bytes (16 gigabytes) per day, it would fill in 44 years.

Normally when a log record is written, it is simply moved into a log buffer. Log buffers are written to disk as soon as one of the following occurs:

- The log is explicitly forced (i.e., all log data up to and including a specified RBA is written to disk).
- The installation-specified maximum number of log buffers are full.

When the log is forced and why it is forced are discussed in subsequent sections of the paper. The amount of storage devoted to the active log is under the control of the installation. By providing sufficient space on DASD for the active log, it is possible (almost) to guarantee that for most situations requiring rapid recovery, only information stored in the active log need be referenced.

Unit of recovery. A "unit of recovery" (UR) is the mechanism used by DB2 to track the progress of an application as it updates data stored in a data base. When an application program first attempts an update operation, DB2 establishes a UR for the application. Application in this context includes both user-written programs and the Query Management Facility[1] (QMF—a separate product that uses DB2) or DB2I[2] (an interactive interface to DB2). The UR lasts until a point of consistency is reached. (Note that an implicit point of consistency exists when the application first starts.) A point of consistency is that point at which, according to the application program logic, all data accessed and modified by the UR is in a consistent state. For example, a bank transaction might transfer funds from account A to account B.

Figure 1 Points of consistency

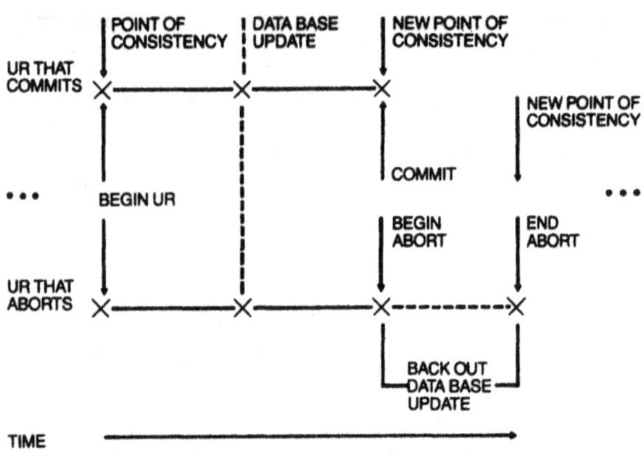

The transaction would first subtract the amount of the transfer from account A and then add the same amount to account B. After the second operation has been completed, the data in the two accounts is consistent. At this point the application can signal DB2 that the data is consistent and the updates are to be committed. When this happens, the UR for the transaction ends. If the transaction continues to run after this point, a new unit of recovery will be established when it next attempts to update the data base.

During the period after the update to A and before the update to B, the data in the two accounts is inconsistent and uncommitted. DB2 does not allow other applications to access uncommitted data stored in DB2 data bases. After the point of consistency has been reached (and the updates have been committed), the two accounts can then be accessed by other applications.

All updates made by a unit of recovery either are completed (and committed) or are aborted, which means the updates are backed out and appear to other applications as though they were never made (Figure 1).

When a UR is initiated, a begin-UR log record is written. All subsequent log records that are generated on behalf of the UR contain the RBA value of the previous UR-related record in the log, thus linking together all log records for a single UR (see Figure 2). When it is determined that a UR is to be committed or aborted, a log record is written (and forced to DASD) indicating the beginning of the commit or abort process. The various phases of the commit process are logged, as is the end of the commit or abort process (which is also forced to DASD). These records are used during restart to determine the state of the UR at the time of system termination.

Commit processing. A single application may involve DB2 and either TSO (the Time Sharing Option of MVS), Information Management System/Virtual Storage (IMS/VS), Customer Information Control System/Operating System/Virtual Storage (CICS/OS/VS), or batch programs. Because DB2 may operate in conjunction with another subsystem (IMS/VS and CICS/OS/VS) that also manages recoverable resources and has a recovery log (separate from the DB2 recovery log), it is necessary to coordinate the recovery activity between DB2 and the other subsystem. For data in the two subsystems to remain consistent, it is necessary that corresponding updates be made in both subsystems or in neither.

During commit processing, one subsystem coordinates the process, which consists of two phases. This subsystem is always IMS/VS or CICS/OS/VS. Neither TSO nor batch programs participate in commit; rather DB2 unilaterally controls the commit process.

The first phase of commit processing is known as the "prepare" phase, in which each subsystem determines that it can continue the commit process. Each subsystem logs this event and forces the log to DASD. The second phase, known as the "commit" phase, is when each subsystem records in the log the fact that the guarantee to commit was made.

Figure 3 shows the two-phase commit process. At point 1, IMS or CICS begins processing a transaction. At 2, a Structured Query Language (SQL) call is issued which attempts to update data, causing 3, a begin-UR event, to be logged in DB2. At point 4, the requested update operation occurs. At 5, IMS/CICS initiates the commit process and notifies DB2, which logs this event, performs its phase 1 processing, logs its completion, and then notifies IMS/CICS (at 7 and 8) that it has completed phase 1. At 9 the irrevocable decision to commit is made by IMS/CICS, and this event is recorded in the IMS/CICS log (on stable storage). At 10, IMS/CICS notifies DB2 that the decision is to commit, and DB2 logs this (11), completes its phase 2 processing, logs the event, and notifies IMS/CICS of the completion (12 and 13). IMS/CICS then completes its phase 2 processing (14).

Note that if either IMS/CICS or DB2 fails before point 9, when the decision to commit (or abort) is recorded in the IMS/CICS recovery log, the UR will be aborted.

Figure 2 UR-related log records

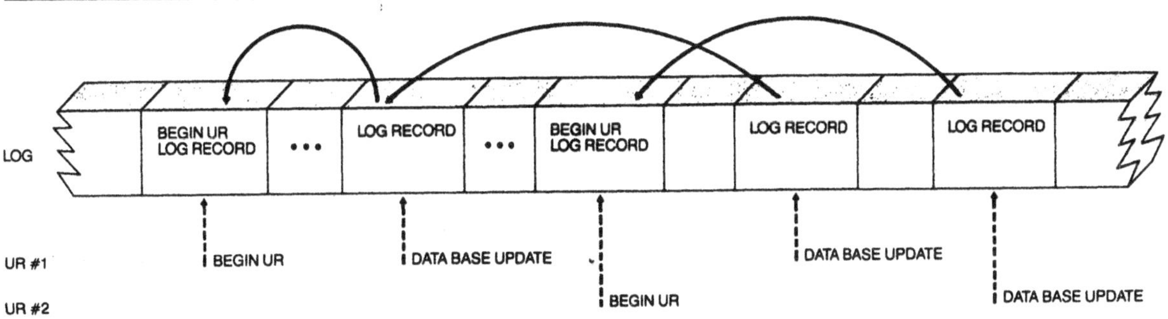

Figure 3 Two-phase commit

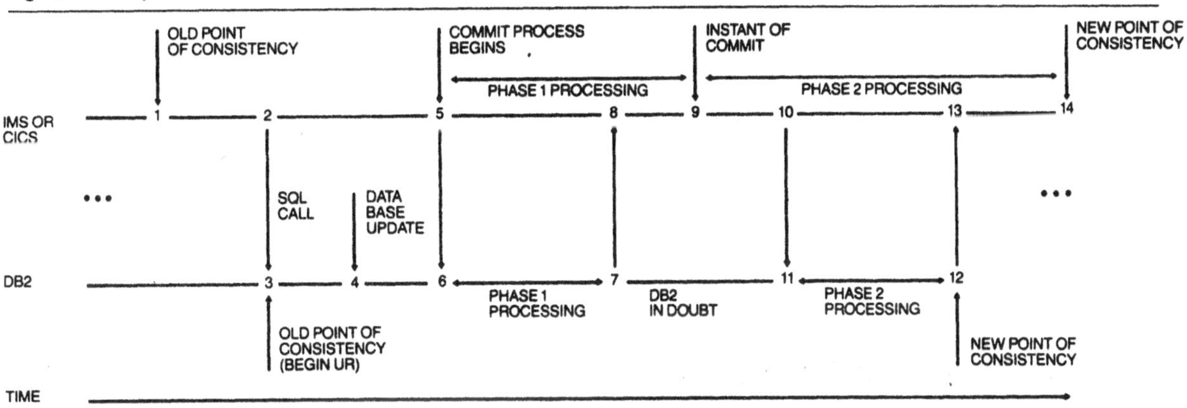

A failure of either system after 9 will result in the UR being committed. If DB2 fails between 7 and 11, the status of the UR is in doubt since DB2 has no knowledge of the decision at point 9. The status of an in-doubt UR is resolved after DB2 restarts and re-establishes communication with IMS/CICS.

DB2 logging

In addition to the UR control log records just described, other information is recorded in the log for recovery purposes. Some of this information is related to a UR (e.g., log records describing the updates performed by the UR), and some is not. Both types play an important part in the recovery process. Understanding what is logged, when it is logged, and why it is logged is necessary to understand data recovery in DB2.

Open/close. Whenever a tablespace (a DB2 object in which one or more tables are stored) or an indexspace (a DB2 object in which an index defined on a table is stored) is opened or closed (the VSAM open or close of the data set(s) that contain the DB2 object), this event is logged. Note that log records of this type are not related to a single UR since DB2 supports multiple users accessing the same data. Logging this information provides a set of delimiters for updates to the data object; i.e., there may be information of interest in the log about an object only for the period between the open log record and the close log record. Included in the open log record is sufficient information to enable the open operation to be performed again. The open log record is used at restart time to perform the open operation if it is necessary. Since all pending I/O activity is completed prior to writing a close log record, this record is used during the restart process to filter out records relating to the closed object.

Checkpoint. At periodic intervals, depending on the amount of log activity and an installation-specified variable, DB2 initiates what is called a checkpoint operation, during which system status information is recorded on the log. This process occurs asynchronously with normal data base activity and does not prevent access to any DB2-managed data. The checkpoint process consists of

DB2 always begins the restart process at the last complete checkpoint.

- Writing a log record that denotes the beginning of the checkpoint.
- Writing a list of active URs in the log. These log records describe the current state of each active UR (in commit processing, in abort, or in neither). This information, along with other UR-related log records, is used at restart time to determine whether or not any recovery actions are required on behalf of active URs and, if so, what type of action.
- Writing information about each open tablespace and indexspace in the log. Included in the log records is sufficient information to perform the open operation at restart time as well as an indication of the earliest point in the log at which an outstanding update operation exists for the DB2 object. An update operation starts when the decision is made to perform the update and completes when the page containing the update has been recorded on DASD.
- Writing a log record that denotes the end of the checkpoint.
- Updating the active log data set information and the RBA of the checkpoint log record in the BSDS.

DB2 always begins the restart process at the last complete checkpoint. The frequency at which checkpoints are taken thus has an effect on the amount of time required to perform restart since it tends to limit the quantity of log data that must be processed. Since the frequency of checkpoints is determined by the amount of information written in the log, the more update activity on a system, the more often checkpoints will occur. The checkpoint process itself writes information in the log (the amount of information is somewhat dependent on the system load) and therefore adds overhead and decreases performance. Yet, if the checkpoint frequency is too large, the restart process may have to access the archive log.

Writing pages to disk. DB2 maintains data base information as rows stored in pages on DASD. DB2 also maintains indexes in pages which are also stored on DASD. When a particular row or index entry is to be accessed, the page containing the row or index entry is read into a buffer in memory. DB2 maintains a pool of these buffers in memory. Since SQL is a set-oriented language, it is possible to update many rows contained in many pages in a data base with a single statement. Also, since DB2 allows more than one index to be defined on a table, it is possible for an update to a single row to cause updates to more than one index. It would not be possible or desirable from a performance point of view to hold all of the updated pages in memory until a commit point is reached; therefore, DB2 will write uncommitted changes back to the data base in order to reclaim buffer pool space. This design then makes it necessary for DB2 to be able to undo uncommitted updates after a system failure.

If a required page is already in the buffer pool, no read operation need be performed. If the page is not in the pool, a synchronous read operation is performed since the process cannot continue until the page can be accessed. Write operations, however, are usually performed asynchronously to the process that performed the modification. Once a page modification is complete, the page becomes a candidate for writing back to DASD.

During the modification process, DB2 writes one or more log records that describe the update operation. All data base modifications are logged as UR-related records. These records contain two types of information (where possible in a single log record):

- UNDO—sufficient information to undo an uncommitted update (e.g., the old value of an updated column)
- REDO—sufficient information to be able to redo an operation (e.g., the contents of a newly inserted row)

These log records also include information that identifies the DB2 object and the page number to which the log record applies.

The RBA of the log record written describing the most recent update is stored in a special location in the page. When it becomes necessary to write a page back to DASD, DB2 checks to see that the log record whose RBA is stored in the page has been written to DASD and, if not, forces the log up to that point before writing the page to DASD. Since the log is always written to DASD prior to the page being written, it is possible for DB2 to back out or undo uncommitted updates using information contained in the log.

Compensation log records describe the redo phase of an undo operation.

Compensation log records. Compensation log records (CLRS) describe the redo phase of an undo operation. Since DB2 write operations are not performed synchronously, it is possible that the undo operation of an uncommitted update which was originally externalized, might itself be lost if DB2 fails before the result of the undo is written to DASD. Consider the following sequence without CLRS:

- A UR updates a row, changing a value in a column from A to B. DB2 writes an undo/redo log record which indicates that the new column value is B and the old column value is A.
- The log is written to DASD.
- The page containing the row is written to DASD.
- The UR aborts.
- The log record describing the update is read, the page containing the row is read, and the update is backed out; i.e., the value in the column is changed from B to A.
- The end abort log record for the UR is written, and the log is forced to DASD.
- The system fails. Note that the page containing the back-out uptake has not yet been written to DASD.

If compensation log records are not written, then when the system is restarted, the restart process will read the log record describing the update of the column from A to B. This action will not cause an update since the row on DASD contains a B. The log record indicating the UR completed an abort will be read indicating that it is not necessary to process this UR. After the restart completes, the row contains an uncommitted update and is thus inconsistent.

Compensation log records correct the problem as follows.

- During the backout operation, a CLR is written which has a new column value of A and an old column value of B.
- The end abort log record is written, and the log is forced (including the CLR just written) to DASD.
- The system fails. The row stored on DASD still contains the value B.
- The restart process will read the first log record describing the update of A to B and not perform an update.
- Next it will read the CLR which will cause it to change the column from B back to A, thus completing the backout of the uncommitted update.

Recovery processes

Any recovery process involves applying either undo log records or redo log records or both. Since these functions are common, the rules for performing them are given below prior to the discussion of the recovery processes themselves.

Undo/redo processing. The RBA value stored in the header of a page uniquely identifies the log record that describes the last update operation made to the page. Therefore, it is possible to determine whether the update described by a log record was made to the page by comparing the RBA in the page to the RBA of the log record. If the RBA in the page is less than the RBA of the log record, the change described by the log record was not applied to the page. If the RBA in the page is greater than or equal to the RBA of the log record, the change was applied to the page.

The redo process simply determines whether the update described by the log record has been applied to the page, and if it has not, performs the update and stores the RBA of the log record in the page to indicate that the update has been made.

The undo process is more complicated. If the update operation was performed, a CLR describing the undo of the update is written, the update is undone, and the log RBA of the CLR is stored in the page to indicate that the undo operation was performed. Even if the update operation was not performed, it is necessary to write a CLR that describes the undo of the update, although the RBA in the page is not modified. This is done so that the update can be undone (after being redone) if media recovery (discussed shortly) is necessary at a later time.

The rules for performing undo operations, including the writing of compensation log records, follow:

- If the log record being processed has only redo information, write an undo-only CLR for the opposite operation.
- If the log record has both undo and redo information, and if the RBA in the page is less than the RBA of the log record, write a redo/undo CLR. The page itself is not modified since the change described by the log record was not applied to the page.
- If the log record has both undo and redo information, and if the RBA in the page is greater than or equal to the RBA of the log record, apply the change to the page, write a redo/undo CLR, and store the RBA of the CLR in the page.
- If the log record has only undo information, and if the RBA in the page is less than the RBA of the log record, write a redo CLR. The page itself is not modified since the change described by the log record was not applied to the page.
- If the log record has only undo information, and if the RBA in the page is greater than or equal to the RBA of the log record, apply the change to the page, write a redo CLR, and move the RBA of the CLR to the page.

These rules assume that the page can always be accessed successfully, which is not always the case (e.g., I/O error); however, compensation log records are always written even if the page cannot be accessed. This is possible because the CLR can be written with only information contained in the log record being processed. It is necessary in order to be able to perform media recovery on the object.

The rules for redo processing are much simpler:

- If the log record contains redo information and the log RBA in the page is less than the RBA of the log record, apply the change to the page and store the RBA of the log record in the page.
- If the log record contains redo information and the log RBA in the page is greater than or equal to the RBA of the log record, do nothing.

Media recovery. Media recovery is generally used to recover from physical errors, i.e., data has been lost due to a media failure (e.g., a bad track, head crash) or from some other error which makes the data unusable. Media recovery consists of starting with a copy of the data (called an image copy) which was made at a known point in the log, and redoing all committed update operations using the appropriate redo information on the log up to the point of failure.

DB2 supports two different types of image copies. The first, called a full image copy, is simply a copy of a tablespace. The second, called an incremental image copy, makes a copy of only the pages that have been updated since the last image copy was made. This is accomplished as follows:

- When a page is first modified, DB2 sets an indicator on corresponding to the data page in another page called a space map page, and sets an indicator on in the data page itself indicating that it has been modified.
- When an incremental image copy is taken, DB2 uses the indicators in the space map to determine which data pages to copy. It resets both the indicator in the data page and the space map indicator when the copy has been made.

An image copy can be made while other users have read-only access to the data or while other users have read/write access to the data. In the case where read-only access is allowed, DB2 saves the log RBA at the point in time when the image copy has completed in the DB2 catalog and saves information about the data set which contains the image copy. In the case where the data may be modified while the copy is being made, the RBA value saved corresponds to one that existed when the image copy process was initiated. The RBA thus saved becomes the starting position in the log for any subsequent media recovery operation that uses the corresponding image copy.

In order to minimize the amount of log that must be processed during media recovery, DB2 remembers the log RBA when the first update is made to a DB2 data object and also remembers the log RBA when the object is closed. This information is stored for each object in a DB2 directory as a list of start/stop RBA values. Media recovery reads the start/stop RBAS associated with the object being recovered and only processes the log within the RBA ranges so defined.

Media recovery involves applying redo log records. These records may be redos of committed updates, and they may also be redos of uncommitted updates, which are always succeeded by CLRs that are redo records for the undo of the update. If compensation log records were not written, it would be necessary to perform update operations, not knowing whether they were committed or not, and then after determining that the UR was aborted, undo all of the updates that had just been made.

Restart. When a hardware/software failure or a power outage causes an abnormal system termination, the state of the data stored on DASD at that time is almost certainly inconsistent with that of data stored at other times because of the way DB2 performs write operations. If DB2 were to be started after a system failure without knowledge of the events in progress when the failure occurred, the data would be exactly as it was at the time of failure.

When DB2 is restarted after a system termination, it uses information recorded in the log to restore the state of the system (including the data bases) to the point where it was at the time of termination, and in fact requires only information stored in the log (i.e., no system directories, catalogs, etc., need be accessed). This capability is important because DB2 maintains system directories and catalogs in data bases of their own, which may themselves require recovery actions during restart processing. If the termination was not normal, e.g., a power failure or system error, the data bases may be in an inconsistent state in that committed updates may not have been stored externally on DASD, and/or uncommitted updates may have been recorded on DASD. If the termination was via a shutdown command, all activity was made quiescent (all URs were completed, all DB2 objects were closed, and all updates were written to DASD) prior to the termination. Therefore, many of the steps below result in no action being taken even though the same restart process is followed.

Figure 4 presents a summary of the restart process that pertains to the following discussion. Note that the figure shows a checkpoint that started but did not complete before the system termination. Any records associated with the incomplete checkpoint are ignored by DB2. The DB2 restart process is outlined as follows:

a. Read the BSDS and determine the RBA of the last complete checkpoint.
b. Beginning at the start of the last complete checkpoint, (phase 1), read the log in a forward direction and (at phase 2).

Figure 4 Summary of restart processing

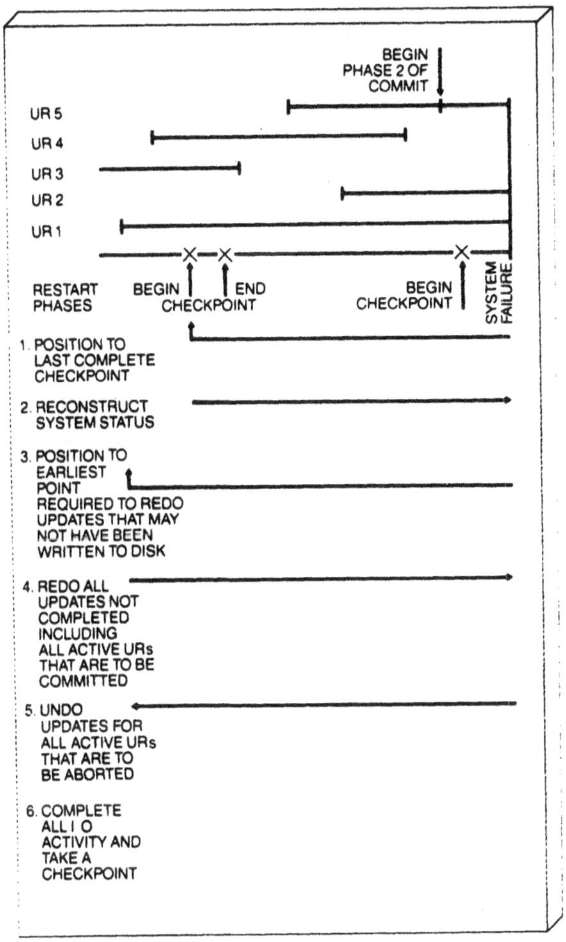

- Establish the status of all URs at the time of the termination (i.e., whether the UR was active, in commit, or in abort) by using the UR information recorded in the checkpoint and updating this information with UR-related information recorded in the log (e.g., begin UR, end UR, etc.). In the figure, URs 1 and 2 are to be backed out since they have not committed, URs 3 and 4 have completed commit, and UR 5 will complete commit processing during restart because it entered phase 2 of commit before the system failure.
- Establish the set of all tablespaces and indexspaces that were open at the time of termination by using checkpoint log records for DB2 objects as well as any open/close log records.

- Determine the earliest point in the log that contains records describing updates that may have to be redone because the pages may not have been written to DASD. This is done by determining the minimum value of the RBAS stored in the checkpoint records for DB2 data objects and the RBAs of any open log records that are found.

c. Start reading the log in a forward direction beginning at the RBA determined in the previous step (3), and redo all updates that have not been completed (4). This process reads to the end of the log.
d. Read the log in a backward direction and undo the updates of all URs that were active or in abort at the time of termination (5).
e. Force all updates to be externalized, and wait for all I/O operations to complete and take a checkpoint (6).

The restart process is not complete until the end checkpoint record has been written to the log. If failure occurs during restart prior to this point, DB2 will terminate abnormally and a subsequent restart will be necessary. Therefore, the restart process must provide for this condition, which introduces additional complexity in the process itself. Consider the following: A UR aborts for some reason, and the system terminates abnormally. During the restart process the updates performed by the UR are undone (including the writing of CLRs), and the UR completes abort processing. All log records that describe this process are written to DASD, and then the system fails again, before the pages which were modified during the undo process could be written to DASD. The resulting inconsistency will be corrected during a subsequent restart (which hopefully completes successfully) because, during the forward recovery phase, CLRs describing the backout will be read and processed.

Additional complications may be introduced when DB2 is connected to IMS/VS or CICS/OS/VS. These complications occur when DB2 fails while connected to one of these subsystems and one or more URs have completed the processing of phase 1 of commit (recorded in the log) but have not started phase 2. The status of a UR in this state is termed "in doubt" because only the commit coordinator (IMS or CICS) knows whether the decision was made to commit or abort the UR. During DB2 restart, all update operations are undone for a UR that has not completed phase 1 of commit. Likewise, all updates for a UR that has begun phase 2 of commit are redone. For a UR that is in doubt, DB2 performs redo processing in anticipation of a decision to commit (which is highly probable because the system failure interrupted the commit process) and locks all of the data accessed by the UR to prevent other users from accessing uncommitted modifications. It is the responsibility of the coordinating subsystem to resolve the situations that are in doubt when it and DB2 reconnect.

DB2 attempts to include both redo and undo information in the same log record.

A further complication arises during the restart processing of a UR that is in doubt when individual undo and redo log records are processed. DB2 attempts to include both redo and undo information in the same log record, but this is not always possible. Consider the case where the redo record for an operation precedes the undo record in the log. Remember that during restart, DB2 performs redo for an "in-doubt" UR and that during the redo process, the RBA of the redo log record applied to a page is stored in the page itself. Later, when the status of the UR is resolved, the decision may be made to abort the UR. Then, when the undo log record is read, it appears to the undo procedure that the update operation was not performed because the RBA of the undo record is greater than the RBA of the redo record which was stored in the page. This problem may be solved as follows: If the RBA of the log record is greater than or equal to the RBA of the page during restart when an undo-only log record is processed for an "in-doubt" UR, the RBA of the undo log record is stored in the page even though no other updates are made to the page. In the case where the undo log record precedes the redo log record in the log, the processing of the redo record results in the RBA of the redo record being stored in the page. Thus, if the decision is made later to abort the UR, the undo process will work properly.

On-line recovery. If the data stored in a page becomes logically inconsistent, DB2 must restore the data to a consistent state. One way in which a page can become inconsistent is because of software failures that result in errors being introduced into the page. If this situation is detected by DB2, it marks the page as logically inconsistent and denies further access to the page. This is necessary to prevent access to inconsistent data until the recovery process completes.

A second way that data in a page can become inconsistent is for a process to be aborted at a critical point in time. Updates to pages are in general not atomic (i.e., all or nothing) since they consist of distinct suboperations. For example, inserting a row into a page requires moving the row into free space within the page, writing a log record describing the insert, updating a page directory to point to the newly inserted record, updating the amount of free space remaining in the page, and storing the RBA of the record in the page. This operation is not atomic because a failure part way through will leave the update partially completed. Another example of a nonatomic operation is space reclamation within a page after rows have been deleted. When space reclamation becomes necessary, all the rows in the page are moved toward the beginning of the page, leaving a contiguous free area at the end. For ease of implementation and for performance reasons, it was decided not to log all of the above actions and thus, if the process is aborted at a critical point, the normal undo process cannot recover the page to a consistent state.

When DB2 detects an inconsistent page, it initiates an internal recovery operation.

To detect this condition, DB2 marks the page (in the page header) as being logically inconsistent at the beginning of the update process and marks it logically consistent again after the update completes. In the insert example given above, the page is inconsistent only after the log record has been written and until the RBA is stored in the page header. Although at first it might seem that the simplest solution might be to throw away the copy of the page in memory, this could cause the loss of committed updates that have never been written to DASD.

When DB2 detects an inconsistent page, it initiates an internal recovery operation which uses the log to perform forward recovery of the page using the version stored on DASD as the base. When the recovery operation completes, the page is marked consistent and can be accessed again. During the period when the page is marked inconsistent, it is unavailable for access, and a user attempting to access the page will receive a resource-not-available return code.

Unavailable data. In certain error situations, DB2 will itself make data unavailable until the data can be recovered.

If DB2 is unable to write a page to DASD because of a write I/O error, the page is added to what is called the write error range. Subsequent requests to access the page are denied, and the user will receive a resource-not-available return code. During abort and restart, if DB2 is unable to read a page because of a read I/O error, the page is also added to the write error range. This is necessary since the page cannot be read and the undo/redo operation cannot be performed.

Other situations in which DB2 will make data unavailable are during restart when a DB2 object (i.e., a tablespace or indexspace) cannot be opened, or when an error is detected (e.g., an addressing error is detected by the CPU) while DB2 is attempting to apply a log record to a page that has been read. In both of these cases, DB2 "stops" the DB2 object (the tablespace or indexspace), thus making it unavailable for access. When the object is stopped by DB2 during the restart process, compensation log records will still be written as discussed earlier.

Data made unavailable by DB2 will be made available again only after having been recovered. In the case of an I/O error, media recovery must be performed. In the case where the DB2 object is stopped, data may be recovered by performing a "deferred restart" or via media recovery. Deferred restart is a process that uses the version of the DB2 object that exists on DASD as the base and then performs redo starting at the point on the log established for the DB2 object from its checkpoint log record or open log record. The method chosen to recover the data depends on the reason why the object was made unavailable. If the problem was caused because a disk pack was not ready or was not mounted, or some similar condition, deferred restart would be chosen (since it would probably require the processing of fewer log records). In the case of such problems as a head crash that damaged a disk pack, or a fallback if deferred restart failed, media recovery can be used to make the DB2 object available again.

Concluding remarks

Both the procedures that write log records and those that perform undo/redo operations based on them are fairly complex. The subjective cost of implementation mentioned by Gray[3] seems about right: "writing a recoverable action is 30 percent harder and requires about 20 percent more code than a nonrecoverable action." The total cost in lines of code for data recovery in DB2 is very close to that of System R, i.e., 11 percent for DB2 versus 10 percent for System R.[4]

Maintaining the active log on DASD allowed us to use the same log to perform undo operations during normal processing, as well as at restart time, and allowed us to use a single log for both undo and redo information.

It is often the case that an operation viewed externally as a single update actually requires that more than one internal update operation be performed. Two approaches can be followed to provide atomicity of an update operation that consists of many lower-level update operations:

- Do things twice—first access and lock all of the data items that have to be modified, and if everything is all right, re-access them and perform the updates.
- Do things once—access, lock, and modify the data, and if anything goes wrong, invoke an internal backout mechanism to undo the updates that have been performed.

The second approach was chosen, not only because it performs better if most operations complete successfully, but also because it was easier to implement because much of the backout mechanism was already required to support abort and restart. This backout mechanism is used internally by DB2 to give the appearance of atomicity to multirow operations; e.g., a multirow update operation either succeeds completely or no rows are updated. It is also used to support updates to multiple indexes. An example of this is a table with three indexes, not all of which allow duplicate key values. The insertion of a row might meet the uniqueness criteria of the first two indexes but fail that of the third, at which time the internal mechanism would be invoked to undo the two successful insertions.

We recognize that improvements can be made in the area of data recovery, and we also recognize the importance of this capability to our users. We expect that as DB2 evolves, additional procedures and techniques will be developed to continue to improve this very important area.

Cited references

1. J. J. Sordi, "The Query Management Facility," *IBM Systems Journal* **23**, No. 2, 126–150 (1984, this issue).
2. K. R. Hammond and M. R. Zimowski, "TSO Attach: A multipurpose communication channel to IBM Database 2," *IBM Systems Journal* **23**, No. 2, 151–164 (1984, this issue).
3. J. Gray, P. McJones, M. Blasgen, R. Lorie, T. Price, F. Putzolu, and I. Traiger, *The Recovery Manager of a Data Management System*, Research Report RJ-2623, IBM Research Division, 5600 Cottle Road, San Jose, CA 95193 (August 15, 1979).
4. M. W. Blasgen et al., "System R: An architectural overview," *IBM Systems Journal* **20**, No. 1, 41–62 (1981).

General references

W. C. McGee, "The information management system IMS/VS," *IBM Systems Journal* **16**, No. 2, 84–168 (1977).

IBM Database 2 General Information, S370-20, IBM Corporation; available through IBM branch offices.

J. P. Strickland, P. P. Uhrowczik, and V. L. Watts, "IMS/VS: An evolving system," *IBM Systems Journal* **21**, No. 4, 490–510 (1982).

Reprint Order No. G321-5217.

Richard A. Crus *IBM General Products Division, Santa Teresa Laboratory, P.O. Box 50020, San Jose, California 95150.* Mr. Crus joined IBM in 1965. He has been involved with the architecture and with the design and development of DB2 since its inception and was the technical team leader for the data manager component of DB2. Mr. Crus is currently an advisory programmer in the DB2 Advanced Development Department. He has a B.A. in mathematics from the University of Utah.

FAULT TOLERANT LOCKING (FTL) FOR TIGHTLY COUPLED SYSTEMS*

Wesley W. Chu and Jung M. An

University of California, Los Angeles

ABSTRACT

To assure data consistency among replicated share data in a tightly coupled distributed system in case of processor, memory or network path failures, a fault tolerant locking (FTL) protocol is proposed in this paper.

A *lock word* is generated and appended to the record or a group of records (segment) that contains the status (free, locked, update-initiated, or failed) of each record (or segment) as well as the accessibility of its replicated copy. The contents of the *lock word* provide information for fault recovery from a replicated copy. Further, a *status table* is created at each processor to indicate the accessibility (good or failed) of each record (or segment). The processor consults its *status table* before accessing the record (or segment).

The FTL protocol was implemented on a tightly coupled multiple-computer testbed for a space defense application. Experimental results present such protocol behavior as overhead, lock-request period and time out period for processor failure detection. Further, it has also been experimentally demonstrated that the FTL is capable of detecting a processor failure during updating and recovering from data inconsistency among record copies.

1. INTRODUCTION

In a tightly coupled distributed processing system, multiple copies of shared files are maintained in different shared memory modules to provide high survivability. To assure *mutual consistency* among the copies, data updates should be applied to all file copies. However, if a processor fails during an update process, some file copies may have updated while others have not, resulting in mutual inconsistency. To recover from this type of failure and assure the transaction is atomic [1], we propose to use the *Fault Tolerant Locking (FTL)* protocol that is implemented on top of the conventional consistency-control protocols FTL detects a processor failure, identifies and recovers inconsistent file copies, and releases the file lock so that other processors may lock and use the file again. FTL also prevents processors from reading and updating out-of-date file copies in case of shared memory modules and/or path failures.

We shall first describe the FTL concept, its implementation and operations. Then we present the time relationship about the lock-holding time. Finally, we discuss some of the FTL experimental results from a multicomputer testbed which provide information about the performance and characteristics of FTL.

2. FTL CONCEPT

To provide the status of a file, a word that indicates the current state (free, locked, update-initiated, or failed) of that file as well as the accessible state (accessible, inaccessible) of the replicated file copies are appended to each file copy in the shared memory modules. File copies are updated one at a time according to a predefined sequence. In this manner, if a processor fails* during a file update, the update status, *(completely* updated, *partially* updated, or *un-updated)* of all the copies of a file can be identified. Based on this status of the copies of a file, the inconsistent copy can be detected and recovered from any of the consistent copies.

When a processor that holds the lock fails, attempts from any other processors to lock this file will, of course, be unsuccessful. Such a processor failure will be detected after a pre-specified unsuccessful number of repeated lock attempts (time-out) by the other processors. To prohibit further accesses to failed copies, each processor maintains a file copy *status table* in its local memory. When a processor experiences a memory and/or path failure while accessing a file copy, it marks the failure on its *status table*.

3. FTL OPERATIONS

3.1 Implementation

To implement the FTL in a tightly coupled system, shared records are duplicated in different shared memory modules (Fig. 1). Each processor maintains a *record status table* (RST) in its local memory which indicates the status (good or failed) of each record copy, or segment, in the shared memory modules. Each record copy, or segment, has a *lock word (LW)* that indicates one of the four possible states of the copy (free, locked, update-initiated, or failed) and the states of the other copies (accessible or inaccessible) (Fig. 2). The status of the copy assures data consistency in case of path failure. Each processor is required to read the *lock word* before accessing the record copy and mark on its record *status table* if either of the record copies is inaccessible.

To simplify our discussion, we assume each file has two copies: a *primary* copy and a *shadow* copy. Before

* This work was supported by the Ballistic Missile Defense Advanced Technological Center under Contract DASG60-85-C-0059.

* A failed processor is also assumed unable to issue any memory reference.

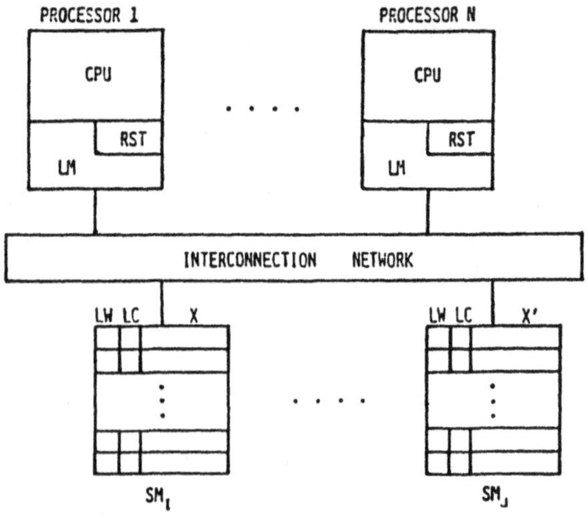

LM: LOCAL MEMORY

SM: SHARED MEMORY

X': SHADOW COPY OF RECORD X

LW: LOCK WORD (FOUR POSSIBLE STATES)

LC: LOCK COUNTER

RST: RECORD STATUS TABLE

Figure 1. A Tightly Coupled Distributed System with FTL

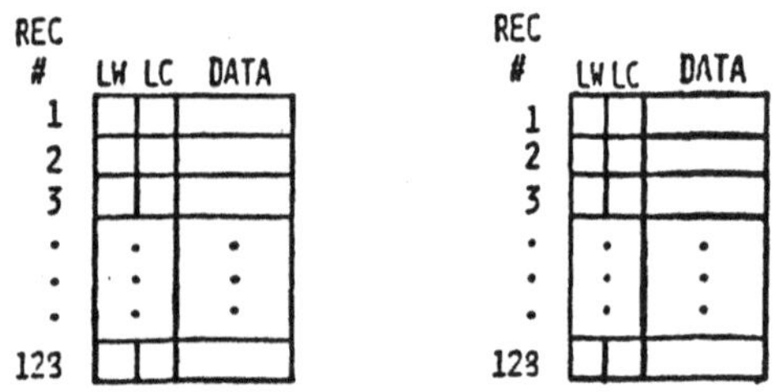

LW = LOCK WORD

LC = LOCK COUNTER

Each lock word indicates:

1) One of four states: *Free*, *Locked*, *Update-initiated*, or *Failed*.

2) Status of the other record copies (accessible or inaccessible)

(a) Duplicated Records In Shared Memory Modules

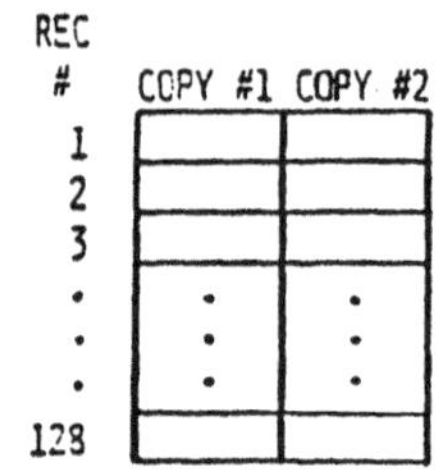

Each entry indicates one of two states: *Accessible* or *Inaccessible*.

(b) Record Status Table (RST) In Each Processor

Figure 2. Duplicated Records and Record Status Table

accessing a record copy,[1] a processor first checks the RST to determine if the copy is accessible. Then it reads the *LW* of the record copy. If the *LW* of the copy indicates 'failed', the processor marks 'failed' on the RST and tries the other copy. If the requested copy is being locked or update-initiated (by some other processor), the processor repeatedly checks the *LW* until the copy becomes free. When the processor finds the copy is free, it locks the copy and does the same process for the second copy. Then it prepares updates in its local memory. When all updates to the record are ready, the processor marks 'update initiated' on the *LW* of the first copy and performs the update. After completing the update onto the second record copy in the same manner, the processor releases the lock for both copies. The FTL update procedures are shown in Figs. 3 and 4 for normal operations with no failure and no lock contention.

3.2 Detection of Processor Failure

When two or more processors request to lock the same record simultaneously, only one of them will obtain the lock grant. Other processors might experience time-out and initiate the recovery process which is undesirable. To prevent this from occurring, a *Lock Counter (LC)* is introduced for each record copy. After a processor successfully locks a record copy, the *LC* of the copy is incremented by one. When a record copy is currently locked, a processor trying to lock the same copy will repeatedly request to lock the copy until it succeeds. When the processor finds that the *LC* of the requested record copy has been incremented while waiting for a lock grant, this implies that the record has been released by its holding processor and locked by some processor again. The processor resets the *time-out counter* and continues requesting for the lock-grant (Fig. 5). If the *LC* remains

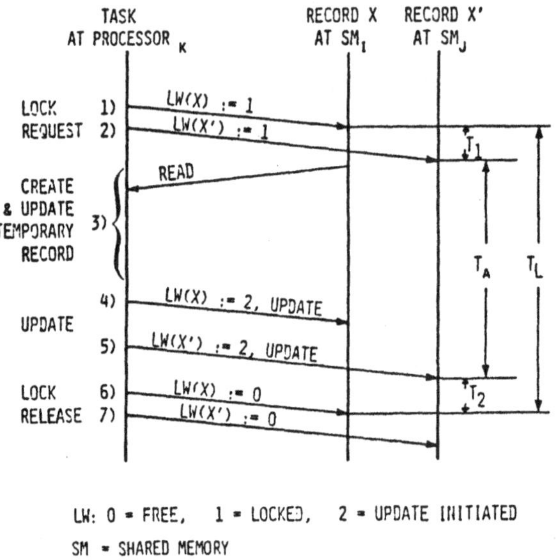

Figure 3. FTL Protocol for Record Update

[1] For simplicity in our discussion, we assumed the record as a unit of data items for locking and recovery. However, to reduce overhead, a group of records (segment) may be used as a unit of data item for locking and recovery.

1) Lock Record X (LW(X): = 1)

2) Lock Record X'(LW(X'): = 1)

3) Create and update temporary record in local memory

4) Mark lock word (LW(X): = 2) and update record X

5) Mark lock work (LW(X') = 2) and update record X'

6) Unlock record X (LW(X): = 0)

7) Unlock record X' (LW(X'): = 0)

LW: 0 = Free, 1 = Locked, 2 = Update-initiated

Figure 4. FTL Protocol for Record Update

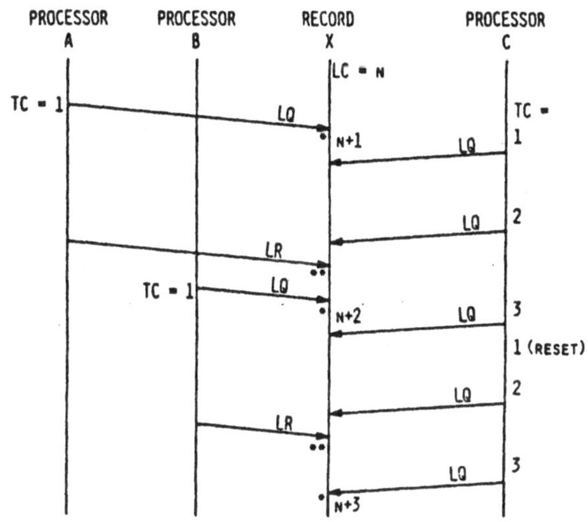

LC: LOCK-COUNTER
LQ: LOCK-REQUEST
TC: TIME-OUT-COUNTER
TC(MAX) = 3
LR: LOCK-RELEASE
•: RECORD IS LOCKED
••: RECORD IS UNLOCKED

Figure 5. Example of the FTL Time-Out Mechanism: No-Failure Case

unchanged after a predetermined number of lock requests (i.e., time-out period), the processor currently holding the lock is considered failed (Fig. 6). The processor that detects the time-out then increments the *LC* of the record copy by one. This prevents other processors from detecting the same failure. To prevent *false* failure detection, the time-out period (determined by the number of repeated lock requests) must be larger than the lock-holding time of any application program.

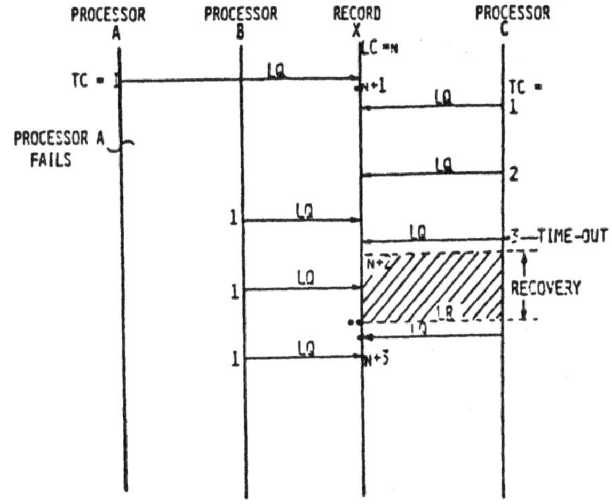

LC: LOCK-COUNTER
LQ: LOCK-REQUEST
TC: TIME-OUT-COUNTER
TC(MAX) = 3
LR: LOCK-RELEASE
•: RECORD IS LOCKED
••: RECORD IS UNLOCKED

Figure 6. Example of the FTL Time-Out Mechanism: Failure Case

3.3 Technique for Reducing the Time-Out Period for Performance Improvement

To provide rapid failure detection, the time-out period should be short. However, a short time-out period may cause false failure detections. To avoid this, the processor that holds the lock can increment the *LC* periodically should it hold a lock longer than the pre-specified time-out period. This will prevent other processors from generating undesirable time-out signals.

3.4 Recovery from a Processor Failure

The processor reads the *LW*s of all copies of the requested record when it detects a time-out for a record. Based on the FTL *status table* as shown in Fig. 7, the processor takes the appropriate recovery action: either discarding the inconsistent record copy and operating in a degraded mode, or copying from the consistent record copy into the inconsistent one.

3.5 Handling of a Shared Memory Failure

When a processor detects a memory failure by hardware detection or diagnostic program, one approach is to notify all the other processors of the failure. Whenever the processor accesses a record copy in a shared memory, it needs to check message boxes which requires large processing overhead. Further, two or more processors may detect the same memory failure independently and may receive duplicate failure messages. Therefore, such a message passing technique requires high overhead.

To avoid such message passing overhead, we propose the following technique for handling memory failure: When a processor requests a record from a shared memory module

LOCK STATUS TABLE

LW X	LW X'	RECOVERY REQUIRED?	INCONSISTENT RECORD COPY	UPDATE COMPLETED?
0	0	NO	N/A	N/A
1	0	NO	N/A	NO
1	1	NO	N/A	NO
2	1	YES	X	NO
2	2	YES	X'	YES
0	2	NO	N/A	YES

Figure 7. FTL Recovery Procedures for a Processor Failure

and detects a memory failure, it marks 'inaccessible' on its local RST (without notifying the other processors). It also marks 'inaccessible' on the *LW* of the record copy if the *LW* is still accessible. When a second processor finds that the *LW* on its requested record copy is marked 'inaccessible', this second processor marks the 'inaccessible' of that record in its RST. If the *LW* of that record copy is inaccessible, then this record copy can not be accessed by any processors which assures data consistency.

3.6 Handling of a Path Failure

A single point failure in the crossbar network or in the multiple bus system may prevent one or more processors from accessing a particular memory module.* This will prevent record updating in that memory module. However, the records may be accessed by other processors that are not blocked by that single point path failure, and cause data inconsistency. This can be avoided by maintaining the status of the other record copy in the *LW* of each record copy. When a processor detects a record is inaccessible, it marks the 'inaccessible' of that record on its RST and on the *LW* of the accessible copy. When another processor accesses the accessible copy, the *LW* will reflect the inaccessibility of the other copy. The processor should then mark that information on its RST to avoid further accesses of that inaccessible copy of that record.

4. RECORD LOCK-HOLDING TIME

Let us present the record lock-holding time as a function of various system parameters. This may shed light on the interrelationship among the number of retries for locks, the retry period for lock-request, FTL overhead, and response time.

The *lock-holding time*, T_L as shown in Figs. 3 and 8, is the sum of the time for locking record copy X', T_1, the execution time for an application process (including read and update of record copies), T_A, and the time for releasing record copy X, T_2. That is,

$$T_L = T_1 + T_A + T_2 \qquad (1)$$

Since the FTL requires reading a record copy (before copying the record into the local memory) and updating the primary and shadow copies, there are three memory accesses for each record update. Thus,

$$N_m = 3\,N_r$$

where

N_r = Record size in words,

N_m = Number of memory cycles for accessing a record

The execution time for an application process, T_A, is the sum of the execution time of that process without memory conflict and the additional delay due to memory conflict. Thus,

$$T_A = T_a + (1 + P_c)\,N_m = T_a + 3(1 + P_c)N_r \qquad (2)$$

where

T_a = Execution time of a process without memory conflict,

P_c = Probability of memory conflict for each memory cycle.

Substituting (2) into (1) we have,

$$T_L = T_1 + T_a + 3(1 + P_c)N_r + T_2 \qquad (3)$$

5. FTL EXPERIMENTS

In this section, we shall present a few experiments via a multi-micro computer testbed to characterize the behavior of FTL protocol. The experiments for the FTL protocol were implemented on the Crossbar Multicomputer Testbed [2, 3]. The locking used by the application program is on record level. This section describes the testbed, the application program, the implementation of the protocol on the testbed, and experimental results.

5.1 Crossbar Multi-Microcomputer Testbed

The testbed contains six processors connected to twelve 32K byte memories by means of a crossbar network (Figure 9). A global clock allows processes on separate microcomputers to have a common time base for performance measurement. A global hardware flag register is used to synchronize accesses to shared data made by the processor set. For more detailed information, the the interested reader should refer to [2].

5.2 Application Program

The Application Program is a distributed implementation of a generic low-altitude space defense system in which one processor is dedicated to a simulated radar and radar return assimilation program, four processors execute three fundamental space defense task threads, and a sixth processor executes radar scheduling tasks. The software makes use of the multiported shared memory. A common data file, the track file, is maintained in the shared memory. The track file is accessed by the processors with the record locking technique.

The simulated space defense process runs three radar control loops: Detection, Track Initiation, and Track. Radar detections are simulated using an arrival rate based on an 82 - re-entry vehicle and 629 - decoy threat targeted for simultaneous impact. The application scheduler in each of

* Assuming the failure does not cause network partitioning; that is, two processors having access to only one of the two copies, but not the same one.

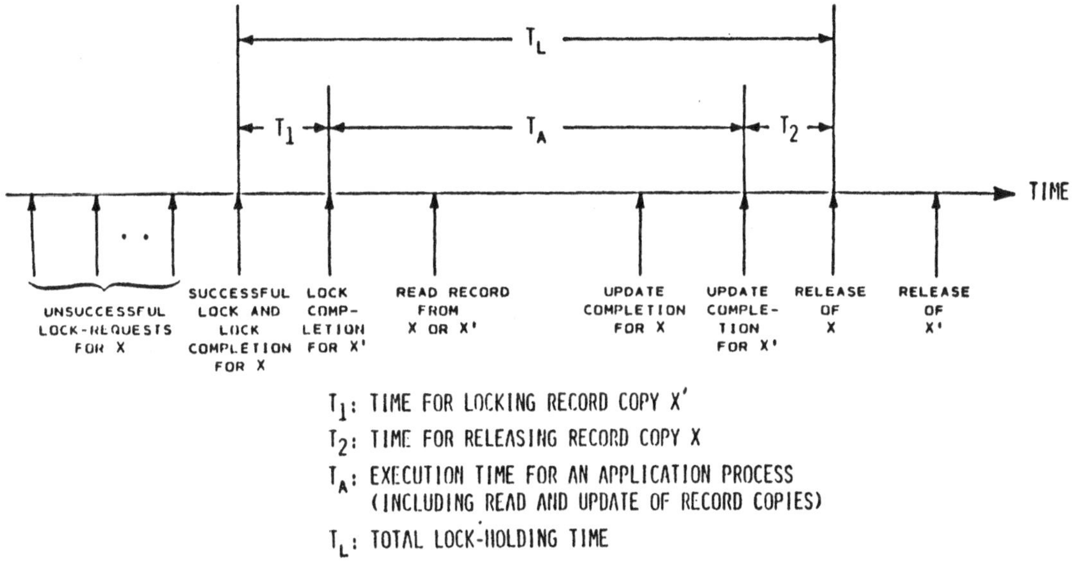

Figure 8. FTL Lock-Holding Time for a Record

the four space defense task processors polls three radar return queues in a round-robin fashion. When a nonempty queue is detected, the scheduler activates the appropriate task to process the data.

5.3 Implementation of FTL Protocol

The Track file was duplicated and placed in shared-memory modules of the testbed. When a task needs to modify a record in a shared-memory, it first locks the record copies in sequence in order to avoid deadlock situations. A local copy is then created, and a synthetic load is executed simulating an update to the local copy. After the update is completed, the primary record copy is marked update-initiated and the local copy written to it. If a task cannot lock both copies of a record in an allotted amount of time, the processor holding the lock is considered to have failed and a recovery procedure is initiated on the record (Figure 10). The allotted time to lock the record copies is measured by iterations of unsuccessful lock attempts in the lock procedure. When a predetermined number of iterations are attempted, the processor attempting to lock the record transfers control to a recovery procedure that examines the lock states from the LW of the two record copies to determine if they are consistent with each other. If inconsistency exists, the lock states are used to determine which copy is inconsistent so the consistent copy may be written over the inconsistent copy. The lock states of both record copies are set to 'free' and the processor returns to the thread of processing.

5.4 Experimental Results

A set of experiments was performed for evaluating the feasibility of the FTL protocol via the Crossbar Multicomputer Testbed. Three experiments characterize the FTL protocol under no-processor-failure situation, in terms of 1) overhead of the FTL protocol, 2) choice of lock-request retry period, and 3) choice of time-out period for processor failure detection. Another experiment studies the FTL protocol recovery time in the presence of processor failures. These experiments were performed at SDC [3] and we shall present and discuss these results.

5.4.1 Overhead of the FTL Protocol

Concurrency-control with the FTL protocol needs to perform additional lock and update to the second copy of each record. Therefore, it requires more processing resources than without FTL (baseline system). For the particular application, we note from Fig. 11 that FTL requires 24.2% more CPU resources of which 7.8% is used to lock the second record copy, and 16.4% is used to execute the FTL code. As a result, the lock-holding time of the FTL system is longer than the baseline system. Because of larger processor utilization for the system using FTL, the port-to-port times are also increased. From Fig. 12 we note that for this application, using FTL increases the Track Thread response time by 19.7%.

5.4.2 Lock-Request Retry Period

When a processor fails to obtain a lock grant for a record, it retries repeatedly until it receives a grant or reaches a time-out (i.e., detects a processor failure). If the period between retries (retry period) is too short, the number of shared memory conflicts increases. If the retry period is too long, the processor may be waiting for a lock even though

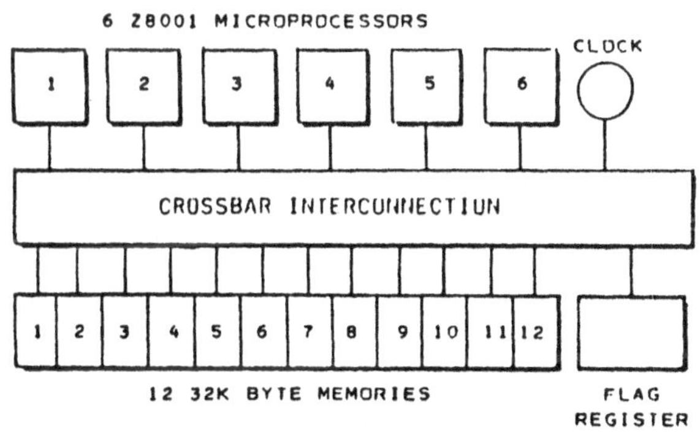

Figure 9. The SDC Corssbar Multicomputer Testbed

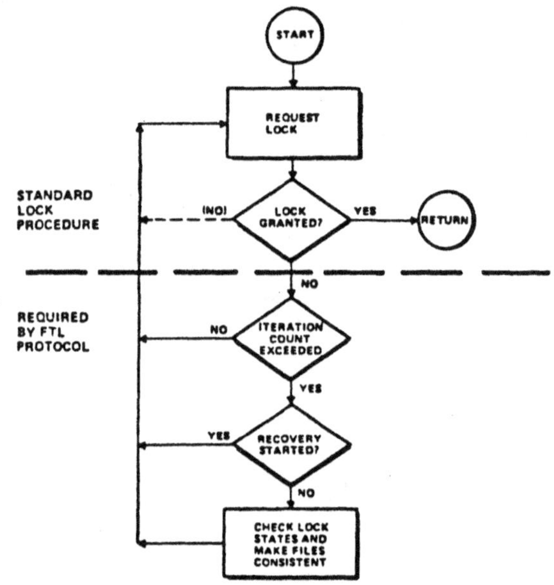

Figure 10. Flow Diagram of FTL for Handling Processor Failure

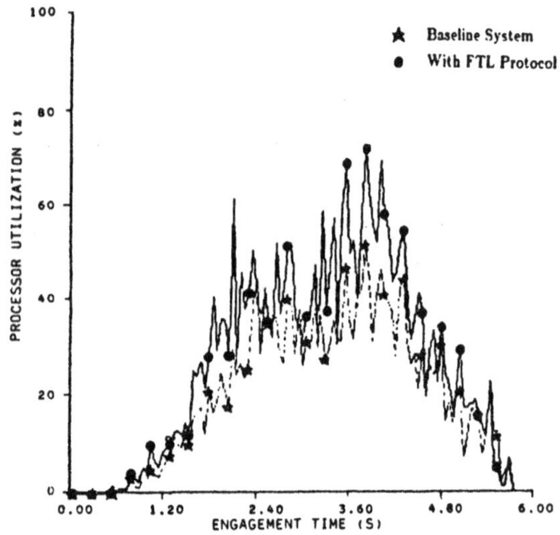

Figure 11. Processor Utilization

the record is 'free.' [1] For the given application example a delay loop is inserted in the lock procedure. The retry period can be controlled by varying the number of the loop iterations. Each loop (retry) iteration is about 0.95 μs. Fig. 13 displays the lock-grant time as a function of the retry period. We noted that the lock-grant time is rather insensitive to the retry period. A slightly lower average lock-grant time occurred at ten loop iterations (9.5 μs simulated time).

[1] Queuing of lock requests is not feasible since memory modules do not have enough intelligence for queuing handling. Queuing handling at the processor would be costly because of the required interprocessor communication (IPC) among processors.

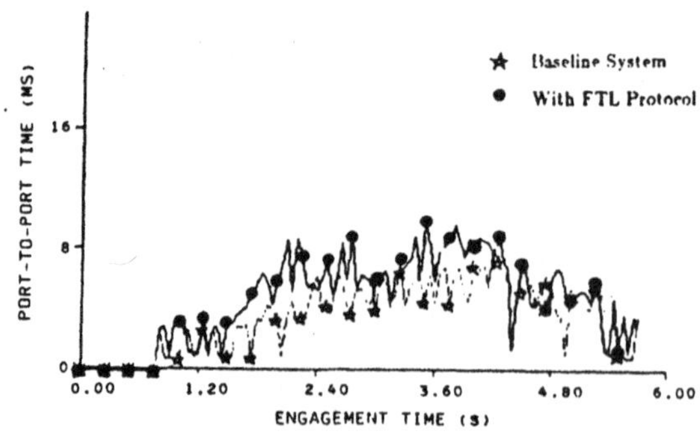

Figure 12. Maximum Port-to-Port Time for the Track Thread

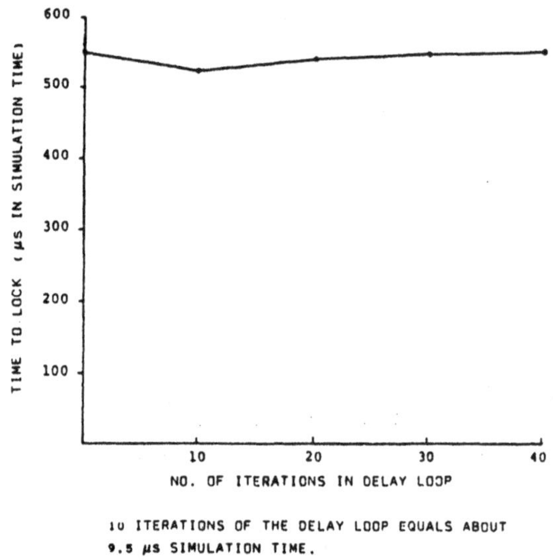

Figure 13. Lock-Request Retry Period vs. Lock-Grant Time

5.4.3 Time-Out Period for Processor Failure Detection

The time-out period for detecting a processor failure during a record update should be longer than the maximum lock-holding time for any task. The time-out period is measured as the maximum number of lock requests for a record. If the time-out period is too long, a processor would issue unnecessary requests for a lock that is held by a failed processor. On the other hand, if the time-out period is too short, the processor would initiate unnecessary recovery processes. Again, the time-out period is implemented by executing loop iterations. Each iteration runs for about 54 μsec. For the application example, the experiment shows that 13 iterations (corresponding to 650 μs) is the lowest number that yields no false time-out detection as shown in Fig. 14.

5.4.4 Performance of the FTL Protocol With Processor Failures

This set of experiments study the time required to detect and to recover from a processor failure. To emulate a failure, the processor is forced into an infinite loop while it

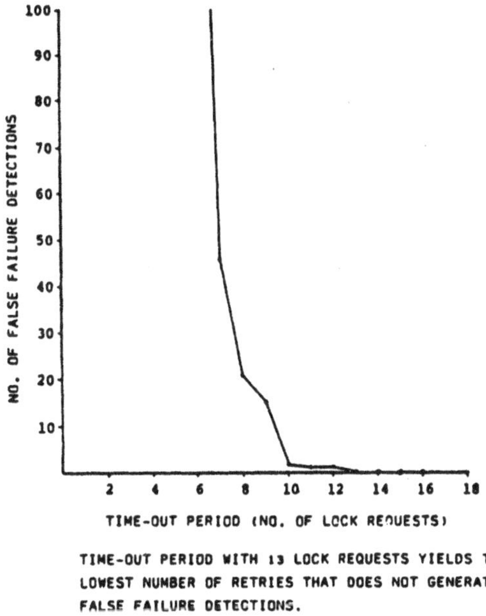

Figure 14. Time-Out Period vs. False Failure Detection

holds a lock. It was shown that the time for detecting the failure and completing the recovery is within 2 to 10 ms for a task with a maximum allowable of 40 ms port-to-port time.

6. CONCLUSIONS

A Fault Tolerant Locking protocol has been presented for tightly coupled distributed systems for maintaining data consistency in case of failure during updating replicated record copies. The FTL implementation requires a *lock word* that specifies the status of that record as well as the accessibility of its copies, and a *record status table* at each processor to specify the accessibility of each record. Based on the status of the LW and RST, FTL can recover and assure data consistency from processor and memory failure. To assure data consistency in case of network path failures, the FTL prohibits further accesses to those record copies that are inaccessible by some processors.

The FTL protocol has been implemented on a multicomputer testbed for a space defense application. Experimental results reveal that the FTL is capable of detecting a processor failure during update and recovering from data inconsistency between record copies. The overhead for performing the fault tolerant locking protocol depends on the lock frequency, and its application. The testbed experiments reveal that the overhead is within an acceptable range for the application example. The set of parameters that may affect the system performance are: Time-out period, lock granularity (record or a group of records) and lock protocol (.e.g, exclusive lock for write and shared for read, or reserve, upgrade or exclusive lock). Further research and experimentations in these areas are desirable for characterizing and improving the performance of FTL.

7. ACKNOWLEDGEMENT

The authors wish to thank G. Barnett and W. C. McDonald of System Development Corporation for implementing the FTL protocol on their testbed and performing the experiments.

8. REFERENCES

[1] B. W. Lampson, "Atomic Transactions," Chapter 11 of *Distributed Systems: Architecture and Implementation*, Springer-Veritag, 1981.

[2] W. C. McDonald and R. Wayne Smith, "A Flexible Distributed Testbed for Real Time Applications," *IEEE Computer*, Vol. 15, No. 10, Oct. 1982.

[3] G. Barnett, "Fault Tolerant Locking Protocol Experiment Results - Volume I," System Development Corporation, TM-HU-311/204/00, November 1984.

A RESILIENT COMMIT PROTOCOL FOR REAL TIME SYSTEMS*

Jung Min An and Wesley W. Chu

Computer Science Department
University of California, Los Angeles
(213) 825-2047

Abstract

A low cost resilient commit protocol is presented which is *non-blocking* and *tolerant to multiple failures*. In this commit protocol, sites are linearly numbered and updates are broadcast in one phase according to this number sequence. Failures are recovered by the smallest numbered surviving site. Applying this commit protocol to existing concurrency control techniques and their procedures for site recovery are discussed.

1. Introduction

The survivability of distributed systems can be improved with multiple copies of files. When an update is performed at a site, this update should be delivered to those sites that have a replicated file. All file copies should be identical. This is referred to as *mutual consistency*. File copies may, however, differ temporarily during update propagation. If a site fails during an update broadcast, only a part of the file copies may be updated, resulting in mutual inconsistency.

Posting a file update in a system is known as a *commit*; which implies that the posted update will not be backed out [GARC82]. The site that broadcasts an update to other sites is known as the *coordinator* and the receiving sites of the update are the *participants*.

Two-phase commit is a well known method which ensures mutual consistency among file copies in case of failures [KOHL81]. It is also called a *blocking commit* because when a coordinator site fails during an update broadcast, other sites are blocked from using the file copies until the failed coordinator recovers and completes the unfinished commit work [SKEE81]. The time interval required for the commit process is relatively short as compared with the time needed to prepare update data at a coordinator site. Thus, it is less probable that a failure would occur during the commit interval resulting in blocking of the file. This technique has been implemented in several prototype systems such as INGRES [STON79] and LOCUS [WALK83]. Both of these are non-real time systems.

A two-site resiliency scheme for error detection and recovery for non-blocking commit was presented in [ALSB76]. Expanding such a scheme to n-site resiliency would be very costly. Skeen [SKEE81] proposed a *three-phase commit* protocol by adding another buffer state to the two-phase commit. When a coordinator fails, one of the participants is elected to be the new coordinator and complete the suspended commit process based on its local state. In the *back-up coordinator* method, [HAMM80], each file has a preassigned set of back-up coordinators. These back-up coordinators communicate with the coordinator during commit processes and take its place in case of coordinator failure. All of the above methods require excessive communications and therefore are not suitable for real time applications.

In this paper, we shall first present a low cost resilient commit protocol that is *non-blocking* and *tolerant to multiple failures*. Next, we show how to incorporate this commit protocol into existing concurrency control techniques such as EWP [CHU85] and PSL [STON79]. Finally, we discuss the procedure for site recovery.

2. Assumptions

We restrict our discussion to distributed systems that consist of multiple computers connected via an interconnection network. Further, we assume the following:

1. ***The topology of the communication network is designed such that site partitioning does not occur even in the presence of link failures.***

2. ***A message sent by a site will eventually be received by a destination site as long as the destination is alive.*** This can be assured by exchanging a positive acknowledgement in the network subsystem for every message delivery. Based on this assumption, there would be no lost or out-of-sequence messages.

3. ***"I am alive" messages are periodically exchanged among the sites for failure detection.*** With this assumption, acknowledgement messages and time-out detection mechanisms are eliminated from our resilient commit protocol.

4. ***Failed sites are not allowed to rejoin the system.*** In real time systems, files are usually stored in volatile memories (e.g., MOS dynamic RAMs) and a site failure causes a total loss of data, making the site recovery infeasible within real time constraints. However, in section 5, the site recovery issues will be addressed under the assumption that all files are stored in non-volatile media.

5. ***All the files that are required to perform a transaction reside at the transaction site.***

* This work was supported by the Ballistic Missile Defense Advanced Technology Center under Contract DASG60-8[illegible]-C-00[illegible]

3. Resilient Commit Protocol

The basic concept of our resilient commit protocol is that if an update is posted at any operating site, all other operating sites that keep a copy of the file will eventually receive the update despite multiple failures. Thus, mutual consistency among the file copies is preserved for an update. (When more than one site performs updates simultaneously, the commit protocol does not necessarily maintain mutual consistency. Concurrency control protocols provide file consistency by controlling simultaneous updates from different sites.)

In the commit protocol, sites are numbered for a given file. Updates are broadcast *according to this number sequence*. If only a subset of operating sites receives an update after a failure occurs, mutual inconsistency is resolved by having the smallest numbered operating site retransmit the last update received from the failed site. This retransmission must be done *in the number sequence* so that a failure of the smallest numbered site will have the next smallest numbered site redo the retransmission. Thus, the commit protocol is resilient to multiple failures.

In the commit protocol, exchanges of acknowledgement messages are eliminated by relying on the network subsystem at each site for failure detection. However, network subsystems require an acknowledgement for every update delivery.

Let us now summarize the operation of the proposed commit protocol:

1. For each file, sites are numbered and updates are sent in this number sequence.

2. Updates are posted immediately after being received. Further, each site should save the last updates *from all other sites* for update retransmissions in the event that it should become the smallest numbered surviving site.

3. When a site failure is detected, the smallest numbered surviving site retransmits the last update received from the failed site *in the number sequence*.

During the recovery from a failure, duplicate updates may be sent to a site, which would be detected by examining the update sequence number (SN). [1] The operations for the SN are listed as follows:

- For each file, every copy maintains a SN. Initially, all copies have the same SN (e.g., SN=n as shown in figure 1).

- When a coordinator finalizes an update, it increments its local SN by one and broadcasts the update with the new SN to other sites.

- An incoming update with a SN less than or equal to the local SN of the receiving site is discarded.

- When an update is posted, the local SN is replaced with the new value.

Figure 1a shows the no-failure case where site 3 broadcasts an update according to the number sequence. Note that no extra communication is required. In figure 1b, site 3 fails after sending an update to the first two sites. At the detection of the failure,

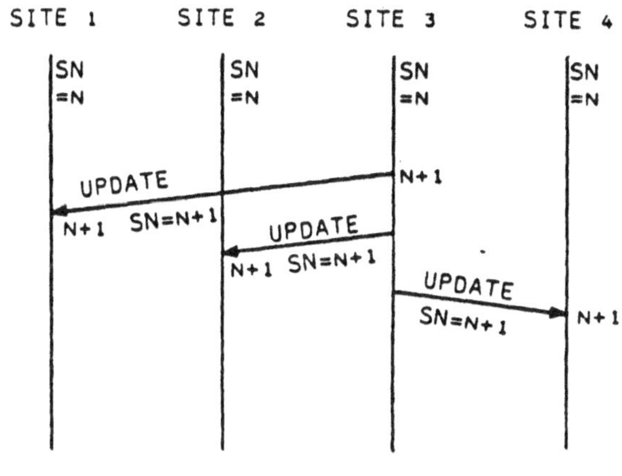

1a. No-Failure Case

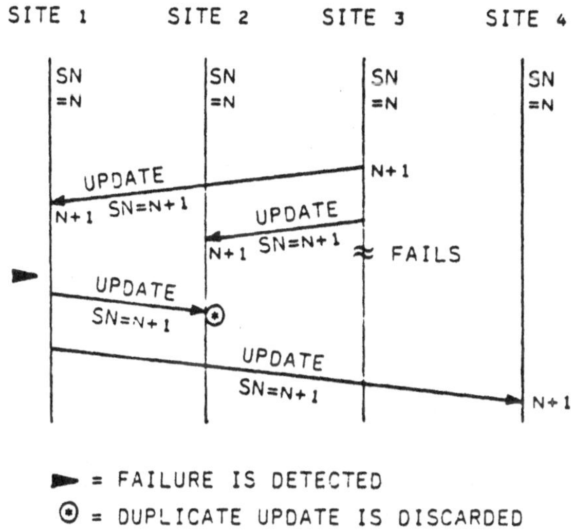

1b. Recovery from a site failure

Figure 1. The Resilient Commit Protocol

the smallest numbered site (site 1) retransmits the update. By comparing the SNs, site 2 detects and discards the duplicate update.

Reducing Messages for Failure Recovery

Suppose a site fails after all other sites have received its last update. Our commit protocol requires that the smallest numbered surviving site always retransmits the last update from the failed site. In this case, all sites will receive this update twice. To eliminate these duplicate updates during the recovery, a coordinator could indicate the completion of each update broadcast. This procedure is described as follows:

1. A coordinator sends an update-complete (UC) message to the smallest numbered site after completing an update broadcast.

2. When a site receives the UC message, it discards the saved update.

[1] The SN concept was also used in the EWP to detect conflicts among concurrent update requests [CHU85]

For systems with infrequent updates, the above approach is appealing since the additional overhead due to UC messages will be small and it is less probable that a site fails during an update broadcast. Moreover, real time systems usually require that real time constraints should be met even when failures occur and therefore it is desirable to reduce unnecessary overhead during a recovery.

4. Resilient Concurrency Control Techniques

For a set of concurrent updates generated from different sites, the commit protocol itself does not necessarily maintain mutual consistency. Concurrency control produces the relative order for multiple accesses to a file and provides internal and mutual consistency among file copies [BERN81].

Many concurrency control protocols have been introduced. The *primary site locking (PSL)* protocol [STON79] is accepted to be a low cost locking method. The *exclusive writer protocol (EWP)* has a very low overhead with no transaction restarts, database rollbacks, or deadlock. Although it provides limited serializability, the EWP has great appeal for distributed real time systems since strict serializability is usually not required in real time systems [CHU85].

In this section, we shall discuss how to incorporate the resilient commit protocol into EWP and PSL to preserve internal and mutual consistency in the presence of failures.

4.1 Resilient Exclusive Writer Protocol

In the *Exclusive Writer Protocol (EWP)*, a file is written by only one predetermined site, called the *exclusive writer (EW)*, which does not change during system operation. Non-EW sites send update-request messages to the EW. Then, the EW broadcasts the update to all other sites (see figure 2a).

For the EWP to be resilient, sites are numbered and the site with the smallest number is designated as the EW. Since updates are broadcast only by the EW site, failures of non-EW sites do not cause any file inconsistency. When the EW site failure is detected, the next smallest numbered site becomes the new EW and retransmits the last update received from the old EW since the old EW may have failed during the broadcast of the last update.

The operations for the resilient EWP are summarized as follows:

1. Sites are numbered and the site with the smallest number is selected as the EW.

2. The EW sends an update to other sites *in the number sequence* (i.e., lowest numbered site first, highest numbered site last).

3. Each non-EW site should save the last update received from the EW.

4. When the EW fails, the site with the next smallest number becomes the new EW and retransmits the last update received from the old EW *in the number sequence.*

Figure 2a shows the no-failure case. Site 3 sends an update-request message to the EW which then broadcasts the update. The EW site fails during an update broadcast in figure 2b. The next smallest numbered site (site 2) becomes the new EW and resends the last update. A duplicate update is received and discarded by site 3.

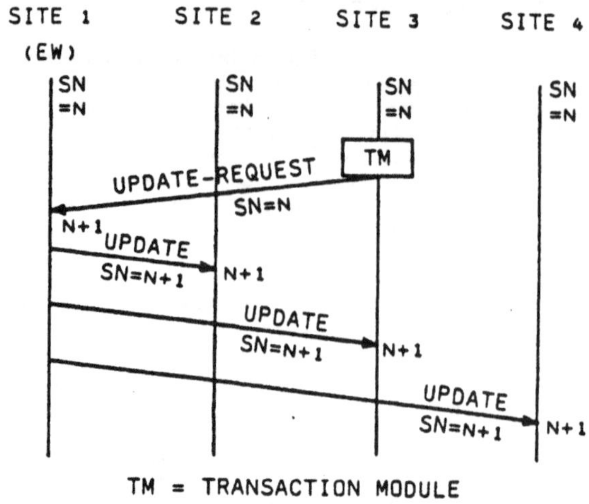

2a. No-Failure Case

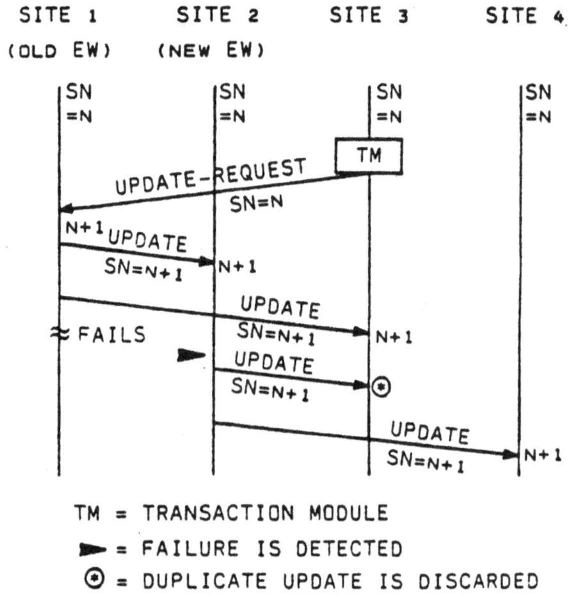

2b. Recovery from the EW Failure

Figure 2. The Resilient EWP

If the EW site fails right after receiving an update-request but before sending out the update, the update-request will be lost. This is similar to a conflicting update request that is discarded in the EW site.

As explained in section 3, to eliminate unnecessary update retransmissions during the recovery from the EW failure, the EW may send an UC message to the next smallest numbered site after each update broadcast.

4.2 Resilient Primary Site Locking Protocol

In the resilient PSL protocol, similar to the resilient EWP case, sites are numbered and the smallest numbered site is designated as the primary site (PS). When the PS fails, the next smallest numbered site becomes the new PS. Since the new PS does not know whether the lock was being held by any other site and whether any lock-request was queued in the old PS, the new PS requests the file status of all other sites. Also a site that issued a lock-request, but has not received a lock-grant from the old PS must resend a lock-request to the new PS.

In contrast to the EWP case, failures of non-PSs must be considered since non-PSs broadcast updates directly. In addition, non-PSs may fail while holding a lock or while their lock-requests are being queued in the PS, which must be resolved by the PS. The operations for the resilient PSL protocol are summarized below:

1. Sites are numbered and the site with the smallest number is the PS.

2. Updates are broadcast *in the number sequence.*

3. Each site saves the last updates *from all other sites.*

4. When a non-PS failure is detected: if the failed site is holding a lock, the lock is released by the PS; if the failed site has made a lock-request, the lock-request is discarded by the PS; otherwise the PS broadcasts the last update received from the failed site *in the number sequence.*

5. When the PS fails: the site with the next smallest number becomes the new PS; the new PS broadcasts the last update received from the old PS *in the number sequence* and requests the lock-status of other sites; if a site was waiting for a lock-grant from the old PS, it makes another lock-request to the new PS.

Figure 3a shows the no-failure case for the resilient PSL protocol. Site 3 issues a lock-request to the PS (site 1). After receiving a lock-grant, site 3 broadcasts an update. Figure 3b depicts the recovery procedure when a non-PS fails while broadcasting an update. The last update from the failed site is rebroadcast by the PS to ensure mutual consistency among the file copies. When the PS fails in figure 3c, site 2 becomes the new PS and requests the lock-status of other sites and site 3 responds that it is holding a lock. The dotted lines show the case where another site (site 4) which has made a lock-request to the old PS makes another lock-request to the new PS. After receiving an update from site 3, the new PS grants the lock to site 4.

In the resilient PSL protocol, the update-complete (UC) message can also be employed to reduce messages for the recovery from a failure. The non-PSs send a UC message to the PS each time an update broadcast is completed and the PS sends the UC to the next smallest numbered site.

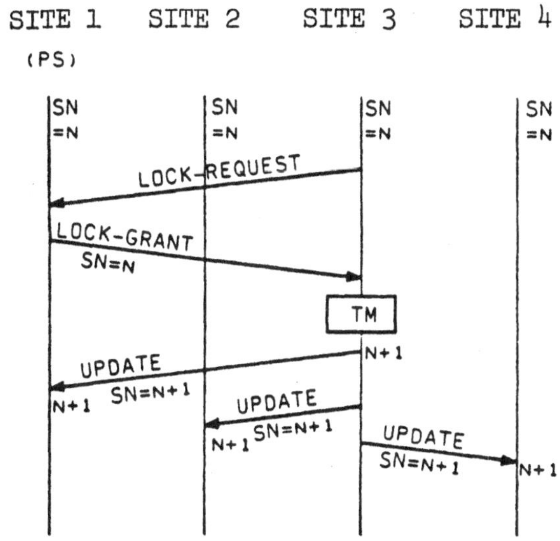

TM = TRANSACTION MODULE

3a. No-Failure Case

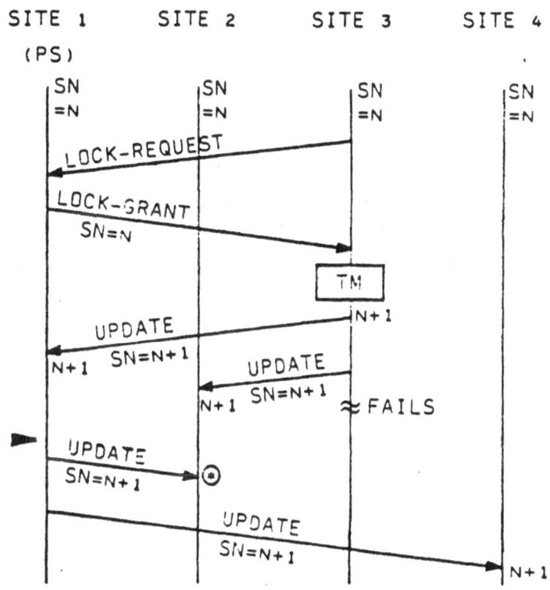

TM = TRANSACTION MODULE

► = FAILURE IS DETECTED

⊙ = DUPLICATE UPDATE IS DISCARDED

3b. Recovery from the non-PS Failure

Figure 3. The Resilient PSL (continued to the next page)

5. Site Recovery

So far, we have assumed that failed sites are not allowed to rejoin the system. In this section, we introduce a method for having failed sites rejoin the system, assuming that all files are stored in non-volatile media.

In our commit protocol, failures are recovered by the smallest numbered surviving site. The recovering site should not be the smallest numbered surviving site until it is fully recovered. Thus, the recovering site is given a number larger than any of the surviving site numbers. The operating sites should store all the updates to be sent to the failed site. The updates are delivered to the recovering site according to the update sequence number, *SN*.

When multiple failures occur while an update is being broadcast, the update may be sent only to failed sites, but not delivered to any operating site. During the site recovery, the last update must be undone even though it was completely posted in

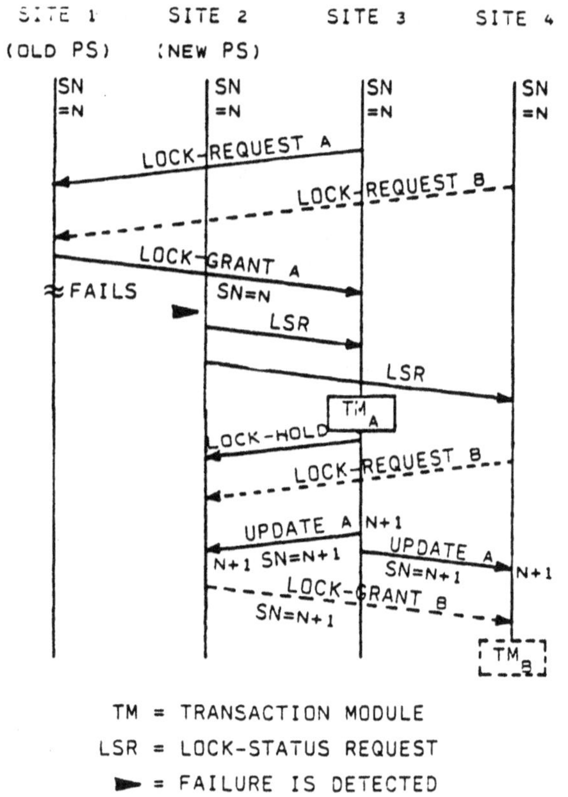

3c. Recovery from the PS Failure

Figure 3. The Resilient PSL

that site. Therefore, all sites should save previous values of the last posted update.

The detailed procedure for site recovery is given in the following:

1. The recovering site undoes the last update (whether or not it was completed) along with the SN, and broadcasts an 'I am up' message.

2. When the smallest numbered site receives the message from the recovering site, it determines the site number which is larger than any of the surviving site numbers. The new site number is then sent to all other surviving sites *in the number sequence*. The list of surviving sites and the new site number are sent to the recovering site.

3. When the recovering site receives its new site number with the list of operating sites, an operating site is selected to recover all lost updates. The posting of newly incoming updates is postponed until all lost updates are received. The 'I am up' message is broadcast repeatedly if the new site number is not received within a certain time interval.

Since a recovering site can not send an update until all missing updates are received and posted, a failure of the site during its recovery does not affect file consistency. However, the failure of the smallest numbered site may delay the site recovery until the next smallest numbered site takes over.

6. Conclusions

We have presented a one phase commit protocol with back-up coordinators which ensures mutual consistency among file copies in case of multiple failures. Since the proposed protocol requires additional overhead only when a failure occurs, it has much appeal for real time applications.

The commit protocol can be incorporated into concurrency control techniques, such as the EWP and the PSL protocol, with little additional overhead. Since the EWP only requires the EW site to broadcast updates and does not need locking, the recovery procedure for the EWP is much simpler and has less overhead than that for the PSL protocol.

Acknowledgement

The authors wish to thank Dr. J. Hellerstein of IBM Research Labs for his stimulating discussion and comments in writing this paper.

References

[ALSB76] P. A. Alsberg and J. D. Day, "A principle for Resilient Sharing of Distributed Resourced," *Proceedings of the 2nd International Conference on Software Engineering* 1976, pp. 562-570.

[BERN81] P. A. Bernstein and N. Goodman, "Concurrency Control in Distributed Database Systems," *Computing Surveys*, Vol.13, No.2, June 1981, pp.185-221.

[CHU85] W. W. Chu and J. Hellerstein, "The Exclusive Writer Approach to Updating Replicated Files in Distributed Processing Systems," *IEEE Transactions on Computers*, June 1985, pp. 489-500.

[GARC82] H. Garcia-Molina, "Reliability Issues for Fully Replicated Distributed Databases," *IEEE Computer*, Vol.15, No.9, September 1982, pp.34-42.

[HAMM80] M. Hammer and D. Shipman, "Reliability Mechanisms for SDD-1: A System for Distributed Databases," *ACM Transactions on Database Systems*, Vol.5, No.4, December 1980, pp.431-466.

[KOHL81] W. H. Kohler, "A Survey of Techniques for Synchronization and Recovery in Decentralized Computer Systems," *ACM Computing Surveys*, Vol.13, No.2, June 1981, pp.149-183.

[SKEE81] D. Skeen, "Nonblocking Commit Protocols," *SIGMOD International Conference on Management of Data*, Ann Arbor, Michigan, 1981, pp.133-142.

[STON79] M. Stonebraker, "Concurrency Control and Consistency of Multiple Copies of Data In Distributed INGRES," *IEEE Transactions on Software Engineering*, Vol.SE-5, No.3, May 1979, pp.188-194.

[WALK83] B. J. Walker, et al., "The LOCUS Distributed Operating System," *Proceedings of the 9th ACM Symposium on Operating System Principles (SOSP 83)*, Bretton Woods, NH, October 10-13, 1983, pp.49-70.

Chapter 5

INTERCONNECTIONS AMONG HETEROGENEOUS DATA BASES

There are two kinds of distributed data bases: homogeneous data bases and heterogeneous data bases. In the homogeneous environment, only one kind of data base management system is used at all sites of the computer network. In the heterogeneous environment, several kinds of data base management systems (such as IMS, IDS, TOTAL, System/2000, System R) are used in the network. This kind of heterogeneous data base configuration will become more prevalent as more large private companies and government agencies try to interconnect their existing computers and data bases.

In order to integrate different types of data base management systems, one possible approach is to build a global schema of data. A user in the computer network can use a universal data manipulation language to access data described in the global schema without knowing the exact physical location of the data and its data structure. If we need to move data from one site to another, the data can be converted to a canonical form and then be translated back to the data format suitable for the destination data base management system. The key to this approach is to select a data model which contains sufficient semantic information about the data and can be easily translated into a different data model.

In this chapter, the first paper by Chen discusses the use of the entity relationship approach in describing and maintaining the enterprise view of data. Fundamental operations for changing the enterprise schema are presented. The second paper by Gligor and Luckenbaugh provides an overview of existing approaches of interconnecting heterogeneous DBMS's and discusses the present alternatives for distributed transaction management and structured data transfer protocols. The paper by Cardenas and Pirahesh presents a global conceptual model that is based on the entity relationship model for data base communication in a heterogeneous data base management system. Landers and Rosenberg present an overview of the prototype implementation of the multibase system, which provides access to heterogeneous distributed data bases. The last paper presents the design considerations of a special class of distributed data base systems that are formed from interconnecting one or more large processors with a set of workstations. For more discussion on this subject, see [LYNG 84b, KRIS 84, KING 84, STON 84].

The entity-relationship model— A basis for the enterprise view of data

by PETER PIN-SHAN CHEN
Massachusetts Institute of Technology
Cambridge, Massachusetts

ABSTRACT

The concept of the enterprise view of data is very useful in the database design process and in the construction of conceptual schema. This paper discusses the use of the entity-relationship approach in describing and maintaining the enterprise view of data. Fundamental operations for changing the enterprise schema are presented. Finally, an example is given to show the differences between the entity-relationship approach and the data-structure approach in modeling the enterprise view of data.

INTRODUCTION

The subject of the logical view of data has attracted considerable attention in the past ten years. However, most researchers have focused on the user view of data. The need for studying the enterprise view of data was not recognized until recently. Different users of a database may have different views of the database, but the enterprise should have a unique and consistent view of the database. This is particularly important in designing a logically meaningful and consistent database. The concept of the enterprise view of data is very useful in the database design process and in the design of conceptual schema.

Enterprise view and database design

Database design is a process to organize data into a form which matches the underlying data model of the database management system. There are three major types of database management systems: network, hierarchical, and relational. In the network database management systems, which include Honeywell's IDS and UNIVAC' DMS-1100, data will be organized into different types of records and can be represented by a data-structure diagram[1] (see Figure 1). In the hierarchical database management systems, which include IBM's IMS, data will be organized into a form similar to but more restricted than the data-structure diagram. In the relational database management systems,[2] data will be organized into a set of tables (or "relations"). In general, to design a database is to decide how to organize data into specific forms (record types, tables) and how to access them. Up to now, there are very few tools available to aid the database design process. Usually, the database designer relies on his own intuition and experience. Thus, the resulting database may not satisfy company's objectives and may cause problems in company's operations.

Another related problem in database design is that the output of the database design process—the user schema (a description of the user view of data)—is not a "pure" representation of the real world. One of the reasons is that the database designer is restricted by the limited capabilities of the database management system. For example, the many-to-many relationships between entities are difficult to represent directly in some database systems. Another reason is that the user schema may contain some features related to the storage representation of the database. For instance, it may describe which record types can be directly accessed and how to access other record types. In addition, the user schema is usually designed to be efficient for a certain type of data processing operations. For example, the data about employees may be grouped into two record types, employee-master and employee-detail, to improve the retrieval performance. Therefore, the user schema is usually not a direct representation of the real world. This makes the user schema difficult to understand and difficult to change.

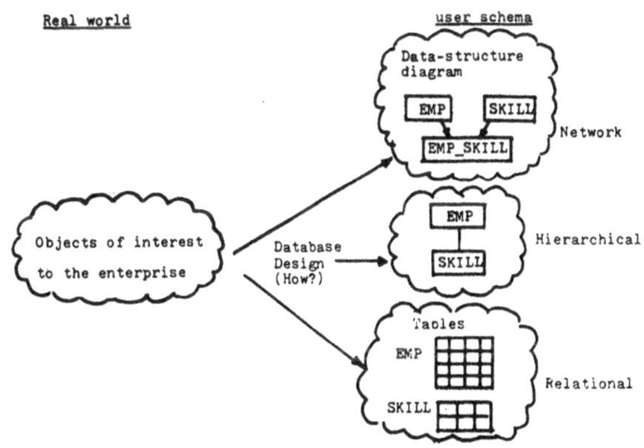

Figure 1—Conventional database design process

A possible solution to the above problems is to introduce an intermediate stage in the database design process: defining the enterprise schema, which is a "pure" representation of the real world and is independent of storage and efficiency considerations. The enterprise schema will then be translated into different types of schemata for different database management systems (see Figure 2). It can also be translated into several schemata for the same database management system to optimize different types of data processing operations. There are several advantages of this approach:

(1) The enterprise schema is easier to understand than a user schema since the former does not have the restrictions of the underlying database management system;
(2) The enterprise schema is more stable than the user schema, since some types of changes in the user schema may not require any change in the enterprise schema. If the enterprise schema needs to be changed to reflect the changes in the enterprise environment, the changes can be performed easily since efficiency and storage issues are not considered.

Enterprise view and conceptual schema

What is the difference between the enterprise schema and the conceptual schema proposed by the ANSI/X3/SPARC group?[3] Basically, they are very similar since both are descriptions of the enterprise view of data. In the SPARC's approach, the conceptual schema serves as the interface between the external schema (user view of data) and the storage schema (physical view of data) (see Figure 3). The requirement of serving as an interface between two other schemata may introduce some undesirable features into the conceptual schema. If this restriction on the conceptual schema is ignored, there is almost no difference between the conceptual schema and the enterprise schema. Therefore, the techniques discussed in this paper are also suitable for describing and maintaining the conceptual schema in the SPARC's architecture.

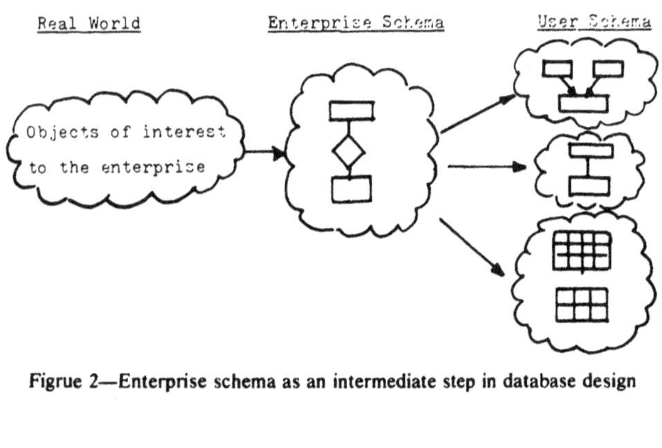

Figrue 2—Enterprise schema as an intermediate step in database design

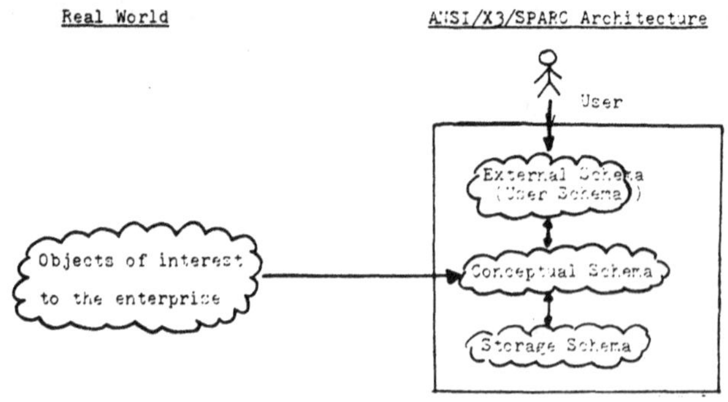

Figure 3—Enterprise view and conceptual schema

Approach used in the paper

In order to describe the enterprise view of data, a mental framework to model the real world is needed. Different people may be used to different mental frameworks. The mental framework used in this paper is the Entity-Relationship (E-R) model.[4,5] The E-R model and similar approaches[6-9] have been found useful in modeling the real world. A diagrammatic technique called the Entity-Relationship (E-R) diagram will be used in this paper to represent the enterprise view of data.

This paper is divided into three parts. The first part discusses how to use the E-R model and diagrammatic technique to describe the enterprise view of data. This is an extension of the work reported in Reference 5. The second part describes fundamental operations for changing the enterprise view of data. This is an area where very little work has been done. The operations proposed in this paper will be useful in maintaining the enterprise schema. The third part uses the E-R approach to analyze an example given by Bachman[10] concerning changes in the conceptual schema.

MODELING THE REAL WORLD USING THE ENTITY-RELATIONSHIP MODEL AND DIAGRAMMATIC TECHNIQUE

In this section, we shall use examples to show how to use the Entity-Relationship (E-R) model and diagrammatic technique to describe the enterprise view of data. A more formal definition of the model can be found in Reference 5.

It is assumed that the responsibility of defining and maintaining the enterprise schema belongs to a person called the *enterprise administrator*. The following is the suggested procedure for the enterprise administrator to define the enterprise schema:

(1) *identify entity sets of interest to the enterprise*
An *entity* is a "thing" which can be distinctly identified. According to the needs of the enterprise, entities can be classified into different *entity types* such as EMPLOYEE, STOCK_HOLDER. An *entity set* is a group of entities of the same type. In the E-R

Figure 4—Entity sets

diagram, an entity set is represented by a rectangular-shaped box (see Figure 4). The terms, "set" and "type," can be interchanged in the E-R diagram. The reader may use either one to interpret the E-R diagram.

There are many "things" in the real world. In addition, different enterprises may view the same thing differently. It is the responsibility of the enterprise administrator to select the entity types which are most suitable for his company.

(2) *identify the relationship sets of interest to the enterprise*

Entities are related to each other. Different *types* of relationships may exist between different types of entities. A *relationship set* is a set of relationships of the same type. For example, PROJ_EMP, which describes the assignment of employees to projects, is a relationship set defined on two entity sets, EMP and PROJ. A relationship set can also be defined on more than two entity sets. For example, PROJ_SUPP_PART is a relationship set defined on three entity sets PROJ, SUPP, and PART. In the entity-relationship diagram, a relationship set is represented by a diamond-shaped box with lines connecting to the related entity sets (see Figure 5). The "m" and "n" associated with the PROJ_EMP relationship in the E-R diagram indicate that the relationship is an m:n mapping. That is, each employee may be associated with several projects, and each project may have several employees. In certain companies, each employee belongs to at most one project, and the PROJ_EMP relationship is a 1:n mapping.

There are many types of relationships between entities. The responsibility of the enterprise administrator is to select the relationship sets (or types) which are of interest to the enterprise. He also has to specify the type of mappings (1:1, 1:n, m:1, or m:n) of the relationships.

(3) *identify relevant properties of entities and relationships (i.e., define value sets and attributes)*

Entities and relationships have properties, which can be expressed in terms of *Attribute-value* pairs. "Blue," and "4" are examples of *values*. Values can be classified into different *types* such as COLOR or QUANTITY. A *value set* is a group of values of the same type. An *attribute* is a mapping from an entity set (or a relationship set) to a value set (or a group of value sets). For example, "address" is an attribute which maps entities in the entity set EMP to values in the value set NAMES_OF_LOC. Note that we relax the constraint imposed in Reference 5 that the mapping from the entity set to the value set has to be a function (i.e., m:1 mapping). In other words, we now allow that an attribute (such as address) can have several values (such as locations) for the same entity (employee). This relaxation in the definition of attribute will make the changes in the enterprise view simpler. This point will become clear in the next section.

In the E-R diagram, a value set is represented by a circle, and an attribute is represented by an arrow directed from the entity set (or the relationship set) to the desired value set(s) (see Figure 6). After selecting entity sets and relationship sets, the enterprise administrator identifies the attributes and value sets which are relevant to the company's operations.

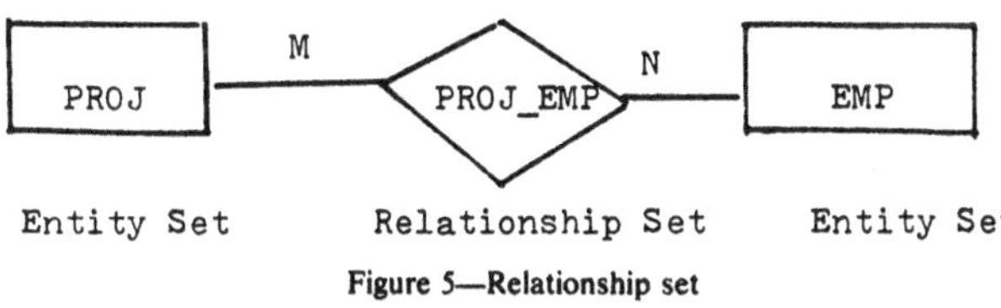

Figure 5—Relationship set

The three steps stated above cover a major part of the enterprise schema. For simplicity, we shall not discuss in this paper other issues related to the enterprise schema such as integrity constraints.

To design a database, the enterprise administrator first draws an E-R diagram such as the one shown in Figure 7. He then drew the attributes and value sets for each entity set and relationship set. The E-R diagram is then translated into a data-structure diagram or a set of tables ("relations") (see Figure 2). The rules and procedures used in the translation process were discussed in Reference 5. Here, we shall investigate how to change the enterprise schema (the E-R diagram) itself.

MODIFICATION OF THE ENTERPRISE VIEW

Although the enterprise schema is more stable than a user schema, it still needs to be changed from time to time

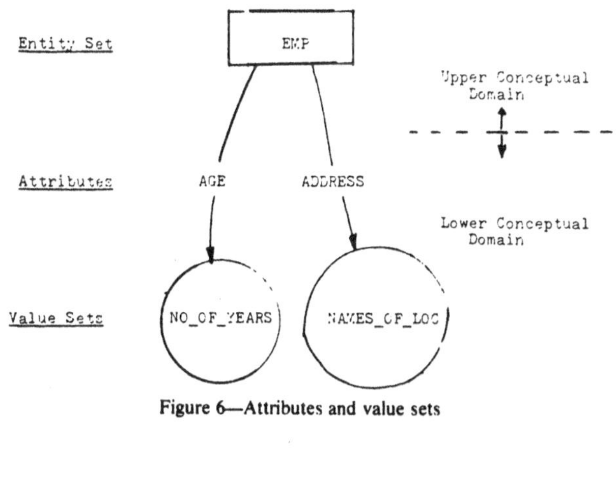

Figure 6—Attributes and value sets

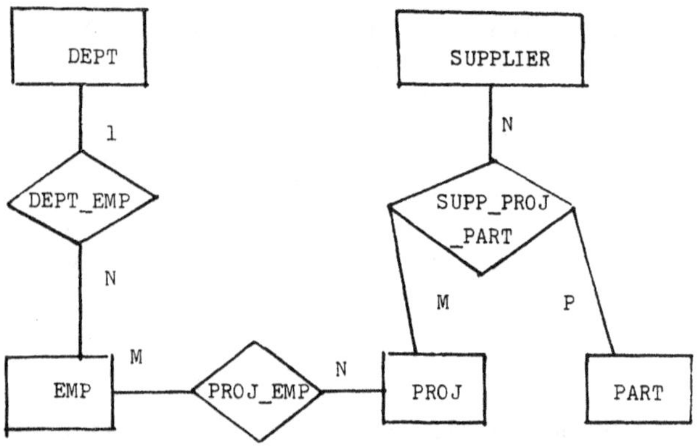

Figure 7—An entity-relationship diagram (with entity sets and relationship sets only)

to reflect the changes in the enterprise environment. Excepting a paper by Bachman,[10] very little work has been done in this area. In this paper, we use the E-R model as a basis for analyzing different types of changes in the enterprise view of data. We not only propose a set of operations but also analyze the consequences of these operations.

There are five basic types of operations: *add, delete, split, merge,* and *shift*. The first four operations are applicable to entity sets, relationship sets, attributes, and value sets. The *shift* operation is used when the enterprise administrator would like to view a value set in the old enterprise schema as an entity set in the new schema or vice versa. It is useful to think that the E-R diagram consists of two conceptual domains: (1) the upper conceptual domain which consists of entity sets and relationship sets; (2) the lower conceptual domain which consists of attributes and value sets. We shall discuss the first four operations in both the upper and lower conceptual domains. Finally, we shall discuss the shifting an entity set from the upper conceptual domain to the lower conceptual domain and the shifting a value set in the opposite direction.

Operations in the upper conceptual domain

The following are the basic operations applicable to entity sets and relationship sets:

(1) *Split an entity into several subsets*
For instance, the entity set EMP in Figure 8a can be split into two entity sets: MALE_EMP AND FEMALE_EMP in Figure 8b. The consequence of this operation is that the relationship sets associated with the entity set may also have to be split. For example, PROJ_EMP is split into PROJ_M_EMP and PROJ_F_EMP (see Figure 8b).

(2) *Merge several entity sets into one entity set*
This is the opposite operation of (1). The consequence is that the related relationship sets may have to be merged.

(3) *Split a relationship set into several subsets*
An example of this operation is: the relationship set PROJ_EMP in Figure 8a can be split into two relationship sets, PROJ_MANAGER and PROJ_WORKER, in Figure 8c. Note that the type of mapping in the new relationships may be different from that in the original relationship. For instance, the mapping in PROJ_MANAGER is 1:n while the mapping in PROJ_EMP is m:n.

(4) *Merge several relationship sets into one set*
This is the opposite operation of (3). Note that these relationship sets have to be defined on the same group of entity sets.

(5) *Add a new entity set*
For example, a new entity set called SUPPLIER may be added to the E-R diagram in Figure 8a. The result is shown in Figure 9a. Note that it is possible to have stand-alone entity sets in the enterprise schema, although in many cases relationships between the new entity set and the existing entity sets are established immediately (see the next operation).

(6) *Add a new relationship set*
We may add a new relationship set for the new entity set such as the relationship set PROJ_SUPP in Figure 9b. We may also add a new relationship set for existing entity sets such as the relationship set PROJ_MANAGER in Figure 9b.

(7) *Delete an entity set*
For instance, after deleting the entity set EMP in Figure 9b, we have Figure 9c. The consequences are: (i) the relationship sets related to the entity set are

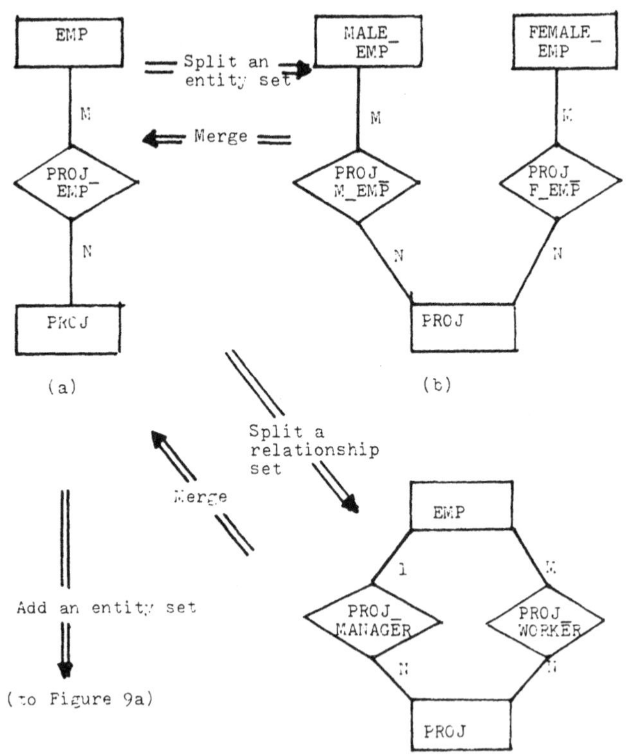

Figure 8—{Split / Merge} {Entity / Relationships} Sets

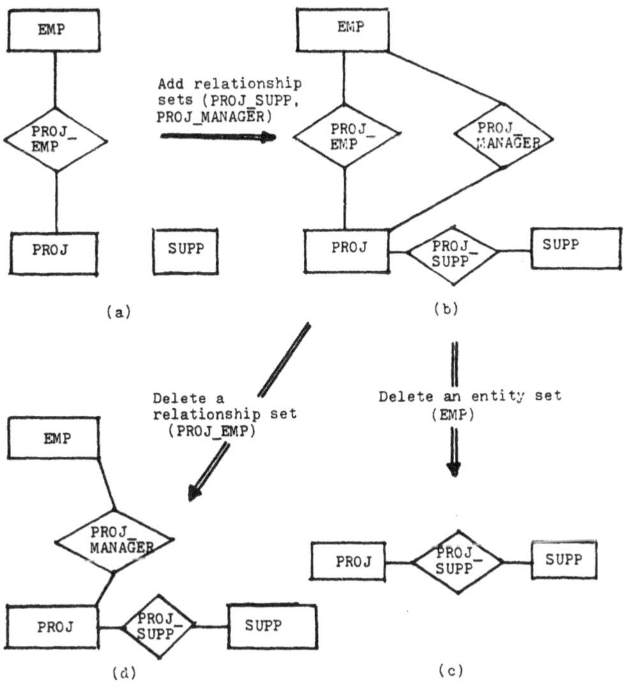

Figure 9—{Add / Delete} {Entity / Relationship} Sets

also deleted; (ii) attributes related to the deleted entity set and related relationship sets are also deleted.

(8) *Delete a relationship set*
An example is: delete the relationship set PROJ_EMP in Figure 9b, and the result is shown in Figure 9d. The consequence of this operation is that the attributes of the relationships are deleted (not shown in Figure 9d).

Operations in the lower conceptual domain

Assume that the entities in the entity set EMP have two attributes, LEGAL_NAME and PHONE, which map the entities to the value sets NAME and PHONE_# (see Figure 10a). We shall use these attributes and value sets as the basis for the discussion of the following operations:

(1) *Add a value set*
For example, a new value set called DOLLARS may be added to Figure 10a. The result is shown in Figure 10b. Usually, this operation is followed by an "add attribute" operation.

(2) *Delete a value set*
After deleting the value set PHONE_# in Figure 10a, we get Figure 10c. The consequence is that all attributes associated with this value set will be deleted.

(3) *Split a value set into several subsets*
The value set NAMES in Figure 10a may be split into two value sets FIRST_NAMES and LAST_NAMES in Figure 10d. The consequence is that attributes related to the value set may have to be adjusted. Although the attribute LEGAL_NAME is not split in Figure 10d, it is possible to split it into two attributes: LEGAL_FIRST_NAME and LEGAL_LAST_NAME. It is the responsibility of the enterprise administrator to make this decision.

(4) *Merge several value sets into a value set*
This is the opposite operation of (3).

(5) *Add an attribute*
For instance, Figure 11b is obtained by adding the attribute OTHER_NAME to Figure 11a.

(6) *Delete an attribute*
Deleting the attribute LEGAL_NAME from Figure 11a, we have Figure 11c. The value set associated with the attribute will be deleted by another operation ("delete value set") if desired. In some cases, the value set may be still associated with other attributes (see Figure 11c).

(7) *Split an attribute into several attributes*
For example, Figure 11d is obtained by splitting the attribute PHONE in Figure 11a into two attributes, OFFICE_PHONE and HOME_PHONE.

(8) *Merge several attributes into one attribute*
This is the opposite operation of (7). The attributes have to be defined on the same entity set (or relationship set).

Operations between two conceptual domains

Assume that there are two entity sets (EMP and PROJ), one relationship set (PROJ_EMP), four value sets (NAMES_OF_PLACES, SOC_SEC_#, PHONE_#, and

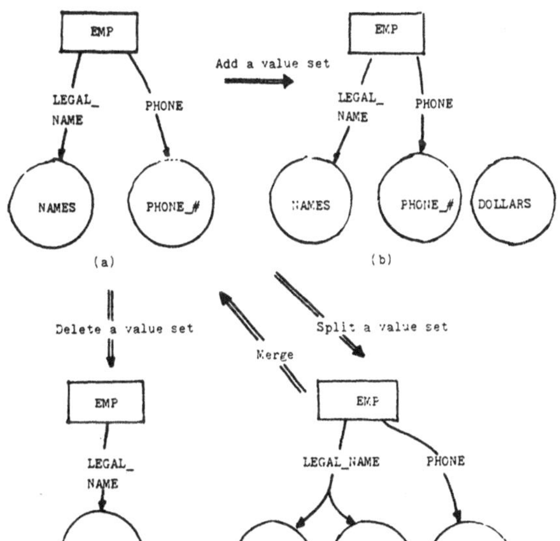

Figure 10—Operations on value sets

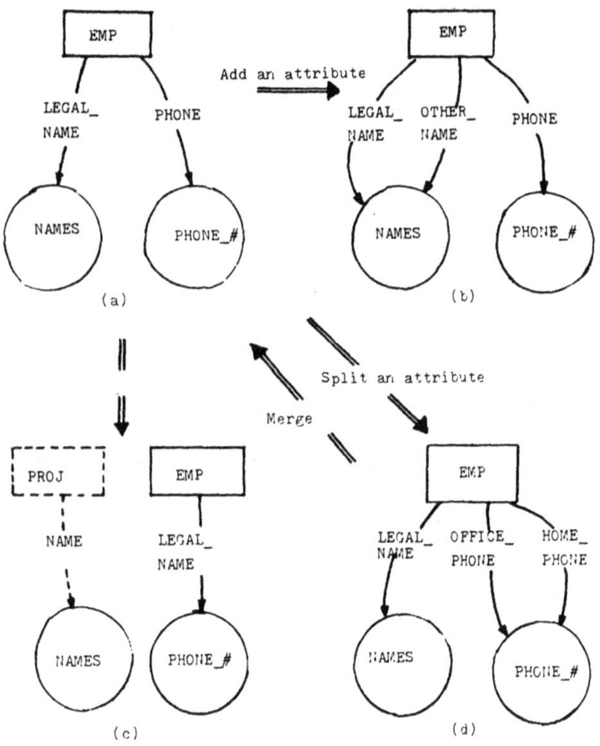

Figure 11—Operations on attributes

PROJ_NAMES), and four attributes (ADDRESS, SOC_SEC_NO, PHONE, and NAME) as shown in Figure 12a. We shall use them as the basis for the discussion on the following operations:

(1) *Shift a value set from the lower conceptual domain to the upper conceptual domain*
When the enterprise environment changes, it may become natural to view PLACE as an entity set instead of a value set. Thus, in Figure 12b "ADDRESS" becomes a relationship set, and "PLACE" has an attribute "NAME" which points to the value set NAMES_OF_PLACES. Since PLACE is an entity set, we may establish new relationships of it with other entity sets such as PROJ or add more attributes and value sets to describe properties of "places."

(2) *Shift an entity set from the upper conceptual domain to the lower conceptual domain*
When the enterprise environment changes again, it may become natural to view PROJ as a value set instead of an entity set. In Figure 12c, PROJ is deleted from the upper conceptual domain, and the relationship set PROJ_EMP becomes the attribute INVOLVED_PROJ. The entity set PROJ in Figure 12b may have been associated with several value sets, but only the value set PROJ_NAMES which is used to identify the entities PROJ remains in the lower conceptual domain.

ANALYSIS OF AN EXAMPLE

In a recent paper, Bachman[10] uses data-structure diagrams to illustrate the changes in a conceptual schema. In this section, we shall first state his example and then use E-R diagrams to interpret his example.

Description of the example using data-structure diagrams

The following is a simplified version of Bachman's example:

(a) In the beginning, the enterprise administrator declared a conceptual schema as shown in Figure 13a. The reader is assumed to have some knowledge of the data-structure diagram.[1] Simply speaking, a rectangular-shaped box represents a record type, and an arrow represents a data-structure-set (i.e., 1:n relationship between record types). In Figure 13a, there are two types of conceptual records, COMPANY and PERSON, and a data-structure-set "a" representing the fact that each person is associated with exactly one company and that each company has a set of personnel.

(b) Later, the enterprise administrator recognized that the personnel of the company were persons in their own right. This fact may be discovered at the merger

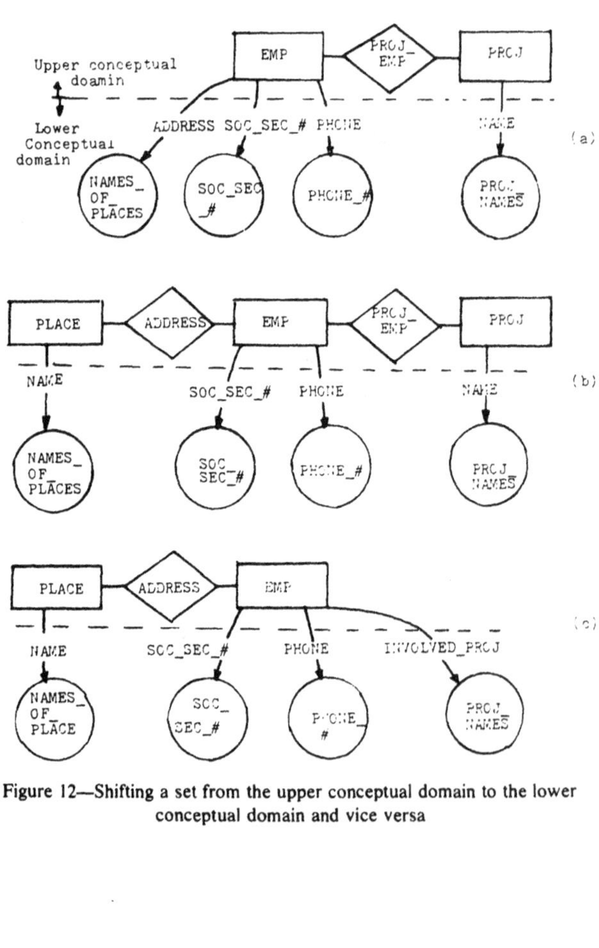

Figure 12—Shifting a set from the upper conceptual domain to the lower conceptual domain and vice versa

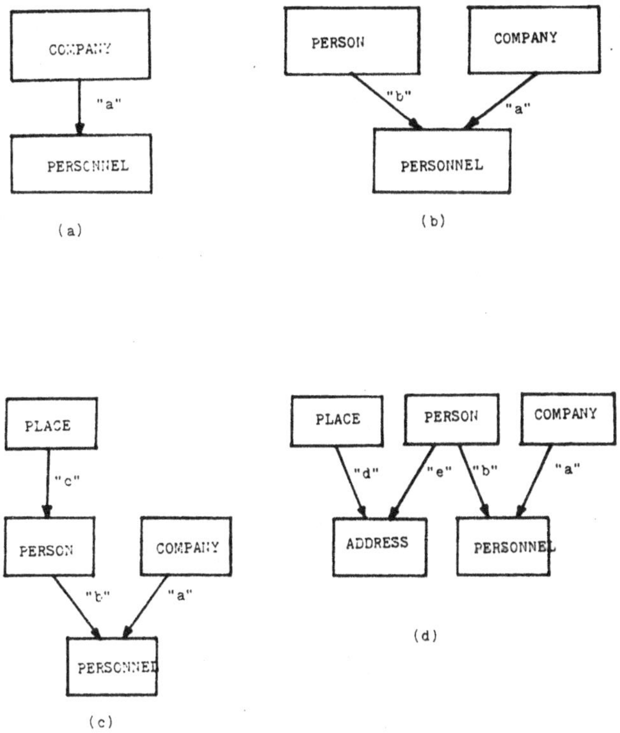

Figure 13—Expressing changes in the enterprise view using data-structure diagrams

of several companies that some of the persons held two jobs and were personnel to two of the merged companies. Figure 13b illustrates the data-structure diagram for the new conceptual schema. Basically, the old personnel type record has been split into two record types, PERSONNEL and PERSON. The "PERSON" has attributes NAME and ADDRESS (not shown in the figure).

(c) After a while, the enterprise administrator decided to factor the address of residence out of the person record. Figure 13c illustrates the addition of the "PLACE" conceptual record type and the data-structure-set type "c." It was also assumed that each person has a unique address (place).

(d) It is now recognized that people move from place to place and that it is desirable to know current address as well as past addresses. Another reason may be: it is discovered that a person may have more than one address. In either case, a new conceptual record type ADDRESS is added to the conceptual schema (see Figure 13d).

Analysis using entity-relationship diagrams

In the following, we shall use E-R diagrams to explain the above example:

(a) The E-R diagram in Figure 14a is corresponding to the data-structure diagram in Figure 13a. There are two types of entities, PERSON and COMPANY, in the enterprise view. Since the mapping between COMPANY and PERSON is 1:n, the relationship set PERSONNEL is represented by a data-structure-set "a" in Figure 13a.

(b) Figure 14b is the corresponding E-R diagram for Figure 13b. Since the relationship set PERSONNEL is an m:n mapping, it is represented by a relationship record type PERSONNEL and two data-structure-sets "a" and "b" in Figure 13b. Note that Figures 14a and 14b have the same entity sets and relationship set in the upper conceptual domain, and the difference is the type of mapping between the entity sets.

(c) Now the enterprise administrator prefers to view "PLACE" as an entity set rather than a value set. Thus, we have Figure 14c. The attribute ADDRESS in Figure 14b becomes a relationship set in Figure 14c. Since the mapping between PLACE and PERSON is 1:n, the relationship set ADDRESS is represented by the data-structure-set "c" in Figure 13c.

(d) The enterprise administrator discovers that the mapping between PLACE and PERSON is an m:n mapping instead of a 1:n mapping. The new enterprise view is represented by Figure 14d. Since the mapping is m:n, the relationship set ADDRESS is represented by the record type ADDRESS and two data-structure-sets "d" and "e." Note that Figures 14c and 14d

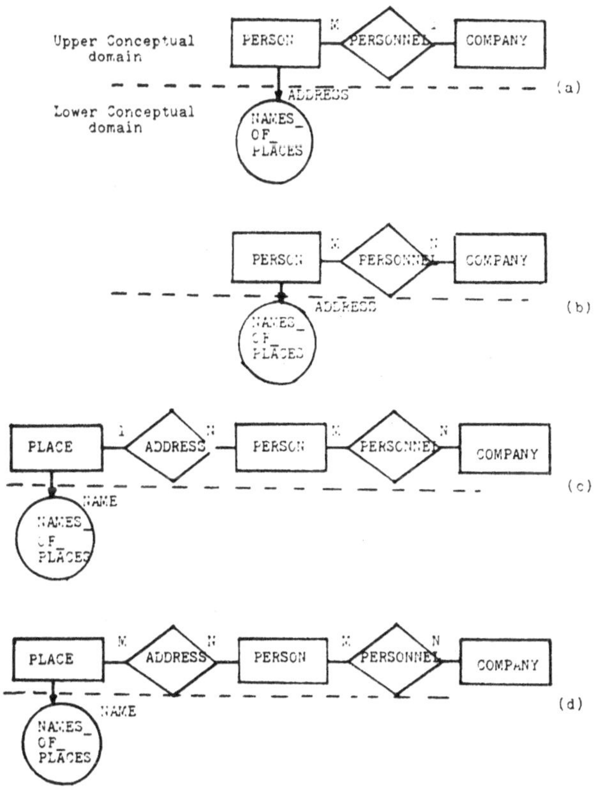

Figure 14—Analysis of Figure 13 using E-R diagrams

are almost the same except that the type of mapping between PLACE and PERSON is different.

In general, the E-R diagram is easier to use to analyze the changes in the enterprise view than the data-structure diagram. Bachman also raised the issue of the ambiguity in Figure 13d: If one wants to modify a person's address, does he have to create a new "address" record or to change the name of the place where the person is living? This question can be easily answered using the E-R approach. Consider Figure 14d. Since the PLACE is an entity set, to change a person's address is to change the relationship between the person and "his place." We should not change the name of the place where the person is living since "NAME" and "NAMES_OF_PLACES" are used to describe a property of the PLACE entities (see Figure 14d).

SUMMARY

The enterprise schema is useful as an intermediate step in database design. In this paper, we have shown how to use the entity-relationship model and diagrammatic technique to describe the enterprise schema. Since the enterprise environment changes from time to time, the enterprise schema will have to change to reflect these changes. Five basic types of operations (add, delete, split, merge, and shift) which are useful in modifying the enterprise schema have been presented, and the consequences of these operations have been discussed. Finally, we have used an example to analyze the differences between the entity-relationship approach and the network approach in modeling the enterprise view of data.

REFERENCES

1. Bachman, C. W., "Data Structure Diagrams," *Data Base 1*, 2, Summer 1969, pp. 4–10.
2. Codd, E. F., "A Relational Model of Data for Large Shared Data Banks," *Comm. ACM 13*, 6, June 1970, pp. 377–387.
3. ANSI, *Interim Report of ANSI/X3/SPARC Group on Database Management Systems*, ANSI, February 1975.
4. Chen, P. P., "The Entity-Relationship Model," (abstract), *Proc. 1st Very Large Database Conf.*, Framingham, Mass., Sept. 1975, ACM.
5. Chen, P. P., "The Entity-Relationship Model: Toward a Unified View of Data," *ACM Tran. on Database Systems 1*, 1, March 1976, pp. 9–36.
6. Moulin, P., J. Randon, M. Teboul, et al., "Conceptual Model as a Database Design Tool," *Proc. IFIP TC-2 Working Conf.*, Jan. 1976, Black Forest, Germany, pp. 459–479.
7. Hall, P., Todd S. Owlett, "Relations and Entities," *Proc. IFIP TC-2 Working Conf.*, Jan. 1976, Black Forest, Germany, pp. 430–458.
8. Deheneffe C. and H. Hennebert, "NUL: a Navigational User's Language for a Network Structured Data Base," *Proc. ACM 1976 SIGMOD Conf.*, Washington, D.C., June 1976, pp. 135–142.
9. Tozer, E. E., "Database Systems Analysis and Design," Technical report, Software Sciences Limited, England, April 1976.
10. Bachman, C. W., "Trends in Database Management—1975," *Proc. AFIPS 1975 NCC*, Vol. 44, AFIPS Press, Montvale, N. J., pp. 569–576.

Today's remote, heterogeneous DBMSs do not effectively communicate with each other. With new application-level protocols and new data and transaction managers, intercommunication would improve.

Interconnecting Heterogeneous Database Management Systems

Virgil D. Gligor and Gary L. Luckenbaugh, University of Maryland

In spite of rapid advancements in the development of communication networks, there is still a great need for the development of improved communication between remote, heterogeneous database management systems, or DBMSs. At present, the lack of effective communication between distributed DBMSs is primarily due to the significant differences between local data managers, local data models and representations, and local transaction managers. A system of interconnected DBMSs that exhibit such differences is called a network of distributed, heterogeneous DBMSs.

In a closer analysis of these differences, it becomes evident that to achieve effective interconnection of remote, heterogenous DBMSs, the users must have uniform, integrated access to the different DBMSs. The importance of such an interconnection has been significantly demonstrated in many large organizations such as those of the US government,[1] which gather and maintain semantically related data in different DBMSs. The fundamental need for uniform, integrated access to such databases arises because users cannot be expected to learn the use of many different DBMSs and the operational differences between them.

This article is dedicated primarily to the analysis of the existing approaches to interconnecting heterogeneous DBMSs, to the review of four experimental DBMS projects in which effective interconnection of such systems was at least partially achieved, and to the discussion of the present alternatives for distributed transaction management and structured-data transfer protocols.

The architectural model

In establishing an overall architectural model as a solution to the problem of interconnecting heterogeneous, remote DBMSs, the features of existing, centralized DBMSs were extended to accommodate distributed systems and networks in a way similar to that used by Gray.[2] The functional requirement for this model was that the processing functions of the global data manager, the distributed transaction manager, and the structured-data transfer protocol be clearly separated.

Common goals. The architectural model for interconnected, heterogeneous DBMSs was derived from three groups of goals that were common to various DBMS application environments in which experimental DBMS projects were being conducted.

The first group of goals aims at achieving the transparency of local DBMSs. These goals emphasize the need for both uniform and integrated access to remote DBMSs. Uniform access to remote DBMSs requires the existence of a common, global user view of all the data; a common, unified language for data manipulation; and a common, unified data dictionary. In addition, the integration of heterogeneous DBMSs requires a distributed data dictionary that includes the data of all local DBMSs and a set of name-resolution rules, and the inclusion of the results of user operations into the common user view.

The second group of goals is concerned with maintaining the autonomy of all DBMS sites. The requirements of this goal are as follows: (1) The local operations of each DBMS site must be unaffected by the addition of new mechanisms so that reprogramming of systems and/or user programs would be unnecessary. It also facilitates in the expansion of the DBMS network as new DBMSs are added; and (2) Each local DBMS optimization, such as that of access paths, must be unaffected by global operations, and global operations must not cause database reorganization.

The third group of goals suggests the use of standard communication protocols and existent networks. However, the need for special database-oriented protocols, such as structured-data-transfer protocols that use network communication protocols, is well recognized. An important operational issue of this group of goals is the allowance of distributed updates to remote DBMSs by global users. This issue has a major impact on the generation of features for both the database and for the database access protocol levels because it presents a number of semantic-integrity problems peculiar to the interconnection of heterogeneous DBMSs.

For example, the global semantic constraints in a system of heterogeneous DBMSs may not be identical to the constraints imposed locally by each data manager. Consequently, the global and the local updates may cause semantic conflicts. Such conflicts do not necessarily appear in distributed homogenous systems or in interconnected heterogeneous systems, where only uniform, remote access to individual DBMSs is allowed. In the latter case, all local constraints can be used to determine the validity of an update. However, if heterogenous DBMSs are integrated for global accessibility by all distributed users, then semantic conflicts may arise; alternatively, changing local constraints to accommodate global ones violates the site autonomy requirement. Such semantic conflicts are illustrated by Kimbleton.[3]

In spite of the complexity of the distributed updates problem, it is important to allow distributed updates through the unified, global user view that do not destroy local DBMS constraints.

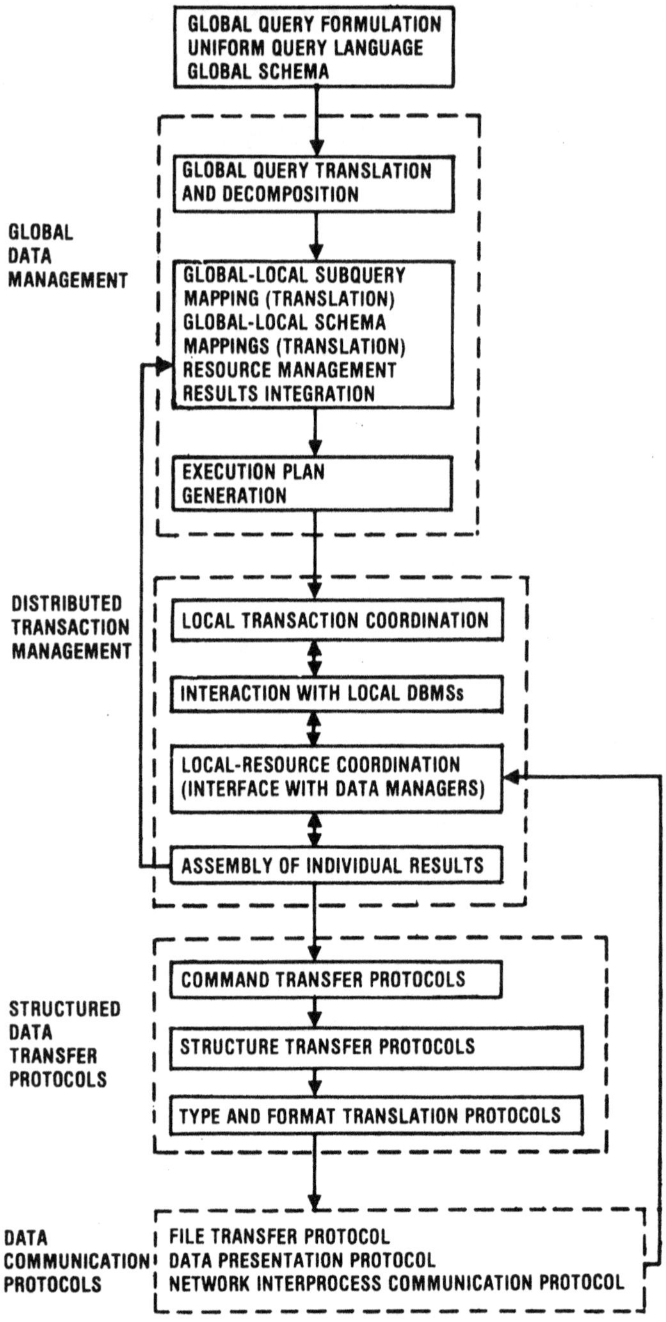

Figure 1. Functional requirement areas.

The model overview. The functional layering of the network of heterogeneous DBMSs, which refers only to the application layer of the ISO reference model described by the International Standards Organization,[4] consists of three sublayers: (1) the global data manager, or GDM, is the top-most sublayer that provides services directly to the end user; (2) the distributed transaction manager, or DTM, is the middle sublayer that supports the services of the GDM, and requires the services of the structured-data transfer protocols; and (3) the structured data transfer protocols, or SDTP, is the lower sublayer that supports the services of the DTM, and requires the services of the data presentation protocol, or DPP, and of other application layers, such as those of the file transfer protocol, or FTP. Each of these sublayers consists of several functional features, illustrated in Figure 1 and discussed in detail throughout the remainder of this article.

Features of the global data manager

The GDM of a distributed DBMS performs both the mappings between the global unified view of the data and the local DBMSs, and all relevant I/O operations.

Input. The initial input to the GDM is either a query or transaction formulated on the global schema. If the query or transaction is directed to an individual DBMS, then it is translated into the local query language and passed to the DTM. If a distributed query or transaction (which requires integrated, multi-DBMS access) is formulated, then the GDM transforms the original query or transaction into a collection of subqueries, each in a format acceptable to one of the local DBMSs.

Output. The GDM generates a plan of subquery execution, and passes these subqueries to the DTM. The DTM presents each subquery to the appropriate DBMS through the communications network and, when the results are available, it returns them to the GDM. Finally, the GDM assembles any individual results to produce the answer to the original query. The final result is presented to the user in terms of the global schema of the distributed DBMS. In this manner, the GDM communicates with the end user and with the DTM.

Functions. A GDM must include the following five functions: (1) global data model analysis, (2) query decomposition, (3) query translation, (4) execution plan generation, and (5) results integration. These five functions, which are illustrated in Figure 1, are basic to the features of a GDM in both heterogeneous and homogeneous distributed DBMSs. However, in heterogeneous systems, the mapping between the uniform global data model and the specific local data models, the query translation, and the results integration are significantly more elaborate than in homogeneous systems.[5,6] As has been illustrated,[7] all distributed DBMSs include these functions in different ways, and the boundaries between these functions are not always distinct. Likewise, frequent interaction between the GDM and the DTM tends to blur the boundary between them in actual DBMSs.

The global data model. The global data model is central to the GDM of a distributed DBMS. It provides the global schema, which is the basis for both the distributed DBMS users' view of the data and the unified data accessing language. The global schema may be stored in a distributed data dictionary along with local schemas and other information about the local DBMS. The distributed data dictionary is frequently consulted by the GDM to provide information about the mapping between the global view of the data and the local DBMS. For instance, the query decomposer consults the dictionary to determine how to fragment the original query into appropriate subqueries, and the query translator consults the dictionary for local schema and naming information needed to translate subqueries properly.

Query decomposition. The query decomposer takes the original global query and fragments it into subqueries. In order to divide the global query into its local subquery components, the GDM uses the distributed data dictionary as a guide. A global query which references only a single local DBMS does not need to be decomposed at the global level, since its decomposition can be done by the local host. In principle, the decomposition strategy does not differ in heterogeneous systems from that of homogeneous ones.

Query translation. Query translation is a language-to-language translation which takes into account underlying data model differences. Query translation can take place at several points in the operation of the GDM. In a system of distributed homogeneous DBMSs, query-to-query translation is not required, since the same language is used for both the local and the global queries. In the heterogeneous case, this translation may be necessary in the following areas:

- global-local query translation,
- subquery translation, and
- subquery results interpretation.

It is assumed that the user issues the global query in the unified global query language. The global query translator may receive the original query that is formulated on a particular external view of the global database, and translate it into a global query that is based on the global schema of the database. After this is done, the translator translates each subquery based on the local schemas, into the appropriate language for the local DBMS. Finally, the subquery results interpreter takes the subquery results and performs the translations necessary for results integration.

For specific examples of global-to-local schema mappings, subquery translations, and results integrations works by Jacobs,[5] Smith,[6] Chiang,[8] and Cardenas should be consulted.

Execution plan generation. The execution plan generator interacts with the DTM by passing subqueries to it. The execution plan generator decides which subqueries can be sent to the local DBMS in parallel, which queries must precede others, and what the relationships are among the intermediate results. The execution plan generator has the same function in both homogeneous and heterogeneous DBMSs.

Results integration. The results integrator combines the individual subquery results and represents them in terms of the global schema. Information from the distributed data dictionary and query decomposer will determine how the local DBMS results will be integrated into the global schema.[6]

GDMs: The approach of four projects

CSIN. The Chemical Substances Information Network,[1] which interconnects a group of remote, heterogeneous data base and file systems, was designed and implemented at Computer Corporation of America. CSIN ties together various existing databases scattered throughout the US with component information systems that are not necessarily general DBMSs. In this configuration, the subquery formulation process must be somewhat restricted, as the local query processors of some of the systems are more limited than those of general DBMSs. Consequently, each CSIN relation must be stored on a single component system. CSIN provides each user with a uniform way to access the individual DBMSs, but does not support the integration of these systems.

The global conceptual model in the CSIN project does not include all the data represented by the conceptual models of the component DBMSs. Certain data can be accessed only through the predefined query facilities or through direct contact with the local system, and not through CSIN's general query facility. The global data dictionary in CSIN, called the information resources directory, or IRD, is logically part of the CSIN processor but is located on a separate computer accessed through the communications network. Along with the global schema and local schemas, the IRD contains information used for query decomposition such as statistics on the local data and limitations of local query processors.

The CSIN query processor performs most of the duties of the global data manager. It uses information about the component systems, such as query capabilities and estimated result sizes, to generate a query execution plan. The CSIN access planner then considers a completely parallel strategy for processing subqueries. Actual execution of the subqueries is done by the component data interfaces.

Query decomposition is somewhat simplified in CSIN by the restriction of relations to a single component. Query translation and results integration are both performed by the CSIN query processor, the latter with the help of the transaction module's own DBMS. In addition, CSIN possesses a Script execution facility for selecting predefined queries or programs that allows a CSIN specialist to compile an optimal execution plan ahead of time, and is particularly helpful to the casual user who inputs a common request.

UCLA. The UCLA DBMS project[9] attempts to provide a uniform user view of a number of heterogeneous DBMSs. The UCLA approach includes both a global conceptual model and an internal model. The global conceptual model used is the entity-relationship model. A data-independent accessing model, modified to incorporate Codasyl syntax, is used for the global internal model. The user's request to this DBMS is based on a global external model known as the virtual database model.

Because of the large number of system layers, there are also many mappings and schemas which must be maintained in the distributed data dictionary, called the network catalog. The network catalog contains the virtual model, or VM, which is the global external model, the uniform global conceptual model, the uniform global internal model, the uniform local conceptual model, the uniform local internal model, and the local logical or data definition language model.

Query translation occurs at several points in the processing of a request. Initially, the query is translated into an appropriate form for the global conceptual and internal models based on the VM. After decomposition, the query translator converts the subqueries into the query or data manipulation language of the local systems.

The UCLA approach to DBMSs includes both a global conceptual model and an internal model, which uses Codasyl syntax.

Query decomposition in the UCLA project must provide for interdatabase relationships, that is, global relations defined over more than one component DBMS. Such relations were forbidden in the CSIN system. Interdatabase relationships in the UCLA project are implemented by explicit access paths reflected at the level of the uniform global internal models.[9]

The execution plan generation in the UCLA project is performed by the global query decomposer and the access path selector. The recomposer performs results integration.

XNDM. The XNDM project, which was initiated at the National Bureau of Standards,[3] interconnects several heterogeneous DBMSs that are running under the Multics, Tenex, and the Tops-10 operating systems through the Arpanet. XNDM uses the relational model as its global model and uses Sequel as the basic framework of the data language.

The distributed data dictionary used by XNDM is called the network wide directory system and is contained within the experimental network operating system of NBS.

The translation process in XNDM is a five-phase process: (1) lexical and syntactic analysis, (2) standardization, (3) static semantic processing, (4) dynamic semantic processing, and (5) code generation.

The two semantic processing phases perform the functions of query decomposition and execution plan generation, while the remaining phases perform the various stages of query translation. XNDM uses a common core translator, which takes custom-tailored front ends and back ends to handle the different translations needed for the different local DBMSs.

The first two phases of the translation process perform global query translation on the experimental network query language global query. The original query is converted to a source syntax tree representation and is put into a standard form for further processing. Each translation phase reshapes the tree until it represents a sequence of subqueries for the target local DBMSs. In the last phase, the code generator performs the subquery translation and outputs the DML statements for the component systems; the subqueries are first interpreted to produce call statements to primitive database operations on the local systems, and then these calls are translated to the appropriate DML statements for the target DBMSs.

Query decomposition begins in the static semantic processing phase with the data item renaming module and the record structure mapping module. This process prepares the tree representation for the decomposition into subtrees, a subsequent process which takes place in the dynamic semantic processing phase.

The dynamic semantic processing sequence module chains the subtrees together and determines the execution plan generation for the subqueries. The execution sequence that is selected will minimize the processing of intermediate records.

Results integration must be performed outside of the translation process of XNDM.

Multibase. The Computer Corporation of America's Mulitbase project[6] to interconnects and integrates preexisting, heterogeneous DBMSs. Multibase does not require any changes to the local databases or DBMSs. The GDM of the Multibase system consists of three main parts: (1) Query Translator, (2) Query Processor, and (3) Local Database Interface.

In Multibase, any of the local DBMS sites may have a global data manager. It is the only system mentioned that uses something other than the relational or the entity-relationship model as its global data model. A functional data model is used to define the global schema, and Daplex is the global query language. In addition to the global and local schemas, Multibase uses an integration schema which provides information used to resolve inconsistencies between the data of different local systems.

The query translator, according to Smith, "translates a global query over the global schema into a global query over the disjoint union of local schemata."[6] The local database interface also performs some query translation by translating local queries generated by the query processor into local queries in the DML of each local DBMS.

Query decomposition is performed by the query processor which decomposes the global query over the disjoint union of local schemata into individual local queries over local schemata. The query processor actually creates a query processing strategy from the query over the disjoint union of local schemata. This query processing strategy consists of a set of local subqueries together with move operations and local queries issued by the query processor. Taking this into consideration, it would be valid to say that the query processor includes the functions of execution plan generation. In addition, with its access planner and execution strategist, the query processor performs query optimization and coordinates local subquery execution.

In the Multibase project, a functional data model is used to define the global schema, and a local database interface is used for translation.

A local database interface stands between the execution strategist and each of the local DBMSs. The LDI may reside either with the GDM or at the local site. Besides translating subqueries, the LDI translates local subquery results into a uniform format for the query processor, which performs results integration.

Features of the distributed transaction manager

The distributed transaction manager is responsible for controlling the execution of distributed transactions in integrated, distributed DBMSs; these transactions will reference data at more than one site in a network.

A primary purpose of a transaction manager, whether it is distributed or centralized, is to help ensure the consistency of the database. In particular, a distributed transaction manager must extend the functions of local transaction managers[2] to maintain the global consistency of the distributed database. To do this, the DTM assumes that whenever a transaction runs in isolation and completes its task, it preserves the consistency of the database. However, when transactions are executed concurrently, or in the event that a system fails, there are two modules of the DTM that are designed to handle serializability and recovery. The concurrency control module makes sure that if transactions *A* and *B* reference shared data and are executed concurrently, the DTM ensures that the results will be the same if *A* was executed before *B*, or *B* before *A*. As it is imperative that intermediate results not be left in the database if the system crashes, the recovery control module makes sure that the distributed transactions will execute to completion, or not at all.

Concurrency control. The concurrency control module must schedule the subtransactions of concurrently executing transactions. This makes the concurrent execution of transactions equivalent to a serial or sequential execution of the transactions. There have been many algorithms published to solve this problem for centralized and homogeneous distributed systems.[10] However, very little work has been done to solve this problem in a heterogeneous, distributed environment. There are two basic alternatives for concurrency control in a heterogeneous, distributed DBMS.

Alternative 1. The first alternative is to coordinate the concurrency control mechanisms of the local transaction managers, or LTM. This requires that the LTMs be modified to recognize and respond to other LTMs.

This alternative is not an acceptable solution for two reasons. First, there are literally thousands of variations of concurrency control algorithms.[10] In order for this alternative to be useful, one would have to develop a general scheme for coordinating any combination of these algorithms; this would be very difficult, if not impossible. Second, the autonomy of the local DBMSs would be violated, as the local transaction managers would require extensive reprogramming in order to recognize and communicate with the other LTMs.

Alternative 2. The second and more appropriate alternative is to provide a hierarchy of concurrency control. This alternative to concurrency control does not violate the autonomy of the local DBMSs since the local systems are not modified in any way. All software is added on top of the existing systems whenever needed. The LTMs are not modified and are assumed to provide concurrency control for local transactions at each of the sites. The DTM, like the GDM, can view a distributed transaction as a collection of subtransactions, each of which runs on a single site.

The DTM is responsible for scheduling these local subtransactions for execution. Subsequently, it is the LTMs responsibility to schedule the individual operations of each sub-transaction. For example, suppose that there are two distributed transactions *A* and *B* that reference some of the same data and that there are two local DBMS sites. In order for the execution of *A* and *B* to be equivalent to the sequential execution of *A* and *B* in some arbitrary order, the DTM must ensure that either *A* effectively precedes *B*, or that *B* effectively precedes *A* at both sites. Let Ai (or Bi) represent the subtransaction of *A* (or *B*) that runs at site *i* and let → stand for "effectively precedes." In order for *A* and *B* to be serializable, the following condition must be satisfied: $(A1 \rightarrow B1)$ and $(A2 \rightarrow B2)$ or $(B1 \rightarrow A1)$ and $(B2 \rightarrow A2)$.

In this description, we have defined → as "effectively precedes" for two reasons. First, the requirement that $A \rightarrow B$ means that the net results must be the same as if *A* was executed to completion prior to executing *B*. However, the local transaction manager may execute *A* and *B* concurrently as long as the net results are the same as executing A and then B. Second, if A and B do not share any data, then the requirement $A \rightarrow B$ is met, since any order of execution will produce identical results. For example, suppose A and B are two distributed transactions that run at sites 1 and 2. Further suppose that $A1$ and $B1$ share some of the same data, but $A2$ and $B2$ do not share any data. The concurrency control condition can be trivially satisfied at site 2, since executing $A2$ and $B2$ in any order or concurrently will produce the same results.

A large number of algorithms have been published in the literature for concurrency control on such topics as two-phase locking, timestamping, and serialization graph checking.[10] The concurrency control mechanisms of the DTM can be based upon any variation of these algorithms. The only requirement is that the DTM must be able to tell which objects are being referenced by the subtransactions so that it can properly determine when synchronization between transactions is necessary. In centralized and homogeneous distributed systems, this information is usually provided by the local data managers. However, in a heterogeneous distributed system this information must be provided by the GDM so that the local data managers will not need to be modified.

For concurrency control, we can either coordinate the control mechanisms of local transaction managers—a nearly impossible task—or provide a control hierarchy.

Both distributed and centralized algorithms can be used by the DTM. Distributed algorithms are those whose components exist at several sites within the network. A centralized DTM would exist at only one site in the network. A distributed DTM would not necessarily violate the autonomy of the local DBMSs, since the DTM components would run on top of the local system as part of an application protocol.

The requirement for autonomy does place one minor restriction on the form that subtransactions may take. In order not to violate the autonomy of the local DBMSs, it must be possible to execute local transactions at the local sites without the DTM being aware of their existence. Furthermore, the DTM must continue to maintain the global consistency of the database even through it is unaware of these local transactions. This means that the DTM must serialize the distributed transactions together with the invisible, locally originated transactions. For example, suppose two subtransactions $T11$ and $T12$ are executed at site 1 on behalf of distributed transaction T, and that a locally originated transaction L is also being executed on site 1. There are two possible legal execution sequences: $L \rightarrow T11 \rightarrow T12$ and $T11 \rightarrow T12 \rightarrow L$.

It would be incorrect to allow the execution sequence $T11 \rightarrow L \rightarrow T12$, since inserting L between the two subtransactions of T may cause data inconsistencies.[2] The solution to this problem is to require that no more than one subtransaction per distributed transaction be executed at any given site. In other words, $T11$ and $T12$ in the preceding example would have to be packaged into one transaction $T1$. With this restriction, there would be no way that an invisible local transaction could become inserted into the middle of a distributed transaction.

Recovery control. The purpose of recovery control is to provide data protection and recovery procedures for all transactions. Because it is desirable to build recovery mechanisms on top of the recovery mechanisms of the local DBMSs, we assume that all of the local systems provide methods for recovering local transactions in the event of system failure. The responsibility of the DTM is to provide such means of recovery for distributed transactions. In short, the DTM makes sure that either all of the subtransactions complete or that they all abort. The DTM does this by utilizing the two-phase commit protocol described by Gray[2] and by Lampson.[11]

In brief, this protocol relies upon a process that coordinates the completions of the subtransactions. The coordinator process goes through two phases. During the first phase, it prepares all the subtransactions, and during the second phase, it completes them all. In order for this scheme to work, the coordinator must be crash resilient.

Each subtransaction exists in one of four states: active, aborted, prepared, or committed. An active transaction is one that is running and contains no updates permanently stored in the database. An aborted transaction is one that has been terminated and has had all of its updates removed from the database. If the coordinator finds that a subtransaction has aborted due to a system crash, then it will abort the remaining subtransactions. A committed transaction is one that has terminated and has had all of its updates permanently stored. A prepared transaction is one that has had all of its updates saved in a safe place. This type of transaction can be either committed or aborted but, in the event of a system crash, can still be committed when the system recovers.

A major problem appears if this two-phase commit protocol is used in a heterogeneous DBMS. Most local DBMSs provide an external view of transactions as being in either an active, committed, or aborted state. There is usually no prepared state. Consequently, the local transaction managers would have to be modified in order to support this new state. Unfortunately, there does not appear to be a way around this problem. The most practical recovery algorithms for distributed systems are based on the two-phase commit protocol. Even so, it seems highly unlikely that a recovery algorithm could be designed that would not rely upon the existence of something like a prepared state.

Further problems can appear if the local systems do not provide full recovery measures in the event of a system failure. For example, many time-sharing systems provide data recovery measures only when a single file is being updated. Multiple file updates may not be recoverable. There does not appear to be an effective solution to this problem that would circumvent the modification of local transaction managers.

Summary of distributed transaction management. In summary, the DTM views a distributed transaction as a set of subtransactions. At most, only one subtransaction is allowed per site in the network. The DTM must make certain that two or more distributed transactions that reference shared data will execute in the same effective order at all sites in the network. This task can be done using existing algorithms such as two-phase locking, timestamping, and serialization graph checking.[10] We have not recommended any particular algorithm, or suggested that the DTM should be distributed. At the expense of throughput, the DTM could simply execute all distributed transactions in sequential order. This approach may be appropriate for distributed systems that must be brought on line quickly.

The most suitable recovery control algorithm is the two-phase commit protocol. However, the local DBMSs must be extended to allow transactions to exist in a

In distributed transaction management, a transaction is viewed as a set of subtransactions, with only one allowed per site in the network.

prepared, but not committed, state. Alternatively, the distributed system designer could choose not to support the data recovery measures that have been described.

The experimental systems developed to date[7] show that little research has been done on DTM in heterogeneous, distributed DBMSs. There are at least three reasons for this: (1) Some of the systems surveyed do not allow distributed updates or synchronized retrievals such as repeatable reads.[2] Without these features, there is no need for global recovery or concurrency control; (2) Some systems emphasize uniform access to individual DBMSs rather than integrated, distributed access. In other words, transactions reference only one remote site, and the LTMs can consequently ensure consistency without the help of a DTM; and (3) Most of the distributed, heterogeneous DBMSs are experimental in nature, and distributed transaction management was simply not included as part of the scope of the research project.

Features of the structured data transfer protocols

SDTPs are application-level protocols required for the interconnection of remote heterogeneous DBMSs.[12] The SDTPs are used by protocols and programs at higher levels which implement the interconnection of the remote DBMSs. These protocols and programs belong to the GDM and to the DTM. The SDTPs themselves use the data communication protocols. In fact, the SDTPs can be seen as extensions of the Data Communication Protocols, or DCPs, particularly since some of the DCP layers such as the file transfer protocol and the data presentation protocol layers assume the existence of the SDTPs. (The National Bureau of Standards draft proposals for the FTP and the DPP assume that the transformation of a file format from the file's native mode into the network-wide, virtual file format is performed externally at a level above them.)

The areas that are covered by the SDTPs are the command transfer protocols, the structure transfer protocols, and the type and format translation extensions to DPPs. The command transfer protocols deal with the transfer of commands to remote DBMSs. These protocols are particularly useful in cases where some of the transaction and data management protocols are implemented as remotely located servers rather than as application-protocol layers. As with the other SDTPs, the command-transfer protocols use a cannonical command format for command transfer across the network. Higher levels such as the GDM will perform the translation between local command formats and the cannonical form.

The most important SDTPs are the structure transfer protocols. A structure can be a Pascal or a Cobol record, a PL/I , or a C structure. It can contain a set of basic types such as integers, reals, and pointers, or it can contain other structures. The structure itself may have a specific type and, therefore, the types of a structure form a directed, acyclic graph. An example of a directed, acyclic graph in which a file is the base structure is shown in Figure 2.

The structure transfer protocols include two basic kinds of protocols: (1) protocols for pointer*- free structures, and (2) protocols for structures with pointers. The structure transfer protocol layer is a direct user of the FTP and DPP layers since files are most likely to be the representation type for most structures with or without

*"Pointer" is a generic term for the identifier of another structure. Pointers can identify structures within a host or structures located within remote hosts.

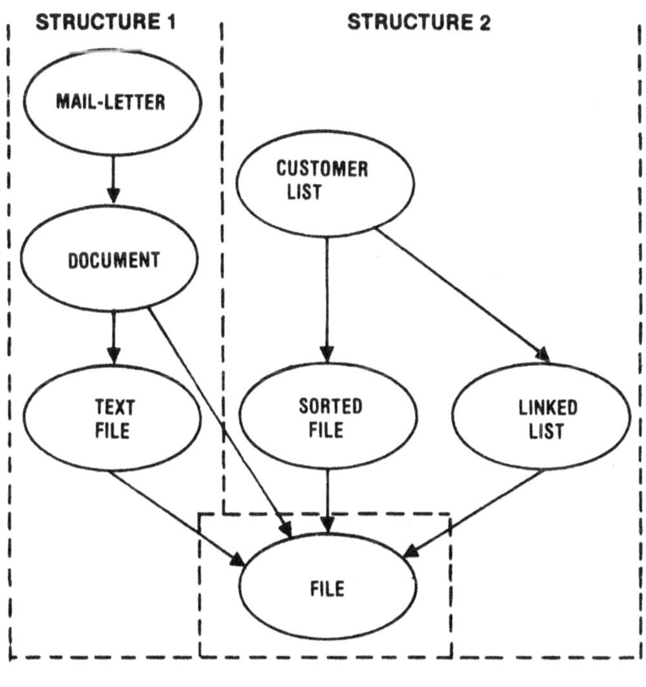

Figure 2. Two acyclic directed graphs illustrating the interrelationships among the types of two structures.

pointers. It is safe to assume that the protocols for the transfer of structures with pointers are significantly more complex than those which handle pointer-free protocols.

Other protocols for structure management, such as those used for space allocation and deallocation, are actually part of the data management protocols and are not considered at this level.

Type and format translation protocols are necessary for types of objects not included at the DPP level. Some structures may contain only basic types, such as integers, reals, characters and binary strings. Some other structures may contain other types, such as relations, documents, and lists, whose translation are not currently handled at the DPP level. Consequently, the structured transfer protocols require that the DPP level must be extensible, that is, the DPP must be prepared to handle a large variety of types in addition to the four that are currently specified.[13]

The need for SDTPs. The principal role of the SDTPs is the preservation of the meaning of transmitted data. The need for SDTPs is apparent, since the only potentially viable alternative to the use of SDTPs for communication among remote, heterogeneous DBMSs is that of using DCPs in various stylized ways. There are three alternatives for using DCPs as substitutes for SDTPs. However, none of the alternatives are adequate substitutes for SDTPs. A fourth alternative, which came close to being a specialized SDTP, is also presented together with its advantages and disadvantages are also discussed.

Alternative 1. First, the DCPs may be used as they are currently proposed, that is, the FTP, the DPP etc. Such use would require (1) that all structured data and commands of remote DBMSs be stored in the files of the various hosts, and (2) that the DCPs transfer the structures and commands as files across the network. The problem with this approach is illustrated in Figure 3. By storing a structure in a file, the meaning of the structure is lost, as the type "structure" is coerced downward to the type "file." Although the file may be delivered correctly from host H_i to host H_j, and although the representation of the file in host H_j would be correct because the DPP and FTPs were used, the DCPs (in this case, the FTP) cannot convert the file at host H_j into the correct structure at host H_j. In short, the DCPs cannot coerce the file at H_j into the structure at H_j because they do not understand the meaning and format of such things as structures and pointers. They are also unable to recognize the differences between the types "structure at H_i" and "structure at H_j." Consequently, direct reliance on DCPs to substitute for SDTPs is an inadequate way of bypassing the need for SDTPs.

Note that the implicit assumption in Figure 3 is that each host is equipped with the file presentation protocol which (1) transforms files at host H_i into the virtual file format (as expected by FTP/DPP), and (2) transforms the virtual files into files at host H_j. These transformations would be provided by SDTPs or directly by the architecture.

Alternative 2. Second, existent DCPs, such as those used by Telnet, may be augmented with mechanisms that could potentially eliminate the need for SDTPs. For example, each component DBMS can be equipped with a translator, like the CDI in CSIN,[1] which converts commands, messages, and structured data into terminal-oriented character strings (for example, strings ending with CR characters). As shown in Figure 4, these strings

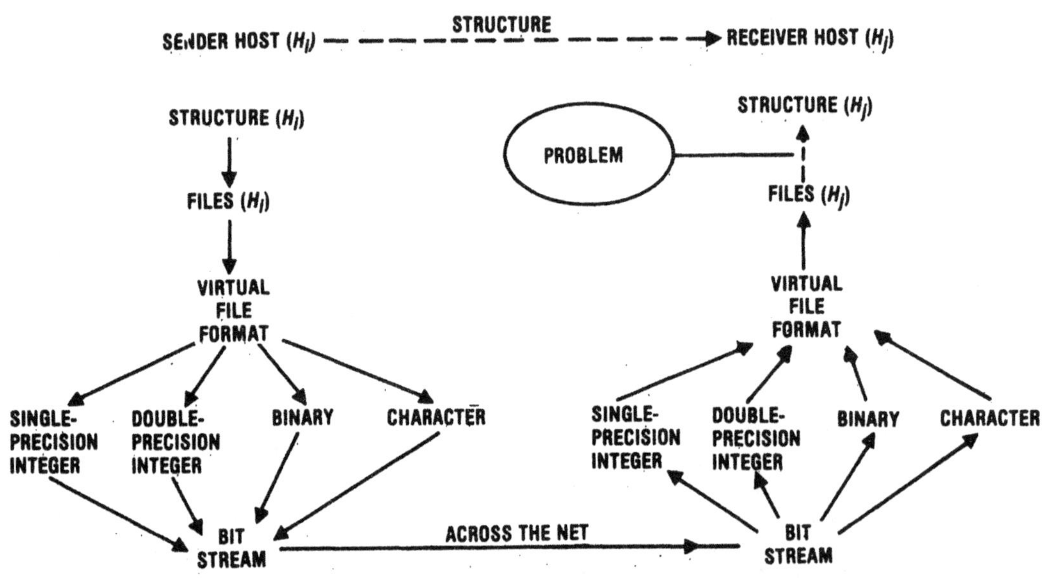

Figure 3. An example of the problem with alternative 1. Using standard DCPs, a structure at host H_i can be transported as a file to host H_j. At host H_j the file cannot become a structure.

would form the input to the Telnet protocols. Next, the Telnet protocols deliver the character strings to remote hosts where translators convert the character strings into commands, messages, and structured data.

In this approach, the translator parses the message strings using string-matching algorithms, performs data translation, and error detection and handling functions. This approach has the major disadvantage of imposing substantial translation overhead. The translators must convert complex data structures and types, commands, and messages into character strings intended for human-user inspection and processing. The more complex the data types to be transferred, the more overhead the translation process would impose. Such translation is necessary if DCPs such as those of Telnet are to be used, thereby making this second approach an inadequate substitute for the SDTPs.

Alternative 3. Third, the features of the DCPs may be augmented with selected mechanisms found in SDTPs. This approach differs from the second in that the augmentation is done internally to the DCPs, not externally. For example, the NBS draft proposal for the FTP* includes some nontransfer management functions that belong to SDTPs and higher level DBMS protocols. These functions include file management such as file space allocation on different hosts, file renaming, access-control modifications, and possibly file moves (as opposed to file copies or transfers). However, other management functions that belong to SDTPs, such as the transfer and recomputation of file indexes for index-sequential accesses, are not included.

Of course, significantly more complex functions performed by SDTPs could be included within various layers of DCPs. For example, the DPP layer might handle the transfer of more data types rather than just characters, or single- or double-precision integers and binary strings.

Further augmentation of DCPs with SDTP functions would not be beneficial for at least three reasons. First, further augmentation of DCPs with SDTP and DBMS functions would clutter the DCPs specifications with infrequently used, higher level functions. Second, this would also result in poor DCP layering and separation of concerns, and would violate the ISO model.[4] Third, further augmentation of DCPs would result in increased implementation cost and overhead. For these reasons, the augmentation of DCPs with SDTP functions is apparently an inadequate substitute for SDTPs.

Alternative 4. Let us assume that the translator of alternative 2 translates all structured data to and from a common format, called the structured data interchange form.[8] The SDICF then replaces the terminal-oriented character string as the common data format, which is transported across the network.

The SDICF is a file that consists of the structural data occurrences and a description of the structured data being interchanged among heterogeneous databases. The

*It must be noted, however, that the designers of the NBS draft proposals for the FTP and DPP have never suggested, nor intended, to replace the SDTPs by using DCPs.

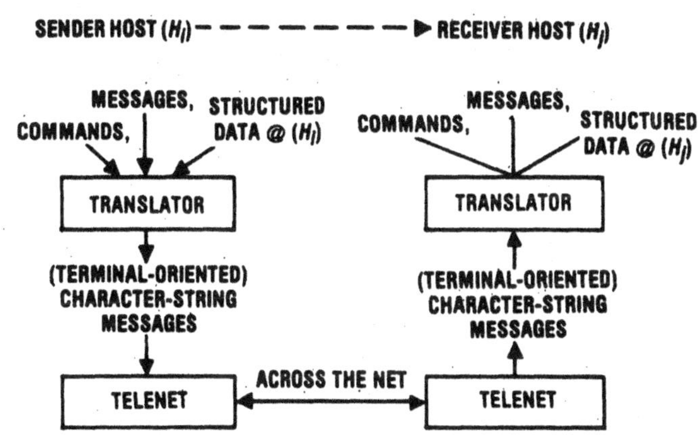

Figure 4. An example of alternative 2 illustrating the CSIN approach to the substitution of SDTPs with DCPs.

description section of the SDICF also defines the structure of the various data sections. A data section of the SDICF file contains the attribute values and additional information to allow the reconstruction of the structured data or of the database subsets within remote databases.

The translator transforms any portion of a DBMS into an SDICF file at a source DBMS host. The SDICF file, which is transported across the network by an FTP-like protocol, is translated by the remote host translator into a corresponding portion of the remote DBMS. Subsequently, the translated data is integrated within the remote DBMS.

Some details of the SDICF file contents and of the various components of what we call the "translator" are provided by Chiang.[8] Also provided are some examples of how structured data of a DBMS, which uses one data model, are transported and integrated into another DBMS, which uses a different data model.

This alternative is more suitable than the other alternatives for the transfer of structured data among remote heterogeneous DBMSs. However, it is not entirely suitable as a substitute for SDTPs for the following reasons. First, this alternative shares a major drawback with alternative 1. The SDICF is a structure itself; therefore, if it is coerced into a "sequential stream of ASCII characters,"[8] a mechanism or some protocol is required to make sure that the remote host is able to correctly coerce the sequential stream of ASCII characters back into the SDICF structure. No FTP can ensure the proper preservation of the meaning of the SDICF structure stored within a file. Consequently, some specialized protocol is still needed between the SDICF mechanism and the FTPs.

Second, this alternative does not seem to deal with the more complex problem of transferring structured data with pointers. The semantics for the transfer of structures with pointers (which may point to data located in remote hosts) are not defined, and the problems which appear in the transfer of such structures are not addressed.

Third, the SDICF format does not appear to be suitable as a canonical form for the transfer of commands, and for the transfer of subqueries to remote hosts. However, the SDICF may be adapted to that function. Whether the SDICF is the most suitable form for the transfer of structured data remains to be determined by future projects. Few of the experimental systems developed to date[7,12] include specific SDTPs that are distinct from the more traditional data communication protocols.

The need for a canonical format. There are several techniques available for translating data in a heterogeneous computer network. These include translation by the sender, the receiver, a centralized translation server, and translation by both the sender and the receiver through the use of a network wide canonical format.

The use of a canonical format appears to be the most appropriate method for translation. The primary reason is the ease with which a new host can be added to the network. The new host must have software written which can translate its internal representation for data to and from the canonical format. However, none of the other hosts in the network will be affected. Using this method each host needs two translators to translate to and from the canonical format. Consequently, if there are n dissimilar machines, only $2n$ translators are needed. On the other hand, translation only by the sender or by the receiver necessitates the use of $n(n-1)$ translators. The canonical format approach also has a minimal amount of host overhead, a minimal amount of message overhead, and is very reliable.[14]

The NBS draft proposal for the DPP provides data translation services between two communicating heterogeneous computer systems. The DPP entities operating on each host computer are responsible for translating local data to and from the network-wide canonical format. The DPP must be extensible to recognize any number of data types that might appear in different environments. The DPP is required to recognize these data types so that it could support the interconnection of remote, heterogeneous DBMSs.

Most DBMS systems make use of complex data structures containing pointers. It is desirable to allow these data structures, and fragments of a data structure, to be copied from one host to another. This permits a data structure to be distributed throughout the system.

As a result of data structure distribution, there must be a way to copy pointers from host to host, and to allow the pointers to point to structures located across machine boundaries. As currently specified in the NBS draft,[13] the DPP provides no services for handling pointers. Therefore, an additional protocol, such as the structure transfer protocol, is necessary for handling data structures with pointers. The structured transfer protocols are responsible for translating pointers just as the DPP is responsible for translating data. Pointers must be translated because of the differences in addressing architectures. Even if pointers are not allowed to point across machine boundaries, and all pointers are implemented as simple offsets into the data structure being copied, it is still necessary for them to be translated. Pointer translation is necessary because the length of the data items in the structure may change due to translation. Consequently, the pointer offsets must be adjusted to compensate for these changes.

The best method for translating pointers is through the use of a canonical pointer format. The canonical format for pointers consists of the pointer itself and the context that is used for the pointer resolution. A context is a mapping from a pointer to an object. Thus, the canonical format of a pointer is a pair <integer, context>. The integer is a displacement within the context object which selects either a local object or a system-wide name (pointer). The system-wide name consists of a unique identifier of the remote context and an integer displacement within the remote context. The unique context identifier is usually structured as a <unique host identifier, context identifier>.

A detailed discussion of the various alternatives for contexts and for systemwide names is presented by Gligor[12] and Sollins.[15] Specific features of the protocols for the transfer of structures with pointers are also presented. The specific features are derived (1) from the canonical format for structure with pointers, (2) from the meaning of the transfer operation (such as copy vs. move operations), and (3) from the ability to preserve the sharing of components within the same structure with pointers.[12,15] The reader must be aware, however, that very few protocols exist for the transfer of structures with pointers. More experience with such protocols is necessary for the generation of a stable set of specific features.

An architectural framework that separates the activities of global data management, distributed transaction management, and structured-data transfer protocols is suitable for the analysis of existing systems as well as the design analysis of new systems. However, uniform, integrated access to autonomous, local DBMSs using standard communication protocols has been only partially achieved to date. Although the provision of a common, uniform user view of the database is fairly well understood, it is not as simple to integrate the systems to support distributed updates without violating the autonomy of the distributed DBMSs. The use of standard data communication protocols is always possible, provided that protocols such as those of the SDTP layer are added. However, very few real systems have provided such protocols because relatively little research has been done in DTMs and SDTPs. ■

Acknowledgments

This work was supported in part by the National Aeronautics and Space Adminstration at the University of Maryland under contract NAS 5-27378, and by the National Bureau of Standards at International Software Systems, Inc., under contract NB80SBCA0367.

References

1. "A Prototype Chemical Substances Information Network," *Computer Corporation of America,* tech. report CCA-79-19, Cambridge, Mass., Aug. 21, 1979.
2. J. N. Gray, "Notes on Database Operating Systems," in *Operating Systems: An Advanced Course*, R. Bayer et al., eds., Vol. 60, Springer-Verlag, New York, 1978, pp. 394-481.
3. S. R. Kimbleton and P. Wang, "Application and Protocols", in *Distributed Systems: Architecture and Implementation,* Lecture Notes in Computer Science, Paul Lampson and Siegert, eds., Vol. 105, Springer Verlag, New York, 1981, pp. 308-370.
4. "Data Processing—Open Systems Interconnection—Basic Reference Model," *Int'l Standards Organization, ISO/TC97/SC16/537* rev., ANSI, New York, Dec. 1980.
5. B. E. Jacobs and T. E. Jacobs, "On the Functional Requirements of a Global Data Manager for a Set of Distributed Heterogeneous Databases I and II," University of Maryland tech. reports TR-1068 and TR-1069, Oct. 1981.
6. J. M. Smith et al., "Multibase-Integrating Heterogeneous Distributed Database Systems," *AFIPS Conf. Proc.*, Vol. 50, 1981 NCC, pp. 487-499.
7. V. D. Gligor and E. Fong, "Distributed Database Management Systems: An Architectural Perspective," *J. Telecommuncation Networks,* Vol. 2, No. 3, Nov. 1983, pp. 249-270.
8. W. P. Chiang, D. DeSmith, D. Leder, D. K. Nguyen, R. Perreault, and J. Fry, "Draft Specification for a Structured Data Interchange Form," University of Michigan Database Systems Research Group, working paper 80 DI 2.6. Feb. 1981.
9. A. Cardenas and M. H. Pirahesh, "Data Base Communication in a Heterogeneous Data Base Management System Network," *Information Systems,* Vol. 5, No. 1, 1980, pp. 55-79.
10. P. Bernstein and N. Goodman, "A Sophisticate's Introduction to Distributed Database Concurrency Control," *Proc. Eighth Conf. Very Large Databases,* Mexico City, Sept. 1982, pp. 62-76.
11. B. W. Lampson and H. Sturgis, "Atomic Transactions," *Distributed Systems: Architecture and Implementation,* Lecture Notes in Computer Science, Paul Lampson and Siegert, eds., Vol. 105, Springer Verlag, New York, 1981, pp. 246-265.
12. V. D. Gligor, "Features of Structured-Data-Transfer Protocols for Networks of Heterogeneous Database Management Systems," *Proc. Workshop on Self-Describing Data,* N. Roussopoulos, ed., University of Maryland, College Park, Md., Oct. 1982, pp. 229-270.
13. S. E. Clopper, "Features of the File Transfer Protocol (FTP) and the Data Presentation Protocol (DPP)" Institute for Computer Sciences and Technology, National Bureau of Standards report ICST/HLNP-80-6, Washington, DC, Sept. 1980.
14. P. Levine, "Facilitating Interprocess Communication in a Heterogeneous Network Environment," MIT Laboratory for Computer Science, tech. report TR-184, Cambridge, Mass., July 1977.
15. K. R. Sollins, "Copying Complex Structures in a Distributed System," MIT Laboratory for Computer Science, tech. report TR-219, Cambridge, Mass., May 16, 1979.

Virgil D. Gligor is a research associate professor of electrical engineering at the University of Maryland. Since 1981, he has been a consultant with International Software Systems, Inc., in the area of distributed systems. Between 1977 and 1981, he was associated with the Computer Systems and the Federal Systems groups of Burroughs Corporation. He has lectured at the University of California at Santa Barbara and at the Institutul Politechnic Bucuresti in Romania. His research interests include reliability and integrity of operating systems, computer architecture, and distributed database systems.

Gligor received BS, MS, and PhD degrees in electrical engineering and computer science in 1972, 1973, and 1976, respectively, from the University of California, Berkeley.

Gary L. Luckenbaugh is a consultant with International Software Systems, Inc., in the area of distributed systems. Currently, he is a PhD candidate in computer science at the University of Maryland, College Park. His research interests include the formal specification and verification of real-time systems, distributed operating systems, and database management systems.

Luckenbaugh received a BS in electrical engineering from the University of Delaware in 1979. While at Delaware, he worked on various research projects, including distributed file systems design and implementation.

Questions about this article can be directed to Virgil D. Gligor, Dept. of Electrical Engineering, University of Maryland, College Park, MD 20742.

DATA BASE COMMUNICATION IN A HETEROGENEOUS DATA BASE MANAGEMENT SYSTEM NETWORK

ALFONSO F. CARDENAS† and MIR HAMID PIRAHESH
Computer Science Department, University of California, Los Angeles, CA 90024, U.S.A.

(*Received* 12 *February* 1979; *in revised form* 10 *August* 1979)

Abstract—An architectural approach is outlined toward the long range goal of a far-reaching data base communication system capable of supporting a network in which any user in any network node can be given an integrated and tailored view or schema (e.g. hierarchical, relational), while in reality the data may reside in one single data base or in physically separated data bases, managed individually by the same type of GDBMS (e.g. CODASYL, IMS, relational) or by different GDBMS. A series of data base model layers and mappings or translations between these layers are proposed. The entity-relationships model is fundamentally used for the highly logical model layers of the integrated system and a modified DIAM is used for the physical distribution and access path oriented layers. A comprehensive example of an integrated network of heterogeneous data bases is outlined, showing for a set of queries their formulation through different layers of the system from the virtual user realm to the physical data bases. Major challenges and issues are discussed.

1. INTRODUCTION

The use of different generalized data base management systems (GDBMS) has mushroomed in recent years. These various GDBMS are significantly different, except for those that follow the proposed CODASYL DBTG standard, and are unable to communicate effectively with each other. There are significant syntactic and semantic differences among them. GDBMS may be classified into four categories: hierarchical, such as IMS; network, which includes TOTAL and all systems following the CODASYL DBTG architecture; inverted hierarchical, such as System 2000, and inverted network, such as ADABAS and DATACOM/DB; and the relational systems being advocated. The problem that we address herein is communication between different data bases, each one perhaps under a different GDBMS. This is a challenging problem posed by the proliferation of data bases.

The major concerns are the following. First, the effective communication between physically separated data bases, managed individually by the same type of GDBMS (e.g. CODASYL systems), communicating through a network facility. There is the need for a system to give each user an integrated model or schema of the various data bases participating in the network as if it were one centralized data base, thus providing the user independence from the physical distribution of the participating data bases. Second, communication between separated data bases each one managed individually by a different type of GDBMS. The user should be provided with independence from the syntax and semantics of each participating GDBMS, except perhaps from that of the special GDBMS in primary use at the user's node; in other words, the user should be able to access any data base in the network as if it were under the GDBMS of interest. Third, even in distributed data base environments where the same type of GDBMS is used each node should be able to tailor its data organization and its logical view of the data base in the way that it is more appropriate for its applications. The schema desired by users residing at other nodes of the network might be different. This brings the idea of virtual data bases which we will pursue. The term "heterogeneous data base environment" denotes any of the situations indicated in this paragraph.

In summary, the long range goal is to have a far reaching data base communication system capable of supporting a network in which any user in any node can be given an integrated and tailored view or schema, while in reality the data may reside in one single data base or in physically separated data bases, managed individually by the same type of GDBMS or by different GDBMS. No network with such capabilities is operational today. There are no data base/data communication systems that permit supporting such a complex network. Yet, the need for such networks is becoming evident. Just as there was the need for data base systems to evolve and facilitate integration of various files, so there is the need for a system to facilitate integration of the growing number of different and related data bases in the manner discussed herein. The thrust of this paper is to outline an architectural approach towards fulfilling this need.

In heterogeneous data base environments there should be the flexibility of providing different types of logical views, perhaps in different data base models, for different users. The information involved in the answers to user queries could reside in an actual data base with a view of data different to that of the model on which the query is formulated. The view on which the query is originally formulated is called the *virtual data base*. For example, the virtual view could be relational while data is in an IMS data base or in a DBTG data base.

A number of authors have addressed heterogeneous data bases. The main proposals have been to restructure each data base into a common structure under a given GDBMS and converting and migrating the entire data base from the GDBMS to the given GDBMS. In some situations a conversion is appropriate because the

†Present address: Boelter Hall 3731, University of California, Los Angeles, CA 90024, U.S.A. Part of this work was supported by the National Science Foundation, Grant MCS 78-16754.

GDBMS is being replaced by another one. This is further addressed in Section 7. Much work has been done in this direction, much of it generally termed "data base conversion", by Soshani[1]; Housel, Shu and Lum[2–4]; and Su[5]. Our interest is to maintain the original data base and provide an effective information interchange among the different systems without incurring mass migration of data. This is what we proposed originally[6] in view of the emergence of the possibility of networks of computers and heterogeneous data bases. This has been proposed also by Adiba and Delobel[7, 8]. A growing number of other practitioners are pursuing such possibility. The major functional characteristics, and attractions to this approach are that:

(1) The application programs interacting with the original data base will not have to be changed, thus avoiding costly reprogramming.

(2) The data bases can be kept distributed and thus obtain the benefits of truly distributed systems.

(3) Each data base can be optimized locally for its major applications.

Our approach entails a *global conceptual model* of data and a *global internal model* of data. The global conceptual model is a highly logical model of the information content of the integrated system. It is used as a vehicle in the process of understanding user queries and decomposing them to extract information from individual data bases. The global conceptual model is the union of the conceptual models of each participating data base in the integrated system. The global internal model is the access-path oriented model of the structure of the integrated system showing precisely the data structures and access paths actually available (e.g. chains, inverted indexes, etc.). The global internal model is the union of the internal models of each participating data base. It is used as a vehicle in the process of identifying the specific access paths through the different data bases that should be followed to answer user queries, while shielding the user of this level from the need to know the intricacies of the physical storage of data.

The Entity–Relationship (E–R) model proposed by Chen[9] is fundamentally used for the conceptual level. In a similar context Adiba and Delobel[7, 8] have chosen the model by Abrial[10]. Our model for the internal level is basically that proposed by Nahouraii, Brooks and Cardenas[6]; it is essentially a modified version of DIAM (Data Independent Accessing Model[11, 12]) incorporating the syntax proposed by the CODASYL SDDTG (Storage Data Definition and Translation Group)[13].

In Ref. [6] we detailed the local and global internal modeling of data bases toward effective communication for the case of different logical data bases managed by the same GDBMS and for the case of different data bases managed by different GDBMS; the capability and adequacy of our internal model is demonstrated therein. In this article we (1) introduce a complementary local and global conceptual level and (2) outline and illustrate our proposed overall macroscopic architecture and methodology toward effective communication in a heterogeneous data base environment.

Section 2 outlines the general architectural approach and building blocks toward permitting the definition of virtual data bases and directing queries to them, while underneath there is in reality a heterogeneous data base environment. Section 3 outlines briefly the basic E–R model and the basic DIAM–SDDTG model. Section 4 illustrates the correspondence between the DIAM–SDDTG model, the E–R model and the data models of available GDBMS. Section 5 presents a comprehensive example of an integrated network of heterogeneous data bases, involving IMS, CODASYL DBTG and relational data bases. Section 5 traces the formulation and translation/processing of queries, through the various layers of the integrated system. Section 6 presents the possibility of relationships between entities residing in different data bases. Section 7 provides further discussion and compares different approaches. Section 8 concludes this work.

A number of important issues and problems in physically distributed data base management are addressed elsewhere by Rothnie and Goodman[14] and are not addressed herein. Our architectural approach and methodology focuses on the challenging problems of effective communication between heterogeneous databases.

2. APPROACH TO COMMUNICATION IN A HETEROGENEOUS DATA BASE ENVIRONMENT

Figure 1 shows the proposed system architecture through which communication in a heterogeneous data base environment is possible. Several data bases under different GDBMS are involved. Whether the data bases are geographically distributed or not is of no major further concern. The problem is still the same. The *global query translator* processes the query initially submitted by a user and, with the knowledge of the virtual data base model associated with that query, translates it to the form acceptable by the global conceptual model and global internal model. The query is then decomposed by a *query decomposer* and *access path selector*, a translator, into the appropriate subquery(ies). The subquery(ies) will then have to be translated into the query language or data manipulation language of a specific GDBMS, so as to then be processed by the corresponding node(s) to extract the information from the specific physical data base(s) involved. The answers to the subquery(ies) are then joined together and reformatted by the *query recomposer*, a translator, according to the virtual data base model. The result is the answer to the original query based on the user's virtual model.

There will be of course many users who will confine their queries locally to a given physical data base managed by a given GDBMS. They will probably constitute the majority of the bulk volume applications. In this case the local GDBMS will process their queries directly and completely. The global query translator, the query decomposer and access path selector, and the query composer will not be needed for such cases.

A number of important catalogues or directories and mapping or data definition translation procedures are necessary. Figure 2 shows the different layers of the proposed architecture and their associated models. The

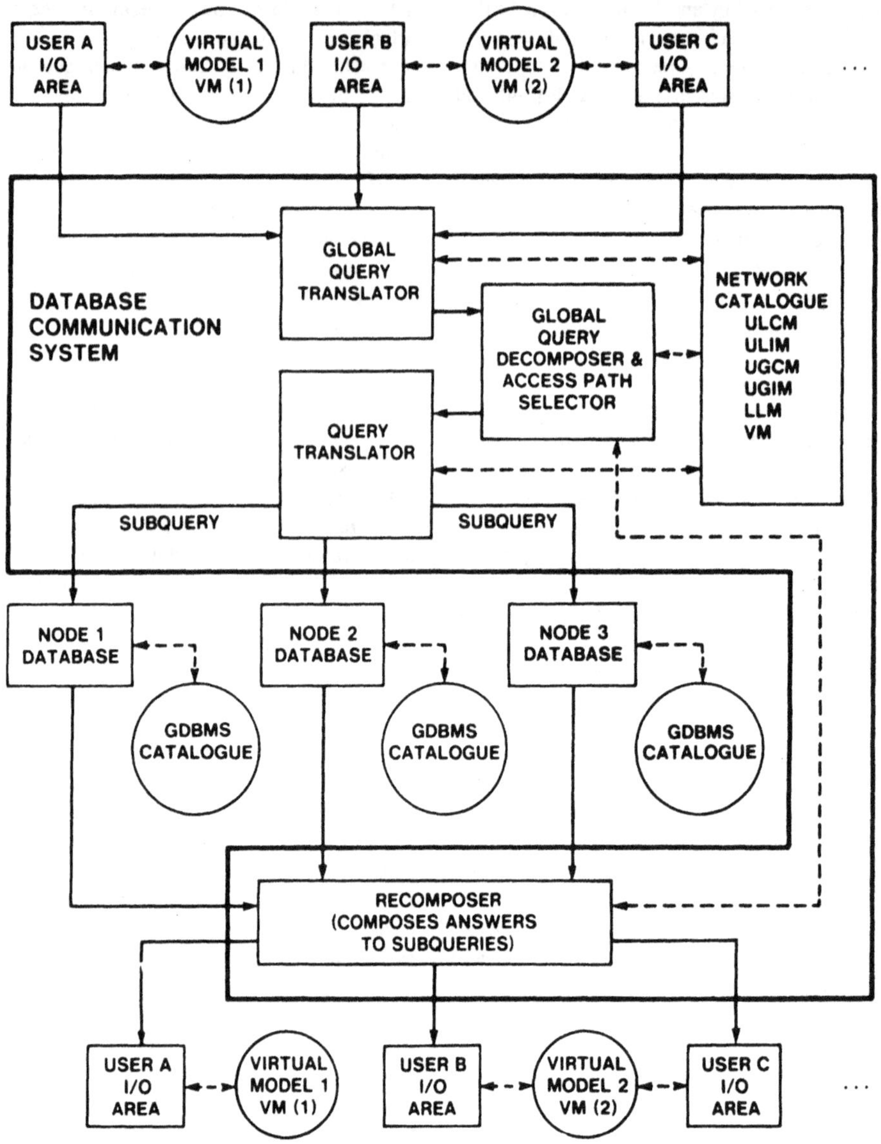

Fig. 1. System architecture and building blocks to support communication in a heterogeneous data base environment.

innermost circle contains the physical data bases actually stored. The outermost layer is the collection of virtual data bases as seen by the users of the heterogeneous data base network. The user deals with the outermost level, called the *virtual model* (VM), and the system should handle all the necessary mapping to extract information from the local physical data bases, represented by the *local physical data base* (LPDB). The definition of the layers and the mappings in between is assumed to be a manual process to be done by a network data base administration group. The other layers involved are:

(a) The local logical model, LLM, of the local data base in terms of its own GDBMS DDL (data description language). For example, in CODASYL DBTG it is the schema/subschema definition. In IMS it is the "physical data base description", or the "logical data base description" if IMS "logical relationships" or multiple physical data bases, all under the covers of IMS, are involved.

(b) The *unified local internal model*, ULIM, which is the equivalent of the LLM in terms of the DIAM-SDDT string model.

(c) The *unified local conceptual model*, ULCM, which is the conceptual model of the local data base in terms of the Entity–Relationship model.

(d) The *unified global internal model*, UGIM, which is the internal model of the integrated data base. The UGIM is the union of the ULIM's plus any inter data base access paths (discussed in Section 6).

(e) The *unified global conceptual model*, UGCM, which is the conceptual model of the integrated data base. The UGCM is the union of the ULCM's plus any interdata base relationships (discussed in Section 6).

Let us address each of these levels and their role in mapping between the VM and the LPDB levels:

The LLM is the logical description of the information stored in the local physical data base, and the definition

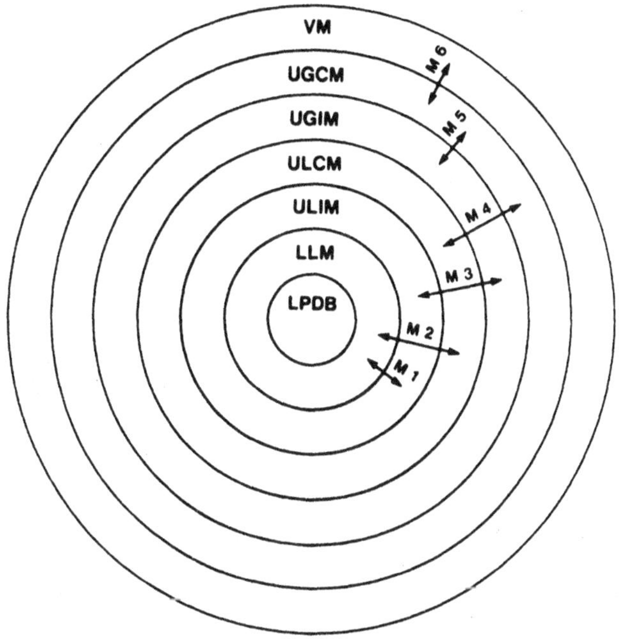

Fig. 2. Diagram of the different layers of the system and their associated models and mappings.

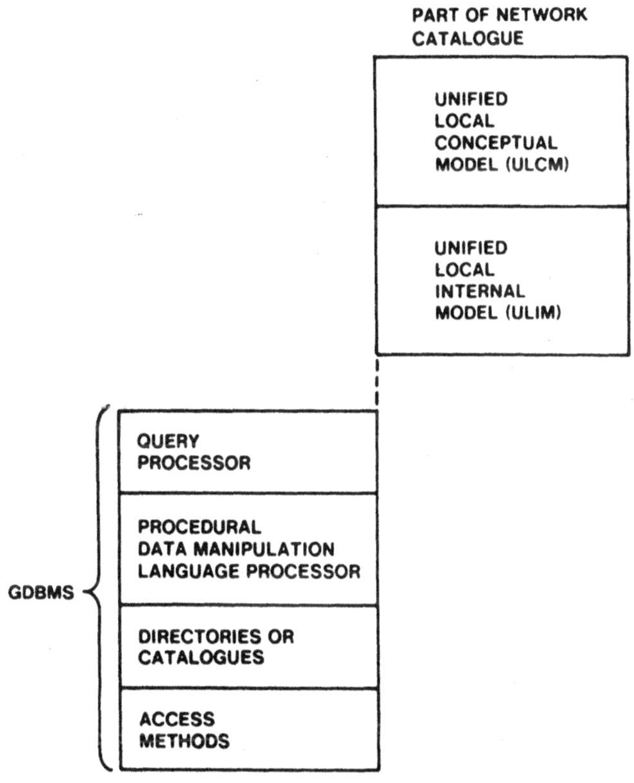

Fig. 3. Functional constituents of a GDBMS and associated catalog with ULCM and ULIM.

of the access paths available. Communication with the physical data base can be done through the LLM interface where the queries are manipulated by the local GDBMS. The other alternative to answer a query (the term query will refer to a command in a high level query language, such as System 2000 immediate access language, or in a more procedural and access-path oriented language, such as IMS DL/1 or CODASYL's DML) is to by-pass the LLM and deal directly with low-level physical data structures. This is a matter of simplicity against optimization of physical access. This has been discussed already[6] and our choice is for simplicity and more independent layers. LLM will be involved only with the logical level of the query language or of the procedural language interface.

Figure 3 shows the important functional constitutents

of a GDBMS. Unfortunately for us, the syntax, semantics and physical organization of commercial GDBMS may differ at each of the levels, except for CODASYL DBTG systems. Hence we resort to a unified logically oriented conceptual model, ULCM, and to a unified access-path oriented model, ULIM, equivalent to LLM. Both the ULCM and the ULIM should provide the simplicity and uniformity desired to represent the various LLM's of the heterogeneous data bases involved. Neither the ULCM nor the ULIM contain new information compared to LLM. There will be a mapping procedure M1 that will map between a given type of LLM (e.g. CODASYL DBTG GDBMS) and ULIM. A query issued at the virtual level will be translated through several layers first into the equivalent searching commands at the ULIM level, rather than directly into the commands of each specific GDBMS. This is advantageous because the data base searching algorithms are complex enough even when working with a nnified model such as ULIM, and because if any new GDBMS is added to the network then the searching algorithms through the ULIM do not have to be modified and only a new mapping is needed. The ULIM is used to provide a formal description in the common DIAM-SDDT string model of what access paths a particular database has available to answer queries, independent of the model used by the GDBMS managing the data base. The access path selector, Fig. 1, will analyze a query and decide what access path(s) at the ULIM level can be followed to answer it. If for each GDBMS there is a table in the network catalog indicating how the access paths (DIAM strings) are implemented and their cost, then the appropriate specific access requests for the specific GDBMS can be generated. Ghosh, Senko and Astrahan have proposed optimal access path searching in the DIAM framework [20, 21].

Although the ULIM is the internal model of the local data base, in some cases it is not enough to show clearly the entities, relationships and their attributes, particularly M:N relationships. As we will show in the following section there are different ways that an M:N relationship and its attributes can be implemented, so given a ULIM one might get different conceptual models and vice versa. ULCM is an unambiguous representation of the conceptual model and should be derived by a specialized data base administration (DBA) group from the LLM.

The UGCM is the conceptual model of the integrated data base. It is formed by the union of the ULCM's and any interdata base relationships. A VM can be derived only from the UGCM so that a VM is independent of the organization or physical disposition of the underlying data base(s). The queries made by a user on a VM should be translated to the equivalent queries at the UGCM level, then at the UGIM level, then at the ULIM level and finally at the LLM level for processing by the particular GDBMS involved; the answer is then composed or reformatted to adhere to the original VM level. Figure 4 outlines these translation steps to be performed transparent to the user and automatically by the network system. This translation in a few cases may be more like reformatting. Thus a number of crucial mappings or translation procedures are needed. Figure 5 indicates them. They should be kept in the system catalog(s). In this article we do not detail these translation algorithms that would be needed to implement our proposed architecture. Such algorithms are the subject of on-going research. In this article we propose, illustrate and attempt to justify the overall architecture. Hence here we only indicate functional characteristics and major issues of such translation algorithms in terms of what the inputs and outputs from them should be.

By using the UGCM and other layers as a bridge between VM and an internal model, a strong data and physical placement independency is achieved. However, there is a tradeoff between independency and optimization of access path searching. If the DBA is to define VM's for users in such a way that efficiency is high, then not only the conceptual model but the internal model must be considered too by the DBA. If the structure of the VM is not too different from the structure of the internal model, then the translation process will be easier and efficiency will tend to be higher. The mapping M6 becomes more complex as the dissimilarity between VM and UGCM increases.

Where should the catalogs and mapping procedures reside physically? In a centralized approach they would reside in a central repository. In a decentralized approach the catalog and procedures for ULIM and ULCM would reside next to the corresponding LLM; the UGIM UGCM and VM would be in a central repository and the VM would also reside at the node where its user is (the mapping M6 between UGCM and VM would be done at the central repository). Detailed analysis of this important placement issue is not taken up herein; Chu and Nahouraii[19] provide an analysis of the tradeoffs.

Adiba *et al.*[7, 8] propose a global architecture rather similar to ours, Fig. 1. They use only Abrial's semantic model[10] for describing local data bases and also the global view. An access path oriented model of the robustness and completeness of the DIAM-SDDT model in expressing precisely access paths actually available (inverted indexes, chains, etc.) is not identified therein; it is our opinion that such modeling level is necessary for cost effective communication. In Ref.[8] they focus on communication problems and protocols. Their work is analogous and complementary to ours.

The work by Schneider[22] is another analogous significant effort toward communication in distributed heterogeneous data bases. He proposes providing users with a third normal form relational view of every data base, and then compiling queries in a relational query language into sets of optimized relational subqueries, to be eventually translated into search programs to access the actual data bases. The compilation into relational subqueries is outlined in Ref.[22]. The efforts of Adiba, *et al.*; Schneider; and ours have been independently conducted.

3. THE ENTITY-RELATIONSHIP (E-R) MODEL AND THE DIAM-SDDT MODEL

According to the accepted definition in practice, the "conceptual model" should represent the facts or information content of the data base, while the "external

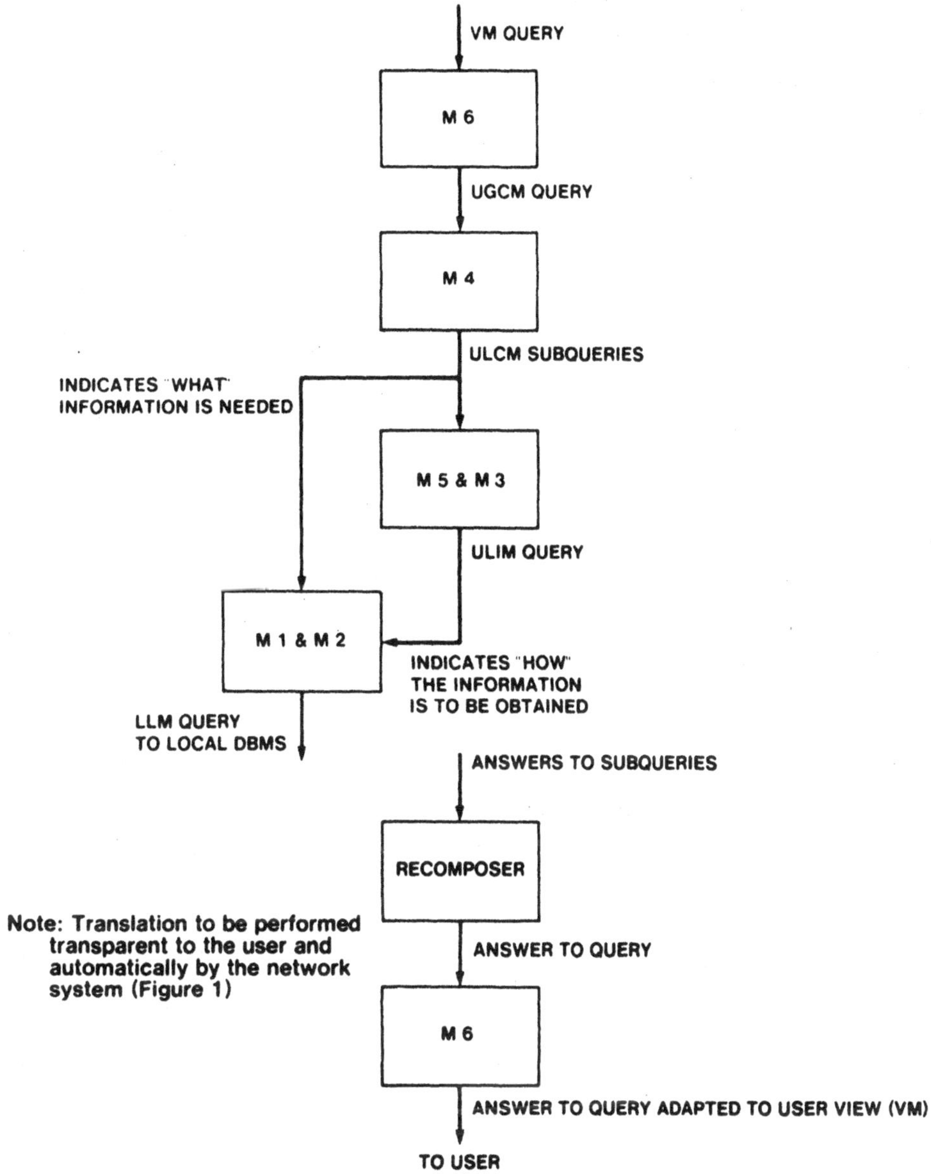

Fig. 4. Translators involved in processing a query.

MAPPING PROCEDURE	BRIDGE BETWEEN THESE MODELS
M1	LLM and ULIM
M2	LLM and ULCM
M3	ULIM and UGIM
M4	ULCM and UGCM
M5	UGCM and UGIM
M6	UGCM and VM

Fig. 5. Mapping procedures involved in the network system.

model" (which we call here the "virtual model") should be an appropriate view for the user. The external model and conceptual models might be very different. In the available GDBMS there is almost no such flexibility and so external models usually look like a subset of the conceptual model. Pelagatti *et al.*[15], Miles[16], Navathe[17, 18], Abrial[10] and Chen[9] have done work in this area. We have chosen the Entity–Relationship (E–R) model proposed by Chen[9] to represent the conceptual model. It is sufficient as a conceptual model for ordinary data bases (managed by ordinary GDBMS), although the generic structure proposed by Miles[16] shows finer granularity than the E–R model.

The E–R model consists of a set of *objects* of type *entities* or *relationships* which are structured in a certain way. The entity objects represent the things that are thought to be independently recognizable in the real world, and relationships show the association between the instances of the entities. Figure 6 diagrams entity types E1 and E2 and the relationship *R* between them. The relationship *R* is a mapping between instances of E1 and E2. The map *R* accepts one instance of E1 as input argument and returns one or several instances of E2. Conversely, *R* accepts one instance of E2 and returns one or several instances of E1. Thus the implementation

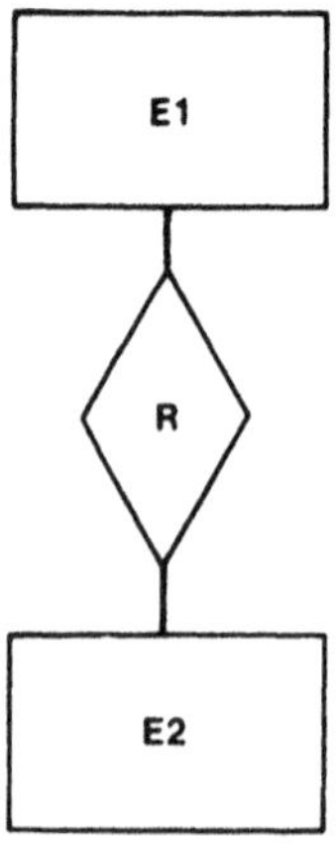

Fig. 6. Entities and their relationship in the E–R model.

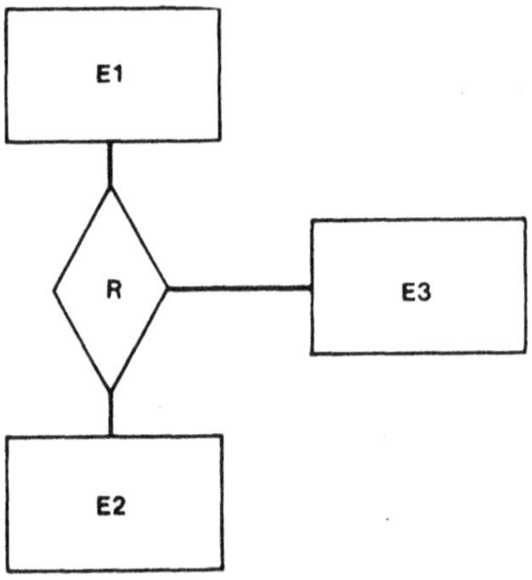

Fig. 7. A trinary relationship in the E–R model.

of *R* contains two mapping functions, one from E1 to E2 and one from E2 to E1. One of the mappings might be missing or not explicitly implemented. We shall address later various implementations of *R*. Categorization of relationships as 1:1, 1:M, M:1, and M:N are interpreted as type of mappings. For example, 1:M means that the mapping from E1 to E2 is 1:M and from E2 to E1 is 1:1. Relationships can be among several entities. Figure 7 diagrams a trinary relationship between E1, E2, and E3. Each instance of *R* associates one instance of E1, E2, and E3 to each other. For convenience, where clear, we shall use "entity" to denote "entity type".

We will classify E–R relationships as *hierarchical* or *non-hierarchical*. This is a modification to the original E–R model. If an instance of an object is uniquely specified by using its relation with another entity (entities) then that relationship is hierarchical; if not, then the relationship is non-hierarchical[17]. If a relationship is hierarchical then it should be 1:M or 1:1. A hierarchical relationship associates occurrences of two or several entities such that at least one of the entities needs the primary keys of other entities to specify it uniquely. An example might be the hierarchical relationship between the entity parent and the entity child. Although the *hierarchical* relationships are defined for binary relationships[17], they can be defined for relationships of higher dimensionality.

If the entities and relationships can be decomposed into simpler ones, using functional dependencies, then they are *composite entities* or relationships. Decomposition as normally discussed for the relational model is applicable to the E–R model as well.

The original definition of the DIAM string model is due to Senko *et al.*[11]. A modification of this model was used by Nahouraii Brooks and Cardenas[6] in detailing our approach for data communication between different LLM's or GDBMS at the unified internal model level. The CODASYL SDDTG proposal is a further development of the DIAM string model and introduces a different syntax. We will adhere to the CODASYL syntax in this paper and refer to our model[6] as the DIAM–SDDT model. The constructs of our internal model are:

(a) Elements, attributes, fields (they are all synonyms).

(b) Group (A-string in DIAM), which is an aggregation of elements. Thus a record in a conventional file, a DBTG record and an IMS segment are represented. A group is used to represent the E–R entity, which consists of its entity key and its attribute values.

(c) Collection (E-string in DIAM), which is a homogenous gathering mechanism over instances of a group, collection or aggregate. Thus a conventional file, a set of DBTG record occurrences, a set of IMS segment occurrences, and a single entry or variable entry TOTAL data set are represented by a collection. Which instances of a construct belong to the collection is specified as a parameter of the collection.

(d) Aggregate (L-string in DIAM) which is a non-homogeneous gathering mechanism over elements, groups, collections or aggregates. A matching criteria parameter is used to specify which instances of the participating constructs belong to an aggregate. Thus an aggregate may represent a DBTG set and an IMS segment hierarchy.

Collections and aggregates are used to implement the relationships among groups. Figure 8 shows different ways to implement a relationship between two entities and its representation using collections and aggregates, depending on whether the relationship is 1:1, 1:M, or M:N. The DIAM–SDDT constructs are diagrammed as follows: a circle for a group, a rectangle for a collection and a triangle for an aggregate. Note in Figure 8 that in an M:N relationship a link group GR is needed to keep the attributes of the relationship (e.g., the attribute "amount supplied" in a supplier-part M:N relationship).

The constructs (DIAM strings) are fully described (as opposed to pictorially outlined in Fig. 8) in an internal model catalog (DIAM string catalog) which contains the construct name, type and its parameters. The parameters are comprised of a construct list, the constituents on the construct, how the construct is composed and on which construct the given construct participates. The syntax used to define the internal model in terms of the above mentioned constructs is defined in detail by the SDDTG[11]. The development of the internal models for different data bases under one

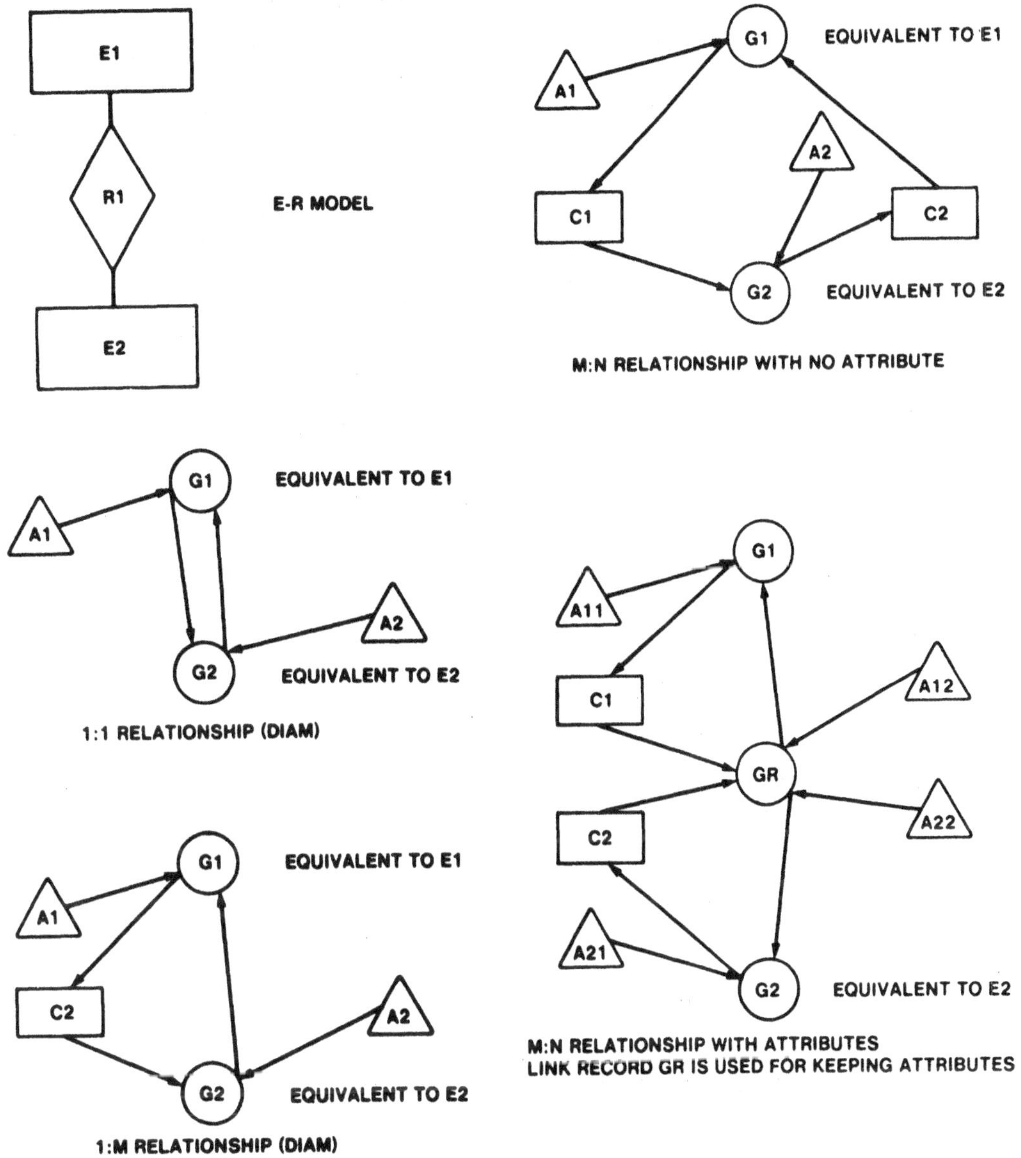

Fig. 8. Implementation of an E–R relationship and its representation in the DIAM-SDDT internal model.

GDBMS, for equivalent data bases but structured differently (i.e. different logical views of the same data) under one GDBMS, and for different data bases under different GDBMS has been amply detailed and illustrated elsewhere[6]. However, for clarity and convenience we provide the following illustrations of the mapping between DIAM, E–R and the main types of available GDBMS.

4. CORRESPONDENCE BETWEEN DIAM-SDDT, E-R AND AVAILABLE GDBMS

Let us outline the correspondence between the main data base models of available GDBMS and the DIAM-SDDT and E–R models, i.e. the mapping M1 between the LLM and ULIM and M2 between LLM and ULCM.

Relational model

The relational model of a data base consists of a set of tables or relations. Both entities and relationships of the E–R model are translated into tables and are treated in the same way. The representation of entities is the same in the E–R and relational models. The E–R relationship is defined as a table which contains the mapping between instances of the participating entities. For example, Fig. 9 shows two translations of the E–R model comprised of the entities PART (P#, PD) and SUPPLIER(S#, SD) and their M:N relationship which has the attribute QTY "quantity supplied":

(a) Three relations T1, T2 and T3, Fig. 9(a). T1 and T3 represent the entities. T2 represents the relationship which contains the keys of PART and SUPPLIER and QTY.

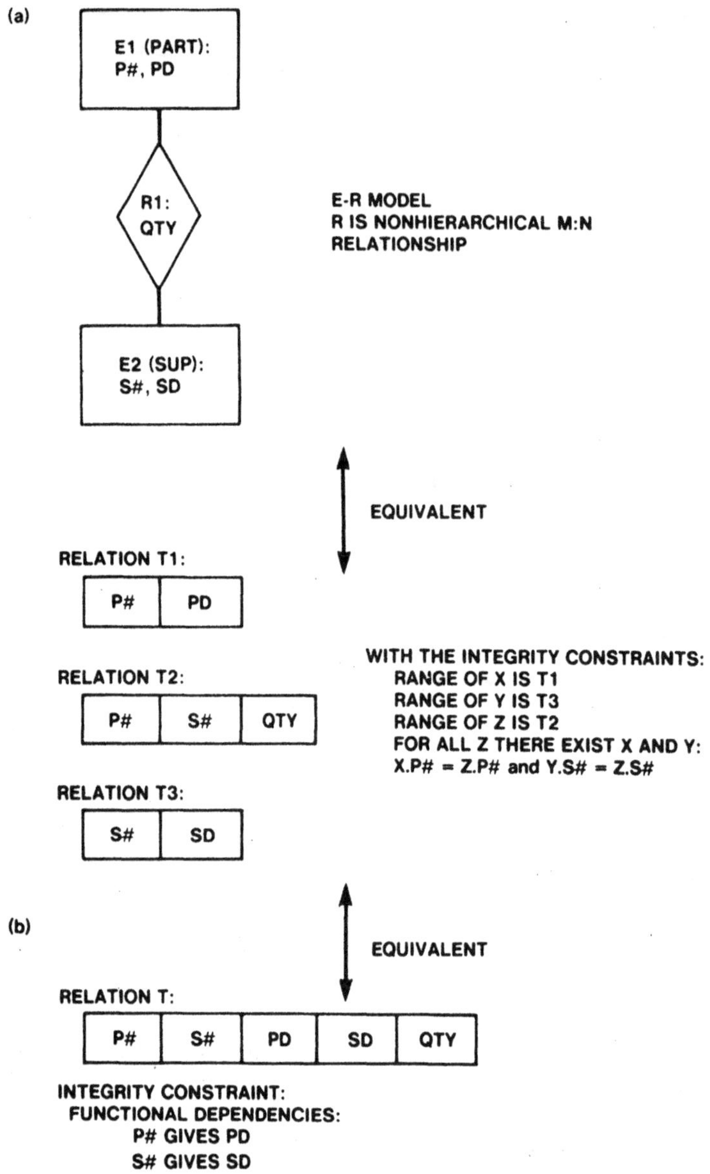

Fig. 9. Translation of a non-hierarchical relationship to its equivalent in the relational model.

(b) One relation T, Fig. 9(b). Using functional dependencies *T* decomposes into T1, T2 and T3.

Note how the information about the relationship *R* may be hard to visualize if one resorts to Fig. 9(b). Another alternative might be two relations: PART(P#, PD) and PSQ (P#, S#, SD, QTY).

In the case of 1:N and 1:1 relationships which are non-hierarchical different translations are possible.

Hierarchical relationships are translated in a different way. In Fig. 10 the child entity can be translated to one relation only by including also the key E# so that all tuples are unique. The hierarchical relationship is 1:N for which different forms of the relational model equivalents were treated in the previous paragraph.

Since given a relational data base different conceptual models (E-R model) can be found then at the time of defining the map between LLM and ULCM, one conceptual model should be chosen to avoid ambiguity. Judicious judgement will guide to the entity object, the relationship object and their attibutes. This will be a crucial responsibility of the DBA specialist in charge of integration of the system as per Figs. 1 and 2.

In a multidata base environment a goal is the consistency of the representative conceptual models. Efforts should be exercised to identify the same entities and relationships among the different conceptual models if the associated data bases contain the same objects. In the case of composite entities or relationships in the ULCM's of the local data bases, efforts should be exercised to decompose them to get identical entities and relationships. This is

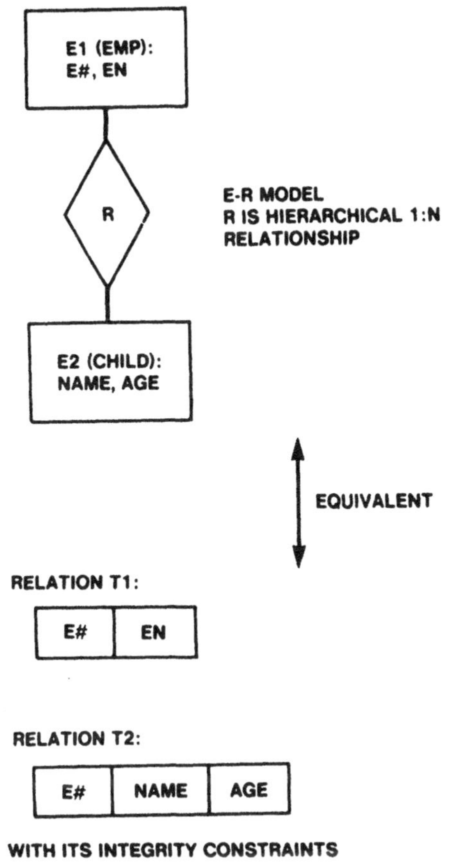

Fig. 10. Translation of a hierarchical relationship to its equivalent in the relational model.

necessary to achieve in the process of merging ULCM's to build the UGCM. To achieve this probably it is necessary to convert some of the relationships to entities and vice-versa. An example of this process for an IMS case is given later in this section.

Since relationships are not shown explicitly in the relational model, then in its DIAM-SDDT ULIM there are no access paths and tables are translated into groups. However, there could be the interpretation that an access path will exist between two relations when two fields are in common.

Network

The correspondence between the network model and the E–R is discussed in detail by Chen[9]. By network model we refer to any CODASYL DBTG GDBMS, Cincom's TOTAL or HIS' IDS. The mapping is usually simple because in the network model, in contrast to the relational model, entities and relationships are separated explicitly. M:N relationships are represented through link records.

The derivation of the DIAM-SDDT model of a network data base is straight forward[6]. We will exemplify it in the following section.

IMS

The data structure used in IMS "physical data bases" is hierarchical. The relationship between two segments, in terms of the E–R model, can be hierarchical or non-hierarchical depending on the IMS child segment. A problem with non-hierarchical relationships is that in an IMS "physical data base" it is not possible to have a child segment without having a parent for it, which is the case in E–R non-hierarchical relationships. However, a "logical relationship" can be established between different physical data bases. Then the relationship is non-hierarchical, and can be 1:N or M:N. The attributes of the relation are held in the IMS pointer segment or intersection segment.

Because of the hierarchical data structure used in IMS a set of integrity contraints are needed for the conceptual and internal models.

This algorithm is envisioned to find the E–R model of an IMS database (this algorithm should be followed by a data base administration group and it is a manual process):

S1—Do for all physical databases.
- S1.1—Do for all parent segments starting from root segment.
  - S1.1.1—Define an entity (equivalent to parent segment), determine the key.
  - S1.1.2—Determine the type of relationships with its children, hierarchical, and nonhierarchical (1:N, M:N).
  - S1.1.3—Determine the attributes of each relationship.
  - S1.1.4—Formulate the integrity constraints.

S2—Find the relationships between physical databases.
- S2.1—Determine the type of relationship (nonhierarchical 1:M, M:N).
- S2.2—Determine the attributes of the relationship.
- S2.3—Formulate the integrity constraints (deletion, insertion, and replacement rules, which can be physical, logical or virtual).

S3—If the resulting E–R model is satisfactory in global environment then STOP.

S4—Decompose the composite entities and relationships to achieve compatibility among E–R models of local databases. The Entities and relationships may be interchanged.

S5 Go to S3.

The derivation of the DIAM-SDDTG model of an IMS data base is straight forward[6]. We will exemplify it in the following section.

5. EXAMPLE OF AN INTEGRATED NETWORK OF HETEROGENOUS DATA BASES

In this section we chose three heterogeneous data bases: in the relational model, IMS hierarchical model and DBTG network model. The ULIM and ULCM and the required mappings are defined for each one. The UGCM and UGIM and the associated mappings are formulated. Two user views (VM views) in relational and hierarchical models are built. A set of queries are presented and their formulation is traced through different layers of the system from the virtual realm to the physical data bases. It is assumed that the reader has some familiarity with the data definition facilities of IMS and DBTG.

5.1 *Data base* 1 (*DB*(*1*)), *relational*

DB(1) contains the inventory and bill of materials information of parts in different warehouses:

The internal model of this data base does not contain any information about access paths, presumably because the physical organization and access paths are not known, at least initially.

5.2 *Data base* 2 (*DB*(2)), *IMS*

DB(2) contains the information about the warehouse and inventory of parts. It is arbitrarily implemented in IMS with two "physical" segments: one for Part information as IMS root segment and one for Warehouse as child segment. The IMS DDL is provided below. Notice that since the relationship (E–R model) between Part and Warehouse is M:N then there will be duplicate segment instances of Warehouse (with the same W# and WD). An integrity constraint should be added to express this fact.

```
DBD NAME = DB(2)
SEGM NAME=PART,BYTES=37
FIELDS NAME=(P#, SEQ) , BYTES=16, START=1
FIELD NAME=PD, BYTES=20, START=17
FIELD NAME=CLASS, BYTES=1, START=37
SEG NAME=WH, PARENT=PART, BYTES=27
```

Rel PART(P#, PD, CLASS)
    part information:part number, part description, its class
Rel WH(W#, WD)
    warehouse information (Part-Warehouse relation):
    Warehouse number, warehouse description
Rel PSTR(P#A, P#C, QTY–USED)
    product structure (bill of material): assembly part number, component part number, quantity used per assembly
Rel PW(P#, W#, QTY)
    Part-Warehouse relation: part number, warehouse number, quantity of the part in that warehouse
INTEGRITY CONSTRAINTS:
    All the part numbers in the WH, PW and PSTR relations must be in the PART relation too. And all W#s in PW must be in the WH relation. The formal definition of integrity constraints is as follows:
        Ranges of X1 and X2 are PART
        Range of Y is WH
        Range of Z is PW
        Range of W is PSTR
        For all Z, there exists an X1 and there exists a Y : Z.P# = X1.P# & Z. w# = Y. W#
        For all W, there exists an X1 and there exists an X2 : W. P#A = X1. P# & W. P#C = X2. P#

The mappings M1 and M2 are the following:

Mapping M1:	<u>ULCM elements</u>	:	<u>LLM elements</u>
	Entity E11		Relation PART
	Entity E12		Relation WH
	Relation R11		Relation PW
	Relation R12		Relation PSTR
			For PSTR and PW some integrity constraints would have to be enforced

Mapping M2:	<u>ULIM elements</u>	:	<u>LLM elements</u>
	Group G11		Relation PART
	Group G12		Relation WH
	Group G13		Relation PW
	Group G14		Relation PSTR

FIELD NAME=(W#, SEQ), BYTES=5, START=1
FIELD NAME=WD, BYTES=16, START=6
FIELD NAME=QTY, BYTES=6, START=22, TYPE=BINARY
Integrity constraint is that if two instances of WH have the same W# then their WD should be the same.

The mappings M1 and M2 are the following:

Mapping M1:	ULCM elements	:	LLM elements
	Entity E21	:	segment PART with all fields
	Entity E22	:	segment WH [W#,WD], projection of WH segment over (W#, WD)
	Relation R21	:	WH is the "physical child" of PART (the relationship between parent and child) R21.QTY:QTY field in WH segment

Mapping M2:	ULIM elements	:	LLM elements
	Group G21	:	segment PART with all its fields
	Group G22	:	segment WH with all its fields
	C21,A211,A212	:	WH is the child of PART with hierarchical and physical parent pointers

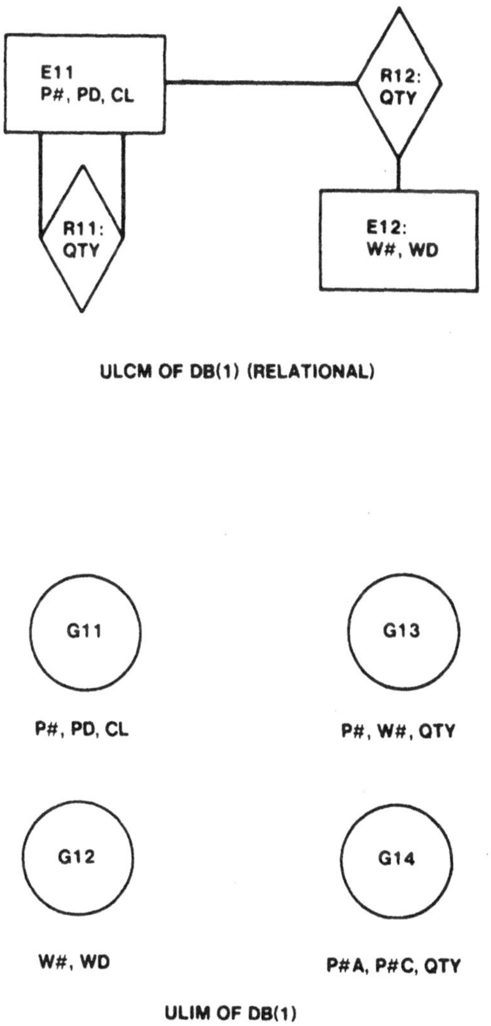

Fig. 11. ULCM and ULIM of data base DB(1), relational.

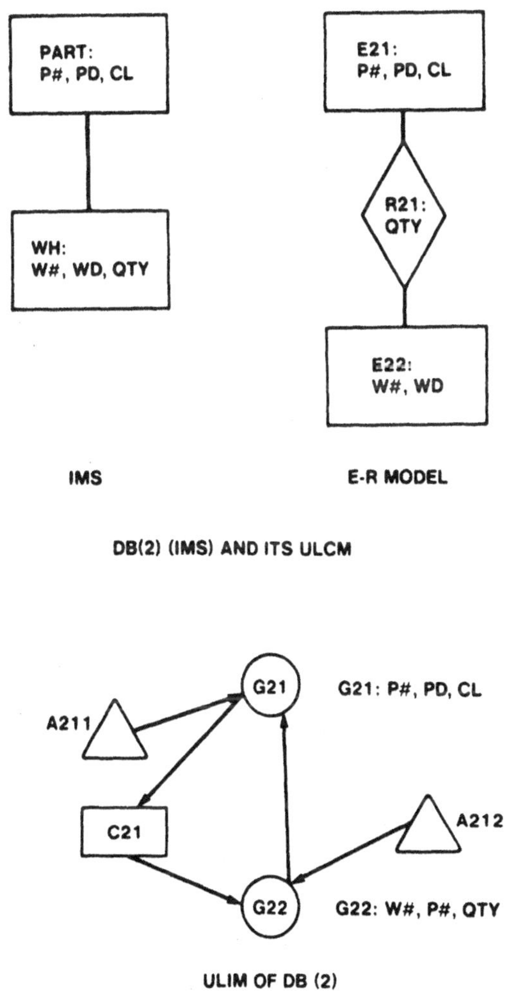

Fig. 12. ULCM and ULIM of data base DB(2), IMS.

The detailed definition of the ULCM and of the ULIM appears in Appendix A. This is to be stored in the network catalog. For simplicity reasons from here on we will not provide this level of details.

5.3 *Data base* 3 (*DB*(3)), *IMS*

DB(3) is the bill of materials data base in IMS shown in Fig. 13. It consists of the PART as root segment and an IMS "logical" relationship with quantity per assembly as intersection data. The parts can be the same as those in DB(1) and DB(2). But it is assumed that if two parts are the same in DB(1) and DB(2) then their bill of material should be identical. The definition of DB(3) in IMS-DDL is:

```
DBD NAME=PRODSTR
SEGM NAME=PART, BYTES=37
LCHILD NAME=(COMP-ASSMB, PRODSTR), PAIR=ASSMB-COMP
FIELD NAME=(P#, SEQ), BYTES=16, START=1
FIELD NAME=PD, BYTES=20, START=17
FIELD NAME=CLASS, BYTES=1, START=37
SEGM NAME=ASSMB-COMP, POINTER=(LPART, TWIN, LTWIN),
            PARENT=((PART), (PART, PHYSICAL, PRODSTR))
FIELD NAME=(P#, SEQ)
FIELD NAME=QTY
SEGM NAME=COMP-ASSMB, POINTER=PAIRED, PARENT=PART,
            SOURCE=((ASSMB-COMP, PRODSTR))
FIELD NAME=(P#, SEQ)
FIELD NAME=QTY
```

The mappings M1 and M2 are diagrammed in Fig. 13 and are the following:

Mapping M1:	ULCM elements:	LLM elements
	Entity E31	PART segment and its attributes
	Relation R31	ASSMB-COMP segment and its logical relationship
Mapping M2:	ULIM elements:	LLM elements
	Group G31 :	PART segment and its attributes
	Group G32 :	ASSMB-COMP segment and its attributes
	A311,C31,A312 :	Child-twin pointers and physical parent pointers
	A321,C32,A322 :	Logical child-twin pointers and logical parent pointers

5.4 *Data base* 4 (*DB*(4)), *CODASYL DBTG*

DB(4) is the same as DB(2) implemented in a CODASYL type GDBMS. DB(4) may have the same parts which are in DB(1), DB(2), or DB(3) or new parts. The definition of DB(4) in terms of the CODASYL DDL is:

```
SCHEMA NAME IS PART-WAREHOUSE

AREA NAME IS DATA-AREA

RECORD NAME IS PART,
    LOCATION MODE IS CALC HASH-P# USING
    P# IN PART DUPLICATES ARE NOT ALLOWED;
    WITHIN DATA-AREA.
    02 P#; TYPE IS CHAR 16.
    02 P0 ; TYPE IS CHAR 20.
    02 CLASS; TYPE IS CHAR 1.

RECORD NAME IS WH;
    WITHIN DATA-AREA.
    02 W#; TYPE IS CHAR .5.
    02 WD; TYPE IS CHAR 16.
    02 QTY; TYPE IS DEC 6.
```

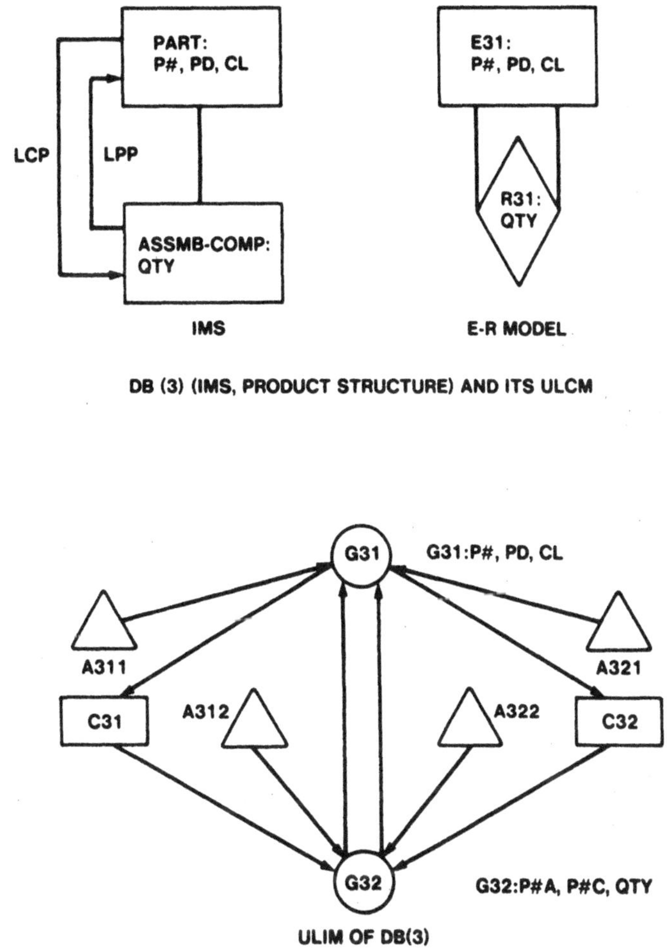

Fig. 13. ULCM and ULIM of data base DB(3), IMS.

```
SET NAME IS INVENTORY;
    OWNER IS PART.
    MEMBER IS WH.
    MANDATORY AUTOMATIC;
    ASCENDING KEY IS W# IN WH;
    DUPLICATES ARE ALLOWED;
    SET OCCURRENCE SELECTION IS THRU LOCATION MODE OF OWNER.
```

The ULCM is the same as the ULCM for DB(2). The ULIM is also the same as the ULIM for DB(2) (see Fig. 12).

5.5 Building the unified global conceptual model UGCM

The UGCM is formed by joining the equivalent entities and relationships of the ULCM's involved. This is the mapping M4, Fig. 2. A partitioned global conceptual model is an E–R model whose entities are partitioned and each partition belongs to a ULCM. Figure 14 shows the UGCM formed by joining the ULCM of DB(1) through DB(4) introduced in Sections 5.1–5.4 and illustrated in Fig. 11–13. It can be easily seen that entities E11, E21, E31, and E41 are equivalent. Note the other equivalent components in Fig. 14:

E1 is the union of entities E11, E21, E31 and E41 with all their attributes
E2 is the union of entities E12, E22, and E42
R1 is the union of relations R11 and R31
R2 is the union of relations R12, R21 and R41

Constraints: If two parts in DB(1) and DB(3) have the same part# then their product structure should be the same.

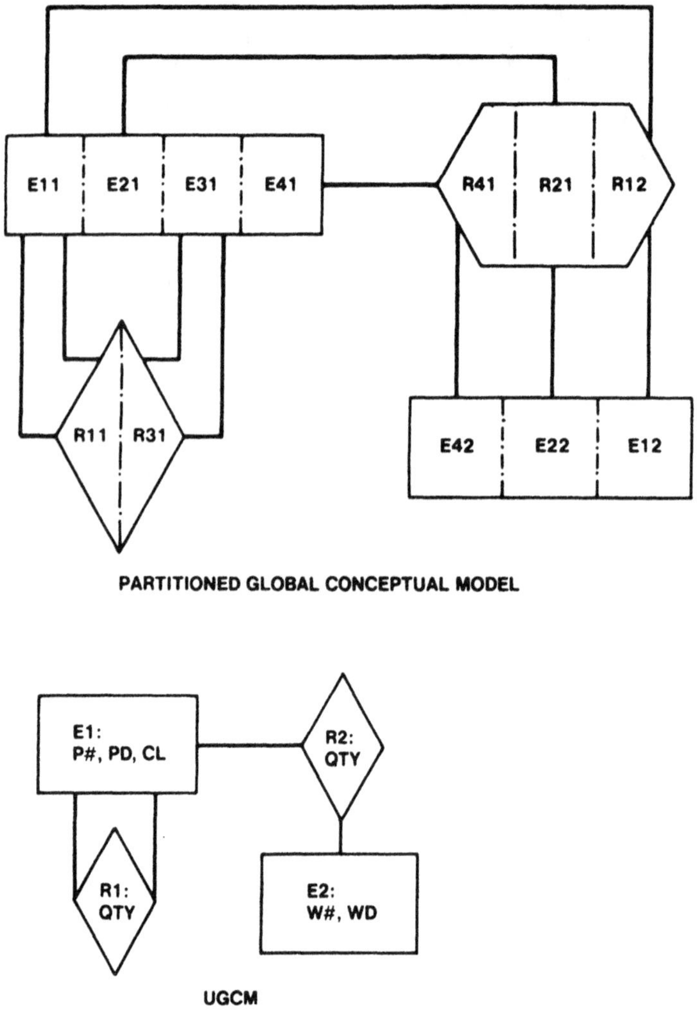

Fig. 14. The unified global conceptual model (UGCM) formed by joining the ULCM of DB(1)–DB(4) shown in Figs. 11–13.

This can be written as:

Range of X1 is E11
Range of X2 is E11
Range of Y1 is E31
Range of Y2 is E31
for all X1 if X1.P#=Y1.P#, then for all X2.P#, such that (X1,X2) belongs to R11, there exists Y2.P# such that Y2.P# = X2.P# and (Y1,Y2). QTY = (X1,X2).QTY and vice versa

Each conceptual model of a local data base must be a subset of the global conceptual model. Proper union of ULCM's to form the UGCM should guarantee this.

5.6 *Building the unified global internal model UGIM*

UGIM is formed by the union of all internal models. There is no interdatabase access path in our example. An interdatabase access path links instances of entities in two different local data bases. There is no such path in our example, and hence the mapping M3 between UGIM and the ULIM's is one-to-one and the catalogue entry for the UGIM is the union of the catalogue entries for the ULIM's.

5.7 *Building virtual models (VM)*

Different virtual models can be derived from the UGCM. We shall derive in this example VM's in the relational model and in IMS, and thus illustrate mapping M6. It is important to keep in mind that there is a trade-off between data independence and efficiency. For example, an IMS data base view (a VM) can be built with root segment equivalent to WH and dependent segment equivalent to PART. However, all physical data base accessing to PART first is easier and faster since that is the way that it is structured internally, DB(2) in Fig. 12. To access a segment which is not the root segment either a secondary index in IMS should be used or sequentially oriented traversal of the hierarchy should be done.

5.7.1 *Relational VM*(1). The first virtual model VM(1) shall consist of two relations: PROD-STR for bill of materials and INVENTORY for inventory shown in Fig. 15. PROD-STR contains the assembly part number P#A and its description PDA, the component part number P#C and its description PDC, and the quantity per assembly QTY. The INVENTORY relation contains warehouse number W# and its description WD and the part number P# of the part in that warehouse with its quantity. Both relations could be decomposed to simpler ones. Note that the local data bases in the network do not contain such relations. Rather all four local data bases are used to support such relations of VM(1).

The M6 mapping is as follows:

Mapping M6: <u>VM(1) elements</u> : <u>UGCM elements</u>

PROD-STR — Range of X is E1
Range of Y is E2
Rel (X.P#,X.PD,Y.P#,Y.PD,
(X,Y).QTY):(X,Y) belongs to R1

INVENTORY — Range of X is E1
Range of Y is E2
Rel (Y.W#,Y.WD,X.P#,(X,Y).QTY):
(X,Y) belongs to R2

5.7.2 *IMS VM*(2). The second virtual model VM(2) is an IMS "logical" data base, Fig. 15. PART is the root segment. The bill of material information is represented as QTY-ASSMB (for "components" of an assembly (PART)) and QTY-USED (for "where used", i.e. of what other assemblies it is a component). The inventory information is in the WAREHOUSE segment. Through VM(2) a union of information in local data bases is accessed. The definition of VM(2) in terms of the IMS DDL is as follows:

```
DBD VM2
SEGM NAME=PART, BYTES=36
FIELD NAME=(P#, SEQ), BYTES=16
FIELD NAME=PD, BYTES=20, START=17
SEGM NAME=QTY-ASSMB, PARENT=PART,
        BYTES=22
FIELD NAME=(P#C, SEQ), BYTES=16, START=1
FIELD NAME=QTY, BYTES=6, START=17
```

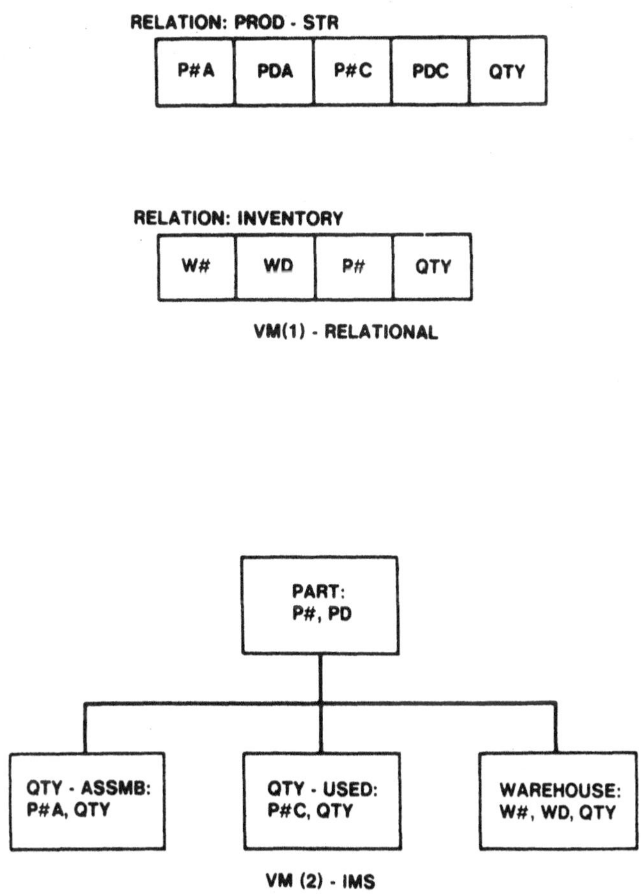

Fig. 15. Virtual models (User Views) VM(1) and VM(2) derived from the UGCM of Fig. 14.

```
SEGM NAME=QTY-USED, PARENT=PART, BYTES=22
FIELD NAME=(P#A, SEQ), BYTES=16, START=1
FIELD NAME=QTY, BYTES=6, START=17
SEGM NAME=WAREHOUSE, PARENT=PART, BYTES=27
FIELD NAME=(W#, SEQ), BYTES=5, START=1
FIELD NAME=WD, BYTES=5, START=6
FIELD NAME=QTY, BYTES=6, START=22, TYPE=BINARY
```

Integrity constraint: all part numbers in QTY-ASSMB and QTY-USED segments should be in PART segment

The M6 mapping is as follows:

VM(2) elements	
PART segment	E1[P#,PD]
QTY-ASSMB segment	The occurrence of each P#=pi is found as follows: Ranges of X, Y, are E1 Relation (Y.P#,(X,Y).QTY): (X,Y) belongs to R1 and X.P#=pi; then sorted on Y.P#
QTY-USED segment	The occurrence of each P#=pi is found as follows: Ranges of X,Y are E1 Relation (X.P#,(X,Y).QTY): (X,Y) belongs to R1 and Y.P#=pi and mapping from X to Y gives QTY per assembly; then sorted on X.P#

5.8 *Queries and their formulation at different layers of the system*

Figure 4 has summarized the translators involved in processing a query. Let us take the following arbitrary queries made by users of VM(1) and VM(2) and show their formulation at different layers of the system (Figure 2) step by step.

Query 1 (Q1): Find the stock status of the part with P#=112

Query 2 (Q2): Find the stock status of the components of the assembly whose P#=500

For query 2 each component is stored in several warehouses. All the components and their warehouses should be included in the output. The significance of this query is that it uses both the bill of material information and the inventory information, that is, different local data bases need to be accessed to obtain the answer.

5.8.1 *Formulation of queries at the VM level, Fig.* 15

For VM(1)

```
Q1: Range of X is INVENTORY
    Get (X.P#,X.W#,X.QTY): X.P#=112

Q2: Range of X is PROD-STR
    Range of Y is INVENTORY
    Get (Y.W#,Y.P#,Y.QTY): X.P#A=500 and X.P#C=Y.P#
```

For VM(2)

The VM(2) user is in an IMS environment using DL/1 as a data manipulation language

```
Q1: GU PART (P#=112)
       WAREHOUSE;
    DO WHILE (STATUS=FOUND);/*print WAREHOUSE from I/O area*/
    GNP WAREHOUSE;
    END;
```

Q2: In the following program it is assumed that the multipositioning feature of DL/1 is defined in the PCB (so there is one unique position pointer for each hierarchical path)

```
GU  PART (P#=500)
    QTY-ASSMB;
DO  WHILE (STATUS=FOUND);
GU  PART (P#=QTY-ASSMB.P#A)
    WAREHOUSE;
```

```
DO WHILE (STATUS=FOUND); /*print WAREHOUSE from I/O area*/
GNP WAREHOUSE;
END;
GNP QTY-ASSMB;
END;
```

5.8.2 *Formulation of queries at the UGCM level, Fig.* 14. The formulation of queries at the UGCM level is the same independent of whether originally the user came from the VM(1) or VM(2) environment. Translation of the original queries to the following must be done by the translator responsible for mapping M6, Fig. 2.

```
Q1: Range of X is E1
    Range of Y is E2
    GET (X.P#,Y.W#,(X,Y).QTY): X.P#=112 and
        (X.Y) belongs to R2

Q2: Range of X is E1
    Range of Y is E1
    Range of Z is E2
    GET (Y.P#,Z.W#,(Y.Z).QTY):X.P#=500
     and (X,Y) belongs to R21 and (Y,Z) belongs to R2
```

5.8.3 *Formulation of the queries at the UGIM level and ULIM level.* The translation of queries from the UGCM level is independent of the original VM. The major issues that must be considered by any algorithms that translate into the UGIM and ULIM levels are:

(A) Where the answers to queries are really stored. The mapping M4 is used for this purpose.

(B) How to communicate with data bases that contain the desired information. This is specified when the ULIM is built.

(C) What are the best access paths if several alternative ones are available. Mapping M5 should be used to translate the query to the internal level and M3 to decompose the query to the local level (see Fig. 2). If there are no usable interdatabase access paths then searching should be done and optimized separately for each database; this is the case in our example. If there are interdatabase access paths then searching should be optimized globally and then the query should be decomposed to take advantage of such access paths. Searching could start in one local data base and the interdatabase access path be used to traverse to another local data base.

Let us trace the translation process for our example.

Query 1

The stock status of part P#=112 may be found in DB(1), DB(2) and DB(4). Mapping M4 is consulted for this. There are no interdatabase access paths; therefore the query should be processed against DB(1), DB(2), and DB(4) individually. With the aid of mappings M5 and M3 the corresponding decomposed queries for each individual local data base are as follows:

DB(1), Fig. 11: Since the internal model ULIM(1) is just four groups without any access paths among them (as it is considered in this case), then a query like in the relational calculus should be formulated:

```
Range of X is G13
GET (X.P#,X.W#,X.QTY): X.P#=112
```

DB(2), Fig. 12:

T1–Find the instance of G21 using P#=112
T2–Find all instances of G22 under C21 using A211 associated to the instance of G21 (found in T1) and C21

DB(4), depicted also by Fig. 12:

T1–Find instance of G41 using P#=112
T2–Find all instances of G42 under C41 using A411 associated with the instance of G41 (found in T1) and C41

Query 2

The information may be stored in DB(1), DB(2), DB(3) and DB(4). If the part with P#=500 is found in DB(1), then there is no need to search for it in DB(3). If DB(3) has this part its bill of material should be the same as the one in DB(1). This was the constraint asserted for mapping M4 in Section 5.5. If the part can not be found in DB(1), then DB(3) should be searched to find the bill of material.

Since there are no interdatabase access paths, the search should be done separately. However, the information of what are the components of P#=500 has to be extracted first from DB(1); this information is then used to search DB(1), DB(2) and DB(4).

The corresponding decomposed queries for each local data base are as follows:

DB(1), Fig. 11:

```
Range of X is G14
GET in PART-LIST (X.P#A):X.P#A=500 /*PART-LIST is a temporary GROUP*/
Range of Y is PART-LIST
Range of Z is G13
GET (Y.P#,Z.W#,Z.QTY): Y.P#=X.P#
```

DB(2), Fig. 12: The list of components of P#=500 (PART-LIST) found in DB(1) is used to find the stock status in DB(2).

T–Do for each P#=pi in PART–LIST
  TI–Find the instance of G21 with P#=pi
  T2–Find the instances of G22 using A211 associated with G21 (found in T1) and C21

DB(4) depicted also by Fig. 12: The query is similar to the previous one for DB(2).

5.8.4 *Formulation of queries at the LLM level.* The queries formulated at the UGIM and ULIM levels should be translated to equivalent queries at the LLM level. Since the major optimization is envisioned to be done by algorithms at the UGIM level, further optimization may not be necessary. The queries at the LLM are as follows:

Query 1

```
DB(1):  Range of X is PW
        Get (X.W#,X.QTY): X.P#=112

DB(2), Figure 11:
        GU    PART (P#=112)
              WAREHOUSE
        DO    WHILE (STATUS=NOT FOUND);
                /*print WAREHOUSE*/
        GNP   WAREHOUSE;
        END;
```

Note that in this case the query at the DL/1 LLM level is identical to the original DL/1 query at the IMS VM level. The translators of the network system should detect from the beginning that this may happen and thus that it may be unnecessary to actually translate the original query through all the stages shown in Fig. 4. In this case translation from the VM(2) level is necessary only for DB(1) (a relational data base) and DB(4) (a DBTG data base).

```
DB(4), a DBTG data base depicted also by Fig. 12:
MOVE '112' to P# OF PART.
FIND PART RECORD.
IF INVENTORY SET EMPTY GO TO FINISH.
FIND NEXT RECORD OF INVENTORY SET.
DO WHILE (STATUS=NOT FOUND).
move and print record from I/O area
FIND NEXT RECORD OF INVENTORY SET.
END.
```

Query 2

Derivation of the actual query(ies) for the data base(s) involved is left as an exercise for the enthusiastic readers!

6. INTERDATABASE RELATIONSHIPS AT THE LEVEL OF THE UNIFIED GLOBAL CONCEPTUAL MODEL (UGCM)

During the systems analysis stage of the information systems development cycle, entities and relationships are identified. In a multidata base or heterogeneous data base network environment entities and relationships are identified separately. When data bases are integrated as proposed herein, many other meaningful and useful relationships may be visualized and defined. These new relationships at the conceptual level of the integrated system are those that may be defined between entities whose instances occur in different local data bases. Such relationships shall be called *non-local* or *interdatabase relationships*.

Figure 16 shows examples of relationships that are local to a data base and relationships that are non-local. Non-local or interdatabase relationships are implemented by interdata base access paths that would be reflected at the UGIM level.

Let us return to our example of the previous section. The relationship R1 in the UGCM in Fig. 14, which covers bill of material, is local because for each part the bill of material structure is the same no matter where it is stored. Each local data base that contains bill of materials has all instances of relationships necessary to obtain the components of a part. After integration of DB(1) (a relational data base) and DB(2) (an IMS data base) it may be that it is realized that there is a part P4 in DB(2) which may be also available from warehouse W1; however, this warehouse information is only in DB(1). There is no association between P4 and W1 because they belong to different local data bases.

Thus, there is the need for the implementation at the internal model level of an association between the instance P4 in DB(2) and the instance W1 in DB(1). This would be an interdatabase relationship (see Fig. 17).

This is a simple illustration of a situation that may present itself as (1) different data bases are integrated to complement each other, as proposed herein, or (2) as a data base is decentralized and geographically distributed. In the frontiers of decentralization and geographically distribution is the possibility of going even beyond having different but related entities and relationships geographically distributed: instances of entities geographically distributed or in different data bases and related to each other as illustrated in Fig. 17. No commercial GDBMS provides effective support for this situation even when the data bases involved are of the same kind, i.e. all IMS, all TOTAL, etc. Further into the future is the possibility of a network system capable of supporting interdatabase relationships between instances of entities residing in distant data bases and each data base under a different GDBMS. Yet, this is an upcoming situation with the proliferation of data bases under different GDBMS and with the interest of establishing data base networks.

6.1 *Implementation*

Interdatabase relationships should be implemented by explicit interdatabase access paths. Aggregates are proposed to be used to link one ULIM group in one local data base to another ULIM group or collection in another local data base. Figure 18 illustrates this, showing an aggregate A12 between the group G12 (which at the LLM level is a tuple of the relation WH (W#,WD) in DB(1)) and the collection of group G21 (which at the LLM level is the segment PART with its field P#, PD and CLASS in the IMS DB(2)). Similarly, aggregate A21 may be envisioned; the explanation is left up to the enthusiastic reader. Note the capability that we envision for the UGIM catalog or directory of the network:

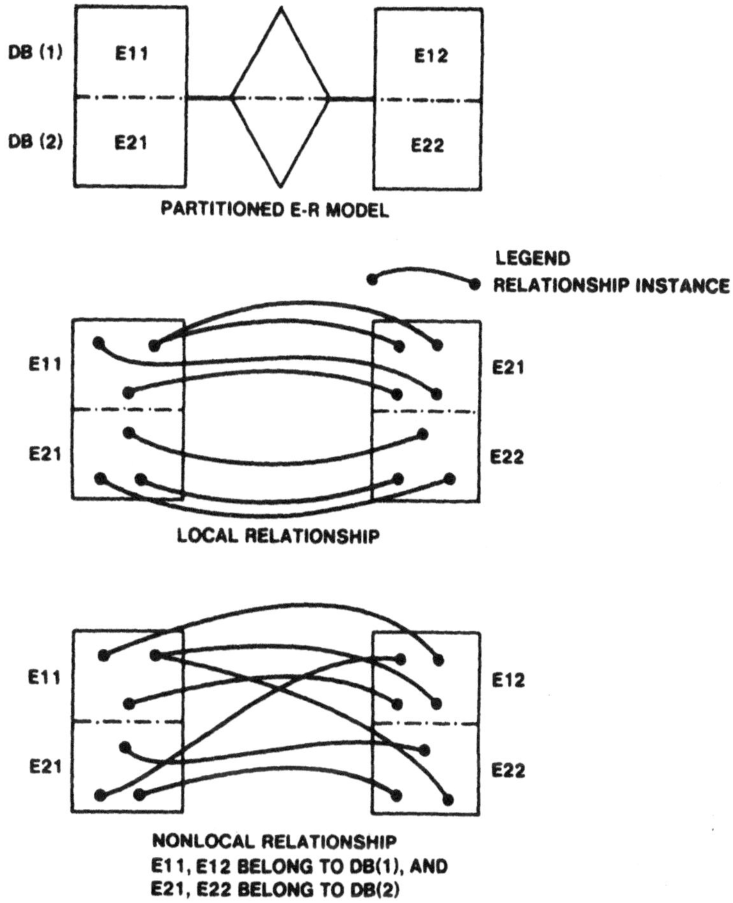

Fig. 16. Example of local and non-local relationships.

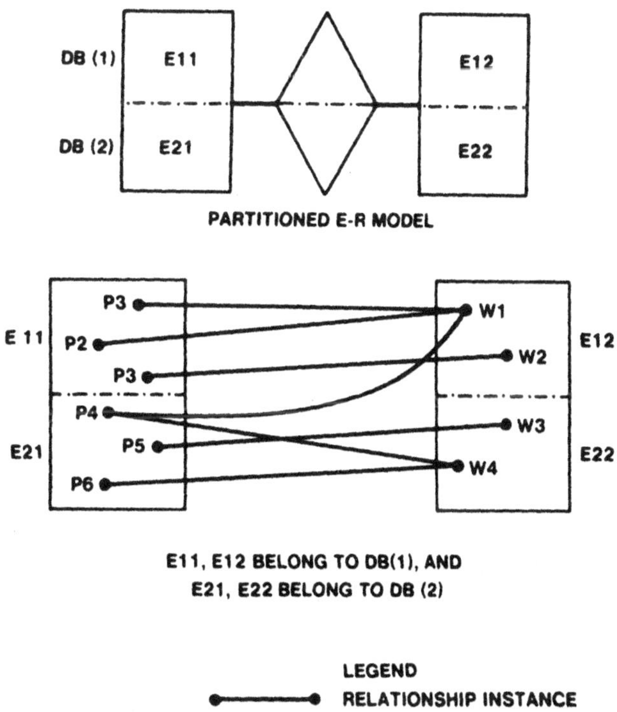

Fig. 17. Integration of DB(1) and DB(2) illustrating non-local or interdatabase relationships.

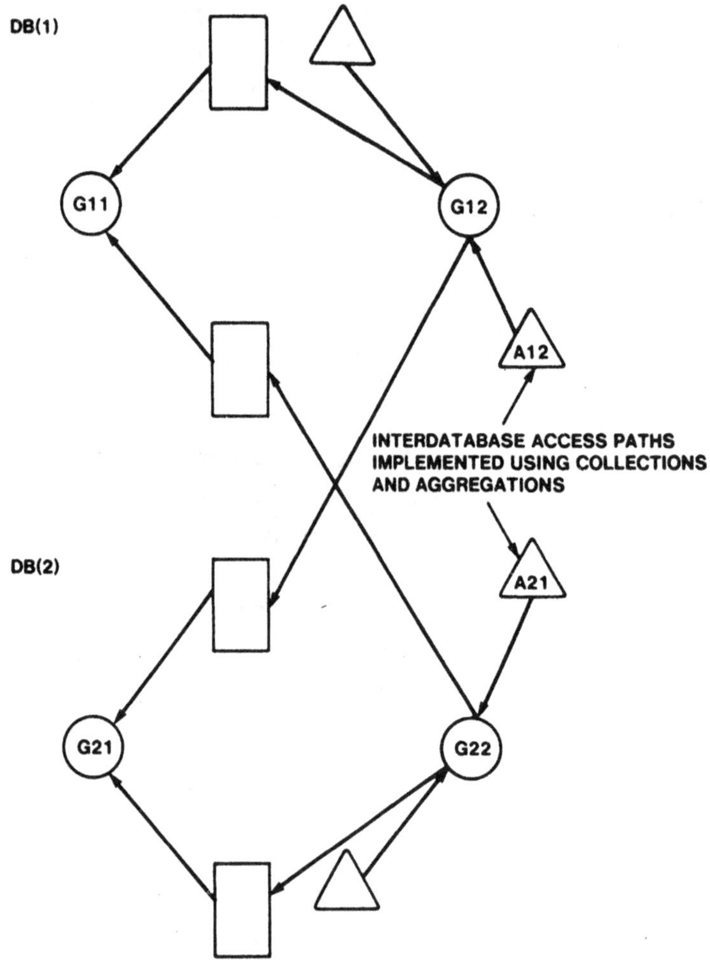

Fig. 18. UGIM of the data base in Fig. 17 with interdatabase access paths.

complete representation through a common framework of the various access paths, regardless of the logical data base structure (relational, IMS, System 2000, etc.) and of the locality or physical distribution of the data base(s). This is a challenging capability indeed.

Another type of interdata base access path that can be implemented at the UGIM level is between counterpart instances of groups that belong to the same entity at the level of the UGCM. This type of access path does not have a corresponding relationship at the level of the UGCM. The usage of counterpart interdatabase access paths is in the following cases:

(1) One data base has some attributes of an entity that are not stored in the equivalent entity in another data base. For example, in Fig. 18 suppose that G11 were made up of P#, PD, CLASS, WEIGHT and COLOR while G21 were made up of P# and PD. The interest is in reducing data redundancy by actually not storing weight and color in G21, and resorting to the counterpart interdatabase mechanism to provide a virtual view. The needed counterpart interdatabase access path would be in addition to the ones already shown in Fig. 18. This redundancy saving would have to be weighted against the possibly large access time cost for users fairly local to DB(2) and interested only in G21. The communications cost between DB(1) and DB(2) is a considerable cost incurred in materializing G21 for a user interested only in G21. This is the same old question of physical fields/records versus virtual fields/records.

(2) Two data bases have counterpart entities, and in addition in one data base there are normal access paths to other groups with related information while in the other there is no such information. For example, the IMS DB(2) in Fig. 12 does not contain bill of material information, but by using a counterpart access path the group instance in DB(1) that is a synonym to a group instance of interest in DB(2) may be located, and then its bill of material can be found. This will be a most useful capability as small and more limited data bases are tied in the future to a network with bigger and more encompassing data bases holding more information.

The possibility of and the justification for interdata base access paths between different groups in different ULIM's remains to be investigated.

7. FURTHER DISCUSSION AND COMPARISON OF DIFFERENT APPROACHES

In this section the performance of the proposed architecture in different environments is discussed. It is shown in what circumstances the method of interpretation is advantageous over the conversion. Large amount of mapping is inappropriate for some cases. The trade-offs are discussed. The homogeneous data base communication is examined. At the end the problems of directory management and integrity are treated.

7.1 *Interpretation (query translation) vs conversion*

As discussed in section 1, if data base conversion is done once then there is no need for subsequent translation of a query from one GDBMS language to another. The cost of conversion is mainly in reprogramming of the application and training of the people to deal with the new environment. The cost of interpretation is much lower but is should be done for every query to be processed. Assume that C1 is the cost of conversion and C2 is the cost of interpretation and N is the number of times a query is initiated in the lifetime of data base. Then if C1 is greater than N*C2 then conversion is less cost effective.

The need for a data base communication system exists even if the conversion method is adopted. The interpretation does not go away either. Refer to Section 7.5 for more detail.

7.2 *Discussion on number of layers of the system model*

The problem of data base communication is relatively complex and not investigated broadly. The lack of enough knowledge and complexity requires a step by step approach to attack the problem. This is done by introducing different layers in the model which accomplish relatively independent tasks. The advantages of layering are:

—to reduce the complexity,

—to prevent the changes in one layer to proliferate in the other layers of the system,

And the disadvantage is the inefficiency due to large amount of mappings required. This approach is not new in science and particularly computer science. For example a DBMS which is built on top of the operating system is undoubtedly several orders of magnitude slower than one that would work with the bare machine. But the advantage is its machine independency and less complexity.

In the proposed system model, the conceptual model is separated from the internal model because they have different objectives. The bulk of the mapping is between these two models. The mapping between VMs and UGCM can be very complex if the corresponding models are very different. The other mappings are fairly simple and there is little overhead associated with them. As a result there is a tendency to remove the internal model (UGIM,ULIM) from the communication management directory because of its overhead. This issue is discussed in the next section. The stability of the UGIM and ULIM is much less than the UGCM and ULCM. This makes the directory maintenance more expensive for UGIM and ULIM.

7.3 *Discussion on internal models (ULIM,UGIM)*

The inclusion of the internal model layers in the system model should be examined carefully due to the large amount of overhead associated with it. The overhead is discussed in subsequent paragraphs.

The need for these layers arises in the following major conditions:

(A) Highly redundant distributed data bases, i.e., environments in which the same information appears in different local data bases. The cost of searching and of access paths can be included in an internal model. This cost would be the basis to decide which local data base should be used to answer the request of the subquery resulting from the UGCM query. This decision is meaningful if there are several choices due to the redundancy in distributed data bases.

(B) The interface language of the local data base is highly procedural and low level, such as IMS–DL/1 or DBTG–DML. The data model of these systems is close to their data structures. Translation of the query from the conceptual model to the LLM model can be done in two steps, which reduces the complexity. However, if complexity is not a problem then UGIM and ULIM can be removed. If there is a low level of redundancy and the interface to the local data base is through a very high level language, such as a relational model language, then there is no need for internal model layers. Once the query is decomposed it can be sent to the local data base.

In the case that the local data base management is very intelligent (for example System R) the internal layer is not appropriate. Future DBMSs are expected to change the internal model of data base dynamically, at least to some extent for needed performance. As a result there would be a lot of overhead to keep the global directory up-to-date. The searching algorithms involved would be very complex and it would be difficult for the data base communication manager to understand the behavior of the local data base. This includes mostly the category of relational model type data bases. In this situation somehow the cost function should be kept in a global directory to select the appropriate local data base if the distributed data bases are redundant. For example the cost can be associated to the number of tuples in the relation. In this case there is less accuracy in the cost function but there is less overhead too. This problem is the same as the query decomposition and processing in a relational model, a subject of current research.

Let us now examine the overhead associated with the internal models (DIAM) in the system directory. This overhead can be justified in the situations previously discussed. The overhead is mostly due to the relatively large amount of data for the internal model and its instability. DIAM models the objects at the "type" level rather than "instance" level. The number of internal model objects: groups, collections and aggregates are much more than the conceptual model. The conceptual model is relatively stable and changes when semantic requirements of data change. However, the internal model changes due to: reorganization, modificantion in file structures and access paths. Every time the internal model changes the system directory should be changed. This causes a great deal of overhead in large distributed data base environments.

7.4 *Distribution of directory*

The system directory by itself is a data base. The user of this data base is mainly the query interpreter. This user reads the directory data base. When a local data base is changed by the DBA, this will necessitate that the system directory be updated. This change can be in conceptual model or internal model or virtual model (VM). The optimum distribution of directory depends on the volume of each type of traffic. If update traffic volume is low, then the directory should be distributed. But if update traffic volume is high, then update of multiple copies becomes very expensive and a more centralized directory approach should be chosen. A comprehensive treatment of the problem of distribution of directory can be found in CHU [23].

7.5 *Homogeneous data base communication*

The general requirement of this special case is discussed in Section 1. Basically

—different local DBMSs are linked,

—query interpretation is required.

The data base communication system should get the nonlocal queries and decompose them and send them to other local data bases. This is done in the same manner as the heterogeneous case.

The query interpretation is necessary because of different structuring of data models involved. For example if all of the DBMSs are IMS, in one local data base S1 could be the root segment but in the other one it could be a child segment; each of these data base configurations needs a different DL/I command for access. Another example can be the case when all DBMSs are relational. A relation, say R1 exist in one local data base as one independent relation, but it is embedded in another relation, say R2, in some other local data base. The query which is written for R1 should be modified to access R1 embedded in R2. This brings up the issue that there is a need for a semantic model that represent the data in one way. This is the UGCM in the system model.

By resorting to data base conversion one can make data models exactly the same. This will eliminate the interpretation since there is no incompatibility among data models. However it is not clear that this method is always possible because it does not give any choice to local data base administrators to tailor the data models according to the local needs.

In the homogeneous environment the number of mapping procedures is less. For example just one mapping procedure between LLM and ULCM is needed. In heterogeneous cases for each DBMS type a separate mapping procedure should exist.

7.6 *Integrity*

There are several issues associated with the updating of data base objects. One is the fact that VM has a subset of UGCM information. A user probably should not be able to update any object in a data base without some limitations because it may affect some other objects which are not in his VM. This is the classical problem of updating through subschemas.

The second issue is associated with locking. There are different granularities and modes of locks in the local DBMSs. If a transaction makes a lock request according to its VM, that lock should be translated to the locks acceptable to the local DBMS. This can be done in the same way that a query gets translated.

The task of global transaction management is the responsibility of the data base communication system. Different distributed locking schemes can be employed. For example the communication system can make a request for the locks from the local data bases when the subqueries are going to be sent. Then after the acknowledgements come back from all of them the subqueries are sent to the local data bases.

There are similar issues associated with the incompatibility among modes of the locks and crash recovery, which are not addressed here.

8. CONCLUSION

We have proposed and illustrated through a comprehensive example an architecture and a methodology for communication between different data bases, each one under a different GDBMS and perhaps geographically distributed. The long-range goal is to provide future network users with:

(1) Independence from the syntax and semantics of each participating GDBMS, except perhaps from that of the special GDBMS in primary use at the user's node;

(2) Independence from the physical distribution of the participating data bases, giving each user an integrated model or schema of the various data bases participating in the network as if it were one centralized data base.

(3) Flexibility of tailoring the logical view of the data base in such a heterogeneous GDBMS environment.

Figure 1 outlines the system architecture proposed and the necessary building blocks. Central to the approach is a series of architectural layers and associated models and mapping procedures between the models, as shown in Fig. 2. These models and mappings will reside in a highly protected network catalog, transparent to the user.

Our approach entails deriving a global conceptual model and a global internal model of the integrated system. The global conceptual model is used as a vehicle in the process of understanding user queries and decomposing them to extract the information from the individual data bases. The global conceptual model is the union of the conceptual models of the data bases participating in the network. The global internal model is the access-path oriented model of the structure of the integrated system. The global internal model is the union of the internal models of the participating data bases and interdata base access paths. It is used as a vehicle in the process of identifying the access paths through the different data bases that should be followed to answer queries, while shielding the user from the need to know the intricacies and distribution of the available access paths. The Entity-relationship model is fundamentally used for the conceptual level. The DIAM-SDDT model is fundamentally used for the internal level.

A network DBA will have the task of developing both the conceptual and the internal models for each data base under each GDBMS and arriving at the global conceptual model and the global internal model. From the global model the DBA can derive and tailor the virtual view desired by a user at a given node. User queries originate at this user view.

The DBA derives the models from the schema descriptions in the DDL of each GDBMS, although detailed access-path and performance oriented information not appearing in the schema description may need to be gathered for network optimization reasons (e.g. inverted indexes available and their speed). This is a crucial network design task highly unlikely to be automated. We have outlined the tasks and methodology through a comprehensive example in Section 5 involving a relational data base, two IMS data bases and a DBTG data base.

User queries originate at the virtual user level and it is up to the system to automatically process them. Various translation steps are necessary, as summarized in Fig. 4. The construction of the necessary translators is the subject of future work. These are necessary for effective operation of any heterogeneous data base network. Manual transformations by either users or DBA would be exceedingly intricate and time consuming. Section 5 traced the formulation and processing of queries through our comprehensive case.

As different but related data bases are integrated into a network, the possibility of non-local or interdatabase relationships arises. These are relationships that may be defined between entities whose instances occur in different local data bases, as shown in Fig. 17. Thus the possibility of user views actually including not only different entity types distributed throughout the network but also instances of the same entity type but residing in different data bases must be addressed. The definition and use of such complex schemas and relationships must be controlled by the network DBA.

A number of important issues in physically distributed data base environments addressed elsewhere by Rothnie and Goodman [14] are not addressed herein. For example, the actual location of the catalogs containing the models and the mapping procedures, and the problem of communication costs and delays between physical locations. The problems and issues addressed herein and the architectural approach and solutions proposed remain, independent of whether the data bases are actually geographically distributed or not.

Acknowledgement—We dedicate this work to the late Michael E. Senko of IBM, a great friend who suffered such a premature death. His ideas lead to DIAM and influenced CODASYL's SDDT model and our approach to the heterogeneous data base management challenge. Many thanks are due to Peter Chen and to the three anonymous reviewers for their valuable criticisms.

REFERENCES

[1] A. Soshani: A logical-level approach to data base conversion. *Proc., SIGMOD Conf.*, pp. 112–122. San Jose, California, 1975.
[2] N. Shu, B. Housel and V. Lum: CONVERT, a high level translation definition language for data conversion. IBM Corporation, *Rep. RJ 1500*, San Jose, California, Jan. 1975.
[3] N. Shu, V. Lum and B. Housel: An approach to data migration in computer networks. IBM Corporation, *Rep. RJ*1703, San Jose, California, Jan. 1976.
[4] N. Shu, B. Housel, R. W. Taylor, S. P. Ghosh and V. Lum: EXPRESS: a data extraction, processing and restructuring system. *ACM Trans. Data Base Systems* **2**(2), June 1977.
[5] S. Y. W. Su: Application program conversion due to data base changes. *Proc., 2nd Int. Conf. on Very Large Data Bases*, pp. 143–157. Brussels, Belgium, Sept. 1976.
[6] E. Nahouraii, L. O. Brooks and A. F. Cardenas: An approach to data communication between different GDBMS. *Proc., 2nd. Int. Conf. on Very Large Data Bases*, Brussels, Belgium, Sept. 1976.
[7] M. Adiba and C. Delobel: The cooperation problem between different data base management systems. *IFIP-TC2 Working Conf.*, Nice, France, Jan. 1977.
[8] M. Adiba and D. Portal: A cooperation system for heterogeneous data base management systems. *Inform. Systems* **3**(3), 209–215 (1978).
[9] P. Chen: The entity relationship model: toward a unified view of data. *ACM Trans. Data Base Systems* **1**(1) (1976).
[10] J. R. Abrial: Data semantics. *IFIP-TC2 Working Conf.*, Cargese, Corsica, April 1974.
[11] M. E. Senko, E. B. Altman, M. M. Astrahan and P. L. Fehder: Data structures and accessing in data base systems. *IBM Systems J.* **12**(1) (1973).
[12] M. E. Senko: DIAM as a detailed example of the ANSI/SPARC architecture. *IFIP-TC2 Working Conf.*, Freudenstadt, Germany, Jan. 1976.
[13] SDDTG of CODASYL Systems Committee, A stored data definition language for the translation of data. *Inform. Systems* **2**(3) (1977).
[14] J. B. Rothnie and N. Goodman: A survey of research and development in distributed database management. *Proc., 3rd Int. Conf. on Very Large Data Bases*, Tokyo, Japan, Aug. 1977.
[15] G. Pelagatti, P. Paolini and G. Bracchi: Mapping external views to a common data model. *Inform. Systems* **3**(2), 141–151 (1978).
[16] J. Miles Smith and D. Smith: Data base abstraction: aggregation and generalization. *Trans. Data Base Systems* **2**(2), 105–133 (1977).
[17] S. B. Navathe: Schema analysis for data restructuring. IBM Corporation, *Rep. RJ*2225, San Jose, California, April 1978.
[18] S. B. Navathe and J. P. Fry: Restructuring for large data bases: three levels of abstraction. *ACM Trans. on Data Base Systems*, **1**(2), 138–158 (1976).
[19] W. Chu and E. Z. Nahouraii. File directory design considerations for distributed data bases. *Proc. of the 1st Int. Conf. on Very Large Data Bases*, Framingham, Massachusetts, 1975.
[20] S. P. Ghosh and M. E. Senko: String path search procedures for data base systems. *IBM J. Res. Devel.* **18**(5), 408–422 (1974).
[21] S. P. Ghosh and M. Astrahan: Translator optimizer for obtaining answers to entity set queries from an arbitrary access path network. *Information Processing*, 1974. North-Holland, Amsterdam (1974).
[22] L. S. Schneider: A relational query compiler for distributed heterogeneous databases. *IFIP TC 2.6*, NASWG, Jan. 1977.
[23] W. Chu: Principles of distributed data base design. In *Computer Communications: State of the Art and Directions for the Future*, Vol. 2 (Edited by W. Chou). to be published by Prentice-Hall, Englewood Cliffs, New Jersey.

APPENDIX A

Unified Local Conceptual Model (ULCM) and Unified Local Internal Model (ULIM) for the IMS Data Base DB(2).

```
E21 REGULAR ENTITY RELATION
    ATTRIBUTE:  P#, PD, CLASS
    PRIMARY KEY:  P#
```

E22 REGULAR ENTITY RELATION
ATTRIBUTE: W#, WD
PRIMARY KEY: W#

R21 NONHIERARCHICAL RELATIONSHIP RELATION
ROLE/ENTITY-RELATIONSHIP.PK/MAX-NO-OF-ENTITIES
E21/P#/m
E22/W#/n (m:n mapping)
ATTRIBUTE: QTY

INTEGRITY CONSTRAINTS:
Range of X is E21
Range of Y is E22
for all Y there exists an X : (X, Y) belongs to R21 /* an instance of E22 can not exist unless an instance of E21 exists, which is its parent in the IMS database */

ULIM(2):

Local internal model ULIM(2) (see Fig. 12):

INTERNAL MODEL OF DB(2)
Entries are: G21

LOGICAL GROUP IS G21
DEFINED OVER: P#,PD,CLASS
KEY IS: P#

LOGICAL GROUP IS G22
DEFINED OVER: W#,WD,P#(virtual),QTY
KEY IS: (W#,P#)
VALIDATION IS:
Range of X is G22
Range of Y is G22
for all X and for all Y : If X. W# = Y. W# then X. WD = Y. WD

LOGICAL COLLECTION IS C21
DEFINED OVER: G22 SUBSET IS UNIQUE VALUE OF P#
ORDER IS: W#

LOGICAL AGGREGATE A211
DEFINED OVER: G21, C21
MATCH IS G21.P# = C21.P#

LOGICAL AGGREGATE A212
DEFINED OVER: G21, G22
SYMMETRIC OF A211

AN OVERVIEW OF MULTIBASE

Terry Landers
Ronni L. Rosenberg*

Computer Corporation of America
575 Technology Square
Cambridge, Massachusetts 02139
U.S.A.

This paper describes the prototype implementation of MULTIBASE -- a software system that provides a uniform, retrieval interface through a single query language and database schema to data in pre-existing, heterogeneous, distributed databases. MULTIBASE efficiently executes queries that may require data to be retrieved from different databases that have different schemata, data models, and query languages. This is accomplished without making any changes to the pre-existing databases, their database management systems, or their application programs. MULTIBASE presents the user with the illusion of a single, integrated, nondistributed database. To do this, MULTIBASE assumes complete responsibility for knowing the location of the local databases, accessing the data at each of the local database management systems, resolving data incompatibilities, and combining the data to produce a single result.

----

*Writer

This research was jointly supported by the Defense Advanced Research Projects Agency of the Department of Defense (DARPA) and by the Naval Electronics System Command (NAVELEX) under contract N00039-82-C-0226. The views and conclusions contained in this document are those of the authors and should not be interpreted as necessarily representing those of DARPA, NAVELEX, or the U.S. government.

1. INTRODUCTION

MULTIBASE is a software system that provides a uniform, integrated interface for retrieving data from pre-existing, heterogeneous, distributed databases. It was designed to allow the user to reference data in these databases with one query language over one database description (called a schema). By presenting the illusion of a globally integrated system, MULTIBASE allows the user to access data in multiple databases quickly and easily. Because there is an integrated schema and a single query language, the user has to be familiar with only one, uniform interface instead of numerous, local system interfaces. MULTIBASE does not require any changes to the pre-existing databases, their database management systems (DBMSs), or their application programs.

Distributed, heterogeneous databases occur in many organizations, for several reasons. First, many databases were created before the benefits of data integration were well understood. Second, the lack of a central database administrator (DBA) has encouraged individual groups within an organization to create and maintain separate databases that satisfy their own requirements; typically, these databases are not globally integrated. Third, the distribution of data across several sites is essential in some environments to handle large volumes of data processing.

Many organizations have a pressing need to access all their data rapidly and reliably. This need is very difficult to satisfy when the data that are important to the organization are stored in many, independent databases. Formulating and implementing queries that require data from more than one database requires knowing where all the data are stored, mastering all the necessary interfaces, and correctly combining partial results from individual queries into a single answer. MULTIBASE overcomes these difficulties by allowing users to access all relevant data uniformly, while providing an automated system that performs the necessary, underlying operations.

As an example of the kind of application where MULTIBASE is useful, consider a university that uses four different databases implemented with three different data models (illustrated in Figure 1.1). The databases were developed independently for the personnel and course registration offices at the main and branch campuses of the university, and they contain data tailored to the needs of these groups. For instance, each campus stores the value of the salary paid to an employee for work done at that campus. To answer the question "Which instructors teach math classes at both the main and the branch campuses and earn more than $25,000 a year?", a programmer must retrieve information from all four databases. To execute this query successfully, the programmer must:

1. Know the location of the necessary data, the data formats, and the query languages of the local DBMSs.

2. Decompose the question into subqueries that can be executed at each database. In this example, the query would be decomposed into four subqueries that would identify instructors who teach at the main campus (executed at the MAIN campus database), identify instructors who teach at the branch campus (executed at the BRANCH campus database), retrieve the annual salary for main campus employees (executed at the MAIN EMPLOYEE database), and

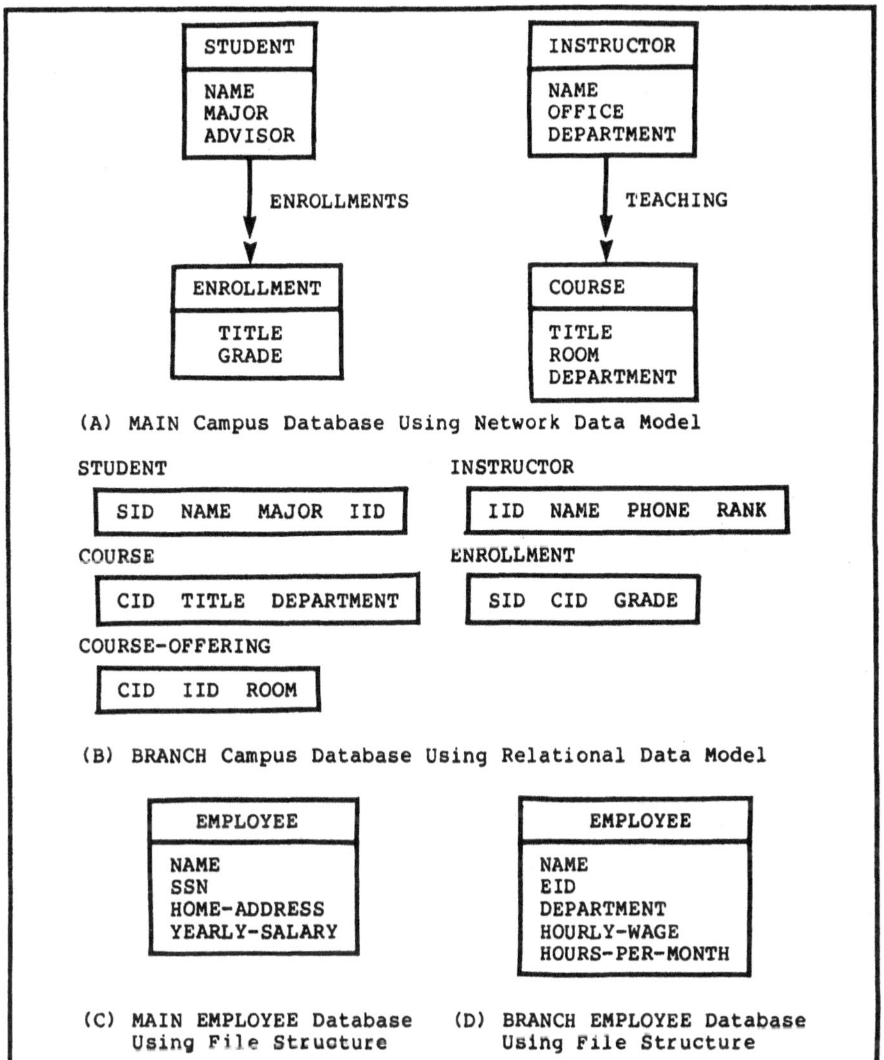

Figure 1.1 University Databases

retrieve the annual salary for branch campus employees (executed at the BRANCH EMPLOYEE database). Note that the third subquery would retrieve the data item YEARLY-SALARY while the fourth subquery would have to retrieve the expression (HOURLY-WAGE * HOURS-PER-MONTH * 12).

3. Arrange for the partial results to be accumulated at one database site. The programmer could choose to accumulate all the results of all the subqueries at one of the four sites. Other

query processing strategies are possible and might be more efficient (e.g., might require less data movement).

4. Write a program to extract from this accumulated data a complete response to the original question. In this example, the programmer could first write a program to extract the data that lie at the intersection of the partial results from the two INSTRUCTOR subqueries. For each of these INSTRUCTORs, the annual salary would be computed as the sum of the two campus salaries and would then be compared to 25,000 to yield the desired results.

Without an integrated interface, this procedure is time consuming and error prone. In contrast, MULTIBASE will answer this kind of multi-database query quickly and correctly.

1.1 Capabilities of MULTIBASE

MULTIBASE is designed to provide a logically integrated, retrieve-only, user interface to a physically nonintegrated environment. It provides a single interface through a single query language to data in all the databases. Through this interface, MULTIBASE presents the user with the illusion of a single, integrated, nondistributed database. The system assumes complete responsibility for knowing the location of the local databases, accessing the data at each of the local DBMSs, resolving data incompatibilities, and combining the data to produce a single result.

To correctly and efficiently execute multi-database queries, MULTIBASE has to solve problems including the following: transforming a query expressed in the user's global query language into a set of subqueries expressed in the different languages supported by the local DBMSs; formulating an efficient plan for executing a sequence of subqueries and data movement steps; implementing an efficient program for accessing the data at a single local site; moving the results of subqueries among local sites; resolving incompatibilities between the databases, such as differences in data types and conflicting schema names; resolving inconsistencies in copies of the same information that are stored in different databases; and combining the data into a single answer.

Before local databases can be accessed through MULTIBASE, the local host systems must be connected to a communications network. This network can be local or geographically distributed. MULTIBASE is then connected to the same communications network, as illustrated in Figure 1.2. After this, a global user can access data in the local databases through a single interface -- MULTIBASE -- using a single query language. Each local site maintains autonomy for local database update. Local application programs can continue to operate using the existing local interfaces, as before.

MULTIBASE does not provide the capability to update the data in the local databases or to synchronize read operations across several sites. To implement global concurrency control mechanisms for read or update operations, the global process must request and control specific services offered by the local systems (e.g., locking local database items). These services are required to insure consistency across the databases. Most systems do not make available to an external process the services necessary to implement global

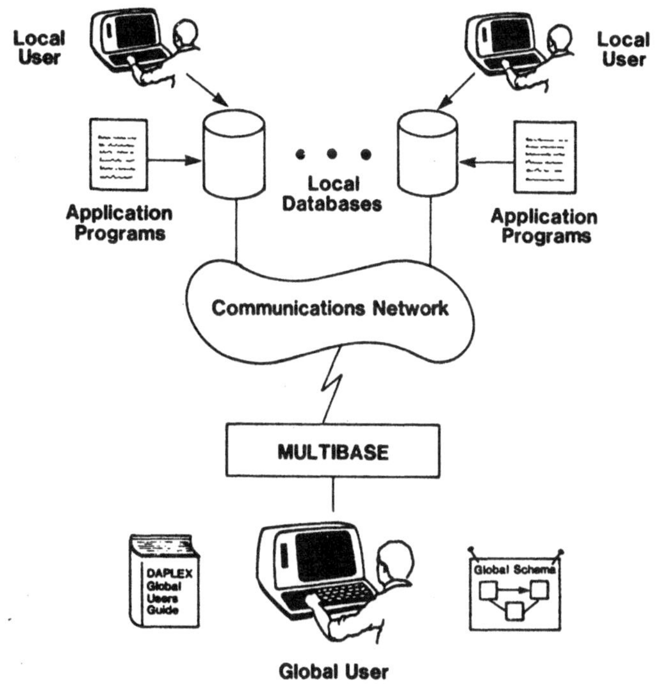

Figure 1.2 Communications Network Connects MULTIBASE and its Global Users with Local Systems

concurrency control. Since MULTIBASE is designed to operate without requiring modifications to existing systems (see Section 1.3), the tools needed to insure consistency across databases are not globally available. Thus, autonomy for database update is maintained locally, and MULTIBASE provides the global user with the same level of data consistency that the local host DBMSs provide to each local database user.

1.2 DAPLEX and the Functional Data Model

The language provided to global users by MULTIBASE is DAPLEX, a data definition and manipulation language for database systems. DAPLEX is based on the functional data model [1]. A fundamental goal of DAPLEX is to provide a conceptually natural, database interface language; the DAPLEX constructs used to model real world situations are intended to closely match the conceptual constructs a human being might employ when thinking about those situations.

The basic constructs of the functional data model are entities and functions; these correspond to conceptual objects and their properties. Entities with similar properties are grouped together to form entity sets. Entity functions can be single-valued or multi-valued. When applied to a given entity, a function returns a specific property associated with that entity. Each property is represented by either a single value or a set of values.

1.3 Design Objectives

MULTIBASE has three key objectives: generality, compatibility, and extensibility. To satisfy the first objective, MULTIBASE has been designed to be a general tool, capable of providing integrated access to various database systems used for various applications. MULTIBASE not been engineered to be an interface for a specific application area.

The second requirement of MULTIBASE is that it co-exist and be compatible with existing database systems and applications. No changes or modifications to local databases, DBMSs, or application programs are necessary to interface MULTIBASE with systems already in operation. The local sites retain full autonomy for maintaining the databases. All local access and application programs can continue to operate without change under MULTIBASE.

The third design objective is that it must be relatively easy to couple a new local system into an existing MULTIBASE configuration.

All these objectives are achieved by designing a modular architecture for MULTIBASE and by making the system largely "description driven." MULTIBASES's modular architecture isolates those parts of the system that deal with specific aspects of a local system. Because of this, a MULTIBASE configuration can be expanded to include a new DBMS in a short period of time and with little impact on the existing MULTIBASE software. Descriptions are used throughout MULTIBASE to tailor general modules for specific applications, users, and databases. These descriptions are written by the person(s) responsible for tailoring MULTIBASE to integrate access to the local databases. Throughout the rest of this paper, this person is referred to as the Database Administrator (DBA). Since descriptions are easily modified, both responses to local database changes and access to new databases can be provided quickly. How these key design objectives are met is discussed further in the remainder of this paper.

1.4 Organization of this Paper

The basic schema and component architectures of MULTIBASE are presented in Section 2. Section 3 describes how MULTIBASE processes multi-database queries. Section 4 explains the use of views (global schemata derived from existing databases) to achieve integration and to handle incompatible data. Section 5 presents MULTIBASE's approach to local and global query optimization. The paper concludes with a summary in Section 6.

2. BASIC ARCHITECTURE

The basic architecture of MULTIBASE is structured to facilitate achievement of the key objectives of generality, compatibility, and extensibility. In the following two sections, the schema and component architectures are discussed.

2.1 Schema Architecture

The major technical challenge in supporting heterogeneous, distributed databases is to provide the user with an integrated, coherent, global view of the data stored in the local databases. The user of the global database must be insulated not only from the location of the data, but also from local system details like data model, data description, and access language. The approach followed in MULTIBASE is to separate the issues of incompatible data handling and database integration from issues related to the "homogenization" of the heterogeneous local databases. This is done by defining a global schema over DAPLEX representations of the local host schemata. Incompatible data handling and database integration are handled at the level of the global schema; homogenization of the local databases is handled at the level of the DAPLEX representations. This multi-level schema architecture is shown in Figure 2.1, and its components are discussed below.

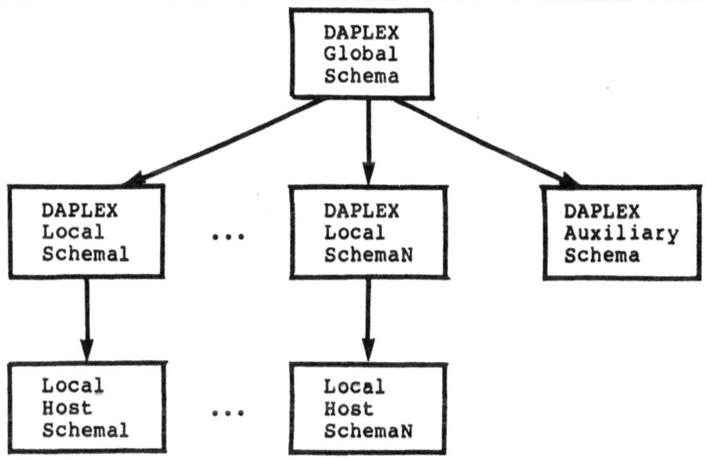

Figure 2.1 MULTIBASE Schema Architecture

The _local host schemata_ are the original, pre-existing schemata defined in the local data models and used by the local DBMSs. For instance, the university example has network (MAIN campus database), relational (BRANCH campus database), and file (EMPLOYEE databases) schemata. When a new database is incorporated into a MULTIBASE configuration, its schema can be adopted without change as a new local host schema.

The DAPLEX local schema is a DAPLEX-equivalent of the local host schema for each local DBMS. Figure 2.2 illustrates the DAPLEX local schemata for the university databases shown in Figure 1.1. Because local schemata are expressed in a single data model, higher levels of MULTIBASE need not be concerned with differences in data models among the local DBMSs. Because handling of local system differences is isolated at the DAPLEX local schema level, the addition of a new database into a MULTIBASE configuration does not significantly affect higher levels of the system.

DAPLEX's flexible modeling capabilities make it easy to emulate a variety of data models. For example, a DAPLEX local schema for the relational data model describes each relation as an entity and each domain as a single-valued, scalar function. A DAPLEX local schema for the network data model describes each record type as an entity; each data item as a single-valued, scalar function; and each set as a multi-valued function that returns the corresponding set of member entities.

The DAPLEX auxiliary schema describes a DAPLEX auxiliary database that is maintained at the Internal DBMS within MULTIBASE. The auxiliary database stores additional data that are not available in any of the local databases and data that are needed to resolve incompatibilities. The Internal DBMS is described more fully in Section 3. An example of an auxiliary database schema is in Section 4.

The DAPLEX global schema is an integrated view of the data in the underlying, nonintegrated DBMSs, including the auxiliary database. It is designed to present data in a way that is convenient for some group of global users. MULTIBASE can support several different global schemata for the same underlying DBMSs. A powerful mapping language describes how to achieve these views using the DAPLEX local and auxiliary schemata.

To the user, a global schema appears as if it were the schema for an integrated DBMS. In issuing DAPLEX global queries against the global schema, the user need not be aware of the location of the required data or the differences in schemata and data models among the local DBMSs. Thus, MULTIBASE presents users with the illusion of a homogeneous and integrated database, without requiring that the local databases be physically integrated.

A specification of a global schema that integrates the MAIN and BRANCH databases is in Section 4.

```
type COURSE is entity
     TITLE : string;
     ROOM : string;
     DEPARTMENT : string;
end entity;

type ENROLLMENT is entity
     TITLE : string;
     GRADE : string;
end entity;

type INSTRUCTOR is entity
     NAME : string;
     OFFICE : string;
     DEPARTMENT : string;
     TEACHING : set of COURSE;
end entity;

type STUDENT is entity
     NAME : string;
     MAJOR : string;
     ADVISOR : string;
     ENROLLMENTS : set of
                     ENROLLMENT;
end entity;
```

(A) DAPLEX Local Schema for MAIN Campus Database

```
type COURSE is entity
     CID : integer;
     TITLE : string;
     DEPARTMENT : string;
end entity;

type ENROLLMENT is entity
     SID : integer;
     CID : integer;
     GRADE : string;
end entity;

type INSTRUCTOR is entity
     IID : integer;
     NAME : string;
     PHONE : string;
     RANK : string;
end entity;

type STUDENT is entity
     SID : integer;
     NAME : string;
     MAJOR : string;
     IID : integer;
end entity;

type COURSE-OFFERING is entity
     CID : integer;
     IID : integer;
     ROOM : string;
end entity;
```

(B) DAPLEX Local Schema for BRANCH Campus Database

```
type EMPLOYEE is entity
     NAME : string;
     SSN : integer;
     HOME-ADDRESS : string;
     YEARLY-SALARY : float;
end entity;
```

(C) DAPLEX Local Schema for MAIN EMPLOYEE Database

```
type EMPLOYEE is entity
     NAME : string;
     EID : integer;
     DEPARTMENT : string;
     HOURLY-WAGE : float;
     HOURS-PER-MONTH : integer;
end entity;
```

(D) DAPLEX Local Schema for BRANCH EMPLOYEE Database

Figure 2.2 DAPLEX Local Schemata for University Databases

2.2 Component Architecture

The component architecture of MULTIBASE is illustrated in Figure 2.3. There are two types of modules: a global data manager (GDM) and a local database interface (LDI). All global aspects of a query are handled by the GDM. All specific aspects of a local system are handled by an LDI. There is one LDI for each local host DBMS accessed by MULTIBASE. Since the Internal DBMS, containing the auxiliary database, is an integral part of the GDM, it is not shown in Figure 2.3.

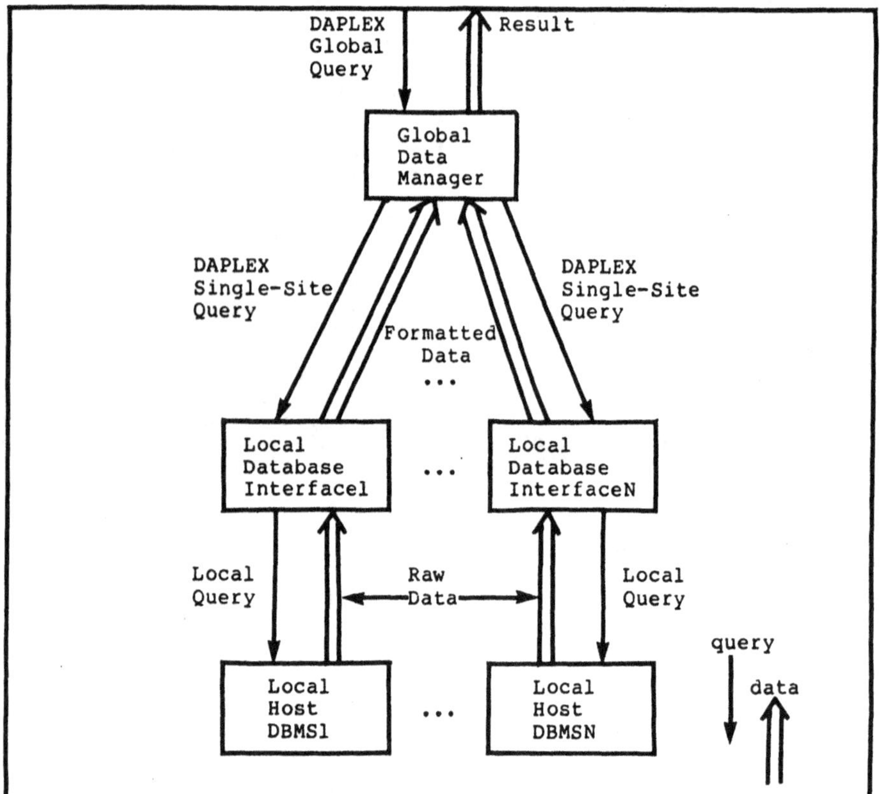

Figure 2.3 MULTIBASE Component Architecture

The component architecture can best be illustrated by following a query through MULTIBASE. A user poses a DAPLEX global query over the global schema. The GDM transforms the DAPLEX global query into a set of DAPLEX single-site queries. Each single-site query is still expressed in DAPLEX, but it is expressed in terms of a DAPLEX local schema and references data at exactly one local host DBMS. An LDI receives a DAPLEX single-site query and translates it into a local query that is expressed in the local query language. This query is then executed at the local DBMS. When query execution is complete, the LDI reformats the data into a standard representation and returns the formatted data to the GDM. The GDM combines the data returned from all the LDIs and presents the user with a single, consistent result.

To satisfy the objective of extensibility, the interface between the GDM and <u>any</u> LDI is standardized. Going from the GDM to an LDI, all single-site queries are expressed in DAPLEX. Going from an LDI to the GDM, all data are returned in an expected format.

Because all knowledge of local host protocols and query language syntax and semantics is isolated within the LDIs, the GDM is shielded from details of local systems. To add a new DBMS to a MULTIBASE configuration, only a new LDI must be designed and implemented. The DBA translates the local host schema into its equivalent DAPLEX local schema and extends the global schema to incorporate the new information. Global queries can then access the data in the newly incorporated DBMS.

3. QUERY PROCESSING

In the previous section, the overall query processing responsibilities of the GDM and LDI were explained. The objective of this section is to describe how these responsibilities are satisfied by the modules internal to the GDM and LDI.

3.1 Global Data Manager (GDM)

The architecture of the GDM is shown in Figure 3.1. How its components process a query is discussed below.

Transformer: This component takes as input the user's query -- a DAPLEX global query that references the global schema. It produces as output a DAPLEX global query that references DAPLEX local schemata and the auxiliary database schema. This transformation is described in more detail in Section 4.

Optimizer: The Optimizer interacts with several GDM components to perform global optimization. The Optimizer examines the global structure of the query to determine an overall strategy before forwarding the query, or separable pieces of it, to the Decomposer. The Optimizer subsequently refines this strategy, after the output of the Decomposer has been processed by the Filter. In some cases, the Optimizer may request several stages of processing by the Decomposer and Filter. The final output of the Optimizer is a global execution strategy that combines local processing and data movement steps. Global optimization is discussed further in Section 5.2.

Decomposer: The decomposer takes a transformed DAPLEX global query and separates it by local database site, thus producing DAPLEX single-site queries. Parts of the global query that reference the auxiliary database or that combine data across sites are collected into queries to be run by the Internal DBMS.

Filter: The Filter may reduce the decomposed queries by removing from them operations that are not supported by the local host DBMS. It is discussed in the next section.

Monitor: The Monitor oversees the execution of the strategy developed by the Optimizer. It initiates the DAPLEX single-site queries at the appropriate LDIs. It sends to the Internal DBMS a final query that may include references to the auxiliary database and operations that compensate for local system limitations (see Section 3.2), combine the data returned by the LDIs, and format the output as requested by the user.

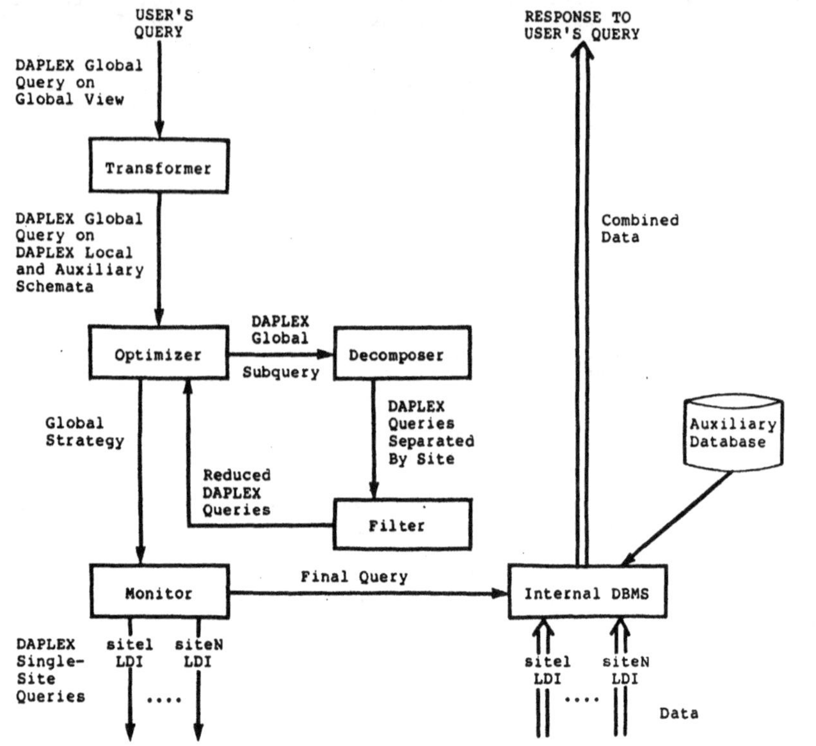

Figure 3.1 GDM Component Architecture

Internal DBMS: This DBMS supports all DAPLEX capabilities. It is used to store the results of the DAPLEX single-site queries and to perform all the required steps of the final query (e.g., combining and formatting the data). The Internal DBMS includes the auxiliary database, which contains information necessary to resolve incompatibilities and inconsistences among data stored at different sites. The use of the auxiliary database is described in Section 4.

3.2 Compensating for Local System Limitations

DAPLEX is a very powerful query language. Many local host systems do not support all the capabilities provided by DAPLEX. For example, many systems do not support arithmetic expressions, and some systems cannot compare two data items. Once the GDM has decomposed the global query into DAPLEX single-site queries, it must insure that each single-site query sent to an LDI can be handled in its entirety by the local host system.

It is the job of the Filter component of the GDM to examine each DAPLEX single-site query to locate operations not supported by the destination host system. The Filter removes all non-supported operations from the DAPLEX single-site query, expands the query to retrieve the additional data that are necessary to perform those operations, and generates an internal query to be run by the Internal DBMS. This internal query uses the data returned by the LDI and performs all operations that were not supported at the local host.

For example, suppose a user posed the query "Which employees in the branch personnel department earn more than $25,000 a year at the branch campus?" and the file system supporting the BRANCH EMPLOYEE database did not support arithmetic expressions. There would be no point in passing the following query to the LDI, since it could not be translated into the query language of the local system:

```
for each E in BRANCH.EMPLOYEE
   where DEPARTMENT(E) = "PERSONNEL"
     and HOURLY-WAGE(E)*HOURS-PER-MONTH(E)*12 > 25000
   print NAME(E);
```

In this example, the Filter would examine the query, determine that the arithmetic expression could not be performed locally, and send a modified query to the LDI requesting that the NAMEs, HOURLY-WAGEs, and HOURS-PER-MONTH for all employees in the personnel department be retrieved. Once the data are sent back to the GDM, the operation involving the arithmetic expression is performed in the Internal DBMS, and only the data requested by the user are presented as the result.

To satisfy MULTIBASE's objectives, the Filter component is description driven. The DBA is provided with a language that allows a local host DBMS to be described in terms of which DAPLEX capabilities it does not support. Thus, no modifications to the GDM software are necessary to incorporate a new local system into MULTIBASE. When incorporating a new DBMS into a MULTIBASE configuration, the description formulated by the DBA tailors the Filter for the capabilities of the new host system.

3.3 Local Database Interface (LDI)

The architecture of an LDI is illustrated in Figure 3.2. How its principal components process a local query is discussed below.

Optimizer: The Optimizer examines the DAPLEX single-site query and determines a local query processing strategy that will rapidly answer the query. If the local DBMS uses a high-level (i.e., set-at-a-time) language such as DAPLEX, query optimization is relatively direct. However, if the local DBMS uses a low-level (i.e., record-at-a-time) language such as CODASYL DML embedded in COBOL, the optimization may be complex. Local optimization is discussed more fully in Section 5.1.

Translator: The translator component provides a uniform interface to all the databases. Two queries that look very similar when expressed in DAPLEX over local schemata may be transformed by the LDIs into dramatically different local queries. For example, consider the university databases whose DAPLEX local schemata were shown in Figure 2.2. A DAPLEX global query asking "Which students

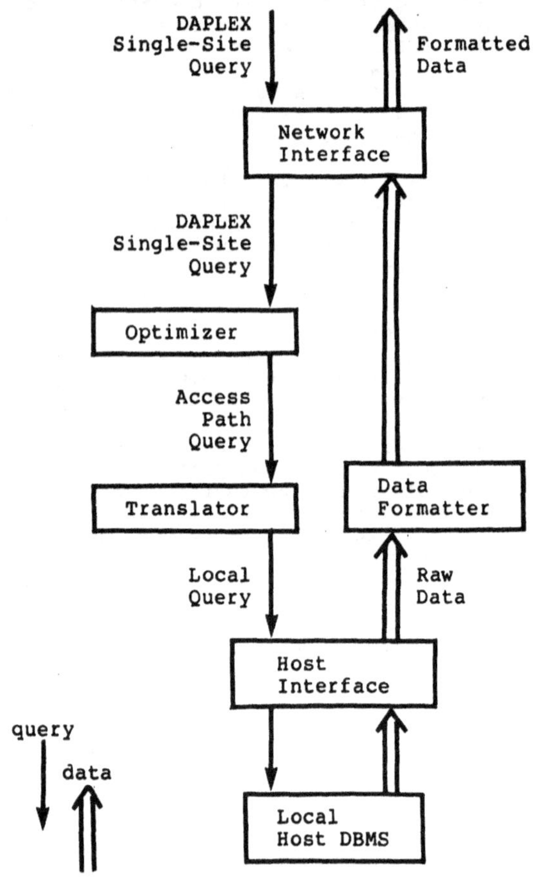

Figure 3.2 Local Database Interface Architecture

are failing at least one course?" would request the same type of data from both the MAIN and BRANCH databases and would look similar when expressed in DAPLEX over both local schemata, as shown in Figure 3.3. The differences in the resulting translations to local queries, shown in Figure 3.4, are striking.

To satisfy the objective of extensibility, the LDIs are designed to be simple processors, not general-purpose DBMSs. Because of this, development of a new LDI takes only 3-6 person months. However, if a local host system provides restricted query capabilities, the system designers may choose to trade a longer LDI development period for a more powerful LDI that compensates for some local limitations. For instance, if a local host system has very limited capabilities, executing a local query at this system might

```
"Which students are failing at least one course?"

          for each S in STUDENT where
            for some E in ENROLLMENTS(S):
               GRADE(E) = "F"
               print NAME(S);

          (a) MAIN Campus Local Schema

          for each S in STUDENT where
            for some E in ENROLLMENT:
               SID(E) = SID(S) AND
               GRADE(E) = "F"
               print NAME(S);

          (b) BRANCH Campus Local Schema
```

Figure 3.3 DAPLEX Single-Site Queries Over DAPLEX Local Schemata

```
OPEN MAIN.
01 FIND FIRST STUDENT RECORD OF STUDENT-SYSTEM SET.
GO TO 03.
02 FIND NEXT STUDENT RECORD OF STUDENT-SYSTEM SET.
03 IF ERROR-STATUS = 326
   OR ERROR-STATUS = 307 GO TO XT.
IF ERROR-STATUS NE 0 GO TO XT.
FIND FIRST ENROLLMENT RECORD OF ENROLLMENTS SET.
GO TO 05.
04 FIND NEXT ENROLLMENT RECORD OF ENROLLMENTS SET.
05 IF ERROR-STATUS = 326
   OR ERROR-STATUS = 307 GO TO 02.
IF ERROR-STATUS NE 0 GO TO XT.
IF GRADE NE "F" GO TO 04.
PRINT NAME.
GO TO 02.

(a) MAIN Campus Implemented with Network Data Model

RANGE OF S IS STUDENT
RANGE OF E IS ENROLLMENT
RETRIEVE (S.NAME) WHERE S.SID = E.SID
                  AND E.GRADE = "F"

(b) BRANCH Campus Implemented with Relational Data Model
```

Figure 3.4 Translations to Local Query Languages

require that large amounts of data be moved to the GDM for further processing. With such a system, a more powerful LDI could eliminate the need for much of this data movement and might be cost effective. In this case, the description written by the DBA (and used by the GDM's Filter) would take into account the combined capabilities of the local host system and the LDI.

4. LOGICAL SCHEMA INTEGRATION

MULTIBASE gives the global user the impression of a single, integrated schema for data distributed across several, independent databases. This logical impression is maintained by the Transformer module of the GDM. This module transforms queries written against the global schema into queries written against the DAPLEX local schemata and the auxiliary schema.

The key idea behind the Transformer is view mapping [2]. View mapping and its application to data integration are described in Section 4.1. While view mapping alone goes a long way towards providing a semantically clean global schema, there are incompatibilities between local databases that it cannot handle. The additional mechanism for handling these cases in MULTIBASE is the auxiliary database. The use of the auxiliary database for handling incompatibliities is discussed in Section 4.2.

4.1 Integration via Views

A global schema or view is a logical description of the underlying databases -- a way of looking at the available data. A view is constructed by MULTIBASE from a view definition and a view derivation. The view definition is a description of the logical data items available to the user, including the entities, functions, and constraints on how the entities in the view may overlap. To the end user, the view or global schema looks exactly like a schema for an integrated database.

Given a view definition and the DAPLEX local schemata, MULTIBASE must be told how data items in the view are related to data items in the local schemata. This is accomplished by a view derivation, which is a set of rules for deriving the view from the underlying databases. These rules are expressed as a DAPLEX query and thus can use all the capabilities provided by the DAPLEX query language. The view derivation is specified once by the DBA and is of no concern to the end user. It incorporates techniques for resolving incompatibilities among the local databases through renaming, restricting, logically restructuring, and generalizing the objects in the underlying databases. Once a view is defined, the user is able to query any of its data objects without regard to the underlying data structures or locations. Since a view is a logical, not physical, description, it can be changed easily and many such views can be defined over the same databases, each tailored for a particular user or application.

A user's query posed over a view is transformed in accordance with the view derivation into a query that references the local schemata. The query over the view definition is mapped into a query over the local schemata by replacing the view objects with the corresponding rules provided in the view derivation, as shown in Figure 4.1.

For example, if we wanted a view of MAIN and BRANCH INSTRUCTORs along with all math COURSEs they teach, we could create the view illustrated in Figure 4.2. The corresponding DAPLEX view definition is shown in Figure 4.3.

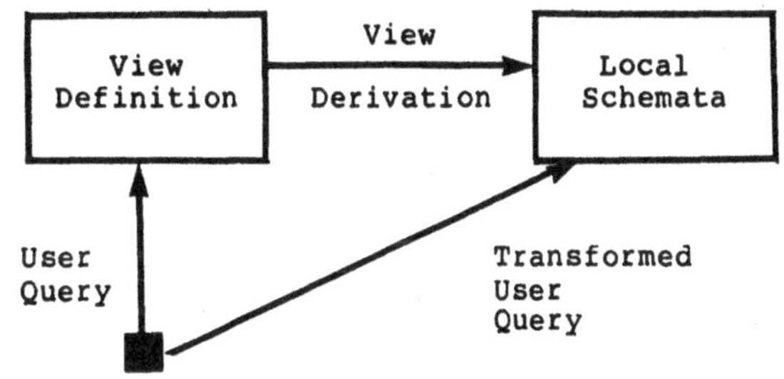

Figure 4.1 Query Transformation

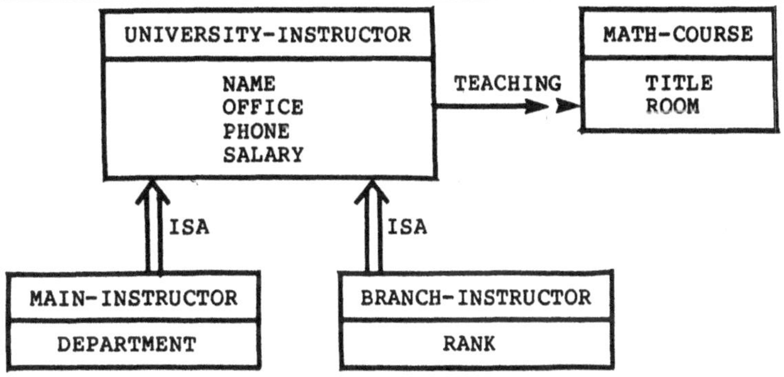

Figure 4.2 A Logical View of University Instructors

In the figures, both entities from the local schemata and their functions are renamed to provide additional semantic information. Only a subset of the available data items are visible to the user of the view. The set of courses is restricted to those from the math department. A general UNIVERSITY-INSTRUCTOR data object is defined to include the data items common to both the MAIN and BRANCH databases (e.g., NAME). Some additional information -- DEPARTMENT and RANK -- that is specific to MAIN and BRANCH INSTRUCTORs, respectively, is also provided in the view. The contain statements declare that all MAIN-INSTRUCTORs are UNIVERSITY-INSTRUCTORs and all BRANCH-INSTRUCTORs are UNIVERSITY-INSTRUCTORs, and thus MAIN- and BRANCH-INSTRUCTORs inherit all data items defined for the generalized UNIVERSITY-INSTRUCTOR object. The share statement declares that MAIN- and BRANCH-INSTRUCTORs can overlap -- an INSTRUCTOR can teach at both the MAIN and BRANCH campuses.

Figure 4.4 shows the view derivations for MAIN-INSTRUCTOR and BRANCH-INSTRUCTOR. These global entities are derived directly from corresponding entities in the local schemata. Figure 4.5 shows the derivation for MATH-COURSE. This global object is a generalization of the MAIN and BRANCH course offerings, restricted to the math

```
type MATH-COURSE is entity
     TITLE : string;
     ROOM : string;
end entity;

type MAIN-INSTRUCTOR is entity
     DEPARTMENT : string;
end entity;

type BRANCH-INSTRUCTOR is entity
     RANK : string;
end entity;

type UNIVERSITY-INSTRUCTOR is entity
     NAME : string;
     OFFICE : string;
     PHONE : string;
     SALARY : float;
     TEACHING : set of MATH-COURSE;
end entity;

contain MAIN-INSTRUCTOR in UNIVERSITY-INSTRUCTOR;
contain BRANCH-INSTRUCTOR in UNIVERSITY-INSTRUCTOR;
share MAIN-INSTRUCTOR with BRANCH-INSTRUCTOR;
```

Figure 4.3 DAPLEX View Definition

department. The derivation for the remaining global entity, UNIVERSITY-INSTRUCTOR, is discussed in the next section.

```
derive MAIN-INSTRUCTOR from
   for each I in MAIN.INSTRUCTOR
      define MAIN-INSTRUCTOR to be
         (DEPARTMENT --> DEPARTMENT(I));
   end loop;
end derive;

derive BRANCH-INSTRUCTOR from
   for each I in BRANCH.INSTRUCTOR
      define BRANCH-INSTRUCTOR to be
         (RANK --> RANK(I));
   end loop;
end derive;
```

Figure 4.4 View Derivation for MAIN and BRANCH INSTRUCTORs

In addition to regular DAPLEX constructs, five key statements are used in specifying the derivation rules: derive, define, case, becomes, and equivalence. These statements are discussed below.

The derive statements introduce a DAPLEX query that describes how to produce the desired view of the data from underlying data objects. The define statements provide DAPLEX expressions that will be substituted for references to data objects in the view definition. The becomes statements in Figure 4.5 define convenient, shorthand references for general DAPLEX expressions, in this case

```
MAIN-MATH becomes (C1 in MAIN.COURSE
          where DEPARTMENT(C1)="MATH");
BRANCH-MATH becomes (C2 in BRANCH.COURSE-OFFERING
          where DEPARTMENT (the(C3 in BRANCH.COURSE
             where CID(C2)=CID(C3)))="MATH");

derive MATH-COURSE from
   for each C in MAIN-MATH + BRANCH-MATH
      case C is
         when MAIN-MATH -->
            define MATH-COURSE to be
               (TITLE --> TITLE(C),
                ROOM  --> ROOM(C));
         when BRANCH-MATH -->
            define MATH-COURSE to be
               (TITLE --> TITLE(the(BC in BRANCH.COURSE
                              where CID(BC)=CID(C))),
                ROOM  --> ROOM(C));
      end case;
   end loop;
end derive;
```

Figure 4.5 View Derivation for MATH-COURSE

for a set of COURSEs in the MAIN database and COURSE-OFFERINGs in the BRANCH database, both restricted to the math department. The *the* operator is used to convert a reference to a singleton set into a reference to the entity contained in that set. The plus sign ("+") in Figure 4.5 is a set union operator. Thus, the *derive* statement declares that for each course in MAIN-MATH and each course in BRANCH-MATH, a MATH-COURSE in the view is defined. The *case* statement provides for conditional definitions based on where the data originate. The *define* statements assert that for courses from the MAIN database, a reference to TITLE and ROOM in the view is to be interpreted as a reference to data items of the same names in the underlying database. For courses from the BRANCH database, a reference to TITLE in the view is to be interpreted as a reference to the TITLE in the COURSE relation where the identifier matches the course identifier for this COURSE-OFFERING.

Figures 4.6 and 4.7 illustrate how MULTIBASE uses these view derivations to transform a DAPLEX query over the view. The DAPLEX equivalent of the question "What are the names and ranks of all branch instructors?" is shown in Figure 4.6(a). The transformation of this DAPLEX query onto local structures is shown in Figure 4.6(b). In this case, the global and transformed DAPLEX queries are almost identical.

Figure 4.7 illustrates global and transformed DAPLEX queries requesting titles and rooms of all math course offerings. The transformation process yields two queries, corresponding to the two alternatives provided in the *case* statement; one query is to be executed against the MAIN database and the other against the BRANCH database. The expressions provided in the *becomes* statements are substituted into the queries for references to MAIN-MATH and BRANCH-MATH. The derivation for TITLEs of BRANCH-MATH courses is used, yielding a reference to TITLE as found in the BRANCH.COURSE relation. In this case, the global and transformed queries are quite different.

```
for each I in BRANCH-INSTRUCTOR
   print (NAME(I), RANK(I));
end loop;

(a) DAPLEX over View


for each I in BRANCH.INSTRUCTOR
   print (NAME(I), RANK(I));
end loop;

(b) DAPLEX Transformed onto
    Local Structures
```

Figure 4.6 "What are the names and ranks of the branch instructors?"

```
for each MC in MATH-COURSE
   print (TITLE(MC), ROOM(MC));
end loop;

(a) DAPLEX over View


for each MC in MAIN.COURSE where DEPARTMENT(MC)="MATH"
   print (TITLE(MC), ROOM(MC));
end loop;

for each MC in BRANCH.COURSE-OFFERING
   where DEPARTMENT(the(C3 in BRANCH.COURSE
                    where CID(MC)=CID(C3)))="MATH"
   print (TITLE(the(BC in BRANCH.COURSE
                    where CID(BC)=CID(MC))),
          ROOM(MC));
end loop;

(b) DAPLEX Transformed onto Local Structures
```

Figure 4.7 "Print the titles and rooms for all math course offerings."

4.2 Handling Data Incompatibilities

The objective in handling data incompatibilities is to reconcile differences that arise when separately developed and maintained databases are accessed conjointly. Incompatibilities include differences in naming conventions, underlying data structures, representations, or scales; missing data; and conflicting data values. The DBA must apply knowledge of the underlying databases to determine what incompatibilities might arise. The DBA must further decide what rules should be used to reconcile these incompatibilities. These rules can be described to MULTIBASE, after which they will be followed automatically in generating the answers to users' queries.

The view mechanism is a natural vehicle for handling many incompatibilities through renaming and logical restructuring. Since the view derivation can include arithmetic expressions, it can perform automatic scale conversion. For example, YEARLY-SALARY is stored in the MAIN EMPLOYEE database while HOURLY-WAGE and HOURS-PER-MONTH are stored in the BRANCH EMPLOYEE database. Although similar information is available in both databases, they cannot be compared directly. The global schema must present one consistent salary value; in our example, the global schema presents annual salary. The view derivation must include a formula for calculating the annual salary for BRANCH INSTRUCTORs from the available data.

Although the view mechanism as described above is a powerful tool, a fixed formula in the view derivation is not always sufficient to reconcile incompatibilities. In some cases, additional data, which may vary over time, is also required. To handle this additional data for incompatibility reconciliation, MULTIBASE provides the auxiliary database. The auxiliary database is maintained in the GDM's Internal DBMS. It is created by the DBA and can contain any data that are useful, given the application and the available databases. The auxiliary database can contain new data that are not available in any of the underlying databases, statistics that are used to determine which data values should be used in case of a conflict, and conversion tables that provide a means of performing data transformations that cannot be done using simple formulas.

For example, the MAIN INSTRUCTOR database provides the INSTRUCTOR's OFFICE while the BRANCH INSTRUCTOR database provides PHONE. To provide both the PHONE and OFFICE, as in our example, the global view must contend with missing values. Since the MAIN and BRANCH INSTRUCTORs do not totally overlap, some OFFICEs do not have corresponding PHONEs and vice versa. Figure 4.8 is a simple auxiliary database schema for this example. This auxiliary database contains the missing locations and phones.

```
type OFFICES is entity
     OFFICE-LOCATION : string;
     OFFICE-PHONE : string;
end entity;
```

Figure 4.8 DAPLEX Auxiliary Database Schema

Given the auxiliary database defined above, the view derivation would reference not only the local DAPLEX schemata but also the auxiliary schema. For example, Figures 4.9 and 4.10 are the full view derivation for the generalized UNIVERSITY-INSTRUCTOR. The equivalence statement (==) defines when an INSTRUCTOR from the MAIN database is equivalent to an INSTRUCTOR from the BRANCH database. The derive statement declares that for each object in MAIN-INSTRUCTOR and BRANCH-INSTRUCTOR, a generalized UNIVERSITY-INSTRUCTOR is defined. The case statement enumerates the three possible INSTRUCTOR partitions, described below. Each partition is defined using the set operators of union ("+"), difference ("-"), and intersection ("*").

```
MI in MAIN-INSTRUCTOR == BI in BRANCH-INSTRUCTOR
   when NAME(MI) = NAME(BI);

derive UNIVERSITY-INSTRUCTOR from
   for each I in MAIN-INSTRUCTOR + BRANCH-INSTRUCTOR
      case I is
         when MAIN-INSTRUCTOR - BRANCH-INSTRUCTOR -->
            define UNIVERSITY-INSTRUCTOR to be
                  (NAME-->NAME(I),
                   OFFICE-->OFFICE(I),
                   PHONE-->OFFICE-PHONE(the(O in OFFICES
                           where OFFICE(I)=
                                 OFFICE-LOCATION(O))),
                   SALARY-->YEARLY-SALARY(the
                            (E in MAIN.EMPLOYEE where
                            NAME(E)=NAME(I))),
                   TEACHING-->MATH-COURSE(TEACHING(I)));

         when BRANCH-INSTRUCTOR - MAIN-INSTRUCTOR -->
            define UNIVERSITY-INSTRUCTOR to be
                  (NAME-->NAME(I),
                   OFFICE-->OFFICE-LOCATION(the
                            (O in OFFICES where
                             OFFICE-PHONE(O)=PHONE(I))),
                   PHONE-->PHONE(I),
                   SALARY-->HOURLY-WAGE(the
                            (E in BRANCH.EMPLOYEE where
                            NAME(E)=NAME(I)))
                          * HOURS-PER-MONTH(the
                            (E in BRANCH.EMPLOYEE where
                            NAME(E)=NAME(I)))
                          *12,
                   TEACHING-->MATH-COURSE(C in
                              BRANCH.COURSE-OFFERING
                              where IID(C)=IID(I)));
```

Figure 4.9 View Derivation for UNIVERSITY-INSTRUCTOR (continued on Figure 4.10)

For those INSTRUCTORs found only in the MAIN database, NAME and OFFICE are directly defined. PHONE is obtained from the OFFICE-PHONE in the auxiliary database, where the corresponding OFFICE-LOCATION matches the MAIN-INSTRUCTOR's OFFICE. SALARY is obtained from the INSTRUCTOR's entry in the MAIN EMPLOYEE database. The set of MATH-COURSEs taught by this INSTRUCTOR is obtained by taking the set of all courses taught by the INSTRUCTOR and applying the view derivation for MATH-COURSE to yield the restricted set of math courses.

For those INSTRUCTORs found only in the BRANCH database, NAME and PHONE are directly defined. OFFICE is obtained from OFFICE-LOCATION in the auxiliary database. SALARY is computed using the HOURLY-WAGE and HOURS-PER-MONTH values found in the BRANCH EMPLOYEE database. The set of MATH-COURSEs taught by the INSTRUCTOR is obtained by taking the set of BRANCH COURSE-OFFERINGs taught by the INSTRUCTOR and applying the view derivation for MATH-COURSE.

```
            when MAIN-INSTRUCTOR * BRANCH-INSTRUCTOR -->
               define UNIVERSITY-INSTRUCTOR to be
                      (NAME-->NAME(I),
                       OFFICE-->OFFICE(I),
                       PHONE-->PHONE(I),
                       SALARY-->YEARLY-SALARY
                                (the(ME in MAIN.EMPLOYEE
                                where NAME(ME)=NAME(I)))
                                + (HOURLY-WAGE(the
                                  (BE in BRANCH.EMPLOYEE
                                  where NAME(BE)=NAME(I)))
                                * HOURS-PER-MONTH(the
                                  (BE in BRANCH.EMPLOYEE
                                  where NAME(BE)=NAME(I)))
                                *12 ),
                       TEACHING-->MATH-COURSE(TEACHING(I))
                                + MATH-COURSE(C in
                                  BRANCH.COURSE-OFFERING
                                  where IID(C)=IID(I)));
         end case;
      end loop;
   end derive;
```

Figure 4.10 View Derivation for UNIVERSITY-INSTRUCTOR (continued from Figure 4.9)

For those INSTRUCTORs found in both the MAIN and BRANCH databases, NAME, OFFICE, and PHONE are directly available in one local database or the other. SALARY is computed as the sum of the two annual salaries. The set of MATH-COURSEs is the union of the courses taught at the MAIN and BRANCH campuses.

Given this complete view definition and derivation, MULTIBASE will automatically resolve incompatibilities with every query. Our original query -- "Which instructors teach math courses both at the main and at the branch campuses and earn more than $25,000 a year?" -- can now be phrased easily and concisely over the global view, as illustrated in Figure 4.11. Figure 4.12 shows the same query after it has been transformed by view mapping onto the local structures and the result has been simplified. A direct transformation would yield three queries, one for each of the INSTRUCTOR partitions provided for in the <u>case</u> statement. Combining the DAPLEX expression (I isin MAIN-INSTRUCTOR and I isin BRANCH-INSTRUCTOR) with the definitions of the INSTRUCTOR partitions shows that two of the three queries would never produce any query results (e.g., there is no INSTRUCTOR such that (I isin MAIN-INSTRUCTOR and I isin BRANCH-INSTRUCTOR and I isin (MAIN-INSTRUCTOR - BRANCH-INSTRUCTOR))). The simplification performed here is the recognition that two of the three queries would never produce any results and the elimination of these two queries from further processing. Rules for simplification are built into the Transformer module of the GDM. The complexity of the transformed query clearly illustrates the advantages of having MULTIBASE assume the burden of reconciling incompatibilities.

Further details on view definition, derivation, and transformation techniques can be found in [3] and [4].

```
for each I in UNIVERSITY-INSTRUCTOR
   where I isin MAIN-INSTRUCTOR
      and I isin BRANCH-INSTRUCTOR
      and SALARY(I) > 25000
   print NAME(I);
end loop;
```

"Which instructors teach math courses both at the main and at the branch campuses and earn more than $25,000 a year?"

Figure 4.11 DAPLEX Query Expressed over View

```
for each MI in MAIN.INSTRUCTOR
  for each BI in BRANCH.INSTRUCTOR
      where NAME(MI)=NAME(BI)
      and YEARLY-SALARY(the(ME in MAIN.EMPLOYEE
                          where NAME(ME)=NAME(MI)))
        + (HOURLY-WAGE(the(BE in BRANCH.EMPLOYEE
                         where NAME(BE)=NAME(BI)))
           * HOURS-PER-MONTH(the(BE in BRANCH.EMPLOYEE
                               where NAME(BE)=NAME(BI)))
           * 12)
          > 25000
    print NAME(MI);
 end loop;
```

Figure 4.12 DAPLEX Transformed onto Local Structures

5. QUERY OPTIMIZATION

Query optimization in a distributed database environment -- particularly a heterogeneous one -- is a complex problem. However, it is important to solve this problem, since solutions can dramatically decrease query response time. The principal cost factors are communications delay in moving partial results between sites and local processing times, which may vary widely from system to system. Typically there are many different query processing strategies that will answer a given query.

MULTIBASE performs query optimization at two levels: global and local. Local optimization deals with minimizing the time to retrieve data from a local DBMS. Local query optimization is discussed in Section 5.1. Global optimization deals with fully utilizing the potential for parallel processing in a distributed system and minimizing communication costs by reducing the amount of data moved between sites. Global query optimization is discussed in Section 5.2.

5.1 Local Optimization Techniques

As mentioned before, each site's LDI translates a DAPLEX single-site query into an equivalent program over the local host schema in the query language of the local host DBMS. The objective of local optimization is to produce programs that minimize processing time. The method of obtaining this objective depends on the nature of the local query language, the physical database organization, and the access paths supported by the DBMS.

An access path is a storage structure that facilitates rapid access to selected data in the database; e.g., hash keys, indices, and pointers. MULTIBASE must interface with a wide variety of DBMSs, some with procedural, navigational DMLs (e.g., IMS and CODASYL), others with high-level query languages (e.g., DAPLEX LDM and relational systems such as INGRES and System R). Because these systems differ substantively in the level of direct control over access path selection that they give to programmers, the LDIs must do different amounts of optimization when dealing with them.

High-level query language systems do access path selection themselves, given a physical database organization. Such systems are equipped with query optimizers whose aim is to produce inexpensive strategies for processing high-level queries [5, 6, 7, 8, 9, 10]. For these "self-optimized" systems, MULTIBASE assumes that no optimization is necessary in the LDI; the LDI merely translates the DAPLEX single-site query into a local query.

Navigational systems require the programmer to specify an appropriate route through the database for processing a query. With navigational systems, the LDI usually has a choice of programs for implementing a given query. Each program consists of a sequence of access path traversals. The cost of a program (i.e., the time required to execute it) is typically a function of which access paths it uses and the sequence in which these access paths are traversed.

The first problem in implementing a local query optimizer is identifying the class of DAPLEX single-site queries that can be effectively optimized at the LDI. There is a trade-off between the amount of work done by the GDM and the software complexity of the LDI. At one extreme, the GDM could decompose the global query into the largest possible DAPLEX single-site subqueries. This scheme would probably reduce the volume of data sent back from the local sites to the GDM, since the data would be restricted by more conditions in the qualification. It would also require less post-processing by the GDM to construct the final answer. However, the more complex the queries sent to the LDI, the more sophisticated the LDI has to be to generate efficient programs for these queries. A practical constraint in MULTIBASE is that the LDI does not have the services of a full-fledged DBMS to manage its local workspace. Thus, for instance, it cannot sort a file, eliminate duplicates, or merge two files. Therefore, it is imperative to keep LDI processing simple.

The other extreme of global query decomposition -- decomposing the global query into the smallest possible units (e.g., one-variable selection queries) for processing at the local databases -- is equally unacceptable. Not only would the communications volume be prohibitive, but the physical access paths available in the local database would not be exploited.

MULTIBASE embodies a compromise solution: the class of DAPLEX single-site queries for which an LDI can generate efficient programs is the class of queries such that no two variables in the DAPLEX single-site query range over the same entity type. (For a detailed definition of these queries, see [11] and [12]). All DAPLEX single-site queries are decomposed by the Filter at the GDM into one or more queries that fall into this class. The GDM sends the resulting queries to the LDI for optimization and processing. The optimizer may further decompose each of these queries into effectively optimizable components by removing all value-based join expressions. Each component is then the unit of optimization. By accepting a larger class of queries at the LDI and optimizing components of each of these queries, the optimizer's task is simplified and, at the same time, the amount of data returned and the amount of work performed by the GDM are reduced.

After receiving a query from the GDM, the LDI optimizer proceeds as follows:

1. Decompose the DAPLEX query into effectively optimizable components
2. Identify the potential strategies for processing each component
3. Compute the cost of executing each strategy for each component
4. Find the minimum-cost strategy for each component
5. Merge the minimum-cost strategies for the components to obtain a strategy for the query
6. Construct a program that implements this strategy

To decompose a DAPLEX single-site query into effectively optimizable components, the optimizer first constructs a graph representation of the query such that (1) each node of the graph corresponds to an entity type referenced in the query and (2) each value-based join expression and each reference to a function that returns another entity as its value constitutes an arc. For example, Figure 5.1 uses the DAPLEX MAIN campus local schema (from Figure 2.2) and shows the DAPLEX single-site query for "Print the names of all students with the titles of all courses that they are failing which are in their major and taught by their advisor." Figure 5.2 illustrates the resulting query graph.

```
      for each S in STUDENT
       for each E in ENROLLMENTS(S) where GRADE(E) = 'F'
         for each I in INSTRUCTOR where ADVISOR(S) = NAME(I)
           for each C in TEACHING(I)
             where MAJOR(S) = DEPARTMENT(C) and
                   TITLE(C) = TITLE(E)
             print NAME(S), TITLE(E);
"Print the names of all students with the titles of all courses
that they are failing which are in their major and taught by
their advisor."
```

Figure 5.1 DAPLEX Single-Site Query over Local Schema

After the query graph is constructed, it is augmented to indicate any additional access paths that are available. The arcs that represent value-based join expressions are pulled off, resulting in one or more optimizable components. Figure 5.3 shows the resulting access path graphs for the example query of Figure 5.1.

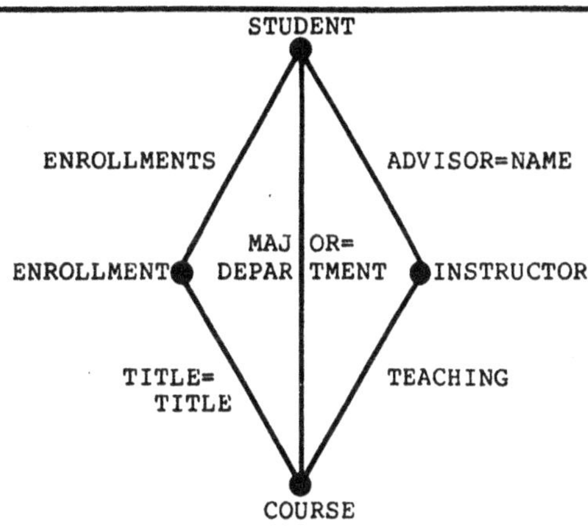

Figure 5.2 Query Graph

The second task of the local optimizer is to identify the potential strategies for processing each component. A strategy consists of an entry point, which assigns the direction of access path traversal, and the order in which the access paths will be traversed. In the example of Figure 5.3, both graphs have two potential strategies. The first graph can use as an entry point either the system pointers or the hash key access path on GRADE. In either case, once the entry point is selected, the direction of traversing the ENROLLMENTS access path, from an ENROLLMENT to a STUDENT or from a STUDENT to many ENROLLMENTs, becomes fixed. In a more complex example -- one containing additional access paths from STUDENT and ENROLLMENT to other entity types -- the order of traversal also would become a factor in selecting strategies.

The access path optimizer uses a cost model to compute the costs of implementing a selected strategy for each query component. Three factors contribute to the cost of a query processing strategy. The first factor is the cost of executing the program that implements the strategy; i.e., local host processing. This cost is determined by the number of disk pages accessed during the execution of the program. The second factor is the cost of shipping the resulting file(s) constructed by the program. This cost is determined by the total size of the file(s). The third factor is the cost of post-processing by the GDM. The least-expensive strategy for processing each component of the query is selected. Local query optimization concludes by merging all the least-expensive component strategies, including the value-based join expressions, and constructing a program that implements the final query strategy.

Full details of local query optimization techniques, including the cost model formulas, can be found in [11] and [12].

In keeping with the design objective of generality, the optimizer has been developed to use parameters provided by descriptions written by the DBA. These parameters include available access paths (e.g. hash fields, indices, sorted order, and pointers -- parent-

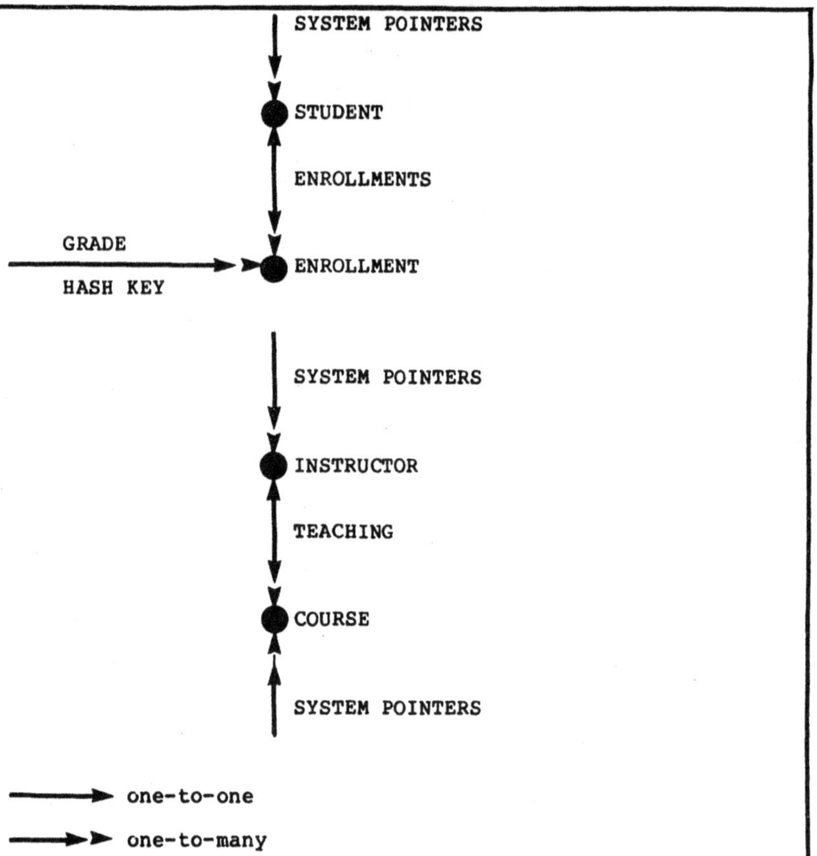

Figure 5.3 Access Path Graphs

to-child, child-to-parent, and sibling-to-sibling), cardinality, connectivity, selectivity, size, and physical clustering. The parameters of the cost model and the formulas for cost estimation are general enough that one implementation of the local query optimizer can be used with most navigational access systems.

5.2 Global Optimization Techniques

Perhaps the most straightforward strategy for processing a global query that references data at more than one site is to decompose the global query into a set of disjoint local queries and move the data from each local site to the GDM's Internal DBMS, where the data can be combined and further restricted as necessary. The major drawback of this approach is that the cost of communications and system resources might be very high, since the amount of data moved might be very large.

A large part of MULTIBASE's global query optimization strategy is based on the data reduction and data movement techniques used in SDD-1 (System for Distributed Databases) [13, 14]. That strategy has been augmented with additional techniques designed to handle generalized objects and partially overlapping data. Since different operations might have to be performed (and thus different data retrieved) based on the sites at which an entity is found, the SDD-1 data movement strategies have been extended with ones that handle entity partitions (such as those provided in the case statement of a view derivation) by exchanging entity identifiers before shipping large volumes of data values.

For example, using the MAIN and BRANCH campus databases, if we had a query that referenced only INSTRUCTORs who taught at both the MAIN and BRANCH campus, we would be interested only in the entity partition equivalent to the intersection of the INSTRUCTOR entities at both databases. Several strategies could be used to solve the query: (1) all data needed from both databases could be shipped to the GDM, where the intersection would be formed; (2) a complete list of INSTRUCTOR identifiers could be exchanged by the MAIN and BRANCH sites, with each performing a local intersection and shipping to the GDM only the data needed; or (3) identifiers could be shipped from one site to the other; in parallel, the sending site could forward to the GDM all data needed, as if all INSTRUCTORS were included in the intersection; and the site receiving the identifiers would perform a local intersection, forwarding to the GDM exactly the data needed.

This extension of the data movement strategies developed for global optimization in homogeneous distributed DBMSs (such as SDD-1) solves only some of the new issues found in a heterogeneous environment. This heterogeneity introduces three additional factors that must be taken into consideration when seeking an optimal strategy.

The first factor is that the costs of performing a local query may differ greatly from site to site and must be incorporated in the overall cost of any strategy. In particular, since the auxiliary database is stored locally to the GDM, restricting data at a foreign site based on data in the auxiliary database will often result in less data movement and thus a large cost savings, while the opposite is seldom true.

The second factor is that the ability to receive and reference "moved" data may vary widely from site to site. Many DBMSs do not support the creation and loading of temporary databases. Some systems provide for reading in data one record at a time from an external disc file, while others do not. If the DBMS does not support either temporary databases or reading in data from an external file, data cannot be moved directly to effect a data reduction. If the amount of data that would be moved is small, a query modification technique can be employed. For example, consider a query that contains a join expression across sites; e.g., SITE1.F1 = SITE2.F1, where the number of data values for SITE2.F1 is small. A query can be run first at SITE2 to retrieve the data values for SITE2.F1. After being modified, the query sent to SITE1 would read as follows: SITE1.F1 = constant-value1 or SITE1.F1 = constant-value2....

The third factor is local query capabilities, as described in Section 3.2. Some global optimization strategies might have to be rejected due to limitations of the local system; i.e., even if the data were already local, the operations required to effect data reduction might not be supported locally. Full details of global query optimization techniques, including the cost model formulas, can be found in [15]

Again, in keeping with the design objective of generality, the global query optimizer has been designed to operate based on a set of parameters provided by descriptions that include overhead for local query execution, ability to create temporary databases, and ability to reference external files.

6. SUMMARY

This paper has presented an overview of the prototype MULTIBASE system, which provides access to heterogeneous distributed databases. MULTIBASE has been designed to be a general, easily extendable system, relying heavily on descriptions to tailor configurations for specific applications. MULTIBASE provides facilities for:

1. Uniform query access to dissimilar DBMSs
2. Logical schema integration
3. Data incompatibility handling
4. Local query optimization
5. Global query optimization

MULTIBASE is more than halfway through a four-year effort. In the effort to date, the research investigation has been completed and a breadboard version of MULTIBASE has been designed and implemented. This breadboard provides uniform query access, logical schema integration for non-overlapping data, techniques for handling incompatible data, and a local query optimizer. The breadboard demonstration system provides integrated access to two disjoint ship databases, one a CODASYL database and the other a hierarchical database.

In the remaining time, a prototype version of MULTIBASE will be designed and implemented. This version will be robust enough for standalone test and evaluation experiments in various applications. The implementation language will be ADA* and so the system is expected to be portable. A great deal has been learned from experience with the construction and operation of the breadboard version, and substantial design changes are being incorporated into the prototype version.

---

*ADA is a registered trademark of the ADA Joint Program Office -- U.S. Government.

7. ACKNOWLEDGEMENTS

The authors wish to express their appreciation to the following people who have contributed to the work reported in this paper: Philip Bernstein, Umesh Dayal, Nathan Goodman, Randy Katz, Ken Lin, Kenneth Olson, James Rothnie, Dave Shipman, Diane Smith, John M. Smith, Eugene Wong, and Laura Yedwab. The principal researchers on the MULTIBASE project were Umesh Dayal, Nathan Goodman, and Randy Katz. Kenneth Olson and Laura Yedwab contributed substantially to the implementation.

The authors also wish to thank Deborah Edmiston for her assistance with the original organization of this paper and John Smith for his assistance with editing the paper.

8. REFERENCES

[1] Shipman, David, The Functional Data Model and the Data Language DAPLEX, ACM Transactions on Database Systems, 6, 1 (March 1981) 140-173.

[2] Stonebraker, Michael, Implementation of Views and Integrity Constraints by Query Modification, Proceedings ACM SIGMOD Conference (1975).

[3] Katz, Randy; et al., Database Integration and Incompatible Data Handling in MULTIBASE -- A System for Integrating Heterogeneous Distributed Databases, Technical Report CCA-81-06, Computer Corporation of America (28 May 1981).

[4] Dayal, Umesh; and Hwang, H.-Y., View Definition and Generalization for Database Integration in MULTIBASE -- A System for Heterogeneous Distributed Databases, Proceedings Berkeley Workshop on Distributed Data Management and Computer Networks (1982).

[5] Wong, Eugene and Youssefi, K., Decomposition -- A Strategy for Query Processing, ACM Transactions on Database Systems, 1, 3 (September 1976) 223-241.

[6] Youssefi, K. and Wong, Eugene, Query Processing in a Relational Database Management System, Proceedings Very Large Databases Conference (1979) 409-417.

[7] Selinger, P.G.; et al., Access Path Selection in a Relational Database Management System, Proceedings ACM-SIGMOD International Conference on Management of Data (May 1979) 23-34.

[8] Stonebraker, Michael; et al., The Design and Implementation of INGRES, ACM Transactions on Database Systems, 1, 3 (September 1976) 189-222.

Design Considerations for Shared Integrated Database Systems (SIDS)[1]

Wesley W. Chu
University of California, Los Angeles

J. Patrick Haverty
System Development Corporation

ABSTRACT A shared integrated database system (SIDS) consists of an integrated database (IDB) interconnected with a set of workstations that contain fragments of the IDB. Thus, a SIDS is a special class of a distributed database system. This paper presents three types of SIDS configurations: non-partitioned SIDS, partitioned SIDS, and replicated partitioned SIDS. Some of the key SIDS protocol design issues for presentation and application layers of the open system interconnection model are discussed. A special SIDS example is also given.

1. Introduction

With the advent of low cost computer communication and VLSI technology, it has become common to connect many remotely located terminals and computers via a communication network. Such interconnected systems provide the capability for sharing computing resources such as databases. Sharing databases provides numerous advantages. However, the integration of several individual databases into a shared database raises many design issues including file distribution, directory design, concurrency control, deadlock management, fault recovery, data translation, and interface design.

A shared integrated database system (SIDS) consists of an integrated database (IDB) interconnected with a set of workstations that contain fragments of the IDB. The IDB is the union of all the local databases of the workstations. Through the IDB, each user at a workstation is able to share and update the IDB. Therefore, a SIDS is a special class of distributed database system. With the explosive growth in the use and availability of personal computers, workstations, and local area networks, many SIDS will be designed and implemented in the future.

This paper will first describe the architectures of three SIDS classes, then present the SIDS protocol design issues, and finally describe a special SIDS in which workstations do not initiate updates.

2. Shared Integrated Database System Configurations

A shared integrated database system can be classified into three types: non-partitioned, partitioned, and replicated partitioned. These are described below.

2.1. Non-Partitioned Integrated Database System. This system consists of a non-partitioned shared integrated database (IDB)

[1]This research is supported in part by the NSF contract number IST80-02671.

and multiple workstations with their own local databases as shown in figure 1. There is a dictionary at each workstation which describes the data schemes, formats, data ranges, security, file access rights, integrity constraints, and concurrency information. The dictionary also contains such physical characteristics as size, keys, default values, display format, etc. There is a directory at the IDB site which combines all the dictionary information from all the workstations and the current status of the shared files. File updates made on the local databases by the user at the workstation are periodically forwarded to the IDB. In turn, the IDB updates the local databases of the relevant workstations.

Should a requested data item not reside at the local database, it is transferred from the IDB to the requesting site (provided there is enough storage space available). Should the requested data exceed the workstation storage capacity, then the user communicates with the IDB to transfer only the relevant data (e.g., a subrelation) for his application.

The protocol diagrams for data transfer and file update for a nonpartitioned SIDS are shown in figures 2 and 3 respectively.

2.2 Partitioned Shared Integrated Database System. The non-partitioned SIDS is simple to implement, but it suffers from (1) long response times for IDB accesses; and (2) the single point failure of the IDB. To remedy this, the IDB may be partitioned and stored on several computers (see figure 4). This allows processing transactions in parallel to improve response time. Also, instead of a single large computer, several small computers can be used to manage the large integrated database. Furthermore, such a system does not have a single point failure, thereby permitting graceful degradation. However, such flexibility results in the following design complexities.

1. Database partitioning and file allocation [7, 5, 18, 20] affect system performance and optimal allocation is highly dependent on the operating environment and applications.
2. Directory management is more complex for the partitioned SIDS since a transaction may involve several partitioned IDBs, thereby requiring coordination overhead. Furthermore, the directory of the partitioned IDB may be partially replicated. Therefore, to

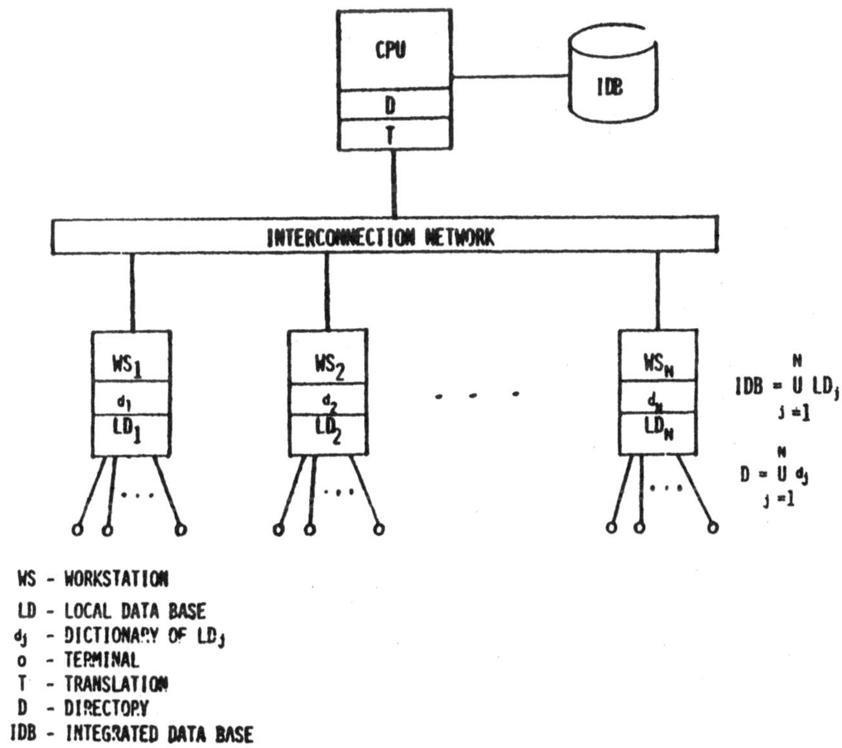

Figure 1. Non-partitioned shared integrated database system.

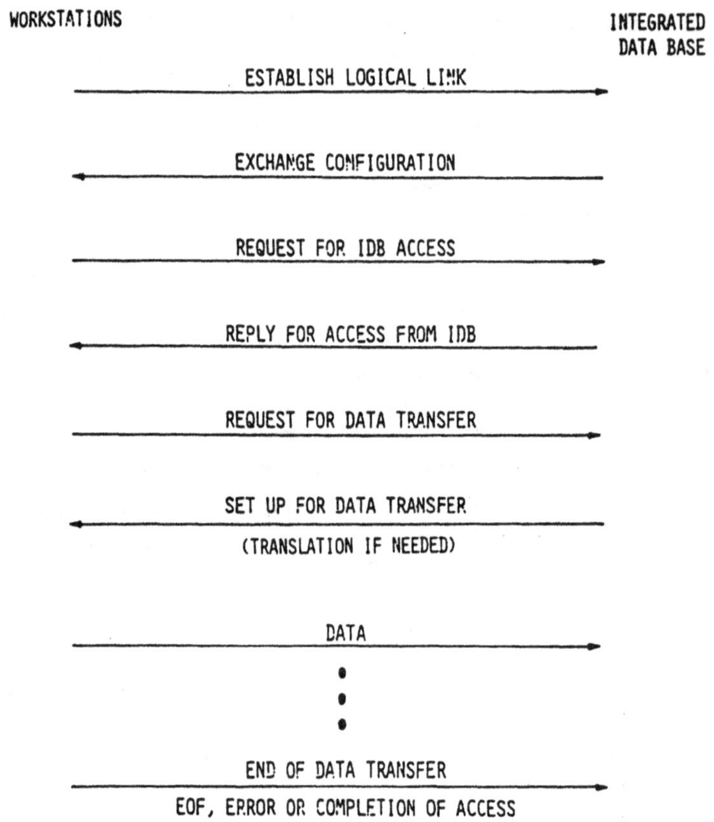

Figure 2. Protocol Diagram for Data Transfer in a Non-Partitioned SIDS.

ensure consistent directory update, concurrency control (locking, timestamps) is needed for directory updates.

3. IDB updates are more complex in the partitioned SIDS since updating the local database of the workstation may involve updating several partitioned IDBs.

4. Deadlock management in the partitioned SIDS requires coordination among the partitioned IDB sites which increases overhead.

5. In a partitioned SIDS, processing a transaction may require retrieving and updating data from several partitioned IDB computers. Thus, a query analyzer is needed to decide the location as well as the sequence for query processing [29, 15, 11, 5]. Query optimization is further complicated by its dependence on data base partitioning and allocation.

6. The fault recovery procedure for the partitioned SIDS is more complex than for the non-partitioned SIDS, because the failure of one site can affect files at other sites [2]. Ensuring data consistency when the network is partitioned (due to malfunction) is a rather complex problem [22].

2.3 Replicated Partitioned Integrated Database System. This system is similar to the partitioned SIDS except that file copies and their directories are replicated to improve availability and to reduce read response time (see figure 5). However, multiple file copies and directories require concurrency control and, hence, complicate data management. Furthermore, the recovery strategy of replicated copies of files is more complicated than that of the non-replicated partitioned SIDS.

2.4. Homogeneous and Heterogenous SIDS. The SIDS could be homogeneous or heterogeneous. In a homogeneous system, all workstations are identical, and they use the same syntax (e.g., same file structures and data

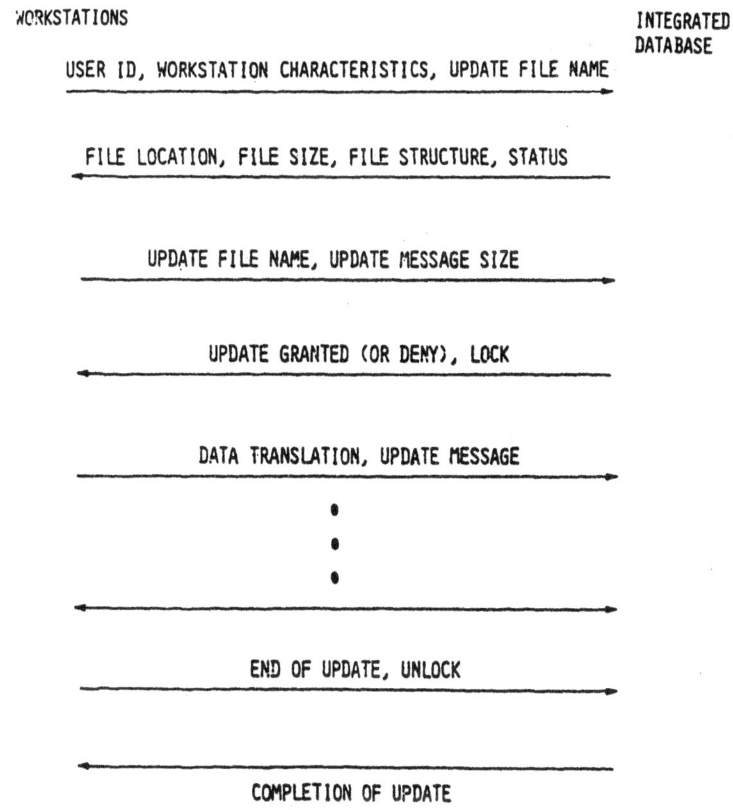

Figure 3. File Update in a Shared Integrated Database System.

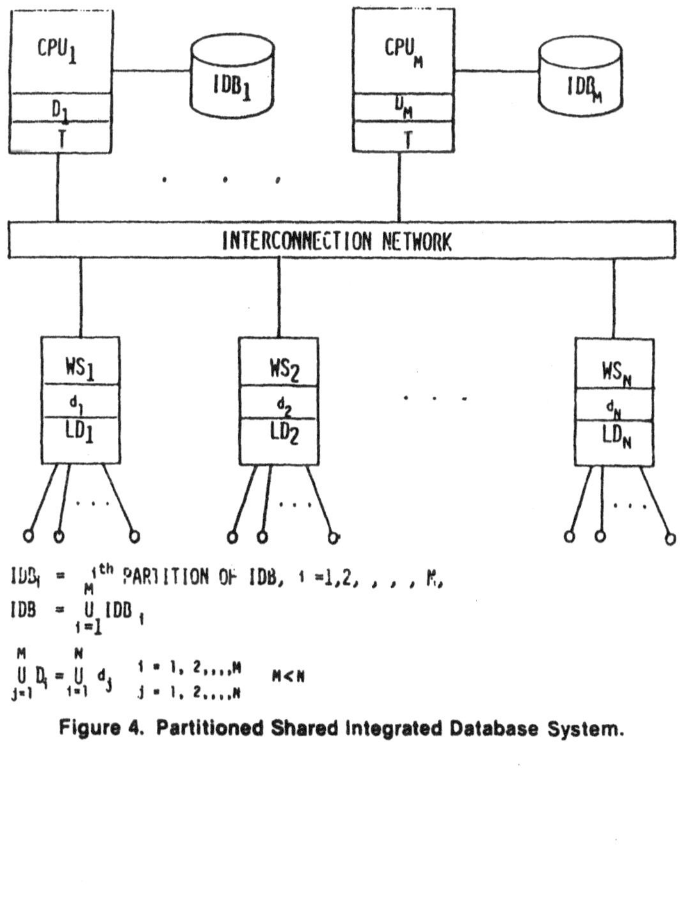

$IDB_i = i^{th}$ PARTITION OF IDB, $i = 1, 2, \ldots, M$,

$$IDB = \bigcup_{i=1}^{M} IDB_i$$

$$\bigcup_{j=1}^{M} D_i = \bigcup_{i=1}^{N} d_j \quad \begin{matrix} i = 1, 2, \ldots, M \\ j = 1, 2, \ldots, N \end{matrix} \quad M < N$$

Figure 4. Partitioned Shared Integrated Database System.

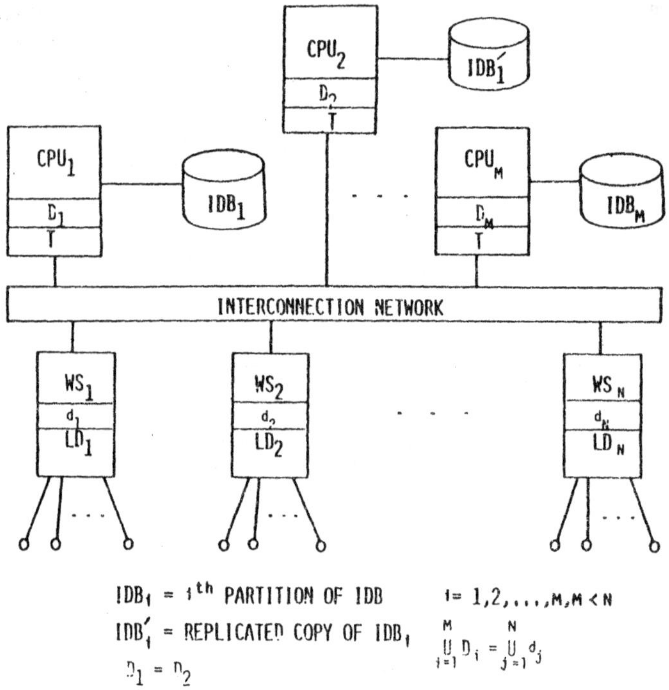

Figure 5. Replicated Partitioned Shared Integrated Database System.

formats). As a result, no translation is needed to transfer files between the IDB and the local database of the workstations.

In a heterogeneous system, the workstations may differ in terms of word lengths, bit order, operating system, file operations, programming languages used, and communications capability. Therefore, when files are transferred between a workstation local database and the IDB, data translation is required.

In many cases, IDB data may consist of data that were originally planned for local use only. Thus, there may be a wide variety of file structures and data models in the SIDS which complicates data management and translation. Yet, most of the distributed database systems for the coming years will be of this type. This is because there is a need for connecting and sharing the existing databases, even when they have different structures and formats.[2]

[2]For example, Digital Equipment Corporation defines a file transfer protol called Data Access Protocol (DAP) for use with its DECNET product [Pas 77]. In the DAP system, all the computers in the network may be different; however, they are made by the same manufacturer, and the DEC Record Management Service (RMS) is able to translate the data format of one computer to that of another.

3. SIDS Protocol Design Issues

To provide for communication among database systems, it is desirable to use standard formats and protocols. The OSI (Open System Interconnection) reference model consists of seven layers as shown in figure 6. Layers 1 through 4 (physical, data link, network, and transport) are concerned with data communication. Layers 5, 6, and 7 are the session, presentation, and application layers.

In addition to other services, these protocol layers provide specific services for communication among database systems. The ***session layer*** provides the means for the cooperating presentation entities to organize and synchronize their dialog and manage their data exchange. The ***presentation layer*** provides the services that allow application processes to interpret the meaning of the information being transferred. The ***application layer*** directly serves the application processes by providing access to the OSI environment and by providing the distributed information services to support the application process and manage the communication [21, 13].

There are many issues pertaining to the ***application*** and ***presentation*** layers that need to

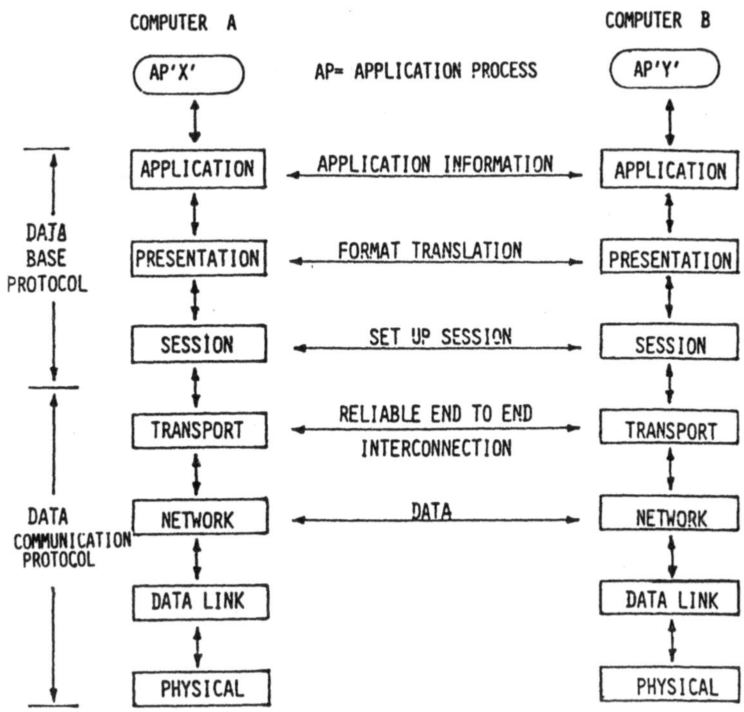

Figure 6. Open System Interconnection Model.

be considered and resolved in designing the SIDS. Since these layers are currently being developed and refined, this discussion should serve as a basis and framework for further research and development.

3.1. Application Layer. The OSI reference model identifies three categories of services elements for the application layer: management service element, application-specific service element, and user-specific service element [21].

The management service elements provide for OSI communication which is independent of the nature of the specific application such as directory look up, control of access, commitment, and concurrency control. The application-specific elements are required by certain categories of applications to support the functions of the information transfer process such as file transfer, virtual terminal, job transfer, and manipulation. The user-specific service elements apply to the functions that are unique to the specific application area such as banking or order entry systems. Therefore, for a specific transaction, all three service elements may be invoked.

In this section, some of the SIDS design issues for the management service elements of the application layer are discussed.

3.1.1. Concurrency Control. To allow SIDS users to modify their databases, concurrency control is needed to manage concurrent file updates. Locking and timestamping are commonly recommended techniques for concurrency control [3]. However, we proposed the following protocol that is more efficient for the SIDS.

When an update is initiated at a workstation, it performs its local update and then sends the update together with the time of the update (timestamp) to the IDB site for confirmation. The local update will not be finalized until it is confirmed. To further reduce the concurrency control overhead, we let the IDB distribute the update to the workstations periodically[3] rather than instantaneously.

In the case where there are multiple updates to a file during an updating period (known as

[3]The updating period affects the response time and, therefore, depends on the operating environment and user requirements; it could range from seconds to hours.

an update conflict), the IDB can detect such conflicts and based on certain predetermined criteria (e.g., update time, priority, etc.) select one update. (Workstations are notified if their updates were rejected.) All the rejected updates will be cancelled, and the selected update will be performed. Since concurrent updates to the same data item should be infrequent, the overhead of this approach should be lower than that of locking protocol and conventional timestamp methods [17].

For the non-partitioned SIDS, the IDB site should also be the update confirmation site. This reduces network traffic since the update will be performed at the IDB. Likewise, for the partitioned SIDS, the files that are stored at an IDB site should have that site designated as the update confirmation site for those files. All the updates that are performed locally at the workstations have to be confirmed by the respective IDB sites. An IDB site periodically sends the confirmed updates to all the relevant workstations. Conflicting updates can be handled in the same manner as that of the non-partitioned SIDS.

For the replicated SIDS, each file should select an IDB site as its primary update confirmation site. The primary sites confirm update requests from all the workstations. Whenever an update is initiated at a workstation, the update is first performed locally at the workstation, and then is forwarded to its primary site for confirmation. The primary site periodically sends the confirmed updates to the replicated IDBs as well as to all affected workstations. Update conflicts are handled in the same manner as that of the non-partitioned SIDS.

3.1.2. Directory System. The directory system provides physical, logical, and operational status information about the shared files on the SIDS. The organization, distribution, and content of the directory system are key design issues [9, 27, 1, 25]. The SIDS directory consists of the location, status (used, locked, up, down), dictionaries (data format, data model, accessibility to various users, etc.) of the shared files at local databases and characteristics of the workstations (memory size, word size, file management systems, programming language used, and support etc.).

For the non-partitioned IDB, there are two possible approaches. One is to install a directory locator at each workstation which provides the list of shared files, their location, and accessibility. This allows a workstation to negotiate access to remote files residing at other workstations but doing so requires high communication overhead as well as extra workstation software. Another approach is to install the directory at the IDB site and have workstations communicate with IDB to update or retrieve shared files. This approach requires less communication when a transaction involves several files at different workstations, and also less software overhead at the workstations, but the approach may have problems with reliability.

For the partitioned SIDS, the IDB is divided into several fragments. There are three approaches to the directory design:

1. Create a centralized directory which is controlled by one of the IDB sites, and operate in the same manner as the non-partitioned SIDS.
2. Assign a sub-directory at each partitioned IDB site. The sub-directory consists of all the required directory information about the partitioned IDB. Every sub-directory also contains the location of all the sharable files and their associated sub-directories. (The directory of the entire system can be obtained by combining all the sub-directories.) If the content of the sub-directories is not overlapped or partially replicated, then updating the content of a sub-directory does not affect the contents of the other sub-directories. However, should a transaction involve shared data among several partitioned IDBs, coordination is required.
3. Replicate the entire directory and store it at each of the partitioned IDB sites. This approach reduces read response time and increases availability; however, it increases the complexity of concurrently updating the replicated copies of the directory.

3.1.3. Deadlock Management. Deadlock can be managed either by avoidance, detection, or prevention [8, 26, 19, 24]. Deadlock avoidance is practical only if program file accesses are known in advance, which is unusual in current database systems.

Using deadlock detection, transactions are only restarted when a deadlock actually occurs. Deadlock prevention forces a transaction to restart when the danger of deadlock exists. Deadlock detection causes transactions to block more frequently than deadlock prevention. But deadlock prevention creates more transaction restarts, which are extremely expensive. Thus, deadlock detection has greater appeal.

Deadlocks are detected by explicitly constructing the waits-for graph of the system and searching for cycles. If a cycle is found, one of the transactions on the cycle has to be aborted, thereby breaking the deadlock. The main difficulty in implementing deadlock detection algorithms in a distributed system is efficiently constructing the waits-for graph, since arcs may span site boundaries (e.g., site A holds a lock on a file at site B) [19]. For the non-partitioned SIDS to reduce communication overhead, deadlock detection should be located at the IDB site. For the partitioned SIDS, each IDB site should provide deadlock detection for those files from several IDB sites, then coordination among the IDB sites is required to construct a global waits-for graph.

Furthermore, caution is required when a layered protocol is used, since layering makes higher layers (e.g., application) dependent on the sources of lower layers (e.g., presentation). If a dependency also exists from a lower layer to a higher layer (e.g., waits-for memory), then deadlock will result. Some examples are cited in [14].

3.1.4 Fault Recovery. Should an update be aborted prior to modifying all replicated copies, mutual consistency will be lost. The two phase commit protocol [16] can be used to ensure mutual consistency in the presence of failures.

The first phase is to notify all affected workstations (and IDBs for the partitioned SIDS) that there is a file update forthcoming, and these sites reply with a guarantee commit message if they are prepared for the update. After receiving these messages from all affected sites, the sender transmits (second phase) the update messages to all affected sites. Should a committed site detect a failure (by timeout) during the second phase, it contacts the sender or another committed site. This permits the system to recover after a site failure and guarantees the consistency of replicated file copies.

Let us now discuss fault recovery in SIDS. The database of the crashed site must be made internally consistent as well as mutually consistent with other file copies. There are two major problems: 1) having the crashed site perform all the updates that occurred while it was down; and 2) completing any update transactions that were initiated by the crashed site and were interrupted by the crash.

Let us first discuss the fault recovery for workstations. The failed workstation can recover all the updates that occurred while it was down if a history file is maintained at the IDB in which all updates to the local database are recorded and marked to indicate the times when reconfigurations (crashes or recoveries) occurred. When a crashed workstation resumes operations, the IDB sends a copy of the portion of the history file made between the time of the crash and the time of recovery.

To recover from a workstation crash during an update transaction, the workstation should keep a list of updates in its local database that can survive any crash. When the workstation resumes operation, this list will be checked for outstanding updates so that the IDB can be made consistent with the recovered workstation.

Let us now discuss the fault recovery for the IDB. If the IDB crashes before completing an update transaction, we have two consistency problems to contend with: (1) the IDB may have broadcast update messages before modifying its own database; and (2) the IDB may have completed the updating but had not yet begun to send update messages to the workstations. Problem (1) can be dealt with using the history file technique described above. For problem (2) we can require IDB to record the updates to be made for a transaction before beginning to modify its own database. This list of recent updates must survive any crash. When the IDB recovers, this list will be checked for outstanding updates so that the surviving workstations can be made consistent with the IDB.

When the IDB is down, the workstations no longer communicate among themselves. All the updates performed at the workstations are temporary and must be confirmed when the

IDB recovers. For the partitioned SIDS, only the workstations that interact with the failed partitioned IDB will be affected. Therefore, a partitioned SIDS provides a greater availability. For replicated partitioned SIDS, the back-up IDB can automatically switch over when the primary IDB fails. Thus, such a system provides higher availability as well as avoiding time consuming transaction rollbacks.

3.2. Presentation Layer. In this section, possible approaches of data translation for SIDS are discussed. There are three ways to perform data translation. The first scheme is to do direct conversions between site pairs (or negotiate a translation strategy [23]). The second scheme is to convert data from the host-site format to a standard representation (e.g., Entity-Relational format [6]) and then to translate from this canonical representation to the target-site format [4, 28]. The first scheme may be suitable for a system with very few numbers of different database management systems or systems which have similar characteristics. The second scheme is logically more appealing but usually more costly because it provides a canonical data format for translations, and, thus, is suitable for a system with a variety of database models. The third scheme is hierarchical translation [10]. Unlike canonical translation (second scheme), all workstations and local databases that do not require translation are placed into one group. Thus, translations are only required between different groups. The hierarchical approach avoids the higher overhead of canonical translation and yet provides a more structured way to perform translation than the direct conversion.

To provide the user with an integrated, coherent global view of the shareable database in all the workstations in the SIDS, the IDB site needs to provide facilities to resolve incompatible data handling and database integration. The homogenization of local databases can be handled either at the IDB site or at the workstation sites. The IDB should provide an integrated view of all the shareable databases which gives a user the illusion that SIDS has a homogeneous integrated database.

Since data translation could be very complex and costly, careful consideration should be given to selecting a translation scheme for a SIDS based on the characteristics of the workstations, data models, applications software language models, and operating environment. Much more research work is needed in this area.

4. Special Case: Workstations That Do Not Require Updating

When none of the workstations in the system requires updating capability, concurrency control is not required. Further, if the workstations are all identical, translation is not required either. The Federal Aviation Agency (FAA) has such a system currently under operation. The integrated database periodically broadcasts relevant information to the databases of each of the workstations. A pilot can query the workstation for weather information, air traffic conditions of a specific route, time of flight, etc. Should the pilot request information outside the local database (e.g., weather conditions in Europe), the workstation forwards the query to the IDB. Query response time from the local database is within a few seconds. Queries that require processing at the IDB take about 30 seconds. Since such queries are infrequent, response times are satisfactory for the users.

The system consists of about 150 workstations. Each workstation consists of dual Z-80 microcomputers with dual floppy disks, one for storing the local database and the other for storing application programs. Each workstation consists of twenty-four terminal ports and three printers, one for error log, one for hard copy, and one for emergency reports from the FAA integrated database.

A generalization of the above system is to replicate the IDB and store it on several computers. Such a system should provide higher availability as well as shorter response times. However, it introduces more complexity in directory design, concurrency control for updating the replicated IDB, and procedures for fault recovery.

5. Summary and Conclusions

In this paper, three shared integrated database system (SIDS) architectures are presented: non-partitioned SIDS, partitioned SIDS, and replicated partitioned SIDS. Several implementation issues of SIDS protocol for the presentation and application layer have been presented.

In a shared integrated database system (SIDS), each workstation has its local database which stores fragments of the IDB. Such systems represent a special class of distributed database systems with replicated files. To reduce overhead in synchronization, a periodic updating concurrency control technique with timestamp is proposed. Other design issues such as directory, deadlock management, fault-recovery, and data translation are also presented.

Since there are many workstations and databases already in existence, and these databases have been developed independently, the logical first step is to integrate these databases to form a non-partitioned integrated database system. As we gain more experience and understanding of SIDS characteristics and user requirements, more advanced SIDS architectures (such as the partitioned and replicated SIDS) will be implemented to improve system performance and availability.

References

1. Allen, F.W., Loomis, E.S. and Mannino, M.V. "The Integrated Dictionary/Directory System," *Computing Surveys*, Vol. 14, No. 2, June 1982, pp. 245-86.
2. Alsberg, P. and Day, J., "A Principle for Resilient Sharing of Distributed Resources," *COMPCON Proceedings*, San Francisco, 1978.
3. Bernstein, P. and Goodman, J., "Concurrency Control in Distributed Data Base Systems," *ACM Computation Systems*, Vol. 13, No. 2, June 1981, pp. 185-221.
4. Cardenas, A.F. and Pirahesh, M.H., "Data Base Communication in a Heterogeneous Data Base Management System Network," *Information Systems*, Vol. 5, 1980, pp. 55-79.
5. Casey, R.G., "Allocation of Copies of a File in an Information Network," *SJCC 1972*, AFIPS Press, Vol. 40, 1972.
6. Chen, P.P., "The Entity Relationship Model—Toward a Unified View of Data," *ACM Transactions on Data Base System*, Vol. 1, No. 1, March 1976.
7. Chu, W.W., "Optimal File Allocation in a Multiple Computer System," *IEEE Transactions on Computers*, October 1969, pp. 885-89.
8. Chu, W.W. and Ohlmacher, G., "Avoiding Deadlock in Distributed Data Bases," *Proceedings of the ACM National Symposium*, Vol. 1, March 1974, pp. 156-60.
9. Chu, W.W., "Design Consideration of File Directory Systems for Distributed Data Bases," *State of the Art Report*, Distributed Data Bases: 2, 1979, pp. 73-87.
10. Chu, W.W. and To, Victor, "A Hierarchical Conceptual Data Model for Data Translation in a Heterogeneous Database System," *Proceedings of the International Conference on Entity-Relational Approach to Systems Analysis and Design*, Los Angeles, December 10-12, 1979.
11. Chu, W.W. and Hurley, P., "Optimal Query Processing for Distributed Data Base System," *IEEE Transactions on Computers*, Vol. C-31, No. 9, September 1982, pp. 835-50.
12. Day, John, "Terminal, File Transfer, and Remote Job Protocol," *Protocol and Techniques for Data Communication Networks*, F.F. Kuo, ed., Prentice-Hall, 1981.
13. DesJardins, R., "International Standards for Open Systems Interconnection," *SIGCOMM 83 Tutorial*, University of Texas, Austin, March 1983.
14. Hellerstein, J. and Chu, W.W., "Some Potential Deadlocks in Layered Communications Architectures," *AFIPS Proceedings*, Vol. 50, 1980, pp. 137-40.
15. Hevner, A.R. and Yao, S.B., "Query Processing in Distributed Database Systems," *IEEE Transaction Software Engineering*, Vol. SE-5, No. 3, 1978, pp. 177-87.
16. Lam, B., and Sturgis, H., "Crash Recovery in a Distributed Data Storage System," *Internal Report, Xerox* Palo Alto Research Center, 1976.
17. Lin, K.W., Nolte, J., Bernstein, P.A., and Goodman, N., "Distributed Database System Designer Handbook," Technical Report, *Computer Corporation of America*, January 1983.
18. Mahmoud, S. and Riordon, J.S., "Optimal Allocation of Resources in Distributed Information Networks," *ACM Transactions on Data Base Systems*, Vol. 1, No. 1, March 1976, pp. 66-78.
19. Menasce, D.A., Popek, G.J., and Muntz, R.R., "A Locking Protocol for Resource Coordination in Distributed Databases," *ACM Transactions on Data Base System*, Vol. 5, No. 2, June 1980, pp. 103-38.
20. Morgan, H.R. and Levin, K.D., "Optimal Program and Data Locations in Computer Networks," *Communications of the ACM*, Vol. 20, No. 5, May 1977, pp. 315-22.
21. OSI Data Transfer, "A Tutorial on the Open System Interconnection Reference Model," *OMNICOM Information Service*, Vienna, Va., Transmission No. 1, June 1982.
22. Parker, D.S. et. al., "Detection of Mutual Inconsistency in Distributed Systems," *IEEE Transactions on Software Engineering*, Vol. 9, No. 3, May 1983.
23. Passafiume, J.J. and Wecker, S., "Distributed File Access in DECNET," *Proc. 2nd Berkeley Workshop on Distributed Databases and Networking*, Lawrence Berkeley Laboratory, Berkeley, Cal., 1977.
24. Ries, D.R., and Smith, G.C., "Nested Transactions in Distributed Systems," *Proceedings of the Symposium on Reliability in Distributed Software and Database Systems*, July 1981, pp. 117-23.
25. Reis, D.R., (ed.), "An Architectural Framework for Database Standardization," *Computer Corporation of America*, July 1982.
26. Rosenkrantz, D.G., Streans, R.E., and Lewis, P.M., "System Level Concurrency Control for Distributed Database Systems," *ACM Trans Database System*, Vol. 3, No. 2, June 1978, pp. 178-98.
27. Small, Dana L., and Chu, W.W., "A Distributed Data Base Architecture for Data Processing in a Dynamic Environment," *Digests of Papers*, COMPCON 79, February 1979, pp. 123-27.
28. Smith, John, et al., "Multibase-Integrating Heterogeneous Distributed Database Sys ems," *Proceedings of National Computer Conference*, 1981, pp. 487-99.
29. Wong, E., "Retrieving Dispersed Data from SSD-1: A System for Distributed Databases," *Proceedings of the Second Berkeley Workshop on Distributed Data Management and Computer Networks*, May 1977, pp. 217-35.

Chapter 6

CASE STUDIES OF DISTRIBUTED DATA BASE SYSTEMS

There are several distributed data base systems that have been implemented. In this chapter, we shall present three experimental distributed data base systems, and two commercial systems.

The first two papers present the R* distributed data base which consists of a confederation of voluntarily cooperating sites, each supporting the relational model of data and communication via IBM's CICS. A key feature of the architecture is to maintain the autonomy of each site. The third paper presents the SIRIUS-DELTA, a distributed data base system that is a cooperation of heterogeneous local data base systems. The fourth paper discusses the Mermaid system which provides the design of a common front end which integrates to heterogeneous data bases. The fifth paper by Norman and Anderson presents an application that uses the distributed data base system Tandem computers. The paper discusses the application requirements, the architecture of the data base and the algorithms used for updates and inserts. The last paper by Chan, *et al.*, presents an overview of a distributed data base manager that supports Ada programming language.

For additional information on case studies of distributed data base management systems, the interested reader is referred to [ROTH 80, STON 77].

R*: AN OVERVIEW OF THE ARCHITECTURE.

R. Williams, D. Daniels, L. Haas, G. Lapis, B. Lindsay, P. Ng, R. Obermarck, P. Selinger, A. Walker, P. Wilms and R. Yost.

IBM Research, San Jose, Ca. USA.

R* is an experimental distributed database system being developed at IBM Research to study the issues and problems of distributed data management. R* consists of a confederation of voluntarily co-operating sites, each supporting the relational model of data and communicating via IBM's CICS. A key feature of the architecture is to maintain the autonomy of each site. To achieve maximum site autonomy SQL statements are compiled, data objects are named and catalogued, and deadlock detection and recovery are all handled in a distributed manner. The R* architecture, including transaction management, commit processing, deadlock detection, system recovery, object naming, catalog management, and authorization checking is described. Some examples of the additions and changes to the SQL language needed to support distributed function are given.

1. TRENDS IN DATABASE AND DISTRIBUTED PROCESSING SYSTEMS

There are several factors leading to the development of distributed database management systems. People and organizations share data because of its intrinsic value; indeed corporations regard their data as a major asset. The number of computer installations is increasing due to declining costs of hardware. Users of these installations need to share data to do their work, and now that computers can easily be interconnected by electronic networks, distributed systems are evolving for data exchange. Database systems provide consistent views of data, concurrency control for multiple users and recovery in case of failures by using the notion of transaction processing. A database management system can therefore be expanded into a distributed database management system, DDBMS, to supply the same application features to a network of users potentially able to share all the data at all the sites.

Each site should retain local privacy and control of its own data. It is also very desirable to present data to programs and users at a site in the network as if that site were the only one. Furthermore to achieve best

Improving Database Usability
and Responsiveness

performance programs should run locally if all the data for the program is local to the site. Specifically there should be no central dependencies in the network; no central catalog, no central scheduler, no central deadlock detector or breaker, etc. We call this concept of maximum independence "site autonomy" [LINDSAY 80a].

With these goals in mind, we have designed a DDBMS, called R*, using the relational database technology. It is a follow-on project from System R [ASTRAHAN 76, BLASGEN 79]. The SQL language [CHAMBERLIN 76] has been extended where necessary to allow for new functions but existing SQL programs that ran in System R should also run in R*.

The paper describes the environment in which R* runs and the data forms to be supported by R*. The skeletal architecture of R* is described by following the processing of a query entered at one site; query processing in R* is basically similar to the query processing in System R. The major issues and processes are:

- Environment and Data Definitions
- Object Naming
- Distributed Catalogs
- Transaction Management and Commit Protocols
    - Transaction Number
- Query Preparation
    - Name Resolution
    - Authorization Checking
    - Access Path Selection and Optimization
    - Views
- Query Execution
    - Concurrency
    - Deadlock Detection and Resolution
    - Logging and Recovery
- SQL Additions and Changes

R* is partially implemented (see Status section 9).

2. ENVIRONMENT & DATA DEFINITIONS FOR R*

R* consists of several database sites that communicate via CICS, an IBM software product [CICS 78], as shown in Figure 1. CICS was chosen as the communication medium to minimize our prototyping efforts so that we could concentrate on distributed database, DDB, issues. Any network configuration and interconnection topology allowed by CICS can be used in R*; CICS communications is used merely as a transport medium. R* also considers the communications medium to be unreliable, i.e., message delivery is not guaranteed, however when messages are delivered to the database software they are assumed to be delivered intact in order and without duplication. R* runs in a CICS address space, and CICS handles terminal I/O, program and task management. Note that sites in R* would

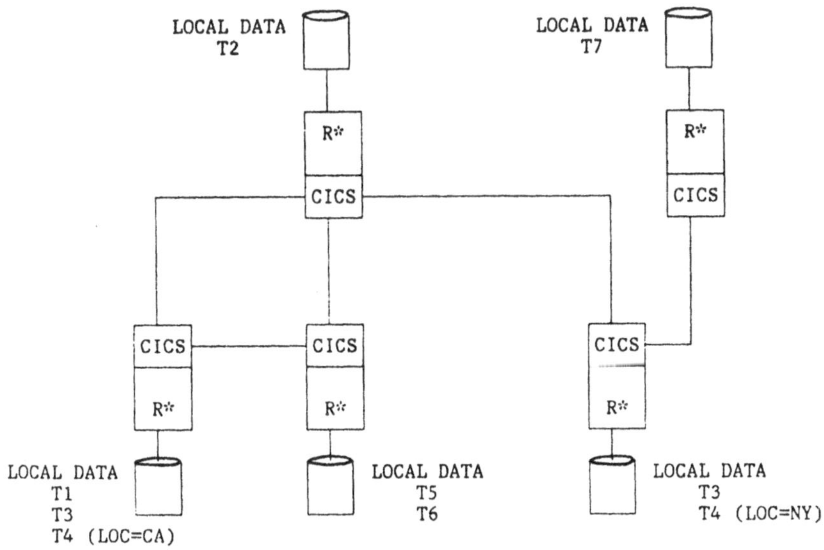

T1, T2, T5, T6, T7 : Dispersed Data
T3 : Replicated Data
T4 : Partitioned Data (by tuples with LOC=CA or LOC=NY)

Figure 1. R* Distributed Database Configuration.

typically be physically separate computer systems, but sites need to be only logically distinct, not physically distinct, especially for initial development purposes (there are already enough problems using one machine for debugging complex software)!

Data in R* is stored in tables (relations) that may be dispersed, replicated or partitioned. Combinations of these distributions are supported also; for example partitioned data may be replicated. Dispersed data means that tables T1,....Tn are uniquely stored at the various sites S1,......Sk; e.g., T1,T2 at S1; T3 at S2 etc. Replicated data means that copies of a table exist and are guaranteed to be identical at all times. All copies are updated synchronously, using a two-phase commit protocol. Partitioned data is logically one table, part of which is stored at one site, and another part(s) at another site(s). In horizontal partitioning some rows (tuples) are stored at one site, some at another site according to some disjoint separation criteria based on column values (e.g. store values 1 to 100 in site 1 and all the rest in site 2). In vertical partitioning, some columns are stored at one site, some at another, according to some column separation criteria. The vertical fragmentation must be lossless so that the original relation can be created from the vertical partitions [AHO 79] and therefore all partitions must have a set of common columns that determine the values of all columns in the complete relation, or a virtual column created artificially by the DDBMS to enable a one-to-one match of the fragmented tuples during reconstruction. Partitioned data can also be replicated. The end-user of the database need not be aware of the data distribution for query execution or for application programming. Data consistency, reassembly of partitions and access of remote data is performed by the DDBMS itself and is transparent to the end-user.

The SIRIUS/DELTA DDBMS also allows partitioned and replicated data forms [LeBihan 80]. The Polypheme prototype went further and allowed for heterogeneous database systems in its design. The technique was for all systems to employ a standard relational form for communications to other sites, and a mapping to the internal form at each site [Adiba 80a]. CICS supports distributed data processing through function shipping using the

Inter-Systems Communications feature [CICS 78]. Also using function shipping, TANDEM systems support distributed data, with an emphasis on availability, but few technical papers exist on their systems [Tandem].

In R*, some tables can be snapshots of other tables [ADIBA 80b]. Snapshot data is a copy of a relation(s) in which the data is consistent but not necessarily up-to-date. Snapshots are read-only and are intended to provide a static copy of a database (e.g. Friday's sales figures). They are not updated when the base relation is updated. They may however be periodically refreshed by recopying the data from the base relations (e.g. every Friday at 6 p.m.). Programs that only need snapshot data might run more efficiently from snapshots than from current relations. For example relations that are locally stored snapshots derived from a remote operational database would allow local programs to run much faster from the snapshots than from the operational data. Availability is increased also for transactions that use snapshot data.

3. OBJECT NAMING

The naming problem in distributed systems is to allow data sharing but without undue restrictions on an end-user's choice of names. For autonomy reasons we don't want to have a global naming system, nor do we want to force users to choose unique names. Furthermore adding a new site with a previously defined database to a previously established network would lead to terrible renaming problems.

Names used in SQL statements are names chosen by end-users writing ad-hoc queries or application programs. Network details must be transparent to such users, so that programming is as simple as possible and also so that the same programs will work correctly when entered at any site.

We solve the problem by mapping end-user names, which we call "print names", to internal System Wide Names, "SWN". An SWN has the form:

USER USER_SITE.OBJECT_NAME BIRTH_SITE

The BIRTH_SITE is the site in which the object was first created. Because site names are chosen to be unique outside of the system, an SWN is unique.

Name completion rules for adding default parts to print names and synonym mapping tables for each user are used to convert a print name to an SWN. For example if BRUCE logs on in SAN_JOSE and accesses a table he calls T, which was locally created and stored in San Jose, then the SWN:

BRUCE SAN_JOSE.T SAN_JOSE

is generated.

This mapping mechanism allows different end-users to reference either the same object with different print names or different objects with the same print names. Objects may be stored and moved without impacting user code (see catalogs in section 4) and this location transparency mechanism permits site autonomy. A more complete discussion can be found in [LINDSAY 80b].

4. DISTRIBUTED CATALOGS

In the SDD-1 system [Rothnie 77, Rothnie 80], the catalog is logically a single table, which can be fragmented and replicated. This allows catalog entries to be replicated and distributed among the data module sites. However, this also implies that local objects may have their catalog entries at a remote site and that data definition operations may not be totally local. SDD-1 does cache catalog entries to aid performance but this also adds overhead for updating purposes. A distributed version of INGRES [Stonebraker 77, Epstein 80] distinguishes between local relations (accessible from a single site) and global relations (accessible from all sites). The name of every global relation is stored at every site. Creation of a global relation involves broadcasting its name (and location) to all sites of the network, but cached catalog entries are supported. Thus both SDD-1 and INGRES implement a global catalog and therefore restrict site autonomy and complicate system growth. For a large network any operation requiring unanimous participation will create difficulties, and may require complex recovery mechanisms.

R* uses a distributed catalog architecture. Catalogs at each site keep and maintain information about objects in the database, including replicas or fragments, stored at that site. In addition the catalog at the birth site of an object keeps information indicating where the object is currently stored and this entry is updated if an object is moved. Cataloging of objects is done in this totally distributed manner to preserve site autonomy. An object can be located by the system from its SWN and no centralization is necessary.

For performance reasons, a catalog entry can be cached at another site so that a reference to it can be as efficient as a local reference e.g., for compiling (see section 6). A cached entry may become out-of-date if another transaction has changed the structure of or the access paths to the object after the cached entry is made; this fact is discovered during a later processing step and then the cached entry is updated from the correct catalog entry and the initial processing must be restarted. This discovery is made because entries have version numbers which are checked during subsequent processing against version numbers store in the real catalog entries to determine if the cached entry used at an earlier stage was valid. Restarting in this way is not expected to occur very often because catalog entries are relatively static.

The catalog entry for an object includes the object SWN, type and format, the access paths available, a mapping in the case of a view to lower level objects, and various statistics that assist query optimization. Each entry is identified by the SWN of an object. To find an object's catalog entry, first the local catalog, (plus the local cache), then the birth-site catalog and then the site indicated by the birth-site catalog are checked in that order, stopping when the catalog entry is found. This gives the best efficiency together with site autonomy.

5. TRANSACTION MANAGEMENT AND COMMIT PROTOCOL

5.1 Transaction Number

The DDBMS must support the notion of a transaction. A transaction is a recoverable sequence of database actions that either commits or aborts. If the transaction commits, all of its changes to the database take effect, but if the transaction aborts, none of its actions have any effect upon the database state. In SDD-1 and in INGRES each statement is a transaction whereas in System R one can define a transaction to be any number of SQL statements.

A transaction starts at the site where it is entered. Subsequently agents may be created at other sites to do work on behalf of the transaction. Both synchronous and asynchronous execution can be performed to take advantage of parallelism or pipelining during the compilation and execution of the transaction.

Any request to the DDBMS is given a transaction number that is made up from the site name and a sequence number (local time of day may be better) Each site is unique and the sequence is increased for each new transaction. Therefore the transaction number is both unique and ordered in the R* network. Uniqueness is necessary for identification purposes, for acquiring resources, breaking deadlocks etc. For example if a transaction starts at site A, sends work to site B, which in turn sends work to site A then it is necessary for A to know that both pieces of work are on behalf of the same transaction so that locks on data objects can be shared.If such locks could not be shared a deadlock would occur and make processing the query impossible. Ordering is used to provide a means of knowing which transaction to abort in the case of a deadlock between different transactions. R* aborts the youngest, largest numbered, transaction.

5.2 Transaction Commit Protocol

Whenever a transaction's actions involve more that one database site, the DDBMS must take special care in order to insure that the transaction termination is uniform: either all of the sites commit or all sites abort the effects of the transaction.

The so called "two phase" commit protocol [LAMPSON 80a, GRAY 78, LINDSAY 79, MOSS 81] is used in order to insure uniform transaction commitment or abortion. The two phase commit protocol allows multiple sites to coordinate transaction commit in such a way that all participating sites come to the same conclusion despite site and communication failures. There are many variations of the two phase commit protocol. In all variations there is one site, called the coordinator, which makes the commit or abort decision after all the other sites involved in the transaction are known to be recoverably prepared to commit or abort, and all the other sites are awaiting the coordinator's decision.

When the non-coordinator sites are prepared to commit and awaiting the coordinator's decision, they are not allowed tc unilaterally abandon or commit the transaction. This has the effect of sequestering the transaction's resources, making them unavailable until the coordinator's decision is received. Before entering the prepared state, however, any site can unilaterally abort its portion of a transaction. The rest of the sites will also abort eventually. While a site is prepared to commit, local control (autonomy) over the resources held by the transaction is surrendered to the commit coordinator.

Some variations of the two phase commit protocol sequester resources longer than other variations. Rosenkrantz, Stearns, and Lewis [ROSENKRANTZ 78] require all sites other than the single active site of the transaction to be prepared at all times. The linear commit protocols described in [GRAY 78] and [LINDSAY 79] have a commit phase with duration proportional to the number of sites involved.

R* actually uses a presumed-to-commit protocol. The number of messages required in the usual two phase commit protocol is 4(N-1), where N is the number of sites involved in the transaction, but by assuming the commit succeeds the number of messages can be reduced to 3(N-1). If a failure requiring transaction abort occurs, then all 4(N-1) messages are needed. The improvement is obtained by removing the need for acknowledging the commit message. The coordinator logs the start of the transaction commit processing and then sends messages to the other sites (called apprentices) involved in the transaction. An apprentice is a site that does work at the request of another site, which then is called the master. Each apprentice still has to log its decision and reply to the coordinator who logs the resulting decision. Therefore the apprentice has to await commit/abort instructions from the coordinator, during which time its resources are tied up. Lost commit messages are detected by a time-out, but to avoid the very long outages that could occur if a network breaks down, operator intervention must be permitted.

This presumed-to-commit protocol minimizes the duration of the commit protocol. Other variations, notably those proposed for SDD-1 [HAMMER 79], provide mechanisms for circumventing the delay caused by coordinator failure, by sending extra messages (to nominate a backup coordinator) which prolong the commit phase in the normal case. It does not appear possible to completely eliminate the temporary loss of site autonomy during the commit procedure [LAMPSON 80b].

6. QUERY PREPARATION

6.1 Name Resolution

When an SQL statement is first seen by R*, it is parsed and then undergoes name resolution in which all SQL print names are resolved into SWNs. Then it is possible to determine if catalog entries for each database object are available locally. If any entries are missing because they are stored at remote sites and not in the local cache then a message has to be sent to the remote site to fetch catalog information for the remote objects from the birth site as described in section 4.

6.2 Authorization Checking

After name resolution the authorization of the user to perform operations indicated by the SQL statement on local data is checked. Because all sites are cooperating in R* voluntarily, no site wishes to trust other sites with respect to authorization. Therefore authorization checking for a remote access request must be done at the site that stores the data and all controls for accessing data must be stored at the same site as the data being controlled. It is possible to control all access to local data locally without the need to contact another site, thus preserving site autonomy. Each site is responsible for maintaining its own site authorization using passwords etc. Authorization for data access is checked for each user, but remote sites authenticate on a site-to-site basis when responding to a request for data. A remote site is trusted to have validated its own users. If this breaks down the damage is limited to the aggregate of privileges held by the users at that site.

Thus the authorization entity in R* is a user at a site, and user level authorization semantics are enforced using site level authentication [WILMS 81]. For example, PAT SAN_JOSE is different from PAT YORKTOWN. An object owner, initially the creator, can grant access rights to any other user, local or remote, and that person can pass on access rights to other users if the original grant permitted subsequent grants (included the grant option). This is the same as in System R [GRIFFITHS 76]. For site to site authentication in networks see encryption techniques [NEEDHAM 78, KENT 76].

6.3 Compilation and Plan Generation

Just as with programming languages, it is possible to compile rather than interpret the database language. Compilation offloads from execution time to compile time much of the overhead of operations needed to set up the data request and thus improves the performance of repetitively executed data access requests.

For conventional programming languages, compilation is a binding process in which high level constructs are mapped to a low level instruction set, which is fixed by the machine on which the compiled code is to be run. Analogously, in a database system access requests expressed in a very high-level database language, such as SQL, can also be compiled into an access program which uses low level objects [CHAMBERLIN 76]. This compilation includes a binding process in which the requests are bound to required authorizations, data objects, and the paths to access them. However, one of the primary differences between the compilation of programs written in conventional programming languages and the compilation of programs written in database languages lies in the fact that the latter depends on objects that are subject to change. Between compile time and execution time, a relation may be deleted or moved, an access path may be dropped, or a required privilege may be revoked. Recompilation or invalidation is necessary when such items change.

In a DDBMS data objects accessed and access paths used may reside at a remote site and the question as to where binding should be done arises.

The approaches can be grouped into three classes:

- All binding for every request can be done at a chosen site;
- All binding can be done at the site where the request originates;
- Binding can be done in a distributed way, at the sites where data objects are accessed.

The first approach would not function well because it is a centralized approach and suffers from poor efficiency and lack of resiliency to failure. It would require a centralized catalog and therefore an excessive amount of communications in the network. The advantages offered by a DDBMS would be mostly lost if a centralized compiler had to be used for all compilations; it would become a system bottleneck. Site autonomy would be lost in this approach of course.

The second approach is not good either. First, to preserve each site's autonomy, it should not be necessary to get agreement from all sites at which requests have been compiled before another site can change an access path for its locally stored relation. Secondly, the compiling site should not need to remember and record the physical details of data access paths at other sites since individual databases may be changed, for example by adding a new access path. Thus if a program depends on a relation that has been changed at a remote site we do not want to do a global recompilation for the whole program if we can avoid it by doing a local recompilation at the remote site for part of the program. Also, to protect data in a high level DDBMS, a user at a certain site may choose only to grant access to a view which is an abstraction of underlying physical data objects, rather than granting access to the objects themselves, which means that the entire compilation and binding cannot be done at the originating site.

The third approach overcomes the drawbacks mentioned above and offers additional advantages. The master site can decide inter-site issues and perform high-level binding and the local sites can decide local issues and do a lower-level binding (e.g. for access path selection). When compilation is distributed and the portion of program to access and manipulate a site's data objects is generated at the same site, it follows naturally that if recompilation has to be done due to changes of local objects, it can be done on a local basis. Thus distributed compilation allows for local control in apprentice sites, which preserves site autonomy. However, global optimality becomes more difficult to obtain after local changes have occurred and it is desirable to be able to do a complete global recompilation, optionally, to improve execution efficiency in some cases. Other advantages of distributed compilation are that failure resiliency is also improved by limiting the scope of actions to a local site when possible. Also different versions or releases of system code could exist at different sites and it would still work correctly.

The INGRES DDBMS [STONEBRAKER 77] seems to be moving towards a compilation approach of preparing queries for execution but most distributed systems still use interpretive methods. R*, using the third approach above, performs distributed compilation [DANIELS 82, NG 82]. In R* the site where the SQL query enters becomes the master site and to compile a request for data at mutiple sites, the overall global plan for executing the program has to be created at the master and then communicated to the apprentices. The difficulty in the design of distributed compilation arises because we want to compile programs to achieve global optimality for execution but retain local site autonomy. The master site may not have complete and up-to-date knowledge of the data objects and access paths available at the apprentice sites, therefore it may make poor decisions and generate very inefficient code if it did the complete compilation. Incorrect decisions can be detected by an apprentice site by checking the version number of the information on which the decision was based, but the extra overhead of correct but distributed compilation is the cost incurred for site autonomy and data protection. The overhead in this case is to redo the entire compilation. The solution is that the master chooses the execution plan, join order, which sites do work etc. and apprentices choose how to access local data.

The global plan is a structural skeleton of the access strategies and is generated at the master site using the information available at the master site. If the master has insufficient catalog information about data objects at other sites, it can request the necessary information and cache it for later use. The global plan specifies the invocation sequence of the participating sites and the order of parameters. If the SQL statement requires a join, the global plan would also specify the join order and join methods.

The global plan is a high level representation of the decisions made by the master site with regard to the execution of the SQL statement. The optimal choice of access paths is discussed later in section 6.4. A global plan should be globally optimal if the information used in access path selection is correct. In addition to the global plan, the compiler at the master site also generates a set of local execution strategies for the local data objects accessed. This includes, for example, which index to use and whether sorting is done. The selection of the global plan and the local execution strategies is termed the "path selection" phase.

The global plan together with the SQL statement is sent to those remote databases that contain the data needed for this SQL statement. This processing phase is termed the "plan distribution" phase. In the global plan, references to data objects are made in terms of their relative positions in the SQL statement. The use of the SQL statement for the expression of the action needed, together with the fact that the global plan is a high level representation, solves the problem of version incompatibility of system code among DBMS's at different sites.

At the remote apprentice sites the first task performed is to check the validity of the catalog information that the master used. If an out-dated version was used, an error message is returned to the master site and the global plan is re-generated by the master using updated information.

Compilation in an apprentice site follows the same pattern as at a master site except that no name resolution is needed. The decisions made by the master site concerning the interfaces among sites to execute this SQL statement will be followed. However, the apprentice is free to change the sequence of the local operations. For example, if the SQL statement requires a join, then the apprentice site can change join orders and join methods for local relations as long as the result tuples are presented in the order prescribed, if any, in the global plan. The apprentice may also use access paths unknown to the master. The access path selector in the apprentice site also generates a set of local execution strategies, which, in turn, undergo the code generation phase to produce local subsections. Figure 2 shows the compilation process.

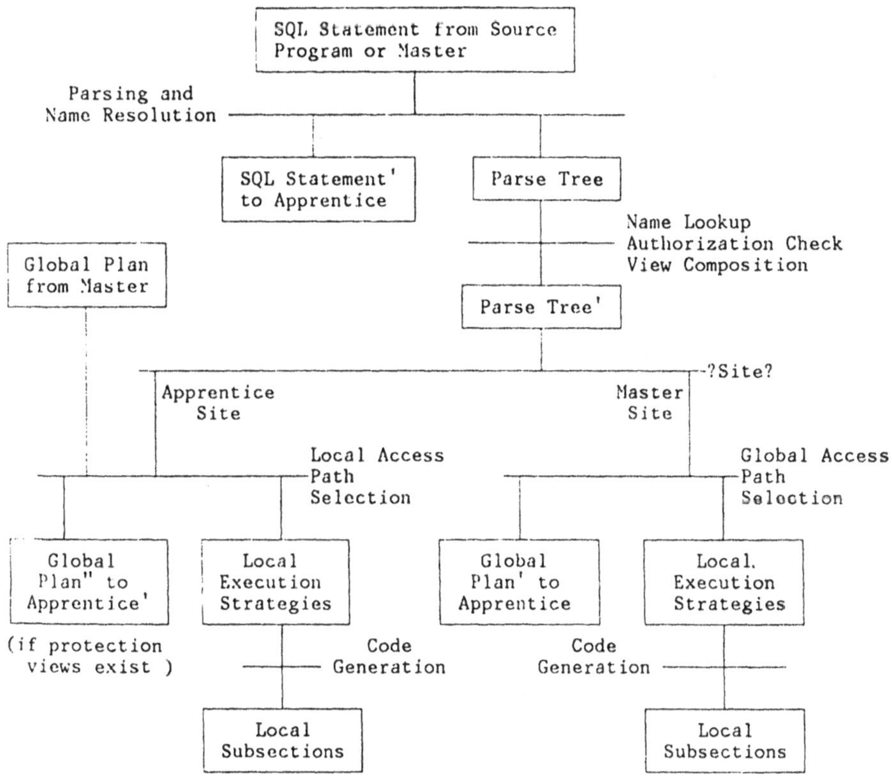

Figure 2. Skeleton of Distributed Compilation.

Just as in a programming language compiler, there is a code generation step. Code is generated at the master site and at each apprentice site involved in the distributed compilation; each piece is called a subsection. Each subsection contains code both for calling its local Research Storage System,RSS, which performs local data management, and for passing data and control to other sites according to the overall plan.

The whole compilation for a SQL program or query is processed itself as a transaction. After all the subsections have been generated in the involved sites for every SQL statement in the program being prepared and no errors are detected, the master commits the compilation transaction using the two phase commit protocol. Upon receiving the "prepare" command, each apprentice stores the subsections into an access module. Besides the access module, the SQL statements and the global plans are also stored for recompilation purposes. During execution, subsections call one another as subroutines or coroutines, or they may be executed in parallel.

6.4 Access Path Selection and Optimization

To execute a query efficiently it is necessary to select access paths to data that minimize the total processing time of the query. Epstein studied this problem for distributed INGRES [Epstein 78] and Selinger for SYSTEM R [SELINGER 79]. The SYSTEM R work has been extended for R*.

During compilation the access paths to data objects are selected and the access path selector in R* tries to minimize total predicted execution time of a SQL statement by exploring a search tree of alternatives and estimating the cost of each [SELINGER 80]. Three components are included to model the execution costs of SQL statements for different access paths in R*: I/O cost , CPU cost and message cost. The cost formulae have the form:

TOTAL_COST = I/O_COST + CPU_COST + MESSAGE_COST

I/O_COST = I/O_WEIGHT * NUMBER_OF_PAGES_FETCHED

CPU_COST = CPU_WEIGHT * NUMBER_OF_CALLS_TO_RSS

MESSAGE_COST = MESSAGE_COST * NUMBER_OF_MESSAGES_SENT + BYTE_COST * NUMBER_OF_BYTES_SENT

As in System R, the cost of an access plan is calculated as the weighted sum of the components. NUMBER_OF_CALLS_TO_RSS represents the estimated number of tuples retrieved; and MESSAGE_COST consists of a per message cost and a per byte cost. Both the number of messages and the amount of data moved are minimized together.

In order to take into account the added cost component and the variety of data forms (partitoned and replicated data) that can be created, the access path selector in R* is considerably more complex than that in System R. The cost of accessing a horizontally partitioned relation is the sum of the costs of accessing its components. Note that not all of the components need to be accessed if the path selector can exclude some components by examining the partitioning criteria. The cost of accessing a vertically partitioned relation is the cost of joining the components. Again, the partitioning criteria may reduce the cost. The cost of accessing a replicated relation for read is the minimum of the costs of accessing the replicas. For updates, it is the sum [SELINGER 80].

The situation is more complex in choosing an optimal path for a join of relations which reside at different databases. In addition to the join order, output tuple order, and join method, the join result location becomes another parameter, thereby increasing the branching factor of the search tree. To join the inner relation B residing at site N to the outer relation A residing or produced at site M, R* considers five possibilities:

- All the qualified tuples of the inner relation B are sent to site M and stored in a temporary relation. The join is performed at site M.

- Qualified tuples of the outer relation A are sent to site N.one at a time. Matching qualified inner relation tuples are retrieved and joined to the outer relation tuple, at site N.

- Outer relation tuples are retrieved. For each qualified tuple, a request containing the values of the outer relation's join column(s) is sent to site N. Then matching qualified inner tuples are retrieved and sent back to site M, where the join is performed. This way of obtaining inner relation tuples is termed "fetching as needed."

- All the qualified inner relation tuples are sent to a third site, site P, and stored in a temporary relation. Then (matching) qualified outer relation tuples are sent to site P to perform the join using the temporary relation. This is a combination of the first and second approaches above.

- Outer relation tuples are sent to a third site, site P, and for each of these outer relation tuples, a request is sent to the inner relation site to retrieve the matching tuples. The join is performed at site P. This is a combination of the second and third approaches above.

In executing a chosen join method, advantage is taken of the parallelism and pipelining available in processing an SQL statement. For example, fetching tuples from site A and other tuples from site B can be done in parallel. As another example while inner tuples from site A that match an outer tuple from site B are joined at site A, the next outer tuple can be fetched from site B.

6.5 Views

A view in R*, as in System R, is a non-materialized virtual relation defined by an SQL statement. It is defined in terms of one or more tables or previously defined views and during processing a view is materialized from its component objects. Views can be used as shorthand notation for reducing the amount of typing required when frequently executing complex queries, or they can be used as a protection mechanism for hiding rows or columns in underlying tables from the user of the view.

Unlike in System R, in R* view component objects may be at different sites. Therefore to provide data protection between sites a protection view is materialized only at the site owning the view. This scheme prevents sending sensitive data to a node where no user is authorized to see it. Therefore during compilation the master site generates a plan for processing the view as if it were a physical table and sends the plan and SQL statement to the apprentices where the view will be processed (and where view records will eventually materialize.) An apprentice site may itself decompose a view component in terms of other views on tables at yet other sites. In that case the apprentice acts as a master to other apprentices and must generate a plan and send subplans to its apprentice sites. The plan distribution progresses in this way until all views are resolved and may even loop back to a site that has already participated in the compilation.

7. QUERY EXECUTION

Queries are executed by running the compiled code generated during query preparation. The local subsection is loaded and executed and it calls remote subsections as needed. Messages are sent to execute remote-procedure-like calls. Local and remote sections of code call the Research Storage System RSS, which is the same as in System R. The RSS returns one record at a time when it is called; joins and other multiple record handling operations are carried out at a level above the RSS. Therefore the only new features required in the RSS are begin and end transaction functions associated with each unique transaction number. Transaction management and commit protocols to synchronize database changes at the end of a transaction were covered in section 5.

7.1 Concurrency

Distributed transaction processing requires database concurrency control mechanisms [ESWARAN 76, GRAY 78] in order to avoid interference among concurrently executing transactions. The concurrency control mechanism should not require centralized services for resource allocation or deadlock detection. Distributed concurrency control algorithms, including distributed deadlock detection, which do not impact site autonomy have been developed, [OBERMARCK 80] and [MENASCE 78]. The R* techniques used for deadlock detection and resolution are different from those in System R (section 7.2), but the concurrency control mechanisms used in R* are the same as those used in System R.

7.2 Deadlock Detection and Resolution

The SDD-1 system has an interesting technique for reducing deadlock occurrences. It attempts to analyze the read and write sets of queries and group them into classes that require disjoint sets of resources. Then one query in each class can be run without interference and so no deadlock should occur. However, for unpredictable data references during query execution this technique would not work.

The distributed deadlock detection algorithm in R* attempts to maximize site autonomy, minimize messages and minimize unnecessary processing or other bottlenecks [OBERMARCK 80]. The basic idea is that each site does periodic deadlock detection using transaction wait-for information gathered locally or received from other sites. Real deadlock cycles are resolved and potential cycles are converted to transaction wait-for 'strings'. Each 'string' is sent to the next site along the path of the (potential) multi-site deadlock cycle only if the first transaction number in the string is less than the last transaction number in the string. This is an optimization to reduce the number of messages sent. Note also that other orderings could be chosen. This process continues until a cycle is found. The cycle will be found at one site only (due to the transaction ordering) and only sites involved in the transaction will be involved in finding it. This is usually 2 or 3 sites only in what is potentially a very large network. When a deadlock cycle is discovered a standard deadlock cycle breaker program is run and the deadlock is broken by aborting one of the transactions (such as the one that has done the least work so far). The other sites involved in the chosen transaction will be told subsequently to abort the transaction.

An example distributed deadlock is shown in Figure 3. There are three sites 1,2,3 and three transactions X,Y,Z each of which has an agent waiting for resources at a remote site. The algorithm for breaking the deadlock can be understood by following the messages sent from site to site until the cycle is found at site 3.

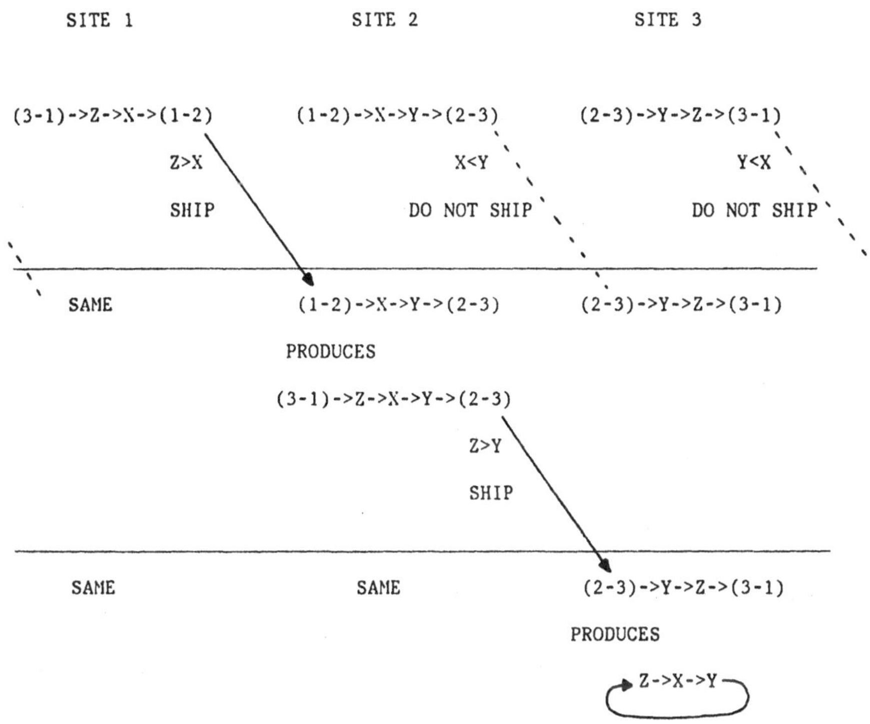

X, Y, Z ARE TRANSACTIONS

-> MEANS "WAITS FOR"

(I-J) MEANS REMOTE CALL FROM SITE I TO SITE J

Figure 3. Global Deadlock Detection.

7.3 Logging and Recovery

The mechanisms used for logging are the same as in System R. As previously discussed each site involved in a transaction has to log data changes and commit decisions during two phase commit. If a site or communications link fails during query execution before two phase commit, time-outs will occur at the calling site and the called sites and the transaction will be aborted at all sites. No resources will be sequestered after time-outs have occurred. If a failure occurs after a site has entered phase one of the two phase commit then its resources are held by that transaction until communications are re-established and the in-doubt transaction status is resolved and the database made consistent.

8. SQL Additions and Changes

The SQL database language [CHAMBERLIN 76] developed for System R has been extended for R* and some example extensions are given below. These extensions are not the only ones needed, nor because of space limitations, can each be fully explained. However it is hoped that they give the reader an idea of the kind of high-level non-procedural language statements needed in a distributed database system like R*.

```
DEFINE SYNONYM <relation-name> AS <System-Wide-Name>

DISTRIBUTE TABLE <table-name> HORIZONTALLY INTO
   <name> WHERE <predicate> IN SEGMENT <segment-name site>
    .
    .
   <name> WHERE <predicate> IN SEGMENT <segment-name site>

DISTRIBUTE TABLE <table-name> VERTICALLY INTO
   <name> <column-name-list> IN SEGMENT <segment-name site>
```

```
   <name> <column-name-list> IN SEGMENT <segment-name site>


DISTRIBUTE TABLE <table-name> REPLICATED INTO
   <name> IN SEGMENT <segment-name site>
   .
   .
   <name> IN SEGMENT <segment-name site>


DEFINE SNAPSHOT <snapshot-name> (<attribute-list>)
       AS <query>
       REFRESHED EVERY <period>;


REFRESH SNAPSHOT <snapshot-name>


CREATE INDEX <name> ON <table-name>
DROP INDEX <name> FOR <table-name>


MIGRATE TABLE <table-name> TO <segment-name site>
```

9. STATUS OF R* AND FUTURE PLANS

As of November 1981, when this paper was written, large sections of R* have been coded and tested as an experimental prototype system. The transaction management, communications environment and system interfaces for CICS running under VM or MVS have been coded and run in a single processor. The compiler, optimizer and access path selector have also been written. Code generation from the R* compiler is just beginning. R* has just started sending the first messages for remote catalog look-up and for distributed compilation. The RSS data management, deadlock detection, commit/abort processing, logging and recovery have been tested.

Future work includes linking the coded subsystems together once they are all written, the generation of code from the compiler and the execution and testing of "distributed queries" running, at first, in a single machine environment. Then we will bring up physically separate machines and test actual distributed processing with real message traffic using the CICS/ISC (Inter-Systems-Communications) facility. Next different kinds of data distributions will be examined. By that time we should be able to examine the overall behaviour of R* and to make improvements to the optimizer and to the system code to improve the performance and possibly the design too. R* is a large experimental project and we are under no illusions that we have got it all just right!

10. CONCLUSIONS

We have presented the overall architecture of R*, emphasizing those issues that affect the autonomy of the sites participating in the distributed database. A key ingredient of site autonomy is careful distribution of function and transaction management responsibility among the participating sites. Avoiding global and centralized data and control structures is required, not only to enhance local autonomy, but also to facilitate graceful system growth, data protection and failure resiliency.

Data access authorization is managed by the site holding the data and remote access requests are authenticated. Local control and stand alone processing capabilities require that all relevant catalog structures be locally stored and managed. Distributed query compilation was developed to support local site autonomy. Local representation of compiled query fragments allows local invalidation of the query if local objects or authorizations are modified. Although local control must be surrendered to the coordinator site during the transaction commit protocol, careful selection of a distributed commit protocol can minimize the duration of the loss of local control.

The R* architecture supports several kinds of data distribution. Attention has been given to efficient execution of programs by the compilation and optimization of users queries and SQL programs.

Unlike other DDBMS (e.g. INGRES [STONEBRAKER 77] and SDD-1 [ROTHNIE

80]), R*'s emphasis on site autonomy has led us away from shared control and globally managed or centralized catalog and name resolution structures. At the same time, R* provides transparent remote data definition and manipulation facilities, distributed transaction management, and distributed concurrency control which should simplify data sharing for both ad hoc query users and application programmers. Existing single site SQL programs and queries can be run against distributed data without modification in an R* environment and programmers can continue to develop programs without having to worry about network issues.

ACKNOWLEDGMENTS

The following people have contributed to the R* work also, and we would like to acknowledge their main contributions: M. Adiba who developed snapshots, J. Gray who worked on the architecture, recovery and commit, F. Putzolu who developed the RSS data management, and I. Traiger who worked on several distributed systems issues and the RSS data management.

REFERENCES

[Adiba 80a] M.Adiba, J.M.Andrade, P.Decitre, F.Fernandez and Nguyen Gia Toan, "Polypheme: An Experience in Distributed Database System Design and Implementation", Proc. of the International Symposium on Distributed Databases, Distributed Databases, North Holland Publishing Company, Paris, March 1980.

[Adiba 80b] M.E.Adiba and B.G.Lindsay. "Database Snapshots", IBM Research Report RJ2772, San Jose, CA. March 1980.

[Aho 79] A.V.Aho, C.Beeri and J.D.Ullman, "The Theory of Joins in Relational Databases", ACM Transactions on Database Systems, Vol.4, No.3, September 1979, p.297.

[Astrahan 76] M.M.Astrahan, M.W.Blasgen, D.D.Chamberlin, K.P.Eswaran, J.N.Gray, P.P.Griffiths, W.F.King, R.A.Lorie, P.R.McJones, J.W.Mehl, G.R.Putzolu, I.L.Traiger, B.Wade, and V.Watson, "System R: A Relational Approach to Database Management", ACM Transactions on Database Systems, Vol.1, No.2, June 1976, p.97.

[Blasgen 79] M.W.Blasgen, M.M.Astrahan, D.D.Chamberlin, J.N.Gray, W.F.King, B.G.Lindsay, R.A.Lorie, J.W.Mehl, T.G.Price, G.R.Putzolu, M.Schkolnick, P.G.Selinger, D.R.Slutz, I.L.Traiger, B.W.Wade, and R.A.Yost, "System R: An Architectural Update", IBM Research Report RJ2581, San Jose, CA, July 1979.

[Chamberlin 76] D.D.Chamberlin, M.M.Astrahan, K.P.Eswaran, P.P.Griffiths, R.A.Lorie, J.W.Mehl, P.Reisner, and B.W.Wade, "SEQUEL 2: A Unified Approach to Data Definition, Manipulation, and Control", IBM Journal of Research and Development, November 1976, p. 560. (Also, see errata in January 1979 issue.)

[CICS 78] CICS Inter System Communication,
"CICS/VS System/Application Design Guide", Chapter 13, Version1, Release 4, IBM Form Number SC33-0068-1, June 1978, pp.379-412.
"CICS/VS Introduction to Program Logic", Chapter 1.6, Version 1, Release 4, IBM Form Number SC33-0067-1, June 1978, pp.83-110.

[Daniels 82] D.Daniels, "Query Compilation in a Distributed Database System", Masters Thesis in preparation, Department of EECS, MIT, Cambridge, Mass. For January 1982.

[Epstein 78] R.S.Epstein, M.Stonebraker and E.Wong, "Distributed Query Processing in Relational Database Systems". Proc. 78 ACM SIGMOD Conference on Management of Data, Austin, Texas, May 1978.

[Epstein 80] R.Epstein and M.Stonebraker, "Analysis of Distributed Database Processing Strategies." International Conference on Very Large Data Bases, Montreal , October 1980.

[Eswaran 76] K.P.Eswaran, J.N.Gray, R.A.Lorie, and I.L.Traiger, "The Notions of Consistency and Predicate Locks in a Database System", Communications of the ACM, Vol.19, No.11, November 1976, pp. 624-633.

[Gray 78] J.N.Gray, "Notes on Data Base Operating Systems", in Operating Systems An Advanced Course, Lecture Notes in Computer Science 60, (ed. Goos and Hartmanis), Springer-Verlag, 1978, pp. 393-481.

[Griffiths 76] P.Griffiths and B.Wade, "An Authorization Mechanism for a Relational Database System", ACM Transactions on Database Systems, Vol.1, No.3, September, 1976, pp. 242-255.

[Hammer 79] M.Hammer and D.Shipman, "Reliability Mechanisms for SDD-1: A System for Distributed Databases", Computer Corporation of America Technical Report, July 1979.

[Kent 76] S.T.Kent, "Encryption-Based Protocols for Interactive User-Computer Communication", Masters Thesis, Laboratory for Computer Science TR-162, Massachusetts Institute of Technology, Cambridge, Mass., May 1976.

[Lampson 80a] B.W.Lampson and H.E.Sturgis, "Crash Recovery in a Distributed Data Storage System", Communications of the ACM, to appear.

[Lampson 80b] B.W.Lampson, "Replicated Commit", Workshop on Fundamental Issues in Distributed Systems, Pala Mesa, CA. Dec. (paper dated November 24), 1980.

[LeBihan 80] J.Le Bihan, C.Esculier, G.Le Lann, L.Treille, "SIRIUS-DELTA: Un Prototype de systeme de gestion de bases de donnees reparties". Proceedings of the International Symposium on Distributed Databases, Paris, March 1980.

[Lindsay 79] B.G.Lindsay, P.G.Selinger, C.Galtieri, J.N.Gray, R.A.Lorie, F.Putzolu, I.L.Traiger and B.W.Wade, "Single and Multi-site Recovery Facilities", Distributed Data Bases, Edited by I.W.Draffan and F.Poole, Cambridge University Press, 1980, Chapter 10. Also available as "Notes on Distributed Databases", IBM Research Laboratory RJ2571, San Jose, CA., July 1979.

[Lindsay 80a] B.G.Lindsay and P.Selinger, "Site Autonomy Issues in R*: a Distributed Database Management System", IBM Research Report RJ 2927, San Jose, CA., 1980.

[Lindsay 80b] B.G.Lindsay, "Object Naming and Catalog Management for a Distributed Database Manager", Proceedings 2nd International Conference on Distributed Computing Systems, Paris, France, April 1981. Also: IBM Research Report RJ2914, San Jose, CA., August 1980.

[Menasce 78] D.A.Menasce and R.R.Muntz, "Locking and Deadlock Detection in Distributed Databases", Proc. 3rd Berkeley Workshop on Distributed Data Management and Computer Networks, August 1978, pp. 215-232.

[Moss 81] J.E.B.Moss, "Nested Transactions: An Approach to Reliable Distributed Computing", Ph.D. Thesis, Report MIT/LCS/TR-260, Department of EECS, MIT, Cambridge, April 81.

[Needham 78] R.M.Needham and M.D.Schroeder, "Using Encryption for Authentication in Large Networks of Computers", Communications of the ACM, Vol.21, No.12, December 1978, pp. 993-999.

[Ng 82] P.Ng, "Distributed Compilation and Recompilation of Database Queries", Masters Thesis in preparation, Department of EECS, MIT, Cambridge, Mass., for January 1982.

[Obermarck 80] R.Obermarck, "Global Deadlock Detection Algorithm", IBM Research Laboratory RJ2845, San Jose, CA., June 1980.

[Rothnie 77] J. B. Rothnie and N. Goodman, "An Overview of the Preliminary Design of SDD-1: A System for Distributed Databases", Proc. 2nd Berkeley Workshop on Distributed Data Management and Computer Networks, Lawrence Berkeley Laboratory, University of California, Berkeley, CA, May 1977, pp. 39-57.

[Rothnie 80] J.B.Rothnie, Jr., P.A.Bernstein, S.Fox, N.Goodman, M.Hammer, T.A.Landers, C.Reeve, D.Shipman, and E.Wong, "Introduction to System for Distributed Databases (SDD-1)", ACM Transaction on Database Systems, Vol.5, No.1, March 1980, p. 1.

[Rosenkrantz 78] D.J.Rosenkrantz, R.E.Stearns, and R.M.Lewis, "System Level Concurrency Control for Distributed Database Systems", ACM Transaction on Database Systems, Vol.3, No.2, June 1978, pp. 178-198.

[Selinger 79] P.G.Selinger, M.M.Astrahan, D.D.Chamberlin, R.A.Lorie and T.G.Price, "Access Path Selection in a Relational Database Management System", Proceedings of the ACM SIGMOD Conference, June 1979.

[Selinger 80] P.G.Selinger and M.Adiba, "Access Path Selection in Distributed Database Management Systems". Proceedings of International Conference on Databases, University of Aberdeen, Scotland. July 1980. pp.204-215.

[Stonebraker 77] M.Stonebraker and E.Neuhold, "A Distributed Data Base Version of INGRES", Proc. 2nd Berkeley Workshop on Distributed Data Management and Computer Networks, Lawrence Berkeley Lab, Univ. of California, Berkeley, CA., May 1977, pp. 19-36.

[Tandem] See sales literature. Tandem Corp., Cupertino, CA.

[Wilms 81] P.F.Wilms and B.G.Lindsay, "A Database Authorization Mechanism Supporting Individual and Group Authorization". Second Seminar on Distributed Data Sharing Systems June 1981, to be published by North Holland Publishing Company, April 1982.

R*: A Distributed Data Sharing System

Robert A. Yost
Laura M. Haas

IBM Research Laboratory
San Jose, California 95193

ABSTRACT: R* is an operational, experimental, distributed database management system which supports the Structured Query Language (SQL). It was designed and implemented at the IBM Research Laboratory, San Jose, California. This paper describes some of the facilities in R* which simplify the sharing of data in a network of interconnected database sites. It also describes various ways that workstations might be useful in this distributed environonment.

INTRODUCTION AND HISTORY

R* is an operational, experimental, distributed database management system which supports the Structured Query Language (SQL). It was designed and implemented at the IBM Research Laboratory, San Jose, California.

R* uses the relational model of data which was pioneered by IBM Fellow E. F. Codd in the early 1970s and prototyped by the System R project team (IBM Research, San Jose) in the mid- and late-1970s. More recently, IBM has introduced program products derived from this technology, namely the Structured Query Language Data System (SQL/DS) for use on the DOS/VSE and VM/CMS operating systems, and Database 2 (DB2) for use on the MVS operating system.

This paper briefly describes some of the characteristics of the R* system, which represents an evolutionary extension to the current IBM relational technology. Those interested in more information are invited to read some of the more than 30 publications which describe R* in considerable detail. A bibliography identifying some of these publications is included at the end of this paper.

AS WITH ALL EXPERIMENTATION DONE AT THE IBM RESEARCH DIVISION, THERE CAN BE NO GUARANTEE THAT ANY OF THE FUNCTIONS DESCRIBED HEREIN WILL EVER BE AVAILABLE IN A PROGRAM PRODUCT.

R*: THE BASIC IDEA

In R*, there may be one or more database sites that are located at geographically dispersed locations. Figure 1 on page 2 illustrates how R* might be configured at a company that manufactures widgets in Los Angeles and has regional sales offices in San Francisco, New York, Chicago and Seattle. Given this database network topology, an application program could be run at Los Angeles which would produce a report based on information stored at any or all of the database sites. This application program would contain SQL database requests but would have no data communication requests. The R* system would handle all data communication and would return the results to the application. This ability to share geographically dispersed data is what R* is all about.

In the current implementation of R*, the granularity of data distribution is a single table. In other words, each table is located at precisely one location in the database network. In future distributed DBMSs there may be finer levels of data fragmentation whereby either horizontal and/or vertical subsets of tables could be individually dispersed in the network.

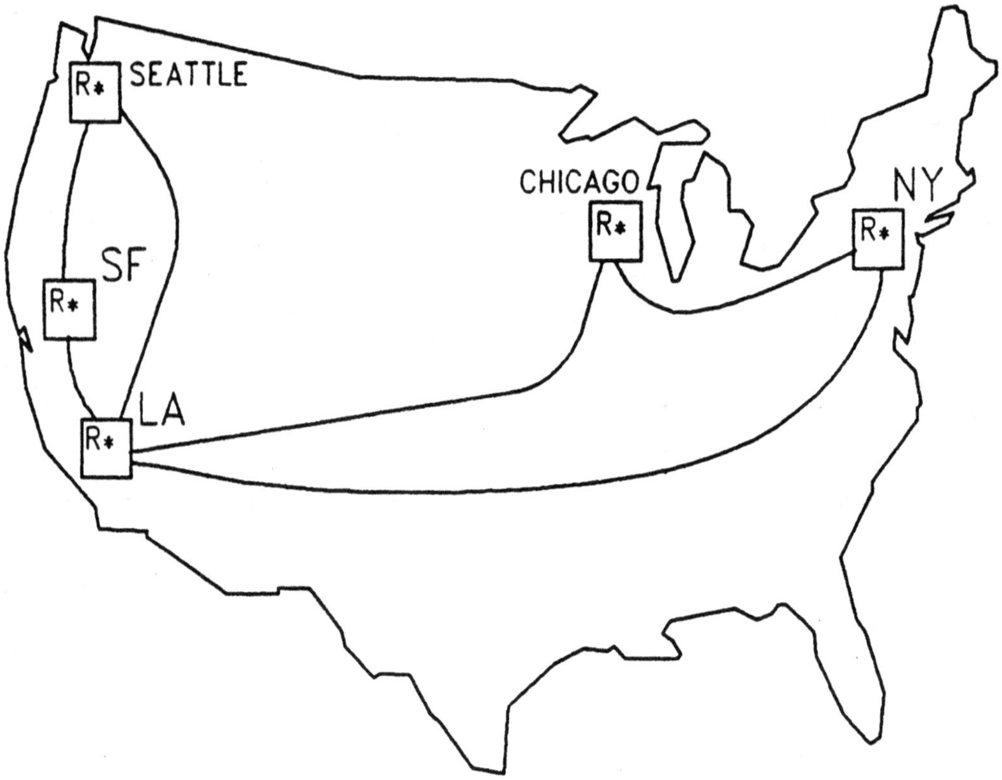

In R*, database objects may be stored at geographically distant database sites. In this illustration, a suitably authorized user at the Los Angeles site may access data objects located at any database site in the network.

Figure 1: R*: The Basic Idea

WHAT PROBLEM DOES R* SOLVE?

In a centralized database management system, such as DB2 or SQL/DS, each database instance is located at a single geographic site. These centralized systems simplify the job of sharing data by providing a high-level database language (SQL), unit-of-work (i.e., transaction) management, concurrency management, authorization services and more. But what happens to data sharing when an enterprise has more than one of these centralized DBMSs? For applications that access only local data, there is no data sharing problem. However, for applications that need to access data at one or more remote databases, there is a data sharing problem and current centralized DBMSs do little, if anything, to help.

Figure 2 illustrates this problem. Assume that widget salespeople in New York need to access both sales information located in their local database and inventory information located at the manufacturing plant in Los Angeles. They need this information in order to produce a report which predicts their ability to supply future demand for widgets in the New York area. There are several ways for the salespeople in New York to access the data located in Los Angeles: 1) They could telephone someone at Los Angeles and ask them to query the database and describe the results; 2) They could connect a terminal located in New York to application programs running against the Los Angeles database; 3) They could extract a data file containing the relevant inventory information from the Los Angeles database and transmit it to New York. Regardless of which of these methods is used, the inventory data obtained from Los Angeles would then have to be combined with the sales data from New York by the application program or the salespeople themselves to produce the desired report. There are numerous variations on how one might overcome the difficulties created by the fact that some of the required data is stored in a remote database; but each variation adds complexity for either the application designer or end-user that would not be necessary if all the data were located in a single DBMS.

A distributed DBMS, such as R*, dramatically simplifies this data sharing problem by permitting application programs to access data objects stored in a network of interconnected database sites by simply issuing database requests. Assume for a moment that R* is installed at both Los Angeles and

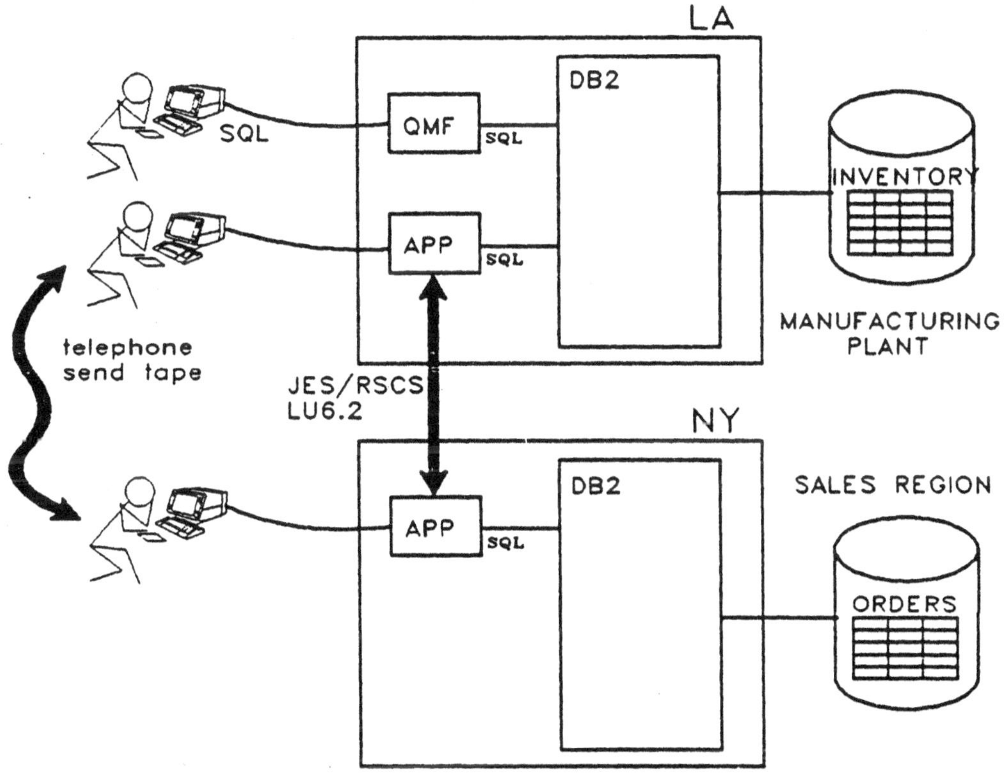

Figure 2: Application design is difficult

New York (see Figure 3). Assume also that the custodians of the Los Angeles database have entered appropriate SQL commands to authorize access to portions of the inventory tables to the salespeople at New York. An application program could then be written that contains SQL statement that reference the sales information tables located in the New York database and inventory information tables located in the Los Angele database. The salespeople could then run the application at New York and generate the report.

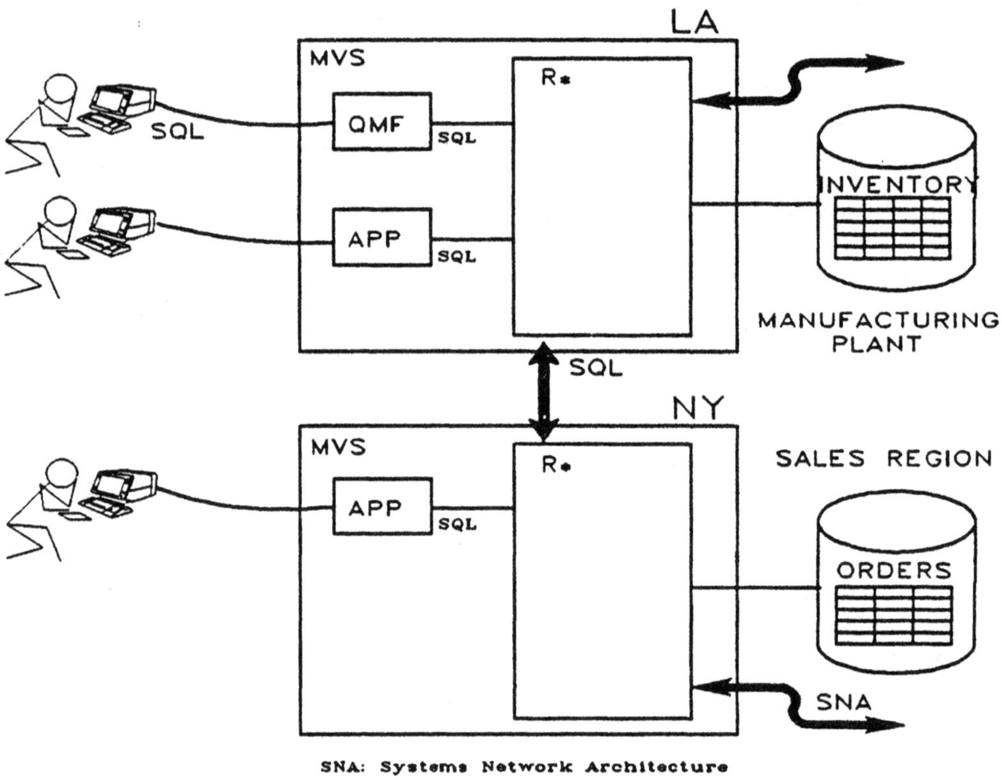

Figure 3: Application Design is Simplified

R* PROTOTYPE ENVIRONMENT

Figure 4 on page 5 shows the environment and various components of the R* prototype. The prototype runs in an MVS operating system in conjunction with TSO (Time Sharing Option) and CICS/VS (Customer Information Control System). Each R* System runs in an MVS address space under control of CICS/VS. There can be more than one such R* system in a single MVS system, and each can support

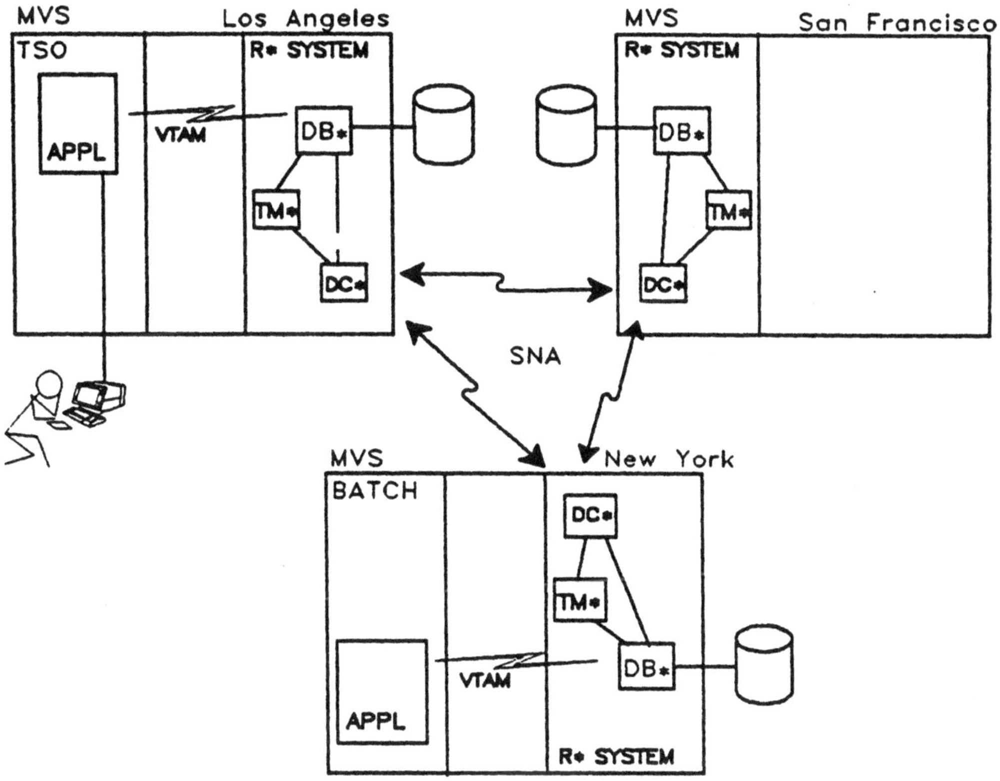

Figure 4: R* Prototype Components

multiple "database sites". This ability to run multiple "database sites" in a single machine has proved invaluable in the implementation and testing of the R* function.

Applications that use R* may be written in PL/I, System/370 Assembler Language or COBOL. As in the DB2 and the SQL/DS program products, these applications contain embedded "EXEC SQL" statements which define the database requests. The applications execute in a user's TSO address space. Requests for database function are sent to an R* system address space. A modified version of QMF (Query Management Facility) allows TSO users to make ad-hoc queries and produce reports. The R* system uses the ISC (Inter-System Communication) capabilities of CICS to communicate with "database sites" located in other R* systems.

R* OBJECTIVES AND DESIGN ASPECTS

R* was designed to satisfy three design objectives: it should (1) be easy to use, (2) be capable of autonomous operation, and (3) provide good performance. To satisfy these objectives, many difficult design choices were addressed such as query decomposition, optimal site and access path selection, transaction consistency, locking and deadlock detection, recovery and resilience with respect to site failure.

The first objective is **ease of use**. R* is easy to use because application program developers and end-users can use SQL to access data objects just as they do today in SQL/DS or DB2. In fact, someone familiar with either DB2 or SQL/DS should feel right at home with R*. The reason that R* users can use SQL is that R* supports the notion of **data location transparency**. The database worries about where an object is currently stored, not the application programmer or end-user. In fact, in R* a single application program can be written which executes at many different database sites in the network. At each site, a specially tailored access plan is developed by the database to optimize access to the database objects defined in the application, given its execution location and the current locations of the database objects that it references.

The second R* objective is **site autonomy**. One way to characterize a distributed system is the degree to which a single node in the system can operate when connections to all other nodes fail. In R*, this ability to operate autonomously is considered vital. Sites should also be administered independently. They should be able to add new users to their system, switch to new releases, etc., without consulting any central authority. To achieve this degree of autonomy, each database site must be entirely self-sufficient; it cannot rely on any form of central service such as a central name server or a central point for detecting deadlocks. Autonomy also implies that individual sites do not have global knowledge about what operations are taking place at other sites and that individual sites will continue database processing despite site and/or communication failures.

The third, and final, R* objective is **good performance**. There are many things in R* that were done to promote good performance; only two will be mentioned here. First, as in SQL/DS and DB2, SQL statements are **compiled** (as illustrated in Figure 5 on page 7) into access modules. During compilation, database object names are resolved, access paths are determined, authorization rights are validated, and access plans are distributed to all involved database sites. This early binding makes it unnecessary to repeat many of these time-consuming operations each time the application program is actually executed. The second thing that leads to good performance is that R* enables users to place copies of data in their local system to avoid the overhead of using the communication system when their applications are executed. This concept is called **locality of reference** and is vital to good performance in any distributed system which utilizes relatively slow and unreliable communication devices. A user can invoke the new MIGRATE TABLE statement to physically move a table from a remote database site to the local database site. Alternatively, a user can create a **snapshot** of data. A snapshot is a stored database object, like a table, but it is for read-only access and is periodically refreshed from the base objects in its definition. The definition of a snapshot is in the form of an arbitrary SQL SELECT query. Figure 6 on page 8 shows three snapshots of a single base table located in Los Angeles. The R* implementation of snapshots is particularly attractive when the snapshot definition is on a single base table. In that case, the refresh process sends only the differential information to the snapshot site, rather than simply re-executing the entire query.

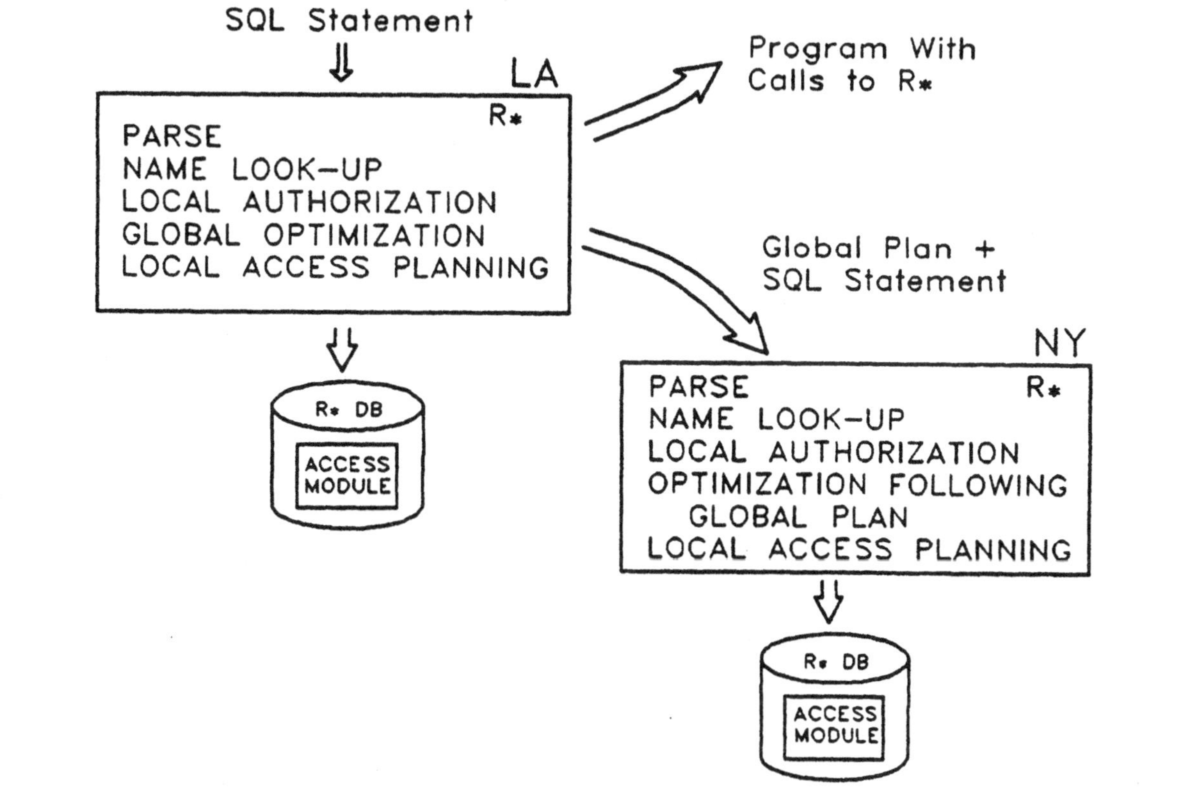

Figure 5: Compilation of SQL is Distributed

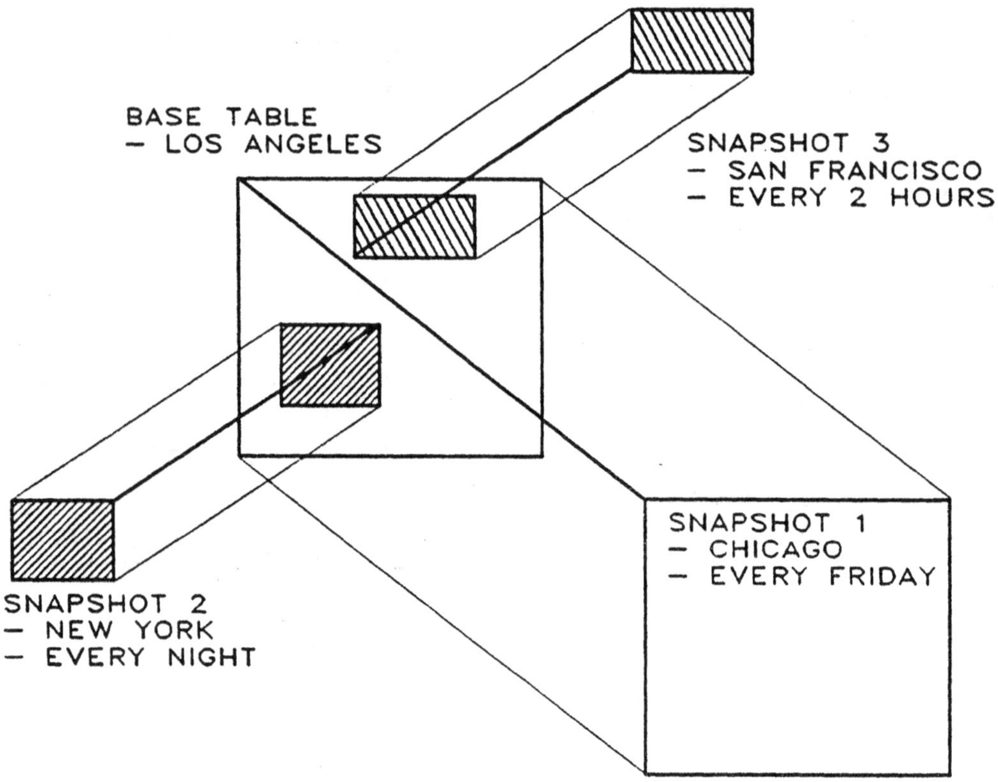

Figure 6: Snapshots: Read-only Copies of Data

When a snapshot is defined on a single base table, then the refresh process will transmit differential information to each snapshot site; it will not re-execute the snapshot definition.

PROTOTYPE STATUS

Most SQL functions and system services are supported by the R* prototype in a location-transparent manner. The compiler, optimizer, access path selector, plan selector and access structure generator are all operational. SQL data manipulation statements for SELECT, INSERT, UPDATE, DELETE, multi-table joins, subqueries, INSERT FROM subquery, various data aggregation services (e.g., SUM, MAX, AVG, etc.), ORDER BY and duplicate elimination all work. Authorization checking works. In addition to authorization based on user identification, R* supports the notion of GROUPs of users. Users are assigned to GROUPs and then either users or GROUPs are authorized access to database objects. VIEWS and snapshots are operational. The SQL data definition commands are supported so that, for example, remote tables can be CREATED and DROPPED. The MIGRATE function works; this new SQL command is used to move snapshots as well as tables from one database site to another. The INTRODUCE

DATABASE function also works; this new SQL command is executed at each of two database sites before data can be shared.

Solutions to the difficult problems involving distributed computation and recovery management are operational. A unit-of-work (i.e., a transaction) is always uniform and atomic regardless of machine or communication failures. R* uses commit protocols designed to reduce commit overhead (both messages and log writes). If, during database restart, "in-doubt" transactions are present on the R* log, then the resources used by the transaction are locked until the coordinating site resolves whether the transaction should be committed or aborted.

A distributed deadlock detection mechanism detects and resolves deadlocks among processes in either the same or different sites. Transaction management, communication services, data management, deadlock detection, logging and recovery are all operational. In fact, there are only two major SQL functions missing from R*: support for UNION and support for LONG FIELDs that exist in tables stored at remote locations. There are no significant technical problems in implementing these functions.

CURRENT FOCUS

The new focus of the R* project is to address the role of intelligent workstations in the distributed SQL environment hypothesized by R*. The first step will be to build a new, experimental database management system supporting the SQL language, yet small enough to run in an IBM Personal Computer (PC). This system will be prototyped initially for PC/DOS but will be portable so that it should be easy to move it to other operating systems and processors. Figure 7 on page 10 shows the proposed new R* workstation DBMS. It will support concurrent transactions, transaction recovery, compilation and eventually many of the distributed characteristics of the mainframe R* system.

At the same time, work will proceed on various ways of connecting application programs running in workstations with SQL databases, wherever those databases might reside. Several possible configurations are being considered. Figure 8 on page 10 shows an application program running in a workstation connected by a communication link to a mainframe that has an R* database. Associated with this application is an **SQL Stub** that performs communication services, blocking/deblocking and field conversion. Since the database is R*, the application running in the workstation can access SQL data objects stored in either LA or NY, subject to authorization constraints.

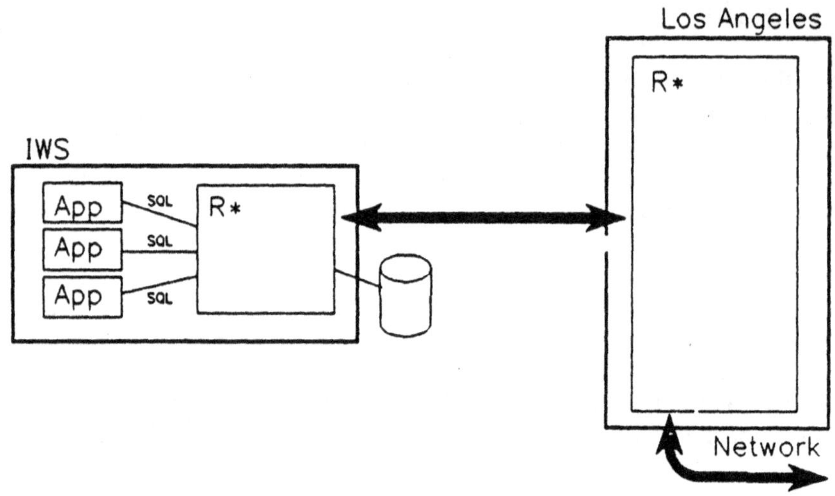

Figure 7: A Personal R* Database

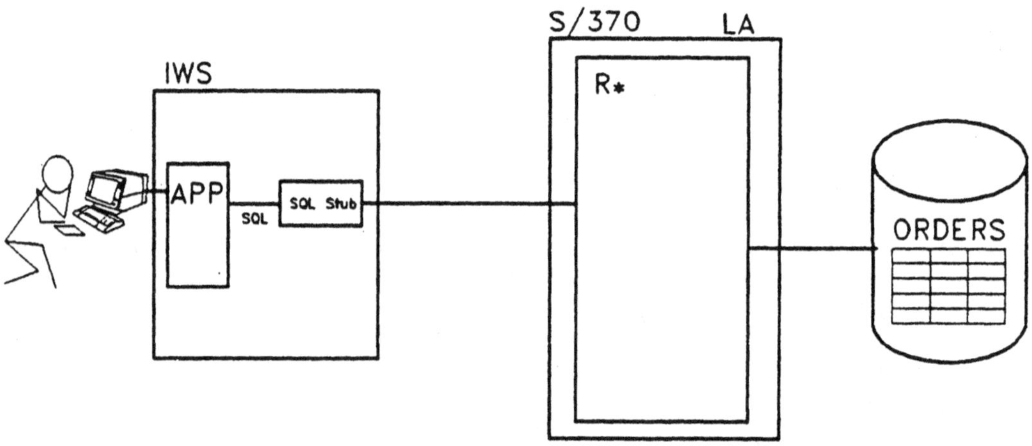

Figure 8: SQL Applications Running Outboard of Host

Figure 9 on page 11 shows the proposed new R* workstation database operating as a database server, perhaps a departmental database. In this configuration there are two intelligent workstations connected to the database server via a local area network (LAN). One of the workstations is running a multi-tasking system (e.g., TOPVIEW) that has two applications concurrently connected to the database server. Since the database server is an R* node, which is connected to a functionally superior R* running on a host, the applications running on the workstation can use SQL to access data objects located elsewhere in the database network.

These are but a few of the configurations which are possible. Other configurations include personal databases and database servers interconnected **without** hosts. There is much room for research in this arena. Many of the design decisions made originally for mainframe, peer-to-peer, systems need to be reconsidered for the workstation/host environment.

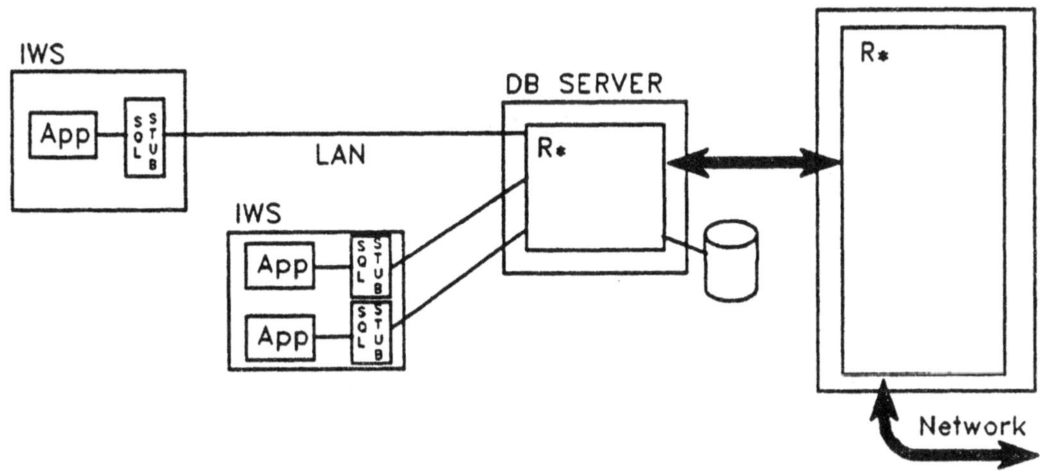

Figure 9: SQL Database Server is the Host

CONCLUSION

The R* prototype has demonstrated that it is possible to build a distributed SQL system that is easy to use, can run autonomously and has good performance. It appears likely that workstation databases can be incorporated into the R* design and can thereby increase the degree of potential data sharing. Instead of just a few dozen large hosts sharing data, there may be thousands of workstations connected together or connected to a back-bone host database network. The level of potential data sharing in such a network is mind-boggling. Much research needs to be done to understand the various design alternatives and to understand how to configure and administer such distributed database networks.

Since the principal purpose of database management systems is to promote the sharing of data, and since enterprises are opting for multiple systems environments, it seems likely that many DBMSs of the future will be of the distributed variety. To the extent that these distributed systems are able to promote even greater data sharing than today's centralized DBMSs, they will have contributed substantially to the field of database management.

ACKNOWLEDGEMENTS

The implementation of R* has not been a simple exercise. It has required the efforts of many researchers to achieve the current level of function. The authors wish to thank all of those who have contributed, especially Pat Selinger, who formed the project and managed it for many years, Bruce Lindsay, who has been a principal architect of R* from the very beginning of the project, and Irv Traiger (our manager), who was instrumental in the recent expansion of R* into the workstation arena.

The current R* project members who are making contributions to the workstation R* effort are Walter Chang, Bill Cody, Laura Haas (manager), George Lapis, Bruce Lindsay, Guy Lohman, Lothar Mackert (visiting scientist), John McPherson, C. Mohan, Paul Wilms and Robert Yost (manager).

BIBLIOGRAPHY

AdLi80 Adiba, M., Lindsay, B. *Database Snapshots*, **Proc. 6th International Conference on Very Large Data Bases**, Montreal, October 1980.

BeHL83 Bertino, E., Haas, L., Lindsay, B. *View Management in a Distributed Database System*, **Proc. 9th International Conference on Very Large Data Bases**, Florence, Italy, October-November 1983. See Also IBM Research Report RJ3851, April 1983.

BeOb81 Beeri, C., Obermarck, R. *A Resource Class Independent Deadlock Detection Algorithm*, **Proc. 7th International Conference on Very Large Data Bases**, Cannes, France, September 1981.

DSHLM82 Daniels, D., Selinger, P., Haas, L., Lindsay, B., Mohan, C., Walker, A., Wilms, P. *An Introduction to Distributed Query Compilation in R**, In **Distributed Data Bases**, H.J. Schneider (Ed.), **Proc. 2nd International Symposium on Distributed Data Bases**, Berlin, September 1982, North Holland Publishing Company. Also IBM Research Report RJ3497, 1982.

HSBDL82 Haas, L.M., Selinger, P.G., Bertino, E., Daniels, D., Lindsay, B., Lohman, G., Masunaga, Y., Mohan, C., Ng, P., Wilms, P., Yost, R. *R*: A Research Project on Distributed Relational DBMS*, **Database Engineering**, Vol. 5, No. 2, December 1982.

LDHKS84 Lohman, G., Daniels, D., Haas, L., Kistler, R., Selinger, P. *Optimization of Nested Queries in a Distributed Relational Database*, IBM Research Report RJ4260, April 1984.

LHMWY84 Lindsay, B., Haas, L., Mohan, C., Wilms, P., Yost, R. *Computation and Communication in R*: A Distributed Database Manager*, **ACM Transactions on Computer Systems**, Vol. 2, No. 1, February 1984. Also in **Proc. 9th ACM Symposium on Operating Systems Principles**, Bretton Woods, October 1983. Also IBM Research Report RJ3740, January 1983.

Lind81 Lindsay, B.G. *Object Naming and Catalog Management for a Distributed Database Manager*, **Proc. 2nd International Conference on Distributed Computing Systems**, Paris, April 1981.

LiSe80 Lindsay, B.G., Selinger, P.G. *Site Autonomy Issues in R*: A Distributed Database Management System*, IBM Research Report RJ2927, September 1980.

LMHDL84 Lohman, G., Mohan, C., Haas, L., Daniels, D., Lindsay, B., Selinger, P., Wilms, P. *Query Processing in R**, Forthcoming as a chapter in **Query Processing in Database Systems**, W. Kim, D. Reiner, and D. Batory (Eds.), Springer-Verlag, 1984. Also IBM Research Report RJ4272, April 1984.

LSGGL80 Lindsay, B., Selinger, P., Galtieri, C., Gray, J., Lorie, R., Putzolu, F., Traiger, I., Wade, B. *Single and Multi-Site Recovery Facilities*, In **Distributed Data Bases**, I.W. Draffan and F. Poole (Eds.), Cambridge University Press, 1980. Also Available as *Notes on Distributed Databases*, IBM Research Report RJ2571, San Jose, July 1979.

Moha84a Mohan, C. *Recent and Future Trends in Distributed Data Base Management*, **Proc. NYU Symposium on New Directions for Data Base Systems**, New York, May 1984. Also IBM Research Report RJ4240, 1984.

Moha84b Mohan, C. **Tutorial: Recent Advances in Distributed Data Base Management**, ISBN 0-8186-0571-5, IEEE Catalog Number EH0218-8, IEEE Computer Society Press, 1984.

MoLi83 Mohan, C., Lindsay, B. *Efficient Commit Protocols for the Tree of Processes Model of Distributed Transactions*, **Proc. 2nd ACM SIGACT/SIGOPS Symposium on Principles of Distributed Computing**, Montreal, Canada, August 1983. Also IBM Research Report RJ3881, June 1983.

MoSF83 Mohan, C., Strong, R., Finkelstein, S. *Method for Distributed Transaction Commit and Recovery Using Byzantine Agreement Within Clusters of Processors*, **Proc. 2nd ACM SIGACT/SIGOPS Symposium on Principles of Distributed Computing**, Montreal, Canada, August 1983. Also IBM Research Report RJ3882, June 1983.

Ng82 Ng, P. *Distributed Compilation and Recompilation of Database Queries*, IBM Research Report RJ3375, January 1982.

Ober82 Obermarck, R. *Distributed Deadlock Detection Algorithm*, **ACM Transactions on Database Systems**, Vol. 7, No. 2, June 1982.

SeAd80 Selinger, P.G., Adiba, M. *Access Path Selection in Distributed Database Management Systems*, **Proc. International Conference on Databases**, Aberdeen, Scotland, July 1980.

TGGL82 Traiger, I.L., Gray, J., Galtieri, C.A., Lindsay, B. *Transactions and Consistency in Distributed Database Systems*, **ACM Transactions on Database Systems**, Vol. 7, No. 3, September 1982.

WiLi81 Wilms, P.F., Lindsay, B.G. *A Database Authorization Mechanism Supporting Individual and Group Authorization*, In **Distributed Data Sharing Systems**, R.P. van de Riet and W. Litwin (Eds.), **Proc. 2nd International Seminar on Distributed Data Sharing Systems**, Amsterdam, June 1981, North Holland Publishing Company.

Wilm80 Wilms, P. *Qualitative and Quantitative Comparison of Update Algorithms in Distributed Databases*, **Proc. International Symposium on Distributed Data Bases**, Paris, March 1980. In Distributed Data Bases, C. Delobel, and W. Litwin (Eds.), North Holland Publishing Company.

WiLS83 Wilms, P.F., Lindsay, B.G., Selinger, P. *"I Wish I Were Over There": Distributed Execution Protocols for Data Definition in R**, Proc. **SIGMOD 83**, May 1983.

Will82 R. Williams, D. Daniels, L. Haas, G. Lapis, B. Lindsay, P. Ng, R. Obermark, P. Selinger, A. Walker, P. Wilms, R. Yost, *"R*: An Overview of the Architecture"*, **Improving Database Usability and Responsiveness**, (Procs. International Conference on Databases, Jerusalem, Israel, June 1982), P. Scheuermann, ed., Academic Press, New York, 1982, pp. 1-27. Also available as IBM Research Laboratory RJ3325, San Jose, Calif., December 1981.

The SIRIUS-DELTA Architecture: A Framework for Co-Operating Database Systems

Christian ESCULIER
56 rue Jenner, 75013 Paris, France

SIRIUS-DELTA is a distributed database system which is aimed at co-operation of heterogeneous local database systems. It illustrates how the Open Systems approach has been used in the context of distributed database systems, mainly in its architecture and its Data Manipulation Protocol. It also illustrates that distributed databases is an area where co-operation between ISO/TC97/SC5 Programming Languages and ISO/TC97/SC16 Open Systems Interconnection sub-committees is of a major importance for future developments.

Keywords: Distributed databases, open systems, standardization, data manipulation protocol, distributed execution plan.

Christian L. Esculier is an Independent Consultant, international expert in databases. An important part of his activity is related to standardization. He is a member of the three ISO/TC97/SC5 groups working on databases: WG3 (conceptual level), WG5 (co-ordination and architecture) and the Expert Group on database languages (network DDL and DML, relational). He is a member of the AFNOR database comittee and represents the French Bureau d'Orientation et de Normalisation en Informatique (BNI) in the database area. His links with experts in interconnected systems are mainly based on five years of activity on Distributed Databases in the context of the Pilot Project SIRIUS.

1. Introduction

SIRIUS-DELTA is one of the prototype systems designed and built within the framework of SIRIUS project. Its purpose is to integrate results obtained in the course of the first phase of the project by IGOR, FRERES, POLYPHEME,... prototypes and fundamental research work. After a description of SIRIUS-DELTA system principles (Section 2) and architecture (Section 3), we discuss each functional level of the system: SILOE (Section 4) dealing with distributed data management functions, SCORE (Section 5) which insures distributed data consistency and resiliency, SER (Section 6) whose function is to manage process execution on several processors.

SIRIUS-DELTA design started in 1977 and the final version of the prototype was operational in 1982 [10,15]. It is interesting to link this work to the SC5 and SC16 activity during the same period of time, and to consider the relationship between their technical domains in respect of problems met in distributed databases.

2. SIRIUS-DELTA Principles

SIRIUS-DELTA has been designed on the following basis:

* the relational model has been used for set-oriented database manipulation, at the external level and for inter-systems exchanges. The Data Manipulation Protocol is relational [5].
* the distributed executive uses a data flow approach and is oriented toward a high degree of parallelism.
* the Open Systems approach is the fundamental philosophy of the system for all aspects concerning co-operation and communication [9].

From a functional point of view, SIRIUS-DELTA provides high-level services which can be

described in terms of transparencies (for a user of SIRIUS-DELTA):
· data distribution transparency
· data replication transparency
· concurrent access transparency
· components heterogeneity transparency.

From an operational point of view, existing software and hardware products have been used as much as possible so as to allow us to focus on issues specifically related to distribution.

The essential work has been conducted in two domains:
– distributed database definition and manipulation
– distributed executive.

As a result of this work, SIRIUS-DELTA provides:
· distributed data base description functions
· distributed data base manipulation functions
· distributed concurrency control functions
· distributed execution functions.

Some mechanisms and techniques developed in SIRIUS-DELTA are very general and can be used in other distributed systems (process monitoring systems, office systems, etc.). This is specially the case for distributed concurrency control and distributed execution mechanisms [11].

3. SIRIUS-DELTA Architecture and Functionalities

SIRIUS-DELTA general architecture is described in terms of:
– the global/local duality
– a functional layering [15].

3.1. Global / Local Duality

A distributed system may be viewed at:
· a global level, which provides a unified view of the system
· a local level, which interacts with the components of the system.

As regards data, the global level is the one where the Distributed Database (DDB) appears as one single Database (DB). The local level corresponds to the database storage components where we find the actual data (local databases).

As regards transaction processing, the global level is the one where a process (producer) submits local action requests, the local level corresponding to those processes (consumers) which process the requests.

3.2. Main Functional Layers

Five basic functional layers can be defined in a Distributed Database System (D-DBS) [1], providing:
· database conventional management functions
· distributed data management functions
· distributed control functions, especially concurrency control
· distributed execution functions
· transport functions.

In SIRIUS-DELTA, the implementation of the first and last layers has taken advantage as much as possible of existing products: the REALITY database system and a point-to-point communication facility. Original software has been developed for the other three layers which are:
SILOE : distributed data management
SCORE : distributed concurrency control
SER : distributed execution.

These three layers will be described in the following sections, but some attention should be paid to the modular structure of SIRIUS-DELTA, especially concerning the distributed executive.

3.3. Distributed executive architecture and functionalities

The executive which runs SIRIUS-DELTA is implemented as a set of cooperative and local instantiations of a global executive. Cooperation among local executives does not rely on any specific (and unique) entity. In particular, such functions as scheduling of transactions and actions, concurrency control and data transfer are based on decentralized control mechanisms (see sections 5 and 6).

SIRIUS-DELTA distributed executive includes two basic layers which are:
– the task scheduling layer (SER); this achieves synchronized execution of actions for every submitted transaction (intra-transaction synchronization) which happens to run on several processing components [13]
– the concurrency control layer (SCORE); this achieves synchronization of concurrent and conflicting transactions (inter-transaction synchronization) as well as reliable termination or

abort of transactions (atomicity property) [15].

Depending on the system to be implemented, one may choose to include the SCORE layer or not to do so. For instance, SCORE would not be needed in an information retrieval system.

The basic service provided by SIRIUS-DELTA executive is the enforcement of atomic and reliable transactions in a distributed and failure-prone environment. For example, SILOE is offered such primitives as "initiate transaction", "abort transaction", "commit transaction". SIRIUS-DELTA executive guarantees that all transactions are kept atomic under all circumstances i.e.:

- modifications to be performed on behalf of a transaction are either all completed or not executed at all;
- intermediate modifications performed by a transaction are not visible to other transactions.

Transaction content is transparent to the executive. This approach offers reasonable flexibility as regards the type of application software to be implemented on top of SIRIUS-DELTA executive.

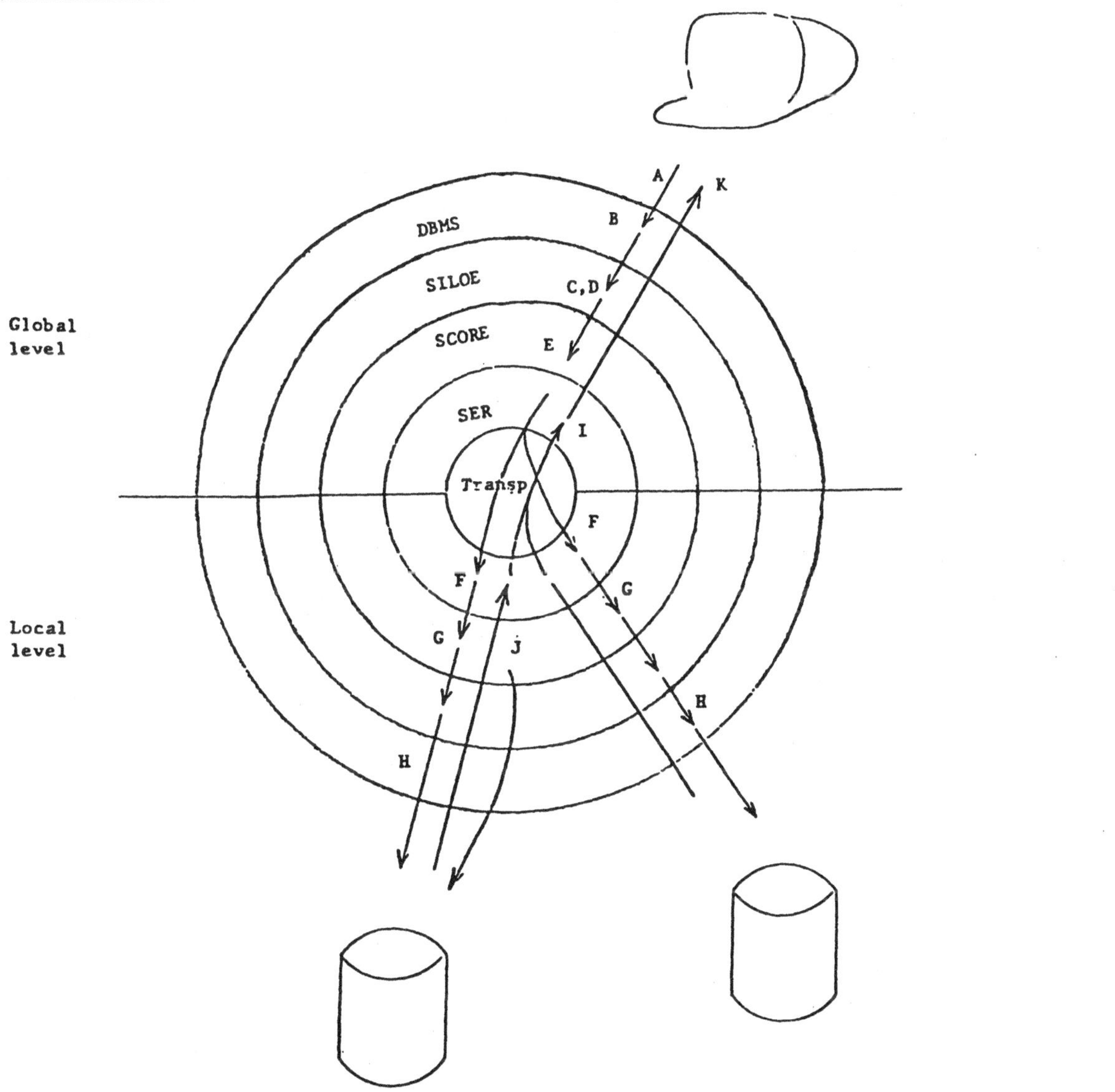

Fig. 1. SIRIUS-DELTA General Architecture.

3.4. General Architecture

SIRIUS-DELTA general architecture contains the five functional layers introduced in the previous section, both at the global and at the local level. Figure 1 gives a representation of this general architecture. Arrows indicate in what way a request goes through the system [3].

Entry (A): a request is entered by a user at the global level, using a DBMS external language which depends on an external conventional schema.

Syntactic-Semantic Analysis (B): at the global level, the DBMS validates and analyzes the request, using the user global external schema and the global conceptual schema.

Localization (C): SILOE locates data needed for processing the request. It infers local actions to be carried out and associated scenarios.

Distributed Execution Program Optimization and Production (D): if several scenarios are possible, a cost and performance evaluation is made, leading to the selection of a distributed execution program.

Transaction initialization (E): global-SCORE assigns a unique identifier to the distributed execution program (a ticket).

Local Actions Activation (F): SER activates local actions contained in the distributed execution program, on indicated sites, when activation conditions are met.

Concurrent Access Control (G): local-SCORE achieves concurrency control (access to one same data item by several local actions): compatible local actions are executed, the other ones are made to wait according to the ordering defined by a circulating sequencer.

Local Bases Utilization (H): local-SILOE and the DBMS manage local bases, with local-SILOE being mainly used as an adaptor/translator. This is local actions effective execution.

Results Transport (I): SER performs results transfers (intermediate or final) and associated synchronization.

Transaction Termination (J): for an updating transaction which completes normally, a commit protocol is triggered which involves global-SCORE/local-SCORE, with local-SILOE carrying out – via the DBMS – final writes.

Answer to User (K): the results or an execution code is returned to the user by the DBMS at the global level.

4. SILOE

SILOE in the SIRIUS-DELTA sub-system providing data localization and requests distributed evaluation.

4.1. Global SILOE

Global SILOE offers two types of functions:
- it provides global internal schema management and therefore, offers to the DDB administrator tools for the definition and validation of distribution,
- it provides for each transaction data localization, production of the associated distributed execution program and monitoring of its execution.

4.2. Local SILOE

A module interfaces each local DBMS to adapt commands to the external schema associated to the local base.
Local SILOE translates the sub-request for the associated DBMSs and completes functionalities offered by local DBMSs in order to get homogeneity of functions between processors.

4.3. Data Manipulation Protocol (DMP)

Exchanges between SILOE layers are defined using a protocol which is oriented towards relational databases manipulation. The DMP uses a control language which is close to QUEL, and results are flat sequential files representing intermediate relations.

All the local database systems must conform to this protocol. Experiments shown that heterogeneous systems can co-operate using this protocol with a limited software development for the associated adaptator in local-SILOE.

5. SCORE

SCORE is the name given to the level (and to the software) corresponding to "Système de COntrôle REparti" (Distributed Control System) which provides also for a COnsistent and REsilient handling of the SIRIUS-DELTA database.

The consistency of a data base may be threatened for many reasons, in particular:

(1) interferences between simultaneous accesses to common data items
(2) failures of system components.

SCORE's purpose is to provide mechanisms needed to maintain SIRIUS-DELTA in a consistent state. That is, not only should the database be kept consistent but so should the state information used by the distributed executive in order to process user activities correctly [4,7,11]. To this end, it is necessary to identify all the actions which the executive must associate with any given user transaction so that every "transformed" transaction is actually implemented as an atomic operation.

In order to reach this goal, SCORE includes the following three mechanisms:
(1) a decentralized synchronization mechanism, called the Circulating Sequencer
(2) locking/unlocking protocols
(3) a two-phase commit protocol.

6. SER

SER is the SIRIUS-DELTA sub-system which provides distributed execution functions over the whole set of interconnected processing components (see Fig. 2)

Services provided by SER are essentially:
- activation of remote processes
- scheduling of processes according to conditions specified by SILOE in a distributed execution program

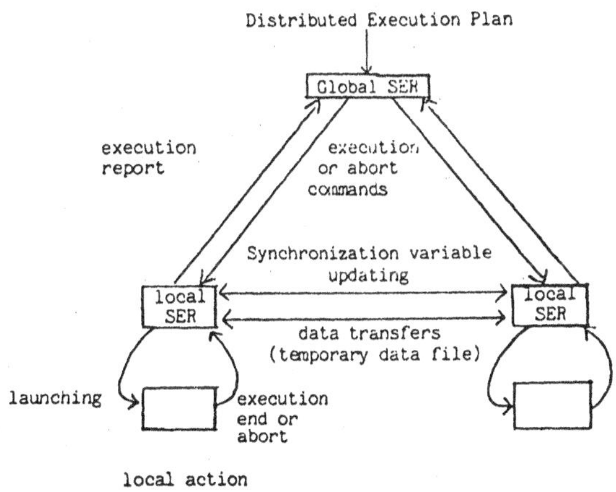

Fig. 2. SER Distributed Execution Structure.

- data transfers between processes within a distributed execution program
- logical expression and computing of process activating conditions; those conditions can be related to the results of other processes
- as far as possible, use of the parallelism provided by the set of interconnected processing components
- detection and signal of failures and of normal or abnormal end of processes execution. This is an essential service for SCORE reliable commitment protocol.

SER operation is characterized by a fully distributed execution control relying on three basic entities: Local Action, Synchronization Variable and Temporary Data File. These three entities are not only used in an internal way in regard to SER, but also by SILOE for the formulation of distributed execution program and by SCORE for resources acquisitions.

Each server SER provides for each local action context:
· preparation of its initiation, i.e. the evaluation of its activation condition
· Effective activation in connection with local operating system, making available data needed for execution
· local control of execution as well as control of normal or abnormal end, leading to end expression evaluation and eventual updating of remote synchronization variables.
· storage of data for transfer.

7. Conclusion

The SIRIUS-DELTA experiment has been profitable in various domains. In particular, it has helped us to gain:
- insight into problems which look important to the future of the computing industry in general
- practical experience in implementing, observing and debugging a distributed system
- understanding of the trade-offs to be made for future D-DBS and distributed systems intended for specific application areas.

Results concerning the layering approach and some distributed algorithms seem general enough to be used in other networking contexts (with an Ethernet-like bus for example).

Many efforts were necessary during

SIRIUS-DELTA design and development because no standards were defined for co-operation of database systems. As an example, the lack of database language standards made the definition of the Data Manipulation Protocol more difficult in terms of control language choice. The absence of any guideline for distributed executive systems has been a big problem too. The fuzziness of the three upper layers of OSI proposal has been another difficulty.

Nowadays, distributed databases systems are proposed as commercial products (see the recent ECC study on D-DBMSs available in Europe) and International Standards are an urgent need for future developments. We need from SC5 international standard database languages, and a database reference model for their harmonization.

We need from SC16 an extended OSI proposal for various kinds of networks and a basis for a distributed executive. And we need, from a common SC5/SC16 work, guidelines for all domains which overlap, and which concern most of the D-DB problematic: architecture, DMP, transaction control, execution control, etc.

SIRIUS-DELTA shows how much SC5 and SC16 domains overlap in distributed databases, and the importance of co-ordinated international standards in the area.

Acknolwedgements

The author would like to gratefully acknowledge: J. Le Bihan, G. Le Lann and L. Treille for their contribution to the production of this article, Pr. Langsford and F. Genuys for their advised comments, W. Litwin and Zabeth Baqué for their logistical support.

References

[1] M. Adiba, J.C. Chupin, R. Demolombe, G. Gardarin, J. Le Bihan, Issues in distributed data base management systems: a technical overview, Proceedings of 4th VLDB, September 1978, 89–110.

[2] ANSI: ANSI/X3/SPARC study group on database management systems, Interim report, FDT, Bulletin of ACM-SIGMOD, Vol. 7, no 2, February 1975.

[3] J. Boudenant, P. Rolin: Modeling of the transaction distribution algorithm in SIRIUS-DELTA, Symposium on distributed software and database system, July 1981, 169–176.

[4] J. Boudenant: Some solutions for distributed database recovery in SIRIUS-DELTA, Distributed data sharing systems, North-Holland publication, June 1981, 55–65.

[5] E.F. Codd: A relational model of data for large shared data banks, CACM, Vol. 13, no 6, June 1970, 377–387.

[6] Ng. X. Dang, G. Sergeant: Expression of paralle'ism and communication in distributed network processing, Proceedings of the international on parallel processing, Bellaire, Michigan, 1977.

[7] G. Ferran: Distributed checkpoint in a distributed management system, Real-time systems Symposium, December 1981.

[8] G. Gardarin, W. Chu: A distributed control algorithm for reliably and consistently updating replicated database, IEEE Transactions on Computers, Dec. 1980, Vol. C-29/N12.

[9] ISO: Information processing system – open systems interconnection, ISO/TC97/SC16/N719, February 1982, see also *Computer Networks* 5 (1981) 81–118.

[10] J. Le Bihan, C. Esculier, G. Le Lann, W. Litwin, G. Gardarin, S. Sedillot, L. Treille: SIRIUS: A French nationwide project on distributed data bases, Proceedings 6th VLDB, Montreal, October 1980, 75–85.

[11] G. Le Lann: A distributed system for real-time transaction processing, IEEE Computer, Vol. 14, no 2, February 81, 43–48.

[12] W. Litwin: Logical model of a distributed data base, 2nd Int. Seminar on distributed sharing systems R.P. Van de Riet-W. Litwin (Eds), North-Holland, June 1981, 173–207.

[13] G. Sergeant, L. Treille: SER: a system for distributed execution based on decentralized control techniques, Proceedings of the ICCC, Atlanta, 1980.

[14] S. Spaccapietra: Problematical conception of distributed databases management systems, PhD Thesis, Paris VI University, November 1978 (in french).

[15] SIRIUS Coordination: SIRIUS Systems for distributed management, 2nd International Symposium on Distributed Data Bases, September 1–3, 1982, Berlin.

An Introduction to AIDA - A Front-end to Heterogeneous Databases

M.Templeton, D.Brill, A.Chen, S.Dao, E.Lund, R.MacGregor, P.Ward

System Development Corporation
Santa Monica, CA.

ABSTRACT

AIDA (Architecture for Integrated Data Access) is a system that allows the user of one or more existing databases stored under one or more relational DBMSs to access the data using a common language, either ARIEL or SQL. It makes the complexity of manipulating data in distributed heterogeneous databases under various DBMSs transparent to the user. AIDA includes two components that have been presented in earlier papers, the Mermaid testbed and the ARIEL language and translator. The Mermaid portion of AIDA supports access to multiple databases. The user query, expressed in either ARIEL or SQL, is formulated within the user support environment, called Nexus, and translated to an intermediate language representation (DIL). The DIL is transmitted to a local or remote Mermaid distributor which includes the optimizer and controller. The optimizer will plan query execution and send commands to the controller. The controller sends messages to Mermaid drivers that reside on each computer that contains a database.

1. INTRODUCTION

Distributed data management (DDM) is a new area that requires the integration of technology from other fields such as database management, operating systems, networks, artificial intelligence (AI), user interfaces, and for Department of Defense systems, security and formal verification. SDC has developed a prototype DDM system that operates as a front-end to three relational DBMSs that runs on a network of computers connected with an Ethernet. This prototype has demonstrated the feasiblity of the concepts and has been used to experiment with different optimization algorithms and system control strategies. The basic system is now being developed into a product while research continues on extensions in the areas of nonstructured data, computer security, and integration with a deductive inference engine.

The AIDA system is a front-end which integrates existing DBMSs to provide a user with a single language to manipulate data in one or more databases that may be stored on different computers under different operating systems. The long term research goal is to develop a front-end to distributed data, text, image, voice, and knowledge objects that can satisfy future requirements for integration and sharing among loosely coupled nodes (which may be workstations) on a LAN, between LANs, or on a long haul network. The work is directed toward future evolutionary systems in which new DBMS and object management technology will constantly be replacing older technology and in which it is not only necessary but desirable to separate front-end user oriented functionality from the backend management of object resources.

Integration of data from different databases is currently done manually or by replicating data in different databases. Two factors moving the field toward distributed data management (DDM) are the development of networks which make DDM possible and the migration of users away from large central CPUs toward powerful workstations. In the future, users will need not only local personal data, but also data in other databases in order to solve a specific problem. Data may reside in different computers for many reasons such as ownership, security classification, performance, or size. Data may be stored redundantly in different computers for reliability or survivability. In addition, hardware or software upgrades may create a need for integrated access to both old and new databases or for a tool to aid data migration from an old to a new system.

We would like to stress that AIDA is a front-end system and *not* a distributed data management system (DDBMS) although it may appear to the user to be a DDBMS. The difference is the split architecture. Integrated distributed data management systems are being developed to handle databases that are designed as distributed databases. The first commercial DBMS of this type is the Tandem ENCOMPASS system [TAND81]. This homogeneous approach has many benefits. The functions of each level (DBMS, network, and operating system) can be clearly defined so that all necessary functions are performed only once. Special operations that may be needed in a distributed environment such as data transfer between databases are built into each local DBMS.

This approach works as long as the entire computer system is acquired and run as a unit. However, when databases with their associated application programs already exist, databases are managed by different DBMSs, or a variety of hardware is in use, this approach cannot be used.

Figure 1 shows a "split architecture" in which a distributor operates on top of a DBMS which can also be used independently. The distributor may or may not be part of a network operating system.

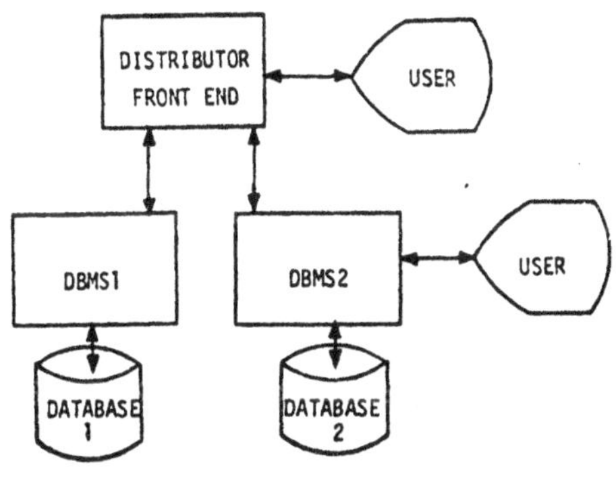

Figure 1. Split Architecture

The advantage of this approach is that each DBMS may operate autonomously when it is not participating as a node in the network. There may be complete local control over access, accounting, and resource allocation, and computers of different types may be used to run the various DBMSs.

The current AIDA configuration consists of four computers running UNIX 4.2 and connected with an Ethernet. Each computer contains a DBMS: a VAX11/780 which is host to a backend Britton-Lee IDM database machine [BRIT84], a Sun 120 with Ingres [SUN84], a Sun 170 with Ingres, and a Sun 120 with Mistress [RHOD82].

Section 2 of this paper discusses similar efforts in this area and previous SDC work in developing an independent front-end to DBMSs. Section 3 examines the AIDA system in detail, Section 4 shows an example of operation, and Section 5 discusses future plans.

2. RELATED TECHNOLOGY

Many technical problems must be solved in order to provide a front-end system which can provide transparent access to existing databases. The AIDA project has made maximum use of related technology. The related technologies may be categorized as:

- Standard user language and data model
- Query optimization
- Distributed operating systems

2.1 STANDARD USER LANGUAGE AND DATA MODEL

Transparent access to a variety of DBMSs requires the definition of a data model and data manipulation language which can be used to mediate between different DBMSs. The language and model need to be broad enough to cover all potential models used in target DBMSs and all functionality of the target language, or at least a subset of the target language which will be supported in the distributed system.

There are two stages of solution to the problem of multiple database access. The first is to provide a standard view of single databases stored under different DBMSs and to provide access to a single database at a time through a standard query language. The second is to provide an integrated view of multiple heterogeneous databases and to provide the capability to access and integrate data from several databases to answer one query. The AIDA system is addressing both parts of the problem.

The solution to the first problem, that of a common language, is being addressed by the DODIIS NQL-DD/D Project [TEMP85a], the SAFE Project [SAFE], the ADAPT Project [LOGI78], and FOCUS [FOCU]. The DODIIS (Dept. of Defense Intelligence Information System) contract was awarded to SDC in September, 1983. SDC is developing a DODIIS Query Language (DQL) and a common data dictionary and directory (DD/D) for locating data. The goal is to provide a common functionality and language that includes some features not found in the target systems, and it does not attempt to provide all features found in all target systems. This project is drawing on the technology developed by the AIDA System.

The SAFE Project is providing a complete environment for the intelligence analyst including many postprocessing tools. The common query language, SUL (SAFE User Language) is a composite of the target DBMS languages. ADAPT, an older system designed in 1976, was also designed for use by intelligence analysts. The language, UDL (Uniform Data Language), requires that the user understand the structure and access paths of each database being accessed. The functionality is close to what is supplied by the DBMS where the data is stored.

FOCUS is a product that started as a DBMS with a query language and many user interface support tools. It expanded to access other DBMSs and access methods through the same query language. Currently, it supports access to QSAM, VSAM, ISAM, IMS, IDMS, TOTAL, and ADABAS files.

The next step beyond common access to a single database at a time is common access to multiple databases. There are relatively few other efforts in this area. CCA (Computer Corporation of America) developed the language ADAPLEX [SMIT81a] and the system Multibase [SMIT81b,LAND82] which is a front-end distributor to heterogeneous DBMSs. Their goals are the same as those for AIDA although their implementation differs significantly. CCA actually built their own DBMS, called the "Local Data Manager" that manipulates data and does postprocessing. AIDA uses one or more existing DBMSs to do manipulation and postprocessing. CCA has put more emphasis on access to nonrelational DBMSs and translation than AIDA has and less emphasis on query optimization. Another difference is that AIDA is stressing a separation of the data model, the user query language, and the intermediate language. All communication between AIDA processes is via an intermediate language which is independent of the user language and the semantic model of the data.

Another system, NDMS, is being developed at CRAI in Italy [STAN83]. Its goals and architecture are very close to those of AIDA. NDMS uses SQL for the user language and has the concept of an intermediate language, although the intermediate language is very different from the one used in AIDA. The user model is the relational data model with semantic extensions, and schemata of the underlying databases are integrated into a federated schema with different user views. The local DBMS is used for local query processing. Communication between processes is done through mail messages sent between computers connected with a network that uses the X.25 protocol.

The US Air Force has sponsored development of a prototype heterogeneous front-end system called IISS (Integrated Information Support System, also known as "I squared S squared") [IISS]. It has a goal of accessing databases on three types of hardware (VAX, IBM, and Honeywell) and many DBMSs. It currently accesses data in Oracle on the VAX and IMS on the IBM. Their approach is batch oriented. There is no ad hoc query language and all retrieval requests must be precompiled.

2.2 QUERY OPTIMIZATION

Access to data in multiple databases requires careful planning to control the time that is required to process the query. This is important in local DBMSs, but it becomes even more important when data must be moved across a network. The query optimization algorithms developed for distributed data management systems (DDBMS) such as SDD-1 [BERN81], Ingres [EPST78], Encompass [TAND81], and R* [WILL81,LOHM84] can be partially used in a distributor front-end. However, there are differences which require adaptation. One difference is that these systems assume that they are operating on a homogeneous network where there is a constant network transmission time between any two nodes. Another difference is that, when operating as a front-end to a DBMS which already contains a query optimizer, it may be beneficial to send the DBMS query fragments containing selects, projects, and joins rather than executing the query in smaller steps. A third difference is that replicated and fragmented relations aren't supported except by INGRES.

The Mermaid system started with ideas from SDD-1 and distributed Ingres when developing the optimization algorithm that is currently running.

2.3 DISTRIBUTED OPERATING SYSTEMS

We have found very little related work in the areas of distributed debugging and retrofitting distributed operating system functions on top of existing operating systems and network protocols. BBN has developed a prototype called Cronus [SCHA85]. Cronus provides a level above host operating systems that appears to be a distributed operating system to application programs. It provides uniform mechanisms for operating system functions including communication, access control, naming, and data storage and retrieval.

The IISS sytem has an operating system component called "NTM" for Network Transaction Manager [IISS]. The NTM is started as an operating system above the existing operating systems and supports the generated application programs.

3. AIDA ARCHITECTURE

3.1 ARCHITECTURAL ASSUMPTIONS

AIDA is expected to operate in an environment where there is a federation of pre-existing databases. Ad hoc users and application programs will access individual databases directly, and AIDA will be used primarily for ad hoc access to the federation.

Mermaid must provide a query optimization algorithm which can adjust to a wide variety of data distributions. In some environments, there may be closely coupled databases in which a relation from one database may be replicated in another database or in which some relations may be fragmented with fragments stored in different databases. In other environments, the databases may be basically disjoint, although there must be some attributes that can be used to join relations across the databases or there would be little reason to treat them as a federation.

It is assumed that processing costs and communication costs will not be uniform. There will be different data management systems which will have different operational characteristics even when running on the same hardware, and there will be different types of computers. The network will also be nonuniform. There may be multiple local networks, possibly different types of networks, connected by gateways. Communication between the gateways may be on lines as slow as 1200 baud.

Both processing time and communication time need to be considered in developing the optimization algorithm. Even within a very fast local area network, there is a significant overhead for every message because data must be retrieved from the sending database and stored in the receiving database.

Since it is assumed that users of AIDA will tend to be using it interactively, minimization of response time is important. The response time includes the time to develop the plan for answering the query as well as the time to execute it. Therefore, a major objective has been to design an optimization algorithm that runs quickly even if the plan is not necessarily the optimum. Plans are not compiled and saved because ad hoc use is expected, but, in the future, plans could be saved if queries are saved in the canned query library or executed from application programs.

Since relational databases are becoming prevalent and relational interfaces are being developed for nonrelational DBMSs, AIDA has emphasized access to relational DBMSs. AIDA assumes the existence of a local optimizer which determines which indices to use, how to perform a join, and the order of joins if multiple joins are required.

AIDA uses the underlying databases for processing. Joins and semijoins between relations in different databases are done by moving data from one database into another and building a temporary relation. This requires at least one DBMS in the federation which can build temporary relations, perform ad hoc joins, and where the user has write permission. There is a concept of "level 1" and "level 2" DBMSs. A "level 1" DBMS is one which is used by AIDA while answering the query, and a "level 2" DBMS is one from which data is only extracted.

AIDA must operate above the pre-existing databases without changing the DBMS or the design of the databases. AIDA cannot require changes to the database structure for compatibility of data types or for optimizations such as the replication of relations.

Most of the expected users will not be doing updates through AIDA. The majority of updates will be made by existing application programs. Some updates may be made interactively, but the updates will be made by the owner of the data to a single database. We expect few conflicting updates, little need for transactions that cross databases, and little demand for instantaneous consistency between replicated copies of relations. The initial implementation of AIDA, therefore, does not support updates, although an update capability has been designed and is being implemented.

3.2 OVERVIEW

The development of Mermaid started in 1982. It was initially implemented on a single VAX running UNIX 4.1. The emphasis the first year was on query optimization and translation of queries to IDL which is the language of the IDM database machine. The ARIEL language and user interface environment was added in 1983. The Ethernet was acquired in 1984 and the entire system was moved to UNIX 4.2 and the network of Suns as well as the original VAX.

The AIDA architecture, when running above a single database, is shown in Figure 2. This example shows the Ingres DBMS which resides on the same computer as the user.

```
          +-------------+
          | NEXUS       |
          +-------------+
          | ARIEL,SQL   |
User      +-------------+
host      | QUEST       |    USER INTERFACE
          +-------------+
          | Ingres PI   |
          +-------------+
          | Ingres DBMS |
          +-------------+
```

Figure 2. Single Database AIDA

The modules are the same as those described below for the distributed architecture.

When AIDA is running as a front-end to a remote database or several remote databases, it includes the Mermaid components as shown in Figure 3. Each of the steps is mentioned here and described in more detail in subsequent sections.

The major processes in the system are:

- the user interface process that resides in the user host computer. The environment is Nexus with an embedded ARIEL or SQL parser and a QUEST (QUEry and Schema Translator) translator that produces DIL (Distributed Intermediate Language). This translator may also be called the "front-end" translator. The process also contains the "Proc.Int." or "Procedural Interface" that is a set of subroutines used to call the Mermaid distributor. Each process contains the "ULP" ("Upper Level Protocol") that is a set of subroutines for interprocess communication.
- the distributor process that resides on the Mermaid host. It contains the Mermaid optimizer and the controller as well as the ULP routines.

The user host and the Mermaid host could be the same computer, but the software will be identical whether the processes are on the same or different computers.

- one driver process for each database to be accessed that resides on the computer with the DBMS. If one computer has multiple databases, there will be multiple driver processes on that computer, one per database. The driver also contains the QUEST translator that translates from DIL to the DBMS query language. It interfaces to the DBMS through a DBMS supplied procedural interface.

```
          +------------+
          | NEXUS      |
          +------------+
          | ARIEL,SQL  |
User      +------------+
host      | QUEST      |    USER INTERFACE
          +------------+
          | Mermaid PI |
          +------------+
          | ULP/TCP/IP |
          +------------+
               | ^
    msg: cmd   | | reply
               V |
          +------------+
          | ULP/TCP/IP |
          +------------+
Mermaid   | optimizer  |
host      +------------+    DISTRIBUTOR
          | controller |
          +------------+
          | ULP/TCP/IP |------------------+-+
          +------------+                  | ^
               | ^                        | |
    msg: cmd   | | reply        msg: cmd  | | reply
      or cntl  | |             or cntl    | |
               V |                        V |
          +------------+            +------------+
          | ULP/TCP/IP |<---------->| ULP/TCP/IP |
          +------------+    data    +------------+
          | Driver     |            | Driver     |
DBMS      +------------+    DBMS    +------------+
host A    | QUEST      |    host B  | QUEST      |
          +------------+            +------------+
          | Ingres PI  |            | IDM PI     |
          +------------+            +------------+
          | Ingres DBMS|            | IDM DBMS   |
          +------------+            +------------+

                         DRIVERS
```

Figure 3. AIDA Distributed Architecture

The processes communicate through the "ULP" whether they are on the same host or on different hosts. The ULP is built on top of the TCP/IP protocol that is supplied as part of UNIX 4.2. All of the code currently operates under UNIX 4.2* on a VAX or a Sun.

All information about schemata, databases, users, host computers, and the network is contained in a DD/D (Data Dictionary/ Directory) which is stored in a database and accessed through a special driver. In the diagram in Figure 3, either of the drivers shown could be the DD/D driver. The QUEST modules and the optimizer access the DD/D in order to do translation and query planning.

* UNIX is a trade mark and trade secret of AT&T.

The following paragraphs will describe the flow of a query through the system. The user builds an ARIEL or SQL query in the Nexus query window. ARIEL is a nonprocedural language developed at SDC [MACG85]. Nexus calls the QUEST front-end to parse and validate the query and, if the query is valid, it is translated from ARIEL or SQL to DIL. DIL is a highly structured language that is designed for communication between processes. The query, now in DIL, is then forwarded to the Mermaid procedural interface which packages the query into a message to be passed through the Upper Level Protocol to the Mermaid distributor.

The Mermaid controller reads the message and passes the DIL query to the optimizer which plans the execution. The optimizer sends DIL subqueries to the controller to be put into messages for one or more drivers. The controller then waits for responses from the site driver/s.

Each site driver will process the DIL (sub)query by calling the QUEST translator to process the query and retrieve the result. QUEST will translate the query into the DBMS query language, send the query to the DBMS, read the status (tuple count, error messages), and then retrieve the response if any. The result returned to the driver may be just a status if the operation does not retrieve data, it may be an unformatted report, or it may be a relation that must be sent to another driver. Status and unformatted reports are sent back to the controller. If a relation is to be sent to another driver, a connection is opened through the ULP and messages are sent to the receiving site or sites as fast as buffers can be filled. When the entire relation has been transfered, the connection is closed and a status message is sent to the controller.

When the controller receives a message from the driver, it reads the message and takes appropriate action. Status messages are processed by the controller which may then send another request to the driver, send a tuple count to the optimizer, or take error correcting action. If the message contains an unformatted report, it is sent back to the user interface where the QUEST module formats a report that is then returned to Nexus for display.

We will now briefly describe each of the modules mentioned above.

Nexus allows the user to create, save, and edit queries and then to transmit the queries to a selected DBMS. Nexus allows selection of a single DBMS or access to a distribued database through Mermaid. Mermaid is "just another" DBMS to Nexus.

The QUEST translator translates from any of three input languages, ARIEL, SQL, or DIL, to any of four output languages, DIL, IDL, QUEL, or SQL. For a given query, the translator does syntactic and semantic checking (called validation), performs transformations to convert the query into an equivalent query (or queries) in the appropriate output language, and then interacts with the back-end DBMS to produce an output result. The Nexus/QUEST process can run without Mermaid to provide local access to a single database in which case QUEST would translate the user language to the target language. When running with Mermaid, the user language is translated into DIL, the DIL is processed by Mermaid, and the QUEST within the driver translates the DIL to the target language.

The DIL representation of the query is put into a message which is sent to the Mermaid program on the same host or another host via the procedural interface (PI) and the Upper Level Protocol (ULP). The PI is a set of subroutines which can be called to interface to Mermaid in much the same way that a program can interface to the IDM or Ingres. All of the Mermaid-specific code such as journaling, knowledge of the message structures, and interface to the ULP resides in the PI routines.

The ULP is used to communicate between the processes: the Mermaid distributor, the drivers, and the user interface. It operates as a layer above the UNIX 4.2 network services code which is above the TCP/IP protocol which is above the Ethernet protocol. We are using a 10 megabit Ethernet. The ULP is used for communication between processes on the same computer or across the network which allows processes to communicate with other processes using the same calls whether they are local or remote.

The Mermaid distributor process has two main components, the query optimizer and the controller. The optimizer plans the execution of the query and sends DIL commands to the controller which packages the commands into messages, sends the messages to driver processes, and waits for responses. The controller schedules the commands so that no remote process is executing more than one command at a time, and it monitors the execution of the system.

Each database is controlled by a driver process that is logged in as the user of the database under the login id of the user of Mermaid and Nexus. It receives a DIL command and executes it. The command may be executed only in the driver or it may require access to the DBMS. If the DBMS is to be accessed, the QUEST translator is called to translate the query and send it to the DBMS. The output is returned to the driver which writes a message back to the controller signalling successful completion or an error. If the command is to retrieve a report, the driver at the user's site displays the report, although this will be changed in 1985 to perform translation of the data to global units and to send the report back to Nexus.

Driver processes may also communicate with other driver processes in order to copy data between databases. The drivers are instructed by the controller to set up a temporary connection (using the ULP) and then move some relation from one database to one or more other databases. Databases may reside on different hosts and different DBMSs, but it is not required that they be on different hosts and different DBMSs. All databases could reside on the same host as the distributor.

The architecture is flexible and highly modular so that a combination of processors, workstations, and database machines can be used. In Figure 3 we show two "sites" or "target hosts", each of which contains a database. Two "sites" may be on two different computers, as shown here, or they may be two databases on the same computer.

If multiple users are on the system, each will have his own copy of the distributor and a site process for each database that he accesses. UNIX allows code to be shared and maintains separate data space for each copy.

4. EXAMPLE TO ILLUSTRATE OPERATION

We will trace the operation of one query to illustrate the operation of the system. First, we will show how the query is answered using the semijoin algorithm, and then we will show the same query using the replicate algorithm.

4.1 SEMIJOIN ALGORITHM

In this example, we will be concerned with three relations in a naval database, namely, the ship, weapon, and install relations. The first two describe various characteristics of the ships and weapons systems in the database, and the third specifies which weapons are installed on which ships. There are four sites, S2, S3, S6, and S7, each of which corresponds to a fleet. The ship relation is fragmented at all four of these sites. Thus ships in the second fleet, for example, are described in the fragment at S2. The install relation is also fragmented at the four sites, and it is dependent on ship. That is, install tuples at a given site can only join with ship tuples at the same site. The weapon relation is replicated in its entirety at two sites, S2 and S3.

Our sample query is "Which US destroyers carry Harpoon weapons?". The user might express this query in ARIEL as follows:

```
retrieve name of ship
where type = "DD"
and flag = "USA"
and name of weapon = "Harpoon"
and ship.num = install.shipid
and install.weapon = weapon.id
```

The NEXUS user interface translates the ARIEL query into DIL, the internal language of the AIDA system:

```
BEGIN
VARIABLES
    ship IS ship,
    install IS install,
    weapon IS weapon
RETRIEVE
    name (ship.name)
SELECT
    ship.type = "DD",
    ship.flag = "USA",
    weapon.name = "Harpoon"
MERGE
    ship.num == install.shipid,
    install.weapon == weapon.id
END
```

The user interface sends this DIL query to the distributor. The first stage in the optimization process is site selection. Because the ship and install relations are fragmented at sites S2, S3, S6, and S7, all four of these sites must be chosen. Furthermore, the copy of weapon at S2 is chosen over the one at S3 because S2 is the result site where the user resides.

The goal of the semijoin algorithm is to reduce the size of relations as much as possible before assembling them at the result site. This is accomplished in the local and global reduction stages of the optimization process. In the local reduction step, single relations are reduced. In the global reduction step, semijoins are used to reduce one relation by another relation within the same database or across databases. For this query, there are two local reduction operations, which we refer to as LOCAL1 and LOCAL2, and two global reduction operations, GLOBAL1 and GLOBAL2. Table 1 demonstrates the progressive reduction of all the relevant relations at the four sites. For example, the ship fragment at S2 initially contains 370 tuples, but after LOCAL1 it is reduced to 20 tuples. Similarly, there are initially 772 tuples in install at S2, but the GLOBAL1 and GLOBAL2 operations reduce this fragment to 111 and then 14 tuples.

		INITIAL	LOCAL1	LOCAL2	GLOBAL1	GLOBAL2
S1	ship	370	370	20	20	20
	install	772	772	772	111	14
	weapon	51	1	1	1	1
S3	ship	361	361	22	22	22
	install	763	763	763	109	16
S6	ship	140	140	5	5	5
	install	184	184	184	13	0
S7	ship	140	140	4	4	4
	install	181	181	181	14	0

Table 1. Progressive Reduction

In the local reduction phase, the selection clauses found in the user's query are applied to the relations, and these relations are then projected on their joining and target attributes. The LOCAL1 operation reduces the weapon relation. It is accomplished by sending the following command to the driver at site S2:

```
retrieve into weapon1 (weapon.id)
where weapon.name = "Harpoon"
```

After the driver returns an acknowledgment, the distributor proceeds to reduce ship. The LOCAL2 operation involves sending the following command to the drivers at S2, S3, S6, and S7:

```
retrieve into ship1 (ship.name, ship.num)
where ship.type = "DD"
and ship.flag = "USA"
```

This command is executed in parallel at the four sites, and the distributor waits until all acknowledgments have been received before proceeding. Unlike ship and weapon, install is not modified by local reduction. This is because there are no select clauses referring to install and because this relation only has two attributes, both of which are used for joining.

In the global reduction stage, semijoins are used to further reduce relations. Initially, four semijoins are possible. These are:

```
SEMIJOIN ship BY install
SEMIJOIN install BY ship
SEMIJOIN weapon BY install
SEMIJOIN install BY weapon
```

The cost and benefit of each of these semijoins is computed, and the most profitable over a certain threshold is selected for execution. This turns out to be reducing install by weapon. Normally, performing the semijoin would require projection of weapon onto its joining attribute, weapon.id. In this case, however, the projection has already been done in LOCAL1. Therefore, weapon1 can be copied directly to the other sites at which install is fragmented:

```
COPY weapon1 @ S2 -> weapon1 @ S3, S6, S7
```

Now, in operation GLOBAL1, we actually perform the semijoin by sending the following command to S2, S3, S6, and S7:

```
retrieve into install1 (install.shipid, install.weapon)
where install.weapon = weapon1.id
```

This command is executed in parallel at the four sites and acknowledgments are sent to the distributor. After they are all received, the distributor examines the remaining semijoins. There are now three possibilities:

```
SEMIJOIN ship BY install
SEMIJOIN install BY ship
SEMIJOIN weapon BY install
```

This time the cost/benefit analysis determines that install should be reduced by ship. Because install and ship are fragmented at all four sites and a placement dependency exists between them, it is not necessary to project off the ship.num attribute or to copy this attribute between sites. Instead, the semijoin operation GLOBAL2 is achieved by simply sending the following command to S2, S3, S6, and S7:

```
retrieve into install2 (install1.shipid, install1.weapon)
where install1.shipid = ship1.num
```

Again, the semijoins are executed in parallel and each driver returns an acknowledgment. At this point, two further semijoins are still possible, but the distributor decides that neither is worthwhile. Thus, the global reduction phase is over. The install relation has been twice reduced and, in fact, Table 1 shows that the fragments at S6 and S7 have no more qualifying tuples at all.

The next stage in the semijoin algorithm is assembly. We build a complete copy of the reduced ship relation at result site S2 by copying the remote ship fragments to S2 and appending them to the fragment already there. This assembly process is then repeated for the install relation. Note that there are only two non-null fragments of install after global reduction. Also, we do not need to assemble weapon because S2 already contains a complete copy of that relation.

```
COPY ship1 @ S3 -> ship1 @ S2
COPY ship1 @ S6 -> ship1 @ S2
COPY ship1 @ S7 -> ship1 @ S2

COPY install2 @ S3 -> install2 @ S2
```

After all relevant relations have been reduced and assembled at the result site, a report is produced and sent to the user interface. This is done by sending the following command to the driver at S2:

```
retrieve (ship1.name)
where ship1.num = install2.shipid
```

The select clauses in the original query are absent here because they have already been applied during local reduction. Also, it is unnecessary to specify the join between install and weapon because GLOBAL1 reduced install by weapon as completely as possible.

After the user has received the report, the final step is to send each driver a command to destroy all the temporary relations that have been built during processing. The distributor then waits to receive the next query from NEXUS.

While the semijoin algorithm produced satisfactory results in the above example, it should be noted that an even better strategy could have been followed. This would have been to reduce ship by install in GLOBAL2 instead of reducing install by ship. Doing so would have made it unnecessary to move any fragments of install to S2 during assembly. This is because install does not contain target attributes and it could have no further reductive effect on ship during the report stage. Thus, the command to generate the report would simply be:

```
retrieve (ship1.name)
```

There are two reasons why this preferred strategy was not followed. First, to compensate for ignoring processing costs, we are currently using a benefit threshold in selecting semijoins. That is, we will not perform a semijoin that can only eliminate a few tuples because its DBMS cost usually outweighs its data transmission benefit. Thus, ship was not further reduced because its largest fragment only contained 22 tuples. Second, the algorithm did not recognize the advantage of reducing ship because it was unable to look ahead to the assembly stage. During global reduction, semijoins were chosen for their immediate benefit and the longer-range possibility of eliminating unnecessary assembly steps was missed. These problems will be addressed in future versions of the optimizer.

4.2 REPLICATE ALGORITHM

In order to contrast the operation of the semijoin and replicate algorithms, we will use the same query and database environment as above.

The first stage in the replicate algorithm is site selection. This involves choosing a relation (or class of relations) to remain fragmented, and then deciding which of the sites containing these fragments will be used for processing. Table 2 shows the initial distribution of the relations at the four sites, with the symbol F denoting fragments and C denoting copies. The size of each fragment and copy is given in tuples. (To simplify our example, we assume the relations have unit width.) Table 2 also shows weights that are used in choosing the processing sites.

	ship	install	weapon	WEIGHT.
S2	F 370	F 772	C 51	-1142
S3	F 361	F 763	C 51	-1124
S6	F 140	F 184		-273
S7	F 140	F 181		-270

Table 2. Site Selection

Because there is a placement dependency between the ship and install relations, these two relations form a class. Normally the largest class is chosen to remain fragmented but, in this case, there is only one possibility (since weapon is not fragmented). Therefore its members, ship and install, will remain fragmented at some subset of their initial four sites.

Each site that is chosen for processing needs to contain a copy of the weapon relation. If weapon does not already exist there, it has to be sent from another site. We will select the set of sites that minimizes data transmission. This could be done by calculating the total transmission cost for every subset of the four sites, but it is more efficient to compute a single weight for each site. These weights represent the size difference between the fragmented data already at a site and the other data needed there. Table 2 shows that all the weights are negative, and therefore all four sites are chosen to be processing sites.

The next stage of this algorithm is replication. Each processing site must have complete copies of all relations except the one that is to remain fragmented. In this case, we send a copy of weapon to sites S6 and S7:

```
COPY weapon @ S2 -> weapon @ S6, S7
```

Once all necessary data is present at the processing sites, the query can be executed in parallel at each of these sites. This is accomplished by sending the following command to the drivers at S2, S3, S6, and S7:

```
retrieve into result (ship.name)
where ship.type = "DD"
and ship.flag = "USA"
and weapon.name = "Harpoon"
and ship.num = install.shipid
and install.weapon = weapon.id
```

Execution of this command results in a partial answer at each processing site. After receiving acknowledgments from all of these sites, the distributor gathers the partial answers into a single complete answer at the result site.

```
COPY result @ S3 -> result @ S2
COPY result @ S6 -> result @ S2
COPY result @ S7 -> result @ S2
```

The next stage in the replicate algorithm is to produce the report at the result site and write it to the user interface. We do so by sending the following command to S2:

```
retrieve (result.name)
```

Finally, as in the semijoin algorithm, the distributor destroys all the temporary relations it has created and then waits for another query.

Since the above example is fairly simple, we should briefly consider a more complex case. Referring to Table 2, suppose the fragments of ship and install at S7 contained only 20 tuples each. Then we would obtain a non-negative weight at S7 and this site would not be selected for processing. That is, it would be more costly to move weapon to S7 than to move the fragments at S7 elsewhere and do the processing at three sites. This latter option, then, is exactly what is done. The fragments of ship and install at S7 are sent to S2 and unioned with copies of S2's ship and install fragments. Then weapon is sent to S6 and the query is executed in parallel at the three processing sites, S2, S3, and S6.

5. PROJECT PLANS

The current AIDA prototype is being modified to make it a product that can be installed by the end of 1987. The main changes between the prototype and product are:

- Support for updates.
- Download of data into new relations in the user's workstation or in private relations within the underlying database.
- New query optimizer that combines the semijoin and replicate algorithm.
- More user interface features such as a forms/menu interface.
- Provision of a program interface.
- Development of a schema design tool to support the user when building the global view of the databases from existing schemata.

6. CONCLUSION

The long term research goals of the AIDA project are to explore the issues in developing a front-end prototype system that can support integration and sharing of data, text, voice, graphics, images, and knowledge objects among loosely coupled nodes on a LAN, between LANs, and over long haul networks. The AIDA project is working with state-of-the-art DBMSs and looking ahead to determine what characteristics are necessary and desirable for an object manager to be easily integrated into the AIDA loosely coupled system.

AIDA is an operational testbed system which has demonstrated the feasibility of operating as a front-end to existing relational databases and DBMSs, and the UNIX operating system. It has proven useful for testing and improving distribution algorithms. A single front-end user language, ARIEL, has been defined which incorporates basic relational functionality with relaxed syntax (compared to relational languages such as QUEL, SQL, IDL), and extended semantics. An internal language DIL (Distributed Intermediate Language) has been implemented to support basic relational functionality and network commands.

The current effort includes further language development, definition and implementation of a semantic model, improvement of distribution algorithms, plan for phased development in incorporating workstation databases into AIDA, and implementing update capability.

7. REFERENCES

[BERN81] Bernstein, P., N.Goodman, E.Wong, C.Reeve, J.Rothnie, "Query Processing in a System for Distributed Databases (SDD-1)", in *ACM Transactions on Database Systems*, December 1981.

[BRIT84**] Britton Lee Inc, "IDM 500 Software Reference Manual", Version 1.7, November 1984.

[BRIL84] Brill, D., M.Templeton, and C.Yu, "Distributed Query Processing Strategies in Mermaid, A Frontend to Data Management Systems", *Proceedings of IEEE Data Engineering Conference*, Los Angeles, April 1984.

[EPST78] Epstein, R., M.Stonebraker, E.Wong, "Distributed Query Processing in a Relational Database System", ACM SIGMOD, Austin, Texas, May 1978.

[FOCU] "FOCUS General Information Guide", Information Builders Inc., 1985.

[IISS] "Integrated Information Support System (IISS) - An Evolutionary Approach to Integration", AF Wright Aeronautical Laboratories, 1985.

[LAND82] Landers, T., R.Rosenberg, "An Overview of Multibase", in *Proceedings of the Second International Symposium on Distributed Database*, ed. Schneider, 1982.

[LOGI78] Logicon Inc., "ADAPT I, Final Functional and System Design Specificaton", 76-C-0899-2, January 1978.

[LOHM84] Lohman, G., C.Mohan, L.Haas, B.Lindsay, P.Selinger, P.Wilms, "Query Processing in R*", IBM research report RJ 4272 (46860) 4/23/84.

[MACG85] MacGregor, R., "ARIEL - A Semantic Front-End to Relational DBMSs", *Proceedings of VLDB 85*, Stockholm, August 1985.

[RHOD82**] Rhodnius Inc., "Mistress: The Query Language", Version 2.2, July 1982.

[SAFE] "SAFE Project User Interface Requirements Specification," TRW CE-7200E, 14 February 1983.

[SCHA85] Schantz, R., R.Thomas, "The Architecture of the Cronus Distributed Operating System", BBN Laboratories, April 1985.

[SMIT81a**] Smith, J. et al., *ADAPLEX Reference Manual*, Computer Corporation of America, Jan. 1981.

[SMIT81b] Smith, J., P.Bernstein, U.Dayel, N.Goodman, T.Landers, K.Lin, E.Wong, "Multibase- Integrating Heterogeneous Distributed Database Systems", *AFIPS Conference Proceedings*, Vol 50, 1981.

[STAN83] Staniszkis, W., M.Kowalewski, G.Turco, K.Krajewski, M.Saccone, "Network Data Mangement System - General Architecture and Implementation Principles", *Proc. of the Third International Conference on Engineering Software*, Imperial College of Science and Technology, London, England, April 1983.

[SUN84**] "Sun MicroINGRES Documentation", Sun MicroSystems, Version 2.0, 1985.

[TAND81**] "Distributed Data Base Management", Tandem Computers Inc., 1981.

[TEMP83] Templeton, M., D.Brill, A.Hwang, I.Kameny, E.Lund, "An Overview of the Mermaid System - A Frontend to Heterogeneous Databases", *Proceedings of IEEE EASCON83*, Washington, September 1983.

[TEMP85a] Templeton, M. and J.Kendall, "Solving the DODIIS Database Interoperability Problem", presented at AFCEA Conference, San Diego, March 1985.

[TEMP85b] Templeton, M., D.Brill, A.Chen, S.Dao, E.Lund, "Mermaid - Experiences with Network Operation", to be presented at IEEE Data Engineering Conference, February 1986.

[WILL81] Williams, R., et al., "R*: An Overview of the Architecture", IBM Research Report RJ3325 (40082) 12/2/81.

[YU85] Yu, C.T, C.C.Chang, M.Templeton, D.Brill, E.Lund, "Query Processing in a Fragmented Relational Distributed System: MERMAID", *IEEE Transactions on Software Engineering*, August 1985.

[YU84a] Yu, C.T., K.C.Guh, C.C.Chang, C.H.Chen, M.Templeton, and D.Brill, "Placement Dependency and Aggregate Processing in a Fragmented Distributed Database Environment", *Proceedings of IEEE COMPSAC*, Chicago, November 1984.

[YU84b] Yu, C.T., K.C.Guh, C.C.Chang, C.H.Chen, M.Templeton, and D.Brill, "An Algorithm to Process Queries in a Fast Distributed Network", *Proceedings of Real Time System Symposium*, Austin, December 1984.

[YU83] Yu, C.T., C.Chang, M.Templeton, D.Brill, E.Lund, "On the Design of a Query Processing Strategy in a Distributed Database Environment", in *Proceedings of ACM SIGMOD83*, San Jose, May 1983.

[**] Not available as an open publication.

EMPACT™: A distributed database application

by ALAN NORMAN and MARK ANDERTON
TANDEM Computers Incorporated
Cupertino, California

ABSTRACT

EMPACT™, TANDEM Computers' manufacturing information control system, is an application that uses a distributed database. The requirements of the system include supporting multiple sites, providing continuous availability to the data, and controlling updates to communal information. The approach taken to satisfy these needs involves the use of both partitioned and replicated data. Presented in this paper is a discussion of the application requirements, the design and architecture of the database, and the algorithms used for updates and inserts.

INTRODUCTION

EMPACT™, TANDEM Computers' manufacturing information control system, is an application that makes use of a distributed database. The requirements of the system include

1. Supporting multiple sites of independently managed machines.
2. Providing the continuous availability of communal information.
3. Permitting decentralization both of control of the application and management of the data.
4. Allowing for centralized development of the application.

This paper discusses the application requirements, the design and architecture of the database, and the methods used for maintaining the database.

APPLICATION REQUIREMENTS

Application Functions

EMPACT was developed to satisfy the data processing requirements of TANDEM Computer's manufacturing division. It was initially designed as a centralized online application that would support a single manufacturing site. The functions contained within EMPACT pertain to all the standard assembly manufacturing needs. These functions are as follows:

1. Parts master
2. Bills of material
3. Inventory control
4. Purchasing/receiving
5. Work in process
6. Master scheduling
7. Materials requirement planning
8. Interplant material transfer (MART)
9. Job/lot tracking

Database Size and Service Levels

EMPACT was implemented on a TANDEM T/16 computer using TANDEM's distributed data management system, ENCOMPASS. The database size and the required service levels for the initial design were moderate—

1. Single manufacturing site
2. Database of approximately 120 megabytes
3. Database containing 500+ data elements and over 40 record types
4. A user community of 150 persons using 55 terminals
5. Monthly transaction rates: 15,000 against the entire database, with 4,500 update transactions against the bill of material files and 1,000 against the item master file.
6. A 6:1 ratio of reads to writes against the item master and bill of materials files.
7. Hardcopy batch reports generated nightly to supplement the online inquiry capabilities; these reports were created using ENFORM, TANDEM's query language.

Business Environment

TANDEM, as a company, anticipated high growth rates over the next several years. This meant that the size of the user community, the transaction volume, and database requirements were expected to increase accordingly. Furthermore, the manufacturing management decided to decentralize its operations. The plan was and is to disperse the manufacturing effort into several plants, all performing similar operational functions although geographically distant. A growth rate of one new plant every 9 months was predicted.

This need to support geographically distributed sites placed some new demands upon EMPACT. As a business requirement, communal data such as item master or bill of materials information would have to be continuously available; the day-to-day business of the individual sites is highly dependent on this information. Also, owing to the decentralized management structure of TANDEM's manufacturing organization, the sites required as much autonomy as possible; the daily business of one site could not adversely affect or be affected by events or circumstances at other sites. Each site was also to be responsible for and have control over the data stored there.

Initial Development Approach

The conceptual approach taken was to divide the elements of the database into two major categories, global data and local data, and one additional category that must be acknowledged but does not enter into this analysis, private data—

1. Global data are information that would be common to and shared by all sites. Examples of global data are the list of parts that determine TANDEM's parts catalog (item master file) or the records that describe TANDEM's product structure (bill of materials file).
2. Local data are information that is uniquely important to the individual site using it but accessible by all sites.

Examples of local data are stock status and work-in-process data. Local data have the same format as the corresponding data at other sites.

3. Private data are information that is only used by the individual site and is not visible to other sites. This data consists of reports and data outside the EMPACT system.

Global and local data are each segregated into record units that are themselves either global or local. This segregation is not a requirement of the distributed application but a means of simplifying certain aspects of the application.

Figure 1 shows the division of the EMPACT database into global and local portions. As previously stated, the major requirement addressed by distributed EMPACT was site responsibility for the maintenance of local information and providing equal shares of control and responsibility for the maintenance of global information.

Global data are necessarily replicated because of the requirement for site independence. If global data are not replicated at all EMPACT sites, then disconnecting any nonglobal site from the network would mean that business activities at that site would be interrupted until the site rejoined the network. Any scheme of centralized global data suffers from this unacceptable possibility.

By our early reckoning, data would be either global (replicated at all sites) or local (single-site resident). However, another condition surfaced that called for only partial replication of data. The interplant material transfer function, known by the acronym MART, permits a request by one site for material from another to be placed and processed, and monitors the subsequent transfer of material. The process requires that all data and status information pertaining to the request be resident at both sites. However, the information is unnecessary to any third party. Such data is classified as semi-global since it only requires partial replication.

The next section provides a brief description of the TANDEM software products that are the foundation of distributed EMPACT.

TANDEM'S SOFTWARE ENVIRONMENT—AN OVERVIEW OF ENCOMPASS-EXPAND

The expansion of EMPACT to support multiple sites was implemented using ENCOMPASS, TANDEM's data man-

```
                       +===============+
                       | Item Master   |
                       +===============+
    +============+                              +===========+
    | Bill of    |                              | Inventory |
    | Materials  |                              |           |
    +============+          ************        +===========+
                           *    Data     *
 +=============+          *  Dictionary   *       +===========+
 | Purchasing  |          *               *       |  Work in  |
 | Receiving   |          *   Programs    *       |  Process  |
 +=============+           *             *        +===========+
                            ************
    +=============+                              +============+
    | Master      |                              | Job/Lot    |
    | Schedule    |                              | Tracking   |
    +=============+                              +============+
                        +=============+
                        |    MART     |
                        +=============+
```

Global Data	Local Data	Semi-Global Data
Bill of Materials	Inventory	MART
Item Master	Master Schedule	
Global data dictionary	Purchasing	
Global programs	Work in Process	
	Job/Lot Tracking	

Figure 1—Structure of the EMPACT database

agement system, and EXPAND, TANDEM's network software. ENCOMPASS is a conglomerate of several major software products, included in which are ENSCRIBE, DDL, ENFORM, PATHWAY, and TMF, the transaction and recovery manager.

ENSCRIBE is a relational-database manager that supports three types of structured-file organizations: key-sequenced, relative, and entry-sequenced. Within these file types, data are organized into logical records. EMPACT restricts itself to fixed-length records and key-sequenced files.

DDL is a data definition language used to define the data elements and record structures that make up an application. The output generated by DDL is stored in a data dictionary that is used by ENFORM, a high-level nonprocedural query language, to generate reports against the application database.

PATHWAY provides a terminal-oriented interface for transaction design and control. Its primary components are a terminal control process (TCP) that provides screen formatting and control, user-written programs, known as *servers,* that access and update the data files using ENSCRIBE procedures, and PATHMON, a monitor process that dynamically manages and allocates application resources.

An application's interface to the end-user is a set of program modules, or *requestors,* that are written in Screen-COBOL (a COBOL-like language with extensions for screen manipulation). The Screen-COBOL programs are interpreted by the TCP to perform screen sequencing, data mapping, and transaction control. The Screen-COBOL programs communicate with the servers by exchanging request and reply messages, hence the names requestor and server.

The servers are single-threaded programs that

1. Read a request message
2. Perform the database function requested
3. Reply

They must be *context-free,* meaning that they do not need a memory of past requests in order to execute the current request.

A server is known to the requestor programs by its *server class name.* A *server class* is a group of server programs that perform identical functions. When a TCP needs to establish communication with a particular server class, it requests a 'link' to an individual server within the given server class from PATHMON (see Figure 2). PATHMON responds by sending the TCP the process name of an already existing server or of a newly created one. How PATHMON decides to respond depends on parameters established when the system is started up. This is one aspect of the load balancing and resource management that PATHMON performs.

Transactions in ENCOMPASS are defined as multistep operations that change the database from one consistent state to another. They are processed via the requestor/server relationship. The end user initiates a transaction request at a terminal; the requestor module responds by sending a series of one or more requests to a set of servers; the servers perform the application function against the database; replies are re-

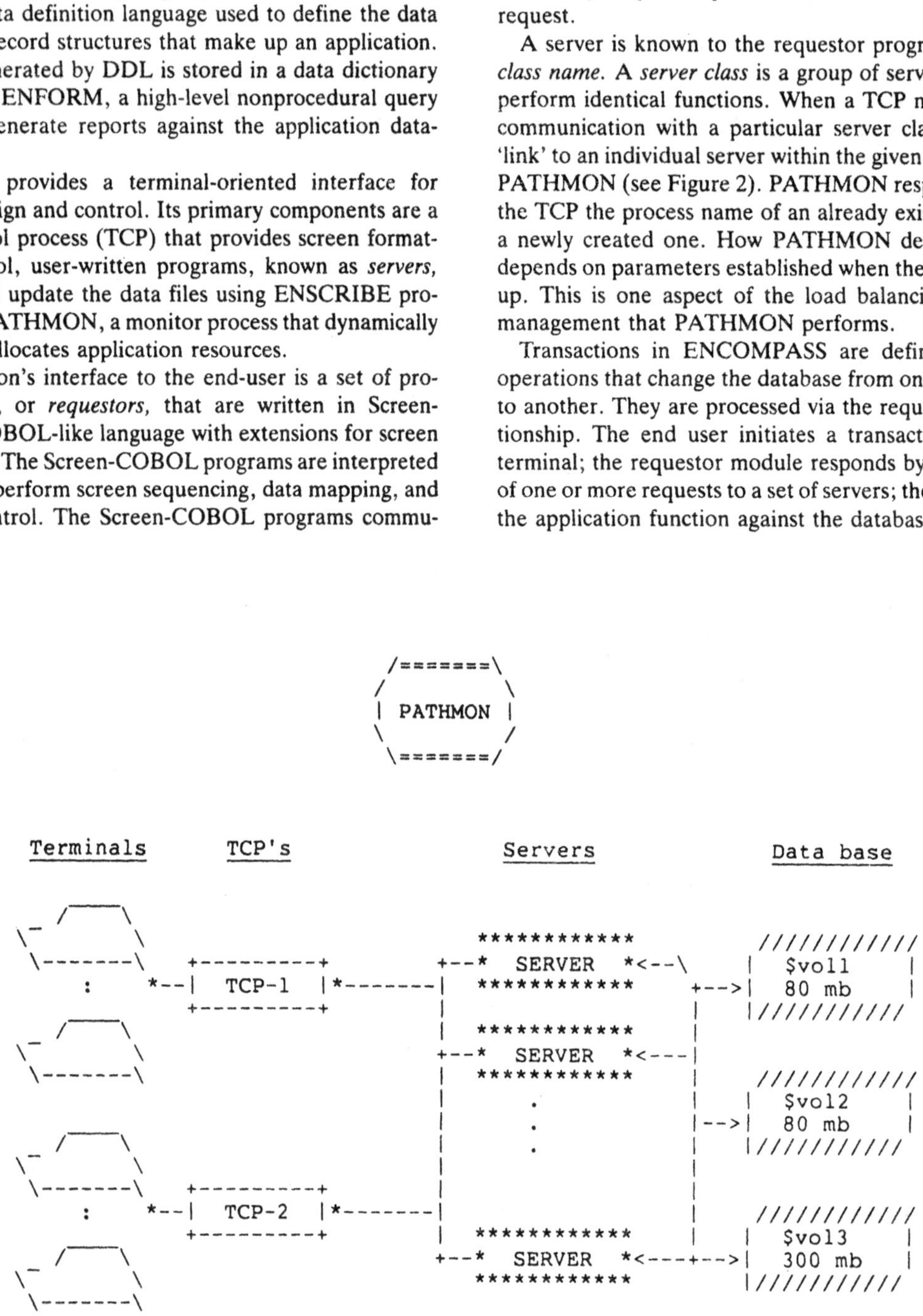

Figure 2—Pathway configuration for EMPACT at a single site

turned to the requestor; and the end user is notified of the result at the terminal. Smith discusses the requestor/server relationship in more detail.[4]

TMF guarantees the consistency of the database by ensuring that precisely all or none of the changes that a transaction attempts to make are permanent. For a more detailed discussion on TMF, refer to Borr's report.[1]

EXPAND, TANDEM's network software, has several features relevant to application design. Control is decentralized; it is characterized by the lack of a network master. Access to geographically distributed system resources is transparent to the system user. In fact, local and remote requests to servers or files look the same to those programs initiating the requests. Nodes in EXPAND network are defined by their system name, for example \LA or \SANFRAN. Interprocess communication across the network requires only that the system name be specified, all other aspects being managed by the operating system. The design of the EXPAND network is described in more detail by Katzman and Taylor.[2]

ENVIRONMENT—EMPACT

EMPACT PATHWAY Configuration

EMPACT, prior to becoming distributed, had over 120 requestors and 40 server classes. There were over 200 transaction types and approximately 100 different reports. Typically, each subsystem, for example, bill of materials, would have three server classes associated with it: one for updates, one for online queries, and one for report generation. Figure 2 shows the EMPACT PATHWAY configuration.

Application Development

The program development environment consisted of a centralized team of programmer/analysts working with management and manufacturing personnel throughout the company. It was agreed that the development of software that could modify the EMPACT database should be controlled by the central team in order to prevent inconsistent alterations to the database. However, all other software, for example, for reports, could be developed anywhere and fall under the control of the intended end user. All released software is archived in a central and controlled repository; this decision aimed to protect the integrity of the released software.

Preliminary Designs

At the time the design for EMPACT's distribution was being considered, TANDEM had a 50-site corporate network. EMPACT is just one client of this corporate network, which is also used for electronic mail, text processing, program development, and many other EDP applications at TANDEM. The network has now grown to 150 sites and is expected to grow accordingly. Each manufacturing site was to have its own system. The question that faced EMPACT's designers was how best to utilize this network to support multiple sites.

The available options were:

1. Remain centralized, have one central database under the control of a single PATHWAY system with remote users accessing the system over the network.
2. Partially distribute the database, have a small number of geographically dispersed *master* sites running independent but identical versions of EMPACT that supported users on sites within a defined region.
3. Fully distribute the database and application: have complete copies of the database and software running at each site.

The first option violated the requirement for continuous availability of the database. Despite TANDEM NonStop™ system design, long-haul communications media are still subject to occasional interruption.

The second option was a compromise solution; vulnerability to significant communications interruptions might, arguably, be reduced, but the principle of site autonomy would not be satisfied. Some individual site or sites would still be dependent on a particular master site. Furthermore, given the geographic dispersion of manufacturing sites, it was unclear whether sites would ever congregate in sufficient numbers to afford nonmaster sites.

These considerations led to the decision to select the third option as the basis for implementing distributed EMPACT. The next section of this paper describes the specific approach taken.

DISTRIBUTION APPROACH

Data Qualification

The primary components of the design of distributed EMPACT are (see Figure 3)

1. Each site has an independent PATHWAY system running identical applications.
2. The database structure for global and local data—as opposed to the data themselves—is global, hence identical at each site.
3. The global portion of the database is replicated at each site, that is, both the structure and the data of files with global information are identical at all sites.
4. The local portion of the database is partitioned over the network, that is although the structure of files containing local information is identical at all sites, Austin stores the Texas data and Neufahrn stores the Germany data.

Database Consistency Solutions

This design satisfies some of the objectives of continuous availability and site autonomy. Because a user is concerned only with his/her portion of the local data and because the global portion is replicated everywhere, query access to the

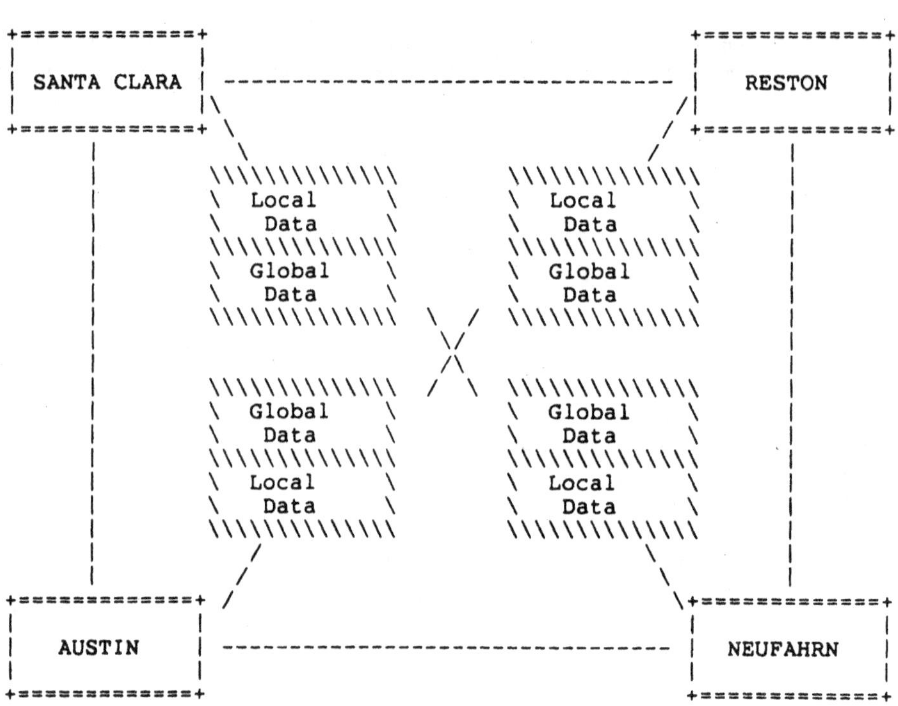

Figure 3—Example of EMPACT network and database structure

database is guaranteed regardless of the status of other sites in the network or the status of the network itself. However, the issue remains how to provide similar guarantees for update access to the global data yet still maintain consistency among the files.

Maintaining the consistency of replicated files requires that any changes to an individual copy be made to the corresponding copies elsewhere in the network. Furthermore, the changes must preserve the consistency of the files in the event of failure.

Preliminary Broadcast Transaction

One method proposed was to modify the existing servers updating global files to *broadcast* the updates to all the sites in the network as a single transaction. The transaction would be performed under the auspices of TMF, hence there would be a guarantee, through the BACKOUT and/or ROLLFORWARD mechanisms of TMF, that the consistency of the database would be maintained in the event of failure.[1]

This proposal, however, has three drawbacks: servers that perform updates against global files require knowledge of the whereabouts of the file replicas; there is a long response time at the user terminal during an update to global data; and updates to the global files can only take place when all sites are available.

Owing to the fact that the EMPACT sites have a variety of hardware and system configurations, the naming of global files (system name, volume, subvolume) is unique to each site. Because it accesses them directly, the server that performs updates to global files needs to know the names of all global-file copies to be updated. Sites in the network have to keep current with the naming changes of all other sites—a problem that becomes considerably worse as the number of EMPACT sites increases.

The terminal response time is unacceptably long because an update to global data involves updating a larger number of file copies. On the basis of operator wait-time, daily business requests cannot rely exclusively on this method of update propagation.

The availability of all sites is necessary because by design the broadcast transaction requires access to all affected files at the same time. Data integrity demands an all-or-nothing update. Entrusting the daily business of a site to this method alone sacrifices site autonomy, since legitimate global activity would have to be interrupted until communications were regained. Figure 4 shows the structure of the preliminary broadcast transaction.

Broadcast Transaction

A refinement to this proposal defines servers at each site, known as *associate* servers, that upon receiving a request from an updating server at an initiating site, perform the updates against their copies of the global files. Furthermore, a new global file, known as the node file, contains a list of all EMPACT nodes in the network and thus serves as a network map. A broadcast transaction now involves sending a request to servers at each of the sites listed in the node file. The servers at remote nodes have knowledge of all physical file placement

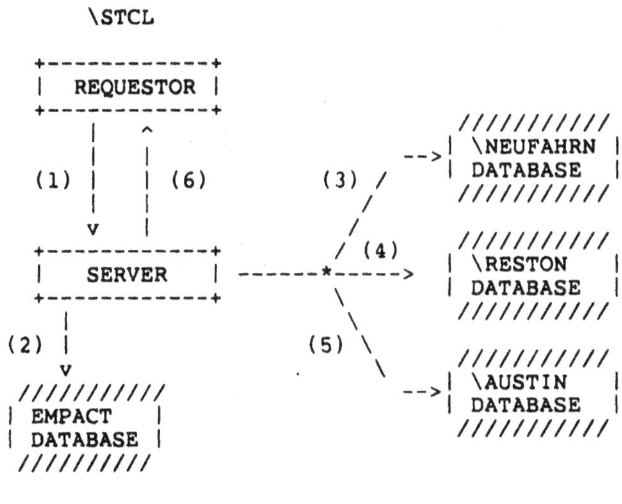

Figure 4—Preliminary broadcast transaction: (1) Requestor sends transaction-request message to server; (2) server updates local copy of database; (3)–(5) server updates all known remote databases; (6) server replies to requestor.

at their respective sites. TMF guarantees the consistency of the database by covering each broadcast. Figure 5 presents the structure of a broadcast transaction with node file and remote server.

This method of broadcasting transactions resolves the problem of naming, but it still violates the requirements of site autonomy and short terminal response time. A transaction that updates global data can only be performed when all sites in the network are available. Furthermore, as the number of sites in the network becomes large, the response time on the terminal becomes unreasonably long.

Suspense Transaction

The selected solution to both of these problems was to sacrifice the absolute consistency of the replicated files in exchange for site autonomy and short terminal response times by using a *suspense* mechanism to maintain database consistency.

Instead of immediately broadcasting the transaction to all sites in the network, the server at the site where a global transaction is initiated first updates its copy of the global file and then posts the transaction message to a suspense, or queue, file. A dedicated process, known as the suspense monitor (SUSMON), asynchronously polls the suspense file for transactions and on an as-soon-as-possible (ASAP) basis sends the transaction messages to appropriate servers at remote sites, one at a time, as separate logical TMF transactions. The database is completely consistent only when the suspense files at all the sites are empty. Figure 6 shows the structure of a suspense transaction.

The requirement of site autonomy is satisfied because updates to global files can be initiated regardless of the status of other sites in the network. The problem of unsatisfactory response time at the user's terminal is resolved because the server at the initiating site has only to update the local database before sending a reply back to the TCP. The propagation of the update to remote sites is performed asynchronously by SUSMON. All update and insert activity involving the suspense file is covered by TMF.

Data Ownership and Key Ranges

As with the broadcast method, TMF guarantees the consistency of the database. However, with TMF, unlike the broadcast method, because the suspense mechanism introduces a time delay in the propagation of updates to remote sites, the

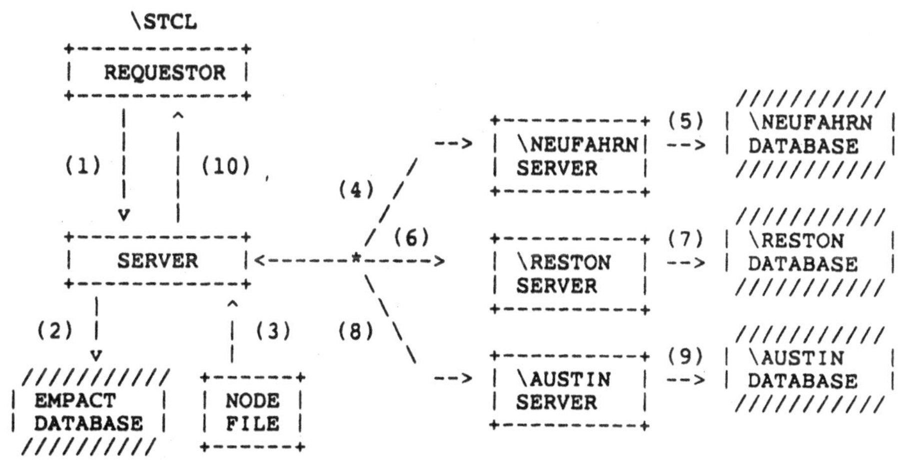

Figure 5—Broadcast transaction: (1) Requestor sends request message to server; (2) server updates local copy of database; (3) server reads node file to determine where else to send transaction; (4), (6), (8) server sends request to associate servers at remote sites; (5), (7), (9) associate servers perform update; (10) servers reply to requestor.

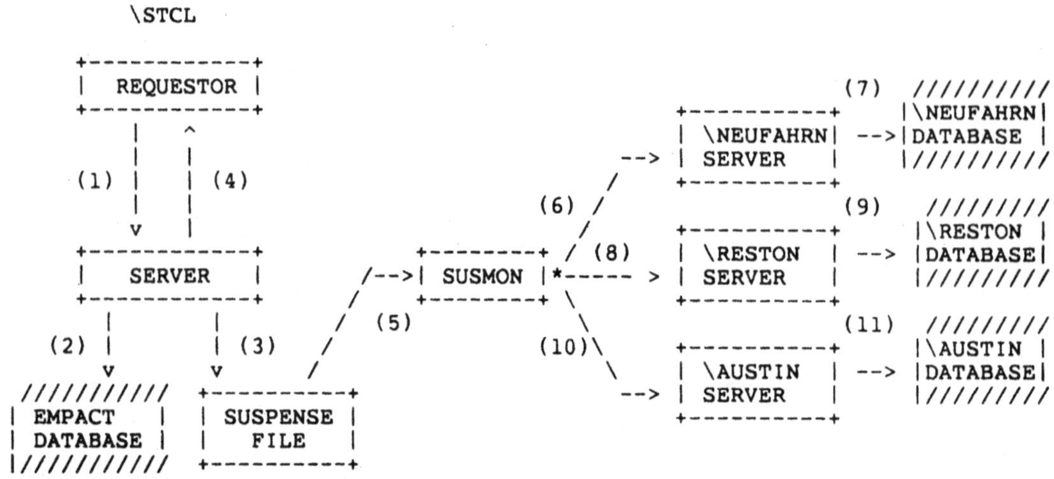

Figure 6—Suspense transaction: (1) Requestor sends request message to server; (2) server updates local copy of database; (3) server posts message in suspense file; (4) server replies to requestor; (5), (7), (9) SUSMON asynchronously sends transaction to remote servers; (6), (8) (10) remote server attempts update at remote database and responds to SUSMON.

possibility of *conflicting* adds and updates among the sites becomes a problem.

Conflicting updates occur when two or more sites update their copies of the same data simultaneously. Similarly, conflicting adds occur when two or more sites add records to a global file with the same key value, but different data. For example, a conflicting add would occur if Reston and Austin were to simultaneously add the same part number to their copies of the item-master file, but have different physical items associated with that number.

To prevent this possibility, ownership (by site) is assigned to global records and the initiation of updates is restricted to only the owning site. To prevent conflicting adds, the ranges of key values are preassigned to the various sites and adds are limited to those ranges.

Although only one site at a time can have add or update rights to a particular record or range of records, these rights could be given away to another site. The user community did not find this an unreasonable limitation.

Stale Data

Another problem introduced by the suspense mechanism is the problem of *stale* data. Stale data occur when an out-of-date copy of a global file is read. The data are out-of-date because an update to the file has been posted at a remote site but has not yet been propagated to the local site. However, because the propagation time for suspense updates is considerably less than the time the user community takes to act on the update, temporary staleness is not a problem.

Before the implementation of distributed EMPACT, the various manufacturing sites were using shared information that was updated and reconciled on a weekly basis. In distributed EMPACT the elapsed time for the propagation of a transaction to all sites in the network is less than a minute; in the worst case, such as a catastrophic network line failure, it is several days. This is viewed as a major improvement. It was also pointed out that if indeed the most current information were absolutely needed, the read could be directed to the copy at the owner site. If a business emergency were to occur that could not wait on the suspense delay, an outside mechanism such as a phone could be used.

In short, the approach taken to satisfy the simultaneous requirements of site autonomy and database consistency is to replicate communcal information, use an ASAP update scheme to maintain the concurrency of the replicated information, and rely on the notion of record ownership to prevent conflicting updates. The favorable relation of propagation time to action time permits brief periods of stale data.

The next section of this paper discusses some of the details related to the implementation of this approach.

IMPLEMENTATION

The conversion of EMPACT from a centralized application to a distributed application required

1. Specific modifications to the structure of the database
2. Developing the suspense-processing utility SUSMON
3. Identifying data consistency algorithms
4. Developing a means to serialize transactions
5. Deciding upon standard update and record-locking protocols
6. Handling processing variations and exceptions
7. Error processing

Database Restructuring

The existing database was reorganized so that the local, global, and semiglobal information reside in distinct sets of files that themselves are solely global, local, or semiglobal. As was mentioned earlier, this restructuring simplifies the organization and reduces the complexity of the update servers. The logic that updates global information can be separated from the relatively simpler logic that updates local information, easing the task of program conversion and maintenance. This conversion is necessary for all programs that access global data.

Suspense File Monitor

The SUSMON process at each site, as shown in Figure 6, is designed to propagate any transaction posted in its suspense file to other sites in the network. Each site has its own suspense file and copy of SUSMON. SUSMON, in conjunction with the servers that update global data, maintains the consistency of replicated data.

SUSMON's map of the network is the node file, which is replicated at all the EMPACT sites. This file contains the Guardian system names and statuses of all sites.

Records in the suspense file contain a copy of the request message, the name of the server class that receives and acts on the message, and a *bit mask* that is matched against the list of sites in the node file to identify where the transaction has been sent or needs to be sent.

SUSMON polls the suspense file looking for work. When finding a transaction that needs to be sent to a remote site, SUSMON performs the following actions:

1. Invokes TMF monitoring—initiates the transaction.
2. Establishes communication with the appropriate server class at the remote site.
3. Sends the request message to the server.
4. Waits for a reply.
5. If the reply is affirmative, updates the bit mask to indicate that the site has processed the transaction successfully.
6. If some site is not available, either because a network link was down or because a system is unavailable, the algorithm defers, intending to try again at a later time.
7. When the bit mask indicates that all necessary sites have received the transaction, the process deletes the record from the suspense file.
8. Ends TMF monitoring—commits the transaction.

Figure 7 diagrams the information flow during suspense processing.

Data Consistency Algorithms

Given the restructured database and the development of SUSMON, the conversion task was directed towards modifying those servers that update global files. The design of a new update algorithm was required to resolve concurrency problems and to provide a guarantee of data consistency within the replicated files. The original update algorithm, a protocol that was designed for a single-site application, plays an extended role in the distributed scheme; we will now describe it before moving on to its modifications.

A standard two-step protocol of *check* and *update* is used for update transactions. As part of the first step, an end user

```
Initiating                                    Remote
  Site                                         Site(s)

+-----+                                     +------+
|     |                                     | A  S |  (3)
|  S  |                                     | S  E |-------> ////////////
|  U  |       (2)        ------------------>| S  R |-------> | EMPACT   |
|  S  |-------------\                       | O  V |-------> | DATABASE |
|  M  |                                     | C  E |-------> ////////////
|  O  |                  -------------------| I  R |
|  N  |<------------\        (4)            | A    |
|     |                                     | T    |
+-----+                                     | E    |
   ^  |                                     |      |
(1) |  | (5)                                +------+
    |  v
+----------+
| Suspense |
|  file    |
+----------+
```

Figure 7—Suspense processing: (1) SUSMON obtains transaction from suspense file; (2) SUSMON establishes communication with server at remote site and sends request message; (3) server updates local copy of database—may involve multiple records; (4) server replies to SUSMON; (5) SUSMON updates bit mask of record in suspense file.

```
+-----------------------------+
|                             |
|     R E Q U E S T O R       |
|                             |
+-----------------------------+
      |    ^         |      ^
  (1) |    | (3) (4) |      | (7)
      v    |         v      |
   +----------------------+
   |    S E R V E R (S)   |
   +----------------------+
      ^ ^       ^ ^    ^ ^
  (2) | |   (5) | |    | | (6)
      v v       v v    v v
    //////////////////////
    | EMPACT DATA BASE   |
    //////////////////////
```

Figure 8—Check and update protocol: (1) Requestor sends check message; (2) Server accesses database and verifies validity of transaction; (3) server replies; (4) requestor initiates update step; (5) server performs validity checks; (6) server updates database; (7) reply is returned to requestor. Note that each access to the database—steps (2), (5), and (6)—may be multiple.

might access a screen and make a request to update a certain record or piece of information in order to add a component part to an existing bill of material structure. The requestor module servicing the end user then sends the appropriate server class a request for the record or piece of information specified. Next, the server verifies that such an update is possible or permitted, and it replies with the requested data. (See Figure 8.)

To add a new component, the server needs to verify, among other things, that the assembly exists, that the component to be added is an existing part, and that the assembly is not a component of the component—bills of materials cannot be recursive.

After the user is satisfied with the data entry, the requestor module initiates the second phase of the update process: a request to a server (not necessarily the process that handled the first request) asks that the update be performed against the database. The updating server again verifies that the update is possible, repeating the validity checks that were used in the first step. If all validation is affirmative, the database is updated, a successful reply is sent to the requestor, and ultimately to the end user. In the event of error, a negative reply is returned.

The purpose of this two-step check and update protocol is to provide a reasonable level of user friendliness and concurrency. The check allows the user to find out prior to performing potentially unnecessary data entry whether or not a given change is actually needed and possible. A higher level of concurrent processing is achieved because data locks, which are handled at the record level, are only held while the actual update is being performed by the server, and not while data are being entered.

Conflicting updates within a site are prevented because an *old-data/new-data* comparison is performed before update. If the current copy of the data in the database matches the old copy of the data in the update request message, then the new updated data are written to the database. Otherwise the update request is rejected because a legitimate update has taken place between the time the check request was issued and the time the update request was made.

This two-step method for performing updates still applies within the environment of suspense processing. The check portion of the transaction remains unchanged, but the update portion requires additional logic to make use of SUSMON.

Upon successful completion of an update, instead of simply replying affirmatively to the requestor, the updating server first writes a copy of the update request message to the suspense file, then replies. SUSMON asynchronously sends the message, as posted, to identical servers at each of the remote sites. These servers perform the same processing logic that is performed at the initiating site, including validity checks; however, no copy of the message is posted in the local suspense file, since the destination of the update has been reached.

Using identical versions of the update server to process a given request at both the initiating site and the receiving nodes minimizes program maintenance; there is no need for multiple servers with nearly identical logic. Moreover, the consistency of the replicated copies of the data is continually being verified. If a replica becomes inconsistent, this mechanism will detect the circumstance.

This second feature, however, places several additional constraints on the structure of updates to global data. SUSMON sends requests to remote sites serially, that is, requests are sent to remote nodes one at a time and only after the previous one has successfully completed. Because the validity checks are also being performed at remote sites, the success of a global request at a remote node is guaranteed only if the transactions processed at the initiating site are serializable.

Transaction Serialization

A set of transactions is considered serializable even though it is processed in an interleaved or concurrent fashion, if there exists some serial order that will produce equivalent results.

The method chosen to accomplish this ordering at a node initiating global updates is a counter called the SUSMON-TRANS-ID. The counter is a 32-bit field residing on a single record in the database. Initially the counter is set to zero. Servers processing global transactions are required to read, lock, and increment the counter prior to posting the request message in the suspense file but subsequent to the completion of all standard processing.

Serialization is achieved using the SUSMON-TRANS-ID if

1. All records read and written are locked from the time of access to the time that the transaction is committed.
2. All records written (added, updated, or deleted) are locked prior to the write operation.
3. All records read are global.

This last clause simply implies that there can be no dependencies on nonglobal information, because the condition of non-

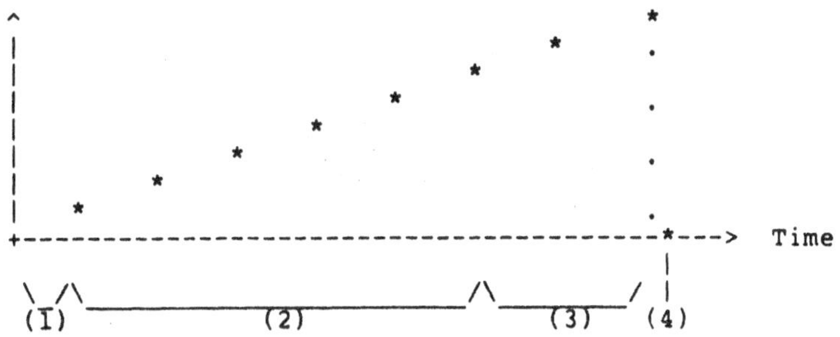

(1) TMF transaction initiated.

(2) Reads and writes performed for standard processing, all locks held.

(3) Obtain SUSMON-TRANS-ID and post message in suspense file. (Only one transaction per site is in this step at one time)

(4) Commit transaction and release locks.

Figure 9—Resource acquisition as a function of time during a global transaction

global data, by definition, may vary from site to node. Figure 9 charts the resource acquisition required for serialization.

The suspense file is key sequenced. The value obtained by incrementing the SUSMON-TRANS-ID counter determines the relative position of the record in the suspense file; this value is used as the primary record key. The order derived is the order in which the transactions will be propagated to other nodes.

Record-Locking Protocol

The first step of the locking protocol requires that all global records that are read also be locked; this ensures data consistency through the duration of database accesses. The second step of the locking protocol requires that the SUSMON-TRANS-ID be locked by any server process that uses the suspense file; this guarantees serialization of outbound transactions. The TMF Transid, however unique, is not capable of being used to serialize transactions; it is acquired at the time that the transaction is initiated, and not at the time that the suspense file is written to. Figure 9 clarifies this point.

Variations and Exceptions

The majority of the transactions in EMPACT easily adhere to this structure. There are three notable exceptions, however: the deletion of a part from the item-master, the addition of new global records, and the interplant transfer of material.

Part information in EMPACT resides in the item master record, which is defined to be global. Deleting an individual part from the database involves deleting the associated record from the item master file, but only after inactivity for the part has been established. A part is considered active if inventory records show a stock quantity for the item, or if the part is called out by any assemblies in the bill of materials records. In short, the activity of a part is defined by both global and local information, and it is this dependence on local information that undoes the algorithm outlined above.

The resolution to this problem was the implementation of part deletion as a broadcast transaction. Because the frequency of this transaction is historically low and because the day-to-day business of the individual sites does not depend on their being able to perform this transaction, the fundamental vulnerabilities of broadcast transactions are acceptable. The lesson learned by the designers of EMPACT was that if a particular transaction did not fit the structure required for suspense processing, broadcasting could serve to perform it.

The decision to assign ranges of key values in order to prevent conflicting adds was also the result of an informative debate. Replication requires a common recognition of a record's global uniqueness; for example, a part number can only identify one kind of part throughout the system. If any site were permitted to add a global record by means of a suspense transaction, then the possibility would exist of simultaneous and independent additions of the same record at different sites. On the other hand, if the addition of global data were performed through broadcast transactions, then a critical aspect of daily business, the addition of a new part, would depend on the availability of all sites.

The solution reached was the creation of a range file that restricts the add capability of any site to a nonoverlapping set of values. The range file is replicated at all sites, and adds can be performed using the suspense mechanism so long as the key value falls within a valid range. Following our example, each site is permitted to add parts within a unique range of part numbers.

The range file is maintained using broadcast transactions.

```
 Initiating                                   Remote
    Site                                      Site(s)


  +-----+                                   +------+
  |     |                                   | A  S |
  |  S  |                                   | S  E |          ////////////
  |  U  |      (2)      ----------------->| S  R |  (3)     | EMPACT   |
  |  S  |--------------\                    | O  V |-------> | DATABASE |
  |  M  |                                   | C  E |          ////////////
  |  O  |               -------------------| I  R |
  |  N  |<-------------\        (4)         | A    |
  |     |                                   | T    |
  +-----+                                   | E    |
    ^  |                                    |      |
(1) |  | (5)                                +------+
    |  v
+--------------------------------------------------------------+
| Suspense |      Suspense record key         |      msg        |
|   file   |Counter value   Sequence Number   |                 |
|          |     n               0            | New Trans       |
|          |     n+1             0            | New Trans       |
|          |     n+2             0            | New Trans       |
+--------------------------------------------------------------+
```

Figure 10—Suspense processing: (1) SUSMON obtains transaction $n0$ from the suspense field; (2) SUSMON establishes communication with server at remote site and sends transaction message; (3) server updates local copy of database; (4) server replies to SUSMON; (5) SUSMON updates the bit mask of $n0$ in the suspense file and begins processing transaction $(n + 1)0$.

```
 Initiating                                   Remote
    Site                                      Site(s)


  +-----+                                   +------+
  |     |                                   | A  S |
  |  S  |                                   | S  E |          ////////////
  |  U  |               ----------------->| S  R |          | EMPACT   |
  |  S  |--------------\                    | O  V |-------> | DATABASE |
  |  M  |      (2)                          | C  E |          ////////////
  |  O  |               -------------------| I  R |
  |  N  |<-------------\                    | A    |
  |     |                                   | T    |
  +-----+                                   | E    |
    ^  |                                    |      |
(1) |  | (3)                                +------+
    |  v
+--------------------------------------------------------------+
| Suspense |      Suspense record key         |      msg        |
|   file   |Counter value   Sequence number   |                 |
|          |     n               1            | New Trans       |
|          |     n               2            | 2nd request     |
|          |     n               3            | 3rd request     |
|          |     n+1             0            | New Trans       |
+--------------------------------------------------------------+
```

Figure 11—Suspense processing: (1) SUSMON polls the suspense file and observes that the sequence number in the suspense key of the first record identifies the first record of a multirequest transaction; SUSMON recognizes that the unit of work demanded in this case requires that all entries for transaction n be processed before completion is reached; (2) SUSMON processes the requests serially in the usual manner; (3) if the server has replied successfully to all requests involving transaction n, completion has been reached, the bit mask of $n1$ is updated and SUSMON begins processing transaction $(n + 1)0$.

Paired with suspense processing, the range file concept satisfies all requirements for uniqueness, site autonomy, and user friendliness.

The interplant transfer of material posed a somewhat different problem. As noted earlier, the interplant transfer data are considered semiglobal because the information is relevant only to the sites involved in the exchange of material, which may be two or more sites but need not be all. The events of a typical interplant transfer of material are as follows: one site requests material from another in the form of a requisition; the supplying site acknowledges the requisition and determines whether there is sufficient available inventory to fulfill the request; if so, the supplying site ships the requested material, and upon receipt the requisition is closed.

A decision was made to implement the interplant transfer functions, or MART subsystem, by replicating the interplant transfer data at the sites involved in the transaction and using the suspense mechanism to move the data from one site to the other.

Suspense transactions in the MART application are composed of potentially multiple requests. The proper processing of these requests at the destination site requires a precise sequencing at the sending site. The internal serialization of a multiple-request transaction can be obtained by incorporating a sequence number into the key of the suspense record; the key is now formed by a counter that contains the value of the SUSMON-TRANS-ID and a sequence number that directs internal order. SUSMON then treats all records associated with a particular counter value as a single transaction but sends the requests, one at a time, to a specified server. The result of these modifications was the evolution of SUSMON from a tool intended solely for broadcasting transactions to a general-purpose transport mechanism.

Figures 10 and 11 describe the differences between a standard SUSMON transaction and a MART SUSMON transaction in terms of the SUSMON-TRANS-ID.

Error determination and handling in a distributed environment requires a level of clarity and coordination that may be unnecessary in a nondistributed setting. A distributed database without a strategy for identifying and resolving errors is singularly vulnerable. SUSMON was chosen as central coordinator of error detection within the distributed EMPACT.

Error Processing

SUSMON's interpretation of error conditions determines the subsequent suspense processing to be followed. SUSMON identifies an error as belonging to one of two distinct categories; either the error is retryable or nonretryable. The selection of a category is based on the following criteria:

1. Retryable.—The error was caused by an unanticipated system restriction or problem. Possibilities include communications disruption between SUSMON and a remote server, site unavailability, or isolated system failures within the remote system.
   Solution.—The sending SUSMON will report the problem, defer any suspense processing to that site for an ordained amount of time, continue processing to other sites, and eventually retry the transactions.
2. Nonretryable.—The error was related to data inconsistency and was reported by the remote server that had attempted to satisfy the request. Possibilities include failure during the remote server's old-data/new-data check or any other consistency evaluation, or media damage such as an uncorrectable parity error within a record accessed by the remote server.
   Solution.—The remote server will report the problem on the remote site, and the sending SUSMON will do likewise locally. SUSMON will indefinitely suspend all activity directed to the site reporting the failure. Resolution of the problem will require a degree of human intervention.

Any problem reporting is done to a hard-copy logging console. It is, moreover, essential that SUSMON suspend all activity to any site that is in error; the serial interdependence of transactions requires the serial processing of any suspense file requests destined to a site. A nonretryable failure of a single transaction to a site effectively interrupts the serial flow of data. Processing to all unaffected sites can continue, since the situation does not imply an error condition outside that reported in the problem site.

EXPERIENCE

The development schedule for distributed EMPACT spans a period of 2 years. The project was commissioned in January 1981 and it was not until September of that same year that the preliminary design was agreed upon. External and internal specifications were completed 3 months later, and in January 1982 coding began.

The development of SUSMON and the conversion of MART to use SUSMON were completed in April 1982. The conversion of the item master subsystem and bill of materials subsystem, along with the restructuring of the database are scheduled to be finished in December 1982. MART and SUSMON were installed in May 1982 for limited production use. Until the final conversion effort is completed, weekly tapes are being sent to all the sites to maintain concurrent copies of the global information.

The results of the limited production use of MART and SUSMON are encouraging. The software has responded well to the demands placed on it, and the assumptions made during the design phase have proven accurate. Operationally, however, the need for a centrally located network management function has become apparent; events that require the cooperation of all the different sites, such as the addition of a new site to the network, are very difficult to manage manually in a distributed environment.

This need was evidenced during the first attempt to quiesce a three-site EMPACT network. Quiescing a network requires that all servers across the EMPACT network be denied access to their suspense files, and that each SUSMON empty its suspense file of any outbound transactions.

The strategy chosen for this first attempt was to coordinate the activity over the telephone. The exercise demonstrated that the operational complexity of a distributed application demands a high level of training and skill at both the system manager and computer operator positions.

To relieve these difficulties, software was developed to aid in the management of the network, especially in the areas of control and configuration. Its capabilities include

1. The addition and deletion of sites to and from the network
2. The quiescing of all global transactions
3. Inquiry into the status of global-transaction processing throughout the network .

It should be noted that SUSMON was used to implement the network management software.

CONCLUSIONS

Distributed EMPACT is an example of an application where the requirements of a business call for a distributed solution. The application is considered successful because the structure and organization of the database and software closely parallel the structure and organization of TANDEM's business environment.

The design of distributed EMPACT illustrates some of the techniques that can be used in a distributed database application, and the actual implementation of distributed EMPACT demonstrates the feasibility of developing a truly distributed application on the TANDEM T/16 system.

ACKNOWLEDGMENTS

We would like to acknowledge the contributions of Vince Sian and Jim Gray to the initial design of Distributed EMPACT. Further thanks are due to Betty Buhr, Rick Burgess, Bob Plummer, Kathy Welch, and to the entire Manufacturing Information Systems staff for their ideas and advice. We also wish to recognize Carl Goldman and Mike Sanders for the management support that they provided. We are grateful for the help and guidance given us by many members of the TANDEM Software Development and Software Education groups, particularly Andrea Borr, Bob Jones, and Jim Collins. Finally, we would like to thank Jim Gray and Rikki Westerschulte for their editorial advice.

REFERENCES

1. Borr, A. "Transaction Monitoring in ENCOMPASS: Reliable Distributed Transaction Processing," TANDEM Technical Report TR 81.2, 1981.
2. Katzman, J., and R. Taylor. "GUARDIAN/EXPAND, a Nonstop Network," TANDEM Technical Report, 1978.
3. Selinger, P. "Replicated Data." In I.W. Draffan and F. Poole (Ed), *Distributed Data Bases, An Advanced Course.* Cambridge: Cambridge University Press, 1980, pp. 223–231.
4. Smith, L. "Designing a Network-Based Transaction Processing System." SEDS-002, TANDEM Computers Incorporated, 1982.

Overview of an Ada* Compatible Distributed Database Manager

Arvola Chan
Umeshwar Dayal
Stephen Fox
Nathan Goodman**
Daniel R. Ries
Dale Skeen***

Computer Corporation of America
Four Cambridge Center
Cambridge, Massachusetts 02142

Abstract

Adaplex is an integrated language for programming database applications. It results from the embedding of the database sublanguage DAPLEX in the general purpose programming language Ada. This paper provides an overview of the DDM: a distributed database manager (DDM) that supports the use of Adaplex as an interface language. The important technical innovations we have incorporated in the design of this system include:

1. An advanced data model that captures more application semantics than conventional data models.
2. Support for flexible data distribution options that improve locality of reference and efficiency of query processing.
3. Extensive query optimization that combines compile time access path optimization with run time site selection.
4. Efficient transaction management that reduces transaction conflicts and improves the resiliency of replicated data.
5. Robust, incremental recovery management that provides for automatic recovery from certain "catastrophic" failure conditions.

1. Introduction

Many military computer applications require access to information stored in databases. In the future, these applications will be implemented by programs written in the DoD's new programming language, Ada. Therefore, it is essential that database management capabilities that are closely coupled to Ada be made available. Toward this end, Computer Corporation of America (CCA) has designed Adaplex, the Ada-based composite language for programming database applications. Adaplex results from embedding in Ada the database sublanguage Daplex [SHIP81]. Two systems that support the Adaplex language are currently being developed at CCA. The implementation of a centralized DBMS, called the Local Database Manager (LDM), has been underway since October '81, and it is scheduled for completion in March '84. The LDM has been designed as a high-performance stand-alone system for managing local data [CFLR81] [CFLN82] [CDFL82]. The design specifications of a distributed DBMS, called the Distributed Database Manager (DDM), which interconnects multiple LDMs in a computer network, recently has been completed [CDFG82] [CDFG83]. Implementation of the DDM began in October '82.

Functionally, the DDM provides the same capabilities that one expects of any modern centralized DBMS. Like the LDM, the DDM supports applications written in either Daplex or Adaplex. Each user interacts with a distributed database precisely as if he were accessing a single-user, centralized, integrated database. The DDM shields users from all complexities introduced by data distribution, replication, and potential site failures. More specifically, the DDM provides the following important facilities:

1. An integrated global schema that encompasses data stored at all sites. The DDM maintains a global directory in order to keep track of the distribution and replication of data. It automatically maps transactions on the global schema into subtransactions on data stored at individual LDMs.

---

*Ada is a trademark of the Department of Defense (Ada Joint Program Office).

**Nathan Goodman's current address: Aiken Computation Laboratory, Harvard University, Cambridge, MA 02138.

***Dale Skeen's current address: Computer Science Department, Cornell University, Ithaca, NY 14853.

This project is supported jointly by the Advanced Research Projects Agency of the Department of Defense (DARPA) and the Naval Electronics Systems Command (NAVELEX) under contract N00039-82-C-0226. The views and conclusions contained in this paper are those of the authors and should not be interpreted as necessarily representing the official policies, either expressed or implied, of DARPA, NAVELEX, or the U.S. Government.

2. Complete physical data independence. The database administrator (DBA) is free to tune parameters involving the physical distribution, replication, and organization of the stored data, without affecting the external view of the database.

3. Mutual consistency of replicated data. Users deal with logical data only. The propagation of updates to redundant copies of updated data is managed by the DDM.

4. Continued operation in spite of site failures. Users can continue to perform update operations on redundantly stored data, even though some copies may be temporarily inaccessible. These latter copies are brought up to date by the DDM before being used for processing subsequent transactions.

5. Interleaved executions of multiple transactions. The DDM guarantees "atomicity" for each transaction. No partial effects of one transaction will be seen by another; and if a transaction is unable to complete, all of its effects on the database are undone automatically.

6. Efficient access to replicated data. The DDM will optimize the selection of sites that are used for accessing replicated data. This selection takes into consideration the availability of sites at run time and the actual data requirements of a given transaction.

7. Dynamic integration of new sites into the system. No quiescence of on-going activities is necessary for reconfiguration of the system.

In the following sections, we give an overview of the DDM's mechanisms for handling distributed and replicated data. Section 2 summarizes the database management facilities provided by the system. Section 3 outlines facilities for distributed database administration. Section 4 sketches the decompilation approach we employ for supporting the Adaplex language. Section 5 highlights our strategies for optimizing Daplex transactions. Section 6 summarizes our mechanisms for synchronizing concurrent transactions. Section 7 identifies our innovations in the area of recovery management. Finally, Section 8 reports the implementation status of the system.

2. The Adaplex Database Languages

The core language for the definition and manipulation of databases, both in the DDM and in the LDM, is called Daplex [SHIP81]. Daplex supports the notions of entities, functions, and generalization hierarchies [SS77]. These high level concepts provide more modelling capabilities than conventional hierarchical, network, or relational data model. Daplex has been extended to provide two user interfaces:

1. The Adaplex Programming Language Interface is designed primarily for application programmers. It integrates the complete programming language Ada with Daplex.(1) In addition to data definition and manipulation facilities, the Adaplex Programming Language Interface also provides access to a report writer utility. Furthermore, database administrators can define views, Ada procedures, and computed functions for controlling access to data.

2. The Interactive Language Interface is designed for use by both application developers and database administrators. Interactive users have complete access to the Daplex language. They also can create temporary databases, interface with a report writer utility, a bulk load utility, and a test data generator utility. In addition, database administrators can enter database authorization specifications and interface with a database reorganization utility.

3. Distributed Database Design

An important design goal of the DDM is to realize the advantage of locality of reference, by storing data items where they are most frequently used. In order to achieve locality of reference for retrieval transactions, it is often desirable to introduce replication. At the same time, replication is needed for improving data availability in the presence of site failures. Flexible options for database fragmentation and replication are supported in the DDM.

3.1 Fragmentation and Grouping

In order to provide efficient support for Daplex's function inheritance semantics(2) without introducing undue complexity, it is preferable to keep all information about a conceptual object at one place. Therefore, we do not consider the vertical fragmentation of properties of any given entity across sites. At the same time, Daplex allows for "direct" pointers that point from one entity to another. In order to facilitate the maintenance of such pointers, we introduce the notion of a <u>fragment group</u> (FG) for collecting together related entities. That is, we put related fragments from different generalization hierarchies together into groups, and we use these FGs as units for physical design. We expect that most databases can be designed in such a way that frequently followed inter-entity references, from entities within

---

(1) No changes whatsoever have been made to the existing Ada language. New (non-Ada) constructs have been introduced in ways that clarify their similarities to (and differences from) existing Ada constructs. The objective has been to make Adaplex easy to learn by trained Ada programmers.

(2) That is, a subtype inherits all functions applicable to its supertypes. In processing an entity of a given type, the Adaplex language allows for access to functions of all relevant supertypes.

a given FG, can be made self-contained (i.e., local to the FG). This will eliminate the cumbersome maintenance of nonlocal pointers. It is important to note that we do not require FGs be defined in such a way that all interentity references are localized. However, interentity references that span FG boundaries have to be processed through (more expensive) value-based join operations on distributed data.

Since we have ruled out the possibility of vertically partitioning the functions (attributes) of individual entities across sites, all fragmentation definition must be on the base types of generalization hierarchies. Partitioning of entities within a subtype can be implicitly defined through partitioning of the corresponding base type. Each fragment of a base entity type is defined in terms of a conjunction of conditions. Each condition can specify subtype membership, subtype nonmembership, or value for a single-valued function. Since fragments are required to be disjoint, their corresponding definition predicates must be non-overlapping.

In addition to fragmentation based on local properties of entities, we also support fragmentation based on associations. (In relational terminology, we support fragmentation based on join conditions.) The fragmentation of a generalization hierarchy can be made dependent on that of another generalization hierarchy. (This dependence must be induced by a single-valued function mapping entities from the former hierarchy to entities in the latter.) For example, assume there is a single-valued function mapping person entities to department entities. If a department fragment D_1 for storing department entities that are located on the first floor has been defined, then the specification of a corresponding person fragment P_1 for storing person entities that reference department entities in D_1 also is permissible. However, the fragment P_1 is required to be stored in the same FG as the fragment D_1.

3.2 Fragment Group Organization

Each group of logically related fragments is treated as a unit for replication, distribution, and physical organization. We distinguish two kinds of replicated copies of an FG. Let X be an FG that is to be replicated n times, at sites $S_1, \ldots, S_n$. The DBA can designate k (less than or equal to n) of these as regular sites for the FG. The remaining (n-k) sites are then treated as backup sites for the FG. Regular sites are intended for storing copies to be used during normal transaction processing; backup sites are used to improve resiliency in the presence of site failures. (The treatment of replicated data on transaction update and site recovery is discussed in Sections 5 and 6.)

The physical organization for each FG is specified in the same way as physical organization is specified for a local database in the LDM. For implementation simplicity, we require that all copies of an FG be organized identically. Discussions on the physical design options available in the LDM can be found in [CDFL82].

The DBA is free to change the replication, distribution, and physical organization parameters at any time. The DDM is designed to accommodate all reorganization of a physical nature (i.e., including changes in distribution and replication parameters) without incurring the overhead of rewriting or recompiling application programs.

4. Implementing the Adaplex Language

For the purpose of portability, A Preprocessor is used to translate an Adaplex program into a modified, pure Ada program with embedded calls to the underlying DBMS. One complication arises from the tight coupling of Daplex with Ada. While this tight coupling enhances the ease of use of the resultant composite language, it often will not be efficient to perform the database access operations in the order specified. In order to facilitate access path optimization, the Preprocessor employs a decompilation strategy. It first isolates the database access (Daplex) component of an Adaplex transaction specification from its general purpose computation (Ada) component. It then converts the Daplex component into a nonprocedural internal representation, called an envelope, which is in a form more amenable to optimization. The envelope is passed on to the DBMS to describe the data that is needed for running the entire transaction.

4.1 Decompilation Advantages

Decompilation is intended to yield two important performance advantages: it reduces synchronization overhead in the system; it also reveals opportunities for access path optimization.

4.1.1 Synchronization Reduction

In many database management systems, the task architecture shown in Figure 1 is employed. All data management functions, such as concurrency control and actual physical data access, are carried out by a separate DBMS task. This architecture

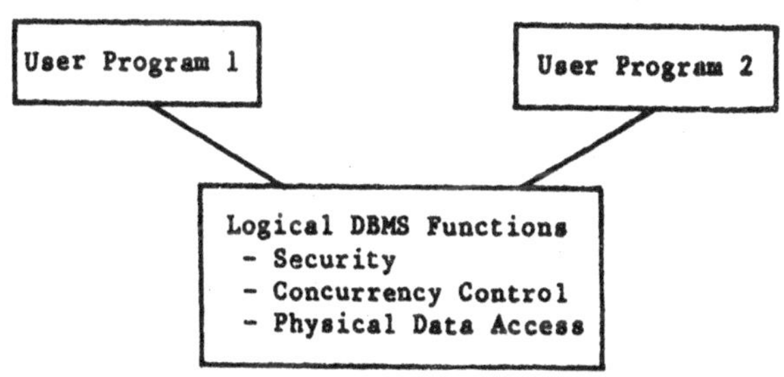

Figure 1. DBMS Architecture

serves to prevent undue corruption of shared data by erroneous user programs. The use of such a task architecture, in a DBMS that supports only record-at-a-time retrievals and updates, will result in two context switches between the user's task and the DBMS task for each accessed record. The expense of this communication, as compared to using high-level DBMS commands that manipulate sets of records, has been discussed in [RS81].

If the LDM/DDM simply translates the "for each" loops in an Adaplex program into "get first" and "get next" operations, the same excessive communication overhead will result. Instead, the Preprocessor converts a number of nested "for each" statements into a non-procedural set-oriented expression called an envelope. The result of executing an envelope is a sequence of hierarchically related records that correspond to entities selected from the database. The modified, pure Ada program makes a single invocation on the underlying DBMS to obtain the collection of data described by an envelope. Either the entire set or a suitably buffered subset of the required data is returned to the user task with a single context switch.

4.1.2 Access Path Optimization

The separate identification of a required set of data permits the DBMS to perform more thorough optimization. The decompilation of Adaplex, in fact, allows for more optimization than is normally found in embedded relational query language systems like Pascal/R [SCHM77] and RIEGEL [RS79]. These latter systems optimize relational expressions that govern the execution of individual iteration loops only. Decompilation in the LDM/DDM, on the other hand, identifies a set oriented expression that describes the data required in a number of arbitrarily nested loops constituting all or part of a database transaction.

The need for access path optimization is illustrated by the query in Figure 2.

This query retrieves the names of students who have taken 4-credit courses, along with the titles of those courses. The obvious approach for process-ing this query is to follow the control structure of the program: a student entity is retrieved; then a course entity in which the student is enrolled is retrieved; if the course is a 4-credit one, then the student's name and the course's title are printed. The retrieval of course entities is repeated until all of the courses for the given student have been exhausted. Next, another student entity and the corresponding course entities are retrieved and processed. This is repeated until all of the student entities have been considered. If the database contains many student entities, and comparatively few 4-credit course entities, and there exists direct access paths for locating the 4-credit courses, then an alternate approach may be better. First, the 4-credit courses are retrieved. Next, the students who are taking those courses are retrieved. This can be done by exploiting available auxiliary structures that represent the inverse of the enrollments function, or by performing a relational join operation. Finally, the name and title pairs are grouped by student. This can be achieved by sorting on the internal identifiers of student entities. An important purpose of decompilation is to decouple the data selection requirements from the output format requirements, in order to uncover such optimization opportunities.

```
for each S in STUDENT
 loop
  for each C in ENROLLMENTS(S)
   where CREDITS(C) = 4
    loop
     PRINT(NAME(S), TITLE(C));
    end loop;
 end loop;
```

Figure 2. An Adaplex Program Segment

4.2 Preprocessing

An Adaplex program goes through a preprocessing stage in order to prepare for multiple run-time invocations. Preprocessing results in a pure Ada program with embedded procedure calls to the underlying DBMS and embedded procedures for unbuffering data retrieved from the database. During the preprocessing stage, the envelopes for defining the data needed by the program are identified; the strategy for obtaining data prescribed by each envelope is also optimized. The description of the optimized execution steps are stored away as <u>access plans</u> that can be invoked at run-time.

In the modified, pure Ada program, the original data manipulation constructs are converted into two basic types of procedure calls. The first type of procedure call initiates the execution of a corresponding access plan. The second type of procedure call obtains data needed for each iteration of an Ada looping construct. The Preprocessor generates both types of procedure calls and the looping constructs. It also generates the descriptions for the Ada record structures for holding the scalar values that are used inside the looping constructs.

The run-time execution of an Adaplex program invokes the Ada procedures described above. An envelope invocation procedure will first initialize parameters from values of run-time Ada program variables, if necessary. The underlying DBMS then retrieves the corresponding access plan for execution. The procedures that access data needed by the modified Ada loops will unbuffer the returned data, and will store the database values in the appropriate Ada records, as expected for the execution of the set of statements within each loop.

5. Envelope Optimization

The objective of envelope optimization is to minimize total processing cost, which is computed as a weighted sum of the costs of intersite data movement and local processing. We have extended distributed query optimization techniques used in existing systems like SDD-1 [BGWR81] and R* [SELI80]. Both SDD-1 and R* focus on conjunctive queries (i.e., queries involving only selections, projections, and joins). SDD-1's strategy is to reduce data by a sequence of semijoins, then transfer the reduced data to a single site, where the result is produced by a final series of join operations. As in R*, the DDM considers mixed join and semijoin strategies. We differ from SDD-1 and R* in the handling of horizontally partitioned data. Consider, for example, the query $R \bowtie S$, where R is horizontally partitioned into R_1, R_2, and S is horizontally partitioned into S_1, S_2. Both SDD-1 and R* replace the original query by the union of four subqueries, $R_i \bowtie S_j$, $1 <= (i,j) <= 2$. Algebraically, this is equivalent to distributing joins over unions. This is not always a good strategy. It is sometimes cheaper first to construct R and S by unions, and then to join them. In the DDM, we consider the tactic of distributing joins over unions only if it is profitable. (Left distribution, right distribution, and both left and right distribution, are all considered.)

Additional extensions to the DDM's optimizer are necessitated by the richness of Adaplex, compared to the relational interfaces supported by SDD-1 and R*. The implications of the richness of the Adaplex language on query processing in a centralized environment have been detailed in [RCDF83]. The extensions developed there also are applicable to the distributed environment. We sketch a few important extensions here. More details can be found in [DAYA83b].

First, the DDM attempts to optimize several nested "for each" loops in a query simultaneously. Many embedded relational query language systems, such as Pascal/R [SCHM77] and RIGEL [RS79], optimize the qualification of one "for each" loop at a time. Optimization over several loops allows the DDM to consider more join strategies, and it can reduce the communication and synchronization overhead between a user program and the DDM. The <u>unidirectional outer join</u> operation(3) is used to model nested iteration loops with embedded output statements in an Adaplex program. A straightforward approach to processing queries containing unidirectional outer joins would be to process all the regular joins before any unidirectional outer join, since these two types of joins do not commute in general. We could restrict the strategy space to only strategies that correspond to join sequences in which all regular joins precede all unidirectional outer joins. However, in order to increase the strategy space for optimization, we define a new operation, called a <u>partial join</u>, with the property that a unidirectional outer join followed by a partial join is equivalent to a regular join followed by a unidirectional outer join [RCDF83]. All three kinds of joins are in fact special cases of the graft operation introduced in [DAYA83b]. In essence, a larger number of join order permutations for an envelope is permissible, provided regular joins are replaced by partial joins, where appropriate.

Second, the DDM optimizes queries with nested quantifiers. In [DAYA83a], it is shown that queries that have mixed quantifiers can be processed using a two-phased technique. In the first or <u>graft</u> phase, all edges representing universal quantification are turned into unidirectional outer join edges, and the resultant query is processed using graft operations. In the second or <u>prune</u> phase, the result of the graft phase is processed to account for quantifications. This graft and prune strategy is potentially more efficient than those based on Codd's Reduction Algorithm [CODD72] [PALE72] [JS82]. The DDM optimizer constructs a good strategy for the graft phase. The result of the graft phase is made available at the transaction's home site, where the prune phase is executed locally.

Third, the DDM optimizer takes advantage of the explicit entity-to-entity functions that are specified in the functional data model. These are implemented by pointers and serve as direct access paths for performing joins between the pairs of entity types that are linked. In case the target entities are stored within other fragment groups, the sets of pointers from the source entities can first be collected in order to pinpoint the set of fragment groups that contain the target entities.

The overall optimization technique employed in the DDM is the following. First, localize selections.(4) Next, collapse joins that can be performed at the same site. Then, enumerate join orders using a leveled hill climbing search strategy: the user can specify an optimization level, N; the optimizer then enumerates join sequences of length N at each stage of the optimization process. When N is one, this heuristic is similar to the "greedy strategy" of INGRES [WY76]. When N is equal to or larger than the number of joins in the query, this heuristic resembles System R's exhaustive enumeration strategy. For a given (partial) join order, and for each join of horizontally partitioned entity sets, determine whether it is cost-effective to distribute the join over the union. For each nonlocal operation, select a site for performing the operation and determine whether it is cost-effective to do semijoin reductions before each join.

In order to amortize the overhead of decompilation and access path optimization, a two-step optimization approach is taken. Access path optimization is performed during the preprocessing stage (i.e., when a repetitive class of transactions is first defined). It involves the ordering of high level database operations and the selection of available access structures to efficiently process these operations. Optimization in this phase does not take into consideration the presence of replicated data. Each fragment group is treated as a distinct logical site, and the cost of an explicit

---

(3) This is similar to one of the dissymmetric joins discussed in [LP76].

(4) The distribution of selection over union is always possible and desirable.

transfer is always included for an operation whose operands are obtained from different fragment groups. The objective of access path optimization at compile (preprocess) time is to minimize total processing cost, using a worst case assumption about data distribution. Run time optimization is performed when an instance of a repetitive transaction class is to be executed. Materialization selection is carried out in this phase. That is, logical sites are bound to physical sites. It takes into consideration the availability of sites, as well as the locality of replicated data that needs to be accessed, in order to select the set of sites for running the transaction. The objective of this phase is to minimize intersite data transmission. Heuristics for materialization selection are discussed in [CDFG83].

6. Concurrency Control

The concurrency control mechanisms for the DDM are generalizations of those used in the LDM [CFLR81] [CFLN82]. We extend the LDM's two-phase locking mechanism in order to synchronize transactions that access distributed and replicated data. We also augment the LDM's multi-version mechanism in order to permit each read-only transaction to read a consistent snapshot of the database, without having to synchronize with concurrent update transactions.

6.1 Update Synchronization

The DDM's concurrency control mechanism for update transactions is based on distributed two-phase locking. In the following discussions, we speak of a distributed transaction as being coordinated by a single coordinator and serviced by a number of distributed agents. The agent of a transaction at a given site is responsible for acquiring locks for the transaction at that site. The processing that needs to be done by an agent is described to the agent nonprocedurally at the envelope level by the transaction's coordinator. The agent then executes the access plan for the envelope and sets locks incrementally as necessary. These locks are set at the page level and are held until the end of the transaction. Because of the incremental locking strategy, deadlocks are possible. They are detected and resolved on a periodic basis, both at the local and global levels.

Each replicated FG copy can be in one of three states: <u>online</u>, <u>offline</u>, or <u>failed</u>. Online copies are accessible and up to date. Offline copies are accessible but out of date. Failed copies are inaccessible. Let X be an FG that is to be replicated at n sites. Let k of these sites be regular sites designated by the DBA. Where possible, the DDM will endeavor to maintain k online copies for FG X. Under normal circumstances, the copies at the k regular sites are kept online. When a regular site that stores an online copy fails, an appropriate offline copy at a backup site is rolled forward and brought online. This is done in order to sustain the degree of resiliency and availability specified by the DBA. Similarly, when a regular site for FG X that has previously failed recovers, its copy is rolled forward and brought online. (A backup site that is storing an online copy will demote its copy to offline status, if appropriate.)

In general, online copies are updated synchronously; offline copies are updated in a background fashion. All online copies of an FG are treated as equals for the purpose of transaction processing. The transaction's coordinator selects a single agent in order to perform read and write operations on a single online FG copy. In case an FG copy is updated, the agent is responsible for propagating the updates to other online copies of the FG. This is done when the agent receives the "End of Transaction" indication from the coordinator. An agent sends positive acknowledgement to the coordinator only when it receives positive acknowledgements from the replication sites that store all the other online copies. Each site that stores a copy of an FG maintains a fragment group status table for that FG. This table identifies the sites that contain online copies of that FG, and it is used by a transaction's agent to determine the set of sites to which updates on the FG must be propagated.

6.2 Multiversion Mechanism

The LDM's multiversion scheme [CFLN82] is extended for operation in the distributed environment. The extended scheme guarantees that each distributed read-only transaction sees a semantically consistent snapshot of the database. Its salient features include:

1. Conflicts between read-only transactions and update transactions are completely eliminated.

2. Read-only transactions never have to be rolled back.

3. Garbage collection of old versions of data objects can be carried out efficiently.

At each LDM, the stored data is organized as a collection of segments. (Each segment is a collection of consecutively numbered logical pages.) There is a single common pool of pages, called the <u>version pool</u>, which is used for storing the old versions of segment pages that are potentially needed by in-progress transactions. Update transactions synchronize by using two-phase locking at the segment page level. Before performing in-place update to a segment page, an update transaction is required to first copy the current version of the page to the version pool. Thus, the multi-version mechanism deals with multiple versions of logical pages. Old versions in the version pool serve dual purposes: rolling back update transactions that have to be aborted, and providing consistent snapshots to read-only transactions.

Consider the example illustrated in Figure 3. The read-only transaction T_r needs to read logical pages P_1 and P_2. T_r has read P_1 when T_u comes along and updates P_2, causing the old version of P_2 to be copied to the version pool. When T_r tries to

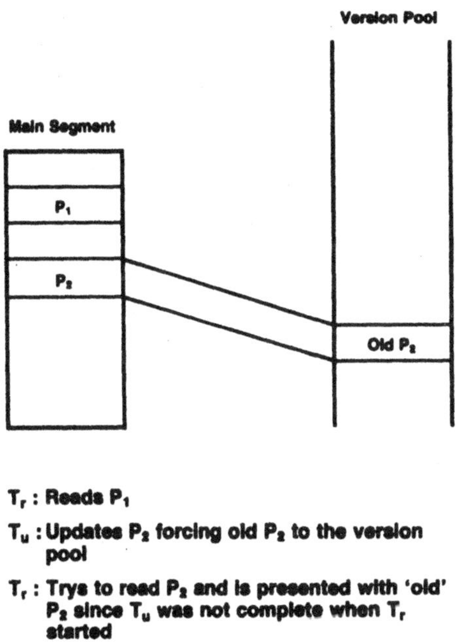

Figure 3. Elimination of Conflicts

read P_2, it still can be made to see a consistent snapshot of the database if it is presented with the old version of P_2, instead of the latest version created by T_u.

The consistent snapshot to be seen by a read-only transaction is defined in terms of a <u>completed transaction list</u> (CTL) that identifies the set of transactions that already have finished execution when the read-only transaction initiates.(5)

An important prerequisite for implementing the multi-version reading algorithm is that it be possible to determine exactly what transactions have completed execution at a given point in time. This is a trivial problem in a centralized environment. For a distributed read-only transaction that reads from multiple sites, the problem is more formidable. The local CTLs are potentially incomplete with respect to transaction dependencies. That is, an update transaction might be added to a CTL at a site before the transactions that it depends upon are added. Our solution for the distributed environment requires the coordinator of the distributed read-only transaction to retrieve the CTLs from sites where the read-only transaction is to perform reading. The coordinator computes the union of retrieved CTLs and retransmits the union-list to the reading sites for use with the multi-version reading algorithm. Some additional requirements are imposed on the atomic commitment protocol: potential transaction dependency information must be propagated during the execution of the commit algorithm. Such dependency information is piggybacked on messages already needed for achieving atomic commitment. Thus, no additional messages will be introduced. Details of the distributed multiversion algorithm can be found in [CG83].

7. Recovery Management

The goals of the recovery management subsystem in the DDM provide for extremely high data availability and resilient transaction processing. The recovery management subsystem consists of three components:

1. The <u>fragment group manager</u> (FGM) provides the desired level of availability for each FG copy, and maintains mutual consistency among copies of an FG.

2. The <u>transaction manager</u> (TM) provides atomic commitment of transactions, even in the presence of failures.

3. The <u>enhanced network</u> (EN) provides the network services required by the other two components.

<u>7.1 The Enhanced Network</u>

The enhanced network layer effects a clean separation between the communication network level and the higher-level managers. In addition to message transmission, it provides services that facilitate failure recovery of TMs and FGMs:

1. It maintains a <u>site status table</u> (SST) that stores the lastest known status of each site in the network (i.e., whether the site is up or down). Higher layers are allowed to query this table.

2. It implements a <u>watch</u> facility whereby a process can register a "recovery watch" or a "failure watch" on a specified site. If the enhanced network layer observes the recovery (failure) of the watched site, it interrupts the registering process.

---

(5) In the DDM, a global transaction identifier can be represented in terms of an originating (coordinating) site identifier, along with a chronologically assigned number that is unique within that site. Thus, a CTL will be made up of a number of sublists. Each sublist is associated with one site and represents completion information for transactions that have been initiated from that site. A sublist can in general be represented by three components: a base number, an exception list, and a bit-map. The exception list identifies transactions whose numbers are below the base number that are still in-progress. The bit-map identifies completed (i.e., committed or aborted) transactions whose numbers are above the base number. The sublist information is periodically recompacted by changing the base number and the corresponding exception list and bit map.

The SST is implemented by a set of Reliable Status Control Protocols. The goals of these protocols are to propagate failure information (and to a lesser extent, recovery information) in a timely, low-cost fashion. An entry in the SST consists of a unique site identifier, the site's incarnation number, and information indicating whether it is up or down. A site's incarnation number is incremented every time it recovers. By labeling a message with both the sender's id and its incarnation number, it is possible to determine during which of the site's operational periods a given message was sent.

The watch facility is implemented by observing changes in the local SST and it does not require the sending of messages to the watched sites. It eliminates the need for high-level timeouts. A straightforward implementation of watches associates a list of local processes with each site in the SST. The list identifies processes that will be interrupted whenever the SST entry for the corresponding site changes. With this implementation, the watch facility is almost free.

The Reliable Status Control Protocols consist of two components: a component that detects failures and recoveries, and a component that propagates failure/recovery information. The CONTROL protocol lies at the heart of the detection component; the CHANGE protocol lies at the heart of the propagation component.

The CONTROL protocol is essentially the one proposed in [WALT82], modified slightly to interface with our CHANGE protocol. A major difference between the CHANGE protocol used in the DDM and the one proposed in [WALT82] is that we have a "primary" site which is given the responsibility of actually disseminating the status change information. (The use of a primary site provides an efficient means for precluding the anomaly of a message affected by the failure of a site, say A, arriving at another site, say B, before the new SST reporting A's failure arrives at B. This anomaly, if allowed to occur, would lead to errors in our concurrency control algorithm. In order to support the primary site mechanism, the Site Status Table is augmented with an ordering field and a unique version number. The ordering field imposes a linear ordering among the operational sites and determines the order of succession if the current primary should fail. The version number designates the primary site and a number that is assigned in strictly increasing order by the primary site.)

The CONTROL protocol uses a static virtual ring. Each site asynchronously and periodically sends a HI message to its nearest operational successor in the ring and to all of the failed sites in between. A failure of a predecessor is detected when a HI message is not received after the elapse of an interval dependent on the sending rate of HI messages and the maximum message delivery time. Once a failure has been observed, the observer should find and notify the current primary, which is responsible for propagating the failure information.

Our mechanism for the propagation of status change information combines an active component and a passive component. The active component requires that each observation of a failure (recovery) be broadcasted to all sites. It is remotely based on the CHANGE protocol proposed in [WALT82]. The passive component piggybacks recent failure information on messages that may have been influenced by the failure, by appending the version number of the sender's SST to each message. At the receiving site, the Enhanced Network delays delivery of a message until its own version of the SST is at least as recent as the sender's. Thus, failure information is guaranteed to be delivered to sites that might be influenced by the failure, at a rate determined by the intensity of the message traffic.

7.2 Fragment Group & Transaction Management

At the conceptual level, a (replicated) FG is managed by an abstract process known as its fragment group manager. Such a process can be accessed directly from a number of different sites and is extremely fault-tolerant. A given FGM provides facilities to read and update one FG. Physically, an FGM is a closely-coupled confederation of processes (at least one process executing at each site that contains a copy), communicating among themselves in order to maintain mutual consistency. Each of these processes watches out for the failure of the others. Each is responsible for deciding, in a decentralized fashion, if its stored copy of the FG should be brought online or offline. It communicates with other processes within the confederation in order to decide what portion of the recovery log stored at one site should be sent over to the other, in order to roll-forward an out-of-date FG copy. Thus, recovery of replicated FG copies at a recovering site is performed in an incremental fashion [ABG82], one FG at a time, at the initiative of the recovering site. As soon as the locally stored copy of an FG has been rolled forward, it can be made accessible to new transactions. Thus, the availability of data stored at a recovering site is improved.

The execution and commitment of a transaction is managed by an abstract process called the transaction manager. The TM interacts with the managers of all FGs involved in the transaction. With respect to recovery management, its primary responsibility is to commit the transaction atomically at all involved FGMs. Like the FGM, a TM is physically implemented as a closely-coupled confederation of processes that span multiple sites in order to achieve high fault tolerance.

Our design for the FGM and TM in the DDM solves a number of reliability problems not addressed in previous prototypes like R* [WDHL82] and SDD-1 [RBFG80]. R* uses a two-phase commit protocol [GRAY78] that is liable to block if the site that is coordinating the commitment fails. SDD-1 makes use of backup coordinators in order to improve resiliency [HS80]. However, no provision is made in SDD-1 to allow for recovery from the situation wherein the primary coordinator and all its backups fail simultaneously. The DDM uses an improved version of SDD-1's commit algorithm in order to permit automatic recovery from such commit catastrophes. Whereas R* handles no replication, SDD-1 makes use of a spooler mechanism to collect update messages destined to a nonoperational site in order to facilitate the site's recovery [HS80]. When all spoolers for a given site fail at the same time, a spooler catastrophe is said to occur, and human intervention becomes necessary for recovery. The DDM makes use of the audit trails at replication sites in order to recover a failed site. It is designed to recover automatically from a total failure situation wherein all replication sites of a given FG have failed simultaneously.

8. System Status

The design specifications for the DDM recently have been completed. Implementation is now underway. In order to ensure the portability of the resulting system, Ada is being used as the implementation language. The initial system is targeted for Digital Equipment Corporation's VAX 11/780 running the VMS operating system. A two-phase implementation is planned. The first phase is scheduled for completion in September '84. It will not include implementation of the Adaplex Language Preprocessor, the Report Writer, the View Mapping Processor, and the Reorganization Utility. These latter modules are to be implemented in the second phase.

9. References

[ABG82]
Attar, R., B. Bernstein, and N. Goodman, "Site Initialization, Recovery, and Back-up in a Distributed Database System," Proceedings of the Berkeley Workshop on Distributed Data Management and Computer Networks, 1982.

[BGWR81]
Bernstein, P. A., N. Goodman, E. Wong, C. Reeve, and J. B. Rothnie, "Query Processing in a System for Distributed Databases (SDD-1)," ACM Transactions on Database Systems, Vol. 6, No. 4, December 1981.

[CDFG82]
Chan, A., U. Dayal, S. Fox, N. Goodman, D. Ries, and D. Skeen, "DDM Design Specifications," Computer Corporation of America, 1982.

[CDFG83]
Chan, A., U. Dayal, S. Fox, N. Goodman, D. Ries, and D. Skeen, "DDM: An Ada Compatible Database Manager," COMPCON Digest of Papers, 1983.

[CDFL82]
Chan, A., S. Danberg, S. Fox, W. K. Lin, and D. Ries, "Storage and Access Structures to Support a Semantic Data Model," VLDB Conference Proceedings, 1982.

[CFLN82]
Chan, A., S. Fox, W. K. Lin, A. Nori, and D. Ries, "The Implementation of an Integrated Concurrency Control and Recovery Scheme," ACM SIGMOD Conference Proceedings, 1982.

[CFLR81]
Chan, A., S. Fox, W. K. Lin, and D. Ries, "The Design of an Ada Compatible Local Database Manager (LDM)," Technical Report CCA-81-09, Computer Corporation of America, November, 1981.

[CG83]
Chan, A., and R. Gray, "Implementing Distributed Read-only Transactions," submitted for publication.

[CODD72]
Codd, E. F., "Relational Completeness of Database Sublanguages," in R. Rustin (ed.) Database Systems, Courant Computer Science Symposium, Prentice Hall, Englewood Cliffs, N.J., 1972.

[DAYA83a]
Dayal, U., "Processing Queries With Quantifiers: A Horticultural Approach," Proc. ACM SIGACT-SIGMOD Symposium on Principles of Database Systems, March 1983.

[DAYA83b]
Dayal, U., "Query Optimization in the Distributed Database Manager (DDM)," Technical Report, Computer Corporation of America, Cambridge, Mass., in preparation.

[GRAY78]
Gray, J. N., "Notes on Database Operating Systems," Operating Systems: An Advanced Course, Spring-Verlag, 1978.

[HS80]
Hammer, M., and D. Shipman, "Reliability Mechanisms for SDD-1: A System for Distributed Databases," ACM Transactions on Database Systems, Vol. 5, No. 4, December 1980.

[JS82]
Jarke, M., and J. W. Schmidt, "Query Processing Strategies in the Pascal/R Relational Database Management System," ACM SIGMOD Conference Proceedings, 1982.

[LP76]
Lacroix, M., and A. Pirotte, "Generalized Joins," ACM SIGMOD Record, Vol. 8, No. 3, September 1976.

[PALE72]
Palermo, F. P., "A Database Search Problem," IBM Research Report RJ 1072, July 1972.

[RBFG80]
Rothnie, J. B., Jr., P. A. Bernstein, S. Fox, N. Goodman, M. Hammer, T. A. Landers, C. Reeve, D. W. Shipman, and E. Wong, "Introduction to a System for Distributed Databases (SDD-1)," ACM Transactions on Database Systems, Vol. 5, No. 1, March 1980.

[RCDF83]
Ries, D., A. Chan, U. Dayal, S. Fox, and W. K. Lin, "Decompilation, Optimization, and Pipelining for Adaplex: A Procedural Database Language," Technical Report, Computer Corporation of America, in preparation.

[RS79]

Rowe, L. A., and K. A. Schoons, "Data Abstraction, Views and Updates in RIGEL," ACM SIGMOD Conference Proceedings, May 1979.

[RS81]

Rowe, L. A., and M. Stonebraker, "Architecture for Future Database Systems," ACM SIGMOD Record, Vol. 11, No. 1, January 1981.

[SCHM77]

Schmidt, J. W., "Some High Level Language Constructs for Data of Type Relation," ACM Transactions on Database Systems, Vol. 2, No. 3, September 1977.

[SELI80]

Selinger, P. G., and M. Adiba, "Access Path Selection in Distributed Database Management Systems," Proceedings of the International Conference on Databases, University of Aberdeen, Aberdeen, Scotland, 1980.

[SHIP81]

Shipman, D., "The Functional Data Model and the Data Language Daplex," ACM Transactions on Database Systems, Vol. 6, No. 1, March 1981.

[SS77]

Smith, J. M., and D. C. P. Smith, "Database Abstractions: Aggregation and Generalization," ACM Transactions on Database Systems, Vol. 2, No. 2, June 1977.

[WALT82]

Walter, B., "A Robust and Efficient Protocol for Checking the Availability of Remote Sites," Proceedings of the Sixth Berkeley Workshop on Distributed Data Management and Computer Networks, 1982.

[WDHL82]

Williams, R., D. Daniels, L. Haas, G. Lapis, B. Lindsay, P. Ng, R. Obermarck, P. Selinger, A. Walker, P. Wilms, and R. Yost, "R*: An Overview of the Architecture," Proceedings of the 2nd International Conferences on Databases: Improving Usability and Responsiveness, 1982.

[WY76]

Wong, E. and K. Youssefi, "Decomposition -- A Strategy for Query Processing," ACM Transactions on Database Systems, Vol. 1, No. 3, September 1976.

REFERENCES FOR ADDITIONAL READING

[ADIB 78a] Adiba, M., and D. Portal, "A Cooperation System for Heterogeneous Database Management Systems," *Information Systems*, Vol. 3, No. 3, pp. 209–215, 1978.

[ADIB 78b] Adiba, M., et al., "Issues in Distributed Data Base Management Systems: A Technical Overview," *Proc. 1978 VLDB*, pp. 89–100, Sept. 1978.

[AJMO 83] Ajmone Marsan, M., et al., "Modeling Bus Contention and Memory Interference in a Multiprocessor System," *IEEE Transactions on Computers*, Vol. C-32, No. 1, pp. 60–72, Jan. 1983.

[ALLE 82] Allen, F.W., M.E.S. Loomis, and M.V. Mannino, "The Integrated Dictionary/Directory System," *Computing Surveys*, Vol. 14, No. 2, pp. 245–286, June 1982.

[ALSB 76] Alsberg, P.A., and J.D. Day, "A Principle for Resilient Sharing of Distributed Resources," *Proc. 2nd International Conference on Software Engineering*, pp. 562–570, 1976.

[APER 84] Apers, P., and G. Wiederhold, "Transaction Classification to Survive a Network Partition," Stanford University Technical Report, STAN-CS-85-1053, Aug. 1984.

[APER 80] Apers, P.M.G., "Data Allocation and Distributed Query Processing," *Proc. ACM Pacific Conference*, San Francisco, 1980.

[AVIZ 78] Avizienis, A., "Fault-Tolerance: The Survival Attribute of Digital Systems," *Proc. IEEE*, Vol. 66, No. 10, pp. 1109–1125, Oct. 1978.

[BADA 80] Badal, C.Z., "The Analysis of the Effect of Concurrency Control on Distributed Database System Performance," *Proc. 6th International Conf. on VLDB*, pp. 376–383, Oct. 1980.

[BARN 81] Barnes, G.H., and S.F. Lundstrom, "Design and Validation of a Connection Network for Many-Processor Multiprocessor Systems," *Computer*, Vol. 14, No. 12, pp. 31–41, Dec. 1981.

[BASK 77] Baskett, F., J.H. Howard, and J.T. Mantague, "Task Communication in DEMOS," *Proc. 6th ACM Symposium on Operating System Principles*, published as *Operating Systems Review*, Vol. 11, No. 5, pp. 23–31, Nov. 1977.

[BERN 84] Bernstein, P., and N. Goodman, "Algorithm for Concurrency Control and Recovery in Replicated Distributed Databases," *ACM Transactions on Database Systems*, Vol. 9, No. 4, Dec. 1984.

[BERN 81a] Bernstein, R., and D. Chiu, "Using Semijoins to Solve Relational Queries," *Journal of the ACM*, Vol. 28, No. 1, pp. 25–40, 1981.

[BERN 81b] Bernstein, P., N. Goodman, E. Wong, C. Reeve, and J. Rothnie, "Query Processing in a System for Distributed Databases (SSD-1)," *ACM Transactions on Database Systems*, Vol. 6, No. 4, pp. 602–625, 1981.

[BIRR 83] Birrell, A.D., and B.J. Nelson, "Implementing Remote Procedure Calls," *Proc. 9th Symposium on Operating Systems Principles*, Vol. 17, No. 5, 3 pp., 1983.

[BIRR 82] Birrell, A.D., R. Levin, R. Needham, and M. Schroeder, "Grapevine: An Exercise in Distributed Computing," *Communications of the ACM*, Vol. 25, No. 4, pp. 260–274, April 1982.

[BOKH 79] Bokhari, S.H., "Dual Processor Scheduling With Dynamis Reassignment," *IEEE Transactions on Software Engineering*, Vol. SE-5, No. 4, pp. 341–349, July 1979.

[BRYA 81] Bryant, R.M., and R.A. Finkel, "A Stable Distributed Scheduling Algorithm," *Proc. 2nd International Conference on Distributed Computing Systems*, April 1981.

[CARD 83] Cardenas, A., *Data Base Management Systems*, Chapter 10, Second Edition, Allyn and Bacon, Inc., Boston, MA, 1983.

[CASE 72] Casey, R.G., "Allocation of Copies of Files in an Information Network," *AFIPS Spring Joint Computer Conference*, Vol. 40, AFIPS Press, pp. 617–625, 1981.

[CENS 78] Censier, L.M., and R. Feautrier, "A New Solution to Coherent Problems in Multicache Systems," *IEEE Transactions on Computers*, Vol. C-27, No. 12, pp. 1112–1118, Dec. 1978.

[CERI 86] Ceri, S., G. Gottlob, and G. Pelagatti, "Taxomony and Formal Properties of Distributed Joins," to appear in *Information Systems*, Vol. 11, Nov. 1, 1986.

[CERI 84] Ceri, S., and G. Pelagatti, *Distributed Databases, Principles and Systems*, McGraw-Hill, New York, 1984.

[CERI 83a] Ceri, S., and S.B. Navathe, "A Methodology for the Distribution Design of Databases," *IEEE*, pp. 426–431, 1983.

[CERI 83b] Ceri, S., S. Navathe, and G. Wiederhold, "Distribution Design of Logical Database Schemas," *IEEE Transactions on Software Engineering*, Vol. SE-9, No. 4, pp. 487–504, July 1983.

[CHAN 82] Chang, J., "A Heuristic Approach to Distributed Query Processing," *Proc. 8th International Conference on VLDB*, Mexico City, VLDB Endowment, Saratoga, CA, pp. 54–61, 1982.

[CHEN 84] Chen, P.P., "An Algebra for a Directional Binary Entity-Relationship Model," *Proc. International Conference on Data Engineering*, pp. 37–40, April 1984.

[CHEN 80] Chen, P.P.S., and J. Akoka, "Optimal Design of Distributed Information Systems," *IEEE Transactions on Computers*, Vol. C-29, No. 12, pp. 1068–1080, Dec. 1980.

[CHEN 76] Chen, P.P., "The Entity-Relationship Model: Towards a Unified View of Data," *ACM Transactions on Database Systems*, Vol. 1, No. 1, pp. 9–36, March 1976.

[CHIU 80] Chiu, D.M., and Y.C. Ho, "A Methodology for Interpreting Tree Queries into Optimal Semijoin Expressions," *ACM Transaction on Database Systems*, Vol. 5, No. 4, pp. 169–178, Dec. 1980.

[CHOU 82] Chou, T.C.K., and J.A. Abraham, "Load Balancing in Distributed Systems," *IEEE Transactions on Software Engineering*, Vol. SE-8, No. 4, pp. 401–412, July 1982.

[CHU 86] Chu, W.W., and L. Lan, "Task Allocation and Precedence Relations for Distributed Real-Time Systems," submitted to *IEEE Transactions on Computers*, for publication, 1985.

[CHU 84b] Chu, W.W., "Distributed Data Base Systems," *Handbook of Software Engineering*, Chapter 13, Vick and Rahmoorthy, eds., 1984.

[CHU 79] Chu, W.W., and V. To,"A Hierarchical Conceptual Data Model for Data Translation in a Heterogeneous Database System," *Proc. International Conference on Entity-Relational Approach to Systems Analysis and Design*, Los Angeles, pp. 647–648, Dec. 10–12, 1979.

[CHU 78] Chu, W.W., D. Lee, and B. Iffla, "A Distributed Processing System for Naval Data Communication Networks," *AFIPS Proc.*, Vol. 47, pp. 783–793, 1978.

[CHU 74] Chu, W.W., and G. Ohlmacher,"Avoiding Deadlocking in Distributed Databases," *Proc. ACM National Symposium*, Vol. 1, pp. 156–160, March 1974.

[CODD 70] Codd, E.F., "A Relation Model of Data for Large Shared Data Banks," *CACM*, Vol. 13, pp. 377–387, 1970.

[COFF 81] Coffman, E.G., Jr., et al., "Optimization of the Number of Copies in a Distributed Database," *IEEE Transactions on Software Engineering*, Vol. SE-7, No. 1, pp. 78–84, Jan. 1981.

[DAVI 84] Davidson, S., "Optimism and Consistency in Partitioned Distributed Database Systems," *ACM Transactions on Database Systems*, Vol. 9, No. 4, Dec. 1984.

[DESJ 83] DesJardins, R., "International Standards for Open Systems Interconnection," *SIGCOMM 83 Tutorial*, University of Texas, Austin, March 1983.

[DIAS 81] Dias, D.M., and J.R. Jump, "Packet Switching Interconnection Networks for Modular Systems," *Computer*, Vol. 14, No. 12, pp. 43–53, Dec. 1981.

[DOWD 82] Dowdy, L.W., and D.V. Foster, "Comparative Models of the File Assignment Problem," *Computing Surveys*, Vol. 14, No. 2, pp. 287–313, June 1982.

[EFE 82] Efe, K., "Heuristic Models of Task Assignment Scheduling in Distributed Systems," *Computer*, Vol. 15, No. 6, pp. 50–56, Dec. 1984.

[ELLI 77] Ellis, C.A., "A Robust Algorithm for Updating Duplicate Databases," *Proc. 2nd Berkeley Workshop on Distributed Data Management and Computer Networks*, 1977.

[ELMA 85] Elmasri, R., J. Weeldryer, and A. Hevner, "The Category Concept: An Extension to the Entity-Relationship Model," *Data Knowledge and Engineering*, Vol. 1, No. 1, pp. 75–116, June 1985.

[EPST 78] Epstein, R., M. Stonebraker, and E. Wong, "Distributed Query Processing in Relational Database Systems," *SIGMOD Proc.*, pp. 169–180, May 1978.

[ESWA 74] Eswaran, K.P., "Placement of Records in a File and File Allocation in a Computer Network," *Information Processing 74*, IFIPS, North Holland Publishing Co., 1974.

[ESWA 76] Eswaran, K.P., et al., "The Notions of Consistency and Predicate Locks in a Database System," *Communications of the ACM*, Vol. 19, No. 11, pp. 624–633, Nov. 1976.

[FERR 82] Ferrier, A., and C. Stangret, "Heterogeneity in a Distributed Database Management System SIRIUS-DELTA," *Proc. 8th International Conf. on VLDB*, Mexico City, Sept. 8–10, pp. 45–53, 1982.

[GARC 82] Garcia-Molina, H., and G. Wiederhold, "Read-Only Transactions in a Distributed Database," *ACM Transactions on Database Systems*, Vol. 7, No. 2, pp. 209–234, June 1982.

[GARC 78] Garcia-Molina, H., "Performance Comparisons of Two Update Algorithms for Distributed Databases," *Proc. 3rd Berkeley Workshop on Distributed Databases and Computer Networks*, Aug. 1978.

[GARD 80] Gardarin, G., and W.W. Chu, "A Distributed Control Algorithm for Reliably and Consistently Updating Replicated Databases," *IEEE Transactions on Computers*, pp. 1060–1068, Dec. 1980.

[GARY 78] Gary, J.N., "Notes on Database Operating Systems," *Operating Systems: An Advanced Course, Lecture Notes in Computer Science 60*, Goos and Hartmanis, eds., Springer-Verlag, pp. 393–481, 1978.

[GAVE 76] Gaver, D.P., S.S. Lavenberg, and T.G. Price, "Exploratory Analysis of a Data Base Management System," *IBM Journal of Research and Development*, Vol. 20, No. 5, Sept. 1976.

[GELE 78] Gelenbe, E., and K. Sevick, "An Analysis of Update Synchronization for Multiple Copy Databases," *Proc. 3rd Berkeley Workshop on Distributed Data Management and Computer Networks*, pp. 69–90, Aug. 28–31, 1978.

[GOOD 86] Goodman, J.R., "Cache Memory Optimization to Reduce Processor/Memory Traffic," submitted for publication to *ACM Transaction on Computer Systems*, Jan. 31, 1985.

[GRAY 81] Gray, J., "The Transaction Concept: Virtues and Limitations," *Proc. 1981 VLDB*, pp. 144–154, Sept. 1981.

[GYLY 76] Gylys, V.B., and J.A. Edwards, "Optimal Partitioning of Workload for Distributed Systems," *Proc. COMPCON Fall 76*, pp. 353–357, Sept. 1976.

[HAAS 82] Haas, L.M., et al., "R*: A Research Project on Distributed Relational DBMS," IBM Research Report RJ 3653, San Jose, CA, Oct. 21, 1982.

[HABE 69] Haberman, A.N., "Prevention of System Deadlocks," *Communications of the ACM*, Vol. 12, No. 7, pp. 373–377, 385, July 1969.

[HAMM 80] Hammer, M., and D. Shipman, "Reliability Mechanisms for SDD-1: A System for Distributed Databases," *ACM Transactions on Database Systems*, Vol. 5, No. 4, pp. 431–466. Dec. 1980.

[HAMM 78] Hammer, M., and D. Shipman, "An Overview of Reliability Mechanism for a Distributed Database," *Proc. COMPCON 78*, pp. 63 65, March 1978.

[HELL 80] Hellerstein, J., and W.W. Chu, "Some Potential Deadlocks in Layered Communications Architectures," *AFIPS Proc.*, Vol. 50, pp. 137–140, 1980.

[HEVN 85] Hevner, A.R., O. Wu, and S.B. Yao, "Query Optimization on Local Area Networks," *ACM Transactions on Office Information Systems*, Vol. 3, No. 1, pp. 35–62, Jan. 1985.

[HEVN 79] Hevner, A.R., and S.B. Yao, "Query Processing in Distributed Database Systems," *IEEE Transactions on Software Engineering*, Vol. SE-5, No. 3, pp. 177–187, May 1979.

[HOLT 72] Holt, R.C., "Some Deadlock Properties of Computer Systems," *Computing Surveys*, Vol. 4, No. 3, pp. 179–196, Sept. 1972.

[HOPK 78] Hopkins, A.L., Jr., T.B. Smith, III, and J.H. Lala, "FTMP — A Highly Reliable Fault-Tolerant Multiprocessor for Aircraft," *Proc. IEEE*, Vol. 66, No. 10, pp. 1221–1239, Oct. 1978.

[IEEE 78] "Special Issue on Fault-Tolerant Digital Systems," *Proc. IEEE*, Vol. 66, No. 10, Oct. 1978.

[IRAN 82] Irani, K.B., and K.W. Chen, "Minimization of Interprocessor Communication for Parallel Computation," *IEEE Transactions on Computers*, Vol. C-31, No. 11, pp. 1067–1075, Nov. 1982.

[JENN 77] Jenny, C.J., "Process Partitioning in Distributed Systems," *Proc. NTC 1977*, pp. 31:1-1–31:1-10, 1977.

[JONE 79] Jones, A.K., et al., "A Multiprocessor Operating System for the Support of Talk Forces," *Proc. 7th Symposium on Operating System Principles*, pp. 159–165, Nov. 1980.

[JONE 79] Jones, L.B., and D.V. Foster, "Toward a Multiple Copy File Assignment Model for Files in a Computer System," *Proc. 17th Annual Southeast Regional ACM Conference*, Orlando, FL, April 1979.

[KATS 78] Katsuki, D., et al., "Pluribus — An Operational Fault-Tolerant Multiprocessor," *Proc. IEEE*, Vol. 66, No. 10, pp. 1146–1159, Oct. 1978.

[KATZ 79] Katzman, J.A., "A Fault-Tolerant Computing System," *Proc. 11th Hawaii International Conference on System Science*, 1978.

[KERS 82] Kerschberg, L., P.D. Ting, and S.B. Yao, "Query Optimization in Star Computer Networks," *ACM Transactions on Database Systems*, Vol. 7, No. 4, pp. 678–711, 1982.

[KING 84] King, R., and S. Melville, "Ski: A Semantics Knowledgeable Interface," *Proc. 1984 VLDB*, pp. 30–33, Aug. 1984.

[KING 73] King, P.F., and A.J. Collmeyer, "Database Sharing — An Efficient Mechanism for Supporting Concurrent Processes," *Proc. 1973 National Computer Conference and Exposition*, Vol. 42, pp. 271–275, June 1973.

[KRIS 84] Krishnamurthy, R., and S.P. Morgan, "Query Processing on Personal Computers — A Pragmatic Approach," *Proc. 1984 VLDB*, pp. 26–29, Aug. 1984.

[KRUE 84] Krueger, P., and R. Finkel, "An Adaptive Load Balancing Algorithm for a Multicomputer," Technical Report #539, Computer Sciences Dept., University of Wisconsin, Madison, April 1984.

[KRUS 83] Kruskal, C.P., and M. Snir, "The Performance of Multistage Interconnection Networks for Multiprocessors," *IEEE Transactions on Computers*, Vol. C-32, No. 12, pp. 1091–1098, Dec. 1983.

[LAMP 82] Lampson, B., and H. Sturgis, "Crash Recovery in a Distributed Data Storage System," Technical Report, Xerox Palo Alto Research Center, Palo Alto, CA, 1979.

[LAMP 81a] Lampson, B., "Atomic Transactions," *Distributed Systems — Architecture and Implementation, Lecture Notes in Computer Science 105*, Springer-Verlag, pp. 246–264, 1981.

[LAMP 81b] Lampson, B., "Ethernet, Pub and Violet," *Distributed Systems — Architecture and Implementation, Lecture Notes in Computer Science 105*, Springer-Verlag, pp. 446–484, 1981.

[LIN 83] Lin, K.W., J. Nolte, P.A. Bernstein, and N. Goodman, "Distributed Database System Designer Handbook," Technical Report, *Computer Corporation of America*, Jan. 1983.

[LYNG 84a] Lyngbaek, P., and D. McLeod, "A Personal Data Manager," *Proc. 1984 VLDB*, pp. 14–25, Aug. 1984.

[LYNG 84b] Lyngbaek, P., and D. McLeod, "An Approach to Object Sharing in Distributed Database Systems," *Proc. 1984 VLDB*, pp. 364–375, Aug. 1984.

[MA 82] Ma, P.Y.R., E.T.S. Lee, and M. Tsuchiya, "A Task Allocation Model for Distributed Computig Systems," *IEEE Transactions on Computers*, Vol. C-31, No. 1, pp. 41–47, Jan. 1982.

[MAHM 76] Mahmoud, S., and J.S. Riordan, "Optimal Allocation of Resources in Distributed Information Networks," *ACM Transactions on Database Systems*, Vol. 1, No. 1, pp. 66–78, March 1976.

[MENA 78] Menasce, D.A., and R.R. Muntz, "Locking and Deadlock Detection in Distributed Databases," *Proc. 3rd Berkeley Workshop on Distributed Data Management and Computer Networks*, pp. 215–234, Aug. 28–31, 1978.

[METC 76] Metcalfe, R.M., and D.R. Boggs, "D.R. Ethernet: Distributed Packet Switching for Local Computer Networks," *Communications of the ACM*, Vol. 19, No. 7, pp. 395–404, July 1976.

[MINO 82] Minoura, T., and G. Wiederhold, "Resilient Extended True-Copy Token Scheme for a Distributed Database System," *IEEE Transactions Software Engineering*, Vol. SE-8, No. 3, pp. 173–189, May 1982.

[MORG 77] Morgan, H.L., and K.D. Levin, "Optimal Program and Data Location in Computer Networks," *Communications of the ACM*, Vol. 20, No. 5, pp. 315–322, May 1977.

[NAVA 84] Navathe, S., S. Ceri, G. Wiederhold, and J. Dou, "Vertical Partitioning Algorithms for Database Design," *ACM Transactions on Database Systems*, Vol. 9, No. 4, Dec. 1984.

[PADM 83] Padmanbhan, K., and D. Lawrie, "A Class of Redundant Path Multistage Interconnection Networks," *IEEE Transactions on Computers*, Vol. C-32, No. 12, pp. 1099–1107, Dec. 1983.

[PASS 77] Passafiume, J.J., and S. Wecker, "Distributed File Access in DECNET," *Proc. 2nd Berkeley Workshop on Distributed Databases and Networking*, Lawrence Berkeley Laboratory, Berkeley, CA 1977.

[PATE 82] Patel, J., "Analysis of Multiprocessors with Private Cache Memories," *IEEE Transactions on Computers*, Vol. C-31, No. 4, pp. 296–304, April 1982.

[POPE 81] Popek, G., et al., "Locus: A Network Transparent, High Reliability Distributed System," *Proc. 8th Symposium on Operating Systems Principles*, Pacific Grove, Ca, Dec. 1981.

[RAO 79] Rao, G.S., H.S. Stone, and T.C. Hu, "Assignment of Tasks in a Distributed Processing System with Limited Memory," *IEEE Transactions on Computers*, Vol. C-28, No. 4, pp. 291–299, April 1979.

[RAVI 83] Ravishankar, C.V., and J.R. Goodman, "Cache Implementation for Multiple Microprocessors," *IEEE*, pp. 346–350, 1983.

[RENN 84] Rennels, D.A., "Fault-Tolerant Computing — Concepts and Examples," *IEEE Transactions on Computers*, Vol. C-33, No. 12, pp. 1116–1129, Dec. 1984.

[RIES 81] Ries, D.R., and G.C. Smith, "Nested Transaction in Distributed Systems," *Proc. Symposium on Reliability in Distributed Software and Database Systems*, pp. 117–123, July 1981.

[RIES 82] Ries, D.R., ed., *An Architectural Framework for Database Standardization*, Computer Corporation of America,July 1982.

[RODR 76] Rodriguez-Rosell, J., "Empirical Data Reference Behavior in Data Base Systems," *Computer*, Vol. 9, No. 11, Nov. 1976.

[ROTH 80] Rothnie, J.B., Jr., et al., "Introduction to a System for Distributed Databases (SDD-1)," *ACM Transaction on Database Systems*, Vol. 5, No. 1, pp. 1–17, March 1980.

[SARR 84] Sarrazin, D.B., and M. Malek, "Fault-Tolerant Semiconductor Memories," *Computer*, Vol. 17, No. 8, pp. 49–56, Aug. 1984.

[SELI 80] Selinger, P.G., and M. Adiba, "Access Path Selection in Distributed Database Systems," IBM Research Report RJ 2883, San Jose, CA, Aug. 1980.

[SIEG 81a] Siegel, H.J., and R.J. McMillen, "The Multistage Cube: A Versatile Interconnection Network," *Computer*, Vol. 14, No. 12, pp. 65–76, Dec. 1981.

[SIEG 81b] Siegel, H.J., and R.J. McMillen, "Using the Augmented Data Manipulator in PASM," *Computer*, Vol. 14, No. 2, pp. 25–33, Feb. 1981.

[SIEW 84] Siewiorek, D.P., "Architecture of Fault-Tolerant Computers," *Computer*, Vol. 17, No. 8, pp. 9–18, Aug. 1984.

[SIEW 78] Siewiorek, D.P., et al., "A Case Study of C.mmp, Cm*, and C.vmp: Part I — Experiences with Fault Tolerance in Multiprocessor Systems," *Proc. IEEE*, Vol. 6, No. 10, pp. 1178–1199, Oct. 1978.

[SIEW 78] Siewiorek, D.P., V. Kini, R. Joobbani, and H. Bellis, "A Case Study of C.mmp, Cm*, and C.vmp: Part II — Predicting and Calibrating Reliability of Multiprocessor Systems," *Proc. IEEE*, Vol. 66, No. 10, pp. 1200–1220, Oct. 1978.

[SKEE 82] Skeen, D., "A Quorum-based Commit Protocol," *Proc. 6th Berkeley Workshop on Distributed Data Management and Computer Networks*, pp. 69–80, May 1982.

[SKEE 81] Skeen, D., "Nonblocking Commit Protocol," *SIGMOD International Conference on Management of Data*, Ann Arbor, MI, pp. 133–142, 1981.

[SMIT 82] Smith, A.J., "Cache Memories," *Computing Surveys*, Vol. 14, No. 3, pp. 473–530, Sept. 1982.

[SPEC 85] Spector, A.Z., D. Daniels, D. Duchamp, J. Eppinger, R. Pausch, "Distributed Transactions for Reliable Systems," Technical Report CMU-CS-85-117, Carnegie-Mellon University, Sept. 1985.

[STAN 84] Stankovic, J.A., "A Perspective on Distributed Computer Systems," *IEEE Transactions on Computers*, Vol. C-33, No. 12, pp. 1102–1115, Dec. 1984.

[STON 84] Stonebraker, M., and L. Rowe, "Database Portals — A New Application Program Interface," *Proc. 1984 VLDB*, pp. 3–13, Aug. 1984.

[STON 82] Stonebraker, M., et al., "Performance Analysis of Distributed Data Base Systems," *IEEE Database Engineering*, Vol. 5, No. 4, pp. 58–65, 1982.

[STON 77] Stonebraker, M., and E. Nenhold, "A Distributed Data Base Version of INGRES," *Proc. 2nd Berkeley Workshop on Distributed Data Management and Computer Networks*, Lawrence Berkeley Laboratories, Berkeley, CA, pp. 19–36, May 1977.

[SVOB 81] Svobodova, L., "A Reliable Object-Oriented Data Repository For a Distributed Computer," *Proc. 8th Symposium on Operating Systems Principles*, Dec. 1981.

[SWAN 77] Swan, R.J., S.H. Fuller, and D.P. Siewiorek, "Cm* A Modular Multi-Microprocessor," *Proc. National Computer Conference*, pp. 636–644, June 1977.

[TANE 81] Tanenbaum, A.S., and S.J. Mullender, "An Overview of the Amoeba Distributed Operating System," *Operating Systems Review*, Vol. 15, No. 3, pp. 51–64, July 1981.

[TANG 76] Tang, C.K., "Cache System Design in the Tightly Coupled Multiprocessor System," *Proc. National Computer Conference*, pp. 749–753, 1976.

[THOM 78] Thomas, R.H., "A Solution to the Concurrency Control Problem for Multiple Copy Databases," *Proc. COMPCON 78*, pp. 56–62, March 1978.

[THOM 73] Thomas, R.H., "A Resource Sharing Executive for the ARPANET," *ARIPS Proc.*, Vol. 42, NCC, pp. 155–163, 1973.

[TRAI 82] Traiger, I.L., J. Gray, C.A. Galtier, and B.G. Lindsay, "Transactions and Consistency in Distributed Database Systems," *ACM Transactions on Database Systems*, Vol. 7, No. 3, pp. 323–342, Sept. 1982.

[VANT 84] van Tilborg, A.M., and L.D. Wittie, "Wave Scheduling — Decentralized Scheduling of Task Forces in Multicomputers," *IEEE Transactions on Computers*, Vol. C-33, No. 9, pp. 835–844, Sept. 1984.

[WAH 80] Wah, B.W., "An Efficient Heuristic for File Placement on Distributed Databases," *IEEE COMPSAC*, pp. 462–468, 1980.

[WAH 84] Wah, B.W., and Y. Lien, "The File-Assignment and Query-Processing Problems in Local Multiaccess Networks," *Proc. International Conference on Data Engineering*, Los Angeles, pp. 228–235, April 1984.

[WENS 78] Wensley, J.H., et al., "SIFT: The Design and Analysis of a Fault-Tolerant Computer for Aircraft Control," *Proc. IEEE*, Vol. 66, No. 10, pp. 1240–1254, Oct. 1978.

[WONG 83] Wong, E., "Dynamic Rematerialization: Processing Distributed Queries Using Redundant Data," *IEEE Transactions on Software Engineering*, Vol. SE-9, No. 3, pp. 228–232, 1983.

[WONG 76] Wong, E., and K. Youssefi, "Decomposition — A Strategy for Query Processing," *ACM Transactions on Database Systems*, Vol. 1, No. 3, pp. 223–241, 1976.

[YEN 82] Yen, W.C., and K.S. Fu, "Coherence Problem in Multicache System," *1982 International Conference on Parallel Processing*, pp. 332–339, 1982.

www.ingramcontent.com/pod-product-compliance
Lightning Source LLC
LaVergne TN
LVHW082022200926
848481LV00010B/2902
* 9 7 8 0 8 9 0 0 6 2 1 3 5 *